Virginia

& the Capital Region

Including the best of DC, Maryland & Delaware

Lonely Planet –

travel guidebooks	in-depth coverage with background and recommendations
shoestring guidebooks	for those with plenty of time and limited money
walking guidebooks	covering the world's best walks
Pisces diving & snorkeling guidebooks	full-color destination coverage
phrasebooks	including unusual languages and two-way dictionaries
TV series and videos	stories from on the road
Journeys travel literature	great reading for armchair explorers
city maps	durable maps covering the world's great cities
travel atlases	country maps in sturdy, convenient book form
website	for chat, background, upgrades, opinion, and up-to-date information
Images	online image library

Download free guidebook Upgrades at:
http://www.lonelyplanet.com/upgrades

'Full marks to Lonely Planet for a good read and priceless information.'
– *The Times*

'For tens of millions of globetrotting readers, the Lonely Planet guides are the gospel of adventure travel.'
– *New York Times Magazine*

ISBN 0-86442-769-7

9 780864 427694

USA	**$21.99**
UK	**£13.99**
France	**159,00 FF**

1st Edition

Virginia
& the Capital Region

Randall Peffer

Jeff Williams

Kap Stann

LONELY PLANET PUBLICATIONS
Melbourne • Oakland • London • Paris

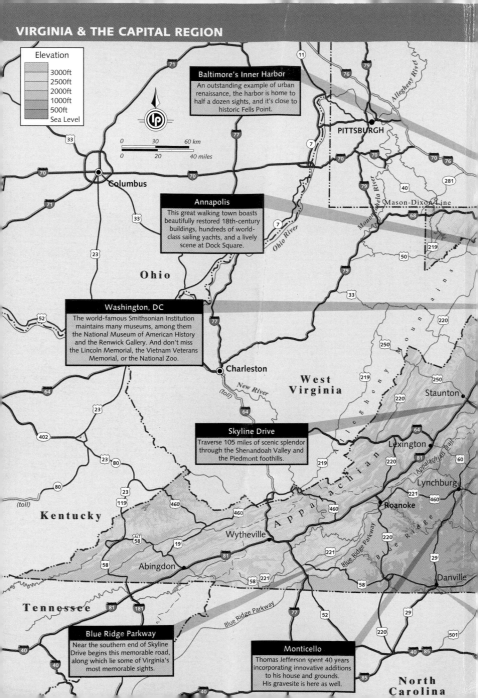

VIRGINIA & THE CAPITAL REGION

Elevation
3000ft
2500ft
2000ft
1000ft
500ft
Sea Level

0   30   60 km
0   20   40 miles

Baltimore's Inner Harbor
An outstanding example of urban renaissance, the harbor is home to half a dozen sights, and it's close to historic Fells Point.

PITTSBURGH

Mason-Dixon Line

Annapolis
This great walking town boasts beautifully restored 18th-century buildings, hundreds of world-class sailing yachts, and a lively scene at Dock Square.

Columbus

Ohio

Ohio River

Washington, DC
The world-famous Smithsonian Institution maintains many museums, among them the National Museum of American History and the Renwick Gallery. And don't miss the Lincoln Memorial, the Vietnam Veterans Memorial, or the National Zoo.

Charleston

New River
(toll)

West Virginia

Staunton

Skyline Drive
Traverse 105 miles of scenic splendor through the Shenandoah Valley and the Piedmont foothills.

Lexington

Lynchburg

Kentucky

Roanoke

Wytheville

Appalachian

Blue Ridge Parkway

Danville

Abingdon

Tennessee

Blue Ridge Parkway
Near the southern end of Skyline Drive begins this memorable road, along which lie some of Virginia's most memorable sights.

Blue Ridge Parkway

Monticello
Thomas Jefferson spent 40 years incorporating innovative additions to his house and grounds. His gravesite is here as well.

North Carolina

Allegheny River

Monongahela River

Appalachian Trail

Blue Ridge

Winterthur
This 100-room chateau on 1000 manicured acres houses a fabulous decorative-arts collection.

Historic New Castle
With enough colonial vestiges to send you back in time, this village is blessed with good restaurants and B&Bs.

Lewes & Cape Henlopen
Where the Delaware Bay joins the Atlantic lies this maritime town, adjacent to giant sand dunes.

St Michaels
Soak up Eastern Shore culture while downing beer and chomping your way through crab.

Mount Vernon
George and Martha Washington's estate and final resting place lures visitors with immaculately maintained grounds and a 19-room mansion.

Civil War Sites
Some of the most poignant include those in Petersburg, Fredericksburg, Danville, and the surrender site at Appomattox.

Berkeley Plantation
Site of the first Thanksgiving, this James River plantation was ravaged by Benedict Arnold during the Revolutionary War and was a base for General McClellan during the Civil War.

Newark
NEW YORK
Trenton
Harrisburg
Pennsylvania
Gettysburg
Susquehanna River
PHILADELPHIA
New Jersey
Wilmington
Cumberland
Maryland
New Castle
Frederick
Mason-Dixon Line
BALTIMORE
Chestertown
Dover
Winchester
Delaware Bay
Annapolis
Delaware
Arlington
WASHINGTON, DC
St Michaels
Easton
Lewes
Alexandria
Rehoboth Beach
Culpeper
Ocean City
Harrisonburg
Fredericksburg
Solomons
ATLANTIC OCEAN
Charlottesville
Potomac River
Waynesboro
James River
Onancock
Chesapeake Bay
Richmond
Appomattox
Petersburg
Williamsburg
Newport News
Hampton
NORFOLK
Virginia Beach
Portsmouth
Emporia
South Boston
John H Kerr Reservoir (Buggs Island Lake)
Great Dismal Swamp
Albemarle Sound
Rappahannock River
Roanoke River
Nottoway River
Virginia

Virginia & the Capital Region
1st edition – September 2000

Published by
Lonely Planet Publications Pty Ltd A.C.N. 005 607 983
192 Burwood Rd, Hawthorn, Victoria 3122, Australia

Lonely Planet Offices
Australia PO Box 617, Hawthorn, Victoria 3122
USA 150 Linden St, Oakland, CA 94607
UK 10a Spring Place, London NW5 3BH
France 1 rue du Dahomey, 75011 Paris

Photographs
Most of the images in this guide are available for licensing from
Lonely Planet Images.
email: lpi@lonelyplanet.com.au

Civil War photographs courtesy of the Library of Congress

Front cover photograph
House in early morning fog, Blue Ridge Parkway near Galax, VA
(Bryan Yarin/Index Stock)

Title page photographs
Washington, DC (Dennis Johnson)
Virginia (Philip Game)
Maryland (Maryland Department of Tourism)
Delaware (Delaware Tourism Office)

ISBN 0 86442 769 7

text & maps © Lonely Planet 2000
photos © photographers as indicated 2000

Printed by Colorcraft Ltd, Hong Kong

**Although the authors
and Lonely Planet try
to make the informa-
tion as accurate as
possible, we accept
no responsibility for
any loss, injury or
inconvenience sus-
tained by anyone
using this book.**

Contents

VIRGINIA'S CHESAPEAKE BAY 304

COLONIAL VIRGINIA (HISTORIC TRIANGLE) 319

HAMPTON ROADS 342

THE PIEDMONT 374

SHENANDOAH VALLEY & RANGES 399

SOUTHWEST & BLUE RIDGE HIGHLANDS 435

FACTS ABOUT MARYLAND 460

4 **Contents**

NORTHERN DELAWARE

CENTRAL DELAWARE

DELAWARE SEASHORE

ACKNOWLEDGMENTS

INDEX

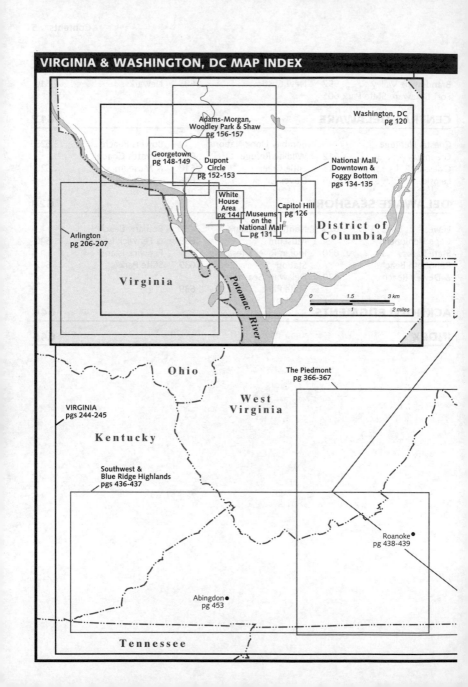

VIRGINIA & WASHINGTON, DC MAP INDEX

Ohio

West
Virginia

Kentucky

Tennessee

0   1.5   3 km
0   1   2 miles

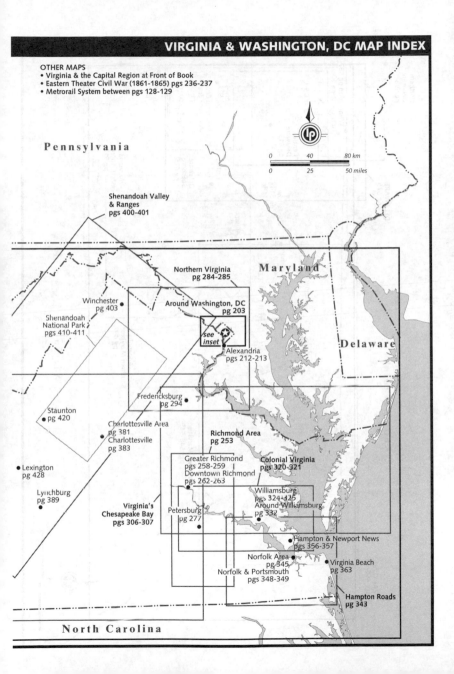

VIRGINIA & WASHINGTON, DC MAP INDEX

OTHER MAPS
• Virginia & the Capital Region at Front of Book
• Eastern Theater Civil War (1861-1865) pgs 236-237
• Metrorail System between pgs 128-129

Pennsylvania

0   40   80 km
0   25   50 miles

Shenandoah Valley
& Ranges
pgs 400-401

Maryland

Northern Virginia
pg 284-285

Winchester
pg 403

Around Washington, DC
pg 203

Shenandoah
National Park
pgs 410-411

see
inset

Delaware

Alexandria
pgs 212-213

Fredericksburg
pg 294

Staunton
pg 420

Charlottesville Area
pg 381
Charlottesville
pg 383

Richmond Area
pg 253

Lexington
pg 428

Greater Richmond
pgs 258-259
Downtown Richmond
pgs 262-263

Colonial Virginia
pgs 320-321

Lynchburg
pg 389

Williamsburg
pgs 324-325
Around Williamsburg
pg 332

Virginia's
Chesapeake Bay
pgs 306-307

Petersburg
pg 277

Hampton & Newport News
pgs 356-357

Norfolk Area
pg 345

Virginia Beach
pg 363

Norfolk & Portsmouth
pgs 348-349

Hampton Roads
pg 343

North Carolina

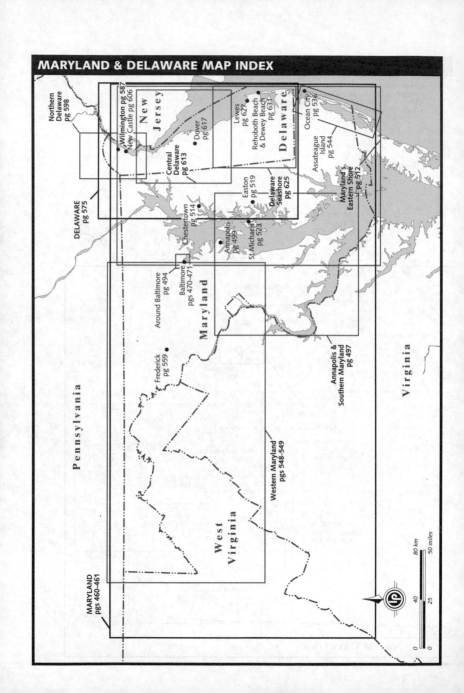

MARYLAND & DELAWARE MAP INDEX

Northern Delaware pg 598

Wilmington pg 587
New Castle pg 606

New Jersey

Dover pg 617

Lewes pg 627

Rehoboth Beach & Dewey Beach pg 631

Delaware

Ocean City pg 536

DELAWARE pg 575

Central Delaware pg 613

Assateague Island pg 544

Maryland's Eastern Shore pg 512

Easton pg 519

Delaware Seashore pg 625

Chestertown pg 514

Annapolis pg 499

St Michaels pg 523

Baltimore pgs 470-471

Around Baltimore pg 494

Baltimore pg 494

Maryland

Pennsylvania

Annapolis & Southern Maryland pg 497

Frederick pg 559

Virginia

West Virginia

Western Maryland pgs 548-549

MARYLAND pgs 460-461

Virginia

80 km
50 miles

0   25   40
0   25

The Authors

Randall Peffer

As a boy, Randy hopped a freight train out of his hometown of Pittsburgh, Pennsylvania, in search of the King of the Hoboes. He's been traveling ever since. Those travels have taken him into jobs as a commercial pilot, a research-schooner captain, and a teacher in a naval prison. Virginia and the Capital Region have enthralled him since he caught his first blue crab at Virginia Beach as a six-year-old. As a teenager, he became addicted to the DC club scene. And as a young adult, he lived on the Eastern Shore and worked as a Chesapeake Bay waterman.

A widely published feature writer, Randy has contributed to *National Geographic*, *Smithsonian*, *Islands*, *Travel Holiday*, *Sail*, *Reader's Digest*, and most of the major metro dailies in the US. He is the author of *National Geographic*'s driving guide to New York, New Jersey, and Pennsylvania. Randy's nonfiction narrative *Watermen*, about Chesapeake fishermen, won the *Baltimore Sun*'s Critic's Choice award. He also recently published his memoir of a maritime exploration of the Massachusetts coast, *Logs of the Dead Pirates Society*.

Randy wrote Lonely Planet's *Puerto Rico* and is currently writing *Virgin Islands*. He lives with his wife, Jackie, and his sons, Noah and Jacob, at Phillips Academy in Andover, Massachusetts, where he teaches literature and writing.

Jeff Williams

Jeff is a Kiwi from Greymouth, on New Zealand's wild west coast. He currently lives on the west coast in a chook house (fowl enclosure) and hopes that one day he will learn how to use an automatic washing machine (after mastering in-line skating).

Jeff has written or contributed to more than 20 Lonely Planet titles, including *USA*, *West Africa*, *South Africa*, *Middle East*, *Australia*, *Western Australia*, and *New Zealand*. All these places have seen him as a temporary visitor, with either subsequent kudos or derision. But his ambition is to amble on, searching for 42, somewhere right beside you, now.

Kap Stann

A native New Yorker who now lives in California, Kap traveled to Washington, DC, almost every year of her childhood. In addition to those starched-shirt school field trips through the Capitol, she also enjoyed long beach vacations at the Eastern Shore, where she watched the wild horses run on Assateague Island.

Kap has contributed to Lonely Planet's *USA* and *Deep South*, and she has written guides to Georgia and South Carolina. She lives in Berkeley with her daughter, Cory.

FROM THE AUTHORS

Randall Peffer First of all, thanks to my co-authors, Jeff Williams and Kap Stann, for their enthusiasm in getting off the beaten track and uncovering fresh, unseen corners of Virginia and Maryland. And double thanks to them for turning in copy ahead of deadline. Jeff's boundless wit throughout this project kept me emotionally afloat while I was adrift in a sea of computer files: Go Broncos!

Our senior editor, Laura Harger, and project editor, Suki Gear, were equally supportive and went above and beyond the call of duty, reading manuscript drafts and offering suggestions to enrich the text. Cartography manager Alex Guilbert and his minions have proven themselves wizards at their tasks. Thanks also to Susan Noble and her staff of research librarians at Phillips Academy's Oliver Wendell Holmes Library for their magical ability to unearth rare and valuable sources at lightning speed. My field research would not have been as trouble-free nor as much fun without the support of Donna Desormeaux at the Washington, DC Convention and Visitors Association and Jennifer Hastings of the Delaware Economic Development Office.

Most importantly, thanks to my family – Jackie, Jacob, and Noah – for giving me the time, space, and support to finish this project. The adventure of travel writing would be hollow indeed without having my family to share it.

Jeff Williams Jeff would like to thank his magnificent son, Callum, who lives in Brisbane, Australia; the incredible staff at the Richmond CVB; the hard workers at Pamplin Historical Park Museum of the Civil War Soldier; the Petersburg Crater Club (and Lee), the beautiful people of Floyd County (Virginia), and the staff at Tuggle's Gap; and the extended Lonely Planet family of Suki Gear, Laura Harger, and Carolyn Hubbard in Oakland, California.

This Book

Much of the information in *Virginia & the Capital Region* was based on *Washington, DC & the Capital Region* (1997) by Kap Stann, Jeff Williams, Randall Peffer, and Eric Wakin.

Randall Peffer was the coordinating author and wrote the Washington, DC, Delaware, and introductory chapters. Jeff Williams wrote the Virginia chapters as well as The Civil War and Activities. Kap Stann wrote the Maryland chapters and contributed to Around Washington, DC.

FROM THE PUBLISHER

Within the red-brick walls of Lonely Planet's historic Oakland office, *Virginia & the Capital Region* was handled with care by many people. Suki Gear was the project editor and saw the book through all the production stages. Wendy Taylor-Hall swiftly and skillfully edited many Virginia chapters, and Maia Hansen chipped in on the Delaware chapters. Michele Posner helped edit Maryland and guided the book in its early stages. Suki, Wendy, and Valerie Sinzdak proofread, with help from Kevin Anglin and Christine Lee. Ken DellaPenta was the indexer.

Thanks to senior editor Laura Harger, managing editor Kate Hoffman, and publishing manager Mariah Bear for stepping in with their wisdom and sound advice during the project.

Over in mapland, cartographer Patrick 'Red Bull' Huerta redrew and fine-tuned the 60+ maps, with much help from Connie Lock and assistance from Matthew DeMartini, Chris Gillis, Guphy Gustafson, Heather Haskell, Kimra McAfee, Patrick Phelan, and Andy Rebold. Senior cartographer Monica Lepe kept things running smoothly.

Upstairs on the designer mezzanine, Ruth Askevold put together the lovely color pages, laid out the entire book with savvy, and blessed the whole crew with her dry humor. Rini Keagy designed the misty cover. Beca Lafore coordinated the illustrations and created the groovy chapter ends. The book's illustrations were created by Mark Butler, Hugh D'Andrade, John Fadeff, Hayden Foell, Rini Keagy, Justin Marler, Hannah Reineck, Jennifer Steffey, Lisa Summers, and Wendy Yanagihara. Design manager Susan 'Two-Cupper' Rimerman kept the design crew in line (nicely).

And finally, thanks to the Crotty brigade: Olga Crotty, for enthusiastically researching wineries in the Shenandoah Valley and other hotspots in the area; Paul 'Homeboy' Crotty, for writing the much-needed piece on John Waters; and David Crotty, for his insight and suggestions for improving the Virginia and DC portions.

Foreword

ABOUT LONELY PLANET GUIDEBOOKS

The story begins with a classic travel adventure: Tony and Maureen Wheeler's 1972 journey across Europe and Asia to Australia. Useful information about the overland trail did not exist at that time, so Tony and Maureen published the first Lonely Planet guidebook to meet a growing need.

From a kitchen table, then from a tiny office in Melbourne (Australia), Lonely Planet has become the largest independent travel publisher in the world, an international company with offices in Melbourne, Oakland (USA), London (UK) and Paris (France).

Today Lonely Planet guidebooks cover the globe. There is an ever-growing list of books, and there's information in a variety of forms and media. Some things haven't changed. The main aim is still to help make it possible for adventurous travelers to get out there – to explore and better understand the world.

At Lonely Planet we believe travelers can make a positive contribution to the countries they visit – if they respect their host communities and spend their money wisely. Since 1986 a percentage of the income from each book has been donated to aid projects and human-rights campaigns.

Updates Lonely Planet thoroughly updates each guidebook as often as possible. This usually means there are around two years between editions, although for more unusual or more stable destinations the gap can be longer. Check the imprint page (following the color map at the beginning of the book) for publication dates.

Between editions, up-to-date information is available in two free newsletters – the paper *Planet Talk* and email *Comet* (to subscribe, contact any Lonely Planet office) – and on our website at www.lonelyplanet.com. The *Upgrades* section of the website covers a number of important and volatile destinations and is regularly updated by Lonely Planet authors. *Scoop* covers news and current affairs relevant to travelers. And, lastly, the *Thorn Tree* bulletin board and *Postcards* section of the site carry unverified, but fascinating, reports from travelers.

Correspondence The process of creating new editions begins with the letters, postcards and emails received from travelers. This correspondence often includes suggestions, criticisms and comments about the current editions. Interesting excerpts are immediately passed on via newsletters and the website, and everything goes to our authors to be verified when they're researching on the road. We're keen to get more feedback from organizations or individuals who represent communities visited by travelers.

Lonely Planet gathers information for everyone who's curious about the planet – and especially for those who explore it firsthand. Through guidebooks, phrasebooks, activity guides, maps, literature, newsletters, image library, TV series and website, we act as an information exchange for a worldwide community of travelers.

Research Authors aim to gather sufficient practical information to enable travelers to make informed choices and to make the mechanics of a journey run smoothly. They also research historical and cultural background to help enrich the travel experience and allow travelers to understand and respond appropriately to cultural and environmental issues.

Authors don't stay in every hotel because that would mean spending a couple of months in each medium-size city and, no, they don't eat at every restaurant because that would mean stretching belts beyond capacity. They do visit hotels and restaurants to check standards and prices, but feedback based on readers' direct experiences can be very helpful.

Many of our authors work undercover; others aren't so secretive. None of them accept freebies in exchange for positive write-ups. And none of our guidebooks contain any advertising.

Production Authors submit their raw manuscripts and maps to offices in Australia, the USA, the UK or France. Editors and cartographers – all experienced travelers themselves – then begin the process of assembling the pieces. When the book finally hits the shops, some things are already out of date, we start getting feedback from readers and the process begins again....

WARNING & REQUEST

Things change – prices go up, schedules change, good places go bad and bad places go bankrupt – nothing stays the same. So, if you find things better or worse, recently opened or long since closed, please tell us and help make the next edition even more accurate and useful. We genuinely value all the feedback we receive. Julie Young coordinates a well-traveled team that reads and acknowledges every letter, postcard and email and ensures that every morsel of information finds its way to the appropriate authors, editors and cartographers for verification.

Everyone who writes to us will find their name in the next edition of the appropriate guidebook. They will also receive the latest issue of *Planet Talk*, our quarterly printed newsletter, or *Comet*, our monthly email newsletter. Subscriptions to both newsletters are free. The very best contributions will be rewarded with a free guidebook.

Excerpts from your correspondence may appear in new editions of Lonely Planet guidebooks, the Lonely Planet website, *Planet Talk* or *Comet*, so please let us know if you *don't* want your letter published or your name acknowledged.

Send all correspondence to the Lonely Planet office closest to you:

Australia: PO Box 617, Hawthorn, Victoria 3122
USA: 150 Linden St, Oakland, CA 94607
UK: 10A Spring Place, London NW5 3BH
France: 1 rue du Dahomey, 75011 Paris

Or email us at: talk2us@lonelyplanet.com.au

For news, views and updates, see our website: www.lonelyplanet.com

HOW TO USE A LONELY PLANET GUIDEBOOK

The best way to use a Lonely Planet guidebook is any way you choose. At Lonely Planet, we believe the most memorable travel experiences are often those that are unexpected, and the finest discoveries are those you make yourself. Guidebooks are not intended to be used as if they provided a detailed set of infallible instructions!

Contents All Lonely Planet guidebooks follow the same format. The Facts about the Country chapters or sections give background information ranging from history to weather. Facts for the Visitor gives practical information on issues like visas and health. Getting There & Away gives a brief starting point for researching travel to and from the destination. Getting Around gives an overview of the transport options available when you arrive.

The peculiar demands of each destination determine how subsequent chapters are broken up, but some things remain constant. We always start with background, then proceed to sights, places to stay, places to eat, entertainment, getting there and away, and getting around information – in that order.

Heading Hierarchy Lonely Planet headings are used in a strict hierarchical structure that can be visualized as a set of Russian dolls. Each heading (and its following text) is encompassed by any preceding heading that is higher on the hierarchical ladder.

Entry Points We do not assume guidebooks will be read from beginning to end, but that people will dip into them. The traditional entry points are the list of contents and the index. In addition, however, some books have a complete list of maps and an index map illustrating map coverage.

There may also be a color map that shows highlights. These highlights are dealt with in greater detail later in the book, along with planning questions and suggested itineraries. Each chapter covering a geographical region usually begins with a locator map and another list of highlights. Once you find something of interest in a list of highlights, turn to the index.

Maps Maps play a crucial role in Lonely Planet guidebooks and include a huge amount of information. A legend is printed on the back page. We seek to have complete consistency between maps and text, and to have every important place in the text captured on a map. Map key numbers usually start in the top left corner.

Although inclusion in a guidebook usually implies a recommendation, we cannot list every good place. Exclusion does not necessarily imply criticism. In fact, there are a number of reasons why we might exclude a place – sometimes it is simply inappropriate to encourage an influx of travelers.

Introduction

From the Blue Ridge Mountains to the Chesapeake Tidewater, the mid-Atlantic states of Virginia, Maryland, and Delaware, along with the District of Columbia, constitute a geographically and culturally distinct region joining the traditions of North and South. Its people are Southerners or Quakers or watermen, faintly Elizabethan or Appalachian or Republican, diplomats, Redskins fans, hunters, and hikers. Here is a place that cherishes its considerable links to American history, from George Washington to George Bush, from Pocahontas to Monica Lewinsky. No other place in the US brings the turbulent history of the American nation so much into the foreground of everyday living. To explore Virginia and the Capital Region and engage its citizens is to feel in full force the restless energy and drama that have long characterized this land and the nation that was born and came of age here.

Washington, DC, lies at the heart of the Capital Region. And today, DC is a beautiful city, studded with monuments, memorials, colossal architecture, and inviting public spaces. Its museums and galleries – most notably the always-free Smithsonian – offer unparalleled access to some of the world's best art, artifacts, and cultural touchstones. But DC is far from being solely ornamental: As one of the seats of global power, Washington pulses to the beat of the latest international controversy or national scandal. With some of the best informed, most intelligent, opinionated, and politically savvy residents on the planet, DC guarantees that you're never far from spirited debate on topics ranging from public policy to which Eritrean restaurant serves the best injera in town.

Some of the country's earliest heritage is rooted in Virginia. Nearly every river landing, mountain pass, field, and town tells stories of English colonies, American independence, or the Civil War. You can visit Jamestown, the first successful English settlement in the New World; the Yorktown battlefield; and Richmond, the former capital of

the Confederate States. Travelers can tour the graceful estates of Monticello (the home of Thomas Jefferson) and Mount Vernon (George Washington's manor). Small reservations still retain some traditions of early Native American nations.

Throughout the state, from tidy lawns to wild woods, you can see the flowering landscapes for which the South is famous, hear the languid Southern dialect, and

15

sample grits, hush puppies, collards, and pecan pie.

The southern Appalachian traditions of the Blue Ridge Mountains in western Virginia reflect a distinct heritage. Bluegrass music fills country stores on Saturday nights, and hand-sewn quilts hang for sale from the porches of tin-roof mountaineer cabins. The Appalachian Trail is the most famous of many footpaths through beautiful backcountry, but even without leaving your car, you can take in stunning vistas along the Blue Ridge Parkway and Skyline Drive.

The Chesapeake Bay defines the Tidewater region that dominates Maryland; nearly every family has a boat for exploring bay waters and its many tributaries. Visitors can easily sample the bay's bounty by ordering a plate of softshell crabs, oysters, or Maryland rockfish. And the state's major cities are right on the bay: Baltimore offers a new waterfront development, and Annapolis, the capital, is where sailors converge amid a colonial setting.

Maryland's Eastern Shore features rural towns surprisingly unaffected by their proximity to the urban corridor; stable communities of farmers and watermen here trace their lineage back to British, African, and Native American roots.

Delaware tops the Delmarva Peninsula (portions belong to DELaware, MARyland, and VirginiA), offering some of the best Atlantic Coast beaches in the region, including the popular resorts at Rehoboth Beach and Bethany Beach. Northern Delaware prides itself on the 'chateau country' of the Brandywine Valley, with its regal estates, formal gardens, and outstanding art collections.

Across the Capital Region, you'll find outdoor recreation in each season, from surfing at Atlantic Coast beaches to skiing on Appalachian Mountain slopes. In between, by boat or on foot, you can discover the tidal lowlands and wooded uplands that led Captain John Smith (of Pocahontas fame) to exclaim about the region, 'Heaven and earth never agreed better to frame a place for man's habitation.' Those were certainly romantic days, and there's plenty in the Capital Region to take you back.

Facts about the Capital Region

HISTORY

Few places in the world can claim to have spawned more dramatic history and myth than Virginia and the Capital Region. To follow the paths of history through this corner of America is to discover the places and people who bring to life the essential stories of the birth and the coming-of-age of the nation known as the United States of America.

Here you can follow the trails forged by a Native American empire and the first European discoverers of the region through a maze of tidewater tributaries and over pale mountain ridges. Within an hour's drive of the US Capitol, you will find the sites of military catastrophes such as the Battle of Brandywine in the American Revolution and the Civil War's Battle of Antietam...as well as the places where warriors laid down their weapons at Yorktown and Appomattox to end the slaughter of those wars.

In the Capital Region, you will tread the land of Pocahontas, Captain John Smith, George Washington, Dolley Madison, Abraham Lincoln, and Harriet Tubman. And, of course, this is the place that seems to engender an almost endless list of juicy scandals, from the romantic adventures of Thomas Jefferson and his slave mistress Sally Hemings to Edgar Allan Poe's fatal attraction for his 11-year-old cousin – not to mention the recent Bill Clinton–Monica Lewinsky affair.

But what is remarkable about the Capital Region is not simply that it has been a locus for such extraordinary goings-on. Along the shores of the Chesapeake, in the pubs of DC, and among the forest hollows of the mountains, you will meet a lot of people who will be proud to tell you their personal or familial roles in the American fairy tales and soap operas.

Prehistory of the Americas

Nearly 20,000 years ago, when the accumulated ice of the great polar glaciers of the Pleistocene lowered sea levels throughout the world, the ancestors of Native Americans crossed from Siberia to Alaska via a land bridge across the Bering Strait. Over millennia, subsequent migrations distributed the population southward and eastward through North and Central America and down to the southern tip of South America.

Native Peoples

The first inhabitants of North America were nomadic hunter-gatherers who lived in small bands. Some of the earliest evidence of human habitation on the continent – dating back as many as 11,500 years – have been unearthed in the Capital Region. At the Williamson site in southern Virginia (just north of the North Carolina border), archaeologists have found a variety of tools used to shape projectile points – indispensable weapons against such ancient large game as mammoth and bison, which were present in the Paleo-Indian period. Researchers also concluded that in addition to large game, such early communities relied heavily on small game and vegetable foods, and that they held some notion of an afterlife – but without strong evidence, these claims remain speculative.

Farther south, the development of pottery around 8000 BC is often considered a hallmark of the Archaic period that followed, but inhabitants of the mid-Atlantic region continued to shape containers out of steatite (soapstone) throughout the Archaic period. Steatite is a soft, easily worked mineral that is readily found in the region – in fact, one soapstone quarry can be seen right in Washington, DC's northwest district, in Soapstone Valley Park. During this time, increased efficiency in hunting and gathering techniques enabled Archaic communities to pursue more than subsistence tasks, and adornments and ritual objects began to appear.

Around 1000 BC, a transition period occurred during which woodland hunting and gathering traditions grew, supported by the rudiments of agriculture. Nuts and seeds were among the first foods to be collected and cultivated, and for the first time, they were stored in underground pits for later use. With the help of such developments, settlements grew more sedentary, and communities constructed relatively permanent housing and discovered the utility of banding together in organized chiefdoms.

These were the prehistoric antecedents to the Native American nations of the modern period. The mid-Atlantic region became the southernmost territory of the great Algonquin Nation that stretched north to New England along the eastern seaboard. The Iroquois Nation presided over areas farther inland. When survivors of smaller bands in the region fled the decimation wrought by European-borne diseases, the Iroquois Nation absorbed many and grew in strength and number. Fear of the stronger Iroquois may have been a compelling factor in forcing the Algonquin tribes into later alliances with the arriving English.

At the time of European contact, many native peoples lived at the water's edge, around cornfields and gardens of squash, beans, and potatoes – as they had for many centuries. Villages consisted of longhouses constructed from bent branches and woven grass mats, and the tribes depended heavily on fish and shellfish for their diet. They dressed in deerskin decorated with seashells, bones, porcupine quills, and paint, and used paints and tattoos to decorate their skin. For religious rituals, they wore headdresses made of snakeskin stuffed with grass and shook hollow gourds filled with pebbles. They called their god Okewas and for generations prophesied that strangers from across the sea would come and destroy their people.

Captain John Smith was the first European to reach the navigable head of the Potomac River (a name derived from the Algonquian word meaning, variously, 'place to which tribute is brought' or 'trading place'). The hostile reception Smith received, his subsequent capture, and his ultimate rescue by Pocahontas (daughter of the tribal leader Powhatan) today make up a favorite American legend.

Early Exploration

The Chesapeake Bay found its way onto the map of European exploration six years after Christopher Columbus landed at San Salvador. Englishman John Cabot sailed past the Virginia capes in 1498 as he searched for the fabled Northwest Passage. That same year, Italian Amerigo Vespucci sailed northward on his own mapping expedition.

During the next century, dozens of other European expeditions (mostly Spanish) passed the entrance to Chesapeake Bay as they followed the trade winds along the Gulf Stream up the North American coast and back to Europe. Some of these mariners' accounts called this great inland sea the 'Madre de Aguas' (Mother of Waters), which some historians believe is a corruption of the Algonquian words for the region, possibly 'Chesupioc,' which is often translated as 'great shellfish bay.' But in spite of regular visits to the great estuary, no serious efforts to colonize the area occurred until 1585, when English adventurer Sir Walter Raleigh established his famous lost colony of Roanoke just south of the Chesapeake in modern North Carolina. Although the colony vanished within a year (probably due to Native American attacks), Raleigh's name for the region stuck. He called this tidewater region 'Virginia' for Queen Elizabeth, the virgin queen, and England eventually called all its eastern seaboard territory by that name. From that expanse England would carve smaller colonies such as Maryland and Delaware, and the area known as Virginia would shrink.

First Colonies

During the European Age of Exploration (the 16th and 17th centuries), the nations of Western Europe subscribed to the political-economic philosophy of 'mercantilism.' Mercantilists believed that the nations of the world were in an unstoppable struggle to define and assert their national identities at the expense of rival nations. A nation furthered its interests by creating a network of economically dependent colonies that might supplement the national treasury, industry, army, and navy.

Portugal and Holland took a strong early lead by establishing trading colonies in Africa and the East Indies, but after Columbus' discovery of America, Spain hit pay dirt by wresting gold and silver mines from the native peoples of Mexico and South America. Fear of Spain's potential domination of the world spurred northern European countries like France, Holland, England, and Sweden to redouble their efforts at colonizing the New World. Everybody wanted a piece of El Dorado (the fabled city of gold).

On April 10, 1606, King James I granted the Virginia Company the right to establish settlements of English colonists in America. The Virginia Company comprised two subgroups: the London and Plymouth Companies. The London Company was allowed to colonize the southern half of the grant, and the Plymouth Company the northern half. A number of other conditions applied. Provisions were made for a president to be elected annually and for a constitution by which the settlers and their children 'would forever...enjoy all liberties, franchises and immunities enjoyed by Englishmen in England.'

Sir Thomas Smith, treasurer of the London Company, supervised arrangements for the colonization. Led by Christopher Newport, 104 English colonists sailed for America and arrived at Cape Henry (near modern-day Virginia Beach) on April 26, 1607, after a four-month voyage on three small ships (*Susan Constant*, *Godspeed*, and *Discovery*). After an initial exploration of Chesapeake Bay, Newport and his colonists entered the James River and on May 14 founded Jamestown, the first permanent English settlement in America (named after England's king). Although the stockholders, as well as some of the 100 men who sailed with Newport, claimed to be on a mission to deter Spanish and Roman Catholic domination of the New World, the men of the Virginia Company hoped that the Jamestown venture would make them all rich.

Newport left his colonists at Jamestown and returned to England, and at first, the colonists were sorely disappointed. Life went badly at Jamestown for a multitude of reasons, chief among them the 'entitled'

attitude of the colonists. More than a third of the original settlers, and an even greater number of subsequent arrivals, were gentry; most of the other colonists were personal servants to the gentry. Local tribes under the powerful chief Powhatan warned the colonists that they would need to plant corn to sustain them through the cold months when hunting and fishing were difficult, but few of the colonists had the inclination or skill to plant, tend, and harvest corn. The Jamestown colony verged on starvation many winters.

Instead of planting corn, colonists like the legendary Captain John Smith fussed about in boats looking for gold, silver, and the Northwest Passage and antagonized the Chesapeake's Native Americans until regular guerrilla skirmishing defined the relationship between the two camps. By the time Newport returned to the colony on January 12, 1608, only 38 of the 100 colonists remained. One of these was John Smith, who became president of the colony in 1608. The following year, the newly incorporated London Company expanded to include even more territory. The charter fixed the boundaries of Virginia at 200 miles north and 200 miles south of Old Point Comfort, and west and northwest from sea to sea. Additionally, government was now vested in the treasurer and council of the company in London.

On July 30, 1619, the first representative assembly in the New World, the House of Burgesses, was elected by free colonists. The king revoked the London Company's charter, and Virginia became a royal colony – England's first – in 1624.

Tobacco: The 'Sot Weed' Factor

Low on funds and without direction and initiative, the Jamestown colony was verging on collapse when John Rolfe, who had married Powhatan's famous daughter Pocahontas, discovered that the weed his father-in-law dried and smoked held an addictive charm for European libertines looking for a new thrill.

With the arrival of the trading ships that resupplied the rum lockers of the Jamestown gentry every spring, Rolfe received news that the British were paying big money for tobacco that the ship captains purchased from West Indian planters who could only supply small quantities. The captains encouraged Rolfe to supply some native weed for the folks back home, but the quality of the local variety did not meet the standards of Europe's growing legion of 'sot weed' connoisseurs. Rolfe obtained seeds of the preferred West Indies plants and planted them in the rich tidewater soil. Voilà! Good smoke.

Suddenly, ship captains were begging Virginians to plant the sot weed and were paying three shillings a pound. While tobacco profits couldn't meet the expectations of gold-hungry investors, a man who tended 1000 tobacco plants a year might get rich. He might even get rich in a hurry if he could locate cheap labor – once a planter drove off the Indians, the land for tobacco plantations was limitless, but the labor supply was not.

The population of the colony amounted to some 4000, including indentured servants, apprentices, and a handful of petty criminals dispatched by an increasingly hostile king.

Colonists sent to England offered to pay passage for anyone willing to work on a tobacco plantation for some years (typically five to seven) in exchange for room and board. After working the contracted years, the indentured servant gained his or her freedom and received a parcel of land to grow corn and tobacco. Tobacco plantations began spreading all along the shores of the southern Chesapeake and its tributaries. Thousands left England for Virginia, seeking fortune and a new life; however, the influx of people still did not meet the demand for plantation labor.

Slavery

In the early colonial period, Europeans tried enslaving Indians as a cheap source of labor, but many escaped back into familiar terrain. Indentured servants were then lured from Europe, and after serving their time, they easily blended into the colonist population.

In 1619, a Dutch merchant ship sailed to Jamestown with a load of indentured English servants to 'sell' to local plantation owners striving to produce more tobacco. On board the ship were 20 Africans the captain had picked up in his travels, and the Virginians bought them as indentured servants too. The Africans found it nearly impossible to escape their servitude due to their distinctive appearance and unfamiliarity with local languages and terrain, and planters soon surmised they could be ruthlessly exploited beyond the years of their servitude. As an oversupply of tobacco began to lower prices and cut into profits, planters conspired to keep servants in bondage so that the servants couldn't start their own farms.

From here, the transition to outright slavery was swift; the first laws addressing slave labor appeared in 1662. In the following decades, tens of thousands of Africans were captured, deported, and enslaved to fuel the ambitions of colonial planters. This practice continued unabated over the next century, and Africans soon made up half of the colonial population. For example, by 1800, Maryland had more than 107,000 slaves, and Virginia recorded more than 339,000 slaves – 45% of the state's population. Only Delaware began to rid itself of slavery after the American Revolution, reducing its slave population to fewer than 1800 by the outset of the Civil War in 1861.

Because slaves were expensive – a skilled worker might cost more than a prized racehorse in a farming community where few even owned mules – slave owning was beyond the reach of the great majority of Southern farmers. The overwhelming number of farms – more than two-thirds – held no slaves. Of those that held slaves, the greatest proportion held only one slave. The popular image of huge plantations with hundreds of slaves (such as in *Gone With the Wind*) actually accounted for only a small number of Southern farms. Yet enriched by slave labor, the members of this elite ruling class dominated the economy, society, and political life of the South far out of proportion to their numbers.

Lord Baltimore & the Religious Idealists

Not every European who came to the Chesapeake in the early 17th century came specifically for profit. In 1634, George Calvert

(Lord Baltimore), having received a grant from the king for vast lands in Northern Virginia, encouraged his brother Leonard Calvert to gather a group of religiously tolerant families to start a society founded on religious freedom in the New World. No doubt Baltimore saw the potential for profits in such a colony, but having suffered religious persecution in England because of his Roman Catholic faith, Baltimore also saw that his royal grant and wealth gave him the opportunity to establish a utopian community free from the persecution and prejudice common in England.

The Slave Trade

The gruesome slave trade that brought millions of Africans (estimates vary from at least 10 million to upward of 20 million) to the New World (South America, the Caribbean, and North America) reached its height in the 18th century, yet its legacy continues to shape (and haunt) contemporary society throughout the Americas.

From the 15th century through the 19th century, the slave trade operated from Africa's west coast, in the region stretching from Senegal to Angola but principally in the central 'Gold Coast' area (now Ghana, Togo, Benin, and Nigeria). At first, captives were largely prisoners of local wars sold by the chieftains of victorious tribes. Later, as demand soared, raiders throughout West Africa kidnapped men, women, and children and drove them to the coast, where they were held in stockades before being loaded onto ships bound for the Americas. An overwhelming number – 95% – were brought to the Caribbean and Central and South America; the remaining 5% arrived in North America.

During the 'Middle Passage' across the Atlantic, captives were packed shoulder-to-shoulder in inhumane and unsanitary conditions for six to 12 weeks before reaching shore. One-third of the captives did not survive the ordeal (sharks commonly followed slave ships in anticipation of the bodies thrown overboard). The ones who did endure were fattened as they reached port and oiled upon arrival to appear healthy for auction.

In addition to being exploited for labor, the slaves saw their most basic human liberties denied. In the American South, clans and families were separated, slave marriages were not recognized, and women were routinely sexually exploited. African culture was likewise suppressed: The slaves were strictly prohibited from speaking in their native languages and from participating in any religious worship or cultural rituals. It was a crime to teach a slave how to read. Though some slaves rose in stature by learning trades or by becoming house servants, the great majority were field workers whose legal status was roughly equivalent to that of domestic animals.

It would take centuries and the costliest war the country has ever fought before slavery was abolished in the US. One century later, full civil rights for the descendants of slaves were legally affirmed. But it may take a century more before the crippling consequences of slavery are fully overcome.

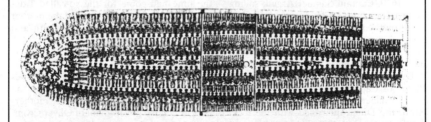

In 1634, Leonard Calvert and about 200 religious idealists – Catholics, Puritans, and Anglicans – sailed up the Chesapeake to an island they called St Clements. They prayed and negotiated with local Native Americans to occupy a great hill overlooking the horseshoe bend in a tributary of the Potomac River. They called this settlement St Mary's City and immediately set about putting their religious tolerance into practice and law. They also cleared the land and planted corn and tobacco. Calvert named the new colony 'Maryland' after Queen Henrietta Maria, wife of King Charles I. It wasn't long before more shiploads of immigrants came to this colony on the Chesapeake north of the Potomac River to pursue religious freedom and plant the sot weed. Slave traders came too, and trade was brisk in agricultural boom towns like Port Tobacco, Oxford, and Annapolis.

The Dutch & the Swedes

Not to be outdone by the British colonial initiatives, the Dutch and the Swedes sent mapmakers and colonists to North America as well, and they too focused on the area of the mid-Atlantic coast that the English called Virginia. Sailing under the Dutch flag, Henry Hudson reached the mouth of Delaware Bay, 100 miles north of the Virginia capes, in 1609 while scouting New World territory for Holland. Finding the bay shallow and rough, Hudson sailed northeast and found the river that today bears his name. It proved a more welcoming place to begin the colony of New Amsterdam, but destiny was to bring the Dutch back to Delaware 45 years later.

In 1610, Captain Samuel Argall, sailing aboard the pinnace *Discovery* from the Jamestown colony, anchored in Delaware Bay and named it for the governor of Virginia, Lord De La Warre. But the English did not return here for years. In 1631, 28 Dutch whalers built a fishing colony in the lee of Cape Henlopen and named the place Zwaanendael. Less than a year passed before the Dutch quarreled with the local Nanticokes, who killed the intruders and scattered the bones of the men and their cattle over present-day Lewes.

In 1638, a shipload of Swedes braved the Delaware and built Fort Christina at the site of today's Wilmington. They claimed an area that stretched from south of Wilmington to near Philadelphia as 'New Sweden,' which included 1000 Swedish and Finnish colonists (their remarkable 400lb governor Johan Prinz was known as the 'Big Tub'). Accomplished farmers and millers, they found the northern shores of the Delaware Bay and River a good place to grow grains that they could process at water-driven mills along the swift-flowing Brandywine Creek.

In 1655, jealousy of the Swedish colony on the Delaware reached its peak among the Dutch at New Amsterdam. They charged up Delaware Bay with ships and armed men under the direction of Peter Stuyvesant and intimidated the Swedes into surrender. A few years later, a British naval vessel sailed within firing range of the Dutch settlement at Fort Casimir (later New Castle); the Dutch surrendered without a fight. Now the shores of a second great bay along America's mid-Atlantic coast were under English control. The English did not drive out the earlier settlers; they simply absorbed them and made them pay taxes. The proud settlers, Swedes and Dutch alike, consoled themselves with the conviction that the British were just another wave of brash immigrants who had yet to prove themselves.

New English immigrants arrived and began clearing plantations south of the old Swedish/Dutch colonies on the Delmarva Peninsula. The English tried raising tobacco, and they introduced slavery. British kings and politicians, watching from afar, thought the time had come for the so-called Tidewater colonies to begin carrying the mother country toward a position of wealth and power on the world stage.

Early Rebellions

Relations between the New World colonies and England became strained under the political troubles and turmoil in the motherland. When the government of Oliver Cromwell replaced the monarchy of Charles I at the end of the Great Rebellion of England, the colony of Virginia mounted a very brief resistance. (That was soon put down when a fleet was sent to quell any trouble in 1652.) The House of Burgesses played a major role in the development of the colony and on occasion exercised its independent streak – the legislators determined that it was the colony, and not Britain, that had the right to elect its own officers.

When the Commonwealth collapsed in England in 1660, ensuing events angered a number of colonists. After being restored to the throne, Charles II introduced the burdensome Navigation Acts, encouraged the slave trade, and showed considerable favoritism in the form of large land grants to his cronies. He appointed Sir William Berkeley governor of the colony of Virginia. Much to the dismay of colonists, Berkeley refused to dispatch soldiers to protect the colony's frontier from Indians, and the Virginia government was controlled by a privileged few who levied intolerable export duties. The right to vote was determined by a property qualification.

All this led to a popular uprising of Virginian farmers, servants, and slaves spearheaded by Nathaniel Bacon, a plantation owner and democratic member of the Governor's Council who had arrived in the colony in 1673. (See the Bacon's Rebellion boxed text in the Colonial Virginia chapter for more information.) Many historians see Bacon's rebellion as the forerunner of the American Revolution.

Following this moderately successful rebellion, Virginia became a channel of expansion into the 'wilderness' – the region beyond the Blue Ridge Mountains – and even as far as the Ohio Valley.

Colonial Struggles

In addition to political squabbles, the Tidewater colonies were also subject to the economic troubles rooted in the overproduction and falling prices of tobacco. Throughout the region, more and larger plantations competed for decreasing tobacco profits. England exacerbated the situation by requiring the colonies to sell their tobacco to the mother country and pay import duties on crops. These economic problems led to a series of confrontations between Marylanders and Virginians, Puritans and Catholics, planters and laborers, and Indians and Europeans.

One major border dispute erupted after William Penn won his grant to Pennsylvania, an area north of Maryland in 1681. Over time, the debate between Maryland and Pennsylvania over territory grew so heated that in 1763 the Crown called in the famous English astronomers Mason and Dixon to settle the conflict. The resulting border – the Mason-Dixon Line – has been popularly considered the dividing line between North and South in the US ever since. (This notion would later be reinforced by the Missouri Compromise, which used the line to divide slaveholding states from free states.) Mason and Dixon also established firm borders for Delaware. Maryland had wanted to annex Delaware, but Delaware's citizens had enjoyed basic autonomy under William Penn's aegis for more than half a century and wished to be fully independent.

In spite of the economic and regional problems, colonists tried to transform their frontier culture into a civilized society that mirrored England's. The colonies established assembly-style governments (with an appointed governor, an appointed chamber of deputies, and an elected representative assembly), a vigorous constable/magistrate system to uphold the laws, strong churches, and rigorous schools and colleges. Health conditions in the colonies improved, longevity increased, and the population of the colonies reached more than one million before the start of the 18th century.

In 1699, the Virginia capital was moved from Jamestown to Middle Plantation (now Williamsburg) after a major fire (and also because the new site was far more suitable). For the next 70 years, the colony prospered with the capital as its social and cultural hub. The number of slaveholding plantations increased.

Prelude to Revolution

As a second century of English colonization began, many planters in Maryland and Delaware reacted to the diminishing returns on tobacco by converting their farms to the production of corn and wheat. They also planted orchards and financed their own merchant fleets in order to overcome their dependence on European and New England shippers. However, England continued to retard the growth of an American infrastructure by prohibiting the use of gold and silver money in the colonies and reducing colonial businesses to barter or trade in paper script of questionable value.

To the north, the French alliance with the native Huron and Algonquin peoples, as well as its fur-trading empire (extending from eastern Canada south to the valley of the northern Ohio River), led France and Britain into four wars between 1689 and 1764.

The last of these wars, called the 'French and Indian War' in America and 'King George's War' in England, erupted in 1754 and lasted nine years, during which the colonists assisted the British. The French were establishing outposts in the Ohio Valley when a small force led by young George Washington was dispatched by the governor of Virginia to warn the French to keep off British claims. In the first clash of the war, in July 1754, Washington surrendered Fort Necessity in western Pennsylvania. When the British commander Edward Braddock was defeated at Fort Duquesne in 1755, Washington was appointed commander of Virginia's army on the frontier, which the colonial army successfully defended. The colony had found in Washington an able commander, and the colonial forces had proved themselves in the campaigns with minimal help from the British.

During this time, English colonists and militia, some under the leadership of young George Washington, fought protracted battles in the Appalachian Mountains north and west of Maryland against Native Americans organized and armed by the King of France. Britain finally prevailed when General James Wolfe captured Quebec in 1759. But when the war ended in 1763, England found itself nearly bankrupt from the fighting.

The war and the terror it had inspired did a lot to realign Americans' patriotism with Britain, but Britain, which had dug deep into the colonial coffers to support its war against the French, was desperate to replenish the national treasury and did so with a series of new taxes that undercut the colonists' patriotism. And in a time of economic hardship, the British Parliament set about to enforce the old Navigation Acts, which restricted colonies in their trade with other nations.

In the course of the next 18 years, the British government imposed new taxes on imports to America, including everything from sugar to tea. In 1765, the British Parliament passed the Stamp Act to defray the costs of maintaining a British defense force in the colonies. This revenue-raising measure required that just about all paper documents issued in the colony had to bear stamps sold by the British. Protest against this act, seen as a form of 'taxation without representation,' was almost instantaneous. In Virginia, Patrick Henry delivered his 'If this be treason, make the most of it' speech, inspiring the General Assembly to oppose many provisions of the act. The Virginia Resolves stated emphatically that Virginians could only be taxed by their own legislature.

Yielding not so much to the colonists but to the demands of their own merchants, the British repealed the act in 1766. The Crown continued to legislate for the colonies, however, and in 1767 passed the Townshend Acts, another revenue-raising measure that included the abhorred tax on tea. Colonists protested against 'taxation without representation,' but the English government did not listen. King George III simply ordered his governors to grow more persistent in collecting the taxes and sent more companies of armed British 'Red Coats' to stand as visible reminders of the royal authority.

The American Revolution Begins

By 1773, the colonists had had enough. To protest English taxes on American imports, they threw a shipload of English tea into Boston Harbor. After word reached Maryland that Bostonians had filled their harbor with British tea, Marylanders staged 'tea parties' of their own in 1774, when they burned the tea ship *Peggy Ann* in Annapolis and ransacked another tea ship in Chestertown.

In subsequent revolutionary events, Virginia played a pivotal role. In 1774, the British Parliament passed a series of laws aimed at punishing the people of Massachusetts for their defiance. These restrictive measures, known as the Coercive or Intolerable Acts, aroused the sympathy of the other colonies, and at a revolutionary convention held at Raleigh Tavern in Williamsburg in 1774, representatives from Virginia called for a meeting of the 13 colonies (and Canada) to discuss the issue of colonial rights. (The Virginia legislature had previously been dissolved by Governor Dunmore, who was infuriated by the continuous revolutionary utterances from the House of Burgesses.)

In response to Virginia's call, representatives of the colonies met at the First Continental Congress, held in Philadelphia in September 1774. In attendance were Virginia's Richard Henry Lee, Patrick Henry, George Washington, and four others – all representatives of the former Virginia legislature. The delegates to the First Continental Congress petitioned King George III to ensure that their rights as Englishmen be maintained, and they also resolved to meet again in May 1775.

A second revolutionary convention met in Richmond, Virginia, in March 1775. At this gathering, Patrick Henry delivered a fiery speech to give impetus to the arming of a colonial militia. He concluded with the now famous words: 'Is life so dear or peace so sweet as to be purchased at the price of chains and slavery? Forbid it, Almighty God! I know not what course others may take, but, as for me, give me liberty or give me death!' The convention delegates established a committee, headed by Henry, to prepare Virginia's military defense.

Less than a month after Patrick Henry uttered his famous plea, the war commenced in Massachusetts. In mid-April 1775, the British moved to prevent the colonial militia from stockpiling munitions at Concord, 18 miles from Boston. The British advance guard bumped into the militia at Lexington

on April 19, and eight Americans died in the fight. At Concord, the militia ('minutemen'), alerted by mounted messengers such as Paul Revere, resisted and turned the British advance into retreat. The Americans, joined by more militia forces, pursued and boxed up the British force in Boston.

In Virginia, colonists hurriedly formed committees of safety and militias. In April 1775, Dunmore, Virginia's royal governor, seized the colonial powder supply in Williamsburg and transferred part of it to the warship *Magdalen*. After a near riot in the Virginia legislature, Dunmore fled to the awaiting man-of-war *Fowey*, anchored in Chesapeake Bay. The burgesses saw his flight as a virtual abdication, and with him went the last royal government in Virginia.

On May 10, the Second Continental Congress met in Philadelphia as planned. Now the colonies were at war, and the deliberations of the congress reflected the new crisis. The congress proclaimed itself the government of the 'United Colonies of America,' heightened the conflict near Boston by adopting the colonial forces as the 'Continental army,' and unanimously chose George Washington as commander-in-chief.

On this same day, May 10, a northern contingent of American forces surprised and captured the British Fort Ticonderoga on Lake Champlain and proceeded throughout the summer to invade Canada and seize Montreal before being turned back at Quebec. Meanwhile, Washington sought to train, organize, and reinforce the main body of his troops as they squared off with the large British force in Boston. At the end of 1775, among Washington's troops was a Maryland militia of well-disciplined soldiers called the Old Line (earning Maryland the nickname 'The Old Line State'). In addition, more than 250 privateers sailed from Chesapeake ports to cripple British shipping and keep the British hemmed in at Boston.

The Declaration of Independence

Eventually, Washington had the soldiers, supplies, and heavy artillery he needed, and he drove the main British force from Boston in March of 1776. But Washington and other

American patriots knew that England's King George III would not give up his lucrative colonies so easily. The patriots predicted that a fresh and strengthened British force would return by summer, probably with a plan to take New York as a means of dividing the northern and southern colonies.

While Washington tried to solidify his military defenses at New York, the Virginia Convention met in Williamsburg in June 1776 to prepare the American colonies psychologically for what promised to be a protracted war. The intellectuals had been hard at work, and the first fruits of their labor came from the work of George Mason. His revolutionary Virginia Declaration of Rights (later described as the embryonic 'Bill of Rights') was adopted, and Virginia's representatives to the next Continental Congress were told to forward it as a proposal for independence. In his declaration, Mason proposed that 'all men are created free and independent, and have certain inherent rights' that include 'the enjoyment of life and liberty, and the means of acquiring and possessing property' (as well as a number of other now-accepted freedoms).

Thomas Jefferson then went to work and, with enhancements to Mason's declaration, produced the Declaration of Independence. The Continental Congress met in Philadelphia and on July 4, 1776 adopted a Declaration of Independence emphasizing that the colonies 'are of right and ought to be free and independent states.'

The Americans Escape Defeat

As the Americans were proclaiming their independence, a British armada with 30,000 troops, including 8000 Hessian mercenaries from Germany, hovered off the coast of New York, and on August 22, they came ashore. During the next three months, the British pushed the Americans back through Long Island, Manhattan, and New Jersey. Finally, in early December, Washington's army retreated across the Delaware River to Pennsylvania. In the face of these defeats, the Continental army shrank to about 3000 ill-equipped, poorly fed soldiers, and the British might have easily have put an end to

the revolution had they pursued the colonists into Pennsylvania. But instead the British chose to wait out the rough winter weather. This is when Washington struck back. Under the cover of a snowstorm, he led his troops east across the Delaware River on Christmas Eve to surprise and overwhelm 900 Hessians who were camped at Trenton. Slightly more than a week later, he drove the British from Princeton back to New York City and set up camp on the heights of Morristown, New Jersey, where the Americans could watch all of the English movements in New York.

As spring turned into summer in 1777, the British once again pursued their divide-and-conquer strategy. They landed a force of about 7000 soldiers in Canada with the aim of sending this force south along Lake Champlain to join with the New York forces in the Hudson Valley, thereby isolating New England from the rest of the colonies. At first, the British won impressive victories as they headed south, but the Americans took the offensive, defeating the British in a skirmish in Vermont and in two major battles at Saratoga, New York, where the British finally surrendered their army.

These American victories bolstered confidence in the American independence movement, gaining Washington more clandestine aid from France (which had been backing the Americans secretly from the outset of the revolution) and spurring army enlistment at home. But the British were far from ready to concede the colonies. In September 1777, under General Howe, the British sailed up the Chesapeake, invaded Delaware, and marched across the state on their way to attack Philadelphia. The British met a band of American patriots south of Newark at Cooch's Bridge, where they skirmished on September 3. Forty Delaware men fell dead before the Delaware forces retreated, and the British pressed forward into Pennsylvania. Eight days later, the British went on to defeat George Washington at the Battle of Brandywine, just across the Pennsylvania border. On September 12, the English returned to Delaware and occupied Wilmington. Two weeks later, the English army occupied the city of Philadelphia as well.

As this British offensive unfolded, British naval ships patrolled the Delaware Bay and River, making the rebellious Delaware colony vulnerable to attack at any time. Tory sympathizers (colonists who supported British rule) in New Castle County systematically raided the farms of those who favored independence. Because of these threats, Delaware moved its capital away from riverside New Castle to safer, southern, inland Dover in Kent County. Meanwhile, Washington and his continentals licked their wounds and tried to survive the bitter winter of 1777–78 in the camp at Valley Forge, west of Philadelphia.

France Brings a Turning Point

In February 1778, France openly recognized the independence of the colonies and declared war on England, hoping to regain some colonies and trading partners that were formerly lost to the British. Two months later, a French fleet sailed toward America to help General Washington. When the British got word of the French fleet's plans, they evacuated Philadelphia and retreated to New York, fearing that the French might try to trap the English forces on the shores of the Delaware Bay and River with no way to resupply the army.

With the large British force fortified at New York and the Yanks watching them from outposts on the western banks of the Hudson River, neither side had the strength, opportunity, or initiative to pursue new military campaigns in the mid-Atlantic colonies for the rest of 1778. To some degree, both sides were waiting to see how England's war against France would play out in Europe before committing more lives and money to the American conflict. Basically, military strategists in all of the camps realized that England did not have the resources to wage war on both sides of the Atlantic.

The Southern Campaign & English Defeat

But despite the military case against sustaining the war in America, in addition to the average English citizen's more acute concerns for the closer-to-home war with France, King George III doggedly refused to give up the American colonies. To this end, he charged his military leaders to come up with a plan that would save him at least a piece of the American pie – the southern colonies. Consequently, a British force came ashore at Savannah, Georgia, shortly after Christmas 1778 and seized the city. For more than a year, the British and the Americans sparred for control of Georgia and South Carolina, but in May 1780, a large British force from New York attacked Charleston, South Carolina, and drove the Americans out.

The Americans fought back, scoring a series of victories throughout the Carolina colonies. In the first half of 1781, the British brought the war to Virginian soil, when the main British force in the South under General Cornwallis moved north from the Carolinas, attacked Richmond (three times), and fortified its position at Yorktown, between the Gloucester and York Rivers on the southern Chesapeake Bay.

But the English were hardly safe. On August 30, 1781, a French fleet arrived at the mouth of the Chesapeake and drove the inferior British fleet to sea, severing the English supply lines. Thereafter, the French fleet combined with Washington's Continental army (reinforced by 6000 French troops) to lay siege to Yorktown from land and sea. Finally, on October 19, after several failed attempts to break out of the trap, Lord Cornwallis' army, which constituted a third of the British troops in America at the time, surrendered (see the boxed text Victory at Yorktown in the Colonial Virginia chapter).

Hostilities on American soil were effectively over, but it was not until the signing of the Treaty of Paris in September 1783 that the British finally accepted the independence of its old colonies, now known as the United States of America. Washington, wishing at that stage to retire quietly from public office, resigned as commander-in-chief in December at Annapolis. But in April 1789, this Virginian was persuaded to be the first president of the new democracy. (See the introductions to the state chapters for history beyond the signing of the Constitution.)

GEOGRAPHY

The contour of the Capital Region slopes downward from the rounded summits of the Appalachian Mountains in the west to the central Piedmont Plateau and on to the flat Coastal Plain region of tidewater and beach at the Atlantic Coast.

Appalachian Mountains

The Appalachian Mountains run along the eastern seaboard, from Maine to Alabama. Historically, the mountains served as a wilderness frontier. Although it is threatened by encroachment, and despite its proximity to one of the most densely populated urban corridors in the US, the range maintains a wild spirit even today.

In the Capital Region, the southern Appalachians consist of three geological provinces. The front range is the famed Blue Ridge Mountains, a region of legendary beauty and rich folk history and heritage. This land of forested coves, rounded summits, and waterfalls can be easily seen on a scenic drive along the Blue Ridge Parkway and Skyline Drive or explored on foot. One of the most popular trails is the Appalachian Trail, the 2086-mile route that runs along the spine of the Appalachians through Virginia and Maryland. The Trail Conference headquarters is located in Harpers Ferry, at the juncture of West Virginia, Virginia, and Maryland – see the Activities and Western Maryland chapters for more information.

To the west is the Ridge-and-Valley province, a fertile belt between the Blue Ridge and the Allegheny Mountains. In Virginia, this lush region holds the celebrated Shenandoah Valley.

Piedmont Plateau

The Piedmont Plateau, named by early settlers who likened it to the 'foot of the mountain' regions of southern Europe, is a large undulating plateau that holds most of the urban development along the eastern seaboard. It is separated from the lower Coastal Plain region by the 'fall line' – the point at which mountain rivers drop from the plateau to the plain in a series of waterfalls, beyond which they are easily navigable to the

Atlantic Ocean. The plateau's convenient access to both the interior and the sea attracted humans from the earliest Paleo-Indian settlements on. Today, the plateau is home to the region's biggest cities – including Richmond, Baltimore, and Washington, DC.

Coastal Plain

The low, flat, 100-mile-wide Coastal Plain of the Capital Region lies between the fall line and the Atlantic Coast. The plain is dotted with marshy wetlands. The best of these, the Great Dismal Swamp in Virginia's southeast corner, is a national wildlife refuge harboring an impressive variety of fauna, particularly birds. Yet this mid-Atlantic region of the plain is mostly dominated by the ecology and riparian history of its two famous bays, the Chesapeake and the Delaware.

The Chesapeake Bay, more accurately described as an estuary (where saltwater and freshwater mix), is in a long, wide delta of 48 navigable rivers and countless smaller streams that together create an area known ecologically and culturally as the Tidewater.

The Atlantic Coast in Virginia, Delaware, and Maryland is protected by a series of narrow barrier islands. Some parts of this coastline are developed as beach resorts, while others are primitive and inaccessible.

CLIMATE

Seasons are distinct in the Capital Region. In the Piedmont Plateau and Coastal Plain, summers are hot and humid; many residents escape to the cooler mountains and beaches for a respite. In the winter, snow opens ski resorts in the mountains, and even Piedmont cities such as DC may receive an accumulation of snow for days at a time from December to February.

The best times to visit are the long spring and fall seasons. In both, temperatures are generally mild; in spring, wildflowers burst forth in profusion, and in fall, the leaves take on spectacular shades of red, orange, and yellow. Expect rain in the spring as well as days that vary from hot one day to frosty the next. The early fall is more consistently dry, and warm summer temperatures linger long into mid-October.

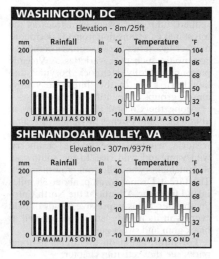

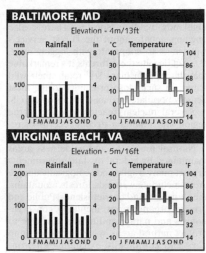

The entire region experiences measured precipitation about 115 days per year. General precipitation is variable, ranging from 36 to 50 inches annually (and an average of 44 inches), with by far the most occurring in the southwest and south-central areas. In winter, snowfall, which rarely stays on the ground for long except in the mountains, ranges from about 10 inches at the coast to 30 inches in the western mountains.

The region's highest-ever recorded temperature (110°F) occurred at Balcony Falls, Virginia, and the lowest (-40°F) was recorded at Oakland in western Maryland. But the expected annual range is nowhere near that. The lowest temperatures occur in January, with an average daily temperature of about 34°F. The region is at its hottest in July, when daily temperatures average 77°F.

The climate in the western upland areas of the region is cooler, with more snow in winter. On any given day, average temperatures in the eastern and western Capital Region differ by about 10°F. In the summer, the coast is generally about three or four degrees cooler than inland areas.

ECOLOGY & ENVIRONMENT

People have been predicting the demise of the Chesapeake Bay environment since colonial times, when the raw-sewage contamination of bay waters resulted in high mortality rates for Tidewater residents. Today's threats come principally from agricultural runoff and urban expansion around DC and Baltimore. Oysters, crabs, and geese have been among the animal populations threatened by bay pollution, but things are now looking up. Returning to the bay area are osprey, eagles, and a near-extinct striped bass know locally as 'rock fish.' Oyster sloops have also recently expanded operations. Fortunately, the bay is defended by such strong advocates as Save the Bay and the Chesapeake Bay Foundation (headquartered on Kent Island, Maryland). As long as forces that preserve it can counteract the forces that threaten it, the Tidewater region will continue to thrive.

Similarly, the Delaware Bay was a mess 20 years ago, but a cleanup mandated by the Coastal Management Act has effectively returned it to a healthier state. Nevertheless, industry along the Christina River and the upper Delaware River – a mix of heavy industry and oil refineries – still threatens a serious environmental accident. Even a small spill from a cruising tanker could wipe out as many as 40,000 wading birds a day in the vast marshlands of the Delaware Bay.

Sprawling urban development encroaches on the Appalachian Mountains' wilderness, which most sadly limits the range of large highlands wildlife species. There's also ongoing debate about the Forest Service's willingness to cooperate with logging interests. Yet despite these threats, it's remarkable that the Appalachians still retain their wild nature in such close proximity to the most densely populated urban corridor of the US.

Several nuclear reactors operate in the region and maintain decent records of responsible operation.

Natural preserves and wilderness areas maintained by federal or state governments protect many fragile and ecologically unique areas, including wetlands, forests, mountains, the shoreline, and barrier islands. Public and private organizations, including conservationists and nature enthusiasts, advocate to protect natural areas, spearheading cleanup days and continually expanding environmental awareness.

FLORA

Blessed with an incredible variety of plant types, the area is most noted for its exceptional profusion of flowering varieties (more than a thousand), which created an Eden-like impression on early European visitors.

As the meeting place of northern and southern varieties, the southern Appalachian forest has more tree types than Europe (130 and 85, respectively), and the beauty of its colorful deciduous cycle (wildflowers in spring, bright foliage in fall) has few rivals in the world.

One notable variety that signals spring throughout the region is the dogwood – a small tree rarely taller than 30 feet that is recognizable by its delicate white or pink blossoms. Smaller white blossoms are found on such flowering shrubs as rhododendron, azalea, and mountain laurel, which reach tree-size heights in thick dells found throughout the mountains, surrounded by pine, poplar, wild cherry, and hemlock.

Hardwoods predominate in the Piedmont Plateau; red maple, black oak, and redbud can be found throughout the region. In Maryland, varieties such as ash, black locust, and American elm thin as you go south, while pine and cedar varieties increase. In

Virginia, you'll find sassafras, persimmon, redbud, tulip, and sweet gum trees as the forest makes a transition from the deciduous northern varieties to the southern conifers – commonly such pine varieties as Virginia pine and loblolly. Hemlock, borvitae, and hawthorn grow in the limestone valleys among groups of beautiful wildflowers.

Along the Coastal Plain, pines grow in abundance, and birches thrive near streams. In Virginia, you will also find alder, holly, wisteria, trumpet vine, myrtle, cranberry, wild yam, and wild rice. In the southwest, walnut, hickory and chestnut grow in groves. The Great Dismal Swamp, about 30 miles inland from the Atlantic at the North Carolina border, holds impressive stands of bald cypress in its moody landscapes, as well as black gum and sweet gum trees.

For information on the area's national parks, see the Activities chapter.

FAUNA

A remarkable diversity of fauna lives in the Capital Region, which is surprising considering the area's proximity to the large cities on the eastern seaboard. The Shenandoah Valley, for instance, has 1100 species.

When the Great Valley of Virginia was first settled by Europeans in the 1730s, herds of bison grazed along the Shenandoah River, but these have long since disappeared. Current large species of animals include the black bear *(Ursus americanus)* in the mountains and in the Great Dismal Swamp area, as well as Virginia white-tailed deer *(Odocoileus virginianus)*.

More common are the small mammals found in abundance throughout the region – opossum, raccoons, muskrats, gray squirrels, striped skunks, eastern cotton-tailed rabbits, and bats. You may also come across gray and red foxes or the more elusive wildcats. Beavers, otter, and mink are present but uncommon (there are only three active beaver dams in Shenandoah National Park).

The many wetland environments of the Coastal Plain harbor such amphibians as snapping turtles and many varieties of frogs, toads, and newts. Of course, the most feared inhabitant of the wetlands is an insect:

the mosquito. As for feared reptiles, poisonous copperheads are present but rarely encountered.

The Tidewater region of the Chesapeake and Delaware Bays is a primary winter haven for migratory waterfowl; Canada geese and snow geese arrive in the Tidewater each fall in numbers exceeding hundreds of thousands. Wading birds, such as egrets and many varieties of heron, are common species in the summer.

Ruffed grouse, wild turkeys, bobwhites (quail), ducks, and geese are among many game varieties present throughout the year. The many songbirds include the cardinal. Raptors (birds of prey) include owls, hawks, and the golden and American bald eagles.

Anglers find such freshwater fish as pike, catfish, bream, and carp, or such saltwater varieties as the rock fish (striped bass), menhaden, bluefish, weakfish, butterfish, herring, and shad. The Chesapeake Bay is rich in blue crabs, clams, and oysters.

See the Activities chapter for information about the region's excellent national parks.

Endangered Species

Rare and threatened plants and animals include the dwarf trillium, pirate bush, rockcress, the Virginia big-eared bat *(Corynorhinus townsendii virginianus)*, the northeastern beach tiger beetle, the grizzled skipper, the regal fritillary, the flypoison borer moth, and the Shenandoah salamander *(Plethodon shenandoah)*. The main culprits endangering these species? Sewage and agricultural runoff, among other pollutants.

GOVERNMENT & POLITICS

The USA has a federal system with a president and a bicameral Congress, consisting of the 100-member Senate and the 435-member House of Representatives. Each of the 50 states has two senators, as well as congressional representatives, the number of which is determined by the size of the state's population.

The president, whose term is four years, is chosen by individual electors of the Electoral College. Each state has a number of electors equal to its number of senators and

congressional representatives. A candidate receives all of a state's electoral votes if he or she wins a simple majority of the popular vote. An elector publicly pledges to vote for a certain candidate but is not legally bound to do so in most states. Over the years, the Electoral College has been the subject of controversy because it can potentially misrepresent the public's will. For example, Benjamin Harrison beat Grover Cleveland in the 1888 presidential election because he had the majority of electoral votes, but he did not have a majority popular vote. To be elected, the president must obtain a majority of 270 of the total 538 electoral votes. (The District of Columbia, which has no voting representatives in Congress, has three electoral votes.) If no candidate receives a majority of the electoral vote, the vote goes to the House of Representatives. The president may only serve two terms. The next presidential election is scheduled to occur in 2000. Washington, within the federal enclave of the District of Columbia, is the seat of the US government.

As for the states, a governor presides over state government, and a bicameral legislature consisting of a senate and a house delegation enacts laws.

ECONOMY

In spite of the economic stagnation or recession plaguing much of the world during the final years of the 20th century, the US has been able to buck the trend, producing steady growth, decreased unemployment, surpluses in the federal budget, and an annual inflation rate of about 2.5%. In addition, the US has

Democrats and Republicans do their dance.

produced the largest annual gross national product in the world ($7.61 trillion), and Americans now claim the highest per capita income ($28,600) of any national group. Meanwhile, the USA's national debt, created by a spate of overspending that began in the 1970s, stands at roughly $5.6 trillion and keeps growing, despite the recent annual budget surpluses. A trade deficit of $187 billion also remains a point of concern.

US citizens pay taxes on a sliding scale, with the poorest paying around 15% of personal earnings and the richest fifth paying around 40%. Average Americans can expect to pay out 20% of their earnings.

Although TV programs and Hollywood movies foster an impression that Americans are flashy and wealthy, the US is as diverse in its economic circumstances as it is in its cultures. Whole regions of the USA are wealthier than others, and within a city, the standard of living can vary considerably from neighborhood to neighborhood. The poorest 20% of the population receives only 4.4% of the national income distribution, while the top 5% receives 17.6%. In the Capital Region, some of the most disadvantaged communities are in the inner city of the nation's capital itself; the rest of the region has its pockets of poverty but is on the whole one of the most developed and economically stable regions in the nation.

During colonial times, the economic mainstay of the region was tobacco. Since the 18th century, the region has diversified its agricultural produce, and today, important cash crops include corn, apples, dairy products, poultry, livestock, peanuts, and Virginia ham. Within the urban corridor of the region, high-tech industries predominate; Maryland is the home of an enormous electronics industry, and Delaware is the base for the giant chemical producer DuPont. The military, as well as federal and state governments, is among the largest employers.

POPULATION & PEOPLE

The greatest proportion of the region's population resides in an urban corridor stretching along the Piedmont – a portion of the larger urban crescent of development concentrated along the mid-to-northern part of the eastern seaboard. In these areas, both in the suburbs and the cities, you will find a wide mix of people, most particularly in the nation's cosmopolitan capital, with its many international influences. This ethnic diversity decreases considerably outside these areas.

As a whole, the region is more than two-thirds white and slightly less than one-third African American, with other races accounting for much smaller proportions (figures vary drastically from place to place; DC, for example, is more than two-thirds African American). The same racial/class dynamics at work in the nation at large are also at work here, which is to say that centuries of oppression and discrimination against non-white people continue to take their toll. Fortunately, visitors intent on accessing the riches of diverse cultures can do so without too much trouble. For example, black-heritage tours provide an alternative perspective on mainstream history, as well as insights into the local culture. Ethnic festivals also offer a chance to explore multicultural activities – from Scottish Highland games to Greek dancing.

Remnants of the region's original Native American communities survive today. In Virginia, there are two state reservations: the Mattaponi and Pamunkey in King William County (see the Virginia's Chesapeake Bay chapter for more information on the Mattaponi); five other Native American communities do not have trust land – the Rappahannock, Upper Mattaponi, Chickahominy, and groups in Amherst County and Person County. In Maryland, a few thousand people on the lower Eastern Shore claim Pocomoke and Assateague ancestry; south of DC in Waldorf, the Piscataways gather for big powwows at Maryland's Indian Cultural Center each June and September. In Delaware, a small but strong community of Nanticokes lives along the Indian River (see the Delaware Seashore chapter).

EDUCATION

While the literacy rate of Americans stands at 97%, public elementary and secondary education in all but affluent suburban areas of the Capital Region is commonly underfunded (as is the case in many areas of the US). As parents increasingly opt out of the system in favor of private education, the gap between the haves and have-nots widens. With far fewer minority families able to choose private education, underfunded public education exacerbates de facto segregation between the races as well.

Beyond the many well-regarded private independent schools and traditional parochial schools in the region, Virginia in particular has lately seen conservative Christian groups funding a constellation of private academies. These schools are often criticized for their lack of tolerance and diversity.

Students who flourish despite these pitfalls face better options in the region's higher-education system. Many public and private colleges and universities thrive in the region. Affirmative action (a policy mandating systematic approaches for achieving a diverse student body and faculty) is hotly debated on many campuses.

Among the best known schools in Virginia are the College of William and Mary in Williamsburg (the second-oldest college in the nation, founded in 1693) and the University of Virginia in Charlottesville (Thomas Jefferson's model 'academical village,' founded in 1819). The state's largest academic institution is Virginia Tech in Blacksburg. Dating to before the emancipation of the slaves, Hampton Institute (in Hampton) is a preeminent black college that counts Booker T Washington among its graduates.

In Maryland, Annapolis is the home of not only the US Naval Academy but also St John's College, known for its 'Great Books' curriculum. Baltimore is the site of the prestigious Johns Hopkins University, and the University of Maryland is located outside of DC in College Park. In Delaware, the mammoth state-run University of Delaware is located in Newark.

Of the many colleges and universities located in the District of Columbia, among the most distinguished are Georgetown University (the first Roman Catholic university in the nation), American University, George Washington University, Catholic University, historic Howard University (largely African American), and Gallaudet College (the world's only liberal-arts school for the deaf).

SOCIETY & CONDUCT

The USA is not a social minefield, but everyone is expected to be polite and considerate and to show respect for the country and its symbols.

The USA is a very well-ordered society, and generally speaking, people stand in line, obey the rules, and follow the instructions. You should be punctual for any business or social occasion and come appropriately dressed – this could mean anything from a bikini to a dark suit, so ask first if you're not sure. People dress a little more formally in the East.

Both men and women shake hands, while family and friends embrace and kiss with varying degrees of visible affection. Straight men don't usually hug or kiss each other. Unless you're introduced to someone as a Mr, Ms, Miss, or Mrs, it's usually OK to use first names. Police and other officials are an exception – they call people 'sir' and 'ma'am' in a very assertive fashion and prefer to be addressed as 'officer.'

Self-confidence and a positive outlook are highly valued in the USA, so if someone asks 'How are you?,' the correct answer is 'Fine, thanks,' 'Very well,' or something even better. Polite understatement is rarely called for and may be interpreted as a regrettable lack of enthusiasm. 'Have a nice day' is a common way of saying good-bye and is seldom meant to be irritating. Another social nicety is saying, 'You're welcome' after being thanked – 'No problem' is a current alternative.

The level of overt patriotism in the USA is very high, and the culturally sensitive visitor will go along with it. The national flag, known as 'The Stars and Stripes' or 'Old Glory,' flies over every school, library, and government office, outside many businesses, and in front of many private houses. It's more than a revered symbol – Americans actually swear allegiance to the flag and are taught to never let it touch the ground.

Though the flag is often displayed on baseball caps and bumper stickers, it might be seen as disrespectful to have it on the seat of your pants.

The national anthem is played at public occasions. Everyone stands, and many people place a hand on their heart (many reveal a poor grasp of anatomy). Those in uniform salute, while civilian men remove their hats (this may be the only time some baseball caps are removed). Most people join in the singing. There's usually a lot of mumbling during the difficult, high-pitched fourth and fifth lines (about the rocket's red glare), but everyone comes in strongly for the rousing chorus about the land of the free and the home of the brave.

Underneath all this is a very real sense of national pride, and it's good to be aware of it when discussing political and social issues. Freedom of speech is one thing, but critical comments, especially from a foreigner, might be interpreted as a slight to national honor and can provoke a very negative reaction. Some other topics of conversation should also be avoided, at least until you're quite sure about the point of view of the person you're talking to. Gun control is a dodgy subject because some surprisingly mild-mannered people are gun owners and cherish their right to bear arms. Religion is risky because many people have fundamentalist beliefs and don't accept scientific notions of geological time or human evolution. The abortion/right-to-life issue is the touchiest subject of all.

Some other don'ts for foreign visitors include the following:

• Don't assume that Americans know anything about your country, but allow for the possibility that some will be extremely well informed.

• Don't expect Americans to answer for US foreign policy in your part of the world.

• Don't smoke anywhere unless it's clearly permitted.

• Don't discard any litter, except in a bin.

• Don't swim or sunbathe nude or (for women) topless – it's unacceptable at all but a few beaches and resorts.

• Don't forget to tip 15% to 20% in restaurants, bars, and taxis.

RELIGION

While today the region can claim a wide variety of religious communities (dominated by Protestant sects such as Baptists, United Methodists, Presbyterians, and Episcopalians), the religious origins of Virginia, Maryland, and Delaware are very distinct.

Virginia has strict Anglican roots – all nonconformists were strongly encouraged to take up residence elsewhere. Maryland was founded in part as a refuge for persecuted Roman Catholics from Europe. Delaware's earliest European settlers – Swedes and Finns – were Lutherans. Dutch immigrants were members of the Reformed Church. Later immigrants were mostly Quakers – a group whose views on ethnic pluralism, slavery, and liberty were a sharp contrast to the beliefs of many slaveholding Anglicans. Subsequent English immigrants belonged to the Church of England and later reorganized as Episcopals. Jesuits brought Roman Catholicism to Maryland and Virginia, but the real increase in Catholics (as well as Jews and Greek Orthodox) came with the 19th-century European immigrants.

Today, Protestants dominate in numbers in the region as a whole. Roman Catholics are the single largest religious denomination in Maryland, although Protestant sects together outnumber Roman Catholics. Amish and Mennonites call southern Maryland and Delaware home, and in Virginia there are Mennonite communities in Dayton (near Harrisonburg) and in Stuarts Draft (west of Charlottesville). The majority of Delaware's citizens identify themselves as Christian (85%); those who claim no religion account for 7.2%, and Jews make up 1.4%.

In general, people in this part of the country take their religion very seriously – Virginia is an intrinsic part of the conservative Southern 'Bible Belt' – and many attend church services (note business closures and 'blue laws' restricting alcohol sales on Sunday). Respectfully attending a local service offers insight into local culture and will usually gain visitors fast friends – and you may hear good gospel music besides. You'll want to dress well and check with an usher about participating in the communion ceremony (generally, this is OK at Protestant churches, but Catholics restrict the ritual to Catholics). Attend services at Washington, DC's National Cathedral for the most modern, diverse, and 'religiously correct' ceremony; the program walks visitors through the expected etiquette.

LANGUAGE

In the late 18th century, a Pennsylvanian offered this description of a gentleman from Maryland: 'He has the softest voice – never pronounces the R at all.' Distinctive regional dialects and speech patterns can be heard in great variety throughout the region. From the black dialect and bureaucratese heard in urban DC, to the gentrified drawl of Tidewater Virginia, to the faintly Elizabethan strains of Eastern Shore Maryland, to the Appalachian twang, the variations of English spoken within this compact geographical region are dramatic. Many locals can readily pinpoint a particular local accent down to a 50-mile radius. Yet few non-English-speaking minorities exist in the region beyond the rich diplomatic community and multicultural neighborhoods of DC.

Tricky pronunciation of place names may further confuse visitors – for example, Suffolk (**suf**-fik), Staunton (**stan**-ton), Chincoteague (**shin**-cuh-teeg), Baltimore (**balm**-er), and Tilghman (**till**-mun).

Facts for the Visitor

THE BEST & THE WORST
The following are some of the places, sights, and experiences that make the Capital Region so special – and some that make it not so special.

The Best
Washington, DC
- Galleries and museums such as the Smithsonian, with their unparalleled free access and some of the world's best art, science, historical, and cultural exhibits
- Memorials such as the larger-than-life Lincoln, the poignant Vietnam Memorial, and the changing of the guard at the Tomb of the Unknowns at Arlington National Cemetery
- The highly charged political atmosphere you can feel when you tour government buildings such as the Capitol and the White House, or while eating and drinking in the surrounding restaurants and bars

Virginia
- Colonial Virginia, with an astonishing variety of almost-sacred sites: Williamsburg, Jamestown, Yorktown, Berkeley Plantation on the James River, Mount Vernon near Alexandria, the George Washington birthplace on Northern Neck, and sublime Monticello (the zenith of Jefferson's achievements) near Charlottesville
- Civil War sites, including New Market in the Shenandoah Valley, Petersburg (both town and surrounds), Fredericksburg (the stone wall in town and Chatham House across the river), Sutherlin House (the last capitol of the Confederacy) in Danville, and the surrender site at Appomattox
- Shenandoah National Park, one of the most pristine places you could ever visit, and Skyline Drive, stretching 105 miles from Front Royal in the north to Waynesboro in the south, with vistas from the summits of the Blue Ridge Mountains

Maryland
- Annapolis, Maryland's capital, with its extensive collection of 18th-century buildings and its sailing scene, including the US Naval Academy and thousands of yachts, and Dock Square's collection of restaurants, bars, and musical entertainment

- Baltimore's Inner Harbor, an outstanding example of urban renaissance, with attractions such as the National Aquarium, museums, historic watercraft, food courts, shopping, and a waterfront promenade
- St Michaels on the Eastern Shore, with the Chesapeake Bay Maritime Museum exhibits, lectures, and collection of watercraft offering a vivid picture of the bay's maritime culture
- Assateague Island National Seashore – 37 miles of untouched coastal wilderness rife with snow geese and wild horses

Delaware
- Winterthur Museum, with 1000 acres of manicured fields and forest, a 100-room chateau, the world's best collection of American decorative arts, and grounds that make for great hiking and excellent picnicking
- Historic New Castle, with the look and feel of colonial America in a breathing, working village (not a living-history museum) that offers terrific restaurants, elegant B&Bs, and few tourists
- Lewes and Cape Henlopen, poised at the foot of giant sand dunes at the junction of Delaware Bay and the Atlantic Ocean – home to 300 years of maritime tradition, including whalers, fishermen, and Delaware Bay pilots

The Worst
Washington, DC
- Waiting in long lines (unless you travel during the winter off season) to see Washington, DC's most popular attractions – make the most of the advance-ticket option, bring a hat or an umbrella to shield yourself from the sun, and carry snacks and water
- The 'Mint,' alias of the Bureau of Engraving and Printing – it's just a big print shop

Virginia
- Virginia Beach, the state's biggest city, an agglomeration of high-rises along a beleaguered strand of coast, 'theme-park' mini-golf courses, paint-ball shooting galleries, amusement parlors, expensive souvenir shops, and tacky wax museums
- Theme parks, with their pastiche European villages and 'adrenaline rides' overshadowing places of historic interest such as Jamestown, Yorktown, Williamsburg, and Richmond

Maryland

- Waldorf, once a country town in rural southern Maryland, now 5 miles of malls, traffic lights, and gridlock on Route 301
- Kent Island, buried under a collection of outlet malls, roadhouses, and marinas, most adorned with images of blue crabs – a victim of the Annapolis Bay Bridge, which crosses the water to this rural Eastern Shore community

Delaware

- Traffic straight out of your nightmares on Route 13 between I-95 & the C&D Canal – lots of trucks, a fog of exhaust vapor, every fast-food chain known to humankind, and traffic lights every half-mile (take scenic Route 9 along Delaware Bay or the newly opened thruway, Route 1)

SUGGESTED ITINERARIES
One Week

You will need three days in DC even if you are a sprinter. Use your mornings for visiting the monuments and government buildings of your choice. You can catch the museums after lunch or get away from the crowds by taking a stroll on the Mall, around the Tidal Basin, or on the back streets of Capitol Hill. Don't miss the Smithsonian's various museums (especially the Air and Space Museum and the National Museum of American History), as well as the National Gallery of Art. Spend your evenings and nights sampling the restaurants and entertainment of Adams-Morgan, Dupont Circle, Georgetown, and Capital Hill.

On Day 4, take a day trip to Mount Vernon and neighboring Virginia plantations or head for Annapolis to take in the colonial architecture, yachting scene, and Naval Academy. To pursue an evening of shopping, dining, and clubbing in a colonial atmosphere, take the Metro across the Potomac River from DC to Old Town Alexandria in Virginia.

On Days 5, 6, and 7, spend two days traveling south through Richmond, Jamestown, and Williamsburg for a glimpse of colonial and Civil War Virginia. Try to visit one of the James River plantations.

If you are already in Annapolis, cross the bridge over Chesapeake Bay and head to the Eastern Shore to explore colonial towns such as St Michaels, Easton, or Chestertown. Don't miss the watermen's villages and wildlife refuges.

For the ambiance of rural fields, upland forests, rushing water, and the Civil War, head north to Antietam National Battlefield and Harpers Ferry. Take time to hike a piece of the C&O Canal towpath or the Appalachian Trail.

Two Weeks

Fourteen days is a much more reasonable length of time to visit if you really want to see the Capital Region, because now you can slow down and spend time smelling the black-eyed susans (a local flower). On this itinerary, you can afford to spend five days in DC and, with this extra time, allow yourself the leisure of a long stroll in Rock Creek Park, a visit to the National Zoo, and the experience of a professional sporting event or concert.

On Days 6, 7, and 8, head east for a day in Annapolis, move on to explore the Eastern Shore of the Chesapeake, and then continue over to the ocean side of the Delmarva Peninsula. Here you can spend a night at the beach at Ocean City (if you want a major-league resort scene) or move farther south to spend a day with the wild horses and waterfowl on pristine Assateague Island or the fishing village of Chincoteague, Virginia.

On Days 9, 10, and 11, continue south on Virginia's eastern shore and cross the mouth of the Chesapeake using the bridge-tunnel. From here, you can work your way back north to DC with visits to the region that cradled both the birth of the nation and many battles of the Civil War. Jamestown, Williamsburg, the James River plantations, and Richmond are all must-sees, and you have time to detour into the western hills to see Thomas Jefferson's Monticello and the University of Virginia at Charlottesville.

On Days 13 and 14, before you end your stay, choose an overnight excursion northwest to either Antietam National Battlefield or Harpers Ferry (see One Week), or head northeast to tour the chateaux of Delaware's Brandywine Valley before stopping for a night to immerse yourself in the shopping, restaurants, and nightlife of Baltimore's Inner Harbor and historic Fells Point. Don't miss the National Aquarium at Baltimore Harbor and a ride aboard a passenger schooner or a water taxi.

One Month

In Week 1, take your time getting to know DC. With a week in the city, you can not only see a lot of the monuments, museums, historic sites, and entertainment districts, but you can also kick back in the cafes of Dupont Circle, Adams-Morgan, and Georgetown and get to know (and act like) the locals.

In Week 2, head off to Annapolis and Maryland's Eastern Shore, visit Assateague Island, and then head north through Ocean City to discover the relatively quiet Delaware beach resorts such as Rehoboth and Lewes, with their collection of gourmet restaurants and large gay community. Linger at the beach, especially Delaware's seaside state parks. Eventually, work your way up the rural coast of Delaware Bay to the historic enclaves of Dover, Odessa, and New Castle, with their restored Federal-period houses. Then it's on to the chateaux of the Brandywine Valley and a two-day stop in Baltimore so you can explore its historic sites, including Fort McHenry and the B&O Railroad Museum, as well as the Inner Harbor area and two exceptional art museums.

In Week 3, you can wallow in Virginia hospitality, exploring Richmond and lingering in the Williamsburg area. Then head for Appomattox (where Robert E Lee surrendered and ended the Civil War) and the foothills and mountains beyond. Once you reach Roanoke, you can take two of the most spectacular mountain drives in the USA by following the Blue Ridge Parkway and Skyline Drive north, paralleling the Shenandoah Valley. Eventually, you will arrive at Harpers Ferry and Antietam National Battlefield, having passed through a host of villages where the Civil War seems like only yesterday.

Week 4 is a week to pack with wilderness adventures. Western Maryland is home to the rugged Allegheny Mountains and almost virgin territory for the traveler. Come in warm weather for whitewater rafting, trekking on the Appalachian Trail, exploring the backcountry of immense state forests, canoeing the Potomac River, or hiking the 185-mile towpath of the C&O Canal, once the 'gateway to the West.' In winter, the downhill and Nordic ski areas open in this snowbelt. You will find all of these adventures outlined in this book. Have at 'em!

PLANNING

As with many destinations, a trip to the Capital Region is best made with some advance planning, especially if you are heading for popular resorts or cities during the high season. You'll want to be aware of the climate, as well as local holidays and events that can enhance your trip if you plan to participate or that may impede a trip designed around a different purpose. And of course, extensive backcountry travel or backpacking always requires advance preparation.

When to Go

Spring and fall are the most temperate and scenic seasons regionwide, though many visitors are naturally drawn to beaches in the summer and mountain ski areas in winter (the mountains are also a cool destination in summer). The tourist season in Washington, DC, runs from late March (early-spring cherry blossoms kick off the high season) through July, and it's wise to purchase advance tickets to popular attractions whenever possible to avoid long lines. DC business travel slumps dramatically during the summer, and vacationers can find good lodging bargains if they can tolerate the heat. Weekend rates for city accommodations are generally lower across the region. Of course, the opposite is true at beach and mountain resort areas.

What Kind of Trip

This guide is largely intended for travelers planning their own trips. Those looking to participate in outdoor activities such as hiking, biking, and backpacking should refer to the Activities chapter, where we list relevant organizations and tour groups.

Visitors interested in group tours of the Shenandoah Valley, colonial Williamsburg, and other historic areas should contact Wayfaring Travelers (☎ 410-666-7456), 27 Sunnyview Drive, Phoenix, MD 21131, which organizes two-week trips.

Maps

Maps of excellent quality are available throughout the USA. Depending on your interests and the way in which you intend to travel, there are many sources. Two good map companies to contact for all kinds of maps are MapLink (☎ 805-692-6777, fax 805-692-6787, ✉ custserv@maplink.com), 30 S La Patera Lane #5, Santa Barbara, CA 93117, and Omni Resources (☎ 336-227-8300, 800-742-2677, ✉ custserv@omnimap .com), 1004 South Mebane St, PO Box 2096, Burlington, NC 27216.

Lonely Planet's Washington, DC City Map (full-color, fold-out design) is a handy resource for navigating the capital city.

Highway Maps The American Automobile Association (AAA) issues the most comprehensive and dependable highway maps, which are free with AAA membership (see Useful Organizations, later in the chapter) and available for a price to nonmembers. These range from national, regional, and state maps to very detailed maps of cities, counties, and even relatively small towns.

Topographic Maps You can purchase topographic maps from the US Geological Survey (USGS; ☎ 703-648-4090), Map & Book Sales, Denver, CO 80225. USGS is an agency of the federal Department of the Interior and publishes detailed topographic maps of the entire country at different scales up to 1:250,000. Maps at 1:62,500, or approximately 1 inch:1 mile, are ideal for backcountry hiking and backpacking. Fortunately, some private cartographers are producing updated versions of old USGS maps at 1:62,500, which give hikers a much clearer notion of mountain terrain. Many book-

stores and outdoor equipment specialists carry a wide selection of topographic maps.

Atlases The DeLorme Mapping series of atlases and gazetteers includes state atlases containing detailed topographic and highway maps at a scale of 1:250,000. Readily available in good bookstores for about $20 each, these are especially useful for car and mountain-bike travel off the main highways.

What to Bring

When packing, bear in mind that this is a fairly conservative part of the country. Casual dress is fine for beach areas, but you'll stand out less and earn the gratitude of locals if you trade in shorts and T-shirts for something slightly less casual. City folk wear jackets and closed shoes even in the sweltering summer, and no matter where you are, exceptionally revealing or sloppy dress (sleeveless, backless, too short or strappy, patched) will attract negative attention from local citizens. It may be wise to pack a dressy outfit for any unexpected business, church, or formal social encounter. You might also make use of a rain jacket or parka, depending on the season.

For health precaution items, see Health, later in the chapter. For camping items, see the Activities chapter.

TOURIST OFFICES
Local Tourist Offices

Tourist promotion and information is handled by states, cities, and local areas, not by the federal government. Every state has a tourist office, which will send out promotional materials on request, mostly aimed at domestic tourists and holiday vacationers. In this book, the address of each state's main tourist office is given in the introductory text for that state. Many cities also send out information and promotional material, and most have websites.

Tourist information services in individual towns and cities vary in style and usefulness. A lot depends on the staff you talk to – the enthusiastic amateurs in small offices are often much more helpful than tourism professionals giving the official line. Tourist offices can tell you about any special events in town and what attractions are operating. Look for discount coupons to local attractions.

Many cities have an official Convention & Visitors Bureau (CVB) that provides tourist information services, but its main function is to promote the city and attract the conference trade. Most aren't really set up to assist independent travelers, but some are very helpful. CVBs distribute the usual tourist literature but don't usually have accommodations information or make referrals. Generally, they keep standard business hours and close on weekends.

Some state governments maintain 'welcome centers,' found on the main highways as you enter a state or approach a city. They are usually open long hours and on weekends, especially during holidays. Pick up the cheap-looking booklet with discount coupons for motels on the main highways.

For information about federally managed sites and lands as well as helpful federal offices, call the Federal Information Center (☎ 800-688-9889, ☎ 703-440-1713 in Virginia).

Tourist Offices Abroad

The USA currently has no government-affiliated tourist offices in other countries. Contact a travel agent for tourist information or hop online to review the extensive websites for Washington, DC, and the states of the Capital Region (see Internet Resources, later in the chapter).

VISAS & DOCUMENTS

All foreign visitors (other than Canadians) must bring their passports. Canadians must have proof of citizenship, such as a citizenship card with photo identification, or a passport.

If you have a non-US passport, you must complete an Arrival/Departure Record (form I-94) before you reach the immigration desk. It's usually handed out on the plane along with the customs declaration. It's a rather badly designed form, and lots of people take more than one attempt to get it right. Answers should be written *below* the questions. For question 12, 'Address While in the United States,' give the address where you will spend the first night. Complete the

Departure Record (the lower part of the form), giving exactly the same answers for questions 14 to 17 as for questions 1 to 4.

The INS officers have absolute authority to refuse admission to the USA or to impose conditions on admission. Their main concern is to exclude those who are likely to work illegally or overstay, so visitors will be asked about their plans and perhaps about whether they have sufficient funds for their stay. It's a good idea to have an itinerary that will account for the period of time you want to stay, as well as proof that you have $300 or $400 for each week of your intended stay. An onward or return ticket helps. These days, a few major credit cards will go a long way toward establishing 'sufficient funds.' Don't make too much of having friends, relatives, or business contacts in the USA – the INS official may decide that this will make you more likely to overstay.

Passport

Your passport should be valid for at least six months longer than your intended stay in the USA, and you'll need to submit a recent photo (37x37mm) with the application (plus a fee of about US$35). Documents of financial stability, a return or onward ticket and/or endorsement by a US resident are sometimes required, particularly for those from developing countries.

Visas

Apart from Canadians and those entering under the Visa Waiver Program (see below), foreign visitors need to obtain a visa from a US consulate or embassy. In most countries, the process can be done by mail or through a travel agent. The relevant authority is the US Immigration & Nationalization Service (INS), not noted for its easygoing attitude. For detailed information about visas, immigration, etc, check the US State Department Internet site at http://travel.state.gov/visa_services.html.

Visa applicants may be required to 'demonstrate binding obligations' that will ensure their return back home. Because of this requirement, those planning to travel through other countries before arriving in the USA are generally better off applying for a US visa while they are still in their home country, rather than while on the road.

The most common visa is a Nonimmigrant Visitors Visa, type B1 for business purposes, B2 for tourism or visiting friends and relatives. A visitor's visa is good for one or five years with multiple entries and specifically prohibits the visitor from taking paid employment in the USA. The validity period depends on what country you are from. The length of time you'll be allowed to stay in the USA is determined by the INS at the port of entry.

If you're coming to the USA to work or study, you will likely need a different type of visa, and the company or institution to which you are going should make the arrangements. Other categories of nonimmigrant visas include an F1 visa for students undertaking a recognized course; an H1, H2, or H3 visa for temporary employment; a J1 visa for exchange visitors in approved programs; a K1 visa for the fiancé or fiancée of an American citizen; and an L1 visa for intracompany transfers. Allow six months for processing the application.

Visa Waiver Program Under the Visa Waiver Program, citizens of certain countries may enter the USA without a US visa for stays of 90 days or less. Currently these countries are Andorra, Argentina, Australia, Austria, Belgium, Brunei, Denmark, Finland, France, Germany, Iceland, Ireland, Italy, Japan, Liechtenstein, Luxembourg, Monaco, the Netherlands, New Zealand, Norway, San Marino, Slovenia, Spain, Sweden, Switzerland, and the UK.

Under this program, you *must* have a roundtrip or onward ticket that is nonrefundable in the USA, and you may be required to show evidence of financial solvency. You will be asked many of the same questions as on the nonimmigrant visa application form, and the same 'grounds for exclusion' apply, except you will have no opportunity to appeal the grounds or apply for an exemption. If the INS doesn't admit you under the Visa Waiver Program, you will have to use your onward or return ticket on the next available flight.

Grounds for Exclusion & Deportation The visa application form asks, among other things, if you are a drug trafficker, whether you seek to enter the USA to engage in terrorist activities, or if you have ever participated in a genocide. If you admit to being a subversive, smuggler, prostitute, junkie, or ex-Nazi, you may be excluded. You can also be refused a visa or entry to the USA if you have a 'communicable disease of public health significance' or a criminal record, or if you've ever made a false statement in connection with a US visa application.

In many cases, the INS will grant an exemption ('a waiver of ineligibility') to a person who would normally be subject to exclusion, but this requires referral to a regional INS office and can take some time (allow at least two months). If you're tempted to conceal something, remember that the INS is strictest of all about false statements – they will often review favorably an applicant who admits to an old criminal charge or a communicable disease, but they're extremely harsh on anyone who has ever attempted to mislead them, even on minor points. After you're admitted to the USA, any evidence of a false statement to the INS is grounds for deportation.

Any prospective visitors to whom grounds of exclusion may apply should consider their options *before* applying for a visa. For immigration law information and referrals to immigration advocates, contact the National Immigration Project of the National Lawyers Guild (☎ 617-227-9727), 14 Beacon St, Suite 602, Boston, MA 02108.

The INS has a very broad definition of 'criminal record.' If you've ever been arrested or charged with an offense, you have a criminal record, even if you were acquitted or discharged without conviction. In these days of computer databases and high-security awareness, you should assume that US authorities can find out anything that may have generated an official record.

Visa Extensions & Re-Entry If you want, need, or hope to stay in the USA longer than the date stamped on your passport, go to the local INS office (call ☎ 800-755-0777,

HIV & Entering the USA

Like tuberculosis and the Ebola virus, HIV (human immunodeficiency virus) is regarded as a communicable disease and is grounds for exclusion from the USA. The INS doesn't test people for HIV, but if you answer yes to the question 'Have you ever been afflicted with a communicable disease of public health significance?' you will probably not be granted a visa unless you apply for an exemption to the general exclusion of HIV-positive visitors.

INS officials at the point of entry may question anyone about their health. They can exclude anyone whom they believe has a communicable disease, perhaps because they are carrying medical documents, prescriptions, or AIDS/HIV medicine. Being gay is not grounds for exclusion. Being an IV drug user is. Visitors may be deported if the INS finds they have HIV but did not declare it. For more information, contact the Immigrant HIV Assistance Project, Bar Association of San Francisco (☎ 415-267-0795), 685 Market St, Suite 700, San Francisco, CA 94105.

or look in the local white pages under US Government) to apply for an extension *before* the stamped date. Calling any time after that will usually lead to an unamusing conversation with an INS official, who will assume you want to work illegally. If you find yourself in that situation, it's a good idea to bring a US citizen with you to vouch for your character. It's also a good idea to have some verification that you have enough money to support yourself.

It's easy to make trips across the border to Canada or Mexico, but upon return to the USA, non-Americans can be subject to the full immigration process. Always take your passport when you cross the border. If your immigration card still has plenty of time on it, you will probably be able to re-enter with the same one, but if it has nearly expired, you will have to apply for a new card, and border control may want to see your onward air ticket, sufficient funds, and so on.

Citizens of most Western countries won't need a visa for Canada, so it's no problem to cross to the Canadian side of Niagara Falls, detour up to Quebec, or pass through on the way to Alaska. Foreigners in Canada who are crossing into the USA are often hit with a US$6 entry fee. Travelers entering the USA by bus from Canada can be closely scrutinized – a roundtrip ticket that takes you back to Canada will make the INS feel less suspicious.

Travel Insurance

No matter how you're traveling, take out travel insurance that covers you not only for medical expenses and luggage theft or loss but also for unavoidable cancellation or delays in your travel arrangements. In addition, everyone should be covered for worst-case scenarios, such as an accident that requires hospital treatment and a flight home. Coverage varies from policy to policy, so ask both your insurer and your ticket-issuing agency to explain the finer points. STA Travel offers a variety of travel-insurance options at reasonable prices. Keep a photocopy of your ticket separate from the original.

Buy travel insurance as early as possible. If you buy it the week before you fly, you may find, for instance, that you're not covered for delays to your flight caused by strikes or other industrial action that may have been in force before you took out the insurance.

If you plan to travel for a long time, the insurance may seem very expensive – but if you can't afford it, you certainly won't be able to afford a medical emergency in the USA.

Driver's License & Permits

An International Driving Permit (IDP) is a useful accessory for foreign visitors in the USA. Although your foreign driver's license *is* valid in the USA and the major car-rental companies are used to seeing foreign licenses, local traffic police are more likely to accept an IDP as valid identification than an unfamiliar document from another country. Your national automobile association can provide one for a small fee (usually valid for one year). Note that an IDP is not a license but rather an official translation of yours (you still need to carry your license).

Hostel Card

Most hostels in the USA are members of Hostelling International/American Youth Hostels (HI/AYH), which is affiliated with the International Youth Hostel Federation (IYHF). You can purchase membership on the spot when checking in, although it's a good idea to purchase it before you leave home. Most hostels allow nonmembers to stay but charge them a few dollars more.

Student & Youth Cards

If you're a student, get an international student identification card (ISIC) or bring along a school or university ID (not as good) to take advantage of student discounts. You can get an ISIC from Council Travel offices around the world with proof of enrollment. The ISIC can get you substantial discounts at museums and tourist attractions and on some airfares.

Seniors' Cards

All people over the age of 65 get discounts throughout the USA. All you need is ID with proof of age in case you are carded. There are organizations such as AARP (see Senior Travelers, later in the chapter) that offer membership cards, often good for further discounts, to Americans and citizens of other countries.

Automobile Association Cards

If you plan on doing a lot of driving in the USA, it would be beneficial to join your national automobile association, or you can join the American Automobile Association (AAA) in the USA. See Useful Organizations, later in the chapter.

Photocopies

All important documents (your passport data page and visa page, credit cards, travel insurance policy, air/bus/train tickets, driver's license, etc) should be photocopied before you leave home. Leave one copy with someone at home and keep another with you, separate from the originals.

EMBASSIES & CONSULATES

US diplomatic offices abroad include the following:

Australia
(☎ 2-6270-5000), 21 Moonah Place, Yarralumla ACT 2600
(☎ 2-9373-9200), Level 59 MLC Center, 19-29 Martin Place, Sydney NSW 2000
(☎ 3-9526-5900), 553 St Kilda Rd, Melbourne, Victoria

Canada
(☎ 613-238-5335), 100 Wellington St, Ottawa, Ontario K1P 5T1
(☎ 604-685-1930), 1095 W Pender St, Vancouver, BC V6E 2M6
(☎ 514-398-9695), 1155 rue St-Alexandre, Montreal, Quebec

France
(☎ 01 42 96 12 02), 2 rue St Florentin, 75001 Paris

Germany
(☎ 228-33-91), Deichmanns Aue 29, 53179 Bonn

Ireland
(☎ 1-687-122), 42 Elgin Rd, Ballsbridge, Dublin

Israel
(☎ 3-517-4338), 71 Hayarkon St, Tel Aviv

Japan
(☎ 3-224-5000), 1-10-5 Akasaka Chome, Minato-ku, Tokyo

Netherlands
(☎ 70-310-9209), Lange Voorhout 102, 2514 EJ The Hague
(☎ 20 310-9209), Museumplein 19, 1071 DJ Amsterdam

New Zealand
(☎ 4-722-068), 29 Fitzherbert Terrace, Thorndon, Wellington

UK
(☎ 020-7499-9000), 5 Upper Grosvenor St, London W1
(☎ 31-556-8315), 3 Regent Terrace, Edinburgh EH7 5BW
(☎ 232-328-239), Queens House, Belfast BT1 6EQ

Your Own Embassy

As a tourist, it's important to realize what your own embassy – the embassy of the country of which you are a citizen – can and can't do. Generally speaking, your embassy won't be much help in emergencies if the trouble you're in is remotely your own fault.

Remember that you are bound by the laws of the country you are in. Your embassy will not be sympathetic if you end up in jail after committing a crime locally, even if such actions are legal in your own country.

In genuine emergencies, you might get some assistance, but only if other channels have been exhausted. For example, if you need to get home urgently, a free ticket home is exceedingly unlikely – the embassy would expect you to have insurance. If you have all your money and documents stolen, your embassy might assist in getting a new passport, but a loan for onward travel is out of the question.

Embassies & Consulates in the USA

Just about every country in the world has an embassy in Washington, DC (call ☎ 202-555-1212 for embassy phone numbers). Many countries also have consulates in other large cities – look under Consulates in the yellow pages. Most countries also have a national delegation that represents the country's interest at the United Nations in New York City.

Here is a list of some of the most-visited embassies and consulates in DC (visa services are generally available on weekdays during hours listed):

Australia (☎ 202-797-3000)
1601 Massachusetts Ave NW, 20036
open 8:30 am to 12:30 pm
Ⓜ Dupont Circle

Canada (☎ 202-682-1740)
501 Pennsylvania Ave NW, 20001
open 9 am to noon
Ⓜ National Archives/Navy Memorial

France (☎ 202-944-6000)
4101 Reservoir Rd NW, 20007
open 8:45 am to 12:15 pm
Ⓜ Dupont Circle

Germany (☎ 202-298-4000)
4645 Reservoir Rd NW, 20007
open 8:30 to 11:30 am
Ⓜ Foggy Bottom or Dupont Circle

Ireland (☎ 202-462-3939)
2234 Massachusetts Ave NW, 20008
open 9 am to 1 pm
Ⓜ Dupont Circle

Israel (☎ 202-364-5500)
3514 International Dr NW, 20008
open 9:30 am to 1:30 pm
Ⓜ Van Ness/UDC

Japan (☎ 202-238-6700)
2520 Massachusetts Ave NW, 20008
open 10 am to noon and 2 to 4 pm
Ⓜ Dupont Circle

Mexico (☎ 202-736-1002)
2827 16th St NW, 20006
open 8:30 am to 1 pm
Ⓜ Dupont Circle

The Netherlands (☎ 202-244-5300)
4200 Linnean Ave NW, 20008
open 10 am to noon
Ⓜ Van Ness/UDC

New Zealand (☎ 202-328-4800)
37 Observatory Circle NW, 20008
open 8:30 am to 5 pm
Ⓜ Dupont Circle

UK (☎ 202-588-6500)
3100 Massachusetts Ave NW, 20008
open 8 to 11:30 am
Ⓜ Dupont Circle

CUSTOMS

US Customs allows each person over the age of 21 to bring 1 liter of liquor and 200 cigarettes duty free into the USA. US citizens are allowed to import $400 worth of gifts from abroad duty-free, and non-US citizens are allowed to bring in $100 worth.

US law permits you to bring in, or take out, as much as $10,000 in US or foreign currency, traveler's checks, or letters of credit without formality. Larger amounts of any or all of the above must be declared to customs (there are no limits).

MONEY
Currency

The US dollar is divided into 100 cents (¢). Coins come in denominations of 1¢ (penny), 5¢ (nickel), 10¢ (dime), 25¢ (quarter), and 50¢ (the rare half-dollar). Quarters are the most commonly used coins for airport luggage-cart machines and for vending machines and parking meters, so it's handy to have a stash of them (self-service laundries have change machines that dispense quarters).

Notes, commonly called bills, come in $1, $2, $5, $10, $20, $50, and $100 denominations – $2 bills are rare but perfectly legal. All bills are the same size and color. There is also a $1 coin that the government has tried to bring into mass circulation; you may get some of these as change from ticket and stamp machines. Be aware that they look similar to quarters.

Exchange Rates

At press time, exchange rates were as follows:

country	unit		US dollars
Australia	A$1	=	$0.63
Canada	C$1	=	$0.69
European Union	€1	=	$0.99
France	FF1	=	$0.15
Germany	DM1	=	$0.50
Hong Kong	HK$1	=	$0.10
Japan	¥100	=	$0.91
New Zealand	NZ$1	=	$0.50
United Kingdom	UK£1	=	$1.61

Exchanging Money

Most banks will exchange cash or traveler's checks in major foreign currencies, though the process may take some time. Banks in outlying areas rarely exchange cash, so it's less of a hassle to exchange foreign currency in larger cities. Additionally, Thomas Cook, American Express, and exchange windows in airports offer exchange (although you'll get a better rate at a bank).

Cash Though carrying cash is more risky, it's still a good idea to travel with some for the convenience. Cash is useful to pay tips, and some smaller, more remote places may not accept credit cards or traveler's checks.

Traveler's Checks Traveler's checks offer the possibility of a refund in the event of theft or loss, and traveler's checks in US dollars are almost as convenient as cash. American Express and Thomas Cook are widely accepted and have efficient replacement policies.

Keep a record of the check numbers you purchased and of those you have used, and keep the record separate from the checks themselves. The numbers are necessary for obtaining a refund of lost checks.

Bring traveler's checks in US dollars, for these can be used at most restaurants, hotels, gas stations, and big stores as if they were cash; get them in $50 and $100 denominations. Traveler's checks in a foreign currency can only be changed at a bank or at one of the few exchange counters. This can be inconvenient; you may not get a good exchange rate, and you may have to pay an exchange fee. If you're reluctant to buy US-dollar traveler checks up front because you think your currency might soon appreciate against the dollar, it would be better to rely on credit cards and/or ATM cards.

ATMs Automated teller machines are available 24 hours a day at almost every bank, as well as at shopping centers, airports, grocery stores, and casinos. You can withdraw cash from an ATM using a credit card (such as Visa or MasterCard), which will usually incur a fee. Alternatively, most ATMs are linked with one or more of the main ATM networks (such as Plus, Cirrus, Exchange, or Accel), and you can use them to withdraw funds from an overseas bank account if you have a card affiliated with the appropriate network. This is usually cheaper than a credit card transaction. The exchange rate on ATM transactions is usually as good as you'll get.

Check with your bank or credit card company for exact information about using its cards at ATMs in the USA. If you will be relying on ATMs, bring more than one card and keep them separate. Remember your personal identification number (PIN) – don't write it on the card. Contact your bank if you lose your ATM card.

Credit & Debit Cards Major credit cards are accepted at hotels, restaurants, gas stations, shops, and car-rental agencies throughout the USA. It's almost impossible to rent a car or make phone reservations without one. Even if you prefer to rely on traveler's checks and ATMs, we highly recommended that you carry a credit card for emergencies, rentals, and reservations. If you're planning to rely primarily upon credit cards, bring more than one and include a Visa or MasterCard in your deck, as other cards aren't as widely accepted.

Places that accept Visa and MasterCard are also likely to accept debit cards. A debit card deducts payment directly from the user's bank account, and users are charged a small fee for the transaction. Check with your bank to confirm that your debit card will be accepted in the USA.

Carry copies of your credit card numbers separately from the cards. If you lose a credit card or it gets stolen, contact the company immediately. Following are toll-free numbers for the main credit card companies:

American Express	☎ 800-528-4800
Diners Club	☎ 800-234-6377
Discover	☎ 800-347-2683
MasterCard	☎ 800-826-2181
Visa	☎ 800-336-8472

International Transfers You can instruct your bank back home to send you a draft. Specify the city, bank, and branch to which you want the money directed, or ask your home bank to tell you where a suitable one is and make sure you get the details right. The procedure is easier if you've authorized someone back home to access your account.

Money sent by telegraphic transfer should reach you within a week; by mail, allow at least two weeks. When it arrives, it will most likely be converted into local currency – you can take it as cash or buy traveler's checks.

You can also transfer money by American Express, Thomas Cook, or Western Union, though the latter has fewer international offices. All these services are expensive.

Security

Usually, there's nothing to worry about, but if you're being cautious, don't carry more cash than you need for the day. Carry it in an inside pocket, a money belt, or your socks, rather than in an outside pocket or a handbag. It's a good idea to divide your money and credit cards and stash them in several places. Most hotels and hostels provide safekeeping, so you can leave your valuables with them. Hide, or don't wear, any expensive jewelry. Using a safety pin or key ring to hold the zipper tags of a daypack together can also help deter theft.

Costs

The cost of accommodations – whether in the city or out in the country – may vary by season and day of the week and will almost always be higher during special holiday or festival periods. At all but the ski areas, prices are generally lowest in winter. The cheapest motel rates are usually around $25 to $35. Rustic camping is inexpensive, at only about $5 per night, but only costlier formal sites (from $15 to $25) offer such amenities as hot showers.

Food prices may seem reasonable by European standards, but DC prices are higher than in most other American cities outside New York. A splurge at a first-rate restaurant in the Capital Region costs anywhere from $25 to $50 per person, but good restaurant meals can be found for $10 – half that at lunch. Purchase food at markets to get by even more cheaply.

Intracity public transportation is relatively inexpensive; buses and subways cost anywhere from 80¢ to $1.50, depending on distance and the system. Owning or renting a car is much less expensive than in other parts of the world. In some areas, a car is the only way to get around. Rentals are fairly inexpensive in large cities, and gasoline costs a fraction of what it does in Europe and most of the rest of the world. (For more information on purchasing and operating a car, see the Getting Around chapter.)

Tipping

Tipping is expected in restaurants and upscale hotels, and by taxi drivers, hairdressers, and baggage carriers. In restaurants, waitstaff are paid minimal wages and rely upon tips for their livelihood. Tip 15% unless the service is terrible (in which case a complaint to the manager is warranted) or up to 20% if the service is great. Never tip in fast-food, take-out, or buffet-style restaurants where you serve yourself.

Taxi drivers expect 10%, and hairdressers get 15% if their service is satisfactory. Baggage carriers (skycaps in airports, attendants in hotels) get $1 for one bag and 50¢ for each additional bag. In budget hotels (where there aren't attendants anyway), tips are not expected.

Taxes

Almost everything you pay for in the USA is taxed. Occasionally, the tax is included in the advertised price (eg, plane tickets, gas, drinks in a bar, and entrance tickets for museums or theaters). Restaurant meals and drinks, accommodations, and most other purchases are taxed, and this is added to the advertised cost. Unless otherwise stated, the prices given in this book don't reflect local taxes.

When inquiring about hotel or motel rates, be sure to ask whether taxes are included.

In Virginia, a 4.5% state sales tax is added to most purchases, and in some places 0.5% is added to this, bringing it up to 5%. In hotels, you are likely to pay an additional 5% hotel tax, meaning the total tax on a bill amounts to about 10%. Restaurant taxes are applied in some areas (fortunately not all), and meal and drink bills may reflect 8% to 10% tax.

In DC, the sales tax is 5.75%, the restaurant tax is 10% (as it is for rental cars and liquor), and the hotel tax is 14.5%. Maryland sales tax is 5%, and the room tax is 10%. Delaware has no sales tax, but room tax is 8%.

Special Deals

The USA is probably the most promotion-oriented society on earth. Though the bargaining common in many other countries is not generally accepted in the US, you can work angles to cut costs. For example, when you're staying at hotels in the off season, casually and respectfully mentioning a competitor's rate may prompt a manager to lower the quoted rate. Artisans may consider a negotiated price for large purchases. Discount coupons are widely available – check circulars in Sunday papers, at supermarkets, tourist offices, and chambers of commerce.

POST & COMMUNICATIONS
Postal Rates

Postage rates increase every few years. At the time of writing, rates for 1st-class mail within the USA are 33¢ for letters up to 1oz (22¢ for each additional ounce) and 20¢ for postcards.

International airmail rates (except to Canada and Mexico) are 60¢ for a half-ounce letter, $1 for a 1oz letter, and 40¢ for each additional half ounce. International postcard rates are 50¢. Letters to Canada cost 46¢ for a half-ounce letter, 52¢ for a 1oz letter, and 40¢ for a postcard. Letters to Mexico cost 40¢ for a half-ounce letter, 46¢ for a 1oz letter, and 35¢ for a postcard. Aerogrammes are 50¢.

The cost for parcels airmailed anywhere within the USA is $3.20 for 2lb or less, increasing per pound up to $6.50 for 5lb. For heavier items, rates differ according to the distance mailed. Books, periodicals, and computer disks can be sent by a cheaper 4th-class rate.

For 24-hour postal information, call ☎ 800-275-8777 or check www.usps.com. These services give zip (postal) codes for any given address, the rules about parcel sizes, and the location and phone number of any post office.

Sending Mail

If you have the correct postage, you can drop your mail into any blue mailbox. To buy stamps, weigh your mail, or send a package 1lb or heavier, go to a post office. There are branch post offices and post-office centers in many supermarkets and drugstores. For the address of the nearest, call ☎ 800-275-8777. Post offices in main towns are usually open 8 am to 5 pm weekdays and 8 am to 3 pm Saturday.

If you wish to send items that require packaging, consider using the services of local packaging stores such as Mail Boxes Etc. In addition to fax, mailbox, and shipping services, these stores pack items and also sell packaging materials. Check the yellow pages under Packaging Services.

Receiving Mail

General delivery mail (or poste restante) can be sent to you c/o General Delivery at any post office that has its own zip code. Mail is usually held for 10 days before it's returned to the sender; you might ask your correspondents to write 'Hold for Arrival' on their letters. You'll need picture identification to collect general delivery mail. In some big cities, general delivery mail is not held at the main post office but at a postal facility away from downtown.

Alternatively, have mail sent to the local representative of American Express or Thomas Cook, which provide mail services for their customers. Stores such as Mail Boxes Etc (see Sending Mail, above) also receive and hold mail for customers.

Telephone

The US phone system comprises numerous regional phone companies (many are Bell subsidiaries) plus competing long-distance carriers plus lots of smaller mobile-phone and pay-phone companies. Technically, the system is very efficient, but it's geared to the needs of local users, and for foreign visitors it's inconvenient and often expensive. Try to bring a telephone card from your home phone company – it may not be the cheapest call option, but it will probably offer better information and service than a US pay-phone company or a phone debit card.

Telephone Numbers & Area Codes If you're calling from abroad, the international country code for the USA is ☎ 1.

All phone numbers within the USA consist of a three-digit area code followed by a seven-digit local number. If you are calling a number within the same area code, just dial the seven-digit number. If you are calling long distance, dial ☎ 1 plus the area code plus the phone number.

Because of increasing demand for phone numbers, some cities and states are being subdivided into more telephone areas, and new codes are being added and changed in patches all over the country.

The 800 and 888 prefixes are for toll-free numbers. These calls are free, though sometimes the toll-free number is not available from the same locality or state or outside the state. Some can be used in Canada, while a few can be used in other foreign countries. To find an organization's 800 number, call ☎ 800-555-1212.

The 900 prefix is designated for calls for which the caller pays a premium rate – phone sex, horoscopes, jokes, etc.

This guide lists the local area code with every phone number. Here are the major codes in the region; if you need the code for another location, dial 0 for an operator:

Washington, DC	☎ 202
Virginia	
Arlington	☎ 703
Hampton and Richmond	☎ 804
Norfolk and Williamsburg	☎ 757
Roanoke	☎ 540
Maryland	
Annapolis	☎ 443
Baltimore	☎ 410
Bethesda	☎ 240
Western Maryland	☎ 301
Delaware	☎ 302

Area codes for places outside the region are listed in the front of telephone directories. That's where you'll find country codes as well.

Directory Assistance For local directory assistance, dial ☎ 411. For directory assistance outside your area code, dial ☎ 1 plus the three-digit area code of the place you want to call plus 555-1212 (this is charged as a long-distance call to that area). Area codes are listed in telephone directories, but make sure you're looking at a recent edition.

To find a number in another country, call the international operator at ☎ 00. Note that international directory assistance can be very expensive from a pay phone.

International Calls To make an international call direct, dial ☎ 011, then the country code (found in the front of most phone directories), followed by the area code and the phone number. You may need to wait as long as 45 seconds for the ringing to start. International rates vary depending on the time of day and the destination. Call the operator for rates. The first minute is always more expensive than those that follow.

Call Charges Most local calls can be made for free from a private domestic phone and for a flat fee from a pay phone. Calls made to numbers within the same area code but outside the local calling zone (typically about 15 miles) are charged by the minute. Long-distance charges vary depending on the destination and the telephone company you use – call the operator (☎ 0) for rate information. Don't ask the operator to put your call through, however, because operator-assisted calls are much more expensive than direct-dial calls.

Generally, nights (11 pm to 8 am), all day Saturday, and 8 am to 5 pm Sunday are the cheapest times to call (60% discount). Evening calls (5 to 11 pm, Sunday to Friday) are mid-priced (35% discount). Daytime calls (8 am to 5 pm, Monday to Friday) are full-price within the USA.

Many hotels (especially the more expensive ones) add a service charge of 50¢ to $1 for each local call made from a room phone, and they have hefty surcharges for long-distance calls. They even charge you for calling 800 numbers. It's cheaper to use a pay phone in the hotel lobby.

On the other hand, many cheaper hotels and motels avoid the hassle of billing for phone calls altogether – they offer free local calls, and any other calls must be collect or billed to a phone card.

On a pay phone, local calls usually cost 25¢ or 35¢. You can use nickels, dimes, or quarters, though phones don't give change. Local-call charges usually only apply to a very small area – if you try to call a number outside the local calling zone or with a different area code, a synthetic voice will tell you to insert more money for the first three minutes. Calling from pay phones can be very expensive. You can pump in coins, call collect, or, on modern phones, use a phone card or credit card.

Phone Cards Phone cards are now almost essential for travelers using the US phone system. There are two basic types. A phone credit card allows you to make calls that are billed to your home phone number. Some cards issued by foreign phone companies will work in the USA – inquire before you leave home. When using a phone credit card, be aware of people watching you, especially in public places such as airports and bus stations. Thieves

will memorize numbers and use them to make calls at your expense. Shield the telephone with your body when punching in your credit card number.

A phone debit card is a good alternative for travelers and widely available from vending machines in airports, bus stations, hotel lobbies, and other locations. You purchase the card with a specified value, for example $5, $10, $20, or $50 for 18, 38, 80, or 220 'units.' To call, you access the company through an 800 number and key in your personal identification number (PIN); a synthetic voice will tell you how many domestic or international minutes your card is good for. The cost of calls is immediately debited from the value of the card. A unit is good for a call of one minute within the USA, half a minute or less for overseas calls.

Rates vary among the debit cards, and the cheapest are generally competitive with rates charged by a US phone company on a domestic phone. Some phone debit cards allow you to add extra value by billing an additional amount to your regular credit card. If you use a phone debit card from a pay phone or a hotel, many systems will debit two units from your card for the initial connection. If you have several calls to make, use the card's follow-on option to save the connection fee and the hassle of repeating your PIN.

Lonely Planet's eKno Communication Card (see the insert at the back of this book) is aimed specifically at travelers and provides cheap international calls, a range of messaging services, free email, and travel information. For local calls, you're usually better off with a local card. You can join online at www.ekno.lonelyplanet.com or by phone from the USA by dialing ☎ 800-707-0031. Once you have joined, to use eKno from the USA, dial ☎ 800-706-1333. Check the eKno website for joining and access numbers from other countries as well as updates on budget local access numbers and new features.

Fax & Telegram

Fax machines are easy to find in the USA – at shipping companies such as Mail Boxes Etc, photocopy services such as Kinko's, and hotel business-service centers, but be prepared to pay high prices (more than $1 a page). Telegrams can be sent from Western Union (☎ 800-325-6000).

Email & Internet Access

If you want to surf the web or send the occasional email message, most public libraries have a computer with Internet access. Other options are an Internet cafe, a copy center (such as Kinko's, which charges about $10 per hour), or a hotel that caters to business travelers. Some hostels even offer Internet access to their guests. The cheapest way to have email access while traveling is to get a free web-based email account – from Hotmail (www.hotmail.com), Yahoo (www.yahoo.com), or Netscape (www.netscape.com), for example – that you can access from any online computer with a browser.

INTERNET RESOURCES

The World Wide Web is a rich resource for travelers. You can research your trip, hunt down bargain airfares, book hotels, check on weather conditions, or chat with locals and other travelers about the best places to visit (or avoid!).

There's no better place to start your web explorations than the Lonely Planet website (www.lonelyplanet.com). Here, you'll find succinct summaries on traveling to most places on earth, postcards from other travelers, and the Thorn Tree bulletin board, where you can ask questions before you go or dispense advice when you get back. You can also find travel news and updates to many of our most popular guidebooks, and the subWWWay section links you to the most useful travel resources elsewhere on the web.

Capital Region websites of various kinds number over 10,000. The following are a few sites that we have found useful.

Washington, DC

Try the Washington, DC Convention and Visitors Association (www.washington.org). This is the big enchilada for travelers interested in DC, with maps, photos, site lists, accommodation lists, restaurants, current events, and general information.

Virginia

Start with www.virginia.org – the official state site – which allows quick access into a host of related sites. Log on to www.state.va.us/~dcr/ for all the information you need on the state and national parks in Virginia. You can use this site in conjunction with www.nationalparks.org.

If you plan on visiting Williamsburg, check out www.colonialwilliamsburg.org, the online guide to the country's biggest historical theme park.

Maryland

The folks at Maryland's Office of Tourism Development have gone over the top, upgrading their site (www.mdisfun.org) in the last couple of years with photos, music, maps – everything for the traveler.

Delaware

The Delaware Tourism Office website (www.state.de.us) is still a little primitive in light of what you get on some state and city websites, but it does have useful maps, photos, attraction lists, and accommodations information.

BOOKS

Most books are published in different editions by different publishers in different countries. As a result, a book might be a hardcover rarity in one country while it's readily available in paperback in another. Fortunately, bookstores and libraries can search by title or author, so your local bookstore or library is the best place to find out about the availability of the following recommendations.

Lonely Planet

If you are planning to travel north of the Capital Region, check out Lonely Planet's *New York, New Jersey & Pennsylvania*. Pick up *USA* for a portrait of the entire country in a nutshell.

Guidebooks

The Smithsonian's Historic America series on Virginia and the Capital Region contains the most exhaustive architectural review of regional historic sites, along with luxurious color photographs. *Maryland: A Guide to the Old Line State* by the Federal Writer's Project (reissued in 1976) provides the most comprehensive guide to the state.

Virginia's Shenandoah Valley by Greg Mock is a word-and-photograph tour of the valley with a focus on history and attractions. *Blue Ridge Parkway: The Story Behind the Scenery* by Margaret Rose Rives tells you all you need to know about the history and construction of the parkway, along with tours you can take (it includes maps). Published by the US National Park Service, the *Guide to Shenandoah National Park and Skyline Drive* is known as the bible for those visiting this national park. It includes descriptions cross-referenced to milepost markers.

The Guide to Black Washington by Sandra Fitzpatrick provides comprehensive information about DC's African American heritage. Bookworms should look through *Literary Washington* by David Cutler.

History & Politics

The first American literature consisted of accounts of exploration and discovery in the New World. Captain John Smith's *The Generall Historie of Virginia, New-England, and the Summer Isles* (1624) displays the largeness of vision and vigorous style of Elizabethan writers. The works of William Byrd (1674–1744), a Virginia plantation owner, were among the first to exhibit an emerging provincialism. His diaries, published as *Secret Diary* and *Another Secret Diary* (in 1941 and 1942, respectively), have been compared to the works of the great English diarist Samuel Pepys.

Great pieces of political writing, remembered for their felicity rather than imaginative content, are Jefferson's *Declaration of Independence* (1776) and *Notes on the State of Virginia* (1787). Alexis de Toqueville's *Democracy in America* describes what a radical experiment in social and political systems the founding of the United States represented in its time.

Even today, *Colonial Virginia* (two volumes, 1960) remains one of the best accounts of the history of an American colony. *Patriotic Gore* by Edmund Wilson is an absorbing account and narrative of Civil War literature.

For more recent DC history, read Woodward and Bernstein's *All the President's Men*, which offers nitty-gritty details on the Nixon administration's Watergate scandal.

Fawn M Brodie's *Thomas Jefferson: An Intimate Portrait* shows a side of this great intellectual's private life. It includes some surprising discussions on his relationships with some of his slaves. For more in-depth coverage of this statesman, Dumas Malone's *Jefferson and His Times* (six volumes) is a monumental work by a Pulitzer Prize winner.

Douglas Southall Freeman's *George Washington* (seven volumes) and *Lee* (four volumes), both Pulitzer Prize winners, survey the lives of two of Virginia's most famous personages. (Both works have been abridged into more digestible single-volume histories.) The Lee biography is especially important, as Lee never penned his own memoirs, but it has come under considerable criticism in recent years.

The diaries of Mary Chesnut, gathered in the 400,000-word *Diary from Dixie* (1905), were considered one of the greatest personal eyewitness accounts of the war and life in the Confederacy until recently. Many historians now contend that much of it may have been 'remembered' and written during Reconstruction. Historian C Vann Woodward edited the diaries and published them as *Mary Chesnut's Civil War* in 1982, an effort that earned him a Pulitzer Prize. Despite the controversy, the end result is captivating.

Booker T Washington's autobiography, *Up from Slavery* (1903), focuses on the life of this great black educator who was born into slavery in Virginia and rose to become one of the first African American reformers.

The Life of John Marshall by Albert J Beveridge is a Pulitzer Prize–winning book that examines the life of the powerful Virginia politician who served as the nation's chief justice for 34 years.

General

A good natural history is Jane Scott's *Between Ocean & Bay: A Natural History of Delmarva*. Christopher P White's *Endangered and Threatened Wildlife of the Chesapeake Bay Region* deals more with the Maryland Eastern Shore but has some Delaware coverage.

Richard C Davids' *The Man Who Moved a Mountain* recounts the life and work of the Reverend Bob Childress and the people of Buffalo Mountain and other parishes in the Blue Ridge Mountains, where he served for many years.

For a look at the Maryland watermen and their quarry, read Randall Peffer's *Watermen* or William Warner's *Beautiful Swimmers*. Tom Horton's *Bay Country* is a readable reflection on the environmental issues challenging the Chesapeake and its people.

Read Gore Vidal's *Washington DC, Burr*, or *Lincoln* to put you in the mood for a DC visit. Elliott Roosevelt, FDR's son who died in 1990, wrote a series of murder mysteries in which First Lady Eleanor Roosevelt solves crimes committed inside the White House during the Great Depression.

Though a fictionalized account, William Styron's *The Confessions of Nat Turner* was a bestseller and won the Pulitzer Prize. The novel has been widely praised for its narrative construct (in which the white author puts himself in black Nat Turner's shoes) but criticized for its somewhat stilted view of the African American.

James Michener lived for years on Maryland's Eastern Shore, where he wrote the bestseller *Chesapeake*. Anne Tyler's popular novels, such as *The Accidental Tourist*, unfold the bittersweet world of contemporary Baltimore.

Delaware Discovered by Kevin Fleming (Portfolio, 1992) is a terrific coffee-table book of photographs capturing the First State and its residents in all their glory.

The latest book from longtime Chesapeake Bay author/photographer Robert De Gast is *Five Fair Rivers*, a tale of solo exploration on the bay's main tributaries by small sailboat.

FILMS & TV SHOWS

Renting a film at the video store or catching a few episodes of a popular TV series is often an entertaining way for travelers to build a private image bank to fuel their imaginations about a forthcoming trip. If you want to see vignettes of the Capital Region, Hollywood has a lot to offer. Here are some favorites.

Washington, DC

This is one town whose images – at least the monuments and buildings such as the Capitol and White House – are flashed around the globe constantly by the media.

Among the political thrillers, a few get our blood humming: *No Way Out* with Kevin Costner, *A Few Good Men* with Jack Nicholson and Tom Cruise, *In the Line of Fire* with Clint Eastwood, and *True Lies* with Arnold Schwarzenegger, which features a car chase through Georgetown.

Wag the Dog with Robert De Niro and Dustin Hoffman is the darkly comic tale of a President who creates an imaginary war to escape a sex scandal, a story that rings frighteningly true to life. Frank Capra's 1939 classic *Mr Smith Goes to Washington*, starring Jimmy Stewart, is still a powerful drama about an innocent senator who stands up against corrupt government.

Stanley Kubrick's *Dr Strangelove* is a painfully funny satire about the US government during the Cold War. Romantics enjoy Rob Reiner's *An America President*, a story about a widowed President (Michael Douglas) falling in love. Horror-film aficionados remember that *The Exorcist* took place in Georgetown.

Virginia

The Old Dominion has been all over the silver screen since 1937, when the Blue Ridge Mountains provided the setting for the classic film *Trail of the Lonesome Pine* with Henry Fonda. If period pieces are your thing, catch the Civil War–era film *Sommersby* with Jodie Foster and Richard Gere. Foster also came to Virginia with Anthony Hopkins to make *Silence of the Lambs* at Quantico.

For a video trip through the Blue Ridge and Shenandoah Mountains, you might ask your video store to order you *National Parks of the Appalachians*.

Maryland

Baltimore and its surroundings frequently appear in TV and film. For a suburban view of the city, check out *The Accidental Tourist* and *The Seduction of Joe Tynan*. Cult film guru John Waters has made all of his tacky masterpieces in and around Baltimore, using local talent such as the transvestite Divine in films including *Pink Flamingos* and *Cry Baby*. For a view of life in a small Eastern Shore town, you can watch the romantic comedy *Runaway Bride* with Julia Roberts and Richard Gere.

Delaware

The First State has rarely appeared in feature films, but Delaware locations have frequently doubled for other sites. For example, *Dead Poets Society*, starring Robin Williams, pretends to take place in New England but was actually shot in Delaware. The film shows Delaware's colonial and rural ambiance. St Andrews School in Middletown is the major location, but the crew shot the drama scenes in the Middletown Theater. Many of the exterior town scenes took place in New Castle, and Wilmington also provided a number of sets.

For some visual images of southern Delaware, take a look at *Violets Are Blue* with Sissy Spacek and Kevin Cline, which was filmed around Assawoman Bay and Fenwick Island.

NEWSPAPERS & MAGAZINES

The dominant regional news source, the *Washington Post*, is also one of the nation's most respected newspapers. In addition, the *Wall Street Journal*, *USA Today*, and the *New York Times* are readily available. Larger city newsstands sell some international newspapers, including the *International Herald Tribune*. See the regional chapters for information on local alternative and cultural presses.

RADIO & TV

All rental cars have radios, and travelers can choose among hundreds of stations. Most radio stations have a range of less than 100 miles, and in and near major cities, scores of stations crowd the airwaves with a wide variety of music and entertainment. In rural areas, be prepared for a predominance of country & western music, local news, and 'talk radio.' Public radio stations carrying news-oriented National Public Radio (NPR) can usually be found in the lower numbers of the radio band.

All the major TV networks have affiliated stations throughout the USA. These include ABC, CBS, NBC, FOX (all commercial stations), and PBS (noncommercial). Cable News Network (CNN), a cable channel, provides continuous news coverage. There are many other cable stations such as ESPN (sports), HBO (mainly movies), and the Weather Channel. Almost all hotel rooms have TVs (most with cable), although many B&Bs do not.

PHOTOGRAPHY & VIDEO

Museums and galleries may prohibit or restrict photography and videography – check their policies before shooting.

Film & Equipment

Print film is widely available at supermarkets and discount drugstores. Color print film has a greater latitude than color slide film; this means that print film can handle a wider range of light and shadow than slide film. However, slide film, particularly the slower speeds (under 100 ASA), has better resolution than print film. Like black-and-white film, slide film is rarely sold outside of major cities, and when available it's expensive.

Film can be damaged by excessive heat, so don't leave your camera and film in the car on a hot summer day and avoid placing your camera on the dashboard while driving.

It's worth carrying a spare battery for your camera to avoid disappointment when your camera dies in the middle of nowhere. If you're buying a new camera for your trip, do so several weeks before you leave and practice using it.

Drugstores are a good place to get your film processed cheaply. If you drop it off by noon, you can usually pick it up the next day. A roll of 100 ASA 35mm color film with 24 exposures will cost between $6 and $10 to be processed.

If you want your pictures right away, you can find one-hour processing services in the yellow pages under Photo Processing. The prices tend to creep up to the $11 scale, so be prepared to pay dearly. Many one-hour photo finishers operate in the larger cities, and a few can be found near tourist attractions.

Video Systems

The USA uses the National Television System Committee (NTSC) color TV standard, which is not compatible with other standards (PAL or SECAM) that are used in Africa, Europe, Asia, and Australia unless converted.

Airport Security

All passengers on flights must pass their luggage through X-ray machines. Today's technology doesn't jeopardize lower-speed film, so you shouldn't have to worry about cameras going through the machine. If you are carrying high-speed (1600 ASA and above) film, you may want to carry film and cameras with you and ask the X-ray inspector to check your film visually.

TIME

The Capital Region operates on Eastern Standard Time. When it is noon in DC, it is 5 pm in London, 3 am in Sydney, and 9 am in Los Angeles. Daylight Saving Time (one hour ahead of standard time) is in effect from 2 am on the first Sunday in April until 2 am on the last Sunday in October.

ELECTRICITY

In the USA, voltage is 110V, and the plugs have two (flat) or three (two flat, one round) pins. Plugs with three pins don't fit into a two-hole socket, but adapters are easy to buy at hardware and drugstores.

WEIGHTS & MEASURES

Distances are in feet, yards, and miles. Three feet equal 1 yard (.914m); 1760 yards, or 5280 feet, equal 1 mile. Dry weights are in ounces (oz), pounds (lb), and tons (16oz equal 1lb; 2000lb equal 1 ton), but liquid measures differ from dry measures. One pint equals 16 fluid oz; 2 pints equal 1 quart. The quart is a common measure for liquids such as milk, which is also sold in half gallons (2 quarts) and gallons (4 quarts). Gasoline is dispensed by the US gallon, which is about 20% less than the imperial gallon. Pints and quarts are also 20% less than imperial ones. There is a conversion chart on the inside back cover of this book.

LAUNDRY

You will find self-service, coin-operated laundry facilities in most towns of any size and in better campgrounds. Washing a load costs about $1 and drying it another $1. Some laundries have attendants who will wash, dry, and fold your clothes for you for an additional charge. To find a laundry, look under Laundries or Laundries – Self-Service in the yellow pages. Dry cleaners are also listed under Laundries or Cleaners.

TOILETS

Public toilets are normally free and found in shopping malls and parks. People often use the facilities in restaurants and gas stations when necessary. Toilets are commonly called bathrooms or restrooms in the USA. In cheaper restaurants, or ones near heavily trafficked areas, there may be a 'customers only' policy in place – a sign will usually say so at the front door. Fear not – even in these places, a polite request of 'May I use your bathroom, please' will more often than not lead to permission.

HEALTH

For most foreign visitors, no immunizations are required for entry, though cholera and yellow fever vaccinations may be required of travelers from areas with a history of those diseases. There are no unexpected health dangers in the Capital Region, excellent medical attention is readily available, and the only real health concern is that a collision with the medical system can cause severe injuries to your financial state.

Hospitals and medical centers, walk-in clinics, and referral services are easily found throughout the region. In a serious emergency, call ☎ 911 for an ambulance to take you to the nearest hospital's emergency room. But note that ER charges in the USA are incredibly expensive.

Make sure you're healthy before you start traveling. If you are embarking on a long trip, make sure your teeth are in good shape. If you wear glasses, take a spare pair and your prescription. You can get new spectacles made up quickly and competently for well under $100, depending on the prescription and frame you choose. If you require a particular medication, take an adequate supply and bring a prescription in case you lose your medication.

Health Insurance

A travel insurance policy to cover theft, lost tickets, and medical problems is a good idea, especially in the USA, where some hospitals will refuse care without evidence of insurance. There are a wide variety of policies, and your travel agent will have recommendations. International student travel policies handled by STA Travel and other student travel organizations are usually a good value. Some policies offer lower and higher medical expenses options, and the higher one is chiefly for countries like the USA, where there are extremely high medical costs. Check the fine print.

Some policies specifically exclude 'dangerous activities' such as scuba diving, motorcycling, and even trekking. If these activities are on your agenda, avoid this sort of policy.

You may prefer a policy that pays doctors or hospitals directly, rather than your having to pay first and claim later. If you have to claim later, keep *all* documentation. Some policies ask you to call back (reverse charges) to a center in your home country for an immediate assessment of your problem.

Check whether the policy covers ambulance fees or an emergency flight home. If you have to stretch out, you will need two seats and somebody has to pay for it!

Food & Water

Care in what you eat and drink is the most important health rule; stomach upsets are the most common travel health problem

(between 30% and 50% of travelers experience them during a two-week stay), but the majority of these upsets will be relatively minor. US standards of cleanliness in places serving food and drink are very high.

Bottled drinking water, both carbonated and noncarbonated, is widely available in the USA. Tap water is usually OK to drink; ask locally.

Everyday Health

Normal body temperature is 98.6°F or 37°C; more than 4°F or 2°C higher indicates a 'high' fever. The normal adult pulse rate is 60 to 80 beats per minute (children 80 to 100, babies 100 to 140). You should know how to take a temperature and a pulse rate.

Respiration (breathing) rate is also an indicator of illness. Count the number of breaths per minute: Between 12 and 20 is normal for adults and older children (up to 30 for younger children, 40 for babies). People with a high fever or serious respiratory illness (such as pneumonia) breathe more quickly than normal. More than 40 shallow breaths a minute usually indicates pneumonia.

Travel & Climate Problems

Motion Sickness Eating lightly before and during a trip will reduce the chances of motion sickness. If you are prone to motion sickness, try to find a place that minimizes disturbance – for example, near the wing on aircraft or near the center on buses. Fresh air usually helps. Commercial anti-motion-sickness preparations, which can cause drowsiness, have to be taken before the trip commences; once you feel sick, it's too late. Ginger, a natural preventative, is available in capsule form from health-food stores.

Jet Lag Jet lag occurs when a person travels by air across more than three time zones (each time zone usually represents a one-hour time difference). It occurs because many of the functions of the human body are regulated by internal 24-hour cycles called circadian rhythms. When we travel long distances rapidly, our bodies take time to adjust to the 'new time' of our

Medical Kit Check List

If you're going off the beaten path, it's wise to take a small, straightforward medical kit. This should include the following:

❑ **Aspirin or paracetamol** (acetaminophen in the USA) – for pain or fever

❑ **Antihistamine** (such as Benadryl) – to treat allergies (eg, hay fever), to ease the itch from insect bites or stings, and to prevent motion sickness

❑ **Cold and flu tablets, throat lozenges, and a nasal decongestant**

❑ **Multivitamins** – consider for long trips, when dietary vitamin intake may be inadequate

❑ **Antibiotics** – consider including these if you're traveling well off the beaten track; see your doctor, as antibiotics must be prescribed, and carry the prescription with you

❑ **Loperamide or diphenoxylate** – 'blockers' for diarrhea

❑ **Prochlorperazine or metaclopramide** – for nausea and vomiting

❑ **Rehydration mixture** – to prevent dehydration, which may occur during bouts of diarrhea, for example; it's particularly important when traveling with children

❑ **Insect repellent, sunscreen, lip balm, and eye drops**

❑ **Calamine lotion, sting relief spray, or aloe vera** – to ease irritation from sunburn and insect bites or stings

❑ **Antifungal cream or powder** – for fungal skin infections and thrush

❑ **Antiseptic** (such as povidone-iodine) – for cuts and grazes

❑ **Bandages, Band-Aids (plasters), and other wound dressings**

❑ **Water purification tablets or iodine**

❑ **Scissors, tweezers, and a thermometer** – note that mercury thermometers are prohibited by airlines

destination, and we may experience fatigue, disorientation, insomnia, anxiety, impaired concentration, and loss of appetite. These effects will usually be gone within three days of arrival, but there are ways of minimizing the impact of jet lag:

• Rest for a couple of days prior to departure; try to avoid late nights and last-minute dashes for traveler's checks or your passport.

• Try to select flight schedules that minimize sleep deprivation; arriving in the early evening means you can go to sleep soon after you arrive. For very long flights, try to organize a stopover.

• Avoid excessive eating (which bloats the stomach) and alcohol (which causes dehydration) during the flight. Instead, drink plenty of noncarbonated, nonalcoholic drinks such as fruit juice or water.

• Make yourself comfortable by wearing loose-fitting clothes and perhaps bringing an eye mask and earplugs to help you sleep.

Sunburn Most doctors recommend sunscreen with a high protection factor (SPF) for easily burned areas such as your shoulders and – if you'll be on nude beaches – areas not normally exposed to sun.

Heat Exhaustion Dehydration or salt deficiency can cause heat exhaustion. Take time to acclimatize to high temperatures and make sure you get enough liquids. Salt deficiency is characterized by fatigue, lethargy, headaches, giddiness, and muscle cramps. Salt tablets may help. Vomiting or diarrhea can also deplete your liquid and salt levels. Anhydrotic heat exhaustion, caused by the inability to sweat, is quite rare, but unlike the other forms of heat exhaustion it is likely to strike people who have been in a hot climate for some time, rather than newcomers. Again, always carry – and use – a water bottle on long trips.

Heat Stroke Long, continuous periods of exposure to high temperatures can leave you vulnerable to this serious, sometimes fatal condition, which occurs when the body's heat-regulating mechanism breaks down, and body temperature rises to dangerous levels. Avoid excessive alcohol intake or strenuous activity when you first arrive in a hot climate.

Symptoms include feeling unwell, lack of perspiration, and a high body temperature of 102° to 105°F (39° to 41°C). Hospitalization is essential for extreme cases, but meanwhile get out of the sun, remove clothing, cover with a wet sheet or towel, and fan continually.

Hypothermia Changeable weather at high altitudes can leave you vulnerable to exposure: After dark, temperatures in the mountains can drop from balmy to below freezing, while a sudden soaking and high winds can lower your body temperature too rapidly. If possible, avoid traveling alone; partners are more likely to avoid hypothermia successfully. If you must travel alone, especially when hiking, be sure someone knows your route and when you expect to return.

Seek shelter when bad weather is unavoidable. Woolen clothing and synthetics, which retain warmth even when wet, are superior to cottons. A quality sleeping bag is a worthwhile investment, although goose down loses much of its insulating qualities when wet. Carry high-energy, easily digestible snacks such as chocolate or dried fruit.

Get hypothermia victims out of the wind or rain, remove their clothing if it's wet and replace it with dry, warm clothing. Give them hot liquids – not alcohol – and high-calorie, easily digestible food. In advanced stages, it may be necessary to place a victim in a warm sleeping bag and get in with them. Do not rub victims. Place them near a fire or, if possible, in a warm (not hot) bath.

Fungal Infections Occurring with greater frequency in hot weather, fungal infections are most likely to occur on the scalp, between the toes or fingers (athlete's foot), in the groin (jock itch or crotch rot), and on the body (ringworm). You get ringworm (which is a fungal infection, not a worm) from infected animals or by walking on damp areas such as shower floors.

To prevent fungal infections, wear loose, comfortable clothes, avoid artificial fibers, wash frequently, and dry carefully. If you do get an infection, wash the infected area daily with a disinfectant or medicated soap and water, and rinse and dry well. Apply an antifungal powder and try to expose the infected area to air or sunlight as much as possible. Change underwear and towels frequently and wash them often in hot water.

Infectious Diseases

Diarrhea A change of water, food, or climate can all cause 'the runs.' Diarrhea caused by contaminated food or water is more serious, but it's unlikely to happen in the USA. Despite all your precautions, you may still get a mild bout of traveler's diarrhea from exotic food or drink. Dehydration is the main danger with any diarrhea, particularly for children, who can become dehydrated quite quickly. Fluid replacement remains the mainstay of management. Weak black tea with a little sugar, soda water, or soft drinks diluted 50% with water are all good. With severe diarrhea, a rehydrating solution is necessary to replace minerals and salts. These solutions, such as Pedialyte, are available at pharmacies.

Hepatitis This is a general term for inflammation of the liver. There are many causes of hepatitis: Poor sanitation, drugs, alcohol, contact with infected blood products or with an infected person are but a few. The symptoms are fever, chills, headache, fatigue, and feelings of weakness and aches and pains, followed by loss of appetite, nausea, vomiting, abdominal pain, dark urine, light-colored feces, and jaundiced skin. The whites of the eyes may also turn yellow. Hepatitis A is the most common strain.

You should seek medical advice, but there is not much you can do apart from resting, drinking lots of fluids, eating lightly, and avoiding fatty foods. People who have had hepatitis should avoid alcohol for some time after the illness, as the liver needs time to recover. Viral hepatitis is an infection of the liver, which can have several unpleasant symptoms or no symptoms at all, and infected people may not know that they have the disease.

HIV & AIDS HIV (the human immunodeficiency virus) develops into AIDS (acquired immune deficiency syndrome), which is a fatal disease. Any exposure to blood, blood products, or body fluids may put an individual at risk. The disease is often transmitted through sexual contact or dirty needles – vaccinations, acupuncture, tattooing, and body piercing can be potentially as dangerous as intravenous drug use.

Fear of HIV infection should never preclude treatment for serious medical conditions. One good resource for help and information is the US Center for Disease Control AIDS hotline (☎ 800-342-2437, 800-344-7432 in Spanish). AIDS support groups are listed in the front of phone books. Also see the HIV & Entering the USA boxed text, earlier in the chapter.

Cuts, Bites & Stings
Skin punctures can easily become infected in hot climates and heal slowly. Treat any cut with an antiseptic such as Betadine. Where possible, avoid bandages and Band-Aids (plasters), which can keep wounds wet.

Bee and wasp stings and nonpoisonous spider bites are usually painful but not dangerous. Calamine lotion will give relief, and ice packs will reduce the pain and swelling. You can best avoid bites by not using your bare hands to turn over rocks or large pieces of wood.

Ticks are parasitic arachnids that may be present in brush, forest, and grasslands, where hikers often get them on their legs or in their boots. The adults suck blood from hosts by burying their head into skin, but they are often found unattached and can simply be brushed off. To remove an attached tick, use a pair of tweezers, grab it by the head and gently pull it straight out – do not twist it. (If no tweezers are available, use your fingers, but protect them from contamination with a piece of tissue or paper.) Do not touch the tick with a hot object like a match or a cigarette – this can cause it to regurgitate noxious gut substances or saliva into the wound. And do not rub oil, alcohol, or petroleum jelly on it. If you get sick in the following couple of weeks, consult a doctor.

WOMEN TRAVELERS
Women often face different situations when traveling than men do. If you are traveling alone, it's not a bad idea to get in the habit of traveling with extra awareness of your surroundings.

In general, you must exercise more vigilance in large cities than in rural areas. Try to avoid the 'bad' or unsafe neighborhoods or districts; if you must go into or through these areas, it's best to go in a private vehicle (car or taxi). It's more dangerous at night, but in the worst areas crime can also occur in the daytime. If you are unsure which areas are considered unsafe, ask at your hotel or telephone the tourist office for advice. Note that tourist maps can sometimes be deceiving, compressing areas that are not tourist attractions and making the distances look shorter than they are.

While there is less to watch out for in rural areas, women may still be harassed by men unaccustomed to seeing women traveling solo. Try to avoid hiking or camping alone, especially in unfamiliar places. Hikers all over the world use the 'buddy system,' not only for protection from other humans, but also for aid in case of unexpected falls or other injuries or encounters with rattlesnakes, bears, or other potentially dangerous wildlife.

Women must recognize the extra threat of rape, which is a problem not only in urban but also in rural areas, albeit to a lesser degree. Conducting yourself in a commonsense manner will help you avoid most problems. For example, you're more vulnerable if you've been drinking or using drugs than if you're sober, you're more vulnerable alone than if you're with company, and you're more vulnerable in a high-crime urban area than in a better district.

If you are assaulted, call the police (☎ 911). In some rural areas where 911 is not active, just dial ☎ 0 for the operator. The cities and larger towns have rape crisis centers and women's shelters that provide help and support. They should be listed in the telephone directory; if not, the police should be able to refer you to them.

Men may interpret a woman drinking alone in a bar as a bid for male company, whether you intend it that way or not. If you don't want the company, most men will respect a firm but polite 'no thank you.'

Don't hitchhike alone, and don't pick up hitchhikers when you're driving alone. If you get stuck on a road and need help, it's a good idea to have a premade sign to signal for help. At night, avoid getting out of your car to flag down help; turn on your hazard lights and wait for the police to arrive. Be extra careful at night on public transit, and remember to check the times of the last bus or train before you go out at night.

To deal with potential dangers, many women protect themselves with a whistle, mace, cayenne pepper spray, or some karate training. If you decide to purchase a spray, contact a police station to find out about regulations and training classes. Laws regarding sprays vary from state to state and town to town, so be informed based on your destination. It is a federal offense to carry defensive sprays on airplanes.

Organizations

Check the yellow pages under Women's Organizations and Services for local resources. Women's bookstores, found in the yellow pages under Bookstores, are good places to find out about gatherings, readings, and meetings, and they often have bulletin boards where you can find or place travel and short-term housing notices.

The following two organizations have affiliates nationwide:

National Organization for Women (NOW)
(☎ 202-331-0066), 1000 16th St NW, Suite 700, Washington, DC 20036
This is a good resource for any women-related information; the main office can refer you to state and local chapters.

Planned Parenthood
(☎ 212-541-7800), 810 Seventh Ave, New York, NY 10019
The staff can refer you to clinics throughout the country and offer advice on medical issues.

GAY & LESBIAN TRAVELERS

There are gay people everywhere in the USA, but by far the most visible communities are in the major cities. In the big cities and on both coasts, it is easier for gay men and women to live their lives with a certain amount of openness. As you travel into the middle of the country, it is much harder to be open. Gay travelers should be careful, *especially* in the rural areas, where holding hands might get you bashed.

Gay travelers will particularly enjoy the lively and open gay community in Washington, DC (see the Washington, DC chapter for gay media, bookstores, bars, clubs, and businesses welcoming gay travelers). Baltimore and Wilmington also have vital gay scenes. Rehoboth Beach in Delaware is a popular beach resort for gay/lesbian singles and couples, with many gay-owned and gay-friendly establishments. (See the sections on Baltimore, Wilmington, and Rehoboth, later in this book, for more details.)

Apart from the Virginia cities close to Washington, DC, Charlottesville and Richmond are about the only other places in the state that have good services for gay and lesbian travelers.

Organizations & Resources

Women's Traveller, with listings for lesbians, and *Damron's Address Book*, for men, are both published by Damron Company (☎ 415-255-0404, 800-462-6654), PO Box 422458, San Francisco, CA 94142. Ferrari's *Places for Women* and *Places for Men* are also useful. These can be found at any good bookstore, as can guides to specific cities.

Another good resource is the Gay Yellow Pages (☎ 212-674-0120), PO Box 533, Village Station, NY 10014, which has a national edition and also regional editions.

These national resource numbers may prove useful:

Lambda Legal Defense Fund (☎ 212-809-8585 in New York City, ☎ 213-937-2728 in Los Angeles)
National AIDS/HIV Hotline (☎ 800-342-2437)
National Gay/Lesbian Task Force (☎ 202-332-6483 in Washington, DC)

In Charlottesville at the University of Virginia, the Lesbian, Gay & Bisexual Union (LGBU) helpline number is ☎ 804-982-2773; it operates 7 to 10 pm Sunday to Wednesday. The University of Delaware in Newark also has a helpline (☎ 302-831-4114) for the lesbian, gay, and bisexual community.

For more information, check out the boxed text Gay & Lesbian DC in the Washington, DC chapter, Gay & Lesbian Charlottesville in the Piedmont chapter, and Gay & Lesbian Rehoboth in the Delaware Seashore chapter.

DISABLED TRAVELERS

Public buildings (including hotels, restaurants, theaters, and museums) are required by law to be wheelchair accessible and to have available restroom facilities. Public transportation services (buses, trains, and taxis) must be made accessible to all, including those in wheelchairs, and telephone companies are required to provide relay operators for the hearing impaired. Many banks now provide ATM instructions in braille, and you will find audible crossing signals as well as dropped curbs at busier roadway intersections.

Some of the larger private and chain hotels (see Accommodations, below, for listings) have suites for disabled guests. The main car rental agencies offer hand-controlled models at no extra charge. All major airlines, Greyhound buses, and Amtrak trains allow service animals to accompany passengers and frequently sell two-for-one packages when attendants of seriously disabled passengers are required. Airlines will also provide assistance for connecting, boarding, and deplaning the flight – just ask for assistance when making your reservation. (Note: Airlines are required to accept wheelchairs as checked baggage and have an onboard chair available, though some advance notice may be necessary on smaller aircraft.)

Of course, the more populous the area, the greater the likelihood of facilities for the disabled, so it's important to call ahead to see what is available.

Organizations & Resources

A number of US organizations and tour providers specialize in the needs of disabled travelers:

Access-Able Travel Source
(☎ 303-232-2979, fax 303-239-8486, www.access-able.com), PO Box 1796, Wheat Ridge, CO 80034
This group's excellent website has many links.

Mobility International USA
(☎ 541-343-1284, fax 541-343-6812, ✉ info@ miusa.org), PO Box 10767, Eugene, OR 97440
This organization advises disabled travelers on mobility issues and runs an educational exchange program.

Moss Rehabilitation Hospital's Travel Information Service
(☎ 215-456-9600, TTY 215-456-9602)
1200 W Tabor Rd, Philadelphia, PA 19141

Society for the Advancement of Travel for the Handicapped (SATH)
(☎ 212-447-7284, ✉ sathtravel@aol.com)
347 Fifth Ave No 610, New York, NY 10016

Travelin' Talk
(☎ 931-552-6670, fax 913-552-1182, ✉ trvlntlk@ aol.com), PO Box 3534, Clarksville, TN 37047
This international network provides assistance to disabled travelers.

Twin Peaks Press
(☎ 360-694-2462, 800-637-2256), PO Box 129, Vancouver, WA 98666
This press offers a quarterly newsletter and several useful handbooks for disabled travelers, including *Travel for the Disabled* and the *Directory of Travel Agencies for the Disabled*.

SENIOR TRAVELERS

Though the age where benefits begin varies with the attraction, travelers 50 years old and up can expect to receive cut rates and benefits. Be sure to inquire about such rates at hotels, museums, and restaurants.

Visitors to national parks and campgrounds can cut costs greatly by using the Golden Age Passport, a card that enables US citizens ages 62 and over (and those traveling in the same car) free admission nationwide and a 50% reduction on camping fees. You can apply in person for any of these at any national park or regional office of the USFS or NPS, or call ☎ 800-365-2267 for information. (See Useful Organizations, later in the chapter.)

Organizations

Some national advocacy groups that can help in planning your travels include the following:

American Association of Retired Persons
(AARP; ☎ 800-424-3410, www.aarp.org), 601 E St NW, Washington, DC 20049
AARP is an advocacy group for Americans who are at least 50 years old and is a good resource for travel bargains. US residents can get one-year/three-year memberships for $8/20. Citizens of other countries can get the same memberships for $10/24.

Elderhostel
(☎ 877-426-8056), 75 Federal St, Boston, MA 02110
This is a nonprofit organization that offers seniors the opportunity to attend academic college courses throughout the USA and Canada. The programs last one to three weeks and include meals and accommodations (open to people 55 years old and up, as well as their companions).

Grand Circle Travel
(☎ 617-350-7500, 800-597-3644, www.gct.com), 347 Congress St, Boston, MA 02210
This group offers escorted tours and travel information in a variety of formats and distributes a free useful booklet, 'Going Abroad: 101 Tips for Mature Travelers.'

TRAVEL WITH CHILDREN

Children receive discounts on many things in the USA, ranging from motel stays to museum admissions. The definition of 'child' varies widely – some places count anyone under 18 eligible for children's discounts, while other places only include children under six.

Many hotels and motels allow children to share a room with their parents for free or for a modest fee, though B&Bs rarely do and some don't allow children at all. More expensive hotels can arrange baby-sitting services or organize 'kids' clubs' for younger children. Restaurants offer inexpensive children's menus with a limited selection of kid-friendly foods at cheap prices, only for patrons under 12 or 10 years of age.

Airlines offer discount children's tickets, but these are often more expensive than the cheapest economy adult tickets. Most buses and tours have discounted children's prices, though the discounts aren't substantial. Car rental companies provide infant seats for their cars on request.

Various children's activities are mentioned in appropriate places in the text. For information on enjoying travel with the young ones, read *Travel with Children* by Lonely Planet cofounder Maureen Wheeler.

USEFUL ORGANIZATIONS
American Automobile Association (AAA)

The AAA, with offices in all major cities and many smaller towns, provides useful information, free maps, and routine road services such as tire repair and towing (free within a limited radius) to its members. Members of its foreign affiliates, such as the Automobile Association in the UK, are entitled to the same services; for others, the basic membership fee is about $46 per year with a one-time $10 sign-up fee (still an excellent investment for the maps alone, even for non-motorists). Its nationwide toll-free roadside assistance number is ☎ 800-222-4357 (☎ 800-AAA-HELP). Also see Car in the Getting Around chapter.

National Park Service (NPS)

The NPS, part of the Department of the Interior, administers national parks, monuments, historic sites, and a few other areas. Visitors can often camp and hike in the bigger areas, but hunting and commercial activities such as logging are prohibited in these protected sites. All have visitor centers with information (exhibits, films, park ranger talks, etc) about why that particular site has been preserved for posterity.

National parks surround spectacular natural features and cover hundreds of square miles. Lodges within parks, and motels and campgrounds near them, are privately owned, by and large. National park campground and reservations information can be obtained by calling ☎ 800-365-2267 or writing to the NPS Public Inquiry, US Dept of the Interior, 18th and C Sts NW, Washington, DC 20013. Also check out the NPS website at www.nps.gov. General information can be obtained from the NPS Public Information Officer (☎ 202-208-4747), US Dept of the Interior, 1100 Ohio Drive SW, Washington, DC 20242. Contact individual parks for more specific information. Also, visit GORP (Great Outdoor Recreation Pages), a handy resource, at www.gorp.com.

Most NPS areas charge entrance fees, valid for seven days, of $4 to $10 per vehicle (usually half-price for walk-in or biking visitors). A few are free, and some don't collect entrance fees during periods of low visitation (usually late fall to early spring). Additional fees are charged for camping and some other activities, depending on the park.

Golden Passports Golden Eagle Passports cost $52 annually and offer one-year entry into all national parks to the holder (and anyone in the holder's car). You can buy one at any NPS fee area, and it is valid immediately, so you can use it for your first visit to any national park and all visits to all NPS sites for the next year – a great deal!

Golden Age Passports cost $10 and enable permanent US residents ages 62 and older unlimited free entry to all NPS sites, plus 50% discounts on camping and other fees. It must be purchased in person at any NPS fee area.

Golden Access Passports are free and give free admission to US residents who are medically blind or permanently disabled. (You must show proof of medically determined disability at any NPS fee area.)

US Forest Service (USFS)

The USFS is part of the Department of Agriculture. National forests are less protected than parks, allowing commercial exploitation in some areas (usually logging or privately owned recreational facilities). Forests are multi-use, with recreational activities such as hunting, fishing, snowmobiling, 4WD use and mountain biking permitted in many areas, unlike the NPS parks, where these activities are infrequently permitted. There are many forest campgrounds, which vary from simple sites with a fire-ring and a pit toilet but no water to campgrounds with showers and sometimes limited Recreational Vehicle (RV) hookups. Most sites are $6 to $12; a few without water are free.

Entrance into national forests is often free, although in 1997 the USFS introduced a new experimental program was introduced in which some of the most popular roads through the forest cost $2 to $5 (per vehicle) to use. These fees were normally valid for several days, and Golden Passports were accepted in some, but not all, cases. This fee-collecting program is expected to go through various changes over the next few years.

National forest campground and reservation information can be obtained by calling ☎ 800-280-2267 (☎ 800-280-CAMP).

Bureau of Land Management (BLM)

The BLM, as it is commonly called, manages public use of federal lands. This is no-frills camping, often in untouched settings. Each state has a regional office located in the state capital. Look in the blue section of the local white pages directory under US Government, Department of the Interior, or call the Federal Information Center (☎ 800-688-9889).

Fish & Wildlife Service (FWS)

Each state has a few regional FWS offices that can provide information about viewing local wildlife. Their phone numbers appear in the blue section of the local white pages directory under US Government, Department of the Interior, or you can call the Federal Information Center (☎ 800-688-9889).

DANGERS & ANNOYANCES
Personal Security & Theft

In urban areas here as well as around the world, it is wise to exercise caution to avoid trouble. Muggings can occur, and even smaller cities such as Richmond, Virginia, and Wilmington, Delaware, have drug problems. Stay out of dangerous districts (see individual chapters for details), and check with your hotel staff or the visitor center to identity which areas are safe to visit and travel through and which are not. Secure your cash in a front pocket, money belt, or hotel safe; leave other valuables home. Maintain an awareness of your surroundings and try not to look hopelessly lost and confused (even if you are). Of course, you will likely find more friendly people eager to help you than people trying to take advantage, so be prepared for both – trust your instincts.

Always lock cars and put valuables out of sight, whether leaving the car for a few minutes or longer, and whether you are in a town or in the remote backcountry. Rent a car with a lockable trunk. If your car is bumped from behind in a remote area, it's best to keep going to a well-lit area or service station if possible.

In hotels, don't leave valuables lying around your room. Use safety-deposit boxes or at least place valuables in a locked bag. Don't open your door to strangers – check the peephole or call the front desk if unexpected guests try to enter. Throughout the region, call ☎ 911 in an emergency.

Street People

The USA has a lamentable record in dealing with its most unfortunate citizens, who often roam the streets of large cities in the daytime and sleep by storefronts, under freeways, or in alleyways and abandoned buildings. Street people and panhandlers may approach visitors in the larger cities and towns; nearly all of them are harmless. It's an individual judgment call whether it's appropriate to offer them money or anything else.

Guns

The USA has a widespread reputation as a dangerous place because of the availability of firearms. This reputation is partly deserved, but it's also propagated and exaggerated by the media. In rural areas, do be careful in the woods (wear bright colors) during the fall hunting season, when unsuccessful or drunken hunters may be less selective in their targets than one might hope.

Recreational Hazards

In wilderness areas, the consequences of an accident can be very serious, so inform someone of your route and expected return. Backcountry adventurers should be prepared for sudden changes in weather conditions; carry emergency survival equipment and know the symptoms of and treatment for hypothermia. Avoid driving after heavy snowfalls; surprisingly few local drivers have developed the expertise of driving in these conditions.

A major summer annoyance in the Tidewater (especially Chincoteague, Assateague, Ocean City, Rehoboth, and the Eastern Shore) are the swarms of mosquitoes and 'no-see-ums.' Make sure you bring plenty of insect repellent (some locals swear by an Avon product with repellent qualities called Skin So Soft, readily available locally).

EMERGENCY

Throughout most of the USA, dial ☎ 911 for emergency service of any sort. In large cities or areas with substantial Latino populations, Spanish-speaking emergency operators may be available, but other languages are less likely. This call is free from any phone. A few rural phones might not have this service, in which case dial ☎ 0 for the operator and ask for emergency assistance – it's still free. Each state also maintains toll-free numbers for traffic information and emergencies.

If important documents get lost or stolen, call your embassy. You can find your embassy's telephone number by consulting the Embassies & Consulates boxed text, earlier in the chapter, or by dialing ☎ 202-555-1212 (directory inquiries for Washington, DC).

Always carry a photocopy of your passport separately from your passport. Copy the pages with your photo and personal details, passport number, and US visa. If it is lost or stolen, this will make replacing it easier. Similarly, carry copies of your traveler's check numbers and credit card numbers separately. If you lose your credit cards or they get stolen, contact the company immediately. (See Credit & Debit Cards under Exchanging Money, earlier in the chapter, for company phone numbers.) Contact your bank if you lose your ATM card.

LEGAL MATTERS
If you are stopped by the police for any reason, bear in mind that there is no system of paying fines on the spot. For traffic offenses, the police officer will explain your options to you. Attempting to pay the fine to the officer is frowned upon at best and may compound your troubles by resulting in a charge of bribery. Should the officer decide that you should pay up front, he or she can exercise their authority and take you directly to the magistrate instead of allowing you the usual 30-day period to pay the fine.

If you are arrested for more serious offenses, you are allowed to remain silent. There is no legal reason to speak to a police officer if you don't wish, but never walk away from an officer until given permission. All persons who are arrested are legally allowed (and given) the right to make one phone call. If you don't have a lawyer or family member to help you, call your embassy. The police will give you the number upon request.

The drinking age is 21, and you need an ID (identification with your photograph on it) to prove your age if anyone asks for it. Stiff fines, jail time, and penalties could be incurred if you're caught driving under the influence of alcohol. During festive holidays and special events, road blocks are sometimes set up to deter drunk drivers. It's illegal to drive with open containers of alcohol in the car. Public drinking is officially prohibited outdoors, but a discreet bottle of wine with a picnic is generally overlooked. Some outdoor venues allow alcohol but prohibit glass containers.

For information on driving laws, car rental, insurance, and other automobile-related concerns, see the Getting Around chapter.

BUSINESS HOURS
Generally speaking, business hours are 9 am to 5 pm, but there are certainly no hard and fast rules. In any large city, a few supermarkets, restaurants, and the main post office are open 24 hours. Shops are usually open from 9 or 10 am to 5 or 6 pm, but in shopping malls they're often open until 9 pm, except on Sunday, when hours are noon to 5 pm.

Post offices are open 8 am to 4 or 5:30 pm weekdays, and some are open 8 am to 3 pm Saturday. Banks are usually open from either 9 or 10 am to 5 or 6 pm weekdays. A few banks are open 9 am to 2 or 4 pm Saturday. Basically, hours are decided by the individual branch, so if you need specifics, call the branch.

PUBLIC HOLIDAYS
National public holidays are celebrated throughout the USA. Banks, schools, and government offices (including post offices) are closed, and transportation, museums, and other services operate on a Sunday schedule. Holidays falling on a Sunday are usually observed the following Monday.

January
New Year's Day January 1 is a federal holiday.

Martin Luther King Jr Day Observed on the third Monday, this holiday celebrates this civil rights leader's birthday (January 15, 1929).

February
Presidents' Day Held on the third Monday, this day commemorates the birthdays of Abraham Lincoln (February 12, 1809) and George Washington (February 22, 1732).

May
Memorial Day On the last Monday in May, Americans honor the war dead (this day also marks the unofficial first day of the summer tourist season).

July
Independence Day Held on July 4, Independence Day (also called the Fourth of July) commemorates the adoption of the Declaration of Independence on that date in 1776; it's celebrated throughout the country with parades, fireworks displays, and a huge variety of other events.

September

Labor Day Observed on the first Monday, this holiday honors working people (and also unofficially marks the end of the summer tourist season).

October

Columbus Day The second Monday of the month commemorates the landing of Christopher Columbus in the Bahamas on October 12, 1492. Though it is a federal holiday, many Native Americans do not consider this event to be cause for celebration.

November

Veterans Day On November 11, Americans honor war veterans.

Thanksgiving Held on the fourth Thursday, this holiday commemorates the Jamestown colonists' first harvest. It's one of the most important annual family gatherings, celebrated with a bounty of food, parades, and televised football games. The following day is the biggest shopping day of the year – everyone burns off pumpkin pie by running shopping relays through the malls in search of Christmas presents and sales.

December

Christmas This major holiday falls on December 25. The night before (Christmas Eve) is as much an event as the day itself, with church services, caroling in the streets, people cruising neighborhoods looking for the best light displays, and stores full of procrastinators.

CULTURAL EVENTS

Besides the public holidays above, the USA celebrates a number of other events. Retailers remind the masses of coming events with huge advertising binges running for months before the actual day. Because of this tacky overexposure, some of these events are nicknamed 'Hallmark Holidays' after the greeting card manufacturer. In larger cities with diverse cultures, traditional holidays of other countries are also celebrated with as much, if not more, fanfare. Unlike the above, however, most businesses stay open for the following:

January

Chinese New Year Festivities last two weeks, beginning in late January or early February. The first day is celebrated with parades, firecrackers, fireworks, and lots of food.

February

Valentine's Day February 14 is a day dedicated to love. No one knows why St Valentine is associated with romance in the USA, but this is a day of roses, sappy greeting cards, and packed restaurants. Some people wear red and give out candies imprinted with the invitation to 'Be My Valentine.'

March

St Patrick's Day On March 17, the patron saint of Ireland is honored by all those who feel the Irish in their blood and by those who want to feel Irish beer in their blood. Everyone wears green (or you may be pinched), stores sell green bread, bars serve green beer, and towns and cities put on lively parades of marching bands and frolicking community groups. Wearing orange on this day may earn you hard stares.

Passover This Jewish holiday takes place in either March or April, depending on the Jewish calendar. Families get together to honor persecuted forebears, partake in the symbolic seder dinner, and eat unleavened bread.

Easter This Christian holiday falls on the first Sunday in spring after a full moon, in either March or April. Those who observe the holiday may go to church, eat a holiday meal, dye eggs, eat chocolate eggs, or do any combination of the above. Travel during this weekend is usually expensive and crowded. Good Friday (the Friday before Easter) is not a public holiday.

May

Cinco de Mayo Held on May 5, this began as a commemoration of the day the Mexicans wiped out the French army in 1862, and it's now the day all Americans get to eat lots of Mexican food and drink margaritas.

Mothers Day On the second Sunday in May, Americans honor moms with lots of cards, flowers, and dinners out (many of the nicer restaurants are packed for early family dinners).

June

Fathers Day Held on the third Sunday, this day pays tribute to fathers.

October

Halloween On October 31, kids and adults dress in costumes. In safer neighborhoods, children go 'trick-or-treating' door to door for candy. Adults go to parties to act out their alter egos.

November

Day of the Dead Observed on November 2 in areas with Mexican communities, this is a day for families to honor dead relatives and make breads and sweets resembling skeletons, skulls, and such.

Election Day The second Tuesday of the month offers US citizens the chance to perform their patriotic duty. Even more flags are flown than on July 4, and signs with corny photos of candidates decorate the land.

December

Chanukah This eight-day Jewish holiday commemorates the victory of the Maccabees over the armies of Syria and the rededication of their temple in Jerusalem. The date of Chanukah changes from year to year, as it's tied to the Hebrew calendar, a nonlunar system.

Kwanzaa Held from December 26 to January 1, this African American celebration is a time to give thanks for the harvest.

New Year's Eve On December 31, people celebrate with few traditions other than dressing up and drinking champagne or staying home and watching the festivities on TV. The following day, people stay home to nurse their hangovers and watch college football.

SPECIAL EVENTS

With such a rich history, the Capital Region has no shortage of anniversaries, centennials, and regular festivals. A trip to this area at any time will enable you to witness at least one or two. Local celebrations are described with the towns and cities in this guide, but some are worthwhile enough to merit special consideration. See the state chapters for expanded lists.

Washington, DC

Dr Martin Luther King Jr's Birthday On the third Monday in January, DC celebrates on the steps of the Lincoln Memorial, where King gave his famous 'I Have a Dream' speech.

Black History Month Every February, the festivities include special events and exhibits at the Smithsonian Institution, intertwined with wreath-laying celebrations on the birthdays of emancipator Abraham Lincoln (February 12) and abolitionist Frederick Douglass (February 14).

Smithsonian Kite Festival On the last weekend in March, hundreds of kite builders and flyers descend on the Mall for a competition that draws tens of thousands of spectators.

Cherry Blossom Festival For the first two weeks in April, blossoming cherry trees ring the tidal basin south of the Mall, but events take place all around town. They include a beauty contest, road race, rugby tournament, craft fair, and parade.

White House Easter Egg Roll During the Easter weekend, the President and the First Lady invite children ages three to six to gather on the South Lawn to roll eggs and listen to entertainment.

Memorial Day Weekend Concerts On the last weekend in May, the National Symphony performs a free concert on the West Lawn of the Capitol.

Smithsonian Folklife Festival For 10 days preceding July 4, this extravaganza brings arts, crafts, and foods featuring selected nations and US states to the Mall.

Independence Day On July 4, the USA celebrates its birthday with dramatic readings, colonial military maneuvers, a food fair, entertainment, a parade, and a free evening concert on the Capitol's West Lawn by the National Symphony as fireworks burst overhead.

Marine Corps Marathon Held on October 24, this popular road race starts at the Iwo Jima Memorial, circles around DC and the Mall, and ends up back where it started.

National Christmas Tree Lighting Pageant of Peace Held in early December, the ceremony begins at 5 pm (come early) on the White House Ellipse. Festivities include caroling, seasonal music, choral performances, and lots of lighted trees. The President pulls the switch to light up the big guy.

Virginia

Lee-Jackson Day On the third Monday in January, this holiday marks the birthdays of Robert E Lee (January 19) and Stonewall Jackson (January 21). It's celebrated throughout Virginia but with special emphasis in Lexington.

Washington's Birthday In late February, Alexandria hosts a parade, complete with Revolutionary War reenactments (the holiday is also celebrated in Fredericksburg and at Mount Vernon).

Historic Garden Week Celebrated throughout Virginia in late April, this holiday sees private houses opened to the public for ogling.

Tour Du Pont Held in early May, this famous cycling event passes through Fredericksburg, Richmond, Emporia, Roanoke, Salem, Blacksburg, and Bristol.

Shenandoah Apple Blossom Festival This four-day celebration in early May attracts more than 250,000 visitors with parades, arts and crafts, live music, races, and even a circus. Many concurrent activities take place in nearby valley towns.

Folklore Week Held at Smith Mountain Lake State Park near Roanoke in early June, this festival includes displays of Appalachian arts and crafts.

Virginia Indian Heritage Festival In mid-June, this event at Jamestown Settlement brings together the state's original inhabitants in a celebration of song and dance.

Virginia Highlands Festival In late July, this event in Abingdon celebrates all that is Appalachia (arts, crafts, livestock, antique sales, and good ol' country music).

Manassas (Bull Run) Reenactments In late August, you can witness reenactments of the two Civil War battles that took place at Manassas.

Virginia State Fair Held during the last week of September and first week of October, this state tradition at Strawberry Hill (Richmond) entertains with carnival rides, exhibitions of livestock and produce, and a variety of food.

Virginia Festival of American Film In late October, Charlottesville hosts recent releases with stars in attendance.

Waterfowl Week During the last week of November, the national wildlife refuge in Chincoteague opens nature trails to the public so people can observe the southward migration of Canada and snow geese.

Thanksgiving at Berkeley Plantation On December 4, Virginia celebrates the original holiday (in 1619) at Charles City with a reenactment involving music and performances.

Maryland

Maryland Hunt Cup Race On the third weekend in April, this steeplechase in Glyndon attracts some senators, congressional representatives, and Presidential cabinet members if the weather is good.

World Championship Wildfowl Carving Competition In late April, Ocean City sees thousands of decoys at this event.

William Paca House & Garden Tour Held in late May, this tour offers the best chance all year to go behind the scenes and into Annapolis' historic homes.

Annapolis Rotary Club Crab Feast Late July offers the chance to eat crabs and drink beer with 10,000 people in a football stadium.

Rocky Gap Music Festival Held in early August, this event in Cumberland is the Woodstock of bluegrass music and draws a host of young people to dance, sing, foot-stomp, swim, camp, and party on. Make plans early.

Maryland State Fair In a state that still likes to think of itself as rural, this is a great state fair, held in Timoniumin in late August.

National Hard Crab Derby It's difficult to believe that crab racing can attract a cast of tens of thousands, but here's the proof. Held on the first weekend in September, the derby at Crisfield is a weird hybrid of carnival, rodeo, and feast – locals love it.

United States Sailboat and Powerboat Shows Annapolis' equivalent to Mardi Gras takes place in the first two weeks of October, when hundreds of demo boats are in view in the waters around City Dock. The event draws legions of boat lovers for eating, drinking, and merrymaking.

Waterfowl Festival In early November, people from around the country go to Easton to buy decorative duck decoys, see master decoy carvers at work, and see or compete in retrieving-dog trials.

Baltimore's New Year's Eve Extravaganza A great fireworks display lights the sky on December 31.

First Night Annapolis On December 31, citywide fine-arts and music entertainment at nominal prices draws thousands to this big booze-free function (of course, the city pubs are packed – as usual – with First Night dropouts).

Delaware

Tour Du Pont In early May, great athletes flock to Wilmington for the official start of this premier cycling competition. Also see Virginia, earlier.

Clifford Brown Jazz Festival Held from mid-June to July, this festival keeps Wilmington's downtown jumping.

Delaware State Fair In late July, families descend on Harrington to enjoy this enormous event.

Nanticoke Powwow In early September, you can find traditional dances, storytelling, food, and crafts at this powwow in Millsboro, but it does have a commercial atmosphere.

Artists' Open Studio Tour Many artists make their homes in Wilmington. From mid-November through December, this event offers a festive way to see their work and get out on the town for wine, cheese, and conversation.

Festive Christmas in Old New Castle Enjoy holiday festivities in mid-December: candlelight, carolers, extended shopping hours, decorated evergreens, mulled cider, and hot, spiced wine.

WORK

Seasonal work is possible in national parks and other tourist sites, especially ski areas. For information, contact park concessionaires or local chambers of commerce. The beach resorts of Ocean City, Maryland, and Rehoboth Beach, Delaware, hire lots of young people to work in hotels, restaurants, and beach attractions. If you are in search of temporary summer employment in a setting with good daytime and nighttime attractions, consider the beach.

If you're not a US citizen, you need to apply for a work visa from the US embassy in your home country before you leave. The type of visa varies depending on how long you're staying and the kind of work you plan to do. Generally, you need either a J-1 visa, which you can obtain by joining a visitor-exchange program, or an H-2B visa, which you get after being sponsored by a US employer. The latter is not easy to obtain because the employer has to prove that no US citizen or permanent resident is available to do the job; the former is issued mostly to students for work in summer camps. (See Visas & Documents, earlier in the chapter, for more information.)

ACCOMMODATIONS
Camping

In general, camping is the cheapest approach to a vacation. Visitors with a car and a tent can take advantage of hundreds of private and public campgrounds and RV parks at relatively low prices. The downside is having to hunker down amid the monster RVs that German-speaking visitors eloquently call *Campingschiffe* (camping ships). Fortunately, some campgrounds segregate tent and RV sites.

AAA's annually updated *Mid-Atlantic Camp Book* covers public and private RV and tent sites in Delaware, Maryland, Virginia, and West Virginia; it's free to AAA members (see Useful Organizations, earlier).

Public Campgrounds These are on public lands such as national forests and national and state parks (also see Useful Organizations in the Activities chapter).

To make a reservation for sites in national forests, call ☎ 800-280-2267. For sites in national parks, call ☎ 800-365-2267. You must pay with Visa, MasterCard, or Discover.

Free dispersed camping (meaning you can camp almost anywhere), also called backcountry camping, is permitted in many public backcountry areas. Sometimes you can camp right next to your car along a dirt road, especially in national forest areas (expect no facilities other than a bush). In other places, you can hike your gear in to a cleared campsite. Information and detailed maps are available from many local ranger stations (addresses and telephone numbers are given in the text) and may be posted along the road. A free camping permit is sometimes required in national forests and often necessary in national parks.

Camping in an undeveloped area, whether from your car or backpacking, entails basic responsibility. Choose a campsite at least 200 yards (approximately 70 adult steps) from water and wash up at camp, not in the stream, using biodegradable soap. Dig a 6-inch-deep hole to use as a latrine, and cover and camouflage it well when leaving the site. Burn toilet paper unless fires are prohibited. Carry out *all* trash. Use a portable charcoal grill or camping stove; don't build new fires. If there already is a fire ring, use only dead and fallen wood or wood you have carried in yourself. Make sure to leave the campsite as you found it.

Most basic developed areas usually have pit toilets, fire pits (or charcoal grills), and picnic tables. Many have drinking water (noted in the text), but it's always a good idea to have a few gallons of water when venturing out to the boonies. These basic campgrounds usually cost about $5 to $7 a night.

Better-developed sites usually have flush toilets, fire pits, picnic tables, and water, and some may have showers and/or RV hookups. These cost several dollars more than basic sites. On the whole, national forest campgrounds tend to be of the less-developed variety, and national park and state park campgrounds are more likely to have showers or RV hookups available. The less-developed sites are often available on a 'first-come, first-served' basis, so plan on an early arrival. Note that if you arrive early on Saturday or around a holiday, you may find campgrounds already full with people who arrived on Friday and are spending the weekend. Better-developed areas may accept or require reservations. In popular parks, reservations are a good idea.

Costs given in the text for public campgrounds are per site. A site normally accommodates up to six people (or two vehicles). If there are more of you, you'll need two sites; however, some campgrounds have group sites. Public campgrounds often have seven- or 14-night limits.

Private Campgrounds These are on private property and are usually close to or in a town. Most are designed with RVs in mind; tenters can camp, but fees are several dollars higher than in public campgrounds. Fees given in the text are for two people per site. There is usually an extra-person charge of $1 to $3 each. In addition, state and city taxes apply. However, there may be discounts for week or month stays.

Facilities often include hot showers, a coin laundry, a swimming pool, full RV hookups, a games area, a playground, and a convenience store. Kampgrounds of America (KOA; ☎ 406-248-7444) is a national network of private campgrounds with sites usually ranging from $12 to $15, depending on hookups. You can get the annual directory of KOA sites by calling or writing KOA, PO Box 30558, Billings, MT 59114.

Hostels

The US hostel network is less widespread than in Canada, the UK, Europe, and Australia, and it's predominately in the north and coastal parts of the country. In the Capital Region, you can find hostels in Washington, DC, including the HI headquarters; in Virginia at three locations (Virginia Beach, Bluemont, and Galax); and in Baltimore, Maryland. Not all of them are affiliated with Hostelling International (formerly American Youth Hostels). Those that are offer discounts to HI/AYH members and usually allow nonmembers to stay for a few dollars more. Dormitory beds cost about $10 to $12 a night. Rooms are in the $20s for one or two people, sometimes more.

HI/AYH hostels expect you to rent or carry a sheet or sleeping bag to keep the beds clean. Dormitories are segregated by sex, and curfews may exist. Kitchen and laundry privileges are usually available in return for light housekeeping duties. There are information and advertising boards, TV rooms, and lounge areas. Alcohol may be banned.

Reservations are accepted and advised during the high season, when there may be a three-night limit. Get further information from HI/AYH (☎ 202-783-6161, fax 202-783-6171, ✉ hiayhserve@hiayh.org, www.hiayh.org), 733 15th St NW, Suite 840, Washington, DC 20005, or use their code-based reservation service at ☎ 800-909-4776. (You need the access codes for the hostels to use this service, available from any HI/AYH office and listed in their handbook.)

Independent hostels have comparable rates and conditions and may sometimes be better. They often have a few private single/double rooms available, sometimes with private bathrooms. A kitchen, laundry, bulletin board, and TV are usually available. *The Hostel Handbook* by Jim Williams is a 66-page listing of all hostels and is available for $5, payable to the author at 722 St Nicholas Ave, New York, NY 10031 (☎ 212-926-7030, ✉ infohostel@aol.com).

The Internet Guide to Hostelling (www.hostels.com) lists hostels throughout the world.

Guesthouses

You could travel all over the Capital Region and stay in a different guesthouse, often called a 'bed & breakfast' or 'B&B,' every night. For ambiance and intimacy, these accommodations are a good option. You get to meet local citizens and usually receive a monster of a breakfast that sets you up for the day.

European visitors should be aware that many North American guesthouses and B&Bs are not quite the casual, inexpensive sort of accommodations found on the continent or in Britain. While they are usually family run, many if not most B&Bs require advance reservations, though some will be happy to oblige the occasional drop-in. A large majority of B&Bs prohibit smoking, at least in guests' rooms. B&B rates usually include a substantial breakfast, but lighter continental breakfasts are not unheard of.

Beyond the similarities mentioned above, B&Bs vary tremendously. The cheapest establishments, with rooms in the $30s and $40s, may have clean but unexciting rooms with a shared bathroom. Pricier places have rooms with private baths and, perhaps, amenities such as fireplaces, balconies, and dining rooms with enticingly grand breakfasts and other meals. They may be in historical buildings, quaint country houses, or luxurious urban townhouses. Most B&Bs fall in the $70 to $110 price range, but some cost much more. The best are distinguished by owner-hosts who evince a friendly attention to detail and who can provide you with local information and contacts.

Reservation services include Amanda's B&B Regional Reservation Service (☎ 410-225-0001, 800-899-7533), 1428 Park Ave, Baltimore, MD 21217. In Virginia, you can use the Division of Tourism reservation service (☎ 800-934-9184) to book country inns and B&Bs. In DC, try Bed & Breakfast Accommodations (☎ 202-328-3510), PO Box 12011, Washington, DC 20005, along with hotels listed in the Washington, DC chapter. Also check out two online services with a plethora of detailed listings and pictures of DC and Capital Region inns: www.bnbaccom.com and www.bbchannel.com/USA.

Motels & Hotels

Motel and hotel prices vary tremendously from season to season in the Capital Region. A hotel charging $40 for a double in the high season may drop to $25 in the low season and may raise its rates to $55 for a special event when the town is overflowing. Prices in this guide can only be an approximate guideline at best. Also, be prepared to add room tax to prices (see Taxes, earlier in the chapter). Children are often allowed to stay free with their parents, but rules vary.

Some hotels allow children younger than 18 to stay free with parents, others allow children younger than 12, and others may charge a few dollars per child. You should call and inquire if traveling with a family.

The prices advertised by hotels are called 'rack rates' and are not written in stone. If you simply ask about any specials that might apply, you can often save quite a bit of money. Booking through a travel agent also saves you money. Members of AARP or AAA can qualify for a 'corporate' rate at several hotel chains (see Senior Travelers and Useful Organizations, both earlier in the chapter).

Hotels hike up the price of local calls by almost 200%, and long-distance rates climb by 100% to 200%. The best plan of action is to use a pay phone for all your calls.

Special events and conventions can fill up a town's hotels quickly, so call ahead to find out what will be going on. The town's visitor center is always a good resource.

If you are on a tight budget, motels with $20 rooms are found generally in small towns on major highways and in the motel strips of larger towns. However, what may be a bottom-end motel in one town may pass for a mid-range hotel in another.

Rooms in the cheap places are usually small, and beds may be soft or saggy, but the sheets should be clean. A minimal level of cleanliness is maintained, but expect scuffed walls, atrocious decor, old furniture, and strange noises from your shower. Even these places, however, normally have a private shower and toilet and a TV in each room. Most have air-conditioning and heat.

Some of even the cheapest motels may advertise kitchenettes. These may cost a few dollars more but give you the chance to cook a simple meal for yourself if you are fed up with restaurants. Kitchenettes vary from a two-ring burner to a spiffy little mini-kitchen and may or may not include utensils. If you plan on doing a lot of kitchenette cooking, carry your own set.

The top-end, full-service hotels, with bellhops and doormen, restaurants and bars, exercise rooms and saunas, room service and concierge, are found in the main cities.

Chains There are many motel and hotel chains in the USA. The level of quality and style tends to be repeated throughout the chain. If you plan to stay at hotels of the same chain, investigate the chain's frequent-guest program – discounts and guaranteed reservations are offered to faithful guests.

The cheapest national chain is Motel 6. Rooms start in the $20s for a single in smaller towns, in the $30s in larger towns. Motel 6 usually charges a flat $6 for each additional person.

Motel chains in the next price level start in the $30s in the smaller towns, in the $40s in larger or more popular places. The main difference is the size of the room and the quality: firmer beds, cable TV, free coffee. If these sorts of things are worth an extra $10 or $15 a night, you'll be happy with the Super 8 Motel, Days Inn, or Econo Lodge.

Stepping up to chains with rooms in the $45 to $80 range (depending on location), you'll find noticeably nicer rooms. Cafes, restaurants, or bars may be on the premises or adjacent to them. The swimming pool may be indoors, with a spa or exercise room also available. The Best Western chain offers good rooms in this price range. Less widespread but also good are Comfort Inns and Sleep Inns.

Reservations The cheapest bottom-end places may not accept reservations, but at least phone from the road to see what's available. Even if they don't take reservations, they'll often hold a room for an hour or two.

Chain hotels will all take reservations days or months ahead. Normally, you have to give a credit card number to hold the room. If you don't show and don't call to cancel, you will be charged the first night's rental. Cancellation policies vary, so find out when you book.

Also make sure to let the hotel know if you plan on a late arrival – many motels will give your room away if you haven't arrived or called by 6 pm. Chains have toll-free numbers, but their central reservation system might not be aware of local special discounts. Booking ahead, however, gives you the peace of mind of a guaranteed room when you arrive.

The reservation numbers of some of the best-known chains are as follows:

Best Western	☎ 800-528-1234
Comfort Inn	☎ 800-221-2222
Days Inn	☎ 800-329-7466
Econo Lodge, Quality Inn, and Rodeway Inn	☎ 800-228-2000
Howard Johnson	☎ 800-446-4656
Motel 6	☎ 800-466-8356
Ramada Inn	☎ 800-272-6232
Super 8 Motel	☎ 800-800-8000
Travelodge	☎ 800-578-7878

Condominiums

Like house and apartment rentals, these self-catering accommodations turn up in beach and ski resort areas. While they are often very expensive, several people can stay for the same price, so condos can be more economical than motels or hotels for larger groups. Contact the chamber of commerce in resort towns for information on condominium listings.

FOOD

Throughout the region, the cuisine ranges from plentiful and cheap fast-food choices (as little as $2 for a meal but not necessarily a very nutritious or tasty one) to elaborate steak houses where a three-course meal and wine cost $50 and up per person. The more distinctive cuisine of the region is served at the coast and around the Tidewater, where seafood and fish specialties predominate, and farther south into Virginia, where you'll find Southern cuisine.

Restaurants generally serve breakfast from around 6 to 11 am. Some budget motels put out a simple complimentary breakfast bar (juice, pastries, cold cereals) from around 7 to 9 am, and this can be a good way for you to save time and money. Standard breakfast choices range from a bagel (a disk-shaped bread product made from heavy dough that has been boiled and then baked) and coffee for under $2 to a full Southern-style breakfast of eggs, breakfast meat (bacon, ham, or beef), 'grits' (a hot cereal of ground hominy seasoned with butter and salt), and biscuits and gravy (around $7 for everything, including juice and coffee). Several fast-food coffee-shop chains, such as the Waffle House, offer breakfast around the clock.

Lunch is served from around 11:30 am to 2 or 3 pm (in cities, the office-worker rush is from noon to 1 pm). Sandwiches, salads, hamburgers, and other short orders go for around $4 to $5. At better restaurants, many

Chesapeake Blue Crabs

When the sallys (young female blue crabs) and jimmys (male blue crabs) molt their hard shells in spring, starting at about the first full moon in May, they become a highly sought-after delicacy. As would be expected, the smaller female crabs are the sweetest and most tender. Forget buying soft-shells in the city – the best place to get them is from the sheds of the watermen of Chesapeake Bay, who will give you tips on the best ones (definitely alive) that you should select.

And where do ya get 'em? Any of these places should see you right.

In Virginia, try the following:

Lowery's Seafood (☎ 804-443-5715),
  in Tappahannock
Payne's Crab House (☎ 804-758-5301),
  in Urbanna
Pearson's (☎ 804-224-7511, 610 Colonial
  Ave), in Colonial Beach
Sea Products (☎ 804-453-6433), in Reedville
Shore Seafood (☎ 757-824-5517), in Saxis

In Maryland, try the following:

Buddy's Crabs & Ribs (☎ 410-626-1100,
  100 Main St), in Annapolis
Cantler's Riverside Inn (☎ 410-757-1311,
  458 Forest Beach Rd), in Annapolis
Harris' Crab House (☎ 410-827-9500,
  433 Kent Narrows Way North), in Grasonville
Port Side Seafood (☎ 410-228-9007,
  201 Trenton St), in Cambridge
PT Hambleton (☎ 410-745-5181),
  in Grace Creek, Bozman
Woodfield's (☎ 410-867-3421), in Galesville

lunch menus are identical to dinner menus, but lunch entrees cost about half (a $7 pasta plate at lunch might go for $12 at dinner). Many restaurants also serve all-you-can-eat lunch buffets, which are a good value for larger appetites.

Dinner is the largest (also the most expensive, most formal, and most varied) meal of the day. It's served from around 6 to 10 pm. (Dinners start later in the cities, but some restaurants offer bargain 'early bird' specials to fill seats around 5 pm.) Traditionally, Sunday dinner is eaten as early as midday in the South (typically after church services, so the dress is semiformal). In many cities, a large Sunday brunch served from 10 am to 2 pm has supplanted this tradition; many hotels and restaurants offer elaborate brunch buffets from which people graze for hours.

Budget travelers will want to seek out farmers' markets, such as those in DC and Baltimore, for the freshest produce at the lowest prices. Many of these markets also offer prepared foods, deli meats, and bread, and some have inexpensive restaurants or cafeterias on-site. Grocery stores and deli counters also commonly have prepared foods for cheap take-out food. Restaurants often offer discounts on meals for children and seniors.

Most restaurants have both nonsmoking and smoking areas; some prohibit smoking.

Seafood Specialties

The Tidewater and coastal regions are famous for fleet-fresh fish and shellfish. The two most famous regional specialties are crab cakes – small tasty patties of crabmeat lightly browned in oil – and Chesapeake Bay oysters served on the half-shell with a wedge of lemon. At a typical Maryland crab house, plates of uncracked shellfish – oysters, crabs, clams, mussels, and shrimp – are served to tables covered with brown paper or newsprint. You'll be offered cracking tools and plastic bibs, and when you're done, the server will collect the whole mess in the paper and toss it away in one quick swipe. (See The Art of Eating a Steamed Crab boxed text in the Annapolis chapter.)

A newer local tradition is the 'raw bar,' typically situated in a saloon, where you can sample local shellfish at a per-item cost.

Southern Cuisine

Classic Southern country cookin' means heaps of crispy fried chicken, a thick slice of baked Virginia ham, or hickory-smoked barbecue ribs, all served with several vegetables and your choice of biscuits or cornbread (called 'hush puppies' in golf-ball-size form or 'corn pone' if it's cylindrical or triangular). If you can forgo the meat, you can order an inexpensive 'vegetable plate' with your choice of three or four vegetables – fried okra, corn on the cob, black-eyed peas, and collard greens are typical selections. (Strict vegetarians should ask if the vegetables have been cooked with meat products.)

Southerners have more of a sweet tooth than other Americans. You will find such wonderful desserts as pecan pie, banana pudding, and peach cobbler. Some popular meats and vegetables are also laced with sugar (honey-roasted ham and sweet-potato soufflé are typical examples).

Not only is Southern food unique and the portions large, the style of service may also differ in the South. Luncheon and dinner buffets are much more common (cafeterias are also much more popular), and many restaurants serve 'family-style,' seating unrelated groups at the same table and having patrons pass plates around and serve themselves. Note that many Southern families may say a prayer before eating; restaurant patrons would not be expected to join in (guests *would* be expected to do so at a family's home), but it's respectful to wait until they're done before serving or eating. You may also notice that many Southerners prefer food served less that piping hot, and many restaurants oblige. Server tips are slightly lower at buffet-style and family-style restaurants (around 10%); at cafeterias, it's kind to leave a tip for the table clearer (a dollar or two).

Traditional soul food, the ethnic cuisine of African Americans, includes all the above plus exotic meats (the preparation of which began in slavery days). Common examples include chitterlings (fried tripe, called 'chitlins') and pigs' feet. Okra was brought to the US from Africa by slaves.

Barbecue (BBQ) is a particularly revered Southern cuisine; pork is the He-Man meat of choice (offered chopped, sliced, or in ribs), but BBQ chicken and beef are also available. 'Cue is served with either a mustard, vinegar, or tomato-based sauce, along with a slice of white bread and a side of coleslaw or baked beans. The classic venue is a no-frills roadside stand with long picnic tables out front and a hickory-scented smoking chimney out back.

Packages of gift-wrapped Southern foods make inexpensive souvenirs – you'll easily find fancy stone-ground grits in small canvas sacks, jars of local fruit preserves and syrups daintily topped with calico-print fabric, and colorful pickled relishes made of corn, cucumber, and red pepper.

DRINKS
Nonalcoholic Drinks

Most Americans start the day with a cup of coffee, and this ritual has expanded in recent years to include the full array of European choices – espresso, cappuccino, and caffe latte (though Americans prefer weaker roasts than Europeans). Beware of popular 'gourmet' coffees strangely flavored with such things as mint, anise, hazelnut, and cinnamon. Brewed decaffeinated coffee is widely available in restaurants.

Orange juice often comes with breakfast. Iced tea, sweetened or unsweetened and topped with a slice of lemon, is a popular nonalcoholic drink considered the 'house wine' of the South. This is what a server will bring if you ask for 'tea' in Virginia. In Delaware, the same request will get you hot tea, so be sure to specify which you want. Sugared sodas – Coca-Cola, 7-Up, root beer, and the like – are also common nonalcoholic choices. Lemonade is a popular noncarbonated summer drink. Milk comes in 'whole' or low-fat varieties. Restaurants serve iced tap water (safe to drink) on request at no charge with a meal.

Alcoholic Drinks

Wine is commonly served at dinner but not exclusively so. In the South in particular, it's not uncommon for iced tea to be the dinner beverage. Microbrewed beer is growing increasingly popular, and you'll find brewpubs in most cities. Hard liquor is widely available, but less commonly consumed than beer and wine. Travelers will learn that most of the cities in the northern part of the region have reputations as 'party towns.' If you are in the mood to get your party on, you will find a lot of kindred spirits in DC, Annapolis, Baltimore, Ocean City, and Delaware's beach resorts.

Beverage laws vary from state to state, and liquor sales in stores and restaurants may be restricted on Sunday throughout the region. In Maryland and Delaware, only official liquor stores sell alcoholic beverages. In Delaware, the sale of spirits on Sunday is limited to establishments serving food. In DC and Virginia, beer and wine are sold at most markets, convenience stores, and even at gas stations; hard liquor is sold in liquor stores.

Note that people under the age of 21 (minors) are prohibited from consuming alcohol in the USA. Carry a driver's license or passport as proof of age to enter a bar, order alcohol at a restaurant, or buy alcohol. Servers have the right to ask to see your ID and may refuse service without it. Minors are not allowed in bars and pubs, even to order nonalcoholic beverages. Unfortunately, this means that most dance clubs are also off-limits to minors, although some clubs have solved the under-age problem with a segregated drinking area. Minors are, however, welcome in the dining areas of restaurants where alcohol may be served.

ENTERTAINMENT

Drama, music, and just plain old merry-making are time-honored pastimes in the Capital Region. You can watch costumed 18th-century drama in colonial Virginia towns such as Williamsburg, which feature old English plays and dance in keeping with the town's historic character.

On the other hand, the Capital Region is the birthplace of musicians such as Duke Ellington and Billie Holiday, and you can feel the strong influence of African Americans in the urban citizens' obsession with playing,

listening and dancing to live jazz, hip hop, and reggae. Clubs such as DC's Georgia Brown's are popular nightspots in all the major cities. In addition, DC has a vibrant Latin scene, especially in the clubs of Adams-Morgan.

To sample a different tradition entirely, head to one of the summer music festivals in the mountains of Virginia or Maryland. Events such as the Rocky Gap Music Festival in western Maryland showcase the region's most homegrown music. Appalachian bluegrass music (a descendent of Elizabethan jigs) is played by a small band using a frenzied fiddle, banjo, and dulcimer. For rhythm, the musicians use a pair of pork rib bones clapped together and a 'gut bucket' (kind of a home-string bass built out of a pole and a washtub) to keep time (for more information on this genre of music, watch the documentary film *High Lonesome* – considered by some to be the equivalent of Bluegrass 101). Along with this music, you may hear mainstream country & western music and see square dancing or a regional form of flatfootin' called clogging.

In the Capital Region, DC features the most impressive variety of nationally and internationally renowned arts and artists, led by the programs of the John F Kennedy Center for the Performing Arts. The symphony, opera (led by Placido Domingo), and ballet are all tops in their fields. The large theaters downtown run long seasons of mainstream Broadway theater and musicals, while a small alternative theater district offers more experimental productions. Political satire and comedy by groups such as the Capitol Steps are also popular diversions in the politically driven capital.

Throughout the region, larger cities host their own symphonies, ballet, and theater companies – some of which are quite good – along with cultural arts programs and venues. Many universities and colleges also offer a full calendar of performing-arts events and lectures open to the public.

There are more dynamic pubs and clubs in this region than even a sybarite could utilize in a decade. See the Entertainment sections in specific chapters for details.

SPECTATOR SPORTS

American sports developed separately from those played in the rest of the world. Consequently, baseball (with its clone softball), football, and basketball dominate the sports scene, both for spectators and participants. Football and basketball are sponsored by high schools and universities, which give them a community foundation that reinforces their primacy.

Baseball is so embedded in the American psyche that, despite complex rules and labor-management conflicts at professional levels, it continues to flourish. Many of the most meaningful metaphors in American language and political discourse come from the sport – such as 'getting to first base' and 'three strikes and you're out.'

Building on the success of the US-hosted 1994 Men's World Cup and the 1999 Women's World Cup (played partially in Maryland), soccer continues to make inroads in the US with lots of youth teams. And DC has produced a professional men's soccer team, DC United, which plays at RFK Stadium.

Many other professional major-league teams have fanatic followers in the region. Fans love the Baltimore Orioles (baseball) ands the Washington Redskins and Baltimore Ravens (football). Crowds come to DC's MCI Center to watch the tough Washington Capitals (ice hockey) and the basketball teams – the Washington Mystics (women) and the Washington Wizards.

The Baltimore-Annapolis-DC triangle is the most enthusiastic and skilled region in the US for lacrosse, a fierce game played with a ball and sticks with basketed ends for passing the ball to teammates and shooting for goals. Almost all of the high schools in the area field teams of men and women. College games at the University of Maryland, Johns Hopkins University, the Naval Academy, and Georgetown University draw enormous crowds who follow their teams like holy pilgrims.

SHOPPING

The region's many urban areas offer almost anything you might need (necessities or luxuries or such specialty items as recreational equipment) at a wide variety of stores and shopping malls, but the region is not known for exceptional bargains or unusual goods.

Among the most distinctive items the region has to offer are Appalachian crafts made in the mountains and on the Eastern Shore. Highland crafts that are well known for quality workmanship include woodwork, quilts, basketry, and folk art. Checking out small cabin shops and meeting artisans selling their wares are some of the pleasures of traveling in the mountains. Visitors restricted to the DC area can find high-end Highland crafts at Appalachian Spring stores, one of which is at Union Station. When you visit Easton on Maryland's Eastern Shore, look for shops and crafters around Easton who specialize in making extraordinary carvings of all manner of waterfowl.

Southern food specialties – stone-ground grits, smoked country hams, handmade fruit preserves, local berry wines – are also popular souvenirs from Virginia and parts of Maryland.

Activities

History may well be the biggest draw in the Capital Region, but the active traveler will not be disappointed with the wide range of outdoor activities available. Throw in the Appalachian Trail, Shenandoah National Park, the Blue Ridge Mountains, and the Allegheny Mountains for hiking, bicycling, and camping; the James, Shenandoah, Maury, and Youghiogheny Rivers for rafting, tubing, and kayaking; the world-class sailing center of Annapolis; fishing and boating possibilities on Chesapeake Bay; bird watching at Chincoteague and Assateague Islands; and horseback riding in Hunt Country and along many mountain trails – just to mention a few possibilities – and you will soon realize the diversity of activities.

Read the suggestions in this chapter and then refer to the regional chapters for specific details, such as how to get to the parks and sites and what facilities to expect there.

USEFUL ORGANIZATIONS

See the Facts for the Visitor chapter for phone numbers and more details on the following organizations.

National Park Service (NPS) administers the use of parks, including many of the national monument sites in DC. The *Guide to National Park Areas: Eastern States* by David L and Kay Scott describes all the major parks east of the Mississippi and has 80 maps. You can apply in person for several types of passes – Golden Eagle, Golden Age, and Golden Access Passports – at any national park or regional office of the US Forest Service or the NPS.

The US Forest Service (USFS) administers the use of national forests. For current information about national forests, contact local ranger stations, which are also listed under individual locations throughout this book.

Each state has a few regional Fish & Wildlife Service (FWS) offices, which can provide information about viewing local wildlife.

PARKS & WILDERNESS AREAS

The Capital Region is well endowed with parks and wilderness areas, some of which see few visitors, compared to parks in other heavily populated states in the US. The major ones are covered here. For more details, you can check out the Area Parks Network at www.areaparks.com. This website is a guide to every national park in the United States and even includes information on some national monuments.

Virginia

According to this state's tourism industry, Virginia is for lovers. Whether or not that's true, it can't be disputed that nature lovers have plenty of wilderness to explore and natural beauty to behold here.

National Parks Within Virginia lies Shenandoah National Park (the country's most visited national park) and two huge national forests.

Virginia has a very enlightened environmental policy. The state includes a network of Natural Area preserves designed to protect rare habitats and species, more than 900 conservation sites protecting one or more communities, and wilderness areas (most lying within the two major national forests).

Assateague Island National Seashore (☎ 757-336-6577) and **Chincoteague National Wildlife Refuge** (☎ 757-336-6122) can be reached from Route 13 via Route 175. At these places, you can go bird watching, fishing, boating, hiking, or bicycling – and you might even catch glimpses of wild horses in the process.

Blue Ridge Parkway (☎ 540-298-0398) is 214 miles of commercial-free road in Virginia (and it extends another 255 miles into North Carolina). In addition to soaking up some history and taking in the beauty of wildflowers, you can go bicycling, mountain biking, camping, hiking, and fishing.

George Washington & Jefferson National Forests (☎ 540-265-5100, www.fs.fed.us/gwjnf) has several points of access from I-81 and the Shenandoah Valley. There are more than 2000 miles of trails and the Mount Rogers National Recreation Area to explore, offering opportunities for hunting, fishing, boating, mountain biking, cross-country and downhill skiing, and horseback riding.

Shenandoah National Park (☎ 540-999-3500) is reached from Skyline Drive. Possibilities including hiking on the Appalachian Trail, camping, hang gliding, horseback riding, and bicycling along Skyline Drive.

State Parks Virginia has about 40 state parks and natural areas. For information, contact the Division of Parks and Recreation, 203 Governor St, Suite 302, Richmond, VA 23219. The better-known parks include the following:

Breaks Interstate Park (☎ 540-865-4413) is on the Kentucky-Virginia border and can be reached from I-81. (From Abingdon, take Route 19 to Route 80; and from Marion, take Route 16 to Route 460.) It features the deepest gorge east of the Mississippi, with opportunities for hiking, swimming, and whitewater rafting.

Claytor Lake (☎ 540-643-2500) is off I-81 near Pulaski. Here, you can go camping, hiking, boating and swimming.

Douthat (☎ 540-862-8100) is off I-64. (Take Route 629, then head 7 miles north.) In addition to swimming and fishing here, you can enjoy the beautiful mountain scenery.

Fairy Stone (☎ 540-930-2424) is accessible from Route 57 from Bassett, or Routes 58, 57 and 8 from the Blue Ridge Parkway. You can enjoy swimming, fishing, and boating in the lake here, or you can choose to hike the wooded trails and camp in log cabins.

First Landing (☎ 757-412-2300), off Route 60 at Cape Henry, has hiking and bicycling trails, an interesting coastal habitat, and the Chesapeake Bay Center.

Grayson Highlands (☎ 540-579-7092) is on Route 58 (near the border with North Carolina). Here, there are alpine peaks and horse trails, as well as camping and hiking facilities.

Kiptopeke (☎ 757-331-2267) is accessible from Route 13 via Route 704. Here, you can go bird watching, fishing, hiking, and swimming.

Natural Tunnel (☎ 540-940-2674) is accessible from I-81. (Take Route 23 north to Gate City, then take Route 871 east for 1 mile.) The natural tunnel is 850 feet long, and there are camping and swimming facilities.

Pocahontas (☎ 804-796-4255) is accessible from I-95. (Take Route 288 north, then Route 10 east

to Route 655.) Here, you can go boating, bicycling, camping, hiking, and swimming in pools.

Shot Tower and New River Trail (☎ 540-699-6778) is a 57-mile greenway that follows an abandoned railway. You can go hiking, bicycling, horseback riding, camping, and fishing here.

Smith Mountain Lake (☎ 540-297-6066) is accessible from Route 460. (Take Route 122 south to Route 608 east, then Route 626 south.) Here, you'll find the second-largest freshwater lake in the state, and you can partake in hiking, camping, and myriad water activities.

Westmoreland (☎ 804-493-8821) is north of Montross, off Route 3. Here, you can go boating, swimming, and fishing on the Potomac River.

Maryland

The state of Maryland has more than 25 state parks and recreation areas. Popular ones include the following:

Assateague State Park & National Seashore (☎ 410-641-2120, NS 410-641-1441) is south of Ocean City on Route 611 south, off Route 50 east. In addition to bird watching and spotting wild ponies, you can partake in primitive camping, boating, and fishing.

Blackwater National Wildlife Refuge (☎ 410-228-2677) is 13 miles south of Cambridge and is known for its migratory-bird life.

Catoctin Mountain Park (☎ 301-271-3180) is on Route 77W, off Route 15. The park has 25 miles of trails leading to natural features.

Chesapeake & Ohio Canal National Historical Park (☎ 301-739-4200) is opposite Harpers Ferry and offers camping and plenty of history.

Green Ridge State Forest (☎ 301-478-3124) is east of Flintstone off I-68 and features wildlife and hiking trails.

Gunpowder Falls State Park (☎ 410-592-2897) is north of Perry Hall and follows the Little and Big Gunpowder Rivers. There are 100 miles of hiking trails, and you can go camping, fishing, and paddling.

Point Lookout State Park (☎ 301-872-5389) is on Route 5 near Scotland. This park features camping, boating, fishing, and hiking on the peninsula.

Savage River State Forest (☎ 301-895-5453) is south of Route 50 and New Germany. This is Maryland's largest state forest, and you can partake in hiking, horseback riding, and mountain biking here.

Delaware

There are more than a dozen state parks in Delaware; visit www.destateparks.com for more details. Popular recreational areas include the following:

Bombay Hook National Wildlife Refuge (☎ 302-653-6872) is on Route 9, 2 miles north of Leipsic, and features migratory birds and nature trails.

Brandywine Creek (☎ 302-577-3534) is off I-95, 9 miles northwest of Wilmington, and features hiking and horse trails.

Cape Henlopen (☎ 302-645-8983) is on Route 9, 1 mile east of Lewes, and features camping, fishing, and bird watching.

Delaware Seashore (☎ 302-227-2800) is on Route 1, between Dewey and Bethany Beaches, and features camping, surfing, fishing, and boat charter (fishing).

White Clay Creek (☎ 302-368-6900) is off Route 896, 2 miles north of Newark, and features horse and hiking trails.

CAMPING

With the huge choice of parks and wilderness areas in this scenic region, finding a great camping spot is rarely a problem. The following is some basic information on how to contact the organizations that can help you make reservations or give you more details.

Virginia

For camping and cabin reservations in any of Virginia's parks, call ☎ 804-225-3867, 800-933-7275, TDD 804-786-2121, or check www.state.va.us/~dcr/. Another good source of information is the Virginia Campground Association (☎ 804-288-3065, 800-552-2225), 2101 Libby Ave, Richmond, VA 23230.

Maryland

For information, contact the Dept of Natural Resources, State Forest and Park Service (☎ 608-327-3600, 888-432-2267), Tawes State Office Building E-3, 580 Taylor Ave, Annapolis, MD 21401. Alternatively, check www.dnr.state.md.us/publiclands.

Delaware

For information, contact the Division of Parks and Recreation (☎ 302-739-4702), 89 Kings Highway, PO Box 1401, Dover, DE 19901, or the Delaware Campground Association, PO Box 156, Rehoboth Beach, DE 19971 (ask for 'Delaware Discoveries'). Also, try visiting www.destateparks.com/camping.htm.

HIKING & BACKPACKING

The beauty of hiking in this region is the easy accessibility of the trailheads. The 300 miles of trails in Shenandoah National Park can all be easily reached from Skyline Drive. But for these hikes, and those in the national forests and recreation areas, you are going to need your own car, as there is very little public transportation away from the main cities. In the southwestern part of the region, there are useful shuttle services catering mainly to mountain bikers (and their bikes).

Some of the trailheads in the national forests are hard to find, but the NPS in these areas provides plenty of information, free maps, and, occasionally, personal advice.

Chris Camden's *Backpacker's Handbook*, published by Ragged Mountain Press, is a beefy collection of tips for the trails. More candid is *A Hiker's Companion* by Cindy Ross and Todd Gladfelter, who hiked 12,000 miles before sitting down to write. Lonely Planet's *Hiking in the USA* includes several hikes around the Appalachian Trail. *How to Shit in the Woods* is Kathleen Meyer's explicit, comic, and useful manual on wilderness toilet training for adults.

A good map is essential for any hiking trip. NPS and USFS ranger stations usually have topographic maps that cost $2 to $6. In the absence of a ranger station, try the local stationery store, hardware store, or bookstore.

Longer hikes require two types of maps: USGS Quadrangles and US Department of Agriculture-Forest Service maps. To order a map index and price list, contact the US Geological Survey, PO Box 25286, Denver, CO 80225. For general information on maps, also see the Facts for the Visitor chapter; for information regarding maps of specific forests, wilderness areas, or national parks, see the appropriate regional chapters in this book.

The major forces to be reckoned with while hiking and camping are the weather (which is uncontrollable) and your own frame of mind. Be prepared for unpredictable weather, especially in the mountainous areas – Maryland's Alleghenies, the Blue Ridge Mountains, and other areas of the Appalachians, such as Mount Rogers. Carry a rain jacket and light pair of long underwear at all times; in spring and fall, take this precaution even on short afternoon hikes. Backpackers should have a pack-liner (heavy-duty garbage bags work well), a full set of rain gear, and food that does not require cooking. A positive attitude is helpful in any situation. If a hot shower, comfortable mattress, and clean clothes are essential to your well-being, don't head out into the wilderness for five days – stick to day hikes.

The most stringent safety measures suggest never hiking alone, but solo travelers should not be discouraged, especially if they value solitude. The important thing is to let someone know where you are going and how long you plan to be gone. Use sign-in boards at trailheads or ranger stations. Travelers looking for hiking companions can inquire or post notices at ranger stations, outdoors stores, campgrounds, and youth hostels.

Fording rivers and streams is another potentially dangerous, but often necessary, part of being on the trail. In national parks and along maintained trails in national forests, bridges usually cross large bodies of water (this is not the case in designated wilderness areas, where bridges are taboo). Upon reaching a river, unclip all of your pack straps – your pack is expendable. Avoid crossing barefoot – river cobbles suck body heat right out of your feet, numbing them and making it impossible to navigate. Bring a pair of lightweight canvas sneakers to avoid sloshing around in wet boots for the rest of your hike.

Although cold water will make you want to cross as quickly as possible, don't rush things: Take small steps, watch where you are stepping, and keep your balance. Using a staff for balance is helpful, but don't rely on it to support all your weight. Don't enter water higher than mid-thigh; when water is higher than that, your body gives the current a large mass to work against.

If you should get wet, wring your clothes out immediately, wipe off all the excess water on your body and hair, and put on any dry clothes you (or your partner) may have. Special synthetic fabrics and wool retain heat when they get wet, but cotton does not.

People with little hiking or backpacking experience should not attempt to do too much too soon, or they might end up being nonhikers for the wrong reasons. Know your limitations, know the route you are planning to take, and pace yourself accordingly. Remember, there is absolutely nothing wrong with turning back or not going as far as you originally planned.

Backcountry areas are composed of fragile environments and cannot support an inundation of human activity, especially any insensitive and careless activity. Most conservation organizations and hikers' manuals have their own set of backcountry codes, all of which outline the same important principles: minimizing the impact on the land, leaving no trace, and taking nothing but photographs and memories. Above all, stay on the main trail, stay on the main trail, and, lastly, even if

Appalachian Trail

The Appalachian Trail (also known as the AT) has assumed legendary status among hardy hikers, and those that complete its 2160-mile length (about 150 people each year out of about 1500 who set out) have reason to feel satisfied. Some people mistakenly assume that the trail is an old one, used for centuries by Native Americans and explorers. Certainly parts of it were, but it was really the idea of a Massachusetts regional planner – Benton MacKaye, who wanted to preserve the Appalachian crests as an accessible, multipurpose wilderness belt – that led to its inception in 1921. It was designed, constructed, and marked by volunteer hiking clubs, brought together by the Appalachian Trail Conference, in the 1920s and 1930s.

The trail runs from Katahdin, Maine, to Springer Mountain, Georgia, and about one-quarter of its length (some 544 miles) is in Virginia. The direction of the trail through Virginia and Maryland is northeast-southwest, but it zigzags across I-81 in a number of places. It passes through 14 states, eight national forests, and two national parks, and it crosses 15 major rivers. The lowest point is near sea level, at the Hudson River in New York, and the highest is the 6642-foot Clingman's Dome in the Great Smoky Mountains. In 1968, the national Trails System Act made the AT a linear national park and authorized funds to buy up the remaining private lands along the trail.

In Maryland, it follows the mountain ridges of South Mountain State Park from the Pennsylvania border to Harpers Ferry, West Virginia. Harpers Ferry has special significance to hikers not only as the near midpoint of the AT but also as the headquarters of the **Appalachian Trail Conference**, or ATC, at Washington and Jackson Sts. The ATC command center, open seven days a week April to October, provides up-to-the-minute weather reports, information on trail conditions and detours, maps, and other critical resources for hikers. The ATC also sells gear, guides, and other backpacking provisions.

The lengthy Virginia section starts near Harpers Ferry and follows the state border in a south-westerly direction to Bluemount and then to Shenandoah National Park, where it adjoins Skyline Drive. (About 100 miles of the trail pass through Shenandoah National Park, and it crosses Skyline Drive 32 times.) South of Waynesboro, the trail roughly parallels the Blue Ridge Parkway, passing through George Washington and Jefferson National Forests. North of Roanoke, it strikes west across I-81 to Jefferson National Forest, then heads southwest to just south of Tazewell. Here, it heads southeast, again across I-81, into the Mount Rogers National Recreation Area (where the highest point on the trail in Virginia is the summit of Mount Rogers, at 5729 feet) and emerges at Damascus, where it crosses the Tennessee border. At Damascus, Trail Days are celebrated every May; contact the Damascus town hall (☎ 540-475-3831) for information.

Backpackers who attempt to hike the length of the trail are a breed apart. Called 'thru-hikers,' these hearty souls adopt trail names by which they are known for the extent of their journey (the

★★★★★★★★★★★★★★★★★★★★★★★★

it means walking through mud or crossing a patch of snow, *stay on the main trail*.

Virginia

Virginia, without doubt, is one of the nation's best hiking areas, offering more than 2000 trails of varying levels of difficulty and a good mix of coastal, foothill, and mountain regions to suit hikers of all abilities. In addition to the famous Appalachian Trail, there are myriad other opportunities for hiking and backcountry camping in Virginia. Shenandoah National Park has more than 300 miles of trails, and the extensive network of trails in the George Washington and Jefferson National Forests is almost limitless. Peak-baggers scramble up the sides of Mount Rogers (5729 feet), Virginia's highest peak, and up the sides of many other southwestern Virginia peaks.

Appalachian Trail

likes of 'Eagle Feather,' 'King of Spain,' 'Weasel'). Perhaps the best known is Earl Shaffer, who became the first person to hike the length of the trail in 1948 and who repeated the feat at age 77 in 1998. Thru-hikers often share an immediate and lifelong bond with fellow veterans as they trade horror stories about inclement weather, Pennsylvania boulder fields and foot sores, along with wonderful tales of serendipitous 'trail magic.' Thru-hikers often start in Georgia in early spring, reaching Harpers Ferry around May and taking four to six months to complete the entire journey.

Information For general trail information, contact the Appalachian Trail Conference (☎ 304-535-6331, www.atconf.org), PO Box 807, Harpers Ferry, WV 25425, or the Appalachian National Scenic Trail (☎ 304-535-6331), Harpers Ferry Center, PO Box 50, Harpers Ferry, WV 25425-0897. The ATC distributes and publishes guidebooks and maps covering every section of the trail, as well as the 'Appalachian Trailway News.'

The Potomac Appalachian Trail Club (PATC; ☎ 703-242-0315, fax 703-242-0968), 118 Park St SE, Vienna, VA 22180, sells a great range of maps ($5, or $20 per packet) of the Appalachian Trail and also publishes the 'Potomac Appalachian' newsletter. A good book is the *Appalachian Trail: Guide Book 7 – Shenandoah National Park and Side Trails* ($9). The *Appalachian Adventure: from Georgia to Maine* is also an excellent reference.

The Roanoke Appalachian Trail Club (RATC), PO Box 12282, Roanoke, VA 24024, maintains 113 miles of the trail, and the Mount Rogers ATC, 24198 Green Spring Rd, Abingdon, VA 24211, maintains 56 miles of the trail, which passes through Mount Rogers and Grayson Highlands State Parks. Their friendly members are always willing to take out-of-towners on hikes.

The trail is marked with 2-by-4-inch vertical white paint blazes; a double blaze indicates that a junction or turn is coming up. Blue blazes mark side trails to shelters and water supplies. In Virginia, a permit is required only if you wish to camp in Shenandoah National Park.

Camping Appalachian Trail hikers can use a number of primitive, open, three-sided shelters with stone fireplaces. Placed at approximate day-walk intervals, these shelters are reserved for hikers with three or more nights in different locations stamped in their permits ($1 per night) and are not for casual campers.

In Shenandoah National Park, the following are maintained by the PATC: Gravel Springs (Mile 17.6), Pass Mountain (Mile 31.6), Rock Spring (Mile 48.1), Bearfence (Mile 56.8), Hightop (Mile 68.6), Pinefield (Mile 75.2), and Blackrock (Mile 87.2). The PATC has six fully enclosed cabins in backcountry areas of Shenandoah National Park (see the Shenandoah Valley & Ranges chapter).

You should be carrying your own food. There are plenty of towns in Maryland and Virginia, close to the trail, where you can get a meal if you have tired of 'dehy,' soups, and gorp.

The eastern shore of Virginia and Maryland includes many fine coastal walks. Near Virginia Beach, better known for fleshy displays than for getting away from it all, there are a few great, undeveloped natural areas for hiking and backcountry camping, among them False Cape and Seashore State Parks, the Great Dismal Swamp, and Back Bay National Wildlife Refuge. Cross the Chesapeake Bay Bridge-Tunnel, and you find even more great coastal wilderness hiking in the beautiful Assateague Island National Seashore, accessible from both Virginia and Maryland.

Books & Maps There are plenty of books describing the hiking possibilities in Virginia; for those relating to the Appalachian Trail, see the Appalachian Trail boxed text; for Shenandoah National Park and other major hiking areas, see the relevant chapters. And you can always just ask at an outdoor gear shop – the staff will guide you to the best and most current publications.

One good general book on Virginia stands out: Allen de Hart's *The Trails of Virginia: Hiking the Old Dominion*. And Jay Abercrombie's *Walks & Rambles on the Delmarva Peninsula* is also a good choice. If you have trouble finding it, contact Countryman Press (☎ 800-245-4151), PO Box 175, Woodstock, VT 05091.

A handy compendium of topographic maps can be found in the *Virginia Atlas & Gazetteer*. If you have trouble finding it, contact DeLorme Mapping Company (☎ 207-865-4171), PO Box 298, Freeport, ME 22312.

Organized Tours If you'd rather venture into the woods in good company, a number of operators can help:

All Adventure Travel (☎ 303-440-4160, 800-537-4025), 5589 Arapahoe, Suite 208, Boulder, CO 80303, offers six-day hiking/bicycling tours to the Shenandoah Valley and the wine country near Charlottesville.

Hiking Holidays (☎ 802-453-4816), PO Box 750, Bristol, VT 05443, runs five-day, five-night hiking trips in the Shenandoah National Park and along beautiful sections of the Blue Ridge Parkway.

New England Hiking Holidays (☎ 407-778-3806, 800-869-0949), PO Box 164B, North Conway, NH 03860, has five-day hiking trips in the Shenandoah National Park and Blue Ridge Mountains.

North Wind Touring (☎ 800-496-5571), PO Box 46, Waitsfield, VT 05673, advertises five-day hiking trips in the Blue Ridge Mountains and Rockfish Valley, with some hiking along the Appalachian Trail.

Maryland

Head north and west of Harpers Ferry (West Virginia), and you will find yourself entering Maryland's rugged sector of the Allegheny Mountains. The Alleghenies and their trails can take you a long way from civilization into pristine mountains and valleys. Green Ridge State Forest and Rocky Gap State Park are two popular trailheads in Allegany County. Farther west is the Savage

River State Forest, south of Grantsville. Flatland hikers love to follow segments (or all) of the Chesapeake & Ohio (C&O) Canal bed that leads 185 miles along the edge of the Potomac River from DC to Cumberland, Maryland.

The 144-mile Tuscarora Trail runs from Shenandoah National Park through the George Washington National Forest and parts of West Virginia to Hancock, Maryland. It was once known as 'The Big Blue.'

The Potomac Appalachian Trail Club (☎ 703-242-0315, fax 242-0968), 118 Park St SE, Vienna, VA 22180, publishes *The Big Blue: A Trail Guide*.

Delaware

Delaware's flat, marshy terrain is not conducive to backcountry hiking. Those who are in the know escape civilization in small boats.

BICYCLING & MOUNTAIN BIKING

Many of the popular hiking trails in the region are either partially or wholly open to cyclists, but there are notable exceptions. It pays to check with the authorities before gearing down and steering your bike along a tempting path.

You can get information on bicycling and mountain biking from most visitor centers. A couple of useful contacts are the Adventure Cycling Association (☎ 406-721-1776), PO Box 8308, Missoula, MT 59807, and the United States Cycling Federation – Virginia/DC District (☎ 757-547-7905), 946 Shillelagh Rd, Chesapeake, VA 23323.

Virginia

Virginia is a real gem, with all types of bicycling terrain and a comprehensive network of trails.

Trails The state is crisscrossed by three major bicycling routes: sections of the Trans-America Bicycle Trail from Oregon to Virginia (500 miles from Breaks Interstate Park, on the Kentucky border, to Yorktown); the Maine to Virginia Bicycle Route (150 miles from DC to Richmond, Virginia); and the Virginia to Florida Bicycle Route (130 miles from Richmond to Suffolk, Virginia, near the border with North Carolina). Maps are available from the Adventure Cycling Association (see above).

In addition to these long routes, you can ride on the 105-mile Shenandoah Skyline Drive, 214 miles of the Blue Ridge Parkway, the 22-mile Colonial Parkway, the 17-mile Mount Vernon Trail, the 33-mile Virginia Creeper Trail, the 128-mile Heart of Appalachia, and a 20-mile route around the Fredericksburg battlefields. The latter is one of nine rails-to-trails bikeways statewide. Many overnight bicycling adventures are offered by national tour companies, including the Berkeley, California–based Backroads (☎ 510-527-1555, 800-462-2848, fax 510-527-1444, ✉ backtalk@backroads.com).

The Heart of Appalachia Bike Route is an interesting route that snakes its way along Virginia backroads for 128 miles – from the Guest River Gorge, just east of Norton, to Burkes Garden. Various side trips are suggested, including an 18-mile circuit of Burkes Garden. At one point, the Bike Route crosses the Trans-America Bike Route (Route 80). For information, call ☎ 888-798-2386.

Mountain bikers can go 'wild' in Virginia's two national forests, in the Grayson Highlands State Park and the Mount Rogers National Recreation Area, and just about anywhere along some of the mountain roads. The 57 miles of the New River Trail, in the state park of the same name, would be manageable for someone used to clicking 21 gears (there is a good map and a user's guide to the New River Trail).

DC and nearby Arlington County have a good collection of bicycle routes. The 45-mile paved Washington and Old Dominion (W&OD) Trail runs from the Potomac River to Leesburg through the Virginia towns of Falls Church, Vienna, and Herndon.

For more information, contact the State Bicycle Coordinator (☎ 804-786-2964) by writing to the Virginia Dept of Transportation, 1401 E Broad St, Richmond, VA 23219. Alternatively, you can visit www.vdot.state.va.us/info/vabiking/default.html for more about biking in Virginia. The address of the Metropolitan Washington Council of Governments (☎ 202-962-3200) is 777 North Capitol St NE, Suite 300, Washington, DC 20002.

Books & Maps Local bike shops have the best information on bike routes and conditions – the staff will tell you about places to go (and not to go) and about local regulations, as well as sell you maps. If you wish to avoid traffic, the secondary routes (those numbered more than 600) are the best choices. Maps of county routes are available from the Virginia Department of Transportation (see the preceding paragraph for contact information), which can also provide you with the very informative 'Virginia Bicycling Guide.'

Look out for Elizabeth and Charlie Skinner's *Bicycling the Blue Ridge*, Randy Porter's and Nancy Sorrells' *A Cyclist's Guide to the Shenandoah Valley*, and Kurt B Detwiller's *Bicycling through Civil War History*.

Mountain bikers will find good ideas in Scott Adams' *Mountain Bike Virginia*, which has detailed maps. The numerous southwestern Virginia trails, including the huge ups and downs of the single tracks of Mount Rogers, are covered in Lori Finley's *Mountain Biking the Appalachians: Northwest North Carolina/Southwest Virginia*. Also look for Randy Porter's *Mountain Bike! Virginia*.

DC routes are indicated on the map 'Bicycle Routes in the Washington Area,' which is available from tourist offices in the region. The *Greater Washington Area Bicycle Atlas* is published by the Washington Area Bicyclist Association (☎ 202-628-2500) in conjunction with American Youth Hostels.

Organized Tours Companies that offer organized, multiday rides include the following:

Laughing Dog Shuttle & Guide Service (☎ 888-595-2453, www.AdventureDamascus.com), in Damascus, organizes a three-day Highlands-to-Shenandoah Valley road ride.

Old Dominion Bicycling Tours (☎ 804-598-1808, www.olddominionbike.qpg.com), 3620 Huguenot Trail, Powhatan, VA 23139, runs a variety of tours, including a cross-state James River basin tour.

Bike & Hike Tours (☎ 888-610-4004) features supported rides along the Blue Ridge Parkway, Skyline Drive, and C&O Canal.

Maryland
Maryland is also an excellent state for bike touring and mountain biking.

Trails Some of the best tours pass through Kent and Talbot Counties on the Eastern Shore and through Calvert and St Mary's Counties in southern Maryland.

Wisp Ski Resort in McHenry is a good place for summer mountain biking. Lots of off-road bikers follow the C&O Canal path and camp at designated sites along the way. (See the Western Maryland chapter.)

Books & Maps John R Wennersten's *25 Bicycle Tours on Delmarva* provides helpful touring suggestions. To obtain a copy, contact Countryman Press (☎ 800-245-4151), PO Box 175, Woodstock, VT 05091.

The free 'Maryland Bicycle Map' is invaluable, as it shows the Northern Central Railroad Trail (20 miles), the Baltimore/ Washington International Trail (14 miles), the Western Maryland Rail Trail (20 miles), and the lengthy Chesapeake & Ohio Canal Trail (184 miles), as well as the Anacostia tributary system.

You can also check the county-by-county maps in 'Best Bike Routes in Maryland: A County-by-County Guide,' available from tourist offices in the region or from Virginia's Department of Transportation (☎ 800-252-8776). Also useful is *Bicycling in Maryland: A Quick Reference Guide*.

Delaware
The Coastal Heritage Greenway passes through historic New Castle and the farms and marshlands of Delaware Bay to the south. This is historic and scenic flatland bicycling, but plan your itinerary carefully so you can end your day at a B&B or campground.

Bicycle Route 1 runs from northern Delaware to the beaches, following a mix of quiet country roads, busy highways and the spectacular Delaware seashore; check

www.state.de.us/deldot/bike for details. The South Delaware Heritage Trail (☎ 302-875-7015) suits those wishing to bike 'inn-to-inn.'

SKIING & SNOWBOARDING
In this region, no ski terrain rivals Jackson Hole or Aspen, but in winter, it does snow! Keen skiers not willing to board a plane to live out their fantasies can find ample satisfaction in Virginia's Appalachians and Maryland's Allegheny Mountains.

Virginia
Usually snow-covered from December to March, Virginia offers the most choices for downhill and cross-country skiers, as well as snowboarding enthusiasts. There are five main areas: Bryce, the Homestead, Massanutten, and Wintergreen for lift-assisted snow play (as well as half-pipes for the snowboarders); and Mount Rogers National Recreation Area for the most sublime 'skinny' skiing, comparable to anywhere in the world when conditions are right (see the relevant chapters for more information). And snowboarders, once the pariahs at many resorts, are much loved in Virginia.

All of these ski areas have a wide range of accommodations and conduct special races. The four downhill areas have state-of-the-art snowmaking equipment. As for DC, you may well get the perennial 'snow job,' but nothing you can ski on! For more information, contact the Ski Club of Washington, DC (☎ 703-536-8723). For more Virginia skiing information, call the Virginia Ski Hotline at ☎ 800-843-7669.

Occasionally, the East sneaks into *Ski* and *Skiing*, both widely available travel magazines published year-round, and you can always find the latest statistics in *Snow Country*, which assesses the difficulty of runs and describes ski-school facilities, lodging, and dining.

Maryland
Although western Maryland has some dramatic mountains and sees significant snowfall, you can't count on sustained periods of cold weather. Downhill skiing and snowboarding

in the Allegheny Mountains tend to rely on snowmaking machines, and it is expensive, crowded, and only moderately challenging there. Wisp Ski Area at Deep Creek Lake (☎ 301-387-4911, www.gcnet.net/wisp) is a popular option.

There are good cross-country ski-touring trails in and around Herrington Manor, New Germany, Deep Creek Lake and Swallow Falls State Parks.

ROCK CLIMBING & CAVING

Climbing is potentially a hazardous activity, though serious accidents are more newsworthy than frequent; driving to the climbing site can be more dangerous than the climb itself. Nevertheless, climbers should be aware of hazards that can contribute to falls and very serious injury or death.

Weather is an important factor, as rain makes rock slippery and as lightning can strike an exposed climber; hypothermia is an additional concern. In dry weather, a lack of water can lead to dehydration.

Many climbers are now following guidelines similar to those established for hikers to preserve the resources on which their sport relies. These include concentrating impact in high-use areas by using established roads, trails, and routes for access; dispersing use in pristine areas and avoiding the creation of new trails; refraining from creating or enhancing handholds; and eschewing the placement of bolts wherever possible. Climbers should also strive to respect archaeological and cultural resources, such as rock art, and refrain from climbing in such areas.

A couple of handy publications are the *Climbers' Guide to Great Falls of the Potomac*, which is available readily and covers both the Maryland and Virginia shorelines of the Potomac, and *Carderock, Past and Present: A Climbers' Guide* (the latter is available from local outdoor-equipment shops).

Virginia

The keen climber can ferret out the odd vertical challenge. Sadly, a number of the modern climbs are in gyms, but there are still a few routes, exposed to the elements, that attract a slower group.

Virginia has a few climbing areas (although the choicest routes are in neighboring West Virginia, at such spots as Seneca Rocks). Notable are those near Great Falls on the Potomac, along Skyline Drive, and in Arlington County. In Richmond, you'll find good practice routes on the old Manchester Bridge ruins on the south side of the James River. For more information on climbing, contact Outdoor Insights (☎/fax 540-456-8742), 6370 Midway Rd, Crozet, VA 22932. Artificial climbing walls in Virginia include the Wall at Bodyworks in Fredericksburg and the Rock Gym in Virginia Beach.

Adventure-caving possibilities abound, even in a state heavily pockmarked by commercial caverns. A couple of good Virginia caving contacts are Highland Adventures (☎ 540-468-2722), PO Box 151, Monterey, VA 24465, and Richmond Area Speleological Society (☎ 804-673-2283), 5300 W Marshall St, Suite 10, Richmond, VA 23230.

Maryland

You'll find a number of good technical climbs and an extensive network of caves in the vicinity of Cumberland in Allegany County. To locate these climbs and caves and to get up to speed on local conditions, consult Allegany Expeditions (☎ 301-722-5170, 800-819-5170) in Cumberland.

There are climbing or caving possibilities in Harford County's Rocks State Park, Frederick County's Sugarloaf Mountain, Patapsco State Park, and Annapolis Rocks near Hagerstown.

For artificial walls in Maryland, try the City of Rockville Climbing Gym and the Baltimore Clipper City Rock Gym.

HORSEBACK RIDING & HORSERACING
Virginia

Horseback riding is extremely popular in Virginia's mountainous areas, where you'll find many liveries and enjoy access to trails of all levels of difficulty. Probably the most famous area is 'Hunt Country' in Northern Virginia, a region crisscrossed with many miles of public trails. The Virginia Horse Council (☎ 540-382-3071), PO Box 72,

Riner, VA 24149, publishes the free 'Virginia Horse Riding Trail Guide,' a list of public horse trails with useful contact numbers and addresses, as well as notes on types of trails.

The George Washington and Jefferson National Forests have many designated and unmarked trails. You'll find stables in Shenandoah National Park and in the Shenandoah Valley. The Magnolia Center for Special Equestrians (☎ 804-273-0813) near Richmond organizes programs for people with disabilities.

It is in the southwest part of the state, however, that you'll see experienced riders trailering their horses. In this region are the New River and Virginia Creeper Trails, as well as the famous Virginia Highlands Horse Trail (with special horse camps that have hitching and watering facilities) in the Mount Rogers National Recreation Area and Grayson Highlands State Park.

Horseracing is popular in Hunt Country, especially point-to-point and steeplechase races. On the first Saturday in May, the Virginia Gold Cup is run at Great Meadow near The Plains; Great Meadow also hosts the International Gold Cup on the third Saturday in October. At Foxfield, near Charlottesville, two major steeplechase meetings are held each year (late April and late September); contact the Virginia Steeplechase Association, PO Box 1158, Middleburg, VA 22117.

Another equestrian sport is combined training (also called three-day eventing and horse trials). You can watch this at the Virginia Horse Center at Lexington, at Morven Park in Leesburg, and at Glenwood Park at Middleburg. The whole horsey gamut is rounded off with polo at Middleburg and endurance riding near Front Royal.

In Virginia, jousting tournaments are held at the Natural Chimneys Recreation Area (June and August).

Maryland
Believe it or not, Maryland's state sport is jousting. The knights in shining armor are long gone, but the modern-day jousters need a fair amount of skill to catch rings of decreasing size with their lances.

The Maryland Hunt Cup Race, held in Glyndon (north of Baltimore) on the last weekend in April, is perhaps America's most challenging steeplechase, and the nine-minute race attracts thousands. (See the Baltimore chapter for more information.)

RAFTING, KAYAKING & CANOEING
The Capital Region is blessed with plenty of free-flowing rivers and streams to satisfy all types of paddlers. There are also huge estuaries (Chesapeake Bay is the nation's largest) and hundreds of miles of coastline for canoeists and sea kayakers. Rivers are rated from class I (the easiest) to class VI (dangerous and only to be attempted by the most skilled of paddlers).

Virginia
In spring and late fall, when the river flows are greatest in Virginia, whitewater rafters hurtle down the James River (at Scottsville, to the south of Charlottesville, and right within the city limits of Richmond); the Maury River near Goshen Pass; the Shenandoah River south of Front Royal; and, farthest west, the Russell Forks River in the Breaks Interstate Park on the Kentucky border (see detailed entries in the relevant chapters).

In summer, when the river flows are much less, tubing (floating downstream on inner tubes) is a popular local pastime. Sometimes, tubers tow along a 'refreshment' tube stacked with drinks.

Not-so-well-known places for whitewater kayaking in Virginia are the Moormans River, the Rappahannock watershed, streams in Carroll County, the New River near the North Carolina border, the Chickahominy and North Anna Rivers, and streams on the slopes of the Blue Ridge Mountains.

For a slightly less gung-ho experience, kayakers, tubers, and canoeists head for the Potomac and Shenandoah Rivers near Harpers Ferry and navigate toward DC. This trip is not without rapids, but it's nothing like the 115-feet-per-mile descents you get on the Youghiogheny (see Maryland, below).

Books & Maps For detailed descriptions of some canoe and kayak trips, contact the Virginia Professional Paddlesport Association (☎ 888-423-5628), 352 Shenandoah Heights Rd, Front Royal, VA 22630, which can advise on the most suitable guidebooks and maps. 'Coastal CaNews' (outfitters should have copies) has information on current coastal and sea-kayaking activities.

Organized Tours There are 15 or so outfitters and trip operators in Virginia; many of them are mentioned in the Virginia chapters. If you plan to stick to familiar waters, many outfitters will provide canoes and kayaks, paddles, life jackets, maps, and shuttle service – short trips cost $30, and all-day trips cost around $40 ($45 on weekends).

For more information, contact the Virginia Professional Paddlesport Association, 352 Shenandoah Heights Rd, Front Royal, VA 22630. One company in particular, Atlantic Canoe & Hire Company (☎ 800-297-0066), PO Box 405, Oakton, VA 22124, runs kayaking tours and trips to parts of the Northern Neck and the Assateague and Chincoteague Islands on the Eastern Shore.

Maryland

The Youghiogheny River, which threads its way between the mountains of Pennsylvania and Maryland, offers world-class whitewater. The Upper Yough has a 5-mile stretch of 20 class IV and class V rapids near Friendship and has been the site of numerous national and international kayaking events. The lower parts of the river are a bit tamer (class I to III), as are the rapids of the nearby Savage River.

All of the tidal tributaries of the Chesapeake make for excellent canoe and sea-kayak adventuring. Favorite Maryland cruising grounds are the St Mary's and Patuxent Rivers in southern Maryland, the Tred Avon River around Oxford, the Chester and Sassafras Rivers on the upper Eastern Shore, and the Pocomoke River on the lower Eastern Shore.

Working with a number of outfitters in Ohiopyle, Pennsylvania, you can plan a rafting adventure to meet your personal skills and courage. The offices of the rafting companies are in the village, on or near Route 381. Rates are lower during the week and vary according to the season.

Laurel Highlands River Tours (☎ 800-472-3846, www.laurelhighlands.com) conducts guided trips on the Middle Yough and Upper Yough (trips include lunch). Other companies offering guided trips are Wilderness Voyageurs (☎ 800-272-4141), Mountain Streams (☎ 800-723-8669, www.mtstreams.com), River & Trail Outfitters (☎ 301-695-5177, www.rivertrail.com), River Riders (☎ 304-535-2663, www.riverriders.com), Upper Yough Expeditions (☎ 301-746-5808), and White Water Adventurers (☎ 724-329-8850, 800-992-7238).

Delaware

This state has scenic, but rarely dangerous, waters for kayaking, canoeing, and tubing along the Brandywine River from Chadds Ford, Pennsylvania, southward, almost to Wilmington. More serene sites for canoeing lie along the hundreds of miles of tidal rivers, such as the Leipsic, that wind through extensive coastal marshes and wildlife refuges on the fringe of Delaware Bay.

In the southern part of the state, you can explore the Indian River, Rehoboth Bay, and Assawoman Bay with a canoe or sea kayak. On weekends and in summer, these waters can get congested with speedboats, Jet Skis, and water-skiers. But you'll only share the place with migratory waterfowl in September or May. There is a canoe trail on the Broadkill River near Milton (☎ 302-684-3425).

Delmarva Dennis Kayaking Adventures (☎ 302-537-5311), in Ocean View, operates a great trip with an emphasis on wildlife spotting.

SCUBA DIVING

There are many opportunities for wreck diving and certification in and around Chesapeake Bay and the Eastern Shore. The best dive conditions typically occur May through October. Regardless, you'll need a full 7mm wet suit or dry suit year-round.

Dive-boat services operate out of Arlington, Prince George, Portsmouth, Norfolk,

Hopewell, and Virginia Beach; in Maryland, the Piney Point underwater dive park includes the wreckage of a German Black Panther submarine, *U-1105*. Diving in Maryland's freshwater lakes is also popular.

SURFING & WINDSURFING
The Capital Region has a few hot spots for surfers and windsurfers.

Virginia
Virginia Beach, with eight dedicated areas nearby, is the hub of surfing in this region and is the host of the annual East Coast Surfing Championships. Restrictions limit where you can take your board, and it must be leashed at all times; an untethered board can earn you a $50 fine. For a surf report, call Wave Riding Vehicles (☎ 757-422-8823).

Windsurfing is fast growing in popularity. Popular centers in Virginia are Belle Haven Marina (☎ 703-768-0018) near Alexandria and Fort Belvoir and Mason Neck State Parks along the Potomac River. At Virginia Beach, you can get lessons and rentals at the Chick's Beach Sailing Center (☎ 757-481-3067); also, those up to wave jumping can try Wave Riding Vehicles (see the above paragraph). In DC, you will see windsurfers at the Washington Sailing Marina.

Maryland
Ocean City in Maryland also has a big surf scene.

Legal surfing beaches change daily, but you'll probably find the best surf and riders around the pier and inlet at the south end of town before 8 am, when the offshore breeze is shaping and glassing off the waves.

The Chesapeake Bay's rivers, coves, and harbors can be superb venues for windsurfing, particularly in the spring and fall, when the wind is up and the sea nettles (stinging jellyfish) are south of the Potomac River. At these times of year, Sandy Point State Park is a popular site for windsurfing. In Ocean City, head for Assawoman Bay.

Delaware
The windsurfing crowd congregates at Dewey Beach around Rehoboth Bay. Surfing is not nearly as popular in Delaware as it is in Ocean City, Maryland, because the beach breaks around Rehoboth and Dewey often close out in a hurry.

SAILING
The Department of Natural Resources' 'Cruising Guide to Maryland Waters' is available from tourist offices throughout the state.

Virginia
Virginia shares the waters of Chesapeake Bay, and there are many opportunities for sailing in the state; a good place to start is the Chesapeake Sailing Association (☎ 757-588-2022) at Willoughby Harbor in Norfolk; it offers five-day 'learn to sail' packages. Chick's Beach Sailing Center (☎ 757-481-3067) at Virginia Beach is a good place to rent a boat.

Don't be surprised if you see some large sailing craft in the inland lakes, such as Smith Mountain, Buggs Island, and Claytor Lakes.

Maryland
Annapolis, Maryland, is the sailing capital of the US in title and in fact. There are thousands of racing and cruising sailboats berthed at the marinas that line the city's shores (and more than 200,000 registered boaters). If you know your way around a sailboat, you can probably find a place aboard someone's boat for the Wednesday-evening or weekend races. Making such acquaintances can lead to an

invitation for some vacation cruising to the backwaters of the Eastern Shore.

Annapolis also has a large collection of 'head boats' (which charge per person) to carry tourists on daylong sails. More than a dozen yacht charter companies rent bareboats (boats without crews) out of Annapolis. Other places to find bareboats for charter are Rock Hall (near Chestertown, on the upper Eastern Shore), Oxford (on the central Eastern Shore), and Solomons Island (in southern Maryland).

SALTWATER FISHING

The Chesapeake Bay and the Atlantic Ocean offer great saltwater fishing.

Virginia

From July through September, the wealthy are in pursuit of the white marlin. The poorer anglers could probably afford to potter around Wachapreague or Chincoteague on the Eastern Shore. Wachapreague, the so-called flounder fishing capital, is also a good place to chase black and red drum, kingfish, spot, gray trout, bluefish, and croaker. The seaward beaches of the Barrier Islands, accessible only by boat, are great for surf casting. Knowledgeable anglers reckon that the Sea Gull Fishing Pier on the Chesapeake Bay Bridge Tunnel is one of the hottest spots in the state – you will still have to pay the $10 crossing fee.

You do not need to have a license for saltwater fishing in Virginia, and this applies to the bay, ocean, and everywhere up to the freshwater line. This is good news, as there are nearly 20 catchable species in the bounds of Chesapeake Bay, including the seasonal cobia, black and red drum, bluefish, and striped bass (which can be caught year-round). A valuable resource is the *Guide to Virginia Saltwater Fishing*, published by the Virginia Saltwater Fishing Tournament (☎ 757-491-5160), 968 S Oriole Drive, Suite 102, Virginia Beach, VA 23451.

Maryland

Oddly, Maryland's saltwater-fishing regulations differ from Virginia's. Even nonresidents used to be able to fish the Chesapeake

without a license, but those days are gone. However, you can buy a five-day Chesapeake fishing permit for $4 at almost any bayside venue. The catches are similar to those in Virginia waters. Ocean City is the place to go if you want to head offshore for marlin, tuna, mako, or swordfish. Within range of the surf angler on Assateague Island are sea bass, flounder, and tautog. Head for the northern bay if you're after striped bass. Off Tilghman Island, you will find bluefish, rockfish, and the huge (35 to 60lb) drum fish.

Delaware

As in Virginia, you don't have to pay a thing to fish in the saltwater of Delaware Bay or in the ocean. Currently, bluefish, summer flounder, and weakfish have been strong throughout the bay. Look for tautog around wrecks and rock piles in the ocean and in the mouth of the bay. In recent years, strong runs of yellowfin tuna and white marlin have been seen offshore.

FRESHWATER FISHING

Virginia

This state is an ideal destination for the keen angler; more than 25 freshwater species live in state waters. And there is no shortage of idyllic rivers, streams, and lakes where the canny quarry can be snagged – nearly a million trout are annually released into more than 180 trout streams, which stretch for 2800 miles.

Look for brown and rainbow trout, largemouth and smallmouth bass, and crappie in Lake Moomaw; striper (including the state's largest, at more than 45lb), smallmouth bass, and walleye in Smith Mountain Lake; crappie, bream, and channel cats in the Rivanna Reservoir, just outside Charlottesville; flathead catfish and white bass in Claytor Lake, southwest of Roanoke; catfish and smallmouth bass in the Rappahannock; and largemouth bass, crappie, and bluegill in Hungry Mother State Park.

Residents pay $5 for five consecutive days of fishing in rivers not stocked with trout ($12 more if they are after trout); nonresidents pay $6 (and an extra $30 for trout fishing). The first weekend in June is a free fishing period throughout Virginia. For information, contact Virginia Dept of Game & Inland Fisheries (☎ 804-367-1000), 4010 W Broad St, Richmond, VA 23230.

For general information, read the *Virginia Fishing Guide* by Bob Gooch. If it's trout you are after, check out *Virginia Trout Streams* by Harry Slone.

Maryland

A freshwater permit for five days will cost the traveler $7 ($5 extra for a trout stamp). The lakes and slow-moving streams of western Maryland are well stocked with largemouth bass. The faster streams have pike, walleye, and trout. The Gunpowder River in Baltimore County may have the best brown- and rainbow-trout fishing in the state.

Local tourist offices will provide information on popular fishing spots and on places to purchase permits.

Delaware

You'll have to buy a Delaware fishing license to fish for trout in freshwater streams, such as Brandywine Creek. More than four dozen inland lakes are well stocked with crappie, perch, trout, bass, and bluegill. A seven-day nonresident freshwater license costs $5.50.

For information, contact Delaware Division of Fish & Wildlife (☎ 302-739-3441), 89 Kings Highway, PO Box 1401, Dover, DE 19901.

CHARTER FISHING
Virginia

If you wish to head out to sea in search of the big fish (in Virginia waters), you will find operators at Wachapreague and Chincoteague on the Eastern Shore, at Reedville and Smiths Point on the Northern Neck, and at Norfolk and Virginia Beach. You can get on board a head boat for about $300 per day; triple this if you are after marlin.

Maryland

Head for Ocean City, but expect that a half day on the water will cost you $400 to $500 for the boat and tackle. For about half that

price, you can go fishing on the Chesapeake Bay. There are large fleets of charter fishing boats working out of Chesapeake Beach and Solomons and Tilghman Islands.

Solomons Charter Captains Association (☎ 888-591-7222) and Chesapeake Beach Fishing Charter (☎ 301-855-0784) are two decent companies to contact for charters.

Delaware

Important billfish tournaments bring a host of fancy sport-fishing rigs to Lewes, and you can charter one of these boats if you don't mind spending more than $1000 a day. Lewes also has some head boats that fish around the mouth of the bay. Check at Fisherman's Wharf (☎ 302-645-8862) in Lewes for half- and full-day fishing trips.

For bargain bay fishing, take one of the boats out of North Bowers Beach for the day. The fishing for blues, weakfish, and flounder is good. Fishing for the whole day will cost you less than $30, and you will never forget the woebegone look of this town, presided over by the ruins of Heartbreak Hotel.

CLAMMING & CRABBING

Virginia has its share of spots along the Chesapeake shore – when you find them, however, reveal them to no one!

Clamming and crabbing for personal consumption require no license in Maryland. If you are at the Atlantic shore, try Assawoman Bay for both activities. Clams love intertidal sand flats, and crabs like brackish water. Any dock, pier, or seawall along the Chesapeake will likely have a colony of catchable blue crabs.

In Delaware, from May to November, the shores of Indian River and the Little Assawoman and Rehoboth Bays are all good places to look for clams and crabs (no license is required). You will also find blue crabs in the tidal rivers of Delaware Bay.

GOLF
Virginia

Virginia's golf courses have played a huge part in world affairs – this recreation has given a number of presidents the chance to slip a friendly word of advice into the ears of foreign visitors. It may not exactly constitute an adventure sport, but it is certainly popular, as is evident on the state's more than 150 courses in the state, including some of the nation's finest: those at The Homestead (Cascades is rated among America's 100 best golf courses), the Shenandoah Country Club, Meadows Farm in Orange County, Tides Inn, the courses at the Williamsburg Inn and Kingsmill Resort (home of the PGA Michelob Championship), Honey Bee and Hell's Point in Hampton Roads, and the Country Club of Virginia in Richmond.

For more information, contact the Golf Resorts Association (☎ 800-932-2259) and Virginia State Golf Association (☎ 804-378-2300, www.vsga.org). Get a copy of the free annual 'Virginia Golf Guide' by stopping at tourist information centers or by calling the 800 number for the Golf Resorts Association, above.

Maryland

This state has more than 200 courses, many frequented by presidents. The TPC at Avenel hosts the annual Kemper Open. The 'Maryland Golf Guide' contains all you need to know, and you can obtain a copy by calling the Maryland Office of Tourism at ☎ 800-634-7386.

Delaware

The McDonald's LPGA Championship (www.mcdslpgachampionship.com), one of four major tournaments on the women's tour, takes place at the Du Pont Country Club.

BIRD & WILDLIFE WATCHING

During the fall, winter, and early spring, the Chesapeake, located right on the Atlantic Flyway, is host to one of the world's greatest collection of waterfowl, including Canada geese, snow geese, and swans. Visiting the website www.audubon.org/campaign/refuge can be an excellent way to obtain more details.

Virginia

Great 'twitching' areas are the Chincoteague, the Eastern Shore, the Plum Tree Island and Back Bay National Wildlife Refuges, Assateague Island, and the Great Dismal Swamp. The Caledon Natural Area on the Potomac River has one of the East Coast's greatest concentrations of bald eagles.

Many bird species, as well as other wildlife, can be seen in Shenandoah National Park, Assateague Island, the Great Dismal Swamp, and in the many forests and recreation areas of the mountainous southwestern part of Virginia.

Maryland

Maryland's biggest collections of waterfowl, as well as fish hawks and eagles, gather at Eastern Neck National Wildlife Refuge near Chestertown, the Blackwater National Wildlife Refuge near Cambridge, and Point Lookout in southern Maryland.

Delaware

The Bombay Hook and the Prime Hook National Wildlife Refuges have immense populations of snow geese in season. Fort Delaware/Pea Patch Island is a good place to look for large populations of waders, including snowy egrets.

Both the Nature Conservancy (☎ 302-369-4144) and the Delaware Nature Society (☎ 302-239-2334) organize bird-watching trips to the state's wildlife areas.

Getting There & Away

Most travelers arrive in the Capital Region by air, bus, train, or private vehicle. The following information is a very general summary of these options. We strongly recommend that you take out travel insurance before you leave. (See Visas & Documents in the Facts for the Visitor chapter for more information.)

AIR

Even if you are continuing immediately to another city in the USA, the first airport you land at is where you must carry out immigration and customs formalities. If your baggage is checked from, for example, London to Phoenix, you will still have to take it through customs if you first land in Chicago. Passengers from Asia will go through immigration and customs in Honolulu if their flights stop there on the way to California.

Passengers aboard the airplane are given standard immigration and customs forms to fill out. After the plane lands, you'll first go through immigration. There are two lines: one is for US citizens and residents, the other for nonresidents. After immigration, you collect your baggage and pass through customs. If you have nothing to declare, you'll probably clear customs quickly and without a baggage search, but don't count on it. For details on customs allowances and the procedure for foreigners entering the USA, see the Facts for the Visitor chapter.

If your flight is continuing to another city, or you have a connecting flight, it is your responsibility to get your bags to the right place. Normally, there are airline representatives at counters just outside the customs area who will help you. Most airports will have pay phones and car rentals, but other facilities can be pretty minimal. Don't count on a foreign exchange office, tourist information desk, or left-baggage service. US airports are run for the benefit of airlines, not travelers, and some are very user-unfriendly.

Airports

There are three major airports in the Capital Region; all three are within 35 miles of Washington, DC. (See later chapters for regional airports and local transit information.)

Baltimore-Washington International Airport (BWI; ☎ 410-859-7111, 800-435-9294) is located in Linticum, Maryland, 10 miles south of downtown Baltimore and 30 miles northeast of Washington, DC. From BWI, you can find limousine, van shuttle, taxi, and train service to both cities and beyond.

Washington-Dulles International Airport (pronounced **dull**-ess; ☎ 703-661-2700) is in Herndon, Virginia, 25 miles west of DC. From here, limousine, van shuttle, and taxi service is available to downtown DC; shuttles also connect with outlying Metro subway stations.

By far the most convenient airport for DC visitors flying to/from other US destinations is the Ronald Reagan Washington National Airport (☎ 703-417-8000), which is right on the Potomac River near Arlington National Cemetery. A terminal subway station offers easy access to all Metro points; you can also find quick shuttle and taxi service to downtown.

Travelers heading straight for Delaware, especially Wilmington, should consider flying into Philadelphia International Airport (☎ 215-492-3181), 8 miles southwest of downtown Philadelphia. It is served by direct flights from Europe, the Caribbean, and Canada and offers connections to Asia, Africa, and South America. There is shuttle-bus service to Wilmington (see the Wilmington chapter).

Airlines

Most major airlines offer service to the Capital Region. Here's a partial list of the ones with toll-free telephone numbers (free within the US). Major domestic carriers are noted with an asterisk.

Air Canada	☎ 800-776-3000
Air France	☎ 800-237-2747
Air New Zealand	☎ 800-262-1234
American Airlines*	☎ 800-433-7300
British Airways	☎ 800-247-9297
Canadian Airlines	☎ 800-426-7000
Continental Airlines*	☎ 800-525-0280
Delta Air Lines*	☎ 800-221-1212
Japan Airlines	☎ 800-525-3663
KLM Royal Dutch Airlines	☎ 800-374-7747
Northwest Airlines*	☎ 800-447-4747
Qantas Airways	☎ 800-227-4500
Southwest Airlines*	☎ 800-435-9792
TWA*	☎ 800-221-2000
United Airlines*	☎ 800-241-6522
US Airways*	☎ 800-428-4322
Virgin Atlantic	☎ 800-862-8621

Buying Tickets

Numerous airlines fly to the USA, and a variety of one-way, roundtrip, and Round-the-World fares are available. It pays to do a bit of research first. Start by perusing travel sections of magazines such as *Time Out* and *TNT* in the UK, or the Saturday editions of newspapers such as the *Sydney Morning Herald* and *The Age* in Australia. Ads in these publications offer cheap fares, but don't be surprised if the tickets happen to be unavailable or sold out when you contact the agents. They're usually low-season fares on obscure airlines with conditions attached.

Start shopping for a ticket early – some of the cheapest tickets must be bought months in advance, and some popular flights sell out early. Talk to recent travelers, contact a few travel agents, and look in newspapers and magazines for special offers. Online travel agencies now list some of the cheapest fares available (see below), but as with bucket-shop advertisements, the best fares are often unavailable or sold out. To start, try www.etn.nl. Airlines themselves can supply information on routes and timetables, but unless there's a price war, they won't offer the cheapest tickets.

High season for most of the USA is mid-June to mid-September (summer). May and October are often 'shoulder' periods, with low season being November through March, except for the week before and the week after Christmas, which are peak periods. In winter, ski resorts and destinations in Florida and Hawaii have high-season prices and can book up well in advance.

Airlines often have competitive low-season, student and senior citizens' fares, but the fares often have complicated conditions and catches. Find out about the fare, the route, the duration of the journey, and any restrictions on the ticket.

Cheap tickets are available in two distinct categories: official and unofficial. Official tickets have a variety of names including 'APEX,' 'excursion,' 'promotional,' and 'advance-purchase' fares. Unofficial tickets are simply discounted tickets that the airlines release through selected travel agencies (not through airline offices). The cheapest tickets are often nonrefundable and require an extra fee for changing your flight (usually $50). Many insurance policies will cover this loss if you have to change your flight for emergency reasons. Return (roundtrip) tickets usually work out cheaper than two one-way fares – often *much* cheaper.

Air Travel Glossary

Baggage Allowance This will be written on your ticket and usually includes one 44lb (20kg) item to go in the hold, plus one item of hand luggage.

Bucket Shops These are unbonded travel agencies specializing in discounted airline tickets.

Bumped Just because you have a confirmed seat doesn't mean you're going to get on the plane (see Overbooking).

Cancellation Penalties If you have to cancel or change a discounted ticket, there are often heavy penalties involved; insurance can sometimes be taken out against these penalties. Some airlines impose penalties on regular tickets as well, particularly against 'no-show' passengers.

Check-In Airlines ask you to check in a certain time ahead of the flight departure (usually one to two hours on international flights). If you fail to check in on time and the flight is overbooked, the airline can cancel your booking and give your seat to somebody else.

Confirmation Having a ticket showing the flight and date you want doesn't mean you have a seat until the agent has checked with the airline that your status is 'OK', or confirmed. Meanwhile you could just be 'on request'.

ITX An ITX, or 'independent inclusive tour excursion,' is often available on tickets to popular holiday destinations. Officially, it's a package deal combined with hotel accommodations, but many agents will sell you one of these for the flight only and give you phony hotel vouchers in the unlikely event that you're challenged at the airport.

Lost Tickets If you lose your airline ticket, an airline will usually treat it like a traveler's check and, after inquiries, issue you another one. Legally, however, an airline is entitled to treat it like cash; if you lose the ticket, it's gone forever. Take good care of your tickets.

MCO An MCO, or 'miscellaneous charge order,' is a voucher that looks like an airline ticket but carries no destination or date. It can be exchanged through any International Association of Travel Agents (IATA) airline for a ticket on a specific flight. It's a useful alternative to an onward ticket in those countries that demand one and is more flexible than an ordinary ticket if you're unsure of your route.

In some places, especially the UK, the cheapest flights are advertised by obscure bucket shops whose names haven't yet reached the telephone directory. Many such firms are honest and solvent, but some will take your money and disappear. If you feel suspicious about a firm, don't give agents all the money at once – leave a deposit of 20% or so and pay the balance on receiving the ticket. If they insist on cash in advance, go elsewhere. And once you have the ticket, call the airline to confirm that you are booked on the flight. You may decide to pay a little more than the rock-bottom fare and opt for the safety of a better-known travel agent. Established firms such as STA Travel (www.sta-travel.com) and Council Travel (www.counciltravel.com), both of which have offices internationally, and Travel CUTS in Canada (www.travelcuts.com) offer good prices to most destinations.

Once you have your ticket, make a copy of it, and keep the copy separate from the original ticket. This will help you get a replacement if your ticket is lost or stolen. Remember to buy travel insurance as early as possible to protect yourself against any penalties for an unavoidable cancellation. (See Visas & Documents in the Facts for the Visitor chapter for details.)

Air Travel Glossary

No-Shows These are passengers who fail to show up for their flight. Full-fare passengers who fail to turn up are sometimes entitled to travel on a later flight. The rest are penalized (see Cancellation Penalties).

On Request This is an unconfirmed booking for a flight.

Onward Tickets An entry requirement for many countries is that you have a ticket out of the country. If you're unsure of your next move, the easiest solution is to buy the cheapest onward ticket to a neighboring country or a ticket from a reliable airline that can later be refunded if you do not use it.

Open Jaw Tickets These are return tickets on which you fly out to one place but return from another. If available, these can save you backtracking to your arrival point.

Overbooking Airlines hate to fly with empty seats, and since every flight has some passengers who fail to show up, airlines often book more passengers than they have seats. Usually, excess passengers make up for the no-shows, but occasionally somebody gets bumped. Guess who it is most likely to be? The passengers who check in late.

Point-to-Point Tickets These are discount tickets that can be bought on some routes in return for passengers waiving their rights to a stopover.

Reconfirmation At least 72 hours prior to departure time of an onward or return flight, you must contact the airline and 'reconfirm' that you intend to be on the flight. If you don't do this, the airline can delete your name from the passenger list, and you may lose your seat.

Restrictions Discounted tickets often have various restrictions on them – such as advance payment, minimum and maximum periods you must be away (eg, a minimum of two weeks or a maximum of one year), and penalties for changing the tickets.

Standby This is a discounted ticket that only allows you to fly if there is a seat free at the last moment. Standby fares are usually available only on domestic routes.

Travel Periods Ticket prices vary with the time of year. There is a low (off-peak) season and a high (peak) season and often a low-shoulder season and a high-shoulder season as well. Usually, the fare depends on your outward flight – if you depart in a high season and return in a low season, you pay the high-season fare.

Online Purchase Most airlines have their own websites with online ticket sales, often discounted for online customers. To buy a ticket via the Web, you'll need to use a credit card – this transaction is straightforward and secure, as card details are encrypted. Commercial reservation networks offer airline ticketing as well as information and bookings for hotels, car rental, and other services. Networks include the following:

Atevo Travel	www.atevo.com
Biztravel.com	www.biztravel.com
CNN Interactive's Travel Guide	www.cnn.com/Travel
Excite Travel by City.Net	www.city.net
Internet Travel Network	www.itn.net
Microsoft Expedia	www.expedia.com
Preview Travel	www.previewtravel.com
Priceline	www.priceline.com
Travelocity	www.travelocity.com

There are also online travel agencies that specialize in cheap fares:

1-800-Airfare	www.1800airfare.com
Cheap Tickets	www.cheaptickets.com
LowestFare.com	www.lowestfare.com
Yahoo Travel Specials	travel.yahoo.com/destinations/specials

Round-the-World Tickets RTW tickets can be a great deal if you want to visit other regions as well as the USA. Often they work out to be no more expensive, or even cheaper, than a simple roundtrip ticket to the USA, so you get the extra stops for nothing. They're of most value for trips that combine the USA with Europe, Asia, and Australia or New Zealand. RTW itineraries that include South America or Africa are substantially more expensive.

Official airline RTW tickets are usually put together by a combination of two or three airlines, and they permit you to fly to a specified number of stops on their routes as long as you don't backtrack. Other restrictions are that you usually must book the first segment in advance and cancellation penalties apply. The tickets are valid for a fixed period, usually one year. An alternative type of RTW ticket is one put together by a travel agent using a combination of discounted tickets.

Most airlines restrict the number of sectors that can be flown within the USA and Canada to three or four, and some airlines 'black out' a few heavily traveled routes (such as Honolulu to Tokyo). In most cases, a 14-day advance purchase is required. After the ticket is purchased, dates can usually be changed without penalty, and tickets can be rewritten to add or delete stops for $50 each.

From Australia, Qantas, British Airways, and American Airlines offer a Global Explorer pass (enabling you to fly from Sydney to the US to Europe to Asia and back to Australia for A$1880 to A$2400).

From New Zealand, a RTW ticket via North America, Europe, and Asia on Air New Zealand (and some other airlines) will cost about NZ$2300.

Courier Flights Businesses often need to send urgent documents or freight securely and quickly. Courier companies hire people to accompany the package through customs. In effect, what the companies do is ship their freight as your luggage on regular commercial flights. This is a legitimate operation, but there are two shortcomings – the short turn-around time of the ticket (usually not longer than a month) and the limitation on your luggage allowance. You may have to surrender all your allowance and take only carry-on luggage. Courier opportunities are not easy to come by, and they are unlikely to be available on other than principal routes. In London, try Bridges Worldwide (☎ 0189-546-5465).

Travel Passes & Add-On Fares Some deals for inexpensive air, bus, and train travel within the USA can only be purchased overseas in conjunction with an international air ticket. These include Visit USA air passes, Greyhound's International Ameripass, and some Amtrak rail passes. Also, you can often get super-cheap domestic flights within the USA as an add-on to your international airfare. Think about your travel connections within the USA when you're shopping for your air ticket. (See the Getting Around chapter for details.)

Travelers with Special Needs

If you have special needs of any sort – a broken leg, dietary restrictions, dependence on a wheelchair, responsibility for a baby, serious fear of flying – you should let the airline know as soon as possible so it can make arrangements accordingly. You should remind the airline when you reconfirm your reservation (at least 72 hours before departure) and again when you check in at the airport. It may also be worth calling around the airlines before you make your reservation to find out how they can handle your needs.

Airports and airlines can be very helpful, but they do need advance warning. Most international airports can provide escorts from check-in desk to plane where needed, and there should be ramps, elevators (lifts), accessible toilets, and reachable phones. Aircraft toilets, on the other hand, are likely to present a problem; travelers should discuss this with the airline at an early stage and, if necessary, with their doctors.

Guide dogs for the blind often have to travel in a specially pressurized baggage compartment with other animals, away from their owners, though smaller guide dogs may be admitted to the cabin. Guide dogs are not subject to quarantine as long as they have proof of being vaccinated against rabies.

Deaf travelers can ask that airport and in-flight announcements be written down for them.

Children younger than two years old travel for 10% of the standard fare (or free on some airlines), as long as they don't occupy a seat. (They don't get a baggage allowance, either.) 'Skycots' should be provided by the airline if requested in advance; these will hold a child weighing up to about 22lb. Strollers can often be taken on as hand baggage. Children between two and 12 can usually occupy a seat for one-half to two-thirds of the full fare, but they do not get a baggage allowance. Sometimes there is a children's rate on a discounted fare, sometimes not – it can be cheaper for a child to fly on an adult discounted fare than on a child's fare at two-thirds the full adult rate. For pricing purposes, the child's age is reckoned at the time of departure on the first leg of the flight.

Departure Taxes

Taxes for US airports are normally included in the cost of tickets bought in the USA or abroad. There's a $6 airport departure tax on all passengers bound for a foreign destination and a $6.50 North American Free Trade Agreement (NAFTA) tax on all passengers entering the USA from a foreign country, both added to the purchase price of your air ticket. See Visas & Documents in the Facts for the Visitor chapter for information on entry requirements.

Baggage & Other Restrictions

On international flights, the usual baggage allowance is 20kg (44lb), but on flights from the USA, the limit is commonly higher; check with the airline. On most domestic flights, you are limited to two checked bags, or three if you don't have a carry-on bag. There could be a charge if you bring more or if the size of the bags exceeds the airline's limits. A ski bag, snowboard, or a packed bicycle is usually OK, but a surfboard or a Windsurfer may cost extra. Again, check with the airline to be sure.

If your baggage is delayed upon arrival (which is rare), some airlines will provide you with a cash advance to purchase necessities. If sporting equipment is misplaced, the airline may pay for rentals. Should the baggage be lost, it is important that you submit a claim. The airline doesn't have to pay the full amount of the claim; instead it can estimate the value of your lost items and reimburse you accordingly. Note that it may take the airline anywhere from six weeks to three months to process the claim and pay you.

Items that are illegal to take on a plane, either as checked or carry-on baggage, include aerosols of polishes, waxes, etc; tear gas and pepper spray; camp stoves with fuel; and divers' tanks that are full. Matches should not be packed in checked baggage. Mercury thermometers are also prohibited.

During check-in, you may be asked questions about whether you packed your own bags, whether anyone else has had access to them since you packed them, and whether you have received any parcels to carry. These questions are asked for security reasons, and jokes are definitely not appreciated.

Smoking is prohibited on all domestic flights and on most international flights to and from the USA. Most airports in the USA prohibit smoking except in designated areas.

The USA

New York and Los Angeles still have the greatest number of cheap flights to and from overseas destinations. These hubs also have a lot of competition on domestic air routes (hence low fares) and excellent access to the nation's rail and bus networks. If you are planing to visit a number of cities in the USA, you may want to book your roundtrip ticket in and out of one of these two hubs, then city-hop by buying inexpensive fares aboard one of the domestic discount air carriers such as Southwest Airlines.

Southwest Airlines is a terrific bet if you are headed to or from the Capital Region, as BWI Airport is a Southwest hub. With 14 days advance purchase, you can fly roundtrip to BWI from Los Angeles on Southwest for $327; from Islip, New York (not far from JFK International Airport) for $88; from Providence, Rhode Island (a 45-minute train ride from Boston) for $88; and from Fort Lauderdale, Florida (22 miles from Miami) for $185. Such fares represent a good value, considering that train fares roundtrip from New York to DC cost $40 more than the Southwest fare.

US Airways' Metrojet has started competing on many of these routes, so prices should remain low.

Canada

Travel CUTS has offices in all major cities. The *Toronto Globe & Mail* and *Vancouver Sun* carry travel agencies' ads. The magazine *Great Expeditions*, PO Box 8000-411, Abbotsford, BC V2S 6H1, is also useful. There are daily flights to all the big US cities from Vancouver and Toronto, and many smaller Canadian cities have connections as well. But commuter flights to cities such as New York and DC can be expensive. At the time of publication, United Airlines offered a roundtrip fare of $179 between Toronto and DC.

Australia & New Zealand

There are some direct flights from Sydney to Los Angeles and San Francisco and from Melbourne to Los Angeles, with quite a few more going via Auckland. Flights to other US cities will usually involve a stop in Los Angeles, San Francisco, or Honolulu, but Los Angeles is the main gateway. Qantas, Air New Zealand, and United Airlines are the main airlines on the route. Air New Zealand has regular flights from Auckland direct to Los Angeles, with connections to DC. Flights from Christchurch and Wellington require a plane change on one of the Pacific Islands or are routed through Auckland. Fares from Melbourne, Sydney, Brisbane, and sometimes Adelaide and Canberra are 'common rated.' From Hobart and Perth, there's always an add-on fare.

In Auckland, STA Travel (☎ 09-309-0458), 10 High St, and Flight Centre (☎ 09-309-6171), National Bank Tower, 205-225 Queens St, are the main discount travel agencies,

with other offices all over Australia and New Zealand. They usually offer comparable rates for flights to the USA, within a few dollars of each other, and will often match a lower fare offered by the other agency. It's also worth checking the online agency www.travel.com.au. Low season is roughly February, March, October, and November. High season is mid-June to mid-July and mid-December to mid-January. The rest of the year is considered shoulder season.

Some of the cheapest fares are with Japan Airlines and involve indirect routes and a night's layover in Tokyo. The savings really aren't worth it if your time is limited. The cheapest tickets often have advance-purchase requirements and minimum- and maximum-stay provisions. Full-time students can get an extra discount of A$80 to A$140 on some roundtrip fares to the USA.

At press time, United Airlines' NZ$2510 was the best fare out of Auckland. It also had the lowest fare out of Sydney: A$2105.

The UK & Ireland

One of the busiest, most competitive air corridors in the world is the UK to the USA, with hundreds of scheduled flights by British Airways, American Airlines, United Airlines, Delta Air Lines, Northwest Airlines, Continental Airlines, Kuwait Airways, Air India, TWA, and discount specialist Virgin Atlantic.

London is arguably the world's headquarters for bucket shops (see Buying Tickets, earlier). Check the ads in magazines such as *Time Out*, plus the Sunday papers, *Exchange & Mart*, and the free magazines distributed all over London. Most British travel agents are registered with the ABTA (Association of British Travel Agents). If you have already paid for a flight sold by an ABTA-registered agent who then goes out of business, ABTA will guarantee a refund or an alternative. Unregistered bucket shops are riskier but sometimes cheaper.

Two large, well-established and reliable agents for cheap tickets in the UK are STA Travel (☎ 020-7361-6262), 86 Old Brompton Rd, London SW7; and Trailfinders (☎ 020-7937-5400), 215 Kensington High St, London W8. STA Travel has offices in most of the UK's main cities. Trailfinders has offices in Manchester (☎ 0161-839-6969), Glasgow (☎ 0141-353-2224), and Dublin (☎ 01-677-7888).

Other reputable agencies include Flight-bookers (☎ 020-7757-2000), 177 Tottenham Court Rd, London W1; and Council Travel (☎ 020-7437-7767), 28A Poland St, London W1. The Globetrotters Club, BCM Roving, London WC1N 3XX, publishes a newsletter called *Globe* that covers obscure destinations and can help you find traveling companions.

From UK regional airports, cheap discounted flights may be routed via London, Paris, or Amsterdam and will probably not fly direct to smaller US cities such as Las Vegas or Denver.

High season occurs at various times between April and October, and most of the rest of the year is considered low season. Note that there's also a 'super peak' season from December 12 to 24, when fares are even higher than in high season.

Virgin Atlantic is an airline with consistently low fares, such as 21-day-advance-purchase deals from London to Washington-Dulles International Airport for about £249. Student travel agencies might be able to offer a small discount to travelers with proof of student status. United Airline's fare from Heathrow to DC is about £367. Other carriers charge even more.

Continental Europe

There are nonstop flights to many US cities, but many of the discounted fares involve indirect routes and changing planes. The main airlines between Europe and the USA are Air France, Alitalia, British Airways, KLM, Continental, TWA, United, American, Delta, Scandinavian, and Lufthansa. Sometimes an Asian or Middle Eastern carrier will have cheap deals on flights in transit to the USA, if you can actually get a seat. Also try Icelandair connections via London.

The newsletter *Farang*, La Rue 8 á 4261 Braives, Belgium, covers exotic destinations, as does the magazine *Aventure du Bout du Monde*, 116 rue de Javel, 75015 Paris.

The most common route to the Capital Region is through DC or via New York. If

you're interested in heading east with stops in Asia, it may be cheaper to get a Round-the-World ticket instead of returning the same way.

France Council Travel (☎ 01 44 55 55 44) is at 22 rue des Pyramides, 75001 Paris. Nouvelles Frontières (☎ 08 03 33 33 33) and Havas Voyages (☎ 01 53 29 40 00) both have branches throughout Paris. Some of the cheapest advertised fares, low-season round-trip from Paris, start around 2300FF to New York, 3200FF to Miami, and 3300FF to Los Angeles. At press time, United Airlines offered a 5103FF roundtrip fare from Paris to Washington, DC.

Germany For discount fares, try STA Travel (☎ 69-43-01-91), Bergerstrasse 118, 60316 Frankfurt; or Council Travel (☎ 211-36-30-30), Graf Adolf Strasse 64, 40212 Dusseldorf, and (☎ 089-39-50-22), Adalbert Strasse 32, 80799 Munich. Cheap advertised fares, low season roundtrip from Frankfurt, start around DM700 to New York, DM900 to Miami, and DM1000 to Los Angeles.

Netherlands Amsterdam is one of the best places to get cheap airfares, and its Airport Schiphol is excellent. The official student agency, NBBS (☎ 020-624-0989), Rokin 38, is good but may not have the very lowest prices, so check some of the discount travel agencies along Rokin. Other established agencies include Budget Air (☎ 020-556-3333), Singel 21, and Flyworld/Grand Travel (☎ 020-657-0000), at Airport Schiphol, which does everything by phone and fax. Some of the cheapest advertised fares for low-season roundtrips start around f1950 to New York, f1400 to Miami, and f1450 to Los Angeles.

Africa

The USA is becoming a popular destination for young South Africans. The student fares from STA Travel are the cheapest option. STA Travel has several offices in Johannesburg, including the University of the Witwatersrand (☎ 11-716-3045), and in Cape Town (☎ 21-418-6570). The Flight Centre has opened in South Africa, with offices in

Johannesburg (☎ 11-880-2361), and some other discount travel agencies such as Seekers are starting to appear. Rennies Travel is about the largest and most established travel agency in the country, with several offices in Johannesburg.

At press time, there were no nonstop flights between Africa and the Capital Region. Direct connecting flights are available through major international carriers. British Airways, for example, flies daily from its London (Heathrow) hub to seven cities in Africa, including Nairobi, Cape Town, and Johannesburg. Its standard rate for a flight between Baltimore-Washington International Airport and Nairobi runs around US$2800. American Airlines offers the Nairobi-to-DC flight for US$3161.

Asia

Bangkok, Hong Kong, Kuala Lumpur, Singapore, Seoul, and Tokyo all have good connections to the US West Coast on high-quality national airlines that then connect with US carriers, which go to the Capitol Region's airports. Many flights to the USA go via Honolulu and allow a stopover. Bangkok is the discounted-fare capital of the region, though its bucket shops can be unreliable. Hong Kong, Kuala Lumpur, and Singapore are also very competitive.

STA Travel has branches in Hong Kong, Tokyo, Singapore, Bangkok, and Kuala Lumpur. Ask the advice of other travelers before buying a ticket. At press time, both American and Continental were offering a US$814 fare from Bangkok to DC.

Central & South America

The main gateway to Central and South America is Miami, but there are also many direct flights via New York, Houston (Texas), and Los Angeles. Check the international flag-carrier airlines of the countries to which you want to connect (for example, Aerolineas Argentinas, LanChile, and Varig), as well as US airlines such as United and American. Continental has flights from about 20 cities in Mexico and Central America, including San Jose, Guatemala City, Cancún, and Mérida.

BUS

Greyhound (☎ 800-231-2222 for fares and schedules, ☎ 800-822-2662 for customer service, www.greyhound.com) is the major long-distance bus company, with routes throughout the USA and to the Canadian cities of Montreal, Toronto, and Vancouver.

Greyhound runs buses several times a day along major highways between large towns, stopping at smaller towns that happen to be along the way. Towns not on major routes are often served by local carriers, and Greyhound will usually have information about them – the name, phone number, and sometimes fare and schedule information as well. Local phone numbers for Greyhound and other carriers are listed under their respective cities and towns throughout this guide.

Peter Pan Trailways (☎ 800-343-9999), Capitol Trailways (☎ 800-444-2877), and Martz Trailways (☎ 800-432-8069) provide bus services in the northeast region of the country, competing with Greyhound.

The frequency of bus service varies, but even the least popular routes will have one bus per day. Main routes will have buses every hour or so, sometimes around the clock. Buses are reasonably fast, traveling mostly on the interstate highways, but bus trips can still be very long because of the great distances. Nonexpress buses will stop every 50 to 100 miles to pick up passengers, and long-distance buses stop for meal breaks and driver changes. A cross-country trip from New York to Los Angeles will take about 70 hours.

Generally, buses operated by Greyhound and its main competitors are clean, comfortable, and reliable. Buses have air-conditioning, onboard lavatories, and reclining seats. Smoking is not permitted. The buses stop for meals, usually at fast-food restaurants or cafeteria-style truck stops. Most baggage has to be checked in and should be properly labeled. Larger items, such as skis and bicycles, can be transported, but there may be an extra charge. (Call first to be sure.) Don't leave hand baggage on the bus during rest stops.

Bus travel is often the cheapest way to cover long distances, and those who rely on bus travel represent a wide cross-section of the population. However, many people in the USA consider buses to be transportation for the poor, and they are put off by the possibility that fellow passengers may be from the lower strata of society. Bus stations can be depressing places, often in unsafe areas of big cities. But by the standards of most countries, US bus services are very good, and the unvarnished view of American life is a travel experience you won't get on the airlines.

Tickets & Fares

Tickets can be bought over the phone with a major credit card (MasterCard, Visa, American Express, or Discover) and mailed to you if purchased 10 days in advance, or you can pick them up at the terminal with proper identification. Greyhound terminals also accept traveler's checks and cash. Note that only by purchasing a ticket can you reserve a seat. You can buy a ticket as late as 15 minutes before departure, but the bus company will only fill the number of seats on the bus – no standing allowed. Buy your ticket in advance, if possible, to ensure that you get a seat and perhaps a better price.

The cost of bus travel varies tremendously. Sometimes you can get discounted tickets if you purchase them seven or 21 days in advance. Sometimes a roundtrip ticket costs twice the price of a one-way ticket; at other times, roundtrips are cheaper than two one-ways. Special promotional fares are sometimes offered (eg, 'Anywhere Greyhound goes for $99,' or 'Anywhere in California for $45'). Other promotions include Greyhound's $59 one-way unlimited mileage ticket, which can be a bargain if you're looking for a cheap way to cover a long distance. If you're traveling with a friend, ask about Greyhound's companion fares, where two can travel for the price of one (roundtrip journeys only). As with regular fares, these promotional fares change from season to season – call Greyhound for current details.

Tickets for children ages two to 11 are half price. Senior citizens are entitled to a 15% discount. A disabled passenger and a companion can travel together for the price of one. Student discounts are available occasionally on specific routes during certain times of the year (call Greyhound).

Passes

Passes can be economical if you want to travel a lot in a short period, but they also can be an inducement to cover too much ground in an attempt to get value out of the pass. The passes are for unlimited travel on consecutive days (see below), not for a number of days spread over a longer period. Greyhound stamps your pass the first time you use it, and the days start from then. Two short-term passes cost more per day but may better suit your itinerary.

The pass is valid on dozens of regional bus lines as well as Greyhound and includes side trips to Montreal, Toronto, and Vancouver. Passholders can call ☎ 888-454-7277 in the USA for information, but seat reservations must be made in person at a bus station.

The Ameripass can be purchased in the USA and costs $179 for seven days of travel, $289 for 15 days, $399 for 30 days, $599 for 60 days. Buy one by phone or at any Greyhound station.

The International Ameripass is available from travel agents in the UK at £85 for five days of travel, £110 for seven days, £170 for 15 days, £230 for 30 days, £340 for 60 days. A £75 four-day pass is good for travel between Monday and Thursday.

In Australia, New Zealand, and elsewhere, passes are usually priced in US dollars, and you pay the current equivalent. The pass will cost about $159 for seven days of travel, $239 for 15 days, $319 for 30 days, $499 for 60 days. The International Ameripass is available in the US to foreign students staying less than one year; buy one by phone from the Greyhound International Office in New York City (☎ 212-971-0492, 800-246-8572).

Stations

Some larger towns and cities such as Richmond, Virginia, have a bus station shared by Greyhound and other bus lines, but sometimes Greyhound and other companies have separate stations. Better ones have clean bathrooms, luggage lockers, information boards, pay phones, and snack bars. Some bus stations are in unattractive, even dangerous, parts of town, so it's better to avoid arriving at night. Budget for a taxi to and from the station.

In many small towns, Greyhound no longer maintains a bus station but stops at locations along the route, such as a McDonald's or a post office. To board at these stops, know exactly where and when the bus arrives, be assertive when you flag it down, and be prepared to pay the driver with exact change.

TRAIN

Amtrak (☎ 800-872-7245, www.amtrak.com) has an extensive rail system throughout the USA, with Amtrak Thruway buses providing convenient connections to and from the rail network to some smaller centers and national parks. The advantages of train travel include comfort, sociability, great scenery, and the pleasure of arriving in an elegant station in the heart of a city such as New York, Chicago, Boston, or DC. Besides that, American railroads have a great tradition, and rail travel still has a special romance, especially for rail enthusiasts, who will also enjoy many historic rail routes, restored steam trains, and railroad museums.

Train travel is quicker than bus travel, but the time saved may be offset by less convenient departure and/or arrival times. Traveling by train is usually more expensive than by bus on the same route, but some special deals may make train travel competitive. On a busy, long-distance connection, it's often possible to find an airfare that's cheaper than a train ticket. In short, trains are rarely the quickest, cheapest, or most convenient option, but they can be close on all counts, and people enjoy them for the travel experience.

Long-distance trains run most routes daily, though some routes are covered only three to five days per week. Commuter trains provide very fast and frequent services on shorter routes, especially along the Northeast corridor – Boston, Hartford, New York, Philadelphia, Baltimore, DC, and Newport News. Metroliner trains in this region are especially fast and comfortable but more expensive.

Tickets & Fares

It can be difficult to get useful information about Amtrak services and prices – try a travel agent who specializes in train travel. Reservations can be made any time from 11 months in advance to the day of departure. Because space on most trains is limited, it's a good idea to reserve as far in advance as you can. This also gives you the best chance at getting a discount fare.

Various one-way, roundtrip, and touring fares are available, with discounts of 15% for seniors age 62 and over, 50% for children ages two to 15, 25% for military, and 15% for disabled travelers. Fares vary according to type of seating; you can travel in coach seats or in various types of sleeping compartments. Low-season fares are offered on all tickets from early January to mid-June and from late August to mid-December. Amtrak also offers a variety of all-inclusive holiday tour packages.

International Gateway Fares are discount fares that can be purchased overseas in conjunction with an international air ticket for specific one-way trips in the Northeast, including New York to DC ($46); Metroliner express service to DC ($56), and New York to Boston ($37).

The Amtrak website has lots of information about Amtrak services, but it won't give general information about fares. You have to nominate a date and a route and pretend to book a ticket; it will give a fare for that time and route only. If you go to a train station, the actual fare will probably be different from the amount quoted on the website. Despite the company's monopoly on rail travel, Amtrak's prices are as complex as the ultracompetitive air-travel industry. Generally, the earlier you book a ticket, the cheaper the price.

Passes

The USA Rail Pass is available from travel agents outside of North America, but foreign-passport holders can purchase it from Amtrak once inside the USA. The pass offers unlimited coach-class travel within a specific region for either 15 or 30 days, with the price depending on region, number of days, and season traveled. Currently, the 30-day East Coast pass is $275 in high season, $225 in low season.

Present your pass at an Amtrak office to buy a ticket for each trip. Reservations should be made as well, as far in advance as possible. You can get on and off as often as you like, but each segment of the journey must be booked. At some rural stations, trains will only stop if there's a reservation. Tickets are not for specific seats, but a conductor on board may allocate you a seat. Sleeper or 1st-class accommodations cost extra and must be reserved separately.

A new option offered by Amtrak in conjunction with Canada's VIA Rail, the North America Rail Pass offers unlimited travel on US and Canadian railways for 30 consecutive days for US$450 in the off-peak season, or US$645 in the peak season (from June 1 to October 15).

CAR & MOTORCYCLE

Most people get around the region (and the rest of the nation) by private automobile. For information on buying or renting a car, or using a drive-away (driving a car for someone else), see the Getting Around chapter. Drivers of cars and riders of motorcycles will need the vehicle's registration papers, liability insurance, and an international driver's permit in addition to their domestic license. Canadian and Mexican driver's licenses are accepted.

If you're considering shipping a car, note that air-cargo planes do have size limits, but a normal car or even a Land Rover can fit. For motorcyclists, shipping the bike by air is probably the easiest option; you may be able to get a special rate for air cargo if you are flying with the same airline. Start by asking the cargo departments of the airlines that fly to your destination. Travel agents can sometimes help as well.

Getting Around

Though private automobile remains the most common way to traverse the Capital Region beyond city-to-city connections, air, train, and bus service is readily available throughout the region.

AIR

The major domestic carriers servicing the Capital Region's main airports are as follows:

American Airlines	☎ 800-433-7300
Continental Airlines	☎ 800-525-0280
Delta Air Lines	☎ 800-221-1212
Frontier Airlines	☎ 800-432-1359
Northwest Airlines	☎ 800-447-4747
Southwest Airlines	☎ 800-435-9792
TWA	☎ 800-221-2000
United Airlines	☎ 800-241-6522
US Airways	☎ 800-428-4322

Beyond the three major international airports (Baltimore-Washington International, Washington-Dulles, and Ronald Reagan Washington National – see the Getting There & Away chapter), many smaller airports serve parts of Delaware, Maryland, and Virginia. In this book, regional airports are discussed under the cities and towns that they service.

Several airlines run short commuter flights between the major airports and smaller regional airports. If you're coming from outside the Capital Region, they may prove useful, but they aren't necessarily the most practical way to travel inside the region nor the most economical. US Airways (☎ 800-428-4322) is the main carrier, with commuter services from all three major airports. For example, it flies from BWI to Richmond three times a day; the lowest fare is $188 roundtrip if you fly over a weekend. Also contact United Express (☎ 800-241-6522) or Continental Express (☎ 800-525-0280). Shuttle America (☎ 888-999-3273) operates a limited number of scheduled flights in and out of the New Castle Regional Airport, 5 miles south of Wilmington, Delaware. Currently, flights run between this airport and Norfolk, Virginia; Hartford, Connecticut; and Buffalo, New York.

BUS

Buses are the budget alternative for getting to many smaller cities not served by air or rail service (but check car rental rates and packages to compare costs). Nearly every city of any size has its Greyhound bus station or stop; Trailways is another bus line that often uses the same terminals. See Getting There & Away for more information about bus transit, special fares, and toll-free numbers for route and schedule information.

Some popular routes are as follows:

DC-Baltimore
20 times a day; $9 one way

DC-Richmond
8 times a day; $16 one way

Richmond-Norfolk
9 times a day; $16 one way

Baltimore-Wilmington
14 times a day; $16 one way

TRAIN

Amtrak's Metroliner route carries passengers from New York City and other cities along the eastern seaboard to destinations throughout the region, from Delaware to Virginia's Atlantic Coast, including major stops in Wilmington, Baltimore, BWI Airport, DC, and Richmond. For more information on train travel, special fares, and toll-free phone numbers, see Getting There & Away.

Some of the most popular routes are as follows (fares listed are one way):

DC-Baltimore
28 times a day; $19 to $28 on Amtrak, but under $6 if you take a MARC train on a weekday

DC-Richmond
five times a day; $24 to $30

Richmond-Newport News (Norfolk)
twice a day; $22 to $25

Baltimore-Wilmington
28 times a day; $29 to $37

CAR

The Capital Region is well served by major interstate freeways. I-95 runs north-south along the eastern seaboard and connects with major east-west routes in Baltimore, DC, and Richmond. Around major cities, a three-digit interstate extension bypasses the central city for through-travelers (in Baltimore it's I-695; in DC it's the I-495 Beltway).

The region offers two exceptionally scenic two-lane highway routes for leisurely driving adventures: the Appalachian route through Maryland and Virginia via the Blue Ridge Parkway and Skyline Drive (most scenic, and most crowded, during the fall foliage season); and the old Atlantic Coast Hwy (Route 17), which detours from the urban corridor and runs through the old-time beach towns of the Delmarva Peninsula, the 18-mile-long Chesapeake Bay tunnel, mainland Virginia's corner coast, and Dismal Swamp before continuing south to Florida.

For information on road conditions, call ☎ 800-367-7623 in Virginia, ☎ 800-541-9595 in Maryland, ☎ 800-732-8500 in Delaware, and ☎ 202-727-5745 in DC.

If you're looking for someone to ride along and share the cost of fuel, ask around, put up a notice in hostels, check the ride boards at universities, and look at newspaper classified ads. Hostels can be especially good places to find riders, not only for long trips but also for local day trips when you're looking for someone to share the cost of a rental car.

Road Rules

The use of seat belts and child safety seats is required throughout the Capital Region. Drive on the right side of the road.

The speed limit is generally 55 or 65mph on highways, 25mph in cities and towns, and as low as 15mph in school zones (strictly enforced during school hours). It's forbidden to pass a school bus when its lights are flashing. On the interstate highways in designated rural areas, the speed limit is 65, 70, or even 75mph. Always watch for posted speed limits.

Most states have laws against littering – if you are seen throwing anything from a vehicle, you can be fined $1000 and be forced to pick up what you discarded.

In winter conditions, you may have to carry snow chains and fit them if there is snow on the road. Many cars are fitted with steel-studded snow tires for winter driving.

Penalties are very severe for DUI, driving under the influence of alcohol and/or drugs. Police can give roadside sobriety checks (making you touch your nose, walk in a straight line, etc) to assess if you've been drinking or using drugs. If you fail, they'll

---

Accidents Do Happen

In an auto-dependent country like the USA, accidents are fairly common. It's important that a visitor knows the appropriate protocol when involved in a 'fender-bender':

- DON'T TRY TO DRIVE AWAY! Remain at the scene of the accident; otherwise, you may spend some time in the local jail.

- Call the police (and an ambulance, if needed) immediately and give the operator as much specific information as possible (your location, the number of vehicles involved, whether injuries were sustained). The emergency phone number is ☎ 911.

- Get the other driver's name, address, driver's license number, license plate number, and insurance information. Be prepared to provide any documentation you have, such as your passport, international driver's license, and insurance documents.

- Tell your story to the police carefully. Refrain from answering any questions until you feel comfortable doing so (with a lawyer present, if need be). That's your right under the law. The only insurance information you must reveal is the name of your insurance carrier and your policy number.

- Always comply with a request that you undergo an alcohol breathalyzer test. If you refuse, you'll almost certainly find yourself with an automatic suspension of your driving privileges.

- If you're driving a rental car, call the rental company promptly.

require you to take a breath test, urine test, or blood test to determine the level of alcohol or drugs in your body. If you refuse to be tested, you'll be treated as if you'd taken the test and failed. The maximum legal blood alcohol concentration is 0.08%. During festive holidays and special events, road blocks are sometimes set up to deter drunk drivers. In some states, it is illegal to carry 'open containers' of alcohol in a vehicle, even if they are empty. Containers that are full and sealed may be carried, but if they have been opened, they must be carried in the trunk.

Also see Legal Matters in the Facts for the Visitor chapter for more information.

Driver's License

Visitors can legally drive in the USA for up to 12 months with their home driver's license. An International Driving Permit (IDP) is a very useful adjunct (see Visas & Documents in the Facts for the Visitor chapter).

It's much easier and less expensive to get car insurance if you have a local driver's license. In most states, it is not difficult or expensive to get one – call the state Department of Motor Vehicles for details. It usually involves a simple multiple-choice test of the highway codes and an undemanding driving test. You'll need a birth certificate or passport and proof of residence (an address) in the state. You may also need to get a Social Security card, which can involve some Social Security Department bureaucracy. (The card is stamped 'not valid for employment.') Getting a license can be a revealing look at US public administration.

Insurance

Every owner or driver of a motor vehicle must 'maintain financial responsibility' to protect the health and property of others in case of an accident. The easiest way to do this is to have auto liability insurance, and most states specify a minimum level of coverage. For rental cars, the company will arrange insurance if you're not already covered – it may cost almost as much as the rental.

If you buy a car, you must take out liability insurance, and this can be difficult if you don't have a local license (see Driver's License, above). A car dealer or AAA (see below) may be able to suggest an insurer. Even with a local license, insurance can be expensive and difficult to obtain if you don't have evidence of a good driving record. Bring copies of your home auto insurance policies if they can help establish that you are a good risk. Drivers under 25, and especially those under 21, will have big problems getting insurance.

AAA Membership

If you'll be doing much driving, whether in your own vehicle, someone else's, or a rental, membership in the American Automobile Association (AAA; ☎ 800-874-7532, www.aaa.com) is highly recommended. Having a AAA (referred to as 'triple A') card entitles you to free 24-hour emergency roadside service anywhere in the USA in the event of an accident, breakdown, or locking your keys in the car. Members are entitled to free service within a given radius of the nearest service center, and service providers will tow your car to a mechanic if they can't fix it. The nationwide toll-free roadside assistance number is ☎ 800-222-4357.

AAA also offers free road maps, tour books, and other travel literature; gives advice on how to buy a used car; and provides travel agency services. It also sells car insurance and issues traveler's checks without commission.

If you're considering buying a used car, some AAA offices have diagnostic centers where mechanics perform vehicle inspections on-site for their own members and those of foreign affiliates.

The AAA membership card will often get you discounts for accommodations, car rental, and admission charges. AAA offices can be found in major cities and in many smaller towns throughout the USA; for addresses, check the AAA website. The cost of membership varies by region, ranging from $46 to $63 for the first year and $36 to $45 per year thereafter.

If you are a member of an automobile association in another country, this will probably entitle you to reciprocal rights in the USA – bring a letter of introduction and proof of membership.

Rental

Car rental prices vary widely from city to city, company to company, car to car, and day to day. Within the Capital Region, you might pay as little as $20 per day or as much as $45. If you're arranging a rental before you get to the USA, check all the options with your travel agent first. If you get a fly-drive package, local taxes may be an extra charge when you collect the car. Several online travel reservation networks have up-to-the-minute information on car rental rates at all the main airports and let you make online reservations (see Buying Tickets in the Getting There & Away chapter). Rates are usually lower in main cities with lots of competing companies, but if there's a big conference or sports event in town, rental cars will cost more for a few days before and after.

Once you're in a city, shop around. Use toll-free numbers to check the big companies, but try the local ones too. Many airports have a courtesy phone and a board with advertisements for car rental agencies. You can spend 30 minutes calling a dozen of them toll-free, select the most suitable, and they'll pick you up and take you to their lot. Be sure to ask for the best rate – discounts may be offered for renting on weekends, for three days, by the week or month, or even for renting a car in one place and returning it to another if the company needs to move cars in that direction. Even if the company doesn't need cars moved, a 'one-way' rental can be useful. The extra drop-off charge ranges from nothing to $200.

Compare the total cost, including insurance and mileage; one company may charge a little less for the car but a little more for the insurance. Also estimate the distance you'll be driving; an 'unlimited mileage' plan works out more economically than a 'cost-per-mile' plan if you'll be driving long distances.

Some companies won't rent a car for more than about four weeks at a stretch or will require you to bring the vehicle in for a mileage check and oil change every four weeks. Arrangements in which car rentals are included as part of a fly-drive package are more likely to permit long-term rentals.

Most rental companies require that you have a major credit card, that you be at least 25 years old, and that you have a valid driver's license (see Driver's License, above). Alamo, Thrifty, Budget, and Rent-A-Wreck may rent to drivers between the ages of 21 and 24 for an additional charge (usually around $20 per day).

There are several types of insurance to consider. Liability insurance is required by law in most states but is not always included in rental contracts because many Americans are covered for rental cars under their regular car liability insurance policy. Check this carefully. You need liability coverage, but don't pay extra if sufficient coverage is already included with the rental. Insurance against damage to the car, called collision damage waiver (CDW) or loss damage waiver (LDW), is usually optional ($8 to $12 per day) but will often require you to pay for the first $100 or $500 of any repairs. This cost, called the deductible, may be removed by paying additional premiums. Some credit cards, such as MasterCard Gold and American Express, will cover your CDW if you rent for 15 days or less and charge the full value of the rental to your card. Check with your credit card company before you leave home to determine if this service is offered and what the extent of coverage is.

The major nationwide car rental agencies are as follows:

Alamo	☎ 800-327-9633
Avis	☎ 800-831-2847
Budget	☎ 800-527-0700
Dollar	☎ 800-800-4000
Enterprise	☎ 800-325-8007
Hertz	☎ 800-654-3131
National	☎ 800-328-4567
Thrifty	☎ 800-367-2277

Rent-A-Wreck (☎ 800-421-7253) offers older vehicles at lower prices. There are also thousands of smaller local companies that sometimes offer better prices than their national competitors. Check the yellow pages under Automobiles.

Purchase

If you'll be driving in North America for more than about three months, you may want to consider buying a vehicle. For periods of two months or less, it would probably be cheaper, and certainly less of a hassle, to rent a car. However, if you want a small van or a camper, rentals are much more expensive, so buying is relatively more attractive.

Cars bought at a dealer cost more but may come with warranties and/or financing options. Dealers are often concentrated in a certain area, so you can look at a lot of vehicles in a short time and compare prices. Buying from an individual is usually cheaper; look in the newspaper classified ads or special ad publications for used vehicles, such as *Auto Trader*. Private sellers are spread all over the suburbs, so you'll usually need a car to look for a car. Check the *Kelley Blue Book* (available at public libraries or online at www.kbb.com) for the average value of the model and year of vehicle you're considering, and have it checked out by a mechanic or diagnostic service before you buy. AAA may be helpful (see AAA Membership, above). Bargaining when buying a used car is standard practice.

The legalities vary a little from state to state. If you buy from a dealer, the dealer should submit to the DMV (Dept of Motor Vehicles) the required forms for the car's registration and transfer. If you buy from an individual, you (the buyer) must register the vehicle with the DMV within 10 days of purchase. To register the vehicle, you will need the bill of sale, the title to the car (the 'pink slip'), and proof of insurance or other financial responsibility. Some states, notably California, require a 'smog certificate' before a vehicle can be registered. It is the seller's responsibility to see that the vehicle passes the smog emission check; don't buy a car without a certificate, or you may face some costly

repairs to bring the vehicle up to standard before you can register it.

Selling a car before you go home can be a desperate business. Dealers will offer a laughably small amount if you're not buying another car, but it still might be your best option – selling to a dealer requires little paperwork from the seller. Or you can put a 'for sale' sign on the car itself and advertise as widely as possible, especially in hostels, colleges, and local papers. Have a phone number where buyers can call you, and be prepared to drop your price for a quick sale. Be sure to notify the DMV that you've sold the vehicle, or you may have to pay someone else's parking tickets later.

Drive-Aways

One option for longer trips is a 'drive-away car' from a vehicle transportation company that needs drivers to move cars from one place to another.

To be a driver, you must be over 21 and be able to present a valid driver's license, personal references, and a $200 to $400 cash deposit that is refunded upon safe delivery of the car. Some companies also require a printout of your driving record and a major credit card or three forms of identification. You pay nothing for the use of the car, but you do pay for the fuel you use. The company pays you nothing to drive the car, but it does pay the insurance. Check the car carefully for damage before you start.

You must deliver the car to its destination at a specified time; the time allotted for a trip usually works out at about six hours of driving per day. The company also stipulates a maximum mileage, so you have to follow the shortest route. Make sure you understand the conditions for deposit refund and how you can cash the refund check.

There may not be cars available when and where you want to go, so it helps to be flexible, to plan ahead, and to contact several companies. Availability depends on demand; coast-to-coast routes are the most available. Some demand is determined by holiday movements; for example, lots of cars need drivers from the Northeast to Florida at the start of winter.

Drive-away car companies are listed in telephone directory yellow pages under Automotive Transport & Drive-Away Companies. They include the following:

AAA Advantage Auto Transport   ☎ 800-480-1733

A-A Auto Transport & Driveaway   ☎ 800-466-6935

A Anthony Driveaway Truckaway   ☎ 800-606-2006

Across America Driveaway   ☎ 800-964-7874

Auto Driveaway Co   ☎ 800-346-2277

Contranz   ☎ 800-862-9999

National Auto Transport   ☎ 800-225-9611

Phone a week or two ahead of when you want to travel.

Parking

Parking is scarce and expensive in many inner-city areas. Metered street parking is geared toward short-term use, with time limits usually from 10 minutes to three hours. Put in enough dimes and quarters to prepay the whole time you'll be parked – you can't extend the time by putting more money in later. That's called 'meter-feeding,' and you can be fined for it. Metered parking spaces are usually free on Sundays and public holidays and outside business hours (8 am to 6 pm).

Commercial parking lots in cities charge $10 per day or more. Many are unattended and require prepayment, either by credit card or by stuffing cash into a paybox. Attended parking garages are the most secure places to park but also the most expensive. Some parking garages offer 'validated parking,' free or discounted parking for customers who spend money at certain stores. Get your parking stub validated – usually with a stamp or a sticker – when you make a purchase. Many hotels charge $12 to $20 for parking, on top of the room rate; ask about any parking charges when you book.

Average penalties for unauthorized parking are $10 for parking in a no-parking zone, $20 for parking at an expired meter, and as high as $300 for parking in a zone reserved for the disabled. Pay parking fines promptly, or you'll be charged even more.

MOTORCYCLE

Riding a bike in America is an almost mythic experience, with a heritage going back beyond *Easy Rider* and *The Wild One*. The biker on the road descends from the cowboy on the range and endures many of the same discomforts, as well as the same sense of freedom and the wide-open spaces.

Much of the information under Car, earlier, applies to motorcycles too. To ride a motorcycle, you need a US state motorcycle license or an International Driving Permit endorsed for motorcycles. A state DMV can give you the rules relating to motorcycle use. Helmets are required in almost every state.

Motorcycle rental and insurance is expensive, especially if you want to ride a Harley-Davidson. EagleRider motorcycle rentals (☎ 800-910-1520), with offices in major cities nationwide, charges $135 per day for a 1340cc Harley, including helmet and liability insurance, but collision insurance (CDW) is extra. Buying a bike would be cheaper if you're staying a few months and if you can take a loss to sell it in a hurry.

BICYCLE

The region's terrain offers a variety of experiences for bike touring, from mountain biking along rugged Forest Service roads and trails through the Appalachian forest to leisurely trips along the two-lane blacktop at the remote peninsular coast. Spare parts and repair shops are readily available. For more information, see the Activities chapter.

If you're flying to the region and bringing your bike with you, ask the airline about requirements, restrictions, and any additional fees before purchasing a ticket.

HITCHHIKING

Hitchhiking is never entirely safe in any country in the world, and we don't recommend it. Travelers who decide to hitchhike should understand that they are taking a small but potentially serious risk. People who do choose to hitchhike will be safer if they travel in pairs and let someone else know where they are planning to go.

WALKING

You can cross the region on foot along the Appalachian Trail, part of the 2159-mile route along the spine of the mountain range. Another well-traveled hike is the 185-mile trail that follows the old Chesapeake and Ohio (C&O) Canal towpath, stretching from DC to Cumberland, Maryland. (See the Activities chapter for more information.) Dedicated city walkers will be most drawn to Washington, DC, for long, safe walks through neighborhoods filled with monuments and notable architecture.

BOAT

The Delaware Bay, Chesapeake Bay, and Atlantic Coast are all connected by the Intracoastal Waterway, the navigable channel along the eastern seaboard. Small craft can traverse the region by following this route and stopping at a plethora of ports, many historic and bucolic, along the way. The government publishes the *Coast Pilot* guide for navigation information, available from government bookstores, by mail order, or from many marine supply shops in the region.

The *Waterway Guide* is the bible for intracoastal travelers. This cruising guide offers essential information about navigation, ports of call, marina facilities, as well as local history. Order this book on the Internet or pick it up at any good yacht chandler, such as Fawcett Boat Supply (☎ 410-267-8681), 110 Compromise St, Annapolis, Maryland.

Hundreds of marinas line the Chesapeake Bay and its fringed waterways. In Maryland, the major yachting centers are in Annapolis and Solomons Island, on the Eastern Shore along the Sassafras River, and in Rock Hall, St Michaels, and Oxford. In Virginia, the main marinas are on the York River and in the Norfolk area. On the Delaware Bay, Lewes is the major yachting center.

LOCAL TRANSPORT

Each city operates its own municipal bus service, and these services vary considerably from system to system in reliability, cost, and safety. Commonly, passengers pay upon boarding, and exact change is required (some modern buses accept paper money). Seats up front are often reserved for disabled or elderly passengers.

Besides the Amtrak service in the region (see the Getting There & Away chapter), regional rail service is also available. Maryland's MARC trains connect with Union Station in DC and BWI Airport, as well as service points in eastern Maryland.

Washington, DC, operates a modern, efficient subway system called the Metro, with service throughout the District, to the airport, and into outlying suburban communities. Baltimore has a Metro as well, and though the system is efficient, it only services a narrow corridor of suburban towns north and south of downtown.

Even small towns usually offer taxi service. Relative to other forms of transit, taxis are an expensive way to get about, but for convenient point-to-point service they can't be beat. In cities like DC, taxis can be the most sensible way for newcomers to get around – fares for short distances may be comparable to the Metro (especially if you share cabs), and driving and parking are sometimes not worth the hassle.

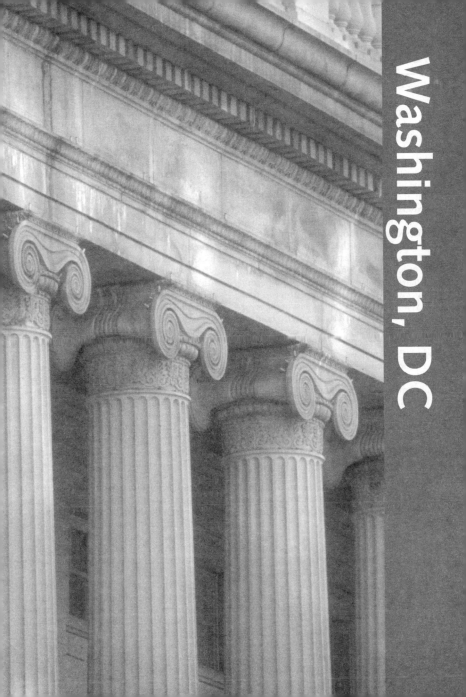
Washington, DC

Facts about Washington, DC

The District of Columbia is a tale of two cities. One tale roots in the monuments, museums, and the 20 million visitors who come every year to bear witness to one of the most powerful cities on Earth. But for a traveler wishing to get behind the scenes, a more lively and often-neglected story beckons from the District's multicultural neighborhoods. Here, you will find a rainbow of faces in a city where seeking pleasure is as much an addiction and art form as the political deal.

From the top of the 555-foot Washington Monument (the tallest point in DC), you can see miles of the long, flat Potomac River basin, which patriots selected for the permanent seat of the US government more than 200 years ago. About 2 miles east of the river, the land rises to form a low shelf, a contour the city's chief architect Pierre L'Enfant recognized as 'a pedestal awaiting a monument'; today, it's known as Capitol Hill.

Broad avenues radiate from the stately Capitol like spokes on a wheel, intersecting at geometric angles with an alphabetized grid and roundabouts designed for defense. The corridor from the Capitol to the river forms a vast green centerpiece, a national lawn called the Mall. The great majority of the city's world-famous sights – the White House, the Lincoln Memorial, the National Gallery, and the Smithsonian museums – are located around this compact area. You could walk it in 30 minutes flat or spend days exploring these icons of American culture and democracy.

Downtown DC surrounds the Mall with neoclassical federal buildings, courthouses, bureaus, and libraries. Around these buildings lie landscaped courtyards, squares, and plazas rife with statues, fountains, and flowers that lure local citizens and travelers to call 'time out' and enjoy the sun, fresh air, and passing human parade.

The 'other DC' lies beyond downtown in distinctive neighborhoods stretching from the Potomac and Anacostia River waterfronts to the ridges north of the Mall and downtown.

These neighborhoods are not collections of the high-rise, concrete apartment buildings so typical of the world's capitals in the 21st century. To a large degree, Washingtonians – both rich and poor – relish a more genteel existence, raising their families and pursuing their passions closer to street level in brick townhouses, individual homes, and stately apartment buildings along tree-lined streets. Here is a city where citizens still enjoy the neighborliness of a seat on a front-door stoop, a table with friends at an outdoor cafe, block parties, and evening walks.

And when they go out, Washingtonians go with all the fire in the belly of lovers and dreamers with a mission. Just take a stroll among the throbbing street-side cafes around sophisticated Dupont Circle on a sunny Sunday afternoon. Lose yourself in the crowded pubs lining Georgetown's M St on a Friday evening. Or get caught up in a sea of protest marchers roiling toward the steps of the Capitol building. You will feel the hair rise on the back of your neck and – some say – a rhythm like wild hope in your feet.

If you give in to the city's rhythm, your feet will carry you into DC's distinct cultural enclaves – the vibrant gay community, the political activists, the cultural elite, the African American vanguard, the artists, or the international population of diplomats and refugees. Of course, the most exciting spots in the capital city are the ones where these groups mix it up the most.

One place overflowing with energy and a mix of different kinds of people is the ethnic, bohemian district of Adams-Morgan in the northwest quarter of the city. Here, the streets on weekend nights become a parade of the wild at heart swaying to the beats of reggae and salsa that pour from blocks of restaurants, bars, and clubs with outrageous names like Madame's Organ. By day, you will find DC's multicultural stew of citizens and visitors cruising the food courts and shops of Union Station, patrolling the corridors of the national museums, roaming the bike paths and trails in Rock Creek Park, exploring the towpath of the C&O Canal, and dreaming along the shores of the Potomac. But probably no place beats the green plain of the Mall on a warm April or October day, when it seems as if all the children of the world have come to fly their kites.

HISTORY

The US Congress met in a variety of cities – Philadelphia, New York, and Annapolis (Maryland) among them – before the fledgling republic was ready to commit to a permanent seat of government. Congress considered many sites from the St Croix to the St Mary's Rivers (the country's borders at the time) and decided upon the Potomac as a natural midpoint that would satisfy both northern and southern states. (Though this occurred a century before the Civil War, the stark differences between the regions were already apparent.) This spot had the added benefits of being across the river from George Washington's home in Mount Vernon and sitting at a point on the Potomac that positioned it well for commerce (see Geography, later).

Folks started referring to it as 'the city of Washington' around 1791, and the name stuck. Maryland and Virginia agreed to cede land to create the District of Columbia (named for Christopher Columbus), and an area '10 miles square' was laid out by African American mathematician Benjamin Banneker and surveyor Andrew Ellicott. French engineer (and supporter of the American Revolution) Pierre Charles L'Enfant was hired to design the city, and he came up with an elegant plan (based on European Renaissance ideals for a city of 800,000) that would showcase public buildings and monuments. But while L'Enfant's design was widely admired, he quickly ran afoul of local politics. After L'Enfant was fired, Banneker continued to carry out L'Enfant's plans.

Work started on the ornate Capitol in 1793, but it was barely complete when British troops torched it in the War of 1812. Though the Capitol was eventually rebuilt, the city entered a slump that lasted for decades. A dispirited vote to abandon the capital lost by only nine votes.

When to Visit DC

The height of the visitor season runs from April 1 to the beginning of August. But at any time of the year, visitors may have to wait in long lines to see the newest and most popular attractions. In terms of weather, the most comfortable times are spring (when millions of pale-pink cherry blossoms bloom) and fall. Summers can be oppressive, as the daytime temperature sometimes rises over 90° F and the humidity feels like Singapore. Summer nights are only slightly cooler. From December to February, enough snow falls to collect on the ground and snarl traffic for days at a time.

Charles Dickens visited and dismissed DC as 'the City of Magnificent Distances,' complaining about 'spacious avenues that begin in nothing and lead nowhere; streets, mile-long, that only want houses, roads, and inhabitants; public buildings that need but a public.'

The Civil War focused attention on DC, bringing bivouacs, temporary hospitals, and armies to its outskirts. The war's chaos and expense led Washingtonians to wonder whether construction of the elaborate Capitol dome might not be suspended. President Lincoln responded, 'If people see the Capitol going on, it is a sign we intend the Union shall go on.' In the war's aftermath, the Great Emancipator was assassinated in Ford's Theater (a memorial flag remains draped over the theater box shrine today), and the role of the US capital changed from state-led administration to centralized leadership.

In the 1870s, territorial governor Alexander 'Boss' Shepherd overhauled the town's ailing infrastructure, but his extravagant use of federal funds and his penchant for steamrolling anything in his way led to a crackdown by Congress that robbed DC of self-government for another 100 years. For the citizenry, it was a high price to pay for a city beginning to look like it might fulfill L'Enfant's vision of a world-class capital.

Lincoln, the Great Emancipator

A beautification plan at the turn of the century added most of the landscaping, parks, and monuments for which DC is now well known. Nevertheless, until recently DC suffered from its image as a Southern backwater. It was John F Kennedy who so succinctly slammed it as 'a city of Southern efficiency and Northern charm.' The Kennedy Center, established as a 'living memorial' to JFK, did much to bring cosmopolitan culture to the place.

Today, DC's international community of diplomats, lobbyists, journalists, and refugees has representatives from every nation in the world. The city's intense and divisive political climate is downright *romantic* to political activists. Spectacular *free* art is visible at every turn. From a Southern backwater, DC has evolved into a national and international pilgrimage site (as was intended) for legions of Americans and foreign visitors.

Yet DC has long been notorious for troubling problems. Poverty, crime, and racially segregated neighborhoods in the shadow of glorious monuments proclaiming 'equality for all' embarrass those who would hope to

hold up the nation's capital as a model. The city has been scandal-ridden since the days when President Thomas Jefferson refused to give up his affair with his slave Sally Hemings while in office. The end of the 20th century produced even thicker moral clouds than usual over the city. During 1998, the world watched as the embarrassing saga of President William Jefferson Clinton's sexual adventures in the White House, and the subsequent impeachment proceedings unfolded like a soap opera on TV and in newspapers around the globe.

But as DC enters the new millennium, the mood in the city is more hopeful than it has been since the early 1960s, when John and Jackie Kennedy made DC what reporters loved to call 'Camelot.' New corporate commitment to the downtown area has created a spectacular sports arena, the MCI Center, that is engendering urban renewal. Crime is at a 25-year low. New restaurants and clubs are bursting forth all over the city. Meanwhile, a number of once-segregated neighborhoods in the city such as Capital Hill, Shaw, and Adams-Morgan are growing more racially diverse. In DC, people of white, black, Asian, and Latino backgrounds are clearly discovering the excitement (and losing their fears) of living in a multicultural community. Finally, the year 2000 marks the occasion for both presidential and major congressional elections. These elections are the biggest and best opportunity for the renewal of the American democracy in almost a decade, and the optimism surrounding such renewal in this city is palpable.

Washington, DC, is no flawless model of democracy, but it is a microcosm of the grand ideals and sticky realities of the US.

GEOGRAPHY

The topography of DC is both subtle and complex, although the first-time visitor who only sees the downtown monuments around the Mall can be excused for thinking of the US capital as simply a low, level city by a river. The truth is that DC stands at the exact point where the Coastal Plain and the Piedmont Plateau intersect with each other and the Potomac River.

Much of downtown and southeast DC lie on the delta where the small Anacostia River joins the broad Potomac. If you travel up the Potomac along the DC waterfront from the Washington Channel, you can see the 'fall line' (the point at which mountain rivers drop from the plateau to the plain in a series of waterfalls) that marks the border between the coastal lowlands and the piedmont rising in Arlington, Virginia, along the shores northwest of Ronald Reagan Washington National Airport. At the point where this line of hills meets the Potomac, you reach the head of navigation on the river. This fact was important to George Washington when he picked the site for his capital. Seagoing ships could sail the whole way up the Potomac to this point to facilitate the shipment of the important tobacco crop. North of DC, the Potomac is full of boulders and swift currents. The C&O Canal, which begins here on the east bank, was built to facilitate water travel and commercial shipping from here through the Cumberland Gap in the Allegheny Mountains to the western frontier.

On the eastern side of the river, the fall line defines the high ground of the Georgetown University Campus and the surrounding neighborhood of Georgetown. Moving farther east of Rock Creek, you can see that the upper lip of the fall line runs through Adams-Morgan, more or less along Kalorama Rd and east from here along U St.

South of these points, the heart of the city surrounding the Mall is basically coastal lowlands carved out by the erosion caused by the last ice age, as well as by the Potomac and Anacostia Rivers. It's likely that Capitol Hill, the gently sloping focal point on these lowlands, was once the actual meeting point of the Potomac and the Anacostia before erosion caused the rivers to flow farther to the west and south.

Also see Orientation in the Washington, DC chapter.

GOVERNMENT & POLITICS

The municipal government of the District, which is overseen by the federal body, has recently been as scandal-ridden as the federal government. As a federal protectorate, DC has a political life that more closely resembles that of a colony than a state. District residents won the right to vote in presidential elections only in 1961, and their hard-fought struggle for Congressional representation earned them only nonvoting representatives.

Home Rule

Though the USA was founded on the principle of 'no taxation without representation,' residents of the nation's capital still have no voting representatives in Congress. In fact, residents of the District of Columbia only gained the right to vote in presidential elections as recently as 1961.

As a political entity, DC is an anomaly that operates more like a colony or Indian reservation – a reservation of 600,000 people. Congress oversees the District's budget and, on whim, grants and restricts opportunities for DC's self-governance. Considering that the District's population is predominantly African American, charges of paternalism and racism are often issues in the debate.

Congress justifies its decisions by pointing to DC's track record, which is far from sterling. As early as the 1870s, an elected mayor who earned the nickname 'Boss' Shepherd so liberally disposed of federal funds that Congress revoked 'home rule' for another century. More recently, the District has been rocked with scandals of financial mismanagement, drug use, and such irresponsible administration that the nation's capital is left with barely adequate public services, from garbage and snow removal to fire fighting and police protection.

Though advocates have proposed statehood since the 1960s, this history makes it even less likely now than in the past. Because the District overwhelmingly votes Democratic, and statehood would virtually assure the election of two additional Democratic senators, the Republican Congress will predictably oppose the idea at any time. (Also see the Government & Politics section in Facts about the Capital Region.)

Despite calls for statehood, the rise in status seems a long way off – made longer still by the District government's long reputation for inefficiency and fiscal irresponsibility. For example, during the 1990s, longtime mayor Marion Barry was reelected to serve in office after being caught by undercover police smoking cocaine with an ex-girlfriend in a local hotel. In the wake of Barry's reelection, the US Congress systematically stripped him of power until he was little more than a sad figurehead. During the twilight of the Barry administration, a new African American face entered city government as Chief Financial Officer. During his three years in this post, Anthony Williams won general admiration for his intelligence, integrity, and stabilization of the city's precarious financial situation. In the fall of 1998, he won election as DC's mayor and brought a squeaky-clean, can-do image to city government.

ECONOMY

DC's economy largely depends on only two major employers: the federal government and the service industry. In recent years, the gross regional product of the District has hovered around $50 billion. Revenues from the federal, state, and local governments represent more than 36% of the GRP. Service businesses represent almost 42% of the economy, and this percentage continues to grow whereas government percentages have been shrinking during recent years. Leading the growth in the service sector are businesses related to tourism, legal services (lobbyists), education, and engineering/management. Industries such as construction and manufacturing add less than 4% to the economy.

In the last 30 years, DC's economy has become more specialized than ever, and its extraordinary dependence on government and service sectors makes the local economic situation extraordinarily vulnerable to the vicissitudes of the national economy. In other words, DC felt the nationwide recession of the early 1990s more than the surrounding states of Virginia and Maryland. During the robust economy of the late 1990s, DC has experienced a renaissance.

POPULATION & PEOPLE

Today, Washington, DC, – referred to as 'DC,' 'Washington,' or locally as 'the District' – continues to be largely a company town. About a third of its approximately 600,000 residents work for the government (federal or district), and 42% work in supportive service industries. Ultimately, *all* business here is dependent upon government business. A high proportion of metropolitan-area residents are educated through college and beyond, and many are well informed and opinionated about public policy and current events.

There are, however, sharp racial and socioeconomic divisions between black and white and rich and poor. This is typical among American cities, but here the proportions are more dramatic, as DC proper is three-quarters African American, and two-thirds of the DC population earns under $32,000 annually. To be more geographically specific, *three-quarters* of DC is overwhelmingly African American; *one-quarter* – that is, the Northwest – is predominantly white. During the last 30 years, the city has lost 200,000 residents, and middle-class (white and black) flight has sent much of the policy-making population to the affluent suburbs, where taxation earns them Congressional representation. (See the Home Rule boxed text, earlier, for more about DC's anomalous political designation.)

Finally, two other distinctive qualities of the District's population contribute to its character. DC has about 70,000 college students at 10 institutions of higher learning, making DC the third-largest college town in the USA after Boston and New York. And in DC, females outnumber males by a ratio of more than five to four. Some estimates place this ratio as high as two women for every one man if you look solely at the city's workforce.

Approximately 4.4 million people live in the surrounding suburban towns in Maryland and Virginia.

ARTS & ARCHITECTURE

Grand monumental architecture and galleries full of fine arts are some of DC's biggest draws. The city's architecture owes a great deal to the original city plan by chief architect Pierre L'Enfant – the interesting shapes of many buildings arose from his street grid full of diagonals and roundabouts. He intended that no building would rise higher than the Capitol (around 13 stories), and while this has left DC free of modern skyscrapers, it has resulted in many short and squat modern government buildings.

Borrowed Roman and Grecian architectural styles – columns and marble everywhere you turn – reflect the ambition to create a classical capital (the Capitol, Archives, and Lincoln Memorial are examples). You can see the Victorian era reflected in DC's lavish churches and townhouses; the Old Executive Office Building is a fine example of Victorian excess. Many monolithic modern buildings that easily overwhelm their surroundings (such as the Housing and Urban Development building in the southwest quad-

rant) are examples of the post-WWII building boom. The 1978 East Wing of the National Gallery of Art and the National Air and Space Museum, completed in the 1980s, are two premier examples of modern design, as is the John F Kennedy Center for the Performing Arts (1971). The Watergate complex (which includes a hotel, offices, shops, and apartments), on the shores of the Potomac in Foggy Bottom, is in a league of its own, with all its glass and parabolic curves doing a good impression of a lunar space station. At the National Building Museum, travelers can view exhibits that examine DC's unusual architectural choices.

As for arts, DC's galleries hold astounding classical and modern masterpieces (though they're not best known for their innovation); DC's ready and free access to so many collections in such a compact area is nearly unparalleled in the world.

Washington, DC

As in many of the world's great cities, walking is the best way to explore the District of Columbia. Vigorous trekkers will have no problem making the 5-mile hike from Capitol Hill in the east to Georgetown on the western border. And if you walk, the layout of most streets is so straightforward, you may never get lost. But if the weather is hot or you are low on energy, you will probably use DC's Metro to move from neighborhood to neighborhood. In such a case, a clear sense of the city's layout will be your key to navigating underground successfully.

ORIENTATION

Originally, the District claimed territory in the shape of a neat diamond spanning the Potomac River on land ceded by Maryland and Virginia. But over the years, the diamond has eroded on the western edge, and the city returned land west of the Potomac River to Virginia.

Now, the river (across from which lie the Virginian cities of Arlington and Alexandria) bounds the city to the west. Maryland's Montgomery and Prince George's Counties – with their suburban communities (such as Bethesda, Silver Spring, and Seat Pleasant) – border the northern, eastern, and southern sides of the city. The District itself now measures 69 sq miles.

A freeway bypass called 'the Beltway' (I-495) rings the city. Decades ago, the Beltway divided the metropolis from farms and rural communities. Today, the metropolitan area of tightly packed suburban housing developments extends at least 10 to 15 miles beyond the Beltway in all directions. The population boom accompanying this development has rendered the Beltway painfully inadequate (during morning and evening rush hours) as an artery for facilitating commuter traffic.

The Capitol is the center of the District in more than a strictly symbolic way. From the Capitol building, the city divides into four quadrants (northwest, northeast, southeast, and southwest) along axes following N Capitol St, S Capitol St, E Capitol St, and the Mall (the equivalent of W Capitol St). Not only does the Mall divide the western side of the city into north and south, this national lawn (nearly a quarter-mile wide and 2 miles long) is the locus or front yard for most of DC's monuments and museums.

Highlights

- The always-free, always-dazzling Smithsonian museums – not only the heavy-hitters on the Mall but also the Renwick Gallery and Museum of American Art

- The monumental sights – paddleboating by the Jefferson Memorial, the view from the top of the Washington Monument by night, and the poignant Vietnam and Lincoln Memorials

- The political tour – the Capitol Rotunda and Statuary Hall (skip the tour and line), protests outside the Supreme Court, Jackie O's Blue Room in the White House, and the political debate at Irish pubs on the Hill

- Georgetown's historic district, with its collection of restaurants and pubs catering to the young and affluent

- The sidewalk cafes, galleries, boutiques, bookstores, gay scene, and foreign embassies of Dupont Circle

- Adams-Morgan's funky international restaurant and club scene along the 18th St strip

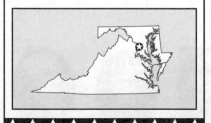

Identical addresses appear in all four quadrants of DC, so you *must* know the directional component of most addresses (11th St NW and 11th St NE, for example, are in opposite parts of town). Most sights of interest to visitors are located around the Capitol, along the Mall, and in the northwest quadrant.

Thoroughfares spread out in a grid of north-south numbered streets and east-west lettered streets (from A to W, with no B, J, X, Y, or Z Sts; note that some businesses and residents call I St 'Eye St'). Addresses on lettered streets generally reveal their cross street; for example, Sholl's Colonial Cafeteria, at 1900 K St NW, lies at the corner of 19th and K, and the main library, at 901 G St NW, sits on G St between 9th and 10th Sts.

Pierre L'Enfant overlaid DC's street grid with broad diagonal avenues named after states in the Union. Pennsylvania Ave is best known as the president's address; it connects the White House and the Capitol; Connecticut Ave is also a major thoroughfare through the northwest quadrant. Massachusetts Ave makes an efficient diagonal across the northern half of Washington, DC. New York Ave is the principal artery for entering town from the northeast, whereas Pennsylvania Ave brings you into town from the southeast. The main east-west arteries through DC are K and M Sts; 16th is a good north-south route. Traffic circles at the intersections of major avenues add to the city's scenic appeal but can make DC a challenging place for outsiders to navigate by car – until they discover the utility of the circles for altering direction without losing oneself in a maze of back streets.

Capitol Hill

The Capitol Hill district is at the east end of the Mall, surrounding the Capitol building. This is the only area with sights in all four quadrants; it's a government, business, and residential area east of the Capitol and is currently in the midst of rapid gentrification. The neighborhood is the site of monumental government buildings (such as the Supreme Court, the Library of Congress, and the Senate and House office buildings),

in addition to the Capitol, the city's last market building, and a number of clubs and bars catering to congressional staffers or gays. Sights of major interest to visitors (including government buildings and Union Station) ring the Capitol building within a radius of four or five blocks. Beyond these public attractions, Capitol Hill's residential streets can be an extraordinary place to stroll amid shade trees and block after block of restored Federal-period townhouses, reviving the days of nearly 200 years ago, when Washington was home to a vanguard experiment in democracy.

Downtown

This is the business district north of the Mall, between the White House to the west and Union Station to the east. For decades, this was one of the saddest areas of the city. After the surrounding office buildings closed their doors for the day, the streets here were home to few but the homeless and visitors scurrying between taxis and a clutch of hotels. However, money has been pouring into downtown redevelopment during the last several years. The biggest byproduct of all this investing is the huge sports arena known as the MCI Center. With the center attracting crowds to pro basketball and hockey events, downtown is becoming a livelier place after hours. The once-minuscule and tawdry Chinatown section, north of the MCI Center, now bustles with patrons drawn to scores of new inexpensive Asian (and other ethnic) restaurants opening in the area, and new pubs are popping up on every block. Some of the District's most popular clubs have opened their doors downtown, some migrating here from traditionally popular entertainment zones such as Dupont Circle and Georgetown.

Foggy Bottom

This area is the headquarters for the Department of State, as well as George Washington University; it is also an upscale residential area that includes the mammoth Watergate complex. While Foggy Bottom is neither an entertainment zone nor loaded with national monuments and museums, it

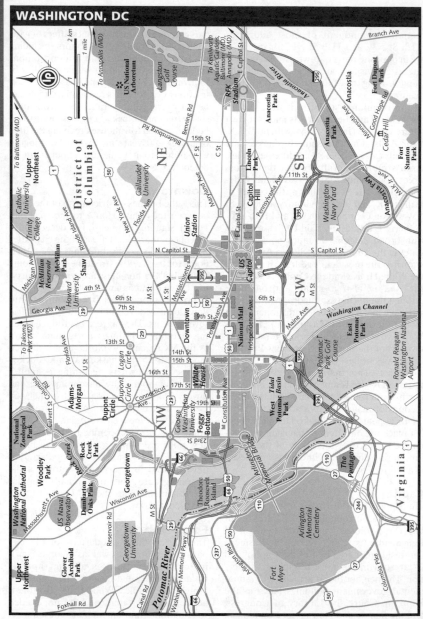

has the subtle charm of quiet, well-kept neighborhoods with a good collection of ethnic restaurants. The Metro stop here is also the closest public-transportation link to the major entertainment zone of Georgetown, which lies a half-mile to the west, across the Pennsylvania Ave bridge over Rock Creek.

Georgetown

Along the Potomac River and C&O Canal at the west end of town, Georgetown is the District's well-preserved historic district, featuring more than 100 restaurants, lively bars and clubs, pristine Federal-period townhouses, and the vast campus of Georgetown University. The area appeals to upscale students, resident professionals, and flocks of suburbanites who flood in from the Virginia suburbs and Bethesda, Maryland, looking for action.

Dupont Circle

This is an upscale business and residential area in northwestern DC (north of Foggy Bottom). Most of the foreign embassies are here, as well as a large gay community with its own well-developed collection of restaurants, bars, clubs, and bookstores. With broad sidewalks and myriad outdoor cafes, Dupont Circle makes for some of the best strolling and people-watching in the city.

Adams-Morgan

This is DC's bohemian, international neighborhood north of Dupont Circle. Although Adams-Morgan is largely an area of Victorian townhouses and apartment buildings drawing an astounding mix of Latino, black, Asian, and white residents, the neighborhood also has a popular business strip along 18th St and Columbia Rd, featuring a rich collection of ethnic restaurants and a cafe, bar, and club scene that rocks like New York's Greenwich Village.

Shaw

Just east of Adams-Morgan, this traditionally African American neighborhood has seen a new influx of other ethnic groups (including whites) drawn to the historically significant stock of Victorian townhouses near Howard University. A very happening club and restaurant scene – largely patronized by African Americans – has developed in recent years along U St.

Southwest

This district on the southwest side of the Mall is being reclaimed by urban redevelopment and gentrification. The promenade, yacht basin, restaurants, and hotel that have developed along the Washington Channel of the Potomac River are now attracting a lot of residents and tourists out for a stroll during fair weather.

Southeast & Anacostia

Although this area of residences and small businesses – located south of Capitol Hill and across the Anacostia River – has some major claims to fame (with places such as the Frederick Douglass National Historic site), the neighborhoods here house the city's poorest and most desperate residents. Drugs and violence are still a common part of the landscape here, and travelers would do well to avoid the area.

Maps

The Map Store (☎ 202-628-2608), 1636 I St NW, is a good source. Lonely Planet offers a color fold-up map of Washington, DC, convenient for navigating the city. Most bookstores sell local maps (see Bookstores, later in the chapter), as do major museum gift shops.

INFORMATION
Tourist Offices

You will find the Washington, DC Convention and Visitors Association (☎ 202-789-7000) at 1212 New York Ave NW, Suite 600, Washington, DC 20005. This office distributes information (including events calendars and an African American heritage guide) by mail or from its 6th-floor offices. It's open 9 am to 5 pm weekdays.

Two visitor centers are to the east of the White House. The White House Visitor Center is located in the Commerce Building, at 1450 Pennsylvania Ave NW. The National

Park Service (NPS) Visitor Pavilion is in the northeast corner of the Ellipse. (See the White House section, later in the chapter.)

The International Visitors Information Service (☎ 703-536-4911) operates from the International Arrivals building at the Washington-Dulles International Airport in Virginia. You can pick up brochures and maps from 8 am to 10 pm. The service also provides a 'language bank' (☎ 202-939-5538) to answer visitors' questions in 42 languages.

Call the National Park Service at Dial-a-Park (☎ 202-619-7275) for information about events in and around DC's parks and monuments. (NPS operates most of the federal sights open to the public in DC.)

Other useful resources include Deaf REACH (☎ 202-832-6681), Disabled Visitors Information (☎ 202-789-7000), and the Gay and Lesbian Hotline (☎ 202-833-3234).

Money

During business hours (9 am to 5 pm), major banks exchange money and cash traveler's checks. Also try American Express, which has two locations: 1150 Connecticut Ave NW, near Dupont Circle (☎ 202-457-1300), and 5300 Wisconsin Ave (☎ 202-362-4000), in the Mazza Galleria, near the Maryland border. The mall location is open until 6 pm weeknights and offers Saturday service from 10 am to 5 pm.

Another reliable exchange is Thomas Cook (☎ 202-237-2229), with currency service desks at 1800 K St NW (weekday business hours only) and in Union Station, across from Gate G (weekend service available). It also has three desks at Washington-Dulles International Airport (☎ 800-287-7362) in the West End, East End, and International Terminal, as well as at Ronald Reagan Washington National Airport (☎ 703-417-3200). Hours vary, but all are open from at least 9 am to 9 pm daily.

At Baltimore-Washington International Airport, go to Travelex America (☎ 410-859-5997), on the upper level at the entrance to Concourse C; it's open 6:30 am to 8:30 pm daily.

Post & Communications

The main post office (☎ 202-635-5300), where all general-delivery mail is directed, is out near the Maryland border at 900 Brentwood Rd NE, Washington, DC 20066 (near the Rhode Island Ave Metro stop). It is open 8 am to 8 pm weekdays, 8 am to 6 pm Saturday, and noon to 6 pm Sunday; holiday hours vary.

The more conveniently located post office at 2 Massachusetts Ave, next to the Postal Museum (across from Union Station), also has the longest hours: 7 am to midnight weekdays and to 8 pm weekends. Throughout town, you can easily find other US post offices, as well as many private mailing outlets (such as Mail Boxes Etc), where you can send faxes and packages via United Parcel Service or FedEx (including overnight delivery). To send a telegram, call Western Union (☎ 800-325-6000) and ask for the nearest office.

The area code for DC is 202. Local calls cost 25¢. Note that some hotels charge guests up to $1 for local calls.

Internet Resources

Travelers can find visitor information at www.washington.org. The Planet Earth home page on the web is nosc.mil/planet_earth/washington.html; there, you can get information on government agencies, the Metro system and area airports, and all that's new in DC. For the update on pressing White House information, check out www.whitehouse.gov. Check out www.ustreas.gov for a virtual tour of the Bureau of Engraving and Printing and save yourself a long wait in line at the real place.

If you need to get online while you're in the city, visit the Cyberstop Cafe. (See Dupont Circle under Bars & Clubs, later in this chapter.)

Travel Agencies

There is a Hostelling International's American Youth Hostel Travel Center (☎ 202-783-4943), at 1108 K St NW, diagonally across from the hostel near Domino's Pizza, as well as a Council Travel (☎ 202-337-6464), at 3301

M St NW in Georgetown. Both specialize in low-budget and student-oriented travel resources. They help find airfare discounts and sell Eurail passes. The Travel Center hosts travel seminars and maintains a library and bookstore as well. It's open 10 am to 6 pm Monday, Tuesday, Thursday, and Friday; to 2 pm Wednesday; and 12 pm to 5 pm Saturday. Council Travel's hours are 10 am to 6 pm weekdays, 11 am to 6 pm Wednesday, and 11 am to 3 pm Saturday.

See the Sunday Travel section of the *Washington Post* for advertisements of discount travel agents in DC and the surrounding suburbs.

Bookstores

Washington, DC's bookstores are more than places to buy books and periodicals. The ones with attached cafes encourage casual meetings and conversation. Many bookstores sponsor readings, open-mike poetry nights, and other literary events; some feature live music, and many are open late. Also see museum bookstores for titles related to their collections.

Dupont Circle has a wonderful selection. Kramerbooks (☎ 202-387-1400), at 1517 Connecticut Ave NW, features the popular Afterwords Cafe and live entertainment. Olsson's Books & Records (☎ 202-785-1133), 1307 19th St NW, sells just what you would expect. Also see Mystery Books (☎ 202-483-1600), 1715 Connecticut Ave NW, and Lambda Rising (☎ 202-462-6969), 1625 Connecticut Ave NW, specializing in gay and lesbian titles. Lammas (☎ 202-775-8218), 1607 17th St NW, bills itself as 'Washington's only feminist bookstore.' The International Language Center (☎ 202-332-2894) and the Newsroom (☎ 202-332-1489) feature books and periodicals in 100 languages; both are located at 1753 Connecticut Ave NW, near S St.

For used books, go to Idle Times (☎ 202-232-4774), 2410 18th St NW. Near the Maryland border in Upper Northwest is Politics & Prose (☎ 202-364-1919), 5015 Connecticut Ave NW, which sponsors author readings and serves great coffee.

In Georgetown, there's Bridge Street Books (☎ 202-965-5200), 2814 Pennsylvania Ave NW; Lantern Bryn Mawr Bookshop (☎ 202-333-3222), 3160 O St NW, for used books; and another Olsson's (☎ 202-338-9544), 1239 Wisconsin Ave NW. Barnes & Noble (☎ 202-965-9880), 3040 M St NW, features literary events, music, and a 3rd-floor cafe overlooking M St.

Pyramid Books (☎ 202-328-0190), 2849 Georgia Ave NW, across from Howard University in Shaw, specializes in Afro-centric books.

On Capitol Hill, you can stop by the Government Printing Office bookstore (☎ 202-512-0132), 710 N Capitol St, between G and H Sts (open weekdays only). Here they sell 15,000 titles published by the US government, including the blockbusters *Selling to the Military* and *Nest Boxes for Wood Ducks*. Near the Capitol, Trover Shops (☎ 202-543-8011), 227 Pennsylvania Ave SE, is a DC institution for books, cards, and gifts. Chapters (☎ 202-347-5495), 1512 K St NW, is a friendly literary bookstore just blocks from the White House that sponsors author events and poetry readings.

Downtown, another Olsson's Books & Records (☎ 202-638-4882), 418 7th St NW, is an extensive full-service bookstore with a well-stocked collection of jazz and blues CDs, as well as the Footnotes cafe. (See Downtown under Places to Eat, later in the chapter.)

Media

DC produces plenty of quality newspapers and offers innovative TV and radio programs, which makes sense considering the swarms of journalists and reporters in the city.

Newspapers Besides being the major local newspaper, the *Washington Post* is one of the top newspapers in the nation. The smaller circulation *Washington Times*, owned by Reverend Sung Myung Moon's Unification Church, is more conservative. The free alternative weekly *Washington City Paper*, distributed throughout the city, scrutinizes District politics and trends and contains excellent entertainment coverage, including listings for the upcoming week's new movies, concerts, exhibits, readings, and special events. If you just want to get a quick view of city nightlife, pick up a free copy of the very useful *Barstool* newspaper in almost any pub. *The Georgetowner* is a weekly tabloid of arts, entertainment, and real estate with a focus on Georgetown events, venues, and personalities.

For news and events of particular interest to the gay and lesbian population, look for the free weekly *Washington Blade* in stores around Dupont Circle and elsewhere. The *Washington Afro-American* is the city's newspaper for African Americans.

TV The federally supported Public Broadcasting System (PBS) based here in DC operates a superior national news program, as well as arts, entertainment, and children's programming. (PBS is not only highly regarded, it's also hotly contested; conservatives who consider it too liberal aim to decimate its budget.) You'll find *The News Hour*, *Sesame Street*, and *Mr Rogers Neighborhood* on WETA Channel 26.

All national networks (ABC, CBS, NBC, and CNN's all-news station) are represented on the dial, and C-SPAN broadcasts live from the floor of Congress (aired at bars across Capitol Hill).

Radio Tune in to locally produced National Public Radio (NPR) at either WAMU (88.5 FM) or WETA (90.9 FM) for the most thoughtful local and national news coverage and features (they also play jazz).

The Voice of America (☎ 202-619-4700) prepares news reports for international broadcast in 44 languages from its studios at 330 Independence Ave SW (enter on C St). Free 45-minute tours are offered weekdays at 10:30 am, 1:30 pm, and 2:30 pm; reservations are required.

Laundry

Many budget hotels and hostels offer coin-operated washers and dryers; higher-priced hotels provide higher-priced laundry and dry-cleaning services. You'll find self-service and wash-and-fold laundries in residential neighborhoods and around college campuses; a few are open 24 hours.

Medical Services & Emergencies

Anywhere in the US, the free number to call for any emergency – police, fire, or accident – is ☎ 911. In DC, *know your quadrant*. Without the correct coordinates, emergency services can easily head to the wrong side of town.

Round-the-clock telephone service is also available from the Traveler's Aid Society hotline (☎ 202-546-3120); drop-in service is available at their desks at branch offices in Union Station (☎ 202-371-1937), Ronald Reagan Washington National Airport (☎ 703-427-3972), and Washington-Dulles International Airport (☎ 703-572-8296). The George Washington University Medical Center is at 901 23rd St NW (24 hours; ☎ 202-994-3211).

Other useful numbers are the DC Rape Crisis Center (☎ 202-333-7273) and Poison Control (☎ 202-625-3333).

Dangers & Annoyances

Washington, DC, has earned a reputation for crime, violence (44 murders per 100,000 residents, the highest of any city in the Americas), and drug use. However, most sections of the city that are of interest to travelers are extremely safe and afford vigilant police protection. These areas include the Mall and Downtown area (by day), Capitol Hill, Foggy Bottom, Georgetown, Dupont Circle, and Adams-Morgan. Even these areas attract a significant number of homeless people (especially in fair weather), and you can expect to be solicited for spare change. For the most part, these panhandlers pose no danger and will not hassle you further if you decline to give them money.

Several sections of the inner city are home to people living in desperate circumstances, and you could be at risk there. Some of these areas are easily identifiable, including all of Anacostia (southeast of the Anacostia River), the northeastern area of the city east of N Capitol St, the southeastern area of the city east of 8th St SE, and south of D St SE to the Navy Yard.

Other dodgy areas are pockets within otherwise safe districts or on their fringes, and unsuspecting travelers may inadvertently wander into these areas and put themselves at risk. Travelers should avoid the area east of 13th St NW at night when visiting the U St entertainment district (Shaw). Likewise, the area east of Chief Ike's Mambo Room on Columbia Rd (Adams-Morgan) is no place to go wandering by yourself at night; nor is Kalorama Rd east of 18th St NW in the same district. Between M and U Sts, 14th St has long been notorious for prostitution and associated street crime (although it seems less so recently, as some prostitution and solicitation has migrated to the Internet). Many residents think it is safer to take a cab after dark from Dupont Circle to the restaurants and clubs of Adams-Morgan instead of making the short, six-block walk uphill along dark and quiet streets.

Standard urban precautions for travelers in DC include the following: leave valuables at home; store your identification and cash securely in a money belt or neck pouch; avoid walking alone through poorly lit areas at night; if you're lost and confused, try not to look lost and confused. Though the city's high-crime reputation should not be downplayed, neither should it be overblown; most violent crime occurs outside tourist areas.

The hot and humid summer weather can be a health concern; exposure and dehydration may cause heat stroke, especially in July and August. This is particularly a concern at the many DC attractions where visitors stand outside in the sun in long lines and at political rallies on the Mall. In these months, plan your travel for the cooler mornings and late afternoons (advance planning can also reduce your time in lines); aim to be inside in air-conditioning through the midday heat; carry water and snacks; and wear hats and loose, light clothing.

CAPITOL HILL

Three years after Thomas Jefferson and Alexander Hamilton decided that Washington should be the nation's capital in 1790, construction began on the grand Capitol that was to grace the hill east of the Potomac. During the Civil War, the rise now known as Capitol Hill was nicknamed 'Bloody Hill' for all the injured soldiers moved into the legislative buildings that were serving as temporary hospitals.

Today, the residential areas east of the Capitol are home to a cross section of Washingtonians – poor living near rich, longtime residents next to transplanted staffers.

As mentioned earlier, travelers should be aware that east of 8th St and south of D St, the neighborhoods become higher-crime areas. Keep your eyes open, go where you feel comfortable, and remember that neighborhoods change over time.

Walking Tour

The US Capitol is the epicenter of Washington, DC; all the city's avenues intersect at an imaginary point under its dome.

Although the Capitol may appear to face the Mall, you actually see its back from the Potomac side. The Capitol opens eastward (note the direction of the Armed Liberty statue up top) onto a small, shady plaza surrounded by monolithic government landmarks.

A particularly nice approach to the Capitol is from **Union Station**. As you exit the station, you see the impressive vista of the Capitol dome framed in the station's huge archways. Walk south past fountains, statues, and an arc of flags from every state along landscaped paths. The **Taft Memorial** on your right houses carillon bells that ring every quarter hour. Circling around the northwestern side of the Capitol, you will spot a shady **grotto** designed by Frederick Law Olmstead (who also designed New York City's Central Park) in 1875.

If you continue to the south of the Capitol or approach it from the Mall, you'll pass the gigantic **Grant Memorial** in front of the reflecting pool. The **US Botanic Gardens** are on the south side of Maryland Ave. Behind the conservatory, on the other side of Independence Ave SW, you'll see the grand **Bartholdi Fountain**.

After touring the inside of the Capitol, depart the Capitol to the east and cross the plaza to climb the marble steps of the **Supreme Court** building. From here, if you

WASHINGTON, DC

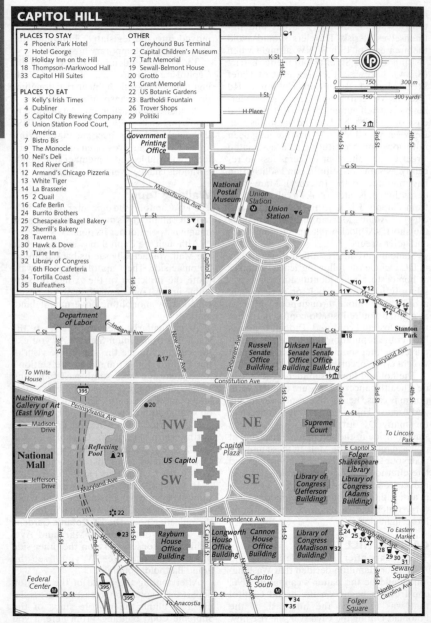

CAPITOL HILL

PLACES TO STAY
4 Phoenix Park Hotel
7 Hotel George
8 Holiday Inn on the Hill
18 Thompson-Markwood Hall
33 Capitol Hill Suites

PLACES TO EAT
3 Kelly's Irish Times
4 Dubliner
5 Capitol City Brewing Company
6 Union Station Food Court, America
7 Bistro Bis
9 The Monocle
10 Neil's Deli
11 Red River Grill
12 Armand's Chicago Pizzeria
13 White Tiger
14 La Brasserie
15 2 Quail
16 Cafe Berlin
24 Burrito Brothers
25 Chesapeake Bagel Bakery
27 Sherrill's Bakery
28 Taverna
30 Hawk & Dove
31 Tune Inn
32 Library of Congress 6th Floor Cafeteria
34 Tortilla Coast
35 Bulfeathers

OTHER
1 Greyhound Bus Terminal
2 Capital Children's Museum
17 Taft Memorial
19 Sewall-Belmont House
20 Grotto
21 Grant Memorial
22 US Botanic Gardens
23 Bartholdi Fountain
26 Trover Shops
29 Politiki

look north across Constitution Ave, you will see the three **Senate office buildings**. The three **House office buildings** and the two buildings of the **Library Congress** lie to the south. (A mini-subway connects Senate and House buildings to the Capitol.) In session, the Hill is the hectic scene of rushed government staffers dangling security passes from their necks, pods of well-dressed school groups, placard-carrying protesters, and microphone-wielding journalists hoping for impromptu interviews.

For a quiet walk through the Hill's historic residential district, follow E Capitol St out past the **Folger Shakespeare Library** to the right and the **Sewall-Belmont House** (home of the National Women's Party) one block to your left. Among the 19th-century row houses, brownstones, and old corner shops, stop by **Jimmy T's** at 5th St for diner coffee. Then head over to **Lincoln Park**, a lively neighborhood center with historic statues and a nice view of the Capitol (unobstructed by trees in winter).

Within the park stand two historic statues: The **Emancipation Memorial** (1876) portrays a kneeling slave (the likeness of Archer Alexander, the last man captured under the Fugitive Slave Law) breaking the chains of slavery as President Lincoln holds his Emancipation Proclamation in an outstretched hand. African American soldiers raised all the funds to erect it, and the statue served as the principal tribute to President Lincoln in DC until the Lincoln Memorial opened. The other statue, the **Mary McLeod Bethune Memorial** (1974), honors the African American educator and founder of the National Council of Negro Women. It was the first statue of an African American woman in DC.

You have many food choices north along Massachusetts Ave or south along Pennsylvania Ave. Your best bet may be **Eastern Market**, at 7th St SE at C St. This colorful market, which dates to 1873, has a popular food counter inside and a choice of restaurants across the street. (Also see Places to Eat, later in the chapter.) The handy Eastern Market Metro stop is a block away, or you could return to the Capitol by walking up Pennsylvania Ave.

Union Station

The most impressive gateway into DC is Union Station (☎ 202-371-9441), 40 Massachusetts Ave NE. The massive 1908 Beaux Arts building was beautifully restored in 1988, transforming it into a contemporary city center and transit hub with Amtrak connections to destinations throughout the East Coast. There is also a Metro station, a cinema (see Entertainment, later in the chapter), and a 200,000-sq-foot complex of shops and restaurants. Many travelers' resources are here – including Travelers' Aid, transit information, currency exchange, and ATMs with late-night and weekend hours.

The huge main hall resembles the Roman Baths of Diocletian. (Strategically placed shields were added to the legionnaire statues lining the 2nd-story balcony.)

The Capitol

William Thornton designed the Capitol (☎ 202-225-6827), Washington DC's most prominent landmark. George Washington laid the cornerstone in 1793, and Congress moved in seven years later. The British nearly burned it to the ground during their 1814 invasion of the city. The dispiriting destruction tempted people to abandon the whole DC experiment altogether, but the government finally rebuilt the Capitol from 1817 to 1819.

The House and Senate wings were added in 1857, and in 1863, a 9-million-pound iron dome was set atop, replacing a smaller one. With a 32½-foot extension of the east face in the late 1950s, the Capitol is now more than twice as large as the original building. Most presidents have been inaugurated on its East Terrace (Reagan preferred the West Terrace).

The House of Representatives meets in the south wing, and the Senate meets in the north wing. When either body is in session, a flag is raised above the appropriate wing. A light in the dome at night means one group is working late.

You enter from the east side (not the Mall side) into the dramatic **Rotunda**. The fresco inside the dome by Italian immigrant Constantino Brumidi, entitled *The Apotheosis of Washington*, depicts Washington as he is welcomed into heaven by 13 angels representing the original 13 states. (The story goes that Brumidi used local prostitutes as models for the angels.) Brumidi and his successors also painted the murals and ceilings in the hallways, which picture the nation's great heroes and their great deeds. (The most recent is a group portrait of the *Challenger* astronauts.) Bare spaces await future heroes and their deeds. Similarly, a marble statue of suffragists has one missing face awaiting the first woman president.

To the right of the Rotunda is **Statuary Hall**, where the House convened until 1857. In 1864, Congress asked each state to send statues of two distinguished citizens for display in this room, but the weight of so much marble was deemed too heavy for the floor, and several of these now grace other parts of the Capitol. What remains is an impressive assemblage of giant stone men in a room of tile and drapery.

The Supreme Court originally met in the Capitol in the **Old Supreme Court Chamber** and then later in the **Old Senate Chamber**. Here the great Senate debates over slavery took place prior to the Civil War.

Free tours of the Capitol stop at the visitors' galleries overlooking the House and Senate floors, but only when they are *not* in session. To watch **Congress sessions**, you must first call to find out when they're occurring (☎ 202-224-3121). American citizens can request passes (good for two years) from their congressional representatives. Foreign visitors can get passes from the Sergeant-At-Arms in Room S-321 for the Senate gallery, or just show their passport at the House gallery for admission. Committee hearings are often more interesting than open session, and some of these are open to the public. Check the *Washington Post*'s 'Today in Congress' notice (in section A) to find an open hearing.

US citizens can meet with their congressional representatives in the House and Senate by calling or writing to request an appointment (as early as three months in advance of your visit).

The Capitol is open 9 am to 4:30 pm daily except New Year's Day, Thanksgiving, and Christmas. You could skip the tour (and another line) by wandering around on your own. There are special tours for those with disabilities (☎ 202-224-4048).

Supreme Court

The Supreme Court (☎ 202-479-3030), directly across the plaza from the Capitol at 1st and E Capitol Sts, holds court in an imposing 1935 building designed by Cass Gilbert and constructed entirely of marble. Gilbert used himself and his friends as models for the justices carved into the building pediment; other marble figures represent Confucius, Solon, and Moses.

The Court is in session from the first Monday in October through June. The justices hear oral arguments and ask questions generally from Monday to Wednesday for two weeks every month, but the schedule varies considerably. Check the *Washington Post* or call before you visit, and get there by 8 am to get a seat (first-come, first-served).

Library of Congress

A block east of the Capitol, the three buildings of the Library of Congress (☎ 202-707-5000) contain approximately 100 million items – including more than 26 million books, 36 million manuscripts, maps, photographs,

National Mall exhibition of the AIDS Memorial Quilt

Hanging out in eclectic Adams-Morgan

Washington Monument

The poignant Vietnam Veterans Memorial

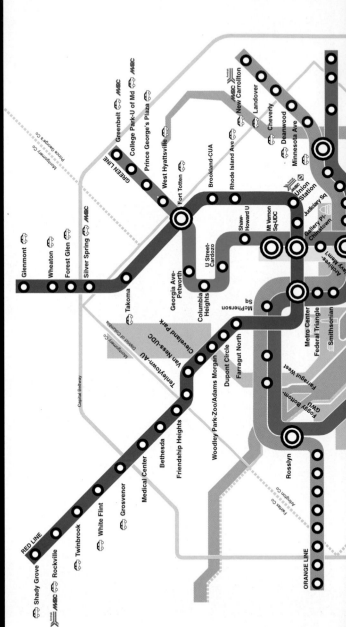

System Map

Legend

- Red Line • Glenmont/Shady Grove
- Orange Line • New Carrollton/Vienna/Fairfax-GMU
- Blue Line • Addison Road/Franconia-Springfield
- Green Line • Branch Avenue/Greenbelt
- Yellow Line • Huntington/Mt. Vernon Sq-UDC

Transfer Station
Parking
Future Station

Commuter Rail
Amtrak
MARC
Virginia Railway Express
Station in Service

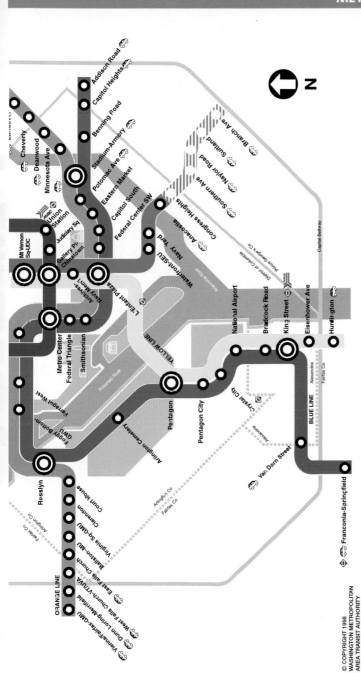

N

ORANGE LINE

Vienna/Fairfax–GMU
Dunn Loring–Merrifield
West Falls Church
East Falls Church–VT/UVA
Ballston–MU
Virginia Sq–GMU
Clarendon
Court House
Rosslyn

Foggy Bottom
GWU
Farragut West
Metro Center
Federal Triangle
Smithsonian
Arlington Cemetery
Pentagon
Pentagon City
Crystal City
National Airport
Braddock Road
King Street
Eisenhower Ave
Huntington

Van Dorn Street
Franconia–Springfield

BLUE LINE
YELLOW LINE

Mt Vernon Sq–UDC
Gallery Pl Chinatown
Judiciary Sq
Union Station
Archives–SEU
Navy Mem'l
L'Enfant Plaza
Federal Center SW
Capitol South
Eastern Market
Waterfront–SEU
Navy Yard
Anacostia
Congress Heights
Southern Ave
Naylor Road
Suitland
Branch Ave

Addison Road
Capitol Heights
Benning Road
Stadium–Armory
Potomac Ave
Minnesota Ave
Deanwood
Cheverly

Alexandria
Fairfax Co
Arlington Co
Fairfax Co
Arlington Co
Prince George's Co
District of Columbia
Capital Beltway
Potomac River
Anacostia River

Rev (08/98)

No Dangerous or
Flammable Materials

No Litter
or Spitting

No Audio or
Video Devices
(without earphones)

No Animals
(except guide dogs)

No Food
or Drinks

No
Smoking

View from the Potomac

Gay Pride march on the Mall

The US Capitol building, a fine example of 19th-century neoclassical architecture

The Smithsonian Castle, now a visitor information center

Springtime flora

Supreme Justice

The US Supreme Court is the highest judicial body in the land. The court consists of nine justices appointed for life terms, and it is referred to by the name of its presiding chief justice, such as the 'Warren Court' or the 'Rehnquist Court.' While the image of stately justices cloaked in black robes is a familiar one, only recently have the faces of women and African Americans appeared.

The rise in stature of the court came with the appointment of John Marshall as chief justice in 1801. Whereas previously justices had given separate opinions, Marshall established the single 'opinion of the court,' which carried much more weight. The Marshall Court issued a number of decisions that upheld the power of Congress over the states and affirmed the court's right to declare unconstitutional actions of the other branches of government.

The most notorious case of the 19th century was *Dred Scott v Sanford* in 1857, a major precursor to the Civil War. In this case, the court ruled that African Americans could not be citizens of the US, and Congress had no right to prevent territories in the American West from allowing slavery.

In 1896, in *Plessy v Ferguson*, the Court upheld the segregation of the 'white and colored races' under a doctrine of 'separate but equal.' In a powerful dissent, Associate Justice and former slave owner John Marshall Harlan of Kentucky wrote 'the white race deems itself to be the dominant race, but the Constitution recognizes no superior, dominant, ruling class of citizens….Our Constitution is colorblind…In respect of civil rights all citizens are equal before the law.' It wasn't until almost 60 years later that the court said in *Brown v Board of Education of Topeka* that 'separate but equal' was not in fact 'equal.'

One of the most important and most controversial rulings of the 20th century was the 1975 *Roe v Wade* decision that negated all laws preventing the right to an abortion in early pregnancy. The opinions of prospective Supreme Court justices on *Roe v Wade* are invariably sought out and considered a condition of appointment.

Today, protesters and advocates continue to gather on the marble steps of the Supreme Court atop Capitol Hill to try to sway judicial and public opinion.

sheet music, and musical instruments – making it the largest library in the world. The British used the books from the original library to burn the Capitol in 1814. Retired President Jefferson sold his collection to the library to rebuild it.

Step into the historic **Jefferson Building** (1897) to see its impressive Main Reading Room and the Great Hall, with vaulted ceilings and ornate decoration; it's the one on the plaza, on 1st St SE between E Capitol St and Independence Ave.

The library's two modern annexes are nearby. The **Adams Building** is behind the Jefferson Building, between 2nd and 3rd Sts SE. Like the Capitol, a series of underground hallways connect these two. The **Madison Building**, located immediately south of the Jefferson Building between Independence Ave and C St SE, holds the library's central visitor center and an inexpensive cafeteria with a view.

The library screens classic films for no charge, and occasionally there are concerts performed on the library's five Stradivarius violins (call ☎ 202-707-8000 for special events and exhibitions information). For reading-room hours, call ☎ 202-707-6400.

Legislative Office Buildings

Members of the House of Representatives and Senate do business in six legislative office buildings surrounding the Capitol. The three Senate office buildings – Russell (its Senate Caucus Room was the familiar scene of the prolonged Watergate hearings), Dirksen, and Hart – are on the north side of Constitution Ave. The three House office buildings – Rayburn, Longworth, and Cannon – are on the south side of Independence Ave.

US Botanic Garden

The conservatory (☎ 202-225-7099) on the far-eastern end of the Mall (downhill from the Capitol) dates from 1931 and resembles London's Crystal Palace; the Botanic Garden's history in other locations dates to 1842. Iron-and-glass greenhouse rooms provide a beautiful setting for displays of exotic and local plants, including cycad trees that produce 50lb cones. This place was closed for renovations during much of 1999 and 2000, but when it reopens, it will be a good place to relax and cool off. Admission is free, and it is open 9 am to 5 pm daily (until 9 pm in summer).

Folger Shakespeare Library

The Folger research library and museum (☎ 202-544-4600, 544-7077 for events), 201 E Capitol St SE, houses the world's largest collection of works by Shakespeare, and sponsors changing exhibits, concerts, and plays. Its theater is modeled after the one at Stratford-upon-Avon. The museum is free and open 10 am to 4 pm Monday to Saturday.

Sewall-Belmont House

The historic house (☎ 202-546-3989) from which Alice Paul and the National Women's Party led the struggle for equal rights for women is at 144 Constitution Ave SE, on the corner of 2nd St. The heroines of the women's rights movement are the focus of historical exhibits, portraits, sculpture, and a library. The 1800 building has been the headquarters for the party since 1929. It's free and open 11 am to 3 pm weekdays, noon to 4 pm Saturday.

Capital Children's Museum

This children's museum (☎ 202-675-4120), 800 3rd St NE at H St, holds three floors of inviting, hands-on, interactive exhibits, including a do-it-yourself TV studio, a cave, a miniature Mexican village, a fire station, a what's-under-the-street exhibit, and the always-popular maze and bubble shroud. It's open 10 am to 5 pm daily; admission is $6 for everyone over the age of two.

The museum is only a three-block walk northeast of Union Station, but the neighborhood is somewhat ragged; you may prefer to take a cab.

The National Women's Party

'If we get freedom for women, then they are probably going to do a lot of things that I wish they wouldn't do. But it seems to me that it isn't our business to say what they should do with it. It is our business to see that they get it.'   **– Alice Paul**

Firebrand Alice Paul was born into a Quaker family in 1885 and gained notoriety as one of the nation's first and foremost feminists. In 1914, Paul co-founded the Congressional Union, an organization that advocated for a Constitutional amendment granting women the right to vote. By picketing Congress and the White House and by staging hunger strikes, the group lobbied for the 19th Amendment, which passed in 1920. It states 'the right of citizens of the United States to vote shall not be denied or abridged…on account of sex.'

Paul and her cohorts went on to form the National Women's Party (NWP) to work for total equality for women. Their primary goal was the Equal Rights Amendment (ERA), first proposed by the NWP in 1923. The most recent version of the ERA – 'Equality of rights under the law shall not be denied or abridged by the United States or any state on account of sex' – was approved by two-thirds of the House of Representatives and the Senate in 1971 and 1972, but it failed to get ratification by the required 38 states and thus never became law.

The National Women's Party is now headquartered in the house of Alice Paul, who died in 1975. Mementos of the women's rights movement throughout the century are on display.

National Postal Museum

In the post office building across from Union Station, the newest Smithsonian museum (☎ 202-357-2991) features Cliff Clavin's postal carrier uniform from *Cheers* and kid-friendly exhibits on postal history such as the Pony Express. There are plenty of philatelic displays of stamps, as well as souvenirs. It's open 10 am to 5:30 pm daily.

NATIONAL MALL

The 400-foot-wide expanse of green stretching 2 miles from the Potomac River to Capitol Hill is called the Mall. Lined with gravel paths and shade trees along its bordering streets (Constitution Ave to the north and Independence Ave to the south), the Mall is home to the capital's most famous monuments and museums.

It has taken on this role only relatively recently. Between 1791 and 1972, the area held a swamp, a cow pasture and slaughter site, a Civil War hospital, a train station, a stagnant canal, and temporary government buildings from WWI.

When Pierre L'Enfant designed it, he imagined the Mall as a grand promenade lined with mansions and embassies, like an American Champs-Elysées, but it evolved in a more American way into a national lawn lined with family-friendly museums. On sunny days, the Mall attracts people who jog, walk dogs, play soccer and Frisbee, and pose for photographs. The Smithsonian's Kite

Festival, in late March, and its Folklife Festival, in June, are two highlights among many popular public events taking place annually on the Mall.

But perhaps the Mall is best known for the political gatherings and rallies held here. Antiwar protesters demonstrated against the Vietnam War during the 1960s, and in 1963, Martin Luther King Jr delivered his world-famous 'I Have a Dream' speech on the steps of the Lincoln Memorial. Three decades later, the Million Man March returned to question how that dream had progressed.

When the Vietnam Veterans Memorial first opened in 1982, it generated tremendous controversy, but its subsequent popularity sparked a monument binge around the Mall, memorializing American military history with congressionally approved monuments (in various states of completion) to WWII, the Korean War, women in Vietnam, black Revolutionary War patriots, African American Union soldiers, and a Japanese American patriots memorial. (Proposals such as a monument to the Army's canine corps did not win congressional approval.)

On the Mall, you're never too far from a stand selling hot dogs, sodas, ice cream, and

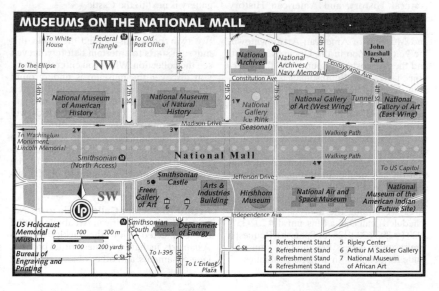

MUSEUMS ON THE NATIONAL MALL

other snack foods. Metro riders can use the Smithsonian station for all Mall sights (though the Mall's north side is actually a bit closer to the Archives/Navy Memorial and Federal Triangle stations).

Smithsonian Museums & Galleries

Among the world's finest research centers, the Smithsonian Institution administers more than a dozen phenomenal museums and galleries in DC, as well as the National Zoo. It maintains a collection so large (138,843,570 pieces at last count) that only 1% of it is ever on display.

In 1826, James Smithson, a Brit who had never been to America, willed £4,100,000 to the US to found an 'establishment for the increase and diffusion of knowledge' in the event that his only heir, a nephew, die childless. That happened six years later, and the gift of $508,318 came when the entire yearly budget of the US was less than $34 million. In 1846, Congress decided to use the funds to create a museum and research center.

Nine of the Smithsonian establishments are on the Mall (listed individually later); families shouldn't miss the Air and Space, Natural History, and American History Museums. (For Smithsonian museums in other districts – such as the Renwick Gallery and Museum of American Art downtown, the National Zoo in the Upper Northwest, and the Anacostia Museum – see those sections, later.) The Smithsonian is also planning the Museum of the American Indian, due to open on the Mall in 2002.

The Smithsonian museums are open 10 am to 5:30 pm (with exceptions noted in text) daily except Christmas. Admission is always free.

Call ☎ 202-357-2700 for general information on any of the Smithsonian museums, or look on the web at www.si.edu. For activity information (concerts, films, and lectures are among the many special events scheduled), call Dial-a-Museum at ☎ 202-357-2020 (☎ 202-633-9126 for Spanish). Request a 'Smithsonian Access' brochure for a museum guide for people with physical disabilities.

Smithsonian Castle The original Smithsonian museum now houses the Visitor Information Center, a clearinghouse for information about the institution. Referred to as the 'Castle,' the turreted red-brick building is on the south side of the Mall at 10th St SW, and it serves as the most recognizable landmark as you surface from the Metro station. Inside, a 20-minute film provides an overview. The 1855 castle also houses the crypt of Smithsonian benefactor James Smithson. The center is open 9 am (an hour before the museums) to 5:30 pm daily.

The small round building directly west is the aboveground access to the largely underground **Ripley Center**. Public lectures, classes, and temporary exhibits take place in the center's classrooms and meeting spaces.

Freer Gallery of Art Named for founder Charles Lang Freer, the Freer Gallery was built in 1923 to hold Freer's collection of American and Asian art, including an extensive collection of paintings by James McNeill Whistler. Its Middle Eastern and Asian exhibits are the most evocative, especially those in the Peacock Room. The gallery is next to the Castle.

National Museum of African Art One of two twin 'bookends' behind the castle, this museum starts to entertain before you even see the collection. When you enter the foyer, you discover the museum is underground (built to conserve open space), and tunnels connect to the three other underground galleries and to the Freer Gallery. (Kids will enjoy tossing pennies three stories down into the fountain.) Devoted to sub-Saharan African art, the museum displays masks, textiles, ceramics, and other examples of the visual traditions of a continent of 900 distinct cultures.

Arthur M Sackler Gallery Twin to the National Museum of African Art above ground and connected below, the Sackler exhibits Asian arts, including Chinese ritual bronzes, jade ornaments, and other objects reflecting the aesthetic heritage of half the world's population – some of which date to the third millennium BC.

Arts & Industries Building This odd little museum beside the Castle houses Victorian Americana, mainly the inventions and products of the 1876 Philadelphia Centennial Exposition. Wurlitzer-era carriages, machinery, and bric-a-brac are displayed with a ghostly carnival-type ambiance; there's also a full-size locomotive. The museum shows performances for children here in the Experimental Gallery and Discovery Theater; check at the desk to see what's playing.

The antique **carousel** in front of the building takes children for old-fashioned rides ($1). It's open 10 am to 5:30 pm.

Hirshhorn Museum East of the Castle, this modern donut-shaped museum with a view of the Mall (enter from Independence Ave) houses the extensive modern- and contemporary-art collection of Latvian American millionaire Joseph Hirshhorn. With one of the largest collections of 20th-century sculpture in the world, the museum displays works by Rodin, Brancusi, Calder, and Henry Moore. Also exhibited are paintings by Dubuffet, O'Keeffe, Warhol, Pollock, Stella, and de Kooning. From September to June, the museum airs independent films and art documentaries. Call ☎ 202-357-3235 for special events.

The museum's sunken **sculpture garden** on the Mall holds a rich collection of works in a beautiful setting, including Rodin's *Monument to the Burghers of Calais*. There's an outdoor cafe nearby in the summer.

National Air and Space Museum Since its bicentennial opening on July 4, 1976, the National Air and Space Museum has grown to be the world's most popular museum. Its cavernous halls hold full-size aircraft and spacecraft, from the Wright brothers' *Flyer* and Charles Lindbergh's *Spirit of St Louis* to the command module of *Apollo IX*. The museum actively engages all visitors big and small. You can touch a moon rock, walk

through a DC-7 and Skylab, or join a volunteer-led tour to hear the stories behind the impressive flying machines on display.

The museum's Langley Theater shows IMAX films on a 50-by-75-foot screen. Of the six shows, the best is still *To Fly*. Get a ticket ($5.50 for adults; $4.25 for seniors, children, and students) as soon as you arrive, enjoy the exhibits, and then see the film later, when you're tired of walking. Or, come back after hours for evening screenings, which are usually at 6 pm.

The **planetarium** presents astronomy programs several times a day for an extra charge. The gift shops sell model planes and spacecraft, personalized dog tags, and freeze-dried astronaut food among other space paraphernalia. The museum cafeteria and restaurant are in a spacious greenhouse-like setting overlooking the Mall. The museum is generally open 10 am to 5:30 pm but may have extended summer hours.

National Museum of Natural History This museum holds many awesome highlights: the 45-carat Hope Diamond; a suspended life-size model of the largest blue whale ever seen; the 13-foot-tall mammoth elephant that greets you at the entrance; dinosaur skeletons; an insect zoo; and a hall of geology, gems, and minerals. Other exhibits examine various ecosystems and Native American cultures. The Johnson IMAX Theater screens nature films; advance tickets (☎ 202-633-7400) cost $5.50 for adults and $4.50 for children and seniors.

The hands-on exhibits in the Discovery Room enable children to closely examine shells, bones, geodes, costumes, and more. The small room is open afternoons only and requires tickets for a specific time; get passes when the Discovery Room first opens for the widest choice of times.

The museum's two windowless cafeterias (one for Smithsonian members only) are among the least desirable of the ready options – at lunchtime, it's better to wander over to the National Museum of American History or up to the Old Post Office Pavilion (see those sections, later in the chapter).

WASHINGTON, DC

NATIONAL MALL, DOWNTOWN & FOGGY BOTTOM

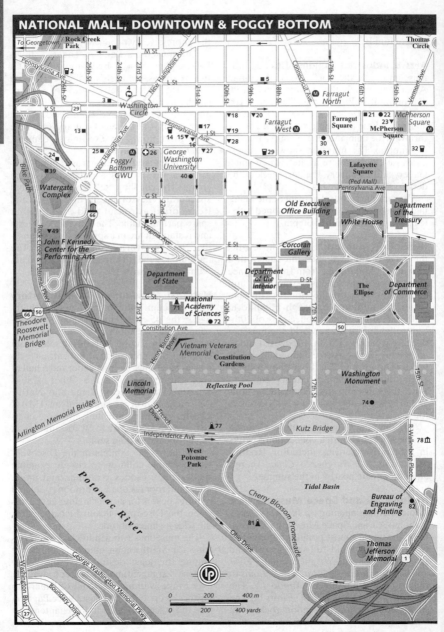

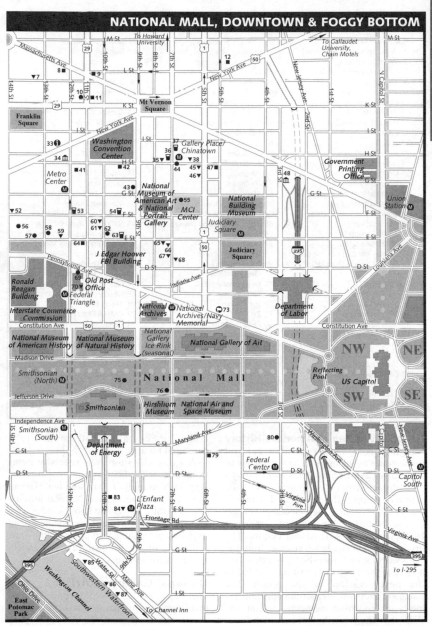

NATIONAL MALL, DOWNTOWN & FOGGY BOTTOM

To Howard University
To Gallaudet University, Chain Motels

Massachusetts Ave

Franklin Square

Washington Convention Center

Metro Center

Mt Vernon Square

Gallery Place/Chinatown

Government Printing Office

Union Station

National Museum of American Art & National Portrait Gallery

MCI Center

National Building Museum

Judiciary Square

Judiciary Square

J Edgar Hoover FBI Building

Ronald Reagan Building

Old Post Office

Federal Triangle

Interstate Commerce Commission

Pennsylvania Ave

Department of Labor

National Archives

National Archives/Navy Memorial

Constitution Ave

National Museum of American History

National Museum of Natural History

National Gallery Ice Rink (seasonal)

National Gallery of Art

Madison Drive

Smithsonian (North)

Jefferson Drive

National Mall

Reflecting Pool

US Capitol

Smithsonian

Hirshhorn Museum

National Air and Space Museum

Independence Ave

Smithsonian (South)

Department of Energy

Maryland Ave

Federal Center

Capitol South

L'Enfant Plaza

Frontage Rd

Southwestern Waterfront

Washington Channel

To Channel Inn

East Potomac Park

Ohio Drive

To I-295

NATIONAL MALL, DOWNTOWN & FOGGY BOTTOM

PLACES TO STAY
1 Washington Monarch Hotel
3 Wyndham Bristol
5 Lincoln Suites Downtown
8 Swiss Inn
9 Morrison-Clark Inn
11 Hostelling International –
 Washington, DC
12 Howard Johnson Inn
13 River Inn
17 Lombardy
21 Sheraton St Regis
24 Howard Johnson's Premier
25 George Washington
 University Inn
39 Swissôtel Watergate
41 Marriott Metro Center
42 Grand Hyatt Washington
47 Red Roof Inn
50 Allen Lee Hotel
64 Hotel Harrington
79 Holiday Inn Capitol
83 Loews L'Enfant Plaza Hotel

PLACES TO EAT
6 Havana Breeze
7 Stoney's Bar & Grill
15 Milo's, Mehran
16 TGI Fridays
18 Tequilla Grill
19 Aroma
20 Sholl's Colonial Cafeteria
23 Georgia Brown's
27 Lindy's Bon Appétit,
 Kinkeads
28 Chalán
35 Chop Sticks, Capital Q

38 China Doll Gourmet,
 Szechwan Gallery,
 Ho Wah Restaurant
45 Go-Lo's
46 Burma Restaurant
49 Roof Terrace Restaurant
51 World Gourmet
52 Red Sage
59 Dean & DeLuca's Deli
60 Mike Baker's
61 Lincoln House Restaurant
 Bar & Deli
65 Austin Grill
66 Jaleo's
67 Footnotes
68 Mark
70 Old Post Office Pavilion
84 L'Enfant Plaza Mall
85 Open-Air Seafood Market
86 Le Rivage
87 Hogates

ENTERTAINMENT
2 One Step Down
14 Froggy Bottom Pub
27 Red Lion
29 Hung Jury
32 Zei Club
36 Fadó
37 Coco Loco
40 George Washington University
 Lisner Auditorium/Ticketplace
53 Polly Esther's
54 The Bank
57 National Theater
58 Warner Theatre
63 The Ritz

74 Sylvan Theater
87 Zanzibar

OTHER
4 Spanish Embassy
10 HI Travel Center
22 Chapters
26 George Washington University
 Medical Center
30 The Map Store
31 Wilderness Society
33 Washington, DC Convention
 and Visitors Association
34 National Museum of Women
 in the Arts
43 Martin Luther King Jr
 Memorial Library
44 Chinatown Friendship Arch
48 National Jewish Historical
 Society of Greater Washington
55 Discovery Channel Store
56 National Place
62 Ford's Theater,
 Lincoln Museum
67 Olsson's Books & Records
69 Observation Tower
71 Albert Einstein Statue
72 Federal Reserve
73 Canadian Embassy
75 Carousel
76 Sculpture Garden
77 Korean War Memorial
78 US Holocaust Memorial
 Museum
80 Voice of America
81 FDR Memorial
82 Tidal Basin Boathouse

National Museum of American History
Ranging from such venerated cultural touchstones as the original American flag to such kitsch Americana icons as Dorothy's ruby slippers from *The Wizard of Oz*, the original Kermit the Frog, and Fonzie's *Happy Days* jacket, the eclectic collection of the National Museum of American History celebrates American culture. The original whites-only lunch counter from the Woolworth's in Greensboro, North Carolina, tells the story of the sit-ins that led to the desegregation of the South. The poignant Vietnam Memorial collection exhibits the touching mementos left at 'the Wall' over the years. And of course, the First

Ladies' inauguration ball gowns are a perennial favorite.

A lively gift shop sells specialty items from all over the US: Vermont maple syrup, Appalachian quilts, Charleston tea, Harlem Boys Choir cassettes, and Navaho jewelry. There are also wonderful books, guides, toys, and trinkets. The recently remodeled cafeteria has an updated menu; the Palm Court restaurant offers sit-down service in an ice-cream parlor setting.

National Gallery of Art
This gallery (☎ 202-737-4215) consists of two buildings: the original neoclassical building across the Mall from the Air and Space

Museum, now called the West Wing, and the modern angular East Wing across 4th St. The two are connected by an underground tunnel.

The **West Wing** exhibits primarily European works from the Middle Ages to the early 20th century, including masterpieces by Rembrandt, Vermeer, El Greco, Renoir, Monet, and Cézanne. It's the only gallery in America that owns a da Vinci (the *Ginevra di Benci)*, and it hosted such blockbuster exhibitions as the Vermeer collection in 1996. You can customize your own tour of the collection with the museum's multimedia computers.

The spacious **East Wing** features a Calder mobile as the centerpiece of its four-story atrium, along with other abstract and modern works.

Though affiliated, the National Gallery is not part of the Smithsonian Institution; note the different hours. It's open 10 am to 5 pm Monday to Saturday and 11 am to 6 pm Sunday. Admission is free. The West Wing operates the Terrace Cafe; a buffet cafeteria and espresso bar is in the tunnel across from the underground fountain. There are big bookshops as well. Check at the desk for a calendar of events such as concerts and lectures.

From November to March, the humble National Gallery **Ice Rink** next to the gallery offers ice skating and refreshments (see Activities, later in the chapter).

US Holocaust Memorial Museum

Opened in 1993, this museum (☎ 202-488-0400, www.ushmm.org) is a hauntingly powerful memorial to victims of Nazi tyranny from 1933 to 1945. The three-floor permanent exhibit traces the rise of Hitler's Germany and graphically documents Nazi atrocities against six million Jews and millions of others – including homosexuals, the disabled, Jehovah's Witnesses, and political dissidents and resistors – with the use of film footage, audio and video recordings, photographs, and recovered personal belongings. The museum's literature recommends the main exhibit for children over the age of 11 and the separate children's exhibit for children eight to 11. However, all the exhibits vividly convey the scope and nature of Holocaust atrocities, and parents would do well to overestimate rather than underestimate the impact of such horrific history on children.

The museum is half a block south of the Mall. Though its official address is 100 Raoul Wallenberg Place SW, you enter from the 14th St side. Admission is free, but crowds necessitate that they hand out admission tickets. The box office distributes all tickets available that day from 10 am until they run out (limit four per person). They admit you that day only at a specific time (for example, at 10 am, you may end up with tickets for admission at 2:30 pm), but once in, you can stay as long as you like. (Visitors may see the children's exhibit, a computer room featuring a multimedia Holocaust encyclopedia, and the memorial room without a ticket.)

The museum is open 10 am to 5:30 pm daily except on Yom Kippur and Christmas. The cafe opens at 9 am for folks waiting in line for tickets.

Bureau of Engraving and Printing

Often mistakenly called the 'Mint,' the bureau (☎ 202-874-3019), at 14th and C Sts SW (one long block south of the Mall), is where they design, engrave, and print all US paper currency. Tour guides lead groups on raised walkways through what is, essentially, a print shop. Kids are excited by it, so many families wait hours in line for their turn. You do learn fun money trivia, and you can buy such souvenirs as shredded money and uncut sheets of $1 or $2 bills.

The bureau is open 9 am to 2 pm weekdays. This is a popular tour, and from July to August, you need to pick up free tickets at the kiosk on 15th St and then go to the 14th St entrance for the tour (tickets are often gone by late morning). The nearest Metro stop is Smithsonian.

Washington Monument

The 555-foot white obelisk rising above the center of the Mall offers a wonderful view of the Potomac basin, especially at night (it's open until midnight from spring to fall). The monument (☎ 202-426-6841) has had a checkered history: Construction began in 1848 but was not completed until 37 years later. The first glitch occurred when Pope

Pius IX contributed a stone that was subsequently stolen by anti-papists, who then undermined fundraising efforts. The project was abandoned during the Civil War; after the war, the Army Corps of Engineers resumed construction. The two separate phases of construction are evident in the slightly different shade of stone you see about a quarter of the way up.

An elevator ride takes visitors to an observation landing inside, where you may stay as long as you like. You can even walk down (on your own or on a ranger-led tour). The inside of the shaft is decorated with plaques from different states and from the Cherokee Nation. The monument is open 9 am to 5 pm September to March and 8 am to midnight April to August. Admission is free, but expect long lines.

You can purchase advance tickets through Ticketmaster (☎ 800-505-5040) for a 'convenience charge' of $1.50 per ticket.

Sylvan Theater

Downhill from the Washington Monument, this outdoor theater (☎ 202-426-6841) features free military (and sometimes big-band) concerts at 8 pm Tuesday to Friday and Sunday from June to August.

Lincoln Memorial

This memorial (☎ 202-426-6841), at the west end of the Mall, is much more than a monument to the 16th US president; its symbolic power became apparent immediately upon its completion in 1922. Invited to speak at the dedication was Dr Robert Moton, president of Tuskegee Institute (a historical African American college in Alabama), yet instead of being seated at the speakers' platform, Dr Moton was ushered to a segregated section across from the white audience. Indignant African Americans protested and transformed the memorial into a symbol of America's commitment to civil rights. From its steps in 1963, Martin Luther King Jr preached, 'I have a dream – that one day this nation will rise up and live out the true meaning of its creed: "We hold these truths to be self-evident, that all men are created equal."'

Designed to resemble a Greek temple, the monument's 36 columns (representing the 36 states in Lincoln's union) tilt slightly inward to avoid the optical illusion of a bulging top.

The hands of the 19-foot-tall marble statue are positioned to read A and L in American Sign Language to honor Lincoln's support for Gallaudet College for the Deaf. Under the memorial is a stalactite-filled cave now closed to the public. The monument is open 24 hours and offers a stirring view of the Mall, Washington Monument, Capitol, and Potomac River at night.

Vietnam Veterans Memorial

Just north of the Lincoln Memorial, two walls of polished black marble that come together in a V shape are inscribed with the names of 58,202 veterans killed as a result of the Vietnam War (including 1150 officially listed as Prisoners of War/Missing in Action, denoted by a cross). The stark, powerful memorial (☎ 202-634-1568) – the most visited memorial in DC – was designed by Maya Ying Lin, a 21-year-old architecture student at Yale University, whose design was selected in a national competition. Names are inscribed chronologically from date of death; alphabetical rosters are available nearby. On request, volunteers will

Martin Luther King Jr

help you get rubbings of names from 'the Wall.' The most moving remembrances are the notes, medals, and mementos left by survivors, family, and friends since the memorial was completed in 1982 (see many such items on exhibit at the Museum of American History). The monument is open 24 hours, and the ranger station is staffed until midnight.

Opponents to the design insisted on a more traditional sculpture, which was added nearby in 1984; a memorial to women who served in the war was recently unveiled as well.

Korean War Memorial

This stone memorial on the south side of the Reflecting Pool near the Lincoln Memorial depicts a troop of soldiers taking a hill. One local speechwriter relates how 'walking among the soldiers early on a rainy morning is spooky…like being in a cinéma vérité before the talkies were invented.'

FDR Memorial

During his historic four-term presidency, Franklin Delano Roosevelt entreated that no memorial be built in his honor 'any larger than his desk.' Despite this request, a 7½-acre memorial with grottos, waterfalls, and large rock palisades opened in 1997 at West Potomac Park near the Jefferson Memorial.

Tidal Basin

A ring of cherry trees, a gift from Japan in the early 20th century, surrounds the Tidal Basin and the Jefferson Memorial. When the trees bloom in late March and early April, the basin's perimeter shimmers with their pale-pink blossoms. The Cherry Blossom Festival is timed to coincide with this event – the first two weeks of April draw 100,000 visitors to DC for the festivities, which climax with the Cherry Blossom Parade.

The Tidal Basin boathouse (☎ 202-484-0206), just south of the Bureau of Engraving and Printing, rents **paddleboats** 10 am to 6 pm daily March to September (weather permitting). The cost is $7 per hour for a two-seater and $14 per hour for a four-seater.

Jefferson Memorial

This memorial (☎ 202-426-6841), south of the Washington Monument and Tidal Basin, honors Thomas Jefferson – the third US president, drafter of the Declaration of Independence, and founder of the University of Virginia. Designed by John Russell Pope to resemble Jefferson's Virginia home, the rounded, domed monument was initially derided by critics as 'the Jefferson Muffin.' Inside, there's a 19-foot bronze likeness, and excerpts from Jefferson's writings are etched into the walls. In spring, you can sit on the steps and admire the cherry blossoms; there's also a beautiful moonlight reflection over the Tidal Basin. The memorial is open 24 hours.

DOWNTOWN

Downtown began in what is now called Federal Triangle, east of the White House and bordered by Pennsylvania and Constitution Aves. This area was a thriving marketplace throughout the 19th century, though by mid-century it became known as 'Hooker's Division' due to the presence of General Hooker's Union troops. The strong commercial district began to decline after WWII, when residents started moving to the suburbs. President Kennedy encouraged a revitalization effort in the 1960s, which resulted in the renovation and transformation of the Old Post Office Pavilion, a Romanesque structure that escaped demolition in the 1930s. Federal Triangle is now characterized by its many red-roofed government buildings – including the National Archives, at its tip.

Since then, downtown has spread north and east. Though definitions vary, its boundaries roughly encompass the area east of the White House to Judiciary Square at 4th St, and from the Mall, north up to around K or M St.

The following downtown section traces a path east from the White House to the Federal Triangle, north to Metro Center, and east to Gallery Place, Chinatown, and Judiciary Square.

The Federal Triangle area (Ⓜ Federal Triangle or National Archives/Navy Memorial) from 14th St east to 6th St includes the

National Archives, the Ronald Reagan Building, and the Old Post Office (an easy place to take a break from touring; food and shops are in an interior courtyard). The FBI building is across the street, and Ford's Theater is about a block north.

The Metro Center area is a bit of an outpost for visitors, within two blocks of the Washington Convention Center and the National Museum of Women in the Arts.

From the Gallery Place/Chinatown area, you can easily access the National Museum of American Art and National Portrait Gallery, as well as the small but growing Chinatown neighborhood. The MCI Center sports complex opened in 1997 between these two places and has brought new life to the whole district. Legions of residents and tourists head here for pro hockey and basketball games, and families come to tour the Discovery Channel Store (which is actually more like a science museum).

Judiciary Square, a compact area across from the National Building Museum, is generally considered the eastern edge of downtown. In the past, many residents and travelers avoided the few blocks of rough borderlands between here and the Capitol Hill district to the east – including 2nd, 3rd, and 4th Sts NW – which seemed to be an oasis for homeless people. With the opening of the MCI Center, the increase of pedestrians, and improved police supervision, this area no longer seems as threatening as it once did, but travelers should still be cautious.

Two other sights worth visiting are the **National Jewish Historical Society of Greater Washington** (☎ 202-789-0900), 701 3rd St NW (Ⓜ Judiciary Square), with an archive and museum open noon to 5 pm Sunday to Thursday; and the **Wilderness Society** (☎ 202-833-2300), 900 17th St NW, with a permanent collection of 70 Ansel Adams photographs on display. It's open 9 am to 4:30 pm weekdays.

Old Post Office

The 1899 landmark Old Post Office (☎ 202-606-8691), at 12 St NW and Pennsylvania Ave (Ⓜ Federal Triangle), has been beautifully restored into a complex of food places and shops called the Pavilion. The impressive, seven-story, glass-roofed courtyard is a nice place to eat, relax, and get out of the weather. Also, the National Park Service operates an elevator here to take visitors up to the 400-foot **observation tower** for a broad view of downtown (find the small NPS office on the lower level in the corner). The elevator ride is free and operates 10 am to 5:45 pm daily (8 am to 10:45 pm in summer). Of course, there's also a functioning post office here.

Ronald Reagan Building

At 3.1 million square feet and sprawling over 11 acres, the Ronald Reagan Building (☎ 202-312-1300), 1300 Pennsylvania Ave, was designed by world-class architects and is the second-largest government building in the US (the Pentagon is larger). It's the new kid on the block, built during the past 10 years for a staggering $800 million.

Aside from government offices and the massive International Trade Center, the building also has an atrium with sculptures and other pieces, a large food court (see Places to Eat, later in the chapter), and tunnels to the Federal Triangle Metro station and Department of Commerce.

National Archives

The grand neoclassical building located on Constitution Ave between 7th and 9th Sts (Ⓜ National Archives/Navy Memorial) houses the National Archives (☎ 202-501-5000). Inside, a dimly lit rotunda displays the original documents upon which the US government is founded – the Declaration of Independence, the Constitution, and the Bill of Rights. Also here is one of four remaining versions of the 1297 Magna Carta, courtesy of Texas billionaire (and erstwhile presidential candidate) H Ross Perot, who purchased it upon its discovery in 1974. These precious documents are sealed in airtight cases filled with helium, which sink nightly into an underground vault to protect them from nuclear attack or theft.

The archives are free and open 10 am to 9 pm daily. You can take guided tours of the 55-ton steel vault and see other documents at 10:15 am and 1:15 pm daily if you make reservations (call at least 10 days in advance). Researchers must first make arrangements with an archivist (☎ 202-501-5400) and enter on the Pennsylvania Ave side. Visitors must pass through X-ray security.

J Edgar Hoover FBI Building

The honeycomb-like FBI building (☎ 202-324-3447), at 10th St and Pennsylvania Ave NW (Ⓜ Federal Triangle or Archives), is officially named the J Edgar Hoover FBI Building in honor of the notorious director who led the bureau for 48 years (1924–72) and transformed it from a tiny force into a huge crime-fighting bureaucracy.

The FBI tour is one of the most popular in DC, and it ends with a bang – actually the many bangs of a live machine-gun demonstration. You also see crime laboratories, DNA testing, and a forfeiture unit (items the FBI has confiscated). Free 45-minute tours run 8:45 am to 4:15 pm weekdays. Line up at the E St entrance between 9th and 10th Sts; people start lining up by 7:30 am in busy seasons.

Ford's Theater

On April 14, 1865, lone gunman John Wilkes Booth assassinated Abraham Lincoln while the President and Mrs Lincoln watched *Our American Cousin* in the Presidential box in Ford's Theater (☎ 202-347-4833), 511 10th St NW. The scene of the crime remains draped with a period flag to this day. You can look around on your own, catch a tour, or, to fully enjoy the beautifully restored theater, attend one of the many live performances the operating theater puts on seasonally. The basement's **Lincoln Museum** maps out the details of the assassination and displays related artifacts.

Across the street, the **Peterson House** is today immortalized as the 'house where Lincoln died.' The tiny, unassuming little group of rooms creates a movingly personal memorial. The national historic area encompassing all three sites is open 9 am to 5 pm daily (the theater may occasionally be closed for rehearsals or matinees). The closest Metro stop is Metro Center, but you

could also take the slightly longer but well-worn path from the Federal Triangle stop.

National Museum of Women in the Arts

This museum (☎ 202-783-5000) is at 1250 New York Ave NW at the corner of 12th St (Ⓜ Metro Center or McPherson Square). In it you'll find a collection of 2600 works by almost 700 women artists from 28 countries, including Judy Chicago, Mary Cassat, and Georgia O'Keeffe. The impressive 1911 building – once a Masonic lodge open only to men – features a grand foyer and cozy mezzanine. (The mezzanine cafe serves such arty sandwiches as the Frida Kahlo – grilled dill havarti and sautéed spinach.) Displays are largely paintings, and mostly portraits at that – not as rich a scope as you might hope. But the museum sponsors a vital series of special lectures, concerts, and shows such as a recent exhibit called 'Defining Eye: Women Photographers of the 20th Century.'

The gift shop sells pottery, jewelry, and other crafts handmade by women. Admission is free ($3 donations encouraged for adults), and hours are 10 am to 5 pm Monday to Saturday and noon to 5 pm Sunday.

Martin Luther King Jr Memorial Library

Washington, DC's main public library (☎ 202-727-1111), 901 G St NW (Ⓜ Metro Center), houses a popular mural portraying the Civil Rights movement and is an important community and cultural center, sponsoring many readings, concerts, films, and children's activities. There's a gift kiosk as well, with specialty periodicals. The library is usually open 10 am to 9 pm Monday to Thursday and 10 am to 5:30 pm Friday and Saturday. See the phone book for the more than two dozen branch libraries around town.

National Museum of American Art & National Portrait Gallery

These Smithsonian museums (☎ 202-357-2700) are housed in the old 1867 US Patent Office building between 7th and 9th and F and G Sts NW (Ⓜ Gallery Place/Chinatown).

You'll recognize them by the gleaming *Vaquero* out front by Luis Jimenez Jr.

One highlight of the American Art Museum is a spirited, colorful collection of American folk art, including a giant bottle-cap giraffe, a Coca-Cola-icon quilt, and James Hampton's 1964 *Throne of the Third Heaven of the Nations Millennium General Assembly* – a room-size shrine constructed from gold and silver tin foil and colored craft paper. The Portrait Gallery contains portraits of important Americans and frequent biographical exhibits. There's a nice little cafeteria with courtyard seating between the two museums.

Note that the museum and gallery will closed for renovations until 2003, but their websites – www.AmericanArt.si.edu and www.npg.si.edu, respectively – are very informative, and much of the artwork can be viewed online.

Chinatown

You enter DC's Chinatown under Friendship Arch, the ornate golden gate on H St at 7th St NW. Constructed in 1986, it's the largest of its kind outside China, and until recently, it was Chinatown's most appealing feature. If you are familiar with the Chinatown sections of New York, San Francisco, or Boston, this neighborhood of Asian restaurants and business seems small indeed. The area was in decay for years, but the arrival of the MCI Center has brought many more visitors and prosperity to the area. Now, many new reasonably priced Asian eateries, as well as other ethnic restaurants and bars (even a new, popular Irish pub), have opened within the several blocks fanning out from the intersection of 7th and H Sts NW.

MCI Center

This monumental sports arena (☎ 202-628-3200), 601 F St NW, came to Chinatown in 1997. The 20,000-seat venue is home to the NHL's Capitols, the NBA's Wizards, and the WNBA's Washington Mystics. The arena also includes a sports gallery, interactive sports display, and memorabilia from famous players, including Babe Ruth, Mark McGuire, and Sammy Sosa.

The **Discovery Channel Store** (☎ 202-639-0908), the flagship attraction for the popular TV station, is also on the premises of the MCI Center. More like a modern science museum than a retail outlet, the Discovery Channel Store has a fascinating collection of displays and includes a great 15-minute film called 'Destination DC,' a 40-foot T-Rex, a TV studio, and the Hubble Observatory. The store is open 10 am to 10 pm Monday to Saturday and to 6 pm Sunday.

You can also get guided walking tours of downtown here. A central feature on the tour is the story of how John Wilkes Booth planned and executed his assassination of President Abraham Lincoln. Tours leave twice daily at 10:30 am and 1 pm. The cost is $7.50 for adults and $5 for seniors and children.

National Building Museum

This museum (☎ 202-272-2448), 401 F St NW (Ⓜ Judiciary Square), takes up an entire city block. The main room is the Great Hall, where rows of massive pink marble Corinthian columns – among the largest in the world – rise 75 feet high. Four stories of ornately ornamented balconies flank the dramatic 300-foot-wide interior courtyard, a grand setting for inaugural balls held here since the Grover Cleveland administration in the late 19th century.

Built in 1887 to house the Pension Office (note the frieze of terra-cotta soldiers outside), the structure now holds a museum dedicated to architectural arts. The showy space easily overshadows the exhibits, but they're provocative nonetheless – the one called 'Washington: City and Symbol' examines the deeper significance and symbolism of DC's architecture. Concerts here make the most of the natural acoustics.

There's also a coffee bar and a museum shop with great furnishings, crafts, and rich coffee-table books. Admission is free; hours are 10 am to 4 pm Monday to Saturday and noon to 4 pm Sunday.

The museum is across the street from the Law Officers Memorial, a stark memorial to police officers slain in the line of duty.

WHITE HOUSE AREA

The site for the White House – originally called the President's House – was selected by George Washington in 1791. The hope was that the president and Congress could keep an eye on one another along the unobstructed sight line of Pennsylvania Ave, but later, the Treasury Building was built immediately east of the White House, blocking the view. Flanking the White House's west side is the Old Executive Office Building, a French Second Empire palace that could have been designed by cartoonist Charles Addams.

Pennsylvania Ave crosses in back of the White House (which faces the Washington Monument). Until recently, it served as a central thoroughfare, but after threats from gunmen in 1995, the portion across from the White House was blocked from car traffic. The concrete blockades and the heightened security presence add an imposing imperial air to the White House; nevertheless, the area is more pleasant as a pedestrian walkway.

Across from the White House to the north, you will find the Renwick Gallery, the Smithsonian museum dedicated to American crafts. Several doors down, there's the 1824 **Blair House** – the presidential-guest quarters since 1948. (Note the plaque out front commemorating the bodyguard who was killed in action while protecting President Truman from the 1950 assassination attempt by Puerto Rican freedom fighters.)

Lafayette Square, named for the Marquis de Lafayette (an American Revolutionary War hero), is the statue-studded park just north of the White House. It's a nice spot to walk around; play chess; or observe tourists, undercover security police, and placard-carrying demonstrators. Once an orchard, the area around the square was lined in the 19th century with the mansions of the rich and powerful.

North of the square, on opposite sides of 16th St, there's the exclusive Hay Adams Hotel to the west and the beautiful **St John's Church** to the east, where pew 54 is reserved for presidential families to worship.

South of the White House, an expansive park called the **Ellipse** borders the Mall and is surrounded by more sights. The southern-most point of the semicircular presidential lawn provides the classic photo opportunity of the front of the White House. The National Christmas Tree is decorated here in December, and whimsical urban visionaries have also proposed the installment of a 'national sofa' here across from a large screen that would allow two-way communication with White House residents. The National Park Service operates a visitor pavilion in the northeast corner of the Ellipse (snacks and restrooms are available).

The elegant row of monumental buildings at the west side of the Ellipse from E St south includes the wonderful Corcoran Gallery (the Octagon House is directly behind), the Red Cross, Constitution Hall, and the Organization of American States at the corner of Constitution Ave.

The **Department of the Interior** (☎ 202-208-4743), on C St NW at 19th St, displays dioramas of American wildlife, maintains a nice garden out back, and runs a gift shop featuring Native American crafts.

On the east side of the Ellipse, the Hotel Washington and Willard Intercontinental hotel bank a power-broker block of Pennsylvania Ave. Here too, **Pershing Park** attracts brown bag lunchtime crowds, and there's an outdoor cafe in summer (and plenty of cart vendors offer fast food nearby).

The **Department of Commerce** building along the Ellipse's east side – at its opening in 1931 the government's largest building – contains two significant resources for tourists: the White House Visitor Center on the north side, which distributes tour tickets, and the humble National Aquarium.

The **National Press Club** and **National Press Building**, at the corner of 14th and F Sts NW, houses journalists from around the world. In the same block, below ground, you'll find food, newsstands, shops, and a place to rest your feet at the **National Place** complex.

White House

Since 1800, every president since John Adams has lived in the White House (☎ 202-456-7041), at 1600 Pennsylvania Ave, and it has grown in size and stature from a presidential residence to a symbol of presidential power.

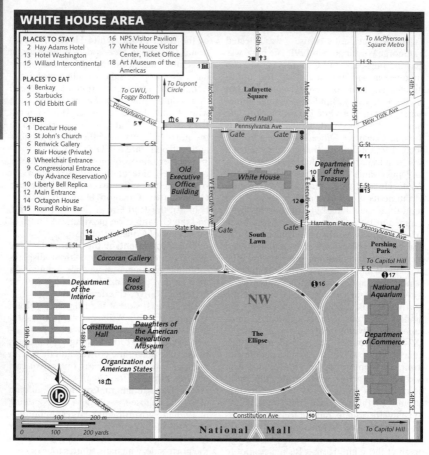

WHITE HOUSE AREA

PLACES TO STAY
2 Hay Adams Hotel
13 Hotel Washington
15 Willard Intercontinental

PLACES TO EAT
4 Benkay
5 Starbucks
11 Old Ebbitt Grill

OTHER
1 Decatur House
3 St John's Church
6 Renwick Gallery
7 Blair House (Private)
8 Wheelchair Entrance
9 Congressional Entrance
   (by Advance Reservation)
10 Liberty Bell Replica
12 Main Entrance
14 Octagon House
15 Round Robin Bar

16 NPS Visitor Pavilion
17 White House Visitor
   Center, Ticket Office
18 Art Museum of the
   Americas

It was torched by the British in 1814 and reopened in 1818. An overhaul in 1950 gutted almost the entire interior, and Jacqueline Kennedy's extensive redecoration campaign in the 1960s replaced the previous hodgepodge with more tasteful furnishings. Presidents have customized the property over time: Franklin Delano Roosevelt put in a pool; Truman installed a 2nd-story porch; Bush added a horseshoe-throwing lane; Clinton put in a jogging track. Some residents never leave: It's said that Eleanor Roosevelt and Harry Truman both sighted the ghost of Abe Lincoln in Lincoln's old study.

On the free self-guided tour, you see a number of interior rooms, including the China Room, Blue Room, and Red Room. The self-guide pamphlet highlights the usual perfunctory details of the decor and history, but it's more interesting to personalize this powerful symbol of American democracy by envisioning the resident personalities who shaped it.

Tours run 10 am to noon Tuesday to Saturday. In fall and winter, just line up at the east entrance; in spring and summer, first obtain tickets (up to four per person) at the White House Visitor Center, at 1450 Pennsylvania Ave (a block southeast of the White House

WASHINGTON, DC

The White House, home to US presidents since 1800

on the ground floor of the Commerce Building). Here you can see a useful video and exhibits that orient you to the White House before you start on your tour. The visitor center is open 8 am to 5 pm daily (7 am to 7 pm June to August). The ticket booth opens at 8 am and distributes all tickets available that day until the supply is exhausted; no advance tickets are available here.

US citizens can shortcut the lines by making an advance request of their congressional representative to be put on one of the early morning congressional tours. Disabled visitors can forgo ticketing and go directly to the Pennsylvania Ave driveway starting at 10 am on tour days.

The White House is also open for garden tours on selected weekends in April and October, and for candlelight tours during the Christmas season. The traditional Easter Egg Roll takes place on the South Lawn – the only time the grounds are wide open to the public (see Special Events, later, for details).

If you would like to find out the president's schedule, call the White House Press Office for the recorded press announcement (☎ 202-456-2343).

Department of the Treasury

The squat monolith of the Treasury (☎ 202-622-0896) occupies a city block next door to the White House at Pennsylvania Ave and 15th St. To end the debate on where to build

it (they hadn't wanted to block the view of Congress), President Andrew Jackson stood on the lawn, stuck his cane in the ground, and declared, 'Here.'

The 1833 Greek Revival landmark (each of the 30 36-foot columns were carved from a single block of granite) is decorated as befits a treasury, with golden eagles, ornate balustrades, and a two-story marble Cash Room constructed with eight types of marble. There's even a **Liberty Bell replica** on the White House side. US currency was printed in the basement here from 1863 to 1880. Free guided tours are offered Saturday mornings only at 10, 10:20, and 10:40 am (call for reservations). The staff is extremely security conscious (your name, birth date, and photo identification are required for admission).

Old Executive Office Building

The imperial-looking 1888 OEOB (☎ 202-395-5895), immediately west of the White House, was designed by Alfred Mullet to house State, War, and Navy Department staff. Two years after the building's completion, Mullet committed suicide after not being paid and facing criticism over its lavish design. Today, the OEOB is used as offices for White House staff. (During the Reagan administration, Colonel Oliver North led covert efforts to raise funds for the Nicaraguan contras from Room 392 in the basement.)

Take a free tour of this beautifully restored French Second Empire building on Saturday mornings by appointment (call Tuesday to Friday 9 am to noon). The Indian Treaty Room murals are worth a look.

Renwick Gallery

The Smithsonian's Renwick Gallery (☎ 202-357-2700), on Pennsylvania Ave at 17th St, invites you up the regal stairs of the 1859 mansion, through its dignified Grand Salon, and then startles you with some really wild pieces of craftwork, whimsy, and abstraction. Don't miss Larry Fuente's *Game Fish* (1988) – a sailfish trophy meticulously adorned with beads, buttons, badminton birdies, Scrabble tiles, dominoes, yo-yos, PEZ dispensers, and more. The gallery's collection focuses on crafts, and after a close look, you can recognize some of the pieces as furniture, jewelry, dishes, and lampshades. It's free and open 10 am to 5:30 pm daily.

Corcoran Gallery

Housed in a beautiful 1897 Beaux Arts building overlooking the Ellipse, the private Corcoran (☎ 202-639-1700), on 17th St NW, houses an esteemed collection of American art – Hudson River School, Ashcan, Pop, Abstract Expressionism – as well as some French and Dutch works. Elegant, contemplative rooms and halls are full of master paintings and sculpture (including *Dancer and Gazelles*, a favorite).

You can hear jazz performances in the atrium Wednesdays at lunchtime, and a jazz/gospel brunch takes place some Sundays (check the current schedule). It's a great place to linger over coffee. There's also an art school out back and occasional student shows. Hours are Wednesday to Monday 10 am to 5 pm (Thursday until 9 pm). Admission is free, but donations are encouraged.

Historic Buildings

Two historic houses near the White House offer a glimpse of the area's early-19th-century residential district. In the 1960s, the government proposed tearing down these historic houses and erecting government buildings, but the appeals of First Lady Jacqueline Kennedy spared the houses – though the modern government monoliths now loom directly behind. Facing Lafayette Square at 748 Jackson Place NW, the 1818 **Decatur House** (☎ 202-842-0920) features mannerly tours detailing the life and lifestyles of the genteel residents, along with architectural and decor highlights. It's open 10 am to 3 pm Tuesday to Friday and noon to 4 pm Saturday and Sunday. Admission is $3.

West of the White House, the **Octagon House** (☎ 202-638-3221), 1799 New York Ave NW, was the temporary home of President and Dolley Madison while the White House was being repaired after being burned by British troops. The 1801 Federal-style mansion now houses the American Institute of Architects, as well as its museum of architecture and the interior arts. Hours are 10 am to 5 pm Tuesday to Sunday. Admission to the exhibition galleries is $3 for adults and $1.50 for seniors and students.

The **Daughters of the American Revolution Museum** (☎ 202-879-3239), 1778 D St NW, contains 33 period rooms and genealogical information dating to the Revolutionary War. Admission is free; hours are 8:30 am to 4 pm Monday to Thursday and 1 to 5 pm Sunday. The adjacent 4000-seat **Constitution Hall** is a popular venue for concerts and performances.

The **Organization of American States** (OAS; ☎ 202-458-3751), on 17th St NW, between C St and Constitution Ave, was founded in 1890 and is dedicated to promoting political and economic cooperation between the nations of North and South America. The OAS's 1910 Beaux Arts building is right next to the small Art Museum of the Americas, entered on 18th St NW. The Aztec Garden lies between them. Admission to the museum is free, and hours are 9 am to 5 pm Tuesday to Sunday.

National Aquarium

Although it would take a considerably spruced-up aquarium to compete with DC's many free museums, you may want to visit this small aquarium (☎ 202-482-2825) in the basement of the Commerce Building (enter on 14th St south of Pennsylvania

Ave). It has a touch tank and a sampling of ecosystems from the Chesapeake Bay to the Pacific Ocean. Staff members feed the piranha and sharks at 2 pm on alternating days. Admission is $3 for adults and 75¢ for seniors and children. It's open 9 am to 5 pm daily.

FOGGY BOTTOM

The city's West End district was nicknamed 'Foggy Bottom' after the emanations of a long-lost gasworks – the term has also been used to metaphorically describe the bureaucratic gobbledygook emanating from the district's government agencies. The area falls roughly between 17th St NW and Rock Creek Park, the Mall to the south, and K or M St to the north, where it bumps up against Dupont Circle. (For sights at the 17th St-Ellipse boundary, see White House Area, earlier.)

Settlers from Hamburg, Germany, came here in the mid-18th century and called the area Funkstown, after its first resident. Some church services are still offered in German. By the 19th century, K St divided the wealthy in north Foggy Bottom from the laboring classes in the south, where the riverside was lined with factories making beer and cement. Many African Americans settled south of K St after the Civil War.

In 1912, **George Washington University** (☎ 202-994-4949) was built here. Today, the university fills several blocks. One of the campus hallmarks is the **Lisner Auditorium** (☎ 202-994-6800), which hosts a full slate of rock concerts, drama performances, and comedy acts. The surrounding neighborhood is a mix of professionals and students.

Department of State & National Academy of Sciences

The Department of State (☎ 202-641-3241), 2201 C St NW, at 23rd St, offers tours of its diplomatic reception rooms by advance reservation only. The National Academy of Sciences (☎ 202-334-2000), facing the Mall on Constitution Ave between 21st and 22nd Sts NW, features an appealing **Albert Einstein statue** set in a shady spot to the west of the building at 22nd St and Constitution

Ave. The larger-than-life smiling figure invites children to climb all over it.

Nearby, the **Federal Reserve** (☎ 202-452-3000), on C St between 20th and 21st Sts, is as close to a central bank as there is in the US. It's only open for a tour, which takes place Thursdays at 2:30 pm (admission and tours are free).

John F Kennedy Center for the Performing Arts

Overlooking the Potomac River, the Kennedy Center (☎ 202-467-4600, www .kennedy-center.org), at 2700 F St NW (Ⓜ Foggy Bottom/GWU), was dedicated as a 'living memorial' to Kennedy in 1964. The center's four stages and theater almost single-handedly turned around DC's reputation as a cultural desert. There are also nice views (particularly at sunset), several shops, a cafe, and the Roof Terrace Restaurant (see Places to Eat, later in the chapter). You could take a tour (☎ 202-416-8341), but the best way to see the center is to attend one of the many performances, festivals, films, and concerts held here year-round.

This site once housed the Christian Heurich Brewery, makers of Senate-brand beer until 1956 (now, 'Old Heurich' is a local homebrew). History- and scandal-lovers will be thrilled to learn that the Kennedy Center's parking garage is where *Washington Post* reporters Bob Woodward and Carl Bernstein met with their Watergate informant 'Deep Throat.'

Watergate Complex

The riverfront Watergate complex, 2650 Virginia Ave NW (Ⓜ Foggy Bottom/GWU), is a posh private community encompassing residential apartments, designer boutiques, the deluxe Watergate Hotel, and the notorious office buildings that gave Nixon's Watergate scandal its name. Here in 1972, a break-in at Democratic National Committee headquarters was linked to CREEP – the Committee to Re-elect the President – leading to the unprecedented resignation of a sitting president. Monica Lewinsky lived here in the mid-1990s while she was having her affair with President Clinton.

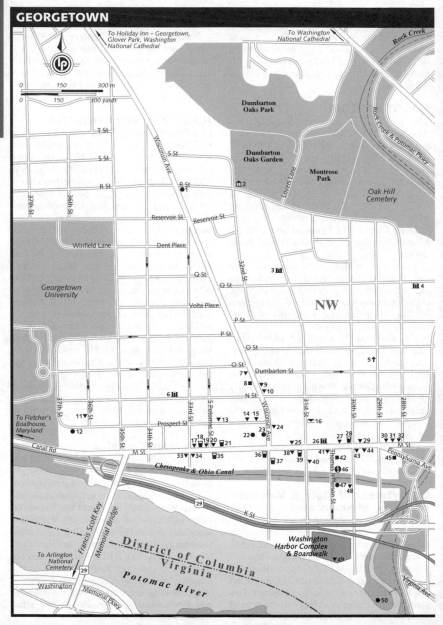

GEORGETOWN

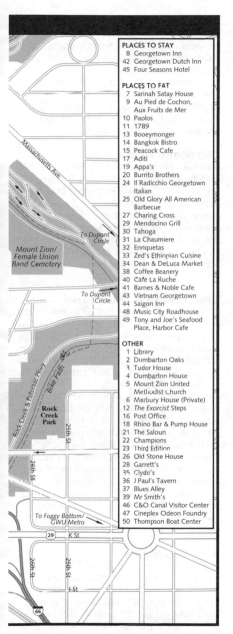

PLACES TO STAY
8 Georgetown Inn
42 Georgetown Dutch Inn
45 Four Seasons Hotel

PLACES TO EAT
7 Sarinah Satay House
9 Au Pied de Cochon,
   Aux Fruits de Mer
10 Paolos
11 1789
13 Booeymonger
14 Bangkok Bistro
15 Peacock Cafe
17 Aditi
19 Appa's
20 Burrito Brothers
24 Il Radicchio Georgetown
   Italian
25 Old Glory All American
   Barbecue
27 Charing Cross
29 Mendocino Grill
30 Tahoga
31 La Chaumiere
32 Enriquetas
33 Zed's Ethiopian Cuisine
34 Dean & DeLuca Market
38 Coffee Beanery
40 Cafe La Ruche
41 Barnes & Noble Cafe
43 Vietnam Georgetown
44 Saigon Inn
48 Music City Roadhouse
49 Tony and Joe's Seafood
   Place, Harbor Cafe

OTHER
1 Library
2 Dumbarton Oaks
3 Tudor House
4 Dumbarton House
5 Mount Zion United
   Methodist Church
6 Marbury House (Private)
12 *The Exorcist* Steps
16 Post Office
18 Rhino Bar & Pump House
21 The Saloun
22 Champions
23 Third Edition
26 Old Stone House
28 Garrett's
35 Clyde's
36 J Paul's Tavern
37 Blues Alley
39 Mr Smith's
46 C&O Canal Visitor Center
47 Cineplex Odeon Foundry
50 Thompson Boat Center

GEORGETOWN

Georgetown was an established town in Maryland before the capital moved in. In fact, its history stretches back much farther: It was the Native American settlement of Tohoga when British fur trader Henry Fleet arrived in 1632.

Once the decision was made to site the new nation's capital between here and the town of Alexandria farther downriver, Georgetown drew DC's gentry and thrived on a flourishing tobacco-exporting industry. Georgetown University, the country's first Roman Catholic university, began in 1789. Many 18th-century buildings remain throughout the campus and district.

Although Georgetown was a Confederate bastion during the Civil War, it was also a stop on the Underground Railroad that smuggled slaves to freedom. An antebellum free black community settled in Herring Hill (between 29th St and Rock Creek Park, north of P St) but was later supplanted by Georgetown's expanding affluent white community. Some historic African American churches remain, and their services continue to draw worshippers from other parts of DC.

In 1871, Georgetown became part of the District of Columbia. During the 1930s, New Deal Democrats bought up much of the housing and reshaped the neighborhood. The Kennedys moved in during the 1950s (to **Marbury House**, on N St NW at 33rd St, exterior view only), and Georgetown grew more fashionable, developing since then into a very popular district for shopping, dining, and entertainment. The largely white, mostly affluent community is a mix of college students and longtime residents.

Georgetown stretches west from Rock Creek Park along the Potomac River and north past T St NW. Its main drag is M St NW, and its epicenter is the intersection of M St NW and Wisconsin Ave. These downtown streets host popular eateries, trendy clothing boutiques, record stores, bookstores, bars, and clubs.

Movie buffs will definitely want to visit **The Exorcist steps**, at 3600 Prospect St (west of 36th St) – that's where the priest goes tumbling down in the 1973 movie.

The community resisted the plan for a Metro station, and as a result, Georgetown is not easily accessible by public transit (though it's a nice walk west along Pennsylvania Ave from the Foggy Bottom station in decent weather). It's often congested – gridlocked at peak times – and street parking can be nearly impossible (off-street parking is both limited and expensive). If you must drive, look for spots on O, P, or Q Sts near Dumbarton Oaks, or on the same streets to the west by Georgetown University.

Georgetown University

Founded in 1789, America's first Roman Catholic college (☎ 202-687-5055), on 37th St NW, was originally directed by America's first black Jesuit. Notable alumni include President Clinton. Its attractive shaded campus of cobblestone lanes retains some of its original 18th- and 19th-century buildings. Enter at O and 37th Sts NW. Today, about 6000 undergraduates pursue degree programs here.

Dumbarton Oaks

In 1944, the agreement to create the United Nations was reached at Dumbarton Oaks (☎ 202-339-6401), 1703 32nd St NW, at S St. The estate has a small but excellent collection of pre-Columbian and Byzantine art. It's open 2 to 5 pm Tuesday to Sunday. A $1 donation 'would be appreciated.'

The 16-acre **Dumbarton Oaks Garden** contains many flowering plants and is also open to the public for a fee of $3 for adults, $2 for seniors and children (free during the winter). Enter through the gate at 31st and R Sts NW. It's open 2 to 6 pm daily.

Dumbarton Oaks is easily confused with **Dumbarton House**, a more modest Federal-period historic house museum (☎ 202-337-2288), at 2715 Q St NW. Tours run 10:15, 11:15 am, and 12:30 pm Tuesday to Saturday. Donations are requested.

Tudor House

This Georgetown mansion (☎ 202-965-0400, www.tudorhouse.org), 1644 31st St NW, between Q and R Sts, was first occupied by Martha Washington's granddaughter in 1794. Her descendants retained the property

until it was opened to the public in 1983. Well kept and with more than 5 acres of grounds, the mansion now functions as a small museum and features furnishings from Mount Vernon.

Admission is $6 for adults, $5 for seniors, and $3 for students. Guided tours take place at 10 am, 11:30 am, 1 pm, and 2:30 pm Tuesday to Friday; also, there are tours on the hour 10 am to 3 pm Saturday.

Old Stone House

This house (☎ 202-426-6851), 3051 M St NW, may be the oldest building in Washington, DC. Built in 1765 by Christopher Layman, a cabinetmaker, it has since been a boarding house, tavern, brothel, and shop. It is now maintained as an example of 18th-century life. The outside appears old, but the inside has been renovated to accommodate sightseeing tourists. It's free and open noon to 5 pm Wednesday to Sunday.

Chesapeake & Ohio Canal

The scenic and historic C&O Canal runs from Georgetown 185 miles upriver to Cumberland, Maryland (see the Western Maryland chapter). In DC, it's a major recreational resource for hikers, cyclists, and boaters (see Activities, later in this chapter).

The canal runs parallel to M St NW in Georgetown's central zone. Travelers can walk south from M St NW on Thomas Jefferson St to find the NPS visitor center (☎ 202-653-5190), which occupies the lower back floor of 1057 Thomas Jefferson St NW. (In winter it's open weekends only.) You can buy tickets here for mule-pulled **barge rides**, which carry passengers through the canal the old-fashioned way. Boats generally run from around April to November (depending on weather). Fares are $7.50 for adults, $6 for seniors, and $4 for children.

Religious Sights

Founded in 1816, the Mount Zion United Methodist Church (☎ 202-234-0148), 1334 29th St NW, is the oldest African American congregation in DC and was once a stop on the Underground Railroad. Nearby, among the overgrown headstones at Mount Zion

Cemetery and the adjacent Female Union Band Cemetery, behind 2515–31 Q St, you can see graves of DC's antebellum free black community. (From Wisconsin Ave, head east on Q St and turn left at the path just before 2531 Q St.)

The 24-acre Oak Hill Cemetery also contains 19th-century gravestones; several of Washington's descendants are buried here (enter at R and 30th Sts).

DUPONT CIRCLE

The Dupont Circle area, north of the White House, was once a marshland called 'the Slashes,' after Slash Creek, which flowed through it. In the early 1870s, a group of developers calling themselves the California Syndicate bought up most of the land, improved it, and named it Pacific Circle. By the early 20th century, the area was home to Washington, DC's wealthiest citizens. Though many were forced to abandon their mansions during the Great Depression, the area later began to regain its luster when many mansions were converted to elegant embassies along the northwest stretch of Massachusetts Ave. As other embassies followed, nearby Sheridan Circle became the center of DC's diplomatic community, now referred to as Embassy Row.

Today, the eclectic neighborhood ranges from plush ambassadorial estates, exclusive art galleries, and refined museums to gay bars, yuppie pool parlors, and anarchist bookstores. It's generally considered the place to go to find a wide variety of restaurants, cafes, pubs, clubs, and trendy boutiques. Patio seating on wide sidewalks, window tables, and park benches offer some of the best people-watching roosts in the city. It's a very lively and safe place to walk around.

The scenic park with the marble statues and fountain inside Dupont Circle is at the intersection of Connecticut and Massachusetts Aves (though when people direct you to Dupont Circle, they're generally referring to the entire neighborhood). The Dupont Circle Metro station underneath the Circle (a modest underground food court designed to resemble train cars) provides the best access to everything in this area.

For a view of the grand architecture of the area, head north up Massachusetts Ave's **Embassy Row** from the Circle to Sheridan Circle, around which you'll see the elegant flag-waving embassies of many countries. Continue north on Massachusetts Ave to see the exceptional Embassy of Japan, the Islamic Center (on Belmont Rd off Massachusetts), and the embassies of Brazil and Great Britain (few of these allow visitors). If you wander up by the Textile Museum, look for the steps leading down S St to 22nd – it's a scenic little spot.

A few blocks north of the White House, you can tour the publishing operations of the *Washington Post* (☎ 202-334-7969), at 1150 15th St NW.

The **Metropolitan AME Church**, 1518 M St NW, was built in 1886 by African Americans. The funeral of Frederick Douglass occurred here in 1895.

More than a dozen **art galleries** throughout the district offer glimpses of art as varied as Tiffany glass, African masks, Inuit carvings, and all-media from artists with disabilities. There's a compact row of galleries on R St between Florida and Connecticut Aves. A 19-member gallery association holds a collective open house the first Friday of each month except in August and September (call ☎ 202-232-3610 for more information).

Phillips Collection

America's first modern-art museum (☎ 202-387-2151), 1600 21st St NW, at Q St northwest of the Circle, exhibits an outstanding collection in a casually intimate setting. From room to room, you can see great works by Renoir (the huge *Luncheon of the Boating Party* is one example), Cézanne, Monet, Degas, van Gogh, Klee, Rothko, O'Keeffe, Diebenkorn, and Jacob Lawrence. You enter through the modern extension wing and work your way back to the Victorian home that originally housed the collection; now there's a small cafe and bookstore.

The galleries are open 10 am to 5 pm Tuesday to Saturday and noon to 7 pm Sunday. Donations are requested during the week; weekend admission is $6.50 for adults,

WASHINGTON, DC

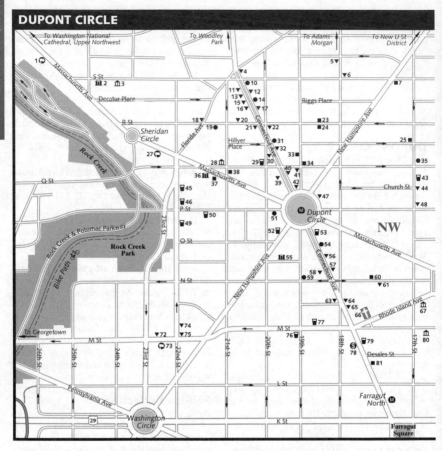

DUPONT CIRCLE

$3.25 for students and seniors, and free for youth under 18. On Thursday night, the museum extends its hours to 8:30 pm and charges $5 for adults. Sunday afternoon concerts and lunchtime lectures are among many scheduled special events.

B'nai B'rith Klutznick Museum

This museum (☎ 202-857-6583), 1640 Rhode Island Ave NW, maintains one of the largest collections of Judaica in the nation, from archaeological artifacts and items from early Jewish American settlements to exhibits on contemporary arts, sports, and culture. The

museum is open 10 am to 5 pm Sunday to Friday. Donations are encouraged.

Textile Museum

Housed in two historic residences, this museum (☎ 202-667-0441), 2320 S St NW, displays handmade fiber art and Asian carpets from its collection of 15,000 textiles from around the world, some dating from 3000 BC. (Find the flaw: Traditional textile artists from Islamic carpet makers to Appalachian quilters often weave an intentional flaw into the pattern so as not to dangerously mimic God's perfection.) It's open Monday

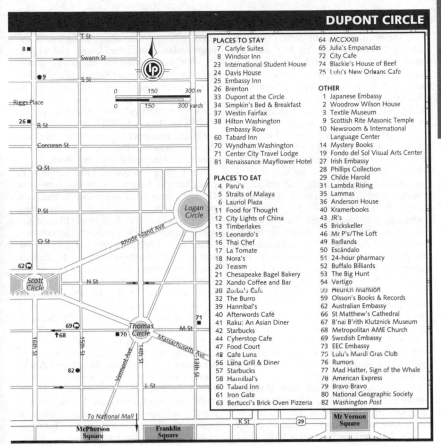

DUPONT CIRCLE

PLACES TO STAY
7 Carlyle Suites
8 Windsor Inn
23 International Student House
24 Davis House
25 Embassy Inn
26 Brenton
33 Dupont at the Circle
34 Simpkin's Bed & Breakfast
37 Westin Fairfax
38 Hilton Washington
Embassy Row
60 Tabard Inn
70 Wyndham Washington
71 Center City Travel Lodge
81 Renaissance Mayflower Hotel

PLACES TO EAT
4 Paru's
5 Straits of Malaya
6 Lauriol Plaza
11 Food for Thought
12 City Lights of China
13 Timberlakes
15 Leonardo's
16 Thai Chef
17 La Tomate
18 Nora's
20 Teaism
21 Chesapeake Bagel Bakery
22 Xando Coffee and Bar
30 Zorba's Cafe
32 The Burro
39 Hannibal's
40 Afterwords Café
41 Raku: An Asian Diner
42 Starbucks
44 Cyberstop Cafe
47 Food Court
48 Cafe Luna
56 Luna Grill & Diner
57 Starbucks
58 Hannibal's
60 Tabard Inn
61 Iron Gate
63 Bertucci's Brick Oven Pizzeria

64 MCCXXIII
65 Julia's Empanadas
72 City Cafe
74 Blackie's House of Beef
75 Lulu's New Orleans Cafe

OTHER
1 Japanese Embassy
2 Woodrow Wilson House
3 Textile Museum
9 Scottish Rite Masonic Temple
10 Newsroom & International
Language Center
14 Mystery Books
19 Fondo del Sol Visual Arts Center
27 Irish Embassy
28 Phillips Collection
29 Childe Harold
31 Lambda Rising
35 Lammas
36 Anderson House
40 Kramerbooks
43 JR's
45 Brickskeller
46 Mr P's/The Loft
49 Badlands
50 Escándalo
51 24-hour pharmacy
52 Buffalo Billiards
53 The Big Hunt
54 Vertigo
55 Heurich Mansion
59 Olsson's Books & Records
62 Australian Embassy
66 St Matthew's Cathedral
67 B'nai B'rith Klutznick Museum
68 Metropolitan AME Church
69 Swedish Embassy
73 EEC Embassy
75 Lulu's Mardi Gras Club
76 Rumors
77 Mad Hatter, Sign of the Whale
78 American Express
79 Bravo Bravo
80 National Geographic Society
82 Washington Post

to Saturday 10 am to 5 pm and Sunday 1 to 5 pm. Donations are encouraged.

Fondo del Sol Visual Arts Center

This artist-run 'alternative' museum (☎ 202-483-2777), 2112 R St NW, at Florida Ave, promotes the cultural heritage and arts of the Americas through such exhibits as pre-Columbian artifacts, *santos* (carved wooden saints), and folk and contemporary art. In late summer, the Caribbeana Festival features salsa and reggae music. It's open 12:30 to 5:30 pm Wednesday to Saturday. Donations are encouraged.

National Geographic Society

Kids will enjoy the National Geographic Society's Explorers Hall (☎ 202-857-7588) at the headquarters at 1145 17th St NW at M St, where there's a simulated orbital flight, a moon rock under glass, an 11-foot globe, and many interactive video displays. It's free and open 9 am to 5 pm Monday to Saturday and 10 am to 5 pm Sunday.

Historic Buildings

The headquarters of the Historical Society of Washington, DC (☎ 202-785-2068) are in the **Heurich Mansion**, 1307 New Hampshire

Ave NW, at 20th St. Docents guide visitors through 14 rooms of the medieval-inspired 1894 Victorian home of local brewing magnate Christian Heurich, but you can wander about on your own if you'd rather (look for the small garden refuge). The society is dedicated to preserving the history of Washington, DC; it operates a library on DC history and sells Washingtoniana in its bookstore. The mansion is open 10 am to 4 pm Monday to Saturday (call for a tour schedule). Admission is $3 for adults, $1.50 for seniors, and free for children under 12.

Founded in 1783, the Society of the Cincinnati (☎ 202-785-2040), 2118 Massachusetts Ave NW, opens the doors of its headquarters for a viewing of the 1902 **Anderson House** and exhibits on the Revolutionary War, the society, and the Anderson family. The Beaux Arts mansion is opulently furnished with European and Asian art. It's free and open 1 to 4 pm Tuesday to Saturday.

The 1915 **Woodrow Wilson House** (☎ 202-387-4062), 2340 S St NW, offers guided hour-long tours of the home of the 28th president (including a 15-minute introductory newsreel). The house is furnished in Roaring Twenties style. It's open 10 am to 4 pm Tuesday to Sunday. Admission is $5 for adults, $4 for seniors, $2.50 for students, and free for children under seven.

The impressive **Scottish Rite Masonic Temple** (☎ 202-232-3579), 1733 16th St NW, patterned after the Mausoleum of Halicarnassus (one of the 'seven wonders of the world'), was designed by John Pope (who designed the Jefferson Memorial) and includes a J Edgar Hoover Room downstairs. It's free and open 8 am to 2 pm weekdays.

St Matthew's Cathedral (☎ 202-347-3215), 1725 Rhode Island Ave NW, a gold-domed sanctuary with rich mosaics and yellow-and-ironwork globes, is where JFK's funeral took place. Catholic masses are offered in Spanish and Latin, as well as English; guided tours are offered 2:30 to 4 pm Sunday. Donations are accepted.

ADAMS-MORGAN

The funky, ethnic, bohemian neighborhood of Adams-Morgan, north of Dupont Circle, is centered along 18th St and Columbia Rd – this winding, climbing route was once a major trail for Native Americans. Before 1955, the neighborhood was called Lanier Heights, but after DC became the first major city to integrate its public schools voluntarily, residents elected to change the name by combining the names of two area elementary schools, historically white 'Adams' and historically African American 'Morgan.' Adding to this blend today are residents from Central and South America, the Caribbean, Central Africa, Southeast Asia, and many other lands.

The lively district is lined with restaurants, cafes, bars, and clubs – a funkier version of Dupont Circle. It's a great place to hang out, people-watch, browse, and eat. The long hilltop blocks of 18th St between Florida Ave and Columbia Rd are packed with new and secondhand bookstores, record stores, retro- and nouveau-clothing boutiques, sidewalk cafes, and rooftop restaurants.

Note that the neighborhood is not too convenient to the Metro, though in decent weather, it's a nice walk from the Woodley Park/Zoo station along Calvert St. At night, you'd be better off in a cab to avoid the hassle of gridlocked streets and limited parking.

Occupying two historic houses near Meridian Hill Park, the **Meridian International Center** (☎ 202-667-6800), 1624 and 1630 Crescent Place NW, presents three-month exhibits focusing on the cultural and artistic heritage of a particular country or region. The International Visitors Information Service operates out of here.

Meridian Hill Park (unofficially dedicated to Malcolm X) scales the slope from the lower Shaw neighborhood (see that section, later in the chapter) to the upper reaches of Adams-Morgan. Some waterfalls grace this contour and provide a needed bit of scenery to an uneven area (for safety's sake, avoid visiting alone or at night).

UPPER NORTHWEST

To the northwest of Adams-Morgan, among the comfortable residential neighborhoods, lie three major sights – the Washington National Cathedral, the National Zoo, and Rock Creek Park. The district ranges from middle class to more affluent along upper Connecticut, Wisconsin, and Massachusetts Aves. It is well served by several Metro stops.

Washington National Cathedral

A national cathedral in a country founded on the separation of church and state is a provocative idea, so you know the National Cathedral (☎ 202-537-6200), on Wisconsin Ave NW at Massachusetts, has to be an unusual place. Architecturally, the massive, high Gothic cathedral (sixth-largest in the world) is intended to rival European scale and majesty, right down to the flying buttresses and individually designed gargoyles. It's home to one denomination – the Episcopal Church – but it strives to cover all the politically correct patriotic bases: There's affirmative action at the altar; a stained-glass window of *Apollo 11*; and each week, prayers are devoted to a different state and religious tradition.

The national church was originally George Washington's idea, but it took 83 years to complete. Martin Luther King Jr gave his last sermon here before being assassinated. Now it's the standard place for state funerals and other high-profile events.

Take the elevator to the **tower overlook** for an expansive view of Washington, DC. The landscaped grounds include a fragrant herb garden and garden shop, and there's a great gift shop downstairs with many wonderful gift icons. Daily tours are offered, but the best way to experience the cathedral is to attend a service – all are invited and made welcome (the program cues you when to sit, stand, and other protocol). There are three services daily (donations are requested). Take the Metro to the Tenleytown station, and then hop on the No 30, 32, 34, or 36 bus to the cathedral.

National Zoological Park

This zoo (☎ 202-357-2700, 673-4800 for a recording), 3000 Connecticut Ave NW, is run by the Smithsonian Institution. It was beautifully designed by Frederick Law Olmsted, who designed New York's Central Park. The zoo follows the natural contour of its woodland canyon setting. The 130 acres hold lions, tigers, bears, and many other exotic residents, mostly in natural-habitat environments set along two sloping paths.

The dozen zoo buildings include the Great Ape House; an aviary; a reptile house; and the newest additions, **Amazonia** (a replica of the Brazilian rain forest), and the **Think Tank**, which explores animal intelligence. From May to mid-September, buildings are open 9 am (some open at 10 am) to 6 pm daily (until 4:30 pm during the rest of the year). The grounds are open longer; you can see the animals outside from 8 am to 8 pm May to mid-September, or 8 am to 6 pm during rest of year. Parking is extremely limited. There is a great 'Zoo Bar' across the street. The closest Metro stop is Woodley Park/Zoo, a nice one-third-mile walk north from the station.

Rock Creek Park

This national park drops a slice of wilderness into the center of urban Washington, DC. The park starts at the Potomac River and extends north through DC, first confined to the narrow corridor of Rock Creek until it expands to wide parkland in the Upper Northwest district. Terrific bike and hiking trails extend along its entire length, but most major recreational services (including park headquarters) are in the zone north of the zoo. Some sights can be reached by foot from a Metro station; most require a car to access easily.

Recreational services include free guided nature walks and astronomy programs at the **nature center** and **planetarium** (☎ 202-282-1063), near Missouri and 27th Sts NW; they're open 9 am to 5 pm Wednesday to Sunday. There are also hiking and biking trails, an 18-hole golf course, tennis courts, and horse rentals (see Activities, later, for details).

Historic sights in the park include the remains of Civil War forts (at Oregon Ave and Military Rd, and at 13th and Quackenbush Sts NW). On the creek at Tilden St, the 1820 **Pierce Mill** (☎ 202-426-6908, Ⓜ Van Ness/UDC) is open to visitors 8 am to 4:30 pm Wednesday to Sunday. The park's western **Soapstone Valley Park** extension

WASHINGTON, DC

ADAMS-MORGAN, WOODLEY PARK & SHAW

PLACES TO STAY
1 Kalorama Guest House at Woodley Park
2 Connecticut-Woodley Guest House
10 Omni Shoreham Hotel
14 Taft Bridge Inn
15 Normandy Inn
16 Washington Courtyard by Marriott
17 1836 California
38 Adams Inn
49 Kalorama Guest House
53 Washington International Backpackers

PLACES TO EAT
4 Lebanese Taverna
5 Acapulco
6 Saigon Inn
7 Tono
8 Jandara
9 Rajaji
13 Florida Avenue Grill
18 El Tamarindo
19 Jolt N' Bolt
22 Julio's
23 U-topia
25 Polly's
27 Ben's Chili Bowl
28 Kaffa House
39 Avignon Frères
41 Meskerem
42 Red Sea
45 Astor
46 Tom Brazil
48 Cafe Riche
51 Cities
52 I Matti
54 New Orleans
55 Rumba
56 Felix
57 Mobay
58 Cafe Lautrec
59 Belmont Kitchen Pantry
60 La Fourchette
63 Roxanne and the Payote Grill
64 Saigonaise
65 Pearl

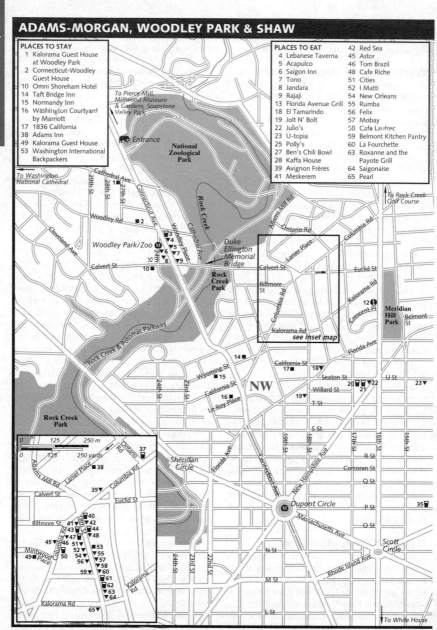

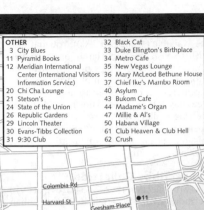

(off Connecticut Ave at Albemarle St) preserves quarries where the area's original Algonquin residents obtained soapstone for shaping cookware.

The park's **Carter Barron Amphitheater** (☎ 202-426-6837), 16th St and Colorado Ave NW, holds summertime concerts. An **Art Barn** studio presents works by local artists. Park headquarters (☎ 202-426-6832), 5000 Glover Rd NW, are located near the nature center (open 9 am to 5 pm daily).

The easiest way to reach the park by public transportation is to take the Metro's Red Line to the Woodley Park/Zoo stop. The park and zoo lie just a block to the east (look for the signs).

National Museum of Health & Medicine

On the grounds of the Walter Reed Army Medical Center, 6825 16th St N (at Aspen, adjacent to Rock Creek Park), this peculiar collection (☎ 202-782-2200) includes such medical oddities as gangrenous bones, a preserved brain, children's skeletons, bone chips from Lincoln's head, and President Garfield's spinal column (along with more conventional medical exhibits). It's free and open 10 am to 5:30 pm daily.

Hillwood Museum & Gardens

Heiress Marjorie Merriweather Post (of Post Toasties fame), once wed to the ambassador to the Soviet Union, amassed an imperial collection of Russian art now on display at her Hillwood estate (☎ 202-686-8500), 4155 Linnean Ave NW. A cafe serves Russian specialties (borsht, blintzes, cabbage) and an English afternoon tea. It's open 9 am to 4:30 pm Tuesday to Saturday. Guided tours are by advance reservation. A $10 donation is requested for adults, $5 for students.

SHAW

Named for Colonel Robert Gould Shaw, a white Bostonian who commanded the famous African American 54th Massachusetts Regiment (as related in the 1990 film *Glory*, in which Matthew Broderick played the role of Shaw) during the Civil War, the Shaw neighborhood stretches south to north from around Thomas Circle to Meridian Hill Park, and east to west from roughly N Capitol St to 15th St NW.

Anchoring the neighborhood is Howard University, a traditionally African American school founded in 1867. The university's elite settled in an attractive adjacent area called **LeDroit Park**, where some fine examples of Victorian homes remain around U St NW between 4th and 5th Sts.

Shaw's heyday was in the 1930s, when it was a high point on the country's renowned 'chitlin' circuit' of African American entertainment centers. Shaw's 'Great Black Way' hosted such celebrities as Ella Fitzgerald, Eubie Blake, and Duke Ellington (born at 1212 T St NW).

One of the highlights of the neighborhood's many contributions to the Civil Rights movement occurred in the 1950s, when Washington's Committee for School Desegregation first met here at **John Wesley African Methodist Episcopal Church**, the 1850s sanctuary at 1615 14th St NW. Their work led to the landmark civil-rights case *Brown v Board of Education* that mandated school desegregation.

In 1968, the DC riots following the assassination of Martin Luther King Jr hit the neighborhood hard; fires destroyed many buildings and devastated the historically strong black commercial district.

Today, the district is undergoing a gradual renaissance, particularly the 'New U' area along U and 14th Sts NW. The reopening of the historic Lincoln Theater and the appearance of many new cafes, clubs, and shops alongside familiar neighborhood joints make this an up-and-coming area in DC. The U St/Cardozo Metro station provides convenient access to the area.

Howard University

Since its founding to educate African Americans in 1867, Howard University (☎ 202-806-6100), 2400 6th St NW, has become one of the nation's most-respected schools. Its distinguished alumni include Supreme Court Justice Thurgood Marshall, the great diplomat Ralph Bunche, and Nobel Prize laureate Toni Morrison.

Today, the university has more than 12,000 students in 18 different schools. Campus tours are available (☎ 202-806-2900). You may also wish to visit the Moorland-Springarn Research Center (☎ 202-806-7239), with the nation's largest collection of African American literature, open 9 am to about 4:30 pm weekdays (free admission). The James Herring Gallery of Art (☎ 202-806-7070) is open 9:30 am to 4:30 pm weekdays (free admission). From the Shaw/Howard U Metro, walk north on 7th St.

Evans-Tibbs Collection

This art collection (☎ 202-234-8164), at 1910 Vermont Ave NW, originated with Lillian Evans Tibbs. She was a celebrated opera diva who toured Europe during the 1920s and '30s and was widely known as Madame Evanti. Her Victorian home near Logan Circle became an informal salon where African American artists and literary figures would gather. She began a tradition of collecting works of art by many of these artists. Her grandson, Thurlow E Tibbs Jr, continued that tradition and significantly increased the collection's aesthetic and historical value.

The gallery exhibits the finest works by African American masters, as well as emerging artists. Exhibit hours are 5 to 8 pm Wednesday and Thursday and 2 to 6 pm Saturday, or by appointment. Donations are encouraged.

Mary McLeod Bethune House

This house (☎ 202-673-2402), 1318 Vermont Ave NW, between 13th and 14th Sts, is a national historic site devoted to African American women's history and is the former home of educator Mary McLeod Bethune (founder of the National Council of Negro Women and the first African American women's college in the US). It's free and open 10 am to 4 pm Monday to Saturday.

Lincoln Theater

This restored theater (☎ 202-328-6000), 1215 U St NW, has regained its position as the preeminent cultural institution of DC's African American community. The best way to see it is to attend one of the many performances held here.

UPPER NORTHEAST
The Upper Northeast district is a residential district with neighborhoods that range from OK to not so great. It's dominated by the large campuses of Gallaudet University to the south and Catholic University farther north. (Trinity College is also nearby.)

Gallaudet University
Established in 1864, Gallaudet University (☎ 202-651-5505, TDD 202-651-5359), 800 Florida Ave NE (enter from 8th St), is the world's only accredited liberal-arts school for the hearing impaired. Student protests here in 1989 led to the appointment of the college's first hearing-impaired president. Few sports fans know that in 1894, Gallaudet football players invented the American football huddle to prevent their opponents from reading the sign language used to call the plays. Tours are available by advance reservation.

National Shrine of the Immaculate Conception
This huge, strange church (☎ 202-526-8300), adjacent to Catholic University at Michigan Ave and 4th St NE, accommodates 6000 worshipers in what is the largest Catholic church in the Western Hemisphere. In addition to the church's unearthly size, the Marian shrine is an eclectic mix of Romanesque and Byzantine styles – from classical towers to a mosquelike dome, and minarets besides. Yet the mosaics, the stained glass, and a little grotto chapel downstairs by themselves are lovely.

The church is open 7 am to 7 pm daily. Take the Metro to Brookland/CUA. When you exit the station, hook back around to Michigan Ave, and walk southwest up the hill until you spot the basilica looming on the horizon.

Franciscan Monastery
This monastery (☎ 202-526-6800), 1400 Quincy St NE, maintains 44 acres of grounds that invite contemplation. In spring, thousands of tulips bloom, and in June, it's roses. Holy sights dot the grounds; there are catacombs too.

The monks in residence lead tours every hour on the hour (except noon) from 9 am to 4 pm Monday to Saturday and 1 to 4 pm Sunday. From the Brookland/CUA Metro station, walk east on Monroe St to 14th St NE; go north on 14th St to Quincy. The monastery is on the right.

US National Arboretum
You can drive, bike, or walk through 440 acres of beautifully landscaped native and exotic plants at the National Arboretum (☎ 202-245-2726), 3501 New York Ave NE, 2 miles northeast of the capitol. Also see the **National Bonsai and Penjing Museum** (open 10 am to 3:30 pm).

The grounds are open 8 am to 5 pm weekdays and 10 am to 5 pm weekends. The flowering season from March to May is the best time to visit. From the Stadium/Armory Metro station, take the B2 or B4 bus to the intersection of Bladensburg Rd and R St, and walk to the gate from there.

Kenilworth Aquatic Gardens
The only national park devoted to aquatic plants, Kenilworth Aquatic Gardens (☎ 202-426-6905) is at 900 Anacostia Drive NE. Displays include a beautiful selection of water lilies and other varieties of aquatic vegetation on more than 40 ponds. The best time to see blooms is mid-July to mid-August; the water-lily festival is the last Saturday in July. Admission is free.

From the Deanwood Metro station, walk along Douglas St to the pedestrian overpass; continue to Anacostia Ave and turn right. By car, take New York Ave (Route 50) east across the Anacostia River; at the highway split, stay right toward Annapolis. Exit at Kenilworth Ave south (Route 295), turn right on Douglas St, and follow the signs.

SOUTHWEST
The original site for the nation's capital was identified as the confluence of the Potomac and Anacostia Rivers. Today, DC's southern riverfront ranges from the upscale waterfront at the Potomac side in southwestern DC to the rough streets of southeastern DC along the Anacostia. Directly east of the Capitol,

along E Capitol St, is RFK Stadium (home of the DC United professional soccer team).

Along the waterfront, a promenade runs along the Washington Channel parallel to Maine Ave SW from around 6th St to around 11th St SW. One side is lined with yachts, sailboats, and houseboats in a narrow marina; the other with park benches (a great spot to watch the sunset), a hotel, and several big and popular seafood restaurants (a few with patio seating). More adventurous visitors continue past the end of the promenade to the open-air **seafood market**, where fisherfolk hawk the day's catch from floating barges. The **Arena Stage**, a popular theatrical venue, is near the southern end of the promenade. The theater is close to the Waterfront Metro stop, but the seafood market is the same distance from the L'Enfant Plaza station. The walk south from the Jefferson Memorial or the Bureau of Engraving and Printing crosses under several imposing freeways and may make travelers targets to muggers (a cab is a better bet).

Across the channel, there's **Potomac Park East**, a long narrow strip of green running from the Jefferson Memorial to the scenic promontory at Hains Point.

The **Washington Navy Yard**, built in 1800, stretches along the Anacostia River from 1st to 11th Sts SE. Here you'll find the Navy Museum, the Marine Corps Museum, and tours of the decommissioned destroyer USS *Barry*. Featuring submarines, guns, uniforms, and scale ship models, the **Navy Museum** (☎ 202-433-6897) is the more interesting of the two museums. It's open 9 am to 4 pm weekdays and 10 am to 5 pm weekends. The **Marine Corps Museum** (☎ 202-433-3534) is open 10 am to 4 pm Monday to Saturday and noon to 5 pm Sunday (possibly extended hours in summer). Both museums are free. From the Navy Yard Metro, exit onto M St and walk east to 9th St to enter.

For an offbeat sight, check out the entombed leg of Colonel Ulric Dahlgren nearby. Dahlgren, son of a Washington Navy Yard commander, lost his leg at Gettysburg. His father made sure his son's leg was given full honors at its interment. A plaque marks the site on Isaac Hull Ave. (From the Navy Museum exit, walk to the right three blocks,

turn right on Isaac Hull Ave, and walk down to the fire hydrant.)

The Eighth & Eye **Marine Corps Barracks** are home to the Marine Corps commandant (☎ 202-433-6060). You can catch a two-hour parade drill here on Friday evenings at 8:45 pm during the summer. Call at least three weeks in advance for reservations, or send a request to the Adjutant, Marine Corps Barracks, Washington, DC 20390, or just show up at the general admission line at 7 pm before the drill. The closest Metro stop (three blocks south) is Eastern Market.

ANACOSTIA

A district of DC across the Anacostia River, Anacostia is named after its Native American inhabitants – recorded by Europeans as Nacothtant or Anaquashtank, the name was later corrupted to Anacostia. A European settlement here predated Washington, DC – in fact, the Native American trading village here drew famed Captain John Smith as early as 1608.

Before the Civil War, the area was the home of a large free black community, and after the war, many freed slaves settled here. The village was incorporated into DC in 1854. In 1877, abolitionist Frederick Douglass moved in (see the boxed text). Parts of Anacostia developed into a middle-class African American community by the end of the century, and a few quiet middle-class neighborhoods remain. Yet years of decline have now earned the district a reputation for violent crime. Use extra caution – you might want to consider an organized tour.

Frederick Douglass National Historic Site (Cedar Hill)

Cedar Hill (☎ 202-426-5960), 1411 West St SE, was the home of abolitionist, author, diplomat, and former slave Frederick Douglass from 1877 until his death in 1895. Here, he wrote *The Life and Times of Frederick Douglass*, and today, the house still contains most of his original furnishings, right down to his wire-rim eyeglasses on the rolltop desk. After his first wife died, Douglass sealed off her room, and he was the last one to use it for 80 years until it was opened again in 1962.

Frederick Douglass: From Slave to Statesman

Born a slave in 1817 on a plantation outside of Easton, Maryland, Frederick Douglass lived a life that eventually led him to prominent government posts such as US Marshall for the District of Columbia and US minister to Haiti. Aside from these prominent positions he held, Douglass is remembered by Americans as the country's most outstanding African American leader during the 19th century.

When he was 21 years old, Douglass escaped wretched treatment at the hands of Maryland planters and established himself as a freeman among a community of sympathetic Quakers in the booming whaling port of New Bedford, Massachusetts. Largely self-educated, Douglass had a natural gift for eloquence. In 1841, he won the admiration of New England abolitionists when he delivered an impromptu speech at an anti-slavery convention, introducing himself as 'a recent graduate from the institution of slavery with his diploma [whip marks] on his back.' Thereafter, abolitionists hired Douglass as an agent for the Massachusetts Anti-Slavery Society, for which he traveled the Free States speaking for the abolition of slavery and energizing the Underground Railroad to carry runaway slaves to freedom.

Douglass so angered the pro-slavery establishment in America that his friends urged him to flee to England to escape seizure and punishment under the recently enacted Fugitive Slave Law. Douglass continued lecturing against slavery in England and became so popular that admirers contributed money to purchase his freedom in the States. After Douglass returned to the US in 1847, he became the self-proclaimed 'station master and conductor' of the Underground Railroad in Rochester, New York. During the decade preceding the Civil War, Douglass worked with other prominent abolitionists, such as Harriet Tubman and John Brown. But Douglass broke with Brown when he learned of the zealot's disastrous plans to attack the federal armory at Harpers Ferry, West Virginia.

In 1860, Douglass campaigned for Abraham Lincoln's election to the presidency. When war broke out, Douglass helped raise two regiments of black soldiers, the Massachusetts 54th and 55th (see the film *Glory*, with Denzel Washington) to fight for the Union cause. After the Union won the war, Douglass went to Washington, DC, to lend his support to the 13th, 14th, and 15th Constitutional Amendments, which abolished slavery; granted citizenship to former slaves; and guaranteed all citizens the right to vote, exclusive of their race or color.

His Anacostia hilltop residence is now a national historic site open to the public and operated by the National Park Service.

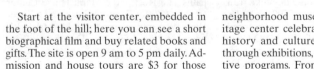

Start at the visitor center, embedded in the foot of the hill; here you can see a short biographical film and buy related books and gifts. The site is open 9 am to 5 pm daily. Admission and house tours are $3 for those over the age of six, and seniors pay $1.50. For reservations, call ☎ 800-967-2283.

From the Anacostia Metro, you can take a B2 or B4 bus right to the house, but the bus stop and route for the return trip is less convenient. (It's better to take a cab.)

Anacostia Museum

This Smithsonian museum (☎ 202-287-3369), 1901 Fort Place SE, expanded from a neighborhood museum to a regional heritage center celebrating African American history and culture in the 'Upper South' through exhibitions, education, and interpretive programs. From the Anacostia Metro stop, take the W1 or W2 bus to the museum. Note that the museum will be closed for renovations through spring 2001.

ACTIVITIES

For outdoor recreation, residents head primarily to Rock Creek Park and the C&O Canal, both to the northwest. You can also enjoy boating activities on the Potomac River and some activities on the Mall.

Bicycling

A 10-mile paved bike path runs from below the Kennedy Center to Pierce Mill, largely along the wooded creek in Rock Creek Park. (The park's Beach Drive between Military and Broad Branch Rds is closed to vehicles 7 am Saturday to 7 pm Sunday.)

The C&O Canal towpath also makes a great bike route, particularly for mountain bikes – it starts in Georgetown and stretches nearly 185 miles northwest to Cumberland, Maryland. (See the Around Washington, DC and Western Maryland chapters.)

Bike rentals are available at Thompson Boat Center (see Boating, later). In Adams-Morgan, City Bikes (☎ 202-265-1564), 2501 Champlain St, next to Ben & Jerry's, has mountain bikes and hybrids for $10 an hour or $25 for 24 hours. Big Wheel Bikes (☎ 202-337-0254), at 1034 33rd St NW in Georgetown, rents racing and mountain bikes at similar rates.

Several good books describe local bike tours, including *Short Bike Rides in and around Washington, DC*, by Michael Leccese (Globe Pequot Press), and *25 Bicycle Tours in and Around Washington*, by Ann M Oman (Backcountry Publications). Another good source is *ADC's Washington Area Bike Map*, by the Metropolitan Washington Council of Governments. You can find this and other good maps and guides at The Map Store (☎ 202-628-2608), 1636 I St NW.

Hiking & Jogging

Fifteen miles of well-marked day-hike trails traverse Rock Creek Park's 2100 acres. The trails range in difficulty from easy to strenuous; loop trips are possible. The C&O Canal National Historical Park has many trails and a towpath (see the Around Washington, DC and Western Maryland chapters); a popular 4-mile roundtrip runs between Fletcher's Boathouse (see Boating, later) and Francis Scott Key Bridge in Georgetown.

The National Mall is also a popular jogging route. Of course, the most exclusive jog in town is the track on the White House lawn, installed at President Clinton's request (no public access). A 1½-mile Parcourse exercise trail runs behind the Omni Shoreham

Hotel (Ⓜ Woodley Park/Zoo), stopping at 18 exercise stations.

Boating

Boaters head to the Potomac River and the C&O Canal. Rent canoes (and bikes) at Thompson Boat Center (☎ 202-333-9543), 2900 Virginia Ave NW (on the Potomac north of the Kennedy Center). It's open 6 am to 8 pm weekdays . It has canoes, rowboats, kayaks, rowing shells, rowing classes, and bikes. You can rent similar equipment at Fletcher's Boathouse (☎ 202-244-0461), upriver at 4940 Canal Rd NW.

Golf

The city has two public golf courses, one near downtown and one in the Upper Northwest district, and both are open dawn to dusk year-round (first-come, first-served). The East Potomac Park Golf Course (☎ 202-554-7660), south of the Jefferson Memorial, offers a par 72, 18-hole course and two nine-hole courses. Greens fees for nine holes are $11, and 18 holes are $16.50; club rental is $6/8. It also offers a driving range and miniature golf. The Rock Creek Golf Course (☎ 202-882-7332) offers two nine-hole courses that may be played as one 18-hole course. Fees for nine/18 holes are $9/15 weekdays, $12/19 weekends; cart rental is $10/17; club rental is $6/9.

Horseback Riding

Rock Creek Park has 11 miles of bridle paths. The Rock Creek Park Horse Center (☎ 202-362-0117), at Military and Glover Rds NW, rents horses for guided trips. It's open 1 to 8 pm Tuesday to Friday and 10 am to 6 pm weekends.

Swimming

Of the 35 outdoor and 11 indoor free public pools in DC, try the one in Georgetown (☎ 202-282-2366) at 34th St and Volta Place NW; the indoor Capitol East pool (☎ 202-724-4495), at 635 North Carolina Ave SE in Capitol Hill; or the Marie Reed pool (☎ 202-673-7771), at 2200 Champlain St NW, near the foot of 18th St in Adams-Morgan. Note that during hot weather these pools can be jammed with people, and the ambiance can be anything but relaxing.

Ice Skating

The small National Gallery Ice Rink (☎ 202-289-2666), on the Mall at Madison Drive and 9th St NW (between the Museum of Natural History and the National Gallery), offers a homey ice-skating scene from about December to April (depending on the weather), generally from 10 am to 11 pm. The rink plays tinny oldies music and attracts languid teens – a pretty whimsical touch to the monumental Mall. Admission is $4 to $5 for adults and $3 to $4 for seniors and children. Skate rentals cost $2.50 per two-hour session.

If the ice is thick enough, you can also skate on the Reflecting Pool and on the C&O Canal in Georgetown; bring your own skates.

Tennis

The city maintains more than 50 free public tennis courts throughout DC; for information and a permit to use the courts, call the DC Department of Parks and Recreation (☎ 202-673-7671), 3149 16th St NW.

ORGANIZED TOURS

Tourmobile Sightseeing (☎ 202-554-5100) regularly runs trams around major monuments and museums; their running commentary focuses on practical information (what it is, when it's open, whether it has food service, how to get elsewhere). Get on and off as often as you like for an all-day fee ($16 for adults, $7 for children – get a day and a half of use by purchasing after 2 pm).

Other general and specialty tours include Gray Line (☎ 202-289-1995), offering a black-heritage tour and the largest number of foreign-language tours (Japanese, French, Italian, German, and Spanish). You might also choose Old Town Trolley Tours (☎ 202-832-9800), with on-off service available, or Scandal Tours (☎ 800-758-8687), which delivers the dirt on DC's infamous sites.

DC Ducks (☎ 202-832-9040) recycles amphibious military vehicles into land/water city tours. For river tours, try Spirit Cruises (☎ 202-554-8000), departing from 6th and Water Sts SW. (It also runs tours to Mount Vernon.) Bike Sites (☎ 202-966-8662) has professionally guided bike tours of the city and surrounding historic sites. You can take the 'da Vinci to Lewinsky' walk for about $12 with Tour DC (☎ 301-588-8999).

SPECIAL EVENTS

The city is best known for its Cherry Blossom Festival in March and April and for the Smithsonian Folklife Festival in June. And of course, Independence Day is always a big event. For a full calendar, contact the Washington, DC Convention and Visitors Association (☎ 202-789-7000).

Here are some highlights:

January

Martin Luther King Jr's Birthday (☎ 202-619-7222) On the third Monday, orators recite King's 'I Have a Dream' speech at the Lincoln Memorial.

Robert E Lee's Birthday (☎ 202-727-1111) Every January 22, Lee's birthday is celebrated with 19th-century festivities, a free tour, and cake at Arlington House (see the Around Washington, DC chapter).

February

Black History Month February brings special events and exhibits at the Smithsonian Institution, intertwined with wreath-laying celebrations on the birthdays of Abraham Lincoln and abolitionist Frederick Douglass (February 14).

Abraham Lincoln's Birthday (☎ 202-619-7222) On February 12, you can hear the Gettysburg Address read at the Lincoln Memorial.

Chinese New Year's Parade In mid-February, dances and firecrackers light up Chinatown.

March

St Patrick's Day Parade Around March 17, revelers parade down Constitution Ave NW.

Smithsonian Kite Festival (☎ 202-357-2700) In late March, kite designers and flyers gather on the Mall for this rite of spring.

April

Cherry Blossom Festival (☎ 202-547-1500) This two-week-long arts and culture fest in early April celebrates the blooming of thousands of DC's cherry trees. It all culminates in a parade extravaganza.

White House Easter Egg Roll (☎ 202-456-2200) During Easter weekend, the Easter Egg roll on the White House grounds is hosted by the First Lady for children three to six. Enter at the East Gate on E Executive Ave.

May

Annual Georgetown Garden Tour The gardens of historic houses are opened to the public, with hostesses at each (the tour starts at 10:30 am at 3224 N St NW).

Memorial Day Commemorative programs are held at Arlington Cemetery and the Vietnam Memorial.

June

Gay Pride Day Gays, lesbians, and their friends and families march through DC (date varies).

Smithsonian Folklife Festival (☎ 202-357-2700) On the last weekend in June and first weekend in July, this popular event is a gathering of American regional groups with crafts, food, music, and dance on the Mall.

July

Independence Day (☎ 202-919-7222) On July 4, colonial troops parade, the Declaration of Independence is read aloud, musicians play concerts, and fireworks explode over the Potomac.

September

Labor Day Concert The first Sunday in September, the national Symphony Orchestra closes its summer season with a free concert on the West Lawn of the Capitol.

October

Marine Corps Marathon On October 24, this popular road race starts at the Iwo Jima Memorial in Arlington National Cemetery (see the Around Washington, DC chapter), circles around DC, and ends up back where it started.

November

Veterans Day On November 11, you can attend special memorial services honoring military veterans at Arlington Cemetery and the Vietnam Veterans Memorial.

December

Kennedy Center Holiday Celebration (☎ 202-416-8000) From December 1 to January 1, the center offers plenty of free seasonal music and activities, including gospel and a *Messiah* sing-along.

National Christmas Tree Lighting Pageant of Peace (☎ 202-619-7222) On the second Thursday in December, the president illuminates the national Christmas tree and lights a menorah on the Ellipse.

PLACES TO STAY

Washington, DC, offers the complete range of accommodations, from dormitory-style hostels to five-star hotels. When inquiring about room rates, travelers should bear in mind that DC is overall a business town, so hotel rates are highest during the business week and drop dramatically (sometimes by as much as half) on weekends and during the summer. Guesthouses or B&Bs, on the other hand, maintain fairly constant rates year-round. The tourist seasons are spring to fall, running roughly from April to September – with a peak start in April for the cherry blossom spell and a drop in August due to the heat. The business season starts earlier in spring and runs later in fall, virtually disappearing in the summer. Play any card for a discounted rate – even museum membership can earn you a discount at some DC motels (mention professional associations, veteran status, any government or NGO affiliation). The city assesses a 13% tax plus $1.50 per room per night on accommodations.

The following section lists lodging at the budget (hostel, guesthouses, and hotels less than $65), mid-range (rates less than $125), and top end ($125 and up) price categories. Some rates include tax, and prices vary depending on shared versus private baths, so categories are approximate. Wherever you choose to stay, proximity to a Metro station greatly increases your ability to get around with ease.

Though downtown accommodations (including Capitol Hill and the Mall area) are convenient to major sites, most become fairly lifeless once the workers have gone home. The northwestern neighborhoods are lively at night, but you'll need transportation to major sights. You could stay around Dupont Circle and seek out the many less-traveled sites right in the area. The Adams-Morgan neighborhood offers the most reasonable rates at several guesthouses not

Hotel & Guesthouse Reservation Services

Seasoned travelers know that reservation services can often get a better rate on accommodations than an individual's calling an inn or hotel directly, so it pays to shop around and check with reservation services before you commit to paying a hotel's rack rate.

DC has an impressive number of services, and they often compete with each other to give you the lowest rates. In addition, while DC has perhaps 100 B&Bs, only a few advertise independently or give out their addresses to strangers. Meanwhile, the reservation services keep their client lists of B&Bs nearly as secret as the location of the Holy Grail.

For citywide B&B lodging, you can find referrals through Bed & Breakfast Accommodations (☎ 202-328-3510) and the Bed & Breakfast League (☎ 202-363-7767). For foreign students, the Foreign Student Service Council (☎ 202-232-4979), 3259 Prospect St in Georgetown, can arrange two- to three-day homestays with American families ($15 processing fee; the council can fax applications). For homestays for $20 a night and up including kitchen privileges, call and drop by the Women's Information Bank (also known as Bed & Bread; ☎ 202-338-1863), at 3918 W St NW, above Georgetown in the Glover Park neighborhood off the D2 bus line, one block southeast of 39th and Benton Sts NW (ring the bell).

For hotels, check Capitol Reservations Inc (☎ 202-452-1270, 800-847-4832), 1730 Rhode Island Ave NW, No 1114. These folks offer discounts on 75 hotels in the city. Washington DC Accommodations (☎ 202-289-2220, 800-554-2220), 2201 Wisconsin Ave NW, provides a similar service. You can save money on package tours by checking in with Capitol Reservations Tour and Travel Services Inc (☎ 202-452-1270, 800-847-4832), 1730 Rhode Island Ave NW.

Accommodations Express (☎ 609-525-0800, 800 974-7666), in Ocean City, New Jersey, and Hotel Reservations Network (☎ 214-361-7311, 800-964-6835), in Dallas, Texas, are services offering discount rates for hotels in DC and other major US cities.

★★★★★★★★★★★★★★★★★★★★★★★★★★

too far from the Metro, but it might be too far out or raggedy for some travelers. The Foggy Bottom district has less of a neighborhood feel, but it's closer in and right on the Metro – and consequently more pricey. Then there's Georgetown, which isn't convenient to the Metro; it's also pricey and quite congested, though this doesn't seem to diminish its popularity. You could also consider budget motels at the outskirts of town.

Capitol Hill & Northeast

Capital Hill, with its large collection of historic homes ripe for development as B&Bs, is an up-and-coming area for accommodations.

Hostels One option is the *Thompson-Markwood Hall (☎ 202-546-3255, 235 2nd St NE)*, at C St, open to women 18 to 34 years old in DC for work or study. The minimum stay is two weeks. The charge of $21 a day ($625 per month) includes two meals a day

(one on Sunday) and covers a small comfortable room with a phone and a shared bath. There's a spacious patio and yard. No alcohol, smoking, or male guests above lobby-level common areas are allowed.

Better yet, India House Too is a fairly new hostel in neighboring Takoma Park (see the Around Washington, DC chapter). It's only four stops away on the Metro's Red Line from Union Station and a 100-yard walk from the Takoma Metro stop.

Guesthouses There are numerous B&B inns populating Capitol Hill, but many can only be accessed through booking agencies (see Hotel & Guesthouse Reservation Services, earlier). Fortunately, several of the most interesting inns do not cloak themselves in the secrecy of a booking agent's client list.

Hereford House (☎ 202-543-0102, 604 South Carolina Ave SE) is an early-20th-century townhouse on a quiet residential

Camping Around DC

You won't find any campgrounds within DC. The nearest one is in *Cherry Hill Park* (☎ 301-937-7116), northeast of town in College Park, Maryland. It has 400 sites and two pools; sites cost $27 for two tent campers ($3 each additional person) and $35 for RVs. It's open year-round; call for reservations in the summer. The minimum drive time into downtown DC is 15 minutes, but expect longer. A better bet is taking a bus from the campground to the College Park Metro stop; both the bus and the Metro run throughout the day.

Greenbelt Park (☎ 301-344-3948, 6565 Greenbelt Rd), a national park 12 miles northeast of DC, operates a 168-site campground (no hookups). Sites cost $10 per night. A city pool and showers are available down the road for a minimal charge.

Duncan's Family Campground (☎ 410-741-9558, 800-222-2086, 5381 Sands Rd), in Lothian, Maryland, lies 21 miles outside the city limits to the east, off Route 50 to Annapolis. The campground offers free van service to a Metro stop, as well as a laundry and a gift shop. There are 300 sites, most with full hookups, going for $29 to $32 depending on the season. You will pay $19 for one of the few sites with no hookups.

street near Eastern Market. British expat Ann Edwards offers six guest rooms in her home, and the decor is definitely reminiscent of the British Isles and wild flowers from Wales, Ireland, and Scotland. Two rooms have private baths. Singles start at $45 in high seasons; doubles start at $75.

You will find *Bull Moose Bed & Breakfast* (☎ 202-547-1050, 101 5th St NE, www.bullmoose-b-and-b.com) nearer to the Capitol building. There are 10 guest rooms in this Victorian townhouse; two have private baths. Rates are in flux, so call ahead.

Maison Orleans Bed 'N Breakfast (☎ 202-544-3694, 414 5th St SE) is an Edwardian (Federal front) row house built in 1902, located halfway between Capitol South and Eastern Market Metro stops. This three-story townhouse has three guest rooms with private baths, as well as a public living room and dining room decorated with family pieces from the '30s and '40s. In addition to the architecture and decor, the patio, with its fountains and fish pond, definitely creates a sense of the French Quarter in New Orleans, where owner Bill Rouchell grew up. Rates range from $90 to $125.

Jim and Mary Pellettieri retired from their day jobs a few years ago to devote their time to hosting guests in *A Capitol Place* (☎ 202-543-1020, 134 12th St SE). The guesthouse is set in a 100-year-old Victorian townhouse and features an eclectic mix of period antiques and traditional 20th-century pieces. Guests can choose a five-room apartment or a single room with private bath. The daylight basement room with bay-front window has a living area, dining area, kitchen, and laundry for guests. Rates start at $95 for couples ($30 for each additional person).

Hotels If you have a car, you're striking out elsewhere, and you don't mind the lousy area, there's a strip of cheap chain motels along the tracks in the northeastern part of the city along New York Ave NE. Predictable offerings include the *Budget Motor Inn* (☎ 202-529-3900, No 1615), with singles/doubles for $49/63; *Super 8 Motel* (☎ 202-543-7400, No 501), with singles/doubles for around $55/65; *HoJo Inn* (☎ 202-546-9200, No 600), with singles starting at $59; and *Days Inn* (☎ 202-832-5800, No 2700), with singles/doubles for $62/68. Note that these are the prices the motels quote when you call them, but during slow seasons, they often have a price war going, and you may see these places advertising rooms for less than $40 if you drive along New York Ave.

Unfortunately, mid-range hotels in DC often charge around $100 a night for a room with private bath (though again, you can find lower weekend rates, special discounts, and packages). Kitchenettes can help you lower the cost of eating out. The *Holiday Inn on the Hill* (☎ 202-638-1616, 415 New Jersey Ave NW) offers rates starting at $99, single or double. It's conveniently close to Union Station.

Capitol Hill Suites (☎ 202-543-6000, 200 C St SE) is a 152-room property right in the heart of the legislative action around the Hill. Some of the rooms here are reserved for congressional interns (from both high school and college) who come to spends months working for Congress and the Senate, giving the hotel a youthful feel. The price is definitely upscale, with rack rates of $139, but you can get weekend and off-season deals for less than $120.

On Capitol Hill across from Union Station, the *Phoenix Park Hotel* (☎ 202-638-6900, 520 N Capitol St NW) offers Irish hospitality along with 88 neatly appointed rooms. It's owned by an Irish firm and features the brogue-filled Powerscourt cafe and the Dubliner pub downstairs. The high 'rack' rate of $149 to $249 drops to $115 for government business, with weekend rates of $89 to $149 depending on availability.

The *Hotel George* (☎ 202-347-4200, 15 E St NW) is the upscale reincarnation of the old Bellevue Hotel. This boutique hotel with 139 rooms stands out for its contemporary styling. The public spaces sparkle with lots of stainless steel, glass, fossilized coral, bold contemporary art, and a centerpiece grand piano. The upscale restaurant here serves French cuisine (see Places to Eat, later). Rooms have all the amenities, including data ports, and there is a fitness center and steam room. Rack rates start at $185, but you should ask about weekend specials, which can be as low as $129.

National Mall Area

Another option is the *Holiday Inn Capitol* (☎ 202-479-4000, 550 C St SW), one block southeast of the Air and Space Museum. It is a newly renovated nine-story hotel with 529 rooms. You get the usual amenities that come with this chain (such as a coffeemaker, ironing board, and hair dryer), plus a fitness center, restaurant, bar, and rooftop pool. Rates start at $125 per room.

The *Best Western Skyline Inn* (☎ 202-458-7500, 10 I St SW), five blocks south of the Capitol building at the intersection of I-395

and S Capitol St, is a large concrete and glass establishment with more than 200 rooms. Don't expect a lot of character or charm here, but the rooms all have air-conditioning and a TV. Rates start at $83.

South of the Mall, *Loews L'Enfant Plaza Hotel* (☎ 202-484-1000, 800-243-1166, 480 L'Enfant Plaza SW) provides upscale family-friendly lodging above the Metro station, two long blocks south of most Smithsonian museums. Daily rates may range from $179 to $299, with $109 winter specials (inquire about packages). The hotel hosts an annual Bark Ball for dogs and gives kids a Back House hotel tour. A heated bubble converts an outdoor pool for year-round use.

Downtown

Hostels The main hostel for the worldwide Hostelling International organization, headquartered in DC, is *Hostelling International – Washington, DC* (☎ 202-737-2333, 1009 11th St NW), at K St. The eight-story hostel (24-hour access) provides dormitory lodging for 300 on men's and women's floors, in eight-bunk rooms. Sleep sacks are required (also available by loan). Facilities include modern and clean bathrooms and kitchens, coin-operated laundry, a tiny store, comfortable common dining and lounging rooms (with TV), and a dank smokers' room in the basement. It's a central gathering place and resource for many traveling students and other HI-types, and it's handicapped accessible, but it's isolated – four blocks north of Metro Center in a nothing-happening area (safe enough). The charge is $19 for members and $22 for nonmembers; reservations and ID are required. From the Metro Center station, go north on 11th St NW to the flag-flying hostel.

Hotels With 260 rooms, the *Hotel Harrington* (☎ 202-628-8140, 800-424-8532), at the corner of 11th and E Sts NW, is a favorite budget choice a block from Ford's Theater north of the Mall. The hotel is popular with scout troops, school groups, marching bands, tourist families, and small-time salespeople. The 11-story hotel generally offers basic rooms with private baths for $84/94 single/double, but you can get specials for $69.

Near the youth hostel, the **Swiss Inn** (☎ 202-371-1816, 800-955-7947, 1204 Massachusetts Ave NW) rents seven rooms in a homey brownstone house in a somewhat isolated area four blocks from Metro Center. Rooms with kitchenettes, private baths, telephones, and TVs rent for less than $70 during the winter. Laundry access and a manager who is bilingual in Swiss-German are other pluses. You may get a 20% discount if you mention Lonely Planet.

The **Red Roof Inn** (☎ 202-289-5959, 500 H St NW) has 179 rooms, a sauna, a coin laundry, free parking, and a plodding elevator (opt for a walkable floor). Singles/doubles start at $79/89; the weekend rate is $59. Both the hotel and the neighborhood were recently undergoing much-needed renovation.

The **Howard Johnson Inn** (☎ 202-546-9200, 600 New York Ave NE) has only 53 rooms and looks a little tired. It is also rather far from the attractions of downtown and the Mall. The rack rate is $99 on weekends in high season for a room with one double bed, but you may get a better deal in the off season.

More centrally located, **Lincoln Suites Downtown** (☎ 202-223-4320, 800-424-2970, 1823 L St NW) was remodeled in 1996 to provide rooms with kitchens, TVs, coffee, and tea. Rates start at $109 with an autoclub discount for singles or doubles. The rate includes a free continental breakfast on weekends and free access to a nearby health club. Lincoln Suites is two blocks west of Connecticut Ave on the border of Dupont Circle.

A few blocks north of the convention center, in a somewhat isolated area, the **Morrison-Clark Inn** (☎ 202-898-1200, 800-332-7898), Massachusetts Ave NW at 11th St, is an elegant historic hotel set in an expansive 1864 mansion with a well-regarded Southern dining room. Its 54 rooms and suites are tastefully appointed with Victorian accents and all-modern conveniences. Singles and doubles cost $135, but ask for a 15% discount during low seasons.

A modern luxury alternative facing the convention center is the **Marriott Metro Center** (☎ 202-737-2200, 775 12th St NW).

There are 456 rooms in this 14-floor property (built in 1989). Here you get the predictability of this international chain and the benefits of restaurants, bars, a fitness center, massage center, and indoor pool. Rates can start as low as $129 but will balloon when availability gets tight.

Nearby, the **Grand Hyatt Washington** (☎ 202-582-1234, 1000 H St NW) also gives you across-the-street access to the convention center, as well as direct access to the Metro Center station. There are 900 rooms, five restaurants, bars, a parking garage, a fitness center, and a pool packed into this gigantic concrete building. Rates start at $199.

The **Sheraton St Regis** (☎ 202-638-2626, 923 16th St NW) is the former Ritz Carlton where, in Room 1012, Special Counsel Kenneth Starr's interviewers interrogated Monica Lewinsky and made the tapes that detailed the intimate goings-on in her affair with President Clinton. You will find more than 200 rooms and suites here with elegant furnishings and a butler on every floor. Rates start at about $325, depending on the season and availability.

White House Area

Many of DC's top hotels cluster north of the Mall in the vicinity of the White House. These hotels cater to dignitaries and the corporate aristocracy; on a walk through their lobbies or at the bar, you may spot celebrity power-brokers sealing deals or you could catch signs of clandestine rendezvous and interrogations.

One landmark on DC's political landscape is across from the White House – the refined **Hay Adams Hotel** (☎ 202-638-6600, fax 202-638-2716, 800 16th St NW), overlooking Lafayette Square. Reportedly, Colonel Oliver North solicited contributions for the Contras while dining here with interested parties. Room rack rates start at $220 weekends and $325 weekdays. This is the price for an interior room; you'll pay about $50 more for a view of the White House. Some winter weekends have specials of $195.

President Grant originally coined the term 'lobbyist' (so the story goes) for the political wranglers hanging out in the lobby of the historic Willard Hotel. Today known as the **Willard Intercontinental** (☎ 202-628-9100, 1401 Pennsylvania Ave NW), the luxuriously restored 1904 marble hotel (the third on this site) has housed 10 American presidents in its various incarnations, including Lincoln, Harding, and Coolidge. Julia Ward Howe wrote the lyrics to the 'Battle Hymn of the Republic' here during the Civil War. The Willard has a great Round Robin Bar, Nest Lounge jazz nights (hotel guests receive jazz CDs), and afternoon tea. It's been recognized for outstanding handicapped access. Standard weekday rates for singles/doubles of $325 can drop to $219 on the weekend.

Foggy Bottom

The **Allen Lee Hotel** (☎ 202-331-1224, 2224 F St NW) offers friendly service and clean rooms with phones, TVs, and worn furnishings. Rates include taxes – singles/doubles with private bath are $49/63; with shared bath, $39/52 (extra cots are $6). From the Foggy Bottom Metro station, go right and walk three blocks south on 23rd St; it's at the corner of 23rd and F Sts.

The former Inn at Foggy Bottom is now the **George Washington University Inn** (☎ 202-337-6620, 824 New Hampshire Ave NW). This centrally located choice has 95 rooms in the heart of the university community. Rates fluctuate according to availability, but expect to pay $89 and up.

You will find similar accommodations at the **River Inn** (☎ 202-337-7600, 924 25th St NW), between I and K Sts. This is an all-suite facility with 126 rooms, full kitchens, a fitness center, and parking. It's an easy walk to the Kennedy Center and the Foggy Bottom Metro station. You can get weekend specials here for $100.

The **Lombardy** (☎ 202-828-2600, 2019 Pennsylvania Ave NW) is right in the mainstream of Foggy Bottom. Largely serving the nearby Department of State and White House, this hotel has 127 well-equipped rooms with rates starting at $109 on weekends.

Located strategically across from the Watergate complex (just across the creek from

Georgetown), **Howard Johnson's Premier** (☎ 202-965-2700, 2601 Virginia Ave NW) is notorious as the 'Plumbers' lookout' (ask for Room 723 to be part of history). Since the major renovation in 1999, rack rates have hovered around $139, but ask about discount rates.

Of the many big-business luxury hotels clustered north of Washington Circle, the **Wyndham Bristol** (☎ 202-955-6400, 2430 Pennsylvania Ave NW) offers some of the best weekend deals, with rates as low as $124, including a full breakfast. This is a 14-story building with 400 rooms and a modern glass atrium stretching from top to bottom. You get valet parking, a fitness center, a restaurant, and a bar.

If you like lodging in the company of political scandal, try the **Swissôtel Watergate** (☎ 202-965-2300, 2650 Virginia Ave NW), which housed the notorious 'Plumbers' of the Watergate scandal in 1972. The modern building is decorated with antiques and checkerboard marble; included are its acclaimed restaurant, a health club, and great service. Rooms start at $99 for January weekends ($150 during the week), but expect to pay more than $240 in warmer weather. Most rooms overlook the Potomac River.

The **Washington Monarch Hotel** (☎ 202-429-2400, 2401 M St NW) offers 415 rooms and a comprehensive health club with a workout pool. The current owners are a group specializing in managing distinctive resort hotels known for exceptional service, elegant decor, and spacious rooms. Guests can enjoy the fancy Bistro restaurant and a large atrium lobby. Weekend packages start at $159 a night; standard weekday rates are more like $265 but sometimes dip to $199, depending on availability.

Georgetown

If you don't mind being about 10 blocks from the entertainment/restaurant district of Georgetown's M St, consider the **Holiday Inn – Georgetown** (☎ 202-338-4600, 2101 Wisconsin Ave NW). This 296-room property backs up against the Dumbarton Oaks Garden section of Rock Creek Park and has its own jogging trail, which gives the hotel something of a town & country feel. Of course, all rooms are fully equipped with the features typical of this chain worldwide. The outdoor pool makes this place particularly attractive to families in warm weather. Room rates start at about $120.

The **Georgetown Dutch Inn** (☎ 202-337-0900, 1075 Thomas Jefferson St NW), just off M St, is an attractive, European-style boutique hotel with 47 suites. Each suite has its own kitchen, brass and crystal chandeliers, colonial reproduction furnishings, and nice flower arrangements. For upscale ambiance, this hotel is a good value, with singles starting at $120 and doubles at $130.

The **Georgetown Inn** (☎ 202-333-8900, 1310 Wisconsin Ave NW), just north of M St, has long been a favorite gathering place for Georgetown University alumni and parents on college weekends. The inn spreads 95 rooms through a collection of restored 18th-century townhouses with elegant decor and service to match. Rates start at about $135, depending on the season and availability.

The lively **Four Seasons Hotel** (☎ 202-342-0444, 2800 Pennsylvania Ave NW) was once declared DC's best hotel by Conde Naste publications. This Five Diamond property with 260 rooms caters to the upscale crowd, but it's less stiff than ritzy hotels downtown. At Sunday brunch, you might find a mix of college couples, blue-blood families in sporty Land's End separates, and international corporate executives. Rack rates start at $370, but weekend rates may dip to $270.

Dupont Circle

One of the most attractive neighborhoods, Dupont Circle is rife with accommodations in all categories.

Hostels Just half a block from Dupont Circle, at 19th and Q Sts (northeast corner), **Simpkin's Bed & Breakfast** (☎ 202-387-1328, 1601 19th St NW) is an 1888 Victorian townhouse and a popular stop for bohemian types and public-interest professionals on a budget. Each of the six guest rooms in this small hostel-style inn have air-conditioning and shared bath. Travelers with passports get a 50% discount. This discount makes the

rate $30 per person per couple in a private room. Singles' rooms run $25 to $45.

Davis House (☎ 202-232-3196, 1822 R St NW) is an older row house with 11 rooms on a quiet residential street. The American Friends Service Committee operates this hostel for international visitors, AFSC staff, and those 'working on peace and justice concerns' (or working for an overseas nonprofit institution). You need advance reservations to stay here. There are no private baths and no kitchen; smoking and alcohol are not allowed. Singles and doubles cost $45; shared rooms are $35.

Across the street, the **International Student House** (☎ 202-387-6445, 1825 R St NW) offers 90 guests an 'in-depth experience in international living.' You're expected to stay a minimum of three months during the summer, and four otherwise. Rates include breakfast and dinner and start at $620 a month for shared rooms with phones (higher for single rooms, a private bath, and parking). There are comfortable common areas (library, piano room) with Tudor accents, and a walled courtyard.

Guesthouses The **Brenton** (☎ 202-332-5550, 1708 16th St NW) is a Victorian row house just north of R St on the west side of 16th street. Manager Ed Eccard has nine rooms decorated with Victorian antiques. Most of the rooms have a shared bath, and the management provides a free continental breakfast and happy hour daily. This is a gay-run inn with a mostly gay clientele. Rooms rent for $79.

Dupont at the Circle (☎ 202-332-5251, 1604 19th St NW) caters to an upscale crowd. This Victorian inn is smoke-free and has six rooms and a suite. All rooms are decorated with Victorian antiques and have a private bath with claw foot or Jacuzzi tubs. One of the specialties of the house is breakfast or fresh fruit and homemade bread. Rates start at $110 for low seasons but can rise to $150 in the spring.

Hotels The **Tabard Inn** (☎ 202-785-1277, 1739 N St NW) retains the original quirky charm of an old Victorian townhouse (separate hot and cold faucets, armoires, iron bed frames, vintage overstuffed couches, and maybe even an old upright piano in the corner of your room). The style is hippie tweed, rustic gentility. You will find 40 rooms upstairs. Downstairs there is a popular restaurant and bar, with a lounge seemingly designed for fomenting armchair revolutions over glasses of vintage port (see Places to Eat, later). Rooms with shared bath cost $65 to $95, and rooms with private bath go for $155 and up.

Center City Travel Lodge (☎ 202-682-5300, 1201 13th St NW) is a budget choice north of Massachusetts Ave, close to downtown. There are 100 well-maintained but uninspiring rooms in this venue. Rates start at $79 and include a free continental breakfast.

The *Embassy Inn* (☎ 202-234-7800, 1627 17th St NW) is a 38-room boutique hotel with the feel of a B&B; it's just a few blocks east of Dupont Circle. They offer a complimentary continental breakfast, newspaper, and afternoon sherry. Rooms are not large, but they are fully equipped, including private baths. Rates usually start at $99, but you may get a discount as low as $55 if you ask.

The *Windsor Inn* (☎ 202-667-0300, 1842 16th St NW) is similar to the Embassy Inn, with 45 rooms farther northeast. Here you will find small, tastefully decorated rooms (including cable TV), free continental breakfast, and afternoon sherry in the lobby. Rack rates run $109 but may dip into the $60 range off season.

In a more removed residential area, the *Carlyle Suites* ☎ 202-234-3200, 1731 New Hampshire Ave NW), at S St, has 175 small suites (some would say cozy, others might think cramped) with kitchenettes, all in an Art Deco style. Downstairs, there's a gleaming cafe/bar. Rates for singles/doubles hover around $119/129 (youth under 18 stay free with parents). They advertise quite a bit in gay newspapers.

Hilton Washington Embassy Row (☎ 202-265-1600, 2015 Massachusetts Ave NW) gives you one of the city's most exclusive neighborhoods and a lot of luxury for the money. The Indonesian Embassy faces the hotel from across the street; the Indian Embassy lies to the rear; and about 20 other embassy mansions line Massachusetts Ave as you head northwest from here. The hotel's 11-story building with 193 rooms looks smaller than it is tucked among the embassy mansions. There is a rooftop pool, outdoor bar, and underground parking garage here. Rates start at $125.

The *Westin Fairfax* (☎ 202-293-2100, 2100 Massachusetts Ave NW) is also tucked away on Massachusetts Ave. The 200 rooms are loaded with everything from minibars to modem ports, and you get a complimentary newspaper and shoeshine daily. The Jockey Club restaurant on the main floor has long been a place for international power-brokers. Conde Naste publications recently voted this place the second-best hotel in DC. Rates start as low as $139.

The claim to fame of the *Wyndham Washington* (☎ 202-429-1700, 1400 M St NW) is that it was where federal agents caught former Mayor Marion Barry (1990s) smoking crack with an ex-girlfriend. Though some weekend rates start at $145, standard weekday rates are around $219 (if that notoriety is worth it to you).

Dating from 1924 but less exclusive than in years past, the *Renaissance Mayflower Hotel* (☎ 202-347-3000, 1127 Connecticut Ave NW) remains a regal landmark south of Dupont Circle. During the Kennedy administration, the Secret Service reportedly knew Suite 812 as 'JFK's playpen.' There's a Starbucks coffee stand in the grand lobby; also check out the inaugural ballroom. During the Clinton impeachment hearings, Monica Lewinsky cloistered herself here with her lawyers (no one is saying which suite). Room rates start at $160 for winter weekends but usually climb above $235.

Adams-Morgan & Woodley Park
These lively districts offer plenty of low-cost accommodations.

Hostels The cheapest place to stay is *Washington International Backpackers* (☎ 202-667-7681, 2451 18th St NW), with no-frills dormitory lodging in a worn walk-up building. There are five small bedrooms (six to eight beds per room, triple bunks, linen provided), three OK bathrooms, a comfortable common room with cable TV, makeshift kitchen facilities, bike rentals ($7), and a small breakfast.

It's upstairs from one of the liveliest blocks in DC (with cafes, stores, and clubs). The cost is $15 a night per person, and there is a $1 onetime charge for linens. You come and go as you please with your own key. Free pickup from the train or bus station is available by advance request.

Guesthouses The *Adams Inn* (☎ 202-745-3600, 800-578-6807, 1744 Lanier Place NW) converted two side-by-side townhouses and a carriage house on a shady residential street into a welcoming guesthouse with cozy common areas (porch, living rooms, patio). Homey rooms are modestly furnished with old Asian carpets, and there are modern bathrooms (but there are no phones or TVs in the rooms). You have access to kitchen facilities, coin laundry, and pay phones, as well as coffee and donuts around the clock. Room prices include continental breakfast and run from $45 for a single/double with shared bath to $60 for private bath. It's half a block from the intersection of Calvert and 18th Sts and is a 10-minute walk from the Woodley Park/ Zoo Metro.

Across Rock Creek Park from Adams-Morgan, the compact Woodley Park neighborhood is convenient to the Metro and zoo and has a dozen places to eat and gather (there's even a popular blues club – see Entertainment, later). Here you will find the old-fashioned *Connecticut-Woodley Guest House* (☎ 202-667-0218, 2647 Woodley Rd NW), looking a little like Grandma's house. This is a large 1920s house with 14 simple but clean rooms for rent. Currently, there is flowery water-stained wallpaper, worn carpets, and sunken twin beds with chenille spreads. (The new owners are on a tear to upgrade the property.) Staff and guests are friendly, and the house overlooks the Sheraton's green lawn. Singles and doubles with shared bath are $46, $57 with a private bath. Group rates are a real bargain: A triple with shared bath is $58.50; a quadruple runs $60. From the Woodley Park/

Zoo Metro station exit, turn around, walk to Woodley Rd, and turn left; the house is on your right. There's free parking here, too.

The *Kalorama Guest House at Woodley Park* (☎ 202-328-0860, 2700 Cathedral Ave NW) has 19 rooms in two Victorian townhouses. Rates run $55 to $105. This inn's companion property, the *Kalorama Guest House* (☎ 202-667-6369, 1854 Mintwood Place NW), lies a few blocks west of 18th St in Adams-Morgan, offering continental breakfast and afternoon sherry, along with comfortable rooms in a brick townhouse with some Victorian frills. There are 29 rooms here, ranging in price from $55 to $105, and half have private baths. Smoking is not permitted.

The *Taft Bridge Inn* (☎ 202-387-2007, 2007 Wyoming Ave NW) opened in 1996 to offer 13 guest rooms in this turn-of-the-19th-century Georgian mansion. Antique furniture, a paneled drawing room, a garden, and six fireplaces highlight the elegance of this inn, which is tucked into a neighborhood that includes the homes of former Presidents Taft, Eisenhower, and Lyndon Johnson. You get a complimentary breakfast, and there is parking and laundry on the premises. Guests can walk from here to the restaurant and club district of 18th St NW, the Dupont Circle Metro, and the zoo. Rates start at $59 for a shared bath and $94 for a private bath.

The *1836 California* (☎ 202-462-6502, 1836 California St NW) has six rooms in this elegant Victorian townhouse on a residential street west of 18th St. The ambiance is Victorian, with period decor throughout. All rooms have queen-size beds, air-conditioning, and TVs. The two suites with private baths rent for $100 for one person; the four rooms with shared baths are $70 (an additional person costs $10 extra).

Hotels The *Normandy Inn* (☎ 202-483-1350, 2118 Wyoming Ave NW), between Connecticut Ave and 23rd St, is a boutique hotel with 75 rooms that appeal to visiting foreign officials. There is a tea room, as well as a small patio, and some evenings feature a wine and cheese reception. Rates start at $105.

The *Washington Courtyard by Marriott* (☎ 202-332-9300, 1900 Connecticut Ave NW), at Le Roy Place, offers 147 rooms on the western border between Dupont Circle and Adams-Morgan. This hotel offers you all the standard features of the Courtyard chain, including an outdoor pool, a small exercise room, and parking. Rooms start at $115.

To put on the ritz, head for the **Omni Shoreham Hotel** (☎ 202-234-0700, 2500 Calvert St NW), adjacent to Rock Creek Park near the Woodley Park/Zoo Metro stop. This is a 700-room resort hotel in the midst of the city, with manicured grounds, tennis courts, a fitness center, and an outdoor pool. The hotel's timeless design dates from 1929, and the building has hosted presidential inauguration balls and celebrity guests such as Marilyn Monroe throughout its career. Rack rates start at $280, but you can occasionally find a weekend deal for as low as $143.

Upper Northwest
North of Adams-Morgan, the **International Guest House** (☎ 202-726-5809, 1441 Kennedy St NW) offers five clean guest rooms with two beds each for $25 per adult and $12.50 for children six to 16. The cost includes a breakfast of cereal and homemade muffins, as well as evening tea. There's a common room, a large backyard, and some off-street parking. But note the early curfew: The house closes at 11 pm and opens back up at 7 am. Sunday it closes midday, 10 am to 2 pm. Alcohol and smoking are not allowed. To get there from the White House area, take the S2 or S4 bus up 16th St to Kennedy Stand (it's a 4-mile bus trip).

Southwest
You'll find **Waterfront Row** (☎ 202-328-3510) in the Tiber Island residential complex, a block from the seafood restaurants, Capitol Hill Yacht Club, and tour boats. This four-story, 30-year-old townhouse is right across the street from the Waterfront/SEU Metro stop on the Green Line and features an eclectic mix of antique, French, Asian, and contemporary furniture and art. There is one guest room on the 2nd floor decorated in Southwestern style, with a queen-size bed, balcony, cable TV, and private bath. The

music room on this floor also can accommodate guests. Low-season rates are $85, and high-season rates are $110.

Set apart at DC's waterfront, the modern **Channel Inn** (☎ 202-554-2400, 650 Water St SW) offers spacious rooms, many with balconies overlooking the channel (particularly nice at sunset) and a seasonal pool. The hotel anchors a strip of seafood restaurants that attracts busloads of senior tourists. Rooms start at $115; weekend rates are $108.

PLACES TO EAT
Relative to other costs, food is fairly expensive in DC – not as expensive as New York, but more expensive than San Francisco. In general, you'd be lucky to find a decent dinner plate of sauced pasta for less than $9, and even take-out deli lunches with a soda can climb to $7 or $8. So you really have to seek out the bargains. Fortunately, plenty of ethnic eateries offer hearty low-priced meals, many of them vegetarian. Consider shopping at markets, and carry your own snacks, water, and picnic tools to keep eating expenses to a minimum.

Since congressional ethics laws designed to blunt the power of lobbyist largess limited DC's revered 'gift lunch' tradition to $10 as of January 1996, you will now find a profusion of entrees in the $9.95 range at restaurants popular with politicos.

DC's farmers' markets are great places to find fresh produce, meats, seafood, and flowers, and they often offer interesting sights besides. You can usually find prepared foods there or nearby. Most open at 7 or 8 am and close around 5 or 6 pm (with shorter hours on Sunday).

Capitol Hill
On Capitol Hill, you will find your greatest food choices in and around Union Station, off Massachusetts Ave NE, along Pennsylvania Ave SE between 2nd and 4th Sts, and around Eastern Market southeast of the Capitol.

Budget & Mid-Range Besides the great food court on Union Station's lower level (cheap eats, from *chiles rellenos* to

Fabulous Food Courts

Although 'food courts' have a bad name in the US (associated with the chain-restaurant junk food found in shopping malls), DC's best food courts are attractive, lively places where you can find a variety of inexpensive food to eat quickly (particularly with kids in tow). You can commonly find vegetarian Indian curries, sushi, burritos, Chinese stir-fry, and fruit smoothies, among more traditional American choices. Downtown, you'll find a number of popular food courts. There is one in the Old Post Office (Pennsylvania Ave at 12th St) and another at the Ronald Reagan Building (enter on Pennsylvania Ave, directly across from the National Theater, or on 14th St). Also try the shops at National Place, in the Press Club Building on 14th St at F St. South of the National Mall, L'Enfant Plaza Metro station also connects directly with subterranean delis, cafes, markets, and shops.

Undoubtedly, the most popular food court in the city is on Capitol Hill at Union Station. There are six self-contained and rather pricey restaurants on the main floor, but the bargain diner's paradise waits on the lower level of this magnificently restored railway station. Here you will find galleries of tables and more than two dozen fast-food vendors serving a variety of American and ethnic cuisine, from pizza to Cajun dishes.

Large government buildings typically have cafeterias designed for their employees that are also open to the public for inexpensive American fare (you may have to pass through security, and the ambiance is usually fluorescent and utilitarian). Exceptional spots include the 6th-floor cafeteria at the Library of Congress Madison Building, catered by different DC restaurants, and the exclusive Senate dining room in the Capitol (obtain passes in advance from your congressional representative). Or befriend a congressional staffer to work your way into the free-appetizers circuit, compliments of one reception or another.

Power and social lunches are a big part of the DC scene, and consequently, restaurants and food courts get very crowded at noon on weekdays. This is particularly true of Union Station's restaurants and food courts between March 15 and June 1, when Congress is in session and tens of thousands of school kids arrive for organized tours of the city. These school groups in particular can descend on the food courts like locusts. If you find yourself amid this youthful feeding frenzy, here's a way to navigate the tumult: Avoid the long lines at the food stalls selling burgers, pizza, and ice cream. The lines at ethnic food stalls such as Ichiban (Japanese) are minimal, and you can get a plate of chicken teriyaki with rice and vegetables for $4.

★★★★★★★★★★★★★★★★★★★★★★★★★★

Chesapeake Bay oysters), upstairs has *America*, a restaurant with seating at the bar, on a narrow mezzanine, or at tables. Regional specialties – such as Mississippi fried catfish or a Midwestern patty melt – run around $10.

Eastern Market (☎ 202-543-7293), 7th St SE at N Carolina Ave, in the Capitol Hill area, has food stalls selling produce, meats, and fish. A crafts and flea market takes place on weekends, and there are cafes all around. People line up with butchers and fishmongers for the greasy-spoon joint inside, serving breakfast and some of the best crab cakes in the city (less than $5).

Among several eateries along 7th St SE across from Eastern Market, *Misha's Deli* (☎ 202-547-5858, 210 7th St SE) serves traditional Russian food – mushroom-caviar dip ($6 a pound), black bread, broccoli-cheese knishes ($2), 'baboushka soup' – all in a stylish deli setting (a skyline silhouette adorns the rafters) for take-out or eat-in.

A lot of the Hill's upscale residents favor *Tunnicliff's* (☎ 202-546-3663, 222 7th St SE). This place is particularly popular for long outdoor lunches on warm-weather weekends when folks want to relax after shopping in the market. The cuisine here is Cajun (blackened catfish is less than $10).

For steaming coffee and espresso, muffins, sweets, and modern sandwiches, there's **Bread and Chocolate** (☎ 202-547-2875, 666 Pennsylvania Ave SE), at 7th St, where you can get a California croissant sandwich with turkey, sprouts, and tomato for about $4 and a double espresso for $1.50.

A lot of tourists and Capitol Hill staffers head for the brewpub atmosphere of the **Capitol City Brewing Company** (☎ 202-842-2337, 2 Massachusetts Ave NE). This cavernous place on the 1st floor of the National Postal Museum is one of the city's few microbreweries. Its greatest assets are the tables near the picture windows that look out on Capitol Hill. Sandwiches such as the catfish club are a bit pricey at $8.

A block west of Union Station, the **Dubliner** (☎ 202-737-3773, 520 N Capitol St), at F St, in the Phoenix Park Hotel, is DC's dark, wood-paneled, classic Irish pub and offers bowls of Irish potato soup ($4). Next door, at **Kelly's Irish Times** (☎ 202-543-5433), you will find all the corned beef and cabbage ($10) or Irish stew ($8) you can eat.

The clump of cafes and restaurants along Massachusetts Ave NE (between 2nd and 4th Sts, getting more expensive as you go east) are near the Senate office buildings and appeal to a lot of Senate staffers – single, under-30, university-educated, Type-A personalities. This crowd gets its take-out at **Neil's Deli** (☎ 202-546-6970, 208 Massachusetts Ave NE), with thick turkey sandwiches for $4.

The staffers pack the booths and cluster around the bar of the **Red River Grill** (☎ 202-546-7200, 201 Massachusetts Ave NE) at lunch and most nights. Tex-Mex entrees are around $7, but you can eat cheaply here if you order chili con queso ($4). **Armand's Chicago Pizzeria** (☎ 202-546-6600, 226 Massachusetts Ave NE) offers build-your-own pizzas and a lunch buffet, with prices starting a $7.

For something a little more upscale, in a formal setting with tablecloths and candlelight, head to the **White Tiger** (☎ 202-548-5900, 301 Massachusetts Ave NE). Indian veggie dishes such as *chana masala* (chickpeas cooked with onions, tomatoes, and

roasted spices) start at $9. Chicken and meat dishes start at $12.

Five blocks east of the Capitol, **Jimmy T's** (☎ 202-546-3646, 501 E Capitol St) is a down-home corner diner that serves breakfast all day (waffles are $4) and other short orders to neighborhood regulars at red Formica tables.

On Pennsylvania Ave SE between 2nd and 3rd Sts, you'll find Mexican food at **Burrito Brothers** (☎ 202-543-6835, 205 Pennsylvania Ave SE), bagels and schmears at **Chesapeake Bagel Bakery** (☎ 202-546-0994, 215 Pennsylvania Ave SE), and meat-and-two-sides plates (around $5) at **Sherrill's Bakery** (☎ 202-544-2480, 233 Pennsylvania Ave), a neighborhood institution.

Between 3rd and 4th Sts, try the Greek dishes, such as vegetarian stuffed peppers ($7.50), at **Taverna** (☎ 202-547-8360, 307 Pennsylvania Ave SE). You can get a cup of miso soup or brown rice for less than $1.50 at the Japanese take-out place called **Good Health Natural Foods** (☎ 202-543-2266, 325 Pennsylvania Ave SE).

For a pub experience with packs of the so-called House-side staffers, head for the **Hawk & Dove** (☎ 202-543-3300, 329 Pennsylvania Ave SE), where dusty hunting trophies decorate the walls. The crab Reuben sandwich costs $7; cheddar potato skins are $4.25. Another popular pub is next door, the **Tune Inn** (☎ 202-543-2725, 331 Pennsylvania Ave SE). Some folks (read: Southern males) come here for a breakfast beer ($1.50) and a greasy cheeseburger and grits ($4).

If you head to the area near the Capitol South Metro stop, a block south of the Cannon House office building, you will find two restaurants popular with the 'House Side' of the Hill: **Bulfeathers** (☎ 202-543-5505, 410 1st St SE) has a clubby political atmosphere. Several entrees, such as the Lobbyist special (chicken breast sautéed in Old Bay sauce and sherry, topped with crab), go for $10. **Tortilla Coast** (☎ 202-546-6768, 400 1st St SE) moved next door a few years ago from a 'Senate Side' location. A lot of local Hill residents come here for the trendy Tex-Mex cuisine and a chance for sidewalk dining and people-watching from the glass-enclosed porch. The decor here is totally Southwestern; burritos cost $8.

Top End If looking for political celebrities is your thing, head for *The Monocle* (☎ 202-546-4488, 107 D St NW), just north of the Senate office buildings. This is another clubby place, and it appeals to US senators, as well as power-brokers. You can get pasta here for about $10, but the seafood and steak entrees can climb over $20.

The rich, famous, and powerful also favor *La Brasserie* (☎ 202-546-9154, 239 Massachusetts Ave NE). Here you can dine on duck confit, salmon, and squid in its own ink for around $15 for lunch (dinner is more). Yet another celebrity magnet is *2 Quail* (☎ 202-543-8030, 320 Massachusetts Ave NE). This place is a bit precious with all the wicker and pillows (very Lady Legislator), but the food is good: One day it's paella, the next it's penne pasta with seafood in spicy macadamia-nut cream sauce (about $16).

One of the few places to go German in the city is *Cafe Berlin* (☎ 202-543-7656, 322 Massachusetts Ave NE). The wiener and paprika schnitzel (about $17) are popular.

DC's beautiful people discovered *Bistro Bis* (☎ 202-661-2700, 15 E St NW) as soon as it opened in late 1998. This ultra-chic hideaway in the Hotel George west of Union Station features French cuisine. If its on the menu, the calamari Basquinaire (seared squid with roasted peppers, chorizo, and cilantro) is worth the risk. Lunches here run $10 to $18, and dinners are $16 to $22.

National Mall Area

Many visitors stick to inexpensive museum cafeterias on the Mall to conserve time for sightseeing. Note that museum food-service hours are generally restricted to lunchtime, and expect crowds. Cafeteria fare costs $3 and up; restaurant entrees are around $7 to $10. You'll find exceptional settings at the Air and Space Museum and the National Gallery's West Wing; the worst is at the Museum of Natural History.

The most trendy, healthy, very noninstitutional food-court menu is at the Museum of American History. (For those who crave a

fat fix, there's also an ice-cream parlor here.) There's an outdoor cafe overlooking the Hirshhorn's sculpture garden in summer and an espresso bar in the tunnel at the National Gallery year-round. (And you have to wonder what possessed them to install a cafe at the Holocaust Museum.) Refreshment stands and hot-dog carts are never far away for cheap snacks.

Downtown

The hordes of workers who descend on downtown from Monday to Friday create a demand for places to eat in all categories, and this neighborhood responds with gusto.

Budget & Mid-Range Scores of inexpensive downtown eateries serving familiar American and deli food cater to office workers. Markets also typically sell prepared food (sandwiches, fruit salads, soup to go) at lower prices than delis, and many also tuck full-blown hot-food buffets and salad bars in the back behind the aisles, where you might find anything from country-fried steak to broccoli chicken. Also see the Fabulous Food Courts boxed text, earlier in the chapter.

At *Sholl's Colonial Cafeteria* (☎ 202-296-3065, 1990 K St NW), in the Esplanade Mall, you pay per item for such regional cafeteria fare as baked chicken ($2.65), liver and onions ($2.35), mashed potatoes and gravy (65¢), desserts, and drinks. For ambiance, little homilies are scattered throughout: 'The family that prays together stays together.' Open daily, Sholl's serves three meals – breakfast 7 to 10:30 am, lunch 11 am to 2:30 pm, and dinner 4 to 8 pm; it's open 8:30 am to 6 pm Sunday.

Near the youth hostel, *Stoney's Bar & Grill* (☎ 202-347-9163, 1307 L St NW) looks like a dive from the outside, but inside, it's a cozy burger joint that draws neighborhood regulars and Secret Service agents from their headquarters across the street for 'dude burgers' ($5.75), half a fried chicken with cornbread ($7.25), Philly cheesesteaks ($6.50), and cheap beer.

Travelers who want some impressive Cuban cooking can head for *Havana Breeze* (☎ 202-789-1470, 1401 K St NW) across from

Franklin Square. A platter of *picante de pollo* (chicken pieces in a tangy Caribbean sauce with rice) costs $6.

If you're looking to eat around Ford's Theater, the **Lincoln House Restaurant Bar & Deli** (☎ 202-683-4008, 504 10th St NW) is directly across the street. This place has been a budget favorite with breakfast and lunch crowds for years. Two eggs and grits go for $2; seafood pasta salad costs less than $4.

Next door, **Mike Baker's** (☎ 202-347-6333, 518 10th St NW) opened in 1998 as a grill with lots of varnished hardwood and tablecloths to appeal to an upscale crowd. Most entrees go for $10 and up, but you can eat light – grilled, marinated veggies are less than $6.

At **Jaleo's** (☎ 202-628-7949, 480 7th St NW), at the corner of E St, you can put together a meal for less than $10 from 40 choices of tapas. It's next door to the Shakespeare Theater.

There are two other memorable places to eat on this same block: **Footnotes** (☎ 202-638-4882, 418 7th St NW) is the cafe you see inside the window at Olsson's Books & Records. This place is rife with the smell of cappuccino ($2), muffins, croissants, and scones. After you buy a book or magazine, step in here to sample the Ernest Hemingway – smoked salmon, cream cheese, red onion, capers, and tomato on a bagel ($6). For upscale dining, with tablecloths, water goblets, a hostess, and all the rest, join the crowd of FBI agents and staffers eating at the **Mark** (☎ 202-783-3113, 401 7th St NW). This place can get a little pricey, with fish and chips running $12, but some sandwiches, such as the tandoori chicken, go for less than $8.

Tex-Mex aficionados will want to check out the **Austin Grill** (☎ 202-393-3779, 750 E St NW). Here, a bowl of Mexican corn soup costs $5; *chalupa* taco salad with smoked chicken and all the rest goes for $8.

Take a trip to the **China Cafe** (2009 K St, 1411 K St, 1018 Vermont Ave, 1990 M St) for convenient, reliable, no-MSG take-out food.

Top End Trendy **Red Sage** (☎ 202-638-4444, 405 14th St NW), at F St, is as acclaimed for its lavish decor as it is for its innovative cuisine. The style here is all Southwestern, with spicy red walls and chili-laced plates. Entrees start at $10; to economize, go for lunch, or opt for its adjacent Chili Bar.

Georgia Brown's (☎ 202-637-2077, 950 15th St NW) offers high-style, low-country cuisine and hospitality particularly popular with the city's African American elite. On Sunday, there's a live R&B brunch ($22).

Chinatown

Not long ago, this area had few attractions, but since the arrival of the MCI Center in the late 1990s, the area has become the city's fastest-growing entertainment zone. Now, if you find yourself near Chinatown, you can choose from among a growing number of inexpensive Asian restaurants (and some non-Asian offerings as well) along H St NW between 5th and 7th Sts.

China Doll Gourmet (☎ 202-289-4755, 627 H St NW) serves dim sum (about $8) for take-out or eat-in on white tablecloths 11 am to 3 pm daily. **Ho Wah Restaurant** (☎ 202-898-0823, 611 H St NW) does a big take-out business. Shrimp and snow peas here cost $7.50.

Chop Sticks (☎ 202-898-1986, 719 H St NW) has an extensive a la carte menu, with dishes that are popular with the local Asian population. A chicken entree will cost about $6.

If you are looking for some place a little more formal in Chinatown, try *Szechwan Gallery* (☎ 202-898-1180, 617 H St NW). You get linen tablecloths with the spicy cuisine, but the prices are not too steep: Szechwan shredded duck runs less than $11, and a lot of other entrees are the same price.

Go-Lo's (☎ 202-347-4656, 604 H St NW) is famous for its barbecued meats. The crispy orange beef in a spicy orange sauce costs less than $12.

Perhaps the only Burmese food in DC is served upstairs at the *Burma Restaurant* (☎ 202-638-1280, 740 6th St NW). This is a quiet place with good prawn appetizers, papaya salad, and Burmese curries (entrees are $6 to $8). It's open 11 am to 3 pm and 6 to 10 pm daily.

You'll find a small Texas ribs joint right in the heart of Chinatown: *Capital Q* (☎ 202-347-8396, 707 H St NW) offers eight different kinds of Texas-style barbecued meats. Sandwiches run $4 and up. A baked potato stuffed with smoke portabella mushroom costs $5.

White House Area

The classic choice near the White House is the *Old Ebbitt Grill* (☎ 202-347-8881, 675 15th St NW), a watering hole dating from 1856 that serves a daily menu of such local grill favorites as Maryland rockfish, crab cakes, steak, and burgers, along with grilled-chicken salad and pasta plates. Entrees run $8 to $16; also check out the Sunday brunch.

Though all-you-can-eat sushi is a cultural oxymoron, you can find buffet-style sushi along with hot entrees downstairs at *Benkay* (☎ 202-737-1515, 727 15th St NW). Though of course it's less fresh than made-to-order sushi, you can't beat the price, the sumo-wrestling on cable TV, and the rare opportunity for sushi gluttony. Lunch is $10.50, and dinner is $13.50; children eat for half price.

Foggy Bottom

For a university neighborhood, Foggy Bottom is not overrun with places to eat. The truth is that when Foggy Bottom's residents and college students want a night on the town, they make the 10-minute walk

north to the restaurants and bars of Dupont Circle, or they cross the Pennsylvania Ave bridge spanning Rock Creek to the bright lights and lively crowds of Georgetown. Nevertheless, Foggy Bottom is not without its dining attractions. You just have to look a little harder to find them.

Budget & Mid-Range On the end of the row of townhouses known as Red Lion Row, you will find a longtime favorite hangout for George Washington University students. They have been descending on *Lindy's Bon Appétit* (☎ 202-452-0055, 2040 I St NW) for decades to get their fill of 22 different take-out burger choices at $3 each. If it's warm outside and you're lucky, you can grab a cafe table out front; in cooler weather, head upstairs to the Red Lion bar.

When the college students crave pizza, they head for *Milo's* (☎ 202-338-3000, 2142 Pennsylvania Ave NW); prices range from $6 to $12, depending on size and toppings. Bands sometimes play here during the school year. For inexpensive Middle Eastern take-out featuring kosher meats, check out *Mehran* (☎ 202-342-0056, 2138 Pennsylvania Ave NW). You can smell the curry simmering from half a block away, and there are different curry specials every day for less than $6.

Another bargain stop is the *World Gourmet* (☎ 202-371-9048), a deli and market at the corner of 19th and F Sts. It sells sandwiches, salads, and Middle Eastern vegetarian dips such as hummus and baba ghanoush, which you can eat at the counter or at outside tables; $5 will get you a soup and sandwich. It's a good coffee stop, too.

For a modestly priced sit-down meal, the locals hit *TGI Friday's* (☎ 202-872-4344, 2100 Pennsylvania Ave NW), where appetizers such as potato skins and jalapeño poppers run about $4, and entrees such as chicken fajitas start at $7.

For purely Indian cuisine at economical prices, many locals head for *Aroma* (☎ 202-833-4700, 1919 I St NW). The beef and lamb platters cost about $10, but you can get veggie platters such as the *paneer makhani* (cheese cooked with tomato sauce, butter, and spices) for around $7.

In a basement setting right across the street, you will find Chilean recipes served at *Chalán* (☎ 202-293-2765, 1924 I St NW). The dark corners, candlelight, and limited seating make Chalán a good out-of-the-way spot for a tryst. You can get ceviche for $7 and a glass of red wine for $4.

A block north on 20th St, tucked in a basement, the *Tequila Grill* (☎ 202-833-3640, 1990 K St NW) looks like a set for a Jimmy Buffett south-of-the-border song, and you can hear Jimmy over the sound system at almost any hour of the day. This grill is a college hangout that draws in the crowds for standard Mexican dishes (burritos are around $7) and lots of beer specials, such as a bucket of six 7oz beers for $5.

For convenience and economy, you could also consider the chains, such as *Au Bon Pain* for sandwiches and bakery items inside the shopping mall at 2000 Pennsylvania Ave NW.

Top End The *Roof Terrace Restaurant* in the Kennedy Center (see Foggy Bottom, earlier in the chapter) has pricey American cuisine, such as Maryland crab cakes and broiled Atlantic salmon. Plan on $18 and up for entrees.

In the mini-mall hidden behind the façades of Red Lion Row, *Kinkeads* (☎ 202-296-7700, 2000 Pennsylvania Ave NW) offers popular, upscale dining. This restaurant is the re-creation of Robert Kinkead, who was named the 1995 James Beard Mid-Atlantic Chef of the Year. He specializes in imaginative seafood recipes, such as roast monkfish with potato gratin and roasted onions in a pinot noir sauce ($18), both served in the lively downstairs tavern and more formal upstairs dining room.

Georgetown

Some travelers find Georgetown a preppie enclave and too self-consciously quaint; others adore the thorough restoration of the large stock of Federal-period townhouses and the village ambiance of this neighborhood. But whatever your final perspective, you would be missing an essential DC experience if you did not come to Georgetown to cruise the streets for a restaurant. Simply

put, Georgetown is like one giant outdoor food court, with more than 100 restaurants and people-watching perches in every storefront eatery along its central arteries of M St and Wisconsin Ave NW. There's no Metro service here, but if you can make your way across Rock Creek (from the Foggy Bottom/GWU Metro), you'll find the commercial zone in a walkable, 10-block area.

Budget & Mid-Range For starters and rest stops, there's the *Coffee Beanery* (☎ 202-337-8121, 3110 M St NW), where espresso costs slightly more than $1 and lattes go for $3.

One of the best places for economical dining in Georgetown is *Appa's* (☎ 202-625-6685, 3291 M St NW). This hole-in-the-wall take-out kitchen has a few tables and a cook who specializes in Peruvian charcoal-grilled rotisserie chicken. A leg and thigh cost about $2.50, a breast and wings cost just pennies more, and a half chicken costs $5. Side orders, such as rice, beans, and potatoes, run less than $1.50.

Next door to one another on M St NW at 30th St are two good Vietnamese restaurants: *Saigon Inn* (☎ 202-337-5588, 2928 M St NW) and *Vietnam Georgetown* (☎ 202-337-4576, 2934 M St NW). Although some patrons swear by one or the other, many diners find these restaurants interchangeable. The Saigon Inn chain is a bit cheaper, at around $5 for lunch (also see Woodley Park, later). Vietnam Georgetown offers bowls of shrimp and rice-noodle soup for $6.

An excellent grocery store and its associated cafe merit mention for wine, cheese, meat, and imported picnic provisions. The cafe at *Dean & DeLuca Market* (☎ 202-342-2500, 3276 M St NW) is pricey ($5 for a latte and a croissant) but full of sumptuous smells and elegant displays of produce. The *Burrito Brothers* (☎ 202-965-3963, 3273 M St NW) serves filling California-style burritos ($5); tacos and quesadillas cost $3.

Popular American diner fare (sandwiches, burgers) is plentiful at *Booeymonger* (☎ 202-333-4810, 3265 Prospect St NW), at S Potomac St. This is a packed, claustrophobic-feeling place where folks line up to order take-out and claim the few tables, but locals swear the food is worth the hassle. They recommend the bacon, turkey, and Swiss cheese on French bread ($5).

If the weather is fair and you fancy a walk down by the Potomac River, consider a stop at the *Harbor Cafe* (☎ *202-944-4330, 3000 K St NW)*, in the Washington Harbor complex. This is the one bargain stop among all the eateries lining the riverside boardwalk of the complex. You can eat in the small cafe area or get a sandwich to go. Ham, turkey, and Swiss cheese on homemade rye runs less than $6.

People say if you like the dark, homey feel of a British pub, you should visit *Charing Cross* (☎ *202-338-2141, 3027 M St NW)*. Surprisingly, the fare here is primarily Italian and relatively inexpensive. A single three-topping pizza from the wood-burning oven costs $5.

Zed's Ethiopian Cuisine (☎ *202-333-4710, 3318 M St NW)* is comparable to the Ethiopian restaurants in Adams-Morgan (that means good). Vegetarian dishes are about $6; meat dishes are $7 to $8. *Aditi* (☎ *202-625-6825, 3299 M St NW)* has tangy Indian food. Budget-conscious fans come for the more reasonably priced lunch instead of the pricey dinner (at lunch, meat curries are $10 and vegetable curries are $7).

Sarinah Satay House (☎ *202-337-2955, 1338 Wisconsin Ave NW)* serves chicken and beef satay with gado gado peanut sauce (about $9) along with other Indonesian dishes for lunch and dinner (closed Monday). *Enriquetas* (☎ *202-338-7772, 2811 M St NW)* may be the city's oldest Mexican restaurant. A loyal and regular clientele keeps the cooks busy making the ever-popular enchiladas (less than $9).

The name says a lot at *Il Radicchio Georgetown Italian* (☎ *202-337-8663, 1211 Wisconsin Ave NW)*. This place is an Italian bargain-lover's delight, with all the spaghetti you can eat for about $8 and more than 20 choices of sauce. *Paolos* (☎ *202-333-7353, 1303 Wisconsin Ave NW)* is an upscale Italian bistro famous for its wine collection; it caters to both the Georgetown preppies and the Euro crowd. The attraction here is the scent of brick-oven baking, an outdoor

patio, and storefront window seats to see and be seen. Entrees such as the pepper-grilled filet mignon salad run about $11.

Relatively new to the scene, the *Mendocino Grill* (☎ *202-333-2912, 2917 M St NW)* is a bistro with a fusion of nouvelle cuisine and a wine bar capturing some of Paolos' crowd who are looking for a new venue. The attractions here are finger foods such as the spicy chicken pizza ($9); entrees, such as crab, asparagus, and mushroom crepes, run $13 and up.

The *Peacock Cafe* (☎ *202-625-2740, 3251 Prospect St NW)* has the advantage of being a block away from all the tourist activity on M St and Wisconsin Ave. In other words, this place is a little-known haven where locals can linger over breakfast and a sandwich. Unlike Booeymonger up the street, the Peacock Cafe has a laid-back feel. But make no mistake, you pay for the civilized ambiance: Pancakes cost more than $5, as do most sandwiches, soups, and salads.

Bangkok Bistro (☎ *202-337-2222, 3251 Prospect St NW)* is in the same building as the Peacock Cafe. This is definitely an upscale Thai place, with iridescent table tops, suspended room dividers, and walls painted in a mix of gold and green. Prices are a little steeper than what you may be used to paying for Thai food: Pad Thai costs $10; *tom yam gong* (spicy shrimp soup) is $4.

Old Glory All American Barbecue (☎ *202-337-3406, 3139 M St NW)* brings the tradition of the Southern rib shack to DC. Picture two floors, a rowdy downstairs bar, long tables, and the scent of ribs in tangy sauces sizzling over a hickory or oak fire. There are six different kinds of barbecue sauce from which to choose. A full rack of ribs goes for $18; a half-rack costs $13, but you can eat for less if you order the pork shoulder sandwich (less than $8) or chicken wings ($6). Don't miss the BBQ shrimp ($8).

You can 'put the South in your mouth' at the *Music City Roadhouse* (☎ *202-337-4444)*, on 30th St NW at the canal, a smoker-friendly saloon in a former foundry offering Southern plates. Most of the time country & western music is the theme, and the decor includes trophies on the wall such as Tanya

Tucker's jeans. But on Sunday, this place rocks out with a popular gospel brunch (about $20), served to the harmonies of Brother Luke and the Sensational All Stars.

Top End Set away from crowds near the canal, *Cafe La Ruche* (☎ 202-965-2684, 1039 31st St) offers a sunny dining room full of colorful tile tables alongside a garden. Caribbean-French entrees, such as moules and *saucisses* (small sausages), start at $10.

Also worth a splurge are *Aux Fruits de Mer* (☎ 202-333-2333, 1335 Wisconsin Ave NW) and *Au Pied du Cochon* (☎ 202-333-5440), at the same address. The seafood starts at $14; land food starts at $12. If you are on a budget, you can still afford these places if you order the crepes with French fries and ratatouille ($7). They're open 24 hours.

1789 (☎ 202-965-1789, 1226 36th St NW) is a quintessential early-American inn tucked into a Federal-period townhouse near the edge of the Georgetown University campus. The ambiance here is oil lamps, china, and antique decorations. The cuisine is classic American with an emphasis on regional seafood and farm fare. One popular standard on the menu is the Summerfield rack of lamb for $32.

Tahoga (☎ 202-338-5382, 2815 M St NW) features contemporary American regional cuisine. Simple elegance is the name of the game here, and you can get outdoor, candle-lit dining on the rear patio and on a 2nd-floor deck. The St Jacque Scallops Provencale costs $15.

Tony and Joe's Seafood Place (☎ 202-944-4545, 3000 K St NW) is a premier riverside people-watching venue, with lots of outdoor-cafe seating on the boardwalk facing the Potomac. This place is packed Friday to Sunday, especially for the Sunday jazz brunch ($24, with free-flowing champagne). Crab-cake entrees run $24.

La Chaumiere (☎ 202-338-1784, 2813 M St NW) has a French country inn atmosphere with a large, free-standing stone fireplace as a centerpiece. If money is no object, consider the Dover sole (deboned and served whole), priced between $24 and $27 depending on weight.

Dupont Circle

For everyone who considers Adams-Morgan too funky and Georgetown too preppie, Dupont Circle is the main restaurant district. It's also the center of DC's gay community. Weekend nights bring in a host of out-of-town license plates from surrounding suburbs. Many restaurants are found along Connecticut Ave NW on either side of the Circle and on side streets all around.

Budget & Mid-Range Attached to Kramerbooks, *Afterwords Café* (☎ 202-387-1462, 1517 Connecticut Ave NW) is a good place to meet up with someone before spending a day or evening in the city; it's also just a great place to hang out and watch people who stroll the sidewalks of Dupont Circle. In the morning, Afterwords is a cafe for espresso ($2) and muffins. In the afternoon, it's an alfresco brunch spot with a mezzanine hideaway. By night, it becomes a bar scene with live music most nights.

Xando Coffee and Bar (☎ 202-296-9341, 1647 20th St NW) is another popular cafe and people-watching venue a block north of Afterwords. There are plenty of tables corralled on the edge of the sidewalk in both the shade and the sun. A large cafe au lait costs less than $2; a shot of almond, blackberry, or mint flavoring is 25¢ extra.

If you've been on the road and are feeling a little out of touch, stop by the **Cyberstop Cafe** (☎ 202-234-2470, 153 17th St NW). There are six computers here in a sort of living-room arrangement where it's easy to chat and kick back while your fingers are surfing or catching up on email. Online time is $5 for a half hour or $7 for an hour. Espresso runs about $2 after tax. Other coffee places in the area are **Hannibal's** and **Starbucks**. There's also a **Chesapeake Bagel Bakery** (1636 Connecticut Ave NW) outlet here.

Scores of restaurants and cafes line Connecticut Ave north of the literal Dupont Circle roundabout. **City Lights of China** (☎ 202-265-6688, 1731 Connecticut Ave NW) is one of the most popular Chinese restaurants in the city. Try the asparagus and crab-meat soup ($3) or spicy eggplant with garlic sauce ($6 at dinner).

Authentic southern Indian vegetarian plates at **Paru's** (☎ 202-483-5133, 2010 S St NW), off Connecticut Ave, include paratha, two curries, a samosa, and a lassi for around $7. Food is served in a small dining room across a counter from the kitchen.

Lauriol Plaza (☎ 202-387-0035, 1801 18th St NW) graciously serves Mexican, Spanish, and South American dishes. A ceviche Peruano appetizer costs $6.50, paella is $16, and fajitas are $7. You'll find Malaysian and Singaporean dishes, such as nasi goreng ($8) and satay ($7) with peanut sauce at the **Straits of Malaya** (☎ 202-483-1483, 1836 18th St NW).

Vegetarian and health-food specialties are in abundance at **Food for Thought** (☎ 202-797-1095, 1738 Connecticut Ave NW); the menu includes sunburgers (patties made of rice and sunflower seeds) for $5.50 and veggie Reubens (Swiss, sauerkraut, green pepper, onion, mushrooms, and tomato on rye) for $7. It's open for dinner daily and for lunch Monday to Saturday.

La Tomate (☎ 202-667-5505, 1707 Connecticut Ave) offers pasta plates and Italian dishes ($9 to $12) in a bright and airy dining room or out on the patio. **Leonardo's** (☎ 202-234-8100, 1724 Connecticut Ave NW) features Italian and American cooking. The seafood salad ($7) is a popular item on the menu.

For Greek specialties, consider **Zorba's Cafe** (☎ 202-387-8555, 1612 20th St NW), off Connecticut Ave, where they serve moussaka for $5 and gyros for $4. There is piped-in Greek music (sit outside).

Get a light bite at **Timberlakes** (☎ 202-483-2266, 1726 Connecticut Ave NW), famous for its burgers (around $6) and fish and chips made with farm-grown catfish ($7). Thai lovers head a few doors over to the **Thai Chef** (☎ 202-234-5698, 1712 Connecticut Ave NW). Soup, such as tom yam gai (spicy chicken), goes for $3. A platter of shrimp pad Thai costs $9.

If you crave Mexican, check out **The Burro** (☎ 202-483-6861, 1621 Connecticut Ave), where you can get a quesadilla for $4. Breakfasts here are economical as well: The frittata (with eggs, feta cheese, grilled veggies, and roast potatoes) costs $3, including a cup of coffee.

For a totally crunchy scene just off Connecticut Ave to the northwest of the Circle, stop by **Teaism** (☎ 202-667-3827, 2009 R St NW). Everything here is organic. You can eat in or get take-out and sit in the sun in front of this two-story townhouse. It has more than 30 varieties of tea (prices start at about $2), including oolong, green, tisane, and Darjeeling. The bento boxes (Asian boxed meals, which may contain teriyaki salmon, ginger salad, rice, and fruit) cost less than $8.

Raku: An Asian Diner (☎ 202-718-8680, 1900 Q St NW) is next to Afterwords (earlier in this section). This is the place to come for reasonably priced sushi – the spicy tuna roll goes for less than $5, and a four-roll assortment costs $13.

If you stray into the West End in lower Dupont, you'll find a few more choices around 22nd and M Sts NW. **Lulu's New Orleans Cafe** (☎ 202-861-5858, 1217 22nd St NW) makes a good turtle soup ($3), catfish and oyster po' boy sandwiches ($8), and decent jambalaya ($8). At night, this place turns into a hopping club (see Entertainment, later).

East of the Circle, **Cafe Luna** (☎ 202-387-4005, 1633 P St NW) features inexpensive Italian fare, such as a mozzarella and tomato sandwich with a side of fruit for less than $6; pasta with garlic and olive oil costs the same.

You will find a number of attractive and moderately priced restaurants along Connecticut Ave south of the Circle. Over at *Bertucci's Brick Oven Pizzeria* (☎ 202-463-7733, 1218 Connecticut Ave NW), you might pay $12 for a pizza, but the soup and salad in this popular chain goes for less than $4, and there is an endless supply of hot, freshly baked rolls.

The *Luna Grill & Diner* (☎ 202-835-2280, 1301 Connecticut Ave NW) is a cheery little storefront operation with a parquet floor and secluded booths. The cuisine is basically American-fusion; a monte cristo sandwich with grilled turkey and cheese costs $7.

South of here, on the same side of the street, stands a great take-out place with one glass table: *Julia's Empanadas* (☎ 202-861-8828, 1221 Connecticut Ave NW) is one of three in the city, which testifies to the popularity of the food. You can get a massive Chilena empanada for $3.

Top End The restaurant in the historic Tabard Inn (see Places to Stay, earlier) offers an arty daily menu of appetizers, such as smoked trout cakes with red-cabbage relish ($7.50); entrees, such as grilled shrimp with fennel garlic cream ($19); and things in puff pastry.

Across from the Tabard, the *Iron Gate* (☎ 202-737-1370, 1734 N St NW) has a storybook setting under trellises outside or inside by the fire. Monday to Saturday, it serves high-end romantic food, such as lamb chops with ruffly paper garters (about $18).

Nora's (☎ 202-462-5143, 2132 Florida Ave NW), at the corner of R St, offers organic gourmet dinners in an elegant, intimate corner bistro.

In the West End part of lower Dupont, *City Cafe* (☎ 202-797-4860, 2213 M St NW) also promotes an organic menu, including fish, seafood salad, spring rolls, and carrot juice (entrees cost up to $14). Steak lovers go to *Blackie's House of Beef* (☎ 202-333-1100), at 22nd and M Sts NW, for large steaks ($20 to $25).

If you are looking to find the city's hip Euro crowd, go to *MCCXXIII* (☎ 202-822-1800, 1223 Connecticut Ave NW), otherwise known as 'Twelve Twenty-Three.' Men will need a jacket, nice slacks, and polished shoes to get past the doorperson; women wear cocktail dresses or business suits. Lunch prices for items such as spinach ravioli start at $12. Dinner entrees can exceed $25. After dinner, this place turns into a popular Euro club (see Entertainment, later).

Adams-Morgan

This restaurant-entertainment district has an amazing concentration of ethnic restaurants, particularly in a three-block stretch of 18th St NW south of Columbia Rd. In DC, the name Adams-Morgan has come to symbolize an international smorgasbord. Here you can find *mee goreng*, *yebeg alecka*, shish kabobs, calzone, jerk chicken, burritos, empanadas, and of course, Happy Meals. Parking on the streets and sometimes even in the surrounding lots can become impossible from dinnertime until after midnight. The menus and ambiance of all these places are budget to mid-range, though you can find selected entrees toward the top end.

For breakfast in this late-to-rise neighborhood, try *Jolt N' Bolt* (☎ 202-232-0077, 1918 18th St NW), it's a great perch for coffee ($1), tea, and bakery treats. Other good breakfast spots are the *Belmont Kitchen Pantry* (☎ 202-667-1200, 2400 18th St NW) and *Avignon Frères* (☎ 202-462-2050, 1775 Columbia Rd NW), where you can get two eggs and a side of grits or hash browns for less than $3.

The small *open-air farmers' market* (☎ 717-573-4527) at Columbia Rd and 18th St NW in Adams-Morgan is open 7 am to 5 pm Saturday year-round and draws an international crowd.

There are a dozen Ethiopian restaurants here (some say Eritrean); many feature live jazz in the evenings. Two good ones are at the top of the hill: *Meskerem* (☎ 202-462-4100, 2434 18th St NW) and, across the street, *Red Sea* (☎ 202-483-5000, 2463 18th St NW). Some local restaurant mavens claim the food at Meskerem is slightly better to match the higher prices; Meskerem also offers authentic seating on camel-hide hassocks at woven-straw drum tables upstairs (don't let them consign you to the basement). If you prefer less exotic seating, go to Red Sea. At both, you can order spicy stews of lamb, beef, chicken, seafood, and lentils, braised and simmered for hours (small portions are less than $5, large portions are less than $10). Meals are commonly served with two vegetable side dishes and a plate of *injera*, a spongy bread used to scoop up food in place of silverware.

For a taste of the Caribbean, head to *Mobay* (☎ 202-745-1002, 2437 18th St NW). This is a happy place, with both indoor and outdoor cafe tables and a young crowd pulsing to the back beat of Bob Marley and his descendants. Try the Chicken Rundown (chunks of chicken smeared in a light, seasoned, coconut custard sauce and covered with fresh coconut) for $9.

For French, *Cafe Lautrec* (☎ 202-265-6436, 2431 18th St NW) is the granddaddy of DC's bohemian cafes. Its two-story, outdoor mural of Parisian singer Aristide Bruant mimicking Toulouse-Lautrec's painting is a neighborhood landmark. Though many come just for the jazz or tap-dancing bartender, you can eat good French food with a Moroccan twist for less than $10.

A less predictable French-Moroccan experience can be had at *Cafe Riche* (☎ 202-328-1881, 2455 18th St NW), if the eccentric bartender/owner Benny ('the Sultan of 18th St') is in the mood to let you in or serve you. Sometimes Benny prices things according to his whim, but menu prices usually keep entrees less than $10. The more predictable French bistro *La Fourchette* (☎ 202-332-3077, 2429 18th St NW) makes a great bouillabaisse (about $11), along with other daily specials.

Cities (☎ 202-328-7194, 2424 18th St NW) changes its 'city' theme every three months or so, re-creating its menu, wine list, and decor in the style of, for example, Rio, Istanbul, Bangkok, Montreal, or Florence (Tuscan specialties cost $14 to $20). There's a disco upstairs; dining is quietest in the back room. The crowd here is upscale, with a lot of 20- to 40-year-old Euro-types.

For Italian, *I Matti* (☎ 202-462-8844, 2436 18th St NW) is a bright and airy spot on the fashionably dark street, with red-tile floors, blond-wood tables, and big picture windows (perfect for people-watching). A locally renowned chef invents pasta plates and modern Italian fare garnished with fried radicchio or fava beans ($12.95 and up) for power-lunchers and dinner crowds.

Another Italian offering is *Pearl* (☎ 202-328-0846, 2228 18th St NW). Entrees, such as sesame-crusted yellow-fin tuna, can run more than $15, but you can also select from the appetizer menu, where a large pot of steamed mussels in tomato sauce runs about $8. There is a DJ after about 9 pm most nights in the bar upstairs.

El Tamarindo (☎ 202-328-3660, 1785 Florida Ave NW) serves excellent Salvadoran and Mexican dishes 24 hours a day in a checkered vinyl-tablecloth setting off 18th St. Enchiladas, tacos, and *flautas* all cost about $7.

Rumba (☎ 202-558-5501, 2443 18th St NW) makes you feel like you have walked into a Cuban bistro. It's decorated with a collection of Latin American guitarlike instruments and religious santos hung on the walls. Here you will eat *yuca frita* (fried yuca root with mojo sauce) while listening to salsa by Celia Cruz and others pumping from the sound system.

You can eat like you're in Rio De Janeiro at *Tom Brazil* (☎ 202-232-4668, 1832 Columbia Rd NW), where *xinxim* (chicken flavored with garlic, spice, and oil) costs about $9.

New Orleans (☎ 202-234-0420, 2412 18th St NW) is Adams-Morgan's extremely popular Cajun restaurant. Crowds gather early here on weekends, so you may have to wait in line for a seat in this restaurant that looks like a bayou crab shack. Prices are very reasonable, with shrimp gumbo running about $6, chicken jambalaya $10.

When Washingtonians crave a taste of the Southwest, they dine at *Roxanne and the Payote Grill* (☎ 202-462-8330, 2319 18th St NW). One popular item on the menu here is Corona-beer-battered shrimp for $8. Vegetarian black-bean chili is $5.

Saigonaise (☎ 202-232-5300, 2307 18th St NW) is the place to come for Southeast

Asian delights. *Canh chua ca tom* (a lemony soup with shrimp, fish cake, sprouts, mushrooms, and pineapple) goes for about $3; curried chicken costs less than $8.

Astor (☎ *202-745-7495, 1829 Columbia Rd NW*) makes a great sandwich stop, especially for vegetarians. Astor offers 10 different veggie platters, such as the falafel (with pita bread, hummus, and Egyptian salad), for less than $5.

The most upscale Italian restaurant in Adams-Morgan is ***Felix*** (☎ *202-483-3549, 2406 18th St NW*). You can get sautéed shrimp with angel-hair pasta, asparagus tips, and a tomato/basil sauce for $18. Choose from cafe tables on two levels of this modern steel and glass emporium that looks rather out of place among the 1920s townhouses typical of Adams-Morgan. This places turns into a popular club after about 10 pm.

Woodley Park

The compact triangle above the Woodley Park/Zoo Metro station is packed with good places to eat. The clientele is a diverse mix of locals and tourists from several neighborhood hotels. All these restaurants are budget to mid-range.

At ***Lebanese Taverna*** (☎ *202-483-3007, 2641 Connecticut Ave NW*), you can make a meal of the many good Middle Eastern appetizers that run less than $5 – baba ghanoush, falafel, moussaka, or tabouleh. Entrees are $11.50 and up.

For Thai cuisine, consider ***Jandara*** (☎ *202-387-8876, 2606 Connecticut Ave NW*), serving several good soups, such as *poh tack* (hot-and-sour seafood with lemongrass), for less than $4 and noodle dishes for less than $8.

The ***Saigon Inn*** (☎ *202-483-8400, 2614 Connecticut Ave NW*) has good Vietnamese food, including clear spring rolls for $3 and skewered lemon chicken for $6 at lunch (dinner prices are higher).

Rajaji (☎ *202-265-7344, 2603 Connecticut Ave*) serves Indian curry dishes (about $8). The cafe seating outside makes for a relaxing dinner during the late evenings in warm weather. There are two other restaurants in this same collection of storefronts, and both venues also have ample outdoor seating.

Acapulco (☎ *202-986-0131, 2623 Connecticut Ave NW*) offers Mexican dining. *Posole* (spicy soup with pork, chicken, and chorizo) costs $2. The chicken enchilada costs $7.

Tono (☎ *202-332-7300, 2605 Connecticut Ave*) is a Japanese restaurant next door. *Tempura zarusoba* (cold buckwheat noodles with shrimp tempura on the side) runs $8.

Also handy are a bakery cafe, an Irish pub, and a gourmet market (all across from the Omni Shoreham Hotel).

Shaw

There's an intriguing mix of great soul-food landmarks and avant-garde cafes within walking distance of the U St Metro. Recent neighborhood revitalization along U St and a bohemian enclave centered at U and 14th Sts make this neighborhood an emerging entertainment zone in DC – anything can happen. All the following are suitable for travelers on a tight budget.

Ben's Chili Bowl (☎ *202-667-0909, 1213 U St NW*) is such a neighborhood institution that it appears on the Metro station maps as a local landmark. The regulars gather here for chili dogs ('Our chili will make a hot dog bark!'), scrapple, milkshakes, TV, and conversation. Prices for hot dogs start at less than $2; chili goes for less than $4. It opens at 6 am every day but Sunday, when it opens at noon; the chili flows until at least midnight every night.

The vanguard collect across the street at the ***Kaffa House*** (☎ *202-462-1212, 1212 U St NW*), a collective named for the region in Ethiopia where the coffee bean was first discovered, according to the owners. Howard University students, poets, and dreadlocked Rastas come for vegetarian soups, muffins, and coffee, as well as for readings and live jazz. Soups are a value here, at less than $3.

U-topia (☎ *202-483-7669, 1418 U St NW*) is one of the neighborhood's new arty restaurants. It serves an assortment of experimental dishes, the most local of which is called U-Street Shrimp-and-Rice (about $9). The colorful abstract interior, out-there patrons, and great bar are big draws.

Polly's (☎ *202-265-8385, 1343 U St NW*) offers morning-after brunches on weekends, with eggs, strong coffee, and mimosas by the pitcher. Prices for brunch start at about $10 if you don't order alcoholic drinks. The *Florida Avenue Grill* (☎ *202-265-1586, 1100 Florida Ave NW*) serves down-home Southern-style breakfasts, lunches, and dinners – grits, meatloaf, and barbecued ribs (entrees are $6 to $9). From the U St/Cardozo Metro station, walk north on 11th St for three blocks.

Julio's (☎ *202-483-8500, 1604 U St NW*) stands about halfway along U St between the entertainment districts of Shaw (around the U St/Cardozo Metro stop) and Adams-Morgan. During fair weather, folks come here early and stay late for the rooftop Sunday brunch that runs from 10 am to 4 pm. The $15 charge covers all you can eat (eggs, grits, corned beef hash, baked ham, waffles, pizza, salad bar), plus an unlimited supply of champagne or mimosas.

Northeast

Look for the *DC Farmers Market* (☎ *202-547-3142*), 5th St and Neal Place NE, open daily year-round; and the *DC Open Air Farmers Market* (☎ *202-728-2800*), at RFK Stadium (Oklahoma Ave and Banning Rd NE), on Thursday and Saturday year-round (also Tuesday July to September).

Southwest

For cheap eats on the water, head south of the Mall to Maine Ave SW and the parallel boardwalk along the Washington Channel. At the spot near where the I-395 freeway passes over these local thoroughfares, you will find the *open-air seafood market*. A handful of barges here sell fresh seafood (with all the smells and tentacles; it's a sensory spectacle even if you don't buy anything). The vendors also sell some prepared foods, such as soft-shell crab sandwiches (in season) for $3 to $5 and fish platters with fries for $5 to $6, and great crab cakes for about $5. Unfortunately, there are no picnic tables, so you must sit on the curb or amble back down to boardwalk benches.

Le Rivage (☎ *202-488-8111, 1000 Water St SW*) lies off Maine Ave on the northern end of the Washington Channel. This is a great dinner-date restaurant with its views of the

sunset framing a backdrop of candlelight and French cuisine. Red snapper in a white-wine sauce will run you $20.

Hogates (☎ *202-484-6300, 800 Water St SW*) is a little farther south along the channel. This seafood restaurant has been a DC institution for more than 50 years. One of the attractions here is dining on the outdoor patio, but bring your insect repellent in warm weather. A 1¼lb Maine lobster costs $20.

ENTERTAINMENT

DC rocks, and the best place to find out what's happening is the weekly tabloid *Washington City Paper*, issued each Thursday afternoon and distributed free in corner racks and at bookstores, restaurants, and clubs around the city. A similar free tabloid publication called *The Bar Stool* comes out every other Tuesday and forecasts the city's nightlife scene for the coming two weeks. A more mainstream resource is the Weekend tabloid that appears in Friday's edition of the *Washington Post*, as well as listings in the *Post*'s daily Style section and Sunday's Show section. The weekly *Washington Blade* tabloid, distributed free at many city outlets, includes events of particular interest to DC's gay community.

For advance planning, you can request a seasonal calendar (produced quarterly) of major cultural events from the DC Convention and Visitors Association (see Information, earlier in the chapter).

Ticketplace (☎ 202-842-5387), 1100 Pennsylvania Ave NW in the Old Post Office Pavilion, and at the Lisner Auditorium at George Washington University, sells tickets to citywide concerts and shows on the day of performance at half price plus 10%. Available tickets are listed on a board at the office. It's open noon to 6 pm Tuesday to Friday, 11 am to 5 pm Saturday. (Tickets for Sunday and Monday shows are sold on Saturday.) Ticketplace accepts cash only; full-price advance sales are also available. You can also check with theaters directly on the day of the performance to see if tickets are available for less than face value.

The John F Kennedy Center for the Performing Arts (see the Foggy Bottom section, earlier in this chapter) is a massive building overlooking the Potomac with four stages hosting operas and concerts as well as a film theater (and a good rooftop restaurant besides). Nationally recognized artists and companies appear here, and film festivals and cultural fairs are also common. Tickets to the main events can be steep; inquire about half-price tickets that are sometimes available on the day of performance.

You can hear jazz outdoors in 4200-seat Carter Barron Amphitheater at Rock Creek Park on summer weekends (see Upper Northwest, earlier in this chapter). Contact the theater (☎ 202-426-6837) or National Park Service (☎ 202-619-7222) for a schedule of current performances.

Theater

The *National Theater* (☎ 202-628-6161, 800-447-7400, 1321 Pennsylvania Ave NW), established in 1835 and renovated in 1984, is DC's oldest continually operating theater. *Les Misérables* has been performed here in the past. The *Warner Theater* (☎ 202-628-1818, 1299 Pennsylvania Ave NW) is a 1924 Art Deco theater that hosts headliner concerts and the annual *Nutcracker*.

Arena Stage (☎ 202-488-3300), at the waterfront on 6th St and Maine Ave SW, is actually three theaters – among them a theater-in-the-round, where they host both mainstream and more experimental performances.

The *Shakespeare Theater* (☎ 202-547-1122, 450 7th St NW) is home to a Shakespearean troupe. Shakespearean and other performances are also held in the Elizabethan theater of the Folger Shakespeare Library (see Capitol Hill, earlier in the chapter).

Ford's Theater (see Downtown, earlier in the chapter) is not only a historic site, it's an inviting performance venue. You sit in wooden chairs downstairs or up in the balcony; the flag-draped box where Lincoln was sitting when he was shot is reserved as a memorial. Expect the likes of the *Fantasticks* and other mainstream performances.

The Lincoln Theater (see Shaw, earlier in the chapter) is another historic theater. The center of the 1930s 'Black Broadway' strip in

Free or Cheap Events

In addition to being free all day, DC's museums also present special evening events, many of which are free. There are many lectures and readings, but there are also wonderful and unusual concerts and performances, from bluegrass jams to art films to puppet shows. Call Dial-a-Museum (☎ 202-357-2020) for an updated recording, or pick up a calendar of events at museum desks. The Library of Congress and DC churches are dramatic venues for regularly scheduled concerts (usually jazz and classical).

Street fairs and festivals provide great local entertainment; they're scheduled throughout the more temperate months (see Special Events, earlier, or check papers for listings).

Note also that many of the major memorials are most dramatic at night, and you can avoid crowds and conserve your time for day-only museums by covering such sights as the Lincoln Memorial, Jefferson Memorial, and Washington Monument in the evening (the elevator goes to the top until midnight from around April to September).

★★★★★★★★★★★

the neighborhood's heyday, the theater was recently renovated by the city.

DC's theater district lies east of Dupont Circle around 14th St NW between P and Q Sts. Here you'll find smaller repertory companies, alternative theater, and cheaper seats. Check the listings for the *Woolly Mammoth Theatre Co* (☎ 202-393-3939, 1401 Church St NW), off 14th St; the *Source Theatre Co* (☎ 202-462-1073, 1835 14th St NW); and *Studio Theatre* (☎ 202-332-3300, 1333 P St NW).

The *Gala Hispanic Theatre* (☎ 202-234-7174, 1625 Park Rd NW), in the Upper Northwest, has been staging four major Spanish-language productions annually for 23 years.

Classical Music & Opera

The National Symphony and the Washington Chamber Symphony perform at the

Kennedy Center (see Foggy Bottom, earlier in the chapter). The symphony also holds summertime concerts at an outdoor amphitheater at *Wolf Trap Farm Park for the Performing Arts* (☎ 703-255-1827), a 40-minute drive away in Vienna, Virginia (see the Northern Virginia chapter).

In town, other classical performances take place at local universities and churches, as well as at acoustically monumental venues such as the National Gallery of Art (see National Mall, earlier), the National Building Museum (see Downtown, earlier), the Corcoran Gallery (see White House Area, earlier), and the Library of Congress (see Capitol Hill, earlier).

The *Washington Opera* (☎ 202-295-2400, 800-876-7372), with offices at 2600 Virginia Ave, is an emerging jewel. Famed tenor Placido Domingo became its conductor in 1996. In the subsequent year, there was talk that the opera would move from the Kennedy Center, where it's been housed for the past 25 years, to a new theater built in the shell of a former downtown department store. But in mid-1998, the opera signed a new 15-year lease with the Kennedy Center to mount a season of 26 weeks in the Kennedy Center Opera House.

Comedy

Running in DC for more than a decade, *Shear Madness* (☎ 202-467-4600), at the Kennedy Center, is an ever-changing, comical whodunit with lots of innuendo about the capital's contemporary political scene.

It is difficult to find comedy clubs in DC, but *Improvisation* (☎ 202-296-7008, 1140 Connecticut Ave NW) is a good one. You will find this club in a basement with about 60 tables. This club books nationally known comics, so be sure to make reservations if you hope to get in on a weekend. The cover runs $12 to $15, and there is a two-drink minimum.

Children and their parents enjoy *Now This* (☎ 202-364-8292, 6950 Oregon Ave NW), a totally improvisational musical and comedy performance. Some shows are geared toward adults, some for kids; call for information.

Gross National Product (☎ 202-783-7271, 1602 South Springwood Drive), just north of DC in Silver Spring, Maryland, is a another comedy group claiming to turn this morning's headlines into this evening's belly laughs.

Capitol Steps Political Satire (see Alexandria in the Around Washington, DC chapter) is a comedy troupe spoofing DC politics.

Bars & Clubs

While there's symphonic music here, and while opera has gotten a huge boost from the leadership of Placido Domingo, DC's music scene really thrives in the bars and clubs. Washingtonians have long had a love affair with jazz and blues, but this is a cosmopolitan city, and you will find an abundance of places to get your groove on to reggae, salsa, techno, and house sounds.

The greatest concentration of nightlife and streetlife for walkable bar-hopping is in Adams-Morgan (mostly 18th St NW between Florida Ave and Columbia Rd) and in Georgetown (mostly M St NW between 29th and 33rd St). There are many bars around Dupont Circle, quite a few catering to gays. Many bars also feature live music, DJs, and dancing. Free or cheap food is often offered to lure patrons.

Capitol Hill A relative newcomer to the area, *Politiki* (☎ 202-546-1001, 319 Pennsylvania SE) has become popular with the under-30 crowd of staffers and locals for its Pacific-islands decor, pool tables, and swing-dancing scene on the 2nd floor, which looks like a set out of a Glen Miller movie. It's a good dance scene Wednesday and on the weekends.

In general, Capitol Hill bars cater to the congressional crowd, and all of the following places in this section can also be found under Places to Eat.

On the Senate Side of the Hill along Massachusetts Ave, look for the Red River Grill. This place is a pickup scene for the young and the politically active. Word has it that the outdoor deck here is the place where White House intern Monica Lewinsky first began hinting to friends about her relationship with President Clinton.

You will also find a number of popular pubs on the House Side of the Hill along Pennsylvania Ave between 2nd and 5th Sts SE. The Hawk & Dove, where dusty hunting trophies decorate the walls, has been an institution since the late 1960s. If Congress is in session, you might see one or two of the younger representatives (such as Congressman Patrick Kennedy, Senator Ted Kennedy's son) in here. Coats, ties, and suits are the scene after work, but by night, the crowd is a bit younger and in jeans, khakis, and polo shirts. Come with the crowds on Friday evening, when a 20oz Bud draft costs less than $2.50 and there are free tacos. It's a good pickup scene if you are under 35.

Right next door, the Tune Inn is also a preppie hangout featuring dead animals on the wall. This place once won an award for being the best dive in DC, and the crowd here is a little younger and rowdier than at the Hawk – but still preppie. A lot of the folks here are congressional interns (that means they are working for free to get college credit). Many are from the South in fact or in spirit. This place is also a popular stop for Capitol Hill softball teams after their games. Friday night rocks.

A few blocks farther to the south, you will spot Tortilla Coast. A lot of local Hill residents, staffers, and tourists come to sit in the street-side booths, where the plate-glass windows are removed in fair weather and you can do some 1st-class people-watching. The crowd here consists of upscale residents and staffers under 35. A lot of women find this a comfortable place to go, and on busy Friday and Saturday nights, groups of women may outnumber the men at the bar.

Bulfeathers has a clubby atmosphere that draws in congressional representatives and staffers. The scene here is largely coat-and-tie country for politicos in the 25-to-40 age group. It's popular with professional women, who find they can sit at the bar without getting hit on by a school of sharky guys.

On the north side of the hill, just beyond Union Station, you can hear some Irish music at the Dubliner. This classic Irish pub fills every afternoon and evening with a mix of local Irish and plenty of middle-aged

Duke Ellington

Born and raised in DC's Shaw district, Edward Kennedy Ellington (1899–1974) developed his keyboard skills while listening to local ragtime pianists. His first piece was the 'Soda Fountain Rag,' composed at age 16. Ellington became successful in DC by the early 1920s and left for New York City in 1923, where he went on to play at Harlem's Cotton Club.

Ellington collaborated with many artists – trumpeters Bubber Miley and Cootie Williams and saxophonists Johnny Hodges and Otto Hardwick were among them. But the most famous of his collaborators was composer Billy Strayhorn, who gave the Ellington Band its theme, 'Take the A Train,' in 1941. Strayhorn worked with Ellington throughout his life and collaborated on later numbers such as 'Such Sweet Thunder' (1957) and 'Far East Suite' (1966).

Ellington is best known for his big-band jazz compositions. But his broad range and huge volume of work – more than 1500 pieces – set him above everyone else in the field. The entire Duke Ellington collection is preserved by the Smithsonian Institution and is occasionally on display.

tourists on a spree to pound a few pints of Harp. Every night, the pub hosts live Irish or American folk music that draws a crowd of 30- to 50-year-olds.

You will find a younger crowd next door at Kelly's Irish Times. The long bar and the booths fill with folks who come for the Guinness on tap and live Irish music Wednesday to Saturday. More than a few Capitol Hill staffers will tell you this was the first bar in the city that served them.

In spite of all the polished brass and hardwood, the Capitol City Brewing Company still feels like the post office it once was, and it has not yet developed much character. Nevertheless, it pulls in a lot of tourists, so this is not a bad place to meet another out-of-towner during the cocktail hour and then head off to some place nearby where you can mix with the locals and the beer is cheaper. The house golden ale runs $4.

Downtown Because this area was all but deserted after dark until the arrival of the MCI Center in the late 1990s, rent was cheap, and dance clubs started popping up in defunct retail and banking spaces. Now, because the dance clubs are still here (but are changing their names and addresses with dizzying speed), because the MCI Center draws crowds to sporting events, and because a lot of new restaurants are opening, downtown is becoming the city's newest entertainment district. The pub scene is not very dynamic yet, but no doubt the pubs will follow the clubs and the restaurants that are already here.

At the moment, one of the hottest clubs is **The Bank** (☎ *202-737-3177, 915 F St NW*). Located in a space vacated by a financial institution, this place is a gigantic New York–style disco with four levels. The music is hip hop, house, funk, and disco. The crowd is multiracial. Designer-style sportswear is the fashion of choice for the under-30 patrons. Some nights you only have to be 18 to get in, but you can't drink. The cover is $5 during the week, $10 on weekends.

Coco Loco (☎ *202-289-2626, 810 7th St NW*), in Chinatown, is a popular restaurant that does a quick change into a hot club similar to what you find in Caracas, where the salsa and merengue sizzle after 11 pm on weekends. The scene is Euro and high fashion, drawing a mix of ages to pack the dance floor. Many locals consider this place among the top two or three Latin clubs in the city. The cover is usually $5.

If you still can't get enough of the original *Star Wars* trilogy, *Gilligan's Island*, or *The Brady Bunch*, head for **Polly Esther's** (☎ *202-737-1970, 605 12th St NW*). This dance club has re-created the last three decades of the 20th century. Take your pick of a '70s dance scene, '80s disco, or '90s Top 40, all on different dance floors. The crowd is totally mixed, and sometimes you get waves of folks in town on conventions. Expect a $5 cover.

The Ritz (☎ *202-638-2582, 919 E St NW*) claims to be the city's largest dance club,

with five different dance floors where you can groove to hip hop, house, old school, and reggae. The club gets packed with a real mix of ages and races on weekends. You'll pay a $10 cover. No sneakers, jeans, or T-shirts are allowed.

Zanzibar (☎ *202-554-9100, 700 Water St SE*), near Hogates restaurant on the Washington Channel waterfront, is a late-night club appealing to the Euro crowd who also favor places like Coco Loco. So ladies, put on your little black dress and heels for this place. You get Caribbean, Latin, and African rhythms for dancing, and sometimes there is a comedy show. The cover is $10, and a strict dress code is enforced.

Zei Club (☎ *202-842-2445, 1415 Zei Alley NW*) is another of DC's New York–style dance clubs and is a major attraction to the Euro crowd. 'Zei' is Greek for 'to live,' and this club claims to be all about living well with style. The club is not for college kids, and don't show up unless you can cop an attitude. The crowd is mostly under 30; the cover is $10.

Fadó (☎ *202-789-0066, 808 7th St NW*) sticks out in Chinatown like James Joyce in Shanghai, and maybe this is a good marketing ploy, because an Irish pub is just what a fair percentage of the crowd is looking for when they want to tank up before and after the sporting events at the MCI Center down the street. The owners dropped a bundle to make every room look like a different place (eg, a cottage, a library) or era (eg, Victorian, Celtic) in Ireland, but the pub feels more like a movie set than a real gin mill. Nevertheless, it packs in the thirsty who are willing to pay $4 and up for the beer on sports nights.

Foggy Bottom In this college neighborhood, George Washington University has some pubs to call its own. For sports, a lot of folks head to the Tequila Grill (see Places to Eat). Mexican-food specials and $1-beer happy-hour specials pull in the students. You get a DJ here Thursday to Saturday. Fall and winter Sundays mean all football, all day.

The *Red Lion* is the pub above the ever-popular Lindy's Bon Appétit burger joint (see Places to Eat). Both despondent and euphoric students wander in nightly for $1.50 shooter specials and hang to watch TV and talk school with their buds.

Froggy Bottom Pub *(☎ 202-338-3080, 2141 Pennsylvania Ave NW)* is another popular GW hangout with a pool table. The big attractions here are grub-and-pub specials, such as 'all you can eat and drink' on Saturday for $10. Happy-hour specials run from 5 pm to midnight. Friday means a free buffet.

One Step Down *(☎ 202-331-8863, 2517 Pennsylvania Ave NW)* is one of the city's hottest jazz spots and draws in out-of-town talent on the weekends. During the rest of the week, you get local artists and a great jukebox. The cover during the week is $5, weekends $12 to $20. Most patrons are yuppies in their mid-20s.

Georgetown With about 40 clubs and bars spicing up the streets of this compact neighborhood, Georgetown is always in party mode. Like the restaurants in the area, the clubs and bars cater to the largely white hordes of college students and professionals who live in the area, as well as suburban types who wish they lived here and visit by night to pretend.

DC really excels in live blues and jazz. And the preeminent ***Blues Alley*** *(☎ 202-337-4141, 1073 Rear Wisconsin Ave)*, in an alley south of M St, has attracted such nationally known artists as Dizzy Gillespie and Ahmed Jamal to its elegant candlelit supper club. The cover charge is steep ($13 to $40) and so are the drinks and Creole specialties. The crowd is largely professional and racially mixed.

For a more casual and less-expensive evening, the under-30 gang favors ***The Saloun*** *(☎ 202-965-4900, 3239 M St NW)*. This place features blues on Saturday and live jazz other nights (slip in before 9 pm to evade the $3 cover). Its clientele is much more varied than the usual M St prowlers.

Old Glory All American Barbecue (see Places to Eat) can be a good alternative to spending a bundle of money on the cover at the other jazz and blues caves in the neighborhood. There is live music (usually blues) here on Tuesday, Thursday, Friday, and

Saturday. The cover is only $2. Folks come in from the 'burbs to kick up their heels, and dress is more casual here than most of G-town, with plenty of tank tops on women.

Garrett's *(☎ 202-333-1033, 3003 M St NW)* is another one of Georgetown's bars on the English-pub theme, with a copper-top bar, wood floors, and limited seating. You can purchase bottled domestic beer for about $1.50 during the evening happy hour, and this place can get packed by 6 pm on Wednesday, Friday, and Saturday. The scene on such nights is definitely a meat market, featuring the young, beautiful, and well-educated types having a fling with their first jobs or grad school in the big city. There are actually three bars here; head for the outdoor patio to escape the smoke.

Mr Smith's *(☎ 202-333-3104, 3104 M St NW)* is kind of a downscale clone of Garrett's in that it is smaller and draws a slightly younger, more collegiate crowd (although you can see a lot of the same folks – often clutches of young women – hopping from one pub to the other looking for their complements). Drinks are cheap during the evening happy hour, with some beers running only $1; there are also 50¢ appetizers. The crowd can be so thick around the front-room bar that you can't help but meet people because it's impossible to drink your suds without rubbing bodies with at least two folks at once. There are live bands on weekends playing indoors or on the back patio, depending on the weather (no cover charge).

Clyde's *(☎ 202-333-9180, 3236 M St NW)* has been a Georgetown institution for more than 35 years, and a lot of us caught our first hangover from this place back in the days when the drinking age in DC was still 18 and this was the neighborhood's first saloon. Times have changed. Clyde's has definitely gone upscale and no longer offers cheap booze at happy hour (although there are half-price entrees). The crowd is mostly yuppies trying to recall their wild and crazy youth in Georgetown. Now they come in for a drink before having a late dinner. The kitchen serves typical pub fare and is open at least until midnight on weekends.

Looking similar and appealing to a slightly younger after-work crowd in pin-striped suits, *J Paul's Tavern* (☎ 202-333-3450, 3218 M St NW) is a fancy, old-style oyster bar. Its Sunday brunches are popular.

Champions (☎ 202-965-4005, 1206 Wisconsin Ave NW) is a sports bar a league or two above your average beer-and-baseball place, fans. The place is decorated with rafts of signed photographs, balls, and uniforms. The crowd here is mostly frat boys and/or jocks from the local universities. A lot of their female counterparts drift in on weekend nights, when the dance floor downstairs gets packed and the whole place turns into a meat market for hard-body types.

Music City Roadhouse (see Places to Eat), has 'cheap bastard' specials that pull in the under-30 crowd for live alternative or blues jams. Curiously, the decor in this converted foundry is pure country & western. The crowd is yuppie and very gregarious. You won't be alone here for long.

Currently, the best place to get your dance on in this part of town is the *Rhino Bar & Pump House* (☎ 202-333-3150, 3295 M St NW). This venue used to be Winston's, which was a notorious dance and grope palace, and while the name has changed, the crowd of mostly college types still leave their inhibitions at the door. The upstairs has a diner/gas-station/pool-hall theme. 'Dark dance pit' is the best description of the downstairs bar.

For a true college bar experience right out of the movies (it was a set in the film *St Elmo's Fire*), catch the scene at the *Third Edition* (☎ 202-333-3700, 1218 Wisconsin Ave NW). Lines start early on weekends. The DJ on the upstairs bar cranks a real mix of dance tunes from hip hop to classic rock to '80s disco. You can head for the patio and the tiki bar out back on the patio for a breather. Weekend cover is usually $5.

Dupont Circle While the Circle has a well-deserved reputation for its gay clubs and bars (see Gay & Lesbian Venues, later), this neighborhood is a happening spot for straight night owls as well.

The Big Hunt (☎ 202-785-0609, 1345 Connecticut Ave NW) advertises itself as the 'happy hunting ground for humans in pursuit of a mate, food & drink' and largely lives up to its name. This is especially true on Monday nights, when the crowd descends (GW students, yuppies in jeans, and government staffers). They come in for happy-hour specials on booze and hang around to munch on 15¢ chicken wings, play pool, get a little crazy, and maybe meet the loves of their lives.

Brickskeller (☎ 202-628-0202, 1523 22nd St NW) claims to have the world's largest collection of beer (more than 800 brands). You might think the Brickskeller is Mecca for the city's beer snobs, but in fact you will find the crowd is a mix of college students and yuppies who usually don't order anything fancier than a bottle of Sam Adams. With beer prices starting at about $2.50 and no happy hour, you've got to be feeling a little flush to drink here, and maybe that's the point. The old townhouse is broken up into a lot of rooms and has three bars.

Childe Harold (☎ 202-483-6700, 1610 20th St NW) is another clubby little pub below street level, appealing to the working gentry (over 30), who show up in coats and ties after work to tell horror stories about their bosses and clients. There's patio seating in the summer. Domestic beer runs about $2 during the evening happy hour.

Buffalo Billiards (☎ 202-331-7665, 1333 New Hampshire Ave NW) is one of the most popular places to cue it up in all of Northwest DC. There are at least 20 pool tables here and six dartboards to attract the college and yuppie crowd to this bright cave. But table prices can be a little steep, with a range of $8 to $14 for two players per hour.

Lulu's Mardi Gras Club (☎ 202-861-5858, 1217 22nd St NW), at M St NW, is party central for this part of town. We are talking eight rooms, two dance floors, seven bars, 50¢ beer before 10 pm, and different dance themes for different nights. On the weekends, you get house and industrial on the downstairs floor and '70s and '80s retro upstairs. Lines start earlier here. Expect a $5 cover. The crowd is under 25. (Also see Places to Eat.)

If you're looking for a dance club that's a bit funkier and drawing more African

Americans and college students, try **Bravo Bravo** (☎ 202-223-5330, 1001 Connecticut Ave NW), an enormous basement place under a pharmacy. There is a raised dance floor, several bars, and either a DJ or live music. Expect to dance to reggae, house, or Ethiopian music. This club admits people over 18.

Some of the Euro crowd also drifts into **Rumors** (☎ 202-466-7378, 1900 M St NW), but this is mostly a college and yuppie meat market for the under-30s gang who plan on getting a little friskier than their comrades partying in Georgetown. The setting is a gin joint posing as an Adirondack boat house, with garage doors that open onto a patio in nice weather. A DJ spins dance classics Tuesday to Sunday.

It seems like the DC-area alumni groups from a host of Big 10 universities and party schools hold regular informal get-togethers at the **Mad Hatter** (☎ 202-883-1495, 1831 M St NW). Check out the free buffet of appetizers midweek and the 50¢ oysters on Friday. DJs generally play rock Wednesday to Friday. If you are over 30 and in the mood to relive your college madness, you will find like-minded souls here to join you.

The local yuppie crowd likes to hang out at the **Sign of the Whale** (☎ 202-785-1110, 1825 M St), alongside the strip joints such as Joanna's and Camelot. This place is a cozy English-style pub complete with a fireplace and high ceilings. The back bar (up some stairs) has dancing to DJ mixes of rock Tuesday to Saturday.

Kramerbooks and Afterwords Café (see Places to Eat) has evolved from a cafe scene into something of a meat market in recent years. For decades, this has been the place to see and be seen in the Circle. The advent of live music on the upstairs stage has gotten the bookniks to abandon their browsing, sip some fermented beverages and mingle, mingle, mingle. Stop in on a Thursday night: You could find your date for the weekend whether you are straight, gay, or bi.

MCCXXIII (see Places to Eat, earlier) is the neighborhood's popular hangout for the Euro crowd who staff the embassies along Massachusetts Ave. Dinner wraps up here by 10:30 pm, and the parade of ladies in tight cocktail dresses and dark men with slick hair and Italian suits begins to flow through the door. Inside, the DJ plays jazz, R&B, Top 40, techno, and disco cuts while folks sip martinis before shimmying onto the dance floor.

Adams-Morgan & Woodley Park In Adams-Morgan, **Asylum** (☎ 202-319-9353, 2471 18th St NW) is a small dungeonlike place (there are fake rock walls, battle axes, and swords around). It's definitely the place to come drink on a Saturday when you're down to your last few bucks. Bottles of Shiner beer (there's a reason you have never heard of it) cost 25¢ before 7 pm, and the price increases 50¢ per hour thereafter. The crowd is definitely under 30 – a mix of local males and young women from the suburbs who come in on a spree as pairs to check out the guys and catch a cheap buzz.

You will find one of DC's other great dives nearly across 18th St at **Millie & Al's** (☎ 202-387-8131, 2461 18th St NW). This bar gets all fired up during happy hour (4 to 8 pm Tuesday to Friday). The crowd is college kids, recent grads, and softball teams who pile in for 99¢ beers. Some folks actually try to watch the constant diet of sporting events playing on the two TVs, but mostly everyone is here to tease and be teased.

On the opposite end of the spectrum, you have Felix (see Places to Eat). Its smoky plate-glass windows, Art Deco cityscape of New York, and martini bar appeal to the yuppie and Euro crowd who want to walk on the wild side but can't quite find their tribes after dinner in most of the gin mills of Adams-Morgan.

Downstairs, the sound system cranks Sinatra, some folks smoke cigars, and most people drink beer or one of about six options of Bordeaux. There is live music seven nights a week (generally mellow blues or jazz) in the upstairs lounge. If you are an over-30 professional type, Felix is a pretty good pickup scene around 9 pm on weekends: you'll meet a lot of folks who have come in from the suburbs for dinner and now are looking for someone to lead on the path to a little debauchery, or at least to a manic dance club. The cover here is $5 at 10 pm on weekends.

Crush (☎ 202-319-1111, 2323 18th St NW) is for the barely legal crowd looking for a hyper dance club. You will find it about a block down the street from Felix, on the other side, and you'll know you are in the right spot because of the line Thursday to Saturday. Some of the city's most popular DJs work the long, narrow dance floor upstairs. The music is a mix of funk, house, soul, and hip hop. The crowd is generally under 25, and you can get in and not drink if you are over 18. Beer is $1 on Thirsty Thursdays.

Madame's Organ (☎ 202-667-5370, 2461 18th St NW) has moved three times in the last six years, but it remains a wonderfully raunchy blues club. Attractive alternative types pack this place after about 9:30 pm Thursday to Saturday, and things can get pretty nasty on the dance floor. You can play pool or whatever upstairs in Big Daddy's Love Lounge and Pickup Joint.

Club Heaven & Club Hell (☎ 202-667-4355, 2327 18th St NW) is a popular venue for the under-30 gang. Heaven is the dance club upstairs in this old townhouse, where you can jam to '80s music. Hell is the basement pub with billiards, where you can look a little rumpled. You will need neater clothes and $5 to get past the gatekeeper (St Peter?) at Heaven. Both places trade on funhouse-style decor and lots of black lights.

Chief Ike's Mambo Room (☎ 202-332-2211, 1725 Columbia Rd NW) caters to a similar age group. But ain't nobody getting dressed up here. This club's intentionally wacky voodoo decor is hot with the post-college gang who hang around DC working as political staffers. There are theme nights, such as mambo Mondays and blues Thursdays; weekends have a DJ who spins everything from disco to hip hop. There is a $3 cover for the dance floor.

Habana Village (☎ 202-462-6310, 1834 Columbia Rd NW) has to be one of the best Latino venues in the city. This old townhouse has a cosmopolitan bar and romantic back-room downstairs, where you can sip a Cuba Libre (rum & cola) and nibble tapas in front of the fireplace on a cool evening. But after 10:30 pm Thursday to Saturday, you will find a scene on the upstairs dance floor that would be hard to duplicate in Havana. A DJ spins out flaming salsa and merengue hits to a packed crowd, which is a mix of Latinos and other Washingtonians. Men are usually 30 to 50 and pay a $5 cover. Women are significantly younger and get in free. Tight dresses are definitely hip. If your dance steps are a little shaky, show up at 9:30 pm on weekend nights for free salsa lessons.

Bukom Cafe (☎ 202-265-4600, 2442 18th St NW) is a West African bar and restaurant with some of the best live reggae in the city. The music starts after about 9:30 pm Wednesday to Saturday, and the place is packed by 11 pm. There is hardly any place to dance, but nobody cares – everybody kind of stands in one place, bounces to the music, and bumps their body against other people. The crowd is 25 to 50 and is a spicy mix of black and white folk who can get down with His Majesty Ja and love to share a tune and a laugh.

In Woodley Park, you will find *City Blues* (☎ 202-232-2300, 2651 Connecticut Ave NW) facing the Woodley Park/Zoo Metro entrance. It occupies an old Victorian town-house, where you can wander from room to room through the smoky haze listening to the blues and nursing your $5 drink (the minimum; a cover charge may also apply). The club is a hot scene for over-30 jazz devotees.

Cafe Lautrec (see Places to Eat), voted best jazz club by local critics, is a small restaurant infamous for its wild bartender, Johne Forget, who tap dances on the bar most weekends. The cafe asks for a $6 food/drink minimum. Preppie types usually stick to the patio here; hip folk dive into the smoky jazz cave ambiance.

Shaw The New U District has some of the city's best venues for alternative music and offers multicultural styles and crowds. The *Chi Cha Lounge* (☎ 202-234-8400, 1624 U St NW) has been voted one of the best bars and meat markets in DC by several of the local entertainment guides. The draw here is the eclectic atmosphere, which might be described as Sultan of Brunei meets Frank Sinatra and Thelonius Monk in Ecuador. For $15, you can buy some potent Arabian tobacco (enough for a group) and smoke it from a hookah at your table on Sunday, Monday, and Tuesday. You can also get Andean food here. There's live jazz on weekends. The crowd is under 30, funky, and hip.

The *Black Cat* (☎ *202-667-7960, 1831 14th St*) hosts hard-core bands such as Girls Against Boys, the Zimmermans, and Jimmie's Chicken Shack; the back room is reserved for poetry readings and other groovy events. The crowd is under 35 and very alternative.

The *State of the Union* (☎ *202-588-8810, 1357 U St NW*) books many of the same artists, and weird DJs run the garagelike back room for dancing. The sickle-studded Soviet decor is a nostalgic look back at the Cold War (there's Russian food too). One of the best things about this place is it attracts one of the most ethnically diverse crowds in the city. Most patrons are under 35.

Another hip scene a few doors down is *Republic Gardens* (☎ *202-232-2710, 1335 U St*). There are five rooms, four bars, and Renaissance furnishings. Hip hop, R&B, and reggae spin from the DJ booth. The crowd is largely African American, well healed, and under 35. The cover ranges from $5 to $10.

So much for the classics. The *New Vegas Lounge* (☎ *202-483-3971, 1415 P St NW*) plays the blues with an anything-goes jam (bring your ax if you want to join the fun) on Tuesday and Wednesday; there's no cover. Greats such as Wilson Pickett have played here, but the scene is a bit strange, as the bands are largely black and the crowd is largely white. Thursday night is college night, when you get in for free with a college ID.

The *9:30 Club* (☎ *202-265-0930, 815 V St NW*) is a popular venue for alternative music. This place has four bars and two levels and holds 1000 rockin' souls. Basically, folks come here to see a show and dance a bit, so the crowd changes according to the band. Call to find out who's playing and what the cover will be.

The *Metro Cafe* (☎ *202-518-7900, 1522 14th St NW*) is another concert venue in the

U St district, but with only 175 seats, this club has an intimate (and smoky) ambiance. You usually get three bands a night (after 10 pm) for a cover of $5. The sound varies from acoustic or ska to Latin or country. The crowd ranges from 20-somethings to over 40, depending on the music.

Stetson's (☎ *202-265-6918, 1619 U St NW*) is your place on U St to catch a buzz and a munch on little money. From 4:30 to 7:30 pm, drafts run $1.50, and sometimes you will find even cheaper specials: On Monday, you can get a mug of Rolling Rock for $1 and a burger for $2. Interestingly, the gang here is largely yuppie (Democrat types) who live in the townhouses just down the hill toward Dupont Circle.

If the club scene is too much to contemplate and you are in the U St district, consider Polly's Cafe (see Places to Eat). This is a longstanding neighborhood pub with a fireplace for raw weather and a small patio for fair days and nights. Polly's is a great place for couples to start out a night on the town by splitting a pitcher of Rolling Rock ($8).

Gay & Lesbian Venues

Dupont Circle and – more recently – Capitol Hill are focal points in the city for the gay and lesbian communities, and both areas offer a lot of entertainment. In the Dupont Circle neighborhood, the bars, clubs, cafes, and restaurants on 17th and P Sts are the heart of the gay scene, and *JR's* (☎ *202-328-0090, 1519 17th St NW*) is at the heart of the heart. This place draws a crowd of professional men ages 20 to 40 and gets packed on weekend evenings. Everyone seems to know each other here, which can be a little daunting to a newcomer. But folks are friendly, and if you hang around for more than a beer, you'll make some acquaintances.

Mr P's/The Loft (☎ *202-293-1064, 2147 P St NW*) appeals to the same age group of men, but here the crowd is more casual and very hip to leather. There are go-go boys, darts, and video.

Almost across the street, *Escándalo* (☎ *202-822-8909, 2122 P St NW*) is a full-service restaurant that also has a bar scene attracting Latino gays and lesbians.

Gay & Lesbian DC

The seat of more than 30 national gay and lesbian organizations and more than 300 social, athletic, religious, and political support groups, DC is one of the safest and most gay-friendly cities in the US. Today, gays and lesbians such as Congressman Barnie Frank, Sabrina Sojourner, and David Catania are respected workers for equal rights on both the national and local level. The *Washington Blade*, the weekly paper for DC's gay community, regularly has more than 100 pages, while the city boasts of more than 35 bars catering to predominantly gay and lesbian clientele.

DC has always had a rich gay scene, but most of it was underground until 1965, when the Mattachine Society organized the first gay picket of the White House. Legends about life in these private clubs date back to diaries from the 1920s of a gay federal employee named Jeb Alexander, including a story about jazz singer Billie Holiday's sizzling close encounter on stage with Miss Kentucky. Other legends date back to the experience of gay black men at Nob Hill in the late 1950s and Frank Kemeny's struggle in the same era to hold onto his federal job after he came out. He never got his federal job back, but he was the first openly gay person appointed to a DC government position (the Human Rights Commission, 1974).

DC's gay community has organized and hosted gay-rights marches in 1979, 1987, 1993, and 2000. The last two marches brought more than 750,000 activists to the capital. Such rallies highlight how gay pride has become an integral quality of DC's character at the outset of the 21st century.

★★★★★★★★★★★

For years, *Badlands* (☎ 202-296-0505, *1415 22nd St NW*), near P St, has had the reputation of being the most steamy gay dance club in the city, and the reputation is well deserved. On weekends, the huge dance floor is a packed, strobe-lit scene pulsing to heavy house sounds. Come early, because lines at the door can get long. The cover is $5.

If you want to make the scene at the oldest gay bar still in operation in America, head for *Nob Hill* (☎ 202-797-1101, *1101 Kenyon St NW*), near Howard University in Columbia Heights. This place opened in 1957 and can still get over-the-top. There are male strippers on Saturdays. The crowd is diverse in both age and race.

For the best-known lesbian bar in the city, head downtown to *Hung Jury* (☎ 202-279-3212, *1819 H St NW*). This place has been popular for almost 20 years. You will meet a lot of college-age women (and some older women). The music is hard-core dance rhythms; the dress is largely jeans and T-shirts. Friday and Saturday nights have a $5 cover, and those 18 to 20 are welcome (for dancing, not drinking).

Phase One (☎ 202-544-6831, *525 8th St SE*) is a popular lesbian bar on Capitol Hill offering pool tables and dancing for a mixed crowd.

Elan (☎ 202-544-6406, *1129 Pennsylvania Ave SE*) is one of the newcomers to the lesbian bar scene on Capitol Hill. This place attracts a mixed group of women to its lounge atmosphere. On Friday night, you will find country & western dancing.

DC's biggest gay club is south of Capitol Hill at *Tracks 2000* (☎ 202-488-3320, *1111 1st St SE*). It's a huge warehouse-turned-disco; the crowd is flamboyant, with a healthy selection of shirtless leather boys, club kids, and trannies. The music is usually throbbing house or industrial, but Sunday afternoons feature line dancing (with lessons). There is sometimes pickup volleyball during good weather. The cover ranges from $5 to $8, depending on what time you arrive. Since Tracks 2000 is in a seedy part of town, take a cab.

Remington's (☎ 202-543-3113, *639 Pennsylvania Ave SE*) is another popular Capitol Hill bar/club. The theme is country & western, and the 30- to 50-year-olds who come here dress the part. The Sunday afternoon tea dance starts at 4 pm and features bottled beer for less than $1.50.

Also on Capitol Hill, you will find **Zieg-field's** (☎ *202-554-5141, 1345 Half St SE*). This restaurant bar appeals to the straight and gay alike and features DC's premier drag shows.

Bachelor's Mill (☎ *202-544-1931, 1104 8th St SE*) rocks with house music and dancing that attract a lot of black men. There are theme nights – some for women, some featuring drag king and queen contests.

The Edge/Wet (☎ *202-488-1200, 52 & 56 L St SE, 2nd floor*) is another hot Capitol Hill bar/club sometimes frequented by gay legislators. There are male go-go dancers and showers for anybody who gets too fired up on the dance floor.

Cinemas

First-run movies play at cinemas throughout DC; for starters, there's the nine-screen **AMC** (☎ *703-998-4262*) at Union Station and the **Cineplex Odeon Foundry** (☎ *202-333-3456*) at the C&O Canal in Georgetown (see the newspaper for complete listings). Alternative and foreign films are regularly shown at the Kennedy Center's **American Film Institute** cinema (☎ *202-785-4600*) and the Cineplex Odeon's **Outer Circle** (☎ *202-244-3116, 4849 Wisconsin Ave NW*) – north on Wisconsin Ave at the DC border. Also check for film showings at museums (the Hirshhorn regularly shows art films) and the Library of Congress (more classic films).

SPECTATOR SPORTS

The popular **Washington Redskins** (☎ *301-276-6060*) play football at the new $160 million, 78,600-seat FedEx Field just east of DC in Maryland. Games are nearly always sold out, but you can buy 'scalped' tickets around the stadium at exorbitant prices, or buy tickets to the two preseason games that usually take place toward the end of summer. From DC, take E Capitol St (Central Ave) to Harry S Truman North, turn right on Lottsford Rd and follow it to Arena Drive. On Metro, get off at Cheverly, Landover, or Addison Road stations and take the shuttle.

The **DC United** (☎ *703-478-6600*) professional soccer team hosts competitions at Robert F Kennedy (RFK) Stadium (☎ 202-547-9077) at E Capitol and 22nd Sts SE (Ⓜ Stadium/Armory). Call RFK Stadium for the current schedule.

The **NBA Wizards**, formerly the too-violent-sounding Bullets, play basketball downtown at the MCI Center (☎ 202-628-3200) and in the suburbs at the USAir Arena (☎ 301-350-3400) in Landover, Maryland (take the Beltway to exit 17A and follow signs). The MCI Center is also the home of the **Capitals** (☎ *202-366-2277*), DC's NHL ice-hockey team, and the WNBA **Washington Mystics** (☎ *202-628-3200*) professional women's basketball team.

DC's favorite college football team is Georgetown's **Hoyas** (☎ *202-687-4692*).

Competitive crew racing attracts large crowds to the shores of the Potomac around the Thompson Boat Center. You can sometimes watch local and embassy teams play soccer, rugby, polo, and cricket on the Mall. Call the National Park Service (☎ 202-619-7222) for dates.

Since the Washington Senators left DC for Texas some 20 years back, the city has had no professional baseball team, and fans have adopted the Baltimore Orioles for hometown-vicinity favorites (see the Baltimore chapter).

SHOPPING

People don't come to DC for the shopping, but you can find some good items nevertheless. Classic DC souvenirs include shredded money from the Bureau of Engraving and Printing, copies of the Declaration of Independence from the National Archives, and stuffed pandas from the National Zoo.

Museum gift shops sell a wonderful selection of things related to their specialties. At the Air and Space Museum, you can buy sophisticated model airplanes and freeze-dried astronaut food. The Museum of American Art sells oddball handmade jewelry. The National Gallery of Art sells prints for as little as $2. The National Building Museum sells arty interior furnishings, the Renwick Gallery sells hand-blown glass and other crafts, and the American History Museum sells products from every region of the US – from Vermont maple syrup and stone-ground Carolina grits to Navaho pottery and Inuit icons. Also look for fun and arty mobiles, great children's toys and trinkets, and, of course, fabulous books on art, architecture, history, science, and culture.

Along 18th St in Adams-Morgan, you'll find great vintage and modern clothing boutiques, music stores, and thrift stores with weird retro finds. Ethnic markets and stores may yield votive candles and frilly crinoline party dresses for little girls. The New U area at U St NW around 14th St has a much smaller but similar collection of shops, several of which specialize in African items such as masks and wooden carvings.

The upscale Dupont Circle district has dozens of art galleries exhibiting paintings, sculpture, and artifacts for sale. This is also where you'll find Benetton, Gap, and Polo.

Georgetown along M St NW (from around 30th to 35th Sts) also has trendy boutiques and national chains such as Urban Outfitters, Victoria's Secret, and the Body Shop. Georgetown Park is a huge shopping mall at 3222 M St NW with Eddie Bauer–type clothing. (President Clinton used to cause a stir by shopping here for his Christmas gifts.)

Shopping complexes downtown are good places to get out of the weather and have a snack, but you'd hardly head there just to shop. However, Union Station does have a few nicer clothing stores as well as an Appalachian Spring store with regional crafts.

Of course, the bookstores – new, used, historical, political, art-related – are wonderful (see Bookstores under Information, earlier in this chapter).

GETTING THERE & AWAY
Air
Flights into Washington, DC, land at one of three area airports: Ronald Reagan Washington National Airport (☎ 703-661-2700), Washington-Dulles International Airport (☎ 703-471-4242), or Baltimore-Washington International Airport (BWI; ☎ 410-859-7034, 800-435-9294). The first is by far the

most convenient; it's just across the river from DC, and the Metro stops right there. Dulles is 26 miles west, and BWI is 35 miles north. Major car rental agencies are well represented at all three airports. Also see the Getting There & Away chapter for specific information on airlines and travel in the region.

Bus
Greyhound buses stop at the Greyhound Terminal (☎ 800-231-2222), at 1005 1st St NE, on the corner of L St near Capitol Hill. Peter Pan Trailways buses (☎ 800-343-9999) also arrive and depart from the Greyhound Terminal. Note that the rundown neighborhood becomes deserted at night, and the nearest Metro station is eight blocks south (via 1st St SE) at Union Station. Cabs are usually available at the station; travelers should hail or call one. Don't try walking across town from the bus station at night.

Train
Passenger trains from around the country arrive directly downtown into Union Station, the 'flagship' terminal of the Amtrak network – it's the best way to arrive in the capital. Located at 50 Massachusetts Ave NE on Capitol Hill, Union Station (☎ 202-371-9441) connects directly to DC's Metro subway system. Call ☎ 800-872-7245 for Amtrak information and reservations, or pick up schedules at Union Station.

Amtrak's express Metroliners travel between DC and New Haven, Connecticut. And in the spring of 2000, the new superfast Acela express trains also started running between New York and DC at speeds in excess of 150mph. Amtrak will get you to major cities in less time for premium fares. It's an extremely civilized way for serious visitors to travel conveniently from downtown Manhattan to downtown DC (around $95 one way unless you hold a discount ticket). See the Getting There & Away chapter.

Also from Union Station, the MARC commuter train (☎ 800-325-7245) runs to Baltimore weekdays only; fares run $6. Other MARC trains serve Maryland's northern suburbs and run up to Harpers Ferry, West Virginia.

Car & Motorcycle

Running north-south to DC, I-95 merges into the I-495 Beltway that surrounds the metro region. Approaching from the northeast, Route 1 leads into Rhode Island Ave, and the Baltimore-Washington Expressway (Route 295) leads to Route 50 and New York Ave.

From the south, I-395 takes you to downtown near the Mall by the Memorial Bridge or the 14th St Bridge. From the west, I-66 runs from Virginia to the Mall area, but you should avoid congested rush hours here unless you have at least two passengers and can use the zippy HOV lane (drivers are ticketed for driving in the carpool lane with fewer than three people per vehicle).

Coming from the north on the Beltway, take the Connecticut Ave exit marked Chevy Chase to get to Adams-Morgan and Dupont Circle, or take the Wisconsin Ave exit to get to Georgetown.

GETTING AROUND

Most major sights and hotel districts are efficiently served by the Metro subway system, and DC's unusual street grid can be difficult to navigate by car (not to mention parking) but wonderful to explore on foot. Given these factors, your best bet is to forget the car altogether or leave it in an outlying neighborhood.

Cabs are plentiful and (relatively) cheap for getting around town day or night. For groups of three or four, taking a cab may be near comparable in price to the sum of Metro fares for each – and a whole lot more convenient. All three major airports can be accessed through a variety of ground-transportation options.

For bicycling information, see Bicycling, under Activities, earlier.

To/From the Airports

To get to town from Ronald Reagan Washington National Airport, follow signs to the Metro station. At the station, take either the westward Blue Line or eastward Yellow Line – both end up downtown. The fare will probably be less than $2, depending on your destination and time of travel. A taxi to or from downtown will cost between $12 and $15. Taxis leaving from the airport tack on an additional $1 fee.

From the Washington-Dulles International Airport, the Washington Flyer Express (☎ 703-417-8400, 888-927-4359) runs shuttle vans to and from the convention center and Dulles Airport. Buses run every half hour weekdays from early morning to around 9:30 pm and less frequently on weekends (call for exact schedule). The fare is $16 one way and $26 roundtrip, payable with cash only. Buses also take people to and from the Metro stop at West Falls Church, Virginia, for $10 one way. A taxi to or from Dulles costs around $47.

There are many options for getting to and from Baltimore-Washington International Airport. For complete information, see the Getting There & Away chapter. A taxi between BWI and downtown DC costs about $57. SuperShuttle vans run 24 hours a day. Call ☎ 800-258-3826 24 hours in advance for reservations and pickup service. The fare is $28 one way and $56 roundtrip.

On weekdays only, you can take the MARC commuter train (☎ 800-325-7245) between DC's Union Station and a terminal near BWI; once there, you'll be shuttled to and from the airport free of charge. The fare is $5 one way and $9 roundtrip. Amtrak also stops at BWI, but the fare from the airport to DC can be as high as $15 if you have to take a reservations-only train. (See the Getting There & Away chapter.)

Metrorail

DC boasts a sleek modern subway network (☎ 202-637-7000 for route information 6 am to 11:30 pm). The Metro runs conveniently to most major sights, hotel and business districts, and out to the Maryland and Virginia suburbs (see the color Metrorail System map). Trains and stations are well marked, well maintained, well lit, climate-controlled, reasonably priced, decently staffed, reliable, and safe. Trains run 5:30 am to midnight weekdays and 8 am to 1 am weekends. Parking is plentiful at certain outlying stations. The time limit for parking is 24 hours, and there's a $2.25 charge between 2 and 10:30 pm (no charge if you arrive before or leave after these times).

The network consists of five color-coded lines – blue, yellow, orange, green, and red – that intersect at a total of seven transfer points. The trickiest part of navigating the system is determining and remembering the final destination of the train you want, because trains and platforms are identified by their outlying terminus (names that are otherwise irrelevant to in-town travelers).

To ride the subway, buy a computerized, paper fare card in any amount from self-service machines inside the station entrance (buy one for each passenger). Keep the card handy; you'll need it to both enter *and* exit Metro stations. To exit, slip your fare card in the slot on the turnstile.

If the card's value is the same as the fare, the turnstile keeps the card and the gates open. If the card's value is greater, the turnstile returns the card to you with the remaining value printed on it and the gates open. If the card's value is less than the fare, the turnstile returns the card to you and the gates don't open; if this happens, you need to use an Addfare machine, which tells you how much money to add. Other machines inside the gates dispense free bus transfers – remember to get these before exiting if you need a bus connection.

Rates are determined by the distance traveled and time of day (there's a premium for traveling at rush hour). The minimum fare is $1.10. The maximum value the machines can dispense is a $20 card. Machines give up to $4.95 change in coins.

A one-day excursion Metrorail pass costs $5, and it's good for unlimited travel weekdays starting at 9:30 am or weekends all day. A Fast Pass is good for one week of unlimited travel and costs $25; for $30, you can get a Fast Pass good on both Metrorail and Metrobus. Senior discounts are available to holders of the free Metro Senior Citizen ID

Card. All these special cards are available from the Sales & Information office in the Metro Center station at 12th and F Sts NW. Call ☎ 202-637-7000 for the nine other branches and information about additional local outlets.

Metrobus

DC's Metrobus system provides relatively clean and efficient bus service throughout the city and to outlying suburbs. Call ☎ 202-637-7000 for route information, schedules, and fares (the minimum fare is $1.10; 25¢ with a Metro transfer). Automatic fare machines accept paper dollars; you need the exact fare or a Fast Pass (see Metrorail).

Some handy routes are the L2, which runs along 18th St in the heart of Adams-Morgan (connecting to Metro stations at Woodley Park and Foggy Bottom), and the D5, which runs from Union Station to Georgetown's central M St strip (you can board along K St downtown).

You can pick up Metrobus route maps at the transit store in the Metro Center station, among other locales.

Car & Motorcycle

All major car rental agencies are represented in town and at the airports, and most have offices at Union Station (refer to the Getting Around chapter for national toll-free numbers). Weekly rates are often the best deal.

Unfortunately for young drivers, most national agencies in DC won't rent to anyone under 25. Some local car rental companies will rent to drivers over 21 with a major credit card, but their rates may not be competitive.

In addition to the city's geometric street pattern and many confusing traffic roundabouts, certain lanes of some streets change direction during rush hour, and some two-way streets become one-way streets. But still, DC's not New York – outside of rush hours, driving around town during the day is no big deal. Finding street parking can, however, be a hassle in certain congested neighborhoods, most notably in Georgetown, Adams-Morgan, and around the Mall.

Taxi

Taxicabs are plentiful in the central city and are generally easy to find; hail them with a wave of the hand. The fare structure works on a zone system: The city is cut into eight concentric zones (zone maps are posted in cabs), and rates are determined by how many zones you cross, and also by the number of passengers and time of day (there's an evening rush-hour surcharge).

You pay $4 to travel in one zone, $5.50 for two zones, and $1.50 for each additional passenger. There are additional fees for extra services (eg, large bags, ordering a cab by phone, traveling during a snow emergency).

Try Diamond (☎ 202-387-6200), Yellow (☎ 202-544-1212), and Capitol (☎ 202-546-2400) – three major cab companies that come when you call.

Around Washington, DC

The District of Columbia is at the heart of a metropolitan region that expands into suburban Virginia and Maryland, and a number of sights closely associated with Washington, DC, lie within the I-495 Beltway that rings the city. Many other attractions lie within a day trip of DC.

One of the DC area's most visited sights is Arlington National Cemetery, which is best known for its Tomb of the Unknowns. The Pentagon, also located in Arlington, is the headquarters of the powerful Department of Defense. The massive five-sided structure – said to be the largest office complex in the world – can be visited on a guided tour designed around security measures.

The city of Arlington offers resources for DC metro-area visitors. In fact, there's a cluster of budget motels off I-495 in Arlington, just south of the Potomac River, that are inexpensive and convenient for visitors traveling by car.

Alexandria is also a popular destination for DC visitors looking for a short day trip

out of the city. The compact riverside 'Old Town' lures walkers with its colonial architecture, beautiful historic houses, churches, storefronts, and taverns alongside modern boutiques, restaurants, and cafes.

In so-called Beltway Maryland, you can sample the hip, upscale restaurant and entertainment scene in Bethesda, or head to Takoma Park for a smaller and funkier selection of places to eat, drink, and sleep. For a rural experience, hikers join the C&O Canal towpath in Georgetown and follow the Potomac River north into the woods of Maryland (see C&O Canal National Historic Park in the Western Maryland chapter). Other attractions inside the Beltway include the Paul Garber Facility (the Smithsonian Air and Space Museum's restoration and storage facility), and the Surratt House, where John Wilkes Booth and his accomplice planned the assassination of Lincoln.

Day trips from DC by train, bus, or car will carry you farther afield to Chesapeake Bay and Allegheny Mountain adventures. For key sites beyond the DC Beltway, see the Maryland and Virginia chapters.

Highlights

- Arlington National Cemetery – the most famous final resting place in the world
- Cobblestone streets and an aura of history in Old Town Alexandria
- The lively restaurant and club scene in Bethesda, Maryland
- *Enola Gay* and other warbirds at the Paul Garber Facility

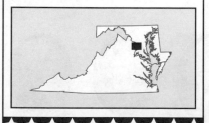

Beltway Virginia

Arlington and Alexandria are both fascinating cities in their own right – the former has the world's most famous cemetery and the Pentagon; the latter has its quaint and well-preserved Old Town. Both also shelter high-tech industries and a fair slice of US brain power (some of it atrophying in bureaucratic service!).

ARLINGTON
When Washington, DC, the nation's capital-district-to-be, was in the planning stages, it was envisaged as the shape of a square, with the Potomac River as a nongeometric but natural dividing line. In 1847, the land south of the river was deemed unnecessary, so the Arlington sector (named after George

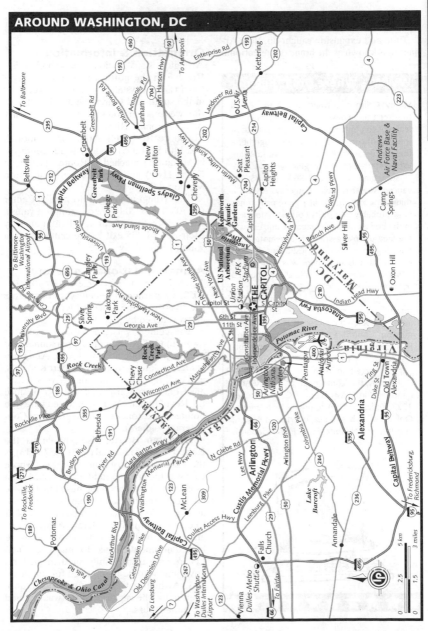

AROUND WASHINGTON, DC

Washington Parke Custis' Arlington House) was returned to the control of Virginia.

Time and expansion caught up. Now Arlington is known as the home of the national cemetery and the Pentagon, the world's most renowned defense facility.

Orientation & Information

Arlington is a collection of neighborhoods – Rosslyn in the north across from Georgetown (DC), Crystal City and Pentagon City in the south, and Clarendon and Ballston in the west. Arlington's northern boundary is the Potomac River, crossed by the Key, Theodore Roosevelt, Arlington Memorial, and 14th St (I-395) Bridges. To the southeast is Alexandria, reached by Route 1 (Jefferson Davis Hwy) and the George Washington Memorial Parkway.

The Arlington Visitor Information Center (☎ 703-358-5720, www.co.arlington.va.us), 735 S 18th St, is near the Pentagon City Metro and I-395 exit 9. The center is open 9 am to 5 pm daily.

Arlington National Cemetery

The 612-acre national cemetery (☎ 703-607-8052, www.arlingtoncemetery.com) is across the river from the Lincoln Memorial and is easily reached by Metro.

The cemetery is the burial ground for more than 225,000 military personnel and their dependents, along with such American leaders as John F Kennedy, Robert Kennedy, and civil rights leader Medgar Evers. Veterans from every war the US has fought since the Revolutionary War are interred here (the pointed headstones mark the graves of Confederate soldiers).

Arlington House, also known as the Robert E Lee Memorial (☎ 703-557-0613), is the former home of Robert E Lee, whose wife was the great-granddaughter of Martha Washington and her first husband (before George). The house and part of the 1100-acre property were confiscated after Lee left to command the Confederate Army of Virginia, and bodies of Union soldiers were buried around the house to spite Lee. When Lee returned, the family sued the federal government to be reimbursed for the property. Arlington Cemetery was born, and, eventually, the historic house was opened for public tours.

WWW – Where Did It Begin?

Sunny California always seems to get all the credit these days for any advances in the realm of computers and the Internet. Truth is, the idea of connecting computers together – the precursor to the modern World Wide Web – started off in Arlington, Virginia.

Sometime in the late 1960s, the US Advanced Research Projects Agency (ARPA), a think tank with heaps of government funds (and probably one of its boffins somewhere in the bowels of the Pentagon) came up with the idea of linking scientists in remote locations together. There was just a hint of paranoia in all this – if there was a net with multiple 'nodes,' it couldn't all be knocked out simultaneously in a nuclear attack.

The brain power of several universities throughout the country was eventually utilized to develop the protocols TCP/IP (Transmission Control Protocol/Internetworking Protocol) – the means by which the computers 'talked' to each other – but the project impetus came from Arlington.

Fittingly, the 'coming out' of the ARPAnet happened in Washington, DC, in October 1972. Today, it is not surprising that America Online (AOL) has its headquarters in Reston, and that the National Science Foundation is also located here.

The **Tomb of the Unknowns** holds an unknown soldier from WWI, WWII, and the Korean and Vietnam Wars. Visitors come to pay their respects and to watch the changing of the guard; soldiers march ritualistically in front of the memorial 24 hours a day. During the day, the guard changes every half hour from April to September, every hour otherwise. At night, it's every two hours, year-round.

Near the eternal flame that marks the **grave of John F Kennedy** lie gravestones for Robert Kennedy, Jacqueline Kennedy Onassis, and her two infant children. Other notable memorials include the Confederate Memorial, the Tomb of Pierre L'Enfant, the mast of the battleship USS *Maine*, the Iwo Jima Memorial, a memorial to 934 journalists killed in action, and the *Challenger* memorial.

Arlington Cemetery is free and opens at 8 am daily. From October to March, it closes at 5 pm; from April to September, it's open until 7 pm. Tourmobiles (☎ 202-554-0614) are a handy way to visit the far-flung sights; they leave around every 15 minutes from the visitor center ($5 for adults, $2 for children).

From Arlington Cemetery Metro, follow signs the short distance up to the visitor center. To get here from DC by car, take the Arlington Memorial Bridge (behind the Lincoln Memorial) across the river to the cemetery entrance. Parking costs $1 per hour for the first three hours.

LEE FOSTER

Arlington Cemetery: Final home of the brave

Women in Military Service for America Memorial

This memorial (☎ 703-533-1155, www .womensmemorial.org), at the entrance of Arlington National Cemetery, honors all women who have served in the armed forces in times of war and peace, from the time of the American Revolution to the present. The memorial includes an education center and theater (free).

The Pentagon

The Pentagon (☎ 703-695-1776), south of Arlington Cemetery, is the home of the Department of Defense. Built during WWII in 16 months, the aptly named building is constructed around a 5-acre courtyard and is by some accounts the world's largest office complex.

Free guided tours take visitors through portions of the building (guides walk backwards to keep a keen eye on you), and a short film is shown. Tours are given weekdays every half hour from 9:30 am to 3:30 pm. US citizens should bring photo identification, and foreigners should bring their passports.

Take the Metro to the Pentagon station, and at the top of the escalator, you will see a window with a sign about tours.

Newseum

The Freedom Forum's fascinating, state-of-the-art, interactive Newseum (☎ 703-284-3700, www.newseum.org) is the second major reason to visit Arlington. Visitors are bombarded from all angles with past and present news and are given ample opportunity to experience how news is made.

In one hall, there is a block-long (126-foot) screen that depicts breaking news from several services. Below it is an 'as it happens' update of news on a Times Square–style teletype screen, and below that are the actual front pages of many of the world's top papers.

There's also an interactive newsroom, a broadcast studio, and the superb News History gallery, which traces the greatest news stories (and the famous journalists who made them news). In the Freedom Park, 1101 Wilson Blvd, reached from the Newseum, is the **Journalists Memorial**, commemorating journalists killed in pursuit of the news.

The Newseum is open 10 am to 5 pm Wednesday to Sunday and is free. There's parking next door, but it's expensive.

Activities

Northern Virginia is ringed and crisscrossed by **hiking** trails, such as the National Scenic Heritage Trail. It's almost possible to walk from DC to Maine or to the Great Smoky Mountains in Tennessee. The 45-mile Washington & Old Dominion Trail (W&OD) follows an old railway bed from Shirlington, in southern Arlington, to Purcellville, in far eastern Loudoun County in the Allegheny foothills of Virginia. From here, it's a short jump to the Appalachian Trail and its 2000 miles of hiking access south and north. **Horseback riding** is permitted on the W&OD from Vienna to Purcellville.

Bicycling is permitted in Arlington National Cemetery along the 17 miles of a paved trail that follow the George Washington Memorial Parkway from Memorial Bridge to Mount Vernon, as well as on the W&OD Trail (check the latter by calling ☎ 703-729-0596). North of the Potomac is the C&O Canal towpath, which goes from central DC to Harpers Ferry (see C&O

ARLINGTON

PLACES TO STAY
34 Arlington/Cherry Blossom Travelodge
37 Ritz-Carlton Pentagon City
39 Days Inn Crystal City
40 Crystal City Marriott
43 Howard Johnson Plaza National Airport Hotel
44 Econo Lodge - National Airport
45 Best Western Arlington Inn & Tower

PLACES TO EAT
1 Red Hot & Blue
2 Star of Siam
3 Tivoli
5 Queen Bee
6 Nam Viet, Cafe Dalat
7 Hard Times Café
10 Xando
11 Sagebrush Grill
33 Stars Restaurant
35 Food Court
36 Skydome Lounge, Penthouse Restaurant
41 Chez Froggy
42 Ruth's Chris Steak House

OTHER
1 Atomic Grounds
4 Newseum, Journalists Memorial
8 Iota, Whitlow's on Wilson
9 Galaxy Hut
12 Medgar Evers Gravesite, General Omar N Bradley Gravesite
13 President William Howard Taft Gravesite
14 Women in Military Service for America Memorial
15 Tourmobile Stop
16 Visitor Center
17 Arlington House (Robert E Lee Memorial)
18 Kennedy Family Gravesite
19 Rear Admiral Richard Byrd Jr Gravesite
20 General Philip H Sheridan Gravesite
21 Pierre Charles L'Enfant Gravesite
22 Confederate Section & Monument
23 Rough Riders Memorial
24 Mast of the Battleship USS Maine
25 Challenger Memorial
26 Audie Murphy Gravesite
27 Amphitheater
28 Tomb of the Unknowns
29 Joe Louis Gravesite
30 Nurses Memorial
31 General of the Armies, John J Pershing Gravesite
32 Rear Admiral Robert E Peary Gravesite
35 Fashion Center at Pentagon City
38 Arlington Visitor Information Center

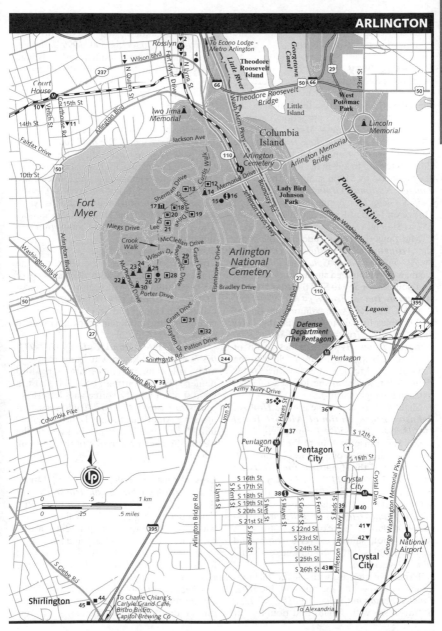

Canal National Historic Park in the Western Maryland chapter), and in the south of the region is Interstate Bike Route 1.

Places to Stay

A comfortable bed in this area (there are more than 30 hotels and motels) will cost much less than one across the Potomac. The Metro gets you to DC's attractions easily.

The **Econo Lodge – Metro Arlington** (☎ 703-538-5300, 6800 Lee Hwy), on the corner of Washington Blvd, has singles and doubles for $70 to $99 in the low season, and they increase by $10 in summer. The **Econo Lodge – National Airport** (☎ 703-979-4100, 2485 S Glebe Rd), 3 miles south of 14th St Bridge on I-395 at Route 120, has rooms for $52 to $119 all year.

Mid-range places include the following: the **Arlington/Cherry Blossom Travelodge** (☎ 703-521-5570, 3030 Columbia Pike), with clean, well-maintained singles for $62 to $69 and doubles for $69 to $72; the **Best Western Arlington Inn & Tower** (☎ 703-979-4400, 2480 S Glebe Rd), with comfortable singles and doubles for $65 to $149; and the **Days Inn Crystal City** (☎ 703-920-8600, 2000 Jefferson Davis Hwy), 1.3 miles south of the 14th St Bridge on Route 1 (close to the Crystal City Metro station), with singles/doubles for $89/99 in the low season ($20 extra in the high season).

Slightly more expensive are the **Howard Johnson Plaza National Airport Hotel** (☎ 703-684-7200, 2650 Jefferson Davis Hwy), which has transportation to the airport included in the rates of $79 low season, $119 high season; the **Comfort Inn Ballston** (☎ 703-247-3399, 1211 N Glebe Rd), which has spacious doubles for $69 in the low season, $106 in the high season; and the **Holiday Inn Arlington at Ballston** (☎ 703-243-9800, 4610 N Fairfax Drive), I-66 exit 71, with a pool, sauna, exercise room, and singles/doubles for $79/89 on weekends and $99/109 weekdays.

Expensive choices, with all the facilities you would expect for the price, are the **Ritz-Carlton Pentagon City** (☎ 703-415-5000, 1250 S Hayes St), with singles and doubles for $129 to $179 on weekends and considerably more on weekdays; and the **Crystal City Marriott** (☎ 703-413-5500, 1999 Jefferson Davis Hwy), 1.2 miles south of 14th St Bridge on Route 1, which has weekend specials for $74 to $135 and weekday singles/doubles starting at $189/209.

Places to Eat

All of the brew pubs mentioned under Entertainment serve meals. The **food court** (☎ 703-415-2400, 1100 S Hayes St), at the Fashion Center at Pentagon City, has just about every sort of fast food imaginable and is open daily.

There are restaurant enclaves at Crystal City, Clarendon, Shirlington, and Rosslyn as well as near the Court House Metro station. The visitor center will add many more to this list.

Shirlington There are good choices at the Shirlington Village, S 28th St, just west of I-395 (southbound exit 7, northbound exit 6). **Charlie Chiang's** (☎ 703-671-4900), specializing in Hunan and Szechuan dishes, just creeps into the moderate bracket with main courses for $12 to $20.

The **Carlyle Grand Café** (☎ 703-931-0777) is a lively bistro with great rotisserie and grilled meals (there are early-bird dinner specials starting at $12). It's also a good spot for a quick coffee and dessert.

Bistro Bistro (☎ 703-379-0300) serves innovative American cuisine. Lunch is served until 5 pm, and if you are lucky with the weather, you can eat at one of the sidewalk tables.

Crystal City Two miles south of the 14th St Bridge, **Ruth's Chris Steak House** (☎ 703-979-7275, 2231 Crystal Drive), in Crystal Park building No 3, is an upscale place for which you have to dress up to eat – a true carnivore's delight – and as you dine, you get magnificent views of the DC skyline. A meal for two will cost well over $60, as entrees are $16 to $30.

Chez Froggy (☎ 703-979-7676, 509 S 23rd St), another Crystal City favorite, is open for dinner daily for less expensive 'Froggy' dishes, such as the ubiquitous legs sautéed in butter and garlic.

A good tip: for some of the finest views of DC by night, try the **Penthouse Restaurant** (☎ 703-416-4100, 300 Army Navy Dr), on the 14th floor of the Doubletree Hotel, and the revolving **Skydome Lounge** above (be warned, entrees are $20 to $40).

The **Stars Restaurant** (☎ 703-521-1900), in the Sheraton National Hotel at the corner of Columbia Pike and Washington Blvd, is another place with great views.

Rosslyn Stop by **Atomic Grounds** (☎ 703-524-2157, 1555 Wilson Blvd), an upscale 'cyberlounge' open daily at 6:30 am.

Red Hot & Blue (☎ 703-276-7427, 1600 Wilson Blvd), at N Pierce St, open daily for lunch and dinner, gets rave reviews from everyone who eats there. Sample Memphis-style wet and dry ribs, chicken, smoked ham, and all the Southern accessories you could wish for; entrees are $7 to $15.

Other Rosslyn delights are the **Star of Siam** (☎ 703-524-1208, 1735 N Lynn St), which has a fabulous selection of Thai curries and seafood dishes, and **Tivoli** (☎ 703-524-8900, 1700 N Moore St), an upscale place serving delectable northern Italian cuisine. The 'Tiv' is expensive, and an entree such as linguine Saracena costs about $25. You are expected to dress appropriately for fine dining.

Clarendon A clone of the branch in DC's Dupont Circle, **Xando** (☎ 703-522-0300, 2050 Wilson Blvd) is the classiest of coffeehouses, with just about every treatment of the brown bean imaginable and plain coffee if you want it that way; it turns into a bar after dark.

Good restaurants in this enclave include **Queen Bee** (☎ 703-527-3444, 3181 Wilson Blvd), **Nam Viet** (☎ 703-522-7110, 1127 N Hudson St), and **Cafe Dalat** (☎ 703-276-0935, 3143 Wilson Blvd) for inexpensive and sumptuous Vietnamese dishes; the **Hard Times Café** (☎ 703-528-2233, 3028 Wilson Blvd) for Tex-Mex chilis, cornbread, and beans (no entree is more than $7); and the **Sagebrush Grill** (☎ 703-524-1432, 1345 N Courthouse Rd),

another inexpensive Tex-Mex place with the most economical lunch specials you're likely to taste.

Entertainment

For fun nighttime activities, check in the Weekend section of the *Washington Post* on Friday, and in the free *Where Washington* and *City Paper*.

Arlington boasts more than half a dozen professional drama companies. The **Washington Shakespeare Company** (☎ 703-418-4808, 601 S Clark St) enacts performances with a twist, such as *The Taming of the Shrew* with an all-female cast. The **Classika Theatre** (☎ 703-824-6200, 4041 S 28th St) is from Russia, and **Horizon Theatre** (☎ 703-243-8550) performs plays covering women's issues.

Recommended Arlington bars are **Whitlow's on Wilson** (☎ 703-276-9693, 2830 Wilson Blvd), near the Clarendon Metro, with 15 brews on tap, a pool table, a jukebox, live music, and an appropriate dark and dank atmosphere; the **Galaxy Hut** (☎ 703-525-4837, 2711 Wilson Blvd), with passable pub grub (American/Continental) and a well-stocked bar of 12 taps; and the **Capitol Brewing Co** (☎ 703-578-3888, 2700 S Quincy St), often voted the best brew pub (and which has two sister establishments over the river in DC).

Iota (☎ 703-522-8340, 2832 Wilson Blvd) is the best place to see live bands. It also has a restaurant, but you'd be better off ordering food at the bar. There's a poetry series every second Sunday ($5 cover).

Getting There & Away

Metrorail From Union Station in DC, you can catch the Metrorail Blue Line to Rosslyn, Arlington Cemetery, the Pentagon, Pentagon City, and Crystal City; the Yellow Line links into Alexandria and connects Arlington destinations with Ronald Reagan Washington National Airport; and the Orange Line heads west through Rosslyn, Court House, Clarendon, and Ballston (all the way to Vienna). For Metrorail details, see Getting Around in the Washington, DC chapter.

Bus Arlington does not have its own bus system, but it is well served by the DC Metrobuses (☎ 202-637-7000). Greyhound/Trailways (☎ 703-998-6312) buses also pass through Arlington on their way to/from DC.

Car Driving within the Beltway can be a real headache – traffic congestion can be maddening, and once you reach a destination, parking is extremely limited.

That said, suburban Virginia and Maryland have a sophisticated road system – I-95 (connecting with the I-495 Beltway) passes to the east and south of the region. A feeder freeway, I-395, cuts north-south through both Alexandria and Arlington to reconnect with I-95S. Route 50W connects the city areas to the northwest, I-66W leads to the west and Shenandoah Valley, Route 29 to Manassas, and Route 1 is a slower but more relaxed alternative to the north-south I-95 (and gives access to many of the historic attractions, such as Mount Vernon).

Just watch out for HOV (high occupancy vehicle) routes: if you find yourself alone in an HOV lane in rush hour, expect a fine.

ALEXANDRIA

'The fun side of the Potomac' is the slogan of this fascinating city (population 120,000), and ongoing archaeological projects are an important part of its allure. The natural barrier of the Potomac allows this now-suburban city to retain a historic charm. In the pre-Revolutionary days, Alexandria was bigger than Georgetown, modern DC's oldest precinct.

Orientation

The main streets dividing the city are north-south Washington St (George Washington Parkway) and east-west King St. Streets are simply divided by the 100 system – eg, Cameron to Queen is the 200 block north.

The historic area, Old Town, is a square marked by the King St Metro in the west, Slaters Lane in the north, the Potomac River to the east, and South St – most historic sights lie to the east of Washington St.

Saturday parking costs $2 all day, or $3 if your car is still there after 6 pm. Visitors can park free at any two-hour parking meter in the city by picking up a pass from the visitor center.

Information

The Alexandria Convention and Visitors Association (☎ 703-838-4200, www.FunSide .com) is in Ramsay House, 221 King St, Alexandria, VA 22314. This is the best place to start a tour of the town, especially for the free 24-hour parking permit. The yellow clapboard Ramsay House was built in 1724 in Dumfries, 25 miles to the south, and was moved here in 1749. The house once belonged to William Ramsay, Alexandria's first Lord Mayor. It is open 9 am to 5 pm daily.

At the visitor center, you can purchase a Market Square block ticket ($9 for adults and $5 for youth under 18), which allows entry to three of Alexandria's attractions: the Stabler-Leadbeater Apothecary Museum, Carlyle House, and Gadsby's Tavern Museum.

Good banks for foreign exchange are Burke & Herbert, on the corner of King and Fairfax (it has ATMs); and Crestar, at 515 King St.

The main post office (☎ 703-549-4201) is at 1100 Wythe St.

Super Crown Books (☎ 703-548-3432), at 501 King St, near the Crestar bank, is a good bookstore for browsing. The aptly named kid's bookstore A Likely Story (☎ 703-836-2498) is at 1555 King St.

There is a self-serve laundry, West End Coin-Op (☎ 703-370-1727), 4623 Duke St, in the Fox Chase shopping center.

Alexandria Hospital (☎ 703-379-3000), at 4320 Seminary Rd, is a 24-hour facility.

Torpedo Factory

This collection of buildings at 105 N Union St was built during WWI for the manufacture of torpedo parts (and reused again during WWII as a munitions factory). Today, it is the centerpiece of a revamped waterfront with marina, shops, parks and walkways, residences, offices, and restaurants. The **Torpedo Factory Art Center** (☎ 703-838-4565) is dedicated to nearly 200 artists and crafters who sell their creations directly from their studios. It's open 10 am to 5 pm daily (free).

Also in this complex is **Alexandria Archae-ology** (☎ 703-838-4399), an interesting place where archaeologists, engaged in a number of local urban digs, clean and catalog the artifacts they have unearthed. The real appeal is seeing the current work in progress; there are also informative videos. It's free and is open 10 am to 3 pm Tuesday to Friday, to 5 pm Saturday, and 1 to 5 pm Sunday.

Fort Ward Museum & Historic Site

Fort Ward (☎ 703-838-4848), 4301 W Braddock Rd, was one of the largest of the 162 Civil War fortifications known as the Defenses of Washington. The northwest bastion of the fort has been completely restored, and the remaining earthwork walls are well preserved to reflect the original state of the defenses. The museum on site has interpretative displays and features exhibits on Civil War topics. Tours, lectures, and living-history programs are offered, and there are services for the disabled.

The museum is open 9 am to 5 pm Tuesday to Saturday and noon to 5 pm Sunday; the historic site is open 9 am to sunset (free).

Gadsby's Tavern Museum

This museum (☎ 703-838-4242), at 134 N Royal St, consists of two tavern buildings built in 1770 and 1792 and named after John Gadsby, who operated them from 1796 to 1808. As the center of political, business, and social life in early Alexandria, they were visited by George Washington and Thomas Jefferson. Lafayette stayed here during a visit in 1824, and the tavern ballroom was the scene of Washington's last two birthday celebrations.

The rooms of the tavern and hotel have been restored to their 18th-century appearance. Look for the **gravestone of the 'female stranger'** who died here in October 1816.

The museum is open 10 am to 5 pm Tuesday to Saturday and 1 to 5 pm Sunday from April to September; otherwise, it is open 11 am to 4 pm Tuesday to Saturday and

1 to 4 pm Sunday. Admission is $4 for adults and $2 for youth under 18. There are guided tours and services for the disabled.

The Lyceum

The Lyceum (☎ 703-838-4994), 201 S Washington St, is Alexandria's history museum. It is housed in a Greek Revival building that was restored in the 1970s. The changing exhibits focus on Alexandria since its founding. There are prints, photographs, ceramics, silver, and Civil War memorabilia on display here.

It is free and is open 10 am to 5 pm Monday to Saturday and 1 to 5 pm Sunday.

Stabler-Leadbeater Apothecary Museum

This museum (☎ 703-836-3713), 105–7 S Fairfax St, is an 18th-century apothecary shop (founded in 1792 by Quaker pharmacist Edward Stabler). It features a fine collection of 900 hand-blown apothecary bottles in their original site. (We have been told chemist conventions visit in droves.) Of greater interest is that here on October 17, 1859, Lieutenant Colonel Robert E Lee (see the boxed text, later) received his orders to move to Harpers Ferry to put down John Brown's insurrection.

The bottles are displayed 10 am to 4 pm Monday to Saturday and 1 to 5 pm Sunday; admission is $2.50 for adults and $2 for youth under 18.

Prince Street

The 100 block of Prince St, called **Captain's Row**, is one of two remaining cobblestone streets in Alexandria. The cobblestones were the ballast of English ships, and the street was possibly laid by Hessian prisoners of war. There are lovely private homes, including one once owned by a Captain John Harper. It is said that his wife died in self-defense after the birth of her 15th child!

Gentry Row is the 200 block of Prince St, named after the number of imposing private dwellings. The pumpkin-colored **Athenaeum** (☎ 703-548-0035), a Greek Revival building at 201 Prince St, is now a museum of fine art. It started as a bank in 1850 and was used as

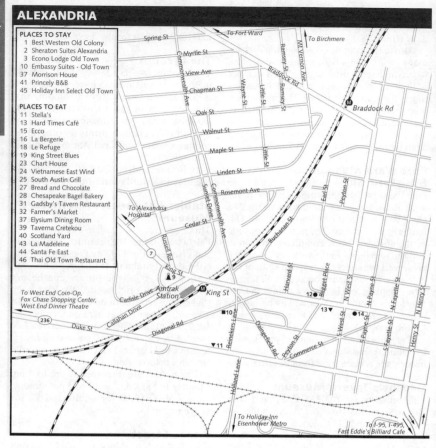

ALEXANDRIA

PLACES TO STAY
1   Best Western Old Colony
2   Sheraton Suites Alexandria
3   Econo Lodge Old Town
10 Embassy Suites - Old Town
37 Morrison House
41 Princely B&B
45 Holiday Inn Select Old Town

PLACES TO EAT
11 Stella's
13 Hard Times Café
15 Ecco
16 La Bergerie
18 Le Refuge
19 King Street Blues
23 Chart House
24 Vietnamese East Wind
25 South Austin Grill
27 Bread and Chocolate
28 Chesapeake Bagel Bakery
31 Gadsby's Tavern Restaurant
32 Farmer's Market
37 Elysium Dining Room
39 Taverna Cretekou
40 Scotland Yard
43 La Madeleine
44 Santa Fe East
46 Thai Old Town Restaurant

a hospital during the Civil War. The museum is free and is open 10 am to 4 pm Tuesday to Saturday and 1 to 4 pm Sunday.

Black History Resource Center

This center (☎ 703-838-4356), 638 N Alfred St, in the Parker-Gray Historical District (entrance on Wythe St), presents lectures, tours, and other activities relating to the accomplishments and history of African American Alexandrians. On display are paintings, photographs, books, and other memorabilia that document black experience in Alexandria and Virginia from 1749 to the present. The center

is open 10 am to 4 pm Tuesday to Saturday (free). There is an annex, the Watson Reading Room, with a wealth of books and documents relating to African American topics.

Christ Church

George Washington, who had a townhouse in Alexandria, purchased a pew in Christ Church. This red-brick Georgian-style church, at the corner of Washington and Cameron Sts, has been in use since 1773.

Robert E Lee was confirmed here, and there is an interesting churchyard cemetery that contains the graves of a number of

WASHINGTON, DC

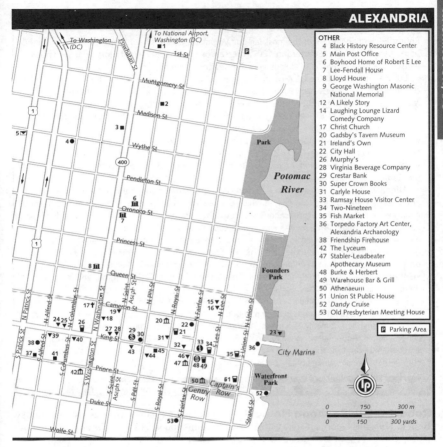

ALEXANDRIA

OTHER
4 Black History Resource Center
5 Main Post Office
6 Boyhood Home of Robert E Lee
7 Lee-Fendall House
8 Lloyd House
9 George Washington Masonic
   National Memorial
12 A Likely Story
14 Laughing Lounge Lizard
   Comedy Company
17 Christ Church
20 Gadsby's Tavern Museum
21 Ireland's Own
22 City Hall
26 Murphy's
28 Virginia Beverage Company
29 Crestar Bank
30 Super Crown Books
31 Carlyle House
33 Ramsay House Visitor Center
34 Two-Nineteen
35 Fish Market
36 Torpedo Factory Art Center,
   Alexandria Archaeology
38 Friendship Firehouse
42 The Lyceum
47 Stabler-Leadbeater
   Apothecary Museum
48 Burke & Herbert
49 Warehouse Bar & Grill
50 Athenaeum
51 Union St Public House
52 *Dandy* Cruise
53 Old Presbyterian Meeting House

P Parking Area

Confederate soldiers. Early in the Civil War, it was here that Lee met with Southern representatives before accepting command of the Rebel army. It's free and is open 9 am to 4 pm Monday to Saturday and 2 to 4 pm Sunday.

George Washington Masonic National Memorial

The best feature of this neoclassical monstrosity, probably Alexandria's most prominent landmark, is the view from the 9th floor, where you can see the Capitol, Mount Vernon, and the Potomac River. Washington, initiated into the Masons in Fredericks-

burg in 1752, later became Worshipful Master of Alexandria Lodge No 22.

The memorial (☎ 703-683-2007), 101 Callahan Drive at King St, is free and is open 9 am to 5 pm daily. There are tours about every 45 minutes and lots of parking.

Lloyd House

This Georgian-style house (☎ 703-838-4577), 220 N Washington St, dates from 1794. As part of the Alexandria library service, it has a collection of rare documents and books that cover the city's history and genealogy. It is open 9 am to 5 pm Monday to Saturday (free).

Robert E Lee

Robert Edward Lee is one of the most famous Virginians, and it is hard to escape his name in this book. Lee was born in Stratford in 1807, the son of Henry Lee – 'Light Horse Harry,' who was himself a representative of an already very distinguished Virginia family.

Lee was educated at the US Military Academy at West Point, where he graduated second in his class (one must wonder, who was first?) as a second lieutenant in the engineers. In the battles of the Mexican War, he distinguished himself and was wounded in the storming of Chapultepec in 1847.

Lee was assigned to the US Military Academy as superintendent and was later promoted to the rank of colonel in the cavalry. In 1861, when he was in command of the Department of Texas and war between the states seemed imminent, Lincoln summoned him to Washington, DC, and offered him command of the Union forces. Lee declined, and on April 21, three days after his beloved Virginia seceded from the Union, he resigned from the US Army and became commander in chief of the Confederate Forces of Virginia.

After a year as military advisor to Jefferson Davis, he assumed command of the Army of Northern Virginia. Many battles followed, in which Lee proved himself a master strategist and a tactical genius with his use of field fortifications and defensive entrenchments to facilitate outflanking maneuvers. In February 1865, he was elevated to commander of all the forces of the South, but two months later, he surrendered to the numerically far-superior Union forces of Ulysses S Grant at Appomattox, virtually ending the Civil War. (He applied for a postwar amnesty, but it was granted posthumously, more than a century later, by an Act of Congress in 1975.) In 1865, he became president of Washington College (now Washington & Lee University) in Lexington, and he remained there until his death in 1870.

Lee was revered by both Southerners and Northerners, and the places he was associated with still attract visitors from both camps in large numbers. In Virginia, these include Stratford Hall (his birthplace), his boyhood home in Alexandria, Arlington House (his antebellum home, now the Robert E Lee Memorial), Appomattox, Washington & Lee University, the Lee Chapel and Museum (where Lee is buried) in Lexington, and a host of battlefields where he brilliantly defied the odds stacked against him. Perhaps the best image of Lee is the portrait by American artist William Edgar Marshall.

Robert E Lee Boyhood Home

Built in 1795, this Georgian-style townhouse (☎ 703-548-8454), 607 Oronoco St, was Lee's childhood home. Lee's father, Henry, a Revolutionary War commander and governor of Virginia from 1792 to 1795, moved his family to Alexandria in 1810. The house is open 10 am to 4 pm Monday to Saturday and 1 to 4 pm Sunday from February to December. Admission is $4 for adults and $2 for youth under 18.

Lee-Fendall House

Across the street from Lee's boyhood home, this house (☎ 703-548-1789), 614 Oronoco St, was built in 1785 and includes furniture that belonged to the Lees. It is open 10 am to 4 pm Tuesday, Thursday, Friday, and Saturday, and 1 to 4 pm Wednesday and Sunday. Admission is $4 for adults and $2 for youth under 18.

Carlyle House

Near the corner of Fairfax and Cameron Sts, by the old Alexandria Bank, is the imposing, Georgian-style Carlyle House (☎ 703-549-2997), built by Scottish merchant John Carlyle between 1751 and 1753. The house is open 10 am to 4:30 pm Tuesday to Saturday and noon to 4:30 pm Sunday; there are tours every half hour ($4 for adults and $2 for youth under 18).

Friendship Firehouse

This Italianate firehouse at 107 S Alfred St, dates from 1855. Local legend has it that

Washington helped found the volunteer fire company and that he served as its captain and even paid for a new fire engine. It's free and is open 10 am to 4 pm Friday to Saturday and 1 to 4 pm Sunday.

Old Presbyterian Meeting House

The red-brick building (☎ 703-549-6670) at 321 S Fairfax St was built in 1774 by a group of Scottish founders. The graveyard holds the Tomb of the Unknown Soldier of the Revolutionary War and the grave markers of William Ramsay and John Carlyle. It's open 9 am to 5 pm weekdays and is free.

Special Events

Alexandria always seems to have something to celebrate or commemorate. The town's associations with Washington and Lee are given thorough annual workouts. Lee's birthday is celebrated in the third week of January, and Washington's birthday is celebrated in February with a much vaunted parade, banquet, and ball.

On the second weekend in June, the Red Cross Waterfront Festival is celebrated with ship tours, art shows, and entertainment. The Scottish nexus is recalled on the fourth weekend of July with the annual Virginia Scottish Games, and in early December with the Scottish Christmas Walk – featuring wailing bagpipes and kilted pipers. Another December event is a candlelight tour of Alexandria – music and food accompany your sojourn – call ☎ 703-838-4200.

Organized Tours & Cruises

There are informative walking tours of Old Town Alexandria conducted daily from late March to November. They commence at Ramsay House (see Information, earlier) at noon daily ($8 per person). There are also ghost tours on weekend nights at 9 pm ($4 for adults, $3 children).

There are several cruises on the Potomac. The Potomac Riverboat Co (☎ 703-548-9000) docks its boats at the city marina behind the Torpedo Factory. The boats operate from April to October. The *Admiral Tilp* sails past Alexandria ($7/6/4 for adults/seniors/children; 40 minutes), the *Matthew*

Hayes heads farther up the Potomac ($14/13/6; nine minutes), and *Miss Christin* sails to Mount Vernon ($22/20/10, including entry to Mount Vernon; two hours).

The *Dandy* (☎ 703-683-6076) is a restaurant/cruise ship renowned for its food and service. On weekdays, lunch is $26; the Sunday champagne brunch is $32; midnight dance cruises start at $23.

Places to Stay

The nearest budget accommodations are at the HI youth hostel in DC (see Downtown, under Places to Stay, in the Washington, DC chapter). The ***Econo Lodge Old Town*** (*☎ 703-836-5100, 700 N Washington St*) is the best close-to-town bet for the budget traveler; doubles cost $70 to $80. The ***Econo Lodge – Mount Vernon*** (*☎ 703-780-0300*), on Route 1, 7½ miles south of the I-95/I-495 Beltway, is a better cheapie; singles and doubles cost $65 to $75. There are dives along this strip, so beware.

Strolling through Old Town Alexandria

DENNIS JOHNSON

The **Holiday Inn Eisenhower Metro** (☎ 703-960-4300, 2460 Eisenhower Ave), just north of I-95/I-495, is handy to the Metro. It has a heated indoor pool and an exercise room. Singles are $69 to $119, and doubles are $79 to $129.

The **Best Western Old Colony** (☎ 703-739-2222, 615 1st St), on the George Washington Memorial Parkway, includes a free breakfast in its year-round rate of $69. The **Sheraton Suites Alexandria** (☎ 703-836-4700, 801 N Saint Asaph St), a block east of Washington St, has doubles starting at $115 in the low season and $135 in the high season.

Princely B&B (☎ 800-470-5588, 819 Prince St) has 30 houses in and around Old Town; expect to pay about $70/80 for a single/double. The **Alexandria & Arlington B&B Network** (☎ 888-549-3415, www .aabbn.com) is a booking service.

The **Embassy Suites – Old Town** (☎ 703-684-5900, 1900 Diagonal Rd), adjacent to King St Metro and the Amtrak terminal, is a trusted favorite, offering all the facilities – indoor pool, sauna, sundeck, exercise room, and restaurant. Rooms are $154 to $204 all year.

The **Holiday Inn Select Old Town** (☎ 703-549-6080, 480 King St), half a block from the City Hall, has a restaurant, gift shop, and area transportation. Some rooms have a balcony overlooking a central courtyard and are the best value. All rooms are $169.

Morrison House (☎ 703-838-8000, 116 S Alfred St) is one of the most expensive choices, but it's worth the luxury if you can afford it. This four-star, boutique-style hotel includes the aid of a butler, two excellent restaurants (see Places to Eat), and a library where afternoon tea is served. The rooms, furnished with Federal-style reproductions, have marble baths and cost $150 to $295 per night.

Places to Eat

There are many eateries in Old Town, most spread out along King St.

If you are short on cash, stock up for the week at the Saturday **farmers' market** (☎ 703-838-4770, 301 King St); cheap fresh produce, baked goods, and meats are sold here.

Bread and Chocolate (☎ 703-548-0992, 611 King St) has a wonderful selection of sandwiches as well as desserts to keep any sweet tooth satisfied. A hearty breakfast will cost $3.50 to $6.50.

The **Hard Times Café** (☎ 703-683-5340, 1404 King St) is inexpensive, casual, and open for lunch and dinner. As one discerning local food critic opined, 'two can eat silly here for $20.' The menu features onion rings for $3, five-way chilis (including Cincinnati with a hint of cinnamon), Mexican dishes ('all-the-way wet' with mucho sauce), and corn bread.

The **Chesapeake Bagel Bakery** (☎ 703-684-3777, 601 King St) has seating for those who like round things with holes in them for breakfast. **Stella's** (☎ 703-519-1946, 1725 Duke St), which has a decor harking back to the 1940s, wins our prize for the best Sunday brunch, with unlimited champagne and a diverse breakfast selection from 11 am to 2:30 pm ($12.95). There is an adjoining beer garden.

The **Vietnamese East Wind** (☎ 703-836-1515, 809 King St), several thousand miles away in terms of flavor, is a good choice for vegetarian lunches (around $7) or steaming pho (beef noodle soup). It's open for lunch weekdays and dinner daily.

Some other lunch possibilities are **La Madeleine** (☎ 703-739-9494, 500 King St), a French bakery/cafe that concocts fresh breads and pastries from its wood-burning oven; and **King Street Blues** (☎ 703-836-8800, 112 N Saint Asaph St), a Southern 'roadhouse' diner, where you can expect beef stew and garlic potatoes, hot salad, and yummy chicken – the lunch special is only $5.

Thai Old Town (☎ 703-684-6503, 300 King St) is testimony to the growing number of Southeast Asian immigrants to the metropolitan DC area and the popularity of their cuisine. Pad Thai here costs less than $10. Sweet-and-sour soups run less than $5 a bowl.

Taverna Cretekou (☎ 703-548-8688, 818 King St) is a delightful eatery and a real slice of Athens – it has an outside grapevine arbor, waiters spontaneously dance for you á la Zorba after supper, and the Sunday brunch is legendary. Expect to pay $20 to $25 for a full meal.

The *Santa Fe East* (☎ 703-548-6900, 110 S Pitt St) and the *South Austin Grill* (☎ 703-684-8969, 801 King St) both have fireplaces and offer good Tex-Mex food for a reasonable price – lunch is $7 to $14 and dinner is $12 to $20.

With the preponderance of French eateries, Lafayette would no doubt be happy. *Le Refuge* (☎ 703-548-4661, 127 N Washington St) is open daily (except Sunday) for lunch and dinner. The early-bird dinner, offered nightly from 5:30 to 7 pm (all night Monday), is $20 and includes salad, a main course, and dessert.

La Bergerie (☎ 703-683-1007, 218 N Lee St), in the Crilley shops, is Alexandria's best dining choice by far. A full meal of their Basque cuisine will cost $20 to $25 for lunch and $35 for dinner. La Bergerie is open 11:30 am to 2:30 pm for lunch and 6 to 10:30 pm for dinner Monday to Saturday.

Ecco (☎ 703-684-0321, 220 N Lee St) serves delicious Italian pizzas, pastas, and sauces (always generous servings) accompanied by hearty salads. It's open daily for lunch and dinner (entrees are $8 to $15).

Gadsby's Tavern Restaurant (☎ 703-548-1288, 138 N Royal St) tries hard to emulate an 18th-century hostelry. Once the finest public house in America, its new life of kitschy charm destroys any such ambiance. The 'tav' is open for lunch 11:30 am to 3 pm and for dinner 5:30 to 10 pm; Sunday brunch is 11 am to 3 pm.

The *Scotland Yard* (☎ 703-683-1742, 728 King St) struggles to create the culinary masterpieces of Scotland, a struggle made especially difficult because (notwithstanding the haggis), there are few such delights! At dinner, the lace curtains, highland menu, and cozy atmosphere (plus tasty 'Bramble Mist' dessert) ring an echo from the glens.

The *Chart House* (☎ 703-684-5080, 1 Cameron St), on the waterfront, has views that justify the considerable cost. Main courses, which include a salad bar of more than 60 items, are $16 to $25. Sunday champagne brunch (11 am to 2:30 pm) is a little more than eggs and bacon for around $18.

The *Elysium Dining Room* (☎ 703-838-8000), a multiaward winner in Morrison House (see Places to Stay), is bloody expensive, but by all reports, it's well worth the hefty check. It's open daily for breakfast and dinner, Sunday for brunch.

Entertainment

The *West End Dinner Theatre* (☎ 703-370-2500, 4615 Duke St) has the largest dinner-theater stage in the area and is only minutes from DC. It features Broadway musicals and comedies. From Tuesday to Sunday, dinner is served at 6 pm and the curtain rises at 8 pm; there are matinees Wednesday and Sunday, with lunch at noon and curtain up at 2 pm ($30 to $35 per person).

Capitol Steps Political Satire (☎ 703-683-8330, 210 N Washington St) is now a DC tradition. This well-established comedy troupe spoofed DC politics throughout the '90s and is now lampooning into the 21st century.

For quiet beers in true drinking environments, try the *Union Street Public House* (☎ 703-548-1785, 121 S Union St), easily spotted because of the big gas lamps out front; the *Warehouse Bar & Grill* (☎ 703-683-6868, 214 King St), with great crab cakes and humorous caricatures adorning its walls; the *Virginia Beverage Company* (☎ 703-684-5397, 607 King St), with its 13 taps, homemade root beer, and huge steaks; and *Fast Eddie's Billiard Cafe* (☎ 703-660-9444, 6220 Richmond Rd), with 26 Brunswick pool tables.

Birchmere (☎ 703-549-7500, 3701 Mount Vernon Ave), just south of Glebe Rd, is the place for bluegrass, folk, and country.

Other live music venues can be found along or near King St: *Murphy's* (☎ 703-548-1717, 713 King St) and *Ireland's Own* (☎ 703-549-4535, 132 N Royal St) both have live Irish entertainment nightly, buckets of Guinness, and champagne brunches on Sunday. *Two-Nineteen* (☎ 703-549-1141, 219 King St), a Creole/New Orleans–flavored place, has jazz nightly.

The *Fish Market* (☎ 703-836-5676, 105 King St), serving reliable seafood meals and providing good music, suits the more mature crowd.

Getting There & Away

For driving details, see Arlington, earlier.

From Union Station in DC (see the Washington, DC chapter), you can catch the Metrorail to Arlington, Alexandria, and points beyond in northern Virginia.

Amtrak passes through Alexandria on its East Coast route. The King St Metro station – which also doubles as the Amtrak station (connected by DC's Metrorail Yellow and Blue Lines) – is the city's main transport hub, and from here you can take Metrorail AT-2 or DASH bus AT-5 directly to the city's visitor center. Other Metrorail stations, connected to the Yellow and Blue Lines, are Braddock Rd and Eisenhower Ave.

Greyhound/Trailways (☎ 703-998-6312) passes through Arlington.

Getting Around

Alexandria's bus transit system, DASH (☎ 703-370-3274), operates daily. The cost of travel is 85¢ for a four-hour pass. The brochure 'DASHing Around Alexandria' explains how to get from sight to sight easily. Buy DASH tokens from the visitor center.

Beltway Maryland

The state of Maryland surrounds three sides of the District of Columbia, but travelers looking at a map or flying over the area en route to Ronald Reagan Washington National Airport may be tempted to dismiss the Maryland towns skirting DC as formless suburbs distinguished only by the differing income levels and racial mixes of their inhabitants. To some degree, such assumptions hold true. Nevertheless, Beltway Maryland contains a number of fetching sites.

BETHESDA

Once a quiet Maryland town, Bethesda has grown since the end of WWII to be one of the largest, most influential, and most affluent suburban communities in the nation. The large campuses of the National Institutes of Health and the National Naval Medical Center (where US presidents receive medical care) dominate the city.

Downtown Bethesda spreads out from the intersection of Wisconsin Ave (a long, straight shot from Georgetown) and Old Georgetown Rd. A Metro station here makes Bethesda a convenient destination from DC. Visitors can walk to a great variety of restaurants, clubs, bookstores, and boutiques within a compact zone along Bethesda Ave, a few blocks south of the Metro and in a knot of lanes off Old Georgetown Rd a few blocks north of the Metro.

But by far, the coolest way to approach Bethesda is via the **Capital Crescent Trail**, which runs a sheltered 10 miles along an old railroad route to Georgetown. The scenic paved trail, which passes over a trestle bridge and through a historic tunnel on its way to meet the C&O Canal towpath along the Potomac (see C&O Canal National Historic Park in the Western Maryland chapter), deposits riders and hikers at restaurant gulches at either end.

Information

Bethesda has no visitor center, but you can get information about the town and most of DC's northern suburbs through the Conference and Visitor Bureau of Montgomery County (☎ 800-925-0880), 12900 Middlebrook Rd, Suite 1400, Germantown, MD 20874.

Places to Stay

Lodging downtown caters to business travelers; rooms start at $100 on weekdays and are discounted by a third or more on weekends.

Prices at the *American Inn* (☎ 301-656-9300, 800-323-7081, 8130 Wisconsin Ave), a decent older motel within walking distance of the Metro, are typical: $130 weekdays and $69 weekends (including continental breakfast and free Internet access). Newer motel chains downtown include the Ramada and Residence Inn by Marriott.

The high-end *Hyatt Regency Bethesda* (☎ 301-657-1234, 800-233-1234, 1 Bethesda Metro Center) is above the Metro station in the heart of downtown Bethesda. The deluxe 12-floor suburban hotel features an atrium lobby and a glass-enclosed penthouse pool ($265 and up on weekdays, $109 and up on weekends).

Places to Eat

More than 170 restaurants offer a variety of cuisine to rival DC's Adams-Morgan district, with more upscale crowds and ample parking. Among the dozens of refined restaurants with linens, goblets, and arty interiors, you can find crab shacks, bagel shops, and plenty of sidewalk cafes. All the following selections are within the compact downtown zone.

The organic grocery **Norman's Farm Market** (☎ 301-215-7533, 4915 Bethesda Ave) has a delicatessen that offers gourmet veggie wraps, prosciutto-and-parmesan pizza, soups, salads, *muffalettas* (a New Orleans–style submarine sandwich), and other overstuffed sandwiches for $6. There's a picnic table outside among stands of designer produce.

From morning beignets to evening etouffee, or $5 gumbo anytime, the **Louisiana Express Company** (☎ 301-652-6945, 4921 Bethesda Ave) prepares fiery Cajun and Creole specialties. Great food, low prices, fast and friendly service, cozy tables, and long hours (7:30 am to 10 pm daily) make this local favorite the hands-down best value in town.

Across the street, **Bethesda Crab House** (☎ 301-652-3382, 4958 Bethesda Ave) preserves a bit of pre-suburban Bethesda: Here, blue-collar workers and old-timers gather around newspaper-lined picnic tables inside and out, chiseling away at crack-your-own crab (platters are $18). It's open 9 am to midnight daily and is smoker friendly.

Among the more modern upscale choices, organic **Thyme Square** (☎ 301-657-9077, 4735 Bethesda Ave) serves mostly vegetarian dishes for $8 and up, along with a grilled shrimp salad, mojo-marinated chicken, and power juices in a colorful, folk-arty, smokefree environment.

The **Mongolian Grill** (☎ 301-654-8811, 7710 Wisconsin Ave) offers distinctive ethnic cuisine from Central Asia. Bethesda's answer to Tex-Mex, the **Cottonwood Cafe** (☎ 301-656-4844, 4844 Cordell Ave) serves high-end Southwestern specialties (fajitas are $10) in a fancy but not stuffy atmosphere.

Cesco Trattoria (☎ 301-654-8333, 4871 Cordell Ave) serves upscale Italian, starting with a warm octopus salad and moving to a classic osso buco. Dinner entrees start at $11. It's closed Sunday.

Quick takes: **Pastry Designs** (☎ 301-656-0536, 4927 Elm St) offers glamorous chocolates and desserts; the classic chrome **Tastee Diner** (☎ 301-652-3970, 7731 Woodmont Ave) is open 24 hours and has an ATM inside, and the **Barnes & Noble** (☎ 301-986-1851, 4801 Bethesda Ave) bookstore, at the corner of Bethesda and Woodmont Aves, has a cafe and a large selection of periodicals on the 2nd floor.

Entertainment

The **Bethesda Theatre Cafe** (☎ 301 656 3337, 7719 Wisconsin Ave) presents second-run films and family matinees in its huge old movie house outfitted with cafe tables, swivel chairs, family-friendly menu, and full bar. There's also a modern *multiplex cinema* downtown on Wisconsin Ave.

For nightlife, **Lewie's** (☎ 301-652-1600, 6845 Reed St), a block west of Wisconsin at Bethesda Ave, is a big friendly club on Bethesda's avant-garde side that hosts R&B artists and bluesy rock bands nightly except Monday.

Uncle Jed's Roadhouse (☎ 301-913-0026, 7525 Old Georgetown Rd) features down-home rock Wednesday to Sunday. A block down, **Flanagan's Irish Pub** (☎ 301-986-1007, 7637 Old Georgetown Rd) hosts Irish folk music.

The **Shark Club** (☎ 202-387-8894, 4915 St Elmo Ave) has swing dancing, cigars, and billiards in its tank-lined basement bar.

Getting There & Away

The Metrorail Red Line services Bethesda at its station on Wisconsin Ave at Old Georgetown Rd. (See the Washington, DC chapter for more details.)

Metrobus (☎ 202-637-7000) Nos 32, 34, and 36 run up and down Wisconsin Ave between Georgetown and Bethesda.

Getting Around

Griffin Cycle (☎ 301-656-6188), at 4949 Bethesda Ave, two blocks from the Capital Crescent Trail, rents bicycles for $15 a day (tagalongs are available; there's an extra charge for helmets). It opens at 11 am weekdays, 10 am Saturday, and noon Sunday. For bike and boat rentals at the southern end of the trail, see Activities in the Washington, DC chapter.

GLEN ECHO PARK

Along the Potomac River, 6 miles north of DC, visitors stumble upon a bygone amusement park, where an old arcade, bumper-car pavilion, and an odd building called the Cuddle Up are scattered around other architectural treasures, including a stone Rapunzel tower, yurts, and a Spanish-style ballroom. In this peculiarly quiet Fantasyland off the Clara Barton Parkway, the National Park Service runs a multifaceted art-and-crafts center (☎ 301-492-6229).

The park has its origins as a Chautauqua retreat center, one of several such centers established in the late 19th century to 'promote

liberal and practical education among the masses.' While the Chautauqua movement continues at other centers, here the retreat gave way to an amusement park made accessible to city families with a trolley line from DC. The popular park had its heyday in the early 20th century and then began a decline in the 1960s (it would appear that desegregation played a role), and the property fell into the hands of the federal government.

Today, the lovely historic **carousel** remains the centerpiece of the park and operates weekends from May through September. The arcade now houses the NPS visitor center (open daily), and an **Adventure Theater** (☎ 301-320-5331), which hosts children's performances. The stone tower is a bookstore and gallery. Yurts hold artist studios, and the ballroom hosts swing and folk dances. Many buildings are used year-round for a wide variety of fine arts and performances for children and adults, but drop-in visitors would get the most out of a visit on weekends, when most buildings and attractions are open to the general public and most events are scheduled.

In a former stable, the **Discovery Creek** center (☎ 202-364-3111) highlights ecological exhibits and activities designed for children ages three to 11. It's open 10 am to 3 pm Saturday and noon to 3 pm Sunday; admission is free for adults and $4 per child.

Across the ravine, at the **Clara Barton Historic Site**, the last home of the founder of the American Red Cross is open daily for guided public tours (☎ 301-492-6245); admission is free.

To reach Glen Echo Park from Bethesda on public transportation, you can take the Montgomery County Ride-On-Bus Service (☎ 240-777-7433) No 29 bus from the Metro station in Bethesda. The bus departs every 30 minutes and costs $1.10 during rush hours (90¢ at other times).

TAKOMA PARK

At the northern tip of the DC border, you will find the city of Takoma Park, DC's first commuter suburb (founded in 1883). Today, Takoma Park is home to an alternative-minded community that is comparable to

Berkeley, California, or Boulder, Colorado. Within the largely residential community there is an attractive youth hostel, several unusual shops, and bohemian hangouts.

Takoma Park Co-op (☎ 301-891-2667), 201 Ethan Allan Ave, serves as an alternative cultural center, where in addition to offering smudge sticks, fair-trade coffee, and organic produce, handbills rally residents to political action, and meetings of the Raw Vegan Support Group of Greater DC are held. It's open daily 9 am to 9 pm.

Within the central village, the **House of Musical Instruments** (☎ 301-270-9090, 800-540-9090), 7040 Carroll Ave, carries an impressive array of instruments from around the world, including harps, concertinas, drums, dulcimers, and flutes. Sample CDs and inquire about Friday-evening jam sessions and other concerts. Other shops include a bookstore and Tibetan-imports store.

The town hosts an annual **folk festival** in its municipal building in mid-September.

Opened in 1997, *India House Too* (☎ 202-291-1195, 300 Carroll St) is the popular newcomer to DC's hostel scene. This is a 100-year-old Victorian house in a safe, village atmosphere. But the hostel has the accessibility of many downtown DC locations because it's only four stops on the Metro Red Line from Union Station and a 100-yard walk from the Metro stop at Takoma Park.

Frequented by waves of English, Australian, Japanese, and even Russian backpackers, this place runs on the laid-back model of Aussie hostels, with no curfew, a backyard barbie, and in-house parties. Angus Chapman (from the UK) and his partners have nine bedrooms, most with four or six bunks ($14) and shared baths. You can get a private double with shared bath for $34. When the house is full, you will find about 40 backpackers here. Public facilities include a full modern kitchen, dining room, and lounge with TV.

Within sight of the Metro, actually on the DC side of the border, *Takoma Station* (☎ 202 829-1999, 6914 4th St NW) is a great tavern with some of the best blues, R&B, and soul music in the DC area. The comfortable, spacious club hosts live entertainment nightly.

The Metrorail Red Line makes Takoma Park an easy destination for DC visitors. From the Metro stop, you can hike a half-mile farther uphill to the small village or take the No 13 Montgomery County Transit bus (☎ 800-732-3327).

COLLEGE PARK

Emerging from farmland as a stop on the well-traveled route between Baltimore and Washington, DC, in the early 19th century, College Park takes its name from Maryland's Agricultural College, established here in 1856. Today, the school has grown to become the flagship campus of the 11-campus University of Maryland system. The university dominates the town of College Park, where student enrollment outnumbers the local population of 25,000. A small village sits at the south end of campus; other commercial development is sprawled along the length of Baltimore Ave/Route 1.

University of Maryland

U of M enrolls more than 32,000 students in 13 colleges and schools on its attractive 1500-acre campus. Its Terrapins ('Terps') play football in Byrd Stadium and basketball in Cole Field House. A new center for the performing arts will open five performance spaces in 2000.

The U of M visitor center (☎ 301-314-7777, www.maryland.edu), off Baltimore Ave south of Paint Branch Parkway, distributes campus maps and local directories.

College Park Aviation Museum

This charming museum (☎ 301-864-6029), off Paint Branch Parkway a mile east of campus, opened in 1998 to commemorate the 'oldest continuously operating airport in the world.' Several historic planes are attractively displayed in a glass-walled hangar overlooking the quiet airfield. An animatronic Wilbur Wright recounts how he came to the field in 1909 to train military officers to fly the first federal airplane. They have many fun-with-flight activities, from flight simulators and model-making to windsocks, goggles, and a Peter Pan Club. An annual Air Fair is held in September.

The museum is open 10 am to 5 pm daily year-round. Admission is $4 for adults, $3 for seniors, and $2 for children. It's a three-block walk from the Metro.

The WWI-aerodrome theme restaurant **94th Aero Squadron** is across the runway from the museum (it has a children's menu).

Places to Stay

Camping is available within wooded **Greenbelt Park** east of town and also at the more commercial **Cherry Hill Park** (see Places to Stay in the Washington, DC chapter).

A local family operates a modest hostel (not HI-affiliated) upstairs in their home within several blocks of campus, downtown, and the Metro. **Norwich House** (☎ 301-779-1137, 4607 Norwich Ave) has three no-frills rooms outfitted with two twin beds each ($30 single, $36 double, $20 to share room).

Most of the lodging available is in nine chain motels that typically charge around $80 to $90 for standard rooms. Of these, the **Quality Inn** (☎ 301-864-5820, 7200 Baltimore Ave) is the closest to the village (rates start at $79). The **Days Inn** (☎ 301-345-5000, 9137 Baltimore Ave) is a bit less expensive at $65/70 for singles/doubles; it's 1½ miles from campus and has a good Korean restaurant downstairs.

The university has a 110-room inn (☎ 301-985-7300), University Blvd at Adelphi Rd, in the Adult Education building at the north end of campus, with rates starting at $99/114 for singles/doubles (closed for two weeks around Christmas).

Places to Eat

On a three-block stretch of Baltimore Ave south of campus, plenty of low-priced eateries cater to college crowds – the likes of Cluck-U Chicken, Smoothie King, and Yogurt Jungle. The laid-back coffeehouse **Sonic Grind** (☎ 301-277-6755, 7422 Baltimore Ave) serves smoked gouda sandwiches and vegan roasted-pepper wraps for $5 and has a menu of espresso drinks and *chai* (tea with milk and spices). The exhibit 'Velvet Paintings: Kitsch, Mass Culture, or High Art?' was on display during a recent visit.

The **Marathon Deli** (☎ 301-927-6717, 4429 Lehigh Rd) offers good Greek dishes; **Seven Seas** (☎ 301-345-5807, 8503 Baltimore Ave) is a good Chinese restaurant; and **RJ Bentley's** (☎ 301-277-8898, 7323 Baltimore Ave) is a local favorite bar and restaurant for standard American food.

On campus across from the visitor center, you can get lunch weekdays in the **Rossborough Inn** (☎ 301-314-8013), which dates from 1804, when it served as a stage stop between Baltimore and DC. There's also a 'dairy' in the visitor center that serves ice cream and light lunches.

Getting There & Away

The College Park rail station, a mile from campus, serves the Metro Green Line to and from DC and the regional MARC commuter trains between DC and Baltimore. Refer to the Washington, DC and Getting Around chapters for more information.

SIX FLAGS AMERICA

The newest branch of the popular 31-site Six Flags amusement theme parks opened in Prince George's County near Largo in spring 1999. Six Flags America (☎ 301-249-1500), 13710 Central Ave, features two roller coasters that tower over the park in a bright green and yellow-orange spiral. 'Gotham City' features two additional roller coasters and a Batman stunt show. The park is open weekends only in shoulder seasons and daily in summer. Admission is $23 for adults, half price for kids under 48 inches tall. It's a 15-minute drive from DC. Take I-495/I-95 to exit 15A, and take Route 214E for 5 miles.

PAUL GARBER FACILITY

The Paul Garber Facility (☎ 202-357-1400), on Silver Hill Rd in Suitland, is the Smithsonian Air and Space Museum's restoration and storage facility. Specialists have restored the controversial *Enola Gay*, the B-29 bomber that dropped the atomic bomb on Hiroshima. The more than 90 other historic aircraft at the facility include warbirds from WWI and WWII, along with spacecraft. Just about anyone who visits here will tell you the Garber Facility is a haunting place – an odd combination of an aircraft cemetery and Dr Frankenstein's lab.

Tours last three hours. The facilities are unheated, and there are no restrooms or drinking water along the way. Since much of the information included in the tour is highly technical, they don't recommend visitation by children under 14. The free tours start at 10 am on weekdays, 10 am and 1 pm on weekends.

SURRATT HOUSE

Once a post office and tavern, this building (☎ 301-868-1121), 9118 Brandywine Rd in Clinton, gained its infamy after the assassination of Abraham Lincoln. Proprietor Mary Surratt was the mother of a co-conspirator of John Wilkes Booth, Lincoln's assassin. Booth and Surratt's son John hid weapons and hatched their murder plot here. Although Mary Surratt probably had no idea what her son and Booth were up to, a military court judged her an accomplice in the presidential assassination and ordered her to be hanged. Mary Surratt was the first woman to die of such punishment in the US. Curiously, her son John, the true Wilkes accomplice, escaped execution.

The Surratt House is open year-round and has hour-long public tours from 11 am to 3 pm Thursday to Friday and noon to 4 pm on weekends. Tours leave every half hour and cost $3 for adults, $2 for seniors, and $1 for youth under 19.

From Washington, DC, take I-495/I-95 to exit 7A, take Route 223W to Brandywine Rd, and turn left.

In April 1861, a divided Union plunged into four dark years of bloody conflict – brother pitted against brother, families divided and often on opposing sides, widespread destruction, and a horrific toll in both military and civilian casualties. Trying to describe the cataclysmic events of 1861–65 in a few pages is an almost impossible task – some 100,000 books and articles have been written about it! But this chapter, in addition to the numerous maps and Civil War snippets located in the chapters where the events took place, may bring you a little closer to an understanding of the war.

The Unraveling Begins...

The path to war was essentially a long and complex struggle to save the Union. The actual state of war represented the boiling over of differences that had been simmering for some time.

One of the clearest factors was sectionalism, occasioned by the very different economic bases of the primarily agricultural South and the increasingly industrialized North. By the end of the 1850s, the South produced nearly all of the world's cotton, and the viability of this one-crop economy was based on cheap black slave labor. How was it, in America, which feted itself as a country founded on the premise of freedom from oppression, that the practice of human bondage won acceptance?

Following the establishment of the Union, there had been opposition to slavery in both the South and North. But opposition in the South had almost vanished by the 1830s, as any abolitionists there were threatened, tarred and feathered, and generally ostracized. In the North, there was a growing abolitionist presence and a definite sense that slavery was contrary to true liberal ideals – all Northern states had outlawed slavery by 1846. A landmark was the publication in 1852 of Harriet Beecher Stowe's

JAMES F GIBSON

Previous page: Allan Pinkerton (secret service organizer), Lincoln, and General John A McClernand at Antietam (October 3, 1862)

PHOTO – ALEXANDER GARDENER

Left: Group of 'contrabands' at Cumberland Landing, Virginia (May 14, 1862)

Right: Storefront in the South advertising 'Auction & Negro Sales'

novel *Uncle Tom's Cabin*, which hardened opposition to slavery in the North but was met with derision in the South.

The 1850s saw a number of developments that strengthened the divisions. A bill sponsored in 1854 by Stephen A Douglas of Illinois introduced the concept that settlers in the new territories, such as Kansas and Nebraska, had the right to choose whether or not their territory would allow slavery. Douglas' bill was passed into law, effectively ending the provisions of the Missouri Compromise, which for 30 years had successfully held the lid on the powder-keg issue of states' rights by allowing for 12 free states and 12 slave states and by forbidding slavery in the Louisiana Purchase area north of 36°30' north latitude.

Once passed, Douglas' act had the very effect its opponents feared. Although Nebraska remained relatively unscathed, Kansas received a torrent of settlers from both the South and North who intended to influence the future of slavery in the territory. The opposing sides were soon at each other's throats, and there were several bloody encounters.

In one week in May 1856, there was an attack on the 'Free-Stater' town of Lawrence, Kansas, which was followed up with an eye-for-an-eye massacre of pro-slavery settlers by a band led by the fanatical

Northern abolitionist John Brown. 'Bleeding Kansas' intensified the divisions between antislavery and pro-slavery lobbies, and, importantly, politicized the issue and polarized the various political groups. In the same week in May, Senator Charles Sumner, an abolitionist from Massachusetts, was beaten senseless with a cane by Congressman Preston Brooks, a pro-slavery supporter from South Carolina, in the Senate chamber. Not long before the beating, Sumner, in a speech to the Senate, had predicted that the fighting in Kansas would spread out from the western plains to a greater stage, 'where every citizen will be not only spectator but actor.'

In the national election of 1856, the new Republican party, which was opposed to the expansion of the number of slaveholding territories, won valuable experience and recognition but failed to gain office. Northern hopes that the issue of states' rights not be settled in favor of the South were dashed with the Southern-dominated Supreme Court's ruling in the Dred Scott case in 1857 – the court effectively ruled that Congress could not interfere with states' determinations in regard to the issue of slavery. The territories would be allowed to decide by 'popular sovereignty'; that is, a vote by the settlers.

Lincoln Enters the Picture

Before hope of resolving these divisive issues on a political level disintegrated, a little-known, rangy politician named Abraham Lincoln entered the picture. In 1858, Lincoln ran against Douglas in a Senate election. He debated the issue of slavery with Douglas; later, he uttered the immortal words, 'A house divided against itself cannot stand. I believe this government cannot endure permanently half slave and half free.' Lincoln was defeated in the Senate election but won the recognition that would set him up for later battles.

In October 1859, John Brown was captured and hung for his raid on the arsenal at Harpers Ferry (see the Western Maryland chapter). Though Virginia slaves did not heed Brown's call for insurrection, his action sharpened the lines of division between the abolitionist North – which saw him as a martyr – and the pro-slavery South – which feared a larger slave revolt.

Election of 1860

All of these issues came to a head in the critical election of 1860, with sectionalism again the most critical divider. At a convention in Chicago, the Republicans nominated Lincoln to run for president, rejecting the distinguished politician William H Seward, whose strong antislavery stance was seen as a liability.

The Democrats were fielding two slates of candidates – after two conventions, they split into Northern and Southern sections. The Southern Democrats found in John C Breckinridge a candidate willing to protect slavery in the territories. Stephen A Douglas, who had mostly Northern and border-state support, had been rejected by Southern Democrats, who felt his notion of 'popular sovereignty' was not clear-cut enough. A third group, the Constitutional Union Party, led by John Bell, gathered in the extremes of the Southern/Northern split.

The November 1860 election resulted in a Republican victory – Lincoln won a plurality of the popular vote (just over 40%) and more than half the electoral college votes (180 to 123) and therefore would take office the following March.

Once it became clear that Lincoln had been elected president, the Union began to fall apart. South Carolina had threatened to secede if this was the result – they feared that the Republicans, predominantly representing non-slaveholding states, would now act to keep slavery out of the territories. To them, Lincoln was the worst type of 'black' Republican, and they had already witnessed his antislavery stance in earlier debates.

At the South Carolina state convention held on December 20, it was declared 'that the Union now subsisting between South Carolina and other states under the name of the "United States of America" is hereby dissolved.' The other states of the lower south were not far behind – by February 8, Georgia, Alabama, Florida, Louisiana, Mississippi, and Texas had joined with South Carolina at a meeting in Montgomery, Alabama, to form the Confederate States. Jefferson Davis (a West Point graduate and senator from Mississippi) was elected president, and Georgian Alexander Stephens vice president.

Between the time of Lincoln's election and inauguration, very little of practical value was done by the then-incumbent president, the Democrat James Buchanan, or his administration to avoid secession. Concerted attempts at compromise failed – even the proposal by John J Crittenden to extend the line of the Missouri Compromise from the Atlantic to the Pacific was rejected. Meanwhile, the Southerners took control of the 11 forts and several other military installations in their territory, which they would need in time of war.

So by Lincoln's inauguration, on March 4, 1861, he had inherited a no-win situation. On one side, the hardened secessionists were unwilling to compromise, and on the other, the successful Republicans were not about to squander the fruits of their electoral victory. Lincoln was willing

Right: Union cavalry after the Battle of Manassas I (Bull Run)

GEORGE N BARNARD

to compromise on all issues demanded by the Southern states except one – the division of the Union. When he learned that his Union troops in Fort Sumter (Charleston Harbor, South Carolina) needed to be supplied or withdrawn, Lincoln ordered that supplies be sent to them. This action provoked the Confederates into firing the first shots of the Civil War on April 12 and 13, 1861.

With those shots, the issues were now crystal clear; those who previously had lingering doubts took sides. More states aligned with the Confederacy – Virginia on April 17, 1861, then Arkansas, North Carolina, and Tennessee a month later. Slave-owning border states, with stronger ties to the Union – Delaware, Maryland, Kentucky, and Missouri – aligned with the North. These developments complicated matters for Lincoln. How could he outlaw slavery without alienating the loyal border states?

After Virginia's secession, the capital of the Confederacy moved to Richmond, and with Virginia went the military genius Robert E Lee. Lincoln had offered Lee command of the Union forces, but the general would not turn his back on his beloved state. Lincoln called for volunteers 'to cause the laws to be duly executed,' and the South did likewise, brandishing the ideals of defense of homeland and white supremacy.

The Political War

Underlying all of the verbal sparring that preceded the war (and the battles to be waged later) was the issue of slavery. Remarkably, when the war started, the two sides appeared to maintain similar stances. Lincoln feared any attempt at emancipation would alienate the Union's slave-holding border states, while the South enshrined the concept of Negro slavery in its new constitution by prohibiting the African slave trade but permitting the interstate trade of slaves. Slowly, Lincoln realized there were distinct advantages to officially opposing slavery. As the correct moral choice, emancipation would perhaps win support for the Northern cause in Europe. It also meant potential black recruits for the Union forces. But he really needed a victory before he could proclaim such a strong stance; otherwise, his actions would be seen as born of desperation. The victory Lincoln was waiting for came at Antietam, Maryland, in mid-September 1862.

As soon as Lee had departed Union soil, Lincoln acted swiftly, and on September 23, he issued his preliminary Emancipation Proclamation, which promised to free all slaves in the Confederacy by January 1, 1863, unless the Rebel states had by then returned to the Union. The border states were not affected – it was thought that after the war, slavery could easily be abolished in these.

This symbolic proclamation had the desired result. By the end of the war, there were nearly 180,000 black soldiers in the Union army, and many had experienced combat. A great number distinguished themselves in battle and joined the list of war heroes. Furthermore, the move was greeted warmly by the European powers. Even in Britain, where textile industries were hungry for the South's cotton crop, sympathy for the Southern cause dwindled.

Toward the end of the war, the South even made moves that faintly resembled a begrudging acceptance of emancipation. In March 1865, bowing to pressure from the Confederate generals, the Confederacy

Right: Captain Horatio G Gibson and officers at Fair Oaks during the Peninsula Campaign (1862)

allowed the recruitment of black regiments. These never really came into play, as the war was concluded swiftly thereafter.

Two victories in July 1863 – at the battle of Gettysburg and in the capitulation of Vicksburg – further strengthened Lincoln's political position. The midterm congressional elections of 1862 had been a rebuff to the Republicans – the Democratic Party, replete with antiwar forces (known as 'Copperheads'), nearly seized control of the House of Representatives. But with these victories on the battlefield, pro-Lincoln sentiment returned. In dedicating the battlefield cemetery at Gettysburg, he enunciated his feelings simply. Regarding the preservation of the Union, he expressed his belief 'that these dead shall not have died in vain, that this nation under God shall have a new birth of freedom, and that the government of the people by the people for the people shall not perish from the earth.'

The election of 1864 loomed, and Lincoln agonized over it. Battle casualties in 1864 had been particularly heavy, and there were elements in the Republican Party that opposed his renomination. The Democrats, with a platform of immediate peace, nominated General George McClellan (who then insisted that peace was dependent on preservation of the Union). Lincoln got the nomination for the Union Party, a loose alliance of Republicans and War Democrats. Thanks to another string of victories on the battlefield (especially Sherman's capture of Atlanta), he won the election of November 1864 with an electoral-college vote of 212 to 12 (but in most states, his plurality was only slightly more than his opponent's). At his inauguration in 1865, he urged the American people to forget about vengeance and to 'do all which may achieve and cherish a just and lasting peace.'

The Congress abolished slavery with the 13th Amendment to the Constitution on January 31, 1865. So at the fall of Richmond, as Jefferson Davis and his cabinet fled south, Lincoln was greeted by hundreds of 'free' slaves. One elderly slave fell to his knees before Lincoln and praised him as a messiah. Lincoln responded, 'Don't kneel to me. You must kneel to God and thank Him for your freedom.'

Lincoln did not live to see the 13th Amendment finally ratified (that happened on December 6, 1865). On April 14, five days after Lee surrendered to General Ulysses S Grant at Appomattox, Lincoln was assassinated in a Washington, DC, theater by the Southern partisan John Wilkes Booth, who believed that 'this country was formed for the white not for the black man.'

The thankless task of Reconstruction and the implementation of the objectives of the Emancipation Proclamation passed to Andrew Johnson, Lincoln's vice president in the 1864 campaign. Reconstruction was made difficult by extremists on both sides, including Radical Republicans (who had opposed Lincoln's sensible Reconstruction plans), the corrupt Northern opportunists (known as 'carpetbaggers'), and the two Southern organizations that had developed in response to the Southern defeat – the Ku Klux Klan and the Knights of the White Camellia. The spirit of the generous terms that Grant and Sherman had offered to the armies of their defeated enemies, Lee and Joseph E Johnston, faded amid calls for retribution. Reconstruction was to be a bitter and painful process.

The Military War

It was never a certainty that the North would bulldoze the South into submission. The North's strength lay in a roughly two-to-one advantage in manpower, greater financial resources, and a far greater capacity to produce munitions (estimated to have been 30 to one). But as defender, the South had the advantage of fighting on a system of interior lines, it had a huge coastline that proved hard to blockade, and there was always the possibility of foreign aid (from cotton-hungry European powers).

The South had Lee and, as they soon discovered, several other brilliant generals, such as Stonewall Jackson (see the Stonewall Jackson boxed text in the Shenandoah Valley & Ranges chapter). And the volunteer Rebels seemed initially to have a far greater sense of brotherhood – the 'brothers-in-arms' strength of the underdog – which united them on the battlefield.

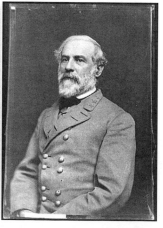

MATHEW B BRADY (GRANT); JULIAN B VANNERSON (LEE)

Far left: General Ulysses S Grant, head of the Union Army (1864–65)

Left: General Robert E Lee, head of the Confederate Army (1862–65) and Grant's main adversary

Early on, the bloodcurdling 'Rebel yell' put the fear of God into the hearts of the opposing Yankees. Only a few definitive victories by the Union forces redressed the balance.

After several minor battles in 1861, the two armies of volunteers, which had been gathering around their respective capitals, clashed in July at Manassas Junction, in Northern Virginia. The victory of the Southern forces in this battle was a precursor of events to come. The North initially suffered heavy losses in the ensuing battles because of poor and hesitant generalship, especially in the eastern theater (centered on Virginia).

The strategy of the war was simple – and certainly never grand. The South was essentially on the defensive, but its early forays into Union territory could have easily been turned into victorious offensives – especially at the point when the North had not yet found a good land-battle commander. The Battle of Antietam, in September 1862, spelled out the horrendous cost in casualties for unsuccessful offensives and also illustrated the difficulties of maintaining a large military force in hostile territory. If there were any doubts, the debacle of Gettysburg, in July 1863, in which the Confederates suffered more casualties than the larger Northern forces, confirmed that further offensive action would be suicidal for the South.

The North's strategy had to be the offensive. It was outlined to a certain extent in May 1861 in the Anaconda Plan of Wilfred Scott, the first supreme commander of the Union forces. Roughly, it proposed that the Confederate coastline be blockaded and control of the Mississippi be wrested, thus surrounding and strangling the South and facilitating Union invasions. The problem was that it took enormous losses and four years to achieve the desired result.

Toward the end of the war, when Grant dogged Lee through Virginia, there is no doubt that attrition came into play. Despite greater losses on the battlefield, Grant maintained the offensive, attempting to isolate his foe from the supply base of Richmond and to sever the interior lines. When Grant eventually trapped Lee in the Confederate capital and the war settled down to a siege, it was only a matter of time before the North won. Interestingly, both sides had to resort to compulsory enrollment of troops – the South in 1862 and the North in 1863.

Lee knew that a set-piece defensive action with no room to maneuver was anathema to an army seasoned to making surprising and bold tactical moves. The biggest army would eventually stretch the defensive perimeter to its breaking point and then move in for the kill. Lee even said that with the Army of Northern Virginia besieged, 'it will be a mere question of time.' And while Lee's troops were bottled up in the Richmond defenses, Union General William Tecumseh Sherman was permitted to wage war in the west (Tennessee) and to eventually march triumphantly through Georgia and the Carolinas.

And of the oft-forgotten naval effort, there is no doubt that the Union navy – called 'Uncle Sam's web feet' by Lincoln – eventually provided a means to help win the war, although its actions and the blockade of the coastline did not really have an impact until the end of 1863. Early in the war, about 10% of the blockade runners were captured, but by the end of 1864, it was about one in three. Toward the end of the Civil War, the only Confederate port that remained open to blockade runners was Galveston, Texas.

And with the Civil War came revolutionary changes in the nature of naval warfare. The most vaunted change at the time was the introduction of ironclad ships – the *Monitor* and *Merrimac/Virginia* battle highlighted this watershed. The use of steam and marine torpedoes ('mines') and the sinking of a battleship by a submarine (the Confederate *Hunley* sank the *Housatonic* in February 1864) presaged the major sea battles of WWI.

There was also a transitional revolution in the nature of land warfare. Innovations that would become de rigueur in later wars included the gathering of military intelligence (albeit there was much misinformation in this war), aerial reconnaissance by balloon (and thus antiballoon measures, such as camouflage and 'anti-aircraft' fire), communication in the field by telegraph, the movement of troops and material by railroad and the use of rail guns (such as those used at the Siege of Petersburg), the establishment of field hospitals and the treatment of diseases in the field, a change in weaponry (repeating magazine rifles, machine guns, shells, and rifled artillery), and the widespread appearance of journalists and photographers on the battlefield.

And what was it all for? For the South, it was probably the defense of its homeland against an invading army; for the North, the preservation of the Union and the survival of a form of democratic government ('of, by, and for the people'), then only 80 years old. Interestingly, before the war, the states were referred to as a plural noun (eg, the United States are…), and after as a singular entity. For the slaves, of course, the war resulted in freedom.

The loss of more than 600,000 lives and the 500,000 or so other casualties was a gaping wound in the Union – a wound that has still not fully healed. The Confederate flags still strewn over the cemeteries of Virginia and other Southern states indicate that the Rebel sentiment is still strong.

Recently, South Carolina has been in the spotlight, as civil-rights activists protest the Confederate flag still flown at the state's capitol, arguing that it symbolizes racism. Pro-flag citizens are rallying back, saying the flag honors South Carolina's heritage and Confederate war

PHOTOGRAPHER UNKNOWN

3242

Left: Post-war Richmond (1865)

dead. Talk to many Southerners and touch on the subject of the war, and you are likely to receive an emotional tirade. Sherman's 'March to the Sea,' Sheridan's razing of the Shenandoah, and the merciless shelling of the civilian populations in Vicksburg and Petersburg are still remembered by the descendants of those who felt the brunt of these actions, and the specter of the emaciated Union prisoners of war in the Confederate prison of Andersonville still arouse intense emotion in the North.

The defeated Lee expressed the purest of hopes when he implored that the sins of the past be forgotten and that Southern supporters should 'make your sons Americans.'

Eastern Theater Chronology

The majority of Civil War battles were fought in the eastern states, and many of those were on Virginian soil. The most intense period of fighting was during the battles of 1864 and 1865, when the armies of Lee and Grant zigzagged through Virginia and Maryland.

1861

The Union won a few minor engagements in northwestern Virginia in June and July. Sizable armies gathered around Washington, DC, and Richmond, and the first major engagement of the war took place on July 21 at Manassas Junction (see Manassas National Battlefield Park, in the Northern Virginia chapter), 26 miles southwest of DC. The result of the Battle of **Manassas I (Bull Run)** was a loss for the Union troops. A stalemate ensued, giving the new Union commander, George B McClellan, valuable time to train his Army of the Potomac. The combined actions of 1861, however, do not equal in losses and size even one day of the later major battles of the war.

1862

On March 9, **USS *Monitor*** and **CSS *Virginia*** (formerly *Merrimac*) dueled in Hampton Roads – the first clash of ironclad vessels in the history of naval warfare. (See the Battle of the Ironclads boxed text, in the Hampton Roads chapter.)

The Confederates under Joe Johnston abandoned their lines around Manassas and moved toward Richmond. McClellan geared up his new army and moved by water to the Union strongholds of Fort Monroe and Newport News. He then mounted his **Peninsula Campaign** on April 4, a march on Richmond to the northwest. Both Confederate resistance and the mud caused by heavy rains slowed McClellan's advance, and he did not come within sight of Richmond for two months.

The Confederates attacked the Union forces at **Seven Pines (Fair Oaks)** from May 31 to June 1, but the Union stood fast. The most significant event was the wounding of Johnston and the subsequent assumption of command by Robert E Lee.

The **Seven Days Battles** raged around Richmond from June 25 to July 1. The fighting seesawed from Beaver Dam Creek (June 26), to Gaines' Mill (June 27), to Savage's Station (June 29), to Glendale and Frayser's Farm (June 30). The Union troops, after several defeats in these battles, successfully disengaged at Harrison's Landing.

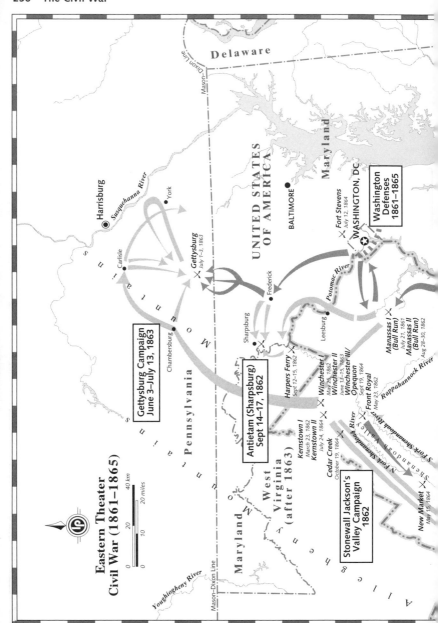

Eastern Theater
Civil War (1861–1865)

Gettysburg Campaign
June 3–July 13, 1863

Antietam (Sharpsburg)
Sept 14–17, 1862

Stonewall Jackson's
Valley Campaign
1862

Washington Defenses
1861–1865

Delaware

Maryland

UNITED STATES
OF AMERICA

Pennsylvania

West
Virginia
(after 1863)

Maryland

Harrisburg

York

Carlisle

Chambersburg

Gettysburg
July 1–3, 1863

Frederick

Sharpsburg

Harpers Ferry
Sept 12–15, 1862

Winchester I
May 26, 1862
Winchester II
June 13–15, 1863
Winchester III/
Opequon
Sept 19, 1864

Front Royal
May 23, 1862

Kernstown I
March 23, 1862
Kernstown II
July 24, 1864

Cedar Creek
October 19, 1864

New Market
May 15, 1864

Leesburg

Manassas I
(Bull Run)
July 21, 1861
Manassas II
(Bull Run)
Aug 28–30, 1862

BALTIMORE

Fort Stevens
July 12, 1864

WASHINGTON, DC

Susquehanna River

Potomac River

Rappahannock River

N Fork Shenandoah River

S Fork Shenandoah River

Shenandoah Valley

Youghiogheny River

Mason–Dixon Line

20   40 km

0   10   20 miles

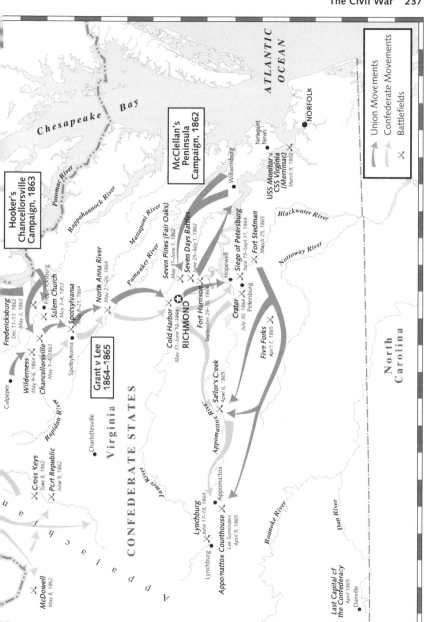

ATLANTIC
OCEAN

Chesapeake Bay

Potomac River

NORFOLK

Newport
News

Williamsburg

USS Monitor v
CSS Virginia
(Merrimac)
March 9, 1862

McClellan's
Peninsula
Campaign, 1862

Hooker's
Chancellorsville
Campaign, 1863

Rappahannock River

Mattaponi River

Pamunkey River

Blackwater River

Nottoway River

Seven Pines (Fair Oaks)
May 31–June 1, 1862

Seven Days Battles
June 25–July 1, 1862

Fredericksburg
Dec 11–13, 1862
May 3, 1863

Fredericksburg
May 3, 1863

Salem Church
May 3, 1863

Spotsylvania
May 8–21, 1864

North Anna River
May 23–26, 1864

Cold Harbor
May 31–June 12, 1864

RICHMOND

Hopewell

Siege of Petersburg
June 15–Sept 31, 1864

Fort Stedman
March 25, 1865

Wilderness
May 5–6, 1864

Chancellorsville
May 1–4, 1863

Spotsylvania

Fort Harrison
September 29–30, 1864

Crater
July 30, 1864
Petersburg

Five Forks
April 1, 1865

Culpeper

Grant v Lee
1864–1865

Rapidan River

Charlottesville

Virginia

CONFEDERATE STATES

James River

Sailor's Creek
April 6, 1865

Appomattox River

North
Carolina

Cross Keys
June 8, 1862

Port Republic
June 9, 1862

Lynchburg
June 17–18, 1864

Appomattox Courthouse
Lee Surrenders
April 9, 1865

Appomattox

Lynchburg

Roanoke River

Dan River

McDowell
May 8, 1862

Last Capital of
the Confederacy
April 1865

Danville

A p p a l a c h i a n

Union Movements

Confederate Movements

✕ Battlefields

Before and during the Peninsula Campaign, the Confederate tactical genius Thomas 'Stonewall' Jackson had played a cat-and-mouse game with Union forces in the Shenandoah Valley. His victories and forays during the **Valley Campaign** successfully prevented the Union forces from reinforcing McClellan's troops around Richmond.

On August 9, Jackson clashed indecisively with the Union forces of General John Pope at Cedar Mountain. When Lee learned that the Army of the Potomac was moving by water to join Pope, he moved to bolster Jackson's forces. The war returned to Manassas, and from August 28 to August 30 the Battle of **Manassas II (Bull Run)** was fought, resulting in another Confederate victory. Lee had, in nine weeks, succeeded in moving the war away from Richmond to the doors of Washington, DC. The Confederate army made an offensive across the Potomac River but was halted in mid-September at the battles of South Mountain and **Antietam (Sharpsburg)** in Maryland (see Antietam National Battlefield, in the Western Maryland chapter).

George B McClellan was relieved of his command on November 7 by Ambrose E Burnside, who prepared for another offensive against the South. In mid-November, the Union army reached Stafford Heights, overlooking Fredericksburg, Virginia, but from December 11 to December 13, the Army of the Potomac was squashed by the defenses of **Fredericksburg** in one of the most one-sided battles of the Civil War (see the Northern Virginia chapter).

Below: Company D, US Engineer Battalion at Petersburg (August 1864)

PHOTOGRAPHER UNKNOWN

1863

After Burnside's indecisive 'Mud March' (January 19–23), Joseph Hooker assumed command of the Army of the Potomac. In April, Hooker led his army upstream in an attempt to slip around Lee's left flank.

Lee's response was swift and deadly, and from May 1 to May 4, he won his greatest victory at **Chancellorsville**. However, in that battle, he lost his most valuable lieutenant, Stonewall Jackson (see the Northern Virginia chapter).

The Confederate army then marched north into Pennsylvania but was followed by the Army of the Potomac, now led by Major General George G Meade. From July 1 to July 3, the Confederates were soundly defeated at the Battle of **Gettysburg**, one of the bloodiest and best-remembered battles of the Civil War. Lee's army retreated into Virginia, and the two armies recuperated. The military lines alternated between the Rapidan and Rappahannock Rivers west of Fredericksburg, and many military personnel from both sides were rushed to bolster operations around Chattanooga in the western theater.

Lee made one more attempt to turn Meade's flank from October 9 to October 22, but he was defeated at Bristoe Station. A move made by Meade in late November, south of the Rapidan, ended in a stalemate at Mine Run.

1864

This was the first year of Ulysses S Grant versus Robert E Lee. After Lincoln conferred the rank of lieutenant general on Grant, giving him total command of Union forces in the field, Grant chose for himself the task of destroying Lee's Army of Northern Virginia and assigned to Major General William Tecumseh Sherman the job of keeping Joe Johnston's Army of Tennessee in check.

The armies of the two generals met up for the Battle of **Wilderness** in tangled thickets on May 5 and 6. The initial battle was a stalemate, and Grant marched toward the vital junction at **Spotsylvania Courthouse**. A battle raged for nearly two weeks, with some of the war's bloodiest fighting (see the Northern Virginia chapter). Grant disengaged again and headed across the **North Anna River** (May 23–26) to **Cold Harbor**. A battle raged there, almost in sight of Richmond, for another two weeks (May 31 to June 12). After some massive, futile frontal assaults, a regretful Grant stealthily disengaged, yet again, and moved toward the strategic rail-junction town of Petersburg.

Grant threw his troops against the Confederates during the **Siege of Petersburg** (see the Richmond chapter) from June 15 to June 18, and the Union forces would have taken the city if they had pressed home their assaults. Lee's army arrived from the north in time to defend Petersburg, at which point a protracted siege of the city began. The Union forces tried to breach a gap in the Confederate lines after the huge explosion of the Battle of the **Crater** on July 30 but were unsuccessful. Lee's defenses were stretched thin as the Union forces peppered away and captured and fortified ground between Richmond and Petersburg, such as at **Fort Harrison** (September 29 and 30), on the James River. Winter brought a halt to major operations, but skirmishing, sniping, and shelling continued.

The year 1864 was an active one in the Shenandoah Valley. First there was the Battle of **New Market** on May 15, in which students from Lexington's Virginia Military Institute participated in charges against the Union lines. Jubal Early's Maryland Campaign began in late June, and after expelling Union troops from the Shenandoah, his forces threatened Washington, DC. They were turned around at the Battle of **Fort Stevens** on July 12.

The Rebels returned to the Valley, but in a series of hard-fought battles against the Union forces of General Philip Sheridan, they were soundly defeated, the last major battle being the Battle of **Cedar Creek** on October 19.

1865

At the beginning of the year, the armies of Grant and Lee still faced each other in entrenchments around Petersburg. In February, Grant dispatched his infantry and cavalry to the south and west of the city in an attempt to outflank the city. Lee, realizing that each passing day increased the likelihood of Union success, attempted to break the impasse by attacking **Fort Stedman** (March 25), to the east of the city. The attack failed, and Lee reported to Jefferson Davis, 'I fear now that it will be impossible to prevent a junction between Grant and Sherman....'

The stretched Confederate defenses were broken at **Five Forks**, southwest of Petersburg, on April 1, and Petersburg fell the next day. Richmond fell on April 3. Lee extricated his forces in the dark of the night, but Grant, rather than savor victory, pursued his old adversary.

After the Battle of **Sailor's Creek** on April 6, the end was in sight. The remnants of the Army of Northern Virginia were cut off at **Appomattox Courthouse** – Lee surrendered to Grant on April 9, and the war was all but over (see the Piedmont chapter). In late May, the Union victory was celebrated with a grand review of Union troops in Washington, DC.

Virginia

Facts about Virginia

At first read, you will find the following chapters replete with history. There will be no apologies, as Virginia oozes history – every town seems to have some association with great events and people. Virginia was the cradle of American civilization and was the predominant battleground of the cataclysmic Civil War between the North and South. Hardly a village, patch of forest, river, or geographical feature escaped the ravages of the war, and there are many mementos left for the traveler to see and reflect on.

Virginia is also endowed with tremendous natural features, from mountains and foothills to coastal beaches, and many of these are covered in detail in the following chapters.

HISTORY

Since the earliest English settlement in the New World, Virginia has played an important and influential role in the shaping of the nation's history – a role disproportionately large for the state's size.

Consolidation of the New Nation

Virginians played a major part in establishing the constitutional basis for the newly independent nation. In fact, four of the first five presidents were born and raised in the state.

In 1778, Virginia abolished further trade in African slaves, but slavery still constituted an important pillar of the state's plantation economy. Many of the nation's leaders – including Washington and Jefferson, who wrote of the importance of individual liberty – still kept slaves. Washington, for example, owned 277 slaves at the time of his death.

The impotent provisions of the Articles of Confederation, which loosely bound the new nation together, needed a thorough re-examination. These matters were considered in detail at a Constitutional Convention that began in Philadelphia on May 25, 1787. Twelve of the 13 states sent representatives (Rhode Island declined), and the convention lasted 16 weeks.

A number of prominent Virginians – George Mason, James Madison, Edmund Randolph, and Washington (who was elected to be the convention's president) – attended. Thomas Jefferson was overseas on government business, and Patrick Henry, who opposed strong central government, did not attend.

After lengthy and sometimes bitter debate, the Virginia Plan was accepted, and a bicameral legislature was established. Throughout the proceedings, both Washington and Madison fought to include a Bill of Rights and ensure the gradual phaseout of slavery. They were unsuccessful but acquiesced to the document in its early form, believing they could introduce these changes later.

On September 17, 1787, the Constitution was signed by 39 delegates and was sent to the states for ratification. The Virginia convention struggled to ratify it after the influential Patrick Henry and James Monroe argued that it was undemocratic. John Marshall and James Madison eventually garnered enough support for the Constitution, and Virginia ratified it by a slim majority. Virginia officially entered the Union as the 10th state on June 25, 1788.

The first Congress of the US met in March 1789 to consider amendments and the two bills of rights forwarded by Virginia and New York. Ten of the amendments (of 12 submitted) were adopted and came to be known as the Bill of Rights. Nine of the amendments are attributable to Madison and one to another Virginian, Richard Henry Lee.

Virginian Presidents

Washington was the first president elected under the terms of the new constitution and was inaugurated in April 1789. He was persuaded to run for re-election in 1792 and served a second term of four years. He declined a third term, preferring to retire to his beloved Mount Vernon on the Potomac River. During his presidency, Virginia ceded part of its territory for the new national

Washington & Jefferson

Two of the greatest Virginians – indeed, two of the greatest Americans – were George Washington and Thomas Jefferson. The first and third presidents were born, lived most of their lives, died, and were buried in Virginia. Washington was born in Westmoreland County in 1732, died in 1799, and is buried at Mount Vernon. Jefferson was born east of Charlottesville at Shadwell in 1743, died in 1826, and is buried at Monticello. There are many other places where they are remembered, and all are covered in this guidebook (as well as many associated annual events).

George Washington

Alexandria – The pew Washington bought for £36 is in Christ Church. A replica of his Masonic lodge is in the George Washington Masonic National Memorial. On his last birthday, he danced with his wife, Martha, in Gadsby's Tavern (see the Around Washington, DC chapter).

Fredericksburg – This is home to another Masonic museum, the place where Washington became a mason. Kenmore, the mansion of his sister Betty, is here. The Rising Sun Tavern was built by his brother Charles, and Ferry Farm is supposedly where he cut down the cherry tree (see the Northern Virginia chapter).

Great Falls – Washington oversaw the construction of the Patowmack Canal here (see the Northern Virginia chapter).

Mount Vernon – This is his estate and final resting place (see the Northern Virginia chapter)

Northern Neck – The George Washington Birthplace National Monument is here (see the Virginia's Chesapeake Bay chapter).

Williamsburg – Many buildings in the historic precinct here, including the House of Burgesses, are associated with Washington (see the Colonial Virginia chapter).

Winchester – This was Washington's headquarters for the French and Indian Wars. His first military office still stands, and he was elected to the House of Burgesses here in 1758 and 1761 (see the Shenandoah Valley & Ranges chapter).

Yorktown – The last battle of the Revolutionary War was fought here (see the Colonial Virginia chapter).

Thomas Jefferson

Barboursville – Located in Orange County, this is home to vineyards and the ruins of a Jefferson-designed mansion (see the Piedmont chapter).

Charlottesville – The University of Virginia, founded in 1819, was Jefferson's ideal 'academical village' (see the Piedmont chapter).

Library of Congress – Jefferson's huge personal collection, donated in 1815, was the cornerstone of this library (see the Washington, DC chapter).

Monticello – This was his crowning achievement (now World Heritage). It is full of his creations and is his final resting place (see the Piedmont chapter).

Natural Bridge – This was purchased by Jefferson (see the Shenandoah Valley & Ranges chapter).

Poplar Forest – A personal retreat near Lynchburg, this place has an octagonal house designed by Jefferson (see the Piedmont chapter).

State Capitol – This Jefferson-designed building was planned in 1785 (see the Richmond chapter).

Tuckahoe Plantation – West of Richmond, this is home to the schoolhouse in which Jefferson studied as a boy (see the Richmond chapter).

Washington, DC – Jefferson was the first to take up the post of president in the new capital.

Williamsburg – Jefferson studied at the College of William and Mary. The House of Burgesses, where he served before drafting the Declaration of Independence, is also here (see the Colonial Virginia chapter).

For more information on Washington, call ☎ 804-786-4484 or check out the website www.gwashington1999.org. For Jefferson, call ☎ 888-293-1776 or try www.monticello.org.

VIRGINIA

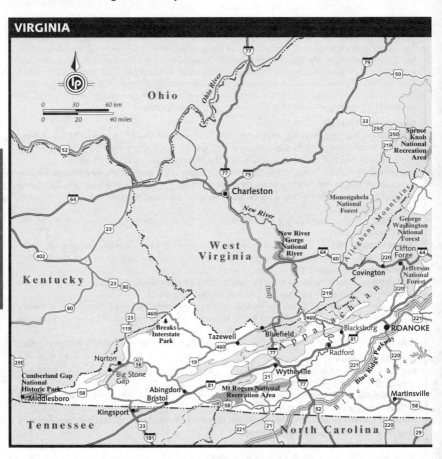

VIRGINIA

Ohio

Ohio River

Charleston

New River

West Virginia

Monongahela National Forest

New River Gorge National River

Spruce Knob National Recreation Area

George Washington National Forest

Clifton Forge

Jefferson National Forest

Allegheny Mountains

Covington

Kentucky

Breaks Interstate Park

Tazewell

Bluefield

Blacksburg

ROANOKE

Radford

Norton

Big Stone Gap

Wytheville

Blue Ridge Parkway

Cumberland Gap National Historic Park

Abingdon

Bristol

Mt Rogers National Recreation Area

Martinsville

Middlesboro

Kingsport

Tennessee

North Carolina

0   30   60 km
0   20   40 miles

capital, which would eventually bear Washington's name.

After the presidency of John Adams (1797–1801), Thomas Jefferson became the second Virginian to be elected president. He served two terms (1801–08) and was the first to take up the post in Washington, DC. Although Jefferson will be remembered more for his intellectual achievements than his deliberations when in office, his purchase of the Louisiana Territory from Napoleon almost doubled the size of the US. He also encouraged the exploration of this new territory, the Mississippi River, and the Southwest, and he carefully steered the nation away from involvement in further damaging wars.

The next Virginian to become president was James Madison. Fully supported by his friend Jefferson, who had declined a third term, Madison took office in 1809. Pressured by hawkish elements in Congress, Madison, unlike Jefferson, was not able to avoid another war, and much of his second term was spent embroiled in the War of 1812. During this war, some Virginian plantations were attacked by British naval forces, and at one stage (in 1814), Madison and his wife had to flee Washington. The city was subsequently

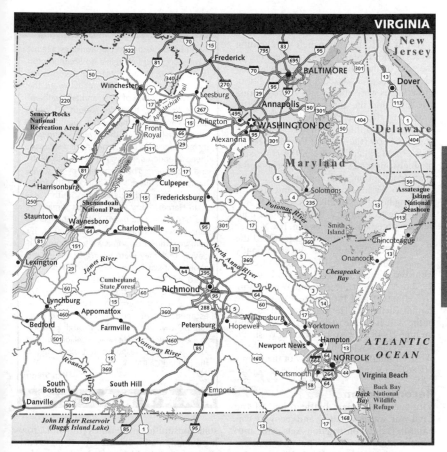

burned by the British in retaliation for the burning of York (now Toronto) in Canada in 1812.

In 1817, the already 'elder' statesman (and Virginian) James Monroe succeeded Madison as president. During his two-term presidency, Monroe oversaw expansion into the West, helped to determine the boundary with British North America (Canada), and signed the Missouri Compromise (which admitted Missouri to the union as a slave-holding state). His most significant achievement (and the first clear statement of US foreign policy) was the Monroe Doctrine, which was deliv-

ered to Congress in 1823. In the 36 years since Washington's inauguration as president, Virginians had occupied the post for 32 years.

The Coming of War

Prior to the Civil War, Virginia was roughly divided into two camps. The eastern camp, based in the Tidewater, was reliant upon slavery to reap the maximum out of its tired soil. The western counties, with a more diverse economic base, were undergoing rapid development.

An attempt in 1830 by democratic forces within the legislature to achieve the gradual phaseout of slavery failed, and with the subsequent failure of Nat Turner's brief slave revolt in 1831, the entrenched slaveholding forces in the legislature won out. Feeding on the fear of the white population, who saw such revolts as a consequence of abolition, these forces were able to pass more oppressive laws, and the antislavery forces in the state were effectively silenced.

Following John Brown's 1859 raid on Harpers Ferry (then part of Virginia; see the Western Maryland chapter), the state surprisingly opposed secession and proposed a peace convention, even dispatching a delegation to Washington with the intention of avoiding hostilities at all costs.

As late as February 1861, the state convention voted against secession. It was after Lincoln's call for troops, which followed the firing on Fort Sumter, that the state finally seceded on April 17, 1861. With Virginia went the military genius Robert E Lee (see the boxed text in the Around Washington, DC chapter) and the future Confederate capital, Richmond. The northwestern portion of the state had little to do with secession and on June 20, 1863, was recognized in Washington as being a separate entity – the state of West Virginia. For an overview of the events of 1861–65, see the Civil War chapter.

Reconstruction

Virginia, as the main battleground of the Civil War, was devastated, and recovery was painful. The Reconstruction Acts came into force in March 1867, and Virginia was designated Military District No 1. Elections for delegates to be sent to a constitutional convention were held in late 1867 – many freed slaves, recent Northern arrivals (called 'carpetbaggers' by the Southerners), and native Unionists ('scalawags') took part, but Confederate sympathizers were barred.

After ratifying the 14th and 15th Amendments to the Constitution (giving former slaves voting rights), the state was readmitted to the Union in January 1870. It was, for long after, plagued with debt and political instability. For much of the period of Reconstruction, the state fought against African American suffrage. Even as late as 1902,

Fighting for Freedom

Two of the most powerful uprisings against slavery occurred in Virginia. In Southampton in August 1831, a 30-year-old slave named Nat Turner led around 70 men toward the county seat's store of arms and ammunition. Along the way, they slew about 60 white masters and their families (they spared a poor white family) before they were suppressed by federal troops. Nat Turner initially escaped, then surrendered; he was sentenced to death and was hung. The nightmare of all slaveowners, Nat Turner's revolt rocked the institution of slavery throughout the South.

In Harpers Ferry (now in West Virginia at the border of Maryland), white abolitionist John Brown further shocked the nation by demonstrating that some whites so opposed slavery that they were willing to die for the abolitionist cause. In 1859, Brown and his band of 22 men attempted to seize the federal arsenal, but they was trapped by US troops. Ten of them were killed, and five escaped; Brown and six others were captured. Brown was executed. Though he failed to incite a region-wide slave rebellion, his raid and the national response to it did prefigure the coming Civil War.

– Kap Stann

state constitutional measures (the 'Jim Crow' legal manipulations) were employed to curb the power of the black vote by the introduction of literacy and property requirements.

The 20th Century

Virginia's economy had, since early times, been based on agriculture – in particular, tobacco production. In the early part of the 20th century, many Virginians left the state to seek work elsewhere. But the network of railroads connecting urban centers expanded, spurring industrial growth and gradually reversing the exodus. The importance of Virginian ports (and the shipbuilding industry) supported industrialization, as steamships carried more and more freight.

By this point, the importance of Virginia as a source of motivating intellectual thought had all but faded. No longer was the state important in the determination of national affairs. In fact, the state seemed to be heading in an opposite direction, clutching to old values fueled by racism and a sense of 'what might have been.' The dominant political force from the mid-1920s until the mid-1960s was Harry Flood Byrd Sr, who was both a governor and senator for Virginia. But more importantly, he was the boss of the 'Organization' – a loose grouping of Democrats who firmly held the reins of state power. During this period, significant reforms were implemented in the fields of city management, state government costs were pruned, and the efficient 'pay-as-you-go' highway program was introduced.

In the late 1950s, the state chose to close schools rather than desegregate, and it was not until the 1960s, under pressure from the federal courts, that Virginians agreed to the necessity of integration and the need for civil rights. Today, with the enfranchisement of African Americans in positions of political and commercial responsibility, this dark period seems to be in the distant past. In fact, many African Americans have made it into local government posts since the 1970s. Richmond's first black mayor was elected in 1977 (when there was also a black majority on the city council). Ironically, in 1989 the first elected black governor in the history of the nation, L Douglas Wilder, moved into the governor's mansion in Richmond – the former capital of the Confederacy.

The new state constitution, adopted in 1971, included some forward-thinking social, educational, and environmental policies. The latter issue came to the fore in the mid-1970s with the Kepone pesticide disaster near Hopewell – a consequence was the introduction of stricter controls over the disposal of toxic waste.

The state's economic renaissance came with WWII, in part because of its new role as the 'military base' for the US. Northern Virginia, the back doorstep of DC, assumed importance as a bedroom community for government employees. Thus, the fastest-growing areas in the state today are the counties near the nation's capital and the area around the many military bases of Hampton Roads, and the large majority of the population is now urban.

GEOGRAPHY

Virginia is roughly triangular in shape, measuring about 200 miles from north to south and 425 miles from west to east. A portion of the state lies on the Delmarva Peninsula and is cut off from the rest of the state by Chesapeake Bay.

The main part of Virginia can be divided into three very distinct topographical regions: the Appalachian Mountains at the western border of the state, the Piedmont Plateau running down the middle, and the Tidewater region – a coastal plain about 100 miles wide that comprises about a quarter of the state. The average elevation of the state is 950 feet.

The Appalachian region is again divided into three parts – the Blue Ridge Mountains, the Allegheny Mountains, and the Great Valley in between. The Blue Ridge Mountains, immortalized in folklore and song, run in a southwesterly direction, vary from 3 to 20 miles in width, and include the highest point in Virginia – Mt Rogers at 5729 feet. These mountains are composed of ancient granitic and metamorphic volcanic formations, some more than one billion years old.

The Blue Ridge Mountains are separated from the Allegheny Mountains by the Great Valley, which varies from 25 to 30 miles in width. It is in turn intersected by five river valleys that drain the high ground to either side. The Allegheny Mountains of Virginia vary from 1500 to 4000 feet in elevation – much of this range is in West Virginia.

The Piedmont, a large undulating plateau, extends from the Potomac River in the north of the state, where it is about 40 miles wide, to the border with North Carolina in the south, where it is about 175 miles wide. At its western edge, the plateau is about 1000 feet in elevation, but it slopes down almost to sea level in the east.

Occupying almost one-quarter of the state and about 100 miles wide is the low-lying coastal plain, or 'Tidewater,' on the eastern fringe. It is about 100 feet in elevation at its western edge and drops to sea level in the often marshy regions in the east. The marshlands are typified by the Great Dismal Swamp, in the state's southeast corner. The general coastline is only 112 miles in length, but if measured to take in all the indentations of bays, inlets, and estuaries, it is more than 3200 miles long.

The state is intersected by a number of rivers, and drainage is in two main directions. The rivers and their tributaries that drain the Piedmont – the Potomac, Rappahannock, James, and York – head into Chesapeake Bay in a southeasterly direction. Most of Virginia's Tidewater region is divided into three peninsulas ('necks') by these rivers.

The one anomaly, the Roanoke River, in the south of the Piedmont, meets the Atlantic Ocean in North Carolina. The main watershed is in the western part of the state. Here, the North Fork of the Holston River and the New River flow in a southwesterly direction, to the south of the Great Valley and into Tennessee.

GOVERNMENT & POLITICS

Virginia's General Assembly is the oldest continuous lawmaking body in the 'New World' – it dates from the House of Burgesses, established in Jamestown in 1619. The General Assembly exercises legislative authority and consists of the 40-member Senate, which has four-year terms and 40 members, and the House of Delegates, which has two-year terms and 100 members.

Currently, the presiding officer of the US Senate (the Lieutenant Governor) is Republican John H Hager, and the Republicans are in majority (21 to 19). In the House of Delegates, the speaker is Thomas W Moss Jr (a Democrat), the majority leader is C Richard Cranwell (a Democrat), and the minority leader is S Vance Wilkins Jr (a Republican).

The state's current governor, the 68th, is James S Gilmore III – a Republican elected to office in November 1997.

ECONOMY

The state's economic base has traditionally been agricultural, with tobacco being the most important crop. And in spite of its recent bad press, the 'sot weed' is still very important, along with other farm produce, such as apples, dairy products, poultry, livestock, peanuts, and the famed Virginia ham.

Virginia's proximity to DC means there are many parts in the north of the state that are inhabited by people who commute to the capital. The military is a major employer in the region near DC (the Pentagon is in Arlington), at Virginia's many forts and military installations, and at Hampton Roads, where the world's largest naval facility is located.

The primary employer is the manufacturing sector, however; transportation equipment, clothes, furniture, and chemicals are important industries. The third- and fourth-largest employers are the wholesale and retail trades and services (the booming travel industry is one of those services).

POPULATION & PEOPLE

The population of the state is approximately 6,800,000, and well over 60% of it is concentrated in an urban corridor that stretches from cities just south of DC, through Richmond, and on to its greatest concentration, in Hampton Roads. This concentration is often seen as an extension of the megalopolis that arches in a crescent from Boston to DC. There are other densely populated areas in the west (in Lynchburg, Charlottesville, and Roanoke). The mountainous southwestern part of the state and much of the Piedmont remain essentially rural enclaves.

There is a mix of people in Virginia. Some 20% of the population is African American, reflecting the time when black slaves played an important part in the development of the region. Many African American sites and Black Heritage walking tours exist throughout the state.

There are around 160,000 Latinos; about 15,000 Native Americans; and approximately 30,000 people each of Chinese, Filipino, Korean, and Vietnamese descent. There is an increasing number of foreign-born people, especially in the region south of DC. The ethnic mix found in these places has created tremendous diversity in the choices of restaurants and entertainment. Generally, relations between the various groups have been much less violent than in other parts of the US, and there seems a conscious attempt for all to work together for the common good.

An interesting series of pamphlets called 'Heritage' focuses on minority groups such as Native Americans, Latinos, and African Americans. It's produced by The Pepper Bird Foundation (☎ 757-220-5761, ✉ PepperBrd@ aol.com), PO Box 1071, Williamsburg, VA 23187. These pamphlets outline pertinent museums, sites, festivals, events, history, and other informational resources, such as publications and organizations. For information on the many Native American powwows and festivals that are open to the public, contact the Virginia Council on Indians, Virginia Department of Health & Human Resources, PO Box 1475, Richmond, VA 23219.

ARTS
Literature

Virginia has a rich literary history, and many of the best works from the state are linked to either the colonial or Civil War period. Perhaps the best-known of Virginian novelists is Ellen Glasgow (1874–1945), who was born into an aristocratic family in Richmond just after the Civil War. In her writings, she eschews her privileged background and attempts to make a realistic assessment of the South and its problems in the period following the war. All of Glasgow's novels mix romantic sensibility and tough reality but give insight into a 100-year period of Virginia's history, particularly as it relates to Richmond at the turn of 19th century. Her most important works are *The Voice of the People* (1900), *Virginia* (1913), *Barren Ground* (1925), *The Romantic Comedians* (1926), *They Stooped*

to *Folly* (1929), and *In This Our Life* (1941), for which she won the Pulitzer Prize.

A contemporary of Glasgow's, Willa Cather (1873–1947) was born in Winchester. Most of her best-known works centered on life on the Midwestern prairie; she received the first Prix Femina Americana in 1933 for her novel *Shadows on the Rock* (1931). *Sapphira and the Slave Girl* (1940) is one of Cather's few novels to include Virginia as a setting.

James Branch Cabell (1879–1958), like Ellen Glasgow, was born in Richmond and came from a distinguished family. He was very prolific, writing more than 50 novels and two collections of autobiographical essays. His first novel was *The Eagle's Shadow* (1904), the first in an 18-volume series called *The Biography of Manuel*, relating the fantastic tales of Manuel in the medieval land of Poictesme.

The famous poet, short-story writer, and essayist Edgar Allan Poe spent some time in the state. After his parents died in his early childhood, Poe was raised for some years by John Allan, a Richmond businessman. He studied in private schools in Virginia during his youth and attended the University of Virginia for one year. (See the Baltimore chapter for more on Poe.)

John William Fox Jr (1863–1919), for many years a resident of Big Stone Gap in the Appalachians, may not have been the most prolific writer, but his novels were certainly popular. Though once described as an 'antediluvian Ozarkian melodrama,' *The Trail of the Lonesome Pine* (1908) was the nation's first novel to sell a million copies. Based on the author's firsthand experiences, this novel paints a sentimental picture of life in the mountains of southwestern Virginia. His fiction has been adapted very successfully for the movies and theater.

Anne Spencer (1882–1975), an African American poet of the Harlem Renaissance period of the 1920s, lived and wrote in Lynchburg. Spencer had an international reputation, and her works have been anthologized in *The Norton Anthology of American Literature*.

VIRGINIA

Fine Arts

Virginia is well represented in all of the fine arts. The first state museum of the arts in the US was the Virginia Museum of Fine Arts in Richmond. The Chrysler Museum in Norfolk has one of the largest art collections south of DC, and Roanoke has the Art Museum of Western Virginia, which has a southern mountain folk art collection.

You'll find all forms of music throughout the state. In the southwest, there is an opera and a symphony in Roanoke; the Garth Newel Music Center, for chamber music, in Bath County; Friday-night mountain music at Floyd Country Store (formerly Cockram's and located in Floyd County, on the Blue Ridge Parkway); and Galax (a town near the North Carolina border), where the fiddle reigns supreme (see the Southwest & Blue Ridge Highlands chapter). Throughout the southwest and Shenandoah areas, performances by square-dance groups and clog dancers keep old forms alive.

Richmond has performances of opera and symphonic music at the Carpenter Center, the Big Gig Musicfest in summer, and a host of choirs. The Richmond Ballet is the state ballet, but the Concert Ballet of Virginia, also based in Richmond, is the state's oldest.

Hampton Roads, the most populous part of the state, is also well served with the fully professional Virginia Opera and the very busy Virginia Symphony.

Jefferson designed the state's architectural gems: Monticello, Poplar Forest, the Rotunda and Academical Village (the University of Virginia), and the state capitol. Other places of interest include the garden layout of Mount Vernon; the Pope-Leighey House (designed by Frank Lloyd Wright) near Mount Vernon; the many Georgian-style plantation mansions; and the preserved colonial city of Williamsburg.

Folk Arts

The Appalachian region is best known for its highly evolved arts-and-crafts traditions – most notably, the craft of woodworking, which ranges from rough-hewn works to fine cabinetry. Appalachia is also renowned for its quilting, basketry, and self-taught artwork.

The music and dancing of the region are distinctive as well – bluegrass music emanates from Highland fiddles, and occasionally, Elizabethan ballads retained from the residents' English ancestry can be heard on Appalachian dulcimers. It is possible to see flatfoot clogging, which is thought to have derived from early-20th-century African American dance, and square dancing is also popular. For those interested in learning more about bluegrass music and Appalachian culture, check out the fascinating documentary film *High Lonesome*, available on video.

Theater

There is a rich tradition of live theater in the state. In 1932, the Barter Theater, so called because produce was traded for admission, was established by out-of-work actors in Abingdon, in the southwest. There, at the oldest professional repertory theater in the US, actors such as Gregory Peck and Ernest Borgnine got their start. Other southwestern theatrical events are the outdoor dramas *Trail of the Lonesome Pine*, in Big Stone Gap, and *The Long Way Home*, in Radford. Another outdoor venue is Lexington's Lime Kiln Theatre, which has a unique setting in a limestone quarry.

The state's second-oldest theater, the Wayside Theatre, is in Middletown, with a season running from May to December. Actors who got their start here include Peter Boyle and Susan Sarandon.

The main cities have quite an assortment of theaters and players. Richmond has the Theatre Virginia (the state's flagship professional company), Theatre IV, and two well-known theater restaurants – Barksdale Theatre and the Swift Creek Mill Playhouse. In Norfolk, the Virginia Stage Company performs in the historic Wells Theatre; Broadway productions are performed at Chrysler Hall.

Film

Virginia has been the setting for American films since the 1930s, with classics such as *Trail of the Lonesome Pine* and, more recently, *Silence of the Lambs*. In spite of this presence in film, the state largely depends on Hollywood for its filmmaking talent and does not have a well-developed movie industry of its own. For more information on movies with settings in Virginia, see Films & TV Shows in the Facts for the Visitor chapter.

INFORMATION
Tourist Offices
Apart from the Virginia Division of Tourism (☎ 800-934-9184), Virginia has 10 'welcome centers' throughout the state on interstate highways. These offices have brochures about regional sites and accommodations in the area, and more specific information. Contact information for these centers is listed under headings that correspond to their locations.

Area Codes
There are four codes: 703 for the area of Northern Virginia around DC; 540 for the Blue Ridge Mountains and Shenandoah Valley; 804 for Richmond and the Piedmont; and 757 for Hampton Roads, Williamsburg, and the eastern shore.

Taxes
In Virginia, a 4.5% sales tax is added to most purchases, and in some places 1% is added to this, bringing the tax up to 5.5%. In hotels, you are likely to pay an additional 5% hotel tax, meaning a total tax of about 10%. There are restaurant taxes applied in some areas (fortunately, not all), and meal and drink bills may run from 8% to 10% in total tax.

Media
All the major cities in Virginia have their own daily newspapers, and these are usually of a high standard. In Hampton Roads, the *Virginia Pilot/Ledger Star* is the pick of the dailies. In Richmond, the *Richmond Times-Dispatch* has a daily circulation of more than 250,000 copies. There are some fine African American weekly papers in Richmond as well. The *Roanoke Times* serves southwest Virginia.

There are radio stations galore, with a smattering of everything on the airwaves, but gospel, country & western, traditional country, and religious music are the most common.

Richmond

Richmond (population 203,000), strategically positioned at the very heart of Virginia, is an intriguing city with a rich past. While the history of the capital (especially the antebellum) is proudly thrust in front of the visitor, there is also a heartening 20th-century feel that is best experienced in The Fan, Shockoe Slip, and Shockoe Bottom enclaves.

Many visitors come expecting a dour, conservative, almost bleak city, but they are soon surprised by its vibrant and multifaceted nature. In addition to its true Southern feel (after all, it was the capital of the Confederacy), there is a real sense that this city is the birthplace of African American entrepreneurship, as a contemplative stroll through the city's revitalized Jackson Ward will reinforce. After wandering through Capitol Square, Shockoe Bottom, Shockoe Slip, the Canal Walk, the Court End, The Fan, Monument Ave, and the Museum District, you'll have a feel for the diversity of neighborhoods, the extraordinary amount of green open spaces, and the vitality and bright future of this city.

HISTORY

Richmond's early colonial history is linked to its strategic position on the James River at the farthest navigable point up the river. The settlement was founded in 1637 as a small outpost, and a fort was constructed there in 1644 as protection against Native American attacks. Richmond had its beginnings as a town when Colonel William Byrd II (the 'Father of Richmond'), a colonial statesman, made projections in 1733; it was later incorporated in 1742. Richmond became the Virginia capital in May 1782 and was chartered as a city in July of that year.

Richmond was important during the American Revolution. As the vulnerability of Williamsburg (then the state capital) became apparent, Virginians seeking independence moved the capital another 50 miles up the James River. It was in this city that Patrick Henry delivered his immortal 'give me liberty or give me death!' speech at the Second Virginia Convention. A month later, the Revolutionary War began. On three occasions during the war, the city was attacked by the British. The second attack was repulsed by Continental Army troops led by Lafayette and von Steuben, but on the other occasions, the town was occupied and burned.

As capital of the Confederacy from 1861 to 1865, Richmond became the prime military objective of the Federal forces. At the commencement of the Civil War, the city had more than 40 tobacco-curing plants and a population of some 100,000. The first major threat to the city – and probably the most serious threat of the entire war – was in 1862. The Federal troops were repulsed in the Seven Days Battles (see the Civil War

Highlights

- The African American heritage of historic Jackson Ward

- The Valentine Museum and myriad other museums – surely one of the country's best historical repositories

- Whitewater rafting on the falls of the James River – a wilderness in the heart of a city

- The lively nightlife of Shockoe Slip, Shockoe Bottom, Carytown, and The Fan

- Petersburg – a fascinating tour through the last major battlefield of the Civil War

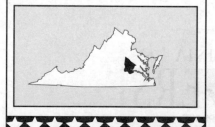

chapter). When Petersburg fell on April 2, 1865, the Confederate government evacuated the city. Its fleeing occupants set fire to most of the warehouses, bridges, and other installations, and the resulting conflagration destroyed much of the old city. On April 4, Abraham Lincoln walked into a city that was still smoldering from the fires. Virginia wasn't readmitted to the Union for another five years following the war, and for two of those years, the city was under military occupation.

The economy boomed in the 1890s with many types of manufacturing – including a stable iron industry and, of course, tobacco. The population grew rapidly in the early 20th century, and banking and finance became a growing industry. During the Great Depression of the 1930s, the number of unemployed people waiting in food lines across the nation with cigarettes in their mouths ensured that Richmond would survive such an economic catastrophe. Now it is a major finance and distribution center boasting 14 of the US's Fortune 500 corporate headquarters.

ORIENTATION

Richmond is at the junction of I-95 (north-south) and I-64 (east-west) and is about a two-hour drive away from DC, Hampton Roads, and the Blue Ridge Mountains. Also bisecting the city east to west is Route 60, and Routes 1 and 301 run through it north to south. I-295 bypasses the city on its eastern side.

The city is bisected by the James River, and most of its attractions lie to the north. The central access to downtown is along Broad St, not Main St, which is three streets to the southwest. The numbered streets that cross Broad St (which divides the city north and south) increase from northwest to southeast. Foushee St, which runs northeast-southwest, is the dividing line for east and west markings.

Richmond's heart is the Court End district, in downtown, which has more than 20 significant old buildings (on the historic register) and museums. Main St, which runs west from the Court End, has most of the banks. Northeast of Broad St is the colorful

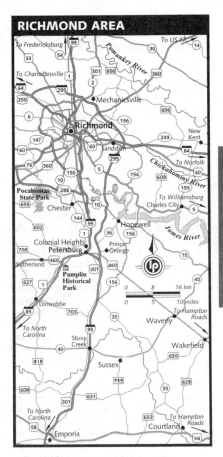

Jackson Ward (see the description under Walking Tour, later in this chapter).

Also fashionable is Cary St. Located between 12th and 15th Sts, this street forms an area of converted warehouses known as Shockoe Slip in the city's oldest mercantile district. The buildings now housing the many shops and restaurants were mostly built between 1868 and 1888, as much of this area was burned to the ground in the Great Evacuation Fire of April 2 and 3, 1865. It is called a 'slip' because of its proximity to the once-bustling Great Turning Basin of the James River Canal (which no longer exists).

Shockoe Bottom is a popular restaurant and nightclub area to the east of Shockoe Slip. The most recognizable feature is Main Street Station, which dominates the warehouses and the 400-year-old 17th St farmers' market, possibly the nation's oldest. Some 15 city blocks between 20th and Pear Sts, along the James River, have been in the process of slow revitalization in the Tobacco Row redevelopment (which started in the mid-1980s). To the north of Shockoe Bottom and perched above the James River are the narrow, shaded streets of Church Hill, where you will find St John's Church, the scene of Patrick Henry's famous speech.

The Canal Walk has revitalized the area immediately adjacent to the James River – points of interest along the 1¼-mile walk relate aspects of the city's history.

To the west of downtown lie the gracious neighborhoods that best reflect Richmond's turn-of-the-19th-century period. The wide Monument Ave is divided by a grassy median strip that has statues of Civil War heroes scattered along it. Fine homes housing the trustees of Virginia's old wealth line either side. Perpendicular to Monument Ave is the Boulevard, where the Virginia Historical Society and the Virginia Museum of Fine Arts are located.

To the south of Monument Ave, a number of streets radiate out in what is known as The Fan district – the western boundary is the Boulevard, and the southern boundary is I-195. An eclectic collection of people live in this gaslit precinct, which features meticulously restored townhouses and traditional brownstones.

The fashionable West End is the area west of the Boulevard, including part of Richmond and part of Henrico County. The area between Thompson St and the Boulevard, which includes the many restaurants, boutiques, and trendy residences of Carytown, is simply called West of the Boulevard. Then comes the elite area of Windsor Farms (with Agecroft Hall and Virginia House), the exclusive Country Club of Virginia, and the University of Richmond. Much farther out, the area west of Parham Rd and beyond the university is called the Far West End.

INFORMATION
Tourist Offices
If you need to find information on a particular attraction, your best bet is the Richmond Information Center (☎ 804-648-3146) in the Old Bell Tower on the Capitol grounds on Capitol Square (corner of 9th and Bank Sts). It's open 9 am to 5 pm Monday to Saturday and on Sunday in the summer from noon to 5 pm.

The Metro Richmond Visitors Center (☎ 804-358-5511, www.richmondva.org), at 1710 Robin Hood Rd, is housed in a converted train depot. To get there, take I-95/I-64 exit 78. There's a gift shop, an informative video, and exhibits. It's open 9 am to 5 pm daily (to 7 pm from June to August).

The Satellite Visitors Center (☎ 804-236-3260), at Richmond International Airport (I-64 exit 197) is open 9:30 am to 4:30 pm weekdays.

The Metro Richmond Convention & Visitors Bureau (☎ 804-782-2777, 800-365-7272) is on the 2nd floor of the 6th St Marketplace, at 550 E Marshall St. Stop by for pamphlets, or call for various tourism-related information.

For lodging reservations and information throughout the metro area, call ☎ 888-742-4666 or visit www.richmondva.org. For a weather report, call ☎ 804-268-1212. There are two Traveler's Aid lines: ☎ 804-643-0279 and ☎ 804-648-1767.

Money
As headquarters of the Fifth Federal Reserve District, Richmond has plenty of financial institutions. The Crestar Bank (☎ 804-343-9262), in the 6th St Marketplace; NationsBank (☎ 804-788-2496), in the 6th and Grace Banking Center; and a wealth of banks on Main St between 10th and 12th all have full facilities. The Central Fidelity National Bank (☎ 804-697-6700), in the James Center at 1021 E Cary St, has a 24-hour ATM.

Post & Communications
The main post office (☎ 804-783-0825), on the corner of 7th and Main Sts, is open 7:30 am to 5 pm weekdays. There are a number of other post offices downtown as

well as places for sending faxes, and there is a business center at the airport.

Internet Resources

Try the following website for the dish on the local scene, including restaurants, music, movies, theater, special events, and the like: richmond.citysearch.com.

A good place to find accommodations and restaurants is www.richmondva.org. For articles about life in the city, try www .discoverrichmond.com. For climate, history, and other fundamental information about the capital, visit www.ci.richmond.va.us.

Travel Agencies

Covington International Travel (☎ 804-344-3244) is in the James Center, at 901 E Cary St. Outside of the downtown area, Travel Agents International (☎ 804-358-5800) is at 5004 Monument Ave. Both agents have a number of other Richmond locations.

Bookstores

Book People (☎ 804-288-4346), 536 Granite Ave, has a motley mix of new and used books but seems to emphasize travel and foreign-language selections. The owner, Ruth Erb, hails from Eastern Europe and has a vast knowledge of the humanities – pick her brain for recommendations. The Valentine Museum has an excellent bookstore as well.

Narnia (☎ 804-353-5675), 2927 W Cary St, in Carytown, is an excellent store for children's books and has a delightful staff. Directly across the street is Carytown Books (☎ 804-359-4831), 2930 W Cary St, the closest thing to an alternative bookstore in Richmond. It has a great magazine section as well as an interesting stock of literature, with a focus on gay and lesbian works. Downtown, Fountain Bookstore (☎ 804-788-1594), 1312 E Cary St, has traditionally catered to the tourist and corporate markets, but the staff are pushing to diversify the stock.

Media

The main daily newspaper is the *Richmond Times-Dispatch*; the Sunday edition's Arts & Entertainment and Sport & Recreation sections are useful.

There are three popular weekly African American papers: *The Voice*, *Richmond Free Press*, and *Richmond Afro-American*. The *Richmond State*, a popular offbeat weekly with heaps of opinion pieces, defies categorization; it's free and available at various city distribution points. *Style Weekly*, for the 'in' crowd wishing to know where it's all happening, comes out on Tuesday and is also free.

There are five local TV stations: Channels 6 (CBS), 8 (ABC), 12 (NBC, the most 'Richmond' of the stations), 23 (PBS), and 35 (FOX).

Probably the most popular of the drive-time radio shows is WRVA's 1140 AM. Also worth tuning in to are WKHK 95.3 FM for continuous country and WTVR 98.1 FM for easy listening. For rock, try WRXL 102.1 FM, and for student news and alternative music, try WDCE 90.1 FM.

Laundry

Main Street Cleaners (☎ 804-644-3310), 1806 E Main St, is open 7:30 am to 6:30 pm weekdays and 9 am to 2 pm Saturday for dry cleaning and laundry. The Lost Sock (☎ 804-358-0646), 1319 W Main St, lets you chug beer while your laundry spins.

Medical Services & Emergencies

The Medical College of Virginia Hospital (☎ 804-828-9000), 401 N 12th St, is open 24 hours. CVS (☎ 804-359-2497), 2730 W Broad St, is a 24-hour pharmacy. The Rape Crisis Center number is ☎ 804-643-0888.

THINGS TO SEE & DO

Richmond has plenty of historic sights and museums to poke around in. And while most travelers rarely imagine a city as the site for a multitude of outdoor endeavors, Richmond defies such stereotypes. Here, you can hike, bicycle, ride horses, fish, golf, and even go whitewater rafting.

Walking Tour

The best place to start a walk through historic Richmond is the Court End, where there are heaps of attractions within eight city blocks – National Landmarks, museums, and other notable buildings. A Historic

Richmond for Kids

So it's time to get rid of the kids – or at least preoccupy them for a while. The **Science Museum of Virginia** has many exhibits that will interest the kids, but perhaps a more suitable choice is the adjacent **Children's Museum of Richmond** (CMOR; ☎ 804-358-6878). This revamped CMOR has plenty of hands-on activities, the 'Great Outdoors Indoors,' an early-childhood center, and it still has a cave (made famous by its predecessor). It is open 10 am to 4:30 pm Tuesday to Friday, to 5 pm Saturday, and 1 to 5 pm Sunday. Admission is $2 for kids and $3 for adults accompanied by a responsible child.

Maymont House & Garden (☎ 804-358-7166), at 1700 Hampton St, in West End, has a children's farm with many animals that are native to Virginia. The grounds are open daily and are free.

About 22 miles north of town on I-95 (Doswell exit) is **Paramount King's Dominion** (☎ 804-876-5000, www.pkdthrills.com), a theme park with all manner of roller-coaster rides, including Volcano – The Blast Coaster, Shockwave, Grizzly, Anaconda, Flight of Fear, Hurler, Outer Limits, and Rebel Yell. There's also simulated whitewater rafting, waterslides, KidZville, and music and dance reviews. Opening times meet the holiday demand: it's open daily June to August and weekends only from April to May and from September to October. Admission is $36 for people ages 7 to 54, $31 for people 55 and over, and $26 for children 3 to 6. Parking costs $6. (They should throw in a nanny for those prices!) This is the most popular attraction in the Richmond area, with some two million visitors annually, so be prepared for crowds. For information on a combined package with Busch Gardens Williamsburg, call ☎ 800-832-1127.

Downtown discount block ticket ($15 for adults, free for children under 7) will get you into more than 30 of these historic places and museums. A ticket is valid for 30 days.

The Museums on the Boulevard block ticket covers six attractions, including Maymont, the Museum of Fine Arts, and the Science Museum. The tickets are $15 for adults and $8 for children two to 12 (valid for 14 days). You can buy the block tickets at the participating attractions or from visitor centers.

Valentine Museum

The Valentine, also known as the Museum of Life and History of Richmond (☎ 804-649-0711, www.valentinemuseum.com), 1015 E Clay St, is a good place to start a tour. Once the home of a 19th-century businessman and arts benefactor, it now features changing exhibitions on American urban and social history, costumes, decorative arts, toys, and architecture. The main emphasis, however, is on the history of the city from the 17th century to the present.

Included in the complex is the stately 1812 **Wickham House**, a Federal-style building built by John Wickham – one of Richmond's wealthiest citizens at the time. Its rare neoclassical decorative wall paintings, Oval Parlor ('one of the 100 most beautiful rooms in America'), and Palette Staircase all indicate the lavish lifestyle of its owner.

The museum is open 10 am to 5 pm Monday to Saturday and noon to 5 pm Sunday; admission is $5 for adults, $4 for seniors, and $3 for children. The tours of Wickham House take place 11 am to 4 pm. Lunch is served on weekdays from April to October in Wickham House's garden cafe.

Museum & White House of the Confederacy

At 1201 E Clay St is the Museum of the Confederacy (☎ 804-649-1861, www.moc.org), one of the more unusual attractions in Virginia. It offers a somewhat odd treatment of the Civil War – the view of the defeated side. It has a great collection of Civil War memorabilia, and a number of subjects one would not expect to see here are treated with sensitivity, such as the role of African Americans in the war and the way in which Southern women mourned their dead. The sword Robert E Lee wore at Appomattox is here, as are a replica of Lee's headquarters; the revered *Last Meeting of Lee and*

Jackson, painted in 1869 by EDB Julio; and many other Confederate artifacts.

Adjacent to the museum is the restored White House (actually painted gray). Its interior looks just as it did during the short existence of the Confederacy. There is a real 'the South will rise again' feel about this place. The upstairs Oval Office is where Jefferson Davis conducted his wartime business, and some rooms in the house contain the Davis family's furnishings. There is an exhibit gallery on the ground level of the White House.

The museum and White House are open 10 am to 5 pm Monday to Saturday and noon to 5 pm Sunday. A combination ticket is $9 for adults, $8.50 for seniors, and $5 for students. For the museum only, tickets cost $6, $4, and $3, respectively; for the White House only, they cost $7, $6, and $4.

John Marshall House

At 818 E Marshall St, on the corner of 9th St, is the house that belonged to former Chief Justice John Marshall. He built it between 1788 and 1790 and lived in it for 45 years, until his death in 1835 – when he was in between posts as the secretary of state and ambassador to France.

The house (☎ 804-648-7998) is open 10 am to 4 pm Tuesday to Saturday; from October to December, it is open until 4:30 pm. Admission is $3 for adults, $2.50 for seniors, and $1.25 for children. Tours take about 20 minutes; there is a gift shop in the wine cellar.

Virginia State Capitol

The Capitol is another example of Thomas Jefferson's prodigious talent. He modeled it in 1785 after a Roman temple (the 1st-century Maison Carrée in Nîmes), and when it was built, it was the first neoclassical building in the New World. The statue of Washington, by Jean Antoine Houdon, was the only one of him completed while he was alive – it is considered to be the most valuable piece of sculpture in the country. It complements the other seven busts of Virginia natives who achieved the nation's highest office. Another interesting room is

the Old House of Delegates Hall, in which Aaron Burr was tried for treason in 1807.

The Capitol (☎ 804-698-1788), in Capitol Square, is open 9 am to 5 pm daily (on Sunday from December to March, it opens at 1 pm). It is free, and tours are offered.

Get all the information you could possibly desire from the Richmond Information Center in the **Old Bell Tower**, which was built in 1824. Also in Capitol Square, to the east of the Capitol, is the **Executive Mansion**, the residence of the state's governors since 1813.

At the corner of 10th and Capitol Sts is the **Old City Hall**, a fine example of Victorian Gothic architecture dating from 1894 – the elaborate interior is worth a look.

Edgar Allan Poe Museum

At 1914–16 E Main St, in Shockoe Bottom, stands the Edgar Allan Poe Museum (☎ 804-648-5523) in the Old Stone House. The four buildings that surround the 'Enchanted Garden' contain Poe memorabilia, a model of Richmond in Poe's time, and the Raven Room, which features James Carling's illustrations that were inspired by Poe's poem *The Raven*. It is the largest collection of Poe publications and artifacts in existence. Although Poe grew up in Richmond, he never actually lived in this house.

The museum is open 10 am to 4:30 pm Tuesday to Saturday and noon to 4:30 pm Sunday and Monday. Admission is $6 for adults and $5 for seniors and students; tours are available. For more information on Poe, see the Baltimore chapter.

St John's Episcopal Church

This colonial church (☎ 804-648-5015), 2401 E Broad St, was built in 1741. It was the site of the rebellious Second Virginia Convention, at which Patrick Henry, on March 23, 1775, uttered the immortal and oft-quoted words 'give me liberty or give me death!'.

The church is open 10 am to 4 pm Monday to Saturday and 1 to 4 pm Sunday. Admission is $3 for adults, $2 for seniors, and $1 for children. There are free Sunday reenactments of Henry's speech at 2 pm (Memorial Day to Labor Day).

VIRGINIA

GREATER RICHMOND

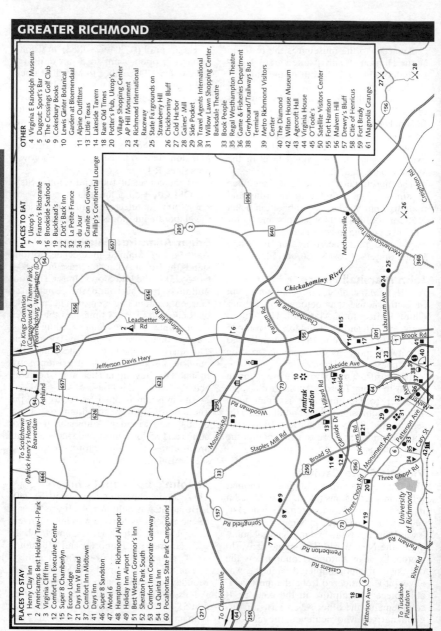

PLACES TO STAY
1 Henry Clay Inn
2 Americamps Best Holiday Trav-I-Park
3 Virginia Cliff Inn
12 Comfort Inn Executive Center
15 Super 8 Chamberlyn
17 Econo Lodge
21 Days Inn W Broad
37 Comfort Inn Midtown
41 Days Inn
46 Super 8 Sandston
47 Motel 6
48 Hampton Inn - Richmond Airport
49 Holiday Inn Airport
51 Best Western Governor's Inn
52 Sheraton Park South
53 Comfort Inn Corporate Gateway
54 La Quinta Inn
60 Pocahontas State Park Campground

PLACES TO EAT
7 Ukrop's
8 Franco's Ristorante
16 Brookside Seafood
19 Buckhead's
22 Dot's Back Inn
32 La Petite France
34 du Jour
35 Granite on Grove,
   Philip's Continental Lounge

OTHER
4 Virginia E Randolph Museum
5 Dugout: Sport's Bar
6 The Crossings Golf Club
9 Cokesbury Books
10 Lewis Ginter Botanical
   Garden at Bloemendaal
11 Alpine Outfitters
13 Little Texas
14 Lakeside Tavern
18 Rare Old Times
20 Potter's Pub, Ukrop's,
   Village Shopping Center
23 AP Hill Monument
24 Richmond International
   Raceway
25 State Fairgrounds on
   Strawberry Hill
26 Chickahominy Bluff
27 Cold Harbor
28 Gaines' Mill
29 Side Pocket
30 Travel Agents International
31 Willow Lawn Shopping Center,
   Barksdale Theatre
33 Book People
35 Regal Westhampton Theatre
36 Game & Fisheries Department
38 Greyhound/Trailways Bus
   Terminal
39 Metro Richmond Visitors
   Center
40 The Diamond
42 Wilton House Museum
43 Agecroft Hall
44 Virginia House
45 O'Toole's
50 Satellite Visitors Center
55 Fort Harrison
56 Malvern Hill
57 Drewry's Bluff
58 Citie of Henricus
59 Fort Brady
61 Magnolia Grange

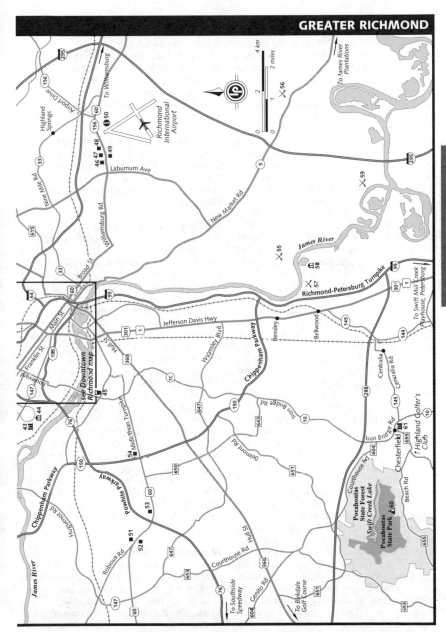

GREATER RICHMOND

Jackson Ward

One of the most fascinating parts of Richmond is Jackson Ward, which at the turn of the 19th century was a thriving African American community at the forefront of cultural, religious, and business progress. Then, it was simply known as 'Little Africa,' but today, the remaining 40 city blocks (or parts thereof) represent the nation's largest National Historic Landmark district associated primarily with African Americans. The best way to see this district, with its many row houses with cast-iron porches, is on foot. Get a copy of the excellent free brochure 'Experience Historic Jackson Ward, Richmond' from the visitor centers.

The best place to start is at the **Black History Museum & Cultural Center of Virginia** (☎ 804-780-9093), in a fine Greek Revival building on Clay St, in the heart of the ward. Highlighting the lives and achievements of black Virginians, it was opened as a repository for oral, visual, and written records relating to African American life in the city and the state. It is open 11 am to 4 pm Tuesday, Thursday, Friday, and Saturday; admission is $2 for adults and $1 for seniors and children.

Southeast of the center, on the corner of Marshall and N 1st St, is the **Consolidated Bank and Trust Co**, the nation's oldest continuously owned African American bank. Northeast of the center, on 'The Deuce' (2nd St), is the **Hippodrome Theater**, 528 N 2nd St, one of the places that gave this ward the nickname 'Harlem of the South.' In this neighborhood, the likes of Bill Robinson ('Mr Bojangles'), Cab Calloway, Lena Horne, Billie Holiday, James Brown, and Nat King Cole honed their skills.

Just to the north of this area is the **Maggie Lena Walker National Historic Site** (☎ 804-771-2017), 110½ E Leigh St, which commemorates the life of a progressive and talented woman who was the daughter of an ex-slave. She was the first black woman to found and serve as the president of a bank (the St Luke Penny Savings Bank, 1903), despite a physical disability and poverty in her early years. The site includes her 22-room brick residence of 30 years (1904–34),

which has been restored to its 1930s appearance. It is open 9 am to 5 pm Wednesday to Sunday; admission is free.

Two blocks west on Leigh St, at the corner of Adams St, is the **statue of 'Mr Bojangles'** (see the boxed text The Happiest Feet in Richmond). Farther down W Leigh St, at No 216, is the **Ebenezer Baptist Church** (1856), where public education for African Americans began. To the northeast, at 114 W Duval St, is the **Sixth Mount Zion Baptist Church** (1867), which was organized by a former slave, John Jasper. Jasper was known for his 'The Sun Do Move' sermon, which he delivered on request more than 250 times during his lifetime.

Hollywood Cemetery

This is an extremely beautiful and historic cemetery perched above the rapids of the James River (☎ 804-648-8501). Statues of winged angels, fresh grave mounds of orange dirt and clay, and brooding hollies set the mood here. The main entrance is near the corner of Albemarle and Cherry Sts. Get a copy of 'Historic Hollywood Cemetery' ($1) from the office – it makes the search through the labyrinthine pathways much easier.

Gravesites to look for are those of presidents James Monroe and John Tyler, Confederate president Jefferson Davis, novelists James Branch Cabell and Ellen Glasgow, sculptor EV Valentine, historian Douglas E Freeman, six state governors, 22 Confederate generals (including JEB Stuart and George E Pickett, who led the ill-fated charge at Gettysburg), 'Pathfinder of the Seas' Matthew Fontaine Maury, and more than 18,000 Confederate soldiers who were buried near a 90-foot-high granite pyramid. This serene cemetery is open 8 am to 5 pm daily.

Monument Avenue

There is no doubt that this tree-lined boulevard is beautiful, but in its role as a shrine to the Confederacy, it cannot help but be controversial. The latest controversy was sparked by the plan to erect a monument to Arthur Ashe, the first African American to

The Happiest Feet in Richmond

The famous dancer and actor Bill Robinson, better known as 'Mr Bojangles,' was born May 25, 1878, on N 3rd St in Richmond's Jackson Ward. There is a larger-than-life aluminum statue of him at the corner of Adams and Leigh Sts, near the intersection to which he once donated a traffic light so that kids from his old neighborhood could safely cross the street. This statue is one of the only major monuments in the city that relates to someone actually born in the Richmond (another is the Arthur Ashe statue, on Monument Ave).

Bojangles was well known for his famous staircase tap routine, which he performed in films of the 1930s. He appeared in six movies with Shirley Temple and in the first African American talkie, *Harlem Is Heaven*. In 1937, he was named the 'outstanding stage and screen star of the year.' Bill Robinson died in 1949. In 1989, the US Congress designated May 25, his birthday, as National Tap Dancing Day.

win the Wimbledon tennis tournament. The other statues commemorate revered personages who, unlike Ashe, were soldiers on a losing side.

From east to west, are General JEB Stuart, facing north; Robert E Lee atop Traveller, the first monument to be dedicated (1890), facing south; Jefferson Davis, by the sculptor EV Valentine; General 'Stonewall' Jackson – like Stuart, facing north, as he died from wounds received in battle; Matthew Fontaine Maury, a scientist and oceanographer; and lastly, but not without a 'swordless fight,' the gentle, quiet achiever, Arthur Ashe.

Some distance north of Monument Ave, at the junction of Laburnum Ave and Hermitage Rd, is a statue of the popular Confederate general AP Hill. His remains were reinterred beneath it. Also, there is a statue of the explorer Christopher Columbus at the northern entrance to William Byrd Park.

Canal Walk

The new 1¼-mile Canal Walk (www.richmondriverfront.com) along the James River is the start of an ambitious redevelopment along the waterfront. So far, the Haxall Canal, from the Tredegar Iron Works to 12th St, and the James River and Kanawha Canal, from 12th St to Triple Cross, have been restored. There are many points of interest along the walk, and the city's history is carefully highlighted. The Tredegar Iron Works houses the Civil War Visitor Center. The best place to begin the Canal Walk is at the park at 12th and Byrd Sts.

The walk was not open long when a controversy arose over the inclusion of a portrait of Robert E Lee at one of the points of interest. As in the Arthur Ashe monument controversy, local opinion was bitterly divided.

Nearby, the 60-acre **Belle Isle**, the site of industry for centuries, is better known for the notorious Civil War prison camp that was established on its east end. It is thought that some 30 Union soldiers (then prisoners) died each day during the harsh winter of 1863–64 as a result of poor shelter and little food. Access is from a pedestrian bridge under Route 1/301 (Lee Bridge). It is open during daylight hours.

Lewis Ginter Botanical Garden at Bloemendaal

This garden (☎ 804-262-9887), 1800 Lakeside Ave, features a new visitor center – a good introduction to what's blooming. For kids, there is a discovery garden, maze, and conservatory.

Lewis Ginter, founder of the American Tobacco Company, established the Lakeside Wheel Club in the 1880s for Richmond's well-to-do. When he died, his niece Grace Arents converted the area for much more humanitarian uses. She set about developing the gardens and changed their name to Bloemendaal, after Ginter's Dutch home. On her death, she bequeathed the gardens to the city of Richmond for everyone to enjoy. The Lora Robins Teahouse on the grounds serves delicious meals. The garden is open 9:30 am to 4:30 pm daily; admission is $4 for adults, $3 for seniors, and $2 for children.

VIRGINIA

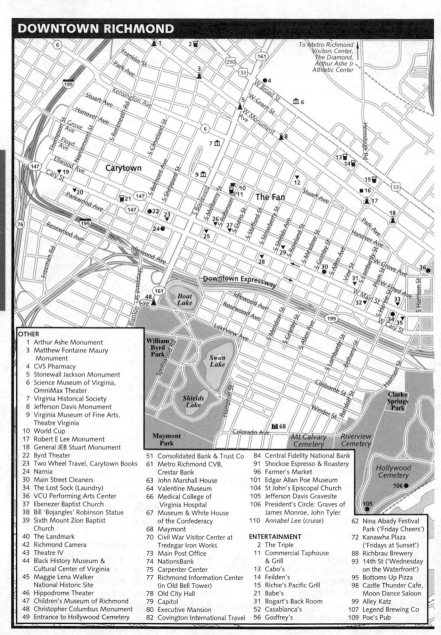

DOWNTOWN RICHMOND

To Metro Richmond
Visitors Center,
the Diamond,
Arthur Ashe Jr
Athletic Center

Franklin St
Park Ave
Stuart Ave
Kensington Ave
Hanover Ave
JR Grove Ave
Thompson St
Floyd Ave
Ellwood Ave
Cary St
Parkwood Ave
Rosewood Ave
Freemann Ave
Idlewood Ave

Carytown

The Fan

W Broad St
W Grace St
W Monument Ave

Downtown Expressway

Boat
Lake

Idlewood Ave
Rosewood Ave
Lakeview Ave

William
Byrd
Park

Swan
Lake

Shields
Lake

Maymont
Park

Colorado Ave

Clarke
Springs
Park

Mt Calvary
Cemetery

Riverview
Cemetery

Hollywood
Cemetery

OTHER
1 Arthur Ashe Monument
3 Matthew Fontaine Maury
   Monument
4 CVS Pharmacy
5 Stonewall Jackson Monument
6 Science Museum of Virginia,
   OmniMax Theater
7 Virginia Historical Society
8 Jefferson Davis Monument
9 Virginia Museum of Fine Arts,
   Theatre Virginia
10 World Cup
17 Robert E Lee Monument
18 General JEB Stuart Monument
22 Byrd Theater
23 Two Wheel Travel, Carytown Books
24 Narnia
30 Main Street Cleaners
34 The Lost Sock (Laundry)
35 VCU Performing Arts Center
37 Ebenezer Baptist Church
38 Bill 'Bojangles' Robinson Statue
39 Sixth Mount Zion Baptist
   Church
40 The Landmark
42 Richmond Camera
43 Theatre IV
44 Black History Museum &
   Cultural Center of Virginia
45 Maggie Lena Walker
   National Historic Site
46 Hippodrome Theater
47 Children's Museum of Richmond
48 Christopher Columbus Monument
49 Entrance to Hollywood Cemetery

51 Consolidated Bank & Trust Co
61 Metro Richmond CVB,
   Crestar Bank
63 John Marshall House
64 Valentine Museum
66 Medical College of
   Virginia Hospital
67 Museum & White House
   of the Confederacy
68 Maymont
70 Civil War Visitor Center at
   Tredegar Iron Works
73 Main Post Office
74 NationsBank
75 Carpenter Center
77 Richmond Information Center
   (in Old Bell Tower)
78 Old City Hall
79 Capitol
80 Executive Mansion
82 Covington International Travel

84 Central Fidelity National Bank
91 Shockoe Espresso & Roastery
96 Farmer's Market
101 Edgar Allan Poe Museum
104 St John's Episcopal Church
105 Jefferson Davis Gravesite
106 President's Circle: Graves of
   James Monroe, John Tyler
110 *Annabel Lee* (cruise)

ENTERTAINMENT
2 The Triple
11 Commercial Taphouse
   & Grill
13 Cabo's
14 Feilden's
15 Richie's Pacific Grill
21 Babe's
31 Bogart's Back Room
52 Casablanca's
56 Godfrey's

62 Nina Abady Festival
   Park ('Friday Cheers')
72 Kanawha Plaza
   ('Fridays at Sunset')
88 Richbrau Brewery
93 14th St ('Wednesday
   on the Waterfront')
95 Bottoms Up Pizza
98 Castle Thunder Cafe,
   Moon Dance Saloon
99 Alley Katz
107 Legend Brewing Co
109 Poe's Pub

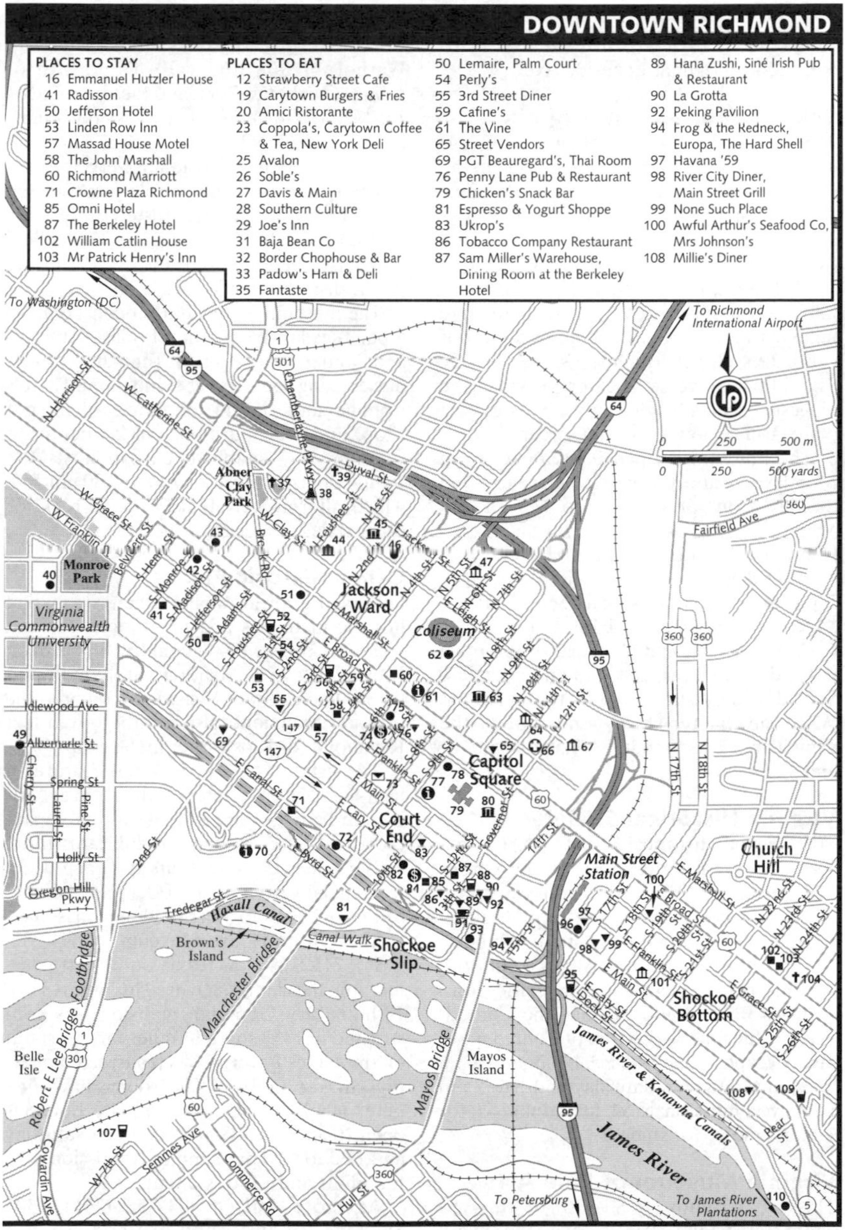

DOWNTOWN RICHMOND
PLACES TO STAY
16 Emmanuel Hutzler House
41 Radisson
50 Jefferson Hotel
53 Linden Row Inn
57 Massad House Motel
58 The John Marshall
60 Richmond Marriott
71 Crowne Plaza Richmond
85 Omni Hotel
87 The Berkeley Hotel
102 William Catlin House
103 Mr Patrick Henry's Inn
PLACES TO EAT
12 Strawberry Street Cafe
19 Carytown Burgers & Fries
20 Amici Ristorante
23 Coppola's, Carytown Coffee & Tea, New York Deli
25 Avalon
26 Soble's
27 Davis & Main
28 Southern Culture
29 Joe's Inn
31 Baja Bean Co
32 Border Chophouse & Bar
33 Padow's Ham & Deli
35 Fantaste
50 Lemaire, Palm Court
54 Perly's
55 3rd Street Diner
59 Cafine's
61 The Vine
65 Street Vendors
69 PGT Beauregard's, Thai Room
76 Penny Lane Pub & Restaurant
79 Chicken's Snack Bar
81 Espresso & Yogurt Shoppe
83 Ukrop's
86 Tobacco Company Restaurant
87 Sam Miller's Warehouse, Dining Room at the Berkeley Hotel
89 Hana Zushi, Siné Irish Pub & Restaurant
90 La Grotta
92 Peking Pavilion
94 Frog & the Redneck, Europa, The Hard Shell
97 Havana '59
98 River City Diner, Main Street Grill
99 None Such Place
100 Awful Arthur's Seafood Co, Mrs Johnson's
108 Millie's Diner
To Washington (DC)
To Richmond International Airport
0 250 500 m
0 250 500 yards
Abner Clay Park
Monroe Park
Virginia Commonwealth University
Jackson Ward
Coliseum
Capitol Square
Court End
Main Street Station
Church Hill
Shockoe Slip
Shockoe Bottom
Haxall Canal
Brown's Island
Canal Walk
Belle Isle
Mayos Island
James River
James River & Kanawha Canals
Robert E Lee Bridge Footbridge
Manchester Bridge
Mayos Bridge
To Petersburg
To James River Plantations
N Harrison St
W Catherine St
Chamberlayne Pkwy
Duval St
W Grace St
W Franklin St
Belvidere St
S Henry St
S Monroe St
S Madison St
S Jefferson St
S Adams St
S Foushee St
S 1st St
S 2nd St
S 3rd St
S 4th St
S 5th St
W Clay St
Brook Rd
N Foushee St
N 1st St
N 2nd St
E Jackson St
N 4th St
N 5th St
N 6th St
N 7th St
N 8th St
N 9th St
N 10th St
N 11th St
N 12th St
E Leigh St
E Marshall St
E Broad St
E Franklin St
E Main St
E Cary St
E Byrd St
E Canal St
Governor St
14th St
15th St
N 17th St
N 18th St
S 17th St
S 18th St
S 19th St
S 20th St
S 21st St
N 22nd St
N 23rd St
N 24th St
S 25th St
S 26th St
E Grace St
Dock St
Pear St
Fairfield Ave
Idlewood Ave
Albemarle St
Cherry St
Spring St
Laurel St
Pine St
Holly St
Oregon Hill Pkwy
2nd St
Tredegar St
W 7th St
Semmes Ave
Commerce Rd
Hull St
Cowardin Ave

To get to the garden, take I-95N to Brook Rd/Route 1N (exit 80), turn left at Hilliard Rd, and turn right at Lakeside Ave.

Science Museum of Virginia

This museum (☎ 804-367-0000, www.smv.org) and the OmniMax Theater are housed in the old Richmond, Fredericksburg & Potomac Railroad station at 2500 W Broad St. The station, with its massive dome, was designed by John Russell Pope and was completed in 1919. There are more than 250 permanent hands-on exhibits covering such diverse fields as aerospace, astronomy, chemistry, computers, electricity, illusions, and physics. The Ethyl Universe Theater provides the biggest spectacle – you can see movies or a planetarium show on a giant screen.

The museum is open 9:30 am to 5 pm Monday to Saturday and 11:30 am to 5 pm Sunday from September to May. From Memorial Day to Labor Day, it's open 9:30 am to 5 pm Monday to Thursday, to 7 pm Friday and Saturday, and 11:30 am to 5 pm Sunday. Admission is $5 for adults, $4.50 for seniors, and $4 for children. The OmniMax shows and planetarium are open in the daytime every day, and on Friday and Saturday, they stay open in the evenings. With one theater show, admission to the exhibit area is $8 for adults, $7.50 for seniors, and $7 for children.

Virginia Historical Society

The Virginia Historical Society (☎ 804-358-4901, www.vahistorical.org), on the corner of Kensington St and the Boulevard, has museum galleries displaying rare Virginia-related treasures and changing exhibits on Virginia history – eg, JEB Stuart's uniform, buttons from Pocahontas' hat, and John Brown's Bowie knife. 'Arming the Confederacy' is the finest collection of Confederate-made weapons in existence. It's open 10 am to 5 pm Monday to Saturday and 1 to 5 pm Sunday; admission is $4 for adults, $3 for seniors, and $2 for students.

Virginia Museum of Fine Arts

This art museum (☎ 804-367-0844, www.vmfa.state.va.us), 2800 Grove Ave, has a superb collection containing a range of works as diverse as Monet's *Iris by the Pond*, Warhol's *Triple Elvis*, Goya's portrait of *General Nicholas Guye*, and Picasso's *Circus Life*. There are many other works representing numerous civilizations, such as a fine collection of Himalayan (Indian, Nepalese, and Tibetan) pieces. Many people come to see the shimmering, jewel-encrusted Easter eggs created by Peter Carl Fabergé. The collection here is believed to be the world's largest public display outside Russia.

The museum is free and is open 11 am to 5 pm Tuesday, Wednesday, Friday, Saturday, and Sunday (until 8 pm on Thursday). Thursday evening tours are at 6 and 7 pm. There's a public cafeteria and sculpture garden, a gift shop, and free parking. On Thursday in summer, the sculpture garden hosts the *Jumpin'* musical events (6:30 to 9:30 pm; $8), which alternatively features jazz, rock, or other styles of music.

Other Historic Places

Outside the downtown area, there are myriad historic mansions and plantations to feast your eyes on. At 1700 Hampton St, between Route 161 and Meadow St, you'll find the 100-acre intact Victorian-Romanesque mansion **Maymont** (also see the boxed text Richmond for Kids earlier in the chapter).

The estate (☎ 804-358-7166) features a high-tech Nature Center (with linked aquariums and a river-otter exhibit), formal Japanese and Italian gardens, a children's farm, carriage rides, and tram tours. It is open 10 am to 7 pm daily from April to October and until 5 pm November to March (admission is free).

The **Wilton House Museum** (☎ 804-282-5936), 215 S Wilton Rd, is on a bluff overlooking the James River. This impressive 18th-century Georgian mansion was constructed in 1753 some 14 miles farther south on the James River; it was resurrected on its present site in 1933. The rooms have fine pine paneling and cornices. The house is open 10 am to 4:30 pm Monday to Saturday and 1:30 to 4:30 pm Sunday. Admission is $5 for adults and $3 for students.

Agecroft Hall (☎ 804-353-4241), 4305 Sulgrave Rd, just south of Carytown, is a

15th-century Tudor manor house uplifted from Lancashire, England, and reconstructed here in 1928 (another transplanted London Bridge or *Queen Mary* perhaps?). The house, furnished with artifacts reflecting the life of Tudor and early Stuart England, is surrounded by 23 acres of lawns, gardens, and woodlands. Agecroft Hall is open 10 am to 4 pm Monday to Saturday and 12:30 to 5 pm Sunday. Admission is $5 for adults, $4.50 for seniors, and $3 for students.

The castlelike **Virginia House** (☎ 804-353-4251), 4301 Sulgrave Rd, is more of the 'transplanted Englishness' that seemed to grip those Virginians who made substantial sums of money in the last couple of centuries. Parts of the original structure date to the English priory of St Sepulchre, but it is the elegant furnishings – a real potpourri of European art, tapestries, and furniture – and the 8 acres of beautiful gardens that make a visit worthwhile. It is open 10 am to 4 pm Monday to Saturday and 12:30 to 5 pm Sunday. Admission is $4 for adults, $3 for seniors, and $2 for students and children.

At 10020 Ironbridge Rd, in Chesterfield, there is the 1822 Federal-style plantation house **Magnolia Grange** (☎ 804-748-1026), which interprets early 19th-century rural life in Virginia. It is open 10 am to 4 pm weekdays and 1 to 4 pm Sunday (closed Saturday). Admission is $2 for adults, $1.50 for seniors, and $1 for students.

The **Virginia E Randolph Museum** (☎ 804-261-5029), 200 Mountain Rd, tells the story of the first supervisor of the 'Jeanes Fund,' an early endeavor to improve black education. It's free and open to the public for tours 1 to 4 pm Monday, Wednesday, Friday, and Saturday and 3 to 5 pm Sunday. Call ahead to make an appointment for a tour.

The **1611 Citie of Henricus** (☎ 804-796-2671), in Chesterfield County and on the banks of the James River, is the site of the second English New World settlement. The short-lived settlement – only 11 years – was decimated in a Native American massacre in 1622. The 'citie' is being reconstructed; when it is completed, it will be open 10 am to 5 pm

Wednesday to Sunday and will include a modern visitor center.

The 18th-century home of Patrick Henry, **Scotchtown** (☎ 804-227-3500), built in 1719 by Charles Chiswell, is near Beaverdam in western Hanover County, about 9 miles northwest of Ashland. The wood-frame house, which was Patrick Henry's home during the Revolutionary War (1771–78), is furnished with period antiques. There are special 'hands-on' tours for children's groups and occasional living-history presentations.

Scotchtown is open 10 am to 4:30 pm Wednesday to Saturday and 1:30 to 4:30 pm Sunday from May to October. Admission is $5 for adults, $4 for seniors, and $2 for children. To get there, take Route 1N through Ashland; turn onto County Rd 738, then County Rd 685.

The **Tuckahoe Plantation** (☎ 804-784-5736), at 12601 River Rd, 7 miles west of Richmond, is an early Thomas Randolph mansion. On the grounds is the school in which Thomas Jefferson studied as a boy. The schoolhouse and exhibit is open 8:30 am to 4 pm and costs $5 per person for groups with fewer than 10 people and $3.50 per person for groups with 10 or more people; admission to the plantation grounds is free.

Hiking

There are more than 200 miles of trails in the Richmond-Petersburg area, including many through the surrounding battlefields. For those who like the terrain a bit tougher, there are many wildlife areas within an hour's drive of the city. For trail information in specific counties, call Richmond (☎ 804-780-5704), Hanover (☎ 804-537-6165), Chesterfield (☎ 804-748-1623), and Henrico (☎ 804-672-5100).

Bicycling

Many of the hiking trails are open to cyclists. The Richmond Area Bicycling Association (RABA; ☎ 804-266-2453) has group rides daily. Two interstate bike routes – the north-south Bike Route 1 and the east-west Bike Route 76 (Trans-America Trail) – pass through Richmond. Also see the Getting Around section, later in this chapter.

VIRGINIA

Horseback Riding

There are more than 270 miles of public trails near the city and some two dozen riding academies and stables. The nearest public equestrian trail is in Pocahontas State Park.

Fishing

The Game and Inland Fisheries Department (☎ 804-367-1000), 4010 W Broad St, provides the brochure 'Fishing Access to the James River in Richmond.' From Covington to the fall line at Richmond, the James River is great for smallmouth-bass fishing. The lower James, which is more tidal and saline, is good for largemouth and striped bass.

Golf

Judging by the many courses in metro Richmond (13 public and 11 private), golf is really popular – probably due to the fact that it can be played year-round. The busy time, of course, is summer and on weekends.

Public courses include Birkdale (☎ 804-739-8800), at 8511 Royal Birkdale Drive, Chesterfield (starting at $25 weekdays); The Crossings (☎ 804-261-0000), 800 Virginia Center Parkway, Glen Allen (starting at $29); and the Highland Golfers' Club (☎ 804-796-4800), 8136 Highland Glen Drive (off Nash Rd), Richmond (starting at $10).

Whitewater Rafting & Kayaking

Richmond has one of the only 'urban' sets of whitewater rapids (up to class V in certain conditions) in the country, thanks to the falls in the James River. The most accessible section of river is near the James River Park (on the south bank, between the Boulevard and Lee bridges).

The Richmond Raft Co (☎ 804-222-7238), 4400 E Main St, offers raft trips, and Adventure Challenge (☎ 804-276-7600, www.adventurechallenge.com) offers kayaking, canoeing, and tubing adventures ($35 to $50, depending on duration). A popular trip is the six-hour day trip on the falls of the James. You can rent canoes and equipment from Alpine Outfitters (☎ 804-794-4172), 7107 W Broad St.

ORGANIZED TOURS

The *Annabel Lee* (☎ 804-644-5700) is a paddlewheel replica offering a variety of two-hour to full-day cruises (lunch, brunch, dinner, and plantation) on the James River from March to December. It's located at the Intermediate Terminal, 4400 E Main St. A plantation cruise costs $45 for adults and $25 for children. On Friday and Saturday, there's a seafood buffet.

Kanawha Cruises (☎ 804-649-2800) has boat rides in and around the new Canal Walk. A tour costs $4 for adults and $3 for seniors and children.

There are a number of good land tours. The Historic Richmond Foundation (☎ 804-780-0107, www.historicrichmond.com), 2407 E Grace St, organizes daily bus and walking tours; the 2½-hour 'Old Richmond Today' tour takes you to the Capitol and historic neighborhoods; it costs $16 for adults and $13 for children.

Richmond Discoveries (☎ 804-795-5781) offers costumed, knowledgeable guides for tours of historic neighborhoods and Hollywood Cemetery (last Sunday of each month March to October).

SPECIAL EVENTS

This is very much a festival city, and Richmonders don't need much of an excuse to turn out for a celebration.

Perhaps the best of all is the '2 Street' Festival in historic Jackson Ward in October. This festival has injected life into the neighborhood every year since 1989. It is centered on 2nd St but spills into a surrounding four-block area. There are tours of historic sites, African American food, and a cacophony of rhythms and sounds – and it's free. Another celebration, in Abner Clay Park in Jackson Ward, is the August Down Home Family Reunion – a large get-together of families who once lived in the Ward but have moved away to different parts of the state or country. Also watch out for the following:

Maymont Flower & Garden Show in midwinter (it offers a great preview of spring)

Easter on Parade along Monument Ave

Races at Strawberry Hill in April

Historic Garden Week at the end of April

Camptown Races at Ashland in May

Arts in the Park at Byrd Park in the first week in May

June Jubilee of Arts & Music in downtown

Big Gig (Richmond's International Festival of Music) in July

State Fair of Virginia at Strawberry Hill in September

PLACES TO STAY
Camping

Richmond is screaming out for a closer campground, and there are no cheap hostels nearby. An entrepreneurial 'planter' with space and vision is needed to trap the burgeoning backpacker market.

The closest campground is in **Pocahontas State Park** (*☎ 804-796-4255, 10300 Beach Rd*). It's a nice place with showers, a large pool, boating, and biking trails. Sites without hookups cost around $11. It is 10 miles south of Richmond; take I-95 exit 6 to Route 10,

then County Rd 655 (Beach Rd) in Chesterfield. You can reserve a site by calling ☎ 804-225-3867 in Richmond, ☎ 800-933-7275 outside Richmond.

The **Americamps Best Holiday Trav-l-Park** (*☎ 804-798-5298, 11322 Air Park Rd*) is about 20 minutes north of the city, just off I-95 exit 89. There are tent sites for $18.25 and full-hookup RV sites for about $23 for two.

The next-closest place is the **Paramount Kings Dominion Campground** (*☎ 804-876-5355, 10061 Kings Dominion Blvd*), in Doswell. It is adjacent to the eponymous theme park (the most popular attraction in the Richmond area – see the boxed text Richmond for Kids), on Route 30, 1 mile east of I-95 exit 98. The campground, which is near all the necessary facilities, is open March to October; sites start at $18 per night (up to five people), and cabins cost $50 for four people.

Guesthouses

The guesthouse and B&B options in the historic quarters are worth trying. The **William Catlin House** (*☎ 804-780-3746, 2304 E Broad St*), a small B&B on Church Hill, is recommended; prices start at $85/95 for singles/doubles. **Mr Patrick Henry's Inn** (*☎ 804-644-1322, 2300 E Broad St*) is similar to the Catlin Inn in most respects; prices there start at $85/95 as well. The restaurant has a local reputation, so reservations are advised (closed Sunday).

The **Virginia Cliffe Inn** (*☎ 804-266-1661, 2900 Mountain Rd*), in Glen Allen, is a grand place on spacious grounds; doubles cost $85 to $125. The **Henry Clay Inn** (*☎ 804-798-3100, 114 N Railroad Ave*), in Ashland, almost doesn't make it into this category, as it has 16 rooms. Doubles with all the creature comforts cost $90 to $145.

The **Emmanuel Hutzler House** (*☎ 804-355-5053, 2036 Monument Ave, www.bensonhouse.com*) is a carefully restored 1914 Italian Renaissance building. Singles cost $85 to $115, doubles $89 to $155.

Hotels

What Richmond lacks in campgrounds it makes up for in hotels and motels.

VIRGINIA

Search along Williamsburg Rd, at the edge of town, and along the Midlothian Turnpike (Route 60), south of the river. If this fails, ask at the visitor center. There are at least 100 accommodations of various sorts in and around Richmond. The cost of a room is inversely proportional to its distance from downtown.

Budget The *Massad House Motel* (☎ *804-648-2893, 11 N 4th St*) is about the best value close to downtown. The rooms are reached by a quaint elevator and are spacious and clean. Singles/doubles cost $38/42.

Motel 6 (☎ *804-222-7600, 5704 Williamsburg Rd*) is 6 miles east on Route 60 and is not far from the airport. You can reach it on Greater Richmond Transit Company (GRTC) bus No 7 (Seven Pines). Singles/doubles in this ubiquitous, reasonably priced stalwart cost $37/43.

The *Super 8 Chamberlayne* (☎ *804-262-8880, 5615 Chamberlayne Rd*) is a quiet place with doubles costing about $50; if you are heading north, you will get a traffic-free start. It's one of seven Super 8 Motels in Richmond. Another, *Super 8 Sandston* (☎ *804-222-8008, 5110 Williamsburg Rd*), near the airport, has rooms for about the same as that on Chamberlayne.

The *Econo Lodge* (☎ *804-262-7070, 8350 Brook Rd*) has doubles starting at $60. The red-brick *Days Inn* (☎ *804-353-1287, 1600 Robin Hood Rd*) is 2 miles northwest of downtown. You enter the rooms (which are adequate) from the parking area; the cost of singles/doubles in low season is $39/45 (otherwise, $50/55). The *Days Inn W Broad* (☎ *804-288-2145, 2100 Dickens Rd*), off I-64 exit 183, close to downtown, is more expensive – doubles cost $63 to $93.

Mid-Range The *Radisson* (☎ *804-644-9871, 301 W Franklin St*), formerly the Holiday Inn Downtown, is popular and has a restaurant with a great view over Franklin St. Doubles cost $70 to $75, and the building is wheelchair accessible.

Outside of downtown, the *Comfort Inn Midtown* (☎ *804-359-4061, 3200 W Broad St*), near The Fan, is a good value, with singles/doubles starting at $65/70 in the low season. The *Comfort Inn Executive Center* (☎ *804-672-1108, 7201 W Broad*), off I-64 exit 183, has singles for $64 to $93 and doubles for $70 to $99 year-round.

South of the river, there are a few mid-range choices. The *Best Western Governor's Inn* (☎ *804-323-0007, 9848 Midlothian Turnpike)* has a restaurant, outdoor pool, and a whirlpool; rooms cost $69 year-round. The *Comfort Inn Corporate Gateway* (☎ *804-320-8900, 8710 Midlothian Turnpike)* has singles/doubles starting at $57/63 in the low season (otherwise, $89/99).

La Quinta Inn (☎ *804-745-7100, 6910 Midlothian Turnpike)* has a pool, restaurant, and handicapped access. Singles/doubles cost $60/69 to $81/88. The *Sheraton Park South* (☎ *804-323-1144, 9901 Midlothian Turnpike)* is much more expensive, but it is a classy place with and an indoor pool, health club, and area transportation. Doubles cost $60 to $120, depending on the season.

Out near the airport, there are a few mid-range places. The *Hampton Inn – Richmond Airport* (☎ *804-222-8200, 5300 Airport Square Lane)* has an outdoor pool and free continental breakfast. Doubles cost $89 to $100. The *Holiday Inn Airport* (☎ *804-222-6450, 5203 Williamsburg Rd)*, the largest of the airport hotels, is about the same price.

Top End Downtown Richmond offers a wide range of upscale accommodations. The *Linden Row Inn* (☎ *804-783-7000, 100 E Franklin St)* is in a group of nice converted antebellum Greek Revival terrace houses. Singles/doubles cost $99/169. The *Berkeley Hotel* (☎ *804-780-1300, 1200 E Cary St)*, in Shockoe Slip, is a small but elegant place with valet parking for guests, a health club, and a renowned restaurant. Singles cost $140 to $170, and doubles cost $155 to $185.

The *Crowne Plaza Richmond* (☎ *804-788-0900, 555 E Canal St)* is in the business district, and all rooms are priced at $119 to $139 year-round. Rooms on one side overlook the river, and on the other side, the city skyline; you may be lucky enough to get a room overlooking both.

The ***Omni Hotel*** (☎ *804-344-7000, 100 S 12th St*) is in the James Center complex, close to Shockoe Slip. The comfortable rooms, furnished in contemporary style, cost $79 for singles or doubles on the weekend and $99 to $159 during the week. Guests can enjoy the restaurants, bar, indoor and outdoor pools, racquetball and squash courts, area transportation, and even an indoor track!

The ***Richmond Marriott*** (☎ *804-643-3400, 500 E Broad St)*, near the 6th St Marketplace, has 400 singles and doubles, many with stunning city views, for $160; there are weekend packages available. A peek into the ostentatious lobby will give you an idea of what this place is about. There are three restaurants, an indoor pool, a nightclub, and a gymnasium with a tanning parlor.

The ***Jefferson Hotel*** (☎ *804-788-8000)*, appropriately on the corner of Franklin and Adams Sts, is the most famous of the downtown hotels, with its magnificent rotunda. Its 26-step staircase was, they say, used as a model for the staircase in the movie *Gone with the Wind*. The rooms live up to the required antebellum splendor but are relatively small. Singles and doubles cost $120 to $265 on weekends and $185 to $265 on weekdays.

The John Marshall (☎ *804-783-1929, 105 N 5th St, www.thejohnmarshall.com)*, which is undergoing gradual renovation, is the town's top place to stay. Contact the hotel for current prices.

PLACES TO EAT

Fortunately, Richmond has plenty of options for dining, and the area around Virginia Commonwealth University is the place to go for cheap student eateries. For good old-fashioned Southern fare, head to downtown. There are plenty of upmarket places in downtown, Shockoe Slip, Shockoe Bottom, and The Fan. Male travelers may occasionally need to dress up with a jacket and tie at some of the fancier places.

The best synopses of eateries are found in 'The Insiders' Guide to Greater Richmond,' written by people who appreciate their food, and in *Style Weekly*.

Downtown & Court End

A convenient way to grab a lunch or snack in downtown is from ***street vendors***, who have their carts set up from 11 am until 3 pm on weekdays. Search along 10th St, and you will 'smell out' carts operated by some of Richmond's popular restaurants. Also, ***Cafine's*** (☎ *804-775-2233, 401 E Grace St)*, known for its homemade focaccias, salads, and pastries, is a great place for a small meal. If you'd like to picnic in a park, however, go to ***Ukrop's*** (☎ *804-379-3663)*, at 10th and Main Sts. It is a distinctly Richmond grocery chain that's revered for both freshness and quality, and it has 15 or so carryout places in the city. Also, try the stores in the Heritage Building or in the Village Shopping Center.

The ***3rd Street Diner*** (☎ *804-788-4750, 218 E Main St)*, a Greek/American restaurant downtown, has a breakfast special for $2.25; it's open 24 hours, and the eclectic staff will draw your gaze away from the food. ***Perly's*** (☎ *804-649-2779, 111 E Grace St)* is another reliable cheapie. It's open 7 am to 3 pm weekdays and is a good choice for breakfast ($1.75 to $5) and lunch ($5 to $8).

The ***Chicken's Snack Bar***, on the lower level of the Capitol building, is a Richmond institution and the haunt of Virginia's hungry legislators. There's a good selection of bagels and sandwiches, but it's the limeade that attracts visitors. Buy one and sip it slowly on the steps of the Capitol.

The ***Penny Lane Pub & Restaurant*** (☎ *804-780-1682, 207 N 7th St)* serves inexpensive English fare (Cornish pasties, shepherd's pie, etc), and there's lashings of it. It's owned by a Beatle-loving Liverpudlian.

The ***Thai Room*** (☎ *804-644-2328, 103 E Cary St)*, upstairs at PGT Beauregard's, is open for dinner 5 to 10 pm Tuesday to Saturday. It serves ginger beef, green-curry chicken, and vegetarian dishes at moderate prices (two can eat for less than $30). The other parts of PGT Beauregard's serve what you'd expect from the old South.

The Vine (☎ *804-648-3501, 550 E Grace St)*, at the 6th St Marketplace, is an elegant place with an outdoor patio. The knowledgeable chef experiments and serves innovative, Southern-influenced 'new' dishes.

Three-course prix-fixe lunches are available, and the Sunday brunch packs them in.

Lemaire (☎ 804-788-8000), in the Jefferson Hotel, is a great dining experience. It has a Southern-inspired menu with regional dishes. It's open 11 am to 10 pm daily. Lunch costs $12 to $20, dinner $25 to $45, and the magnificent Sunday brunch is $27. If you just want to sample the ambiance of this place, have afternoon tea in the Palm Court.

North of downtown, *Dot's Back Inn* (☎ 804-266-3167, 4030 MacArthur Ave), in Bellevue, is a place to meet locals, as it has a real 'neighborhood' feel. The meals are hearty and inexpensive, and the quaint bar is well stocked. It's closed Sunday.

Brookside Seafood (☎ 804-262-5716, 5221 Brook Rd) is the best seafood place north of downtown. During happy hour, you can help yourself to a selection of finger food while enjoying a pre-dinner drink.

Shockoe Slip

In the Riverfront Plaza, *Espresso & Yogurt Shoppe* (☎ 804-782-8619, 951 E Byrd St) is a fine place to enjoy a coffee drink and a cultured dessert. *Shockoe Espresso & Roastery* (☎ 804-648-3734, 104 Shockoe Slip) is another option for caffeine fans.

Sam Miller's Warehouse (☎ 804-644-5465, 1210 E Cary St) is a comfortable place known for its seafood (Maine lobsters, Chesapeake Bay delights) and steaks. It's been around more than 20 years. Sunday brunch is served 11 am to 5 pm.

Peking Pavilion (☎ 804-649-8888, 1302 E Cary St) is for those seeking an inexpensive Chinese meal. The food is superb, with accents on Hunan, Szechuan, and Mandarin, and their lunch platters (about $6) are tops. *Hana Zushi* (☎ 804-225-8801, 1309 E Cary St) is open daily except Sunday for inexpensive Japanese meals such as sushi and sashimi.

La Grotta (☎ 804-644-2466, 1218 E Cary St) is a perfect choice for good old Italian salads, poultry, and pasta, but it's expensive. *Tobacco Company Restaurant* (☎ 804-782-9431, 1201 E Cary St) is immensely popular. Furnished with antiques, it is one of the places to be 'seen' in Richmond. The

menu is extensive, with an accent on contemporary cuisine, and all comers should be well satisfied. If you finish a serving of prime rib, you get the next one free, and no one in the house will say 'Oink, oink.'

Europa (☎ 804-643-0911, 1409 E Cary St) combines a tapas bar and Mediterranean restaurant and has street-level and cellar dining. The 'suits and shoulder pads' clamor for 'little dishes of Spain' as they sip pre-dinner drinks at the busy bar. *The Hard Shell* (☎ 804-644-5341, 1411 E Cary St), next door to Europa, is a popular seafood restaurant known for its oysters and Maine lobsters.

Siné Irish Pub & Restaurant (☎ 804-649-7767, 1327 E Cary St) has very tasty meals and a good selection of beers and stouts. Even though it's a bit too upmarket to have the Irish pub feel, people throng in here in search of the 'blarney.'

Frog & the Redneck (☎ 804-648-3764, 1423 E Cary St) gets its name from its owners, a Southerner and an accomplished French chef. The $35 'tasting menu,' incorporating French touches with regional cuisine, is a good value if your appetite is up to it. Reservations are recommended on weekends.

The *Dining Room at the Berkeley Hotel* (☎ 804-225-5105) has been consistently voted one of Richmond's best restaurants. The food is regional, with American and continental influences, and there's an extensive wine list. Lunch costs $9 to $15, and dinner costs $22 to $30.

Shockoe Bottom & Church Hill

One of Richmond's best restaurants is *None Such Place* (☎ 804-644-0832, 1721 E Franklin St) with an eclectic menu of 'now' Virginia cuisine as well as an enlightened treatment of old favorites, such as salads, steaks, seafood, and mouthwatering desserts. Dinner costs $7 to $20.

Not far from the farmers' market are a handful of consistently good eateries. *Awful Arthur's Seafood Co* (☎ 804-643-1700, 101 N 18th St) is a chain, but it's still awfully good. They have consistently good seafood repasts – steamed crabs, oysters, shrimp, clams, and fish in gigantic portions, especially if you choose the specials (Thursday night is bucket night).

Main Street Grill (☎ *804-644-3969, 1700 E Main St)* has a comprehensive vegetarian menu in the evening (much of the fresh produce is purchased across the road). It's open daily except Monday.

The *River City Diner* (☎ *804-644-9418, 1712 E Main St)* is a good 24-hour alternative, serving hunger-busting hot dogs, hamburgers, and nachos (except Monday, when it's closed).

Mrs Johnson's is part of culinary folklore. From 11 am to 1 pm on weekdays, ladles of Mrs Johnson's prized lunch are dished out. It's hard to find and is untouted, except by those in the know. Look by 18th St behind Awful Arthur's, or follow hungry diners disappearing down alleyways.

Havana '59 (☎ *804-649-2822, 16 N 17th St)* is not for you if you can't stand acrid cigar smoke. But if you have been anywhere that is anywhere lately, you will realize that this is an 'in' place – just look at the pavement outside for the profusion of cigar butts the morning after. (Launder that business suit or sexy black number later – a small price to pay for a top night out.) The food is 'advanced American diner' (steaks, seafood, pasta), the decor transports you to the Caribbean, and it's open until 2 am.

Millie's Diner (☎ *804-643-5512, 2603 E Main St)*, in Church Hill, looks plain from the outside, but you will be happy once you are seated (there is usually a wait, and reservations are not accepted). Large portions of their 'fusion cuisine' (cooked before your eyes), a great wine selection, yummy desserts, and jukeboxes bring locals back to Millie's again and again.

The Fan

Check out *World Cup* (☎ *804-359-5282, 204 N Robinson St)*, serving an aromatic FIFA brand of coffee. *Border Chophouse & Bar* (☎ *804-355-2907, 1501 W Main St)* is a neighborhood stalwart (once called the 'Texas-Wisconsin') and has an eclectic menu. The lunches cost $5.50 to $7, and dinners cost $7 to $11.

Joe's Inn (☎ *804-355-2282, 205 N Shields Ave)* has a bit of a local following based on its modestly priced spaghetti meals. It's very busy at night and is open 7 am to 2 am daily.

Strawberry Street Cafe (☎ *804-353-6860, 421 N Strawberry St)* is another casual place frequented by locals. Its reputation is widespread for an inexpensive 'bathtub' salad bar, burgers, beef, chicken, quiche, and pasta dishes (quiche and burgers are half-price Monday night).

At *Southern Culture* (☎ *804-355-6939, 2229 W Main St)*, the Caribbean, Tex-Mex, Cajun, and Southern food is quite superb and inexpensive. It is fast winning a loyal local following.

There is much more to The Fan than the above, and the adventurous will be well rewarded at *Soble's* (☎ *804-358-7843, 2600 W Main St)*, with its well-stocked raw bar, deli, and bacon cheeseburgers. *Baja Bean Co* (☎ *804-257-5445, 1520 W Main St)* offers California-style and Southwestern specials, as well as a copious selection of wine. *Davis & Main* (☎ *804-353-6641, 2501 W Main St)* serves American 'grilled' cuisine and is open 4 pm to midnight daily, and *Avalon* (☎ *804-353-9709, 2619 W Main St)* has innovative cuisine and microbrews.

If you'd like to simply buy a sandwich and sit and watch the city, try *Padow's Ham & Deli* (☎ *804-354-1931, 1110 E Main St)* or *Fantaste* (☎ *804-355-1642, 1201 W Main St)*, open 24 hours.

Carytown

Stop by *Carytown Coffee & Tea* (☎ *804-355-1955, 2900 W Cary St)*, a great place to sip hot java and chill out. *Carytown Burgers & Fries* (☎ *804-358-5225, 3500½ W Cary St)* serves – guess? Burgers are available at lunch and dinner, Monday to Saturday.

Amici Ristorante (☎ *804-353-4700, 3343 W Cary St)* is expensive but is a good choice for northern Italian cuisine. The decor feebly attempts to re-create a little piece of Italy but is made tolerable by the quality of the food (at dinner, entrees start at $14). Reservations are advised.

Coppola's (☎ *804-359-6969, 2900 W Cary St)* has a good selection of cheap, hearty Italian meals and great sandwiches (for $3 to $6) and heaps of ingredients with which to fashion the perfect picnic lunch. Alternatively, you can dig right into your purchase at indoor or outdoor tables. Also try *New York Deli* (☎ 804-355-6056, 2920 W Cary St) for bagels, deli meats, and fish.

West End
Attracting conservative diners, *La Petite France* (☎ 804-353-8729, 2108 Maywill St) serves mainly formal, and certainly expensive, traditional French cuisine. The house specialty is lobster meat in puff pastry with a whisky sauce, but old favorites, such as chateaubriand, are also served. It's closed Sunday and Monday.

Franco's Ristorante (☎ 804-270-9124, 9031 W Broad St) is the place for authentic, expensive Italian cuisine – good enough to satisfy Frank Sinatra.

du Jour (☎ 804-285-1301, 5806 Grove Ave) is an upscale cafe with sidewalk tables. It describes itself as 'casually sophisticated.' Du Jour has vegetarian sandwiches, and lunch entrees cost about $8; dinner entrees cost $20.

Two favorites, next door to each other, are *Granite on Grove* (☎ 804-288-3600, 5702 Grove Ave), a classy place serving fancy American cuisine, and *Phillip's Continental Lounge* (☎ 804-288-8687, 5704 Grove Ave), a Richmond perennial with classic diner fare.

Buckhead's (☎ 804-750-2000, 8510 Patterson Ave), near the Parham Rd junction, is a very upmarket restaurant known for its prime rib, chops, and huge wine selection. It's open for dinner daily.

ENTERTAINMENT
A visitor to Richmond who thinks the town is representative of the staid old South will be surprised to find that the town buzzes these days. There's a lot going on, and the free *Style Weekly* lists it all.

Theater
On no account should you miss the fabulous old *Byrd Theater* (☎ 804-353-9911, 2908 W Cary St), where the movie is preceded by a concert on an old (but fully functional) Wurlitzer organ that rises like a phoenix from the floor. Shows are an amazingly low

$1; balcony seats are another $2. Another great art-house movie theater is the *Regal Westhampton Theatre* (☎ 804-288-9007, 5706 Grove Ave).

There are a couple of dinner theaters in the Richmond region. The *Barksdale Theatre* (☎ 804-282-2620), in the Willow Lawn Shopping Center on Broad St, was the first of the dinner theaters in the country to put on Broadway musicals, comedies, and drama. It is open 6 to 11 pm year-round.

In Colonial Heights, 11 miles south of downtown on Route 1, is the *Swift Creek Mill Playhouse* (☎ 804-748-4411), another dinner theater – an unlikely mix of Southern fare and Yankee entertainment. The theater is in a 17th-century gristmill, believed to be the oldest in the country.

Theatre Virginia (☎ 804-353-6161, 2800 Grove Rd), in the Museum of Fine Arts, is a professional repertory theater and is probably the best choice for live theater. Its season runs from September to April, and the box office is open 11 am to 5 pm Monday to Saturday; dining is available.

Theatre IV (☎ 804-344-8040), a resident professional outfit, performs in the historic Empire Theatre (the oldest in Virginia), 114 W Broad St, year-round. Performances are at 8 pm, and matinees are at 2:30 pm.

Performing Arts
There is plenty for those seeking the 'yarts.' The *Carpenter Center* (☎ 804-225-9000, 600 E Grace St) is a performing-arts center where you are likely to see or hear opera, ballet, or classical music.

The *Landmark* (☎ 804-780-4213), at the corner of Main and Laurel Sts, also features a range of performances. This architectural incongruity is worth seeing for its Moorish-influenced design, even if no performances are on offer.

The *Richmond Symphony* (☎ 804-788-1212) has built up a substantial reputation in its relatively short 30-year existence. Apart from performances of classical symphonic works, there's a good chamber outfit and the Richmond Pops. The symphony usually performs at the VCU Performing Arts Center, the Carpenter Center, and the Landmark.

The *Virginia Opera* (☎ *804-644-8168*) is based in the Carpenter Center; call the box office between 10 am and 4:30 pm for its season (September to April) schedule.

Ballet lovers have the choice of modern and experimental works performed by the *Concert Ballet of Virginia* (☎ *804-780-1279*) or more classical works by the *Richmond Ballet* (☎ *804-359-0906, 614 N Lombardy St*). The latter has a program of five productions from September to May.

Bars & Clubs

This scene changes daily, but there are always listings in the free *Style Weekly* and in the *Richmond Times-Dispatch*. If you are in Shockoe Bottom, you will have no trouble finding a venue with entertainment. Much of the action is centered on restaurants, because Virginia licensing laws dictate that any place serving drinks must serve food. Shockoe Slip and The Fan are also pretty busy most nights.

Wednesday on the Waterfront (☎ *804-643-2826*), down at the Turning Basin by 14th St, features free music, usually progressive rock, from 5:30 to 7:30 pm; and *Friday Cheers*, in the Nina F Abady Festival Park, is free and features progressive and classic rock 6 to 9:30 pm. Jazz is usually the choice at *Fridays at Sunset*, at the Kanawha Plaza. The music lasts from 6 to 10 pm, and there is a $3 cover.

For folk music, a few venues have a good feel: *Potter's Pub* (☎ *804-282-9999, 7007 Three Chopt Rd*), in the Village Shopping Center; Main Street Grill (see Places to Eat); and *Castle Thunder Cafe* (☎ *804-648-3038, 1724–26 E Main St*). *Poe's Pub* (☎ *804-648-2120, 2706 E Main St*) is open to 2 am nightly (but not for poetry readings); there's acoustic music on weekend nights.

Jazz lovers should head for the cozy *Bogart's Back Room* (☎ *804-353-9280, 203 N Lombardy St*) or *Cabo's* (☎ *804-355-1144, 2053 W Broad St*). Country and bluegrass are likely to be found out in the suburbs. One boot-scootin' choice is *Little Texas* (☎ *804-262-9652, 6922 Staples Mill Rd*).

Rock is featured at a number of venues. The Tobacco Company Restaurant (see Places to Eat) is a haunt for those seeking Top 40 music (there is a $3 cover downstairs). Down by Main St Station is the *Moon Dance Saloon* (☎ *804-343-1757, 9 N 17th St*), featuring acoustic musicians on Wednesday and Thursday nights and blues and rock 'n' roll on Friday and Saturday. *Bottoms Up Pizza* (☎ *804-644-4400, 1700 Dock St*), in Shockoe Bottom, is open until 2 am Friday and Saturday and has live music most days of the week – sometimes on the outside deck.

Alley Katz (☎ *804-643-2816, 10 Walnut Alley*), in Shockoe Bottom, features progressive rock and reggae and attracts a college crowd. *Richie's Pacific Grill* (☎ *804-359-1224, 1847 W Broad St*) has reggae Wednesday and jazz Friday and Saturday.

A happening venue, judging by the nightly lines outside, is Havana '59 (see Places to Eat) – this place really moves, even though the air is thick with cigar smoke.

The locals love their beer and have plenty of bars in which to imbibe. The *Richbrau Brewing Co* (☎ *804-644-3018, 1214 E Cary St*), in Shockoe Slip, is a shrine for those who enjoy microbrews – in this case, Richmond's own 'richbrau.' Other great microbreweries include *Legend Brewing Co* (☎ *804-232-8871, 321 W 7th St*), on the south side of James River and serving vegetarian food, and the *Commercial Taphouse & Grill* (☎ *804-359-6544, 111 N Robinson St*), in The Fan.

There are a few good Irish pubs, including Siné (see Places to Eat); *O'Toole's* (☎ *804-233-1781, 4800 Forest Hill Ave*), which is open for dinner daily; and *Rare Old Times* (☎ *804-750-1346, 10602 Patterson Ave*), which is in West End's Canterbury Shopping Center and has live Irish music nightly except Sunday.

Favorites of travel writers are the *Lakeside Tavern*, on Lakeside Drive, for a bunch of real working-class Richmonders, a game of pool, passable food, cheap beer, and a return to boozy normality; and the *Dugout: Sport's Bar* (☎ *804-266-7883, 1510 Mountain Rd*), in Glen Allen. Other places where you can play pool and billiards are *Side Pocket* (☎ *804-353-7921, 2012 Staples Mill Rd*) and *The Triple* (*3306 W Broad St*) – both are open until late and have full-service bars and full menus.

Gay & Lesbian Venues

One popular gay club is *Feilden's* (☎ 804-359-1963, 2033 W Broad St) – a local remarked, 'By the time you get to Feilden's, you'll have a partner in tow.' It is a members-only club. *Babe's* (☎ 804-355-9330, 3166 W Cary St) is a popular lesbian club (closed Monday). Also, at Cafine's (see Places to Eat) on Saturday is a late-night, gay nightclub 'Boom'; *Godfrey's* (☎ 804-648-3957, 308 E Grace St) has a dance floor and an infamous Sunday drag-queen brunch; and *Casablanca's* (☎ 804-648-2040, 6 E Grace St) is a dark, dingy pick-up joint where you just 'stand and pose.'

SPECTATOR SPORTS

Richmond has no NFL or NBA teams – you will have to go to Baltimore or DC to see those. *The Coliseum* (☎ 804-262-8100), which seats 12,000, is the main venue for a host of other spectator sports, such as ice hockey, basketball, wrestling, and tennis.

The Richmond Braves are a Triple-A farm baseball team for the Atlanta Braves – they play at the 12,500-seat *Diamond* (☎ 804-359-4444, 3001 N Boulevard). Take exit 78 off the I-64/I-95 junction – you can't miss it, as it has a gigantic sculpture of Native American warrior Connecticut peering over a wall. The team's home schedule runs from April to September.

The local soccer team is the *Richmond Kickers* (☎ 804-289-8930), who play in the US Interregional Soccer League, and the local ice-hockey team is the *Richmond Renegades* (☎ 804-643-7825), from the East Coast Hockey League.

The *Richmond International Raceway* (☎ 804-345-7223), in the east at the Virginia State Fairgrounds, between Henrico Turnpike (Meadowbridge Rd) and Laburnum Ave, is a 3/4-mile track that seats 100,000 fans. Each year it hosts the Pontiac Excitement 400, Winston Cup events (early June), the Grand National Autolite Platinum 250, and the Miller 400 (early September).

There must be an abundance of 'revheads' here, because *Southside Speedway*

(☎ 804-744-1275), at Genito Rd in Midlothian, attracts them in droves. On Friday nights, from April to October, expect to find NASCAR short-track races.

SHOPPING

The Very Richmond Shop, in the Jefferson Hotel (see Places to Stay, earlier), has a range of Richmond prints and ephemera. For photography supplies, go to Richmond Camera on W Broad St.

GETTING THERE & AWAY

About a dozen airlines serve Richmond International Airport, which has more than 150 flights daily – these include Delta (☎ 800-221-1212), American (☎ 800-433-7300), United (☎ 800-241-6522), and TWA (☎ 800-221-2000). US Airways (☎ 800-428-4322) is the major regional carrier.

The Greyhound/Trailways bus terminal (☎ 804-254-5938, 800-231-2222) is at 2910 N Boulevard (I-95 exit 78). You will need to take a GRTC bus to get into town.

Richmond is well served by Amtrak (☎ 800-872-7245), but it's some distance away, at 7519 Staple Mills Rd. The station is open 24 hours and has handicapped access. A taxi fare to downtown is about $12. The closest bus is GRTC No 27, which passes Glenside Park 'n' Ride. There are interstate services to New York City ($72), Philadelphia ($52), and Baltimore ($36).

You can reach Richmond via I-95, I-64, Routes 60, 1, or 301. The Highway Helpline (☎ 800-367-7623) has information on the state's major highways.

GETTING AROUND
To/From the Airport

A taxicab to downtown costs $16 to $18. There is no GRTC bus service, but Groome Transportation (☎ 800-222-7222) offers 24-hour service into downtown ($13 for one person, $18 for two, and around $26 for a carload of people).

At the airport, short-term parking is $1 per hour, or $8 for 24 hours; long-term parking is $5 for 24 hours; and satellite parking is $4 per day, with a shuttle running every 10 minutes from the parking area.

All the major car rental companies are located at the airport. In the Richmond area, you can get weather information by calling ☎ 804-268-1212.

Bus

The city bus service is provided by the Greater Richmond Transit Company (GRTC; ☎ 804-358-4782), 101 S Davis St. There are infrequent services out to the suburbs but plenty within downtown. You can get a route map from the basement of City Hall, 99 E Broad St. Most buses leave from, on, or near Broad St. Bus No 24 is a good service for getting south into downtown and Broad St. The base fare is $1.25, and transfers cost 15¢ (request them when you first get on); exact change is required.

GRTC Trolley buses (☎ 804-358-4782) run throughout downtown along two routes 11 am to 11 pm daily except Sunday (25¢ per ride, $1 for an all-day pass).

The Richmond Cultural Connection operates on weekends (10 am to 5:30 pm Saturday and noon to 5:30 pm Sunday) from late May to late November along three routes – Orange (Downtown East), Blue (Boulevard South), and Green (Boulevard North) – passing most attractions every hour ($1 for unlimited rides).

Taxi

There are more than 40 taxi companies in the city. Three 'road-tested' cab companies are Town and Country Taxi (☎ 804-271-2211), Yellow Taxi (☎ 804-222-7300), and Metro Taxi (☎ 804-353-5000). Cabs are metered and charge $1.50 for the first one-fifth mile, and then 30¢ per one-fifth mile thereafter.

Bicycle

Several good bike tours operate in the Richmond area. In Carytown, Two Wheel Travel (☎ 804-359-2453, 2934 W Cary St) does repairs, rents bikes (starting at $15), and provides maps for the region's bike tours.

Another information source is the Richmond Area Bicycling Association (☎ 804-266-7562), which publishes 'Rides Around Richmond,' listing 50 tours.

Around Richmond

Most of the points of interest around Richmond are associated with the Civil War (or peanuts!).

RICHMOND BATTLEFIELD PARK

Richmond was always seen by the Union forces as the main prize of the Civil War, and a few campaigns came within miles of the city. These battles are commemorated in the Richmond National Battlefield Park (☎ 804-226-1981), a collection of 11 sites (altogether more than 760 acres) – including Gaines' Mill, Malvern Hill, Cold Harbor, and Fort Harrison. The new Civil War Visitor Center (☎ 804-226-1981), in the Pattern Storage building, Tredegar Iron Works, is open 9 am to 5 pm daily.

At the small Cold Harbor visitor center is a map of the battle. The Fort Harrison visitor center, open June to August, is close to well-preserved fortifications.

There are interpretative facilities at Chickahominy Bluff, Malvern Hill, Fort Harrison, and Drewry's Bluff. You'll find historical trails at Gaines' Mill (Watt House), Fort Brady, and Drewry's Bluff. There are also tour roads (and picnic areas) at Cold Harbor and Fort Harrison, and an audio cassette is available for a four-hour self-driving tour of the Seven Days Battles. Other sites to visit are Savage's Station, Yellow Tavern, Hanover Junction, Haw's Shop, Howlett and Bermuda Hundred lines, and River Road – ask for a free map at the Civil War visitor center (or at the Museum of the Confederacy).

PETERSBURG

This historic town (population 38,500) on the Appomattox River, 23 miles south of Richmond on I-95, was the scene of the last great battle of the Civil War. When this vital junction center fell to Union troops in early April 1865 after a 10-month siege, the nearby capital of Richmond was evacuated by the Confederates. Much earlier, it had changed hands in the Revolutionary War – it fell in the spring of 1781 to a British force.

VIRGINIA

The Old Towne – the most interesting part of Petersburg with its many fine antebellum buildings – is easy to walk around. In August 1993, a tornado tore through Old Towne, destroying many buildings – locals say it did more damage in five minutes than Grant managed in his entire siege!

The city's many local industries include a large optical-products plant. The giant military installation of Fort Lee is nearby. Recently, the acclaimed actor Tim Reid and his partners established **New Millennium Studios** (☎ 804-371-8204), or 'Hollywood on the East Coast,' in Colonial Heights near Petersburg – eventually there will be studio tours.

Information

The I-95 Petersburg Visitors Center (☎ 804-246-2145) is at the Carson Rest Area on I-95S (20 miles south of the city), and the Petersburg Visitors Center – Old Towne (☎ 804-733-2400, 800-368-3595, www.petersburg-va.org) is at 425 Cockade Alley. Their most fascinating freebie is the pamphlet 'African American

---

Free Black Communities

A small but fascinating sidelight to slavery arose in the antebellum South. Slaves who either bought their freedom or were 'manumitted' (released from slavery) quietly formed small 'Free Black' communities throughout the South. Although their freedom was severely limited, free blacks nevertheless enjoyed liberties denied to their enslaved peers: They organized in largely self-regulated communities, raised families, formed churches, learned trades, inherited property (though most supported abolition, some wealthier free blacks owned slaves), and established a social elite of their own. One such community was located on Pocahontas Island on the north side of the Appomattox River near Petersburg. Although visitors can stroll around the island, no monument or museum recalls the former community.

Historic Sites in Petersburg.' Few know that a group of free blacks left Petersburg in 1829 for Liberia on the West African coast. One of them, Joseph Jenkins Roberts, became that country's first president. He served from 1848 to 1855, and then from 1871 to 1876. There's a marker at the corner of Sycamore and Wythe Sts.

Old Towne

At the **Siege Museum** (☎ 804-733-2400), at 15 W Bank St, you get a glimpse of what life was like for those who were under siege here during the Civil War. The exhibits focus on the civilians rather than the warring troops, and there are several poignant examples of their will to survive. An excellent film evokes a sense of the time. The museum is open 10 am to 5 pm daily. Admission is $3 for adults and $2 for seniors and children.

The intriguing **Trapezium House** of 1817 (☎ 800-368-3595), 244 N Market St, would be a challenge for any modern builder. Its construction is said to have been influenced by Caribbean superstitions that the builder learned from one of his servants. Evil spirits lurked in parallel lines and right angles, the sort that *feng shui* could not remove. It is open 10 am to 5 pm daily from April to October. Admission is $3 for adults and $2 for children and seniors. All tours begin from the Siege Museum.

The **Centre Hill Mansion** (☎ 804-733-2400), on Centre Hill Court, has undergone several remodelings since it was built in 1823. Furnished with Victorian antiques, including a huge 100-year-old Knabe grand piano, it is well worth a visit. It is open 10 am to 5 pm daily, and admission is $3 for adults and $2 for children and seniors.

At 19 Bollingbrook St is the **Farmers Bank** of 1817 (☎ 804-733-2400), one of the oldest bank premises in the nation. It is open 10 am to 5 pm Friday to Monday from April to October. Admission is $3 for adults and $2 for children and seniors. Tours also start at the visitor center.

The historic **Blandford Church**, 319 S Crater Rd, was built in 1735 and is now a

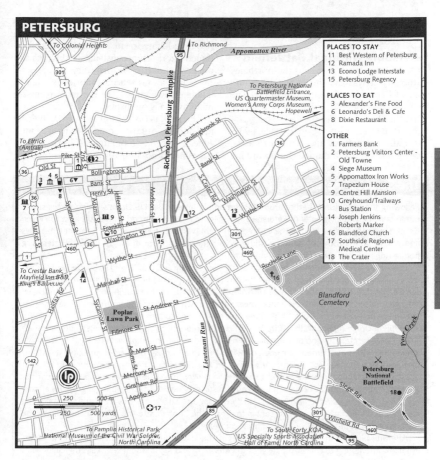

PETERSBURG

To Colonial Heights

To Richmond

Appomattox River

To Petersburg National Battlefield Entrance, US Quartermaster Museum, Women's Army Corps Museum, Hopewell

To Ettrick (Amtrak)

Pike St

Old St

Bollingbrook St

Bank St

Henry St

Market St

To Crestar Bank, Mayfield Inn B&B, King's Barbecue

Marshall St

Poplar Lawn Park

St Andrew St

Fillmore St

Adams-Mars St

Mercury St

Graham Rd

Apollo St

To Pamplin Historical Park, National Museum of the Civil War Soldier, North Carolina

Sycamore St

Adams St

Jefferson St

Madison St

Franklin Ave

Washington St

Wythe St

Richmond Petersburg Turnpike

Bollingbrook St

Bank St

S Crater Rd

Washington St

Sycamore St

Wythe St

Lieutenant Run

Rochelle Lane

Blandford Cemetery

Petersburg National Battlefield

Siege Rd

Winfield Rd

To South Forty KOA, US Specialty Sports Association Hall of Fame, North Carolina

Pine Creek

PLACES TO STAY
11 Best Western of Petersburg
12 Ramada Inn
13 Econo Lodge Interstate
15 Petersburg Regency

PLACES TO EAT
3 Alexander's Fine Food
6 Leonardo's Deli & Cafe
8 Dixie Restaurant

OTHER
1 Farmers Bank
2 Petersburg Visitors Center - Old Towne
4 Siege Museum
5 Appomattox Iron Works
7 Trapezium House
9 Centre Hill Mansion
10 Greyhound/Trailways Bus Station
14 Joseph Jenkins Roberts Marker
16 Blandford Church
17 Southside Regional Medical Center
18 The Crater

memorial to the Confederate soldiers who died during the Civil War. It features 15 stained-glass windows by Louis Comfort Tiffany, 13 of them are memorials donated by the Confederate states.

Let's face it, you probably don't know how Memorial Day got started, do you? Not long after the war ended, Mary Logan, wife of the politician and Union General John Alexander Logan, saw schoolgirls placing flowers on the gravesites of some of Petersburg's war dead near Blandford Church. She saw the observance repeated the following year. Very moved, she told her husband, who was by then head of the Grand Army of the Republic, the major body of Union veterans. At his instruction, Memorial Day was instituted as a national holiday, first celebrated on May 30, 1868, for the purpose of decorating the graves of Civil War dead. The church is open 10 am to 5 pm daily. Admission is $3 for adults and $2 for children and seniors.

The **US Specialty Sports Association Hall of Fame** (☎ 804-732-4099), 3935 S Crater Rd, houses memorabilia of players inducted into the US Slo-Pitch Softball Hall of Fame. It's open daily, and admission is $1.50 for adults and $1 for seniors and students.

Petersburg National Battlefield

This 2650-acre park is just to the northeast of the city. It was the site of the 10-month siege of Petersburg (see the boxed text The Siege of Petersburg).

At the War Room in the Petersburg National Battlefield Visitor Center (☎ 804-732-3531), there are maps and models to assist those going on a self-guided 4-mile driving tour (where you park and walk out to points of interest). There is a living-history program (from mid-June to late August) in which costumed interpreters construct earthworks and portray the life of ordinary soldiers. A 17,000lb Federal seacoast mortar (similar to 'Dictator,' which shelled the town from 2½ miles away) is on display.

The park is open 8 am to 7 pm daily from mid-June to August; from September to mid-June, it's open to 5 pm daily. Admission is $5 per person mid-June to August, $4 otherwise

The Siege of Petersburg (1864–1865)

Following the tumultuous battles around Richmond in June 1864, US Grant's Union forces struck out to take the vital rail center of Petersburg, 23 miles south of Richmond on the Appomattox River. Grant handled the move around the Confederate right with skill. His army stole from their trenches and, thanks to a 2100-foot pontoon bridge across the James River, they got close to Petersburg before Robert E Lee knew what was happening.

Petersburg at that stage was held by a small Confederate force led by PGT Beauregard. Union forces attacked twice but failed to make the most of the opportunity – perhaps because the troops were exhausted. Lee got the Army of Northern Virginia into position just in time, and Grant called off further attacks. On June 20, Grant's forces settled down to a partial siege. It was exactly the situation Lee had hoped to avoid, as his army was now pinned to a fixed position.

In July, a Union regiment, the 48th Pennsylvania, composed largely of coal miners, dug in opposite a Confederate stronghold. Their plan, which was quite a long shot, was to build a 500-foot-long tunnel under the Confederate lines, pack it with 8 tons of blasting powder, and blow it up, thus breaching the Confederate defenses. At dawn on July 30, after a harrowing moment in which a brave soldier crawled into the tunnel to splice the broken fuse, the biggest bang of the war occurred, creating a **150-foot crater** (which you can still see today). Massive bungling by the attacking forces failed to take the advantage, and by midday, the attack was thwarted and the stalemate resumed. A division of black soldiers sent in to breach the Confederate line were butchered, and the hapless General Burnside was removed from command.

After this blunder, the siege continued, and Grant and Meade extended their lines on the southern flank, attempting to cut off supply lines to Petersburg and Richmond. Eventually, the Union lines were more than 50 miles long, stretching from northeast of Richmond in an arc to southeast of Petersburg. In response, Lee stretched his lines taut; his only hope was to break the siege and try to join Joseph Johnston in North Carolina, where his army might have success against Sherman's forces.

Lee's infantry attacked the Union stronghold of **Fort Stedman**, due east of Petersburg, on March 25, hoping to break the Union line in two, but the attack failed, with a loss of about 5000 men. Grant responded swiftly, moving a full corps against the farthest end of the Confederate line and moving Phil Sheridan's cavalry to the crossroads at Five Forks.

The next day, Grant led a concerted assault along Lee's main lines, and on the night of April 2–3, Lee evacuated Petersburg and Richmond to begin his final retreat. Sheridan's cavalry, supported by infantry, chased the retreating Southerners toward Appomattox and the war's end. The next day, Lincoln, transported down the James River by gunboat, walked into a burning Richmond with an escort of sailors and witnessed firsthand the collapse of the Confederacy.

($10 maximum per car). A Petersburg Campaign Pass, which allows access to nine sites, including those in Old Towne, is $15 for adults and $7 for children seven to 16.

To get to the battlefield, take I-95 exit 52 to Route 36 – the entrance is signed.

Pamplin Historical Park

This private park (☎ 804-861-2408, www .pamplinpark.org), 6125 Boydton Plank Rd (County Rd 670, I-85 exit 63A), southwest of Petersburg in Dinwiddie County, is at the site where the Union forces broke through the Confederate defenses on April 2, 1865. Fifteen hours after the breakthrough, Lee was forced to abandon Petersburg.

The **interpretative center**, designed to reflect the shape of the Confederate defensive line at the time, has a fiber-optic battle map; outside is a 1-mile trail that leads to some of the fortifications and to a reconstruction of one of the huts in which Confederate soldiers wintered over in 1864–65.

The **National Museum of the Civil War Soldier** is quite simply one of the best museums in Virginia. First take the audio tour, where you choose from one of 13 soldier comrades (representing both Blue and Gray) who help in interpretation. The tour includes an introduction; camp life (food, diseases, and living conditions); the army on the march; the poignant 'trial by fire' and the illustration of an attack on an electronic map; the soldier's fate (those wounded, imprisoned, or killed); surviving in the field in winter camps; and a 'test of faith.' The displays are being extended all the time – the museum will not be completed until 2011.

Outside, there are cannon-firing and small-arms demonstrations (twice daily, in the morning and afternoon). It is open 9 am to 6 pm during summer; otherwise, 9 am to 5 pm. Admission is $10 for adults, $8 for seniors, and $5 for children six to 11.

Quartermaster Corps Museum

The US Army's Quartermaster Museum (☎ 804-734-4203) is on E Washington St (Route 36), 3 miles east of old Petersburg in Fort Lee. It includes uniforms and equipment dating to 1775, Civil War memorabilia,

Eisenhower's uniforms, President Franklin Pierce's saddles, and General George Patton's jeep, specially fitted out with its Mercedes car seat. The museum is open 10 am to 5 pm Tuesday to Friday and 11 am to 5 pm weekends. It's free; you don't need a pass to enter the fort.

The **Womens' Army Corps Museum** is due to open at Fort Lee in 2000.

Places to Stay

The **South Forty KOA** (☎ 804-732-8345, 2809 Courtland Rd), I-95 exit 41, has more than 100 campsites. In winter, sites start at $21 for two; during peak and summer periods, they start at $26 (an extra person is $3). There are Kamping Kabins for $30 to $40.

There are plenty of cheap chain accommodations, especially near I-95 exit 52/50D and exit 45 near the intersection of I-295. To get to the **Econo Lodge Interstate** (☎ 804-732-2000, 12002 S Crater Rd), take I-95 exit 45 at Route 301; singles and doubles cost $33 to $50. The **Ramada Inn** (☎ 804-733-0730, 501 E Washington St), off I-95 exit 50D northbound and 52 southbound, has a pool and exercise room. Singles cost $43 to $65, and doubles cost $45 to $70.

Also in this enclave is the **Best Western of Petersburg** (☎ 804-733-1776, 405 E Washington St), which has a restaurant. The rooms all have free movies, and the price includes continental breakfast. Singles/doubles cost $40/50 in the low season and $46/50 otherwise.

The **Petersburg Regency** (☎ 804-526-3000, 380 E Washington St) is easily spotted from I-95 – it's the most imposing building around; very comfortable doubles cost $99 to $130.

The **Mayfield Inn B&B** (☎ 804-861-6775, 3348 W Washington St) is an 18th-century brick building. The large rooms, which are furnished with antiques, cost $65 to $70 for a double. To get there, take I-95 exit 52 to Washington St (Route 1/460) and travel west for 3 miles.

Places to Eat & Drink

Visit **Dixie Restaurant** (☎ 804-732-5761, 250 N Sycamore St), an unpretentious place that serves Southern-style fare to poor and rich alike; lunch costs $3 to $5.

Annabelle's (☎ *804-732-0997, 2733 Park Ave*), in a converted barn just off S Crater Rd, serves good old-fashioned American dishes; a steak dinner will cost $8 to $15. *Leonardo's Deli & Cafe* (☎ *804-863-4830, 7 Bollingbrook St*) is a small place serving deli sandwiches for lunch and fine continental fare for dinner.

Alexander's Fine Food (☎ *804-733-7134, 101 W Bank St*) is a cozy, traditional Greek/Italian place open for lunch daily and for dinner Wednesday to Saturday (closed Sunday). Hearty entrees cost $5.95 to $10.95 and come with substantial salads.

King's Barbecue (☎ *804-732-5861, 3221 W Washington St*), off Route 1S, serves beef and pork directly from a dining-room smoking pit. Other Southern favorites are on the menu, and side orders include fried potato cakes and barbecued beans – eat a huge meal here for less than $10. There is another King's: (☎ *804-732-0975, 2910 S Crater Rd*).

In summertime, after work on Thursday, 500-plus locals flock to the grounds of the *Appomattox Iron Works* for Thursday at the Works. A recognized band plays from 5 to 9 pm ($5 entry, first drink free).

Getting There & Away

The closest major airport is Richmond International (see Richmond, earlier, for details). Greyhound/Trailways runs a daily service, and the depot is on the southeast corner of Washington and Adams Sts. The Amtrak stop is in Ettrick, just across the river on Route 36. You'll have to get a taxi to reach accommodations from here (you'll pay about $5 per person).

Petersburg Area Transit (☎ 804-733-2413) serves the city and the surrounding area. A ride is 70¢ (10¢ for a transfer); use exact change. Historic Petersburg Carriage (☎ 804-733-2400) runs tours from Thursday to Sunday ($7 for all passengers; babies are free).

HOPEWELL

The city of Hopewell, north of Petersburg on the James River, is an outgrowth of Old City Point, founded by Sir Thomas Dale in 1613. It was one of the earliest English settlements in America but was wiped out in a Native American attack in 1622. Its strategic location in the Civil War led to its revival. In the mid-1970s, Hopewell was devastated by one of the nation's worst pesticide spills.

The Hopewell Visitors Center (☎ 804-541-2461, www.ci.hopewell.va.us), 4100 Oaklawn Blvd, at the Colonial Corner Shopping Center, is well organized and provides a walking tour map.

The **City Point National Historic Site** (☎ 804-458-9504) was the site of Ulysses S Grant's army headquarters for more than nine months. Included on the site are two rooms with original furnishings, Grant's cabin, and wayside exhibits. At the confluence of the James and Appomattox Rivers, the dozens of other pre–Civil War houses that survived war were used as commissaries, lodgings, and munitions stores for the Union army during the Siege of Petersburg and can be seen in self-guided tours. There is a national cemetery nearby, where many Confederate and Union soldiers are buried. City Point is open 8:30 am to 4:30 pm daily and is free.

Ulysses S Grant: Union general and the 18th US president

On Crescent and Prince George Aves in Crescent Hill-Oakwood, there is a display of the **Sears, Roebuck & Co Houses by Mail** – 44 diverse examples of house-building kits you could order between the 1920s and 1930s. They range from executive housing to English cottages. There is a self-guided tour of the neighborhood, or you can take a 30-minute guided tour (available 9 am to 5 pm; call ☎ 804-541-2461).

The **Weston Plantation** (☎ 804-541-2206), at 21st Ave and Weston Lane (off Route 10), is also worth a visit. The three stories of the house are furnished with antiques, and there are extensive gardens. Particularly interesting is the history in the Civil War journals left by 12-year-old Emma Wood. The plantation is open 10 am to 4:30 pm Monday to Saturday and 1 to 4:30 pm Sunday from April to October. Admission is $5 for adults, $4 for seniors, free for children under 12 .

Five miles north of Hopewell is the **Presquile National Wildlife Refuge** (☎ 804-733-8042), open weekdays 7:30 am to 4 pm. The refuge is home to many waterfowl and wetland species and is an important link in the Atlantic flyway.

The *Pocahontas II* (☎ 800-405-9990) leaves from the marina, 906 Riverside Ave, for tours of the James River from April to November. The shortest cruise is $11 for adults and $6 for children.

There are accommodations close to Hopewell, including a *Holiday Inn Express*, at I-95 exit 61, with rooms starting at $55, and *Hampton Inn (5103 Plaza Drive)*, with rooms starting at $75. For a bite to eat, *Chip's Place* (☎ *804-541-6122, 208 E Cawson St*), open daily except Sunday, is thoroughly pleasant and the source of great club sandwiches ($4.75).

WAVERLY & WAKEFIELD

Peanut-lovers head southeast of Petersburg on Route 460. Some 20 miles from Petersburg is Waverly, home of the 'First Peanut Museum in the USA,' which is housed in the **Miles B Carpenter Museum** (☎ 804-834-3327). It has displays of folk art, machinery, and equipment associated with peanuts. The museum is open 2 to 5 pm daily.

Wakefield, 8 miles farther east on Route 460, is the self-proclaimed 'Peanut Capital of the World.' The reason for a trip that could only be described as 'Nuts!' is the idiosyncratic *Virginia Diner* (☎ *804-899-3106*), which pays homage to the humble goober and which has been open since 1929. The peanuts, cooked in vendor roasters, are free, and a sumptuous breakfast of ham, eggs, hot cakes, omelets, hash browns, grits, biscuits, and sausage costs less than $6. It's open 6 am to 9 pm in summer and until 8 pm in winter.

VIRGINIA

Northern Virginia

At first glance, you could be forgiven for thinking Northern Virginia is just a huge dormitory for the juggernaut of Washington, DC. Sure, its future is linked to the nation's capital, and it is physically connected by the Metro and road bridges across the Potomac River. Also, Washingtonians fan out into nearby counties to relax on weekends. But cross to the south side of the river and you're in Virginia, where people proudly call themselves Virginians.

This chapter covers the main Virginian cities, towns, and counties within an easy drive west, north, and south of the nation's capital, including historic Fredericksburg. Alexandria and Arlington, the largest cities in Northern Virginia, are covered in the Around Washington, DC chapter.

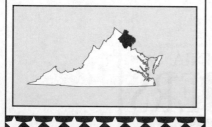

Highlights

- Mount Vernon – home of George and Martha Washington and one of America's most visited estates

- Hunt and Horse Country – a little bit of England in the heart of America

- Manassas Battlefield – the first major battle site of the Civil War

- Historic Fredericksburg – antiques, historic tours, and battlefields

- Spotsylvania, the Wilderness, and Chancellorsville battlefield tours – essential for Civil War buffs

Beyond the Beltway

Travel a little farther beyond the I-495 Beltway into Northern Virginia and you reach Fairfax, Loudoun, Fauquier, and Prince William Counties. These are replete with historical associations, pleasant rural scenery, and such treasures as Mount Vernon and Gunston Hall.

FAIRFAX COUNTY

Fairfax County (population 865,000) has been absorbed into the DC metropolitan area, and life here is dogged by all the attendant inconveniences of living on the edge of a big city. The biggest draw for visitors is Mount Vernon, George Washington's estate.

Fairfax

The Fairfax Museum & Visitors Center (☎ 703-385-8414), 10209 Main St (Route 236), is open 9 am to 5 pm daily. The museum, in an 1873 brick schoolhouse, has exhibits on local, colonial, and Civil War history (free admission).

The **George Mason University Center for the Arts** (☎ 703-993-8788), 4400 University Drive, is a concert hall where symphonies, dance companies, chamber-music groups, and jazz artists perform. There is an adjoining professional theater. The **Fairfax Symphony Orchestra** (☎ 703-642-7200) has a seven-concert Classic Series; check at the box office. The center is open for performances September to May.

The **National Firearms Museum** (☎ 703-267-1600) is in the NRA Headquarters, at 11250 Waples Mill Rd. The museum includes a replica of the Hawken's St Louis (Missouri) shop, where the Hawken rifle, used by mountain men in the 19th century, was created; a Coney Island shooting gallery; and several firearms from the Wild West. It's open 10 am to 4 pm weekdays (free admission).

Fairfax County, so close to DC, has many accommodations. In the town of Fairfax, on

Route 123, is the ***Bailiwick Inn*** (☎ 703-691-2266), a fine restored 19th-century residence. The comforts are not cheap: singles and doubles range from $130 to $295. The dining room is open in the evening Wednesday to Saturday; the prix-fixe menu is $45 weekdays, $55 weekends. Cheaper choices in the Fairfax region are the ***Hampton Inn – Fairfax*** (☎ 703-385-2600), at the intersection of Routes 50 and 29; the ***Holiday Inn Fairfax City*** (☎ 703-591-5500), on Route 123; and the ***Comfort Inn University Center*** (☎ 703-591-5900), on Route 50.

Good dining options are the Tuesday morning ***farmers' market*** (May to November), near Truro Church parking lot, for fresh produce; the ***Black-Eyed Pea*** (☎ 703-352-0588, 3971 Chain Bridge Rd); and ***Havabite Eatery*** (☎ 703-591-2243, 10416 Main St) for home-style cooking.

The City of Fairfax bus (☎ 703-385-7859) runs daily until 9 pm; the fare is 50¢ per sector.

Vienna & Reston

Vienna is a sizable suburban city between Washington-Dulles Airport and DC. Reston, one of the nation's prototypes for a planned community (since 1964), has **Terraset**, the country's first earth-sheltered school, and an interesting town center.

Vienna's **Wolf Trap Farm Park for the Performing Arts** (☎ 703-218-6500), 1624 Trap Rd, is the United States' only national park for the performing arts. During the summer, all types of performances are given in two 18th-century barns, a partial outdoor amphitheater, and the outdoor Theater in the Woods. On Labor Day weekend, an International Children's Festival features local and overseas performers. Why Wolf Trap? Records from 1632 show that wolves caused much damage here, and tobacco was offered as a reward to those who trapped them.

Ticket order forms for events at Wolf Trap Farm regularly appear in the *Washington Post*. In-house shows start at $25; a picnic space on the lawn starts at $17.50. To get there, turn off I-495 onto Route 7. Follow Towlston Rd for 1 mile; the park is on the left and is well marked.

The **Reston Animal Park** (☎ 703-759-3637), 1228 Hunter Mill Rd, is a 56-acre children's zoo with a variety of domestic and exotic animals. There are lots of rides to be had on ponies, horses, and elephants and plenty of fluffy animals to pet, feed, and watch. It opens at 10 am, closing at 5 pm on weekdays and 6 pm on weekends mid-June to Labor Day; the rest of the year, it closes 3 pm weekdays, 5 pm weekends. Admission is $9.95 for adults, $6.95 for seniors and children two to 12.

Also in Reston is the **US Geological Survey** (☎ 703-648-4748), at 12201 Sunrise Valley Drive, where data on minerals and land and water resources are collected and distributed; there are tours Monday, Tuesday, and Thursday year-round.

Sully Plantation

In Chantilly, near Washington-Dulles Airport and well marked with signs, is this plantation (☎ 703-437-1794). Built in 1794, it was once the home of Richard Bland Lee, uncle of Robert E and Northern Virginia's first congressman. The house was saved from bull-dozers expanding Dulles Airport for 'jumbo duty' in the late 20th century. The site is open daily except Tuesday 11 am to 5 pm, to 4 pm in winter. On weekdays, the last tour is at 3 pm and on weekends at 3:30 pm. Tours cost $4 for adults, $3 for seniors, $2 for students and children five to 16. The easiest way here from DC is to take Route 66W and go north on Route 28 until you reach the plantation.

Great Falls

The **Colvin Run Mill Historic Site** (☎ 703-759-2771), 10017 Colvin Run Rd, includes a restored 19th-century gristmill (still producing corn meal and whole wheat flour). It's open 11 am to 5 pm Wednesday to Monday from March to December (the rest of the year, weekends only). Admission is $4 for adults, $2 for seniors and children.

Off the I-495 Beltway at exit 13 and northwest along Route 193 is the scenic 800-acre **Great Falls National Park**. Here, the Potomac River cascades some 77 feet in a series of falls and rapids. A canal system was constructed in 1785 by George Washington's Patowmack Company to circumvent the

VIRGINIA

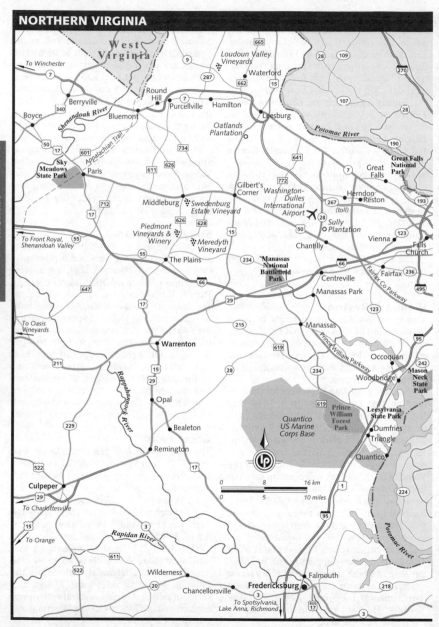

NORTHERN VIRGINIA

West Virginia

To Winchester
7

665
9
Loudoun Valley Vineyards
287
662
Waterford
15
28
109
270

Round Hill
Berryville
340
Bluemont
Purcellville
7
Hamilton
Leesville
107
28

Boyce
50
17
601
Shenandoah River
Appalachian Trail
Oatlands Plantation
641
7
Great Falls
190
Great Falls National Park

Sky Meadows State Park
Paris
734
611
626
Gilbert's Corner
772
Washington-Dulles International Airport
267 (toll)
Herndon
Reston
193

712
Middleburg
Swedenburg Estate Vineyard
626
628
28
Sully Plantation
123
Vienna
Falls Church

To Front Royal, Shenandoah Valley
55
17
Piedmont Vineyards & Winery
15
50
Chantilly
66
236
495

55
The Plains
234
Manassas National Battlefield Park
Centreville
Fairfax
Fairfax Co Parkway

647
66
29
Manassas Park

To Oasis Vineyards
17
215
Manassas
123

Warrenton
95

211
15
29
619
Prince William Parkway
Occoquan
242
Mason Neck State Park

Opal
28
234
Woodbridge

229
Bealeton
619
Prince William Forest Park
Leesylvania State Park

Remington
17
Quantico US Marine Corps Base
Dumfries
Triangle
Quantico

522
Culpeper
29
224

To Charlottesville

15
To Orange

3
Rapidan River
611

522
Wilderness
20
Chancellorsville
Falmouth
218

Fredericksburg
BUS 17
3

To Spotsylvania, Lake Anna, Richmond

0   8   16 km
0   5   10 miles

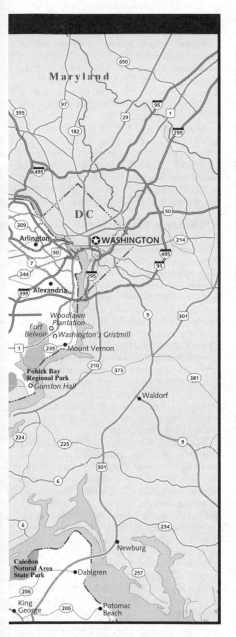

falls – a 3/4-mile stretch of this remains, and you can explore it on foot. Across the river, in Maryland, is the C&O Canal Historical Park. Admission paid at either side permits access to either park for seven days (see the Western Maryland chapter).

The park grounds are open 7 am until dusk daily. Admission is $4 for private vehicles, $2 for pedestrians. The visitor center (☎ 703-285-2966), open 10 am to 5 pm daily, conducts historical programs. Be careful – the slippery rocks on the cliffs around the river are dangerous.

Mount Vernon

A visit to fascinating Mount Vernon (☎ 703-780-2000, www.mountvernon.org), George Washington's home for many years, is a Virginia must-see, and it is second in popularity only to the White House as a visited historic house. The country estate of this quintessential country gentleman has been meticulously restored and affords a glimpse of life as it was when Washington 'took to the farm.' All is not ostentation, however, and there are many glimpses of the farm's working nature and regular living-history presentations.

Much of Mount Vernon's allure has to do with the fact that both George and his wife Martha (neé Custis) are buried here in an enclosure on the south side of the house. The entrance to the family vault bears the brief legend 'Within this enclosure rest the remains of General George Washington.' There are two sarcophagi with the simple inscriptions 'Washington' and 'Martha, Consort of Washington.' George Washington died here in a four-poster bed in the bedchamber on December 14, 1799.

Mount Vernon is pleasantly situated on the banks of the Potomac and has immaculate gardens, a preserved 19-room mansion, and several outbuildings. Work on the main building commenced in 1754, on land that had belonged to the family for 80 years. George and Martha lived here from 1759 to 1775, when George assumed command of the Continental Army. After his eight years as president, he finally retired here in 1797. The Mount Vernon Ladies' Association

VIRGINIA

George Washington: Squire of Mount Vernon

purchased it in 1858 from the Washington family, commenced restoration, and operated it as a national shrine.

The white, colonnaded facade of the main building faces the Potomac, and the kitchen and slaves' and workers' quarters are detached. In the main reception room, you can see the key to the Bastille. The key was presented to Washington by Thomas Paine on behalf of Lafayette (and has only left the building once, when it was taken to Paris for the bicentennial of the storming of the Bastille). The library, with its ornate fireplace, terrestrial globe, and revolving desk chair and secretary desk, exudes an air befitting the nation's first president. There is an adjoining museum that highlights the results of an archaeological dig of the blacksmith's shop and slaves' quarters.

The estate is open 9 am to 5 pm daily in March, September, and October; 8 am to 5 pm from April to August; otherwise, 9 am to 4 pm. Admission is $9 for adults, $8.50 for seniors, $4.50 for children six to 11. In

summer, go early, as there are usually long lines of people waiting to get in.

Mount Vernon is only 16 miles south of DC on Route 235 (the George Washington Memorial Parkway). You can also take Route 1 to Route 235 to reach the south entrance. On public transport, take the Yellow or Blue Metrorail to Huntington, then bus No 11P to the estate.

Mount Vernon Inn (☎ *703-780-0011*), a colonial-style restaurant located on the estate, is a great place to eat. It serves lunch (around $7.50) daily and candlelight dinner Monday to Saturday. Entrees range from $12 to $20. For the inappropriately dressed, there is a snack bar near the entrance to the estate.

Woodlawn Plantation

This plantation (☎ 703-780-4000), in the town of Mount Vernon, features two houses of very different styles, both splendid examples of their respective eras. Woodlawn, a typical plantation home once belonging to Lawrence and Eleanor ('Nelly') Custis Lewis (nephew and granddaughter of George and Martha Washington) was built between 1800 and 1805. The building was supervised by William Thornton, one of the architects of the capitol in Washington, DC. Today, it is furnished with period antiques, and outside, there is a formal garden with a stunning collection of roses. It is open 10 am to 4 pm daily from March to December. Admission is $6 for adults, $4 for seniors and youth six to 18. Tours are conducted on the half hour.

The Frank Lloyd Wright **Pope-Leighey House** – a 1940s middle-class Usonian dwelling of cypress, brick, and glass – is also on the grounds of Woodlawn, where it was moved from Falls Church after being saved from destruction in 1964. Furnished with Wright pieces, the house is utilitarian in structure but quite beautiful. ('Usonian' comes from 'United States of North America'; it was an architectural style developed by Wright to provide affordable, economical housing for people of moderate incomes.) The house is open 9:30 am to 4 pm daily March to December. Admission is $8 for adults, $6 for seniors and students.

To get here, take Route 1 from Washington, DC; the entrance is opposite the turnoff to Route 235.

Gunston Hall

This brick home (☎ 703-550-9220) belonged to George Mason, a contemporary of Washington. Mason penned the lines 'all men are by nature equally free and independent and have certain inherent rights' – words adapted by Thomas Jefferson for incorporation into the Declaration of Independence. One of the main framers of the Constitution, Mason later refused to give the document his support, because it did not include a Bill of Rights, failed to prohibit slavery, and did not provide a system of checks and balances for curbing the power of federal government. He penned the Virginia Declaration of Rights in May 1776, which became the basis for what was later adopted as the Bill of Rights. Unlike Jefferson and Washington, Mason avoided political office, preferring life at Gunston Hall with his family.

Gunston Hall, which dates from 1755, is an architectural masterpiece with elegant carved wooden interiors. It is surrounded by meticulously kept formal gardens with boxwood hedges.

The house is open 9:30 am to 5 pm daily. Admission is $5 for adults, $4 for seniors, $1.50 for students six to 18. It's on a bend in the Potomac River, about a 15-minute drive from Mount Vernon via Route 235, Route 1, and Route 242.

Washington's Gristmill State Historic Park

About a mile west of Mount Vernon on Route 235, this mill (☎ 703-780-3383) was used by Washington when he was a farmer. It is currently undergoing restoration but can be viewed from a distance.

About 4½ miles south of the mill on Route 1 is the Pohick Church, built in the 1770s from plans drawn up by George Washington; the church's interior was designed by George Mason. It is open 9 am to 4:30 pm daily.

Mason Neck State Park

There are a couple of riverfront parks near Gunston Hall. Mason Neck (☎ 703-550-0960) is 7 miles northeast of Woodbridge on Route 242. It has a range of outdoor activities and programs, and many bird watchers come to the adjacent wildlife refuge for the weekend bald-eagle counts.

Pohick Bay Regional Park

This regional park (☎ 703-339-6104) is also northeast of Woodbridge on Route 242 (the Lorton exits off I-95 – No 163 southbound, No 161 northbound). The park has a large pool ($3.50 for adults, $2.75 for seniors and children), boat access to the Potomac, nature trails, and a golf course. Pohick Park is open 8 am until sunset daily ($4 per private vehicle). More than 100 of the 150 sites in the campground have electricity hookups, costing $12 to $14 for four people (available year-round).

LOUDOUN COUNTY

Loudoun County proudly wears the mantle 'Hunt and Horse Country.' Weekends out here can get a little frustrating with ostentatious displays by black-jacketed, jodhpured, leather booted Washingtonians in search of that English brand of finesse and class. Midweek, however, the county is a fascinating destination with several picturesque towns and is replete with history and fine old buildings.

Leesburg

The hub of Loudoun County, Leesburg (population 25,200) is on the Maryland border, to the northwest of Washington-Dulles International Airport, and is one of the oldest towns in Northern Virginia. There are many colonial-era buildings in the town and a number of plantations in the vicinity.

Leesburg was a staging area during the French and Indian War, and it was to here that James and Dolley Madison fled (with copies of the Declaration of Independence and the US Constitution) when the British torched Washington, DC, in 1812. In 1861, a major battle of the Civil War was fought at nearby Ball's Bluff. The Union troops were forced back across the Potomac by the Confederates, and houses on Leesburg's King St were used as hospitals. One of the patients was the young Oliver Wendell Holmes, later a justice of the Supreme Court.

The Leesburg tourist office (☎ 703-777-2420, www.leesburgva.org), inside Market Station at 108-D South St, is open 9 am to 5 pm daily.

Loudoun Museum This museum (☎ 703-777-7427), 16 Loudoun St, covers the time from early Native American settlement through the Civil War to the present. There is a video presentation, and the museum is the starting point of an interesting walking tour. It's open 10 am to 5 pm Monday to Saturday, 1 to 5 pm Sunday. Admission is $1 for adults, 50¢ for children.

Morven Park Just 1 mile north of Leesburg on Old Waterford Rd is a 1500-acre historic piece of property (☎ 703-777-2414) that was once the home of Virginia governor Westmoreland Davis. The Greek Revival mansion, with its manicured boxwood gardens and looking a little like a transplanted White House, is the main reason to visit, but there is also an antique carriage museum with more than 100 horse-drawn vehicles. Admission is $6 for adults, $5 for seniors, and $3 for children six to 12.

Places to Stay There is no real camping option near Leesburg and no nearby budget accommodations. About halfway between Winchester and Leesburg, at Bluemont on the Appalachian Trail, is the spectacularly situated stone lodge *Bears Den (HI-AYH) Hostel (☎ 540-554-8708)*. (To make reservations, write to Postal Route 1, Box 288, Bluemont, VA 22012.) The hostel has a kitchen, a dining room, on-site parking, and a laundry room, and the staff provides information on outdoor activities. Check-in is 5 to 9 pm, and the place is quiet after 10 pm; checkout is by 9:30 am. The hostel charges $10 for HI members ($12 for nonmembers); camping is $4 per person.

From Leesburg, head west on Route 7 for 18 miles, and then turn onto County Rd 601S at the top of the Blue Ridge. Follow this for half a mile uphill to a signed stonegate entrance on the right; follow this road for half a mile. If coming from the Appalachian Trail, take the signed trail to Bears Den Rocks (it's 300 feet to the hostel).

Reliable B&Bs in Leesburg include the renovated, red-brick *Norris House Inn (☎ 703-777-1806, 108 Loudoun St, @ inn@norrishouse.com)*, with singles/doubles starting at $80/95 on weekdays, $90/105 weekends; the *Colonial Inn (☎ 703-777-5000, 19 S King St)*, attached to the Bella Luna Ristorante (see Places to Eat); and *Stonegate B&B (☎ 540-338-9519)*, west of Leesburg on Route 7 in Hamilton.

The *Leesburg Days Inn (☎ 703-777-6622, 721 E Market St)* has budget rooms starting at $42/46 for singles/doubles in low season, $50/54 otherwise.

The *Laurel Brigade Inn (☎ 703-777-1010, 20 W Market St)*, in the town center, is popular and always requires advance booking. (Dating from 1766, it takes its name from a Civil War brigade led by a local colonel.) It has lovely gardens, a restaurant open for lunch and dinner, and pleasantly furnished rooms with no phones; doubles range from $65 to $90.

The *Landsdowne Resort (☎ 703-729-8400, 44050 Woodridge Parkway)* is about a 10-minute drive from Washington-Dulles Airport and 45 minutes from DC via Route 7. Nestled in a secluded spot on the banks of the Potomac, it has a Trent Jones-designed golf course, tennis courts, pools, a fitness center, and restaurants. It's expensive, with singles/doubles costing $149/169 in low season, $40 more in high season.

Places to Eat The *Lightfoot (☎ 703-771-2233, 11 N King St)* is a progressive American bistro with an á la carte, seasonal menu and freshly baked breads. The Laurel Brigade Inn (see Places to Stay) features steak and seafood dishes; lunch entrees start at $10, and a fixed-price dinner is $14. The *Bella Luna Ristorante*, in the Colonial Inn (see Places to Stay), is a cozy little place with classic Italian dishes.

The **Tuscarora Mill** (☎ 703-771-9300), Market Station, occupies the upper level of a turn-of-the-19th-century mill. Hearty lunches at 'Tuskie's' average about $11 and are well worth it; dinner features a number of innovative entrees, and its Sunday brunch is popular.

There are two restaurants in the Landsdowne Resort (see Places to Stay) – the **Landsdowne Grill**, open for dinner only, and the **Riverside Hearth**, open 6 am to 10 pm; dinner costs around $22.

Waterford

This 18th-century Quaker village has established a reputation for being a crafts center – an annual fall tour of local homes, combining a craft fair and those ubiquitous battle reenactments, is held in early October.

The Waterford Foundation (☎ 540-882-3018), in the Tin Shop at Clarkes Gap Rd, 2.4 miles north of Route 9W on County Rd 662, has more information on local walking tours and the craft fair. It's open 9 am to 5 pm daily, but the village is open 24 hours.

Thirsty? Head south from Waterford to Route 9W; the entrance to **Loudoun Valley Vineyards** (☎ 540-882-3375) is 4 miles along on the right. There are great views of the Blue Ridge Mountains, and it is a relaxing place to sit and enjoy European-style wine. The vineyard is open 11 am to 5 pm Wednesday to Sunday.

Oatlands Plantation

Some 6 miles south of Leesburg on Route 15S is the National Trust historic plantation Oatlands (☎ 703-777-3174). The plantation was established by a great-grandson of Robert 'King' Carter, the wealthy pre-Revolutionary planter. The carefully restored Greek Revival-style mansion, which dates from 1803, is surrounded by neat fields that feature in local hunt events such as the Loudoun Hunt Point-to-Point. (You know: the sound of bugles and barking hounds and 'Tailgates down!…Champers, sweetie?') Less pretentious is the Draft Horse & Mule

Day with its associated arts & crafts show, the sheep-dog trials in May, and a Civil War reenactment in August.

The plantation is open 10 am to 4:30 pm Monday to Saturday, 1 to 4:30 pm Sunday, from late March to December. Admission is $6 for adults and $5 for seniors and students 12 to 18.

Middleburg

This quaint little town is right on the border between Loudoun and Fauquier Counties and is fringed with tree-lined roads, horse farms, and wineries. A popular retreat for visitors wanting to escape DC for the day, it is 35 minutes from Washington-Dulles Airport. The Pink Box Visitor Center (☎ 540-687-8888, www.middleburgonline.com), at 12 N Madison St, sells a self-guided walking-tour pamphlet ($1).

Middleburg was established in 1787 by the Revolutionary War soldier Colonel Leven Powell, who purchased the land from George Washington's cousin Joseph Chinn. It had previously been called Chinn's Crossroads (because it is midway between Alexandria and Winchester on the Ashby Gap trade route, now Route 50). The **Windsor House Inn** (1824), on E Washington St, was operated by a Southern sympathizer during the Civil War, but she happily served Union troops when Middleburg was occupied in 1862.

The region has become known for fox-hunting and steeplechasing. Now more than 25 horse meets are held each year, and while the majority are amateur point-to-point races, there are several professional steeplechases. Polo matches (☎ 540-777-0775) are played on Sundays, June to August. Expect to see a well-heeled, genteel crowd loaded up with 'champers' buckets, dainty sandwiches, and pretensions.

A good time to visit is late August, when you have the choice of 'wine, women, mirth, and laughter' at the Middleburg Wine Festival (☎ 703-687-5219). The vintages of at least 20 Virginia wineries are on display, accompanied by entertainment.

The **Middleburg Country Inn** (☎ 540-687-6082, 209 E Washington St) was the former rectory of John's Parish Church. It is a small place, but the rooms are large and furnished with antiques. Singles and doubles range from $95 to $145 weekdays, $185 to $295 weekends. Guests can borrow from the video library, enjoy a country breakfast and afternoon tea, or even chance their hand at croquet.

B&Bs are numerous – there are at least 10 such fine establishments in the area. The *Red Fox Inn* (☎ 540-687-6301, 2 E Washington St, www.redfox.com), formerly Chinn's Ordinary, is believed to be the oldest continuously operating inn in North America (doubles range from $130 to $220). *The Longbarn* (☎ 540-687-4137, 37129 Adams Green Lane) is a 100-year-old renovated barn surrounded by woods, with doubles from $105 to $125.

Middleburg has some fine eateries. The *Upper Crust Bakery* (☎ 540-687-5666, 2 N Pendleton St) has country-style cookies for the kids, as well as healthy sandwiches.

The *Back Street Cafe* (☎ 540-687-3122, 4 E Federal St) always serves what seems a blend of the best American and Italian flavors and dishes made from the freshest of ingredients.

FAUQUIER COUNTY

This predominantly agricultural county of rolling hills, picturesque villages, and vineyards is another hotspot for those lured by the thrill of the hunt. The small junction town of **Warrenton** (population 5300) was established when a trading post, Read Store, opened on the Falmouth-Winchester-Alexandria-Culpeper road.

The Warrenton-Fauquier County Visitor Center (☎ 540-347-4414), 183A Keith St, is open 9 am to 5 pm daily.

The **Old Jail Museum** (☎ 540-347-5525), on Ashby St at Court House Square, has a small eclectic collection. It is open 10 am to 4 pm Tuesday to Sunday (free admission).

Wineries

There are several small wineries in Fauquier and Loudoun Counties. Piedmont Vineyards & Winery (☎ 540-687-5528), south of Mid-dleburg on County Rd 626, has tours and tastings 10 am to 5 pm daily; Meredyth Vineyard (☎ 540-687-6277), south of Middleburg on County Rd 628, has tours and tastings 10 am to 4 pm; Oasis Vineyards (☎ 540-635-7627), north of the junction of Route 211W and Route 522N on County Rd 635, has tours and tastings 10 am to 4 pm; and Swedenburg Estate Vineyard (☎ 540-687-5219), on Route 50 just east of Middleburg, has daily tours 10 am to 4 pm.

Sky Meadows State Park

This park, close to the Appalachian Trail in the northwest corner of Fauquier County, is rich in history. **Mount Bleak House** has been restored to reflect the lifestyle of an 1850s middle-class family. From spring to fall, nature and history programs are offered, and hiking, picnicking, and horseback riding on a bridle trail are all popular. There are primitive walk-in camping sites ($7 per night).

The park (☎ 703-592-3556) is 2 miles south of Paris on County Rd 710W. From DC, take Route 50 to Route 17S, or I-66 to Route 17N.

Places to Stay & Eat

The *Black Horse Inn* (☎ 540-349-4020, 8393 Meetze Rd), in Warrenton, is a gracious old country home with doubles from $100 to $145. *Fat Tuesday's Raw Bar* (☎ 540-347-5757, 573 Frost Ave) is open daily for Creole and Cajun food (and live entertainment most nights).

PRINCE WILLIAM COUNTY

Perhaps the greatest appeal of Prince William County is that it's so close to DC yet so far in terms of feeling – an 'escape' only half an hour from the capital.

Manassas

The city of Manassas (population 29,000) lies south of the battlefield and suffers some of the busiest rush-hour traffic you could ever imagine. The Prince William County/Manassas CVB (☎ 703-361-6599, www .visitpwc.com) is at 4349 Ridgewood Center Drive, in Woodbridge.

The **Manassas Museum** (☎ 703-368-1873), 9101 Prince William St, is the regional history museum for the Northern Virginia Piedmont. The Civil War is emphasized, but there are also collections of photographs, artifacts, and videos covering community history. The museum is open 10 am to 5 pm Tuesday to Sunday. Admission is $2.50 for adults, $1.50 for children six to 17.

There is a daily commuter link between Manassas (9451 West St) and Union Station in DC, via Alexandria and Arlington; for information, contact Virginia Railway Express (☎ 703-730-6664). A one-way ticket to Alexandria costs $5.15, to DC $5.55.

Manassas National Battlefield Park

A visit to this battlefield is an absolute must for keen historians. Arrayed over grassy hills on the very edge of modern DC, there is little left to remind one of the cataclysmic seesawing of the battles of July 1861 and August 1862 – see the boxed text The Battles of Manassas. These battles are referred to as Manassas in the South and as Bull Run in the North. Bull Run is the stream that forms a semicircle around the north and east of the battlefield.

There is a good self-guided tour that commences from the park's visitor center (☎ 703-361-1339). The center also has a number of exhibits, a captivating audiovisual, and a free pamphlet that shows all the points of interest. In August, reenactments of the two Civil War battles of Manassas (Bull Run) are staged.

The park is open daylight to dusk daily. The visitor center is open 8:30 am to 6 pm, except June 15 to Labor Day, when it closes at 5 pm. Admission is $2 per person (free for those under 17). To get to Manassas National Battlefield Park, a 26-mile drive from DC, take I-66W to Route 234 exit 47B; the battlefield is half a mile along this road on the right. Two heavily used highways cross the park, so use caution.

Occoquan & Around

The Prince William County Visitor Center (☎ 703-491-4045) is at 200 Mill St, in Occoquan (the name comes from the Dogue Indian word meaning 'at the end of the water'). The **Mill House** (☎ 703-491-7525), 413 Mill St, is yet another restored 18th-century gristmill. It also houses Historic Occoquan Inc, with local history exhibits, audiovisuals, and a gift shop; it is open 11 am to 4 pm daily (free admission). Occoquan has other treasures, and a visit to this small part of Prince William County can turn into a sojourn of several hours.

Shoppers will love the **Potomac Mills** (☎ 703-643-1855, 800-826-4557, www.potomacmills.com), a value outlet mall (one of the world's largest) at I-95 exit 156. There are more than 220 stores open 10 am to 9:30 pm Monday to Saturday, 11 am to 7 pm Sunday year-round.

The ***Bistro Belgique Gourmande*** *(☎ 703-494-1180, 302 Poplar Alley)* attracts the hungry in droves for its wonderful continental delights.

The ***Lazy Susan Dinner Theatre*** *(☎ 703-550-7384)*, reached from I-95 exit 160 and near where Route 1 crosses the Occoquan River, is known for its Pennsylvania Dutch buffet and theatrical performances. It opens at 6 pm, the dinner buffet is served from 7 to 8 pm, and the curtain goes up at 8:30 pm (an hour earlier on Sunday). Tickets cost $30 for adults and $15 for children. Attached is ***Skinifatz*** *(☎ 703-550-9252, www.skinifatz.com)*, a huge cybercafe where you can surf for free – they get their money from food they sell to passersby.

Prince William Forest Park

This 18,570-acre park consists of pine and hardwood forests in the Quantico Creek watershed. The area was set aside as a national park in 1948 and now offers 37 miles of hiking trails, playing fields, fishing streams, picnic areas, and scheduled naturalist programs run by the staff of the NPS Pine Grove visitor center (☎ 703-221-7181).

The ***Oak Ridge Campground*** *(☎ 703-221-7181)* is 1 mile west of the town of Triangle on County Rd 619 (I-95 exit 150); basic sites are $10 for up to six people. The ***Prince William Travel Trailer Village***

The Battles of Manassas (1861 & 1862)

Not long after the first shots were fired at Fort Sumter, South Carolina, on April 12, 1861, sizable armies of both Union and Confederate troops began to gather around the capitals of Richmond and Washington, DC.

The first significant battle of the Civil War occurred after Confederate soldiers, commanded by PGT Beauregard, camped near the rail junction of Manassas, perilously close to the national capital. The battle that Northerners hoped would end the war, **Manassas I (Bull Run)**, started with an air of ebullience. Under orders from Abraham Lincoln, Brigadier General Irvin McDowell roused his 32,000 poorly trained troops on the afternoon of July 16 and marched to Centreville, 20 miles west of DC. McDowell's men skirmished and scouted near Bull Run, gathering scanty intelligence, and on July 21, the general committed two divisions, including cavalry and artillery, against the Confederate lines.

McDowell's first assault on the right flank was checked by Stonewall Jackson's soldiers and driven back. Then, what was meant to be an organized retreat turned into a rout: The Union troops knew tactical drilling techniques well enough, but they had not been taught the essentials of withdrawal under fire.

On the supposedly 'safe' side of Bull Run, there had been a macabre picnic in progress, with civilians from Washington, DC, coming down to witness the fray. As the soldiers fled in panic, they intermingled with this now-befuddled crowd of onlookers, and there was a melee, especially when a strategic bridge across Cub Run collapsed. When the counting ended, the Confederates, who incurred about 2000 casualties as opposed to McDowell's 3000, could claim victory. Both groups were so ill-trained at this early stage of the war, however, that any advantage could not be followed up.

More than a year later, the war returned to Manassas. Following McClellan's Peninsula Campaign and the Seven Days Battles, Union troops had withdrawn to the safety of DC, and many of McClellan's soldiers were handed over to a new commander, John Pope. By the time Pope was ordered to move against Richmond, Robert E Lee was in command of the Confederates.

Pope advanced south toward the Rappahannock River, and Lee advanced north to confront Pope's troops before they could be reinforced by McClellan. Lee brilliantly split his force and consigned an attack on Pope's supply base at Manassas to Stonewall Jackson's men. Jackson's force came up against a numerically inferior force commanded by Nathaniel Banks at Cedar Mountain, and, after a seesawing battle, the Union troops were forced back with heavy losses.

Pope's main body came up the next day, and **Manassas II (Bull Run)** commenced on August 29, with Pope making heavy but futile attacks on Jackson's troops, who were in defense behind the bed of an unfinished railroad.

The following day, Lee unexpectedly arrived in force with the 30,000-strong force of James Longstreet, which in a devastating flank assault on the Union's left (combined with Jackson's attacks on the other flank) caused a repeat of Manassas I, with the Northerners fleeing back across Bull Run to the security of Washington, DC. At this stage, almost all of Virginia had been returned to the hands of the Confederates.

Pope lost his job when it was revealed that he had lost about a quarter of his force of 70,000 (the remainder of which were then incorporated into the Army of the Potomac), while Lee had lost only 10,000 of his 60,000.

(☎ 703-221-2474, 16058 Dumfries Rd) is 2½ miles north of I-95 (exit 152) on Route 234 – a very busy road. Sites, with electric/water hookups, range from $16.50 to $19.50 for two people.

The park is open dawn to dusk year-round; there is a private vehicle-entrance fee of $4 (valid for seven days). Only campers are allowed in the park in the evenings, unless there is a scheduled public program.

Dumfries

This small town on Route 1 has the **Weems-Botts Museum** (☎ 703-221-3346), 300 Duke St. The museum is the bookstore of Parson Weems, Washington's first biographer and perpetuator of the 'cherry tree' myth. Later, a local attorney named Benjamin Botts used the building as a law office. It is open Tuesday to Sunday (donations are encouraged).

Leesylvania State Park (☎ 703-670-0372) is 2 miles east of Route 1 on County Rd 610 (Neabsco Rd). Once the home of the Lee family, this park is now a popular place for hiking, picnicking, fishing, and boating.

Marine Corps Air Ground Museum (Quantico)

This interesting museum (☎ 703-784-2606), housed in the US Marine base at Quantico (you may remember Quantico from the film *Silence of the Lambs*), shows the development of the US Marine Corps from 1900 to the present.

It is open 10 am to 5 pm Tuesday to Saturday, noon to 5 pm Sunday from April to November (free admission). To get here, take the Quantico exits off I-95.

Fredericksburg Area

The historic town of Fredericksburg, on I-95, is midway between the national capital of Washington, DC, and the state capital of Richmond. In addition to being a great base for exploring the numerous Civil War battlefields, Fredericksburg also makes an ideal base for trips down into the Northern Neck and Middle Peninsula (see the chapter Virginia's Chesapeake Bay), which radiate like two fingers out to the southeast.

FREDERICKSBURG

Fredericksburg (population 20,000) exudes a real sense of history. It once was an important inland port where tobacco and other crops were loaded for transportation down the Rappahannock River – the waterfront is still lined by 18th- and 19th-century buildings.

The site was visited by John Smith as early as 1608, and many luminaries followed

him. Washington spent his childhood, from ages six to 16, at Ferry Farm, just across the Rappahannock River in Stafford County; Mary Washington, George's mother, lived there before she died; and the fifth president, James Monroe, practiced law in the town. It was in Fredericksburg in 1777 that the Virginia Statute of Religious Freedom (which later became the main plank of the First Amendment) was drafted by Thomas Jefferson and George Mason, among others.

During the Civil War, between 1862 and 1864, the town changed hands seven times (see the boxed text The Battle of Fredericksburg, later in this section). Fredericksburg is now a major distribution center and very much an antiquing spot and weekend escape for DC folk.

Orientation

Fredericksburg is split into two parts (no, not Blue and Gray). The old-town area (a 40-block national historic district) has Caroline St as its main access route, where you will find the visitor center and other historic buildings. Places to stay and eat are strewn around the intersection of Route 3 and I-95. Route 1 also passes north-south through the city.

Information

The Fredericksburg Visitor Center (☎ 540-373-1776, 800-678-4748, www.fredericksburgva.com), 706 Caroline St, has maps of walking tours. Its two-part guide for the Battle of Fredericksburg covers the bombardment, river crossings, the tenacious street fighting, and the calamitous Union assault on Marye's Heights. There are also maps for 3-, 9-, and 20-mile bike tours that feature historical attractions.

The center is open 9 am to 5 pm (until 7 pm in summer). You can purchase a Hospitality Pass ($19.75 for adults, $7 for students), which allows entry to seven major historic sites; the Pick Four Pass costs $13.75 for adults, $5.50 for students. (The buildings included are the Fredericksburg Area Museum, Belmont, Rising Sun Tavern, Mary Washington House, Kenmore, Monroe Museum, and the Hugh Mercer Apothecary.)

FREDERICKSBURG

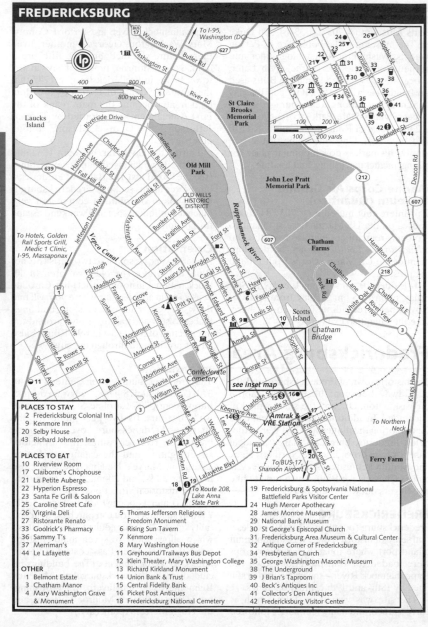

To I-95,
Washington (DC)

Warrenton Rd

Butler Rd

Washington St

River Rd

St Claire
Brooks
Memorial
Park

Laucks
Island

Riverside Drive

Old Mill
Park

OLD MILLS
HISTORIC
DISTRICT

John Lee Pratt
Memorial Park

To Hotels, Golden
Rail Sports Grill,
Medic 1 Clinic,
I-95, Massaponax

Rappahannock River

Chatham
Farms

Chatham Lane

Chatham
Bridge

Scotts
Island

Confederate
Cemetery

see inset map

Amtrak &
VRE Station

To BUS-17,
Shannon Airport

To Route 208,
Lake Anna
State Park

To Northern
Neck

Ferry Farm

PLACES TO STAY
2 Fredericksburg Colonial Inn
9 Kenmore Inn
20 Selby House
43 Richard Johnston Inn

PLACES TO EAT
10 Riverview Room
17 Claiborne's Chophouse
21 La Petite Auberge
22 Hyperion Espresso
23 Santa Fe Grill & Saloon
25 Caroline Street Cafe
26 Virginia Deli
27 Ristorante Renato
33 Goolrick's Pharmacy
36 Sammy T's
37 Merriman's
44 Le Lafayette

OTHER
1 Belmont Estate
3 Chatham Manor
4 Mary Washington Grave
  & Monument

5 Thomas Jefferson Religious
  Freedom Monument
6 Rising Sun Tavern
7 Kenmore
8 Mary Washington House
11 Greyhound/Trailways Bus Depot
12 Klein Theater, Mary Washington College
13 Richard Kirkland Monument
14 Union Bank & Trust
15 Central Fidelity Bank
16 Picket Post Antiques
18 Fredericksburg National Cemetery

19 Fredericksburg & Spotsylvania National
   Battlefield Parks Visitor Center
24 Hugh Mercer Apothecary
28 James Monroe Museum
29 National Bank Museum
30 St George's Episcopal Church
31 Fredericksburg Area Museum & Cultural Center
32 Antique Corner of Fredericksburg
34 Presbyterian Church
35 George Washington Masonic Museum
38 The Underground
39 J Brian's Taproom
40 Beck's Antiques Inc
41 Collector's Den Antiques
42 Fredericksburg Visitor Center

There is also a Virginia Welcome Center (☎ 540-786-8344) on I-95S.

For foreign exchange, try the Central Fidelity Bank (☎ 540-899-0131), 614 Princess Anne St, and the Union Bank & Trust (☎ 540-371-0108), 700 Kenmore Ave.

The Wash & Fold Laundry (☎ 540-899-6515) is at 50312 Jefferson Davis Hwy.

For emergencies, Medic 1 Clinic (☎ 540-371-1664), at 3429 Jefferson Davis Hwy, is open 9 am to 9 pm; call in advance.

Fredericksburg Area Museum & Cultural Center

This museum (☎ 540-371-5668), at 907 Princess Anne St, concentrates on the history of Fredericksburg and the surrounding region. The exhibits are located in the historic town hall/market house, dating from 1816. There are exhibits of prehistory, Native American culture, the colonial period, the Civil War, and recent history. It is open 10 am to 5 pm Monday to Saturday, 1 to 5 pm Sunday from March to November; the rest of the year, it's open 10 am to 4 pm Monday to Saturday, 1 to 4 pm Sunday. Admission is $4 for adults, $1 for students six to 18.

Kenmore

This elegant colonial mansion (☎ 540-373-3381), 1201 Washington Ave, was built circa 1775 for Fielding Lewis and his wife, Betty, the only sister of George Washington. The elaborately carved interiors and decorative plasterwork are considered more lavish than Mount Vernon, and one of the rooms is on a list of America's '100 most beautiful rooms.' Outside, there are lovingly tended boxwood gardens. In the colonial-style kitchen next door, you can sample spiced tea and ginger cookies.

Kenmore is open 10 am to 5 pm Monday to Saturday, noon to 5 pm Sunday from March to December; the rest of the year, it's open 10 am to 4 pm Saturday, noon to 4 pm Sunday. Admission is $6 for adults, $3 for students six to 18.

James Monroe Museum

This museum (☎ 540-654-1043), 908 Charles St, holds the biggest collection of 'Monroe-abilia' in the country – included are White House furnishings, such as the desk on which the Monroe Doctrine was written, books, documents, and decorative arts. Before becoming the nation's fifth president, Monroe practiced law here from 1787 to 1789. The museum is open 10 am to 4 pm daily December to February, 9 am to 5 pm from March to November. Admission is $4 for adults, $1.50 for students six to 18.

Mary Washington House

This house (☎ 540-373-1569), 1200 Charles St, is the 18th-century cottage that Washington purchased for his mother. She lived here for the last 17 years of her life, until she died in 1789 at the age of 81. Once she greeted Lafayette here. The gardens, meticulously tended, reflect the time when Mary arranged them. Her grave and monument are on Washington Ave (west end of Pitt St). The cottage and gardens are open 9 am to 5 pm daily March to November, 10 am to 4 pm December to February. Admission is $4 for adults, $1.50 for students six to 18.

Rising Sun Tavern

This tavern (☎ 540-371-1494), 1306 Caroline St, opened its doors for business in 1760 and has been going strong ever since. Not everyone's 'mug of ale,' it's one of those places (of the type that plague Williamsburg) with 'buxom wench' serving staff. It was built by George Washington's brother Charles. Patrick Henry, Washington, and Jefferson are believed to have met here. Pity, these days you can't buy an ale here – a spiced tea perhaps? It is open 9 am to 5 pm daily March to November, 10 am to 4 pm December to February. Admission is $4 for adults, $1.50 for children; night tours are $5.

Hugh Mercer Apothecary

Not far from the tavern, at 1020 Caroline St, is the Hugh Mercer Apothecary (☎ 540-373-3362), an 18th-century building fitted out to represent the medical office and apothecary shop of one Scottish Dr Mercer, a Revolutionary War brigadier general who was killed at the Battle of Princeton in 1776. Half the fun of this place is finding out about antiquated medical and dental techniques, which will make you think you have walked into a torture chamber, not a doctor's office. The shop is open 9 am to 5 pm daily March to November, 10 am to 4 pm December to February. Admission is $4 for adults, $1.50 for students six to 18.

Belmont Estate

The internationally renowned Detroit painter Gari Melchers (1860–1932) purchased this 18th-century estate (☎ 540-654-1015), at 224 Washington St in Falmouth, when he returned from Europe in 1916, at the time the US entered the war. In the adjoining stone studio, built in 1924, there is an exhibition of Melchers' work, the largest concentration of his impressionist landscape paintings in the US.

The estate is open 10 am to 5 pm Monday to Saturday, 1 to 5 pm Sunday from March to November; the rest of the year, it's open 10 am to 4 pm Monday to Saturday, 1 to 4 pm Sunday. Admission is $4 for adults, $1 for students six to 18.

To get there, take the Route 1 bypass across the river, then Route 17 Business to County Rd 1001 (Washington St).

Chatham Manor

This fine Georgian building (☎ 540-373-4461) at 120 Chatham Lane, across the Rappahannock River from Fredericksburg, was built between 1768 and 1771 by a plantation owner named William Fitzhugh. Many famous people have passed through the house in its 200-year history, including Clara Barton, founder of the American Red Cross, and poet Walt Whitman, who treated the wounded here during the Civil War. Lincoln also met his generals here on two occasions during the war. From the building, there is a superb view of the many-steepled city of Fredericksburg. One of the park staff may relate the history of the battles of 1862 and 1863.

The house, administered by the National Park Service, is open 9 am to 5 pm daily (entry included with $3 pass). To get there, follow William St (Route 3) across the Rappahannock and make the tricky left turn onto signposted Chatham Drive; a loop road in the park returns you to Route 3.

Other Historic Buildings

The **George Washington Masonic Museum** (☎ 540-373-5885), 803 Princess Anne St, relates to the time Washington was active in the Freemasons in lodge No 4 AF & AM in 1752. He was later Worshipful Master of Alexandria Masonic Lodge No 22. The Masonic memorabilia includes a portrait by Gilbert Stuart and the Bible upon which Washington swore his Masonic oath. It is open 9 am to 4 pm Monday to Saturday, 1 to 4 pm Sunday. Admission is $2 for adults, $1 for students (or by secret handshake?).

Not far up the street, at 900 Princess Anne St, is the **National Bank Museum** (☎ 540-899-3243), one of the oldest buildings in the US to have continuously served as a bank. Wander in for a scintillating 30-minute discovery of 200 years of banking – not! It is open 9 am to 1 pm weekdays. Admission is free (unusual for any banking activity).

St George's Episcopal Church, on Princess Anne St between George and William Sts, has a number of famous people buried in its graveyard, including Martha Washington's father and the Revolutionary War generals George Weedon and Hugh Mercer. The **Presbyterian Church**, at the corner of George and Princess Anne Sts, as well as St George's, was hit during the Civil War.

Those retracing the lives of US presidents will undoubtedly make a trip to **Ferry Farm** (☎ 540-373-3381) in Falmouth, which was George Washington's home from age six to 20. He inherited it when he was 11 and kept it until he was 42, a year before he became commander of the Continental Army. This was supposedly the site of the cherry-tree-chopping and coin-throwing incidents. The farm is open 10 am to 4 pm Monday to Saturday, noon to 4 pm Sunday. A donation of $2 for adults, $1 for students is encouraged. To get there, cross the Chatham Bridge and turn right onto Route 3 (which becomes King's Hwy) until you reach the signposted Ferry Rd, and then turn right.

Hiking & Bicycling

For information on, and equipment for, outdoor activities (especially hiking and bicycling), check out Outdoor Adventures (☎ 540-786-3334), 4300 Plank Rd. It's open 10 am to 8 pm weekdays, to 6 pm Saturday, noon to 5 pm Sunday. Bicycles are available for rental (adults only).

Canoeing & Kayaking

Rappahannock Outdoors (☎ 540-371-5085) has kayaks and canoes for hire and offers instruction on canoeing, tubing, rafting, and kayaking. Another canoeing and tubing outfitter is Clore Bros (☎ 540-786-7749), 5927 River Rd. Friends of the Rappahannock (☎ 540-373-3448) offers half-day and two-day canoe tours accompanied by naturalists and historians on the Rappahannock and Mattaponi Rivers.

Golf

The Lees Hill Golfer's Club (☎ 540-891-0111), off Route 1, has an 18-hole public golf course. Meadows Farm Golf Course (☎ 540-854-9890), 4300 Flat Run Rd, boasts the longest hole in the US – the 841-yard, par-6 12th hole.

Organized Tours

Fredericksburg is very much a museum and 'old house' town, and many of the sites are associated with the Washington family. You could spend an entire day here traipsing from one old building to the next. The American History Company (☎ 540-371-6822) has a variety of tours (eg, history and romance walks and 'Feel the Fury' Civil War tours); call them for costs and details.

Special Events

Fredericksburg hosts a number of special events, some honoring past illustrious citizens. In late February, President's Day and George Washington's birthday are celebrated. In late April, it's James Monroe's birthday. Mother's Day, in mid-May, takes on special meaning in Fredericksburg, as George Washington's mother is given top billing. In early June, there is the Arts Festival, which

has been going strong for well over 20 years. Fredericksburg clings tightly to its Gaelic heritage and hosts the Scottish Highland Games and Irish Festival in June.

There are many and varied celebrations at Christmas, including parades, open houses (each with a different theme), and candlelight tours of the historic area.

Places to Stay

Camping There are a number of campgrounds in the region. The *Fredericksburg DC South KOA* (☎ *540-898-7252, 7400 Brookside Lane)*, in Massaponax (exit 126 southbound, exit 118 northbound off I-95) has sites starting at $25 for two people; electricity and water hookups are $2 extra. There are also a few campgrounds on the shores of Lake Anna, just southwest of Fredericksburg (see Around Fredericksburg, later in the chapter).

Guesthouses The *Fredericksburg Colonial Inn* (☎ *540-371-5666, 1707 Princess Anne St)* is inexpensive and exudes the perfect antebellum atmosphere for the Civil War buffs who gravitate to the area. Doubles start at $59; two-room units cost $89.

The *Richard Johnston Inn* (☎ *540-899-7606, 711 Caroline St)*, across from the visitor center, is two 18th-century row townhouses joined together (with a total of nine guest rooms); doubles range from $95 to $135. The inn has parking in the rear, and a few suites open onto a patio.

The *Kenmore Inn* (☎ *540-371-7622, 1200 Princess Anne St)* has 14 rooms furnished with antiques and reproduction furniture (such as four-poster beds). Double rooms (with complimentary sherry) range from $95 to $125.

There are several B&Bs in the region, including the *Selby House* (☎ *540-373-7037, 226 Princess Anne St)*, which has four guest rooms and disabled access.

Hotels & Motels Lodgings are located at all four main exits off I-95 – 118, 126, 130, and 133. The *Econo Lodge Central* (☎ *540-786-8374, 2800 Plank Rd)*, on Route 3 at the

VIRGINIA

junction of I-95 (exit 130B), has low-season singles/doubles for $31/36 (otherwise $35/40). The *Super 8 Motel* (☎ 540-786-8881, 3002 Mall Court), off exit 130B, is ever reliable and economic, as is the *Super 8 Motel* (☎ 540-898-7100, 5319 Jefferson Davis Hwy) off exit 126 southbound; both offer HBO, free local calls, and coffee.

The *Best Western Thunderbird Inn* (☎ 540-786-7404, 3000 Plank Rd) is reached from the same exit off I-95. In winter, singles/doubles cost $39/43 (otherwise add $5). The *Ramada Inn* (☎ 540-786-8361, 2802 Plank Rd) is another place off exit 130B. Singles/doubles in this comfortable, family-owned place start at $45/50 ($5 more in summer).

The *Sheraton Fredericksburg Inn* (☎ 540-786-8321, 2801 Plank Rd) is on Route 3 at I-95 exit 130B. In this large place, in which the rooms have a balcony or patio, there is a pool, wading pool, exercise room, tennis courts, a dining room, and one of the city's most popular lounges (with live entertainment most nights). Singles and doubles cost $89 all year.

The *Best Western Fredericksburg* (☎ 540-371-5050, 2205 William St), reached from I-95 exit 130A, is a two-story motel with a restaurant nearby. A single/double room costs $40/50 in low season, $50/62 in high season.

Places to Eat

The exits off I-95 have a plethora of chain restaurants. In town, *Goolrick's Pharmacy* (☎ 540-373-3411, 901 Caroline St), the oldest continually operating soda fountain in the US, is for nostalgia buffs. They make great milkshakes, soup, and sandwiches, and you should be well satisfied for less than $5.

For regional fare, try the *Virginia Deli* (☎ 540-371-2233, 101 William St) – it has a selection of yummy desserts, an extensive sandwich selection, and Brunswick stew (poultry stew with vegetables, corn, tomatoes, lima beans, and potatoes) for $2.50. The *Caroline Street Cafe* (☎ 540-374-9351, 1002 Caroline St) is a poky, dark but atmospheric place where you get a filling lunch for around $4. Try *Hyperion Espresso* (☎ 540-373-4882,

301 William St) for outside seating – it's a perfect spot for reading the paper, playing chess, or watching the passing parade.

Sammy T's (☎ 540-371-2008, 801 Caroline St) has vegan and vegetarian offerings, economical lunches and dinners, and a friendly bar. A bean and grain burger costs about $4, and a pocket sandwich chock-full of sauteed vegetables is $5. It's also a friendly, relaxed pub.

Ristorante Renato (☎ 540-371-8228, 422 William St), an Italian place in the center of town, is open daily for lunch and dinner. Some of the specials include veal, chicken, and scampi. Entrees cost around $15; the lunch special (includes pasta, salad, and bread) is $6.

The *Riverview Room* (☎ 540-373-6500, 1101 Sophia St), in a setting overlooking the Rappahannock, is known for its sumptuous beef and seafood meals (about $15 to $20 per person).

La Petite Auberge (☎ 540-371-2727, 311 William St) has a strictly French menu that changes daily. There are great early-bird dinner specials (soup, entree, and salad for $13); main courses are about $12.

Le Lafayette (☎ 540-373-6895, 623 Caroline St), housed in a 1771 Georgian-style building, is more upscale. Interesting things are done to local seafood and produce to add a twist to conventional French and continental cuisine. Two could expect to pay about $40 for dinner (without wine).

Claiborne's Chophouse (☎ 540-371-7080, 200 Lafayette Blvd), in the renovated train station, has fast built a local reputation as the place to go for steaks, chops, and seafood. *Merriman's* (☎ 540-371-7723, 715 Caroline St) is similar to Claiborne's (it serves 'creative' American cuisine) but has some vegetarian selections and delicious homemade desserts; it's closed on Monday.

The *Santa Fe Grill & Saloon* (☎ 540-371-0500, 216 William St) is a rowdy venue that specializes in southwestern, predominantly Mexican, food.

J Brian's Taproom (see Entertainment, later) is a popular, buzzing place; the burgers and pizza are good, but many patrons gravitate here for the beer.

The Kenmore Inn (see Places to Stay, earlier) has a predominantly 'surf-n-turf' (fish and meat) daily dinner menu and a hearty brunch on Sunday. There is occasionally live music in The Pub on weekend evenings.

Entertainment

The **Golden Rail Sports Grill** (☎ 540-372-2022), at the corner of 23rd St and Plank Rd, attracts the sedentary who like to flick from screen to screen in pursuit of the ultimate sporting moment. **J Brian's Taproom** (202 Hanover St) is a good place to meet for a beer (also see Places to Eat, earlier).

Live-music venues include **The Underground** (☎ 540-371-9500, 106 George St) for thrashy stuff. A more sophisticated crowd is likely to be seen at the lounge at the Sheraton Hotel (see Places to Stay, earlier), a place that caters to 30-somethings.

The Battle of Fredericksburg (1862)

After the Battle of Antietam (near Sharpsburg, Maryland) in mid-September 1862, Union general McClellan was replaced by Ambrose E Burnside (whose bushy muttonchop hair in front of his ears brought about the term 'sideburns'), one of McClellan's corps commanders at Antietam. Lee's Confederate forces had retreated back into Virginia, and McClellan went home and took no further part in the war.

Burnside, after delaying for a number of weeks, moved his Army of the Potomac, numbering 120,000, through bleak late November weather down the Rappahannock toward Fredericksburg. He reached Falmouth, just across the Rappahannock from the city, where he waited for pontoons to arrive so his army could cross intact. Lee learned of the move and used Burnside's hesitation to his advantage, secreting his troops in Fredericksburg where they occupied the best high ground. On December 11, everything was in place, including the pontoons, and Burnside ordered his engineers down to the river to assemble the bridges.

The Union artillery shelled the town as the Confederate sharpshooters picked off the engineers at the river. The battle seesawed at the river before some of Burnside's infantry began to fan out into the town. The Union army soon moved across the river freely, setting up a bloody endgame on December 13.

In the morning, Burnside committed his army, in a two-pronged attack, to do the impossible. One objective of his attack was to breach the stone wall where the Confederate infantry lay in wait, and the other was to go a mile to the south. Lee looked down from the heights as the morning mist cleared and uttered, 'It is well that we know how terrible war really is, else we would grow too fond of it....'

Burnside's men thrust up against the stone wall, and the survivors of the assault crawled their way back dripping blood, falling, and dying. Burnside, miles away in both distance and realization, sent his divisions forward again and again to be cut to ribbons.

To the south, the Union troops of George Gordon Meade penetrated the defenses but were denied reinforcement. After a spirited counterattack by Stonewall Jackson's troops, the hole in the Confederate line was plugged.

Burnside dreamed of continuing the battle, but reality bit, and the Army of the Potomac retreated in wind and sleeting rain across their pontoon bridges. Many Confederate troops sneaked into the piles of 12,000 dead Union troops (Lee had lost less than half that number) and stole away with their still-warm uniforms.

After the defeat, morale on the Union side was low, and many of the soldiers deserted. Less than a month later, Lincoln replaced Burnside with General Joseph ('Fighting Joe') Hooker, and both armies wintered over near Fredericksburg.

VIRGINIA

VIRGINIA

The Battle of Chancellorsville (1863)

While wintering over after the Battle at Fredericksburg, 'Fighting Joe' Hooker reorganized and re-fitted the Army of the Potomac, now numbering 132,000. On April 27, 1863, Hooker's army (not wishing to repeat Burnside's mistake) skirted around to the northwest of Fredericksburg, crossing the Rappahannock and Rapidan, with the intention of coming around on the Confederate rear. By April 30, three corps of the army had traversed the second-growth timber of the trackless Wilderness and were encamped near the Chancellorsville mansion.

A smaller Union force of two corps under General John Sedgwick began to cross the river near where Burnside had crossed in 1862; they were to form the 'wall' that Hooker would force Lee's Confederates up against. There were another two corps in reserve. On May 1, Fighting Joe confidently moved his forces east toward Fredericksburg. Lee left about 10,000 troops to hold off Sedgwick and turned to meet Hooker's troops head on. This bold move unsettled Hooker and he withdrew his forces into improvised lines around Chancellorsville.

That night, Lee conferred with Jackson and hatched a brilliant and daring plan. On May 2, Jackson's force of 25,000 was to march across Hooker's front and attack the weak Union right flank. Meanwhile, Lee, with a force of 20,000, enacted a charade in front of Hooker's army of 80,000, giving the impression that the Army of Northern Virginia had much stronger offensive capability than it really had at that time.

Just before sundown, Jackson's troops struck and drove the Union corps of Oliver O Howard off in rout. Darkness and the resulting disorganization saved the Union from further destruction. Jackson, accidentally wounded by one of his own men, was carried off to a field hospital, and the Confederate advance was stalled. Hooker still didn't take advantage of the fact that the Confederate army was split in two.

The next morning, Lee went on the offensive again, assigning the cavalier JEB Stuart to command Jackson's forces. Stuart's artillery pounded Chancellorsville and wounded Hooker, literally knocking the fight out of him. Hooker's troops were pushed back to a defensive horseshoe around the Rappahannock bridgeheads.

In Fredericksburg, Sedgwick's men attacked Marye's Heights and drove Jubal Early's Southerners from the defenses that Burnside had failed to take the previous December. Sedgwick then tried to rescue Hooker. Calmly, Lee left a small force to check Hooker's army and moved his weary troops against Sedgwick at Salem Church. Soon he had boxed the Union soldiers into a small bend on the Rappahannock between Fredericksburg and Chancellorsville. These Union forces retreated across the river, lucky to escape.

Not content to call a halt, Lee methodically moved his army back to take on Hooker's main force in Chancellorsville, but Hooker, although he had 40,000 troops in reserve, had crossed the Rappahannock on May 5 and retreated into the camps opposite Fredericksburg. The Union forces had been depleted by 17,000 and the Confederates by about 12,000. But for Lee and the South, victory had a hollow ring – on May 10, one of their finest tacticians, Stonewall Jackson, died of his wounds at Guinea Station.

★★★★★★★★★★★★★★★★★★★★★★★★★★★★★★★★★★★★★

Plays are performed at the *Klein Theater* (☎ 540-654-1124, 1301 College Ave), in duPont Hall at Mary Washington College. A *Blue Light Concert Series* is held on Saturday nights from late June to late August.

Shopping

Many shops in town sell expensive Federal and Victorian antiques. All of the following are on Caroline St, where there are at least a dozen shops.

The Picket Post Antiques (☎ 540-371-7703), at No 602, specializes in Civil War antiques. It's open 10 am to 6 pm Monday to Saturday. Beck's Antiques Inc (☎ 540-371-1776), at No 708, sells rare books on the Civil War and Virginia. It's open 10:30 am to 5 pm Monday to Saturday, 12:30 to 5 pm Sunday. The Collector's Den Antiques (☎ 540-373-2430), at No 717, specializes in old baseball and sports cards. The Antique Corner of Fredericksburg (☎ 540-373-0826), at No 900, also sells Civil War items.

Getting There & Away
The nearest airports are those that serve DC – Ronald Reagan Washington National and Washington-Dulles International Airports. Shannon Airport, reached by Route 17 Business, is for smaller planes.

Greyhound/Trailways (☎ 540-373-2103, 800-231-2222), 1400 Jefferson Davis Hwy, has regular service to DC, Baltimore, and Richmond.

Amtrak (☎ 800-872-7245) has scheduled stops in Fredericksburg at 200 Lafayette Blvd, near the junction of Caroline St and Lafayette Blvd, as part of its East Coast service running from Maine to Florida. There is a commuter link between this station and Union Station in DC, via Alexandria, with several trains daily. For information, contact Virginia Railway Express (☎ 540-373-2890, 800-743-3873, www.vre.org). A single ride to Quantico costs $3.20; to DC, $6.70.

Route 1 and I-95 bisect Fredericksburg in a north-south direction, making it easily accessible by car. But be warned, it is 'cloverleaf hell' and very confusing. Route 17 passes the city on its northern side and continues south through the Middle Peninsula via Hampton Roads all the way to North Carolina. East-west Route 3, the best access to the Northern Neck, also passes through the city.

Getting Around
A public bus service ('Fred') serves the Greater Fredericksburg area and counties; it costs 25¢ including transfer. There are six routes; Fred services operate from about 8 am to 8 pm.

Historic Trolley Tours (☎ 540-898-0737), outside the visitor center on Charlotte St, operate April to December. Fares are $10 for adults and $5 for children for a 75-minute tour.

AROUND FREDERICKSBURG
Fredericksburg's central location, and its closeness to the strategic Potomac and Rappahannock Rivers, made it a vital prize during the Civil War. It is estimated that nearly 100,000 soldiers were killed in and around the city during the course of the war. Some of the bloodiest battles, all complete or partial Confederate army victories – Fredericksburg (December 1862), Chancellorsville (May 1863), the Wilderness (early May 1864), and Spotsylvania (mid-May 1864) – were fought within a 20-mile radius of the city.

On a less gruesome note, Lake Anna State Park makes a lovely outing and is only 25 minutes from Fredericksburg.

Fredericksburg & Spotsylvania National Battlefield Parks
The main visitor center for the Fredericksburg & Spotsylvania National Battlefield Parks (☎ 540-373-6122) sits at 1013 Lafayette Blvd, to the south of Fredericksburg. It is open 8:30 am to 6 pm daily in summer and to 5 pm the rest of the year. There are a number of informative exhibits, and you can rent 2½-hour audio tours of the battlefield sites ($3 for each battlefield tape and a cassette player, $4.25 to buy each tape). Highlights are the Sunken Road, the Kirkland monument, and the national cemetery on Marye's Heights. There is a great bookshop at the Chancellorsville battlefield visitor center (☎ 540-786-2880), on Route 3W.

The NPS provides a good Fredericksburg and Spotsylvania map that has a self-guided 75-mile, 16-stop driving tour. There are many other points of interest you can add to this list, such as Chatham, Guinea Station (the Stonewall Jackson shrine), and Old

VIRGINIA

The Battle of Spotsylvania Courthouse (1864)

On May 4, 1864, Grant's army (as a number of Union armies had previously attempted) surged across the Rapidan and Rappahannock Rivers into the second-growth forest of Wilderness, hoping to fall on Lee's forces in open country before Lee had time to react. In the ensuing and extremely bloody battle, Grant lost more than twice as many men as Lee (18,000 as opposed to 8000), but his army in numbers was still double that of the Confederates. He wouldn't admit defeat and marched his army southeast to the crossroads at Spotsylvania Courthouse to keep the battle alive and to cut Lee off from Richmond.

Lee's advance guards beat Grant to the crossroads, and after the two armies skirmished, a bloody battle ensued. For the next 10 uninterrupted days (May 8–19), Grant repeatedly tried to encircle the Confederates. On May 12, the fight degenerated to hand-to-hand combat at a stretch of Confederate breastworks near the principal road crossing – from then on referred to as the Bloody Angle. There, in torrential rain, the wounded were trodden into the mud, bayonets and clubs were thrust against almost unidentifiable foes, and trees were cut down by the incessant rifle and gunfire.

Nothing but the piled-up logs or breastworks separated the combatants. Our men would reach over the logs and fire into the faces of the enemy, would stab over with their bayonets; many were shot and stabbed through crevices and holes between the logs; men mounted the works and with muskets rapidly handed them kept up a continuous fire until they were shot down, when others would take their places.

– Brigadier General LA Grant, Union forces, Bloody Angle

A lad in Harris' brigade was shot down – a little, smooth-faced fellow, very out of place in this carnage. He raised his eyes, with the sweetest, saddest smile I think I ever saw on earth, and died almost on the instant.

– South Carolinian combatant at Bloody Angle

Grant's force had been depleted by another 18,000 men and gained a mile of useless ground; Lee had lost half that number. Yet these numbers mattered little now as the Army of Northern Virginia could not afford to be in such close contact. Such attrition would ensure the success of the Union army.

The two armies then side-slipped via the North Anna, Pamunkey, and Chickahominy Rivers, toward Richmond, where the war entered its final phases.

★★★★★★★★★★★★★★★★★★★★★★★★★★★★★★★★★

Salem Church (the site of the battle that took place May 3–4, 1863).

A Battlefields Pass for adults costs $3 (free for children) and is good for 10 days. It includes admission to all national park sites in the area.

Lake Anna State Park

Information about Lake Anna State Park, on one of Virginia's most popular lakes, can be obtained from the Lake Anna visitor center (☎ 540-854-5503). The park features a beach, bathhouse, boat ramps, picnic areas, and hiking trails. The visitor center highlights past gold-mining activity and the present natural features of the park. You can pan for gold or join one of the nature programs.

There are a couple of commercial campgrounds on the shores of Lake Anna: ***Rocky Branch Marina*** *(☎ 540-895-5475, 5153*

Courthouse Rd) has tent and electricity/water hookups. ***Dukes Creek Marina*** *(☎ 540-895-5065)* has 50 sites and offers boat launching.

The park is adjacent to County Rd 601 off Route 208 (Lafayette Blvd), 25 miles southwest of Fredericksburg.

Virginia's Chesapeake Bay

Chesapeake Bay looms large both in the present life and in the legends of Virginia. It was to this 'Chesupioc' ('great shellfish bay' is a common translation) that the first English settlers came. The surrounding marshes and saltwater flats are important breeding grounds for wildlife and fish, and the shores are a playground for all manner of water pursuits – fishing, kayaking, water skiing, swimming, and sailing.

The bay is flanked by the southern fingers of Maryland to its north, the peninsulas of Virginia on its west, the low-lying coastal plain ('Tidewater') and Hampton Roads to the south, and the Delmarva peninsula (or 'Eastern Shore') to its east. Several of the region's major rivers – Virginia's Rappahannock, York, and James; Maryland's Patuxent and Anacostia; and the Potomac – drain into this bay, the nation's largest.

The Peninsulas

Three distinct peninsulas – the Northern Neck, the Middle Peninsula, and the Historic Triangle – jut into the western side of Virginia's Chesapeake Bay.

The Northern Neck is a sheer delight, with cozy, sleepy fishing villages, abundant stocks of fresh seafood, plenty of fishing craft for hire, and comfortable B&Bs. It also has several historic sites, such as the birthplaces of Washington and Lee.

The Middle Peninsula is known for its Native American culture, easily witnessed at the Mattaponi and Pamunkey reservations, and for the fishing grounds around Gwynn's Island and Mobjack Bay.

To the south, across the York River, is the Historic Triangle, covered in the next chapter.

NORTHERN NECK
The Northern Neck, a peninsula that extends from Fredericksburg to Chesapeake Bay, is bounded by the Potomac River in the north and the Rappahannock River in the south. Today, it includes King George, Westmoreland, Richmond, Northumberland, and Lancaster Counties.

The poorly maintained Route 3 runs almost through the center of the peninsula, making it the best means of access. There are some interesting historical sites – such as the birthplaces of Washington, Monroe, and Lee – but it is the quiet, rural feel of the peninsula, the numerous quaint fishing villages, and the opportunity for quiet, relaxed hiking that attracts most people.

Highlights

- The birthplaces of George Washington and Robert E Lee

- Northern Neck 'getaways' – Reedville, Smith Point, and Irvington – light years away from DC

- Native American culture and reservations on the Middle Peninsula

- Chincoteague – a compact fishing village that is close to a national wildlife refuge and is great for bird watching

- Assateague Island – one of the country's best national wildlife areas, with remote beaches, endangered species, and wilderness to explore

- Picturesque and historic villages, wildlife refuges, and remote fishing spots along the Eastern Shore's Route 13

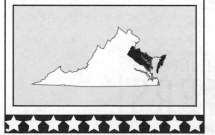

For more information, contact Virginia's Potomac Gateway Travel Center (☎ 540-663-3205) in King George, or Northern Neck Travel Council (☎ 800-393-6180, www.northernneck.org), at PO Box 1707, Warsaw, VA 22572.

Caledon Natural Area State Park

This is bird-watching heaven. In summer, this area of forests and marshes is home to a large concentration of **American bald eagles**. Access to the area is restricted, but ranger-guided tours are offered from time to time – these are immensely popular, so book ahead at the visitor center (☎ 540-663-3861). There are no accommodations in the park, but there are picnic facilities and a self-guided trail.

To get to Caledon from Fredericksburg, take Route 218 east. If you are coming from Route 301, take 218 west. The entrance is a mile or two farther along.

Colonial Beach

Colonial Beach, on the shores of the Potomac River at the northern end of Route 205, is nothing like the beaches you come to expect on the Atlantic Coast. Instead it has some fine restaurants serving traditional Southern-style food and tasty seafood – probably the main reason to make a diversion there.

Overlooking the Potomac, *The Dockside* (☎ 804-224-7260), at The Point, has a great raw bar and serves piles of steamed or broiled seafood; it is closed on Tuesday. *Wilkerson's* (☎ 804-224-7117), on Route 205, is another clever choice, with rockfish, crab cakes, and other seafood. It's open daily, and they serve a sumptuous weekend buffet.

A few miles south of Colonial Beach on Route 205 is James Monroe's birthplace, **Monroe Hall**; it is a private dwelling, so you can look only from outside on the birthplace of the fifth president and one of the fathers of US foreign policy (the Monroe Doctrine was based on his seminal speech, which was delivered to Congress in 1823).

George Washington Birthplace National Monument

Washington's birthplace, in Westmoreland County near Westmoreland State Park, is reached via Route 3 and Route 204. The national monument, which spans 538 acres, is called Pope's Creek Plantation and evokes the spirit of an 18th-century Virginia tobacco farm with its buildings, gardens, groves, livestock, creeks, and rivers. It remains as the young George would have experienced it as he grew from boyhood to maturity. The house in which Washington was born no longer stands, but archaeologists have given us a thorough picture of what it looked like – the foundations are marked by oyster shell.

The visitor center (☎ 804-224-1732) has some interesting exhibits and artifacts and screens a 14-minute film, *A Childhood Place*, about Washington's family history.

It is open daily 9 am to 5 pm (the best time to visit is after 2 pm), and there are regularly scheduled guided tours ($2 for adults, free for youth under 16). The center is accessible to the disabled. After visiting the colonial farm area, you can hike to the beach or through the woods, as Washington may well have once done.

About 2½ miles south of Oak Grove, not far from Washington's birthplace, is the 2500-acre **Ingleside Plantation Winery** (☎ 804-224-8687), which has daily tours and tastings, as well as a picnic area. It is open 10 am to 5 pm Monday to Saturday and noon to 5 pm Sunday; admission is free.

Westmoreland State Park

The campground at this popular park (☎ 804-493-8821), near Lee's Stratford Hall and Washington's birthplace, has a visitor center and hookups for RVs, boat rentals and ramps. Basic sites cost $11; hookups with electricity and water cost $15.50. To get there, follow Route 3 to Baynesville, then turn off onto Route 347; the park is 5 miles northwest of Montross.

VIRGINIA

VIRGINIA'S CHESAPEAKE BAY

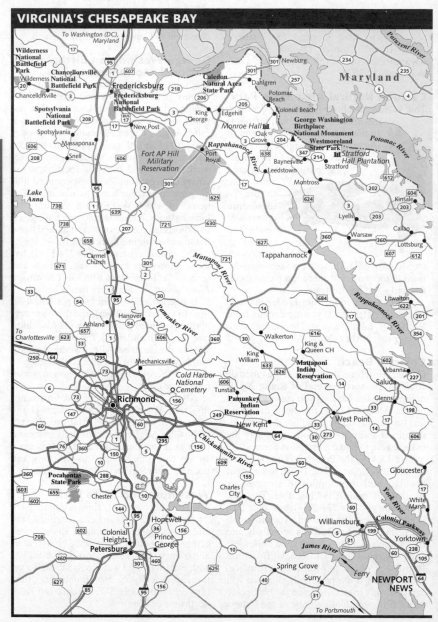

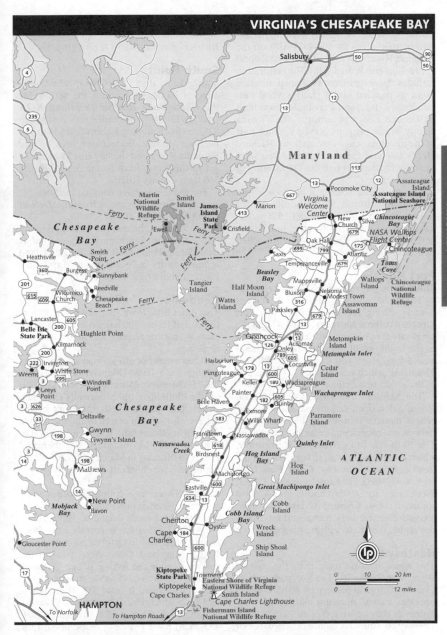

VIRGINIA'S CHESAPEAKE BAY

VIRGINIA

Salisbury
50
90
50

Maryland
4
235
5
13
12
113
12
Assateague
Island
Pocomoke City
667
Assateague Island
National Seashore
Martin
National
Wildlife
Refuge
Smith
Island
James
Island
State
Park
413
Marion
Virginia
Welcome
Center
New
Church
679
Chincoteague
Bay
Chesapeake
Bay
Ewell
Crisfield
Oak Hall
799
175
NASA Wallops
Flight Center
Chincoteague
Heathsville
Smith
Point
695
Saxis
Atlantic
679
Toms
Cove
360
Burgess
Sunnybank
Beasley
Bay
Temperanceville
Wallops
Island
Chincoteague
National
Wildlife
Refuge
201
615
609
Wicomico
Church
Reedville
Chesapeake
Beach
Tangier
Island
Half Moon
Island
Mappsville
Bluxom
Nelsonia
Modest Town
316
Assawoman
Island
Lancaster
605
Watts
Island
Paksley
679
Belle Isle
State Park
200
Hughlett Point
BUS
13
Accomac
Metompkin
Island
Kilmarnock
Onancock
126
Onley
789
605
Metompkin Inlet
222
Irvington
White Stone
200
695
Windmill
Point
Harborton
178
13
Locustville
Cedar
Island
Weems
3
Greys
Point
Pungoteague
600
Keller
180
Wachapreague
Wachapreague Inlet
3
626
Deltaville
Painter
182
605
Belle Haven
Quinby
33
198
Gwynn
Gwynn's Island
Chesapeake
Bay
Exmore
183
Willis Wharf
Parramore
Island
3
14
198
Mathews
Franktown
Nassawadox
Quinby Inlet
ATLANTIC
OCEAN
Nassawadox
Creek
618
Birdsnest
Hog Island
Bay
14
Mobjack
Bay
New Point
Bavon
Machipongo
Hog
Island
Eastville
600
Great Machipongo Inlet
Gloucester Point
634
13
Cobb
Island
17
Cheriton
Oyster
Cobb Island
Bay
Wreck
Island
Cape
Charles
184
Ship Shoal
Island
600
Kiptopeke
State Park
Kiptopeke
Cape Charles
Townsend
Eastern Shore of Virginia
National Wildlife Refuge
Smith Island
Cape Charles Lighthouse
0   10   20 km
0   6   12 miles
HAMPTON
To Norfolk
To Hampton Roads
13
Fishermans Island
National Wildlife Refuge

Stratford Hall Plantation

Dating from the 1730s, this working plantation of 1600 acres (☎ 804-493-8038) on the Potomac River was the birthplace of Robert E Lee – his crib was on display. The restoration includes the magnificent H-shaped mansion (with its paneled Great Hall), several outbuildings, a store, and a gristmill. It was built by Thomas Lee, a governor of the Virginia colony whose progeny played a major part in the development of the nation – Richard Henry Lee and Francis Lightfoot Lee were the only brothers to sign the Declaration of Independence.

Stratford Hall is open 9 am to 4:30 pm daily. Admission is $7 for adults, $6 for seniors, and $3 for youth under 19. There is handicapped access to the reception center and museum only. The plantation is reached by Route 3 and Route 214.

Port Kinsale

This port on the Yeocomico River is reached by Route 202 and was a thriving steamboat landing during the 19th century. The **Port Kinsale Maritime Museum** (☎ 804-472-3001), on Route 608, is a must for those interested in the traditions of the watermen of Chesapeake Bay. Here you can see the skipjack *Virginia W*, which was built in 1904 and is one of the oldest remaining vessels of its type.

The **Skipjack Inn** *(☎ 804-472-2044)*, on Route 203, is open year-round. All of the excellent modern rooms have baths and telephones, and continental breakfast is included. The Skipjack Inn's **Mooring Restaurant**, which overlooks the waterfront, offers all the fresh delights of the bay. **Good Eats Cafe** *(☎ 804-472-4385)*, in Kinsale, opens at 5 pm Wednesday to Sunday and is also a good source of classic Chesapeake fare. They have a comprehensive kids' menu, and on Thursday nights, they have a prime-rib special.

Heathsville

This small, historic town is to the east of Warsaw on Route 360. The Northumberland County Historical Society (☎ 804-580-8581) operates a small **museum** that features the history of the county; it is open 9 am to 4 pm Tuesday to Thursday. Some other places of interest include the courthouse and grounds, St Stephens Church, the old jail, and the Rice's Hotel/Hughlett's tavern grounds.

Smith Point

Smith Point, at the top Chesapeake-bound edge of Northern Neck, is the setting for the **Chesapeake Bay/Smith Island KOA** *(☎ 804-453-3430)*. Its shaded sites cost $20 to $25 for two; Kamping Kabins cost $34 to $44 for four people. Waterfront sites on the Potomac River and the bay cost $5 extra. To get to this camp from Route 3, take Route 360 then County Rd 652.

For those who have cooking facilities, get a sack of pan-ready crabs from the **Deli at Smith Seafood** *(☎ 804-453-3430)*.

See Cruises, below, for information on how to get to Smith and Tangier Islands from Smith Point. Note that Tangier Island is most easily accessed from Maryland's Eastern Shore (see that chapter).

Reedville

This quiet little town (population of 400) at the end of Route 360 has a couple of restaurants, no bars or alcohol, and no traffic lights or police.

It has a number of Victorian-era homes on 'Millionaire's Row' (Main St) and the cute little **Fishermen's Museum** (☎ 804-453-6529) on the diminutive but historically rich main street. The museum tells the story of the fishers who went in search of the menhaden (a small, toothless fish). It is open 10:30 am to 4:30 pm daily May through October, and Friday to Monday in March and April ($2 for adults, free for children).

Cruises There are a couple of cruises available from Reedville and Smith Point to Smith and Tangier Islands. Island & Bay Cruises (☎ 804-453-3430) has a narrated five-hour scenic cruise, May to October, across to Smith Island, Maryland. Once there, you get the chance to tour the fishing village of Ewell, where there are crabbing shanties and a few crusty watermen. It costs $18.50 for adults and $9.25 for children (luncheon is $7 extra).

Tangier & Chesapeake Cruises (☎ 804-453-2628) has a five-hour cruise aboard the

Chesapeake Breeze to remote Tangier Island, with its quaint, narrow streets, gift shops, and unusual local dialect. Cruises run May to October and cost $18.50 for adults and $9.25 for children.

Places to Stay & Eat There are a few fine B&Bs on or near Millionaire's Row; doubles cost $65 to $100. *Cedar Grove* (☎ 804-453-3915, 2535 Fleeton Rd), off County Rd 657, is an elegantly appointed Colonial Revival building; the *Bailey-Cockrell House* (☎ 804-453-5900), on the waterfront, has its own beach; and *The Gables* (☎ 804-453-5209), at the end of Main St, has a built-in, early-19th-century schooner mast.

The *Morris House B&B Inn* (☎ 804-453-7016, 826 Main St), a magnificently renovated 1895 Victorian, has friendly owners and water views from every one of the superb rooms (ask about the waterside cottage).

Elijah's (☎ 804-453-3621, 729 Main St), overlooking Cockrells Creek, is for those who'd rather that others shucked their seafood.

Warsaw & Lancaster
At the junction of Route 3 and Route 360 is Warsaw, a small community with a smattering of historic buildings. The **Richmond County Museum** (☎ 804-333-3607), in the Old Clerk's Office, next to the courthouse, has exhibits highlighting the rural lifestyle.

About 30 miles east of Warsaw, on Route 3, is the town of Lancaster, which has a fascinating historic district. The four buildings of the **Mary Ball Washington Museum & Library** (☎ 804-462-7280), 8346 Mary Ball Rd, focus on the history of the Northern Neck from the colonial period to the present. The museum is open 10 am to 5 pm Wednesday to Friday and 10 am to 3 pm Saturday.

Irvington
This small town, near the southern tip of the Northern Neck and accessible by Route 200, is a popular getaway.

In addition to the famous Tides Inn Resort and Tides Lodge, there is the historic **Christ Church**. This church, which is cruciform in shape, was built around 1735 by Robert 'King' Carter and is Virginia's only colonial church that retains its original structure in an unaltered form. It looks nothing like a modern church, as there is no spire or bell tower. King Carter's descendants include seven governors of Virginia, three signatories to the Declaration of Independence, two Presidents (the Harrisons), several bishops, Robert E Lee, and a chief justice of the US Supreme Court. Interesting features of the church include the triple-decker pulpit tower, enclosed high-backed pews, a marble baptismal font, and Carter family tombs.

The church is open daily, and the reception center (☎ 804-438-6855) is open 10 am to 4 pm weekdays, 1 to 4 pm Saturday, and 2 to 5 pm Sunday roughly from April until November. Admission is free. From Irvington, take County Rds 646 then 709 off Route 200.

The *Tides Inn* (☎ 804-438-5000, 480 King Carter Drive), overlooking the Rappahannock River, has been rated one of the US's top 20 resorts by *Condé Nast Traveler* magazine. You can play golf and tennis, cruise on a yacht, row a small boat, bicycle, swim in the saltwater pool, or dine in either of the two fine restaurants. It is open March to January; singles/doubles start at $195/270 in the low season and rise to $205/300 in the high season.

The *Tides Lodge* (☎ 804-438-6000, 1 St Andrews Lane) is on its own private peninsula and has a marina. It also has just about every amenity imaginable, including a championship golf course, tennis, spa facilities, yacht cruises, and a superb seafood restaurant. It is open April to October, and rooms cost $150 to $170 (add $25 for an extra person).

Activities
There is plenty of opportunity on the Northern Neck to go **fishing** in the rivers or out at sea on Chesapeake Bay. Boats are available for charter, usually between May and December. A popular choice is Captain Billy's Charters at Ingram Bay Marina (☎ 804-580-7292), at the end of County Rd 609 east of Wicomico Church; it supplies charters on *Liquid Assets*, boat rentals, bait, and tackle (a day charter starts at $350). In Reedville, there are a boats to charter – Jim Conner's *Jeannie C* (☎ 804-453-4021),

Pittman's Charters' *Mystic Lady II* (☎ 804-453-3643), and Jim Hardy's *Ranger II* (☎ 804-453-6635). In Lottsburg, there is Chuck's Charters (☎ 804-529-6450).

There are a couple of **canoeing** and **kayaking** liveries in the region. River Rats (☎ 804-453-3064) rents kayaks and small boats and conducts tours; call to make arrangements. Heritage Park Resort (☎ 804-333-4038), 2570 Newland Rd, in Warsaw, rents boats and canoes for $15 a day.

There are many easy and moderate **hiking** and **walking** trails on the Northern Neck, and photographers, birders, or those seeking a quiet hour alone will all find what they're looking for. There are 6 miles of trails in Westmoreland State Park (see that section, earlier); three easy trails in Belle Isle State Park (☎ 804-462-5030), off Route 354 and County Rd 683 near Litwalton; the 1.6-mile Chesapeake-Corrotoman River Nature Trail through upland and marshland terrain, near Lancaster; and a 2-mile jaunt in Hughlett Point Nature Preserve (☎ 804-462-5030), on County Rd 605 off Route 200, north of Kilmarnock.

MIDDLE PENINSULA

The Middle Peninsula is not as isolated as Northern Neck. The defining feature to the north is the Rappahannock River, and in the south, it is the York River and its tributary, the Mattaponi. Rural scenery and glimpses of the waterways are the region's best attractions.

From the Northern Neck, you reach the Middle Peninsula by Route 3, and from Hampton Roads, Route 17 crosses the York River via the Coleman Memorial Bridge, connecting Yorktown to Gloucester Point.

Tappahannock

People come to this small town to go antiquing, and then to eat. The Tappahannock Essex Chamber of Commerce (☎ 804-443-5241) is open 8:30 am to 4:30 pm weekdays .

Rappahannock River Cruises (☎ 804-453-2628) has boats that leave Tappahannock for full-day **cruises** upstream to the Ingleside Plantation Winery (see George Washington

Birthplace National Monument, earlier), where there is a tour and wine tasting; it later makes a stop at Wheatland Plantation. A buffet lunch is available. With luck, you will see bald eagles and many varieties of waterbirds. Cruises operate daily (except Monday), leaving at 10 am and returning at 5 pm, from May to October. Tickets cost $18.50 for adults and $9.25 for children.

Urbanna

This historic port town is well worth visiting, if only to wander nonchalantly around the wharves, where the watermen will be busy unloading their daily catches. It advertises itself as Virginia's 'most beautiful waterfront community,' and we agree it comes close.

About half a mile outside of town via County Rds 602 and 615 is the 66-acre **Hewick Plantation**. The manor house (☎ 804-758-4214, www.hewick.com) was built in 1678 by Christopher Robinson, a member of the Houses of Burgesses and the King's Council. The plantation includes a family cemetery and an archaeological dig. It is open 10 am to 4 pm daily from March to November; there is a nominal entry fee.

In Urbanna, the *Bethpage Camp Resort* (☎ *804-758-4349)*, a campground well suited to RVs, has full hookups starting at $19.95 for two.

Sangraal-by-the-Sea Youth Hostel (HI-AYH; ☎ *804-776-6500)* is near Urbanna. Beds are $14 for members, $15 for nonmembers, and there is a day-use fee of $2. Call ahead to reserve, or write to PO Box 187, Urbanna, VA 23175. They'll transport you to the Saluda and Gloucester bus stations (8 and 10 miles away from the hostel, respectively) during business hours, but the station in Williamsburg is too far away.

To get to the hostel from Williamsburg, take I-64 to the junction of Route 33. Follow this north and cross the York River near West Point. Continue along this road, past Saluda for 10 miles, toward Deltaville. Turn north onto County Rd 626 for about half a mile to a junction. Head to the right and keep following County Rd 626 for 1.4 miles to the Waken post office. Turn left here and follow County Rd 626 to its end; the hostel is beside the Rappahannock.

There are also some great B&Bs: *Hewick Plantation* (☎ 804-758-4214) offers two antique-furnished rooms with private baths at $85 to $150 for two, and *Atherson Hall* (☎ 804-758-2809, 250 Prince George St), in Urbanna, has four rooms at $65 to $75. The *Inn at Urbanna* (☎ 804-758-4852, 250 Virginia St) gets rave reviews for its raw bar; it's open daily.

Mathews County

This county is the smallest in Virginia and is separated from neighboring Gloucester County by North River and Mobjack Bay. Historic sights in the town of Mathews (on Route 14) include the **Courthouse on the Village Green**, which has been in continuous use since 1792. And north of Mathews is **Gwynn's Island**. There is a small museum that, among other things, tells of the flight of the last royal governor, Lord Dunsmore, from the revolutionary army. To the south of Mathews is the restored New Point Comfort **lighthouse**.

The *New Point Campground* (☎ 804-725-5120), 7 miles southeast of the courthouse via Route 14 and County Rd 602, has sites with electricity, water, and sewage hookups for $22 to $24. The *Ravenswood Inn* (☎ 804-725-7272), at Todd's Point, is a good, six-room, moderately priced B&B with rooms starting at $70.

West Point

West Point is a junction town where rivers (the Pamunkey, Mattaponi, and York) and roads (Routes 30 and 33) meet up. The **Mattaponi Indian Museum** (☎ 804-769-2194) includes Pocahontas' necklace and a learning trail. Here you can attend lectures, visit burial grounds and cemeteries, and learn about traditional medicines, dances, pottery, songs, and religion.

It is open 10 am to 5 pm daily by appointment (there is an admission fee). The Mattaponi tribe occasionally has dances that are open to the public. Call the tribal office (☎ 804-769-2229) for dates and sites.

Virginia's Eastern Shore

The slender peninsula that separates Chesapeake Bay from the Atlantic Ocean is a wild, undeveloped, and intriguing destination. It is the southerly finger of Delmarva, the peninsula that also includes Delaware and a sizable chunk of Maryland. Route 13 starts in Wilmington, Delaware, and heads due south to Salisbury, Maryland. It crosses the Virginia border and heads down the center of the southern peninsula and across the Chesapeake Bay Bridge-Tunnel to Hampton Roads.

The peninsula itself is a place to relax, hide in peaceful harbor villages, tour quiet country roads that lead to the bay or ocean, visit pristine and wild Assateague Island and Kiptopeke State Park, watch the famous Pony Penning, or go for a swim. A good guidebook is *Off 13 – The Eastern Shore of Virginia*, by Kirk Mariner – it's available in Chincoteague shops.

The first town located across the Maryland-Virginia state border is **New Church**. For those traveling down Route 13 and the Eastern Shore to Hampton Roads, the Virginia Welcome Center (☎ 757-824-5000), on Route 13 near the Maryland border, is open daily and has a wealth of information on the state.

CHINCOTEAGUE ISLAND

This island (population 1600), just 7 miles long and 1½ miles wide, is one of the highlights of the Eastern Shore. Many people know it from the 1940s novel *Misty of Chincoteague*, by Marguerite Henry, but it has changed markedly from the description in that book. It has developed swiftly and has all the necessary facilities to meet the tourist influx – the road across the causeway has the most prolific billboard collection you are ever likely to see. Still, the island retains a distinct charm, and parts of it, such as some pristine beaches and dilapidated piers, have escaped the auctioneer's gavel and the developer's lack of taste.

In July, wild horses from nearby Assateague Island are herded across the intervening channel to Chincoteague (see the boxed text Wild Horses in the Maryland's Eastern Shore chapter).

Orientation & Information
Main St runs north-south along the western shore, and the main drag, Maddox Blvd (which changes to Beach Rd at the roundabout), continues to the Assateague Channel.

The Chincoteague Chamber of Commerce (☎ 757-336-6161) is in the center of the roundabout on Maddox Blvd. It is open 9 am to 4:30 pm Monday to Saturday and noon to 4:30 pm Sunday from June to October; otherwise, it's open 9 am to 4:30 pm weekdays.

There are 24-hour ATMs on Maddox Blvd at Marine Bank (☎ 757-336-6539) and Shore Savings Bank (☎ 757-336-3144). The Medical Center (☎ 757-336-3682), 4049 Main St, has urgent-care facilities.

Chincoteague National Wildlife Refuge
Just across the Assateague Channel from Chincoteague is the Chincoteague National Wildlife Refuge (☎ 757-336-6122), a thoroughly absorbing area that was set up in 1943 to protect migratory waterfowl. It is now administered by the US Fish & Wildlife Service.

The visitor center (☎ 757-336-6122) is just across the channel bridge on Assateague Island, near where you pay the entrance fee of $5 for cars (valid for a week); it is open 9 am to 5 pm daily. The refuge is open daily 5 am to 10 pm May through September, otherwise, 6 am to 6 pm. Birders will delight in the surprises at the Snow Goose Pool and Swan Cove, or along the quarter-mile Lighthouse, 1.6-mile Woodland, and 3.2-mile Wildlife Loop Trails.

A little farther on is the Assateague Island National Seashore (see that section, later).

Oyster & Maritime Museum
The museum (☎ 757-336-6117), at 7125 Maddox Blvd, has a lot of information on the history of the area, marine life (in particular, the humble oyster), and the seafood industry. It is open 10 am to 5 pm daily in summer, and on weekends only during the spring and fall (closed in winter). Admission costs $3 for adults and $1 for seniors and children.

Refuge Waterfowl Museum
Quite bizarre, but nonetheless popular, this museum (☎ 757-336-5800), 7059 Maddox Blvd, pays homage to the annual slaughter of waterfowl in the nearby refuge and has the paraphernalia of the carnage – weapons, boats, traps, decoys, and 'dead duck' art. It is open daily 10 am to 5 pm from Memorial Day to Labor Day; admission is $2.50 for adults and $1 for children.

Stoney Point Decoys
At 6301 Lankford Hwy in Oak Hall (near Route 13), this decoy factory (☎ 757-824-5621) has hand-painted and decorative ducks. Buy one and take it home so it can't be used to lure the real thing to its doom. The factory is open daily 9 am to 6 pm in summer (otherwise until 5 pm); admission is free.

Fishing
There are a number of fishing charter operators. For trout, croaker, and sea bass on the back bays, call ☎ 757-336-1875, and for overnight offshore safaris aboard the *Tools of the Trade*, contact Hooks & Feathers (☎ 757-336-6812) – a deep-sea trip is $780 for six people. The *Islander* (☎ 757-336-5191) also offers deep-sea trips ($500 for four).

For less serious fishing adventures costing about $30 per person, there are a couple of choices: the Chincoteague View (☎ 757-336-3409), operating from East Side Drive; Captain Bob's (☎ 757-336-6654), 2477 Main St; and Daisey's *Dockside II* (☎ 757-336-3345), operating from Daisey's Dockside Pier, on S Main St.

And there is nothing to stop you from going it alone – Barnacle Bill's Bait & Tackle (☎ 757-336-5188), on S Main St, will rent you the necessaries, provide advice, and let slip the odd secret.

Bird Watching

Because this region is smack on the Atlantic Flyway for migratory species, bird watching is a major outdoor pastime, and it is amazing to see birders with their impressive array of expensive telescopes, photographic zoom lenses, and books (scattered over the hoods of their cars) in search of the buzz twitch.

Kayaking

On the water, kayaking is an ideal way to explore the waterways. Tidewater Expeditions (☎ 757-336-3159), at 7729 East Side Drive, has instruction days when you can learn the skills you need to begin exploring the back bays ($65). They also rent kayaks and canoes (starting at $10 per hour) and have shorter organized trips for $22.50 per person in single kayaks, $39 in doubles.

Bicycling

A great way to see this flat area is on a bicycle. The Bike Depot, at the Refuge Motor Inn (☎ 757-336-5511), rents out good quality bikes. If they have nothing left, try the Piney Island Country Store (☎ 757-336-5188), 7085 Maddox Blvd. And, of course, there is nothing to stop you from walking wherever you want.

Organized Tours & Cruises

You can tour this fascinating region by land or water. Assateague Wildlife Safari Tours (☎ 757-336-6155) has 1½-hour tours of a 7½-mile section of the wildlife refuge. There is a good chance that you will see sika deer, wild horses, many species of shore and song birds, and maybe (only maybe) the endangered Delmarva Peninsula fox squirrel and the piping plover. Call for tour times.

The *Osprey* (☎ 757-336-5511) conducts fully narrated two-hour nature cruises through the Chincoteague channel, passing bird nesting sites. It operates most evenings just before dusk (a good time to spot

birdlife) from Memorial Day to Labor Day. Tickets are $12 for adults and $6 for children, and you need to make reservations. The *Osprey* departs from the town wharf, across from the fire station.

Recommended are Captain Barry's Back Bay Cruises (☎ 757-336-6508), which depart from Landmark Plaza, on Main St. He has a variety of excursions, including a 1½-hour early morning bird-watching cruise ($17.50) and a full morning or afternoon trip on which you look for shellfish and clams ($35).

Special Events

In October, on Columbus Day weekend, the island hosts the Oyster Festival, where you can eat the gooey little gray things in just about every form imaginable – but they are best 'au natural.' There are a limited number of tickets, which must be booked well in advance from the Chamber of Commerce (PO Box 258, Chincoteague, VA 23336). The oysters from Chincoteague are fresh, as this is where they are tonged or dredged.

The famous Pony Penning is held in late July (see the boxed text Wild Horses in the chapter Maryland's Eastern Shore).

Places to Stay

Camping & Cottages Camping is possible right on the beach in *Assateague State Park* (☎ 410-641-3030) in Maryland (see Assateague Island, in the Maryland's Eastern Shore chapter), but not in the Virginia section of the park. On Chincoteague, there are many campgrounds and rental cottages. *Toms Cove Campground* (☎ 757-336-6498, 8128 Beebe Rd), 1½ miles south on Main St, has sites with hookups for $22 to $29 for four people (closed in December); it also has bicycles for rent.

The *Pine Grove Campground* (☎ 757-336-5200, 5283 Deep Hole Rd), reached via N Main St and Maddox Blvd, has sites starting at $18 for four. The *Inlet View Waterfront Campground* (☎ 757-336-5126), in a beautiful waterside location, caters to campers, mobile homes, and travel trailers; rates start at $16. The *Maddox Family Campground* (☎ 757-336-3111, 6742 Maddox Blvd) is a really large campground with well over 500 sites. There are full hookups, a pool, bathhouses, a playground, and a store; rates start at $20 and rise to $28 for full hookups. *Campers Ranch Campground* (☎ 757-336-6371, 4423 Chicken City Rd), in the heart of Chincoteague, has full facilities for tents, trailers and RVs, as well as a swimming pool and a fishing pond.

There are a number of cottages for rent; check at the Chamber of Commerce. To give you an idea, *Snug Harbor Marina & Cottages* (☎ 757-336-6176, 7536 East Side Drive) has them for $56 to $59 in summer, $49 to $53 in fall and spring (their motto: 'Fishing is spoken here'). *Uncle Joe's Cabins* (☎ 757-336-5107) are $55 in summer and drop to $30 at other times of the year. *Vacation Cottages* (☎ 757-336-3720, 6282 Maddox Blvd, www.chincoteagueisland.com) has more than 100 houses and cottages on their books.

Guesthouses The *Watson House* (☎ 757-336-1564, 4240 Main St) is a restored country Victorian residence with tastefully decorated rooms; afternoon tea is provided on the verandah, and bicycle rental is included in the prices of $59 to $89 for singles and $69 to $99 for doubles in the low season (add another $10 in summer). The *1848 Island Manor House* (☎ 757-336-5436, 4160 Main St) consists of two clapboard houses joined by a garden room with a delightful patio. The rooms, tastefully furnished in Federal style, cost $70 to $120 for a double (afternoon tea is included).

Miss Molly's Inn (☎ 757-336-6686, 4141 N Main St) is a gray wooden house; Marguerite Henry wrote *Misty of Chincoteague* in the master bedroom here. There is no smoking, and they don't take credit cards. Rooms range from $69 to $155 for doubles (with breakfast and afternoon tea), and the place is closed January to mid-February.

The *Garden and the Sea Inn* (☎ 757-824-0672, 4188 Nelson Rd) is part of a great little B&B near the Maryland state line. Turn off Route 13 onto County Rd 710 (near the First Virginia Bank) and follow it for a quarter of a mile. It is expensive, but well worth it, with doubles for $60 to $175. Specialties from the kitchen include bouillabaisse, fish from Chesapeake Bay, and scallops.

Hotels & Motels There are plenty of hotels and motels on Chincoteague. The *Beach Road Motel* (☎ 757-336-6562, 6151 Maddox Blvd) is a well-kept place with friendly, helpful owners; singles and doubles start at $35 in the off season, rising to a range of $50 to $75 and $62 to $80 in summer. The *Mariner Motel* (☎ 800-221-7490, 6273 Maddox Blvd) offers singles/doubles for $37/47.

The *Assateague Inn* (☎ 757-336-3738) is just off Maddox Blvd on Chicken City Rd. Bird watchers will love this place, as it overlooks a saltwater marsh and is nestled amongst loblolly pines (each room has access to the balcony). Rooms are reasonably priced, with singles for $40 to $52 and doubles for $54 to $58 in the low season; in the high season, they are $62 to $96 for singles and $106 to $108 for doubles. The *Sea Shell Motel* (☎ 757-336-6589), corner of Cleveland and Willow Sts, has a screened outdoor kitchen; comfortable doubles are $42 to $70 in the low season and $66 to $80 in summer (there is a two-night minimum).

The *Island Motor Inn* (☎ 757-336-3141, 4391 N Main St), on the Intracoastal Waterway, has heaps of views. It is a homey place with a pool, a health-and-fitness room, a restaurant, and an outdoor barbecue – well worth the $68 to $130 for doubles in winter, or $92 to $150 in summer.

The *Waterside Motor Inn* (☎ 757-336-3434, 3761 S Main St) has a great location, with views from private balconies out over Chincoteague Channel. It has a waterfront pool, a fishing and crabbing pier, a tennis court, and a solar health spa with a Jacuzzi; singles and doubles cost $54 to $82 in the low season and $95 to $150 in the summer.

Places to Eat

The best food choices are the fruits of the sea. The *Russel Fish Company* (☎ 757-336-6986), on Main St next to the Coast Guard station, sells fresh fish, live lobsters, and other hot or cold seafood to go. Grab something to eat and sit by the wharf, close to dusk if possible. Magic! Then move the kids down the street to *Muller's Ice Cream Parlor* (☎ 757-336-5894, 4034 Main St) in the historic Cropper

House. They have soda-fountain treats, splits, malts, and Belgian waffles coated in the cold stuff and whipped cream. **Steamers** (☎ 757-336-6236, 6251 Maddox Blvd) serves treats for the kids, as well as 'all-you-can-eat' crab and shrimp platters for adults.

Don's (☎ 757-336-5715, 4113 Main St) has the dubious motto (these are popular on the island) 'If it smells like fish, eat it.' They have an excellent breakfast menu, including a $6.50 crab omelet; clam chowder for $2/3.50 for a cup/bowl; and a seafood platter with fish, shrimp, oysters and clams on the half shell, scallops, and crab cake for $15.

On the bay, **Landmark Crab House** (☎ 757-336-5552), on N Main St, has great views on three sides. Apart from various combinations of crab on offer, there are also beef specials and a large salad bar. Six clams or oysters on the half shell cost $5; a crabmeat cocktail costs $7; hot steamed crabs cost $1.50 each; a crab cake, soft crab, or scallop entree costs $14; and items on the children's menu cost $5.50. The bar in here is reputedly from Al Capone's Chicago speakeasy, and the lighting fixtures are reputedly from *Gone with the Wind* – gazing at them and at beautiful sunsets from the outdoor dining area is free.

Other seafood places include the reliable **Etta's Family Restaurant** (☎ 757-336-5644, 7452 East Side Drive), known for its oyster stew and crab soup; the **Shucking House Cafe** (☎ 757-336-5145, 6162 Main St), next to the Landmark Crab House, has a $10 seafood brunch 11:30 am to 3 pm Sunday. The **Village** (☎ 757-336-5120, 6576 Maddox Blvd) has calamari appetizers and huge seafood platters, and 5 miles west of Chincoteague, in Atlantic, **Wright's** (☎ 757-824-4012) has an 'all-you-can-eat' Crab Galley, where you get clam strips, steamed crab, and Alaskan crab legs.

The **Channel Bass Inn** (☎ 757-336-6148, 6228 Church St), a three-story beige clapboard house and high quality B&B, is open daily for delicious English-style afternoon teas (featuring scrumptious scones).

Entertainment

Chincoteague entertainment is somewhat scanty. **Chattie's Bar** (☎ 757-336-5715, 4113 Main St), on top of Don's (see Places to Eat), has something planned on most nights – comedy, DJs, darts tourneys, or pool competitions.

AJ's...on the Creek (☎ 757-336-5888, 6585 Maddox Blvd) is another place to go for a late-night drink. Most of the locals sneak across the island to **Pony Pines** (☎ 757-336-9746, 7503 East Side Drive) for a quiet drink.

Getting There & Away

From Route 13, turn off at the town of Oak Hall onto Route 175 east, which takes you via a causeway across the channel into the center of Chincoteague. To reach the north side of Assateague Island (in Maryland) from Chincoteague, you must take Route 175 to Route 13 north. Take Route 113 to Route 376, and then take Route 611 to Assateague Island.

ASSATEAGUE ISLAND NATIONAL SEASHORE

Most of this pristine, wildly beautiful, and windswept 37-mile-long barrier island is in Maryland (see the Maryland's Eastern Shore chapter), but the southern portion belongs to Virginia. It can be reached on Route 175 via Chincoteague. It would have to be rated as one of the most remote and alluring wilderness areas in the US, which is to say that a visit is highly recommended. Bird watchers will be well satisfied, as there are around 300 species passing through the area (on the Atlantic migratory pathway), including swans, egrets, and migrant geese.

The Toms Cove Visitor Center (☎ 757-336-6577), operated by the National Park Service (NPS), is on the beach at the south end of the island. This is an information center for the Chincoteague National Wildlife Refuge and Virginia's section of the Assateague Island National Seashore. The visitor center has displays, exhibits, and a small sales area. There are bathhouses near the beach, access to the beach via boardwalks, an off-road vehicle area (for which a permit is required), and the Toms Cove Nature Trail.

If you want to progress north along the beach to the six backcountry camping areas, see the chapter Maryland's Eastern Shore.

Wallops Island, near Chincoteague Inlet, houses the **NASA Wallops Flight Center**, the site of several rocket launchings. There is now a visitor center (☎ 757-824-1344) that highlights current NASA and Wallops space programs; it is across the road from the Wallops Flight Center (the runway encircled by a huge fence), on Route 175. It has space suits, a moon rock, special films of rocket launches, and a videotaped presentation (all of which are popular with the kids).

The exhibit is free and is open 10 am to 4 pm daily from July to Labor Day; otherwise, 10 am to 4 pm Thursday to Monday. There is disabled access.

CENTRAL EASTERN SHORE

Chincoteague and Assateague dominate the Eastern Shore as destinations, but there are a number of interesting things to do and see in the center and in the south of the peninsula – a trip to either side of Route 13 will be rewarding.

Parksley & Accomac

The small Victorian town of Parksley, just off Route 13 on Route 316, is worth a side trip to see the **Eastern Shore Railway Museum** (☎ 757-665-6271), 18468 Dunne Ave, Railroad Square. Here, a 1907 New York, Philadelphia & Norfolk Railroad passenger station, maintenance-of-way tool shed, and myriad artifacts (including seven railcars) have been set out on 10 acres with a pavilion and picnic grounds. The museum is open 10:30 am to 4 pm weekdays and 1 to 4 pm Sunday; admission is $1. The museum also organizes excursions (☎ 800-852-0335).

Accomac, 6 miles south of Parksley, is an historic little town with many examples of restored colonial architecture (a walking-tour guide is available). The **debtor's prison** dates from 1784, when it was built as a jailer's residence, and remains essentially unaltered. Call ☎ 757-787-2462 to arrange a visit; admission is free.

Onancock

This pretty little bayside town (population 1500), once a Native American village, was founded in 1680 as Port Scarburgh. Large ships and ferries plying the route between Baltimore and Norfolk stopped in at the port and added to the town's wealth.

For more information, see the Onancock town office (☎ 757-787-3363) on weekdays.

Things to See & Do Stop by Kerr Place (☎ 757-787-8012), at 69 Market St, a 1799 Federal-period home dating from the shipping boom. Of interest are a museum, research library, and carefully manicured colonial gardens. The museum is open 10 am to 4 pm Tuesday to Saturday year-round; admission is $3 for adults and free for youth under 18.

Also worth a look is Hopkins & Bros (☎ 757-787-8220), 2 Market St, which was built in 1842 and is one of the oldest general stores on the East Coast. It is still operating as a dry-goods store and restaurant.

From early June to mid-September, there are daily five-hour cruises from the town wharf to Tangier Island (lunch is served at the famous Hilda Crockett's Chesapeake House). The tour costs $18 (free for children); contact Tangier Island Cruises (☎ 757-891-2240).

Places to Stay & Eat Five blocks from the marina, the *Colonial Manor Inn* (☎ *757-787-3521, 84 Market St*) dates from 1882. The only telephone is the one that belongs to the number mentioned above, but all rooms have a TV. It is a very reasonable place with friendly owners; double rooms cost $85. The *76 Market St B&B* (☎ *757-787-7600*) is a restored Victorian dwelling close to the shops and harbor; doubles start at $65 in the low season, $85 in high season. The *Spinning Wheel B&B* (☎ *757-787-7311, 31 North St*) is a wood-frame Victorian with comfortable rooms (each with a spinning wheel); rooms cost $75 to $95.

There are a surprising number of quality places to eat, considering the town's size. First visit *Blue Crab Bay Co* (☎ *757-787-3602*) to stock up on chowder, Chesapeake cioppino, cocktail mix, and clam and crab dip kits. These go well with your verandah seafood feasts.

The *Hungry Duck* (☎ 757-787-8700), on the corner of Market and North Sts, is open daily for lunch and dinner and for breakfast on weekends. *Hopkins & Bros Store* (☎ 757-787-4478) is good for seafood and steaks, as is *LJ Street Sports Bar/Restaurant* (☎ 757-787-2144, 20250 Fairgrounds Rd), which is open for lunch and dinner and has bands on weekend nights.

Armando's (☎ 757-787-8044, 10 North St), known for its innovative pasta and seafood dishes, is Argentine-run and is probably the trendiest place on the Eastern Shore; entrees cost $9 to $17.

Wachapreague & Pungoteague

Wachapreague is the self-titled 'Flounder Capital of the World' – don't you just love these 'capitals'? Flounder aside, it's a picturesque fishing village with great views of the waterway between the mainland and the barrier islands, Cedar and Parramore. The village is at the eastern end of Route 180; exit Route 13 at Keller.

From May to October, you can book bird-watching tours and barrier-island **cruises** on *Skimmer I.* At the Wachapreague Marina (☎ 757-787-4110), you can arrange to get dropped off on either Cedar or Parramore Islands for about $60, or they will rent you a boat (and provide fuel and a chart) for $60 so you can select your own fishing spots.

The Hotel Wachapreague, which once attracted the rich and famous keen on hunting and fishing nearby, burned down 20 years ago, but there are still a few accommodations in town. Locals own and run *Hart's Harbor House* (☎ 757-787-4848, 9 Brooklyn Ave); a double here costs $85 to $95. The *Wachapreague Motel & Marina* (☎ 757-787-2105, 15 Atlantic Ave) was once part of the old hotel and has a private beach; doubles cost $40. The *Island House Restaurant* (☎ 757-787-4242) is attached.

In Pungoteague, almost at the western end of Route 180, is the *Pungoteague Junction B&B* (☎ 757-442-3581), housed in an 1869 house with a wraparound porch. They provide toys for your children to play with (a big change when you consider kids aren't welcome at many B&Bs); a double costs $70.

Exmore & Nassawadox

Exmore is 7 miles south of Keller on Route 13, close to Willis Wharf, which gives access to the barrier islands. You could do worse than while away an hour at Willis Wharf learning the delicate and refined art of shucking.

The *Gladstone House* (☎ 757-442-4614, 12108 Lincoln Ave), in Exmore, is a brick Georgian residence with doubles (including breakfast) for $85. *Martha's Inn* (☎ 757-442-4641, 12224 Lincoln Ave), in Exmore, is another grand Georgian-style B&B where singles/doubles cost $60/75. The *Trawler Restaurant* (☎ 757-442-2092), on Route 13, is known for its she-crab soup and sweet-potato biscuits.

The *Anchor Motel* (☎ 757-442-6363), on Route 13 in Nassawadox, has singles/doubles for $37/65 in the low season and $50/72 in summer (there are some efficiencies).

SOUTHERN EASTERN SHORE
Eastville & Cheriton

Route 13 bisects Eastville, a historic 18th-century town well worth a stop, especially to see the old courthouse and debtor's prison. The oldest continuous court records in the US (1632) are stored in the clerk's office, and visitors may inspect them. Not far south of Eastville is the magnificent old house **Eyre Hall**, built in 1735 and extended in 1765.

To the west of Cheriton, on Chesapeake Bay (reached by County Rd 680), is the 300-acre *Cherrystone Family Camping & RV Resort* (☎ 757-331-3063, 1511 Townfields Drive), with every camping facility imaginable, low-season rates are $15 to $24 for two, and high-season rates are up to $31 for two (add $2 for each hookup).

Cape Charles

This 19th-century town, west of Route 13 on Route 184, was once an important railroad terminus. It has delightful residential streets and a downtown with many antique shops.

The *Days Inn* (☎ 800-331-4000, 29106 Lankford Hwy), on Route 13 close to the Chesapeake Bay Bridge-Tunnel, has a swimming pool; singles cost $41 in the low season, more in summer.

VIRGINIA

VIRGINIA

Cape Charles House (☎ *757-331-4920, 645 Tazewell Ave)* is a Colonial-style B&B close to the bay and has a crabbing and fishing pier and boating facilities; singles/doubles are $80/105. Another Colonial-style lodging, **Nottingham Ridge** (☎ *757-331-1010, 28184 Nottingham Ridge Lane)*, borders Chesapeake Bay and serves breakfast on the porch. The *Sea Gate B&B* (☎ *757-331-2206, 9 Tazewell Ave)* also has a porch with spectacular views and bikes for guests; singles/doubles cost $60/75.

The *Bay Avenue Sunset B&B* (☎ *757-331-2424, 106 Bay Ave)* is open year-round and has rooms starting at $75/85 for a double in the low/high season (there is a winter special of $100 for two nights). In nearby Townsend, on County Rd 600 (off Route 13), the clapboard and brick *Picketts Harbor* (☎ *757-331-2212, 28288 Nottingham Ridge Lane)* overlooks sand dunes and has a private beach.

Someplace Else (☎ *757-331-8430)* is a roadside diner known for its seafood and steak dinners.

Kiptopeke State Park

Kiptopeke, just west of Route 13 and a few miles north of the tunnel, is a 375-acre park bordering on Chesapeake Bay that is suitable for families, as there are safe swimming spots. The park (☎ 757-331-2267) is open mid-March to early December, and *campsites* range from $15 for a developed site to $21 for full hookups for six people (it is one of the most expensive state parks, but it's worth it); there is a day-use fee for picnickers.

Eastern Shore of Virginia National Wildlife Refuge

The 651-acre Eastern Shore of Virginia National Wildlife Refuge (☎ 757-331-2760) has a great visitor center, with all sorts of hands-on items for the kids to touch. There are also bird-watching facilities – more than 290 species have been spotted here, as it is one of the major stopovers for migratory birds before they cross the wide mouth of Chesapeake Bay. Also on the premises is a fine collection of waterfowl carvings. There is no admission fee, making this place one of the best value stops on the Eastern Shore (and a great way to rest before or after crossing the bridge-tunnel).

Chesapeake Bay Bridge-Tunnel

This engineering marvel connects Hampton Roads and Virginia's Eastern Shore via Route 13. It is said to be one of the seven wonders of the modern world, and the 17.6-mile two-lane link is the world's largest bridge-tunnel complex. It saves motorists 95 miles of driving and 90 minutes between Hampton Roads and New York City. There is a restaurant, a gift shop, and a fishing pier located on the southernmost of four constructed islands, 4 miles from the southerly end.

The toll facility and fishing pier (☎ 757-624-3511) is open 24 hours year-round; the gift shop is open daily 6 am to 10 pm April 1 to September 30; otherwise, 7 am to 6 pm. The toll of $10 for cars includes a free Pepsi or coffee.

Colonial Virginia (Historic Triangle)

The pearl of 'chronically historic' Virginia is the Historic Triangle, on the peninsula between the York and James Rivers. It consists of Williamsburg, a re-created 18th-century American city; Jamestown Island, the site of the first English settlement in North America; Yorktown, where the closing stages of the Revolutionary War were played out; and the wealthy tobacco plantations to the north of, and along the south banks of, the James River. Williamsburg is a must if you have limited time to visit (it's the biggest historic tourist attraction in the US).

There is more to the Triangle than history, including world-class theme parks such as Busch Gardens and Water Country USA, and a number of factory-outlet shopping malls (all of which far surpass historical sites in visitor numbers).

WILLIAMSBURG

Nowadays, Williamsburg (population 11,500) is a major tourist center, mainly because of the authenticity of its many buildings and numerous historic associations. Some visitors may find the overall treatment 'syrupy' and soon hanker for other parts of the state that are less infested with tourists bedecked with Patriot's Passes, raucous school groups, blasé interpretive staff, and an almost oppressive sense of organization.

But if you want to experience, albeit for a short time, the colonial beginnings of the US, you have to visit. It is, after all, the world's most authentic historic theme park.

History

Here we go again! The area was first settled in 1632 as Middle Plantation. As early as 1676, the rebel Nathaniel Bacon and his followers held a convention here, and a year later, after Bacon had burned the statehouse at Jamestown, the General Assembly met in this town for the first time (see the boxed text Bacon's Rebellion). Because the site, 6 miles inland, was strategically superior to Jamestown (the colony's first capital), it was nominated colonial capital in 1699. Later, it was renamed Williamsburg after the reigning king of England, William of Orange.

The town site was carefully laid out by Royal Governor Francis Nicholson, ensuring that there were public greens and a flourishing mercantile center. Half-acre lots were given to householders for the raising of livestock and for growing vegetables.

The Governor's Palace, completed in 1720, was the residence of royal governors from 1714 to 1775 (when Lord Dunmore was forced to flee). It then housed the Commonwealth of Virginia's first two governors, Patrick Henry and Thomas Jefferson, during the first years of the Revolution. So for

Highlights

- Williamsburg – the nation's best-preserved colonial city

- World-famous theme parks Busch Gardens and Water Country USA – something for the kids to shout about

- Jamestown – site of the country's first English occupation, a fascinating walk or drive through history

- Yorktown – a picturesque town in the heart of the last major Revolutionary War battlefield

- Plantation country – where the stately homes are replete with history

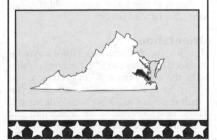

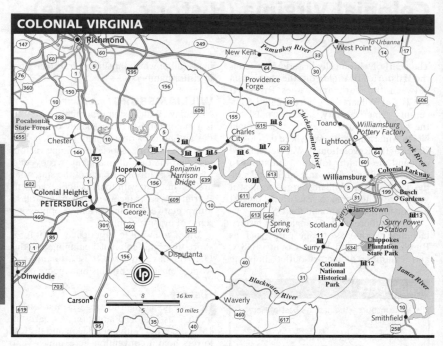

COLONIAL VIRGINIA

81 years, until 1780, the town was Virginia's capital and was definitely the social and cultural center of the colony before Jefferson moved the capital to Richmond, 50 miles west. From the end of the Revolution until the Civil War, it was sleepy, almost forgotten, and stripped of its former importance.

In early April 1862, the Union Army of the Potomac under George McClellan commenced its Peninsula Campaign, then to be the 'last' advance on Richmond. McClellan's army, after besieging Yorktown, ran into a Confederate rearguard near old Williamsburg. After a battle near a line of fieldworks near the city, which did nothing more than produce 2200 Union casualties, Williamsburg fell on May 5.

The city's modern history has much to do with its preservation as a historic district. In the mid-1920s, WAR Goodwin, the local priest at Bruton Parish Church, saw the potential to restore the collection of 18th-century buildings. He had an antipathy toward motor vehicles, seeing them as the bane of American towns. Ironically, he approached Henry Ford for funds but was given the cold shoulder. John D Rockefeller, inspired by Goodwin's vision, contributed some $70 million to the restoration program over the years. He and his wife, Abby Aldrich, even moved into 18th-century Bassett Hall in the mid-1930s so they could see how their legacy was being spent. He established an endowment so that restoration would continue long after he died (in 1960).

Orientation

Roughly, the Williamsburg Historic Area is bounded by Lafayette St in the north, Waller St in the east, Francis St in the south, and Henry St in the west. Just outside of this quadrangle is the College of William and Mary, in a 'V' created by Richmond and Jamestown Rds, and the DeWitt Wallace Gallery and the Abby Aldrich Rockefeller Folk Art Center.

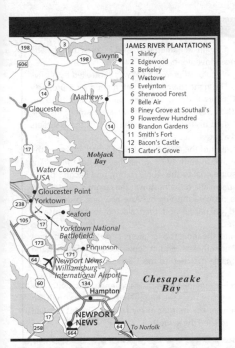

JAMES RIVER PLANTATIONS	
1	Shirley
2	Edgewood
3	Berkeley
4	Westover
5	Evelynton
6	Sherwood Forest
7	Belle Air
8	Piney Grove at Southall's
9	Flowerdew Hundred
10	Brandon Gardens
11	Smith's Fort
12	Bacon's Castle
13	Carter's Grove

The Colonial Parkway passes roughly north-south through the center of the city (via a tunnel), as does Route 60 east-west. Route 5 gives access to the James River plantations to the west, and I-64 passes to the east.

The best way to see this area is on foot or bicycle.

Information

Tourist Offices The Colonial Williamsburg Tourist Visitor Center (☎ 757-220-7645, www.colonialwilliamsburg.org) is 1 mile northeast of the train station, sandwiched between Route 132 and the Colonial Parkway (I-64 exit 238). Upstairs, it sells tickets to Colonial Williamsburg, and downstairs, the Virginia Attractions desk covers the rest of the state. The center is open 9 am to 5 pm weekdays, 8:30 am to 6 pm weekends (extended hours in peak seasons).

Visit the Williamsburg Area Chamber of Commerce (☎ 757-253-0192, www.visitwilliamsburg.com), at 201 Penniman Rd. There is also an information center at Merchants Square, at the west end of Duke of Gloucester St.

Tickets & Passes The first thing you must do in Williamsburg is buy a ticket or pass. These can be purchased from the main visitor center off the Colonial Parkway, or from the office in Merchants Square. The ticket/pass gives you access to the free shuttle bus (you'll want to use this, as local parking is abysmal). You can choose from the following:

Basic Admission – This costs $27/16 for adults/children and is valid for one day only. It allows entry into everything except Bassett Hall, Carter's Grove Plantation, and the Governor's Palace.

Colonist's Pass – This two-day pass is $31/17 for adults/children. It gets you into everything in the Historic Area, the museums (except Bassett Hall), and Carter's Grove.

Patriot's Pass – This unlimited pass costs $35/20 for adults/children, is valid for one year, and gets you into everything in Williamsburg, including the Other Half tour. The pass includes a 20% discount on evening events and entry to History Walks.

Museums Ticket – This ticket is $11/7.50 for adults/children and allows entry to the Folk Art Center, DeWitt Wallace Gallery, and Bassett Hall.

Disabled Travelers The Colonial Williamsburg Tourist Visitor Center provides a guide for the disabled. The disabled can reserve special vehicles by making prior arrangements (☎ 757-220-7644). Some of Williamsburg's buildings are fitted with wheelchair ramps.

Post The post office (☎ 757-229-4668), 425 N Boundary St, is open 8 am to 5 pm weekdays, 10 am to 2 pm Saturday.

Laundry The Town & Country Laundromat (☎ 757-229-4996), 463 Merrimac Trail (Route 143) in the Merrimac Plaza, is open 7 am to 11 pm daily; a drop-off service is available, and there are color TVs for entertainment.

Medical Services The Williamsburg Community Hospital (☎ 757-259-6000, 259-6005 in emergencies) is at 1238 Mount Vernon

VIRGINIA

Bacon's Rebellion

A hundred years before the American Revolution, a Virginian named Nathaniel Bacon led a rebellion that many see as a forerunner to the independence movement.

In the years leading up to the rebellion, Virginia's colonial government was controlled by a privileged few who levied intolerable export duties. The right to vote was determined by a property qualification. White farmers, ignored as King Charles II doled out generous land grants to his cronies, settled Virginia's western frontier, where they were not welcomed by Native Americans. The colony's governor, Sir William Berkeley, demonstrated his indifference to the fears of these settlers by refusing to dispatch soldiers to counter Indian attacks.

Bacon, a plantation owner and democratic member of the Governor's Council, had arrived in the colony in 1673. He assembled his ragtag army of 300 in early 1776, when they fought the Indians on the frontier. The defeat of the Indians was inspirational to the whole colony, and Bacon's popularity was such that he followed up by marching his militia on Jamestown, the colony's capital, and occupying it. As a result, Berkeley was forced to dissolve the Virginia Assembly and order a new election. Bacon, initially arrested, was released on parole and then elected to the House of Burgesses.

Against Berkeley's orders, Bacon marched against the Indians once more. Berkeley raised a force against him, but Bacon marched on Jamestown nonetheless, and in September, he captured and torched it. Just a month later, however – as his militia marched to meet Berkeley's forces – Bacon died of malaria, and his rebellion collapsed.

With no popular leader to oppose him, Berkeley regained power. His revenge was swift – he executed 23 of the rebels, an act that drew this remark from the king: 'That old fool has hanged more men in the naked country than I have done for the murder of my father.' Charles recalled the governor, but Berkeley died before he suffered the king's wrath.

Ave. Urgent Care (☎ 757-220-8300, 565-4801) is at 5251 John Tyler Hwy and 5601 Richmond Rd.

Walking Tour

Walking (or bicycling) is your only choice, as cars have been banned from the Historic Area. Start at Merchants Square, where there's an information center.

The following treatment of attractions assumes that you start at Merchants Square and continue in a roughly counterclockwise direction. You may well ignore this and wander at will, soaking up the atmosphere in your own way. You can get away without paying to see Williamsburg – entry to the Wren Building and Bruton Parish Church is free, for example – but you will largely miss the city's 'interior.'

The buildings in the Historic Area are open 9 am to 6 pm daily April to October,

otherwise 9:30 am to 5:30 pm. You can walk the streets anytime, and the taverns are open at night.

College of William and Mary This is the second-oldest college in the US (it was chartered in 1693; the oldest is Harvard). Jefferson, Monroe, and Tyler were distinguished alumni.

At the west end of Duke of Gloucester St (often referred to as 'Dog St' by locals), the **Sir Christopher Wren Building** is purported to be the oldest academic building in continuous use in America. Although it echoes Wren's style and is similar to buildings in England, the architect never visited the US. Students conduct tours Monday to Saturday.

Also in the college is the **Muscarelle Museum of Art** (☎ 757-221-2700), a fine-arts museum with European and American old-master paintings, colonial Virginia portraits, and contemporary works. It's open 10 am to 4:45 pm weekdays, noon to 4 pm weekends (free admission).

Public Hospital & DeWitt Wallace Decorative Arts Gallery

At the junction of S Henry St (Route 132) and Francis St is the public hospital of 1773 and the modern (1985) structure housing the DeWitt Wallace Decorative Arts Gallery (☎ 757-220-7724). The hospital is a reconstructed insane asylum, the first in North America (isn't Williamsburg just full of firsts and seconds!) and serves as the lobby for the underground gallery. It includes reconstructions of the wretched wire cages in which some of the mental patients were locked.

The gallery is a gem and has a fine collection of furniture, ceramics, and textiles dating from the 17th to 19th centuries. One treasure is the portrait of Washington by Charles Willson Peale, and there are 150 other masterworks. The gallery is open 11 am to 6 pm Wednesday to Monday.

Abby Aldrich Rockefeller Folk Art Center

This is another conventional museum (☎ 757-220-7698) built with the funds of a public benefactor, in this case Rockefeller's wife, Abby. One of the country's finest collections of folk art, it includes household implements, bric-a-brac, children's toys, paintings and sculpture, several of Edward Hick's Peaceable Kingdom paintings, and special exhibitions such as 'Folk Art in American Life.' The center is open 10 am to 5 pm Friday to Wednesday.

Magazine & Guardhouse

At the northwest end of S England St near Market Square is the octagonal 1715 magazine. It was kept busy – first by the British, then by troops of the Continental Army, and later by Confederates during the Civil War. It now houses 18th-century arms and ammunition.

Near the magazine is the guardhouse where troops were stationed to protect the magazine. Inside is the replica **fire engine** (1750), which goes out on Williamsburg's streets in summer. The magazine and guardhouse are on the south side of Market Square, where there was once a regular produce market and occasional slave auctions.

The Capitol

At the east end of Duke of Gloucester St is the imposing Capitol, the 1945 reconstruction of the original 1705 building, which burned down in 1747. The H-shaped building consists of an open-air arcade joining two wings, both with ornate interiors. The **Houses of Burgesses** – the elected house of the colonial government – occupied the east wing, and the **General Court**, where felons were tried, was in the west.

In the House of Burgesses, a guide explains the evolution of English democracy from its parliamentary beginnings (when it was dominated by the landed gentry) to the pre-Revolutionary deliberations seen as the seeds of rebellion.

The justices of the General Court, all appointed by the king, acted as a second legislature, much in the way the Senate and House of Representatives do today. The House of Burgesses and justices would meet in a special conference chamber linking the two wings if there was a need to resolve a deadlocked issue. Thirteen of Blackbeard's pirates were tried here, and the guide tells of the horrendous punishments felons received for now seemingly small offenses.

In the evening, the **fife-and-drum corps** assemble in front of the Capitol before marching down Duke of Gloucester St.

If you have time, from the Capitol turn left down Blair St and follow it to Francis St. Turn left on Francis St and follow it until it kinks and becomes Waller St; on the right-hand side is the 18th-century **Christiana Campbell's Tavern**, now a popular restaurant. Continue up Waller St go and left into Nicholson St to see the **old public gaol**, on the right, about 400 yards along. Then head back to the Capitol.

East End, Duke of Gloucester St

Walk west down Duke of Gloucester St, where you will see taverns and shops, some worth a look but others full of tacky souvenirs of suspect historical authenticity.

VIRGINIA

WILLIAMSBURG

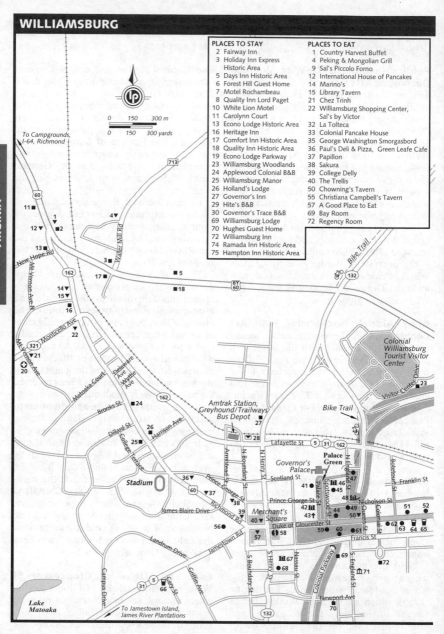

PLACES TO STAY

2　Fairway Inn
3　Holiday Inn Express Historic Area
5　Days Inn Historic Area
6　Forest Hill Guest Home
7　Motel Rochambeau
8　Quality Inn Lord Paget
10　White Lion Motel
11　Carolynn Court
13　Econo Lodge Historic Area
16　Heritage Inn
17　Comfort Inn Historic Area
18　Quality Inn Historic Area
19　Econo Lodge Parkway
23　Williamsburg Woodlands
24　Applewood Colonial B&B
25　Williamsburg Manor
26　Holland's Lodge
27　Governor's Inn
29　Hite's B&B
30　Governor's Trace B&B
69　Williamsburg Lodge
70　Hughes Guest Home
72　Williamsburg Inn
74　Ramada Inn Historic Area
75　Hampton Inn Historic Area

PLACES TO EAT

1　Country Harvest Buffet
4　Peking & Mongolian Grill
9　Sal's Piccolo Forno
12　International House of Pancakes
14　Marino's
15　Library Tavern
21　Chez Trinh
22　Williamsburg Shopping Center, Sal's by Victor
32　La Tolteca
33　Colonial Pancake House
35　George Washington Smorgasbord
36　Paul's Deli & Pizza, Green Leafe Cafe
37　Papillon
38　Sakura
39　College Delly
40　The Trellis
50　Chowning's Tavern
55　Christiana Campbell's Tavern
57　A Good Place to Eat
69　Bay Room
72　Regency Room

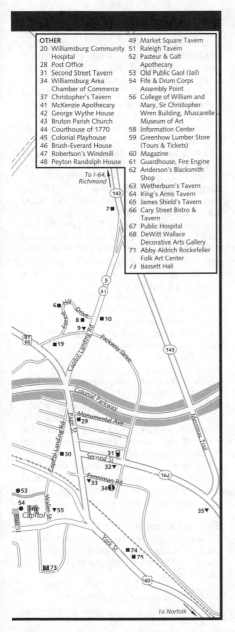

On the south side of the street, near the corner of Blair St, are a couple of taverns. **James Shield's Tavern** is a recent reconstruction of an 18th-century dwelling, and the **King's Arms Tavern** works hard to reproduce the fare Jefferson and Washington would have enjoyed.

Across the road is the **Pasteur & Galt Apothecary** shop. A little ways from that is the **Raleigh Tavern**, where the first meeting of Phi Beta Kappa was said to have been held in the Apollo Room in 1776. The original building burned down in 1859. A bakery, a millinery, and a silversmith are nearby.

Across the road, near the southeast corner of Botetourt St, is **Wetherburn's Tavern**, which dates from 1743 and has been restored to reflect its appearance in 1760. Next door is Tarpley's store. To the right of the tavern is a wigmaker.

Cross Botetourt St, and on the south side is **Anderson's Blacksmith Shop**, where smiths still forge essentials, such as nails and tools, used in the town's reconstruction. Across the road is a printer-bookbinder and colonial post office.

Central Williamsburg At the corner of Queen and Duke of Gloucester Sts is the 1766 **Chowning's Tavern**, a reconstructed alehouse that is the most popular dining place these days, probably because of its location. Opposite Chowning's is Market Square and the magazine and guardhouse (mentioned earlier). There is also the disused **Market Square Tavern**, where Jefferson rented a room when he was studying at the College of William and Mary.

On the north side of Duke of Gloucester St, a few steps from Chowning's, is the site of the original **Courthouse of 1770**. If you did something really bad, you ended up in the Capitol and were probably executed. If you did almost nothing, but incurred the displeasure of the ruling elite, you may have ended up in the stocks here. Today, lots of tourists, who might have done little more than exceed the speed limit on the way to Williamsburg, end up in the stocks for a photo opportunity.

Around Palace Green Wander up the east side of the delightful and broad Palace Green, which runs from Duke of Gloucester St to the Governor's Palace, and take the first right turn onto Nicholson St. On the northeast corner of N England St is the **Peyton Randolph House**, home of a prominent colonist and revolutionary. He was attorney general when the British ruled, but he later became Speaker of the House of Burgesses. From then on, in the eyes of the British, he became a bad boy as president of the first and second Continental Congresses. His house is only open for special, prearranged tours.

Wander up N England St to **Robertson's Windmill**, on the east side near the corner of Scotland St. Barrel-making (coopering), pit sawing, and basketmaking are demonstrated daily.

Head west on Scotland St and you will pass a wheelwright on your right before reaching one of Williamsburg's great attractions, the reconstructed **Governor's Palace** (the original burned down in 1781), nestled in splendor at the far end of Palace Green. A poignant example of the Crown's power, the original palace was built in 1720 by then-governor Alexander Spotswood – it's furnished as it was before the Revolution.

In all, seven British governors lived here, the last being Lord Dunmore, who fled in 1775, leaving behind many of the furnishings you see today. During the Revolution, the palace was home to the Commonwealth's first two governors. There are guided tours through the building, and all your questions on America's 'big start' will be answered. There are also lovely, contemplative surrounding gardens.

Head down the west side of the green, and you will pass the **McKenzie Apothecary**, which is an authentic place deserving a bit of your time (it's free). Strike directly across the green from here to the **Brush-Everard House**, built in 1717 by the gunsmith John Brush. The house's other notable resident, Everard, was twice mayor of the city. It's only open to special tours.

Cross the green (yet again) and walk down to the **George Wythe House**, a large brick building on the corner of Prince George St. Wythe, one of the signatories of the Declaration of Independence, was also mentor to Jefferson.

On the west side of the green, at the northwest corner of Duke of Gloucester St, is the Episcopalian **Bruton Parish Church**, built in 1715. WAR Goodwin, the impetus behind Williamsburg's amazing restoration, preached here. The church is open 9 am to 5 pm daily (donations are encouraged).

From here, return to Merchants Square. Chances are, if you visited all these places, you were on the go all day.

Organized Tours

Interpre-Tours (☎ 757-785-2010), the oldest tour company in Williamsburg, specializes in personal tours. Lanthorn Tours (☎ 757-220-7645) leads night walks that visit selected trade shops at 7 and 8:30 pm. Get tickets from the visitor center or Greenhow Store (see the Williamsburg map). Tours cost $10, or $8 with a Patriot's Pass.

One of the most interesting tours is the Other Half, conducted at 10 am daily from March to September. This tour tells of the experience of African Americans and Africans; a separate ticket is required. Also available from Greenhow Store are carriage and wagon rides, weather permitting.

The Ghosts of Williamsburg candlelight tour (☎ 757-565-4821) takes place nightly (at 8 and 8:45 pm) and is extremely popular; the 90-minute tour costs $7. The Pirates: The Last Walk tour (☎ 757-220-7645) takes place 7 to 8:45 pm Tuesday, Friday, and Saturday ($10 for adults, $8 for children).

There are hour-long guided walks of the Historic Area from Greenhow Store 9 am to 5 pm daily (free if you have a pass – see Tickets & Passes, earlier).

Special Events

Williamsburg is one big year-round historical festival, but there are plenty of other celebrations. Major festivals and events include the following:

Military Through the Ages (mid-March)

President John Tyler's Birthday at Sherwood Forest (March 29)

Garden Week (mid- to late April)

Jamestown Landing Day & Jamestown Weekend (mid-May)

Civil War Weekend (late May)

Independence Day (early July)

Children's Colonial Fair (early July)

First Assembly Day Commemoration (late July)

Yorktown Day & Victory Weekend, celebrating the defeat of the British in October 1781 (mid-October)

Virginia's First Thanksgiving, Berkeley Plantation (November)

Williamsburg's Grand Illumination (early December)

Jamestown Colonial Christmas (late December)

Places to Stay

There are nearly 100 places to stay in the immediate Williamsburg area, so we have provided a small selection to indicate the range, cost, and available services. The nearest budget accommodations are 40 miles away, near Urbanna (see the Virginia's Chesapeake Bay chapter).

For camping and other places to stay in the Williamsburg area, see Around Williamsburg, later in the chapter.

Guesthouses Private guest homes charge about $50 to $60 for two. Local options include *Hughes Guest Home* (☎ 757-229-3493, 106 Newport Ave) and the *Forest Hill Guest Home* (☎ 757-229-1444), on Forest Hill Drive.

There are 20 B&Bs close to Williamsburg. The *Holland's Lodge* (☎ 757-253-6476, 601 Richmond Rd) charges $80 to $90 for two. Four good choices close to the old city are *Governor's Trace B&B* (☎ 757-229-7552, 303 Capitol Landing Rd), with rooms from $115 (with 'eggs in a nest' breakfast); *Hite's B&B* (☎ 757-229-4814, 704 Monumental Ave), with rooms starting at $85; *Applewood Colonial B&B* (☎ 757-229-0205, 605 Richmond Rd), with rooms for $85 to $150; and *Williamsburg Manor* (☎ 757-220-8011, 600 Richmond Rd), with doubles for $95 to $150.

Also see the James River Plantations section, later in this chapter.

Hotels & Motels Chain hotels and motels are sprinkled throughout the region. See the Williamsburg and Around Williamsburg maps for some options.

The Williamsburg Hotel/Motel Association (☎ 757-220-3330, 800-446-9244) will find accommodations for you at no extra charge. The following list progresses roughly from cheaper to more expensive establishments. Hostelries owned, managed, or franchised by chains are generally required to maintain certain standards of quality. For an idea of what to expect from chains, see Accommodations in the Facts for the Visitor chapter.

The *Fairway Inn* (☎ 757-229-8551, 1413 Richmond Rd), a reliable 'cheapie,' and *Carolynn Court* (☎ 757-229-6666, 1446 Richmond Rd), a clean and comfortable place, charge about $27 for doubles in the off-season, rising up to $39 to $47 in high season. The *White Lion Motel* (☎ 757-229-3931, 912 Capitol Landing Rd) is a lovely place to stay, with landscaped gardens, a pool, and a picnic area. Doubles cost $29 to $38 in low season, $46 to $58 in high season. The *Motel Rochambeau* (☎ 757-229-2851, 929 Capitol Landing Rd), also with landscaped grounds, is farther north; doubles range from $26 to $34 in low season, $38 to $48 in high season.

The *Heritage Inn* (☎ 757-229-6220, 1324 Richmond Rd) has low rates, with rooms starting at $40 in low season, $74 in high season. The *Hampton Inn Historic Area* (☎ 757-220-3100, 505 York St) has a heated pool; singles and doubles range from $49 to $59 in low season, $79 to $109 in summer.

The Colonial Williamsburg Foundation (☎ 757-229-1000) operates four accommodations – packages are available for $150 per person for two nights' lodging in restored colonial homes, with meals and admission to the area's attractions. The *Governor's Inn* (506 N Henry St), the least expensive of the foundation's hotels, charges $60 to $90. *Williamsburg Woodlands*, on Visitor Center Drive, is a good choice for families (with nearby eateries and plenty of activities for kids); rooms cost $70 to $125.

The *Williamsburg Lodge* (310 S England St), close to the Historic Area, charges at least $99 for the least expensive doubles in low season, $129 in high season (rooms in the Tazewell and West wings are more expensive). You can dine at the Bay Room restaurant (see Places to Eat). The *Williamsburg Inn* (☎ 800-447-8679 ext 5000, 137 Francis St) is the most luxurious of all and is one of the best hotels in the nation. It charges $185 to $295 for doubles in low season, $245 to $365 in summer. The inn has a fine restaurant, the Regency Room (see Places to Eat), and three golf courses, including the Golden Horseshoe; the latter has attracted many VIPs (golfing presidents) and their guests.

Places to Eat

You'll have no problem finding a variety of cuisines in all price ranges. See Entertainment, later, for taverns that also serve food.

Budget Those strapped for cash should fuel up at the *Williamsburg Shopping Center* (☎ 757-282-1359), on the corner of Richmond Rd and Monticello Ave. Don't hesitate to tear the discount coupons out of the many free publications. Many of these have all-you-can-eat and 'free with the purchase of an entree' specials.

The *Country Harvest Buffet* (☎ 757-229-2698, 1425 Richmond Rd) is one of the best buffets around. All the Southern-style favorites and at least eight seafood items are included in the buffet. Lunch costs $5 for adults, $3 for children; dinner is $10 for adults, $5 for children. The *George Washington Smorgasbord* (☎ 757-220-1410, 500 Merrimac Trail) is also good for sumptuous feasts. All meals include Virginia ham and plenty of choices at the salad bar. Dinner is $16 for adults, $10 for children; Sunday brunch is $10 and $7.

The cafeteria-style *A Good Place to Eat* (☎ 757-229-4370, 410 Duke of Gloucester St) is good for breakfast ($3 to $4) or lunch ($2.50 to $6.50). There is an outdoor dining area, which, on a good day, makes it an even better place to eat. The *International House of Pancakes* (IHOP; ☎ 757-229-9628, 1412 Richmond Rd) is open 24 hours.

Paul's Deli & Pizza (☎ 757-229-8976, 761 Scotland St) is a friendly student place with a huge range of more than 40 subs, *stromboli* (like calzones), and burgers for around $5. The *Green Leafe Cafe* (☎ 757-220-3405, 765 Scotland St), next door to Paul's, serves top sandwiches ($3.50 plus). It has a pub like atmosphere, with a good selection of single malts and Belgian beers. The *College Delly* (☎ 757-229-6627, 336 Richmond Rd) has subs and sandwiches; Greek, Middle Eastern, and Italian choices; and several vegetarian entrees. It delivers free to hotels and motels.

La Tolteca (☎ 757-259-0598, 135 Second St) has great Mexican entrees for $3.25 to $8.75. There's another branch outside of town (☎ 757-253-2939, 5611 Richmond Rd).

Mid-Range Check out *Chez Trinh* (☎ 757-253-1888, 157 Monticello Ave) for delicious, healthy Vietnamese food. Lunch costs less than $5 and starts at 11:30 am daily.

The *Peking & Mongolian Grill* (☎ 757-220-1118), in the Kingsgate Shopping Center off the Route 60 Bypass, offers sumptuous banquets in which you select from more than 50 items; lunch costs $5.50, dinner $7.50 (desserts and salads are included).

Sakura (☎ 757-253-1233, 601 Prince George St) is a Japanese steak and seafood place with *teppan-yaki* tables, where food is prepared on a grill before your eyes. Lunch is $5.50; dinner for two is $27.

For Italian, try *Marino's* (☎ 757-253-1844, 1338 Richmond Rd), offering all-you-can-eat spaghetti and salad for $9; it opens at 4 pm daily.

There are three branches of Sal's. *Sal's Piccolo Forno* (☎ 757-221-0443, 835 Capitol Landing Rd); *Sal's by Maurizio* (☎ 757-229-0337), in the Festival Market Place on Route 60E (see the Around Williamsburg map); and *Sal's by Victor* (☎ 757-220-2641, 1242 Richmond Rd), in the Williamsburg Shopping Center. All serve tasty pizza and traditional pasta dishes and offer take-out service.

Top End Touted as the 'best restaurant in this part of Virginia' by the *New York Times*, *The Trellis* (☎ 757-229-8610) is west of the Historic Area, in Merchants Square. The main chef, Marcel Desualniers, author of a number of cookbooks, has won many awards for his treatments of regional cuisine. A memorable fixed-price dinner costs $25. Reservations are suggested year-round.

Papillon (☎ 757-229-4020, 415 Richmond Rd) is an upscale bistro that features regional seafood. Attached is Christopher's Tavern (see Entertainment).

Chowning's Tavern (☎ 757-229-2141, 100 Duke of Gloucester St), in the heart of the Historic Area, is a reconstructed 18th-century alehouse. It has a selection of old-fashioned food (eg, stew, Welsh rarebit). It's one of the cheaper options in this part of town, especially if you go after 9 pm and dine on sandwiches. At night, you can take part in 'gambols' (traditional board games) and listen to music.

Christiana Campbell's Tavern (George Washington's favorite?), at 120 Waller St, serves seafood and stodgy English-style food. At all four of the Historic Area's taverns, dinner costs $15 to $25; reservations are advised in the high season.

The *Bay Room* (☎ 757-220-7685), in the Williamsburg Lodge, has a huge buffet on weekend nights ($24 for adults, $10 for kids) and a Sunday brunch ($17/11). The *Garden Lounge*, also at the lodge, is the spot for drinks and entertainment.

The *Regency Room* (☎ 757-565-8875, 136 Francis St), in the Williamsburg Inn, is a Mobil five-star winner. The style is classic American (with a French flair), and for the impeccable service and million-dollar atmosphere, lunch is reasonable at $20 to $25, dinner for $50 to $60. After 6 pm, you will need to dress for dinner (coat and tie), and a jacket is mandatory if you wish to visit the Regency Lounge, where cocktails and a light supper are served.

Entertainment

A visit to the taverns is a must for most visitors to Williamsburg. They usually serve colonial-style (English) food, prohibit smoking, and accept casual dress; get information via a central reservations number (☎ 757-229-2141). Three options on E Duke of Gloucester St are Chowning's (see Places to Eat), the *King's Arms* (No 409), and

James Shield's (No 417). Another good one is Christiana Campbell's Tavern (see Places to Eat, earlier).

The *Library Tavern* (☎ 757-229-1012, 1330 Richmond Rd) is immensely popular for lunch, dinner, late-night specials, or a game of pool. Similar are the *Cary Street Bistro & Tavern* (☎ 757-229-2297, 500 Jamestown Rd), which has good food, live music, and a healthy selection of beers; the *Polo Club Tavern* (☎ 757-220-1122, 135 Colony Square Shopping Center), with its long wooden bar and Sunday brunches; and the *Second Street Tavern* (☎ 757-220-2286, 140 Second St), where meals (including hand-patted burgers) are served until 1:15 am, and most sporting events are screened.

Try *Christopher's Tavern* (☎ 757-229-4020, 415 Richmond Rd), attached to Papillon (see Places to Eat). It has a signature lager and more casual, less expensive dining.

The Green Leafe Cafe, Paul's Deli & Pizza, and the College Delly (see Places to Eat) are popular hangouts for college students.

Every evening, there are 18th-century plays, dance, and drama (☎ 757-220-7645) performed in the open-air *Colonial Playhouse* (where the first theater in the country once stood, just south of the Brush-Everard House), out in the streets, or near or in one of the historic buildings. The accent of the company's performances is definitely English and mostly 18th century in character. Check in the 'Visitor's Companion,' a free pamphlet listing current events, available from the main visitor center.

Shopping

There is plenty of shopping in and around Williamsburg. The Prime Outlets (☎ 757-565-0702), 5715 Richmond Rd, has more than 50 designer outlet stores such as Nike, Liz Claiborne, Coach, and Mikasa. Take I-64 exit 234 and drive east on Route 60.

Merchants Square, nestled between the College of William and Mary and the Historic Area, is a collection of 40 distinctive specialty shops (and restaurants) that sell everything from hand-stitched quilts to Christmas decorations.

The Williamsburg Outlet Mall (☎ 757-565-3378), on Route 60, has 55 outlets specializing in clothing and gifts for all ages. It's open 9 am to 9 pm Monday to Saturday, to 6 pm Sunday. Take I-64 exit 234 and drive west on Route 60.

The Williamsburg Pottery Factory (☎ 757-564-3326), about 5 miles northwest of Williamsburg on Route 60, has 32 buildings spread over 200 acres. It offers bargains from all over the world, as well as china and salt-glaze pottery produced on site. Some three to four million people visit annually – compare this to the one million tickets sold annually for Colonial Williamsburg. It's open 8 am to dusk.

Getting There & Away

Air The nearest airport of note is Norfolk International Airport (☎ 757-857-3351), because it has the most incoming flights. An airport shuttle (☎ 757-587-6958) to Williamsburg is $14.

The Newport News/Williamsburg International Airport (☎ 757-877-0221) is in Newport News, 14 miles east. The main service is provided by US Airways (☎ 800-428-4322). A taxi from the airport to Williamsburg costs $15 to $20, and a shuttle can be anything from $9 to $20.

Richmond International Airport (☎ 804-226-3052), 45 miles west, is reached by I-64.

The Williamsburg-Jamestown Airport handles charter flights. Contact Williamsburg Air Charter (☎ 757-220-3141).

Bus Williamsburg is the only site in the Historic Triangle that is easily reached by public transportation. The Greyhound/Trailways depot (☎ 767-229-1460) is in the Transportation Center, on the corner of Lafayette and N Boundary Sts. The ticket office is open 7:30 am to 5:30 pm weekdays, to 3 pm weekends. There are about seven daily trips from Richmond to Norfolk, and these pass through Williamsburg.

Train The Amtrak station (☎ 757-229-8750, 800-872-7245) is at 468 N Boundary St (the Transportation Center). It's open 7:15 am to 9:30 pm Friday to Monday, to 2:45 pm

Tuesday and Wednesday, and to 3:45 pm Thursday.

Car Connecting Hampton Roads with Richmond (51 miles away), I-64 almost passes through Williamsburg. To get to the Colonial Williamsburg Tourist Visitor Center and the Historic Area, the best exit is 238. Colonial Williamsburg, Yorktown (to the east), and Jamestown (to the southwest) are linked by the scenic Colonial Parkway.

Ferry A free ferry service (☎ 800-823-3779) crosses the James River from Jamestown to Scotland, Surry County. The ferry operates 24 hours a day, and the trip takes 15 minutes.

Getting Around

The easiest way to get around Williamsburg is by bus with the James City County Transit (JCCT; ☎ 757-220-1621). The service along Route 60 goes from the Historic Area to Williamsburg Pottery Factory and Busch Gardens. Jamestown and York are not served by JCCT from here. JCCT operates 6:15 am to 6:20 pm Monday to Saturday ($1, plus 25¢ per zone change; exact change needed). If you have a ticket for Colonial Williamsburg, use JCCT's shuttle bus to get around the Historic Area.

The local taxicab service is Colonial Cab (☎ 757-565-1240).

Biking is a good option for getting around the Historic Triangle, especially along the Colonial Parkway to Jamestown or Yorktown. Places to rent bikes include Bikes Unlimited (☎ 757-229-4620), open 9 am to 7 pm weekdays, to 5 pm Saturday, noon to 4 pm Sunday ($10 per day, $5 deposit); and Bikesmith (☎ 757-229-9858). For information, contact Williamsburg Area Bicyclists, PO Box 2222, Williamsburg VA 23187.

AROUND WILLIAMSBURG
Carter's Grove

This plantation (☎ 757-220-7645) is 6 miles east of Williamsburg on Route 60. The site has been settled since 1619, when it was called Wolstenholme Towne, and the mansion was built in 1755 by Carter Burwell, grandson of 'King' Carter, the powerful landowner. The interior of the mansion has intricate carvings and exquisite wood paneling, but the building has undergone many facelifts.

Recently, Carter's Grove has had an extensive archaeological dig that endeavors to discover more of the famous plantation's 400-year history, and the **Winthrop Rockefeller Archaeological Museum** (built into a hillside) is a good place to see the results. There are also reconstructed 18th-century slave dwellings, where guides in costume tell of the role of slaves on the plantations.

Carter's Grove is open 9 am to 5 pm Tuesday to Sunday from mid-March to December. Admission is $18 for adults, $11 for children; free with a Patriot's Pass.

The 7-mile, one-way **Carter's Grove country road** leads back through scenic woods to S England St in Williamsburg; this road is open for cyclists 8 am to 4 pm daily (8.30 am to 3 pm November to December). Another means of getting there is with Williamsburg Limousine (☎ 757-877-0279), which charges $8 per person from the Historic Area.

Busch Gardens Williamsburg

This amusement park (☎ 757-253-3350, www.buschgardens.com), 3 miles east of Williamsburg on Route 60, is divided into 17th-century European nations. People come here for an adrenaline rush on one of the 40 or so rides or to escape, for a moment, 'another bloody historical site.' The kids have persevered with all that historical stuff, so now it's their turn.

Granted, a day at Busch Gardens is nearly as expensive as a year-long Patriot's Pass to the Historic Triangle. But the Triangle hasn't got Apollo's Chariot (where Fabio met the bird), Alpengeist, the Roman Rapids water adventure, Loch Ness Monster and Big Bad Wolf roller coasters, or the unforgettable Escape from Pompeii. For the kids, there is Land of the Dragons, and for all, the Anheuser-Busch Clydesdales.

Busch Gardens opens at 10 am daily mid-March to October; closing times vary. Entrance costs a hefty $37 for adults and most children ($30 for kids three to six); after 5 pm, it's $5 cheaper.

Kids, the History Lesson Is Over

If you've already taken the kids to Busch Gardens and they still need to be entertained, there are other possibilities.

America's Railroads (☎ 757-220-8725), in the Village Shops at Kingsmill, has some 30 model trains operating on the tracks at any one time. Admission is $4 for adults, $2 for children three to 18.

Go Karts Plus (☎ 757-564-7600), 6910 Richmond Rd, northwest of the Williamsburg Pottery Factory, has a Kiddie Land with Space Train, Super Play Port, and battery-powered mini-cars. It's free, but rides cost from one to three tickets ($1.25 each).

You can hire double and single **kayaks** from Explorer Cruises & Kayaks (☎ 757-259-0400), behind the Jamestown Yacht Basin, at the rear of the Jamestown Settlement parking lot. Guided ecotours of the waterways near Jamestown are available.

Afterward, the kids probably deserve a dash of 'the country's best yogurt' from *TCBY* (☎ 757-259-1296, 1673 Richmond Rd), waffles and pancakes from the *Colonial Pancake House* (☎ 757-253-5852, 100 Page St), or fudge from *The Candy Store* (☎ 757-565-1151), across from the Williamsburg Pottery Factory on Route 60W.

★★★★★★★★★★★★★

Water Country USA

This family water park (☎ 757-229-9300, www.watercountryusa.com), at 176 Water Country Parkway, is Virginia's largest, with slides, rides such as the Aquazoid and Big Daddy Falls, pools (including a wave pool with a 13-minute wave period followed by a 10-minute lull), the super-speed-slide Nitro Racer, and various shows.

It opens at 10 am daily Memorial Day to Labor Day; in May and September it's open some weekends. Admission is $28 for adults, $20.50 for children three to six. A three-day, two-park pass (Busch Gardens and Water Country USA) is $55. Water Country USA is about 3 miles east of Williamsburg, just off Route 199, north of I-64.

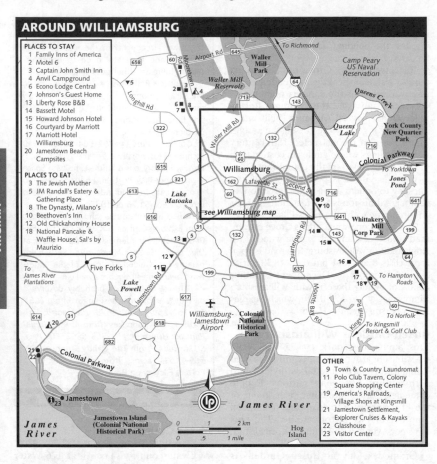

AROUND WILLIAMSBURG

PLACES TO STAY
1 Family Inns of America
2 Motel 6
3 Captain John Smith Inn
4 Anvil Campground
6 Econo Lodge Central
7 Johnson's Guest Home
13 Liberty Rose B&B
14 Bassett Motel
15 Howard Johnson Hotel
16 Courtyard by Marriott
17 Marriott Hotel
   Williamsburg
20 Jamestown Beach
   Campsites

PLACES TO EAT
3 The Jewish Mother
5 JM Randall's Eatery &
   Gathering Place
8 The Dynasty, Milano's
10 Beethoven's Inn
12 Old Chickahominy House
18 National Pancake &
   Waffle House, Sal's by
   Maurizio

OTHER
9 Town & Country Laundromat
11 Polo Club Tavern, Colony
   Square Shopping Center
19 America's Railroads,
   Village Shops at Kingsmill
21 Jamestown Settlement,
   Explorer Cruises & Kayaks
22 Glasshouse
23 Visitor Center

Places to Stay

The following are accommodations in the Williamsburg area. For more options, see Places to Stay under Williamsburg, earlier in the chapter.

Camping The nearest campground is *Anvil Campground* (☎ 757-526-2300, 5243 Mooretown Rd), a small place in a rural setting, 3 miles north of the Colonial Williamsburg Tourist Visitor Center on Route 60. There's a pool, bathhouse, store, and recreation room. Sites are $18 for two people; full hookups are $22.

Jamestown Beach Campsites (☎ 757-229-7609, 2217 Jamestown Rd), on Route 31 (take I-64 exit 242A, then go 5.3 miles west on Route 199), with more than 600 sites, is very close to the settlement and Colonial National Historical Park. Sites range from $18 to $25 for two people; electric/water hookups are $5 extra.

Near the Williamsburg Pottery Factory in Lightfoot, there are four campgrounds near I-64 exit 234. *Kin Kaid Campground* (☎ 757-565-2010, 559 E Rochambeau Drive) is the cheapest, with sites from $10 to $12 for four people; electric hookups cost $1 extra.

The **Best Holiday Trav-L-Park Fair Oaks Family Campground** (☎ 757-565-2101, 901 Lightfoot Rd) has sites for $16 to $22.50 for four (electricity and water are $2.50 extra). It has a pool, playground, fitness trail, and recreation room.

Colonial Central KOA (☎ 757-565-2734, 4000 Newman Rd) has sites for four from $18.95 to $24.95 (more in high season). The **Williamsburg KOA** (☎ 757-565-2907, 5210 Newman Rd) is more expensive; it has all the expected facilities and more, even cable TV hookups – hardly roughing it! Off-season rates for four range from $20 to $28; from May to September, you pay $29 to $33.

Guesthouses The **Johnson's Guest Home** (☎ 757-229-3909, 101 Thomas Nelson Lane) charges about $50 or $60 a night for two people. The 70-year-old **Liberty Rose B&B** (☎ 757-253-1260, 1022 Jamestown Rd, www.libertyrose.com), a four-star place, touted as Williamsburg's 'most romantic B&B,' has delightfully furnished rooms for $135 to $195.

Hotels & Motels The **Bassett Motel** (☎ 757-229-5175, 800 York St), on Route 60 about a mile south of the Historic Area, has large, clean doubles starting at $27 in the off season, rising up to $39 to $47 in high season. The **Captain John Smith Inn** (☎ 757-220-0710, 2225 Richmond Rd) is an economical family place north on Route 60; rooms range from $29 to $39 in winter, $47 to $79 in summer. **Family Inns of America** (☎ 757-565-1900, 5413 Airport Rd) has a heated pool and is close to the factory outlets to the north of Williamsburg. A room, depending on size, facilities, and season, will cost anywhere from $35 to $120 (low family rates are offered).

The **Courtyard by Marriott** (☎ 757-221-0700, 470 McLaws Circle), 2½ miles east of the Historic Area off Route 60, is another great mid-range place. It has a breakfast cafe with full buffet (6 am to noon); doubles range from $59 to $79 in low season, around $145 in summer.

The **Marriott Hotel Williamsburg** (☎ 757-220-2500, 50 Kingsmill Rd), close to Busch Gardens on Route 60E, has heated pools, a health club, racquetball, tennis, a games room, and two restaurants. Rooms in this very classy establishment start at $99 in winter, $139 in summer.

The **Kingsmill Resort** (☎ 757-253-1703, 1010 Kingsmill Rd), a luxurious country-club-style place adjacent to Busch Gardens, has 2900 acres of resort facilities, including three golf courses, tennis courts, indoor and outdoor pools, four dining rooms, activities for the kids, and a free shuttle to Williamsburg. The budget doubles range from $181 to $226 in low season and escalate rapidly from $272 to $346 in summer.

Places to Eat

The **National Pancake & Waffle House** (☎ 757-229-9433), in the Festival Market Place on Route 60E, serves breakfast until 2 pm.

The **Jewish Mother** (☎ 757-565-0085, 2021 Richmond Rd), Virginia Beach's perennial favorite, has set up in Williamsburg, adding some badly needed 'street cred' to a stuffed shirt town; entrées range from $5 to $13.

Beethoven's Inn (☎ 757-229-7069, 467 Merrimac Trail) has beautiful subs (around $4.50), homemade soups, and New York–style deli sandwiches. The **Old Chickahominy House** (☎ 757-229-4689, 1211 Jamestown Rd), corner of Routes 199 and 31/5, a mile out of town, has a $4.50 lunch special.

The **Dynasty** (☎ 757-220-8888, 1621 Richmond Rd) is the best-known of Chinese restaurants in the Williamsburg area. It features Hunan, Cantonese, Mandarin, and Szechuan styles; vegetarian dishes; and a kid's menu. **Milano's** (☎ 757-220-2527, 1635 Richmond Rd), a family place, has all-you-can-eat spaghetti and salad for $9 and also serves thick, juicy steaks.

JM Randall's Eatery & Gathering Place (☎ 757-259-0406, 4854 Longhill Rd) has live music – zydeco, R&B, blues, or folk – most nights starting at 9:30 pm. There is also interactive trivia for those preferring to think rather than listen.

For those touring the plantations on the north side of the James River, there are a few places where you can dine in style. At Berkeley, the **Coach House Tavern** (☎ 804-829-6003) serves lunches ($6 to $12) of sandwiches, salads, and soups; and between Sherwood Forest and Evelynton is the restored Victorian farmhouse *Indian Fields Tavern* (☎ 804-829-5004), where crab cakes, fish, and chicken salads, and a host of other dishes are served for lunch and dinner.

For eateries closer to Williamsburg's Historic Area, see Places to Eat under Williamsburg, earlier.

JAMESTOWN

This historic site at the western end of the Colonial Parkway existed for a relatively short time in the span of history, but it holds an important place in American folklore. The National Park Service oversees visitor centers on Jamestown Island and at Yorktown Battlefield; the state of Virginia operates Jamestown Settlement and the Yorktown Victory Center.

Jamestown was founded in May 1607, when *Discovery*, *Godspeed*, and *Susan Constant* moored in deep waters off the peninsula between the James and York Rivers and 104 boys and men disembarked. It was the first permanent English settlement on the continent but was doomed to failure because of starvation, disease, and attacks by Native Americans.

In 1619, the first representative assembly met, and Jamestown served as Virginia's capital from then until 1699. When the statehouse had been burned for a fourth time, the settlers accepted that they had chosen a poor site, and they moved inland to what is now Williamsburg. At the end of the 19th century, all that was left, after the encroachment of nature, was an overgrown churchyard and church tower.

It is almost 400 years since the town was founded, and the original Jamestown is now a collection of ruins, historical markers, visitor centers, and ongoing archaeological 'digs.' Jamestown Rediscovery, an archaeological search by the Association for Preservation of Virginia Antiquities (APVA), is endeavoring to find the site of the original 1607 fort (they now think they found it) and learn more of the lives of the original settlers and their Algonquin neighbors.

Accommodations and restaurants are located in and around Williamsburg. See Williamsburg and Around Williamsburg, earlier in the chapter.

Jamestown Island (Colonial National Historical Park)

The visitor center here (☎ 757-229-1733) screens a poor film but has decent living-history tours. On site, there are paintings, models, dioramas, and a collection of interesting 17th-century objects unearthed in the many archaeological excavations here. The Jamestown entrance station is open 8:30 am to 5 pm daily in summer, otherwise open to 4:30 pm ($5 per person 17 and over). The visitor center is open 9 am to 5 pm daily.

From the visitor center, there are paths fanning out into 'James Cittie,' where you will find the only standing structure from the 17th-century town, the old **church tower** (dating from the 1640s), which was part of the original brick church. There are a number of statues and monuments, including statues of Pocahontas and John Smith, the Hunt shrine (dedicated to the first Anglican minister), the memorial cross relating to the bleak 'starving time' (winter 1609–10), and Tercentenary and House of Burgesses monuments.

Near the park entrance, there is a reconstructed **glasshouse**, where artisans demonstrate 17th-century glassblowing techniques; their wares make excellent souvenirs.

There are 3-mile and 5-mile **loop drives** around the island (which was connected to the mainland by a narrow isthmus at the time of the original settlement); markers and illustrations relate the early story. For great views of the James River estuary, walk out to Black Point.

Jamestown Settlement

The Jamestown Settlement (☎ 757-253-4838), at the western end of Colonial Parkway just before Jamestown Island, has a museum with changing exhibits, reconstructions of the 1607 James Fort, a Native American (Powhatan) village, full-scale replicas of the three ships that carried the earliest settlers to Jamestown, and living-history demonstrations. It's amazing how many people visit this 'settlement' but do not cross into the original Jamestown to really imbibe history. Advice from many locals is that there is nothing to see on the island, just ruins and swamp – how wrong they are.

Jamestown Settlement is open 9 am to 5 pm daily. Admission is $10.25 for adults, $5 for children six to 12. A combination ticket with the Yorktown Victory Center costs $14 for adults, $6.75 for children.

YORKTOWN

This small town, at the east end of the Colonial Parkway some 14 miles east of Williamsburg, combines all you want in history and, certainly, in isolation. It is a getaway from touristy Williamsburg.

Founded in 1691, when the General Assembly in Jamestown passed the Port Act, Yorktown became a busy tobacco port. In the early autumn of 1781, the most important battle of the Revolutionary War was enacted here – see the boxed text Victory at Yorktown. From here, on October 19, 1781, Washington reported back to the Continental Congress, 'I have the Honor to inform Congress, that a Reduction of the British Army under the Command of Lord Cornwallis, is most happily affected.'

During the Civil War, the town was besieged by Union troops led by George McClellan from April 5 to May 4, 1862. Before the anticipated barrage commenced, the Confederates had stolen away. (At one stage, an elaborate charade by the Confederates under the command of General John Magruder had convinced McClellan that he was facing a much larger force.) Many of the fortifications from this time, and indeed from the Revolutionary War, remain intact.

Today, Yorktown, perched precariously above the York River, basks in the glow of its historical past.

Orientation & Information

Yorktown is at the northeastern apex of the Historic Triangle and at the east end of the Colonial Parkway. It is also reached from the Middle Peninsula via the Coleman Memorial Bridge or from Hampton Roads on Route 17.

The Colonial National Historic Park (☎ 757-898-3400) is open 8 am to dusk daily in summer. The park's visitor center has an intriguing collection of displays and aids that help you understand this last major battle of the Revolutionary War. Included are a 16-minute documentary film, a replica of the quarterdeck of HMS *Charon*, the tent Washington used as his headquarters, a diorama, and a well-constructed electric map. It is open 9 am to 6 pm daily and provides free pamphlets, including one with a simplified town map.

You can also rent a cassette recorder ($2) for the 7-mile battlefield drive and a 10.2-mile Encampment Route (for Washington's and Rochambeau's headquarters); the last tape is rented out at 5 pm. Occasionally, you have to get out of your car on the battlefield route to further imbibe the sense of history, such as at the Grand French Battery, Moore House, and Surrender Field (park entry is $4 per person, free for children under 16).

For regional information, contact the York County Public Information Office (☎ 757-890-3300), 224 Ballard St, Yorktown.

Things to See

The **Yorktown Victory Center** (☎ 757-887-1776, www.historyisfun.org) is a flashier version of the NPS offerings, but it tells essentially the same story. One block from Route 17 and just off old Route 238, the museum has a 28-minute film, *The Road to Yorktown*, and lots of Revolutionary War items. The living-history exhibits, featuring actors dressed as Continental troops and 18th-century farmers, re-create daily life before, during, and after the Revolution. The center is open 9 am to 5 pm daily. Admission is $7.25 for adults, $3.50 for children six to 12. (See Jamestown Settlement for details of combination tickets.)

Three other places in Yorktown proper fall under the aegis of the Colonial National Historical Park: Moore House, the Poor Potter of Yorktown, and the Waterman's Museum. For information on all three, call ☎ 757-898-3400.

Moore House, on Yorktown Battlefield Tour Rd, is the site where the surrender

VIRGINIA

Victory at Yorktown (1781)

The last major battles of the Revolutionary War were fought in and around Yorktown, on the peninsula between the James and York Rivers, during October 1781.

In July 1781, George Washington and French commander Comte de Rochambeau massed their armies and moved toward Sir Henry Clinton's British forces in New York. Washington and Rochambeau had no definite plan of attack; they were counting on the anticipated support of a French fleet under Admiral de Grasse. But then de Grasse informed him that he would only sail with his 3000 troops to Chesapeake Bay and would leave there before the hurricane season began in October. At the same time, Washington learned that Lord Cornwallis and his 9000 troops had established a British naval depot in Yorktown. Washington left half his force to lock up Clinton in New York, and, hoping to pin Cornwallis down with the help of Rochambeau and de Grasse, he began to march the rest of his army to Virginia.

It was the action at sea that made victory at Yorktown possible. De Grasse reached the Chesapeake on August 26 and landed his 3000 troops, where after a few days they joined Americans commanded by Lafayette. The French fleet of Admiral de Barras, equipped with siege artillery, sailed down from Newport, Rhode Island. When the British learned of this move, their fleet set sail from New York to intercept. De Grasse engaged the British navy in the Battle of the Capes on September 5, allowing de Barras to slip into the Chesapeake. The sea battle was inconclusive, but by September 10, the British navy had been forced back to New York. By September 26, the Allied armies were in position, and the French blockade in the Chesapeake prevented any escape by the British by water. The noose could now be tightened around Cornwallis' neck. The siege of Yorktown began on October 6.

Washington was overall commander of a force of 20,000, with formidable siege artillery at his disposal. He was opposed by Cornwallis' army, dug in around Yorktown, as well as a further 1000 troops under Sir Banastre Tarleton across the York River on Gloucester Point. The Continental engineers opened up a parallel opposite the British lines at Yorktown, and the artillery pounded the defenses mercilessly. On October 14, two key British redoubts were stormed at bayonet point, allowing the Continentals to open a second parallel on the night of October 14–15.

Cornwallis attempted to extricate his force to Gloucester Point on the night of October 16–17 but was thwarted by a storm and a shortage of boats. The heaviest cannonade of the war rained down on the British on October 17, and that evening, the British petitioned for terms. On October 20, the British prisoners marched out to the 'Surrender Field,' and England's part in the Revolutionary War was over. The Continentals had lost about 300 men. Washington returned to the Hudson Highlands and remained there for two more years while peace negotiations dragged on. But independence had been won.

★★★★★★★★★★★★★★★★★★★★★★★★★★

terms were negotiated between the French/American force and the British in October 1781. It is open 10 am to 5 pm daily in summer, 1 to 5 pm on weekends in spring and fall (free admission). The Georgian-style **Nelson House**, on Main St, was the former home of Thomas Nelson Jr, a signatory to the Declaration of Independence. It is open 10 am to 4:30 pm mid-June to mid-August (free admission).

The **Poor Potter of Yorktown** is the remains of an 18th-century pottery factory, the largest of its type known to have existed in colonial America. It operated from 1720 to 1745 – a time when British mercantile trade laws made such an operation illegal. It's open 11 am to 4 pm on weekends in spring and fall, daily in summer.

The **Watermen's Museum** (☎ 757-877-2641), 309 Water St, tells of those who have for generations worked along the rivers and tributaries of Chesapeake Bay. It's open 10 am to 4 pm Tuesday to Saturday, 1 to 4 pm Sunday from April to December. Admission is $3 for adults, $1 for children six to 18.

In 1884, more than 100 years after the Revolutionary War, an imposing 98-foot **Victory Monument** with a crowning figure of liberty was completed overlooking the York River; beneath the 13 female figures, symbolizing the 13 colonies, is the inscription 'One Country, One Constitution, One Destiny.'

Places to Stay & Eat
The *Duke of York Motor Hotel* (☎ 757-898-3232, 508 E Water St) has bargain rooms with views of the York River. Singles/doubles are $47/52 in low season and rise to $70 for a double in high season.

The *Yorktown Motor Lodge* (☎ 757-898-5451, 8829 George Washington Hwy), 3 miles south on Route 17, is cheaper, with doubles from $35 in low season, $45 in high season.

The *Yorktown Pub* (☎ 757-898-8793), on Water St, is an absolute delight and the perfect place to take a break between redoubts and fortifications. It has great daily specials, plenty of beer, and is open 11 am to 2 am daily.

Nick's Seafood Pavilion (☎ 757-887-5269), also on Water St, specializes in interesting treatments of fish and shellfish such as seafood shish kebab. Lunch entrees start at $8, but dinner is far more expensive ($20 and up).

Getting There & Away
There is no cheap way to get to Yorktown without your own car, but there are a number of guided tours. If a group of four gets together, Williamsburg Limousine (☎ 757-877-0279) is an option: A morning trip to Jamestown is $20 per person; an afternoon trip to Yorktown is $20; a full day trip to both is $40 (including entry fees).

JAMES RIVER PLANTATIONS
Many of the homes of the slaveholding Virginian aristocracy were built along the banks of the James River. A plantation tour, from Richmond to Williamsburg along Route 5 (John Tyler Hwy), is not that long in distance, but if you visit most of the grand plantations and take time out to relax along the way, expect to fill a day. Block tickets to Shirley, Berkeley, Evelynton, and Sherwood Forest are available from any of these plantations ($28 for adults). Other plantations, south of the James River, are reached by the Jamestown-Scotland ferry.

Shirley
Dating from the 1660s, this plantation (☎ 804-829-5121), 501 Shirley Plantation Rd in Charles City, is the oldest plantation in Virginia. The fine brick outbuildings, which form a Queen Anne forecourt and mansion, have been in the hands of one family, the Carters, for more than 11 generations. Edward Hill, a Carter relative, was the first to settle here, and Robert E Lee's mother, Anne Hill Carter, was born here. Ever since, it has been the preserve of Virginia's wealthy landed gentry.

In 1862, after the battle of Malvern Hill, many of McClellan's wounded troops were treated here by members of the Carter family. This selfless act by loyal Southerners saved the mansion from later destruction by Butler's occupying Federal troops in 1864.

Inside the mansion is the famous carved walnut 'hanging' staircase that goes up three stories with no apparent support, original family furniture, rare books, silver, an old central-heating system (still in use), and portraits. Other original structures are the smokehouse, stable, and dovecote. Look for the diamond scratches on the windows and ask the guide to explain.

Shirley is open 9 am to 5 pm daily, and the last tour is at 4:30 pm. Admission is $8.50 for adults, $7.50 for seniors, $4.50 for children six to 12. It is located off Route 5, on a small peninsula jutting out into the James River.

Edgewood
This Gothic-style house (☎ 804-829-2962), 4800 John Tyler Memorial Hwy, dates from 1849 and is a historic landmark. Particularly beautiful is the Christmas tree display from November 1 to January 1, when women in Victorian garb guide you through the house.

VIRGINIA

The plantation is open 11 am to 5 pm Tuesday to Sunday from February to December. Admission is $8 for adults, $3 for children seven to 10. Admission to the Victorian Christmas is $9 for adults, $5 for children. You can stay overnight here as well. Rooms range from $115 to $190.

Berkeley

Berkeley (☎ 804-829-6018) is southeast of Richmond, off Route 5 along Farm Rd 633. It has many historical associations and was the spot where Thanksgiving was first celebrated in the New World in 1619 (a year before the Pilgrims arrived in New England). President (for a brief period in 1841) William Henry Harrison was born here, as was Benjamin Harrison, a signatory to the Declaration of Independence. (William Henry's grandson, another Benjamin Harrison, was elected president 47 years after his grandfather filled the office.)

During the Revolutionary War, in 1781, the plantation was ravaged by British troops led by Benedict Arnold. During the Civil War, in 1862, Union General George McClellan used the buildings as his headquarters, and one of his subordinate generals, Daniel Butterfield, composed the famous bugle tune 'Taps,' the 'lights out' tattoo, here. Butterfield's bugler, Oliver W Norton, was the first to sound the haunting tune, also at Berkeley – it was then taken up by both Union and Confederate forces.

Another world first was the use of observation balloons, just before the Seven Days Battles around Richmond in 1862. It was here that McClellan was relieved of his command. Also, the first corn whiskey in America was distilled at Berkeley. The house is open 9 am to 5 pm daily, and the grounds open at 8 am. Admission is $8.50 for adults, $7.65 for seniors, $4 for children.

Westover

Westover (☎ 804-829-2882) epitomizes the efforts of the English/American aristocracy. William Byrd II (1674–1744), a member of both the lower and upper colonial legislatures of Virginia (in Williamsburg at the time), had the plantation house built in 1730,

but after it was finished, he spent much of his time away from it, seemingly preferring the high life of London.

Unfortunately, the mansion is only open during Garden Week, in April (or by appointment), but it is worth being there at the right time to see the magnificent interior, with its moldings and carvings and the wrought-iron gates that Byrd brought from England, resplendent with their eagles atop the post aeries. The outbuildings and beautiful gardens are open 9 am to 6 pm daily.

Admission is $2 for adults, $1.50 for children. To get there, take Route 5, then Farm Route 633 to its end.

Evelynton

Once part of the original Westover Plantation land grant, this plantation (☎ 804-829-5075), 6701 John Tyler Memorial Hwy, is named after William Byrd's daughter Evelyn and was believed to have been part of the dowry she never got to use. Since 1847, it has been the home of the Ruffin family, whose patriarch Edmund fired the first shot of the Civil War at Fort Sumter. During the Peninsula Campaign of 1862, many of the buildings were destroyed, and the present colonial-style mansion was rebuilt years later. The house is furnished with antiques, and the surrounding gardens, known for brilliant displays of flowers, are still lovingly tended by descendants of the Ruffin family.

The plantation is open 9 am to 5 pm daily. Admission is $8.50 for adults, $7.50 for seniors, $4.50 for children six to 12. There are tours of the house and gardens, and a gift shop as well. It's located 5 miles west of the Charles City courthouse and is reached by Route 5.

Sherwood Forest

With neither a Sheriff of Nottingham nor a Robin Hood in sight, Virginia's Sherwood Forest instead celebrates a couple of America's famous sons – the ninth president, William Henry Harrison, and his successor, John Tyler. Built in the 1730s, and still owned by Tyler's direct descendants, the house (☎ 804-829-5377), 14501 John Tyler Memorial Hwy, is the longest wooden framed structure remaining in America (300 feet). Harrison once owned it, and Tyler retired here until his death in 1862. He wished to be buried here, but as he died during the Civil War, when the region was occupied by Union troops, he was buried in Richmond's Hollywood Cemetery instead.

The house is surrounded by immaculate grounds and original outbuildings (with an authentic tobacco barn). The grounds are open 9 am to 5 pm daily; admission to the grounds is $3 for adults, $1 children. The house is open 9 am to 5 pm April to December, January to March by appointment ($8.50 for adults, $8 for seniors, $5.50 for students, free for children under five). To get here, take Route 5 through Charles City and New Hope; a sign marks the entrance.

Belle Air

This frame plantation home (☎ 804-829-2431), 11800 John Tyler Memorial Hwy, near Charles City, dates from 1670 and is a Virginian and national historic landmark, the only surviving example of its type in the South. It is furnished with 18th-century antiques and includes an old kitchen, smokehouse, and herb garden. The house is open year-round by appointment only (except for Garden Week, in April). To get here, take Route 5 for 5 miles east of the Charles City courthouse.

Piney Grove at Southall's

Yet another property in James River plantation country, Piney Grove (☎ 804-829-2480), 16920 Southall Plantation Lane, off County Rd 615, is a rare early Tidewater log structure and is the oldest country store in the area (built in 1790). You can stay overnight in the grand, spacious rooms, well worth the $130/160 for doubles/triples and $170 for three in a suite. They have all the touches, right down to fresh mint julips.

Also nearby is the 1857 Ladysmith House and a nature trail. Piney Grove is open year-round by appointment; contact them for entry fees.

Smith's Fort

This plantation (☎ 757-294-3872), at 217 Smith's Fort Lane off Route 31, halfway between Surry Courthouse and the ferry landing, can be reached by the Jamestown-Scotland ferry. It is a brick colonial dwelling on land given by the Indian chief Powhatan to John Rolfe when he married Pocahontas. Included on the site are ruins of the 1609 'new fort' built by John Smith. It's open 10 am to 4 pm Tuesday to Saturday, noon to 4 pm Sunday from April to October. Admission is $4 for adults, $3 for seniors, $2 for students, $1 for children six to 18.

Brandon Gardens

This plantation (☎ 757-866-8486), 23105 Brandon Rd in Spring Grove, was originally a large land grant to John Martin, companion of Captain John Smith. It is a magnificent example of a James River estate (designed by Thomas Jefferson), with superb gardens spanning from the mansion to the river. The gardens are open 9 am to 5:30 pm daily ($5); you can visit the house by appointment or during Garden Week (in April).

To get there from Williamsburg, take the Jamestown-Scotland ferry to Surry County. Take Route 31, and turn northwest onto Route 10. Follow this into Prince George County and take County Rd 611 north to Brandon Gardens.

SOUTH OF JAMES RIVER

There is a real potpourri of attractions in this region, making it well worth a visit. The Surry County Chamber of Commerce (☎ 757-294-0066), the Isle of Wight Visitors Center (☎ 757-357-5182), at 130 Main Rd, in Smithfield; and the Hopewell Visitors Center (☎ 804-541-2461), 4100 Oaklawn Blvd, are good sources of information.

Bacon's Castle is the oldest documented brick house (1665) in English-speaking North America and is the only surviving high-Jacobean structure. It is surrounded by a sophisticated garden, believed to be the oldest on the continent. The castle (☎ 757-357-5976), 6½ miles east of Surry Courthouse, off Route 10 on County Rd 617, is open 10 am to 4 pm Tuesday to Saturday, noon to 4 pm Sunday from April to October (weekends only in March and November). Admission is $6 for adults, $3 for seniors, $4 for children six to 18.

VIRGINIA

Pocahontas

Thanks to the Walt Disney Co, the Historic Triangle now has the ultimate attraction to keep kids amused – the story of Pocahontas. Her appeal may actually inspire them to begin to understand a small aspect of Native American heritage. It is not uncommon to see parents cajoling their preschooler through the Jamestown site with promises such as 'There is a statue of Pocahontas here, can you help us find her?'.

The following account of Pocahontas' life is extracted from the narrative by Nancy Elgoff, a member of the staff of Jamestown Settlement.

The real Pocahontas (meaning 'playful one' or 'little wanton'; she was formally called Amonute and Matoaka) was born about 1596, the daughter of the powerful Powhatan, potentate of more than 30 Algonquian-speaking tribes in the coastal Virginia region.

When she was about 11, she met John Smith near the York River in 1607. Fiction probably blends with history in the account of how she saved Smith's life when she 'got his head in her armes, and laid his owne upon his to save him from death.' The following year, Pocahontas took food to the settlement at Jamestown in an effort to secure the release of Indian prisoners, and the next year, she warned Smith of a plot to take his life.

In 1613, she was kidnapped by one Samuel Argall for ransom. It took Powhatan some time to agree to the terms of the ransom, and the result was that Pocahontas remained with the English, was converted to Christianity, and baptized with the name of Rebecca. Soon after conversion, in 1614, she was married to the planter John Rolfe, who introduced tobacco as a cash crop in Virginia.

In 1616, Pocahontas, John Rolfe, and their son, Thomas, traveled to England in an effort to recruit more colonists for Virginia. While there, she was feted. She became ill on the return trip and died in March 1617. (Thomas returned to Virginia in the 1630s.)

Pocahontas now 'lives' as the most famous Native American (more famous even than Sitting Bull or Geronimo), and your knowledge of her life better be up to scratch or your kids will let you know! There are many 400th anniversary events associated with Pocahontas – yes, it was about 400 years ago that she was born – so there will be something for the kids to see. There are several interpretations of the way she looked: see the portraits by Mary Ellen Howe (1994), Jean Leon Ferris (c 1921), Robert Matthew Sully (1850s), and the Walt Disney Co (1994). The latter bears no resemblance, with her eyes well removed from her nose, but it is the one kids now recognize.

The **Chippokes Plantation State Park** (☎ 757-294-3625), on County Rd 633 off Route 10, includes one of the oldest continuously farmed plantations in the US, an 1854 manor house, formal gardens, and a Farm and Forestry Museum (in which a rooter and a bull-tongue plow take pride of place). It's open 1 to 5 pm Wednesday to Sunday from Memorial Day to Labor Day. Mansion admission is $3 for adults, $1.50 for children; the museum is $2/1. There are bicycles for hire and a swimming pool.

More unusual is the **Edwards' Smokehouse** (☎ 800-222-4267), 11381 Rolfe Hwy in Surry, where you can see Virginia hams being made (tours twice daily weekdays). Those fascinated by glowing carbon rods, two-headed fish, and Charles Burns' mutants should check out the **Surry Power Station** (☎ 757-357-5410), north of the Chippokes Plantation State Park.

An interesting archaeological excavation, **Flowerdew Hundred** was founded in 1619. The archaeological site (☎ 804-541-8897), at 1617 Flowerdew Hundred Rd, off Route 10 near Hopewell, now includes a museum, a detached plantation kitchen, and intriguing outdoor excavations. It is open 10 am to 5 pm Tuesday to Sunday from April to November; on Monday, you may visit by appointment only. Admission is $6 for adults, $4 for seniors, $3 for students.

There is a combination ticket for sites south of the James River. Included are Smith's Fort Plantation, Bacon's Castle, Chippokes Plantation mansion and museum, and the Edwards' Smokehouse, as well as a number of Hopewell attractions to the west ($17). Contact the Hopewell Visitors Center or Surry County Chamber of Commerce.

Most people visiting the plantations and sights south of the James River stay in or near Williamsburg (see Williamsburg and Around Williamsburg), but there are some good accommodations south of the river, including those in nearby Smithfield (see the Hampton Roads chapter).

The **Surrey House** (☎ 757-294-3389, 11865 *Rolfe Hwy*), in the heart of Surry, offers traditional Southern-style and Virginia dining. The menu here features the state's famous smoked ham, peanut soup, crab cakes, and peanut-raisin pie.

Hampton Roads

The extended region of Hampton Roads, from Williamsburg down to Virginia Beach, contains some 1.5 million people and includes Chesapeake, Hampton, Newport News, Norfolk, Portsmouth, Poquoson, and Suffolk. You will likely hear locals refer to Norfolk, Portsmouth, and Chesapeake as being on the 'south side' and Newport News and Hampton being on the 'peninsula.'

Hampton Roads is the name of the waterway that is the outlet of the James, Nansmond, and Elizabeth Rivers into the Chesapeake Bay and, by proximity, of the land around that waterway. The area is a bustling maritime area pocked with military bases, but don't come expecting just a conglomeration of concrete towers, overcrowded ports, and the incessant roar of powerful military jets. The cities of Hampton Roads are fringed by beaches and tidal wetlands, and the region has some charming historic precincts dating from the time of the first English settlement.

The *Susan Constant*, *Godspeed*, and *Discovery* first landed on the southern shore of Chesapeake Bay in 1607 before sailing up the James River to where Jamestown was established. This important connection with ships and the sea continues today.

The Revolutionary War highlighted the importance of the region and its proximity to the sea. On New Year's Day of 1776, more than two-thirds of Norfolk was destroyed in a fire set by the British. Later, the rest was destroyed at the order of the Revolutionaries so the British could not use it, and only the brick walls of St Paul's Church remained. In 1779, the British returned to ransack Portsmouth.

Norfolk was reconstructed after the war and resumed its status as an important world port. A yellow fever outbreak in 1855 lasted for more than four months, and 100 residents succumbed to the disease each day.

In 1861, Virginia seceded from the Union, and the Hampton Roads region was embroiled in war again. The historic battle between *Monitor* and *Merrimac* was fought in March 1862 (see the boxed text Battle of the Ironclads), and a month later the region was the focus of McClellan's Peninsula Campaign (see the Civil War chapter).

Reconstruction commenced in earnest after the war, and Norfolk prospered again. It was linked by rail to other states and, importantly, to the coal fields of western Virginia. The two world wars added to the prosperity of the port – the shipbuilding facilities of Hampton Roads were expanded, more military bases were established or refurbished to respond to the changes of

Highlights

- Norfolk – a buzzing city with a great waterfront and the superb space-age Nauticus museum

- In Hampton, the Virginia Air & Space Center as well as the Casemate Museum, Fort Monroe, and a host of African American heritage sites

- The small historic town of Smithfield – a perfect getaway with many nearby historic attractions

- Boat trips in Hampton Roads and out onto the expansive Chesapeake Bay

- Virginia Beach – for those seeking sun, sand, surfing, and nightlife

- The Great Dismal Swamp, which is really not so dismal

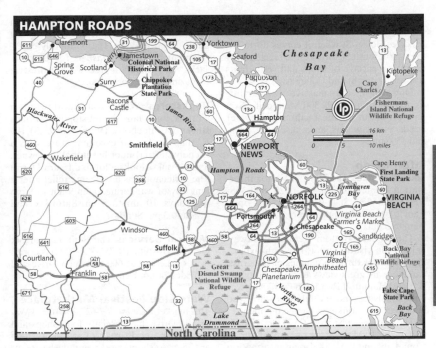

HAMPTON ROADS

modern warfare, and many wartime workers remained in the region.

The Cold War facilitated further development of the military installations, and the populated area expanded. Bridge, tunnel, and road links were built to connect dormitory suburbs to places of work. If anything, Hampton Roads now reflects the United States' new role as a peacekeeper and enforcer in the post–Cold War world. It was from here that some 40,000 military personnel embarked for the Middle East in 1991 during the Gulf War, as well as many to Kosovo in the Balkans in 1998–99.

NORFOLK

Norfolk (population 261,500), on the broad waters of Hampton Roads, has a vibrant city skyline and a wealth of attractions, such as the Waterside Festival Marketplace and the futuristic Nauticus – a late-20th-century equivalent of the Louvre (in its own technocratic way).

Transcending the fleshy delights of nearby Virginia Beach, Norfolk is enlivened by a revitalized downtown and the fashionable restaurant and shopping precinct of Ghent. It's a pity that most travelers pass through Norfolk rather than stopping off in a 'real' destination that oozes history.

Orientation

Norfolk is the hub of the Hampton Roads metropolitan area. On its north shore is Ocean View; across Hampton Roads waterway are Newport News and Hampton; to the east is Virginia Beach; and to the southwest, Portsmouth.

The main access routes are I-64 and I-664 (and the two bridge-tunnels) from Richmond and Williamsburg, Route 13 from the Eastern Shore and major cities to the north (via the Chesapeake Bay Bridge-Tunnel), Route 17 from North Carolina, Route 460 from Petersburg and Richmond, and Route 44 (which becomes I-264) from Virginia Beach.

Most of the attractions are arrayed along the east-west Waterside Drive, which becomes Boush St when it curves north. At the top of Boush St, turn west to reach trendy Ghent, an enclave of shops and restaurants (especially 21st St and Colley Ave).

Downtown, the massive MacArthur Center Shopping Mall, 300 Monticello Ave, has just about all the facilities a traveler needs, plus cinemas, an amusement park, and 150 stores.

Information

Tourist Offices The Norfolk Visitor Information Center (☎ 757-664-6620, 800-368-3097), 4th View St (I-64 exit 273), is open 9 am to 6 pm daily in the summer; otherwise, 9 am to 5 pm.

The Monkey Bottom Wetland Walkway, behind the visitor center, is worth exploring – it passes through patches of sea grass, and there are great views across Willoughby Bay and Hampton Roads. The walkway was once low-lying, and the families who lived here kept pet monkeys – hence the name.

The downtown Norfolk CVB (☎ 757-664-6620), 232 E Main St, is open 8:30 am to 5 pm daily, and there is also an information booth in the Waterside Festival Marketplace. Nauticus has an information desk open 10 am to 5 pm Tuesday to Saturday, and the MacArthur Center has one as well.

You can also check out the following website for the scoop on Norfolk: www.city.norfolk.va.us.

Money Two handy banks offering foreign exchange are Crestar Bank (☎ 757-624-5552), at the corner of Commercial Place and E Main St, and NationsBank (☎ 757-441-4707), at the corner of Atlantic and E Main Sts.

You will find convenient ATMs in the MacArthur Center and in the Waterside Festival Marketplace.

Post The main post office (☎ 757-640-8777) is at 600 Church St, at the corner of Brambleton Ave. There is another post office (☎ 757-622-4751) at 126 Atlantic St, on the corner of E Main St.

Newspapers & Magazines The main daily, the *Virginian-Pilot*, has a Friday gig guide called Preview. The bimonthly entertainment magazine *Flash* is for 'Jumpin' Jacks,' and there's a free weekly lifestyle magazine called *Port Folio*.

Bookstores While touring downtown Norfolk, book fans should stop in to Prince Books & Coffeehouse (☎ 757-622-9223), 109 E Main St. It's an excellent store with a friendly staff. (Rumor has it that the owner, Sarah Pishko, looks a lot like Laura Dern.) The coffeehouse is a welcome relief after a long day of wandering, open 9 am to 8 pm weekdays, 10 am to 8 pm Saturday, and 11 am to 3 pm Sunday.

Medical Services The Sentara Norfolk General Hospital (☎ 757-727-7000) is northwest of the city at 600 Gresham Drive and provides 24-hour emergency facilities.

Waterside Festival Marketplace

This marketplace (☎ 757-627-3300), 333 Waterside Drive, has specialty food shops and restaurants (see Places to Eat, later). There are 75 or so shops, kiosks, and pushcarts offering varied shopping. It is open year-round; the two lively nightclubs stay open until 2 am.

The **Town Point Park**, next to the marketplace, hosts more than 45 festivals and special events, more than 100 concerts annually, and a regular visit by tall ships – all events are free. Get a free calendar of events from the visitor centers.

The **Armed Forces Memorial**, in the park, is particularly moving. It has 20 inscriptions from letters written home by US service personnel killed in wartime. The letters are scattered on the ground as though they have been blown about by the wind. Included is that of Sarah Rosetta Wakeman, who fought in the Civil War disguised as a man, Lyons Wakeman.

Nauticus

Nauticus (National Maritime Center), an imposing 'battleship' of a museum (☎ 757-664-1000, 800-664-1080, www.nauticus.org), 1 Waterside Drive, on the downtown Norfolk

NORFOLK AREA

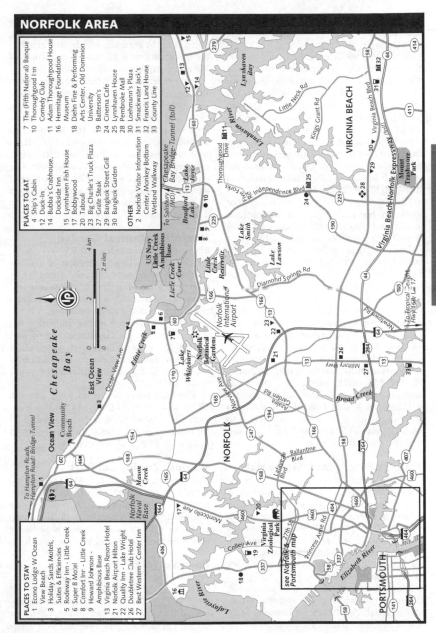

PLACES TO STAY
1 Econo Lodge W Ocean View Beach
3 Holiday Sands Motels, Suites & Efficiencies
5 Rodeway Inn - Little Creek
6 Super 8 Motel
8 Comfort Inn - Little Creek
9 Howard Johnson - Amphibious Base
13 Virginia Beach Resort Hotel
21 Norfolk Airport Hilton
22 Quality Inn - Lake Wright
26 Doubletree Club Hotel
27 Best Western - Center Inn

PLACES TO EAT
4 Ship's Cabin
12 Duck-In
14 Bubba's Crabhouse, Dockside Inn
15 Lynnhaven Fish House
17 Bobbywood
20 Tabouli
23 Big Charlie's Truck Plaza
27 Grate Steak
29 Bangkok Street Grill
30 Bangkok Garden

OTHER
2 Norfolk Visitor Information Center, Monkey Bottom Wetland Walkway
7 The (Fifth Natior al) Banque
10 Thoroughgood Inn Comedy Club
11 Adam Thoroughgood House
16 Hermitage Foundation Museum
18 Diehn Fine & Performing Arts Center, Old Dominion University
19 Batterson's
24 Cinema Cafe
25 Lynnhaven House
28 Pembroke Mall
30 Loehmann's Plaza
31 Smackwater Jack's
32 Francis Land House
33 County Line

VIRGINIA

waterfront, is a magnet for old and young alike and has many ingenious exhibits and entertaining shows.

Attractions include the first-ever 'group' of virtual-reality experiences; a submarine ride; the Aegis Theater, a multimedia naval battle show in which you participate in the defense of a ship (oops, didn't see that incoming projectile!); the Nauticus theater, a film presentation on a giant screen that rises to reveal the harbor outside; and touch pools. There are also one-of-a-kind computer and video interactive exhibits: a navigational sonar sub hunt, oil drilling, time travel, reef diving, flight simulators, and more.

The adjacent 600-foot deep-water pier hosts US Navy, foreign, and commercial vessels and also features spectacular laser shows (with music) on summer nights.

The new **Tugboat Museum** (☎ 757-627-4884) features the Tug *Huntington*, a '30s tugboat anchored alongside Nauticus. Admission is $2 for adults, $1 for children.

Nauticus is open 10 am to 5 pm daily from Memorial Day to Labor Day. It's open 10 am to 5 pm Tuesday to Saturday and noon to 5 pm Sunday the rest of the year. Admission is $7.50 for adults, $6.50 for seniors, and $5 for children.

The **Hampton Roads Naval Museum** (☎ 757-322-2987), within the Nauticus complex, interprets the naval history of Hampton Roads from the Revolution to modern times. It's open and 10 am to 5 pm Tuesday to Sunday and 9 am to 4 pm Monday; admission is free.

Douglas MacArthur Memorial

The MacArthur Memorial, in landscaped MacArthur Square in downtown Norfolk, is a site of four buildings. General MacArthur, the son of a soldier, had no real hometown. He chose to call Norfolk home because his mother was born here. Strange choice – a Navy town for a well-known Army soldier – but there would have been competition for adulation in Arlington!

There are several exhibition galleries. A 25-minute film, which glosses over the often-controversial life of General Douglas MacArthur, is screened here. The museum proper

(☎ 757-441-2965) is in Norfolk's stately 19th-century city hall. MacArthur's final resting place is in the rotunda, which, converted to his specifications, is filled with mementos of life and conquest in far-flung places.

Nine galleries around this add more fuel to the legend. The museum's extensive collection includes military and personal artifacts: 19th- and 20th-century medals, flags, paintings, weapons, equipment, the Japanese instrument of surrender that ended WWII, as well as MacArthur's distinctive corncob pipe, ostentatious military cap, and sunglasses. The gift shop houses his 1950 Chrysler Imperial staff car. The museum is free and is open 9 am to 5 pm Monday to Saturday and 11 am to 5 pm Sunday.

Norfolk Botanical Garden

These delightful gardens (☎ 757-441-5830), which include a large collection of azaleas, rhododendrons, camellias, and roses, are a great place to relax. The 12 miles of pathways can be covered on foot or by trackless train; there is also a canal-boat tour.

Adjacent to the Norfolk International Airport on Azalea Garden Rd (I-64 exit 279B), the gardens are open year-round from 9 am until sunset daily. Admission is $4 for adults, $3 for seniors, and $2 for youth under 19.

The boat tours and train tours operate 10 am to 4 pm mid-March to October. Individual tickets are $2.50 for adults and $1.50 for children, and combination boat and train tickets are $4 and $3, respectively.

Virginia Zoological Park

This 55-acre zoo (☎ 757-441-5227), 3500 Granby St, has more than 300 animals, a horticultural conservatory, an Okavango River delta exhibit, and a nearby park. It is open 10 am to 5 pm daily. Admission is $3.50 for adults, $3 for seniors, and $1.75 for children.

Fort Norfolk

At 810 Front St, on the banks of the Elizabeth River near Ghent, is a military fort (☎ 757-625-1720 on weekends) first commissioned by George Washington in 1794. The original brickwork and buildings date from

1810, and the powder magazine was built in 1854 by the Navy.

Today, the fort represents one of the best preserved and most original War of 1812 sites in America, and it is the oldest fort in the Hampton Roads area. Military reenactments are held here annually. The fort is open 1 to 4 pm Sunday. A donation of $2 per person or $5 per family is requested.

Moses Myers House

This 18th-century brick building (☎ 757-664-6283), 331 Bank St, combining late-Georgian and early-Federal architectural styles, was built in 1792 by a wealthy Jewish resident and shipping magnate. The majority of the furnishings are original and include rare pieces from England and China. The Myers family, who kept the house for six generations, were prominent members of Norfolk society.

The house is open 10 am to 5 pm Tuesday to Saturday and noon to 5 pm Sunday. Admission is $4 for adults and $2.50 for seniors and children. A combination ticket with the Willoughby-Baylor House, the Adam Thoroughgood House, and the Chrysler Museum of Art is $8.

Willoughby-Baylor House

This red-brick townhouse (☎ 757-664-6283), at 601 E Freemason St, built in 1794 by Captain William Willoughby, also combines Georgian and Federal architectural styles. It is furnished with period furniture (not original to the house) and is enhanced by a garden of herbs and flowers.

The house is open by appointment only 10 am to 5 pm Tuesday to Saturday. Admission is $4 for adults and $2.50 for seniors and children.

St Paul's Episcopal Church

St Paul's (☎ 757-627-4353), 201 St Paul's Blvd, was built in 1739 on the site of an earlier church that was built in 1641. It was the only building of note left after the burning of Norfolk on New Year's Day, 1776, by Lord Dunmore's troops. A cannonball fired from a British ship is still embedded in the wall. The graveyard is interesting; the church itself has been added on to over the years, representing a number of styles.

The church is open 10 am to 4 pm Tuesday to Friday; donations are requested.

Chrysler Museum of Art

Five minutes from Waterside, at 245 W Olney Rd in Ghent, is the superb Chrysler Museum of Art (☎ 757-664-6200), a fine collection of paintings, photographs, sculpture, drawings, and decorative arts. Included are paintings by Gainsborough, Renoir, Picasso, and American artists such as Jackson Pollock and Andy Warhol. One of the finest collections of glass (8000 pieces) in the country is displayed in the Institute of Glass.

The museum is open 10 am to 4 pm Tuesday to Saturday and 1 to 5 pm Sunday. Admission is $5 for adults and $3 for seniors and youth under 19.

Hunter House

This 1894 Victorian/Romanesque brick townhouse (☎ 757-623-9814), 240 W Freemason St, once belonged to a doctor. It now features stained glass, original furnishings, and a collection of early 20th-century medical memorabilia. The house is open 10 am to 3:30 pm Wednesday to Saturday and Sunday 12:30 to 3:30 pm from April to December. Admission is $3 for adults, $2 for seniors, and $1 for children.

Hermitage Foundation Museum

About 3 miles north of downtown Norfolk, this museum (☎ 757-423-2052), 7637 North Shore Rd, on 13 wooded acres alongside the Lafayette River, was once owned by a textile tycoon. The Tudor-style mansion, built in 1908, houses one of the largest private collections of Oriental art in the country and has several fine examples of decorative arts. The museum is open 10 am to 5 pm Monday to Saturday and 1 to 5 pm Sunday year-round. Admission is $4 for adults, $1 for youth under 19.

d'Art Center

This center (☎ 757-625-4211), 125 College Place, is your chance to see art in the making. It consists of studios where 40 artists create,

NORFOLK & PORTSMOUTH

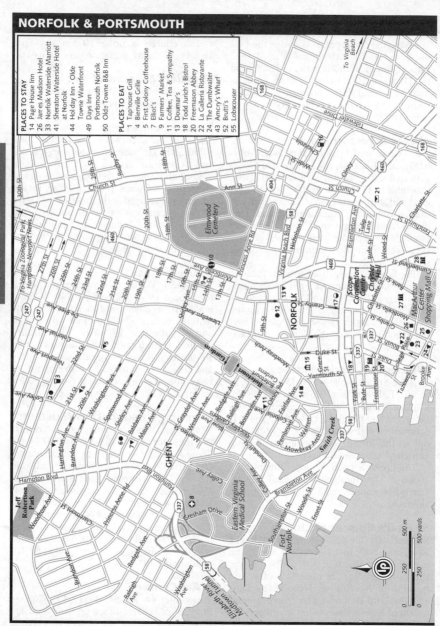

PLACES TO STAY
14 Page House Inn
26 Jarres Madison Hotel
33 Norfolk Waterside Marriott
41 Sheraton Waterside Hotel
44 Hol day Inn - Olde
    Towne Waterfront
    at Norfolk
49 Days Inn
50 Olde Towne B&B Inn
    Portsmouth Norfolk

PLACES TO EAT
1   Tap-house Grill
4   Bienville Grille
5   First Colony Coffeehouse
7   Elliot's
9   Farmers' Market
11 Coffee, Tea & Sympathy
13 Doumar's
18 Todd Jurich's Bistrol
20 Freemason Abbey
22 La Galleria Ristorante
24 The Dumbwaiter
43 Amcry's Wharf
52 Brutti's
55 Lobscouser

NORFOLK & PORTSMOUTH

P Parking Area

OTHER
2 Sudsy s Wash & Pub Laundry
3 Mang's
6 Naro Expanced Cinema
8 Sentara Norfolk General Hospital
10 Main TRT Office
12 Harrison Opera House
15 Chrysler Museum of Art
16 Mark IV Lounge & Restaurant
17 Greyhound/Trailways Bus Depot
19 Hunter House
21 Main Post Office
23 d'Art Center
25 Wells Theatre (Virginia Stage Company)
27 Moses Myers House
28 Willoughby-Baylor House
29 Nauticus, Hampton Roads
   Naval Museum, Tugboat
   Museum, Tug Huntington
30 Armed Forces Memorial

31 Waterside Festival Marketplace
32 Norfolk Visitor Information Center
34 TRT Terminal
35 NationsBank
36 Post Office
37 Douglas MacArthur Memorial
38 Crestar Bank
39 St Paul's Episcopal Church
40 Harbor Tours
42 The Boathouse
45 Hill House
46 Portside Visitor Information Center
47 Olde Towne Trolley
48 Elizabeth River Ferry, Carrie B Landing
51 Lightship Portsmouth
53 Virginia Sports Hall of Fame
54 Commodore Theatre
56 Children's Museum of Virginia
57 Portsmouth Visitor Information Center
58 Portsmouth Naval Shipyard Museum

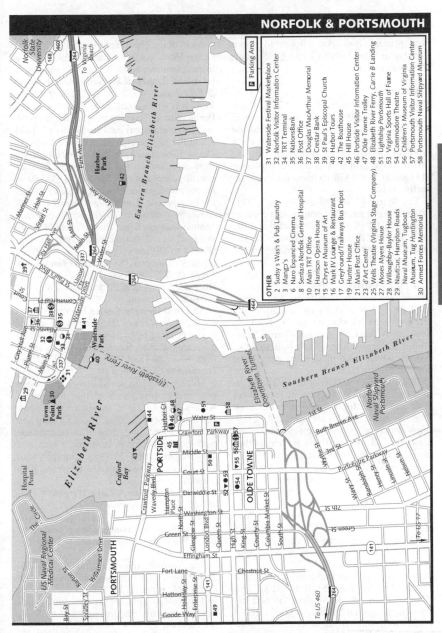

VIRGINIA

display, and sell their original artwork – drawings, paintings, ceramics, jewelry, and photography. It's open 10 am to 6 pm Tuesday to Saturday and 1 to 5 pm Sunday; admission is free.

Cruises

The *American Rover* (☎ 757-627-7245), a magnificent 135-foot, three-masted topsail schooner, cruises Hampton Roads and the Norfolk naval base. These trips depart daily April to October from Waterside and last two to three hours. A two-hour trip costs $14 for adults and $7 for children; call for departure times.

The *Spirit of Norfolk* (☎ 757-627-7771) offers daytime narrated cruises and evening dinner cruises of Hampton Roads and the naval base; it departs from Waterside and costs $20 to $49 for adults, depending on the meal.

Special Events

In mid-April, Norfolk hosts the Azalea Festival (☎ 757-664-2523) to celebrate the city's role as headquarters for NATO's Supreme Allied Commander Atlantic. It includes a parade and an air spectacular. Events, which take place throughout the city, are usually free.

In early June, the Harborfest/Seawall Festival (☎ 757-441-2345) is held at Town Point Park and along the downtown waterfront. There is music, food, entertainment, a tall-ships display, air shows, nautical races, and fireworks – all are free. There are many other festivals in and around Hampton Roads; check the 'Norfolk Visitors' Guide,' available at various lodgings and visitor centers.

Places to Stay

Across from the Chrysler Museum, the *Page House Inn* (☎ 757-625-5033, 800-599-7659, 323 Fairfax Ave, www.pagehouseinn.com) is in a restored Georgian home with magnificently furnished suites (check out the cappuccino machine, imported from Italy). Classy doubles cost $120 to $200. The *Bianca Boat & Breakfast*, owned by the same people and located at the Norfolk/Portsmouth Waterfront, is extremely popular. For more information, contact the Page House Inn.

Most of the cheap hotels and motels are at Ocean View, which is a considerable distance from downtown Norfolk and is considered 'a bit rough.' The *Holiday Sands Motel, Suites & Efficiencies* (☎ 757-583-2621, 1330 E Ocean View Ave), 4 miles east of the Hampton Roads Bridge-Tunnel, is on the beach and has a pool; in the low season, rooms are $45 to $70 (add $25 in the high season). The *Econo Lodge W Ocean View Beach* (☎ 757-480-9611, 9601 4th View St), close to the fishing piers, has off-season singles/doubles for $46/50 ($55/60 in the high season) and efficiencies for $57 to $69 for four people. The *Super 8 Motel* (☎ 757-588-7888, 7940 Shore Drive), off Route 60, is another budget choice. Rooms cost $44 to $49 in the off season; during the high season, rates are $54 to $63 for singles and $59 to $69 for doubles. Close by is the *Rodeway Inn – Little Creek* (☎ 757-588-3600, 7969 Shore Drive). Rooms start at $32 in the low season and cost $60 to $90 in summer.

The *Best Western Center Inn* (☎ 757-461-6600, 235 N Military Hwy), a block north of the junction of I-264 and Route 13, is a good mid-range choice. Rooms cost $50 to $60 in the low season (add $10 in the summer). The *Doubletree Club Hotel* (☎ 757-461-9192, 880 N Military Hwy), in the Military Circle shopping center just south of the junction of Routes 58 and 13, is an impeccable place and is justifiably popular. There's a pool and a dining room, and they offer homemade cookies (the recipe is kept under lock and key). Singles cost $75 to $88, doubles $90 to $98, in the low season (add $7 in the high season).

The *Quality Inn – Lake Wright* (☎ 757-461-6251, 6280 Northampton Blvd) has a lounge, restaurant, pool, tennis courts, and a golf course and driving range. Rooms cost $69 to $79 in the winter and $85 to $95 in the high season.

The *Norfolk Airport Hilton* (☎ 757-466-8000, 1500 N Military Hwy), at Route 13 and Route 165, is near a lot of corporate offices, and its restaurants are known for award-winning cuisine. Singles cost $84 to $134; doubles cost $94 to $139.

The downtown area has a few upmarket accommodations. The **Sheraton Waterside Hotel at Norfolk** (☎ 757-622-6664, 777 Waterside Drive) is on the promenade next to the Waterside Festival Marketplace. The lounge looks out over the water, and there is al fresco dining in the restaurant. Singles and doubles cost $90 to $145, not including parking.

The **Norfolk Waterside Marriott** (☎ 757-627-4200, 235 E Main St) is across the road from the downtown visitor center. The hotel has al fresco dining, an upstairs restaurant with an adjoining piano lounge, a rooftop pool, and a health club. Singles and doubles cost $125 year-round.

The **James Madison Hotel** (☎ 757-622-6682, 345 Granby St), near the MacArthur Center, is a superb and luxurious boutique hotel with disabled facilities, a lounge, and a coffee shop. Standard rooms cost $79 to $149, and suites cost $109.

Places to Eat

Look for the *Port Folio* Dining listings, which indicate price-range information and whether a place has won a Golden Fork or Hall of Fame status. The **Farmers' Market** (☎ 757-625-2897, 1400 Granby St) has heaps of seasonal produce and is the place for self-caterers.

Coffee, Tea and Sympathy (☎ 757-622-8933, 612 Colonial Ave) may very well be what you need; it's open for all meals daily. **First Colony Coffeehouse** (☎ 757-622-0149), on Colonial Ave, has been around for a long time. It's open daily for inexpensive meals (and coffee), and there are live folk and acoustic performances some nights.

For an old-fashioned ice cream on a cone, check out **Doumar's** (☎ 757-627-4163, 919 Monticello Ave), home of the world's original ice-cream-cone machine. Abe Doumar invented the cone at the St Louis Exposition in 1904, and today his nephew still makes cones with the old machine at his drive-in. Doumar's is open year-round except Sundays. There are tours at 10 am and 3 pm or by appointment. The $2 fee for the tour includes an ice cream with…the cone! Favorite flavors are chocolate, butter pecan,

vanilla, strawberry, and lime and orange sherbet. There's also curbside service.

North of downtown, **Tabouli** (☎ 757-627-1143, 4140 Granby St) is one of the best choices for vegetarian cuisine – it has falafel, tabouli, tahini, and mint tea – as well as Mediterranean meat dishes. Belly dancers perform some nights.

Also north of downtown, **Bobbywood** (☎ 757-440-7515, 7515 Granby St) is a husband-and-wife affair that is painted neon green and has an open kitchen and stone hearth oven from an old bakery. The food is 'fun' nouvelle American – such as soft-shelled crab, great mashed potatoes, thin fried onions, pasta, and gourmet pizza.

The **Bienville Grille** (☎ 757-625-5427, 723 W 21st St) has a great dinner menu that incorporates crawfish, Louisiana oysters, gumbo, and Sunday brunch and is enjoyed by all. The express lunches start at $4.95.

La Galleria Ristorante (☎ 757-623-3939, 120 College Place), a great eatery with a northern Italian menu, has an authentic wood-burning pizza oven. It's open for lunch weekdays and for dinner Monday to Saturday.

The Dumbwaiter (☎ 757-623-3663, 117 Tazewell St), a fun place with a distinctive 'warehouse' decor, has Mississippi-influenced meals (and gourmet meatloaf). It is open for lunch and dinner weekdays and for dinner only on Saturdays. Entrees cost $10 to $15. This place defies further description – check it out.

Elliot's (☎ 757-625-0259, 1421 Colley Ave), in Ghent, is a consistent local favorite, with meatless entrees, seafood, a children's menu, and the great hamburgers on which it has built its reputation. Entrees cost $9 to $14.

The **Taphouse Grill** (☎ 757-627-9172, 931 W 21st St) is open daily for 'beer friendly' food and a fine selection of microbrews. Entrees cost about $10.

Todd Jurich's Bistro! (☎ 757-622-2310, 210 W York St) has those California-trend (contemporary) meals, combined with a little bit of continental, into which are tossed seafood and fresh farm produce. Dinner entrees cost $20 to $30.

Freemason Abbey (☎ 757-622-3966, 209 W Freemason St), in an old renovated (and deconsecrated?) church building, has a traditional American menu that includes seafood platters ($18), lobster ($16), and prime rib ($15). It is open daily for lunch ($5 to $8) and dinner.

East of downtown, the *Grate Steak* (☎ 757-461-5501), in the Best Western Center Inn (see Places to Stay), is one of those places where you pick a steak and cook it yourself (don't burn it, or you will pay for it). A meal for two will cost about $25 to $30.

In Ocean View, *Ship's Cabin* (☎ 757-362-4659, 4110 E Ocean View Ave) is superbly situated with views of Chesapeake Bay. Its famous oysters bingo (sautéed in butter, shallots, and wine), blackened tuna, crab soup and cakes, and whiskey pudding entice the locals to return. A dinner for two costs around $50, but it's worth it.

Entertainment

There is plenty of music in this part of the world, as many of the bands on the way to Virginia Beach stop here. The scene includes jazz, blues, country, folk/acoustic, bluegrass, and rock in all their modern manifestations. For current entertainer and venue listings, see the periodicals listed in Newspapers & Magazines, earlier.

Outside the downtown area, *The (Fifth National) Banque* (☎ 757-480-3600, 1849 E Little Creek Rd) has country & western music and free dance lessons. Also, there's a mixed bag of live music at the Quality Inn – Lake Wright (see Places to Stay, earlier). *Batterson's* (☎ 757-440-1901, 5103 Colley Ave) has rock music Wednesday to Saturday.

For rock music downtown, try *The Boathouse* (☎ 757-671-8100, 119 Bessie's Place), at the Waterside (the cover is $5 to $20); *Mango's* (☎ 757-622-4462, 738 W 22nd St); and Chrysler Hall (see below) for international headliners.

Also downtown, the *Mark IV Lounge & Restaurant* (☎ 757-624-9330, 900 Virginia Beach Blvd) has jazz weekend nights. The *Naro Expanded Cinema* (☎ 757-625-6276),

on Colley Ave, is an excellent place with atmosphere. It screens art-house movies, and there are often live jazz and blues performances here.

There are regular opera performances by the Virginia Opera, one of the top regional opera companies in the country, in the *Harrison Opera House* (☎ 757-623-1223), near the corner of Virginia Blvd and Llewellyn Ave. There have even been world premieres of operas here. The season is October to March, and the box office hours are 9 am to 5 pm weekdays.

There are classical-music performances by the Virginia Symphony at *Chrysler Hall* (☎ 757-664-6464, 415 St Paul's Blvd), which is part of the Scope Cultural and Convention Center complex, and at the Chandler Recital Hall of the *Diehn Fine & Performing Arts Center* (☎ 757-683-4061). The Virginia Symphony has performed for more than 75 years, and its Peanut Butter & Jam family series is very popular.

The *Virginia Stage Company* (☎ 757-627-1234) performs at the Wells Theatre, at the corner of Tazewell St and Monticello Ave, from September to May (performances are Tuesday to Sunday).

Spectator Sports

The Norfolk Tides, a Class AAA baseball farm club for the New York Mets, play at *Harbor Park* (☎ 757-622-2222). Box seats cost about $8, and reserved seats cost around $5.

The Hampton Roads Admirals are part of the East Coast Hockey League, with a 'league' of the most boisterous and vocal fans you can ever hope to hear. They play at *Norfolk Scope* (☎ 757-664-6464, 415 St Paul's Blvd), on the corner of Brambleton Ave. The season commences in October and continues to March.

Getting There & Away

Norfolk International Airport (☎ 757-857-3351) is served by American, Delta, Northwest, Southeast, TWA, United, and US Airways. There is a shuttle service (☎ 757-857-1231) from the airport to town.

The Greyhound/Trailways terminal (☎ 757-625-7500) is at 701 Monticello Ave. From here, there are services to Williamsburg, Richmond, DC, and Maryland via the Chesapeake Bay Bridge-Tunnel.

The nearest Amtrak terminal is 21 miles away in Newport News (see later in the chapter), but there is a free Thruway bus to and from downtown Norfolk.

Getting Around

The Tidewater Regional Transit (TRT; ☎ 757-640-6300) bus system serves all of the south side of Hampton Roads (Chesapeake, Portsmouth, Virginia Beach, and Norfolk). Get a timetable from the main bus office at 1500 Monticello Ave, open 7:30 am to 7:30 pm weekdays, or at the Waterside terminal, which is open daily. The cost within one zone is $1.50, with an extend-a-ride option of 75¢. There are Crossroads connections to the PENTRAN system of Newport News and Hampton.

TRT offers the Norfolk trolley tour throughout downtown and into Ghent. The trolley stops at most city attractions on its one-hour circuit; you can get off and then catch a later trolley. The trolley trundles 11 am to 4 pm daily from late May to early September. Tickets cost $3.50 for adults and $1.75 for seniors and children.

The Elizabeth River Ferry (☎ 757-640-6300) plies between the Norfolk Waterside and Portside daily (see Portsmouth).

PORTSMOUTH

Portsmouth (population 103,500), across the Elizabeth River from Norfolk, is the nation's oldest and largest naval shipyard, with a long and fascinating history. As early as 1620, king's grants were offered to mariners to encourage them to settle here and build ships. By 1636, a ferry linked Portsmouth to Norfolk, and in 1716, William Crawford donated land for a market, church, courthouse, and jail.

The Gosport naval shipyard was established in 1767, and the first warship built here was the *Chesapeake*. In 1801, the Gosport naval shipyard was renamed Norfolk naval shipyard – it was, by then, the largest such facility in the country.

Portsmouth was affected by war on several occasions. During the Revolutionary War, the town was bombarded by British ships. Benedict Arnold set up a line of defenses at Fort Nelson, now Hospital Point (site of the US Naval Hospital). The town was abandoned by the British when Cornwallis moved his headquarters to Yorktown.

In 1861, Union troops captured and burned the port, but it was later recaptured by the Confederates. They raised the sunken *Merrimac*, refitted it as the first ironclad battleship, and renamed it CSS *Virginia* (see the boxed text Battle of the Ironclads).

Orientation & Information

Portsmouth can be reached from Norfolk via the Midtown Tunnel (Route 58), the Downtown Tunnel (I-264), or the Elizabeth River Ferry. Most of the attractions are near Portside; historic 'Olde Towne' is close by.

The Portsmouth Visitor Information Center (☎ 757-393-5111, 800-767-8782, www.ci.portsmouth.va.us), 6 Crawford Parkway, is open daily and has a gift shop. Get a copy of the 'Olde Towne Walking Tour' (with its glossary of architectural terms). There is another information center at Portside.

Olde Towne

There is still a large concentration of noteworthy 18th- and 19th-century dwellings in Olde Towne, but most are not open to the public. The TRT **Olde Towne Trolley Tour** (☎ 757-640-6300), which covers all the major buildings of interest, leaves from near the Portside Visitor Information Center noon to 4 pm daily from late May to early September. Tickets cost $3.50 for adults and $1.75 for seniors and children.

Particularly significant is the **Hill House** (☎ 757-393-8591), 221 North St, an English basement-style house built around 1830. It is open 1 to 5 pm Wednesday and weekends from April to December. Admission is $3 for adults and $1 for children.

The **Virginia Sports Hall of Fame** (☎ 757-393-8031), 420 High St, celebrates athletes born and raised in Virginia. It's open daily except Monday and is free.

The Battle of the Ironclads

When Union forces evacuated Norfolk naval yard in the spring of 1861, they failed to fully immobilize the steam frigate USS *Merrimac*, even though it had been burnt and scuttled. When the Confederates captured the yard, they raised the hulk, covered it with a superstructure of 24 inches of oak topped with four inches of steel plating, and rechristened the steel monster CSS *Virginia*.

After *Virginia* had sunk a few wooden ships and mocked the Union shore batteries, authorities in DC began to panic. But, in one of the war's great coincidences, less than 24 hours after *Virginia* had first run amok, the recently commissioned and unorthodox-looking USS *Monitor*, with its revolving turret sporting two 11-inch guns, steamed into Hampton Roads.

The ensuing battle – on March 9, 1862 – was indecisive; the ships withdrew to opposite sides of Hampton Roads, each with a few dents, but both were still operational.

After their initial battle, the two ironclads faced each other across Hampton Roads for two months, but no shots were fired. *Virginia*, just by being there, paralyzed free movement by Union forces up and down the James River.

Just before McClellan ordered the systematic bombardment of the Norfolk defenses on May 4, 1862, Joe Johnston withdrew the Confederate forces, and since the ship's deep draught prevented escape up the James River, they were forced to abandon *Virginia*. The Confederates blew the ship up on May 10. Not long afterward, the *Monitor* sank in a heavy storm. It was rediscovered only in the last few decades.

These two ships changed the face of naval warfare forever. Because the *Monitor* could have sunk all the wooden ships in the Royal Navy in one engagement, wooden ships in all the world's navies were rendered obsolete, and ironclads became the norm.

Portsmouth Naval Shipyard Museum

This museum (☎ 757-393-8591) near the waterfront has many models of 18th-century warships (including the CSS *Virginia* and the USS *Delaware)* and exhibits on all aspects of shipbuilding. It is open 10 am to 5 pm Tuesday to Saturday and 1 to 5 pm Sunday; admission is $1.

The *Portsmouth* (☎ 757-393-8983), at the London Slip, is a retired Coast Guard lightship (No 101). Used to guide mariners away from dangerous shoals, the ship was commissioned in 1915 – the last of its class – and has been restored to its original condition. Board it 10 am to 5 pm Tuesday to Saturday and 1 to 5 pm Sunday; tickets cost $1.

Children's Museum of Virginia

Kids will be easily entertained at this hands-on participatory museum (☎ 757-393-5258), 221 High St, focusing on science, art, music, and technology. It is open 10 am to 5 pm Tuesday to Saturday and 1 to 5 pm Sunday. Admission is $4 and includes entry to the planetarium.

Cruises

A Mississippi-style paddle wheeler called *Carrie B* departs daily from April to October for a narrated 1½-hour cruise of the naval dockyards and the site of the *Monitor/Merrimac* battle. Carrie B Harbor Tours (☎ 757-393-4735) is at the end of Bay St in Portsmouth. Tickets cost $10 for adults and $5 for children; 2½-hour cruises cost $12 and $6, respectively.

Places to Stay & Eat

The *Days Inn Portsmouth Norfolk* (☎ 757-399-4414, 1031 London Blvd), the best budget option in town, is close to restaurants and the ferry. Singles/doubles cost $45/50 to $99/110 all year.

The *Holiday Inn – Olde Towne Waterfront* (☎ 757-393-2573, 8 Crawford Parkway) is near the waterfront and Olde Towne. The rooms are a good value – $83/89 for singles/doubles (add $10 in the high season) – and some have water views. There is a pool and a restaurant overlooking the Elizabeth River.

Good B&Bs include the **Olde Towne B&B Inn** (☎ 757-397-5462, 420 Middle St), a gracious 1885 Victorian home; for others, ask at the visitor center.

Portsmouth is known for its fine seafood restaurants. **Amory's Wharf** (☎ 757-399-0991, 10 Crawford Parkway) is a family-run place with exceptional water views. There are reasonably priced specials on weeknights. **Lobscouser** (☎ 757-397-2728, 337 High St) is open daily for lunch and dinner; the seafood is fresh and the desserts homemade.

Brutti's (☎ 757-393-1923, 467 Dinwiddie St) is a good cafe in which to while away time and is known for yummy 'bagelnutz' (cream cheese baked inside a bagel).

Entertainment
The restored Art Deco **Commodore Theatre** (☎ 757-393-6962, 421 High St) was built in 1945. You can have a meal there as you enjoy the movie (on the main floor), and there is the usual theater seating in the balcony. It is open for Wednesday matinees at 2 pm and daily in the evenings at 6 and 9 pm. Patrons can ring the kitchen for snacks and drinks.

Getting There & Away
The Elizabeth River Ferry (☎ 757-222-6100) between Norfolk and Portsmouth is a Mississippi-style riverboat that makes the five-minute crossing daily. The ferries leave every 30 minutes or so; tickets are 75¢ for adults, 35¢ for seniors and the disabled, and 50¢ for children.

TRT bus Nos 41, 45, 46, 47, and 50 pass near the visitor centers.

HAMPTON
The city of Hampton (population 134,000), north of Hampton Roads, has a rich history. Two years after the first settlement at Jamestown, a fort was established here. Some say the infamous pirate Blackbeard met his end here in 1718 (or was it at Ocracoke Island, North Carolina?).

Hampton was razed by retreating Confederates during the Civil War, and many of its old buildings were destroyed. Fort Monroe remained in Union hands throughout the war. Today, Hampton has a major NASA research center, the Hampton University Museum, Buckroe Beach, and other interesting attractions.

Orientation & Information
Hampton is easily reached from I-64 and Route 60, as both pass through the city before reaching the Hampton Roads Bridge-Tunnel. Alternatively, access to the peninsula is possible via I-664 and Monitor-Merrimac Bridge-Tunnel (the 'M&M').

The Hampton Visitor Center (☎ 757-727-1102), 710 Settlers Landing Rd (I-64 exit 267), has an audiovisual presentation and a gift shop.

Fort Monroe & Casemate Museum
On the north side of Hampton Roads, on Old Point Comfort, sits Fort Monroe, America's largest stone fort. It was built between 1819 and 1834 with thick brick walls meant to withstand bombardment from the sea and a moat intended to repel ground attacks. Throughout the Civil War, it remained in Union hands, although the surrounding territory was controlled by the Confederates.

Today, its exhibits include the prison cell of Jefferson Davis, in a casemate (chamber) set in the walls, Civil War artifacts (including a description of the *Monitor/Merrimac* battle), and details of the military careers of Robert E Lee and Edgar Allan Poe, both of whom served here in the antebellum period.

The casemate museum (☎ 757-727-3391), in Casemate No 20, on Bernard Rd, is open 10:30 am to 4:30 pm daily and is free. To get there, take Route 258 (an extension of Mercury Blvd) to its end and enter the fort through the fort wall.

Virginia Air & Space Center
This is the official visitor center (☎ 757-727-0800, www.vasc.org) for the NASA Langley Research Center, at 600 Settlers Landing Rd. There are interactive exhibits, suspended

HAMPTON & NEWPORT NEWS

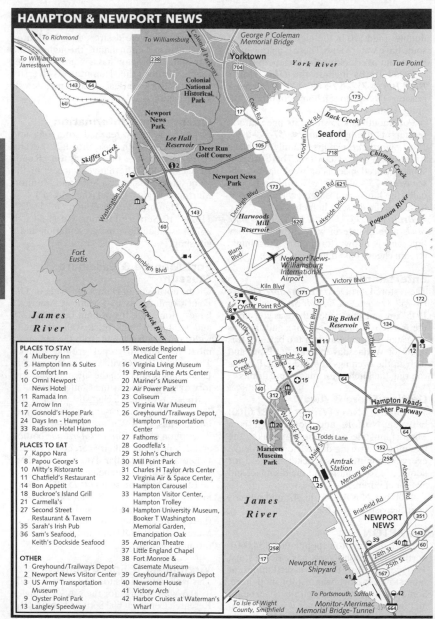

PLACES TO STAY
4 Mulberry Inn
5 Hampton Inn & Suites
6 Comfort Inn
10 Omni Newport
   News Hotel
11 Ramada Inn
12 Arrow Inn
17 Gosnold's Hope Park
24 Days Inn - Hampton
33 Radisson Hotel Hampton

PLACES TO EAT
7 Kappo Nara
8 Papou George's
10 Mitty's Ristorante
11 Chatfield's Restaurant
14 Bon Appetit
18 Buckroe's Island Grill
21 Carmella's
27 Second Street
   Restaurant & Tavern
35 Sarah's Irish Pub
36 Sam's Seafood,
   Keith's Dockside Seafood

OTHER
1 Greyhound/Trailways Depot
2 Newport News Visitor Center
3 US Army Transportation
   Museum
9 Oyster Point Park
13 Langley Speedway

15 Riverside Regional
   Medical Center
16 Virginia Living Museum
19 Peninsula Fine Arts Center
20 Mariner's Museum
22 Air Power Park
23 Coliseum
25 Virginia War Museum
26 Greyhound/Trailways Depot,
   Hampton Transportation
   Center
27 Fathoms
28 Goodfella's
29 St John's Church
30 Mill Point Park
31 Charles H Taylor Arts Center
32 Virginia Air & Space Center,
   Hampton Carousel
33 Hampton Visitor Center,
   Hampton Trolley
34 Hampton University Museum,
   Booker T Washington
   Memorial Garden,
   Emancipation Oak
35 American Theatre
37 Little England Chapel
38 Fort Monroe &
   Casemate Museum
39 Greyhound/Trailways Depot
40 Newsome House
41 Victory Arch
42 Harbor Cruises at Waterman's
   Wharf

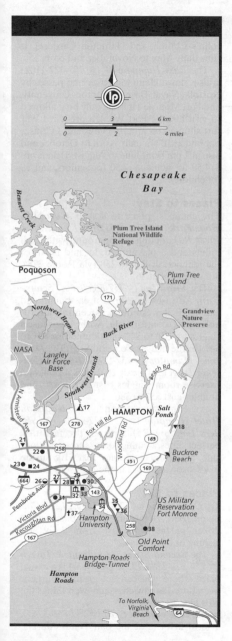

VIRGINIA

aircraft, a space gallery with the *Apollo 12* command module and lunar lander, a Mars meteorite, a moon rock, and a 300-seat IMAX theater. The history of flight and the exploration of space are the themes here. The NASA Langley Motor Tour, which takes you to see the Langley Air Force Base and the NASA research facility, departs from here daily in summer; the cost is included in the admission fee.

The center is open 10 am to 5 pm Monday to Wednesday and 10 am to 7 pm Thursday to Sunday from Memorial Day to Labor Day; otherwise, 10 am to 5 pm daily. It also opens evenings for special events and IMAX films; call ☎ 757-727-0900 for information on scheduled events. For exhibits only, admission is $6 for adults, $5 for seniors, and $4 for children (add $3 for an IMAX show, and add $5 for two IMAX shows). For an IMAX show only, it's $5.50 for adults, $4.50 for seniors and children.

Hampton University Museum
Visiting this museum (☎ 757-727-5308), in the Academy Building of Hampton University campus, is an absolute must. The outstanding collection, started in 1868, has examples of traditional art from African, Asian, Pacific Islander, and Native American cultures.

The university was originally established as a freedmen's school, and an early student was Booker T Washington (see the boxed text in the Piedmont chapter). Today, there are contemporary works by African American artists in the museum and on campus. The museum is open 8 am to 5 pm weekdays and noon to 4 pm weekends; admission is free.

Little England Chapel & St John's Church
There are two churches of note in Hampton. The Little England Chapel (☎ 757-723-6803), 4100 Kecoughtan Rd, was built circa 1879. It is the only known remaining African American missionary chapel in Virginia, and it is both a state and national historic landmark. The chapel's sanctuary holds a permanent exhibit of the religious lives of post–Civil

War African Americans in Virginia. It's open 10 am to 2 pm Tuesday, Wednesday, Friday and Saturday as well as by appointment.

One of the few surviving buildings from the pre–Revolutionary era is St John's Church (☎ 757-722-2567), 100 W Queens Way, in Old Hampton. Built in 1728, it is believed to be the nation's oldest English-speaking parish in continuous use. Of interest is a stained-glass window depicting the baptism of Pocahontas. The church is open 9 am to 3:30 pm weekdays and to noon Saturday; entry is free.

Other Attractions

The city's most bizarre attraction is **Air Power Park** (☎ 757-727-1163), 413 W Mercury Blvd, proof that people still have a macabre fascination for missiles and firepower.

At the other end of the sensibility scale is the **Hampton Carousel**, a beautifully restored wooden 1920 carousel with 48 horses and two chariots, carved by a real melting pot of European immigrants. Having stood at Buckroe Beach Amusement Park for 60 years before restoration, it now revolves at 602 Settlers Landing Rd. It is open 10 am to 8 pm Monday to Saturday and noon to 6 pm Sunday from April to October. Rides cost 50¢.

The **Langley Speedway** (☎ 757-865-1100), 3165 North Armistead Ave, seats 6500 and has the Saturday-night sanction for Winston series races. **Buckroe Beach**, at the eastern end of Route 351, is the haunt of swimmers, and for those not wanting to get into the water, there are parks and picnic facilities.

North of Buckroe Beach is the pristine **Grandview Nature Preserve** (☎ 757-727-6347), an estuarine wildlife refuge that will satisfy the avid birder. Its entrance is at the corner of Beach Drive and State Park Rd.

If you take the Mallory St exit off I-64, you come to **Phoebus**, a fascinating little enclave with bookstores, craft shops, and a couple of great eateries. The 1908 **American Theatre** (☎ 757-727-2787) is being renovated as an arts center. See Places to Eat for the restaurants at Phoebus.

Organized Tours & Cruises

The Hampton Trolley (☎ 757-727-1102) is an authentic reproduction of an 1888 trolley.

It takes you from the visitor center through downtown, past the Air & Space Center, St John's Church, and Hampton Carousel. It runs daily May to November and costs 25¢.

The *Miss Hampton II* (☎ 757-727-1102) cruises down Hampton River and passes by Norfolk Naval Base, Hampton University, and Fort Monroe. (It is the only boat allowed to visit historic Fort Wool, a pre–Civil War fort situated on an artificial island.) Cruises operate at 10 am daily April to October and also at 2 pm from June to August. Tickets are $14.50 for adults, $12.50 for seniors, and $8 for children.

Places to Stay

The cheapest place to stay is *Gosnold's Hope Park* (☎ 757-850-5116, 901 Little Back River Rd), a public campground with flush toilets and a playground, located north of the junction of Route 258 (via Route 278). Sites cost about $6.

The *Arrow Inn* (☎ 757-865-0300, 7 Semple Farm Rd), I-64 exit 261B if eastbound and exit 262B if westbound, is central, affordable, and comfortable, with low-season singles for $36 to $42 and doubles for $41 to $47 (in the high season, add $10). The *Days Inn – Hampton* (☎ 757-826-4810, 1918 Coliseum Drive), I-64 exit 263B, has a pool and exercise room. Singles cost $45 to $80, and doubles cost $51 to $86.

An expensive option is the *Radisson Hotel Hampton* (☎ 757-727-9700, 700 Settlers Landing Rd), with all the facilities, perfect suites, a dining room, and an outdoor cafe. Singles and doubles cost $105 in the low season and $112 in the high season.

Places to Eat

Try *Carmella's* (☎ 757-825-5375, 2123B Coliseum Drive), a bustling Italian place with a dozen pastas to choose from daily and lashing of fresh sauces.

The *Second Street Restaurant & Tavern* (☎ 757-220-2286, 132 E Queen St) is a casual place where you can get gigantic burgers, overstuffed sandwiches, and even things the kids like.

Buckroe's Island Grill (☎ 757-850-5757), a local favorite at the Salt Ponds Marina, serves crab dip and fresh seafood with a delicious variety of toppings.

The following restaurants are at Phoebus (see Other Attractions, earlier): **Sarah's Irish Pub** (☎ 757-722-2373, *38 Mellen St)* is an atmospheric place serving battered shrimp, burgers, fries, and plenty of beer. Down by the waterfront are **Sam's Seafood** and **Keith's Dockside Seafood** – two very good purveyors of the locally caught product.

Entertainment
From May to September, there is live music on Wednesday at Mill Point Park (from 5 to 9 pm), Wine and Jazz at Mill Point Park on Friday (from 5 to 9 pm), and a Block Party in downtown Hampton on Saturday (from 6 to 11 pm).

Fathoms (☎ 757-728-0100) is a dance club attached to the Second Street Restaurant – its motto is 'You never know who you meet 20,000 leagues under the street.' **Goodfella's** (☎ 757-723-4979, *13 E Queens Way)* features acoustic music most nights starting at 9:30 pm.

The **Charles H Taylor Arts Center** (☎ 757-722-2787, *4205 Victoria Blvd)* features local and international performers. See its free magazine for what's on.

Getting There & Away
The Newport News/Williamsburg International Airport is the nearest airport to Hampton (see Newport News, later). A shuttle/taxi to the Coliseum Mall area of Hampton is around $15. The PENTRAN bus leaves from in front of the terminal. The Amtrak station is in Newport News (see below).

Getting Around
PENTRAN (☎ 757-723-3344, TDD 757-722-8427) has 12 scheduled routes in the Newport News/Hampton area. PENTRAN connects with James City County Transit (JCCT) in upper York County (linking Williamsburg) and with TRT in Norfolk, via the Crossroads connection. The latter originates at the downtown Hampton Transportation Center, at 2 Pembroke Ave.

NEWPORT NEWS
The pervading influence here, as in all of the Hampton Roads area, is the sea. Newport News (population 171,000), just off I-64, is equidistant between Williamsburg and Virginia Beach.

The name originates from Christopher Newport, the captain of *Discovery*, who brought with him the 'news' everyone wanted to hear – supplies for the early colonists. Newport News, the fourth-largest city in Virginia, has the world's largest privately owned shipyard (the Navy's aircraft carriers and nuclear submarines are built here), the region's biggest municipal park (8000 acres), and the fine Mariner's Museum. What's more, it gave us the great Ella Fitzgerald.

Orientation
Newport News is on the southern side of the peninsula formed by the York and James Rivers. Route 17 (Jefferson Blvd) and Route 60 (Warwick Blvd) cut through the city north-south; Route 60 turns northeast at the base of the peninsula and joins I-64 to cross Hampton Roads via the bridge-tunnel. I-64 skirts the city on its northern edge – at exit 264, I-664 branches off to Suffolk/Chesapeake via the Monitor-Merrimac Memorial Bridge Tunnel ('M&M').

Downtown (Washington Ave) near the shipyards is an austere place – the attractions are several miles north. The one point of interest here is the Victory Arch, a marble memorial to those who served overseas in the world wars.

Information
The Newport News Visitor Center (☎ 757-886-7777, www.newport-news.va.us), 13560 Jefferson Ave, is open 9 am to 5 pm daily. Foreign exchange is not done easily on the peninsula, so bring traveler's checks.

For medical assistance, the Riverside Regional Medical Center (☎ 757-594-3100) is at 500 J Clyde Morris Blvd.

Mariner's Museum
This fascinating museum (☎ 757-596-2222, www.mariner.org), 100 Museum Drive, has America's most extensive international

VIRGINIA

maritime collection. It includes intricately carved figureheads, steam engines, maps, scrimshaw (whalebone etchings), paintings, ship models (eg, of SS *United States* and RMS *Queen Elizabeth)*, films and videos – designed to put a whiff of sea air in your nostrils – and a display about the *Monitor*. Especially interesting are the tiny carvings by August Crabtree, viewed through magnifying glasses. At the other end of the scale are more than 50 full-size craft, from a Venetian gondola to a WWII Japanese submarine.

The museum is open 10 am to 5 pm daily. Admission is $5 for adults, $3 for students of any age. To get there, take I-64 exit 258A.

War Museum

This museum (☎ 757-247-8523), at 9285 Warwick Blvd, I-64 exit 263A (Mercury Blvd), looks at US military history from 1775 through Operation Desert Storm and the Balkans crisis. There are uniforms, weapons, art (paintings and posters), vehicles, and a special treatment of the role of African Americans and women in war.

It is open 9 am to 5 pm Monday to Saturday and 1 to 5 pm Sunday. Admission is $2 for adults and $1 for seniors and children.

Newsome House

This museum and cultural center (☎ 757-247-2360), 2803 Oak Ave, was once owned by Joseph Thomas Newsome – a prominent black lawyer and editor and the founder of an area church and the Colored Voters League of Warwick County. He was also one of the first black lawyers to represent cases before the Virginia Supreme Court. The house is free and is open year-round by appointment only.

Peninsula Fine Arts Center

An affiliate of the Virginia Museum, this center (☎ 757-596-8175), at 101 Museum Drive, has changing exhibits ranging from national traveling exhibitions to the work of regional artists and craftsmen. It is free and is open 10 am to 5 pm Tuesday to Saturday and 1 to 5 pm Sunday.

Virginia Living Museum

One of the best places to see the state's wildlife, this museum (☎ 757-595-1900, www.valivingmuseum.org), at 524 J Clyde Morris Blvd, has everything from eagles and otters to bullfrogs and bobcats – close up and in natural settings. Kids will love the proximity of the critters, and everyone seems to enjoy the planetarium and aquarium.

The museum is open 9 am to 5 pm Monday to Saturday (plus 7 to 9 pm Thursday night) and noon to 5 pm Sunday from Labor Day to June 9. From June 10 to Labor Day, it is open 9 am to 6 pm Sunday to Wednesday and to 9 pm Thursday to Saturday. Admission is $6 for adults, $5 for seniors, and $4 for children; add $1 for the planetarium. A ticket for the planetarium only costs $2.50.

US Army Transportation Museum

This museum (☎ 757-878-1182) is in Building 300, Besson Hall, Fort Eustis. Trucks, uniforms, differentials, dip sticks, mud flaps, torque, all forms of horsepower and rpm (and a flying saucer), khaki and camouflage, are here. It is open 9 am to 4:30 pm daily and is free.

Special Events

The Celebration in Lights (☎ 757-926-8451) is held in Newport News Park from Thanksgiving to January 1; access to the twinkling displays costs $8.

The Fall Festival, a two-day celebration of traditional crafts, is held in Newport News Park in early October.

In mid-March, there's a reenactment of the naval battle between the *Monitor* and the *Merrimac* at the Monitor-Merrimac Overlook.

Places to Stay

The *Mulberry Inn* (☎ 757-887-3000, 16890 *Warwick Blvd)*, I-64 exit 250A, has a pool and exercise room. Doubles cost $67 in winter, $87 in summer.

There are a couple of reasonable places near I-64 exit 255A: *Comfort Inn* (☎ 757-249-0200, 12330 Jefferson Ave) is a mid-range place. Singles and doubles cost $66 in low season; the rooms cost $75 on weekdays, $85 on weekends in the high season (including breakfast). The *Hampton Inn & Suites* (☎ 757-249-0001, 12251 Jefferson Ave) includes in-room movies and airport transportation. Singles and doubles cost $69 to $109.

The *Omni Newport News Hotel* (☎ 757-873-6664, 1000 Omni Blvd), I-64 exit 258A, has a heated pool and a dining room. Singles and doubles cost $109 in the low season and $129 in the high season. The *Ramada Inn* (☎ 757-599-4460, 950 J Clyde Morris Blvd) also has all the facilities and the in-house Chatfield's Restaurant. In the low season, singles and doubles cost $39 to $69; in the high season, they cost $59 to $89.

Places to Eat
In Oyster Point Square, *Bon Appetit* (☎ 757-873-0644, 11710 Jefferson Ave) has all the pizzazz of a Parisian cafe and blends tasty French and Vietnamese dishes. Lunch costs about $7, and large entrees cost $12 to $18.

Kappo Nara (☎ 757-249-5395, 550 Oyster Point Rd) is a combined sushi bar and Japanese restaurant. Dinner costs about $15. *Papou George's* (☎ 757-269-0501, 303 Oyster Point Rd) is for those who got out of bed late and are hungry, as it serves breakfast until 8 pm. At other times, you can rely on the milkshakes, which are generously thick.

Mitty's Ristorante (☎ 757-873-6664) in the Omni Complex, is the place for an after-dinner drink and live music (usually rock).

Getting There & Away
The Newport News/Williamsburg International Airport (☎ 757-877-0221) is in Newport News. A taxi or shuttle to Newport News is $8 to $15. The PENTRAN bus leaves from in front of the terminal building (see Getting Around, below).

The Amtrak station (☎ 757-245-3589, 800-872-7245), 9304 Warwick Blvd, in Lafayette Square, is the closest station to Hampton Roads. There is a shuttle bus to Norfolk and Virginia Beach from the station.

The Greyhound/Trailways (☎ 757-887-2626) terminal is at 11 Dozier Rd, Fort Eustis, but it also stops at the Hampton

Transportation Center. There are services to most cities on the East Coast.

Getting Around
PENTRAN (☎ 757-723-3344, TDD 722-8427) has scheduled routes in the Newport News/Hampton area. PENTRAN services connect with JCCT in upper York County (going to Williamsburg) and with TRT in Norfolk via the Crossroads service. The latter originates at the downtown Newport News Transportation Center, at 150 35th St.

SMITHFIELD
Across the James River from Newport News is the sizable community of Smithfield, in Isle of Wight County (one of the state's eight original shires). It was once called War-rosquoyacke, after the original Native American inhabitants but was changed, as many of its first English settlers hailed from the Isle of Wight.

It is a pleasant, relaxed option for those visitors who don't mind 'commuting' to the attractions of Hampton Roads. The tourism bureau (☎ 757-357-5182), 130 Main St, is open 9 am to 5 pm daily.

Fort Boykin
In a park at 7410 Fort Boykin Trail, Fort Boykin (☎ 757-357-2291) was built in 1623 to protect settlers against Native Americans and Spaniards. The fort, shaped as a seven-point star, has featured in every major war fought on mainland American soil. It is open 8 am to dusk daily and is free.

St Luke's Shrine
This church (☎ 757-357-3367), 14477 Benn's Church Blvd, is the oldest existing church of English foundation in the country (1632) and is the only surviving example of original Gothic design. It is open 9:30 am to 4 pm Tuesday to Saturday and 1 to 4 pm Sunday from February to December.

Isle of Wight Museum
This museum (☎ 757-357-7459), 103 Main St, has an odd collection focusing on county history – eg, the world-famous Smithfield

hams (the edible variety, not amateur theater). It's free and is open 10 am to 4 pm Tuesday to Saturday and 1 to 5 pm Sunday.

Places to Stay & Eat

The *Smithfield Station* (☎ 757-357-7700, 415 S Church St), on Route 10, has a picture-postcard waterfront setting and overlooks the Pagan River. Single and double rooms in the 'station' cost $69 to $89 in the low season (considerably more in high season), and the suites in the quaint lighthouse cost $175 to $225. The restaurant here is a local favorite and is open daily. There is a Sunday-brunch omelet bar and an outdoor raw bar.

The *Smithfield Inn* (☎ 757-357-1752, 112 Main St) dates from 1752. Singles and doubles in this elegant establishment (with its renowned restaurant) cost $125. The *Isle of Wight Inn* (☎ 757-357-3176, 1607 S Church St) is much cheaper but not lacking in facilities. Singles/doubles cost $52/59 all year.

All the restaurants serve the famous Virginia dry-cured hams, which are made from peanut-fed hogs.

VIRGINIA BEACH

This city (population 431,000) is the fastest-growing on the East Coast (and Virginia's largest). It has been described by some observers as 'the boom town of the 1990s.' Virginia Beach is everything it unashamedly attempts to be – a magnet for young revelers, a carefully-spun web of tackiness, and an almost impenetrable concrete palisade that often prevents the sun's rays from reaching the beach. Its current tag – 'The Redneck Riviera' – seems appropriate.

There has been a concerted attempt near the high-rises to tart up the city and make it more family-friendly. Six miles of crowded beach have been renovated with the addition of parkland, benches, lighting, and a 2-mile bike trail.

So what are the city's good points? Probably its proximity to some truly beautiful parts of Virginia, such as the Great Dismal Swamp, First Landing/Seashore and False Cape State Parks, the excellent Virginia Marine Science Museum, Edgar Cayce's Association for Research & Enlightenment (ARE), and a host of other features removed from the glitz.

You can find your way around Virginia Beach easily. The numbered streets run east and west, and named avenues run north and south, parallel to the beach. See the Norfolk Area map for sites in western Virginia Beach.

History

The first settlement along this strip of coast was at Lynnhaven Inlet in 1621. One of the first settlers' homes from that time, the Adam Thoroughgood House still stands (see later in the chapter). The coast has always been famous for shipwrecks, and the increasing number of tragedies led Congress to establish a lifesaving station here. In 1791, the Cape Henry Lighthouse was built to guide ships into Chesapeake Bay. One of the worst wrecks was that of the *Diktator*, which sunk in March 1891.

The first hotel was built on the oceanfront in 1883, and the Beach quickly developed as a holiday retreat. In 1970, there were 172,000 people living in the city. In 1980, the Beach was 'found,' and in a mere 10 years, the resulting influx of residents doubled the population to 393,000. The population is expected to soon surpass half a million.

Information

The Virginia Beach Visitor Information Center (☎ 757-437-4880, 800-822-3224, www.vbfun.com), 2100 Parks Ave, is at the east end of Route 44 (I-64 exit 284), about half a mile west of the beach on 21st St. The center is open 9 am to 8 pm daily in summer; otherwise, 9 am to 5 pm. There are information kiosks at 17th, 24th, and 27th Sts, on Atlantic Ave.

There is also a Virginia Beach self-guided auto tour; a tape can be rented for $6 (with a $10 deposit) from the visitor information center.

Use the Norfolk International Airport money exchange facilities before coming to the Beach, as the banks charge hefty fees to exchange currencies. NationsBank (☎ 800-880-5454), at the corner of Pacific Ave and

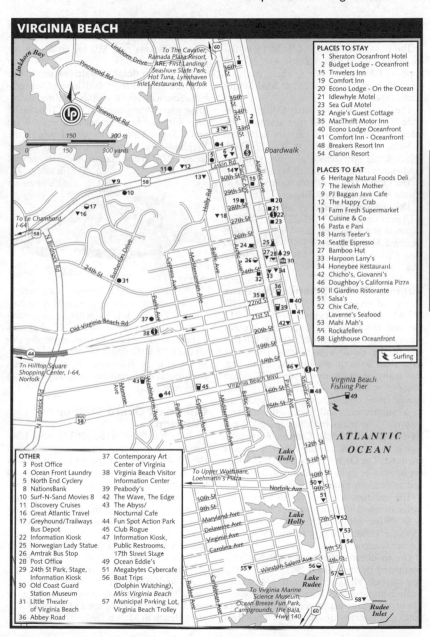

VIRGINIA BEACH

VIRGINIA

Surfing

Atlantic Ocean

Virginia Beach Fishing Pier

31st St (Laskin Rd), is convenient for other banking services.

The post office (☎ 757-428-2821), at the corner of 24th St and Atlantic Ave, is open 8 am to 4:30 pm weekdays. There is also a post office (☎ 757-428-4826) at 33rd St and Arctic Ave.

The Tidewater Community College's Virginia Beach campus has free access to the Internet. Otherwise, you can pay hefty fees at Mebabytes Cybercafe (☎ 757-422-5009), 812 Atlantic Ave, which also has gourmet sandwiches on freshly baked bread.

The Ocean Front laundry is on 32nd St at Arctic Ave, beside the 7-Eleven.

The cheapest emergency medical option is Urgent Care (☎ 757-481-2333), 1120 First Colonial Rd. Close by, the Virginia Beach General Hospital (☎ 757-481-8000), 1060 First Colonial Rd, has 24-hour emergency facilities.

Virginia Marine Science Museum

This great museum (☎ 757-425-3474, TDD 757-427-4305, www.vmsm.org), at 717 General Booth Blvd (Route 60), 2 miles inland from the mouth of Rudee Inlet, is one of the Beach's highlights. There are more than 200 exhibits focusing on the sea, and many of them are hands-on. You can observe waders in a nearby salt marsh, handle crabs, simulate exploration undersea in a submarine, and gaze into endless aquaria. The main building includes the 300,000-gallon **Norfolk Canyon Aquarium**, which has sharks, among other large sea creatures. The Owls Creek Salt Marsh building houses an indoor/outdoor otter habitat and an outdoor aviary.

The museum is open 9 am to 5 pm daily, with extended hours in summer. Admission is $8.95 for adults, $7.95 for seniors, and $5.95 for children. Entry to the IMAX 3D theater is extra.

On an **ocean collections boat trip**, also conducted by the VMSM (☎ 757-437-4949), you can see all types of marine creatures hauled aboard the *Miss Virginia Beach*. These creatures are placed in temporary tanks and then discussed by the knowledge-

able staff. Trips are conducted 12:45 to 2 pm Wednesday between late June and late August. Tickets cost $10 for adults, $8 for children.

You can go **dolphin watching** out at sea with the VMSM from mid-June to September. You will see the pods feeding, swimming, and playing near the shore. Trips in the *Miss Virginia Beach* depart between 9 am and 4:30 pm Monday to Saturday from the Virginia Beach Fishing Center at Rudee Inlet, 200 Winston Salem Ave. Tickets cost $12 for adults, $10 for children.

The bottle-nosed dolphins return here in ever-increasing numbers from May to November. On one July Saturday, in an orchestrated search, there were 407 dolphins sighted. Cape Henry has taken on the deserved title of 'Dolphin Disneyland.' Farther south, at Cape Hatteras, dolphins are seen year-round – this half-year migration has yet to be explained.

Old Coast Guard Station Museum

By the oceanfront in the 1903 Seatack Lifesaving Station, this interesting museum (☎ 757-422-1587), on the corner of 24th St and Atlantic Ave, has many exhibits about local shipwrecks, ship models, and displays of lifesaving equipment. Particularly interesting is the exhibit in the upper gallery relating to the WWII Battle of the Atlantic.

It's open 10 am to 5 pm Tuesday to Saturday and noon to 5 pm Sunday from October to Memorial Day. Admission is $3 for adults, $2.50 for seniors, and $1 for youth under 19.

A block north on the boardwalk is the statue **Norwegian Lady**, commemorating the wreck of the Norwegian *Diktator* off Virginia Beach in March 1891.

Contemporary Art Center of Virginia

This center (☎ 757-425-0000), 2200 Parks Ave, hosts workshops, performances, and exhibitions related to its extensive collection of 20th-century art. The center sponsors the popular June Boardwalk Art Show. It is open 10 am to 4 pm Tuesday to Saturday and noon to 4 pm Sunday. Admission is $3 for adults and $2 for seniors and children.

Adam Thoroughgood House

This brick house (☎ 757-664-6283), 1636 Parish Rd, inland from the bay shore, dates from 1680. It is named after a plantation owner who was an indentured servant who settled in Virginia in 1621. Thoroughgood's grandson probably constructed the small, four-room building. It was built of brick and oyster-shell mortar and made to resemble an English cottage. The house was fully restored in 1957 and is furnished with antiques.

The house is open noon to 5 pm Tuesday to Saturday from January to March; otherwise, 10 am to 5 pm Tuesday to Saturday and noon to 5 pm Sunday. Admission is $4 for adults and $2.50 for seniors and children. A combination ticket ($8) gets you the Moses Myers House, the Willoughby-Baylor House, and the Chrysler Museum (all in Norfolk), as well as this house. See the Norfolk section, earlier, for more information.

Association for Research & Enlightenment

New Age meets the beach at the Association for Research & Enlightenment (ARE; ☎ 757-428-3588), founded by the psychic Edgar Cayce (see the boxed text). The association's building seems an incongruity, tucked away at the corner of 67th St and Atlantic Ave (near the suntanned paradise of the beach), but some revelers may feel the time is ripe for rejuvenation.

Visitors can have their own psychic ability (ESP quotient) tested on electronic equipment, watch an informative video on the life of Cayce, meditate in a tranquil garden or in a 3rd-floor room that overlooks the ocean, attend a lecture, watch a movie on the paranormal, or just practice skepticism. A full library concentrates on Cayce's voluminous philosophies.

The center is open 9 am to 8 pm Monday to Saturday and 11 am to 8 pm Sunday; admission to this 'other world' is free.

Cape Henry Memorial

A stone cross marks the site of the first landing of Jamestown's colonists on April 26, 1607, and where they '...set up a Crosse at Chesupioc Bay.' The memorial, at the northern end of Virginia Beach in Fort Story (☎ 757-898-3400), can be visited 8 am to 5 pm daily.

Edgar Cayce: The Sleeping Prophet

Born in 1877 in Hopkinsville, Kentucky, Edgar Cayce (**kay**-see) is probably best remembered for his dire prophecies of wars and calamities – the outbreak of WWII, the reemergence of Atlantis, the disappearance of the US region west of Nebraska – but these were the smallest part of his work. In fact, of the 14,000 readings he gave from 1923 to 1945, about 65% were on medical problems, and of the rest, only 17 concerned changes to the planet! Cayce claimed that in his sleep he could diagnose an individual's physical state and outline treatment just by knowing his or her name and address (the person could be anywhere in the world).

In 1925, Cayce, 'the 'sleeping prophet,' moved to Virginia Beach following advice received in one of his own psychic readings. In 1932, he reinforced his decision by adding, 'of all the resorts that are in the East Coast, Virginia Beach will be the first and the longest-lasting...the future is good,' well before the Beach took off (pity he wasn't into real estate).

Cayce died in Virginia Beach in 1945 and may reappear in 2158 on the coast of Nebraska.

It's free, but you may need to show photo identification. At the end of a small boardwalk, a relief map indicates the disposition of opposing French and British forces during the Battle of the Capes (see the boxed text Victory at Yorktown in the Colonial Virginia chapter).

Cape Henry Lighthouse

The nearby lighthouse (☎ 757-422-9421), one of the first public works authorized by Congress, operated continuously from 1791 until 1881. It is open 10 am to 5 pm daily from mid-March to October. Admission is $2 for adults, $1 for seniors and youth under 19.

Francis Land House

This historic house (☎ 757-431-4000), 3131 Virginia Beach Blvd, is an 18th-century plantation structure with a fine example of a gambrel roof (a ridged roof with the slope broken on each side). It is open 9 am to 5 pm Tuesday to Saturday and noon to 5 pm Sunday. Admission is $3 for adults, $2.50 for seniors, $1.50 for students, and $1 for children.

Lynnhaven House

At 4405 Wishart Rd, this house (☎ 757-460-1688) is a small, stately, early-18th-century structure that typified middle-class living at the time. From May to October, special events that re-create aspects of 18th-century life are held here. The house is open noon to 4 pm Tuesday to Sunday in the summer. Admission is $3.50 for adults, $1.50 for students, and $1 for children.

Amusement Parks

Some holidaymakers – especially those who choose the Beach for a holiday – seek this sort of entertainment. The **Ocean Breeze Fun Park** (☎ 757-422-4444), 849 General Booth Blvd (Route 60), combines four themes in one – Wildwater Rapids, Motorworld, Shipwreck Golf, and Strike Zone (a baseball simulation). The last thing you would probably want to do after a shipwreck is play golf! The park is open daily. Serving the same market is **Fun Spot Action Park** (☎ 757-422-1401), 962 Virginia Beach Blvd.

There's a plethora of time-wasters along Atlantic Ave between 15th and 30th Sts, and putt-putt golf courses seem to pop up everywhere.

Surfing & Swimming

Surfing is not permitted on the main part of the beach, but skegheads and grommets hang out at the south end, near Rudee Inlet, and on either side of the 14th St pier.

Each year in late August, Virginia Beach is host to the East Coast Surfing Championships (www.surfECSC.com/home2.html), which attracts professionals from all over the world. Wave Riding Vehicles (☎ 757-422-8823) will provide a local surf report and information on the main surf areas.

In the summer, the beach is patrolled by lifeguards from 2nd to 42nd Sts. There are more-remote beaches to the south, at Sandbridge, at False Cape State Park, and at Back Bay National Wildlife Refuge. To get there, take General Booth Blvd (Route 60) then Sandbridge Rd. These places are all signed.

Bicycling

The beach is a great place to bike, as there are many bike paths in the vicinity of the boardwalk or along it. The boardwalk is probably the best place for a visitor to pick up a bike (about $5 per hour; see Getting Around, later in this section).

If you want to venture farther afield (get a bike for a day), the ride south to Sandbridge Beach is recommended and offers a respite from the crowds. Once there, you can bike through to the trail at Back Bay. North of Virginia Beach is First Landing/Seashore State Park, with its Cape Henry bike trail.

Fishing

There are a couple of fishing piers where you may be rewarded for your patience. The Lynnhaven Fishing Pier (☎ 757-481-7071), at Starfish Rd off Route 60 (Shore Drive), and the Virginia Beach Fishing Pier (☎ 757-428-2333), nestled between 14th and 15th Sts, have bait for sale and rent rods and reels – advice is free.

For charters, contact the Virginia Beach Fishing Center (☎ 757-422-5700), at the corner of 5th St and Pacific Ave (half-day trips are $20 for adults, $15 for children), or Fisherman's Wharf Marina (☎ 757-428-2111), Rudee Inlet.

Other Activities

As a resort, Virginia Beach caters to just about every outdoor taste.

For **scuba diving** information, contact the Lynnhaven Dive Center (☎ 757-481-7949, www.ldcscuba.com), Dive Quarters (☎ 757-422-3483, www.divequarters.com), or Wreck-Tec, Inc (☎ 757-491-1135).

Other popular pastimes along the boardwalk are **jogging** and **in-line skating**. For skates, advice, and safety equipment, contact Cherie's Bicycle Rentals (☎ 757-437-8888); there are rental stands at 8th, 22nd, 24th, and 37th Sts.

Also popular is **golf**, and there are several public and private courses. The visitor center has all the details and addresses; all budgets and levels of ability are accommodated. Particularly noteworthy are the Fred Couples–designed course at Heron Ridge (☎ 757-426-3800) and the Rees Jones–designed Hell's Point Golf Club (☎ 757-721-3400).

Tidewater Adventures (☎ 757-480-1999) operates **kayaking** trips from the Cavalier Hotel at 42nd St beach. A 2½-hour trip to see the dolphins costs $40.

Cruises

Virginia Beach Fishing Center/Cruise (☎ 757-422-5700), 200 Winston Salem Ave, operates an oceanfront cruise in the *Miss Virginia Beach* from Rudee Inlet. There are views of the skyline, the old Coast Guard station, Cape Henry, and the lighthouses. They have scheduled sightseeing tours at 11 am and 2:30 pm from Memorial Day to Labor Day. Tickets cost $12 for adults and $10 for children.

Discovery Cruises (☎ 757-422-2900), 600 Laskin Rd, operates scheduled luxury yacht cruises on Virginia Beach's inland waterways (including Broad Bay) from May to October; call for costs.

Special Events

Virginia Beach hosts a number of popular annual events and festivals. In May, there are the Beach Street USA celebrations (from Memorial day on), the Saltwater Fishing Tournament (☎ 757-491-5160), and the Pungo Strawberry Festival.

In June, the Viva Elvis Festival and the Boardwalk Art Show take place. In September, not only is there the Blues at the Beach festival, but also the biggest of the Virginia Beach events – the Neptune Festival (☎ 757-498-0215).

Places to Stay

There are plenty of choices, but most places are expensive. Rates sometimes drop if you book for an extended period (don't be afraid to bargain in the off season). On Atlantic and Pacific Aves, parallel to the beach, you will find most of the accommodations.

Camping The *Virginia Beach KOA Campground* (☎ 757-428-1444, 1240 General Booth Blvd), 2½ miles from the resort, is a quiet place. Basic sites for two start at $15, and hookups start at $18 in the low season ($27 to $70 in the high season); comfortable one-room cabins cost $60.

The *Holiday Trav-L-Park* (☎ 757-425-0249, 1075 General Booth Blvd), almost across the road from the KOA and on 120 acres, is a huge place with some 1200 sites; these start at $15 in the low season and $37 in the high season. Both camps operate free bus services to the Beach.

Northward, the campsites amid the sand dunes and cypresses at *First Landing/ Seashore State Park* (☎ 757-481-2131), just off Shore Drive (Route 60) at Cape Henry, are very popular. The park has standard sites for $10.50, RV sites without hookups for $19.25, and two-bedroom cabins for $80 per night ($510 per week).

Hostels The only reasonably cheap place at the Beach is *Angie's Guest Cottage HI-AYH Hostel* (☎ 757-428-4690, 302 24th St), one block from the beach. The owner, Barbara

Yates, has done a lot to make this one of the best places to stay on the Virginia coast.

In the busy season, from late May to early September, dorm beds cost $11.50 for HI members and $14.50 for nonmembers; otherwise, they cost $8.50 and $11.50. Rooms in the B&B section start at $40/48 for singles/doubles (cheaper in the low season).

Hotels & Motels There are several inexpensive places west of Pacific Ave between 26th and 30th Sts; some are a good value, others are smelly and outrageously expensive in summer.

The *MacThrift Motor Inn* (☎ 757-422-2631, 311 22nd St) has efficiencies and one- and two-bedroom apartments. It is the town's best budget choice, with a pool, free HBO, and microwaves. Rooms cost $29 to $59 in the low season; otherwise, $59 to $99.

The *Travelers Inn* (☎ 757-425-8300, 207 29th St) has spacious rooms and offers deals to those who stay for a week or more. In the low season, rooms cost $39 to $59; in the high season, they cost $69 to $89.

The *Budget Lodge – Oceanfront* (☎ 757-428-4413, 3309 Atlantic Ave) has all the amenities, including a heated pool with a diving board. Rates are $29 to $39 in winter, $82 to $100 in the high season.

The *Idlewhyle Motel* (☎ 757-428-9341, 2705 Atlantic Ave) is utilitarian, but you get a choice of a pool view or ocean view. The rooms are not flashy, but the motel is well located. Prices are similar to the Budget Lodge – Oceanfront.

The *Comfort Inn* (☎ 757-428-2203, 2800 Pacific Ave) includes a free breakfast in its winter rates for doubles. The cost ranges from $45 to $69 (in the high season, $114 to $164). The *Comfort Inn – Oceanfront* (☎ 757-425-8200, 2015 Atlantic Ave) is more expensive – it's on the beach – with winter singles and doubles starting at $49 to $89.

The *Sea Gull Motel* (☎ 757-425-5711, 2613 Atlantic Ave), on the oceanfront, has a rooftop deck and indoor pool. Comfortable double rooms cost $35 to $60 in winter and $110 to $140 in summer.

The *Econo Lodge – on the Ocean* (☎ 757-428-3970, 2707 Atlantic Ave) is a good value,

with winter rates of $49 to $79 and summer rates of $99 to $199; a continental breakfast is included. The *Econo Lodge Oceanfront* (☎ 757-428-2403, 2109 Atlantic Ave) charges the same rates.

The *Clarion Resort* (☎ 757-422-3186, 501 Atlantic Ave) overlooks the ocean and has a heated pool and sauna. It's upmarket, with attractive rooms for $39 to $99 in winter and $139 plus in summer.

The *Breakers Resort Inn* (☎ 757-428-1821, 1503 Atlantic Ave), on the oceanfront, is a small, family-operated place with more than 50 rooms, 15 two-room efficiencies, and a pool. Rooms cost $40 to $50 in winter and $95 to $110 in the high season.

The *Ramada Plaza Resort* (☎ 757-428-7025), on the oceanfront at 57th St, caters to the convention crowd, who expect all the facilities their companies have paid for. Facilities include a restaurant, indoor and outdoor pools, and a fully equipped gym. Singles and doubles cost $60 to $85 in winter and $155 to $210 in summer.

The *Sheraton Oceanfront Hotel* (☎ 757-425-9000), on the oceanfront at 36th St, has all the facilities, including two pools and a dining room. In winter, rooms cost $59 to $69; in summer, $139.

The Cavalier (☎ 757-425-8555, 888-746-2327) resorts, at the corner of 42nd St and Atlantic Ave in a quiet part of town, have just about every facility imaginable and a price tag to match (rooms in summer cost $115 to $195). An old red-brick building – the original 1927 Cavalier Hotel (on 42nd St and Pacific Ave) – combines with an adjacent 1973 high-rise with its own beach. Facilities include restaurants, pools, aerobics facilities, and croquet, tennis, and volleyball areas.

The following are places near the Lynnhaven Inlet Bridge, to the east of the Chesapeake Bay Bridge-Tunnel: *Howard Johnson – Amphibious Base* (☎ 757-460-1151, 5173 Shore Drive), Route 60, has doubles for $40 to $45 in winter and $60 to $85 in summer.

The *Comfort Inn – Little Creek* (☎ 757-460-5566, 5189 Shore Drive), west of Independence Blvd, is a good mid-range choice.

In winter, singles and doubles cost $42 to $48; in the high season, they cost $114 to $164.

The **Virginia Beach Resort Hotel** (☎ 757-481-9000, 2800 Shore Drive) is an expensive choice (but a great one for those who have discovered the Duck-In – see Places to Eat). Singles/doubles start at $99/105 in winter, rising to at least $185/195 in the high season.

Places to Eat

You may at first think there is little else but fast food or junk food in Virginia Beach. But if you look carefully, you'll find healthy, delicious, and elegant alternatives.

For those on a tight budget, the **Virginia Beach Farmers' Market** (☎ 757-427-4395, 3640 Dam Neck Rd) is a good choice. It is open 9 am to 6:30 pm daily (until dusk in winter) and sells dairy products, jams, spices, nuts, meats, and country-style food. The 24-hour **Farm Fresh Supermarket** (521 Laskin Rd) is another good place with a preservative-free salad bar where you can buy fresh fruit and frozen yogurt. The **Heritage Natural Foods Deli** (☎ 757-428-0500, 314 Laskin Rd) has organic salads, sandwiches, and vegetarian entrees. It's open for lunch and dinner daily.

Farther west, **Big Charlie's Truck Plaza** (☎ 757-460-2032, 5792 Northampton Blvd) may not have the healthiest of selections, but it sure is reasonably priced. Its burgers are bloody huge, and it attracts an eclectic crowd in addition to the expected truckers. The **Honeybee Restaurant**, at 24th St and Atlantic Ave, is the Beach's answer for those in search of the old-fashioned, inexpensive breakfast.

The **Jewish Mother** (☎ 757-422-5430, 3108 Pacific Ave) is the first place you should try at the Beach. During the day, it's worth stopping in for the delicious crepes ($5 to $9), pitas ('Frisbees for grandchildren' – $4.50), sandwiches ($4 to $6), salads, and desserts. At night, it metamorphoses into a late-night beer bar, often with free live music (sometimes there's a cover). There is no cover charge at the bar, and the free take-home menu contains a handy guide to Jewish culinary terms.

Salsa's (☎ 757-437-8133, 812 Atlantic Ave) serves, as its name suggests, Southwestern

cuisine. It is open daily for all meals and has specials from 3 to 6 pm, live entertainment on weekends, and a terrible motto: 'Let the spice be with you!'.

Coffeehouses Caffeine addicts can get a fix at several locations. **Cuisine & Co** (☎ 757-428-6700, 3004 Pacific Ave) is open for breakfast, lunch, and dinner daily and offers sandwiches, soup, salads, and delicious homemade desserts. **Seattle Espresso** (☎ 757-425-7650, 301 25th St) has iced drinks and desserts, and **PJ Baggan Java Cafe** (☎ 757-491-8900, 960 Laskin Rd) is open 8 am to 10 pm daily for espresso, sandwiches, and fine wines.

European There are a number of Italian places. **Doughboy's California Pizza** has three Atlantic Ave locations, including one at 17th St (☎ 757-422-6111); use its buy-one-get-one-free coupons after 9 pm. **Chicho's** (☎ 757-422-6011), on Atlantic Ave at 21st St, serves lashings of spaghetti and pizza to a youngish crowd. It too stays open long after the plates have been cleared away, as a popular, frenetic bar.

Il Giardino Ristorante (☎ 757-422-6464, 910 Atlantic Ave) has oodles of noodles and an enormous selection of pizzas and meat dishes; it's classy and thus expensive, as most places with valet parking are. **Giovanni's** (☎ 757-425-1575), 20th St and Atlantic Ave, has been around for more than 30 years and has much cheaper entrees ($6 to $10) and free parking at the rear.

Pasta e Pani (☎ 757-428-2299, 1069 Laskin Rd) wins lots of friends with its great homemade pasta (seasoned with lemon and black pepper), terrific seafood specials, hearty fresh breads, and a tempting tiered dessert cart.

Le Chambord (☎ 757-498-1234, 324 N Great Neck Rd), west of downtown, is a popular institution with French food that is anything but 'institutionalized.' The chef serves up masterpieces, such as sweetbread with lobster sauce and wild-boar tenderloin with marinated dried figs, as well as great desserts. A meal for two with wine costs about $60.

The Bistro and Rotisserie at Le Chambord (☎ 757-486-3636) is a budget version of its neighbor, with a more casual atmosphere. You select from pork, lamb, and chicken rotating in huge glass cases.

Asian Check out *Shogun* (☎ 757-422-5150, *313 Hilltop Square Shopping Center)*, a popular place for sushi and Japanese cuisine that is prepared at your table. Entrees cost $12 to $20.

The *Bangkok Garden* (☎ 757-498-5009), at Loehmann's Plaza, is open for lunch and dinner daily. It serves an excellent *tom yum talay* (a delicious spicy soup). The *Bangkok Street Grill* (☎ 757-498-2439, 4316B Virginia Beach Blvd) specializes in stir-fried noodles. Two people can eat at either place for less than $20.

The *Bamboo Hut* (☎ 757-422-8230), at Pacific Ave and 24th St, is for the really down at heel; its beef or chicken with broccoli is good ($7). *Harris Teeter's*, just off Arctic Ave, has a good selection of *bento* (Japanese lunch boxes) for $6 each.

Seafood This is a logical dining choice in these parts, and there are plenty of opportunities to sample seafood. *Harpoon Larry's* (☎ 757-422-6000, 216 24th St), in the converted rail carriage at the corner of Pacific Ave, is one of the best raw bars around. It is open for lunch and dinner, and most diners will be well satisfied for $12 or less.

Laverne's Seafood (☎ 757-428-6836), at the corner of Atlantic Ave and 7th St, is known for its 'build-your-own' seafood platters, early-bird specials, prime rib, and crab legs for $11.95. *Chix Cafe* (☎ 757-428-8935), at 8th St and Atlantic Ave, has a raw bar and oceanfront beach bar and is somehow related to Laverne's.

Mahi Mah's (☎ 757-437-8030), near the Clarion (see Places to Stay), has burst onto the scene in recent years with its specialty rolls for $6.50, fish dinners for $16, and sushi appetizers for $8. It offers entertainment most nights.

Rockafellers (☎ 757-422-5654, 308 Mediterranean Ave), with its great water views over Rudee Inlet, serves seafood daily for lunch and dinner. Thursday witnesses the 'Maine event' – two 1lb lobsters for $17. Its Sunday brunches start at $4.

The *Lighthouse Oceanfront* (☎ 757-428-7974), at 1st St and Atlantic Ave, is expensive. This place is furnished simply, but all tables have a view of either the inlet or the ocean. Once the food is served (crab, shrimp, scallops, Maine lobsters), the view is secondary. The all-you-can-eat buffet costs $25.

The *Happy Crab* (☎ 757-437-9200, 550 Laskin Rd) is also good – the happiness, we suppose, depends upon the perspective…the crab's or yours. A bucket of crabs costs $25 for two, and a less-threatening seafood platter costs $16.

There are a number of seafood places near the Lynnhaven Inlet. The *Lynnhaven Fish House* (☎ 757-481-0003, 2350 Starfish Rd), at the top of the fishing pier, is good for oysters and chowders. Entrees, such as swordfish and salmon steaks, average about $20.

The *Duck-In* (☎ 757-481-0201, 3324 Shore Drive), at the east side of Lynnhaven Bridge, rates well with the locals. It's good for oysters, chowder (with crab meat, shrimp, and mushrooms), and a host of other tasty seafood dishes (crab cakes included). In summer, dine on the outdoor deck. (Friday evenings are an absolute must – dress as if you have just come from the office.)

Bubba's Crabhouse (☎ 757-481-3513, 3323 Shore Drive), near the Lynnhaven Inlet, is an inexpensive seafood place that has fabulous crab. They have outdoor, waterfront seating. Oh, almost forgot the *Dockside Inn* (☎ 757-481-7211, 3311 Shore Drive) in its marina setting; it's open for all meals daily.

Entertainment

Music Entertainment listings can be found in the free *Port Folio* and in The Daily Break section in Friday's *Virginian-Pilot*. There is a multiplicity of singles bars and flashy clubs between 17th and 23rd St along Pacific and Atlantic Aves. Chicho's (see Places to Eat) is one such place, as is The Edge, nearby.

The Wave, if you are willing to take the plunge, is also between 20th and 21st Sts on Atlantic Ave. The dress code is 'show as much tantalizing flesh as possible without giving the impression that you are near nude.' It is open 4:30 pm to 1:30 am daily, and there's no cover charge. Not far away is *The Abyss/Nocturnal Cafe* (☎ 757-422-0486, 1065 19th St), a double-stage venue.

If you are not in search of Mr or Ms World and just want to enjoy some music, there are a couple of clubs worth checking out: *Ocean Eddie's* (☎ 757-425-7742), on the 14th St pier, has the odd wild bash, where the town's young and not-so-young end up dancing on the tables to the strains of a country/R&B band.

Other rock or pop venues are the Jewish Mother (see Places to Eat, earlier); *Club Rogue* (☎ 757-671-8100), at 17th and Cypress Sts; *Peabody's* (☎ 757-422-6212), 21st St and Pacific Ave, which has a cigar bar and a big dance floor; *The Baja* (☎ 757-426 7748, 3701 S Sandpiper Rd); *Hot Tuna* (☎ 757-481-2888, 2817 Shore Drive), which has a good selection of microbrews; and Mahi Mah's (see Places to Eat).

For country and bluegrass, there's *County Line* (☎ 757-420-2120, 717 S Military Hwy), and for jazz, there's *Tropical Delights* (☎ 757-523-1237, 6220C Indian River Rd). The latter also serves tasty Caribbean food.

Acoustic/folk performances are often the backdrop when having a meal at *Abbey Road* (☎ 757-425-6330, 203 22nd St) and at *Smackwater Jack's* (☎ 757-340-6648, 3333 Virginia Beach Blvd), west of downtown. Headliners play at the *GTE Virginia Beach Amphitheater* (☎ 757-671-8100).

For classical music, the Virginia Symphony occasionally plays at the *24th St Stage*, on the boardwalk.

From April to Labor Day weekend, there is free nightly entertainment at the 17th and 24th St stages. Someone quipped that there is free entertainment – people watching – year-round.

Cinemas There are plenty of cinemas, including the *AMC Lynnhaven 8* (☎ 757-463-2628), next to the mall on Lynnhaven Parkway; the *Cinema Cafe* (☎ 757-499-6165, 758 Dence Blvd), west of town on Route 58; and the *Surf-N-Sand Movies 8* (☎ 757-425-3838, 941 Laskin Rd).

Theater The *Little Theater of Virginia Beach* (☎ 757-428-9233), at the corner of 24th St and Barberton Drive, is the place to see local talent perform theatrical productions ranging from dramas to musicals. Performances are year-round at 8 pm Friday and Saturday evenings, and Sunday matinees are at 3 pm.

For comedy, there are regular shows at the *Thoroughgood Inn Comedy Club* (☎ 757-460-8399, 4801 Shore Drive), west of the Beach near the US Navy Little Creek Amphibious Base, in the Bayside Shopping Center.

Getting There & Away

Virginia Beach is served by Norfolk International Airport (☎ 757-857-3351). A shuttle service (☎ 757-857-1231) runs from the airport to the resort area, which is 15 miles away (30 minutes by car).

The Greyhound/Trailways (☎ 757-422-2998, 800-231-2222) terminal is at 1017 Laskin Rd. When you book your ticket, make sure the Greyhound terminus is specified as Virginia Beach ($22 from Richmond). The downtown Norfolk terminal is not a nice place late at night.

The TRT (☎ 757-428-3388) has only three bus services to the oceanfront/resort area – Nos 20, 33, and 37 – but realize it takes about two hours to get here from Norfolk.

The Amtrak agent in Virginia Beach is Great Atlantic Travel (☎ 757-422-0444), 1065 Laskin Rd, Suite 101. Amtrak does not have a station at the Beach; the nearest is in Newport News (see earlier). There is free bus service from Newport News to the Amtrak shelter at the corner of 24th St and Pacific Ave (you need a valid train ticket to board the bus).

Getting Around

The Virginia Beach Trolley (☎ 757-428-3388) operates in summer, from noon to midnight, from Rudee Inlet to 42nd St. Tickets cost 50¢ for adults and children and 25¢ for seniors and disabled people. There are other trolleys that run along the beach boardwalk, the North Seashore (for First Landing/Seashore State Park), and Lynnhaven Mall.

There is an airport shuttle (☎ 757-857-1231). Car rentals at the Beach include SNAPPY (☎ 757-464-2900) and Budget (☎ 757-486-0050).

Perhaps the best way to get around is by bike. North End Cyclery (☎ 757-428-4235), on the corner of Arctic Ave and Laskin Rd, rents bikes for $4 per hour or $18 per day. Its business hours are 10 am to 7 pm daily. Tom's Bike Rentals (☎ 757-425-8454) will drop off bikes for 24-hour rentals, complete with locks for $17.

AROUND VIRGINIA BEACH

Fortunately, there are many natural areas within easy reach of the bustle of the Beach, and there are several inlets and beaches (eg, Lynnhaven, Broad Bay, and Rudee) where you can fish, swim, boat, or bird watch.

Back Bay National Wildlife Refuge

This 8000-acre refuge (☎ 757-498-2473) was established in 1938 to provide a habitat for migratory birds and other wildlife. It also protects habitats of beach, dunes, woodlands, and marsh. Birders are treated to a variety of species on this major Atlantic flyway. The park is only open during daylight hours, and access is limited to the shore and to designated trails, such as the Dune and Seaside Trails.

You are not allowed to swim or sunbathe on the beach, but surf-casting is permitted. There is a canoe-launching spot for those who want to explore on water, and you can rent canoes at Sandbridge Boat Rentals (☎ 757-721-6210), 3713 Sandpiper Rd.

The entrance to the refuge is at 4005 Sandpiper Rd, Virginia Beach; take General Booth Blvd (Route 60) and follow the signs via Sandbridge to the refuge. It is open sunrise to sunset daily; the visitor center is open 8 am to 4 pm weekdays and 9 am to 4 pm weekends ($4 per vehicle). Remember to bring insect repellent!

False Cape State Park

Not much of the Atlantic Coast has escaped the bulldozer and developer, so it is nice to see this undisturbed 6-mile stretch of beach that is accessible only by bicycle, by boat, or on foot. The park is the southern section of the barrier spit that separates Back Bay from the Atlantic. On the north side is the Back Bay National Wildlife Refuge (5 miles of which you have to walk through if you on foot), and the southern edge is the North Carolina border.

Primitive *camping* (☎ 757-498-2473) is allowed in the park ($7 per site), but you will need to get a permit from the visitor center at First Landing/Seashore State Park – and, most importantly, bring drinking water. Once here, you'll realize it's worth the effort.

First Landing/Seashore State Park & Natural Area

It is such a blessing having this unique environment of sand dunes, salt marsh, and freshwater cypress ponds so close to Virginia Beach. At 2500 Shore Drive, its proximity makes it the state's most visited state park. There are nearly 30 miles of trails (including one accessible to the disabled) within the park. Open from sunrise to sunset, the park encourages visitors to learn a lot about the environment and animal habitats.

The Chesapeake Bay Center (☎ 757-412-2320) is open daily, with educational displays, an ecotourism welcome center, bay lab for nature-based programs, and a gift shop. Daytime visitors can use the picnic areas and the self-guided nature trail. For day use, 8 am to dusk from April to October, there is a parking fee of $3 on weekends, $2 on weekdays.

Bikers have their own 6-mile Cape Henry Trail, which connects to the Beach's numerous other bike paths. For information on camping in the park, see Places to Stay in the Virginia Beach section.

Chesapeake & Suffolk

Chesapeake and Suffolk are included here because they are easily reached from Virginia Beach. The **Chesapeake Planetarium** (☎ 757-547-0153), 300 Cedar Rd, is open 9 am to 4 pm daily (until 8 pm Thursday, when there are free programs).

In nearby Suffolk is **Riddick's Folly** (☎ 757-934-1390), 510 N Main St, a huge Greek Revival house dating from 1837.

Inside is a small museum covering the Civil War. It is open 10 am to 5 pm Tuesday to Friday and 1 to 5 pm Sunday; a donation is requested.

For a bite to eat, *Lock's Pointe at Great Bridge* (☎ *757-547-9618, 136 Battlefield Blvd)*, on the Intracoastal Waterway, is a traditional old seafood house with a large wooden deck outside. Its traditional specialty is lightly baked crawfish cake.

Great Dismal Swamp National Wildlife Refuge

This swamp (☎ 757-986-3705), a national wildlife refuge of 107,000 acres, is anything but dismal. The region is rich in flora and fauna, and exploration – allowed only by day – is rewarding.

Evidence of human occupation of the swamp area dates from some 13,000 years ago, but by 1650, there were few Native Americans in the area. The earliest settlers showed little interest in the swamp until 1665, when William Drummond discovered the lake that still bears his name. In 1728, William Byrd II led a surveying party into the swamp to draw the dividing line between Virginia and North Carolina. Washington examined it in 1763 and then organized the Dismal Swamp Land Co with a view to future draining and logging. It was subsequently logged right through to 1976, and the draining has left the swamp at half of its original size.

There are five major forest types (pine, Atlantic white cedar, maple-blackgum, tupelo bald cypress, and sweetgum-oak-poplar) and three nonforested types of plant communities (remnant marsh, sphagnum bog, and evergreen shrub). The dwarf trillium, found in the northwest section of the swamp, blooms briefly each year for a two-week period in March.

More than 200 species of birds are found in the swamp, and of these species, 93 are nesting. Bird watching is best from April to June (spring migration), when the greatest diversity of species occurs. Local mammals include otters, bats, raccoons, minks, gray and red foxes, and gray squirrels. The white-tailed deer is common, but black bears and bobcats are rarely observed.

There are three species of poisonous snakes (cottonmouth, canebrake, and copperhead) and 18 nonpoisonous species. There are yellow-bellied and spotted turtles and an additional 56 species of turtles, lizards, salamanders, frogs, and toads.

Hiking and biking are options on the many timber roads here; Washington Ditch Rd is the best for bikes. Also near Washington Ditch Rd, the Boardwalk Trail passes through a mile of representative swamp. Boating and fishing are possible on Lake Drummond (a Virginia license is required), and access is via the Feeder Ditch, which connects the lake with the Dismal Swamp Canal. White-tailed deer are legally hunted in the fall.

The refuge is open from 30 minutes before sunrise until 30 minutes after sunset daily, and overnight use is not permitted. To get to the swamp, which is south of Suffolk, take Route 13 to Route 32, and then follow the signs for 4½ miles. To get to the Boardwalk Trail, take White Marsh Rd (County Rd 642) to the Washington Ditch.

In North Carolina, stop off at the Dismal Swamp Canal Visitor/Welcome Center (☎ 252-771-8333, www.icw-net.com/DSCwelcome), 2356 Route 17N, South Mills, NC 27976. For boaters, the refuge is 5 miles from the South Mills Locks.

VIRGINIA IS 4 ♥ ERS
CHESAPEAKE

The Piedmont

Were it not for Charlottesville, the rolling Piedmont Plateau would be the most unsung part of Virginia, an area to be rushed through on the east-west I-64, the north-south Route 29, or the host of other roads that intersect it. Virginia's heartland is sandwiched between, and thus very close to, the scenic Blue Ridge and the historic Richmond and Tidewater regions. (Richmond and Petersburg are also part of the Piedmont – see the Richmond chapter.)

The gem of the area is Monticello, Thomas Jefferson's magnificent home near Charlottesville. The region includes other Jefferson architectural masterpieces, Ash Lawn – Highland (James Monroe's home), the 'real Virginia' cities of Lynchburg and Danville, and many historic monuments and Civil War battlefields, such as Appomattox.

Highlights

- Charlottesville – a pleasant university town with a rich history and sophisticated nightlife

- Monticello – Jefferson's home and greatest architectural achievement

- Lynchburg – the host of historical buildings, monuments, and Jefferson's Poplar Forest

- Appomattox – where the Civil War ended

- Booker T Washington's birthplace – honoring the onetime slave and respected spokesman

There are two Virginia Welcome Centers in the Piedmont, both near the North Carolina border: Skippers (☎ 804-634-4113) is on I-95 (Emporia is to the north), and Bracey (☎ 804-689-2295) is on I-85 near Buggs Island Lake (South Hill is to the north).

CHARLOTTESVILLE

This town (population 38,000) is a Virginia must-see. It has some of the state's finest architectural masterpieces and an altogether Southern feel, with its magnolia-lined streets and the scenic Blue Ridge Mountains as a backdrop.

The locals call it 'C-ville' or 'Mr Jefferson's Country' (a nod to Thomas Jefferson, whose influence is pervasive, especially at the University of Virginia and Monticello). One wag described it as the 'sort of place you like if you like that sort of place,' but it's one of the most delightful and sophisticated destinations in the state. Surrounding the city is the pastoral Albemarle County – a delightful rural area that attracts the rich and famous who can afford to live there.

Orientation

There are two downtowns: The one on the west side, near the university, is called The Corner; the more historic downtown is a mile east of The Corner and is connected to it by University Ave and Main St. In the historic downtown area, 1st St intersects Main St; the streets west of 1st are numbered and are labeled 'W,' and the streets east of 1st are numbered and are labeled 'E' (this means there is a 2nd St E and a 2nd St W, etc).

Information

Tourist Offices The well-signed Charlottesville/Albemarle CVB (☎ 804-977-1783, www.charlottesvilletourism.org) is on Route 20S near I-64, exit 121. To get there, take bus No 8 ('Piedmont College') from the corner of 5th St E and Market St. In addition to arranging accommodations, the bureau can sell you a discounted combination ticket (called a President's Pass) for attractions including Monticello. (Adult combo tickets are $19; for kids, it is cheaper to pay for entry at the individual attractions.)

The 'Thomas Jefferson at Monticello' exhibit, in the north wing of the center's building, is well presented and free. A visit is a must either before or after you go to Monticello. The center is open 9 am to 5:30 pm daily March to October; during the rest of the year, it closes at 5 pm.

At Newcomb Hall (☎ 804-924-3363), on the University of Virginia grounds (reached from McCormick Rd, where there is no parking), students are mustered daily to answer questions and give guided tours of the Rotunda and central grounds. Tours are at 10 and 11 am and 2, 3, and 4 pm daily and are free. More information is available from the University Guide Service (☎ 804-924-3239), off Route 250W – it's well signed.

Money The Wacovia Bank (☎ 804-979-2250), corner of Jefferson and 9th Sts, and the First Virginia Bank (☎ 804-978 3041), on Barracks Rd, are good for foreign exchange.

Post & Communications The downtown post office (☎ 804-978-7648), 513 E Main St, is open 8:30 am to 5 pm weekdays and 10 am to 1 pm Saturday. For faxes, copies, and other business needs, there's a Kinko's (☎ 804-974-6804) at 1350 Seminole Trail; it's open 24 hours.

The Jefferson-Madison Regional Library (☎ 804-979-7151), 201 E Market St, has free public Internet access. The www.catte (☎ 804-964-9254, ✉ surf@cvillecaffe.com), 2036 Rio Hill Center, charges $3.75 for half an hour. The Mudhouse (☎ 804-984-6833), 213 W Main St, also has Internet access.

Internet Resources There is a veritable wealth of information about Charlottesville on the Internet – the city's primary website is probably one of the most accessible and productive in the world. Log on to www.charlottesvilletourism.org and be engrossed; the related 'Hyperville' site gives all the current events. For more performing-arts information and schedules of events, browse through the Charlottesville Guide Online at www.cjp.com/guide.

Travel Agencies Enterprise Travel (☎ 804-296-7500) is at 401 E Market St, at 400 E Main St, and at the airport.

Bookstores New Dominion Book Shop (☎ 804-295-2552), 404 E Main St, focuses on quality literature and art/architecture. Another good choice is the UVa Bookstore – one of the few university stores to maintain its mission as a service to the students and professors rather than as an income-generating machine. Quest Bookshop Inc (☎ 804-295-3377), 619 W Main St, is great for New Age material, and Shenanigan's (☎ 804-295-4797), 2146 Barracks Rd, is a bookstore and toy store catering to the enlightened parent.

Laundry There's Brown's self-service laundry at 1326 E High St, and many motels have laundry facilities.

Medical Services The emergency room at the UVa Hospital (☎ 804-924-2231), on Lee Ave (west of downtown, near The Corner), and the Martha Jefferson Hospital (☎ 804-982-7150), on Locust Ave, east of downtown, have 24 hour facilities.

Monticello

Everybody knows Monticello, Thomas Jefferson's home, probably because it is on the back of the nickel coin (the perfect souvenir?). It is 3 miles southeast of C-ville on Route 53. It is an absolute must to visit if you make it to this part of the world.

And the house is very much the embodiment of its creator, Jefferson, who oversaw all stages of its development over a period of 40 years and incorporated many of his fascinating ideas in the design. Jefferson, the third president of the US and one of the nation's founding fathers, was an intriguing character – perhaps somewhat eccentric, but with a prodigious output. His private chambers were set up so that he got out of the right side of his bed to write and out of the left side to get dressed. This puts a new accent on 'getting up on the wrong side of the bed.'

THE PIEDMONT

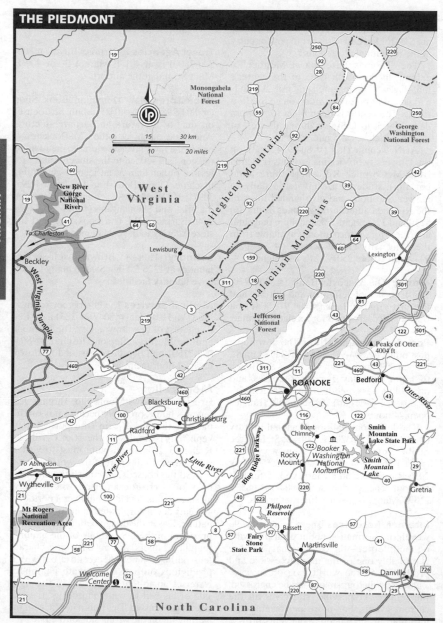

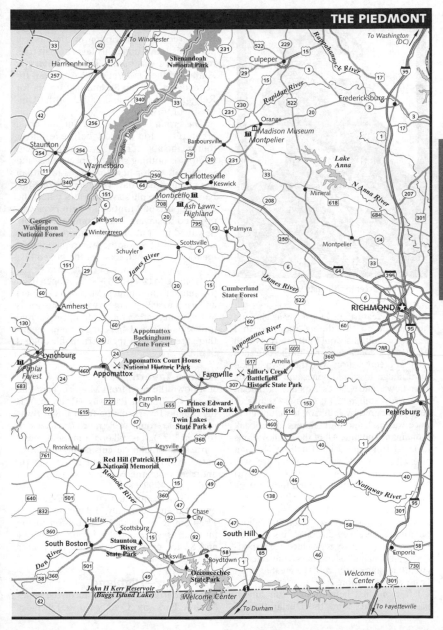

THE PIEDMONT

VIRGINIA

The eccentric Thomas Jefferson

Unusual features include a passage linking the kitchen to the dining room so that weather conditions would not interfere with the meals, a concave mirror in the entrance hall that greets visitors with their own upside down image, fossilized bones and elk antlers from Lewis and Clark's expedition, hidden and narrow staircases (as ordinary staircases were considered by Jefferson to be unsightly space wasters), and outbuildings at the back of the main building. All of these innovations deviated from the usual English Georgian style. (Jefferson's 'essay in architecture' was based on the ancient temple of Vesta in Rome, which is illustrated in the 16th-century *I Quattro Libri*, by Italian architect Andrea Palladio.)

Other inventions are scattered throughout the house – his seven-day clock, his two-pen 'polygraph' (used to reproduce correspondence), and an indoor compass (connected to a weather vane on the roof) he created to indicate wind direction.

Jefferson died here in 1826 (on July 4, exactly 50 years after the Declaration of Independence), and he's buried on the estate in a nearby tomb surrounded by hardwood trees. The inscription on the obelisk above his tomb, under his favorite oak tree, reads: 'Here was buried Thomas Jefferson, Author of the Declaration of American Independence, Of the Statute of Virginia for Religious Freedom, and Father of the University of Virginia.'

The grounds are well laid out and are a great place for a stroll before or after touring the house. The view from the 'mountaintop' is nothing short of spectacular, and visitors often stop here for a day, rather than the planned half day. The remains of Mulberry Row, the old slave quarters, reflect the darker past of Monticello. Jefferson was opposed to slavery – an 'abominable crime' he called it – but he owned more than 200 slaves (one of whom he was reputedly romantically attached to – see the boxed text Dashing Sally: Jefferson's Little Secret).

Monticello (☎ 804-984-9822) is open 8 am to 5 pm daily in summer (March to October) and 9 am to 4:30 pm otherwise. Admission is $9 for adults and $5 for children. The revised tour schedule and ticketing system means there are no longer the interminable queues of old.

Michie Tavern

Just down the road from Monticello, on the Thomas Jefferson Parkway (Route 53), is the Michie Tavern, dating from 1784 (it was moved here from a well-traveled stagecoach route in 1927). It is still operating, and guests can eat colonial-style cuisine in The Ordinary, take a 45-minute tour of the tavern, and check out the Meadow Run Gristmill (built circa 1797).

The tavern museum (☎ 804-977-1234) is open 9 am to 5 pm daily, and lunch is served 11:30 am to 3 pm daily. Admission to the museum is $6 for adults, $5.50 for seniors, and $2 for children. A hearty lunch costs about $11.

Ash Lawn – Highland

James Monroe's 535-acre estate on the James Monroe Parkway (County Rd 795) includes

Dashing Sally: Jefferson's Little Secret

With the release of the film *Jefferson in Paris*, the American public has had to reckon with the possibility that Thomas Jefferson, the 'Father of Independence,' kept a slave mistress, Sally Hemings, for more than 35 years.

The story has been around since Jefferson ran for a second term as president, in 1803. At that time, the opposition press attacked Jefferson's character by accusing him of a sexual liaison with a beautiful mulatto woman, nicknamed 'Dashing Sally,' who was 30 years younger than the president. But Jefferson's cadre of male biographers have ignored, repressed, or dismissed the story for almost two centuries, in spite of circumstantial evidence and Fawn M Brodie's 1974 biography *Thomas Jefferson: An Intimate History*, which details her case for Jefferson's intimate relationship with Hemings.

As the story goes, Jefferson began his liaison with his daughter Mary's slave nurse between 1787 and 1789, while he was America's ambassador to France. At the time, Jefferson was the widowed father of two daughters, a lonely man who had promised his dying wife that he would never remarry. Hemings was the half-sister of his wife – she and Martha shared a father, and her mother was a slave given to Jefferson as a part of Martha's dowry. When the Paris interlude began, Hemings was about 14, and Jefferson was at least 44. And when they returned to Virginia in 1789, Hemings was pregnant. According to the Brodie biography, Jefferson and Hemings continued their relationship until Jefferson died in 1826, by which time there were five children, some of whom bore a striking resemblance to the master of Monticello. These children (but not their mother) were among the handful of slaves Jefferson freed when they became adults. In addition to filmmakers, fiction writers have aired the story – read Barbara Chase-Riboud's *Sally Hemings*.

Given that sexual relations between white planters and slave women, whether by force or by mutual consent, were not a rarity at that time, the Hemings-Jefferson story – if true – might constitute little more than an interesting footnote in a text on American slavery…except for one thing: the persistent tendency among a wide range of writers and commentators to idealize Jefferson.

Until recently, conservative historians have argued staunchly against the existence of any liaison between their hero and Hemings, protesting that such goings-on would be incomprehensible to a man of Jefferson's enlightened moral character. DNA testing of Hemings' descendants has turned up the legendary man's genes, but some argue that it could be the DNA of a Jefferson relative. There is a substantial amount of information on the subject on the Internet; one place to check is www.monticello.org.

Liberal observers have looked at the Sally Hemings story as yet another example that Jefferson was a man ahead of his time, unafraid to sustain a monogamous, interracial romance for decades while living in a racist society. Even Brodie has felt compelled to describe the Hemings-Jefferson relationship as 'a serious passion.' The novels and film show Sally Hemings as the one person who could draw out the emotions of a man who had dedicated his life to worshiping the power of reason. Yet amidst all the romantic speculation, few commentators note that Dashing Sally was a slave child when Tom Jefferson called her to bed, and that she had little choice but to comply.

The researchers of the Thomas Jefferson Memorial Foundation (at Monticello) have assembled a packet of information describing what is and isn't known about the Sally Hemings story and are actively pursuing contacts with African American descendants of Jefferson's slaves in hopes of giving visitors a more complete picture of life at Monticello in Hemings' and Jefferson's day.

VIRGINIA

Monroe's house, farm-craft demonstrations, outbuildings, and boxwood gardens. Jefferson selected the site for his friend and had his gardeners plant orchards there while Monroe was overseas for three years as minister to France. Only 'some' Monroe items are found here. His debts had mounted by the time he retired from office, to a point where he had to sell his farm (on which he had hoped to retire) and many of his possessions.

A colonial crafts weekend, called Plantation Days, is held in early July, and an outdoor summer festival of concerts, family entertainment, dramas, and opera on the grounds is held in late August. The estate (☎ 804-293-9539), administered by the College of William and Mary, is open 9 am to 6 pm daily March to October and 10 am to 5 pm daily November to February. Admission is $8 for adults, $7.50 for seniors, and $5 for children.

University of Virginia

The University of Virginia (UVa) grounds, at the west end of town, include the original Academical Village – which was designed by Jefferson and includes a beautiful Rotunda (a scale replica of the Pantheon in Rome), an original classroom, and a library in the dome room. Jefferson supervised the construction process via telescope from Monticello. Adjacent to the Rotunda are student rooms, faculty pavilions, and gardens. Woodrow Wilson and his absolute antithesis, Edgar Allan Poe, spent student time in the West Range of the village.

The 'Village' (☎ 804-924-7969) is open 9 am to 4:45 pm daily, and tours are free and are at 10 and 11 am and 2, 3, and 4 pm. There is free parking at the Memorial Gym parking lot; otherwise, watch out for parking fines.

Statues of Explorers

On the corner of Ridge and Main Sts in Midway Park is a statue of Meriwether Lewis, William Clark, and Sacajawea, honoring the two explorers of the Louisiana Territory and their Native American guide. On W Main St, east of UVa, is the statue of George Rogers Clark – explorer of the Northwest Territory and older brother of William Clark.

Virginia Discovery Museum

This museum (☎ 804-977-1025), at the east end of the Downtown Mall, is a hands-on place for children and adults alike. There is a permanent 'Jefferson's Corner' display, an 18th-century pioneer log cabin, and plenty of interactive delights.

It is open 10 am to 5 pm Tuesday to Saturday and 1 to 5 pm Sunday. Admission is $4 for adults and $3 for seniors and children. On the first Sunday of the month, entry is free.

Wineries

The 'cognoscenti of the grape' have a good choice in this region. **Jefferson Vineyards** (☎ 804-977-5459), 1353 Thomas Jefferson Parkway, is known for its *vinifera* (American/French varietal) wines; it is open 11 am to 5 pm daily.

The **Oakencroft Vineyard & Winery** (☎ 804-296-4188), 3½ miles west of Route 29 on Barracks Rd (which turns into Garth Rd), has tours and tastings. It is open 11 am to 5 pm daily from April to December and 11 am to 5 pm weekends only in March.

Special Events

In March, there is the Virginia Festival of the Book. For two weeks in April, C-ville celebrates the annual Dogwood Festival, with opening-night fireworks, musical performances, a carnival, and a parade.

Independence Day (July 4) is celebrated at Monticello with a naturalization ceremony. In October, at the Virginia Film Festival, movie stars come to Charlottesville to view screenings of new releases – call ☎ 804-924-3378 for information. In early December, the Charlottesville Tradition includes a grand illumination ceremony, and around Christmas Day, A Merrie Olde England Christmas Festival is held at the Boar's Head Inn Country Resort (see Hotels & Motels under Places to Stay, below).

Places to Stay

Camping The *Charlottesville KOA* (☎ 804-296-9881, 3825 Red Hill Rd) is southwest of the city on County Rd 708 (if eastbound on I-64, take exit 118A to Route 29; if westbound, take exit 121 to Route 20). It is open

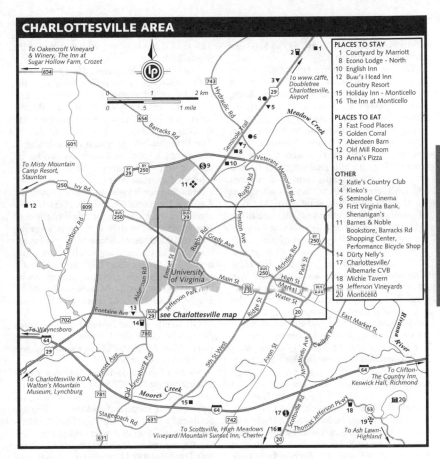

CHARLOTTESVILLE AREA

To Oakencroft Vineyard
& Winery, The Inn at
Sugar Hollow Farm, Crozet

To www.caffe,
Doubletree
Charlottesville,
Airport

Meadow Creek

To Misty Mountain
Camp Resort,
Staunton

University
of Virginia

see Charlottesville map

To Waynesboro

To Charlottesville KOA,
Walton's Mountain
Museum, Lynchburg

Moores Creek

To Clifton-
The Country Inn,
Keswick Hall, Richmond

Rivanna River

To Scottsville, High Meadows
Vineyard/Mountain Sunset Inn, Chester

To Ash Lawn-
Highland

PLACES TO STAY
1   Courtyard by Marriott
8   Econo Lodge - North
10 English Inn
12 Boar's Head Inn
      Country Resort
15 Holiday Inn - Monticello
16 The Inn at Monticello

PLACES TO EAT
3   Fast Food Places
5   Golden Corral
7   Aberdeen Barn
12 Old Mill Room
13 Anna's Pizza

OTHER
2   Katie's Country Club
4   Kinko's
6   Seminole Cinema
9   First Virginia Bank,
      Shenanigan's
11 Barnes & Noble
      Bookstore, Barracks Rd
      Shopping Center,
      Performance Bicycle Shop
14 Durty Nelly's
17 Charlottesville/
      Albemarle CVB
18 Michie Tavern
19 Jefferson Vineyards
20 Monticello

VIRGINIA

from March to November, and there are shady campsites, a pavilion, a recreation hall, and a pool (which is open 10 am to 8 pm Monday to Saturday). It is a good value, with sites/hookups for $19/26 for two and Kamping Kabins for $33.

The ***Misty Mountain Camp Resort*** (☎ 540-456-6409), out on Route 250 toward Waynesboro (8 miles west of C-ville), is an alternative if the KOA is full; sites are $19 to $27 (hookups are $4 extra).

Guesthouses The local B&B private service is Guesthouses Bed & Breakfast, Inc

(☎ 804-979-7264, www.va-guesthouses.com). Most local B&Bs are expensive.

In downtown Charlottesville, there are only a couple choices. ***200 South Street*** (☎ 804-979-0200) consists of two historic houses (one a former house of ill repute) that have been combined. The rooms are $100 to $190 for two (an extra person is $20). The ***Downtown Inn*** (☎ 804-977-3746, 212 E Main St), right on the mall, is small but very atmospheric; the rooms range from $125 to $175 (an extra person is $25).

Outside of downtown Charlottesville, ***The Inn at Sugar Hollow Farm*** (☎ 804-823-7086), on Sugar Hollow Rd, is a quaint little country B&B in a lovely mountain setting; singles are $85 to $130, and doubles are $95 to $160 (an extra person will cost $25).

The Inn at Monticello (☎ 804-979-3593), off Route 20S, is a cozy place with delightful rooms furnished with antiques, canopy beds, and fireplaces. Each room has a private porch; singles/doubles start at $90/135.

Clifton – The Country Inn (☎ 804-971-1800, 1296 Clifton Drive, www.cliftoninn.com), just off Route 250E, 5 miles from C-ville, is a large B&B with all the facilities (pool, heated spa, nature trails, tennis court, and a lake) and additional comforts, such as afternoon tea at 4 pm. In winter, Sunday to Thursday, all rooms are $150; otherwise, they are up to $315. It gets good press – it was rated one of the nation's 'Top 12' by *Country Inns*.

There are a couple of places near Scottsville, south of C-ville off Route 20S. The *High Meadows Vineyard/Mountain Sunset Inn* (☎ 804-286-2218) is set in 50 acres of vineyard. There are nightly candlelit dinners (by prior arrangement) and wine tastings; singles are $80, and doubles are $95 to $185, depending on whether you have a room or suite.

Chester (☎ 804-286-3960, 243 James River Rd, Scottsville), County Rd 726, is a comfortable B&B (with bicycles for guests); all rooms are $140.

Hotels & Motels Strangely, for a university town, there are no budget hostels. There are, however, a couple of value motels downtown on Emmet St (Route 29S). The *Budget Inn* (☎ 804-293-5141, 140 Emmet St) is near the university and the CSXT railway line. Singles/doubles are $40/45, with $2/3 off in winter (an extra person is $5).

The *Econo Lodge University* (☎ 804-296-2104, 400 Emmet St), which is basic but adequate, is open 24 hours; singles and doubles are $45, rising to $70 in summer.

The *Best Western Cavalier Inn* (☎ 804-296-8111, 105 Emmet St N), on Routes 29 and 250 Business, is well within earshot of the railway line. It has a deluxe room special of $65 for a double that includes breakfast, wine on arrival, and a ticket to one of the attractions. Otherwise, singles/doubles are

$60/70 (no frills). It also has a restaurant and an outdoor pool. The *Red Roof Inn* (☎ 804-295-4333, 1309 W Main St) has doubles for $58 to $89.

The *Omni Charlottesville* (☎ 804-971-5500), another hotel trying to marry the colonial with the modern, is at the west end of the Downtown Mall. Single and double rooms are $99 to $134; an extra person is $15 (packages and weekend rates are available). The hotel has all the necessary additions: a restaurant, a spacious lounge on two levels, indoor and outdoor pools, and a fully equipped exercise room.

Heading northward out of downtown, the *English Inn* (☎ 804-971-9900, 2000 Morton Drive), a block south of the junction of Routes 29 and 250 Bypass, combines a motel with the B&B theme. Some of the rooms are furnished in Colonial style, others are more modern in appearance. The full breakfast is enjoyed in the 'olde worlde' dining room. The rooms are worth the money they cost – $56/64 for singles/doubles in winter; otherwise, they start at $67/75.

Off Route 29, the *Econo Lodge – North* (☎ 804-295-3185, 2014 Holiday Drive) has singles/doubles for $40/45 in the low season (an extra person is $5).

South of downtown, the *Holiday Inn – Monticello* (☎ 804-977-5100, 1200 5th St SW), at the junction of I-64 and 5th St, exit 120, has a pool, dining room, and cocktail bar. Singles/doubles in the low season are $61/71; otherwise, they are $66/76. About the same price is the *Courtyard by Marriott* (☎ 804-973-7100, 800-321-2211, 638 Hillsdale Drive), north of downtown off of Route 29. It's a really comfortable place with a large grassy patio (a double is $75, but breakfast is extra).

The *Doubletree Charlottesville* (☎ 804-973-2121, 2350 Seminole Trail), is on Route 29N, 3 miles north of the junction of the Route 250 Bypass and 7 miles from town. Although it is relatively expensive, it is worth the $79 for singles and doubles in the low season. It has a full range of facilities and two restaurants.

The *Boar's Head Inn Country Resort* (☎ 804-296-2181, 200 Ednam Drive, www.boarsheadinn.com), on a 53-acre estate

CHARLOTTESVILLE

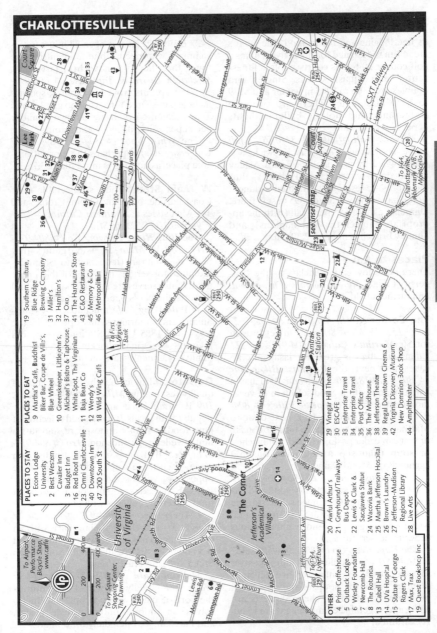

VIRGINIA

PLACES TO STAY
1 Econo Lodge University
2 Best Western Cavalier Inn
3 Budget Inn
16 Red Roof Inn
23 Omni Charlottesville
40 Downtown Inn
47 200 South St

PLACES TO EAT
9 Martha's Café, Buddhist Biker Bar, Coupe de Ville's, Blue Wheel
10 Greenskeeper, Little John's, Michael's Bistro & TapHouse, White Spot, The Virginian
11 Baja Bean Co
12 Wendy's
18 Wild Wing Café
19 Southern Culture, Blue Ridge Brewing Company
31 Miller's
32 Hamilton's
37 Oxo
41 The Hardware Store
43 C&O Restaurant
45 Memory & Co
46 Metropolitain

OTHER
4 Prism Coffeehouse
5 Outback Lodge
6 Wesley Foundation
7 Newcomb Hall
8 The Rotunda
13 Cabell Hall
14 UVa Hospital
15 Statue of George Rogers Clark
17 Max, Trax
19 Quest Bookshop Inc
20 Awful Arthur's
21 Greyhound/Trailways Bus Depot
22 Lewis & Clark & Sacajawea Statue
24 Wacovia Bank
25 Martha Jefferson Hospital
26 Brown's Laundry
27 Jefferson-Madison Regional Library
28 Live Arts
29 Vinegar Hill Theatre
30 ESCAFÉ
33 Enterprise Travel
34 Enterprise Travel
35 Post Office
36 The Mudhouse
38 Jefferson Theater
39 Regal Downtown Cinema 6
42 Virginia Discovery Museum, New Dominion Book Shop
44 Amphitheater

1½ miles west of the junction of Route 29 Bypass and Route 250W, is known both for its fine lodging and for its food. The Boar's Head Inn is designed for the active – it has a golf course, 20 tennis courts, pools, a fitness center, and squash courts. Singles and doubles are $165 to $205 in winter and $179 to $340 in summer. There are two fine restaurants, and hot-air balloon flights depart from the club.

Keswick Hall (☎ *804-979-3440, 701 Club Drive, www.keswick.com)*, in Keswick, was once owned by principals of Laura Ashley (purveyors of wallpapers and fabrics) – thus the rooms are festooned with their products. You'll have to pay $250 to $595 to stay there. Dinner is a mere $55 per head (with the appropriate tablecloths and napkins), and Sunday brunch is noon to 2:30 pm.

Places to Eat
There are a few eating enclaves – the University Corner area, W Main St, Downtown, and farther afield.

The Corner At *The Virginian* (☎ *804-293-2606, 1521 W Main St)* you can get brunch for $6; *Martha's Café* (☎ *804-971-7530, 11 Elliewood Ave)* is great for lasagna, crab cakes, and beer; the *Buddhist Biker Bar* (☎ *804-971-9181, 20 Elliewood Ave)* has a varied menu with a good selection of vegetarian entrees; and *Coupe de Ville's* (☎ *804-977-3966, 9 Elliewood Ave)*, next door to Martha's, has chicken (half a bird) for $6.50, or you can order pasta, seafood, sandwiches, or soup (and see a gathering of PhD eggheads on Monday night).

The *Greenskeeper* (☎ *804-984-4653, 1517 University Ave)* is consistently good and has a great selection of beer, huge salads starting at $4.50, entrees starting at $7, seafood sandwiches starting at $5, and a mountainous brownie dessert for $3.

The *Baja Bean Co* (☎ *804-293-4507, 1327 W Main St)* serves delicious California-style Mexican food. An entree of five delicious taquitos is $3, the soup of the day is $3, burgers start at $4.50, cheap desserts are $3.50, and vegetable chimichangas are $5.50. Ay, caramba!

Cheap places along University Ave bring in the students. *Littlejohn's* (☎ *804-977-0588, 1427 University Ave)* is open 24 hours for insomniacs who need a bite after hitting the town; their hearty sandwiches start at $4. *Michael's Bistro & Taphouse* (☎ *804-977-3697)* is upstairs from Littlejohn's; specials include pan-seared tuna, voodoo gumbo, and Thai coconut curry. It has its own humidor and super-efficient smoke extractors.

The *White Spot* (☎ *804-295-9899, 1407 University Ave)* is perhaps the most affordable place, as nothing is more than $3.75.

W Main Street There's delectable Gulf Coast cuisine, blending Cajun, Creole, and Tex-Mex styles at *Southern Culture* (☎ *804-979-1990, 633 W Main St)*.

The *Blue Ridge Brewing Co* (☎ *804-977-0017, 709 W Main St)* is Virginia's first brewery restaurant (it opened in 1988) and is the place for serious imbibing of the amber fluid. It also serves steak, seafood, pasta, and desserts; the bar is open to 2 am nightly.

A *Wild Wing Café*, much loved by Carolinians and Georgians, has opened in the renovated 1885 Union Station. All the old favorites – beer in the bucket, chicken wings, family-style meals – are on offer.

Downtown This are has the best selection of quality restaurants. *Miller's* (☎ *804-971-8511, 109 W Main St)* is an unpretentious dive popular with locals. It has a good selection of junk food, a smoky atmosphere, and just a hint of veiled sophistication. *Oxo* (☎ *804-977-8111, 215 W Water St)* is an English-run place – hence the name – that is almost the opposite of Miller's and costs twice as much. But for the extra dough you get gourmet food and cushy couches with pillows.

L'Avventura (☎ *804-977-1912, 220 W Market St)* is a classy Italian place with an eclectic menu in keeping with its title, and it is known for its freshly baked sourdough bread and thin-crust pizzas.

Metropolitain (☎ *804-977-1043, 214 W Water St)* is equally as chic as L'Avventura – the sort of place where people call themselves on mobile phones. Posh, pricey, and Parisian, it's open daily for dinner.

Hamilton's (☎ 804-295-6649, 101 W Main St) has 'sort of nouvelle' American cuisine. The cooks are not afraid to mix different flavors; a good entree costs $8 to $16.

The Hardware Store (☎ 804-977-1518, 316 E Main St), a city landmark since 1895, is a must for first-timers to C-ville. Apart from the interesting memorabilia relating to its days as a store and its 'lit up' mall entrance, the place is good for inexpensive meals – barbecued ribs, hamburgers, sandwiches, pasta, fish, salads, and baked potatoes; you can eat well here for less than $10. There's free parking on Water St.

Memory & Co (☎ 804-296-3539, 213 2nd St SW), once a cooking school, now prepares the finest French and classic Italian cuisine with just a hint of Californian influence; the four-course prix fixe meal is worthwhile. There's a popular brunch on Sunday. Smoking is not allowed.

The ***C&O Restaurant*** (☎ 804-971-7044, 515 E Water St) is divided into two parts – a bistro and a more expensive upstairs dining room, both serving innovative French food and wines by the glass. The bistro is open weekdays for lunch and daily for dinner, and the upstairs dining room (where a jacket is required) is open for two seatings, Monday to Saturday, at 6:30 and 9:30 pm. Two diners are likely to spend $50 downstairs and up to $100 upstairs.

Other Locales West of downtown, ***Anna's Pizza*** (☎ 804-977-6228, 115 Maury Ave) is for those craving a pizza (a large is $9.50, a medium is $8, and a small is $6). It is open from 11 am until about 11 pm daily. It also has grinders, calzone, salads, and imported olives.

The ***Golden Corral*** (☎ 804-974-7172, 1185 Seminole Trail) is a buffet place with a great salad bar. ***Wendy's***, the perennial favorite of the impecunious, has two locations: at 416 4th St SW (☎ 804-979-0380) and on Route 29N (☎ 804-973-3324).

The ***Aberdeen Barn*** (☎ 804-296-4630, 2018 Holiday Drive) has a good reputation for consistency and huge portions of steak (meals are $15 to $25).

Tokyo Rose (☎ 804-296-3366, 2171 Ivy Rd), in the Ivy Square (University) Shopping Center, has an excellent sushi bar ($12 is enough for a filling meal). ***Tiffany's Seafood*** (☎ 804 293-5000), also in the same center, has a good reputation as the town's best seafood restaurant, with Maine lobster, soft-shell crabs, and steamed shrimp.

The Boar's Head Inn (see Places to Stay, earlier) has the expensive ***Old Mill Room*** (☎ 804-296-2181), which is housed in an 1834 gristmill. It serves breakfast, lunch, and dinner daily and offers Sunday brunch; reservations are advised.

Entertainment

Get copies of the free *CVILLE Weekly* and *Charlottesville Review* to find out what is on and where. There are heaps of venues for

Gay & Lesbian Charlottesville

With enlightened UVa close by, there are good services for gay and lesbian travelers. The Lesbian, Gay, Bisexual & Transgender Union (LGBTU; ✉ lgbu@virginia.edu) meets at 9 pm every Thursday at the Wesley Foundation, near the corner of Emmet St and Lewis Mountain Rd. The organization's Helpline number is ☎ 804-982-2773 and is available 7 to 10 pm Sunday to Wednesday.

Men2Men (☎ 804-963-8391) is a social group interested in the prevention of HIV/AIDS. The Region 10 24-hour Crisis Hotline is ☎ 804-972-1800.

ESCAFE (☎ 804-296-4789) is a local restaurant that is popular with the gay and lesbian crowd; it is at the west end of the Downtown Mall, near the Omni. Club 216 (216 W Water St) is also a popular meeting place.

Bookstores with gay and lesbian information are Barnes & Noble Bookstore (☎ 804-984-0461), at the Barracks Rd Shopping Center; Quest Bookshop (☎ 804-295-3377), 619 W Main St; and the UVa Bookstore (which stocks *Advocate* and *Out*).

Charlottesville Pride is held for a week in the fall (☎ 804-974-9535).

VIRGINIA

jazz, rock, and just 'chugging.' For current information, call the free daily Happenings Line (☎ 804-980-8000).

Fridays after 5 is free entertainment at the Amphitheater (at the east end of Downtown Mall); the music starts at 5:30 and goes until 8 pm. The *Prism Coffeehouse* (☎ 804-977-7476), at the corner of Gordon Ave and Rugby Rd, is the place for folk and acoustic music.

Cinemas The pick of the cinemas is *Jefferson Theater* (☎ 804-980-1331, 110 E Main St), near the Downtown Mall; new movies can be seen for a mere $2. UVa's *Cinematheque* (☎ 804-924-7900), in the Newcomb Hall Theatre on campus, has a good art-house component. Some other possibilities are the *Vinegar Hill Theatre* (☎ 804-977-4911, 220 W Market St); *Regal Downtown Mall 6* (☎ 804-979-7857), in the Downtown Mall; and *Seminole Cinema* (☎ 804-980-3333, 2306 India Rd), on Route 29N.

Bars & Clubs There are ample nightlife and music venues in C-ville, and many of the restaurants listed earlier feature live music. After all, this is the town where the Dave Matthews Band started out.

Students flock to *Awful Arthur's* (☎ 804-296-0969, 333 W Main St) to hear rock and country (and sample from the extensive raw bar) and also to *Trax* (☎ 804-295-8729, 127 S 11th St), the 'stage that Dave built,' to listen mainly to rock. Goths gravitate toward the darkened depths of *The Dawning*, beneath Tokyo Rose (see Places to Eat, earlier), on weekends, wishing Nick Cave was in town.

Max (☎ 804-295-6299, 120 11th St) is a bit rougher than the other venues, but it has a country & western night for good ol' boys and girls on Wednesday. North of town, *Katie's Country Club* (☎ 804-974-6969), a purely country venue, is in the Shoppers' World Center, out on Route 29N.

Just west of town, *Dürty Nelly's* (☎ 804-295-1278, 2200 Jefferson Park Ave) is very much a locals' hangout, but the people there will welcome travelers into their gritty little tavern. Come for the rock and country and

the well-priced sandwiches, or just come to observe the drunks at the bar.

The *Outback Lodge* (☎ 804-979-7211, 917 Preston Ave), in Preston Plaza, is about the most happening place in C-ville, soundwise, and features local and national acts (the cover charge is $4 to $5).

Performing Arts First get a copy of the free *Charlottesville Arts Monthly*, which lists venues and has a pull-out calendar. Also contact the Artsline (☎ 804-980-3366).

The *Charlottesville and University Symphony Orchestra* (☎ 804-925-6505) plays an annual season.

The *McIntire Department of Music* (☎ 804-924-3984), at UVa, has information about performances by the orchestra, the University Singers, Collegium Musicum, the Jazz Ensemble, and the brass and wind ensembles. These performances are usually in UVa's Cabell Hall, although some are held 'on the lawn' near the steps of the Rotunda.

The *UVa Department of Drama* (☎ 804-924-3376) conducts a variety of performances by local and visiting companies. A good place to see live theater is at *Live Arts* (☎ 804-963-8400), 609 E Market St.

Getting There & Away

US Airways Express, United Express (Atlantic Coast), and Comair: Delta Connection (with three jet flights daily to Cincinnati) serve the Charlottesville-Albemarle Airport, which is 14 miles north of the city on Route 29N. Colgan Air (☎ 800-272-5488) services C-ville from New York.

Regular Amtrak services to New York and Chicago stop at Charlottesville's Union Station (☎ 804-296-4559, 800-872-7245), 810 W Main St. There is a daily New York-to-New Orleans service; C-ville to Richmond, via Washington, DC, is $50.

The Greyhound/Trailways bus terminal (☎ 540-295-5131) is at 310 W Main St, not far from the train station. There are daily buses to Richmond ($18) and Norfolk ($32) and two daily to DC ($28).

Charlottesville is easy to find by car. It is where Route 29 (north-south) meets I-64 (east-west); the latter joins I-95 and I-81.

Getting Around

You have the choice of walking around this pleasant city or renting a bike. A rental from Blue Wheel (☎ 804-977-1870), 19 Elliewood Ave, is about $10 per day. Also check at the Performance Bicycle Shop (☎ 540-963-9161), 1107-E Emmet St.

For a cab, call Yellow Cab (☎ 804-295-4131); a cab out to Monticello will cost about $9. The airport shuttle is Van on the Go (☎ 804-973-7667).

AROUND CHARLOTTESVILLE

The region around Charlottesville is picturesque, with gently rolling hills, wineries, and a number of historical attractions, such as the St Thomas Episcopal Church in Orange, the only surviving example of a Jeffersonian effort at religious architecture.

To the east of Orange County are the Wilderness battlefields, the scene of the first confrontation between Generals Lee and Grant in May 1864. For more information, contact the Orange Visitors Bureau (☎ 540-672-1653), 122 E Main St in Orange.

Waltons' Mountain Museum

Nelson County is best known as the birthplace of *The Waltons* TV series – such is the power of television. This museum (☎ 804-831-2000), on County Rd 617 in Schuyler (**sky**-lar), includes all those oh-so-familiar locales of the series – the Waltons' living room and kitchen, John-Boy's bedroom, and Ike Godsey's store in the rural village where the series was set.

Hollywood screenwriter Earl Hamner Jr based the characters on people from this district whom he remembered from his childhood. The museum, in the old elementary school not far from where Hamner lived as a youngster, is open 10 am to 4 pm March to November. Admission is $5 for adults and $4 for seniors; children are free.

Swannanoa Marble Palace

This palace (☎ 540-942-5161) was built in 1912 and modeled on the Villa de Medici in Italy, with its original Italian frescoes and a Tiffany stained-glass window. It is now the New Age, transcendental University of Science and Philosophy and includes a museum and gardens. The palace is on Afton Mountain, about 20 miles west of Charlottesville on I-64.

Wineries

There are several wineries around Charlottesville, including Afton Mountain Vineyards (☎ 540-456-8667), in Afton, and the Wintergreen Winery (☎ 804-361-2519), in Nellysford. These are open daily in summer and fall for tours and tastings.

North of Charlottesville, near where Route 33 intersects with Route 20, is the Barboursville Vineyard (☎ 540-832-3824). It's open 10 am to 5 pm Monday to Saturday and 11 am to 5 pm Sunday; there are free tours 10 am to 4 pm Saturday.

Governor James Barbour's Mansion

On the same property as the Barboursville Vineyard (see above), and open the same hours, this mansion was designed for Barbour (who was the governor of Virginia from 1812 to 1814) by Jefferson to resemble his own Monticello. It was burned on Christmas 1884; the ruins are now a registered Virginia historic landmark.

James Madison Museum

This museum (☎ 540-672-1776), 129 Caroline St in Orange, commemorates the fourth president of the US (who served during the difficult times of the War of 1812) and the 'father' of the Constitution. The museum also covers the history of the county and has a hall of agriculture with an 18th-century homestead.

It is open 9 am to 4 pm weekdays, 9 am to 1 pm Saturday, and 1 to 4 pm Sunday from March to November; otherwise, 9 am to 4 pm weekdays. Admission is $4 for adults, $3 for seniors, and $1 for youth under 17.

Montpelier

The lifelong home of President James Madison is now owned by the National Trust. The main house of 55 rooms is still undergoing preservation and restoration (it was substantially modified by the du Pont family), but you can see parts of it. The formal garden and grounds overlooking the Blue Ridge Mountains are a real delight. James, Dolley, and other Madisons are interred nearby. It is hoped that Montpelier will one day stand as a monument to Madison, with special emphasis placed on his contribution to the Constitution and Bill of Rights.

The house and grounds (☎ 540-672-2728) are open 9:30 am to 4:30 pm daily April to November and 9:30 am to 3 pm during the rest of the year. Admission, which includes a 10-minute video, a bus tour of the grounds, and a house tour, is $7.50 for adults, $6.50 for seniors, and $3.50 for children.

Montpelier is 6 miles south of Orange on Route 20 at Montpelier Station. In late April/ early May, the Montpelier Wine Festival is held here. The Montpelier Hunt, initiated by Marion du Pont Scott (who built the original steeplechase course) is held in November.

Canoeing

There is really good canoeing on the James River near Scottsville and the chance to fish, explore, and bird watch as you paddle along. For all canoeing, tubing, and rafting equipment, contact James River Runners Inc (☎ 804-286-2338, www.jamesriver.com) at their base camp at Hatton Ferry; it is well signed.

There are 3-, 7-, and 9-mile trips on the James for $16/22/22 per person and overnight trips for $45, all inclusive (the minimum age for canoe trips is 10; for raft or tube trips, it is six). From Route 20S, take County Rds 726 and 625 to Hatton Ferry.

LYNCHBURG

This city and its surrounding area, rightly advertised as the 'real' Virginia, is 60 miles southwest of Charlottesville on Route 29. It was founded by a Quaker named John Lynch, who from 1757 operated a ferry across the James River. In 1785, he built the region's first tobacco warehouse. For the next 100 years, the production of cigarettes and plugs of chewing tobacco ensured the city's prosperity.

During the Civil War, it was a major storage depot, which at one point was saved by the quick thinking of Confederate General Jubal Early. On June 18, 1864, the general, by use of a clever ruse, saved the city from destruction by Union troops. He tricked the enemy by having several trains move along different local rail lines, thus creating the impression that a continuous stream of reinforcements were flowing into the city.

Today, Lynchburg (population 66,000) is a regional center and a college town. It is known as the city of churches, as there are more than 130 of them in the region. It is also a city of very religious people and home to Jerry Falwell's Liberty University.

Orientation

The northeastern boundary of the city is the James River and across the river is Madison Heights in Amherst County. To the southeast of the city is Candlers Mountain, with Lynchburg Regional Airport to the west of that. Two roads divide the city into rough quarters – Route 29 is the north-south artery and Route 501 runs roughly northwest-southeast. Route 460 skirts the city on its southern boundaries.

Information

Tourist Offices The Lynchburg Chamber of Commerce (☎ 804-847-1811, 800-532-7821, www.lynchburgchamber.org) is at 216 12th St, on the corner of Church St. A 10-minute audiovisual is shown, and there are exhibits and a gift shop. It's open 9 am to 5 pm daily. The center also has an information line (☎ 800-732-5821).

Money There are plenty of suitable banks for foreign currency exchange (and other banking necessaries) in The Plaza, at Langhorne Rd and Memorial Ave; River Ridge Mall, 3405 Candlers Mountain Rd; and the Boonsboro Shopping Center, on Boonsboro Rd.

Bookstores On a rainy day in Lynchburg, try Inkling's, at 1206 Main St, across from Percival's Isle; Givens, on Lakeside Drive (Route 221); or The Bookstore (☎ 804-384-1746), in the Boonsboro Shopping Center (on Route 501 Business).

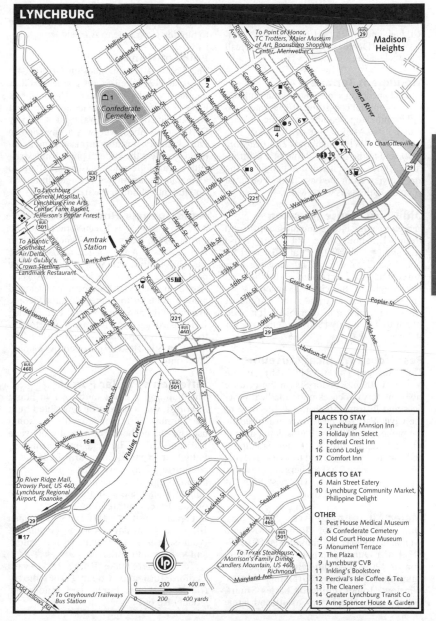

LYNCHBURG

VIRGINIA

PLACES TO STAY
2 Lynchburg Mansion Inn
3 Holiday Inn Select
8 Federal Crest Inn
16 Econo Lodge
17 Comfort Inn

PLACES TO EAT
6 Main Street Eatery
10 Lynchburg Community Market,
Philippine Delight

OTHER
1 Pest House Medical Museum
& Confederate Cemetery
4 Old Court House Museum
5 Monument Terrace
7 The Plaza
9 Lynchburg CVB
11 Inkling's Bookstore
12 Percival's Isle Coffee & Tea
13 The Cleaners
14 Greater Lynchburg Transit Co
15 Anne Spencer House & Garden

0   200   400 m
0   200   400 yards

Medical Services The Lynchburg General Hospital (☎ 804-947-3000), off Tate Springs Rd, has emergency and critical-care facilities. For the Doctor's Answering Service, call ☎ 804-847-4466.

Monument Terrace

This is Lynchburg's most famous landmark – a war memorial consisting of 139 limestone and granite steps leading up to the old city courthouse. At the foot of the steps is a statue of a WWI 'doughboy' *(The Listening Post)*, and at the top is a statue of a Confederate soldier. Even if you don't climb to the top, the view from the base, at the corner of Main and 9th Sts, is worthwhile.

Old Court House Museum

There are many interesting museums in and around Lynchburg. The Old Court House Museum (☎ 804-847-1459), at 901 Court St, in an 1855 Greek Revival building, has a restored Hustings courtroom and exhibition areas depicting the city's 200-year history (including Monacan tribal artifacts, Quaker relics, and Civil War memorabilia). It is open 10 am to 4 pm daily ($1 for adults, free for children).

Pest House Medical Museum

This museum (☎ 804-847-1465), at the corner of 4th and Taylor Sts (in the historic city cemetery), focuses upon medical practices and instruments in use at the time of the Civil War. The pest house was used by the pioneering Dr Terrell to isolate patients with contagious diseases (mainly smallpox) and contains his office and tools used during the period. Some 2200 soldiers are buried in the adjoining cemetery. The pest house is open sunrise to sunset daily.

Maier Museum of Art

On the campus of Randolph-Macon Woman's College, this museum (☎ 804-947-8136), at 1 Quinlan St, houses a fine collection of 19th- and 20th-century American paintings (works by Grandma Moses, Winslow Homer, Gilbert Charles Stuart, Georgia O'Keeffe, Mary Cassatt, and Jamie Wyeth). It is free and is open September to May by appointment and 1 to 5 pm Tuesday to Sunday from June to August.

Point of Honor

The Point of Honor mansion (☎ 804-847-1459), at 112 Cabell St, on Daniel's Hill, is another Lynchburg landmark. The red-brick Federal-style building is so named because it is on the site of a duel. It was built in 1815 by Dr George Cabell, who was a physician to Patrick Henry. It is now furnished and decorated to reflect the Federal period and early-19th-century lifestyles. It is open 10 am to 4 pm daily. Admission is $5 for adults and $1 for students; children are free.

Anne Spencer House & Garden

At 1313 Pierce St is the historic home and garden of the internationally known African American poet Anne Spencer (1903–75). The garden and 'Edankraal' studio, where the poet gained much of her inspiration, was restored in the 1980s. Spencer entertained many famous visitors here, including George Washington Carver and Martin Luther King Jr. The garden is open 10 am to 4 pm Monday to Saturday; donations are requested. The house (☎ 804-846-0517) is open by appointment only.

Jefferson's Poplar Forest

This building, 5 miles south of Lynchburg in Forest, was a retreat designed and built by Thomas Jefferson for his personal use (he stayed here occasionally between 1806 and 1813). The octagonal hermitage, Palladian in style, is unfurnished and is currently being restored – a full-scale archaeological dig is under way. It is a delight, nonetheless, and a must for those on the 'Jefferson trail.'

Poplar Forest (☎ 804-525-1806) is open 10 am to 4 pm daily April to November. Admission is $7 for adults, $6 for seniors, and $1 for youth under 17.

To get there, take Route 221 toward Bedford. Turn off on County Rd 661; the entrance to Poplar Forest is 1 mile along County Rd 661.

Special Events

The city celebrates its river location in June in the James River Bateau Festival with authentic boats ('bateaux'), which once plied the river carrying tobacco and other goods. Call ☎ 804-528-3950 for information.

Places to Stay

Camping The nearest camping areas are close to Appomattox. The **Holliday Lake State Park** (☎ 804-248-6308) has developed sites for $14; it is open from March to early December. To get there, take Route 24 through the national historic park and turn south onto County Rd 626, then take County Rd 692. **Paradise Lake Family Campground** (☎ 804-993-3332) is 6 miles west of Appomattox on Route 460 and adjacent to Paradise Lake. It is open all year, and fully serviced sites cost $14 to $20 for two.

Guesthouses There are a number of reasonable B&Bs in and close to Lynchburg. **Bed & Breakfast Virginia Style** (☎ 804-946-7207) is an association of four B&Bs; contact them for locations and prices.

Some recommended B&Bs include the **Federal Crest Inn** (☎ 804-845-6155, 1101 Federal St), with rooms from $95 to $125, and the **Lynchburg Mansion Inn** (☎ 804-528-5400, 405 Madison St), a Spanish Georgian-style place on Garland Hill ($109 to $144).

Hotels & Motels The **Thomas Motor Inn** (☎ 804-845-2121) on Route 29, 3 miles north of Lynchburg in Madison Heights, is one of the cheapest accommodations; a spacious room with cable TV, bath, and phone is $30, but it's basic.

The **Comfort Inn** (☎ 804-847-9041, 3215 Albert Lankford Drive), just off Route 29, has a pool; the cost for a single/double room in the low season is $60/65; in the high season, it starts at $65/70. The **Econo Lodge** (☎ 804-847-1045, 2400 Stadium Drive), off Route 29, exit 4 if southbound and exit 6 if northbound, has singles and doubles starting at $47.

The **Ramada Inn & Conference Center** (☎ 804-847-4424), near the junction of Odd Fellows Rd and Route 29, has data ports, an airport bus, and a restaurant; singles and doubles are $50 to $55 in the low season but rise considerably in summer. The **Innkeeper of Lynchburg** (☎ 804-237-7771, 2901 Candlers Mountain Rd), just off Route 29S, offers free breakfast, and all rooms have cable TV; singles are $54 to $90, and doubles are $60 to $90. The **Holiday Inn Select** (☎ 804-528-2500, 601 Main St), downtown, is well situated and has comfortable rooms starting at $69 (there is a two-night minimum).

The **Courtyard by Marriott** (☎ 804-846-7900, 4640 Murray Place) is a new place with a pool, whirlpool, gym, lounge, and restaurant; singles/doubles start at $80/85.

Places to Eat

The **Lynchburg Community Market – Bateau Landing** (☎ 804-847-1499), on the corner of Main and 12th Sts, has an excellent selection of fresh food. The market is open 7 am to 2 pm every day (as it has been since 1783), and there is a fine selection of baked goods, ethnic foods, meats, and produce (the perfect place to make up a picnic basket). The **Philippine Delight** (☎ 804-384-5654), in the Lynchburg Community Market, is particularly good for cheap lunches such as chicken broccoli.

The **Farm Basket** (☎ 804-528-1107, 2008 Langhorne Rd) is another inexpensive place to pick up picnic fare and box lunches. It also includes a small and always-packed restaurant where you can get cucumber sandwiches, three-bean salad, Brunswick stew, and delectable gouda cheese biscuits. In addition to a clever name, the **Phila Deli** (☎ 804-384-5972), in the Boonsboro Shopping Center, has sandwiches, hoagies, and salads.

Morrison's Family Dining (☎ 804-237-6549, 3405 Candlers Mountain Rd), in the River Ridge Mall, serves made-from-scratch Southern cooking; you can dine heartily here for less than $10. The **Main Street Eatery** (☎ 804-847-2526, 907 Main St), in the heart of old town, is an elegant place serving medium-price continental and new American cuisine.

There are a number of places for carnivores looking for a huge steak. **TC Trotters**

(☎ 804-846-3545, 2496 Rivermont Ave) serves Tex-Mex for lunch and dinner. The **Crown Sterling** (☎ 804-239-7744, 6120 Fort Ave) is popular with the young professional set and has a cigar and martini bar. The **Texas Steakhouse** (☎ 804-237-3553, 2819 Candlers Mountain Rd), near the Fort Hill shopping plaza, is open for dinner Monday to Saturday; it has a great salad bar, a kids' menu, and the 'house' dinner – rib eye, salad, rice or potato, a glass of wine, and dessert – for $15. The **Landmark Restaurant** (☎ 804-237-1884, 6113 Fort Ave) serves ribs cooked over hickory charcoal, rib eyes, and huge shrimp cocktails.

Meriwether's (☎ 804-384-3311, 4925 Boonsboro Rd), in the Boonsboro Shopping Center, is a gourmet restaurant with a superb wine selection; it's closed Sunday.

There are a number of Asian restaurants. The **China Royal** (☎ 804-385-0011, 205 Gristmill Drive), in the Graves Mill Center, has a sushi bar, and **King's Island** (☎ 804-384-0066, 2804 Forest Rd) serves Chinese and Japanese dishes, including a tasty beef broccoli for $7. The **Kyoto Japanese Steak & Seafood** (☎ 804-237-9134, 2160 Wards Rd), in the Hills Plaza, is one of those places where chicken, steak, and shrimp dishes are prepared at your table.

Entertainment

As far as nightlife goes, this is light on! It was only recently that the city and county revoked a long-standing dry law.

Club Gatsby's (☎ 804-385-5052, 2034 Lakeside Drive) usually has a band and dancing 4:30 pm to 2 am Wednesday to Saturday.

Cattle Annie's (☎ 804-846-2668, 4009 Murray Place) opens at 7 pm Monday to Saturday for live country music. TC Trotter's (see Places to Eat, earlier) advertises the 'best Bloody Marys' in town and has bands on weekends (in summer, they play outdoors).

The Cleaners (☎ 804-847-4909, 1344 Main St) has live rock 'n' roll on weekends (on an outside deck in summer) and a variety of other styles midweek.

The **Drowsy Poet** (☎ 804-846-6604, 3700 Candlers Mountain Rd) has folk music and jazz on Wednesday nights, a menu to suit vegetarians, and a selection of books and board games.

Across from the community market is **Percival's Isle Coffee & Tea** (☎ 804-847-3059, 1208 Main St), a popular meeting spot. There is a wonderful ambiance in this old restored building, which is open 7 am to 10 pm Monday to Thursday and to midnight Friday and Saturday.

The **Lynchburg Fine Arts Center** (☎ 804-846-8451, 1815 Thomson Drive) is a 500-seat theater where drama, dance, and music are performed regularly.

Getting There & Away

Lynchburg's Regional Airport (☎ 804-847-1632) is on Route 29, 8 miles south of downtown. Companies serving Lynchburg include US Airways Express (☎ 800-428-4322), Atlantic Southeast Air/Delta (☎ 804-239-6150), and United Express (☎ 800-241-6522). The taxi/limo service is Airport Limo (☎ 804-239-1777).

The Greyhound/Trailways (☎ 804-846-6614, 800-231-2222) terminal is at the corner of Wildflower Drive and Odd Fellows Rd; there is frequent service to other major centers in Virginia and out of state.

The Amtrak service (☎ 800-872-7245) passes through Lynchburg at really odd hours (the daily Crescent service between New York and New Orleans). Amtrak's station is at the corner of Kemper St and Park Ave.

Getting Around

The Greater Lynchburg Transit Co (☎ 804-847-7771) serves the city and Amherst County; the main terminal is at The Plaza shopping center, at Memorial Ave and Lakeside Drive. The office is on Kemper St.

AROUND LYNCHBURG
Appomattox

Civil War buffs will no doubt make a pilgrimage to this region, where the Court House, now an American shrine, is located (it is some 20 miles east of Lynchburg).

The Appomattox Depot visitor information center (☎ 804-352-2621), in a restored railroad depot on the main street of downtown Appomattox, has information on a walking tour and carriage rides; it is open 9 am to 5 pm daily.

McLean House, where Grant and Lee met on April 9, 1865, and where Lee surrendered the Army of Northern Virginia (and effectively ended the Civil War), is now part of the **Appomattox Court House National Historic Park** (☎ 804-352-8987). The 27 buildings of Appomattox village have been restored to their state at the time of the surrender. McLean House, which was torn down in 1893, with a speculator hope to rebuild it in DC, has since been reconstructed. (Almost unbelievably, Wilmer McLean had moved here in protest after his farm at Manassas/Bull Run had hosted the first major battle of the war!)

There are self-guided walking tours, audiovisual presentations, and help from rangers at the park. The historic park is open 9 am to 5:30 pm daily June to August; otherwise, 8:30 am to 5 pm. Admission is $4 for adults from Memorial Day to Labor Day (during the rest of year, $2), and youth under 17 are free. The courthouse and village are 2 miles north of Route 460 on Route 24.

Red Hill National Memorial

About 26 miles south of Appomattox Court House (or 35 miles southeast of Lynchburg) is Red Hill (☎ 804-376-2044), the final and favorite of the many homes of the Revolutionary War patriot Patrick Henry. The house, restored near an original law office, includes many furnishings provided by Henry's family, and there are outbuildings such as a stable and coachman's cabin. The centerpiece of the museum is the PH Rothermel painting *Patrick Henry before the Virginia Houses of Burgesses*.

Henry, who gave the inspiring 'Give me Liberty or give me Death' speech, is buried

VIRGINIA

Surrender at Appomattox

One of the most poignant events of American history was enacted at Appomattox – the surrender of Robert E Lee's Army of Northern Virginia and the end of the bloodiest war ever fought on American soil.

After Grant had taken Petersburg and Richmond, his Army of the Potomac chased Lee's bedraggled Confederate forces. The Union forces destroyed half the Confederate army at Sayler's Creek, taking many prisoners. General Philip Sheridan's cavalry and a full corps of Union infantry managed to get in front of Lee and block his path. After a sporadic battle, Lee sent a soldier through the lines with a white flag and a letter to Grant.

On April 9, 1865 (Palm Sunday), in the modest house of Wilmer McLean at Appomattox Court House, Lee, resplendent in his best uniform with his sword by his side, sat down to talk with Grant, who was dressed in a private's tunic with lieutenant general's stars pinned to his shoulders. Grant, in an attempt at small talk, mentioned to Lee that they had met before, in the Mexican War, when Grant was a regimental quartermaster, but Lee could not remember him.

Grant spelled out the terms, which were generous and would make it impossible for acts of vengeance to be taken against former Confederate soldiers: Once they had lain down their arms and returned home, they were 'not to be disturbed by the United States authorities so long as they observe their paroles and the laws in force where they may reside.' They made a few changes, and after an exchange of military salutes, Lee returned to his horse, Traveller, and rode away.

When the Union gunners started firing a victory salute, Grant stopped it immediately and then had wagons of Federal supplies moved to the Confederate lines to feed Lee's famished soldiers.

Grant sat down in front of his tent, not outwardly savoring the moment of victory. Lee rode past his troops, many of whom had tears streaming down their faces. In the following days, the once-proud Army of Northern Virginia stacked up its arms, formally surrendered, and wandered away to recommence their shattered lives.

on the property. Two of his 17 children were born here, and two of his daughters were married here. Patrick Henry died here on June 6, 1799, and the simple inscription on his grave reads 'Fame is his best epitaph.'

To get there from Lynchburg, take Route 501 to Brookneal, then follow the signs. The house is open 9 am to 5 pm daily April to October and to 4 pm November to March. Admission is $3 for adults, $2 for seniors, and $1 for children.

Farmville

This is the town where Robert E Lee met Confederate officials in April 1865, in **Jackson House**, not long before the surrender of the Army of Northern Virginia. There is a 27-stop walking tour, which takes in 19th-century warehouse buildings and antebellum churches, as well as Jackson House.

You can get brochures from the Farmville Chamber of Commerce (☎ 804-392-3939). Living up to its name, Farmville has a downtown farmers' market (☎ 804-392-5686) where you can buy produce from local farms (held every Saturday from June to October).

The **Sailor's Creek Battlefield Historic State Park** (☎ 804-392-3435) is north of Route 460 on Country Road 617. It was the scene of the largest pitched battle during Lee's retreat to Appomattox (tune in to 1610 AM for a commentary on the fighting of April 6, 1865). Here, the pursuing Federal troops overtook part of Lee's army and, after three battles, destroyed half of it. More than 7700 Confederates surrendered, and the end for the Army of Northern Virginia was near. The restored **Hillsman House** displays scenes of the fighting.

To the south is **Twin Lakes State Park** (☎ 804-392-3435), which has a loop road running through it. There is also a boat launch, rentals, fishing, and camping (standard sites cost $14 for up to six people); nearby is the pretty **Prince Edward-Gallion State Forest**. The park is 5 miles southwest of Burkeville; take Route 360W to County Rds 621 and 629.

Bedford

Bedford, tucked away in the foothills of the Blue Ridge Mountains, is on Route 460, around 24 miles west of Lynchburg. The **National D-Day Memorial** is in Bedford because this community had the highest per capita loss of lives during the Normandy landing (June 6, 1944).

The **Bedford City/County Museum** (☎ 540-586-4520), 201 E Main St, is housed in an 1895 Masonic Lodge. It has historical exhibits relating to Bedford and the surrounding county. It's a good place to get information and is open 10 am to 5 pm Monday to Saturday. Admission is $1 for adults and 50¢ for youth under 19.

The **Bedford Historic Meeting House** (☎ 540-586-8188), 153 W Main St, is an 1838 Greek Revival building once used as a meeting house for Methodists in the town of Liberty (the name of Liberty was later changed to Bedford) and later as an Episcopal church. The elegant **Avenel**, 413 Avenel Ave, is a fine antebellum mansion that was built in 1838.

And if you can't make it to Israel, then maybe **Holyland USA** (☎ 540-586-2823) is the next best thing. Take Route 122S to Dickerson-Neil Rd (Route 746) and turn right; it's just up the road (follow the star in the east!).

The *Best Western Terrace House Inn* (☎ *804-586-8286, 921 Blue Ridge Ave*), close to downtown Bedford, has singles/doubles starting at $47/51.

Booker T Washington National Monument

About 20 miles southeast of Roanoke, in the Piedmont, is the restored 224-acre plantation where Booker T Washington was born a slave on April 5, 1856 (see the boxed text). By the end of the Civil War, Washington had lived for nine years as a slave on this former tobacco farm.

On this farm, you can now experience first-hand the life and landscapes of people who lived as slaves. There are the restored buildings, tools, livestock and crops, and workers in period costume (in summer) relating to the time Booker T was born here. The big house (the large slave owner's house) is gone; so is the house that Washington was born in.

The monument is free and is open 9 am to 4:30 pm daily. The wheelchair-accessible visitor center (☎ 540-721-2094) has exhibits and a bookstore; a 15-minute audiovisual is screened.

To get to the monument from I-81, take exit 143 to I-581, which becomes Route 220. Follow this south to Rocky Mount, follow park signs, and travel north on Route 122 – the monument is 6 miles east of Burnt Chimney. From Route 29 in Lynchburg, take Route 460W to Bedford, then Route 122S.

SMITH MOUNTAIN LAKE STATE PARK

This extensive state park is on the second-largest freshwater body in the state, with more than 500 miles of shoreline, and was formed to generate power for the Appalachian Power Company. In addition to many water activities, there are hiking trails, bridle trails, primitive camping, picnicking,

Booker T Washington

Booker Talioferro Washington was born on a plantation in Franklin County on April 5, 1856, the son of a slave. He lived on the plantation for nine years, and at the end of the Civil War, his family moved to Malden, West Virginia. Washington then worked in a salt furnace and coal mines, snatching education whenever he could. From 1872 to 1875, he went to a new school for blacks (today called the Hampton Institute) and paid his tuition by working as a janitor. He taught for two years in Malden after graduation. In 1879, he returned to the Hampton Institute as an instructor, and for a time he supervised the training of 75 Native Americans – so successfully that he was selected in 1881 to be an organizer of the Tuskegee Normal School (now Institute) in Alabama.

He developed into a competent public speaker and an important and controversial race leader at a time when racism in the US made it necessary for African Americans to adjust to a new era of oppression. Not all African Americans agreed with Washington's views – especially those expressed in his controversial Atlanta Compromise speech of September 1895, in which he advocated temporary acceptance of his people's inferior social position while they raised their status through vocational training and economic independence.

More importantly, he had the ear of three presidents (William McKinley, Theodore Roosevelt, and William Howard Taft) on educational issues relating to his people. He wrote several books – *The Future of the American Negro*, the autobiographical *Up from Slavery*, and *The Story of the Negro* – and founded organizations designed to advance the position of his people. He died in 1915, probably the most important spokesperson for African Americans at the time.

and a visitor center. When you stop here, consider that the Algonquins were fishing and hunting here long before the advent of electricity.

Smith Mountain Lake Welcome Center (☎ 800-676-8203, www.sml-chamber.com) is at 2 Bridgewater Plaza, Moneta, on Route 122 between Bedford and Rocky Mount. To get to the park from Route 460, take Route 122S to County Rd 608E, then County Rd 626S. If you're interested in fishing for the humongous striper, contact these guides: Spike (☎ 540-297-5611), Bob (☎ 540-297-6334), or Dave (☎ 540-721-5007).

The side-wheeler *Virginia Dare* offers lunch cruises Monday to Saturday ($28.50 per person), dinner cruises Monday to Saturday ($35 to $39), and Sunday brunch ($30); or contact Paddle Wheel Cruises (☎ 800-721-3273). The departure point is off County Rd 853.

In addition to primitive campsites (☎ 540-297-6066) in the state park, which are $7 for up to six, there's the *Crazy Horse Campground* (☎ 540-721-2792), on Blackwater Cove ($30 for sites), reached by County Rd 616.

There are more 'luxurious' accommodations as well. In Rocky Mount, there is a *Comfort Inn* (☎ 540-489-4000, 1730 N Main St), with singles/doubles for $55/62.

Bernard's Landing (☎ 800-572-2048), reached by Route 122 and County Rds 616 and 940, is a new resort on the edge of the lake. It has sandy beaches, a pool, a health club, and handball and tennis courts. If you want a preview, rent the video *What about Bob?*, which stars Richard Dreyfuss and Bill Murray and take place here.

There are a couple of fine restaurants nearby. The *Landing Restaurant* (☎ 540-721-3028), at Bernard's Landing, is the most famous, having earned the title of 'Best Restaurant on the Lake.' All of the meals, even the simplest, are cooked with gourmet flair; the restaurant is open daily, and there is an unforgettable Sunday brunch with savory omelets.

In Moneta, on Route 122 in Bridgewater Plaza, is *The Anchor House* (☎ 804-721-6540), the place for salads, burgers, tacos, and – in the outside Tiki Bar – cocktails.

Nighttime tippling spots, after a day of fishing and swimming, are the *Sportsman's Inn* (☎ 540-297-7532), in Huddleston, and *Moosie's Deli* (☎ 540-721-5255), in the Bridgewater Plaza, Moneta.

MARTINSVILLE

This small city of 16,000, nestled in the Blue Ridge foothills, is named after General Joseph Martin. It was established in 1871 and, thanks to the railway and an industrial boom, its population increased to more than 5000 by 1924. It is now a major manufacturing center of furniture, mirrors, sweatshirts, clocks, and prefabricated homes.

The **Virginia Museum of Natural History** (☎ 540-666-8600), 1001 Douglas Ave, has permanent and traveling exhibits (kids will love the animated triceratops). It is free and is open 10 am to 5 pm Tuesday to Saturday and 2 to 5 pm Sunday.

Martinsville Speedway, on Route 220S between Martinsville and the North Carolina border, hosts four annual races on its 0.526-mile asphalt track – the Winston Cup Series and NASCAR double-headers. The Martinsville Phillies, a minor-league affiliate of the Philadelphia Phillies, is the only professional outfit in Henry County. You can see them 'pitch, catch, and foul out' at Hooker Field, on Commonwealth Blvd.

DANVILLE

Most people would forget Danville if it were not for a train derailment immortalized in a bluegrass song, 'The Wreck of the Old 97.' On September 27, 1903, the Southern Railway's Old 97 express jumped the tracks as it crossed a trestle near the Dan River. It hurtled into the ravine, killing nine (including the engineer) and injuring seven others. There is a marker on Riverside Drive (Route 58W).

Danville (population 56,000) is a real southern industrial town today, but is not without a certain charm. Originally named Wynnes Falls after the first settler, it became Danville in 1793. The main street, dominated by late Victorian architecture ('Millionaires' Row'), dates from the 1890s – a period when textiles and tobacco helped the town recover from the ravages of the Civil War.

Information

The Danville Chamber of Commerce (☎ 804-793-5422, www.danvillechamber.com), 635 Main St, is open 9 am to 5 pm weekdays (unfortunately, it is closed weekends, when most visitors need help!). The staff of the Science Center and Sutherlin Mansion are very helpful and fill the weekend void.

The main post office (☎ 804-792-3766) is at 700 Main St. The Soap Opera Coin Laundry (☎ 804-797-1645) is at 743 Colquohoun St.

Nancy Astor's Birthplace

Nancy Witcher Langhorne (Astor) hails from Danville. A middle-class Southern gal, she skipped a few rungs on the social ladder when she married Viscount William Waldorf Astor in 1906. In 1919, she became the first female member of the British House of Commons and served until the end of WWII. Her verbal spars with the great Winston Churchill were legendary.

Nancy Astor's birthplace is at 117 Broad St – she returned to visit in 1922 and 1946. Stunning Irene Langhorne Gibson, Nancy's sister, was immortalized as the 'Gibson Girl' – the fashion ideal at the turn of the 19th century – by artist/husband Charles Dana Gibson. The modest two-story house, which is being set up as a museum, is open by appointment.

Danville Museum of Fine Arts & History

This museum (☎ 804-793-5644), 975 Main St, is housed in the Sutherlin Mansion, built in 1857. It would be just another stately home turned into a regional museum were it not for the fact that it was, for one week in April 1865, the capitol of the Confederacy.

As the war neared its end, Jefferson Davis and his cabinet fled Richmond for Danville, and the dining room of Sutherlin served as the cabinet room. Here, Davis penned his eloquent plea to the Confederate states to lay down their arms – the original document is on display. The rooms have been restored to reflect the last days of the Confederacy. It is free and is open 10 am to 5 pm Tuesday to Friday and 2 to 5 pm weekends year-round.

Danville Science Center

This center (☎ 804-793-5422), 677 Craghead St, is open daily and is a great kids' retreat, with lots of hands-on activities. It is located in a recently restored Victorian train station (the Amtrak depot) in the heart of the warehouse district. Admission is $4 for adults, $3 for children.

Places to Stay & Eat

The *Howard Johnson Hotel* (☎ 804-793-2000, 100 Tower Drive) is a good stalwart with singles/doubles starting at $71/78. The hotel has a restaurant, bar, and pool and is disabled-accessible.

The *Stratford Inn* (☎ 804-793-2500, 2500 Riverside Drive), just east of Route 29 Bypass, is a great place to stay and is well known to local travelers. It has a pool, whirlpool, and exercise room; singles are $51 to $75, doubles $57 to $85. The *Stratford Inn Dining Room* has hearty lunches (the 'apotheosis of Southern cuisine') for $8.

There are plenty of fast-food joints and diners scattered along Riverside Drive on the north side of the river and on Route 29S on the southern outskirts of town.

Miyako's (☎ 804-799-2599, 2907 Riverside Drive), a Japanese place in the Danville Plaza, is a good choice for seafood and steaks. The *Rock-Ola Café* (☎ 804-793-1848, 140 Crown Drive) is an old-fashioned grill with steaks for $10 to $15, and the *Outback Steakhouse* (☎ 804-792-0781, 111 Enterprise Drive) is one of the successful 'Aussie imitators' with a remarkably good menu.

Joe & Mimma's (☎ 804-799-5763, 3336 Riverside Shopping Center) has a reputation for good pasta. Lasagna, chicken cacciatore, fettuccine, and fresh veal are the specials (specials are not served on Sunday).

Getting There & Away

The Danville Airport, east of the city on Route 360/58 and Airport Rd, is served by US Airways Express (☎ 800-428-4322). You will need to get a cab into Danville; try Danville Taxi (☎ 804-793-5671).

The Greyhound/Trailways depot (☎ 804-792-4722) is at No 302 on Route 58W, near the intersection with Mt Cross Rd. Amtrak

VIRGINIA

has southbound and northbound service stopping at the Science Center at 700 Craghead St. Both of these trains pass through at ungodly hours of the morning.

STAUNTON RIVER STATE PARK

This state park (☎ 804-572-4623), on the banks of Buggs Island Lake (John H Kerr Reservoir), has swimming and wading pools, boat ramps, tennis courts, a children's playground, and a visitor center. A standard campsite is $10.50 (an extra $4.50 for electricity); one-room/one-bedroom/two-bedroom cabins are $55/65/75, respectively. It is 18 miles east of South Boston; from South Boston, take Route 360N for 8 miles, then Route 344E, via Scottsburg, for 9 miles.

The Staunton River Bridge area has been developed into a **battlefield state park** (☎ 804-454-4312), with a Civil War fort, a guided trail, and a museum.

OCCONEECHEE STATE PARK

This state park (☎ 540-374-2210) is named after the Native Americans who lived here for many hundreds of years. It is also on Buggs Island Lake, and facilities include campsites, picnic areas, an amphitheater, and boat ramps. The *campsites* cost $11 to $16 for up to six; electric/water hookups are $4.50 extra.

From Clarksville, head 1½ miles east on Route 58E. The entrance is near the Route 15 intersection. In May, the Native American Heritage Festival and Powwow is held here.

Shenandoah Valley & Ranges

This chapter covers the beautiful Shenandoah Valley and the mountain ranges between the forks of the Shenandoah River – the Blue Ridge to the east of the Valley, the Allegheny Mountains to the west, and Massanutten Mountain to the north – all part of the Appalachians. The river, the region's dominant feature, starts as a stream near Lexington in the south of the Valley. Just west of Front Royal, the two main forks come together, and the Shenandoah 'proper' flows northeast to join with the Potomac River at Harpers Ferry.

The nearly 200-mile-long valley has a rich history. The name 'Shenandoah' has many explanations, but perhaps the most popular is that it's from 'Sherando,' a Native American word meaning 'daughter of the stars,' after the reflected light off the broad surface

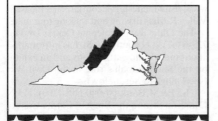
of the river. The first whites to see it were explorers in the mid-17th century, but in the early 18th century, larger groups of Scotch-Irish and German families, who migrated south from Pennsylvania and Maryland, settled in the Valley.

The Valley, 'the breadbasket of the Confederacy,' was very important in the war between the states. Today, there are many reminders of this sad war, and two of the great Civil War generals, Robert E Lee and Stonewall Jackson, are buried in Lexington. Just before the war commenced, the great international statesman Woodrow Wilson was born in Staunton.

The natural wonders of the region include Natural Bridge, near Lexington; the magnificent Shenandoah National Park and the incomparable Skyline Drive to the east of the Valley; and the Alleghenies, scenic Bath County, and Goshen Pass in George Washington National Forest (GWNF), to the west. In all of these areas, there are opportunities for outdoor recreation, such as fishing, hiking, biking, camping, and snow sports.

Visitors interested in group tours of the Shenandoah Valley should contact Wayfaring Travelers (☎ 410-666-7456), 27 Sunnyview Drive, Phoenix, MD 21131. This company organizes two-week trips.

WINCHESTER

Winchester (population 24,000) – the first settlement of the American frontier west of the Blue Ridge Mountains – lies in the northern Shenandoah Valley off I-81, 72 miles from Washington, DC. Initially settled by Scotch-Irish and German settlers in 1732, it played a major part in the French and Indian War. Winchester changed hands 72 times during the Civil War and was the headquarters for both the Confederacy's Stonewall Jackson and the Union's Philip Sheridan. You can visit some of the battlefields – Winchester I, II, and III (May 1862, June 1863, and September 1864, respectively) and Kernstown I and II (March 1862 and July 1864).

VIRGINIA

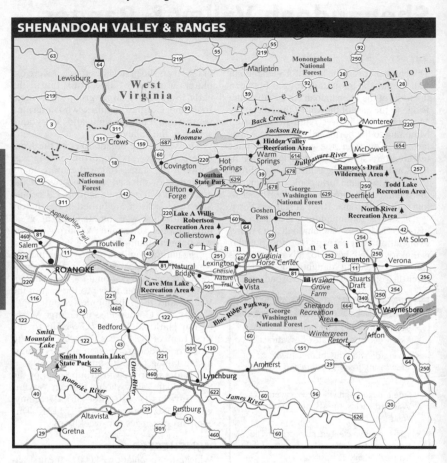

SHENANDOAH VALLEY & RANGES

The town has many associations with the famous. Renowned novelist Willa Cather was born here; country & western singer Patsy Cline spent her childhood here; Revolutionary War hero Daniel Morgan died here; George Washington was elected to his first political office, in 1758, as a member of the House of Burgesses representing Frederick County; and polar explorer Admiral Richard Byrd was also born here.

Winchester is the self-titled 'apple capital of the world' – there are more than 90 orchards in the surrounding area.

Information

The Winchester-Frederick County Visitor Center (☎ 540-662-4135, 800-662-1360, www.visitwinchesterva.com), 1360 S Pleasant Valley Rd, has driving and walking tour maps.

The Olde Town Welcome Center (☎ 540-722-6367), 2 N Cameron St, has information about most Valley attractions and an exhibit on the Shenandoah's role in the Civil War (see Things to See, below).

The F&M Bank (☎ 540-665-4200), 115 N Cameron St, and the Bank of Clarke County in the Apple Blossom Corners shopping center both have foreign-exchange facilities.

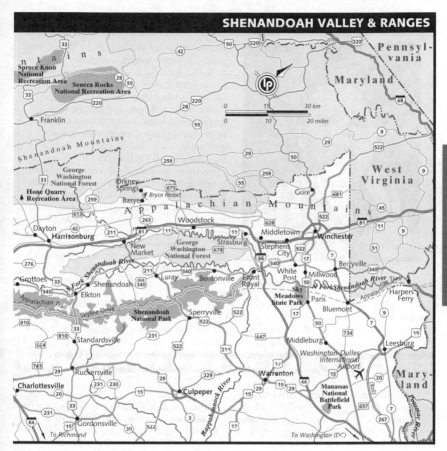

SHENANDOAH VALLEY & RANGES

VIRGINIA

The Soap Factory Coin-Op, a laundry on Berryville Ave, is open 6 am to 11 pm Monday to Saturday, until 9 pm Sunday.

For medical needs, the Urgent Care Center (☎ 540-722-0691), in the Apple Blossom Corners shopping center, is open 9 am to 9 pm; otherwise try the Winchester Medical Center (☎ 540-722-8700), 1840 Amherst St.

Things to See

There are a number of interesting historic, especially Civil War, sites in Winchester. **Stonewall Jackson's headquarters** for part of 1861–62 was in the small house (☎ 540-667-3242) at 415 N Braddock St. Jackson used this house when he came to Winchester to take command of the Confederate army in the Shenandoah Valley. Articles relating to Jackson, the cavalry commander Turner Ashby, and the mapmaker Jed Hotchkiss are on display. (TV star Mary Tyler Moore's great-great-grandfather lent Jackson the house.) It is open 10 am to 4 pm daily April to October; call for hours during other months. Admission is $3.50 for adults, $3 for seniors, and $1.75 for youth under 18.

Patsy Cline

Virginia Patterson Hensley (Patsy Cline), the country & western legend, was born in Gore, Virginia, on September 8, 1932, but spent most of her life in Winchester, where she attended school. She won a talent program in 1957 with the hit 'Walkin' After Midnight,' and the following year, she performed at the Grand Ole Opry. Cline went on to receive national awards in 1961 (for No 1 female artist) and 1962 (for No 1 female artist and for the song 'I Fall to Pieces').

You can retrace her life in Winchester, where there are many sites associated with her: her home (at 608 S Kent St); the house in which she was married (at 720 S Kent St); Gaunt's Drug Store (at the corner of S Loudoun St and Valley Ave), where she was a waitress; WINC Radio (at 520 N Pleasant Valley Rd), where she often performed; and her grave, in the Shenandoah Memorial Park on Route 522S. Also see the Patsy Cline exhibits in the Olde Town Welcome Center and in the Winchester-Frederick County CVB (where you can also pick up a Patsy Cline Nostalgia tour map).

Patsy Cline died in an aircraft accident in Tennessee, at the start of an already brilliant career, on March 5, 1963. She was elected posthumously to the Country Music Hall of Fame in 1973, and long after her death in 1991, she received a triple-platinum award for the album *Patsy Cline's Greatest Hits*.

The **Olde Town Welcome Center** (see Information, earlier) has an exhibit of the Shenandoah's role in the Civil War that gives an overview of the fighting, profiles on important battles, and biographical sketches of the commanders. It is open 10 am to 5 pm Monday to Saturday and noon to 5 pm Sunday. Admission is free (or $3 for the periodic special exhibits). Walking tours of the town depart from here at 10:30 am ($5).

Washington's Office Museum (☎ 540-662-6650), a restored log-and-stone building at 32 W Cork St, was used by then-Colonel Washington when he was building Fort Loudoun during the French and Indian War. It is open 9 am to 5 pm daily from April to October. Admission is $2 for adults, $1.50 for seniors, and $1 for children six to 12.

At 1340 S Pleasant Valley Rd is **Abram's Delight Museum** (☎ 540-662-6650), a limestone house built in 1754 by a Quaker named Issac Hollingsworth. It has been furnished and restored. The 'Delight' is open 9 am to 5 pm daily from April to October. Admission is $3.50 for adults, $3 seniors, and $1.75 for children six to 12.

Glen Burnie (☎ 540-662-1473), at 530 Amherst St, was the home of Winchester's founder, Colonel James Wood, and it has been restored to its exquisite, original splendor. The 14 gardens alone are worth a visit. It is open 10 am to 4 pm Tuesday to Saturday and noon to 4 pm Sunday from April to October. Admission is $8 for adults and $6 for seniors and students seven to 18; it's $5 for the gardens only.

A block entry ticket that includes 'Abram's Delight,' Washington's Office, and Jackson's headquarters is $7.50 for adults, $6 for seniors, and $4 for children six to 12.

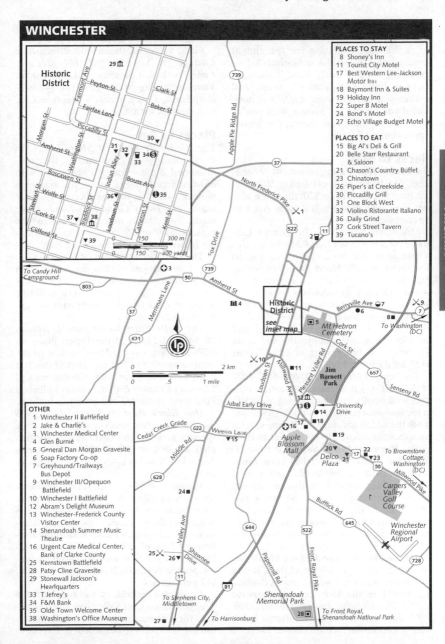

WINCHESTER

PLACES TO STAY
8 Shoney's Inn
11 Tourist City Motel
17 Best Western Lee-Jackson Motor Inn
18 Baymont Inn & Suites
19 Holiday Inn
22 Super 8 Motel
24 Bond's Motel
27 Echo Village Budget Motel

PLACES TO EAT
15 Big Al's Deli & Grill
20 Belle Starr Restaurant & Saloon
21 Chason's Country Buffet
23 Chinatown
26 Piper's at Creekside
30 Piccadilly Grill
31 One Block West
32 Violino Ristorante Italiano
36 Daily Grind
37 Cork Street Tavern
39 Tucano's

OTHER
1 Winchester II Battlefield
2 Jake & Charlie's
3 Winchester Medical Center
4 Glen Burnie
5 General Dan Morgan Gravesite
6 Soap Factory Co-op
7 Greyhound/Trailways Bus Depot
9 Winchester III/Opequon Battlefield
10 Winchester I Battlefield
12 Abram's Delight Museum
13 Winchester-Frederick County Visitor Center
14 Shenandoah Summer Music Theatre
16 Urgent Care Medical Center, Bank of Clarke County
25 Kernstown Battlefield
28 Patsy Cline Gravesite
29 Stonewall Jackson's Headquarters
33 T Jefrey's
34 F&M Bank
35 Olde Town Welcome Center
38 Washington's Office Museum

Historic District

VIRGINIA

Special Events

As the 'apple capital of the world,' Winchester is the natural setting for the annual Shenandoah Apple Blossom Festival (☎ 540-662-3863), held in early May. It includes parades, band competitions, races, and lunches and attracts some 250,000 visitors. And if you believe in finishing what you've started, come back in mid-September for the Apple Harvest Festival.

Places to Stay

The *Candy Hill Campground* (☎ *540-662-8010, 165 Ward Ave*), off Route 50W, has full hookups for $18 to $20; there are also tent sites and showers. It's open April to November.

Motels are abundant. The *Tourist City Motel* (☎ *540-662-9011, 214 Millwood Ave*) is nothing special but is cheap and close to downtown. *Bond's Motel* (☎ *540-667-8881, 2930 Valley Ave*), Route 11, is well maintained and has singles/doubles for $30/32 in the off season, otherwise $32/38. *Echo Village Budget Motel* (☎ *540-869-1900, 3632 Valley Ave*), Route 11, is off the road, and the rooms have air-conditioning and cable TV. Singles/doubles start at $25/32, plus $3.50 for each extra person.

The *Super 8 Motel* (☎ *540-665-4450, 1077 Millwood Pike*) is a trusty, economical stalwart with singles/doubles starting at $40/45 in the low season, $40/49 in the high season. It has the added advantage of having several cheap restaurants nearby (see Places to Eat).

The *Baymont Inn & Suites* (☎ *540-678-0800, 800 Millwood Ave*) has been renovated, and the singles/doubles are a good value, starting at $45/52 in the low season, $52/57 in the high season. *Shoney's Inn* (☎ *540-665-1700, 1347 Berryville Ave*), I-81 exit 315, has a bar, restaurant, exercise facilities, and an indoor pool; singles/doubles start at $45/50.

The *Best Western Lee-Jackson Motor Inn* (☎ *540-662-4154, 711 Millwood Ave*), Route 50, has a pool and restaurant; singles/doubles are $46/51 in the low season, otherwise $52/57. The *Holiday Inn* (☎ *540-667-3300, 1017 Millwood Ave*) is a comfortable hotel, with a restaurant, tennis courts, exercise

facilities, and an outdoor pool; double rooms cost $69 to $89, and an extra person is $6.

Good-value B&Bs include *Brownstone Cottage* (☎ *540-662-1962, 161 McCarty Lane*), with $70 doubles; and *The Inn at Vaucluse Spring* (☎ *540-869-9544, 140 Vaucluse Spring Lane*), in nearby Stephens City, with doubles for $90 to $160.

Places to Eat

The *Piccadilly Grill* (☎ *540-667-4021, 46 E Piccadilly St*) epitomizes the old-fashioned diner – and it's chock-full with old-fashioned diners. Here, the size of a pancake can be the subject of glee for weeks. The *Daily Grind* (*3 S Loudoun St*) might suit those more attuned to the present, as it offers more health-conscious alternatives and a selection of coffees.

The *Cork Street Tavern* (☎ *540-667-3777, 8 W Cork St*), just around the corner from the S Loudoun St pedestrian mall, is a very cozy, casual dining place where a sizable dinner of spare ribs (and other barbecue delights) costs from $12.

The *Belle Starr Restaurant & Saloon* (☎ *540-722-2447*), in the Delco Plaza on Millwood Ave, has good food such as steaks, sandwiches, fajitas, and 'hot' snake bites. It is open 11 am to 2 am daily. *Chinatown* and *Chason's Country Buffet*, both on Millwood Pike, have $6 all-you-can-eat lunch buffets.

One Block West (☎ *540-662-1455, 25 S Indian Alley*) has American fare and daily specials such as crab cakes ($10). *Big Al's Deli & Grill* (☎ *540-678-8774, 107 Weems Lane*) is a New York–style diner with good-value grills.

Tucano's (☎ *540-722-4557, 12 S Braddock St*) is an excellent Brazilian place popular with locals (try the *mugueca baiana*); it is open weekdays for lunch and dinner, Saturday for dinner only. *Violino Ristorante Italiano* (☎ *540-667-8006, 181 N Loudoun St*) has al fresco dining and specializes in contemporary northern Italian cuisine (about $12 per entree).

Pipers at Creekside (☎ *540-662-2900, 136 Creekside Lane*), off Valley Ave, open weekdays for continental meals (dinner only Saturday), is expensive but worth it. Expect to pay $15 to $20 for a main course, about $50 for two people. Make reservations for the previous three restaurants, especially on weekends.

Entertainment

The **Shenandoah Summer Music Theatre** (☎ 540-665-4569, 1460 University Drive), at Shenandoah University, at the intersection of Route 50 and I-81 exit 313, is a professional theater company, performing four musicals each summer from mid-June to early August. Get information from the visitor center or welcome center about performances by **Winchester Little Theater**, in the old Pennsylvania Railroad depot, near the kink in W Boscawen St.

The very casual **T Jefrey's** (☎ 540-667-0429, 168 N Loudoun St) has live entertainment on Friday and Saturday evenings. The Belle Starr (see Places to Eat, earlier) has entertainment nightly, such as R&B, line dancing, and the dreaded karaoke. **Jake & Charlie's** (☎ 540-722-1017, 821 N Loudoun St), a sports club with entertainment, is open daily noon to 1 am.

Getting There & Away

Most people fly into Washington-Dulles International Airport. The Winchester Regional Airport (☎ 540-662-5786) is used only for local flights.

Winchester is served by Greyhound/Trailways (☎ 540-662-4161), the depot of which is near the junction of Berryville and Atwell Aves. A city transit service (☎ 540-667-1815) operates daily except Sunday from outside the Olde Town Welcome Center; the cost of a trip is 50¢ for adults and 35¢ for children.

AROUND WINCHESTER

The region south of Winchester is steeped in Civil War history, and this is highlighted at two excellent battlefield centers – Cedar Creek and Hupp's Hill. There are many rural escapes here as well. If you have time, catch a play at the historic Wayside Theatre (see Middletown, later in this section) or attend one of the many festivals held in the region.

Millwood & White Post

The small town of Millwood, near the Shenandoah River, has the **Burwell-Morgan Mill** (☎ 540-837-1799), at the intersection of Route 255 and County Rd 723. Completed in 1785, it has been restored to the operating condition of a colonial-era gristmill and is open 10 am to 5 pm Wednesday to Sunday from May to October (admission fee).

Out on County Rd 624 is historic **Long Branch** (☎ 540-837-1856), a superbly restored and furnished antebellum mansion built by Robert Carter Burwell (not of the mill fame – that was Nathaniel). It is open 9 am to 5 pm daily April to October. Admission is $6 for adults, $5 for seniors.

White Post, not far from Millwood, has **Dinosaur Land Inc** (☎ 540-869-2222). The kids will deserve a treat after that 'one Civil War site too many,' and 35 life-size replicas of dinosaurs (the names of which will be readily known to your children) are here. Positively Jurassic, this park is open 9:30 am to 5 pm daily in winter, until later in summer. Admission is $4 for adults, $3 for kids.

The white post for which the town was named was erected by the young Washington to mark the way to Greenway Court, Lord Fairfax's estate.

The well-known **L'Auberge Provençal** (☎ 540-837-1375, 800-638-1702), in a 1750s farmhouse on Route 340, is expensive ($145 to $195 for a double including breakfast), but you are paying for perfection. The superb five-course provençal dinner is likely to cost another $55 each.

Middletown

This quaint little town on Route 11 is near the intersection of I-81 (exit 302) and I-66.

Most people deviate off the main drag here to see **Belle Grove** (☎ 540-869-2028), a tasteful stone farmhouse completed in 1794 after Jefferson provided some finishing touches. The farm is still in use today. This was the Union headquarters during the Battle of Cedar Creek in October 1864, and at one stage, the battle spilled over onto the farm. The annual reenactment of the battle, staged in October, attracts 2000 bellicose devotees. Belle Grove is open 10 am to 4 pm

VIRGINIA

Monday to Saturday, 1 to 5 pm Sunday from March to December. Admission is $7 for adults, $6 for seniors, $3 for children six to 12.

The historic **Wayside Theatre** (☎ 540-869-1776), the second-oldest theater in the state, is just off I-81 on Route 11S exit 302. A professional theater company, it presents a range of musicals, dramas, and comedies from May to mid-October and in December. Actors who got a start here include Susan Sarandon, Peter Boyle, and Jill Eikenberry. The box office is open noon to 4 pm Monday and Tuesday, 11 am to 9 pm Wednesday to Saturday, 4 to 8 pm Sunday. The Wednesday and Saturday matinee is $17 (children $7.50), and evening performances are $19 (Saturday night, $23).

The *Wayside Inn* (☎ *540-869-1797, 7783 Main St*) is a beautifully restored 18th-century building with 24 antique-furnished rooms (with four-poster beds) for $95 to $145. The restaurant serves regional American cuisine and is open daily; a dinner for two will cost about $70.

Route 11 Potato Chip Factory (☎ *800-294-7783, 7815 Main St*) is where lovers of potato chips will want to stock up. The chips are made from organically grown potatoes and are cooked in peanut and sunflower oil. Tempt yourself from 10 am to 6 pm Friday and 9 am to 5 pm Saturday.

Strasburg

This upper Shenandoah Valley town has a rich history. During the Civil War, Stonewall Jackson made a raid on Martinsburg in West Virginia and captured a number of Union army railroad locomotives. These were then pulled down the Valley to Strasburg railway station (where the museum is housed today – see below).

For more information on the region, contact the Strasburg Chamber of Commerce (☎ 540-465-3187); it also has an information stand in Strasburg Emporium.

The **Strasburg Museum** (☎ 540-465-3428) focuses on the town's importance as a trading center. On display are farming tools, Native American artifacts, a colonial kitchen, and industrial arts such as coopering and blacksmithing. It is open 10 am to 4 pm daily

May to October. Admission is $2 for adults, 50¢ for children four to 14.

Civil War enthusiasts gravitate toward the **Stonewall Jackson Museum at Hupp's Hill** (☎ 540-465-5884), 33229 Old Valley Pike, northwest of Strasburg on Route 11, which concentrates on the Shenandoah Valley campaigns. Here you'll find a topographical map of the Battle of Cedar Creek, remnants of earthworks dug by Union soldiers, and a well-stocked bookstore. Unlike 'don't touch' places, children are encouraged to try on uniforms and sit in Civil War saddles. The helpful and knowledgeable staff will answer any tricky questions you pose. The museum is open 10 am to 5 pm Monday to Saturday and noon to 5 pm Sunday. Admission is $3 for adults, $2 for seniors and children six to 12.

In the same complex, **Crystal Caverns at Hupp's Hill** (☎ 540-465-8660) is Virginia's oldest documented cave. Admission to the caverns and Stonewall Jackson Museum costs $8 for adults and $6 for seniors and students.

The new **Cedar Creek Battlefield Visitors Center** (☎ 540-869-2064), 8437 Valley Pike, overlooks the battlefield where Phil Sheridan, in the battle against Jubal Early, converted 'crushing defeat...into a splendid victory.'

The **American Presidents Museum** (☎ 540-465-5999) is an unusual but worthwhile collection featuring James Madison's desk (upon which the Constitution was written), portraits of the presidents, and documents signed by Jefferson and Washington. Call for business hours. Admission is $3 for adults and $2 for seniors and children six to 16.

The **Strasburg Emporium** (☎ 540-465-3711), 110 N Massanutten St, which houses more than 100 antique dealers, is open daily.

At the *Hotel Strasburg* (☎ *540-465-9191, 201 Holliday St*), you can stay in antique-furnished Victorian-style single and double rooms for $74 to $165. The adjoining restaurant is open daily for all three meals (delicious salads); main dishes start at $9.

FRONT ROYAL

This sizable town (population 11,500) at the northern end of the Shenandoah National

Park/Skyline Drive is, these days, somewhat of an outdoor center.

Front Royal started out as Lehew Town, a stopover on an important packhorse route. In the mid-18th century, it became known as 'Helltown' because of its raucous reputation. It featured heavily in the battles of the Civil War and was a base for the famous Confederate spy Belle Boyd. Today, Front Royal is an important commercial center, and each May it hosts the **Virginia Mushroom Festival** for fun guys and gals who like fungi. There is a well-preserved historic district along Chester St.

Visit the Front Royal/Warren County Chamber of Commerce (☎ 540-635-3185, www.frontroyalchamber.com), in the old Southern Railroad train station at 414 E Main St, open 9 am to 5 pm daily.

Belle Boyd Cottage

This cottage (☎ 540-636-1446), at 101 Chester St, was the temporary home of the Confederate spy Belle Boyd, who spent time here with her relatives. On one occasion, Belle overheard, through a small hole in the closet floor, a Union general discussing plans with his officers. She wrote the details down in cipher and rode for 15 miles to pass the information on to Stonewall Jackson's Confederate army. The Confederates then moved on Front Royal and captured the town.

The cottage is open 10 am to 5 pm weekdays and 1 to 4 pm weekends from April to October; the last tour is at 3:30 pm. Admission is $2 for adults and $1 for youth eight to 16.

'Warren Rifles' Confederate Museum

Another place with a Civil War theme is this museum (☎ 540-636-6982), at 95 Chester St, which attempts further secular canonization of members of the Confederacy. It is open 9 am to 5 pm weekdays, noon to 5 pm Sunday from April to October. Admission is $2, free for children under 12.

Skyline Caverns

These caverns (☎ 800-296-4545) attract visitors because they house unusual anthodites – spiked nodes or 'cave flowers.'

These formations, unlike stalactites and stalagmites, which grow straight up and down, seem to defy gravity and grow in all directions. They grow an inch every 7000 years. There is also a stream that plunges over 37-foot falls and chambers with predictable names – Wishing Well, Capitol Dome, Cathedral Hall.

The caverns are a mile from the start of Skyline Drive, open at 9 am daily. Admission is $10 for adults, $9 for seniors, $5 for children seven to 13.

Oasis Winery

There are a number of vineyards near Front Royal. This 75-acre vineyard (☎ 540-635-7627), 14141 Hume Rd, off Route 635 in Hume, faces the Blue Ridge Mountains. Known internationally for its sparkling wines, it's open daily 10 am to 5 pm for tours and tastings (tours cost $5). For vineyards in the Shenandoah Valley, see the Virginia for Wine Lovers boxed text.

Canoeing

Bentonville, close to the zigzags of the South Fork of the Shenandoah, south of Front Royal, is the place for serious and not-so-serious paddlers and rafters.

The Downriver Canoe Co (☎ 800-338-1963), Front Royal Canoe Co (☎ 800-270-8808), the Shenandoah River Outfitters (☎ 800-622-6632), and River Rental Outfitters (☎ 800-727-4371) offer a number of trips, from a 3-mile taste of whitewater to ultra-serious trips of 120 miles and longer. A 3-mile trip costs about $36 per canoe, a day trip costs about $49, and a three-day trip costs $137 (there are discounts midweek). Tubing costs about $14 per tube.

These companies operate 9 am to 6 pm weekdays and 7 am to 7 pm weekends from April to October. From Skyline Drive (Mile 20), follow Route 211 west for 8 miles, and then head north on Route 340 – from there, it is 14 miles to Bentonville. From Front Royal, follow Route 340 south to Bentonville.

Horseback Riding

The 4200-acre beef cattle Marriott Ranch (☎ 540-364-2627) offers short and extended trail rides near Front Royal. Costs are $25

VIRGINIA

per person on weekdays, $30 on weekends for a 1½-hour ride.

Golf

The double 18-hole Bowling Green Country Club (☎ 540-635-2883, 635-2024) and the 27-hole Shenandoah Valley Golf Club (☎ 703-635-3588) cater to those willing to chase elusive white balls around the Shenandoah.

Places to Stay

The **Front Royal/Washington DC West KOA** (☎ 540-635-2741), near Skyline Drive (I-81 exit 6), may advertise that it has a 'civil war nearby,' but you shouldn't hear the guns these days. Instead, it's a compact campground with good shady sites, electricity/water hookups for $27 for two, Kamping Kabins for $37, a pool, a playground, and a recreation room.

There are a few good B&B choices. **Killahevlin** (☎ 540-636-7335, 1401 N Royal Ave) is an expensive place ($115 to $185), but it occupies the highest point of Front Royal. **Chester House** (☎ 540-635-3937, 43 Chester St) is another stately place, with doubles for $65 to $120.

South of Front Royal, off Route 522 near Flint Hill, is **Caledonia Farm 1812** (☎ 540-675-3693, 47 Dearing Rd), a lovely farmhouse that has doubles with shared bath starting at $80 and suites starting at $140.

The cheapest motel is the **Center City Motel** (☎ 540-635-4050, 416 S Royal Ave), just north of the junction of Routes 340 and 55, with off-season rates of $32 for doubles; otherwise, rates are $38 weekdays and $44 weekends. The **Super 8 Motel** (☎ 540-636-4888, 111 South St), I-66 exit 13, is a good budget place with off-season singles/doubles for $40/45; otherwise, $45/51.

The **Pioneer Motel** (☎ 540-635-4784, 541 S Royal Ave), on Route 340 near the north entrance to Skyline Drive, is another budget choice. The **Quality Inn** (☎ 540-635-3161, 10 Commerce Ave) is popular and often full in summer. It has a pool and a restaurant with nightly entertainment. Singles/doubles start at $55/65 in the low season, rising to $58/68 in the high season.

Places to Eat

The **Main Street Mill & Tavern** (☎ 540-636-3123, 500 E Main St), a barnlike place a block up from the chamber of commerce, has huge sandwiches starting at $4. Dinners, served with salad, vegetables, and bread, start at $10.

The **Fox Diner** (☎ 540-635-3325, 20 South St), across from the Super 8, is nothing fancy but is a pleasure for aficionados of old-fashioned, honest, home-cookin' establishments. The **Apple House** (☎ 540-636-6329), on Route 55E in Linden, is another of the old diner ilk, serving barbecue, country fare, and donuts daily.

The **14th Street Bistro** (☎ 540-636-8400, 101 West 14th St) offers fine dining, a full bar, and dancing (no smoking). It's open for lunch 11:30 am to 2:30 pm daily and for dinner 5 to 9 pm Monday to Thursday, to 10 pm Friday and Saturday, to 8 pm Sunday.

SHENANDOAH NATIONAL PARK

This park impresses more than one million tourists each year. It was authorized by Congress in 1926 and established in 1935 as a peaceful refuge for nearby urban populations, and most of it has been restored to the way it would have been found by early settlers. It is said by some that Shenandoah means 'daughter of the stars,' and by others, 'river of high mountains.' Whatever interpretation, it deserves any such beautiful appellation.

The rocks that form the Blue Ridge, the backbone of the park, are ancient granite and metamorphic formations, some of which are more than one billion years old. Human inhabitation occupies a mere speck on that timeline, about 11,000 years. Primitive food gatherers (and later, hunters) used the land, but there is little evidence of their passing. Modern settlement of the region began soon after settlers crossed the Blue Ridge, in 1716.

There is something for everyone along the 500 miles of hiking trails, at the 75 overlooks, four campgrounds, seven picnic areas, and in the 30 trout-fishing streams. Through its center winds the spectacular 105-mile Skyline Drive.

Orientation & Information

Skyline Drive (see below) runs through the center of the park. Consequently, most trails and points of interest can be reached from this scenic road.

Visitors can get information by calling ☎ 540-999-3500, checking www.nps.gov/shen, or writing to The Superintendent, Park Headquarters, Shenandoah National Park, 3655 Route 211, Luray, VA 22835. In an emergency only, call ☎ 800-732-0911.

The Dickey Ridge Visitor Center (☎ 540-635-3566), the closest to the northern entrance of the park at Mile 4.6, is open 9 am to 5 pm daily April to November. At Mile 50, in the heart of the park, is the Byrd Visitor Center (☎ 540-999-3283), open the same hours. Both places have exhibits on flora and fauna, pamphlets, weather information, ranger-led activities, and exhibits. Big Meadows, near the Byrd Center, is the park's largest treeless meadow and the place to see wildflowers. There are additional ranger stations at Piney River (Mile 22.1) and Simmons Gap (Mile 73.2) and a private center at Rockfish Gap, outside the park on Route 211, as well as others scattered throughout the park.

The 'Park Guide' costs $2. 'Exploring Shenandoah National Park' is also $2, and 'Guide to Shenandoah Park and Skyline Drive' (called the 'Blue Bible' by the rangers) is $7.50. The latter has all the information you need on accommodations, activities, and hiking trails. ARAMARK, the park concessionaire, provides the free 'Shenandoah National Park.'

When you pay your entrance fee, you receive an excellent map with notes on the park and its mileposts.

Skyline Drive

This superb drive, which follows the main ridge of the Blue Ridge Mountains, covers 105 miles and is the main means of access to Shenandoah National Park. It begins just south of Front Royal (I-66 is 3 miles to the north) and ends in the southern part of the range near Rockfish Gap, near I-64. Two roads, Route 211 (Luray to Sperryville) and Route 33 (Elkton to Stanardsville), cross the park at Miles 31.5 and 65.7, respectively. Mileposts, located on the west side of the drive, begin at the northern end of the drive and help you locate points of interest and facilities.

There are adequate picnic areas along the length of Skyline Drive that have fireplaces, tables, water fountains, and 'comfort stations.' These are at Dickey Ridge (Mile 4.6), Elkwallow (Mile 24.1), Pinnacles (Mile 36.7), Big Meadows (Mile 51.3), Lewis Mountain (Mile 57.5), South River (Mile 62.9), and Loft Mountain (Mile 79.5).

The entrance fee to Skyline Drive is $10 per vehicle ($5 for bikers and hikers), and the pass is good for seven days; disabled people and Golden Age Passport holders (for US citizens over 62) are admitted free. The Shenandoah Passport ($20) is good for one year, and the NPS's Golden Eagle Passport ($52) is also honored. (See the Facts for the Visitor chapter for more information on these 'passports.')

The speed limit is 35mph, and it is strictly enforced.

Activities

There are plenty of options for outdoor enthusiasts, including hiking, biking, horseback riding, fishing, hang-gliding, skiing, and bird and wildlife watching.

Hiking There are many hiking trails and self-guided nature trails. A red-orange blaze indicates a park boundary; a white blaze (the Appalachian Trail is yellow) means the trail is open to hikers and horseback riders; blue means the trail is open to hikers only;

VIRGINIA

VIRGINIA

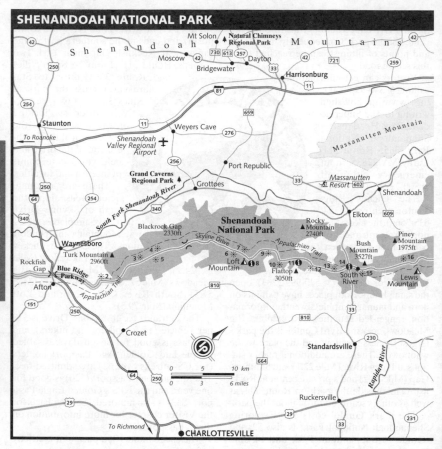

and unblazed trails are nature trails for hikers only (there are no markers).

The following is a selection of some short hiking trails, including location, length, and degree of difficulty:

Fox Hollow (Mile 4.6, 1.2 miles, easy)

Hickerson Hollow (Mile 9.2, 2.2 miles, fairly easy)

Compton Peak (Mile 10.4, 2.4 miles, easy to moderate)

Traces (Mile 22.2, 1.7 miles, easy), through a mature oak forest

Overall Run (Mile 22.2, 6 miles, moderate)

Stony Man (Mile 41.7, 1.6 miles, easy), following a portion of the Appalachian Trail

Whiteoak Canyon (Mile 42.6, 4.6 miles, strenuous)

Hawksbill Mountain Summit, the park's highest peak (Mile 46.7, 2.1 miles, moderate)

Dark Hollow Falls (Mile 50.7, 1.5 miles, moderate)

Story of the Forest (Mile 51, 1.8 miles, easy), emphasizing natural history

South River Falls (Mile 62.8, 2.6 miles, moderate)

Deadening (Mile 79.4, 1.3 miles, easy), climbing to the top of Loft Mountain

Blackrock Summit (Mile 84.8, 1 mile, easy)

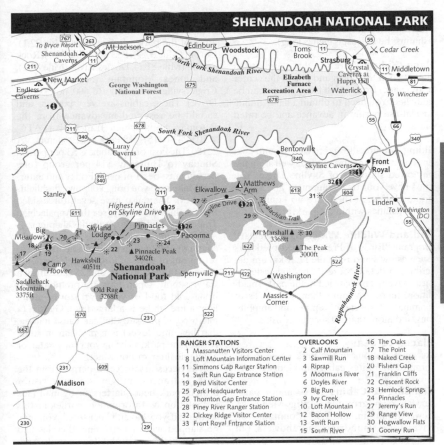

SHENANDOAH NATIONAL PARK

RANGER STATIONS
1 Massanutten Visitors Center
8 Loft Mountain Information Center
11 Simmons Gap Ranger Station
14 Swift Run Gap Entrance Station
19 Byrd Visitor Center
25 Park Headquarters
26 Thornton Gap Entrance Station
28 Piney River Ranger Station
32 Dickey Ridge Visitor Center
33 Front Royal Entrance Station

OVERLOOKS
2 Calf Mountain
3 Sawmill Run
4 Riprap
5 Moormans River
6 Doyles River
7 Big Run
9 Ivy Creek
10 Loft Mountain
12 Bacon Hollow
13 Swift Run
15 South River

16 The Oaks
17 The Point
18 Naked Creek
20 Fishers Gap
21 Franklin Cliffs
22 Crescent Rock
23 Hemlock Springs
24 Pinnacles
27 Jeremy's Run
29 Range View
30 Hogwallow Flats
31 Gooney Run

VIRGINIA

A good guide, *Circuit Hikes in Shenandoah National Park* ($6), describes 32 hikes (ranging from 3 to 20 miles). There is also the free 'Exploring the Backcountry,' available from the visitor centers. For information on backcountry camping, see Places to Stay, later in this section.

Horseback Riding Riding is allowed on designated trails. At Skyland Stables (☎ 540-999-2210), near Mile 41.7, there are guided trail rides (for one or two hours); pony rides are available for children. It is open May to October.

Bicycling This is only permitted on Skyline Drive and on certain public roads. Cycling or mountain biking on backcountry trails and fire roads is not allowed. Normal cycling rules apply along Skyline Drive – use correct lighting at night, travel in single file, and keep to the right.

Fishing About 30 streams stocked with brook trout are open for fishing from the third Saturday in March until mid-October. People ages 16 to 65 must have a valid license ($6.50 for five consecutive days). You must use artificial lures with a single hook only, and the limit is five trout per day (each fish must be at least 8 inches long).

Hang-Gliding There are three authorized sites (two in the north and one in the center of the park) from which hang-gliders can be launched. You need to obtain a hang-gliding special-use permit in advance and be rated Hang 3.

Skiing You are allowed to cross-country ski on some trails and fire roads as well as on the unplowed shoulder of Skyline Drive. You must have your own equipment and appropriate clothing. (There are no equipment-rental facilities within the park.)

Bird and Wildlife Watching In the park programs 'Birds of Prey,' winged predators (such as owls and red-tailed hawks) are described in detail. More than 200 species of birds have been recorded in the park. In addition, there are more than 40 species of mammals, 50 species of reptiles and amphibians, and more than 20 species of fish.

Places to Stay

Accommodations in the park come in the forms of campsites, cabins, and lodges.

Camping & Cabins Three major park-service campgrounds – Big Meadows, Lewis Mountain, and Loft Mountain – all have stores, laundries, and showers, but none have RV hookups. These are open on a first-come, first-served basis. *Lewis Mountain* (Mile 57.6), open April to October, is best for tents ($14); *Loft Mountain* (Mile 79.5), open late May to October, has more than 50 tent sites and some 160 trailer sites ($14); and *Big Meadows* (Mile 51.3), open late May to October, has 40 tent sites and some 160 trailer sites ($17 Memorial Day to the end of October; otherwise, $14).

Mathews Arm (Mile 22.1) doesn't have a store (there's one 2 miles south at Elkwallow); it's open June to October ($14). For reservations, call ☎ 800-999-3500; check site availability at the visitor centers.

There are six fully enclosed cabins (with bunk beds, water, and stoves) in backcountry areas of the park – Range View (Mile 22.1), Corbin (Mile 37.9), Pocosin (Mile 59.5), Rock Spring (Mile 81.1), Doyles River (Mile 81.1), and Jones Mountain (accessible from Criglersville on County Rd 600, not Skyline Drive). These cabins are very popular and should be reserved in advance from the Potomac Appalachian Trail Club (PATC; ☎ 703-242-0315), 118 Park St SE, Vienna, VA 22180. The cost of the cabins is $3 per person Sunday to Thursday, $14 per group (one person must be 21 or over) Friday and Saturday. Make sure you bring your own flashlights (torches). They also have seven three-sided trailside huts for hikers (see the Appalachian Trail boxed text in the Activities chapter).

Free camping is permitted in the back-country. Certain rules apply: Campers have to set up out of sight of a road, trail, overlook, cabin, or other campsite, and 25 yards from a water supply. Open fires are prohibited, so bring cold food or your own stove – don't light a fire (there is a large fine). Giardia (a microscopic parasite that can cause nausea, diarrhea, and fever) is a problem in some parts of the park, so bring your own water, or a suitable filter, or boil water.

It is necessary to get a permit from the park entrances, ranger stations, visitor centers, park headquarters, or by mail (see Orientation & Information, earlier in this section); if you haven't registered, you may be slapped with a hefty fine. Bicycles and motor vehicles are prohibited on trails. And, importantly, carry out what you carry in.

Lodges There are three lodges; for information and costs, contact ARAMARK Virginia Skyline Company (☎ 540-743-5108, 800-999-4714), PO Box 727NP, Luray, VA 22835. *Skyland Lodge*, at the highest point on the drive at 3680 feet (Mile 41.7), is open late March to early December and has rustic cabins that offer magnificent views of the Shenandoah Valley. Single units on weekdays cost $79; one-bedroom suites on weekends start at $126.

Big Meadows Lodge, at 3640 feet (Mile 51.3), is open early May to late October and has a main lodge and rooms in rustic cabins. A main lodge room, on weekdays, starts at $65; a one-bedroom suite on weekends is $134. *Lewis Mountain* (Mile 57.5), open early May to late October, has fully equipped cabins and an adjoining outdoor cooking area, but no phone or TV. The weekday cost for a single-room cabin is $59; on weekends, a two-room cabin is $84.

Places to Eat
The *Panorama Restaurant* (☎ 540-999-2265) is aptly named and serves good traditional Virginia country fare. Sandwiches cost $3.50 to $6; entrees start at $8. It is open 9 am to 5:30 pm daily April to November. There are also dining rooms at Skyland Lodge (late March to December) and Big Meadows Lodge (May to October). Both serve all meals; hours are extended at all restaurants in peak season. On most Fridays from June to September, Skyland hosts the Shenandoah Jubilee Music Show ($12 for adults, $6 for children).

The wayside lunch counters and snack bars located at Elkwallow (Mile 24.1), Big Meadows, Lewis Mountain, and Loft Mountain serve distinctly ordinary snacks and lunches.

Getting There & Away
There's Greyhound/Trailways service to Waynesboro from Washington, DC, every morning ($38), but there are no buses or trains to Front Royal at the north end of the park. A bicycle or car is essential here; hitchhiking would be difficult.

LURAY
This small town has the good fortune of being situated astride two great wilderness areas – Massanutten Mountain, of the George Washington National Forest, and Shenandoah National Park. The Luray-Page County Chamber of Commerce (☎ 540-743-3915, www.luraypage.com), 46 E Main St, is open 9 am to 5 pm daily and until 7 pm in summer.

For the kids, there is the **Reptile Center & Dinosaur Park** (☎ 540-743-4113), with its large reptile collection (plus a few life-size

dinosaur reproductions). Admission is $4 for adults and $3 for children three to 12.

Luray Caverns
These caverns (☎ 540-743-6551), the eastern US's largest and most popular, are 9 miles west of Luray on Route 211 (10 minutes from Skyline Drive). Much of their popularity has to do with a most unnatural feature, a stalactite organ, feted as a 'stalacpipe,' which is played electronically on all tours. In addition, the caverns have crystal-clear pools, monumental columns, and walkways; outside, there is an antique carriage, car, and coach museum.

The caverns are open 9 am to 7 pm daily June 15 to Labor Day and to 6 pm Labor Day to mid-November; otherwise, 9 am to 4 pm weekdays and 9 am to 5 pm weekends. Admission is an exorbitant $14 for adults, $12 for seniors, and $6 for children seven to 13.

Places to Stay & Eat
Three miles east of Luray on Route 211, *Yogi Bear's Jellystone Park* (☎ 540-743-4002) is open March to November. Electric/water hookups cost $23 to $30 for two; camping cabins cost $32 to $48; cabins that are cleaned daily cost $69 to $89. For other camping and cabin options, see Shenandoah National Park, earlier in the chapter.

There are plenty of motels, and Luray is a popular place to stay. The *Luray Caverns Motel East* (☎ 540-743-4531, 831 W Main St), 1 mile west on Route 211 Business, has rooms for $59 to $76 (each extra person is $8). The *Luray Caverns Motel West* (☎ 540-743-4536), 1½ miles west on Route 211 Bypass, has the same prices as its eastern counterpart, but it's older.

The *Days Inn Luray* (☎ 540-743-4521), on Route 211 Bypass, 1.7 miles east of the Route 340 junction, has a restaurant, a pool, and disabled accessibility. Doubles start at $60 in the low season and rise markedly in summer.

Woodruff House (☎ 540-743-1494, 330 Mechanic St) is a B&B with a restaurant and outdoor spa (which is lit by candles at night!). Doubles cost $109 to $185 weekdays and $145 to $215 weekends in the low season.

The *Jordan Hollow Farm* (☎ 540-778-2285) is 6 miles south of Luray in Stanley (just off Route 340 on County Rd 624). There are good rooms in this 200-year-old building constructed of hand-hewn logs. The farm also has a bar, restaurant, and stables. Singles/doubles start at $83/110.

The *Parkhurst Restaurant* (☎ 540-743-6009), on Route 211W, 2½ miles west of Luray Caverns, is a pleasant red-brick place serving American and continental fare. Its dining area, in an enclosed verandah offering great views, is open for dinner daily 5 to 10 pm or later.

SHENANDOAH RIVER, NORTH FORK

The North Fork of the Shenandoah River begins west of New Market, in the George Washington National Forest, and flows north (and to the west of Massanutten Mountain) before joining the South Fork near Front Royal. Route 11 (the original 'Valley Pike') and I-81 parallel this section of river in a southwesterly direction.

Woodstock & Around

Thirty miles south of Winchester, Woodstock is where the Reverend Peter Muhlenberg shouted, 'There's a time to pray and a time to fight' before marching the 8th Virginia Regiment out of his church and off to fight in the Revolutionary War. The Woodstock Chamber of Commerce (☎ 540-459-2542) is at 143 N Main St.

Things to See & Do The Woodstock Museum (☎ 540-459-5518), at 137 W Court St, features early American furnishings, tools, and farm implements used by early Valley settlers. It is open 10 am to 4 pm Thursday to Saturday from May to September (donations are encouraged).

The **Massanutten Military Academy**, 614 S Main St, is in a massive brick building on the main route through town. Behind the academy is a small Civil War cemetery.

The **Woodstock Tower**, located on Massanutten Mountain, offers a panoramic view of Woodstock, the seven bends of the North Fork of the Shenandoah River and sur-

rounding valley, and Fort Valley to the east. From Route 11 in Woodstock, drive east on Mill Rd and go left on Woodstock Tower Rd.

Edinburg, a small community 4 miles south of Woodstock on Route 11, features historic homes, charming B&Bs, quaint shops and galleries, and one of the few remaining pre–Civil War mills in existence. Several shops feature local artisans' crafts – including pottery, stitchery, dried flowers, and handmade baskets. Others specialize in antiques, original oil and watercolor paintings, and folk art.

Midway between Woodstock and Edinburg is Shenandoah Vineyards, a boutique winery in a pleasant country setting (see the Virginia for Wine Lovers boxed text).

Mt Jackson, farther south on Route 11, has the Old Soldiers' Cemetery, with about 400 graves of soldiers representing nine states of the Confederacy.

The area is also known for the **Shenandoah Valley Music Festival** (☎ 800-459-3396), held on weekends from April to Labor Day at nearby Orkney Springs (15 miles west of I-81 and Mt Jackson on Route 263). Classical, symphony, pops, folk, big band, and jazz performances are held outdoors on the grounds of the historic 19th-century Orkney Hotel.

Places to Stay & Eat Right off I-81, the *Ramada Inn* (☎ 540-459-5000, 1130 Motel Drive) has all the trimmings you would expect from this chain, plus a good restaurant; singles/doubles start at $58/66. The nearby Dunkin' Donuts has surprisingly good coffee.

Azalea House (☎ 540-459-3500, 551 S Main St) is a lovely B&B with cozy rooms from $55 to $80 – and on arrival, they serve hot nut bread or homemade cookies and tea or hot cider. The *Inn at Narrow Passage* (☎ 540-459-8000, www.innatnarrowpassage.com), on Route 11 in Edinburg, has been restored to its 18th-century appearance. Rooms furnished with antiques cost $85/110 for singles/doubles.

River'd Inn (☎ 540-459-5369, 800-637-4561, 1972 Artz Rd), several miles down County Rd 663 (off Route 11), sits on one of the famous bends of the Shenandoah. It is expensive, with rooms costing $85 to $325. The restaurant serves continental cuisine, including a prix-fixe dinner ($50) Wednesday to Sunday.

Paisano's (☎ 540-459-8756), in the Wal-Mart Shopping Center (I-81 at Route 42), is an Italian restaurant offering everything from pizza by the slice and sandwiches to meat, seafood, and pasta specialty dishes. It's open 10:30 am to 10 pm Monday to Thursday, 10:30 am to 11 pm Friday and Saturday, and 11 am to 10 pm Sunday.

The *Spring House Restaurant* (☎ 540-459-4755, 325 S Main St) is a local favorite for lunch and dinner (try the excellent Reuben). The pub here is also popular with locals.

Virginia for Wine Lovers

Jamestown settlers were the first to attempt winemaking (unsuccessfully) in the US, many years before the Spanish missionaries placed vines in California soil. Thomas Jefferson planted vines at Monticello, but high humidity and root lice destroyed his crop. Years later, sprays and improved techniques counteracted these conditions, which resulted in great success for vine growing and winemaking in Virginia.

Today, Virginia has a thriving wine industry, with 62 wineries (and more on the way) offering world-class wines and year-round activities. Chardonnay grapes are the most commonly grown in the state, and chardonnay wines are generally considered the region's best.

In the Shenandoah Valley, there are six vineyards:

Deer Meadow Vineyard (☎ 540-877-1919, 800-653-6632), 199 Vintage Lane in Winchester. Open 11 am to 5 pm Wednesday to Sunday from March to December. From Route 50, go south on Route 608 and turn left on Route 629 to Vintage Lane.

Guilford Ridge Vineyard (☎ 540-778-3853), 328 Running Pine Rd in Luray. From I-81, take Route 211 to Business Route 340 south, and take Route 632 for 1 mile. Tasting is by appointment only (minimum of eight people).

Landwirt Vineyard (☎ 540-833-6000), 8223 Simmers Valley Rd in Harrisonburg. Open 1 to 5 pm weekends from April to December and by appointment only January to March. From I-81 exit 257, go south on Route 11 and west on Route 806.

North Mountain Vineyard & Winery (☎ 540-436-9463), 4374 Swartz Rd in Maurertown. Open 11 am to 5 pm Wednesday to Sunday from March to November and 11 am to 5 pm weekends from December to February. From I-81 exit 291, go west on Route 651, south on Route 623, and east on Route 655.

Rockbridge Vineyard (☎ 540-377-6204), 30 Hill View Lane in Raphine. Open noon to 5 pm Wednesday to Sunday from May to December 17 and noon to 5 pm Saturday and Sunday in April. From I-81 exit 205, take Route 606 west.

Shenandoah Vineyards (☎ 540-984-8699), 3659 S Ox Rd in Edinburg. Open 10 am to 6 pm daily March to November and 10 to 5 pm December to February; hourly tours take place from 11 am to 5 pm.

Shenandoah Vineyards was the first winery to open in the Valley and the fifth in Virginia. Emma French Randel and her husband, Jim, planted 5000 vines by hand in 1976 near Emma's family home, and their property has since developed into a flourishing 35-acre vineyard with a lovely view of Massanutten Mountain. Their wines – including cabernet sauvignon, merlot, chardonnay, and Riesling – have won numerous awards.

– Olga Watson Crotty

Bryce Resort

Picturesque Bryce Resort (☎ 800-821-1444, www.bryceresort.com) is in the heart of the Shenandoah Valley near Basye.

Snow skiing is possible from December to early March. There is a vertical rise of 500 feet, and the longest run is 3500 feet (served by two chair lifts and three surface lifts). In addition to ski and snowboard rentals, there is PSIA and SKIwee instruction. A weekday lift ticket (9 am to 4:30 pm) costs $27 for adults and $22 for seniors and children five to 12; on weekends, it's $37/32. There is night skiing 5:30 to 9:30 pm Tuesday to Saturday ($18/15).

Summer activities at Bryce include horseback riding at the TJ Stables (one hour $20), swimming ($3), tennis ($10 per hour), mountain biking ($15 for one to three hours), in-line skating ($20 per day), windsurfing, and grass-skiing ($26 per day).

You can find accommodations at *Stony Court at Bryce Resort* (☎ 800-296-0947), *Sky Chalet Mountain Lodge* (☎ 540-856-2147), and *Chalet High* (☎ 800-848-9858). The two-bedroom Stony Court townhouses start at $120 per night; the Ski Chalet Mountain Lodge has doubles for $35 to $65 weekdays and $50 to $80 weekends; and Chalet High has rooms with two/three beds for around $80/90 weekdays and $138/165 weekends.

To get there, take I-81 exit 273 and follow Route 263 for 11 miles west to Basye and Bryce Resort.

Shenandoah Caverns

These caverns (☎ 540-477-3115) have the usual collection of backlit, colorful stalactites/stalagmites and the ubiquitous Diamond Cascade and Bacon Formations, as well as a constant temperature of 56°F. One big plus is elevator access for the disabled.

The caverns are open 9 am to 5 pm daily in winter, and they stay open later in summer. Admission is $12 for adults, $10.50 for seniors, and $5.50 for children five to 14. The entry fee includes American Celebration on Parade (a tacky exhibit). To get there from I-81, take the Shenandoah Caverns exit (269).

New Market

It is hard to imagine this beautiful valley in the grip of war, but at one time, its peaceful serenity was disturbed by the boom of cannon, staccato rifle fire, and the cries of the wounded. You can learn about the terrible fighting in the Shenandoah Valley at the small but informative museum and other buildings in the **New Market Battlefield State Historical Park** (☎ 540-740-3101). The well-stocked Shenandoah Valley Travel Association (☎ 540-740-3132, www.shenandoah.org) is opposite the battlefield park entrance, on Route 211W (I-81 exit 264).

With a simple stained-glass window, the **Hall of Valor** in the visitor center commemorates the legendary advance by a company of youthful cadets from the Virginia Military Institute (VMI) in Lexington, 10 of whom were killed on the field of battle in New Market in 1864. There is an annual Civil War reenactment in May. Also inside is an excellent chronology of the war. Bushong's farmhouse on the battlefield has been reconstructed and furnished. On the ridge above the Shenandoah River are two spectacular overlooks from which you can see the Alleghenies. The Hall of Valor is open 9 am to 5 pm daily. Admission is $5 for adults and $2 for children. Entry to the farmhouse is free with Hall of Valor admission.

To get to the battlefield park, take I-81 to Route 211W exit 264, and then take an immediate right and drive for about a mile north into the park, passing two other military museums on the way. Ignore the battery of signs and continue to the VMI museum if you wish to see the main battlefield and best exhibits. Tune in to AM 530 for instructions.

The alternative, eclectic **military museum** (☎ 540-740-8065), on the spot where the battle began, has a facade that resembles Arlington, Robert E Lee's house near Washington, DC. It is open daily mid-March to November. Admission is $7 for adults, $5.50 for seniors, and $3 for children.

If you have had enough of the Civil War, you may wish to visit the **Bedrooms of America Museum** (☎ 540-740-3512), 9386 Congress St, just off I-81 exit 264. The furnishings of bedrooms from 1650 to 1930 are on display. The chambers open at 9 am daily. Admission is $2 for adults and $1.25 for children seven to 14.

North of Route 11, 2 miles south of Mt Jackson, is the **Meems Bottom Covered Bridge**, a 204-foot single span across the North Fork of the Shenandoah. It was originally built in 1893 and has been destroyed a few times since; it was last rebuilt in 1979.

The *Budget Inn* (☎ 540-740-3105), just off I-81 exit 264, has doubles for $28 to $38 in winter and $35 to $48 in summer. The *Quality Inn Shenandoah Valley* (☎ 540-740-3141), I-81 exit 264, is a good-size place with a restaurant and pool; singles/doubles are $42/53 in the low season; otherwise, $51/61.

The *Southern Kitchen* (☎ 540-740-3514, 9576 S Congress St), south of Confederate St on Route 11, has good traditional, inexpensive Southern food (peanut soup, barbecued beef, and fried chicken).

Endless Caverns

These privately owned caverns (☎ 540-896-2283), so called because the end to the underground passages has never been found, are not far south of New Market (just off Route 11 on County Rd 793). They can also be reached via I-81 exits 264 and 257. Colored lighting is used to bring out the best in the calcium carbonate, and the 'Snow Drift' is the coup de grace in this subterranean extravaganza. The caverns open at 9 am daily. Admission is $11 for adults and $5.50 for children three to 12.

HARRISONBURG

This market city (population 36,730) was first settled in 1739. It is now an agricultural center (beef, dairy, and poultry) and a college town. In town are James Madison University and the Eastern Mennonite College, and just south of town is the Bridgewater Community College.

You will probably see the incongruous sight of distinctively dressed Mennonites in horse-drawn buggies going about their simple lives in the bustling commercial center of town.

The Harrisonburg-Rockingham County CVB (☎ 540-434-2319) is at 10 E Gay St.

Places to Stay & Eat

The *Harrisonburg-New Market KOA* (☎ 540-896-8929) is near the George Washington National Forest. To get there from Harrisonburg, take Route 11 for 9 miles north and turn east onto County Rd 608 for 3.2 miles. Sites with full hookups cost $17 to $22 in winter and $19 to $25 in summer.

The *Village Inn* (☎ 540-434-7355) is in a rural setting on Route 11, between I-81 exits 240 and 243. Comfortable singles/doubles are $45/50 (an extra person is $5). The *Comfort Inn* (☎ 540-433-6066, 1440 E Market St), I-81 exit 247A, is an award-winner with tidy, comfortable single/double rooms starting at $59/69.

The *Days Inn Harrisonburg* (☎ 540-433-9353, 1131 Forest Hill Rd), I-81 exit 245, has a nearby restaurant, heated indoor pool, and health club privileges; doubles cost $45 to $70. The *Ramada Inn* (☎ 540-434-9981, 1 Pleasant Valley Rd), I-81 exit 243, has a restaurant and a pool; singles and doubles cost $50 to $65 (an extra person can cost $3 to $6).

The *Joshua Wilton House* (☎ 540-434-4464, 412 S Main St) is a delightful late-19th-century house close to downtown. There is a sunroom on the back patio, an upscale restaurant, and an adjacent cafe serving good, moderately priced dinners. The rooms are tastefully furnished with antiques and cost $95 to $105.

The *Health Trek Deli* (☎ 540-433-2359, 451 University Blvd), in Kate's Natural Products, is about the only decent inexpensive vegetarian alternative; it's open 9 am to 6 pm Monday to Saturday. *El Charro* (☎ 540-564-0386, 1570 E Market St) is open every day for good Mexican lunches and dinners.

The *Evers Family Restaurant* (☎ 540-432-0775), on Route 11 (I-81 exit 240), serves an old-fashioned Southern-style buffet. It is open 11 am to 8 pm daily and until 9 pm on Friday and Saturday; a meal costs less than $10.

The *Blue Stone Inn Restaurant* (☎ 540-434-0535, 9107 N Valley Pike), 9 miles north of Harrisonburg on Route 11 (I-81 exit 251), is the place to go for a bit of local color. Open for more than 50 years, it doesn't

VIRGINIA

appear to have changed much. The dining room has a wealth of trophies (animal and fish) mounted on the walls; the ceiling's light fixtures are made from antlers. Large portions of good steak and seafood are its specialties, but you can also go for a drink in the sunroom. It's open 4:30 to 8:30 pm Tuesday to Saturday.

Getting There & Away
The Shenandoah Valley Regional Airport (☎ 540-234-8304) is at Weyers Cave, 10 miles south of Harrisonburg. There is a scheduled US Airways Express service and charter services. Most people traveling in this part of the Shenandoah do so in their own cars.

AROUND HARRISONBURG
Harrisonburg is in a beautiful part of the Shenandoah Valley and is close to a number of interesting towns and attractions.

Dayton
This charming little town (population 900), on Route 42 not far south of Harrisonburg, is set in beautiful rural country.

Just to the north of town is a fortified frontier home, the **Daniel Harrison House** (☎ 540-879-2280). Built circa 1749, it is being restored and redecorated to look as it would if occupied by a well-to-do frontier family. The house is open 1 to 5 pm on weekends from May to October.

The **Shenandoah Valley Folk Art & Heritage Center** (☎ 540-879-2681), at 115 Bowman Rd, concentrates on Valley history and folklife (as do a number of museums in the Valley). It has an electric wall-size map of Stonewall Jackson's 1862 Shenandoah Valley campaign. It is open 10 am to 4 pm Monday to Saturday (except Tuesday) and 1 to 4 pm Sunday from May to October. Admission is $4 for adults and $1 for children five to 18.

The traditional **Dayton Farmer's Market** (☎ 540-879-9885) is 3 miles south of Harrisonburg on Route 42. There are 20 or so shops that sell fresh-baked goods, often prepared by the friendly Mennonite community. The market is open 9 am to 6 pm Thursday and Saturday (to 4 pm Friday).

The **Hone Quarry Recreation Area** (☎ 540-828-2591), 11 miles northwest of Dayton on Route 257, is the cheapest campground in the state – it's free. There are only 10 sites and no services, but this 'heaven' is nestled below the Shenandoah Mountains, on the fringe of the George Washington National Forest. Nearby is the **North River Recreation Area** (☎ 540-828-2591), another basic facility in GWNF with 16 sites (by Elk Horn Lake) and superb views; sites are $3.

Huyard's Country Kitchen (☎ 540-879-2613), in the Dayton Farmer's Market (see above), has inexpensive buffet meals (two can eat for less than $20) and hand-dipped ice cream.

Natural Chimneys Regional Park
The Shenandoah Valley was once the floor of a great inland sea. Eons ago, as the sea receded, natural forces sculpted the Natural Chimneys, towers of solid rock that loom as much as 120 feet above the surrounding pastoral terrain. Viewed from one angle, they resemble enormous chimneys; from another, they take on the appearance of a ruined castle or temple. Perhaps their castlelike appearance has something to do with the site being used for the annual **Jousting Tournament**, held on the third Saturday of August. First held in 1821, it is the oldest continuously held sporting event in North America.

The Natural Chimneys Regional Park **Campground** (☎ 540-350-2510) is open to visitors for day (9 am to dusk) and overnight use. There are 120 campsites with electric/water hookups, hiking and biking trails, picnic shelters, a pool, a store, hot showers, laundry, playgrounds, and self-guided tours (the facilities are limited from December to February). Tent sites cost $9, and RV sites cost $18.50 for four people. A day visit costs $6 maximum per car (or $3 per person; it is $2.50 to use the swimming pool). The visitor center is open 9 am to 5 pm daily April to October.

Stokesville Park (☎ 540-350-2343), west of Mt Solon in George Washington National Forest, has 102 sites and five cabins. The park has a nature trail, a playground, swimming, hiking, fishing, and picnicking. Water, electricity, and sewer hookups are available year-round.

The park is 20 miles northwest of Staunton via Route 250W, Route 42, and County Rds 760, 747, and 730. To get to the Chimneys from Harrisonburg, travel south on I-81 to Route 42S (exit 240) and head west to Bridgewater; follow the signs along Route 42S from there.

Massanutten Resort

This ski resort (☎ 800-207-6277, www.mass resort.com) offers a vertical drop of 1110 feet (the highest in Virginia) and 14 slopes (including the 3400-foot Diamond Jim and 4100-foot ParaDice), most of which are lit at night. There is one quad chairlift, and the field has 100% snow-making capacity.

The field is known for ski racing, and there is a PSIA ski school and SKIwee program. The mid-Atlantic snowboard series is held here in early February. It is open 9 am to 10 pm daily, usually December to mid-March. Weekdays, lift tickets are $30 for adults and $25 for seniors (free for those over 70), and $25 for children six to 12. Tickets are $42 for adults and $34 for seniors and children on weekends (night tickets are $20/15).

To get to Massanutten from Staunton, take I-81 north to exit 247A in Harrisonburg. Head east on Route 33 for 10 miles to County Rd 644; the entrance is on the left. The Guide to Massanutten Mountain ($6) has information on USFS trails, including the Big Blue.

Grand Caverns Regional Park

These caverns (☎ 540-249-5705) are in Augusta County near the appropriately monickered town of Grottoes. They contain one of the largest underground rooms in the East, the Cathedral Hall (70 feet high and 280 feet long). There is some underground graffiti as well, referred to as 'historic signatures' (instead of 'aged vandalism'). Jefferson rode on horseback from Monticello to see the caverns, and Stonewall Jackson let his troops sleep here after the Battle of Port Republic.

The caves are open 9 am to 5 pm daily April to October. Admission is $11 for adults, $10 for seniors, and $7 for children

three to 12. To get there from I-81, take exit 235 onto Route 256. This meets Route 340 at Grottoes; the caverns are nearby on County Rd 844.

A few miles north of Grottoes, just off Route 340, is **Port Republic**, the site of one of the last battles of Jackson's 1862 Shenandoah Valley campaign (see 1862 in the Civil War chapter).

STAUNTON

Staunton (population 25,000) is another old Virginia town exuding history. Pronounced **stan**-tun (and don't forget it!), the town is off I-81 (or off Route 250, 11 miles west of the southern end of Skyline Drive).

There has long been a pathway through this area, originally traversed by Native Americans as they moved up and down the Shenandoah Valley. In 1732, the family of Scotch-Irish immigrant John Lewis built a homestead here, 2 miles east of present-day Staunton. Later, in 1745, the first log courthouse was built (on the site of today's courthouse). Four years after that, Thomas Lewis, son of John, laid out the plans for the town.

It was the seat of government of huge Augusta County, named after the then-Princess of Wales. (In 1738, the county included modern-day West Virginia, Ohio, Kentucky, Illinois, Indiana, and the Pittsburgh area of Pennsylvania.) During the Revolutionary War, the parish church was briefly (17 days in June 1781) capital of Virginia, as Thomas Jefferson and the General Assembly moved here to evade Tarleton's Redcoats.

During the Civil War, the Virginia School for the Deaf and Blind was set up as a military hospital and remained as such for the duration. In 1862, Stonewall Jackson, ostensibly leading his men out of the Valley to Richmond, took them back over the Blue Ridge Mountains into Staunton by train – probably the world's first use of the railway as a military tactic. During the war, Staunton was untouched, and today the town has a fine collection of immaculately preserved Victorian buildings.

Staunton is the birthplace of US president Thomas Woodrow Wilson (1856). There was a huge party in 1922, when the president returned home. Today, Staunton is busily restoring its architectural gems. A visit will be rewarded with engrossing walks.

Orientation

There are five historical districts in town, all easily accessible on foot. Gospel Hill, near the corner of Beverley and Coalter Sts, got its name in the late 1790s, when religious meetings were held here. Today, it's an area of shady streets and elegant homes. The North End, an older neighborhood adjoining Mary Baldwin College (founded in 1842), has lots of historical buildings and steep hills.

Newtown is the oldest residential area and includes the city's first black church. Downtown is a compact area west of Gospel Hill exuding 19th-century charm. Most of the buildings date from 1860 to 1920, Staunton's boom period.

The Wharf historical district dates from the time when the Virginia Central Railroad hit town in 1854. The railroad transformed a sleepy rural village into an important commercial center. Warehouses sprang up around the train depot and supplied everything from fresh produce to wagons and harnesses.

VIRGINIA

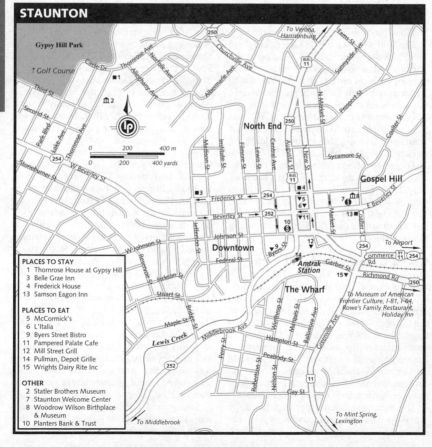

STAUNTON

PLACES TO STAY
1 Thornrose House at Gypsy Hill
3 Belle Grae Inn
4 Frederick House
13 Samson Eagon Inn

PLACES TO EAT
5 McCormick's
6 L'Italia
9 Byers Street Bistro
11 Pampered Palate Cafe
12 Mill Street Grill
14 Pullman, Depot Grille
15 Wrights Dairy Rite Inc

OTHER
2 Statler Brothers Museum
7 Staunton Welcome Center
8 Woodrow Wilson Birthplace
  & Museum
10 Planters Bank & Trust

Information

Stop by the Greater Augusta Regional Chamber of Commerce (☎ 540-886-2351, www.augustachamber.org), at 1303 Richmond Ave, near the junction of I-64, I-81 (exit 222), and Route 250.

The Staunton Welcome Center (☎ 540-332-3971), at Woodrow Wilson's birthplace, 18–24 N Coalter St, is open 10 am to 4 pm January to March and 9 am to 5 pm April to November.

The Augusta Medical Center (☎ 540-332-4000), off I-64 in Fishersville, has 24-hour emergency treatment facilities.

There are no foreign-currency conversion facilities in Staunton, so make sure you have cash before you arrive. Planters Bank & Trust (☎ 540-885-1232), on the corner of Augusta and Johnson Sts, has an ATM.

Woodrow Wilson Birthplace & Museum

Thomas Woodrow Wilson was the 28th president of the US (1913–21) and the eighth Virginian-born president. This stately Greek Revival–style house, built in 1846 and occupied by Wilson's Presbyterian minister father from 1855, has been restored to the splendid condition it was in when Wilson was born here in 1856.

The museum (☎ 540-885-0897), 18–24 N Coalter St, consists of seven exhibition galleries that outline the accomplishments of Wilson, probably the first of the true international American statesmen. Wilson's presidential limousine, a 1919 Pierce-Arrow sedan, is on display. The building is open 9 am to 5 pm daily; winter hours may vary. Admission is $6.50 for adults, $6 for seniors, $4 for students, and $2 for children six to 12. There is a gift shop in the gardens and free parking.

Museum of American Frontier Culture

This wonderful folk museum (☎ 540-332-7850, www.frontiermuseum.org), off I-81 (exit 222) to Route 250, presents life on 18th- and 19th-century farmsteads. Staff in period costume organize demonstrations of daily and seasonal activities, such as tending livestock, planting fields, and doing domestic chores.

One of the farms is typical American, and the three others are European in origin, representing what the early settler-farmers left in England, Ireland, Scotland, and Germany. Full attention has been paid to detail – the thatching on the roofs of buildings imported from Ireland was done by master craftspersons, and the crops represent, as closely as possible, those planted at the time.

The museum is on the Warriors Path used by Indians traveling up and down the Valley. This path later evolved into the County Wagon Road, used by settlers traveling from Pennsylvania to Georgia. The museum is open 9 am to 5 pm daily (10 am to 4 pm December to mid-March). Admission is $8 for adults, $7.50 for seniors, $7 for students, and $4 for children six to 12. The visitor center includes a museum shop.

Statler Brothers Museum

About 2 miles from I-81, at 501 Thornrose Ave, is this unusual museum (☎ 540-885-7297), which is dedicated to the Statler Brothers, a group of country singers, two of them brothers (Harold and Don Reid) who hail from Staunton.

It is full of memorabilia, including music awards garnered by this popular ensemble in their 25-year career, including a platinum award for their contribution to the *Pulp Fiction* soundtrack. Who among the older visitors could forget 'Flowers on the Wall' and 'Bed of Roses'? This free museum, housed in the school the Reid brothers attended, is open 10:30 am to 3:30 pm weekdays. The free tours start at 2 pm.

Places to Stay

There is camping here, as well as plenty of reasonably priced motels and hotels.

Camping The *Shenandoah KOA Kampground* (☎ 540-248-2746) is located along Middle River near Verona, just north of Staunton and 3 miles from I-81. There are 132 shaded campsites, a lake, and electric/water/sewer hookups. It is open March to October, and sites for two cost $22 to $37, depending on the season.

VIRGINIA

Walnut Hills Campground (☎ 540-337-3920, 391 Walnut Hills Rd), in Mint Spring, accommodates travel trailers, motor homes, and tents. There are level sites for RVs with electric/water/sewer hookups; campfires are allowed at the sites. In addition, there is a lake, pool, playground, volleyball net, store, laundry, games room, free showers, and dancing and music on Saturday night. Sites cost $16 to $22 for two (electricity is $3 extra).

Hotels & Motels The *Budget Inn* (☎ 800-216-6835, 816 Greenville Ave), near exit 220, south of the junction of I-81 and I-64 (about a mile from the ramp), has recently been renovated; singles/doubles start at $40/44 and include free continental breakfast. *Shoney's Inn of Staunton* (☎ 540-885-3117) is near the junction of Route 250 and I-81 (exit 222), about half a mile north of I-64. The garden-style rooms have sleeping sofas, whirlpool tubs, and telephones. There's a lounge, a spa, and a restaurant nearby. Singles/doubles start at $52/58.

Other places include the *Econo Lodge* (☎ 540-885-5158, 1031 Richmond Ave) on Route 250, less than a mile west of I-81 (exit 222), with singles/doubles starting at $36/38; the *Super 8 Motel* (☎ 540-886-2888, 1015 Richmond Rd),with off-season doubles starting at $38 to $64 (high-season, $48 to $72); the new *Microtel* (☎ 540-887-0200, 200 Frontier Drive), a good value, with doubles for $40 to $70 in the low season (breakfast included); and the *Best Western Staunton Inn* (☎ 540-885-1112), on Route 250 at I-81 (exit 222), close to Rowe's Restaurant, with singles/doubles starting at $58/65.

The *Comfort Inn* (☎ 540-886-5000, 1302 Richmond Rd), Route 250 (I-81 exit 222), has a pool and singles/doubles starting at $65/70 including breakfast.

The *Holiday Inn Golf & Conference Center* (☎ 540-248-6020), on the Woodrow Wilson Parkway (I-81 exit 225), is a golfer-friendly place where singles and doubles start at $69 in the low season and $89 in the high season. Attached is Mulligan's Irish bar (see Places to Eat & Drink, later).

Inns Staunton is well known for its numerous fine old inns. The *Thornrose House at Gypsy Hill* (☎ 540-885-7026, 531 Thornrose Ave) is a Georgian Revival brick home with a wrap-around verandah. The rooms (infant- and smoke-free) have private baths and air-conditioning and are furnished with antiques. The highlight here is afternoon tea in the parlor. The cost per double of $69 to $89 ($15 per extra person) includes afternoon tea.

The *Belle Grae Inn* (☎ 540-886-5151, 515 W Frederick St) is a romantic old place that comprises closely grouped, carefully restored original Victorian residences, each with decorated guest rooms and suites. It is restricted to adults and well-behaved youth aged 14 or older, and no pets are admitted. The rooms cost $95 to $135 weekdays and $135 to $165 weekends. One of the town's best restaurants is attached (see Places to Eat & Drink, below).

Frederick House (☎ 540-885-4220, 28 N New St), at the corner of Frederick St, is a small hotel and tearoom in the European tradition. It has large rooms and suites with big beds, a private bath, air-conditioning, TV, a phone, and a private entrance; its gourmet breakfasts are prepared year-round. Doubles cost $75 to $150 in the low season; otherwise, $85 to $170.

The *Samson Eagon Inn* (☎ 540-886-8200, 238 E Beverley St) is an antebellum mansion with spacious rooms that have canopied beds, sitting areas, antique furnishings, private bathrooms, queen-size beds, phones, and TVs. Smoking and children are not allowed. The cost for a double ($94 to $125) includes a full gourmet breakfast.

Places to Eat & Drink

One of the best Virginian restaurants is in Staunton – *Rowe's Family Restaurant* (☎ 540-886-1833), just off I-81 exit 222, serves inexpensive, tasty meals. All the homespun Virginia staples are on offer, including mincemeat pies, dishes with Virginia ham, succulent potato soup, breaded catfish, Southern fried chicken, bottomless cups of coffee, and waitstaff fresh out of the 1950s. We love it.

The *Pampered Palate Cafe* (☎ 540-886-9463, 26-28 E Beverley St) is a good choice for vegetarians, with a wide range of fresh-produce sandwiches. There is also a good selection of coffees and local wines. It is open Monday to Saturday for breakfast and lunch.

Shorty's Diner (☎ 540-885-8861, 1013 Richmond Rd) looks like a 1950s jukebox – all stainless steel, neon, and glass – but it has inexpensive American fare, such as burgers and fries for $4.25, and breakfast all day.

Wrights Dairy Rite Inc (☎ 540-886-0435, 346 Greenville Ave), a drive-in restaurant, is a local institution. It has been offering curb service since 1952 and has appeared on a Statler Brothers' album cover (Don and Harold often pull in for a meal).

McCormick's (☎ 540-885-3111, 41 N Augusta St) is open for dinner only, for 'not-quite-fine dining.' But the food is good, and the place has a casual atmosphere, great prime rib, and, occasionally, live entertainment. On Tuesday, there are vegetarian specials for $9, and on Wednesday, there are all-you-can-eat crablegs for $17.

The *Pullman* (☎ 540-885-6612), at the old Staunton C&O station, has a nutritious lunchtime soup-and-salad bar six days a week and brunch on Sunday; it is also open for dinner daily. The *Depot Grille* (☎ 540-885-7332), also in the station, has a 50-foot oak bar where you can enjoy a large selection of beers. Less expensive than the Pullman, it has daily entree specials and a children's menu.

The *Byers Street Bistro* (☎ 540-887-1600, 18 Byers St), in an old warehouse, is a casual, hopping place serving a range of sandwiches, soups, salads, and entrees daily.

The *Mill Street Grill* (☎ 540-886-0656, 1 Mill St) is housed in a converted gristmill and serves delectable ribs grilled with Cajun spices ($12.50), steak, seafood, pasta, Tex-Mex, and a Sunday brunch. For late-night entertainment, there's the adjacent tavern, with pool tables, a good selection of beers, and a colorful crowd.

L'Italia (☎ 540-885-0102, 23 E Beverley St) is a haven for lovers of fine Italian food. It is open 10 am to 11 pm Monday to Thursday and 11 am to 11 pm Friday and Saturday for tasty pastas ($10 to $15) and homemade pastries.

The Belle Grae Inn (see Places to Stay, earlier), features excellent regional cuisine and beverages in a Victorian atmosphere.

Chubby's Sports Bar (1300 Churchville Ave) is open daily for lunch and dinner and has a good selection of inexpensive entrees. *Mulligan's*, attached to the Holiday Inn (see Places to Stay, earlier), is an Irish bar and a popular meeting spot that often features live music.

Getting There & Away

The Shenandoah Valley Regional Airport (☎ 540-234-8304) is at Weyers Cave, 15 miles north of Staunton (take I-81 exit 235).

Greyhound/Trailways (☎ 540-886-2424), 1211 Richmond Rd (Route 250), provides daily service to and from New York and throughout the southern states.

Amtrak (☎ 800-872-7245), on Middlebrook Ave, has trains that pass through on the New York-Cincinnati route (Sunday, Wednesday, and Friday). This train also stops at Clifton Forge for The Homestead resort in Bath County.

WAYNESBORO

The town, settled in 1797 by Irish and German immigrants and named after a Revolutionary War hero, General 'Mad' Anthony Wayne, is well situated 8 miles east of the junction of I-81 and I-64.

For more information on attractions, contact the Waynesboro-Augusta Chamber of Commerce (☎ 540-949-8203), 301 W Main St; it's open 8:30 am to 5 pm weekdays. There is a visitor center (☎ 540-943-5187) on I-64 at Afton Mountain (exit 99) that is open 10 am to 6 pm Monday to Saturday.

Things to See & Do

The P Buckley Moss Museum (☎ 540-949-6473), 150 P Buckley Moss Drive, is a fine-arts museum dedicated to Moss, very much a 'people's artist,' whose subject matter includes the Amish and Mennonite communities. This free museum is open 10 am to 6 pm

Monday to Saturday and 12:30 to 5:30 pm Sunday. There are also four galleries in the **Shenandoah Valley Art Center** (☎ 540-942-7662), 600 W Main St, which is open 10 am to 4 pm Tuesday to Saturday and 2 to 4 pm Sunday (free).

Shoppers will appreciate the selection at the **Waynesboro Village Factory Outlets** (☎ 540-949-5000), 601 Shenandoah Drive, where goods ranging from fine crockery to Hanes underwear can be purchased at bargain prices.

In **Stuarts Draft**, southwest of Waynesboro on Route 340, there are a couple of Mennonite-operated shops. The Candy Shop (☎ 540-337-0298), on County Rd 608, sells homemade apple butter and preserves as well as Hershey products; it's open 9:30 am to 5 pm Monday to Saturday.

Places to Stay & Eat
The *Waynesboro North 340 Campground* (☎ 540-943-9573), on Route 340, 5 miles north of Waynesboro off I-64 exit 94, has sites for $18 to $21 for two (most have electricity and water). *Shenandoah Acres Resort* (☎ 540-337-1911) is on County Rd 660 (off County Rd 608), east of Route 340 in Stuarts Draft, open May to September (10 am to 8:30 pm for swimming). Miniature golf, playground equipment in the water, basketball, volleyball, and other pursuits will keep you amused. Campsites are $30, and cottages (available all year) cost $81 to $125 in summer.

The *Deluxe Budget Motel* (☎ 540-949-8253, 2112 W Main St), 1½ miles west of town on Route 250, has doubles for $30 to $34 in the low season and $40 to $52 in the high season.

The *Iris Inn* (☎ 540-943-1991, 191 Chinquapin Drive) is a modern B&B with all the trappings of fine Southern living; doubles cost $80 to $130 Sunday to Thursday; otherwise, $85 to $140. There is a room equipped for people who are disabled.

Weasie's Kitchen (☎ 540-943-0500, 130 E Broad St) is a simple place known for great breakfasts and inexpensive lunches (around $4); it's open daily for all meals.

The *South River Grill* (☎ 540-942-5567) has moved from downtown to the junction of I-64 and Route 340, and it is well worth seeking out. It has generous vegetable and fruit salads, homemade pasta and sauces, and slow-roasted prime rib; it's open daily for lunch and dinner.

GEORGE WASHINGTON NATIONAL FOREST
The borders of the George Washington National Forest are not much more than 10 miles to the southeast and west from Staunton.

The forest itself is in three parts: Massanutten Mountain, in the north between the north and south forks of the Shenandoah; a larger section that straddles the Blue Ridge Parkway between Charlottesville and Roanoke; and the largest section, which skirts the West Virginia border and includes parts of the Shenandoah and Allegheny Mountains. It is linked to the Jefferson National Forest on both its southwestern and southeastern extremities – the dividing lines being I-64 in the west and Route 501 in the east.

Information
The US Forest Service is the administrator of these forests. The Supervisor's Office is the main headquarters (☎ 540-265-5100, www.fs.fed.us/gwjnf), 5162 Valleypointe Parkway, Roanoke, VA 24019; it provides good maps of the entire forest and detailed brochures. Other ranger district offices include the following:

Deerfield (☎ 540-885-8028), west of Staunton on Route 254

Dry River (☎ 540-828-2591), 112 North River Rd, Bridgewater

James River (☎ 540-962-2214), 810-A Madison Ave, Covington

Lee (☎ 540-984-4101), 109 Molineu Rd, Edinburg

Massanutten Visitors Center (☎ 540-740-8310), New Market

Pedlar (☎ 540-261-6105), 2424 Magnolia Ave, Buena Vista

Warm Springs (☎ 540-839-2521), Route 220S, Hot Springs

Ramsey's Draft Wilderness Area
This wilderness area was designated by Congress in 1980 to preserve a deeply wooded

valley with the last tracts of virgin forest in Virginia. Up in the right prong of the valley are stands of hemlock that have never seen an ax or chainsaw – one that fell had its rings measured and was estimated to be more than 450 years old. The valley is a beautiful, quiet, and moody place. There is a picnic area at Ramsey's Draft, where interpretative signs relate the first battle (McDowell) of Stonewall Jackson's 1862 Valley campaign. There are Confederate breastworks nearby.

You can explore the valley along part of the 32-mile **Wild Oak Trail**; get further information from the USFS. There is a great deal of hiking and cross-country skiing in the area, but mountain bikes are not permitted. Hunting is permitted at certain times, so always wear bright clothing. To get to Ramsey's Draft from Staunton, take Route 250W (it is well signed).

Activities

Covering more than a million acres, the forest offers many activities. There are more than 950 miles of **hiking** trails, more than 60 miles of the Appalachian Trail, rare wildflowers, waterfalls, and interesting geological formations. The highest point in the forest is the 4458-foot Elliott Knob, to the west of Staunton. The Potomac Appalachian Trail Club's *Hiking Guide to the Pedlar District of the George Washington National Forest* ($6), an area near Buena Vista, covers many trails; you can reach the PATC at ☎ 703-242-0315. (See the Activities chapter for more information.)

For **skiing** and **snowboarding**, check out the Wintergreen Resort (☎ 804-325-2100 for ski report), the oldest in the state and 'the South's single best' (according to *Skiing* magazine), high in the Blue Ridge Mountains some 43 miles from Charlottesville. Of the 19 trails, about 20% are beginner, 40% intermediate, 20% advanced, and 20% expert. A 1000-foot vertical drop is served by one double and four triple chairlifts. (Also see Places to Stay, later.)

Massanutten, Bryce Mountain, and Wintergreen have tapped into the burgeoning snowboarding craze. Eastern adherents ('shredders') of soft boots and radical boards have discovered the pleasures of these three places, and the dollar-wise resorts have accordingly added snowboard parks to their slopes. You get a free 1½-hour lesson at Wintergreen when you rent a board. December to March, a weekday lift ticket (9 am to 4:30 pm) costs $33 for adults and $26 for seniors and children six to 12. On weekends and holidays, it's $44/35. There is night skiing 5 to 10 pm Sunday to Thursday ($19/15) and 6 to 11 pm Friday and Saturday ($22/18).

There is **fishing**, with native trout, brook and rainbow trout, small-mouth and large-mouth bass, bluegill, and catfish found in 300 miles of waterways.

Places to Stay

Primitive camping is allowed in most of the forest (no permit is required). Recreation areas are numerous in GWNF. For information, check with the USFS headquarters and ranger offices. The major recreation areas and camping prices are as follows:

Elizabeth Furnace (☎ 540-984-4101; $12) and Little Fort (☎ 540-984-4101; free), southwest of Front Royal on Massanutten Mountain

James River and Cave Mountain Lake (see below), near Natural Bridge (covered later in this chapter)

Lake Moomaw, Blowing Springs (☎ 540-839-2521; $4), and Hidden Valley (☎ 540-839-2521; $4), near Warm Springs and the West Virginia border, off Route 39

Sherando (see below)

Todd Lake (☎ 540-828-2591; $7) and North River, near Elk Horn Lake and southwest of Harrisonburg

Wolf Gap (☎ 540-984-4101; free), to the west of Woodstock

The *Sherando Recreation Area* (☎ 540-261-6105), part of the forest, is east of Staunton, at the foot of the Blue Ridge Mountains, approximately 15 miles south of I-64 via County Rd 664. The 24-acre lake has a small beach and bathhouse and a visitor center. The family campsites are available on a first-come, first-served basis ($10). From April to October, there is water; otherwise, bring your own. The Cliff Trail here takes hikers above the lake. There is also a self-guided nature trail closer to the camping area.

Another great recreation area is *Cave Mountain Lake Recreation Area* (☎ 540-291-2189), an isolated paradise with a 7-acre lake surrounded by hardwoods and pines. It is open from May to early November, and camping is $8 per site. From I-81, take exits 175 or 180 to Natural Bridge and turn onto Route 130. Follow this road for about 3 miles to County Rd 759, and follow it for another 3 miles to County Rd 781. The park is 1.6 miles farther along.

The *Wintergreen Resort* (☎ 800-325-2200, *www.wintergreenresort.com*) has downhill ski slopes (see Activities, earlier), restaurants, a bar, outdoor pools, an indoor pool, tennis courts, 45 golf holes, hiking trails, a riding center, an exercise room and sauna, and the 20-acre Lake Monocan for swimming and canoeing. There are more than 6000 acres of protected forest here and a staff biologist who organizes interpretive walks. All of this does not come cheap. A double room in the resort costs $125 to $165 in summer and $160 to $195 in winter. A round of golf will cost $50 weekdays and $60 weekends, and there are fees for tennis, the Wintergarden spa, guided mountain-bike trips, and horseback riding. Bring a lot of money!

To get here from the north, follow Route 29 south to I-64. Head west on I-64 to Route 250 exit 107. (If coming from the south, turn east on I-64 at the I-81 junction and proceed to Route 250.) Take Route 250 west to Route 151 (Wintergreen is signposted from here); it's 14.2 miles to County Rd 664, then another 4½ miles along this road.

LEXINGTON

This small town (population 7000) in the heart of Shenandoah, 36 miles south of Staunton and off I-81, has a lot to offer the visitor in the way of grace, charm, history, and attractions. It is a perfect place to relax, as the pace of life seems a lot slower here – explore interesting aspects of the Civil War or just wander the streets, where there are horse-drawn carriages and many well-preserved homes. It's a place that hardened

travelers may find after years of nomadic existence and say, 'I could settle down here.'

Lexington was home to Stonewall Jackson before the Civil War and Robert E Lee after – both of these Confederate generals are buried here (not far from their horses, Little Sorrel and Traveller). George C Marshall (Nobel Peace Prize winner for his efforts in the reconstruction of Europe after WWII) and the polar explorer Admiral Richard Byrd both attended the Virginia Military Institute (VMI) here. Sam Houston, commander in the Texan army in the war of independence, was born 5 miles north of Lexington (near Timber Ridge Presbyterian church). More recently, *Sommersby*, set in the time of the Civil War, was filmed in and around Lexington and Bath County.

Orientation & Information

The town is hard to miss if you are coming down the Valley, as Route 11 passes right through it. Lexington is just off I-81 (take exits 195, 188, or 180). The town is cut into four quarters by the east-west Route 60 and the north-south Route 11.

The helpful Lexington Visitors Center (☎ 540-463-3777, www.lexingtonvirginia.com), 106 E Washington St (I-64 exit 55 or I-81 exit 188-B), is open 8:30 am to 6 pm daily June to August; otherwise, 9 am to 5 pm.

The First Union Bank (☎ 540-463-7321) is on S Main St, and Crestar Bank (☎ 540-463-2126) is on the corner of Main and Nelson Sts – both have ATMs.

The post office (☎ 540-463-2822) is on the corner of Nelson St and Lee Ave.

The Stonewall Jackson Hospital (☎ 540-462-1200), off Spotswood Drive, has 24-hour emergency service.

There is a laundry on the corner of Randolph and Henry Sts.

Washington & Lee University

This university, with its picturesque colonnaded campus, is the sixth-oldest college in the country. Founded in 1749 as Augusta Academy, it was renamed Washington College after a donation by the first president. The 'Lee' was added (from Robert E Lee) following the Civil War, as he was

Stonewall Jackson

One of the greatest figures of the Civil War, General Thomas Jonathan Jackson, a true soldier in every sense of the word, was born in Clarksburg, Virginia (now West Virginia) on January 21, 1824. A devout fire-and-brimstone Presbyterian, he had been a professor of natural philosophy for 10 years at the Virginia Military Institute in Lexington when the Civil War broke out.

He was soon in the service of the South, and during Manassas I (July 21, 1861), he earned the nickname 'Stonewall' when his brigade acted as an anchor in a vital part of the battle. Barnard Bee, a Confederate brigadier had shouted: 'There stands Jackson like a stone wall!' – perhaps the most famous phrase of the war.

Jackson proved his tactical genius in the Shenandoah Valley Campaign in the spring of 1862. Although vastly outnumbered, Jackson's force, employing surprise attacks and unusual battle tactics, was able to rid the Valley of Union troops. More importantly, they prevented the reinforcement of the Union armies threatening Richmond. General Richard Taylor, who joined Jackson in May 1862, gives us the best description of Jackson: 'I (saw) a pair of cavalry boots covering feet of gigantic size, a mangy cap with visor drawn low, a heavy, dark beard, and weary eyes – eyes I afterward saw filled with intense but never brilliant light.'

At Chancellorsville, in May 1863, in one of the boldest strokes of the war, Jackson marched his 30,000 men 12 miles westward across the front of General Joseph Hooker's positions and then initiated a surprise attack on the Union army. On the evening of May 2, Jackson rode out to reconnoiter the battlefield. As he returned to his lines, he was shot and mortally wounded by own of his own troops. He died at Guinea Station a week later and was buried in Lexington.

VIRGINIA

college president for a time. Lee's former office has been preserved as he left it. The university is sometimes referred to simply as 'W&L.'

The somber-looking **Lee Chapel and Museum** (☎ 540-463-8768) on campus has a marble statue of a recumbent and contemplative Lee, surrounded by battle flags and memorabilia; it was sculpted by Edward Valentine. Lee, who died at his university home in 1870, is interred downstairs with members of his family. His horse, Traveller, who was with him throughout the Civil War, is buried outside. The chapel is open 9 am to 5 pm Monday to Saturday and 2 to 5 pm Sunday (free).

There is a statue of the inventor and university benefactor Cyrus McCormick on the campus grounds. You can visit **Walnut Grove Farm** (☎ 540-377-2255), 18 miles north of Lexington on County Rd 606, where McCormick was born and later developed the first mechanical wheat reaper. It's open daily 8 am to 5 pm (free).

Virginia Military Institute (VMI)

The huge Gothic campus of this military institute (call ☎ 540-464-7325 for cadet guides) is just to the east of the Lee Chapel. The institute was founded in 1839 and became famous after 10 of its cadets (including cadet Thomas G Jefferson, son of the third president) were killed in battle at New Market in 1864. The institute was virtually destroyed by Union General David Hunter when his troops razed Lexington a month after the Battle of New Market.

At 4:30 pm on most Fridays of the school year, there is a full-dress parade. It's almost a miniature version of the spectacle at West Point and is a great photo opportunity.

At the opposite end of the parade ground is the **George Catlett Marshall Museum** (☎ 540-463-7103), a tribute to the distinguished life of the WWII general and Army Chief of Staff. Marshall was later US Secretary of State and won the 1953 Nobel Peace Prize for his plan for the postwar reconstruction of Europe, the Marshall Plan. The

VIRGINIA

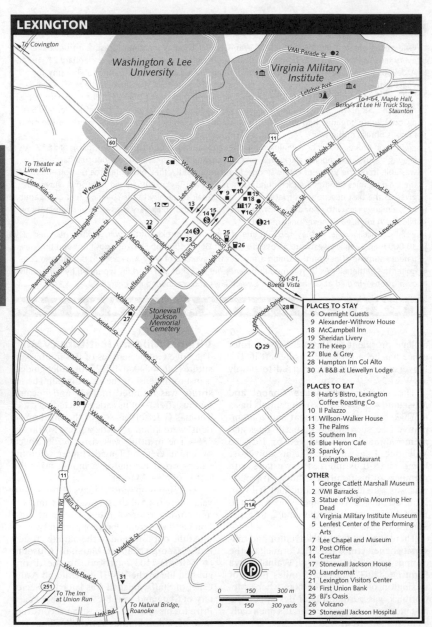

LEXINGTON

PLACES TO STAY
6 Overnight Guests
9 Alexander-Withrow House
18 McCampbell Inn
19 Sheridan Livery
22 The Keep
27 Blue & Grey
28 Hampton Inn Col Alto
30 A B&B at Llewellyn Lodge

PLACES TO EAT
8 Harb's Bistro, Lexington Coffee Roasting Co
10 Il Palazzo
11 Willson-Walker House
13 The Palms
15 Southern Inn
16 Blue Heron Cafe
23 Spanky's
31 Lexington Restaurant

OTHER
1 George Catlett Marshall Museum
2 VMI Barracks
3 Statue of Virginia Mourning Her Dead
4 Virginia Military Institute Museum
5 Lenfest Center of the Performing Arts
7 Lee Chapel and Museum
12 Post Office
14 Crestar
17 Stonewall Jackson House
20 Laundromat
21 Lexington Visitors Center
24 First Union Bank
25 BJ's Oasis
26 Volcano
29 Stonewall Jackson Hospital

museum follows his career from when he was an aide-de-camp to General John Pershing in WWI through to his acceptance of his peace prize, which is on display. Another item displayed is the Oscar won by Marshall's aide Frank McCarthy, producer of the 1970 WWII epic *Patton*. The museum is open 9 am to 5 pm daily. Admission is $3 for adults, $2 for seniors, and $1 for youth seven to 18.

There is a lot of Jackson memorabilia in the **Virginia Military Institute Museum** (☎ 540-464-7232), on the lower level of the Jackson Memorial Hall. Included is his bullet-pierced coat from Chancellorsville and his now stuffed and mounted horse, Little Sorrel. The history of the military institute, including the story of the 250-odd cadets who fought at the Battle of New Market, is also told here. It is open 9 am to 5 pm daily (free).

In the Jackson Memorial Hall, which is the cadet assembly hall, is a painting of the VMI cadet charge at New Market by Benjamin West Clinedinst. It is well worth seeing.

Stonewall Jackson House & Memorial Cemetery

This modest brick structure (☎ 540-463-2552), at 8 E Washington St, was built in 1801. It was home to the VMI's philosophy professor, Thomas Jonathan 'Stonewall' Jackson, for two years before his death (see the Stonewall Jackson boxed text, earlier in the chapter).

The house has been restored and includes many of Jackson's possessions and period pieces. There are tours on the hour and half hour. It is open 9 am to 6 pm June to August and to 5 pm the rest of the year. It is open 1 to 5 pm Sundays year-round. Admission is $5 for adults and $2.50 for children six to 17.

Jackson is buried among hundreds of fellow Confederates, two Virginia governors, and a number of Revolutionary War soldiers at the Stonewall Jackson Memorial Cemetery, on S Main St. The statue above his grave was dedicated in 1891. The cemetery is open from dawn to dusk. Park on S Main St and walk up to the statue and grave. It is often surrounded by Confederate flags, planted by believers in the chant 'The South will rise again!'.

Virginia Horse Center

This $12 million center (☎ 540-463-2194), established by the General Assembly of Virginia in 1985, hosts three-day events, national horse shows, and the annual April Virginia Horse Festival. Entry to most events is free, and there are tours of the facilities. To get to the center from I-81, take exit 191 to I-64W; follow the signs for 2 miles.

Things to See & Do

You can take **horse-drawn carriage tours** conducted by Historic Lexington (☎ 540-463-5647), based at 106 E Washington St. They operate 10 am to 4:30 pm daily April to October, weather permitting. The horses clatter past most of Lexington's main attractions. Tours cost $12 for adults, $11 for seniors, and $7 for children seven to 13. At night, there are 90-minute, candle-lit **Ghost Tours of Lexington** (☎ 540-348-1080); these walks are $8 ($6 for children under 11).

Less sedate but definitely recommended are **canoe trips** on the James and Maury Rivers with the James River Basin Canoe Livery (☎ 540-261-7334, www.canoevirginia .com). The daily fee includes all equipment and a trip map. It's located 1½ miles east of I-81, near exit 188A on Route 60.

There is a good hike on the 12-mile **Chessie Nature Trail**, a stretch of old Chesapeake & Ohio rail bed between Lexington and Buena Vista. It's open daily from dawn to dusk. Bicycles are prohibited, and trail maps are available from the visitor center. Reid's Dam and Lock, 2 miles down the trail on the Lexington side, was built in the 1850s to allow canal boats to pass rapids in the river.

Places to Stay

There are a number of campgrounds and guesthouses around Lexington, as well as motels and hotels north of town.

Camping & Hostels Close to the Virginia Horse Center, *Long's Campground (☎ 540-463-7672)*, on Route 39W (I-64 exit 55), has 45 sites and cabins. In the low season, sites cost $11 for three people ($20 in the high season); cabins are $25 for up to four people.

VIRGINIA

Lake A Willis Robertson Recreation Area (☎ 540-463-4164) is 14 miles west of Lexington, on the eastern slopes of the Alleghenies. It is open 6 am to 10 pm May 20 to Labor Day (fall and spring hours are posted; it's closed in winter); tent sites are $15, and trailer sites are $20 per night. Take Route 251 to Collierstown, and then take County Rd 770.

The *Tye River Gap Campground* (☎ 540-377-6168) is 20 miles northeast of Lexington at Vesuvius, 1 mile from the Blue Ridge Parkway on Route 56. It is open March to November, and the sites cost $15 to $21; there are also cabins.

The most economical place to stay in all of Virginia, apart from camping, is *Overnight Guests* (☎ 540-463-3075, 216 W Washington St). Almost unbelievably, it is only $10 a night for a bed in this six-room, homey place, and it is only four blocks from the visitor center. The hostel started out as a tourist home for out-of-town VMI and W&L events.

Guesthouses Guesthouses are popular and plentiful in and around Lexington – there are nearly 40 such places. Good options include the *Blue & Grey* (☎ 540-463-6260, 401 S Main St), at $105 per couple; *A B&B at Llewellyn Lodge* (☎ 540-463-3235, 603 S Main St, www.Llodge.com), with singles/doubles starting at $60/65 (add $5 in the high season); *Sheridan Livery* (☎ 540-464-1887, 35 N Main St), with luxurious rooms for $75 to $135; and *The Keep* (☎ 540-463-3560, 116 Lee Ave), with doubles for $80 to $115.

The *Inn at Union Run* (☎ 540-463-9715, 325 Union Run Rd) is 3½ miles south of the visitor center on County Rd 674. Nearly all of the rooms have a spa and are filled with Victorian antiques; doubles cost $85 to $115.

The Historic Inns of Lexington (☎ 877-463-2044) – *Alexander-Withrow House* (3 W Washington St), the *McCampbell Inn* (11 N Main St), and *Maple Hall* – all have doubles for $85 to $165. The latter, Maple Hall, is an 1850s country inn located about 6 miles north of Lexington on Route 11N; there are hiking trails, an outdoor pool, tennis court, and even a trout pond. It's open

to the public for dinner. The menu is changed monthly, and local produce is treated in exciting ways, but it's expensive – about $50 for two.

Hotels & Motels There are several places north of town. The *Econo Lodge* (☎ 540-463-7371) is 1½ miles north at the intersection of Route 11 and I-64 exit 55; doubles cost $43 to $45 in the low season. The *Best Western Inn at Hunt Ridge* (☎ 540-464-1500) is not far away; doubles with great views of the Blue Ridge cost $59 to $79 in the low season and $75 to $99 otherwise.

The *Howard Johnson Inn* (☎ 540-463-9181) is 6 miles north of town, at the intersection of Route 11 and I-81 exit 195; singles/doubles start at $40/45 in the low season – otherwise, $50/55. Nearby is a *Travelodge* (☎ 540-463-9131, 2809 N Lee Hwy), where doubles start at $50 ($5 per extra person). Also nearby is the *Ramada Inn Lexington* (☎ 540-463-6400, 2814 N Lee Hwy), which has a heated indoor pool, a restaurant, and some rooms with disabled facilities; singles/doubles start at $52/60.

The *Hampton Inn Col Alto* (☎ 540-463-2223, 401 E Nelson St), close to downtown, combines a modern motel with a 19th-century manor house. A continental breakfast is included in the rates, which start at $72 for doubles in the motel and $150 for the manor house.

Places to Eat

The *Lexington Restaurant* (☎ 540-463-5844, 810 S Main St), a favorite with locals who relish their high-cholesterol breakfast, serves hearty Southern fare; it is open 7 am to 9 pm daily.

Berky's at Lee Hi Truck Stop (☎ 540-463-4478), on Route 11 north of town, is another reliable, inexpensive place (open 24 hours).

The *Blue Heron Cafe* (☎ 540-463-2800, 4 E Washington St) offers a healthy vegetarian alternative to the sometimes prevalent, stodgy Southern cooking found in these parts. It is closed Sunday.

The *Lexington Coffee Roasting Co* (☎ 540-464-6586, 9 W Washington St) has gourmet coffees, fine teas, pastries, cinnamon rolls, and Italian sodas.

Harb's Bistro *(☎ 540-464-1900, 19 W Washington St)* is a lively place serving salads, soups, overstuffed sandwiches, and pasta. It's open daily for breakfast and lunch, and on weekends, it's open for all meals.

The Palms *(☎ 540-463-7911, 101 W Nelson St)* is a local favorite for afternoon drinks and Sunday brunch. They cook great burgers, quiches, and Mexican entrees for around $7 for lunch and $9 for dinner.

Il Palazzo *(☎ 540-464-5800, 24 N Main St)* has traditional Italian fare such as pizza, pasta, and seafood; it's moderately priced and open 11 am to 11 pm daily.

Spanky's *(☎ 540-463-3338, 110 S Jefferson St)* specializes in gourmet deli sandwiches. You can eat in the restaurant or at the popular bar. It's open 8:30 am to 1:30 am daily.

Willson-Walker House *(☎ 540-463-3020, 30 N Main St)* features 'creative American cuisine with regional influences' – for example, the regular greasy burger is replaced by a lean patty on a whole-grain bun and topped with caramelized onions. The restaurant is open Tuesday to Saturday for lunch and dinner; the lunch special is $5, and a dinner sunset special is $11.

The ***Southern Inn*** *(☎ 540-463-3612, 37 S Main St)* is an upscale place with good daily specials and a comprehensive wine list; a top-notch meal costs about $25 per person. It's open Monday to Saturday for lunch and dinner. There's a pub, too – see Entertainment, below.

Entertainment

The happening place for nightlife is the ***Volcano*** *(20 S Randolph St)*, where you can play foosball, sing karaoke-style, shoot pool, and drink until the wee small hours. ***BJ's Oasis*** *(☎ 540-464-4483)*, on E Nelson St, is similar to the Volcano.

The Southern Inn (see Places to Eat, earlier) has a pub open until midnight, and there is live music on Thursday and Friday.

The ***Lenfest Center for the Performing Arts*** *(☎ 540-463-8000)*, at Washington & Lee University, offers a varied program of theatrical and musical entertainment, including performances by the University of Rockbridge Symphony Orchestra. The season runs September to May.

The ***Theater at Lime Kiln*** *(☎ 540-463-3074)*, set in an outdoor lime quarry off Route 60W, produces original works with Shenandoah Valley and mountain themes. It's open Tuesday to Sunday from Memorial Day to Labor Day for evening concert performances that commence at 8 pm. The Sunday concerts are primarily musical, with a range of styles from zydeco to bluegrass.

Getting There & Away

There is no local airport – the nearest large airport is at Roanoke, which is southwest, off I-81.

Greyhound/Trailways *(☎ 800-231-2222)* has a daily service that passes through Buena Vista 12 miles east. The depot is near where Route 11N crosses the Maury River, not far from Main St.

By far, the best way to get around is in your own car, as there are so many good places to visit nearby. In winter, check on road conditions before going into the mountains; call the Department of Highways *(☎ 800-367-7623)*.

Tom's Taxi *(☎ 540-464-8294)* offers a reliable service.

BATH COUNTY

Route 39 winds its way northwest of Lexington and over scenic Goshen Pass to Bath County, through the majestic George Washington National Forest. This peaceful, relaxing corner of the state is tucked up against the border of West Virginia, and town names with the word 'Spring' tell of a time when the good folk of Virginia came to this region 'to take the waters.'

The Bath County Chamber of Commerce *(☎ 540-839-5409)* has a visitor center on Route 220 near the junction with Main St in Hot Springs; it's open 9 am to 5 pm weekdays.

In its heyday, before the advent of the railroad, **Goshen Pass** was the principal stagecoach route to Lexington from the interior. Today, visitors see the landscape much as the early pioneers did, and they can still revel in its beauty, especially in May, when a host of plants (including rhododendrons) are in flower. There is a day-use park where you can raft down the Maury River, fish, swim, or just enjoy a picnic. The oceanographer Matthew Fontaine Maury, who taught at the Virginia Military Institute, thought the pass so beautiful he requested that when he died, his body be carried through the pass when the rhododendrons were in bloom. VMI cadets complied with their professor's wish, in 1873.

The numerous thermal springs are less popular than they were a century ago, but people still come to Hot Springs and Warm Springs (both along Route 220) to bask in the sulfur waters, which range from 77°F to 104°F.

In quaint **Warm Springs**, near the junction of Route 39 and Route 220, is Gristmill Square, a small complex of historic buildings including the Waterwheel Restaurant. The combined smithy's shop and hardware store has been converted into a souvenir shop. Entrance to the clapboard bathhouses of the Warm Springs pools is $7 for one hour.

The **Garth Newel Music Center** (☎ 540-839-5018), between Warm Springs and Hot Springs on Route 220, hosts chamber-music performances in summer. Many people choose to picnic on the grounds before listening to the music in the well-designed Herter Hall.

Three miles west of Covington, just off Route 60, is the only surviving trussed arch in America, the very photogenic **Humpback Bridge**; nearby is a pleasant wayside park. What a contrast this provides to the blight of industry that consumes Covington's river.

Places to Stay & Eat

The closest camping is in *Douthat State Park* (☎ 540-862-8100), and RVs are permitted. There are also boat rentals and ramps, a sandy beach, bathhouse, and picnic areas. Standard sites are $17 for six people. One-room/one-bedroom/two-bedroom cabins are $55/65/75. The park is near Clifton Forge – take I-64 exit 27 to County Rd 629 and head north for 7 miles.

For those who want budget motel-style accommodations, there is the *Roseloe Motel* (☎ 540-839-5373), halfway between Hot Springs and Warm Springs on Route 220, across the road from the Garth Newel Music Center; singles/doubles start at $38/48.

The *Inn at Gristmill Square* (☎ 540-839-2231), in Warm Springs, has some units in the original miller's house for $85 to $140 for a double. In addition, there is a restaurant, bar, sauna, gift shop, and outdoor pool. The Waterwheel Restaurant, part of the inn, dates from the 18th century and is an expensive place decorated with tasteful prints. It serves continental cuisine (trout is a specialty) and has a full wine selection. It's open for dinner and Sunday brunch May to November; entrees start at $18.

There are a number of good B&Bs. *Milton Hall* (☎ 540-965-0196, 207 Thorney Lane), is in Covington not far from the Humpback Bridge. Each bedroom (except the center one) has a private bath. Guests get either a continental or English breakfast and afternoon tea; doubles start at $80. The *Longdale Inn* (☎ 540-862-0892) is just across from the ruins of the ironworks on Longdale Furnace Rd in Clifton Forge. There is a range of rooms in this old 19th-century manor, and depending on the season, you can expect to pay at least $75 for a double.

The *Sam Snead Tavern* (☎ 540-839-7666), in Hot Springs, across from The Homestead, is a great place to enjoy an American-style entree and an ale, as well as live entertainment in the evenings. It's open 5 to 10 pm daily except Tuesday. Corny menu items include water hazards (fish) and the 19th hole (drinks).

The *Hummingbird Inn B&B* (☎ 540-997-9065, 30 Wood Lane, www.hummingbirdinn.com), a Gothic villa off Route 39 Alt, is only a five-minute drive from Goshen Pass. A room is named after the inn's most famous guest, Eleanor Roosevelt. Doubles cost $85 to $135.

The Homestead (☎ 800-838-1776, www.thehomestead.com), in Hot Springs, is one of the oldest and most famous, luxurious, and expensive resorts in the US. It stands like a Loire Valley castle, with the village of Hot Springs arrayed beneath its ramparts. The west wing, east wing, and modern south wing all have rooms furnished in Victorian style, with mahogany bedsteads, a lounge, a writing table, a marble bathtub, and a TV (obviously post-Victorian).

The Homestead attracts those intent on getting the maximum out of the many outdoor pursuits offered. There are three 18-hole golf courses, ski slopes, indoor and outdoor pools, more than 100 miles of riding trails, tennis courts, a bowling alley, trout-stocked streams, spa facilities, and mineral springs. In addition, there are seven restaurants, and one of these has an orchestra and dancing. Expect to pay upward of $230 weekdays and $250 weekends for a standard double in the low season, or $358/396 in the high season (an extra person costs $110).

A game of golf costs at least $45 on The Homestead course in the low season, and the price can go up to $110 on the superb Cascades course in the high season. The recommended mountain-bike trips include Top of the Mountain ($60 with lunch) and a tour to Warm Springs ($75 with lunch). Living is not cheap here! You can rent mountain bikes and explore on your own – again not cheap at $30 for four hours. Hiking and swimming are 'complimentary.'

The Homestead dining room (☎ 540-839-5500) has been turned into a lavish palm court, and it seems to pop out from the pages of a Somerset Maugham novel when the orchestra performs. The meal, featuring regional specialties, is six courses; perhaps the cheapest way to dine here is to take a daily-meals package (about $50) when you book. You are expected to dress for dinner; reservations are essential.

Getting There & Away
Ingalls Airport (☎ 540-839-5326), in Hot Springs, has scheduled service with Colgan Airways. Roanoke is the nearest major airport. Woodrum Livery Service (☎ 540-345-7710) has a shuttle to The Homestead. The closest Amtrak station (☎ 800 872-7245) is in Clifton Forge.

To get to The Homestead and Hot Springs, take Route 39 through Goshen Pass to Warm Springs. There, turn south on Route 220.

NATURAL BRIDGE
This is hardly the seventh wonder of the world, but it is one of the most spectacular sights of the Shenandoah Valley and has been elevated into 'must see' status for visitors to the region. The arch, 215 feet high and 90 feet long, has been eroded out of limestone over the centuries by the seemingly benign Cedar Creek, a tributary of the James River.

The Native American Monocan tribe worshipped it as the 'Bridge of God'; George Washington surveyed it for Lord Fairfax; Thomas Jefferson, impressed by its grandeur, purchased it at one stage; now, it supports a portion of Route 11.

Somehow, the beautiful, natural structure has been incorporated into a macabre complex entitled the **Natural Bridge Inn & Conference Center** (☎ 540-291-2121), which has an attached wax museum, nearby caverns, and lavish accommodations. Commercialism is okay, but only if done tastefully – here, one of the US's great attractions is encircled by kitsch.

Looking up at the 'Bridge of God'

VIRGINIA

JEFF WILLIAMS

To see the Natural Bridge from below (the only real photographic angle) costs $8 for adults, $7 for seniors, and $4 for children six to 15. From June to September, there is an over-the-top sound and light presentation called 'The Drama of Creation,' held every night at 9 and 10 pm. It justifies the $8 admission if only to see the arch by night.

If you are coming from the south, you are probably just beginning to witness 'cavern fever.' It gets worse the farther north you go up the Valley. The **Natural Bridge Caverns** (☎ 540-291-2121) are the equivalent of 34 stories deep. And lurking some 347 feet underground is the Natural Bridge ghost, supposedly a catacomb resident for more than 100 years. The caverns are open 10 am to 5 pm daily March to December; hours vary, so call ahead. Admission is $7 for adults, $6 for seniors, and $3.50 for children six to 15.

If you wish to go into the village (and thus below the arch) and see the **wax museum** and caverns, it will cost $15 for adults and $7.50 for children. Also, the best overlook, Pulpit Rock, has been closed to the public. If enough of you ask, it may be reopened.

The Natural Bridge is 20 miles south of Lexington, just off I-81 (take exit 180 onto Route 11 or exit 175 onto Route 130). The caverns are to the east of Route 11, 1 mile north of Natural Bridge village.

The most beautiful spot in which to camp near Natural Bridge is Cave Mountain Lake Recreation Area (see George Washington National Forest, earlier in the chapter). The *Natural Bridge KOA Kampground* (☎ 540-291-2770), at the junction of Route 11 and I-81 (exits 180 and 180B), has fully serviced sites for $18 to $24 for two people and Kamping Kabins for $32 to $42.

The *Campground at Natural Bridge* (☎ 540-291-2727) is off Route 11 exit 180A and 3 miles along on Route 130E. Sites start at $15, and cabins are available.

The *Budget Inn* (☎ 540-291-2896), on Route 11 (I-81 exit 180), lives up to its name. In the low season, singles/doubles start at $28/32; in the high season, they start at $32/36 Sunday to Thursday and $44/48 weekends.

The Natural Bridge Inn & Conference Center and Stonewall Inn are operated by the *Natural Bridge of Virginia Resort* (☎ 540-291-2121, www.naturalbridgeva.com) – it has a reservations desk at the Natural Bridge ticket office. The low-season rates start at $39 weekdays and $49 weekends for Stonewall Inn; $49/59 for cottages; and $59/79 for hotel rooms ($69/89 in the high season).

The *Colonial Dining Room* on Route 11S in Natural Bridge, is a large place, but the staff manage to serve quality meals. There is a Friday-night seafood buffet and a popular Sunday brunch (about $30 for two).

Southwest & Blue Ridge Highlands

The southwestern part of Virginia is dominated by the Blue Ridge Mountains, and much of its unique culture stems from its isolation and remoteness. An insensitive observer would label the terrain as 'hillbilly country,' but a nature lover or adventurous outdoor enthusiast would see it as 'God's own playground.' In many guides, this region is added as an afterthought; the descriptions of its attractions are scanty, and it is almost dismissed as being part of its oft-forgotten neighbor, West Virginia.

And yet this region is alluring. Roanoke is a surprisingly sophisticated city, Abingdon is a sheer delight, Big Stone Gap is on Virginia's modern frontier, and the many parks of the Appalachians offer myriad outdoor activities. And through much of it runs the scenic Blue Ridge Parkway.

Highlights

- The sophisticated regional center of Roanoke, with its great market, museums, theater, and nightlife
- The best hiking in the state – in Mount Rogers National Recreation Area, Jefferson National Forest, Natural Tunnel State Park, and Burkes Garden
- Abingdon – a great little town with the historic Barter Theatre
- The Blue Ridge Parkway, with Mabry Mill and side trips to unspoiled mountain communities such as Floyd and Hillsville

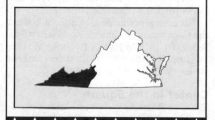

To top it off, the 'mountain people' are among the friendliest you could hope to meet, and when they sing and play bluegrass (and dance), you can add 'talented' to that description.

ROANOKE

Roanoke (**row**-an-oak), with a population of 100,000, is the largest community in western Virginia (and the largest in Virginia west of Richmond) and is easily the main center along the Blue Ridge Parkway. It's a pleasant place to visit, with wide, old streets, a farmers' market, and the Center in the Square mall.

In the 1740s, two Pennsylvania farmers, Mark Evans and Tasker Tosh, settled near some salt licks on land that was crossed by trails used by animals and Native American hunters. In 1834, the area was known as Gainsborough, but it soon became known as Big Lick. When the railway came in 1852, the town was moved to the tracks, and the name Big Lick went with it. The site of the original town then became known as Old Lick. The town of Big Lick was chartered in 1874.

When the Shenandoah Valley Railroad came seven years later, Big Lick was renamed Roanoke to reflect the nearby river and county. The name came from 'rawrenock' – shell beads worn by Native Americans. Another railroad, the Norfolk & Western Railroad, came in 1882. Today, Roanoke is a center for trade, distribution, manufacturing, and health care. It calls itself 'Virginia's festival city' (see Special Events, later in this section).

Orientation

Arrive in Roanoke at night and you will see the Roanoke Star, a 100-foot-high illuminated steel-and-concrete structure that has been a beacon at the top of Mill Mountain for more than 50 years. I-81 is northwest of the city center and is connected to downtown by I-581, which becomes Route 220, running southeast.

SOUTHWEST & BLUE RIDGE HIGHLANDS

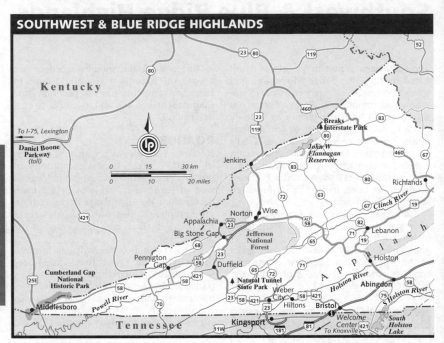

VIRGINIA

The Center in the Square, a cultural precinct, is the hub of downtown. There are five independent cultural organizations housed there and many nearby restaurants.

Information

The Roanoke Valley Visitor Information Center (☎ 540-345-8622, 800-635-5535, www .visitroanokeva.com), 114 Market St, is open 9 am to 5 pm daily. The friendly, enthusiastic staff will screen an eight-minute audiovisual presentation and provide an informative tour map of the city.

The area code for the city and southwestern Virginia in general is ☎ 540.

There are many banks in town where you can exchange currency. A branch of the First Virginia Bank-Southwest (☎ 540-561-8796) is in the Market in the Square, and the main office of the Southwest Virginia Savings Bank (☎ 540-343-0135) is at 302 2nd St SW.

On wet Appalachian days, you can browse at the Dusty Corner Bookstore (☎ 540-362-

5042), 3728 Williamson Rd NW, or Eclectic Bookshop (☎ 540-342-4340), 110 W Campbell Ave. Cantos Booksellers (☎ 540-342-0100), 18 Campbell Ave SE, is in the heart of the tourist area. It is a beautiful store stocked with contemporary literature, esoterica, and books on topics of local interest. Another place to try is Ram's Head Book Shop (☎ 540-344-1237), 2137 Colonial Ave SW, a large independent with a good stock of travel books, children's books, and bestsellers.

Dirty Duds (☎ 540-982-9530), 1101 Gus Nicks Blvd, is a reputable laundry.

For emergency medical treatment, contact the Community Hospital of Roanoke (☎ 540-985-8000), 101 Elm Ave, or Roanoke Memorial Hospital (☎ 540-981-7000), at the corner of Belleview Ave and Jefferson St.

Center in the Square

Three of Roanoke's museums, plus a planetarium and theater, can be found in the restored warehouses of the Center in the

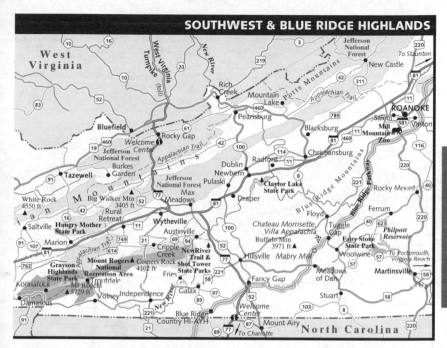

SOUTHWEST & BLUE RIDGE HIGHLANDS

Square. The **Science Museum of Western Virginia** (☎ 540-342-5710) is one of those great places focusing on interactive displays for the kids – natural history, energy resources, and plenty of computer games. The Hopkins **planetarium** has daily shows. The museum is open 10 am to 5 pm Monday to Saturday and 1 to 5 pm Sunday. Admission is $6 for adults, $5 for seniors, and $4 for children; admission to the planetarium costs $1.25.

The **History Museum of Western Virginia** (☎ 540-342-5770) has an odd assortment of exhibits, some of which focus on local Native American culture. It is open 10 am to 4 pm Tuesday to Friday, 10 am to 5 pm Saturday, and 1 to 5 pm Sunday. Admission is $2 for adults and $1 for seniors and children.

The **Art Museum of Western Virginia** (☎ 540-342-5760) has a collection of regional works with an emphasis on Appalachian folk art. The museum is in two parts, with an annex across an alley connected by a 2nd-floor gallery bridge. The gallery of 19th-century American art is particularly good. The museum is free and is open 10 am to 5 pm Tuesday to Saturday and 1 to 5 pm Sunday.

Virginia Museum of Transportation

A short walk from the Market in the Square, at 303 Norfolk Ave, is the Virginia Museum of Transportation (☎ 540-342-5670) – a must for those seduced by steam. Roanoke was once a railway town and is still the base for the Norfolk & Western Railway (once the Norfolk Southern). Exhibits on the Nickel Plate locomotive and other trains built in town are worth a look. It has the largest collection of steam and diesel locomotives in the nation.

It's open 10 am to 5 pm Monday to Saturday and noon to 5 pm Sunday from March to December. Admission is $5 for adults, $4 for seniors, and $3 for youth under 19.

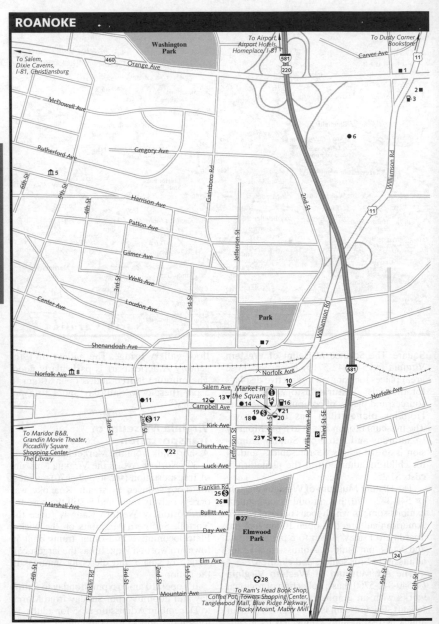

ROANOKE

Washington Park

To Salem,
Dixie Caverns,
I-81, Christiansburg

Orange Ave

To Airport,
Airport Hotels,
Homeplace, I-81

To Dusty Corner
Bookstore

Carver Ave

■ 1

2 ■

3

● 6

McDowell Ave

Rutherford Ave

Gregory Ave

Gainsboro Rd

Williamson Rd

血 5

Harrison Ave

Patton Ave

Jefferson St

Gilmer Ave

Wells Ave

Center Ave

Loudon Ave

Park

Shenandoah Ave

■ 7

Williamson Rd

Norfolk Ave

血 8

Norfolk Ave

● 11

Market in
the Square

10

Salem Ave

9

12 13 ▼

14 ●

15

16

17

19

18 ●

20

21

Campbell Ave

Kirk Ave

To Maridor B&B,
Grandin Movie Theater,
Piccadilly Square
Shopping Center,
The Library

Third St SE

Church Ave

23 ▼

24 ▼

▼22

Luck Ave

Franklin Rd

25

26 ■

Marshall Ave

Bullitt Ave

● 27

Day Ave

Elmwood
Park

Elm Ave

28

To Ram's Head Book Shop,
Coffee Pot, Towers Shopping Center,
Tanglewood Mall, Blue Ridge Parkway,
Rocky Mount, Mabry Mill

Mountain Ave

VIRGINIA

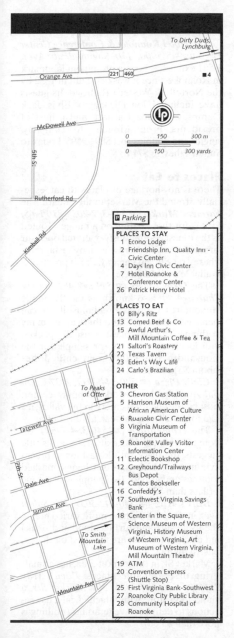

PLACES TO STAY
1   Econo Lodge
2   Friendship Inn, Quality Inn -
    Civic Center
4   Days Inn Civic Center
7   Hotel Roanoke &
    Conference Center
26 Patrick Henry Hotel

PLACES TO EAT
10 Billy's Ritz
13 Corned Beef & Co
15 Awful Arthur's,
    Mill Mountain Coffee & Tea
21 Saltori's Roastery
22 Texas Tavern
23 Eden's Way Café
24 Carlo's Brazilian

OTHER
3   Chevron Gas Station
5   Harrison Museum of
    African American Culture
6   Roanoke Civic Center
8   Virginia Museum of
    Transportation
9   Roanoke Valley Visitor
    Information Center
11 Eclectic Bookshop
12 Greyhound/Trailways
    Bus Depot
14 Cantos Bookseller
16 Confeddy's
17 Southwest Virginia Savings
    Bank
18 Center in the Square,
    Science Museum of Western
    Virginia, History Museum
    of Western Virginia, Art
    Museum of Western Virginia,
    Mill Mountain Theatre
19 ATM
20 Convention Express
    (Shuttle Stop)
25 First Virginia Bank-Southwest
27 Roanoke City Public Library
28 Community Hospital of
    Roanoke

Harrison Museum of African American Culture

This museum (☎ 540-345-4818), at 523 Harrison Ave NW, is also the sponsor of the annual Henry Street Heritage Festival on the last Saturday in September. Lots of exhibits featuring local and regional aspects of African American culture are overseen by the friendliest staff you are likely to meet. It's open 10 am to 5 pm Tuesday to Friday and 1 to 5 pm weekends; admission is free, but donations are welcome.

Special Events

As Virginia's self-styled 'festival city,' Roanoke certainly does live up to its title. Here's a partial list of events to look out for: the Festival in the Park (begins Memorial Day weekend and goes for two weeks), the Henry Street Heritage Festival in the African American enclave of Gainsboro (late September), Conservation Festival and Roanoke Valley Horse Show (both held in mid-June), Vinton's Dogwood Festival (late April), and a Championship Chili Cook-Off and Strawberry Festival (first Saturday in May). Get more information on these events from the Roanoke Valley Visitor Information Center (see Information, earlier).

Places to Stay

There is limited camping around Roanoke, and unfortunately there are no cheap hostels. For campgrounds, see Places to Stay under Around Roanoke, later.

The **Maridor B&B** (☎ 540-982-1940, 1857 Grandin Rd), in Roanoke's Raleigh Court neighborhood, is a pleasant place, with doubles for $95 and two-room suites for $135.

The **Days Inn Civic Center** (☎ 540-342-4551, 535 Orange Ave), I-581 exit 4E, has a pool and tennis courts. Singles and doubles cost $65 to $100, and this includes breakfast. The **Econo Lodge** (☎ 540-343-2413, 308 Orange Ave), I-581 exit 4E, has single/double off season (January to March) rates starting at $37/39; otherwise, $40/45.

The **Friendship Inn** (☎ 540-981-9341, 526 Orange Ave NE), across from the Roanoke Civic Center, has adequate doubles starting at $42.

VIRGINIA

The *Hampton Inn Airport* (☎ 540-265-2600, 6621 Thirlane Rd NW), at the junction of Peters Creek Rd, is close to the airport; well-appointed doubles are $69.

The *Hampton Inn/Tanglewood* (☎ 540-989-4000, 3816 Franklin Rd), across from the Tanglewood Mall, has rooms starting at $60/75 for singles/doubles; a continental breakfast is included.

The *Holiday Inn Hotel Tanglewood* (☎ 540-774-4400, 4468 Starkey Rd), off I-581 at the Franklin Rd/Salem exit, has singles or doubles for $69 to $128. There is a magnificent view of the Blue Ridge Mountains from the bistro.

Add to these, at varying costs, the *Comfort Inn Roanoke – Troutville* (☎ 540-992-5600, 800-628-1957, 2654 Lee Highway South); the *Holiday Inn Airport* (☎ 540-366-8861), at Peters Creek Rd near I-581; and the *Sleep Inn* (☎ 540-772-1500, 4045 Electric Rd), at the Salem exit off I-581.

The *Wyndham Roanoke Airport* (☎ 540-563-9300, 2801 Hershberger Rd NW), I-581 exit 3W, set on 12 landscaped acres, is huge and lavish. The rooms have full amenities and 24-hour room service; the cost is $79 to $154, depending on room size.

The *Clarion Roanoke Airport* (☎ 540-362-4500, 2727 Ferndale Drive NW) is 2½ miles north off I-581 at the Hershberger Rd W exit. There is a restaurant, piano bar, and a club. Singles/doubles start at $69/89 (add $10 for an extra person).

The *Quality Inn – Civic Center* (☎ 540-342-8961, 501 Orange Ave), near I-581 and Williamson Rd, has a restaurant, lounge, and private outdoor pool with courtyard. The rooms are a good value, starting at $49/54 for singles/doubles.

The *Best Western Inn at Valley View* (☎ 540-362-2400, 5050 Valley View Blvd), I-581 exit 3E, is only a mile from Roanoke Regional Airport and is right next to Valley View, Roanoke's largest shopping mall. The hotel has full amenities and a free continental breakfast; singles/doubles cost $69/74 to $92/102.

The *Patrick Henry Hotel* (☎ 540-345-8811, 617 S Jefferson St), close to downtown, is more expensive. There are antiques and kitchenettes in the spacious rooms, which cost $65 to $155 for doubles.

The *Hotel Roanoke & Conference Center* (☎ 540-985-5900, 110 Shenandoah Ave), I-581 exit 5, has been a prominent landmark in Roanoke since it was first built in 1882 by the Norfolk & Western Railroad. Its guests have included Joe DiMaggio, Elvis, Jack Dempsey, Amelia Earhart, and a host of presidents. From Monday to Thursday, singles and doubles cost $89 to $95; Friday to Sunday, they're $71 to $75.

Places to Eat

There is no shortage of places to eat, especially around the Market in the Square. The *Farmers' Market* (☎ 540-342-2028, 310 1st St SW) is for those eating on a budget. Touted as the oldest continuously operated open-air farmers' market, there are many restaurants where you can eat cheaply. Fresh produce is available in abundance.

The *Texas Tavern* (☎ 540-342-4825, 114 W Church Ave), also known as the 'Roanoke Millionaires' Club,' is a real must if you can manage to get a seat (and there aren't many of them). The tiny place is usually packed with locals eager to try (or sample for the thousandth time) the great chili dishes (about $3) on offer.

Cici's Pizza (☎ 540-344-7711, 2037 Colonial Ave), in the Towers shopping center, must be the cheapest eatery in the valley; it's $2/3 for an all-you-can-eat, all-day buffet.

The *Homeplace* (☎ 540-384-7252), on Route 311N near I-81 exit 141, is, as its title suggests, the place for old-fashioned home-style meals (chicken, green beans, mashed potatoes and gravy). Two people will escape for less than $20.

Billy's Ritz (☎ 540-342-3937, 102 Salem Ave), in downtown, has a more varied menu. The usual surf-and-turf (seafood and steak) and chicken teriyaki are featured on the extensive menu.

Market St, in the market area, has a smattering of reasonable places. *Eden's Way Café* (☎ 540-344-3336, 307 Market St), a whole-food store with attached cafe, has selections to delight all vegetarians (nothing is more than $5.50).

Carlo's Brazilian (☎ 540-345-7661, 310 Market St), across the road, serves a variety of international cuisine, including Brazilian dishes. A main course such as *feijoada* (meat stew over rice) starts at $12.50; it's closed Sunday.

Awful Arthur's (☎ 540-344-2997, 108 Campbell Ave), on the corner of Market St, has Roanoke's most extensive raw bar and the freshest of seafood. The crawfish, served by the half-pound and pound, if it is featured on the specials board, is an absolute must. Also in the raw bar are oysters, shrimp, clams, snow crab legs, and mussels.

Saltori's Roastery (☎ 540-343-6644, 202 Market Square) is a New York–style cafe serving all sorts of sandwiches and baked savories, espresso, and cigars (which you can smoke in the cigar lounge).

Mill Mountain Coffee & Tea (☎ 540-342-9404, 112 Campbell Ave) is the perfect place for after-theater coffees and desserts. Mill Mountain also has branches at 17 E Main St, Salem (☎ 540-389-7549) and at 4710-A Starkey Rd (☎ 540-989-5282).

Corned Beef & Co (☎ 540-342-3354, 107 S Jefferson St) is open daily. Lunch is a great value, with 'awesome' salads starting at $4, delicious burgers starting at $4.50, and blackened chicken and pasta for $6.

The Library (☎ 540-985-0811, 3117 Franklin Rd SW), in the Piccadilly Square shopping center and open Tuesday to Saturday, is very upmarket. It's one of Virginia's finest restaurants, and if you weren't here for the tasty seafood or the elegantly presented French cuisine, you could browse through the bookshelves. It's expensive – dinner for two is likely to be around $60.

Entertainment

Roanoke is very much the cultural center of western Virginia. See the Friday *Roanoke Times* entertainment supplement, or the free monthly *City*.

The *Mill Mountain Theatre* (☎ 540-342-5740, 1 Market Square SE), in the Center in the Square, features professional performances year-round, as well as a festival of new works and children's productions. The box office is open 10 am to 6 pm.

The *Roanoke Ballet Theatre* (☎ 540-345-6099) is the focus of performances in spring and fall in town and in other parts of the region. The ballet usually performs at the Mill Mountain Theatre (see previous paragraph).

If you are in Roanoke in July or August, try to catch the Summer-in-the-Park Pops performances of the *Roanoke Symphony* (☎ 540-343-6221). There are also monthly classical performances in January, February, May, September, and October at the Roanoke Civic Center, just off Williamson Rd.

The *Valley Chamber Music Society* (☎ 540-375-2333) performs from October to May at the Olin Theater at Roanoke College, College Lane, Salem.

A cinema-going experience like few others, the *Grandin Movie Theater* (☎ 540-345-6177, 1310 Grandin Rd), reminds us what it was like to go to the movies before there was TV; there are often 99¢ specials.

The *Coffee Pot* (☎ 540-774-8256, 2902 Brambleton Ave) has live bands – bluegrass, rock, blues, jazz, whatever – Wednesday to Saturday. In addition to free pool on Tuesday, this joint serves some of the town's meanest barbecue. The Wednesday buffet is an incredible value at $7.

Confeddy's (☎ 540-343-9746, 24 Campbell Ave), in the heart of downtown, has live music Friday and Saturday night. Billy's Ritz also attracts an energetic crowd, as do Corned Beef & Co and Awful Arthur's (see Places to Eat).

Getting There & Away

Roanoke Regional Airport (☎ 540-362-1999), 5202 Aviation Drive, is 5½ miles north of downtown. It is served by Delta Connection (ASA and Comair), United Express (Atlantic Coast), Northwest Airlink, and US Airways/US Airways Express.

There is no direct airport bus service; a taxi fare from the airport to downtown should be no more than $10. All of the major car rental agencies are represented at the airport.

The Greyhound/Trailways depot (☎ 800-231-2222) is at 17 Campbell Ave (Campbell Court).

VIRGINIA

If you're arriving by car on I-81, switch to I-581 (which becomes Route 220), and you will arrive in the heart of Roanoke.

Getting Around

Roanoke and its satellites, Vinton and Salem, are served by a good bus service, Valley Metro (☎ 540-982-2222, with TDD available). Buses operate 5:45 am to 8:45 pm. The fare is $1.25 for adults and 60¢ for seniors and youth; children under five are free. Transfers are free, and cash fares require exact change. The main interchange is downtown, at Campbell Court.

Taxi companies in the area include Liberty (☎ 540-344-1776) and, for Salem only, Salem (☎ 540-389-8131).

AROUND ROANOKE
Things to See & Do

In nearby Salem, **Dixie Caverns** (☎ 540-380-2085) will leave you whistling when you see the formations and flows of the Wedding Bell, Turkey Wing, and Cathedral Room. Rock hounds will appreciate the nearby mineral shop. The caverns are open 9:30 am to 5 pm daily (until 6 pm in summer). Admission is $5.50 for adults and $3.50 for children. The caverns are at 5753 W Main St (near I-81 exit 132).

The **Mill Mountain Zoo** (☎ 540-343-3241), off the Blue Ridge Parkway, is open 10 am to 5 pm daily. Admission is $5 for adults, $4.50 for seniors, and $3 for children.

To the Rescue Museum (☎ 540-776-0364), in the Tanglewood Mall, 4420 Electric Rd, celebrates the concept of squad rescue, which was developed in Roanoke by Julian Stanley Wise. It is open noon to 9 pm Tuesday to Saturday and 1 to 6 pm Sunday; admission is $2 for adults and $1 for children.

Virginia's Explore Park (☎ 540-427-1800), a re-creation of a pioneer village, is at 3900 Rutrough Rd and is open 10 am to 6 pm (noon to 6 pm Sunday) from April to October. Admission is $8 for adults, $6 for seniors, and $4.50 for youth under 19.

The Roanoke Appalachian Trail Club (☎ 540-387-2347) organizes **hiking** trips in the vicinity. Some 28 miles of the Appalachian Trail cut through the Roanoke Valley. (See the boxed text Appalachian Trail in the Activities chapter.)

There are also **bicycling** opportunities around Roanoke. The Blue Ridge Bicycle Club (☎ 540-774-4678) organizes rides year-round, including the Rockfish Gap ride – a 100-mile per day trek to Waynesboro and back. At Milepost 115, you can rent a mountain bike from Virginia's Explore Park, and then go bicycling on their trails. After you pay park admission, the fee for using the trails is $3, and it's $10/18/28 for a one-hour/half-day/full-day bike rental.

In winter, **cross-country skiing** options are limited only by your imagination and experience. Perhaps the closest 'known' place is Mountain Lake (☎ 540-626-7121), west of Roanoke (see Blacksburg, later in this chapter), but skiers will be seen gliding down the Parkway whenever it's clothed in white.

There is **canoeing** on the James and New Rivers, as well as Craig's Creek. Contact Appalachian Adventures (☎ 540-342-2858), 1122 Wasena St, Roanoke, for canoe rentals ($35/45 for one/two days).

Places to Stay

The *Roanoke Mountain Campground* (☎ 540-857-2490, 2551 Mill Mountain Spur Rd) is on the city's southern limits in Vinton (Mile 120.4 of the Blue Ridge Parkway); it's open May to October, and sites are $9.

In Salem, the *Dixie Caverns Campground* (☎ 540-380-2085, 5753 W Main St), I-81 exit 132, has grassy, shady sites for $10 to $16 for two; there are also electric/water hookups. This is only place near Roanoke that has year-round camping.

Also in Salem, the *Inn at Burwell Place* (☎ 540-387-0250, 601 W Main St, www .burwellplace.com) has vintage bathrooms, is slightly cheaper than Roanoke's Maridor ($80 to $120), and was voted best B&B in 1998 by the *Roanoker Magazine*.

Entertainment

In Salem, *Wits End/Belly of the Beast* (☎ 540-387-3539, 1790 Thompson Memorial Drive), a joint venue (or venue joints?), has bands most nights and live jazz every Saturday.

VIRGINIA

BLUE RIDGE PARKWAY

The Blue Ridge Parkway traverses the ridge of the southern Appalachians for 469 miles, from Shenandoah National Park in Virginia (where it connects with Skyline Drive) to Great Smoky Mountains National Park in North Carolina. The two-lane, paved motor road is marked by concrete mileposts – these begin in the north at Mile 0, near Shenandoah National Park. With more than 17 million visitors per year to various parts of the Parkway, it is the most visited site in the US national park system!

Wildflowers are one of the Parkway's greatest attractions. Look out for wild columbine (red and yellow), trailing arbutus (white to pink), yellow lady slipper, white trillium, white Dutchman's breeches, green jack-in-the-pulpit, and white bloodroot. A great place to see more than 70 species of conspicuous wildflowers (and 20 species of ferns) is along the 2-mile Flat Top Trail; it begins at the Peaks of Otter picnic area, northeast of Roanoke off Route 43. The Parkway is at its best in spring, when the wildflowers bloom. It is also extremely popular in mid-October, when the change in the color of the leaves is most spectacular.

Information

The Parkway can be accessed from several major highways, including I-64, I-81, I-77, I-40, and I-26. There is no fee to enter or use the Parkway. The road is sometimes closed in winter by single-digit temperatures, wind, ice, and snow, but in summer, the temperatures can soar into the 90s. This is understandable when you realize that the elevation of the Parkway varies from 650 feet to 6000 feet.

For emergencies or to learn what to do in the event of a breakdown, call ☎ 808-727-5928. The Parkway speed limit is 45 mph, but this drops to 35 mph in developed areas. At this speed, and with stops, you could reasonably expect to spend two days driving the full length.

In Virginia, Roanoke is the main stop-off along the Parkway, but there are many other visitor centers, campgrounds, and facilities open from May to October.

There are 11 visitor centers (five in Virginia, six in North Carolina), four concessionaires operating lodges and cabins, seven restaurants, and four service stations along the Parkway. There is also a range of activities available – walks vary from simple 'leg stretchers' to extended hikes. In summer and autumn, ranger programs are held at the visitor centers – Humpback Rocks (☎ 540-943-4716), James River (☎ 804-299-5496), Peaks of Otter (☎ 540-586-4357), Rocky Knob (☎ 540-745-9662), and Mabry Mill (☎ 540-952-2947).

There are several free publications that help make the Parkway journey more interesting, including 'The Blue Ridge Parkway Directory,' complete with strip maps and the NPS's 'Official Map and Guide.' The publications are available from any of the concessionaires along the Parkway.

Useful sources are the *Blue Ridge Almanac*, published six times a year ($3 per issue, ☎ 800-877-6026), *Blue Ridge Parkway Guide* (two volumes, $16 per set), *Blue Ridge Parkway: The Story Behind the Scenery* ($8.95), *Bicycling the Blue Ridge* ($10.95), and *Walking the Blue Ridge: A Guide to the Trails of the Blue Ridge Parkway* ($12.95). You can order these books from the Blue Ridge Bookshelf (☎ 800-548-1672), PO Box 21535, Roanoke, VA 24018.

Blue Ridge Institute & Farm Museum

This museum (☎ 540-365-4416) is in the town of Ferrum, based around Ferrum College. Ferrum is not exactly on the Blue Ridge Parkway, but it is easily reached from it. The museum is a living history farmstead that illustrates life in the German-American Blue Ridge settlement in 1800. The costumed interpreters explain the livestock breeds, the gardens, and the gallery exhibits. The museum is free, but farm tours are $4 for adults and $3 for seniors and children.

Fairy Stone State Park

This idyllic little park (☎ 540-930-2424), minutes away from the Parkway, is known for its lucky 'fairy stones.' These stones, formally known as saurolites, range in size from one-fourth of an inch to an inch and are in the form of a Roman, St Andrews, or Maltese Cross. It is said that when the sad tidings of the crucifixion of Christ were related to the fairies, they began to cry. Upon striking the ground, their tears crystallized into these tiny crosses.

The state park offers a lake, beach, pleasure boats, picnicking, and *camping*. Campsites for six with electric/water hookups cost $19; one/two bedroom cabins cost $63/78 (or $68/83 on the waterfront).

To get there, take Route 57W, and then Route 346 from Bassett (northwest of Martinsville), or Routes 8, 57E, and 346 from the Blue Ridge Parkway.

Floyd County

The hills of Floyd County support a counterculture paradise of artists and craftspeople who flourish happily alongside local farming communities. The town of Floyd was once called Jacksonville, after Andrew Jackson, the seventh president, but it was inexplicably named Floyd in the late 1890s. Today, Floyd is a must for those who want to experience the Blue Ridge region as it once was. And that **traffic light** in the town of Floyd – it's the only one in the county.

The place to go is **Floyd Country Store** (☎ 540-745-4563), at 206 S Locust St, especially on Friday night, when there is a Flatfooting Jamboree with locals and guest artists from all over the US. The show starts at 7 pm, and entry to the store is free. There are also Saturday night sessions in summer, with well-known acts such as Wayne Henderson ($7). The rules are the following: No cussin', no moonshine (or other alcohol), no smokin', and no fightin'.

Jacksonville Center (☎ 540-745-2784), the world's largest distributor of bluegrass and old-time music, is nearby.

Mabry Mill

This sawmill and water-powered gristmill (☎ 540-952-2947) is just north of the Meadows of Dan. It is a magnificent old building in a very picturesque setting and is well worth a stop (it has been used on postcards representing a number of other states!).

You can still buy buckwheat flour and cornmeal for those good ol' Southern recipes. It is open 8 am to 6 pm daily May to October (to 7 pm June to August), and it's free.

Meadows of Dan

Apart from its quaint name, there are other attractions near the Meadows. **Chateau Morrisette Winery** (☎ 540-593-2865) is off County Rd 726, west of the Parkway at Milepost 171.5. The winery, a 'thing of stone and wood,' offers tastings, sales, tours, and a monthly jazz festival. It is open 11 am to 5 pm daily year-round. Just over a mile north is **Villa Appalaccia Winery** (☎ 540-593-3100), which produces Italian varietals; it's open 11 am to 5 pm Thursday to Saturday.

The famous Confederate cavalry commander JEB Stuart lived in Patrick County. His former home **Laurel Hill** is in Stuart, 15 miles east of Meadows of Dan. Stuart was born in Ararat, 6 miles south of the Parkway near the North Carolina border.

Galax & Woodlawn

The name Galax comes from a broad, waxy, green leaf plant that produces a long, spiky, white bloom resembling a stream of milk (from *gala*, Greek for 'milk'). If you own a fiddle, chances are you have heard of Galax. In August each year, the **Old Fiddlers' Convention**, the oldest and largest event of its kind in the country, is held here. Rosin up your bow, as there is lots of jollity, dancing, and good music to be had – call ☎ 540-236-8541 for more information.

If you miss the festival, you can still attend the free TGIF (Thank Galax, it's Friday) performances held on the first and third Friday of each month in summer at 7 pm at the Grayson St Stage ($2); otherwise, indoors in the Rex Theatre on Grayson St, 8 to 10 pm Tuesday.

Just northeast of Galax, on Route 58/221 in Woodlawn, the **Harmon Museum** (☎ 540-236-4884) displays Native American objects, guns, and memorabilia from America's wars, and highlights the Carroll County Courthouse shooting (see the boxed text). The museum is open 8 am to 6 pm Monday to Saturday year-round and is free.

The Carroll County Courthouse Incident

Hillsville these days is a quiet mountain community, but it attained international notoriety in March 1912 after a shootout in the Carroll County Courthouse.

In the period leading up to the shooting, two relatives of the prominent Allen family, Wesley and Sidna Edwards, had been arrested for public disturbance. Floyd Allen, an uncle, helped them escape from custody and was himself indicted.

He went on trial on March 13 and was found guilty and sentenced to a year in jail. There were about a dozen members of the Allen family in the courthouse on March 14. Without warning, all hell broke loose, and when the shooting ended, the circuit judge, sheriff, the Commonwealth's attorney, a juror, and a witness were dead, and one member of the Allen family was badly wounded in the thigh.

The Allens scattered, and about 20 detectives from the famous Baldwin-Felts Agency were dispatched from Roanoke to search for the escapees. Eventually, all the Allens either surrendered or were captured. Floyd and his son Claude were tried and executed. Wesley Edwards and his uncle, Sidna Allen, fled to Des Moines, Iowa, but were captured on September 14, 1912, by WG Baldwin, head of the Felts. The agency had been tipped off by Edwards' girlfriend after she had received a letter from Iowa.

Sidna Allen received 35 years and Wesley Edwards 27 years; they were both pardoned by Governor Harry Flood Byrd in 1926. Sidna Edwards, one of those originally arrested, who also received a long jail term, was pardoned in 1922.

★★★★★★★★★★★★★★★★★★★★★★★★★★★★

VIRGINIA

Places to Stay & Eat

Parkway The Parkway has nine campgrounds along its length; four of these are in Virginia and five in North Carolina. The Virginian campgrounds are *Otter Creek* (Mile 61), *Peaks of Otter* (Mile 86), *Roanoke Mountain* (Mile 120), and *Rocky Knob* (Mile 167). They are open from May to October, except Otter Creek, which is open year-round (as is Linville Falls in North Carolina). To make reservations, call the state park system (☎ 800-933-7275).

Campground fees are $9 for families or groups with two adults, plus $2 for each additional person over 18. There are no hookups or showers. There are also 17 picnic grounds in developed areas and tables at some of the overlooks. In Virginia, the picnic grounds are at Humpback Rocks (Mile 6), Otter Creek, James River (Mile 64), Peaks of Otter, Roanoke Mountain, Smart View (Mile 155), and Rocky Knob. Additionally, there are private campgrounds, restaurants, and hotels in communities and towns along the Parkway.

At Mile 86, the *Peaks of Otter Lodge* (☎ 540-586-1081) is open year-round. At this tranquil location, there is a winter special of $45 per person (double occupancy), which includes dinner and breakfast each weekday. There are organized tours to the high points of the Peaks of Otter; a bus departs from the lodge hourly 10 am to 5 pm May to October for the hike to the summit of 3875-foot Sharp Top.

The *Blue Ridge Country HI-AYH* (☎ 540-236-4962) is on the Parkway at Mile 214.5 (a mile north of Route 89) and is reached by a paved driveway on the eastern (right-hand) side. It is a quaint 20-bed place with dormer windows and panoramic views, and a bed costs $13/16 for members/nonmembers. The hostel is closed in January and February. It has a music room, a meeting room, a 'clogging' barn, and nearby hiking, canoeing, rafting, horseback riding, skiing, and mountain biking opportunities. There's a bike-repair shop in Woodlawn, 12 miles away.

The *Doe Run Lodge* (☎ 540-398-2212), at Mile 189 near Fancy Gap, is a mountaintop resort with the most basic of the rooms starting at $87 for two during the low season and $109 in the high season; the log cabin starts at $169. There are tennis courts, a pool, a dining room, and a lounge bar.

Floyd County Just off the Parkway, 6 miles east of Floyd on Route 8, *Tuggle's Gap Restaurant & Motel* (☎ 540-745-3402) is an extremely friendly place. The motel rooms are simple but a good value at $36 for two. The restaurant serves delicious chili and cornbread, as well as hearty breakfasts.

The *Pine Tavern Lodge & Restaurant* (☎ 540-745-4482), 1½ miles north of Floyd on Route 221, has really nice suites that are a superb value at $42 to $52 and a cozy cottage for $65. The restaurant is also excellent, with an innovative menu and attached bar; there is live music on weekends ($4 cover charge). About 1 mile farther down Route 221 is Ray's Rest, a noisy bar that serves passable food.

Floyd, tiny as it is, has some great restaurants. The *Blue Ridge Restaurant* (☎ 540-745-2147, 113 E Main St) is inexpensive and serves fresh pinto beans, hotcakes, and fried squash. *Mama Lazardo's* (☎ 540-745-4242, 110 N Locust St) makes a nice whole wheat pizza crust but then destroys it in a quagmire of gluggy cheese. Without copious cheddar, the pizzas are worth the $3.50/6/8 for a small/medium/large (toppings cost extra).

Meadows of Dan The *Meadows of Dan Campground* (☎ 540-952-2292) is on Route 58 just west of the Parkway; tidy, shaded campsites are $15 to $20 for two.

The *Blue Ridge Motel* (☎ 540-952-2244), just west of the Parkway, has a restaurant, a bar, and clean, quiet rooms (about $70 for a double in summer).

The *Poor Farmer's Market* (☎ 540-952-2670) is a general store, deli, and unabashed gift shop. According to one Roanoke resident, its fried apple pies ($1) are the best ever. The rest of the food is adequate, but the coffee is abysmal.

Galax The *Knights Inn Motel* (☎ 540-236-5117, 312 W Stuart Drive) has tidy doubles

starting at $35 to $37 in the low season and $41 in the high season ($5 per extra person).

BLACKSBURG

Blacksburg (population 35,000) was formerly known as Draper's Meadow and was the first English-speaking colony west of the Alleghenies. Settlers of German, English, Scottish, and Irish origin established a farming community on the surrounding land. In July 1755, a group of Shawnee killed or captured all but four of the settlers in what has come to be known as the Draper's Meadow Massacre. An outdoor historical drama, *The Long Way Home*, performed every summer in nearby Radford (later in this chapter), tells of these events. Colonel William Preston came to the region in 1772, settled on Draper's farm, and built the imposing Smithfield Plantation (see that section, later).

In the 1990s, Blacksburg became the first fully 'electronic village' in the US, with most government services and educational institutions connected by the Internet. The town was rated by Rand McNally as one of the nation's top 20 places for quality of life. The Blacksburg Regional Visitor Center (☎ 540-552-4061), 1995 S Main St, provides information.

Blacksburg Transit (☎ 540-961-1185) operates buses from Main St weekdays only (50¢/25¢ for adults/children).

Museum of Geological Sciences

In Derring Hall at Virginia Tech, the state's largest university, this museum (☎ 540-231-3001) has mineral and fossil displays and a working seismograph. It is free and is open 8 am to 4 pm weekdays and 10 am to 2 pm Saturday year-round.

Museum of Natural History

The Museum of Natural History (☎ 540-231-3001), 428 N Main St, has a number of natural history displays, including one on North American mammals. The specimen research collection has more than one million insects, mammals, and birds. It is open 1 to 5 pm Wednesday to Saturday year-round and is free.

Smithfield Plantation

This plantation consists of a 1774 frame house with stockade and was the home of three governors of Virginia. It is furnished with period pieces, and there is a gift shop (☎ 540-231-3947). The buildings, at 1000 Smithfield Plantation Rd, are open 1 to 5 pm Thursday to Sunday from April to December; admission is $4 for adults and $1.50 for children.

Huckleberry Trail

This 6-mile Rails to Trails Program is being developed on the old Huckleberry Railroad line in Montgomery County. The Merrimac & Provincial Rail line once served coal-mining communities between Blacksburg and Christiansburg. A 3-mile section exists as a component of the Blacksburg Bikeway/Walkway system.

Mountain Lake

This beautiful retreat, northwest of Blacksburg on County Rd 700 just off Route 460 exit 37, is one of those classy old mountain retreats complete with a picturesque lake. It was the setting for the movie *Dirty Dancing*, with Jennifer Grey and Patrick Swayze. There's a hotel and restaurant (see Places to Stay & Eat).

Places to Stay & Eat

The *Comfort Inn* (☎ 540-951-1500, 3705 S Main St) is on Route 460, 3½ miles south of downtown. It is one of the least expensive motels in the region, and the singles/doubles (starting at $55/62) are good values for the money.

The *Clay Corner Inn B&B* (☎ 540-953-2604, 401 Clay St SW) is a quaint B&B with 12 guest rooms (in four houses) – each with bath, TV, and telephone. Singles/doubles start at $74/80 in the low season; in the summer, all rooms cost $90 to $100.

The *Mountain Lake Hotel* (☎ 540-626-7121, 115 Hotel Circle), Pembroke, has a restaurant and bar, nightly entertainment, exercise facilities, and tennis courts. Singles/doubles start at $100/135 in a short low season and at $120/150 on weekdays in the summer. (For directions, see Mountain Lake, earlier.)

In nearby Riner, *River's Edge* (☎ 540-381-4147, 6208 Little Camp Rd, www.river-edge.com) has beautiful grounds and is in a country setting. Breakfast and dinner is included in the doubles price ($130 to $155).

For a bite to eat, *Anchy's* (☎ 540-951-2828, 1600 N Main St) is an inexpensive family spot with an eclectic menu. *Gillie's* (☎ 540-961-2703, 153 College Ave) is a great breakfast spot that is popular with students. *Jacob's Lantern* (☎ 540-552-7001, 900 Prices Fork Rd), in the Sheraton Four Forks Hotel, is more expensive, but is consistently good.

The *Cellar* (☎ 540-953-0651, 302 N Main St), Blacksburg's original underground tavern, serves inexpensive meal specials, has an extensive beer selection, and features local musicians.

RADFORD

A lot of visitors come to this city (population 16,000), southwest of Blacksburg and Christiansburg, to witness *The Long Way Home*, a romanticized play depicting the story of Mary Draper Ingles' capture by the Shawnee in 1755, her captivity, escape, and subsequent 850-mile journey to freedom from Big Bone Lick, Kentucky.

The play is enacted at the Ingles Homestead Amphitheater (☎ 540-639-0679) on Route 232 (I-81 exit 105). The amphitheater is open late June to late August from 4 pm, and there are free 30-minute guided tours of the Ingles' property from 7 pm. Performances are held 8 to 10:30 pm Thursday to Sunday from June through Labor Day. Tickets are $10 for adults, $9 for seniors, and $5 for children.

The *Executive Motel* (☎ 540-639-1664), on Route 11WA, is a cheap, clean place. All of the rooms have two double beds, air-conditioning, a phone, and a color TV; doubles start at $45.

The *Best Western Radford Inn* (☎ 540-639-3000, 1501 Tyler Rd) has tremendous views of the Blue Ridge Mountains. Single/double rooms, colonial in style, start at $61/65 in the low season.

The *Gallery Cafe, Books and More* (☎ 540-731-1555, 1115 Norwood St) is very popular with students who drop in to read, sip brewed coffee, and sample the delicious pastries.

CLAYTOR LAKE & NEW RIVER TRAIL STATE PARKS

Claytor Lake State Park (☎ 540-674-5492) is a good place to relax. The historic Howe House has exhibits about the early settlement of the region. Standard *campsites* cost $11.50, electric/water hookups cost $16, and two-bedroom cabins with waterfront views cost $77. To get there from I-81, take exit 101 near Dublin.

The New River Trail State Park is a 57-mile greenway following an abandoned railroad right-of-way. It's a superb hiking/biking/horseback riding trail. The trail starts in Pulaski in the north, then follows Claytor Lake in its upper reaches before crossing to the true right bank of New River. The direction is then southwest across I-77 to the border of the Mount Rogers NRA. Then it's south to either Fries or Galax.

For more information call ☎ 540-699-6778. There is access from Ivanhoe, Galax, Draper, Pulaski, and the shot tower (see Wytheville, later in this chapter).

PULASKI & NEWBERN

The gritty little town of Pulaski takes its name from a Polish count and Revolutionary War hero. It has a renovated Main St with a number of Victorian-era buildings now housing shops and restaurants. For more information, contact Pulaski Tourism Information (☎ 540-994-8636).

The **Count Pulaski B&B** (☎ *540-980-1163, 821 N Jefferson Ave)* is a moderately expensive place to stay. The comfortable, carpeted smoke-free rooms are a good value ($75 to $95 a double).

Pleasant Newbern, on County Rd 611 (just off I-81) and not far from Pulaski, has a number of interesting 19th-century buildings, 26 of which can be seen from the road. It was a lodging stop for settlers traveling on the Wilderness Road from Pennsylvania and down through the Cumberland Gap to the then-unknown.

The town of Newbern was founded in 1810, and the founder's building, used variously as a post office, store, tavern, and home, is now the **Wilderness Road Regional Museum** (☎ 540-674-4835). It has an interesting, if somewhat jumbled, collection of implements that would have been in daily use 200 years ago. The museum is open 10:30 am to 4:30 pm Tuesday to Saturday and 1:30 to 4:30 pm Sunday; admission is $2 for adults and $1 for children. Not far away from the museum is an interesting shop in which miniature fairground **carousel figurines** are made.

The **Valley Pike Inn** (☎ *540-674-1810)*, Old Wilderness Trail, I-81 exit 98, serves inexpensive country fare, including roast beef, fried chicken, and fruit cobblers.

JEFFERSON NATIONAL FOREST

This massive area of forest (690,000 acres) in west central Virginia extends from the James River and heads in a southwest direction to within 50 miles from the western tip of the state. The forest is mainly Appalachian mixed hardwoods with conifers interspersed, but there are many 'meadow' areas at higher elevation that feature low and flowering vegetation. It has recently been combined with the George Washington National Forest.

As a forest managed for its main resource – timber – there are schizophrenic aspects to both the region and its administration. Recreational activities (which produce little income), although touted as important, take a definite second place. And this is really apparent when you visit one of the administration centers seeking general information! People come to look at the wildlife and trees in one season, to cut down the trees and shoot the wildlife in another.

The information centers, for what they are worth, are as follows:

Supervisor's Office (☎ 540-265-6054), 5162 Valleypointe Parkway, Roanoke

Blacksburg Ranger District (☎ 540-552-4641), 110 Southpark Drive, Blacksburg

Clinch Ranger District (☎ 540-328-2931), Route 3, Box 820, Wise

Williamsburg tavern sign

Richmond's historic downtown

Virginia's Capitol, the first neoclassical building in the US, designed by Thomas Jefferson

Mount Vernon, the estate of George and Martha Washington

Tobacco drying

Historic house in Alexandria

Mabry Mill, on the Blue Ridge Parkway

Re-creation of colonial life on Duke of Gloucester St, Williamsburg

Scenic Great Falls National Park, in Northern Virginia

Cooper at work, Williamsburg

Glenwood Ranger District (☎ 540-291-2189), Natural Bridge Station

Mount Rogers National Recreation Area (☎ 540-783-5196), Route 16, Marion

New Castle Ranger District (☎ 540-864-5195), County Rd 615, New Castle

Wythe Ranger District (☎ 540-228-5551), Route 11, Wytheville

There are a number of developed campgrounds with more than 600 camping units within the forest; all facilities are open May to September, and some remain open in the fishing and hunting seasons.

There are also noteworthy trails passing through the forest: the Appalachian Trail (300 miles of it pass through here); the 4-mile Cascades, the 4-mile Mount Rogers, 1½-mile Roaring Run, and 9-mile Hoop Hole national recreation trails; the Virginia Highlands Horse Trail; the New River Trail; and the Virginia Creeper Trail. Special areas include the James River Face Wilderness, on the northeast end of the forest, and the Mount Rogers National Recreation Area.

WYTHEVILLE

This town, near the junction of I-81 and I-77 and representing the gateway to the southwest highlands of the Appalachians, is surrounded by great mountain scenery.

The Highlands Gateway Visitor Center (☎ 800-446-9670) in Max Meadows, east of Wytheville on Route 121 (take I-81 exit 80), has a plethora of information on sights and activities in the region. There is a wide choice of accommodations and more than 30 restaurants. The Wytheville Area CVB (☎ 540-223-3355, www.wytheville.org) is at 150 E Monroe St.

Things to See & Do

Before doing anything else, drive north of town on Route 52 to the **Big Walker Lookout** in Jefferson National Forest, from where you can see five states. There is a cafe and gift shop (☎ 540-228-4401).

Snoopers Antique & Craft Mall (☎ 540-637-6441), with more than 100 shops, and the **Factory Merchants Outlet Mall** (☎ 540-637-6214), with Black & Decker, Corning,

Audie Murphy Monument

On May 28, 1971, a plane carrying Audie Murphy, the most decorated US soldier in World War II, crashed on the slopes of Brush Mountain in the Jefferson National Forest near Blacksburg. The son of a sharecropper from Kingston, Texas, Murphy died in the crash.

Murphy had joined the infantry at age 18 and served in France. In January 1945, his heroism in action was rewarded with the Congressional Medal of Honor; in all, he was to earn 24 medals from the US, three from France, and one from Belgium. His high profile led to a film career of more than 40 films, in which the diminutive actor usually played a tough cowboy. His memoirs were entitled *To Hell and Back*. Murphy is buried in Arlington National Cemetery in Virginia.

The trail to the crash site is an easy loop walk of 1½ miles. To get there from Blacksburg, follow Main St to Mount Tabor Rd (County Rd 624). Proceed for 12 miles until you pass County Rd 650, then turn left onto a gravel road (Forest Service P188.1). Turn right at the top of Brush Mountain and continue for 3 miles. The drive is a total distance of 17 miles. For more information, contact the Blacksburg Ranger Station (☎ 540-552-4641).

Hanes, and London Fog, are both in Fort Chiswell, at I-81 exit 80.

The architecturally interesting **Haller-Gibboney Rock House Museum** (☎ 540-223-3355), at Monroe and Tazewell Sts, was built in 1823. Furnished with original pieces, it is open 2 to 4:30 pm Sunday from May to September and is free. Some **old log houses** on Main St (Route 11), between 5th and 7th Sts, survived the ravages of the Civil War.

Also reminiscent of times long past, the **shot tower**, near Austinville, south of Wytheville off I-77S, was built in 1807 and produced shot for early pioneers. Lead was melted in a kettle at the top of the 75-foot tower and poured through a sieve. It fell through the tower into another 75-foot shaft below, then into a kettle of water.

VIRGINIA

Nearby are picnic grounds, restrooms and the New River Trail. The tower (☎ 540-699-6778) is open 10 am to 6 pm ($2 per vehicle, self-registration). Visitors may climb the tower.

And trivia buffs – **Dr Pepper** was invented in Rural Retreat, 11 miles southwest of Wytheville, by Dr Pepper, who ran a drugstore in the town.

Places to Stay & Eat

The *Econo Lodge (☎ 540-228-5517, 1190 E Main St)*, on Route 11 a mile west of I-81, is the least expensive place; singles/doubles start at $33/39. The *Super 8 Motel (☎ 540-228-6620, 130 Nye Circuit)*, near the junction of I-81 and I-77, is more expensive ($43/45). The *Days Inn (☎ 540-228-5500, 150 Malin Drive)*, which is moderate in size with 120 rooms, has restaurants nearby; rooms start at $52/55.

The *Holiday Inn (☎ 540-228-5483)*, on Route 11, near the junction of I-77 and I-81, maintains its corporate reliability. There is a restaurant, bar, pool, and disabled facilities; singles or doubles cost $53 to $80.

As a junction town, Wytheville has a plethora of chain eateries; look around the off-ramps at exit 73 off Routes 77, 52, 11 and I-81, or around I-81 exit 70.

Scrooges (☎ 540-228-6622), on Holston Rd near the junction of I-81 and Route 52, features English-style entrees starting at $10 and a kids' menu.

Peking (☎ 540-228-5515, 105 Malin Drive), I-81 exit 73 – a Chinese place, as the name suggests – has a Sunday brunch.

HUNGRY MOTHER STATE PARK

Admit it: Like us, you came here because of the name. Ask someone to explain how this place got its name – it's a good icebreaker.

This state park (☎ 540-783-3422) is known for its beautiful woodlands and peaceful, 108-acre lake, which has a sandy beach, bathhouse, and fishing pier with disabled access. *Camping* sites cost $9.50 for up to six people, electrical and water hookups cost $14, and one-room/one-bedroom/two-bedroom cabins cost $55/65/75, respectively.

To get there, go 4 miles north of Marion on Route 16.

MOUNT ROGERS NATIONAL RECREATION AREA

East of Abingdon, the 115,000-acre Mount Rogers National Recreation Area provides ample hiking and camping opportunities in the hardwood climax forests of the ancient Appalachians. The two highest points in Virginia, Mount Rogers (5729 feet) and White Top (5520 feet), are both within the park.

Outdoor camping is one of the park's attractions (see Places to Stay, later in this section). Fishing is also popular, and there are introduced trout in the many remote mountain streams; a Virginia fishing license is required.

Mount Rogers NRA is part of the Jefferson National Forest (see Jefferson National Forest, earlier in this chapter), so logging still takes place nearby, and hunting is permitted in certain areas. Still, there are many unspoiled portions that make the area a good place to spend some time.

Information

Advance information about this very large area – a wise precaution – is available from the Mount Rogers NRA headquarters (☎ 540-783-5196), Route 16, Box 303, Marion, VA 24254, and from the Highlands Gateway Visitor Center (☎ 540-637-6766), at the Factory Merchants Mall (exit 80) in Max Meadows near Fort Chiswell. Both sell a one-sheet topographic map of the area for $3.

The best way to reach the park headquarters is to take I-81 exit 45 at Marion, then Route 16, 6 miles south of Marion. It is open 8 am to 4:30 pm weekdays Memorial Day to October and 9 am to 5 pm weekends; otherwise, 8 am to 4:30 pm weekdays. There is no fee to drive through the area, but there are day-use fees for some of the recreational sites.

Hiking

This is the biggest attraction in this wilderness region. There is a 64-mile section of the Appalachian Trail that is reserved for walkers only, the 51-mile Iron Mountain Trail, and many other trails that interconnect with either of these. A side trail off the Appalachian Trail leads to the summit of Mount Rogers and provides one of the most popular of the short excursions (for those who want to stand on top of Virginia!).

The **Virginia Creeper Trail** began as a Native American footpath; later, pioneers such as Daniel Boone hiked the trail, but its name stems from the early steam locomotives that wheezed up the steep grades, the last of which ran on March 31, 1977. With 100 trestles and bridges, it was the archetypal mountain railroad. The original creeper engine is in Damascus, near the Straight Creek bridge.

Today, the Creeper is a 34.3-mile, multiple-use trail linking Abingdon with the North Carolina border, 1.1 miles west of White Top Station. It can be used by hikers, bicyclists, and horseback riders, but not by motorized vehicles. About 16 miles of the trail, between Iron Bridge (Mile 18.4) and the state border, is part of the Mount Rogers NRA and Jefferson National Forest. For information, contact the Abingdon CVB (☎ 540-676-2282). Entrance is free.

Get free pamphlets for the following hikes: Rowland's Creek Falls (11.8 miles; moderate to difficult), Whitetop-Laurel Circuit (10 miles; easy to moderate), Four Trails Circuit (9.6 miles; moderate), and Rushing Waters Circuit (15 miles; moderate to strenuous).

Mountain Biking & Horseback Riding

It may seem odd to group these two activities under a single heading, but the fact is that many of the area's trails are open to mountain bikers and horseback riders. Bicyclists should check with the information center to see which trails are open.

A number of bicycle-rental agents serve the region, including Adventure Damascus (☎ 888-595-2453), at 128 W Laurel Ave, Damascus; Blue Blaze Bike & Shuttle Services (☎ 540-475-5095, 800-475-5095), at 727 W Laurel Ave, Damascus; Highlands Ski & Outdoor Center (☎ 540-628-9672), at 302 Green Spring Rd, Abingdon; and Mount Rogers Outfitters (☎ 540-475-5416), at 110 W Laurel Ave, Damascus. Blue Blaze also provides a shuttle service for hikers and bikers to the trailheads.

All services charge roughly the same; for bikers to get to the top of the Virginia Creeper Trail (White Top Station), it's $9 from Damascus ($5 if you have rented bikes from one of the aforementioned companies) and $12 from Abingdon ($7 with rental). Bike rentals are $20/25 with suspension and $15/20 without suspension for a half/full day.

The **Virginia Highlands Horse Trail** (66 miles) connects Elk Garden to Route 94 and is the main route for horse riders. There are many other possibilities for riders – nearly 150 miles – connecting to the New River and Iron Mountain trails. There are horse camps at Fox Creek (off County Rd 603), Hussy Mountain (off Forest Route 14 near Speedwell), and Raven Cliff (just south of County Rd 642 and east of Cripple Creek). All of these camps have toilets for the humans and drinking water for the horses. For more information on horseback riding, contact Mount Rogers High Country Outdoor Center (☎ 540-677-3900), on County Rd 603 near Troutdale.

The moderate to difficult, 10.3-mile **Beartree Bushwacker Bike Route** has been designed specifically for mountain bikes. It runs through the Feathercamp and Beartree areas.

Cross-Country Skiing

In winter (December to March), the trails of the National Recreation Area are great for cross-country skiing, but all precautions must be taken, as the weather in this region can be unforgiving. For more information, contact the Highlands Ski & Outdoor Center (☎ 540-682-9762), on W Main St in Abingdon.

The Forest Service's 'Cross-Country Skiing' booklet lists trails ranging from easy (along the Highlands Horse Trail) to difficult (those that drop steeply in drainage areas off the easier trails; eg, the 5-mile Helton Creek Loop).

Places to Stay

There are five main campgrounds in the NRA; call ☎ 800-628-7202 or 540-783-5196 for information. **Raccoon Branch** is on Route 16 south of Sugar Grove – it has 20 sites, toilets (May to October), and no showers; it's open year-round, and sites are $6. There's a 2½-mile trail to Dickey Knob on the Highlands Horse Trail.

Grindstone is on County Rd 603, west of Troutdale – it has 100 family campsites, toilets, warm showers, and a nature trail; it's open May to December, and sites are $8. There's a trail to the Mount Rogers summit (6 miles).

Beartree is on Route 58, 7 miles east of Damascus – it has 80 individual sites, toilets, showers, year-round fishing, swimming from May to September (10 am to 6 pm in Beartree Lake), and a bathhouse; the day-use fee is $2, and campsites are $10.

Hurricane is 2 miles south of Route 16 on County Rd 650 – it has 29 sites, toilets, showers, and trout fishing; it's open April to September, and sites are $6. The Hurricane Knob Trail (1½ miles) is nearby.

Raven Cliff, on Cripple Creek, is just off County Rd 619 – it has 20 sites, pit toilets, no showers, excellent fishing for trout and smallmouth bass, and picnic shelters; it's open year-round, and sites are $4.

Right in the shadow of White Top, ***Walverton Mountain Escape*** (☎ 540-388-3218, 15123 Highlands Parkway, ✉ jaye@naxs.com) is open April to November. Guests have the use of a fully equipped kitchen, and there's a formal dining room and comfortable lounge; rooms are $95 (there's a two-night minimum).

The ***Fox Hill Inn*** (☎ 540-677-3313), on Route 16 in Troutdale, is a six-room B&B. A double room, furnished in country style, costs $75, including a country breakfast. Kids will love it, as it is a working farm.

GRAYSON HIGHLANDS STATE PARK

Adjoining Mount Rogers NRA, this park (☎ 540-579-7092) lies near Virginia's highest point, Mount Rogers, and provides expansive views of alpine-like peaks of more than 5000 feet. A short section of the Appalachian Trail passes through the park, and there are several horse trails.

The park offers camping, stables, a visitor center, a camp store, and hot showers, but there are no full hookups. Wild ponies were introduced to keep the grass in the meadows down – you may be lucky enough to spot one as they roam the park. In September, the park hosts the Grayson Highlands Fall Festival. ***Campsites*** cost $10.50 for up to six people ($15 with electricity).

To get there from I-81, take exit 45 in Marion, then Route 16S to Volney and go west on Route 58 until you see the signed entrance on Route 362.

ABINGDON

Abingdon (population 10,000) is a real delight and, as somewhat of a festival center, has a wide range of accommodations. Many visitors come to see the Barter Theatre, the state theater of Virginia. There is also a 20-block historic district with fine examples of Federal and Victorian architecture.

The popular Virginia Creeper Trail begins (or ends) here, and there are all sorts of facilities for hikers and mountain bikers, including two laundries, a supermarket, a library, and a (hopefully unneeded) well-equipped hospital.

Information

The Abingdon CVB (☎ 800-435-3440, ✉ acvb@naxs.com), at 335 Cummings St about a quarter-mile from I-81 exit 17, is open 9 am to 5 pm daily. Abingdon is Virginia's second electronic village (after Blacksburg); computers are available at the library for public use.

The Washington County Chamber of Commerce (☎ 540-628-8141, ✉ wccc@naxs.com), 179 E Main St, provides information on local festivals. The free 'Abingdon: A Walking Tour of the Downtown Historic District' interprets 40 landmarks.

Barter Theatre

Abingdon's most famous attraction is the Barter Theatre, founded during the Great Depression by a young, out-of-work actor, Robert Porterfield. It is now the longest-running equity theater in the nation. Struggling with fellow actors in New York, Porterfield had the idea to move to his native southwest Virginia, where there was

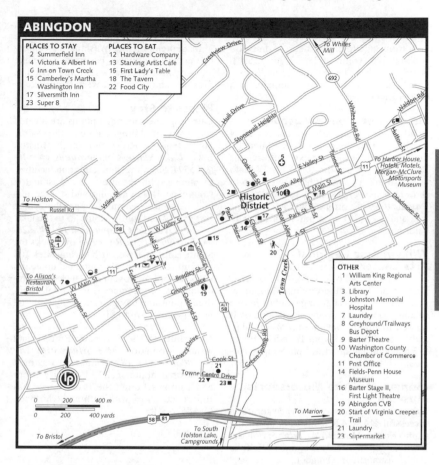

ABINGDON

PLACES TO STAY
2 Summerfield Inn
4 Victoria & Albert Inn
6 Inn on Town Creek
15 Camberley's Martha
    Washington Inn
17 Silversmith Inn
23 Super 8

PLACES TO EAT
12 Hardware Company
13 Starving Artist Cafe
16 First Lady's Table
18 The Tavern
22 Food City

OTHER
1 William King Regional
   Arts Center
3 Library
5 Johnston Memorial
   Hospital
7 Laundry
8 Greyhound/Trailways
   Bus Depot
9 Barter Theatre
10 Washington County
    Chamber of Commerce
11 Post Office
14 Fields-Penn House
    Museum
16 Barter Stage II,
    First Light Theatre
19 Abingdon CVB
20 Start of Virginia Creeper
    Trail
21 Laundry
23 Supermarket

VIRGINIA

an abundance of food, and to 'barter' admission to performances for local food and produce.

The theater opened on June 10, 1933, and admission was 40¢ or the equivalent in produce. With slogans such as 'with vegetables you cannot sell, you can buy a good laugh,' the concept of trading 'ham for Hamlet' caught on quickly. Virginia ham was taken in lieu of play royalties by Tennessee Williams, Thornton Wilder, and Noel Coward, while vegetarian George Bernard Shaw opted for spinach instead. The Barter Theatre has since been a proving ground for

emergent actors including Ernest Borgnine, Gregory Peck, Hume Cronyn, Patricia Neal, Ned Beatty, and Barry Corbin (Maurice Minnifield of TV's *Northern Exposure*).

Porterfield died in 1971, but the theater he inspired has gone from strength to strength: The original Barter Theatre (Main Stage) offers plays in the grand tradition, the Barter Stage II has more exploratory productions, and the First Light Theatre focuses on young audiences.

The Barter Theatre (☎ 540-628-3991, 800-368-3240), 133 W Main St, has live performances (which change every four weeks) from late May to late November nightly except Monday. There are performances for children from June to early August. Admission is about $20 (youth under 17 get $2 off). Perhaps you may be able to persuade door staff to admit you for some pumpkins or a case of Budweiser.

Fields-Penn House Museum
In addition to many arts-and-crafts outlets on Route 11 between I-81 exits 10 and 13, the most notable being Dixie Pottery, this 1860 museum (☎ 540-676-0216), 208 W Main St, is also worth seeing. It has been set up to show how an average family lived in a small Virginia town just prior to the Civil War. It is free and is open 1 to 4 pm Wednesday to Saturday.

William King Regional Arts Center
This center (☎ 540-628-5005), 415 Academy Dr, is an affiliate of the Virginia Museum of Fine Arts. It offers changing exhibits in two galleries, as well as working artists' studios. It is open 10 am to 5 pm Tuesday, Wednesday, and Friday; 10 am to 9 pm Thursday; 10 am to 3 pm Saturday; and 1 to 5 pm Sunday. Admission is free.

Morgan-McClure Motorsports Museum
This museum (☎ 888-494-0404) celebrates a successful NASCAR Winston Cup racing team (Kodak Max No 4), winners of the Daytona 500 in 1991, 1994, and 1995. Take exit 22 just north of Abingdon.

Hot-Air Ballooning
Abingdon has become a ballooning center. Operators include Balloon Virginia (☎ 540-628-6353) and Sky High Balloons (☎ 540-623-2306); flights last an hour on average, and for each foot you get off the ground, expect to pay a dollar!

Special Events
Abingdon hosts many annual festivals. The Virginia Highlands Festival (☎ 800-435-3440), held late July to mid-August, is a celebration of Appalachian cultural heritage.

There is an antique market, arts and crafts, music, food, historic tours, and wine tasting.

In September, the Washington County Fair & Burley Tobacco Festival – more like an agricultural show – features produce, livestock, and country & western music.

Places to Stay
Camping The camping options are located southeast of Abingdon near the scenic South Holston River and South Holston Lake. *Lake Shore Campgrounds* (☎ 540-628-5394) has campsites, sanitation facilities, swimming (plus the use of the Washington County pool), a boat ramp, and storage. It is open April to November. To get there, take I-81 exit 17 and follow Route 75 to the lake.

The *Riverside Campground* (☎ 540-628-5333, 18496 N Fork River Rd) overlooks the South Holston River. It has campsites, full hookups, and some self-contained units, and is open April to November. There is a coin-op laundry, convenience store, a pool, a children's pool, and pay phones. A site with full hookups costs $16 to $19.

Guesthouses There are many B&Bs in and around Abingdon. The *Silversmith Inn* (☎ 540-676-3924, 182 E Main St) was built on the original site of an 18th-century tavern and smithy's home; the brick house has rooms and suites, with bath and whirlpool, for $85 to $105.

The **Summerfield Inn** (☎ 540-628-5905, 101 W Valley St) is Abingdon's oldest B&B and is in the heart of the Historic District. The seven spacious rooms all have baths, air-conditioning, and TV and cost $80 to $130.

The **Inn on Town Creek** (☎ 540-628-4560, 445 E Valley St) has beautiful landscaped gardens that can be enjoyed from covered porches, a Jacuzzi, and a solarium. The rooms, at $85 to $175 for a double, are very comfortable.

The **Victoria & Albert Inn** (☎ 540-676-2797, 224 Oak Hill St) is a magnificent old restored 1892 home with great porches to relax on; the double rooms with gas fireplaces are worth the cost ($85 to $120).

Hotels & Motels The **Alpine Motel** (☎ 540-628-3178, 882 E Main St), off I-81 exit 19, is a small, clean place with nonsmoking rooms and disabled facilities. In this economical place popular with families, doubles are $47 in the low season; otherwise, $54.

The **Empire Motel** (☎ 540-628-7131, 87 Empire Drive), near I-81 exit 19, is a family-owned place, and its owners ensure that it is both clean and comfortable; doubles start at $45.

The **Super 8 Motel** (☎ 540-676-3329), off I-81 exit 17, is an economical place offering a free continental breakfast; singles/doubles are $50/55 weekdays and $55/60 weekends.

The **Comfort Inn** (☎ 540-676-2222, 170 Jonesboro Rd), near I-81 exit 14, has a heated pool, and continental breakfast is included in the tariff; singles/doubles start at $60/72 Sunday to Thursday, $66/76 on Friday and Saturday.

The **Holiday Inn Express** (☎ 540-676-2829), also off I-81 exit 19, has a pool; breakfast is included in the cost of $69/74 for singles/doubles in the low season; otherwise, $75 for either.

Camberley's Martha Washington Inn (☎ 540-628-3161, 800-555-8000, 150 W Main St) is the pinnacle of accommodations in Abingdon (and southwest Virginia). This elegantly furnished inn, dating from 1832, is disabled-accessible. Rooms are expensive (from a rack rate of $159 for a standard, $169 for B&B, $179 for a Barter package, to

$309 for a premier suite), but after a delightful afternoon tea on the porch of the inn, it might all seem worth it.

Places to Eat
Alison's Restaurant (☎ 540-628-8002, 1220 W Main St) is not quite Alice's, but you can still get almost anything you want. It's known for its ribs, gourmet salads, steaks, and fajitas.

The **Starving Artist Cafe** (☎ 540-628-8445, 134 Wall St, Depot Square) is a favorite place to, you know, 'eat your art out.' It has gourmet sandwiches and tasty entrees for lunch and dinner. There is always a selection of the work of local artists on display, and there is outdoor dining in season.

The **Harbor House** (☎ 540-676-3500, 912 E Main St) serves old-fashioned steak, fried and broiled seafood, and chicken dishes (as well as kids' meals) daily.

The Tavern (☎ 540-628-1118, 222 E Main St) is in Abingdon's oldest building (1779). It has been faithfully restored and is open 11 am to 2 pm daily for lunch and 5 to 10:30 pm for dinner. The food is innovative; eg, American trout in herb butter with jalapeño/cilantro mayonnaise ($14 plus).

The **Hardware Company** (☎ 540-628-1111, 260 W Main St), in the center of town, still seems to be the most popular meeting place for locals; it stays open late seven days, when the rest of the town is dead quiet, and has a good selection of food (entrees start at $12, and there are early-bird specials).

The **First Lady's Table** at Camberley's Martha Washington Inn (see Places to Stay, earlier) is the most elegant place in town. Lunch is served 11 am to 4 pm and dinner 5 to 10 pm; reservations are needed, and a jacket is required.

Getting There & Away
Most people arrive here in their own cars. The closest airport is the Tri-Cities Airport, in Tennessee, serving Bristol, Johnson City, and Kingsport.

Greyhound/Trailways has a depot at 465 W Main St, and there are services to Nashville and Washington, DC. There is no passenger train.

BRISTOL

This large town is divided through its center (along State and Goodson Sts, the town's two main thoroughfares) by the Tennessee-Virginia border. More of it is Tennessee than Virginia. It has been named the 'official birthplace of country music,' as the first commercial country music recordings were made here in 1927 by the Victor Talking Machine Co.

In Virginia, the area code is ☎ 540, and in Tennessee, it is ☎ 423 or ☎ 615. There is a Virginia Welcome Center (☎ 540-466-2932) at 66 Island Rd (near I-81 at the Tennessee border). The Bristol CVB (☎ 423-989-4850, www.bristolchamber.org) is at 20 Volunteer Parkway.

On State St, you will find the **Paramount Center** (☎ 423-968-7456), a restored 1931 art deco movie house listed on the National Register of Historic Places. It is open daily, and there are tours available.

The **Bristol International Raceway** (☎ 423-764-1161), a half-mile racetrack south on Route 19/11E, hosts races in the NASCAR series.

Entertainment here is likely to be in the form of 'country.' The **Carter Family Fold** (☎ 540-386-9480) has country music concerts every Saturday in Maces Spring, just to the north of Hiltons. The barn where the 'electronic-free' performances are held is 21 miles west of Bristol (5 miles east of Weber City), off Route 58/421 on County Rd 614. The doors open at 6 pm, and the concerts take place 7:30 to 10:30 pm ($3.50 for adults, $1 for children).

NATURAL TUNNEL STATE PARK

This park is based around an 850-foot-long limestone tunnel believed to have been formed in the dolostone bedrock one million years ago. There is a picnic area, pool, campground, and hiking trails. A chairlift ($2 per person roundtrip) rises to an overlook from which you get great views of the natural tunnel. Travel through the tunnel is prohibited because of railroad safety regulations.

The park (☎ 540-940-2674) is open 8 am to dusk daily, and the cable car operates from 10 am to 5 pm. *Campsites* are $10.50

for up to six people ($15 with electricity). To get there from Duffield, take Route 23 south to County Rd 871; it is 1 mile from the turnoff.

CUMBERLAND GAP NATIONAL HISTORICAL PARK

The Cumberland Gap, a significant break in the Appalachian mountain chain carved by wind and water, is right at the point where Virginia, Tennessee, and Kentucky meet (Virginia's Lee County). It was first crossed by large animals during their major migrations, and later by Native Americans following hunting trails. When the interior was first settled in the late 18th century, some 200,000 pioneers crossed the Gap into 'Kentucke' and beyond. It is still a major thoroughfare.

The national historical park headquarters and visitor center (☎ 606-248-2817), on Route 25E, is open 8 am to 6 pm daily mid-June to Labor Day; otherwise, 8 am to 5 pm (park entry is free). There is also a bookstore and museum.

There are 70 miles of hiking trails, from a quarter-mile loop trail to the 17-mile Ridge Trail along the Cumberland Mountains, and mountain biking is permitted in some places. You can camp at the *Wilderness Road Campground*, where there are 170 primitive sites that are open year-round and cost $8; hot showers are within a short hiking distance. There are backcountry campsites at Gibson Gap, White Rocks, Chadwell Gap, and Martins Fork, which require a use permit, available from the visitor center.

Visitors traveling south on I-81 should take the exit onto Route 25E at White Pine/Morristown, Tennessee. If traveling on Route 23, take the Duffield exit to Route 58, which heads to the Cumberland Gap.

BIG STONE GAP

The main attraction in Big Stone Gap (population 5000) is the rugged beauty of the place. Visitors deviating to this far-flung neck o' the woods for a real feel of the Appalachians won't be disappointed. And for the coal miners' daughters and sons among us, the 'anthracite, lignite, and bituminous' have an irresistible, magnetic power. Choose your weather well – coal fields turn dismal in the mist and rain.

The visitor center (☎ 540-523-2060, ✉ gap tourism@va-village.com) is in the historical 1870 Interstate Railroad car 101, on Route 23 Business near the bridge across the Powell River. It is open daily.

If you have ventured out here, you will have probably heard of the 20th-century novel (and movie) *The Trail of the Lonesome Pine*, by John William Fox Jr. Every year from late June to early September, Thursday to Saturday from 8:15 pm, an **outdoor musical drama** with the same title as the novel is enacted by local performers at the June Tolliver Playhouse (☎ 540-523-1235). The drama depicts the drastic changes in mountain life that followed the Virginia coal boom; otherwise, it is very much a 'naive gal meets worldly guy' tale. Tickets are $10 for adults and $7 for seniors and children. Also on the premises is the historic 1880s **June Tolliver House**, open at intermission during the theater season to sell local crafts; admission is free.

There are three museums near Big Stone Gap that should be visited if you have made it up this far. The **Southwest Virginia Museum** (☎ 540-523-1322) is housed in a Victorian mansion dating from the coal boom of the 1890s. There are many artifacts and exhibits that relate to the history and culture of southwestern Virginia, including furnishings from the mine manager's home. The museum, at the corner of W First St and Wood Ave (just off Alt Route 58), is open daily March to December; from Memorial Day to Labor Day, it is closed Monday. Admission is $3 for adults and $1.50 for children.

The brown cedar-shingled **John Fox Jr Museum** (☎ 540-523-2747), 117 Shawnee Ave, was the home of the author of *The Trail of the Lonesome Pine* and is still furnished as it was when the Fox family lived there in the late 19th century. It is open 2 to 5 pm Tuesday to Wednesday and to 6 pm Thursday to Sunday from Memorial Day to Labor Day; admission is $3 for adults and $1 for children.

The **Harry Meador Coal Museum** (☎ 540-523-4950), 505 E 3rd St, houses a variety of items that illustrate coal mining, past and present. It is open 10 am to 5 pm Wednesday to Saturday and 1 to 5 pm Sunday year-round (donations are requested).

The closest campground is at *Cave Springs Recreation Area* (☎ 540-328-2931), 2½ miles west on Route 58, then 6 miles south on County Rd 621. It is open mid-May to mid-October; sites are $8.

The *Country Inn* (☎ 540-523-0374, 627 Gilley Ave) has singles/doubles for $35/38 and an adjoining camping area. *Stringers' Family Restaurant* (☎ 540-523-5388, 414 E 5th St) serves a hearty country buffet.

NORTON

The city of Norton lies in the center of Wise County, which adjoins the Kentucky border. On Saturday night, 51 weeks of the year (it is closed on the second Saturday in September), **Appalachian Traditions** (☎ 540-523-0891) opens its country cabin from 7:30 to 11 pm for performances of traditional and bluegrass music, cakewalks, and brooms dancing (flatfooting with a broom).

For more information, contact the Wise County Chamber of Commerce (☎ 540-679-0961). The **Heart of Appalachia Bike Route** begins at the Guest River Gorge, just east of Norton – see the Activities chapter for more information on bicycling here.

BREAKS INTERSTATE PARK

The Breaks is a 4600-acre scenic and recreational park with a 5-mile, 1600-foot-deep gorge – 'the Grand Canyon of the South' – as its centerpiece. Here, the Russell Fork River, a tributary of the Big Sandy River, has carved the deepest canyon east of the Mississippi. At one point, the river winds around the 1660-foot Towers – a magnificent pyramid of Paleozoic rocks more than 250 million years old.

Whitewater rafting and kayaking are popular on the Russell Fork, and the best times for these activities depend on when water is released from the John Flannagan Dam. The Catawba rhododendron is in bloom in mid-May, and the rare yellow lady's slipper blooms in early April. There is also scope for fishing, hiking on nature trails, and horseback riding.

The visitor center (☎ 540-865-4413, @ bip@mounet.com) has exhibits and displays of the natural and historical features of the area. The *camping* area (122 sites) is open April to October, and sites are $7; electricity, water, and sewerage are $1 extra for each service. The park is located not far from where Route 460 crosses the Kentucky border. Turn off onto Route 80.

TAZEWELL COUNTY

Near the county seat of Tazewell (once called Jeffersonville) is the **Crab Orchard Museum & Pioneer Park** (☎ 540-988-6755), which depicts the history of the county from prehistoric times to the present. It includes 11 log and two stone structures and a display of horse-drawn equipment.

The museum and park, southwest of Tazewell on Route 19/460, are open 9 am to 5 pm Monday to Saturday and 1 to 5 pm

Sunday (from November to March, it is closed on Sunday). Admission is $6 for adults, $5 for seniors, $3 for students, and $2 for children. To get to Tazewell from I-81, turn off at Marion, near the Mount Rogers NRA, onto Route 16N.

Burkes Garden, northeast of Tazewell on County Rd 623, is 50 sq miles of sylvan farmland encircled by a continuous mountain range with the Appalachian Trail at its edge. It is sometimes referred to as 'God's thumbprint.' Popular myth has it that Cornelius Vanderbilt wanted the 'garden' to build an estate on, but the proud locals refused to sell him the land (instead, he built the famous Biltmore estate in Asheville, North Carolina). A Fall Festival, with produce, arts, and crafts, is sponsored by the Burkes Garden Community Association (☎ 540-963-3385) and is held here in September.

Facts about Maryland

For more than three centuries, the traditions of English gentry and independent bay watermen have governed life here. And while only 20% of Marylanders live the traditional lifestyles of rural gentry, farmers, or watermen, these lifestyles persist in the dreams of Marylanders. Residents here own more thoroughbred horses per capita than people in any other state, and they testify to their romance with the Chesapeake Bay blue crab and the watermen's skipjack by cloning these icons on everything from cocktail napkins to semitrailers. Farms, manors, townhouses, public buildings, railroads, and boats – such as the oystermen's skipjacks – express those traditions and dreams. Nearly obsessed with their heritage, Marylanders have launched into historic preservation of duck decoys, railway locomotives, cannonballs, and tall ships. The number of Maryland's famous

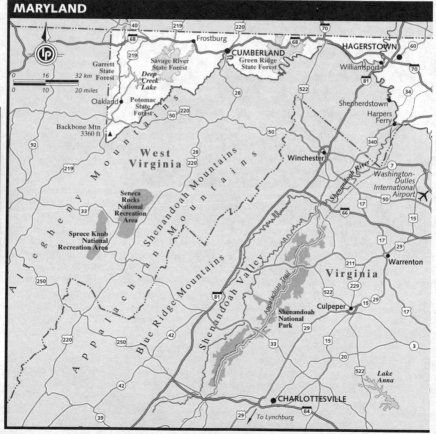

fleet of skipjacks, graceful oystering sloops designed 100 years ago, is on the rise.

The living-history interpreters at Historic St Mary's City and the rebricking of the sidewalks in the historic districts of Annapolis, Chestertown, and Easton are some more obvious signs of Maryland's preoccupation with its past. In response to this nostalgia, the number of B&Bs has exploded over the last 10 years to the point where a traveler can tour the state for two weeks staying in nothing but haunted houses. Visitors will find it easy to join an oysterman or crabber on the bay or to mingle with high society at

horsey affairs such as the Maryland Hunt Cup Race. Best of all, Baltimore, once a seedy industrial port, has emerged as a major cultural center. The city's Inner Harbor is now a popular tourist destination with more waterfront access and attractions than you can find in Boston, San Francisco, or Miami. For many Marylanders, life is something of a romantic adventure, and they love to share it.

HISTORY

One of the original 13 colonies to rebel against England's rule, Maryland cast off its colonial status with almost as much flourish as

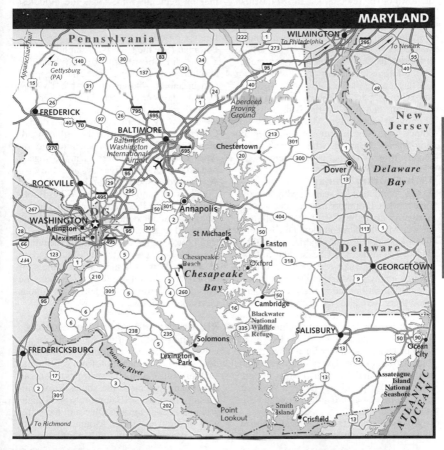

the patriots in Boston. While no Revolutionary battles took place in Maryland, the state was a staging ground for the final campaign against the British. After England surrendered in 1783, the first US Congress ratified the treaty in the Maryland State House in Annapolis. George Washington resigned his commission as commander in chief of the Continental army here in the State House, and Annapolis remained the capital of the new American republic until August 1784.

When war with England started again in 1812, the British fleet sailed up Chesapeake Bay, attacking Maryland ports and burning the town of Havre de Grace. In 1814, British troops drove overland from the Patuxent River to burn Washington, DC. That same year, the British fleet tried to bring an end to the US fleet of privateers by attacking its base in Baltimore. On the morning of September 14, the tattered remnants of a 30-by-42-foot US flag emerged from the mist and gun smoke over Fort McHenry, showing that Americans had repelled the British assault. The event inspired a Maryland lawyer, Francis Scott Key, to write a poem called the 'Star-Spangled Banner,' whose words would become those of the national anthem.

19th-Century Frenzy

As the preeminent US seaport with an active slave market, Baltimore ushered in a wave of prosperity after the War of 1812. Following the war, Marylanders completed the National Pike to Ohio, began the Baltimore & Ohio Railroad, and dug the Chesapeake & Ohio and the Chesapeake & Delaware Canals. Though many of Maryland's tobacco and wheat plantations continued using slave labor, there were also strong abolitionist sentiments afoot in state. Harriet Tubman, an escaped slave, helped form the Undergound Railroad (see the boxed text). In 1859, in an attempt to gain weapons for a slave revolt, John Brown, one of slavery's greatest opponents, conducted his raid on the Federal Armory in Harpers Ferry (now in West Virginia) from a base across the Potomac River in Maryland.

When the southern agricultural states, including neighboring Virginia, seceded from the nation in April 1861, Marylanders strongly voiced hopes for a peaceful restoration of the Union. President Abraham Lincoln imposed martial law to guarantee that Marylanders would stick with the Union and protect the District of Columbia. Caught at the crossroads between the industrial, abolitionist states of the northern Union and the agricultural, slave-holding southern states of the new Confederacy, Maryland became a battleground for the Civil War. The armies of the North and South clashed at Antietam (Sharpsburg). After the smoke cleared, more than 23,000 soldiers lay dead or wounded, making September 17, 1862, 'the bloodiest day in American history.' When it was over, the North had driven General Robert E Lee's Confederate army back across the Potomac. (See the Civil War chapter.)

Lee did not return to Maryland for another year; this time, the Union stopped him in another bloodbath outside a village just over the Pennsylvania-Maryland border – Gettysburg. In 1864, Marylanders voted to abolish slavery, several months before the US Congress did the same with the 13th Amendment. The Confederates surrendered on April 9, 1865, but one last scene in the tragedy had yet to take place. Five days after the Civil War ended, respected Maryland actor and Confederate sympathizer John Wilkes Booth shot and killed President Abraham Lincoln (see the boxed text, later). His flight through Maryland to Bowling Green, Virginia, left a trail of accomplices. After the assassination, Lincoln's body passed through Maryland on its way back to his home state of Illinois for burial; the train followed the same route the President had traveled to deliver his famous Gettysburg Address.

Riding the Industrial Revolution

Maryland's history after the Civil War involves three stories: Baltimore's industrialization, waves of immigration from central and southern Europe, and the struggles of African Americans to achieve the status of full citizenship. Because of Baltimore's good highway and railway links to Ohio and the states west of the Appalachian Mountains, the city boomed as a shipping and manufacturing

Harriet Tubman & the Underground Railroad

Harriet Tubman (1820–1913) was an abolitionist and former slave who became famous before the Civil War because of her role in the Underground Railroad, which helped slaves escape from the South to the North and Canada.

Escaped slaves in the pre–Civil War US could be recaptured and returned to bondage under the federal Fugitive Slave Act of 1793, which was strengthened by the Fugitive Slave Law of 1850. In practice, this meant that under federal law former slaves could be captured in the non-slave North and chained and dragged back to bondage in the South. In opposition to slavery and to fugitive slave laws, some people sought to help slaves to freedom.

One way to free slaves was through the Underground Railroad, which was neither underground nor a railroad. It was 'underground' in the sense of being secret and was a 'railroad' because its members used railroad code words to describe what they did. Routes were 'lines,' stops were 'stations,' guides were 'conductors,' and the fugitives were 'packages' or 'freight.'

The railroad was a loosely organized network of people that included Quakers, Presbyterians, Congregationalists, and, most importantly, free blacks. It was the slaves themselves who often accomplished the most difficult part of the journey from South to North by escaping and heading north, where they were met by Northerners who helped them hide and escape. The most active 'conductors' were Northern free blacks, and of these, Harriet Tubman was the most famous.

Tubman was born in Bucktown, near Cambridge on Maryland's Eastern Shore. As a teenager, she was beaten with an iron weight by a brutal overseer and suffered blackouts throughout her life because of it. She escaped in 1849, leaving behind her parents, siblings, and husband. She returned to the South 19 times to lead more than 300 slaves, including her parents, to freedom.

Tubman traveled with a pistol and faith in God and said, 'I always told God, I'm going to hold steady onto you, and you've got to see me through.' Her pistol was used to defend the slaves and to persuade those who wanted to back out into continuing the journey. At the height of her career as a conductor, Tubman had a $40,000 bounty on her head. She was a friend to abolitionists across the country and helped John Brown plan his raid on Harpers Ferry, West Virginia. Brown called her 'one of the best and bravest persons on this continent – General Tubman as we call her.'

During the Civil War, Tubman worked as a nurse, scout, and spy for the Union army along the coast of South Carolina. She traveled through enemy territory unnoticed and collected information on the location of cotton warehouses, ammunition depots, and slaves. Tubman was paid only $200 for her work over three years and had to support herself by selling pies, gingerbread, and root beer.

After the war, Tubman settled in Auburn, New York, and helped African Americans there. She made her house into the Home for Indigent and Aged Negroes and financed it by selling copies of her autobiography and giving speeches. She was buried with full military honors on March 10, 1913, and is remembered for her words, 'My people must go free.'

MARYLAND

port well into the 20th century. As the westward expansion of the US demanded everything from farm fertilizer and steel to spices and refined petroleum products, Baltimore found ways to import or make them. Over the years, enormous factories, like the Sparrows Point steel mills and oil refineries, grew up along the banks of the Patapsco River. These industries and others created employment for Italian, German, Polish, and Jewish immigrants, as well as for African Americans fleeing lives as sharecroppers in rural Maryland and the deep South.

Assimilation into Maryland life was easier for most immigrants of shared European backgrounds and those sharing the Roman Catholic faith, but the story was different for blacks. 'Jim Crow' segregation laws kept African Americans as 2nd-class citizens until the 1960s, and racial prejudice went unquestioned among the vast majority of the white population. Perhaps in response, some of the strongest black voices to precipitate

social justice in the US came from Maryland: in the 19th century, abolitionists Harriet Tubman and Frederick Douglass; in the 20th century, musical geniuses Eubie Blake and Billie Holiday (see the boxed text in the Baltimore chapter) and the first African American justice of the Supreme Court, Thurgood Marshall.

GEOGRAPHY

About the size of the Netherlands, Maryland is 42nd in land mass among the 50 states, covering about 10,000 sq miles. Its odd shape, like a hand grasping the Chesapeake with the wrist extending into western Maryland, came from a series of border disputes with neighboring colonies. Maryland's northern border is the famous Mason-Dixon Line that has traditionally (and somewhat erroneously) divided the northern industrial colonies from the southern agrarian ones. At its broadest, Maryland extends 250 miles east-west and 90 miles north-south. The

John Wilkes Booth

The man who shot President Abraham Lincoln captured America's imagination with nearly as much vigor as Lincoln himself. Born in 1838 at Bel Air, north of Baltimore, Booth was the son of a respected English actor and seemed destined for celebrity status. As a young man, he distinguished himself as an exceptionally talented Shakespearean actor. By the time he was 25, he may have been the most famous actor on the US stage (judged at the time superior to his brother Edwin, who was later considered America's most gifted Shakespearean).

But theatrical fame was not enough for Booth; he became a violent partisan of the South during the Civil War and once organized an unsuccessful conspiracy to abduct President Lincoln. The actor's boldness led him to make the fateful leap (in which he broke his leg) onto the stage at Ford's Theater to take a bow after shooting the president. After the murder, Booth spent 12 days trying to attend to his broken leg, hide, and escape through southern Maryland. He died in Bowling Green, Virginia, of gunshot wounds (possibly self-inflicted) in a barn.

The assassination of Lincoln remains one of the most famous celebrity murder cases in US history. Handsome, charming, and talented, but egocentric and racist, Booth persists as an icon for the consummate American villain.

Many people relive history with a visit to the Surratt House Museum (☎ 301-868-1121) in Clinton (just southeast of Washington, DC) and other sites that mark the steps on Booth's path as he attempted to escape punishment for the assassination.

On two Saturdays in spring and again in fall, the Surratt Society (named after Mary Surratt, who was hanged as an accomplice to Booth) sponsors a bus trip called the 'John Wilkes Booth Escape Tour,' which spends 12 hours visiting the sites on Booth's flight to Bowling Green.

state rises from sea level in the east to 3360-foot Backbone Mountain in the west.

Three major topographic regions of the eastern USA exist in Maryland – the Atlantic Coastal Plain, the Piedmont Plateau, and the Appalachian region. The bulk of the state lies in the coastal plain, which, along with coastal Virginia is often referred to as the 'Tidewater' area, encompassing all of the land on the Eastern Shore and a lot on the western shore of the Chesapeake. English colonists began settling Tidewater Maryland in 1633 and set up tobacco plantations.

West of the Tidewater is the Piedmont Plateau, an area of low hills and valleys stretching for about 50 miles. The 'fall line,' an area where the land descends 100 feet in several miles, marks the eastern edge of the Piedmont. Here, rivers become unnavigable because of waterfalls and rapids. The Piedmont attracted the first non-English settlers to Maryland – mostly Scotch-Irish and Palatine German. This foothill region remains largely an area of rich farmland, producing corn, soybeans, and hay.

Western Maryland is in the Appalachian Plateau, Ridge, and Valley. Here lie Maryland's share of the Allegheny Mountains and the state's highest peak. The western portion is the most mountainous, especially near the Pennsylvania border. A 10-mile-wide strip of the Blue Ridge Mountains forms a border between the Appalachian region and the Piedmont.

The state's soil makes for rich farmland in the Coastal Plain and Piedmont regions. The soil ranges from light sand loam on the Eastern Shore to clay loam on the Piedmont Plateau. Silt and clay constitute the Appalachian Valley. Limestone and sandstone form the soil base in the western Piedmont area.

Maryland has more miles of navigable rivers than any other state. Some of these, like the Savage and the Youghiogheny, offer superb white-water rafting, canoeing, and kayaking. Most of the western rivers drain into the Potomac River, which borders Virginia. Most of the eastern rivers drain into Chesapeake Bay. Nearly 200 miles long, the

Chesapeake: Loved to Death?

When Marylanders gather to entertain each other with tall tales, a listener will hear stories asserting that in this part of the world people can hardly eat, work, travel, play, worship, or kiss a crab without acknowledging the bay. Almost 200 miles long and 5 to 30 miles wide, Chesapeake Bay is the biggest estuary in the US.

While exploring the Chesapeake and its shores in 1608, Captain John Smith judged, 'Heaven and earth never agreed better to frame a place more perfect for man's habitation.' These days, Smith's remarks ring with irony. Oysters, crabs, and geese are fighting an uncertain battle for survival against the pollution descending on them from agricultural runoff and the urban sprawl of Washington, DC, and Baltimore.

Meanwhile, almost every family in Maryland has a boat with which to get out on the bay and its tributaries – a fact that has prompted more than one environmental journalist to ponder whether the Chesapeake isn't being loved to death. But nobody is planning a funeral. Osprey and eagles have recently returned to the bay area in great numbers. So have the nearly extinct striped bass known locally as 'rockfish.'

bay covers 8000 miles of shoreline, drains a watershed of 65,000 miles in six states, and claims 150 rivers and tributaries. Ninety percent of the Chesapeake freshwater flows from five rivers – the Susquehanna, Potomac, Rappahannock, York, and James.

GOVERNMENT & POLITICS

Although the state government does business in the quiet, colonial capital of Annapolis – as legislators have done for more than 300 years – most of the action happens in the state's largest city. Baltimore city politics often dwarf any news coming out of Annapolis. For example, in 1999 an effort to draft Kweisi Mfume, the president of the

NAACP (the Baltimore-based National Association for the Advancement of Colored People) into the mayor's race, though unsuccessful, made national news.

ECONOMY

Today, Maryland remains a divided state – not by race or class or even Chesapeake Bay, but by lifestyle. More than half of Marylanders work in service jobs or manufacturing, both of which have changed their focus from heavy industries such as steel to electronics and communications. Almost 25% of Marylanders work for the federal or state government, adding more than $9 billion to the state's economy – nearly twice that of manufacturing. Nearly all of these people live in Baltimore or the suburbs between Baltimore, DC, and Annapolis.

The largest and most valuable estuary in the US, Chesapeake Bay produces more food crabs than anywhere else on earth, one-quarter of the nation's oyster harvest, and half of its soft-shell clams.

POPULATION & PEOPLE

Maryland has nearly five million people, making the state the 19th most populous. The areas with the greatest concentrations of people are metropolitan Baltimore and the suburbs surrounding Washington, DC, Annapolis, and Wilmington, Delaware.

A small number of Germans and Scotch-Irish came in the later 1600s, but the largest non-English European population boom – mostly Poles, Russians, Czechs, and Italians – came with the 19th-century industrialization and transportation revolutions. These people settled primarily in the industrial area around Baltimore. Today, Scotch-Irish and German are strong strains in western Maryland, and the central urban populations of the state are fairly homogenous. The people of the Eastern Shore remain largely of British and African descent, and many of the 7000 people claiming Native American ancestry in the state also live in this area.

The current ethnic breakdown is 71% white, 25% black, 2.9% Asian, 2.6% Latino, and 0.27% Native American. About 95% were born in the US.

ARTS

Chicago and New Orleans may have their legions of musicians, California its cult of filmmakers, and Massachusetts its galleries of artists, but probably no state in the Union can compare with Maryland for the number of storytellers.

Literature

Maryland's contributions to American literature include the biography by Reverend Josiah Jensen, a Maryland ex-slave, that inspired Harriet Beecher Stowe to write *Uncle Tom's Cabin*. The writer Edgar Allan Poe lived in Baltimore and his gravesite there now serves as a shrine for literary fans. America's most famous journalist, HL Mencken, was a lifelong Baltimorean.

Today, Maryland native and one of the world's most respected novelists, John Barth, author of *The End of the Road* and *The Sotweed Factor*, teaches at Johns Hopkins University, which boasts the most active university press in the USA.

Visual Arts

Around the shores of Chesapeake Bay, a popular specialty handicraft is the life-size wooden waterfowl carving, an art that draws hundreds of collectors to craft festivals each year. And whereas decoy carving and the other folk arts thrive in rural Maryland, urban Maryland (particularly Baltimore) hosts the fine-arts community. Distinguished art museums such as the Baltimore Museum of Art (BMA) and the Walters Art Gallery, along with dozens of other museums across Maryland, developed as a result of the state's cultured upper classes and its industrial fortunes. Over the centuries, though, few young artistic dreamers have chosen Maryland to inspire them and stretch their talents – until recently.

During the 1980s, Baltimore's Inner Harbor urban-renewal project created a lot of job opportunities for artistic people caught up in the possibilities of redesigning and restoring the heart of a great American city. Many of these young artists and artisans bought derelict row houses in the slums surrounding the Inner Harbor and began restoring them as studios and galleries. For the last decade, more and more artists from the prestigious Maryland Institute of Art and elsewhere have moved into the neighborhoods of Federal Hill and southwest Baltimore (SoWeBo). Now, both neighborhoods have vital communities of working visual artists with annual 'studio days' and fine-arts festivals.

Music

Although the African American sounds of Eubie Blake's jazz and Billie Holiday's blues have been some of Maryland's greatest contributions to the world of music, musical expression isn't limited to the realms of jazz and blues.

Native Marylander Mary Chapin Carpenter dazzles pop-country music fans, while classical music lovers enjoy concerts by the acclaimed Baltimore Symphony Orchestra and the Annapolis Symphony Orchestra, in addition to other symphony orchestras in the state. There is also chamber music at the University of Maryland in College Park, Goucher College, and Loyola University in metropolitan Baltimore. The distinguished Peabody Conservatory of Music at Mount Vernon Square in Baltimore attracts celebrated faculty, guest artists, and students for regular concerts.

Maryland boasts four opera companies and one of the world's greatest gospel ensembles, the Morgan State University Choir. Of course, summer brings a host of local, national, and international musicians to the state for outdoor concerts and music festivals.

Performing Arts

Long before the days when John Wilkes Booth, President Lincoln's nemesis, interpreted Shakespeare, Marylanders had been going to the theater in hordes. Today, the state boasts four opera companies and more than a dozen dance and theater troupes performing in new or elegantly restored theaters in every major city in the state. Touring Broadway shows play at the Baltimore Center for Performing Arts, but there is a lot more than mainstream theater in Maryland.

The Art of Maryland Folktales

Spend more than a few minutes conversing with a Marylander, and you are likely to hear some kind of homespun comical tale of misadventure. Comment to a Chesapeake waterman about the possibility of a thunder squall and a stiff breeze, and you might hear him respond: 'Squall? Blow? Why, you ain't seen blow. One time down to Hooper Straits, I seen it blow so hard that it sunk five boats, drowned 18 men, and blowed a chicken clean into a bottle.'

Visit the town of Easton, on the Eastern Shore, during the annual fall waterfowl festival, and you will find that Marylanders don't just express their folktales in words. Hundreds of carved duck decoys, traditional boat models, quilts, and paintings depict stories of life and death on the Chesapeake. Folk songs abound throughout the state.

George G Carey's *Maryland Folklore* (Tidewater Press, 1989) is a compendium of the kinds of stories Marylanders love best.

The Baltimore Theater Project's avant-garde productions and the African American performances of the Eva Anderson Dancers are just two of many examples of 'alternative' and ethnic live entertainment in Maryland.

Film

Maryland, specifically Baltimore, is currently experiencing a certain celebrity in the filmmaking world. In recent years, Baltimore natives such as director John Waters have set a large collection of both cult and feature films in and around their hometown.

While most of the production and acting folks are imports from Hollywood, Maryland has developed its own stock of professional actors and production people to support the American film industry. For more information, see the section Films & TV Shows in the Facts for the Visitor chapter.

MARYLAND

INFORMATION
Tourist Offices

The Maryland Office of Tourism (☎ 410-767-3400, 800-543-1036), 217 E Redwood St, Baltimore, MD 21298, has statewide guides and maintains a website at www.state.md.us.

Area Codes

Maryland has two area codes, ☎ 410 and ☎ 301 (☎ 410 is in effect for the more populated areas). There may be a new ☎ 443 area code in place by late 2000.

Taxes

Maryland sales tax is 5%. Room tax varies by county, from 5% to 8%.

Media

The state's major newspaper is the *Baltimore Sun*, but most people read the *Washington Post* as well.

You will find NPR radio on WJHV, 88.9 FM. Almost everyone in the Baltimore area listens to 'Rouse and Co,' a comical morning show on WQSR, 105.7 FM.

Baltimore

A tall ship with a lean black hull and two raked masts, Maryland's new flagship has been sailing into Atlantic ports proclaiming the state's virtues for more than a decade. The *Pride of Baltimore II* is a replica of the famous 'Baltimore Clippers,' which made the city, state, and US a major maritime power during the early 19th century. In many ways, the *Pride* is the perfect symbol for this city, which is the largest in Maryland and 13th in the nation.

Baltimore's glory has always been rooted in seafaring. Today, the signs are everywhere. Visit the Inner Harbor and witness the collection of traditional sailing vessels ranging in size from the 200-year-old battle frigate USF *Constellation* to the *Minnie V*, a turn-of-the-19th-century oystering skipjack. Here, people get out on the water in everything from paddleboats, outboards, and yachts to water taxis and excursion vessels.

Nicknamed 'Charm City' because of its hospitality, Baltimore is every bit as proud as it is welcoming. Pride sparkles in the bold designs of the new skyscrapers and museums surrounding the Inner Harbor and the spit-and-polished restorations of 18th-century neighborhoods such as Fells Point. You can sense pride in the elaborate descriptions of entrees on the menus in Little Italy and in the beckoning voices of vendors in the city's lively markets.

Like the *Pride of Baltimore II*, Baltimore tells a story of rebirth. Some years ago, the original *Pride of Baltimore* sank in a storm off the Bahamas; the new ship was built from the memory of the old. By the early 1980s, Baltimore was slipping beneath a sea of urban blight, until then-Mayor Donald Schaefer organized a coalition of government officials, businesspeople, and citizens to revitalize Baltimore. The project began with the leveling of the industrial slums surrounding the Inner Harbor. The area was then filled with parks, galleries of shops, restaurants, a concert pavilion, five-star hotels, new corporate office buildings, a multitude of floating attractions, and continuous musical and cultural events.

The city's primary draws include a convention center, the American Visionary Art Museum, the National Aquarium in Baltimore, the Maryland Science Center, and new stadiums for the Baltimore Orioles and Ravens. The infusion of redevelopment capital and tourist dollars has engendered urban renewal and gentrification in peripheral neighborhoods, attracting a new group of young and talented artists, preservationists, and professionals to the city, which now hosts a population of some 760,000.

Highlights

- Wild and eccentric exhibits at the American Visionary Art Museum
- The lively Inner Harbor – take a water taxi from sight to sight
- The National Aquarium in Baltimore… if you can afford it
- The popular Fells Point bar scene
- World-class art at the Walters Art Gallery
- Sights, smells, food, and camaraderie at the city's unique neighborhood markets
- Edgar Allan Poe's grave – eerie, especially around Halloween
- For traditionalists, an Orioles game at Camden Yards

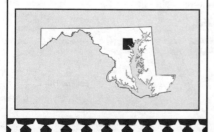

MARYLAND

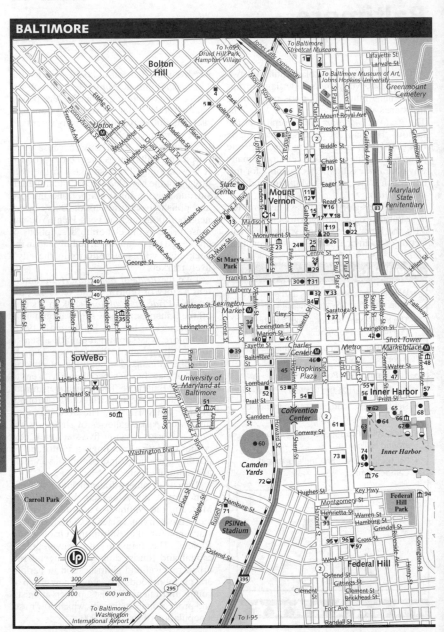

BALTIMORE

BALTIMORE

PLACES TO STAY
4 Betsy's B&B
5 Mr Mole B&B
21 Abbey Hotel
24 Clarion Hotel
29 Mount Vernon Hotel
32 HI Baltimore
52 Holiday Inn
53 Days Inn
56 Renaissance Harborplace Hotel
61 Hyatt Regency Hotel
71 Quality Inn at the Stadiums
73 Harbor Court Hotel
86 Admiral Fell Inn
87 Celie's Waterfront B&B
91 Inn at Henderson Wharf

PLACES TO EAT
9 Brewer's Art
12 Brass Elephant
15 Donna's Coffee Bar
16 Akbar
17 Tony Cheng's
18 Bombay Grill
28 Louie's Book Store Cafe
33 Women's Industrial Exchange & Restaurant
36 Lexington Market
44 Hollins Market
49 Obrycki's
55 Strand Internet Cafe
62 Pratt St Pavilion
63 Light St Pavilion
68 ESPN Zone
69 Amiccis
70 Luigi Petti
79 Dalesio's
81 Broadway Market
82 Ze Mean Bean
83 Nice N' Easy
84 Adrian's Bookstore Cafe
85 Bertha's
88 Daily Grind
93 One World Cafe
94 Joy America Cafe
95 Sisson's South Baltimore Brewing Co
97 Cross St Market

ENTERTAINMENT
1 Club Charles
2 Charles Theatre
6 Lyric Opera House
7 Theater Project
8 Meyerhoff Symphony Hall
10 13th Floor (Belvedere Hotel)
11 Hippo
13 Arena Players
22 Center Stage
34 Mick O'Shea's
40 14 Karat Kabaret
46 Morris A Mechanic Theater
54 Wharf Rat
57 Eubie Blake Cultural Center
59 Orpheus
77 Pier 6 Concert Pavilion
89 Orpheum Cinema
90 Wharf Rat
96 Eight By Ten

OTHER
3 Penn Station (Amtrak, MARC)
14 Maryland General Hospital
19 Mount Vernon Place United Methodist Church
20 Washington Monument
23 Maryland Historical Society
25 Walters Art Gallery, Film House
26 Peabody Conservatory of Music
27 Johns Hopkins Hospital
30 Enoch Pratt Free Library
31 Basilica of the Assumption
35 Edgar Allan Poe House
37 Old St Paul's Episcopal Church
38 Post Office
39 Edgar Allan Poe's Grave, Westminster Cemetery
41 Greyhound Bus Station
42 Baltimore City Hall
43 Jewish Museum of Maryland
45 Baltimore Arena
47 Customs House
48 Port Discovery
50 B&O Railroad Museum
51 Babe Ruth Museum
58 Star-Spangled Banner Flag House & 1812 Museum
60 Oriole Park
64 USF *Constellation* Dock
65 World Trade Center, Top of the World
66 Baltimore Maritime Museum
67 National Aquarium in Baltimore
68 Power Plant
72 Camden Yards Rail Station (Light Rail, MARC)
74 Baltimore Area Visitors Center
75 Carousel
76 Maryland Science Center
78 Baltimore Public Works Museum
80 Baltimore Civil War Museum
92 Bibelot
94 American Visionary Art Museum
98 Baltimore Museum of Industry

MARYLAND

Ensor St
Hoffman St
Preston St
Eden St
Chase St
Eager St
Ensor St
Madison St
Monument St
Johns Hopkins
Broadway
Wolfe St
To Great Blacks in Wax Museum
Orleans St 40
Oldham St
Fayette St
Ann St
Fairmount Ave
Caroline St
Bethel St
Central Ave
Baltimore St
Lombard St
Patterson Park
Pratt St
Little Italy
Gough St
Bank St
Gay St
Aisquith St
Eastern Ave
Fells Point
Fleet St
Aliceanna St
Lancaster St
Market Square
Canton
Boston St
Hudson St
Fell St
Thames St
To Creektown I-695
Water Taxi
Water Taxi
Northwest Harbor
Patapsco River
Key Hwy
Webster St
Boyle St
Key Hwy E
To Fort McHenry National Monument

HISTORY

When the US declared war on Great Britain in 1812, a British admiral proclaimed that 'Baltimore is a doomed town.' The mariner was speaking of his hopes for shutting down America's most prominent seaport and scattering its fleet of armed merchant ships to the wind. The prophecy summarizes Baltimore's recurring predicament throughout its history: Four different times, observers have judged Baltimore doomed, and four times the city has risen, more splendid than before, from its own ruins.

Established as a tobacco and flour-milling center, the settlement took its name in 1729 from George Calvert, Lord Baltimore. The English knight served King Charles I as secretary of state until Calvert's Roman Catholic religious affiliations barred him from center stage in the royal court. Thereafter, Calvert became a 'New World' real estate developer and the first royal grant holder to the lands of Maryland. The current city, only one of three towns named after Lord Baltimore and his sons, prospered early. With a congenial climate most of the year, a fine harbor, and access to first-rate shipbuilding timber, Baltimore developed rapidly as colonial America's shipping and shipbuilding center. Baltimore ships and sailors made up the bulk of the American privateer fleet that disrupted British supply lines, eventually bringing on the British surrender during the American Revolution.

By the end of the Revolution, 45,000 souls lived in Baltimore, and the city's shipyards had begun evolving a new breed of ships – sleek, fast, two-masted schooners with a sharply raked mast – called Baltimore Clippers. But when the British captured scores of merchant vessels from Baltimore, confiscating the ships and cargo as well as enlisting the crews as sailors on British warships and whalers, Baltimore shippers suffered great financial loss, and the city suffered.

The worst of Baltimore's suffering came in 1814, two years after the outbreak of the second war with Britain. After the British burned Washington, DC, they moved to close America's biggest shipping port, and Baltimore reeled under British land and sea attack. Many citizens feared that their city would suffer like Washington, but Maryland troops fought valiantly and repelled the British fleet's dramatic assault on Fort McHenry on September 14. The victory here gave rise to the US national anthem, the lyrics of which recount Baltimore's – and all of America's – escape from the English.

With the end of the British conflict, Baltimore rebounded to become the second-largest city in the USA. For the next three decades, Baltimore prospered as its ships dominated the trade routes to the Caribbean and South America. Meanwhile, Baltimore inventors perfected the steam locomotive, and the Baltimore & Ohio Railroad was built over the Allegheny Mountains, connecting travelers with Pittsburgh, the Ohio River, and the expanding frontier.

Doom struck again with the Civil War. In April 1861, shortly after the Confederate states seceded from the Union, an angry street mob in Baltimore attacked the Sixth Massachusetts Regiment as it marched across the city from one railroad station to another. Four soldiers and 11 citizens died – the first blood letting of the war. Thereafter, President Lincoln imposed military rule over Baltimore. A ring of forts encircled the city with the guns pointed inward. Meanwhile, Baltimoreans divided their loyalties between the Union and the Confederacy, and local men fought and died in great numbers for both opposing armies. Deprived of freewheeling commerce, Baltimore withered even after the end of the Civil War, as government patronage went to seaports that had been clearly loyal to the Union, including Philadelphia, New York, and Boston.

Baltimore eventually bloomed again during the last decades of the 19th century. The railroad brought in massive quantities of grain from the Midwest for milling and shipping; iron and steel factories prospered; the shipbuilding industry flourished; and oyster canning boomed. Then in 1904, a fire broke out in a warehouse and spread before a strong southwest wind. When the conflagration ended, Baltimore's entire business district – 1,500 buildings – lay in ruins. The

MARYLAND

devastation caused $125 million in damage. Less than half of the property was insured.

Undaunted, Baltimore's wealthy refinanced the recovery, and the city bounced back to be the seventh most productive industrial venue in the country. The boom continued until the Great Depression following the stock market crash in 1929. Thereafter, Baltimore struggled in the doldrums of economic stagnation and growing social problems, bred of a densely packed, undereducated, unemployed population. The city's economy recovered during the industrial boom of WWII and the 1950s, but urban decay grew worse.

By the 1960s, citizens fled the city for the suburbs in droves. Crime and sleaze took over; the major downtown tourist attraction became 'The Block,' a neighborhood of striptease palaces, bars, prostitutes, and drug pushers just north of the Inner Harbor. Following the murder of civil rights leader Martin Luther King Jr in 1968, angry mobs burned and looted the city.

For the fourth time in its history, the city began to rise again during the early 1980s. Plans for renewing the Inner Harbor as an urban showcase gained momentum, and the renaissance ensued, making Baltimore's transformation one of the most remarkable success stories in US urban history.

Today, many travelers are drawn to this hard-working, ball-playing, no-nonsense American city for its blockbuster Inner Harbor attractions, comfortable neighborhoods, and ethnic enclaves, all well served by public transit.

ORIENTATION

Rising from the head of the Patapsco River, Baltimore dominates the northern end of Chesapeake Bay. The city lies 100 miles south of Philadelphia and 25 miles north of Washington, DC.

Baltimore's street plan conforms to the cardinal points of the compass. Charles St runs north-south to separate east and west Baltimore. Baltimore St runs east-west, separating north and south Baltimore. Addresses include a compass direction to help with location. For example, N Calvert St is

north of Baltimore St. Except for Eutaw St, most downtown streets are one way.

Immediately north and west of the Inner Harbor is the downtown business district. About half a mile northwest of downtown is the stately Mount Vernon district, home of Baltimore's Washington Monument, the Walters Art Gallery, a centrally located hostel and 'Restaurant Row.' Penn Station, the Amtrak train station, is a mile north of downtown and about half a mile north of Mount Vernon.

Farther north of the downtown business district, the city turns residential surrounding the Johns Hopkins University campus. Southwest Baltimore (SoWeBo) is a rough district west of downtown across Martin Luther King Jr Blvd.

To the east of the Inner Harbor lie Little Italy, Fells Point, and Canton. Immediately south of the Inner Harbor is Federal Hill, where you can get a good view of Baltimore. The top of the Washington Monument and the top of the World Trade Center, on the north side of the Inner Harbor, also offer views.

INFORMATION
Tourist Offices

The Baltimore Area Visitors Center (☎ 410-837-4636, 800-282-6632), 451 Light St, is at the west shore of the Inner Harbor, near the Maryland Science Center. The friendly and knowledgeable staff distribute maps, city guides, and brochures. The center is open 9 am to 5 pm Monday to Saturday, 10 am to 5 pm Sunday, with extended summer evening hours. For information by mail, call the toll-free number to order a city guide.

Money

You will find convenient ATMs at Baltimore-Washington International Airport, Penn Station, and downtown, with several in and around Harborplace (see Inner Harbor, later in the chapter). NationsBank stands at 100 Pratt St (☎ 410-547-4949).

American Express (☎ 410-837-3100, 800-788-3559), 32 South St, operates a currency exchange 8:30 am to 5:30 pm weekdays. For currency exchange at the airport, go to

Travelex America (☎ 410-859-5997), on the upper level at the entrance to Concourse C. It's open 6:30 am to 8:30 pm daily.

Post
The main post office (☎ 410-347-4425), 900 E Fayette St, is where general-delivery mail gets sent. It's open 7:30 am to 9 pm weekdays, to 5 pm Saturday.

Internet Resources
The Baltimore Area Convention and Visitors Association (BACVA) maintains the website www.baltimore.org, with general information and links to hotels, restaurants, and more.

Kinko's (☎ 410-625-5862, fax 410-685-1046), centrally located at 300 N Charles St, provides Internet access and fax services. A more interesting place to check your email is the Strand Internet Cafe (☎ 410-625-8944), 105 E Lombard St, a cybercafe/bar a block from the Inner Harbor.

Bookstores
Bibelot (☎ 410-276-9700), 2400 Boston St, offers the widest selection of books, periodicals, and music in a great location within the historic American Can Company, in the hot new Canton area. (The store hosts an impressive schedule of literary and musical events and contains a Donna's Coffee Bar.) Louie's Book Store Cafe (☎ 410-962-1224), 518 N Charles St, south of the Walters Art Gallery, is a good place to browse for literature, and there's a great neighborhood cafe and bar in back. Adrian's Bookstore Cafe (☎ 410-732-1048), 714 S Broadway in Fells Point, sells many travel titles and periodicals, which you can peruse in the cafe upstairs.

Among specialty bookstores, Lambda Rising (☎ 410-234-0069), 241 W Chase St, sells gay and lesbian books, and Mystery Loves Company (☎ 410-276-6708) is at 1730 Fleet St in Fells Point. There's a Barnes & Noble in the Power Plant (see Inner Harbor, below).

Libraries
The Enoch Pratt Free Library (☎ 410-396-5430), 400 Cathedral St, between Franklin and Mulberry Sts, is the city's main library. It has exhibits on HL Mencken and Edgar Allan Poe.

Media
The daily *Baltimore Sun* aims to cover and depict a broad segment of its market, and with its own foreign correspondents, it has particularly good foreign coverage for a US paper in a city of less than one million.

The *Baltimore Afro-American* covers news of interest to the African American community. The free *Baltimore Alternative* and *Baltimore Gay Paper* serve the gay community. The free weekly tabloid *City Paper* is the source for entertainment listings and more alternative news.

Medical Services
Johns Hopkins Hospital (☎ 410-955-2280) is at 600 N Wolfe St. Maryland General Hospital (☎ 410-225-8100) is at 827 Linden Ave.

Emergency
Travelers Aid (☎ 410-685-3569) operates desks at the airport. Other useful numbers are People Aiding Travelers and the Homeless (☎ 410-685-3569, 685-5874), the Grassroots Crisis Intervention Center (☎ 410-531-6677, 531-6678), the Sexual Assault and Domestic Violence Hotline (☎ 410-828-6390), and the Gay and Lesbian Hotline & Information (☎ 410-837-8888).

INNER HARBOR
The Inner Harbor is the heart of Baltimore. Major tourist attractions here include the waterfront promenade, the aquarium, and several great museums. The Inner Harbor's tourist center is dominated by **Harborplace**, a modern two-story complex on the north shore (restaurants and shops) and west shore (all food), which is near the visitor center and **carousel**. It's very pleasant to stroll around or sit at a patio table and watch the sailing ships, water taxis, and rental paddleboats make their way around the head of the Patapsco River. Many special events are centered at the Inner Harbor plaza throughout the year, and there are often concerts and street performers here.

MARYLAND

The **Power Plant** restoration on Pier 4 holds three more stories of shops and restaurants, including a Barnes & Noble bookstore, a Hard Rock Cafe, and the ESPN Zone restaurant. Pier 6 holds a concert pavilion (see Entertainment, later in the chapter). The following attractions are located clockwise from the northwest corner. The water taxi (see Getting Around, later in the chapter) will take you to all these sights.

USF *Constellation*
Docked at Pier 1, the 176-foot USF *Constellation* (☎ 410-539-1797) is the last surviving ship of the Civil War. Launched in 1854, the sloop-of-war traded fire with pirates, the French, and the British. Some interesting American idioms came from the food served to the non-officers on such ships. For example, 'get the bugs out' comes from the practice of sailors tapping the hardtack (years-old biscuits served at meals) on a ship's deck to dislodge insects. After a $9 million renovation, the ship is open for tours 10 am to 6 pm daily. Tours cost $6 for adults, $3.50 for children six to 15.

Top of the World
You'll see a spectacular view of Baltimore from the 27th floor of the World Trade Center (☎ 410-837-8439), 401 E Pratt St, on the north side of the Inner Harbor. IM Pei designed this building as the world's tallest pentagonal structure. It's open 10 am to 5:30 pm daily, with extended summer hours ($3). Alternatively, you can head to the Belvedere Hotel on N Charles St, where $3 gets you a draft beer as well as a 13-story view (see Entertainment, later in the chapter).

National Aquarium in Baltimore
This modern aquarium (☎ 410-576-3800) is what put Baltimore on the map as a tourist destination when it opened on Pier 3 in 1981. It invites comparison with other phenomenal aquariums in New Orleans, Los Angeles, Chattanooga (Tennessee), and Monterey (California). The structure stretches seven stories high over two piers. Elevators take you to the top in the main building, and then you spiral down from the rainforest habitat

under a towering glass pyramid past circular tanks housing more than 10,000 marine animals, including sharks, rays, venomous aquatic animals, and porpoises. The adjacent Marine Mammal Pavilion features dolphin shows in a 1300-seat amphitheater. There's also a fast-food court.

Admission is $12 for adults, $7.50 for children three to 11. The aquarium is open 10 am to 5 pm daily except Thanksgiving and Christmas, with extended hours in summer. On weekends and in summer, the aquarium can be extremely crowded, and parking and traffic are a challenge all year (your best bet: public ground transit or water taxis). The seal pool outside is free and open to the public.

Baltimore Maritime Museum
This museum (☎ 410-396-3453) on Pier 3 enables visitors to climb aboard three vessels docked next to the aquarium. On exhibit are the *Chesapeake*, a floating lightship; the Coast Guard cutter *Roger B Taney*; and the USS *Torsk*, the last submarine to sink a Japanese ship during WWII. At times, other ships join the exhibit. The museum is open 10 am to 7 pm daily in summer; call for hours the rest of the year. Admission is $5.50 for adults, $4.50 for seniors, $3 for children five to 12.

Baltimore Public Works Museum
On the eastern side of the Inner Harbor, this only-in-Baltimore museum (☎ 410-396-5565), 751 Eastern Ave at President St (enter from the west), explores the practical infrastructure of water, waste disposal, and transportation projects through modest exhibits and a slide show. Outside, underground utilities are displayed above ground. It's open 10 am to 4 pm Wednesday to Sunday. Admission is $2.50 for adults, $1.50 for children.

Baltimore Civil War Museum
In the former 1849 President St train station, this museum (☎ 410-385-5188), 601 President St, tells the story of the 1861 Pratt Street Riot. On April 19, Baltimore secessionists clashed here with Massachusetts volunteers en route to Washington just one week after Fort Sumter, shedding the 'first

blood' of the Civil War. The museum is open 10 am to 5 pm daily. Admission is $2 for adults, $1 for children.

American Visionary Art Museum

Among the most distinctive in the country, this avant-garde museum (☎ 410-244-1900), 800 Key Hwy on the south shore of the Inner Harbor, showcases the raw genius of 'outsider' artists. A small permanent collection of broken-mirror collages, a maniacally embroidered last will, and a 16-foot model of the *Lusitania* made entirely from toothpicks are explained with descriptive captions that attempt to capture each artist's intentions and state of mind. Grand recent exhibits have focused on themes of loss, erotica, and 'Angels & Other Aliens,' and featured works by such provocative self-taught artists as RA Miller, Howard Finster, and Baltimore glass artisan Paul Darmafall. Many works are crafted from scrap wood, tin, thread, and the assorted refuse of an affluent society.

Museum hours are 10 am to 6 pm Tuesday to Sunday. Admission is $6 for adults, $4 for seniors, students, and children. The gift shop has many unusual books, bottle-cap necklaces, goofy toys, and wacky cards. The Joy America Cafe upstairs is a swank place, with a beautiful view of the harbor and innovative, organic fare (see Places to Eat, later in the chapter). Outside, a few sculptures can be seen for free, such as a towering 55-foot whirligig and a twig altar.

Maryland Science Center

This museum (☎ 410-685-5225), 601 Light St, has three floors of colorful interactive attractions designed to entertain children, including a Hubble telescope and exhibits on weather, magnetism, and optics. An IMAX theater shows films on a five-story-high screen.

The center is open 10 am to 5 pm weekdays, to 6 pm weekends. Admission is $9 for adults, $7 for students; films cost extra. Movies are shown in the evening, after the museum galleries are closed.

DOWNTOWN

The financial district is directly north of the Inner Harbor. To either side of this district, from Camden Yards to the west and the I-83 corridor to the east, more attractions can be found within a few blocks of the Inner Harbor. And downtown's Lexington Market is a sight to see (see Places to Eat, later in the chapter). The East/West Trolley runs along Pratt St and Lombard St through downtown and farther west to the railroad museum (see Southwest Baltimore, later in the chapter).

Camden Yards

West of the Inner Harbor, this impressive brick structure occupies an entire city block and houses the Orioles baseball park (see Spectator Sports, later in the chapter). It also serves as a rail terminus for MARC and local light rail trains that run to/from the airport (see Getting There & Away and Getting Around, later in the chapter).

Babe Ruth Museum

Painted baseballs on the sidewalk lead from Camden Yards two blocks northwest to the birthplace of baseball legend Babe Ruth. The museum (☎ 410-727-1539), 216 Emory St off Pratt St, eight blocks west of the Inner Harbor, celebrates the 'Sultan of Swat' with walls full of Ruthian photographs, period-decorated rooms, autographed balls, and an adoring description of each of Babe's 714 home runs.

The museum is open 10 am to 4 pm daily, to 5 pm April to October, with extended evening hours to coincide with Orioles home games. Admission is $6 for adults, $3 for children five to 16, or half-price with your Orioles ticket stub.

Edgar Allan Poe's Grave

The author lies in Westminster Cemetery (☎ 410-706-2072), at the corner of W Fayette and N Greene Sts. If you enter at the gate near the corner, his grave is under a 6-foot-tall white obelisk 5 feet in front of you. An admirer decorates Poe's grave with roses and a bottle of cognac every year on Poe's January 19 birthday. The churchyard is four blocks north and eight blocks west of the Inner Harbor. Street signs lead drivers from here to Poe's house (see Southwest Baltimore, later in the chapter).

Port Discovery

This huge children's museum (☎ 410-727-8120), at President and Baltimore Sts, has turned 80,000 sq feet of the city's old fish market into several inviting habitats: a play house, laboratory, TV studio, and Pharaoh's tomb. When you get tired of reading, there are things to crawl through and climb on. You can easily walk the 2½ blocks here from the Inner Harbor. The museum is open 10 am to 5:30 pm daily. Admission is $10 for adults, $7.50 for children three to 12.

Star-Spangled Banner Flag House & 1812 Museum

In this 1793 house (☎ 410-837-1793), 844 E Pratt St at Albemarle St, Mary Pickersgill sewed the 30 by-42-foot flag (with 15 stars and stripes) that inspired Francis Scott Key to write the poem 'Star-Spangled Banner.' The flag was the last flag with an equal number of stars and stripes (one each for each state). The two extra stars and stripes beyond the original 13 were for Vermont and Kentucky. After this flag was made, all future

Edgar Allan Poe: Prince of Darkness

Poet and scholar Allen Tate put his finger on the enduring appeal of the literature and myth of Edgar Allan Poe when he said the author is like everyone's distressing American cousin who acts out the deepest arrogant, childish, and violent longings hidden in ourselves. In poems such as 'The Raven' and 'The Bells,' and stories such as 'The Fall of the House of Usher' and 'The Pit and the Pendulum,' Edgar Allan Poe (1809–49) gave full voice to the horror that can lurk in the human subconscious.

While a great deal of myth surrounds Poe's life, the truth of his 40 years on earth is quite disturbing enough to have spawned his horrifying literature and self-destruction. Poe was born in 1809 in Boston to a pair of touring actors. After his parents died when he was a toddler, Poe spent most of his childhood in the home of Frances and John Allan, a merchant in Richmond, Virginia. During his youth, Poe studied in England and Scotland for five years and bounced around private schools. He attended the University of Virginia for a year, but in 1827 John Allan pulled him out of college after discovering Poe was gambling and drinking uncontrollably. During the next four years, Poe moved to Boston, published poetry, and served a stint in the US Army. He gained appointment to the Military Academy at West Point but soon found himself dismissed for neglect of duty.

In 1831, Poe settled in Baltimore with his aunt and her 11-year-old daughter, Virginia Clemm. Poe began to fall in love with the girl, which inspired a burst of literary energy, and he turned his attention to writing short stories. While living in Baltimore, his 'MS Found in a Bottle' won him a fiction contest in 1832. When Virginia was 13, Poe married her and moved to Richmond, Virginia. He spent the next decade tending to Virginia's recurrent illnesses (probably tuberculosis). He also perfected the form that would define the modern American short story and drank himself silly. After Virginia died in 1847, Poe's spirit grew even more tortured and haunted (see the autobiographical poem 'Ulalume'). While passing through Baltimore in 1849, Poe got quite drunk and disappeared for days. Someone found him incoherent, and he died soon thereafter of various causes. In 1875, Poe's remains were moved from a pauper's grave to the catacombs of Westminster Cemetery.

Francis Scott Key & the 'Star-Spangled Banner'

Francis Scott Key (1779–1843), a lawyer who dabbled in poetry, had the serendipity to be at the right place during the War of 1812 to receive inspiration for the 'Star-Spangled Banner.'

It was September 1814, toward the end of the War of 1812. After burning Washington, DC, to pay back the Americans for burning York, Canada, the British sailed up Chesapeake Bay to attack Baltimore. On the way north, they captured an American physician named William Beanes. Beanes' friends asked Francis Scott Key, then a lawyer with a profitable Georgetown practice, to intercede with the British and get Beanes released.

Key was allowed aboard a British warship that was preparing to attack Baltimore. The British agreed to release Beanes but had to keep Key aboard until they had completed their attack. Through the night of September 13–14, the warship bombarded Fort McHenry. Above the fort flew the 30-by-42-foot flag sewn by Mary Pickersgill in Baltimore.

'By dawn's early light,' the flag was still flying and the attack on Baltimore had failed. Key was inspired to pen on the back of an envelope the poem that would later become the national anthem. It was soon reprinted and widely distributed as a handbill with the title *Defense of M'Henry*. Within a short time it had been set to music – oddly enough to the tune of the *British* drinking song 'To Anacreon in Heaven.' In 1931, the US Congress declared the notoriously difficult-to-sing, British-drinking-song poem the national anthem of the USA.

flags reverted back to a fixed 13 stripes and a variable number of stars (one for each state).

The house has period pieces, early American art, and an exhibit on the War of 1812. It's open 10 am to 4 pm Tuesday to Saturday; admission is $2. Free parking is available.

Jewish Museum of Maryland

This museum (☎ 410-732-6400), 15 Lloyd St between Baltimore and Lombard Sts (in a marginal neighborhood), opens to the public three historic buildings: the 1845 Lloyd St Synagogue, the 1876 B'nai Israel Synagogue, and the Jewish Historical Society of Maryland headquarters, which houses a collection of photos and artifacts on local Jewish history along with a family exhibit designed for children. Guided tours are offered noon to 4 pm Sunday and Tuesday to Thursday. Admission is $4 for adults, $2 for children.

Other Historic Buildings

The Victorian **Baltimore City Hall** (☎ 410-396-4900), 100 N Holiday St at Fayette St, was completed in 1875. It's made of local marble and has an iron dome and mansard

roof. It's open 8 am to 4:30 pm weekdays only; admission is free.

Inside the **Customs House** (☎ 410-962-2666), 40 Gay St at Lombard St, is the Call Room, where ship captains declared their cargo. Francis Davis Millet painted a mural of the evolution of sea vessels on the ceiling. After his assassination, Abraham Lincoln's body lay in state in the former building on this site, the Merchants Exchange. It's open weekdays at no charge.

Old St Paul's Episcopal Church dates back to 1692. The present sanctuary opened in 1856 at N Charles and Saratoga Sts. It has stained-glass windows by Louis Tiffany and a fabulous pipe organ. Daily services are offered.

MOUNT VERNON

A half-mile northwest of the Inner Harbor, the Mount Vernon district is centered around the Washington Monument in the center of stately Mount Vernon Square. An upscale residential neighborhood with many beautiful homes surround the cruciform park, and the Walters Art Gallery, Baltimore's best art museum, is a block south. So-called Restaurant Row is the stretch of

N Charles St a block south and a block north of the monument. The young brooding folk dressed in black are probably students at the Peabody Conservatory, southeast of the monument.

Bus Nos 3 and 31 run north on Charles St and south on Cathedral St through Mount Vernon, but it's a delightful area to walk around.

Washington Monument

Robert Mills, who later designed the Washington, DC, monument of the same name, designed this monument at Charles and Monument Sts. It's a tall obelisk with a 16-foot George Washington statue on top, right in the middle of Mount Vernon Square, which divides N Charles St in half for two blocks. Climb 228 steps to the top of the obelisk for a city view (Wednesday to Sunday).

Walters Art Gallery

This excellent, must-see gallery (☎ 410-547-9000), 600 N Charles St, houses in three adjacent buildings the private collection that Henry Walters bequeathed to the city. The collection includes ancient, medieval, Islamic, Renaissance, Asian, and contemporary art – essentially a sampling of pieces from 5000 BC to the present. The original 1904 gallery looks like an Italian palazzo, complete with a central courtyard; the three-story mansion houses an Asian art collection. Such traveling blockbuster exhibits as the recent Monet collection are housed in the modern annex. There's also a great atrium cafe here.

The gallery is open 10 am to 4 pm Tuesday to Friday, 11 am to 5 pm weekends. (On the first Thursday of the month, it's also open 5 to 8 pm, and admission is free.) Admission is $5 for adults, $3 for seniors and students 18 to 25, $1 for children six to 17, free 11 am to 1 pm on Saturday.

Peabody Conservatory of Music

The conservatory is at the southeast corner of N Charles St and Mount Vernon Place, across the street from the Walters Art Gallery. It's the oldest classical music school in the USA and is now part of Johns Hopkins University.

Famous graduates include pianist Leon Fleisher, composer Dominick Argento, and opera singer Gordon Hawkins. Don't skip going inside the 1878 library (☎ 410-659-8179), with marble floors and a 60-foot atrium, which is surrounded by marble columns and five tiers of balconies holding the books. It's open regular business hours, or you can call ☎ 410-659-8124 for a schedule of free or inexpensive student recitals.

Mount Vernon Place United Methodist Church

This neo-Gothic church (☎ 410-685-5290), 10 E Mount Vernon Place, dates from 1872. Its facade, though a bit sooty, includes a lot of green serpentine stone. In 1843, Francis Scott Key died in a house where the current Asbury House now stands, to the east of the church. To enter the church, ring the Asbury House bell.

Basilica of the National Shrine of the Assumption of the Blessed Virgin Mary

Benjamin Henry LaTrobe, architect of the nation's Capitol in Washington, DC, designed this dramatic basilica (☎ 410-727-3564), 408 N Charles St, at the corner of Cathedral and Mulberry Sts. It was the first Roman Catholic church in the US to mix Greek revival with Eastern elements and was visited by Mother Theresa and Pope John Paul II. Tours begin Sunday at noon, after the 10:45 am Mass. (The 9 am Mass is offered in Latin.)

Maryland Historical Society

This museum (☎ 410-685-3750), 201 W Monument St at Park Ave, serves as a good introduction to state history, with nicely presented exhibits, many designed for children. Artifacts include a Mason-Dixon mile marker, the original manuscript of the 'Star-Spangled Banner,' and 19th-century period rooms. The gift shop sells some antiques among a small but nice selection of gifts and souvenirs.

The museum is open 10 am to 5 pm Tuesday to Friday, 9 am to 5 pm Saturday, 1 to 5 pm Sunday. Admission is $4 for adults, $3 for students, free for children under 12, free for everyone Saturday morning.

NORTH BALTIMORE

The city grows more residential north of North Ave. Here you will find the Baltimore Museum of Art, the Baltimore Zoo, and Johns Hopkins University. Bus Nos 3, 9, and 11 run to north Baltimore from the Inner Harbor.

Baltimore Museum of Art

This modern art museum (☎ 410-396-7100/7101), at N Charles and 31st Sts, adjacent to the Johns Hopkins campus, houses Maryland's largest collection of art, including paintings and sculpture by Matisse, Picasso, Renoir, Cézanne, van Gogh and Gauguin, along with a wide range of other works from the old masters to Andy Warhol to ancient African masks. (Kids will like following the floor-plan map to find the museum's most coveted treasures.) An elegant branch of Donna's Coffee Bar overlooks the outdoor sculpture garden, and the gift shop has a nice selection of handcrafted objects and even Baltimore kitsch.

The museum is open 11 am to 5 pm Wednesday to Friday, to 6 pm on weekends. Admission is $6 for adults, $4 for seniors, free for anyone under 19.

Johns Hopkins University

One of the most prestigious schools in the nation, Johns Hopkins University enrolls 4600 students at its central campus on N Charles St, about 3 miles north of the Inner Harbor. Founded by a Baltimore financier, Hopkins is known worldwide for its contributions to medicine, international relations, and publishing. The Office of Admissions (☎ 410-516-8171), in Garland Hall, gives free tours on weekdays.

The school opens up two period-furnished historic houses on campus for public tours. The stately Federal-style Homewood (☎ 410-516-5589), 3400 N Charles St, was the home of Charles Carroll Jr, whose father was a signer of the Declaration of Independence. The university campus consists largely of land that was once part of Carroll's estate. Tours are offered 11 am to 4 pm Tuesday to Saturday, noon to 4 pm Sunday. Admission is $6, free for children under 12.

North of the main campus on N Charles St, Evergreen House (☎ 410-516-0895) is on 26 acres, which include the mansion, theater, and gardens of John Work Garett, ambassador to Italy from 1929 to 1933. It's open 10 am to 4 pm weekdays, 1 to 4 pm weekends. Admission is $5 for adults, $3 for students.

Marylanders are fanatic lacrosse players and fans, and they have built a museum honoring the game they adopted from the Native Americans. The Lacrosse Museum and National Hall of Fame (☎ 410-235-6882), 113 W University Pkwy next to the lacrosse field, has exhibits on the evolution of the stick and helmet as well as photos of players. It's open 10 am to 3 pm weekdays year-round. Admission is $3 for adults, $2 for children.

Druid Hill Park

This 674-acre park (☎ 410-396-6106) is one of the country's largest city parks. Inside it is the Baltimore City Conservatory, which is often called the 'Palm House' or the 'Palm Tree Conservancy' because of its tropical plant collection. The conservatory structure is a Victorian domed greenhouse.

The Baltimore Zoo (☎ 410-366-5466), in the middle of the park, is home to 1200 animals. The 6-acre African Watering Hole is inhabited by rhinos, zebras, and gazelles. Here, you will also find perhaps the most innovative children's zoo in the country: Kids can walk through caves, view animals, and pretend they are the animals they see. The zoo is open 10 am to 4 pm weekdays, to 8 pm Saturday, to 5:30 pm Sunday. Admission is $9 for adults, $5.50 for children.

To get to Druid Hill Park, take I-83 exit 7A to Druid Park Lake Dr and follow the signs. The city bus system runs zoo shuttles from the Inner Harbor on weekends.

Great Blacks in Wax Museum

This museum (☎ 410-563-3404), 1601 E North Ave at Broadway, relates the state's distinguished African American history through displays of wax figures of such Maryland natives as Frederick Douglass, Harriet Tubman, and Billie Holiday. It's open 9 am to 5 or 6 pm Tuesday to Saturday (also open most Monday holidays and during Black History Month in February). Admission is $5.75 for adults, $3 to $5.25 for students.

The spectacular hues of western Maryland's fall foliage

Street scene at Baltimore's Inner Harbor (MD)

Naval Academy midshipmen sailing, Annapolis (MD)

Naval officers, Annapolis (MD)

Brandywine Park (DE)

Nemours Mansion & Gardens, in northern Delaware

Market in northern Delaware revealing a bountiful fall harvest

Beachfront houses in Dewey Beach (DE)

Baltimore Streetcar Museum

At this museum (☎ 410-547-0264), 1901 Falls Rd near North Ave, you can view historic displays, tour the streetcar barn, and take unlimited rides aboard vintage Baltimore streetcars built from the 1890s to the 1940s. It's open noon to 5 pm Sunday year-round, as well as noon to 5 pm Saturday from June to October. Admission is $5 for adults, $3 for seniors and children. The museum is under the North Ave Bridge. Go north on Charles St to Lafayette Ave; turn left on Lafayette; drive two blocks and turn right on Jones Falls Rd.

SOUTHWEST BALTIMORE (SOWEBO)

'SoWeBo,' as locals call this area, is a marginal district west of Martin Luther King Jr Blvd, centered around its neighborhood hub at **Hollins Market**. While a small community

of artists has been drawn to the area's low rents, SoWeBo remains a predominantly poor neighborhood that can be dangerous at night. The East/West Trolley runs nearby, along Pratt St and Lombard St from the Inner Harbor to the railroad museum.

B&O Railroad Museum

B&O was the first railroad to sell tickets for passengers in 1823. This museum (☎ 410-752-2490), 901 W Pratt St, is amazing – truly one of the best sights in Baltimore even if you don't like trains. You can see a huge collection of locomotives and passenger cars exhibited in the restored roundhouse, with a 123-foot, cathedral-like ceiling soaring up. You can climb into some of these trains outside in the train yards.

It's open 10 am to 5 pm daily. Admission is $6.50 for adults, $4 for children five to 12.

Billie Holiday: Baltimore's 'Lady Day'

Born Eleanora Fagan in 1915, the singer suffered a poverty-stricken youth in Baltimore's ghetto. But by the late 1920s, she escaped the misery of her early life and began singing professionally in Harlem clubs. Holiday began recording in the 1930s and eventually became a diva, singing with major orchestras led by figures such as Artie Shaw, Count Basie, pianist Teddy Wilson, and sax man Lester Young.

Holiday's career soared during the '40s and '50s with hits such as 'Lover Man,' 'I'll Look Around,' 'Easy Livin',' and 'God Bless the Child.' But her longtime addiction to heroin undercut later performances, and she died in a New York hospital in 1959 while she was under arrest for drug possession.

Her 1956 autobiography and the 1972 film *Lady Sings the Blues* recount the rise and fall of 'Lady Day,' America's best-known blues vocalist.

If you want to listen to Billie on compact disc, pick up *Billie Holiday: Complete Decca Recordings 1944–1950* on MHS Jazz Heritage or *Smithsonian Collection of Classical Jazz – Volume II*.

An excursion train runs weekend rides for an extra charge; call for the current schedule.

Edgar Allan Poe House

In the midst of the southwest Baltimore housing projects, a tiny three-story house built in 1830 on a near-abandoned block is identified by a small plaque as the 1832 home of Edgar Allan Poe (☎ 410-396-7932), 203 Amity St. Poe moved into this house at age 23 and wrote *MS Found in a Bottle* here, in an evocative attic garret up a steep narrow staircase. Furnishings are scarce, but curator Jeff Jerome brings Poe's history to life.

The house is generally open noon to 3:45 pm Wednesday to Saturday in spring and fall; in summer, it's open Saturday only (and may close early from the heat); it's closed from January to March (call to confirm hours). Admission is $3 for adults, $1 for children 12 and under. Inquire about special events around Poe's January 19 birthday and on Halloween. See Downtown, earlier, for information on Poe's grave.

FEDERAL HILL & SOUTH BALTIMORE

The tidy and comfortable middle-class Federal Hill neighborhood draws its name from **Federal Hill Park**, at Battery St and Key Hwy, overlooking the harbor and city. Yet the local **Cross St Market** is the real heart of the neighborhood (see Places to Eat, later in the chapter). It's a half-mile walk over the hill from the water taxi stop for the American Visionary Art Museum.

Baltimore Museum of Industry

In south Baltimore, this old oyster cannery (☎ 410-727-4808), 1415 Key Hwy, contains hands-on exhibits for children, such as an assembly line and 19th-century industrial machines (call to confirm operating schedule). Other exhibits include a garment-making loft, print shop, and tugboat, all from the 19th century.

The museum is open noon to 5 pm Tuesday to Sunday, Memorial Day to Labor Day, with extended hours Saturday morning and Wednesday evening. Admission is $5 for adults, $3.50 for seniors and students, free

for children six and under. The water taxi stops here in summer.

Fort McHenry National Monument

This monument (☎ 410-962-4290) is at the end of E Fort Ave at the eastern end of the peninsula, south of Federal Hill. During the War of 1812, the star-shaped fort protected Baltimore harbor against British attack. British warships shelled the fort on September 13–14, 1814, but failed to dislodge its defenders. Visitors can see a short film and walk around the walls of the fort and inside to see soldiers' quarters, a powder magazine, and bomb shelters. The fort is open 8 am to 7:45 pm daily. Admission is $5 for adults, free for children 16 and under. The water taxi stops here in summer.

FELLS POINT

Fells Point is the waterfront community a mile east of the Inner Harbor, centered along Broadway from Pratt St to the water. Fells Point is one of the oldest maritime communities in the USA. The Fells brothers, from Lancaster, England, settled here in the 1700s, hence the streets named Thames, Shakespeare, Fleet, etc. This neighborhood has been home to the various ethnic communities that worked in the maritime trades. Along the cobblestone streets, you can see the rising tide of gentrification and its accompanying antique shops, vintage-clothing stores, record stores, restaurants, cafes, clubs, and bars.

Most people come here to escape the suburbs, stroll, drink (there are scores of bars) and shop. **Market Square** is a brick plaza at the end of Broadway, where it intersects Thames St at the waterfront. There are often street festivals in the square and always a host of people-watchers. Water taxis deliver passengers to this central square from stops around the Inner Harbor until midnight on summer weekends. (See Getting Around, later in the chapter.)

ORGANIZED TOURS

Harbor City Tours (☎ 410-254-8687) offers daily sightseeing excursions aboard a 20-passenger bus ('women-owned and operated'). African American Renaissance Tours

(☎ 410-728-3837) relates the city's African American heritage by touring such sights as the NAACP national headquarters, at 4805 Mt Hope Dr, and the Billie Holiday statue on Pennsylvania Ave at Lafayette. Among the more offbeat tours, Zippy Larson's Shoe Leather Safaris (☎ 410-817-4141) offers city tours starting at $45 per person (inquire about Wallis Warfield Simpson's connection to the city).

For sailing tours, the *Nighthawk* (☎ 410-327-7245) departs from Fells Point for an evening sail that includes a buffet; tours cost $32.50 per person by advance reservation. (Also inquire about Sunday brunch and murder mystery sails.) Or, try *Clipper City* (☎ 410-539-6277), which leaves from the southwest corner of the Inner Harbor near the Maryland Science Center. For a historical and educational adventure, the Living Classroom Foundation (☎ 410-685-0295) carries passengers on the oyster skipjack *Minnie V*; call ☎ 410-207 6862 for reservations.

SPECIAL EVENTS
Baltimore hosts plenty of events, primarily in its peak summer season. Here's a sampling. The Baltimore Area Convention and Visitors Association keeps track of upcoming events; call ☎ 800-282-6632 to find out more information or to order an events calendar.

April
Billie Holiday Vocal Competition (☎ 410-396-4574) In this mid-April event, contestants vie to inherit the mantle of the late great jazz singer and Baltimore native.

Baltimore Waterfront Festival Music and performances come to the Inner Harbor in late April and early May. (A recent highlight was a kinetic sculpture race.)

May
Center Plaza Concert Series From May to July, the downtown plaza hosts jazz, blues, salsa, and reggae concerts.

Friday Nite Alive Concert Series & Summer Sunday Concert Series Between late May and September, big band, swing, jazz, and other bands perform free concerts at the Pier 6 Concert Pavilion (see Entertainment, later in the chapter). Festivities get under way on Friday nights at 5:30 pm.

July
Hog Calling Contest Fells Point's Market Square (☎ 410-675-6750) hosts this contest, which is just what it sounds like.

Chesapeake Turtle Derby Patterson Park (☎ 410-396-9392), a huge park north of Fells Point, hosts this event – a series of turtle heats named after prominent Baltimoreans.

Artscape (☎ 410-396-4575) This annual celebration of local theater, music, arts, and food takes place in the neighborhood of Mount Royal, north of town.

August
Showcase of Nations Each ethnic group is showcased on different days in this celebration of multicultural Baltimore, held from August to September.

September
Defender's Day Celebration (☎ 410-962-4290) Held on the second Sunday in September at Fort McHenry, this event commemorates the anniversary of the War of 1812's Battle of Baltimore with living-history programs, military drills, and fireworks.

October
Blessing of Baltimore's Work Boats Baltimore's working boats parade through the harbor to be blessed.

PLACES TO STAY
Visitors will need to look beyond downtown for decent lodging under $65 a night. The best bet for budget travelers is to stay at one of the many chain motels that surround the city at interstate exits. The free visitor guide 'Quickguide Baltimore,' available from the visitor center (see Information, earlier), contains discount lodging coupons.

Hostels
The *HI Baltimore* (☎ 410-576-8880, 17 W Mulberry St) is centrally located in an old townhouse between Mount Vernon and downtown, four blocks from the Greyhound station. Run by Hostelling International, it's a large, casual and friendly place featuring a sitting room with a piano, TV, and games. There's a big kitchen as well as laundry facilities. Four dormitory rooms separated by gender contain 80 bunk beds

The hostel underwent extensive repairs in 1999 and was due to reopen in the summer of 2000. Prices are estimated to be $20 a night per person upon reopening. (Call HI headquarters in DC at ☎ 202-737-2333 for updates.)

Guesthouses

For B&B style, *Betsy's* (☎ *410-383-1274, 1428 Park Ave)* has five rooms (starting at $65/85 single/double, including breakfast) in a four-story historic house in the Bolton Hill neighborhood. A higher-end B&B nearby, *Mr Mole B&B* (☎ *410-728-1179, 1601 Bolton St)* offers rooms in a renovated 1870s townhouse for $105 single or double, with a continental-plus breakfast.

You have three good choices in Fells Point if you can spend more than $130 on a room. A half-block from the water taxi stop, *Celie's Waterfront B&B* (☎ *410-522-2323, 800-432-0184, fax 410-522-2324, 1714 Thames St)* offers seven spacious rooms with modern amenities in a townhouse that has been converted to an inn. Despite its name, it's more of a small hotel than a B&B, and it is not exactly *on* the waterfront but faces pier buildings (no complaint – the rooftop view resembles Paris). Some rooms have fireplaces and whirlpool tubs. Rates start at $136 for nice garden-view rooms (two-night minimum on weekends for all rooms), including an ample continental breakfast.

Facing Market Square, the historical *Admiral Fell Inn* (☎ *410-522-7377, 800-292-4667, 888 S Broadway)*, at Thames St, was once a sailors' hotel. Today, the lovely brick hotel offers three floors of guest rooms with Federal-style furniture, four-poster beds, large baths, and some good views. There's also a fine restaurant. Room rates range from $165 to $199, including a continental breakfast.

Also in Fells Points, on the water but a block away from all the action (a better choice for light sleepers), the *Inn at Henderson Wharf* (☎ *410-522-7777, 1000 Fell St)* offers guest rooms in a thoroughly modern hotel carved out of an 1890s tobacco warehouse. Rooms full of brass and brick and nautical prints range from $139 for accommodations overlooking the cobblestone lane to $169 for a harbor view.

Hotels & Motels

The *Abbey Hotel* (☎ *410-332-0405, 723 St Paul St)*, one block east of the Washington Monument in Mount Vernon, gets overflow from the hostel. Despite its good location, it's a flophouse no one could truly recommend even for those on a strict budget. You can rent dilapidated rooms with marginal private baths or filthy common baths by the hour, day, and week, starting at $48/27.50 bath/no bath per night.

A safer bet is an interstate chain motel, such as the modern 36-room *Super 8* (☎ *410-796-0400)*, off I-95 exit 41A in Jessup, about 15 minutes south of the Inner Harbor and 9 miles north of the airport. There's another 75-room *Super 8* (3600 Pulaski Hwy) near I-95 a few miles from the Inner Harbor. Rates at both are around $55 for a single.

The *Quality Inn at the Stadiums* (☎ *410-727-3400, 800-221-2222, 1701 Russell St)*, on a busy thoroughfare several blocks east of the harbor, has standard motel rooms in an older building from $69/74, with a seasonal pool.

The 191-room *Mount Vernon Hotel* (☎ *410-727-2000, 800-245-5256, 24 W Franklin St)* has nine floors of nice, utilitarian rooms in a central location; rates start at $89. Like many more expensive hotels, it offers complimentary shuttle service to the Inner Harbor. The hotel is run by Baltimore International College's business school; the cafe within is run by its culinary school.

The 104-room *Clarion Hotel* (☎ *410-727-7101, 800-292-5500, 612 Cathedral St)*, close to the Washington Monument, is an attractive old property that makes for a classy stay away from the bustle of the Inner Harbor tourist scene. Urbanely outfitted rooms include some nice historic touches, such as towel warmers and high-rise windows that actually open. Standard room rates start at $109, including continental breakfast and access to a health club with a pool; parking is an extra $14. Inquire about special promotional rates as low as $69 double.

Among the cheapest convention-oriented hotels at the Inner Harbor, the 250-room *Days Inn* (☎ *410-576-1000, 800-942-7543, 100 Hopkins Place)* occupies a modern brick building (relatively attractive and subdued for a motel chain), where a standard two-bed room with TV runs around $139; add $9.50 for parking. There's also a seasonal pool. The **Holiday Inn** (☎ 410-685-3500, 301 W Lombard St), a couple blocks west in an older building, has similar rates.

The most expensive hotels in Baltimore ring the Inner Harbor. In all cases, the harbor view is far superior to the city view, so if you can spend more than $200 for a room, get a view. The eight-story **Harbor Court Hotel** (☎ 410-234-0550, 800-824-0076, 550 Light St), overlooking the western side of the harbor, is the city's premier hotel, with excellent views, interiors furnished in marble and lush fabrics, fine dining, and refined service. Your next best bets are the 14-story **Hyatt Regency Hotel** (☎ 410-528-1234, 300 Light St), a few hundred yards north of the Harbor Court, and the 12-story **Renaissance Harborplace Hotel** (☎ 410-547-1200, 202 E Pratt St).

PLACES TO EAT

Baltimore's city markets lead the way in cheap, quick eats. The markets sell a good variety of fresh produce and meat but also have take-out and counter-seating restaurants that serve everything from seafood to Chinese, and most are open until at least 5 pm. Because the markets cover the realm of inexpensive meals so well, the city's restaurants tend to be more formal and expensive than you might think, particularly for ethnic cuisine.

Inner Harbor

At Harborplace, the **Light St Pavilion** is your best bet for a variety of bargain food. A modern, light, and airy two-story food court has tables inside and out on the patio overlooking the harbor. You can eat barbecue, raw-bar seafood, pizza, cheese steak, frozen yogurt, burgers, Mexican, Greek, Chinese, Cajun, Thai, and more; some stands are branches of some of the city's favorite restaurants. There are also gourmet shops selling the likes of imported brie with baguettes and wine.

Both the Light St Pavilion and the **Pratt St Pavilion** hold traditional sit-down restaurants: Phillips Seafood Buffet, Capital City Brewing Company, and California Pizza Kitchen are among the most popular. You'll also find a Donna's Coffee Bar (open early mornings for coffee and treats), Ben & Jerry's ice cream, and Godiva chocolates. Harborplace is open daily, and you will find directories at every entrance.

The Power Plant complex on Pier 5 holds more restaurants, most notably the 35,000-sq-foot **ESPN Zone**, a mega-sports bar with a dozen TV screens and grilled American food.

Joy America Cafe (☎ 410-244-6500, 800 Key Hwy) is to food what the American Visionary Art Museum is to art – radical. On the 3rd floor of the museum, with a harbor view, this fancy restaurant offers an eclectic fusion of Southwestern and Pacific Rim cuisines, all prepared with ultra-organic ingredients. Chefs 'feed the soul' with the likes of achiote-seared ahi tuna with shiitake slaw and wasabi aioli topped with red sesame sauce ($24); they also offer vegetarian entrees. The restaurant serves lunch and dinner Tuesday to Saturday and brunch on Sunday.

Downtown

The **Lexington Market** (☎ 410-685-6169, 400 W Lexington St), at Eutaw St, occupies two square blocks on the same site a city market has stood since 1782. The original food court, Lexington, has more than 140 merchants hawking everything from hog maw and homemade kielbasa to Korean barbecue, Greek salads and jerk chicken. Within, **Faidley's** (☎ 410-727-4898), at the N Paca St entrance, is an institution in itself. Its claim to have the best crab cakes in Baltimore is hard to beat (from $4.50 for a regular serving to $12 for 'all lump' a la carte; platters extra). You can pick fresh fish and have Faidley's cook it, or get crab cakes packaged to go. There's a large happy-hour crowd here on Friday until about 8 pm. With no place to sit, it's an instant party. The market is open 8:30 am to 6 pm Monday to Saturday. Sometimes live bands perform inside; one high school jazz band had people dancing in the aisles.

The **Women's Industrial Exchange & Restaurant** (☎ 410-685-4388, 333 N Charles St) has been in business since 1882 to enable women to earn a livelihood for their handicrafts. You enter through the gift shop, which sells afghans, quilts, knit caps, and many lacy doilies. Out back, there's an anachronistic pale-blue-and-white dining room with a black-and-white linoleum floor. The waitresses are original vintage too, many well over age 60. The menu offers specialties from a bygone era, such as chicken aspic and salmon croquettes. The restaurant also sells more standard sandwich platters for $5, as well as good pie. It's open for breakfast from 7 am and lunch to 3 pm weekdays only.

Across the street, Mick O'Shea's (see Entertainment, later in the chapter) is an Irish pub serving hearty stew and corned beef and cabbage at the bar or at tables in the back. The Strand Internet Cafe (see Internet Resources, earlier in the chapter) is a sleek cafe and bar a block away from the Inner Harbor.

Mount Vernon

Restaurants line Charles St in the Mount Vernon area. Budget diners with big appetites should watch for popular all-you-can-eat buffet lunches on weekdays, usually priced very reasonably for the selection.

Louie's Book Store Cafe (☎ 410-962-1224, 518 N Charles St), south of the Walters Art Gallery, is a Baltimore institution. The atmosphere is relaxing and quiet enough for you to read in peace, and browsers can buy food and drinks (including alcohol) at the back of the bookstore. The bistro-style food is good and fresh; sandwiches start at $6.

The knot of restaurants north of the Washington Monument is considered Restaurant Row. Anchoring the row, the *Brass Elephant* (☎ 410-547-8480, 924 N Charles St) elicits rave reviews for its modern American cuisine, from grilled tuna sandwiches at lunch to $20 pasta plates at dinner (it's cheaper to eat at the bar). The 1860s townhouse in which it's located is decorated with brass fixtures, a fireplace, and chandeliers. It draws an affluent young professional crowd.

Across the street is *Akbar* (☎ 410-539-0944, 823 N Charles St), which offers good Indian specials and attentive service in a

quiet setting tucked below street level (lunch buffet $8). Around the corner, the *Bombay Grill* (☎ 410-837-2973, 2 E Madison) also serves Indian cuisine (some prefer it to Akbar's) for around the same prices.

Tony Cheng's (☎ 410-539-6666, 801 N Charles St) serves spicy Szechuan cuisine (entrees start at $9). The *Donna's Coffee Bar* across the street opens early and closes late.

Brewer's Art (☎ 410-547-6925, 1106 N Charles St), between Chase and Biddle Sts, threatens to unseat the Brass Elephant as the reigning restaurant on N Charles. Spacious dining rooms behind an inviting bar ($1.50 draft beer during happy hour) retain vintage architectural details and are lined with expressive contemporary art. The menu is an equally appealing mix of styles, with such wordy, bordering-on-pretentious entrees as 'freshly made smoked salmon' and 'ricotta ravioli with a beet and roasted garlic cream sauce and wilted spinach' ($13.50 for dinner). Fortunately, the environment is casual enough for families, dates, or single people to feel comfortable. A younger crowd hangs out at the dark catacomb bar downstairs – great make-out rooms. Brewer's Art serves dinner from 4 or 5 pm; it's closed Monday.

Hampton Village

A very Baltimore thing is going on at Hampton Village. This old working-class white neighborhood is being reclaimed and celebrated by a new generation with a finer appreciation of irony. (John Waters is their god – see the boxed text.)

Perhaps the best example of this phenomenon is *Cafe Hon* (☎ 410-243-1230, 1002 W 36th St), the highlight of 'the Avenue' along W 36th St between Falls Rd and Chestnut Ave (take I-83 north to the Falls Rd exit). The name comes from the matronly local habit of calling everyone 'hon'; the cafe sponsors a Big Hair Contest, and patrons boldly call in nasally Baltimorese for the end of the yuppification of Baltimore. The large restaurant is decorated like an old Baltimore kitchen – hard yellow walls, radiators, vintage radios, lunch pails, and pictures of the Pope (the old Pope). Cafe Hon also serves food – fortunately,

John Waters: The Pope of Trash

John Waters' Baltimore is not the one you or I experience. Not the city of Poe or Barry Levinson but a Baltimore of Divine parody, bad hair, stalking stompers, innocence lost, kitsch, coprophagy, teenage delinquency, cross-dressing, tattooed tears, Dreamlanders, serial moms, Sonny Bono, and Patty Hearst. His works have created their own genre using blue-collar Baltimore's heyday as the canvas. Artist, writer, photographer, actor, and – most notably – filmmaker, John Waters is Baltimore's favorite and most famous son.

With 12 films, ranging from *Pink Flamingos* to *Pecker*, John Waters' audience base has increased, as have his budgets, but his work remains shocking, entertaining, and poignant. Unassuming use of pat Hollywood narratives and multiple off-the-wall criss-crossing plots led William Burroughs to dub John Waters 'the Pope of Trash.'

The author of three books and numerous essays for national publications, Waters carries the same unique social commentary from the silver screen to the printed page. His photographs have appeared in Soho art galleries, and he has acted in numerous TV shows and movies, including his own.

Despite an international cult following, John Waters remains a lifelong resident of the city. Baltimore returned the appreciation by declaring February 7, 1985 'John Waters Day.'

– Paul Vincent Crotty

MARYLAND

more modern than their decor – with such offerings as portabella burgers ($9), Atlantic salmon, and Belgian waffles for breakfast.

Other choices down and around the Avenue are *Holy Frijoles* for inexpensive Mexican food, the *Coffee Mill* on Chestnut Ave, a pizza joint, and taverns.

Federal Hill

The *Cross St Market* (☎ 410-727-0074), at the corner of Cross and Light Sts, features a flower mart, delis, Italian food, an inviting square sushi bar and a raw bar, in addition to the usual fresh produce and meat (closed Sunday). On Friday and Saturday evenings, there is a happy hour from 5 to 8 pm at the raw bar at the western end of the market. It's packed on Fridays with people drinking quarts of draft beer and eating steamed shrimp, raw oysters and clams, crabs, and crab cakes.

Most other places are along Cross St, on the north side of the market with a few on S Light St and S Charles St within a block or so of the market. The popular modern microbrewery *Sisson's South Baltimore Brewing Company* (☎ 410-539-2093, 36 E Cross St) serves good Cajun-style dishes, such as blackened strip steak, chicken étouffée, and jambalaya for $14 and up.

Two blocks north of the Cross St Market is one of Baltimore's most trendy cafes, the *One World Cafe* (☎ 410-234-0235, 904 S Charles St). The restored storefront is filled with the smell of pastries and 20 different kinds of coffee. It's a popular place for breakfast, when the offerings include steamed eggs and Belgian waffles served with mimosas and Bloody Marys. Lunches, such as black bean burritos and portabella mushroom sandwiches, include vegan items (most under $5). Local artists display their work here, and there's an upscale pool room upstairs. It's open daily 'very early to very late.'

Fells Point
The popular neighborhood and restaurant district of Fells Point centers around **Broadway Market**. Within two buildings, the market offers fresh produce, breads and pastries, an herb-and-tea shop, freshly made pierogi and piroshki, handmade sausage, and several places to sit down at a counter and eat. The deli grill serves chili dogs and huge glasses of iced tea to a blue-collar crowd.

The longtime local favorite cheap-eats venue in this part of town is **Nice N' Easy** (☎ 410-782-8821, 700 S Broadway), open 24 hours. Ed and Sue Milburn, an extremely gregarious couple, serve a three-egg breakfast or homemade chili for around $2 – there's cheap beer, too.

At **Adrian's Bookstore Cafe** (☎ 410-732-1048, 714 S Broadway), the downstairs is devoted to books and periodicals, and the upstairs is a great squirreled-away cafe where you can get light meals for $5 and watch the street scene below, or hang out for hours lounging on the couch with a cup of joe. Another good cafe is **Daily Grind** (1720 Thames St); it opens early and closes late.

Bertha's (☎ 410-327-5795), at the corner of Broadway and Lancaster St, is a great old bar and grill with wood paneling in the dining room, ceiling fans, bustling servers, and crowds of patrons standing at the smoky bar. 'Eat My Mussels' is the restaurant's motto, and steaming bowls of Bertha's mussels come with a choice of sauces such as garlic butter and capers; spinach, tarragon, and garlic; and creamy mustard ($9). Bertha's also serves salads, sandwiches, and other seafood dishes. You can hear live blues most nights.

Ze Mean Bean (☎ 410-675-5999, 1739 Fleet St) takes Eastern European classics and serves them up lighter and healthier. It's in an avant-garde bistro with tile floors, red walls, loud art, and full-length windows that open to the street – romantic for couples, comfortable for families or singles. The Slavic Sampler features pierogi, cabbage rolls, and thin and crisp potato pancakes served with applesauce and sour cream ($6).

A classical guitarist was performing during a recent visit.

Little Italy
East of the Inner Harbor, Little Italy is largely a quiet residential neighborhood of row houses between Pratt St and Eastern Ave. Its biggest commercial draw is its Italian restaurants along Pratt St and up a three-block stretch of S High St. Here you have a restaurant ghetto in the old style: dark dining rooms with wicker Chianti-bottle candles, accordion music, and cummerbund-wearing valets from the Old Country (parking is scarce). Dinners start at around $15 for pastas (that's *traditional* pastas, not modern lighter fare), around $20 for meat entrees.

A local institution, **Dalesio's** (☎ 410-539-1965, 829 Eastern Ave), at Albemarle St, is perhaps most 'typical' of its breed. **Luigi Petti** (☎ 410-685-0055, 1002 Eastern Ave), at Exeter St, is another local favorite, and it offers rare outdoor seating on a large patio. A quicker, less expensive, and more modern alternative is the casual **Amiccis** (☎ 410-528-1096, 231 S High St), where dinners start at less than $10.

Other Locales
A Baltimore legend since 1944, **Obrycki's** (☎ 410-732-6399, 1727 E Pratt St), at Broadway, is just a few blocks out of comfortable walking distance from Fells Point. People come here to eat steamed spiced crabs at tables that have been covered in brown butcher's paper for easy cleanup. Crabs are priced by the dozen, starting at around $25 and climbing to twice that depending on size.

Haussner's (☎ 410-327-8365, 3242 Eastern Ave) serves traditional German dishes in a large room decorated with table-to-ceiling oil paintings, statues, and ceramic sculptures. The bar – where the men's room is hidden – is labeled 'strictly stag,' and its oil paintings are only of female nudes. The menu has more than 80 entrees, from seafood to traditional German dishes such as saucy hasenpfeffer (marinated rabbit), sauerbraten, and wiener schnitzel (dinners from $8 to $20). Diners tend to wear jackets and ties even at lunch, but the management doesn't turn away casually dressed clients.

Greektown is an old-style ethnic enclave on Eastern Ave, just west of I-895. Here, restaurants, bakeries, and markets carry names like Acropolis, Athena's, and the Olive Leaf and feature authentic Greek cuisine and specialty imported items. One local favorite restaurant is *Ikaros* (☎ 410-633-3750, 4805 Eastern Ave), where (it may be heresy to report) the crab cakes are among the best things on the menu ($14). It's closed Tuesday.

Canton attracts a young population to its up-and-coming neighborhood. Already, pricey harbor-view condos and the big new Bibelot store and shopping center have gentrified the waterfront side of the neighborhood. But tucked a few blocks east is the central square (around O'Donnell St between S Linwood and S Potomac), where locals still feed pigeons from park benches. Several eateries face the square: Start at the *Needful Things Cafe* for breakfast or coffee all day long. Go down the block for *Nacho Mumu's* or across the square to *Helen's Garden* restaurant, set among three pubs.

ENTERTAINMENT
Theater
Baltimore has a host of theater companies. The *Arena Players* (☎ 410-728-6500, 801 McCulloh St) is an African American theater group that hosts performances September to June. There's also the *Children's Theater Association* (☎ 410-366-6403, 121 McMechen St). *Center Stage* (☎ 410-685-3200, 700 N Calvert St), between Monument and Madison Sts, is Maryland's state theater.

The *Morris A Mechanic Theater* (☎ 410-837-3913), Hopkins Plaza at Baltimore and Charles Sts, brings Broadway shows to the city. *Theater Hopkins* (☎ 410-516-7159), Merrick Barn, is the Johns Hopkins University community theater. The *Theater Project* (☎ 410-752-8558, 45 W Preston St) is Baltimore's avant-garde production troupe. The *Eubie Blake Cultural Center* (☎ 410-539-1717, 34 Market Place) is a community arts center.

Performing Arts
The Baltimore Opera Company performs at the *Lyric Opera House* (☎ 410-685-5086), in northern Baltimore between Mount Royal and Cathedral Sts.

The *Meyerhoff Symphony Hall* (☎ 410-783-8000, 1212 Cathedral St) hosts the Baltimore Symphony Orchestra and Chorus, as well as touring performances. The Chamber Music Society of Baltimore plays at the *Meyerhoff Auditorium* (☎ 410-486-1140) at the Baltimore Museum of Art, Charles and 31st Sts. The *Peabody Conservatory of Music* (☎ 410-659-8124, 1 E Mount Vernon Place), offers solo, ensemble, and concert performances by students and others.

National and international musical shows are held at the 4338-seat *Pier 6 Concert Pavilion* (☎ 410-725-8632), at Pratt and Market Sts (Inner Harbor) in summer.

For African and African American dance performances, pay a visit to the *Sankofa Dance Theater* (☎ 410-448-2345, 4900 Wetheredsville Rd).

Bars & Clubs
Downtown, *Mick O'Shea's*, on N Charles St between Saratoga and Mulberry Sts, is a popular Irish pub with Irish music (also see Places to Eat, earlier). Near Mount Vernon, Brewer's Art has a bar with a sophisticated selection of snacks (see Places to Eat, earlier). Farther up N Charles, the *Club Charles* (☎ 410-727-8815, 1724 N Charles St), across from the Charles Theatre, is a great faux-swank art-deco place where you can enjoy martinis.

Baltimore's most active neighborhood for bar hopping is Fells Point, particularly on the east side of Broadway and also on Aliceanna, Lancaster, and Thames Sts to the east of Broadway. One highlight among dozens of bars here is *Wharf Rat* (☎ 410-276-9034, 801 S Ann St). Unlike a lot of the bars, which cater to a college-age crowd, the Wharf Rat draws a mix of folks from mariners and bikers to yuppies and artists. The main attractions are one of the best jukeboxes in town, a pool table, and a selection of nearly 50 microbrews – mostly on tap – including the Rat's own Oliver's Ale. There's another Wharf Rat downtown on Pratt St, across from the convention center.

The Maryland Art Place, on Fayette St between Howard and Eutaw Sts downtown, sponsors the *14 Karat Kabaret (☎ 410-962-8565)* downstairs, a great hideaway bar with a swing seat and a huge clock with carrots for hands. There's a somewhat underground music scene with occasional and uneven performances but very hip and mixed crowds.

In Mount Vernon, the *13th Floor (☎ 410-783-1332)*, in the now-condo Belvedere Hotel (corner of Chase and N Charles Sts), is a lounge bar with a beautiful view. It hosts live music nightly beginning at 9:30 pm – Mambo Combo, Vulgaria, Gumbo Junkyard, and Rumba Club were recently on the bill. It also offers two-for-one beers during happy hour (5 to 9 pm weekdays). *Ottobar (☎ 410-757-6886, 203 Davis St)* features local electronic/punk bands for a cover charge around $7.

Fells Point bars offer dozens of live acts on weekends. Try *Max's on Broadway (☎ 410-675-6297, 735 S Broadway)* for live progressive, alternative, and jazz seven days a week, or go to Bertha's (see Places to Eat, earlier) for live blues.

In Federal Hill, *Eight By Ten (☎ 410-625-2000, 10 E Cross St)*, opposite the north side of the Cross St Market, has live alternative, reggae, blues, and pop music every night. The place jumps, but you've got to love cigarette smoke and cramped spaces.

Gay & Lesbian Venues

Near Restaurant Row in Mount Vernon, *Hippo (☎ 410-547-0069, 1 W Eager St)*, off N Charles St, is the largest gay bar in Baltimore, featuring live shows and dancing. In a tattered area near Little Italy and Fells Point, *Orpheus (☎ 410-276-5599, 1003 E Pratt St)*, at S Exeter St, attracts a Gothic crowd of gays and straights.

Cinemas

The grand *Charles Theatre (☎ 410-727-3456, 1711 N Charles St)*, at Lafayette St, re-opened as a cinema for revival films, art flicks, and documentaries after a lavish restoration in 1999. Over in Fells Point, the *Orpheum Cinema (☎ 410-732-4614, 1724 Thames St)*, east of Broadway, screens revivals and art films.

The *Film House at the Walters Art Gallery (☎ 410-547-9000, 600 N Charles St)* offers an eclectic selection of short films every Friday.

The historic *Senator Theatre (☎ 410-435-8338, 5904 York Rd)*, in north Baltimore, is a large, beautifully renovated theater in which the well-known Baltimore directors John Waters and Barry Levinson often have their premieres.

SPECTATOR SPORTS

Going to a baseball game is a traditional American pastime and one that is particularly enjoyable in Baltimore, though that's largely due to the great Oriole Park at Camden Yards, not to the sometimes erratic performance of the home team, the Baltimore Orioles.

Camden Yards (☎ 410-685-9800), west of the Inner Harbor at Eutaw and Pratt Sts, opened in April 1992 to rave reviews, the cleverest being that it offered the 'joyous possibility that a ballpark might actually enhance the experience of watching the game of baseball.' What this means is that Baltimore designed a retro stadium to recapture the old joys of going to an idiosyncratic ballpark. Camden Yards is asymmetrical and holds a reasonable 48,000 folks in good-size seats, none of which are obstructed by support columns as in other stadiums. It also has a selection of good food (not just the $4 hot dogs and $3 soda monopolies you find at other stadiums).

Baseball season is April to October. The ballpark is within walking distance of the Inner Harbor. The Metro stations at Lexington Market and Charles Center lie within a 10-minute walk of the ballpark, and there is a free shuttle bus from Lexington Market. MARC trains stop right at the park at Camden Station.

In 1996, the powerful Cleveland Browns professional football team accepted Baltimore's invitation to leave Cleveland and come to Baltimore. In the ensuing legal battles, courts approved the team's move to Baltimore but required that the team change its name and uniforms. The team is now called the Baltimore Ravens, after Poe's famous poem, and competes at the new *PSINet Stadium* (☎ *410-261-7283)*, a couple blocks south of Camden Yards.

The Baltimore Spirits (☎ 410-625-2320) play indoor soccer and the Baltimore Thunder (☎ 410-347-2020) play lacrosse at the *Baltimore Arena* (☎ *410-347-2000, 201 W Baltimore St)*, which also occasionally hosts Washington Wizards basketball games as well as concerts and other shows.

SHOPPING
Museum gift stores, particularly at the American Visionary Art Museum and the Baltimore Museum of Art, offer some of the most distinctive gifts, jewelry, and beautiful objects in town.

More than 50 antique stores are clustered along N Howard St between Read and Monument Sts and along nearby Chase St between Park Ave and Charles St, a few blocks north of the Washington Monument. If these seem pricey, you can find less expensive antiques in the many shops at Fells Point, particularly on Fleet and Aliceanna Sts east of Broadway.

Market Center is a collection of 400 specialty shops, including an indoor market area, bordered to the north and south by Saratoga and Fayette Sts and to the east and west by Eutaw and Paca Sts.

Harborplace (☎ 410-837-4636), on the Inner Harbor, and the connecting Gallery Mall across Pratt St are two of the cornerstones in the Inner Harbor redevelopment. With sunlit atriums, fresh air, and great views, these markets draw hordes of tourists and locals to browse 110 specialty shops selling everything from sports-team T-shirts and toys to fine fashions and ship models. Local artisans sell their products at Sam Smith Market, on the upper level of Harborplace's Light St Pavilion.

GETTING THERE & AWAY
Air
Ten miles south of the city center, off Route 295, Baltimore-Washington International Airport (BWI; ☎ 410-859-7111, 800-435-9294) is served by most major airlines. See the Getting There & Away chapter.

Bus
Greyhound (☎ 410-752-1393, 800-231-2222) buses stop downtown at 210 W Fayette St, in a run-down area that's busy during the day. They also stop at the Baltimore Travel Plaza, off I-95, east of town at 5625 O'Donnell St. Sample fares run around $10.50 to Washington, DC; $7 to Annapolis; and $18 to Wilmington, Delaware.

Train
Baltimore's Penn Station is at 1515 N Charles St, between Oliver and Lanvale Sts. Bus Nos 3 and 11 pass the station going north on Charles St and south on Cathedral St. Bus No 61 goes north on Calvert St and south on St Paul St past the station.

Maryland Rail Commuter service (MARC; ☎ 410-539-5000, 800-325-7245 in Baltimore) operates regular train service between Penn Station and Union Station in Washington, DC. Amtrak (☎ 800-872-7245) offers service from other cities along the Northeast corridor – DC, Philadelphia, Trenton, Newark, New York, and points north.

Car
The approach to Baltimore from Washington, DC, is along I-95 north or I-295 north (the Baltimore-Washington Parkway), which becomes Russell St, a road that can slowly take you into town west of the Inner Harbor. Depending on unpredictable rush-hour traffic, an alternative is to take the I-395 exit from I-95. I-395 extends approximately a mile before spilling out as Howard St downtown. Roads between DC and Baltimore can be congested. Another option, which may add 30 to 45 minutes to the normal 45-minute to one-hour trip, is to take Route 29 north from DC until it intersects with Route 40. Then take Route 40 east into Baltimore.

From points north, such as Wilmington, the route is I-95 south. You can avoid the toll at the Fort McHenry tunnel by taking exit 59 west (Eastern Ave) into town. Eastern crosses Broadway in Fells Point and then brings you to the Inner Harbor.

From western Maryland and Harpers Ferry, West Virginia, the approach into Baltimore is along Route 40 (the Baltimore

National Pike), which leads to Mulberry and Franklin Sts downtown. Don't exit off Route 40 onto I-70 east. Although Route 40 and I-70 overlap several times, I-70 ends before it gets to Baltimore. If you end up on I-70, take I-695 south (the Baltimore Beltway) to I-95 north to I-395 onto Howard St.

If you're coming from Annapolis, your best bet is to take I-97 north to I-695 west to I-95 north to I-395 to Howard St. From points farther east, such as Ocean City or the Delaware seashore, the only approach is across the Chesapeake Bay Bridge (Routes 50 and 301). Go across the bridge and then take Route 2 north right into town, where it becomes Hanover St west of the Inner Harbor.

GETTING AROUND

The Mass Transit Administration (MTA; ☎ 410-539-5000) can tell you how to get anywhere in the city by public transportation. The fare system for bus, light rail, and Metro systems is identical: You can travel anywhere within the city for $1.35 with exact change. A weekly pass costs $14, permitting unlimited rides within the city from Sunday to Saturday. You can also buy an unlimited one-day pass for $3. Banks and stores throughout the city sell passes.

The bus system is the most useful for travel within the city. There are about 60 routes throughout Baltimore and into the suburbs. Details on light rail and Metro service are outlined below.

To/From the Airport

The ground transportation desk (☎ 410-691-2045, 800-435-9294) is on the ground level at Concourse C. The cheapest way downtown is by MTA light rail (see above), which goes directly to Lexington Market and Penn Station, among other stops ($1.35) about every half-hour; the ride takes 45 minutes.

Weekday hourly MARC trains (☎ 800-325-7245) make the trip to/from Penn Station in 16 minutes ($3.25), with a free 10-minute shuttle ride between BWI's rail station and the airport. Amtrak runs the same route and is a good option for Amtrak pass-holders, but it's twice as expensive as MARC for everyone else.

SuperShuttle (☎ 800-258-3826) runs van service to the Inner Harbor for around $11 per person; buy tickets at the Concourse C desk. Taxi fares are $20 and up.

Light Rail

This is a one-line train (☎ 410-539-5000) that runs north-south for 22 miles. It runs back and forth from Timonium, north of the city, through the city along Howard St to Glen Burnie, south of the city. Light rail is most useful for commuting to/from the suburbs, although there are six stops more or less downtown (along Howard St) and then five more within the city to the north.

Metro

The Metro subway runs from Charles St Center (at the intersection of Baltimore St) downtown out to Owings Mills. Like the light rail, the Metro is only useful if you want to go to a limited number of places along one line. The stops downtown are along Eutaw St.

East-West Trolley

The East/West Trolley runs along Pratt St and Market St from Port Discovery at Market Place to the B&O Railroad Museum in southwest Baltimore.

Water Taxi

Ed Kane's 11-boat-fleet water taxi (☎ 410-563-3901, 800-658-8947) offers service to more than a dozen stops around the Inner Harbor. The boats run from 11 am to around 6 pm every day year-round, with extended summer hours to 11 pm on weekdays, midnight on weekends; there's also extended service for Orioles home games. (Tell the first mate your destination; not all stops are made every trip.) All-day passes are $4.50 for adults, $2 for children 10 and under, which includes access to the East/West Trolley. In peak summer season, water taxis come about every 15 to 20 minutes; in the off season, they may run every 40 minutes.

Taxi

Local companies are Diamond (☎ 410-947-3333), Sun (☎ 410-235-0300), and Yellow Cab (☎ 410-685-1212).

Around Baltimore

ELLICOTT CITY

City folk like to go antiquing on weekends in historic Ellicott City, a picturesque old mill town that hugs steep hillsides 10 miles west of Baltimore via I-695 exit 13. The 1830 depot is now a rail museum (☎ 410-461-1944). You'll find several serviceable cafes and lots of knick-knacky antique shops here. The local business association (☎ 410-465-1449) produces a historic walking tour map, available at the tiny visitor center, tucked behind the post office in the center of Main St.

HORSE COUNTRY

North of Baltimore on either side of I-83 to York, Pennsylvania, lies more than 100 sq miles of Piedmont fields and forest divided by hedges, white rail fences, and stone walls. Sometimes called the Worthington and Greenspring Valleys after creeks that divide the terrain, this area is a huge collection of fancy horse farms watched over by stately, ancestral manors. Many of Maryland's oldest and wealthiest families have lived on these manors for centuries, and the place is home to legendary figures, including Olympic riders, world champion horses, and Baltimore baseball titan Cal Ripken, who owns an estate here.

Sagamore Farms, the former Vanderbilt estate, is the birthplace of Secretariat, a Triple Crown winner and the highest-earning thoroughbred stud in history.

Country roads that wind through the villages of Worthington, Glyndon, and Shawan to the west of I-83 – and Monkton, Madonna, and My Lady's Manor to the east – make for refreshing tours by bicycle or car and take you past a host of impressive horse farms. The place is awash with colors and scents in April and May, when all the trees and flowers around the manors are in blossom. Sagamore Farms is on the road between Worthington and Shawan.

You'll only get a few chances to see a collection of celebrity owners, riders, and horses in the region. One of the premier events for the horse crowd is the **Maryland Hunt Cup Race**, held in Glyndon on the last weekend in April. This is America's most challenging steeplechase, and the nine-minute race attracts thousands. Spectators arrive around noon dressed in their spring finery – which may include linen dresses and formal attire – to enjoy lavish tailgate parties that have a tendency to put almost everybody in a euphoric state by the late-afternoon race. If you fancy cherry blossoms, mint juleps, and rubbing shoulders with Maryland's aristocracy as well as some of Washington's senators and congressional representatives, the Maryland Hunt Cup may be worth some effort to reserve a parking space.

Reserve parking by April 1 from the Maryland Hunt Cup Association (☎ 410-429-4231) by sending a check or money order to 3535 Butler Rd, Glyndon, MD 21071. Tickets cost $30 per carload for

MARYLAND

Hampton: Not Your Ordinary Horse Farm

To get a taste of life on a Maryland manor, stop at Hampton (☎ 410-962-0688), just off the Beltway (I-695) at exit 27B in Towson. One of the largest late-Georgian houses in Maryland, Hampton is a national park on 60 acres.

The Ridgely family began building the house as the family seat for its horse farm in 1783 and the site for genteel entertainment on a grand scale. Nine rooms in the house are decorated to represent the different periods of Ridgely habitation and include significant antiques and portraits by major painters such as Rembrandt Peale and Thomas Sully. The grounds have exotic trees, shrubs, and flowers, including 200-year-old catalpas. Hampton is open 9 am to 4 pm daily, except in foul weather. Tours run hourly.

AROUND BALTIMORE

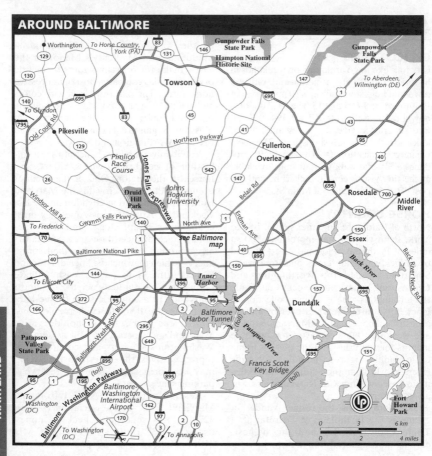

general parking a quarter-mile away; $60 will get you close-in 'patron' parking in a field full of Benzes, Beamers, and Rollses, where the 'in' crowd parties and the chauffeurs do the driving.

The **Timonium State Fair** runs for 10 days around the last week of August and features thoroughbred sales that draw a lot of beautiful animals and beautiful people. Another horsey event that draws a crowd is the **Blessing of the Hounds**, at St John's Church in Glyndon after services on Thanksgiving Day.

ABERDEEN

Northeast of Baltimore, Aberdeen is home to Aberdeen Proving Ground, a large military installation that serves as headquarters of the US Army Ordnance Corps.

On post, the **US Army Ordnance Museum** (☎ 410-278-3602) aims to answer the question 'What the Ordnance Corps has Done for You' with exhibits that reveal the civilian benefits of military research (computers, miniaturization, SUVs, etc). Weapons displays relate the history and development of ammunition. The free museum is open 10 am to precisely 4:45 pm daily; it's closed on national holidays except patriotic or military ones (Memorial Day, Independence Day, Veterans Day). Outside, hundreds of tanks, rocket launchers, and macho commando-style vehicles can be seen around the clock in the Artillery Park.

In town, the **Ripken Museum** (☎ 410-273-2525), in City Hall on Bel Air Ave two blocks east of the train station, traces the famous baseball careers of Bill Ripken and Cal Jr, with family photographs, World Series memorabilia, and a Camden Yards ticket booth. A Cal Jr statue stands in tiny Ripken Plaza outside. A visitor desk here offers local information. The museum is open noon to 3 pm Friday to Monday. Admission is $3 for adults, $1 for students, free for children under 6. From the train station across Route 40, you can catch Amtrak and MARC trains or a taxi cab for the 3-mile trip to Aberdeen Proving Ground (around $6).

For lodging, dining, and other resources in the nearby town of Havre de Grace, see the Maryland's Eastern Shore chapter.

Annapolis & Southern Maryland

ANNAPOLIS

Thirty-five miles south of Baltimore and an equal distance east of Washington, DC, on the western shore of the Chesapeake, Annapolis has been the capital of Maryland since colonial times and now has a population of 35,000. The city, a national landmark, has one of the largest concentrations of 18th-century homes and public buildings (many open to the public) in the country. Although Annapolis is the seat of the state bureaucracy, no modern office buildings mar the skyline or the narrow brick streets.

Home of the US Naval Academy since 1845, Annapolis Harbor and its connecting tidal creeks shelter dozens of marinas where thousands of cruising and racing sailboats tie up. This concentration of recreational sailing

Highlights

- The grounds of the Naval Academy and St John's College
- State House Circle
- People-watching at City Dock, especially from the porch of the Middleton Tavern
- The US Sailboat Show in October
- Crabbing at Chesapeake Beach or Solomons Island
- Fossil-hunting at Calvert Cliffs State Park
- Point Lookout State Park
- Historic St Mary's City – Maryland's first colony

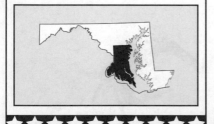

vessels, probably the largest fleet of any city or town in the nation, has earned Annapolis the title of 'Sailing Capital of the United States.' In response to the onshore appetites of the sailing crowd and of visitors who come to immerse themselves in history and the nautical scene, an extensive collection of restaurants, bars, and inns has grown up around the city's waterfront. Today, Annapolis has a well-deserved reputation as a party town.

History

Puritans from Virginia settled Annapolis in 1649 and named their community after Princess Anne Arundel, who became queen of England. From its inception, Annapolis proved an important port and quickly won the distinction of being the seat of government for the Maryland colony. Following the Revolutionary War, Annapolis served as the US capital from November 1783 to August 1784.

With Baltimore eclipsing it as a commercial center during the next two hundred years, Annapolis settled into genteel obscurity for all but Maryland's politicians, local watermen, and midshipmen learning the trade of Captain John Paul Jones. Annapolis was rediscovered as an architectural treasure by the masses fleeing Baltimore and DC in the 1960s and was one of the first municipalities in the state to champion historic preservation. During the last 30 years in particular, the city's historic center has been fastidiously buffed and polished several times. Today, Annapolis blends its historic ambiance with a contemporary enthusiasm for high-tech sailing craft.

Orientation

Annapolis sits on a small peninsula between College and Spa Creeks. The US Naval Academy takes up the northeastern half of the peninsula, and the city constitutes the rest. It's a very compact town – so compact, in fact, that you can walk from one end to the other easily. At the town's center in State Circle is the State House, and west one block

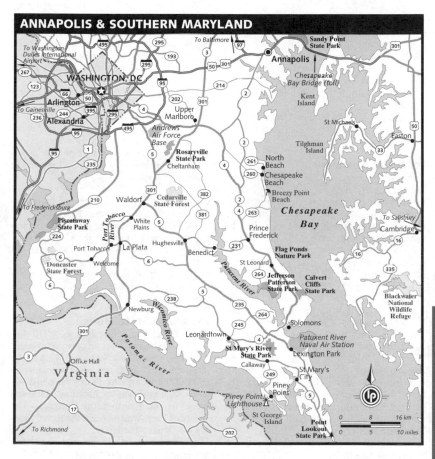

ANNAPOLIS & SOUTHERN MARYLAND

MARYLAND

is Church Circle. The plaza surrounding the Market House (see Places to Eat) is known as Market Space. Running southeast to City Dock from Church Circle is Main St, the major commercial street. Duke of Gloucester St runs southeast from Church Circle to the drawbridge to Eastport, a collection of marinas and residences across Spa Creek.

Information

The Annapolis and Anne Arundel County Conference & Visitors Bureau (☎ 410-280-0445, fax 410-263-9591), 26 West St, is open 9 am to 5 pm daily. From April to October,

an information booth is open at City Dock, where many city tours meet.

A Maryland state visitor center (☎ 410-974-3400) in the lobby of the State House distributes statewide maps and information; it's open 9 am to 5 pm daily.

The post office (☎ 410-263-9292), on Church Circle at Northwest St, is open 8 am to 6 pm weekdays and to noon on Saturday.

The daily newspaper is the *Capital*. Pick up a copy of the giveaway *Inside Annapolis* for information on things happening in town.

The Briarwood Bookshop (☎ 410-268-1440), 88 Maryland Ave, is a great place for used and rare books in a great neighborhood. It's open 10 am to 6 pm daily.

The Avenue Laundromat (☎ 410-267-9092), 74 Maryland Ave, is in a nice area down from Briarwood Bookstore and near a couple of cafes. The laundromat is open daily and provides drop-off wash-fold service on Tuesday.

The Anne Arundel Medical Center (☎ 410-267-1260) is in the historic district at Cathedral and Franklin Sts.

US Naval Academy

The academy began as the Naval School in 1845, although it didn't actually begin awarding bachelor of science degrees until 1932. The federal government pays all tuition, room, board, and medical care for cadets. In exchange, graduates serve in the US Navy or US Marine Corps for six years. If you're interested in applying, stop at the admissions office (☎ 800-638-9156) in Leahy Hall.

Enter through Gate 1 at the intersection of King George, East, and Randall Sts, then walk southeast (right) to the Armel Leftwich Building. Inside is a visitor center (☎ 410-263-6933), which features a video about the Academy, and a gift shop and bookstore. Tours leave from here year-round based on demand (every 15 minutes in the summer). City tours also cover the Naval Academy. Most visitors come to see formation, held daily at 12:05 pm sharp (free), when 4000 uniformed men and women carry on a 20-minute military marching display in the plaza around their massive dormitory – a memorable spectacle.

Midshipman's Room Pass the two cannons aiming at you in Bancroft Hall and head down the hallway to the left to find the designated 'typical midshipman's room.' If you want to see a real midshipman's room though, look in the windows before you go through the gate into the Bancroft courtyard. Real rooms have computers and stereos.

Preble Hall This hall has a museum of naval history, swords, silver settings, a raft on which three men floated for 34 days before being rescued, and artifacts from the battleship

USS *Maine*. On February 15, 1898, the *Maine* blew up in Havana's harbor, killing 266 people onboard. Although it has never been established whether the explosion was an accident or a terrorist act committed by agents of Spain, the popular press whipped the country into a war frenzy with the 'Remember the *Maine*' slogan. Two months later, the US went to war with Spain.

The museum also contains an impressive collection of miniature ships (some several feet long) made of beef and mutton bones by French prisoners of war held for years in England.

Chapel This 1904 sanctuary has many impressive features – bronze doors, an organ, stained-glass windows (one of which depicts the Archangel Michael showing the way through the minefields of Mobile Bay) – but perhaps its most surprising feature is the marble crypt of Revolutionary War naval hero John Paul Jones, kept in the chapel's basement.

Maryland State House

The 1779 Maryland State House (☎ 410-974-3400) is the oldest state capitol in continuous legislative use in the US. George Washington resigned his commission as commander in chief of the Continental army here in 1783, when Annapolis was the national capital and home to the Continental Congress. The Treaty of Paris, which ended the Revolutionary War, was ratified here.

The impressive dome structure includes a newer section completed in 1905. A black line inside along the center hall divides new from old. Visitors are welcome to walk around inside and watch Maryland's senate when it's in session, from January to April. The small, armory-like 1735 **Old Treasury Building** on the grounds of the State House is the oldest official building in the state.

Historic Houses

The 1774 **Hammond Harwood House** (☎ 410-263-4683), 19 Maryland Ave, is a good example of US colonial architecture and is furnished with period pieces. It is open 10 am to 4 pm Monday to Saturday

ANNAPOLIS

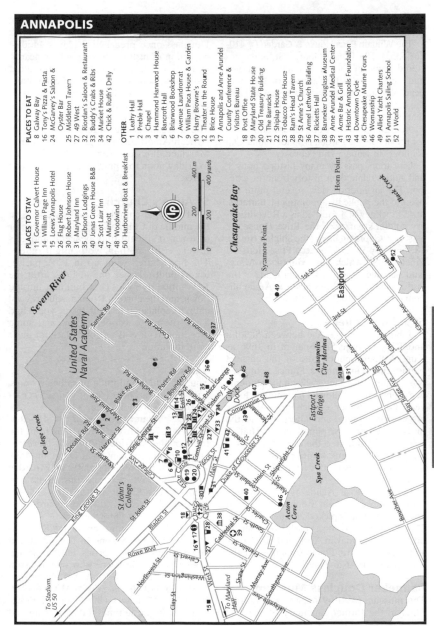

PLACES TO STAY
11 Governor Calvert House
14 William Page Inn
15 Loews Annapolis Hotel
26 Flag House
30 Robert Johnson House
31 Maryland Inn
35 Gibson's Lodgings
40 Jonas Green House B&B
42 Scot Laur Inn
47 Marriott
48 Woodwind
50 Harborview Boat & Breakfast

PLACES TO EAT
8 Galway Bay
16 Tony's Pizza & Pasta
24 McGarvey's Saloon & Oyster Bar
25 Middleton Tavern
27 49 West
32 Riordan's Saloon & Restaurant
33 Buddy's Crabs & Ribs
34 Market House
42 Chick & Ruth's Delly

OTHER
1 Leahy Hall
2 Preble Hall
3 Chapel
4 Hammond Harwood House
5 Bancroft Hall
6 Briarwood Bookshop
7 Avenue Laundromat
9 William Paca House & Garden
10 Harry Browne's
12 Theater in the Round
13 Brice House
17 Annapolis and Anre Arundel County Conference & Visitors Bureau
18 Post Office
19 Maryland State House
20 Old Treasury Building
21 The Barracks
22 Shiplap House
23 Tobacco Prise House
28 Ram's Head Tavern
29 St Anne's Church
36 Armel Leftwich Building
37 Ricketts Hall
38 Banneker Douglass Museum
39 Anne Arundel Medical Center
41 Acme Bar & Grill
43 Historic Annapolis Foundation
44 Downtown Cycle
45 Chesapeake Marine Tours
46 Womanship
49 Allied Yacht Charters
51 Annapolis Sailing School
52 J World

MARYLAND

and noon to 4 pm Sunday; admission is $5 for adults.

The **William Paca House & Garden** (☎ 410-263-5553), 186 Prince George St, is the restored home of former Maryland governor and signer of the Declaration of Independence William Paca (**pay**-ca). Finished in 1765, the structure is a five-part Georgian home that overlooks a garden. Hours are the same as the Hammond Harwood House; admission for the house and garden is $6 for adults. Call for hours in January and February.

City tours pass by many historic houses, and guides relate their history from the exterior. For an interior view, several more are open to the public by appointment: **Barracks**, at 43 Pinckney St, furnished as a Revolutionary soldier's barracks; the **Brice House**, 42 East St, a Georgian home; the **Shiplap House**, 18 Pinckney St; and **Tobacco Prise House**, 4 Pinckney St, which has exhibits on Maryland's tobacco trade. Ask a tour guide at the visitor center or call the Historic Annapolis Foundation (☎ 410-267-7619).

St John's College

St John's, on College Ave between St John and King George Sts, opened in 1696 as King William School, one of the earliest public schools in America. Francis Scott Key was an alumnus. Since 1937, all the students at St John's have followed an identical four-year 'Great Books' curriculum and today are as philosophical and 'alternative' as the midshipmen are disciplined and martial. A 400-year-old tulip tree, the Liberty Tree, was a highlight on campus until recently, but it had to be cut down after irreparable hurricane damage.

In 1982, Naval Academy midshipmen claimed they could beat St John's students at any sport; St John's picked croquet and won. The match has become a yearly event played on the last Saturday in April, and St John's – still – usually wins. For information on the event, call ☎ 410-626-2539.

Banneker Douglass Museum

This museum (☎ 410-974-2893), 84 Franklin St, is in the former sanctuary of the Old Mount Moriah African Methodist Episcopal Church, where Maryland native Frederick Douglass once preached. Today, a modest collection of historic photographs, placards, and artifacts tells compelling stories about distinguished local families and community leaders, as well as the history of efforts to end segregation at St John's College and to achieve equal pay for black Marylanders. The museum is the official repository of African American heritage for the state of Maryland. It is open 10 am to 3 pm Tuesday to Friday, noon to 4 pm Saturday. Admission is free.

St Anne's Church

An Episcopal church, St Anne's stands in the middle of Church Circle near the center of town. It's beautifully peaceful and gets fewer visitors than you might guess. The first church went up in 1704; parishioners built a larger one in 1792, after the Revolutionary War. That building burned down, and the current Romanesque-revival church replaced it in 1859. Inside you'll find a red-tile aisle, wooden floors, and some nice stained glass. It's a good place for quiet contemplation.

Sailing

You can find a multitude of sailing schools, cruises, and bareboat (sail-it-yourself) charters in the Annapolis area.

The schooner *Woodwind* (☎ 410-263-7837) is a 74-foot yacht that sails from the front of the Marriott hotel (see Places to Stay, later in this chapter) at 11 am and 1:30, 4, and 6:30 pm (premium sunset sail) Tuesday to Sunday. Daytime cruises last about two hours and cost $24 for adults, $12 for children under 12. You can also sleep aboard overnight (see Places to Stay, later).

Annapolis Sailing School (☎ 800-638-9192), at 601 6th St, one of the oldest and largest of these enterprises, teaches sailing from April to October. A two-hour lesson aboard a 25-foot sloop costs $25 per person.

The 36-foot *Beginagain* (☎ 410-626-1422, 800-295-1422) leaves City Dock for three-hour cruises three times a day, at 9 am and

1 and 6 pm. The rate is $55 per person. Allied Yacht Charters (☎ 410-280-1522, 800-922-4820), 236 1st St in Eastport, has been a respected name in bareboat charters for decades.

Womanship (☎ 410-267-6661, 800-342-9295), headquartered at 137 Conduit St, is a women-friendly sailing school (signs prohibit shouting) that gets raves from its clients. J World (☎ 410-280-2040, 800-966-2038), 213 Eastern Ave, teaches sailing aboard high-tech sloops in two- to five-day courses.

Bicycling
The Baltimore & Annapolis Trail Park (☎ 410-222-6244) is a 13.3-mile linear trail that follows the old Baltimore & Annapolis Railroad route from Annapolis to Glen Burnie. The southern end of the trail is just north of Annapolis at the intersection of Routes 50 and 450. Downtown Cycle (☎ 410-268-5794), 6 Dock St, rents bicycles.

Organized Tours
A good, easy way to get oriented is on a walking tour. Three Centuries Tours (☎ 410-263-5401) leads two-hour walking tours of town, including Naval Academy sites and the interior of the State House. From April through October, tours leave from the visitor center, 26 West St, at 10:30 am daily and from the information booth at City Dock at 1:30 pm. The rest of the year, tours leave Saturday only, and you may want to call and reserve. Tours cost $8 for adults, $3 for students.

For harbor tours, Chesapeake Marine Tours (☎ 410-268-7601) offers 40- and 90-minute harbor cruises from May to October. (Tour prices start at $6 for adults, $3 for children.) It also sponsors daylong cruises around the harbor and to St Michaels in the summer. Find its ticket booth at the end of City Dock.

The 1928 oyster boat *Half Shell* (☎ 410-216-9529) permits walk-ons at City Dock; inquire about group naturalist excursions.

The Historic Annapolis Foundation store (☎ 410-268-5576), at 77 Main St, offers recorded audio cassette tours of the city, a general tour narrated by Walter Cronkite, and an African American Heritage Tour.

Special Events
You can count on plenty of activity throughout the year in Annapolis. Here's a list of the main events.

May
Chesapeake Bay Bridge Walk & Bayfest (☎ 410-288-8405) This event is held the first Sunday in May. One span of the 4.3-mile bridge is closed for a day, and about 50,000 people walk or ride skateboards and wheelchairs across it. Buses take people over to the Eastern Shore for free, and then people make their way back. The event can tie up traffic on Route 50 for miles.

July
Rotary Club Crab Feast (☎ 410-841-2841) Held in late July or August, this is the world's largest festival of its kind – so big it's held in the Navy-Marine Corps Stadium.

August
Kunta Kinte Festival (☎ 410-349-0338) This festival commemorates the arrival of Alex Haley's slave ancestor, who figures in Haley's book *Roots*, at City Dock – the site of a booming slave market in the 17th and 18th centuries.

Maryland Renaissance Festival (☎ 410-266-7304, 800-296-7304) In nearby Crownsville, this event starts in late August and lasts eight weekends. Highlights include jousting, theater, taverns, buskers, artisans, and food.

October
US Sailboat & Powerboat Shows (☎ 410-268-8828) These shows are the city's equivalents of Mardi Gras, held the first two weekends in October. City Dock and surrounding wharves fill with a fleet of new boats, vendors, food stalls, and what seems like half the world's Jimmy Buffett fans. The streets, bars, restaurants, and inns overflow with crowds of happy (but not totally sober) folk.

MARYLAND

Traffic and parking can be something of a challenge. Another boat show in April heralds the beginning of sailing season; it's slightly saner.

December

First Night Annapolis This event transforms the entire city into a stage December 31, with 250 indoor performances of classical, jazz, blues, folk, dance, and drama. It's a family-oriented arts festival, so there's no booze. Midnight fireworks announce the new year.

Places to Stay

Camping The *Capitol KOA Campground* (☎ *410-923-2771, 800-638-2216, 768 Cecil Ave*), 12 miles away in Millersville, is the closest campground. Sites are $26 without hookups, $31 to $34 with hookups. It's open April to November.

Take Route 50 west to I-97 north, and then take exit 10 (Benfield Blvd); make a right onto Veterans Hwy and follow the signs.

Guesthouses Annapolis has a lovely selection of places to stay within the compact historic district.

Jonas Green House B&B (☎ *410-263-5892, 124 Charles St*), one of the two oldest houses in Annapolis, claims to have had the same family in residence since 1738. Air-conditioned with period furnishings, this B&B welcomes children and pets. Rates start at $100 for a single or double.

Flag House (☎ *410-280-2721, 800-437-4825, 26 Randall St*) contains five rooms and a two-room suite in two connected townhouses; look for the row of international flags out front. Rooms are large with fans, TVs, king-size beds, central air and heat, quilts, and wood furniture. There are two gas fireplaces in the common rooms. Rates start at $120 and include breakfast. The *William Page Inn* (☎ *410-626-1506, 8 Martin St*) offers five rooms in a 1908 home with rates that start at $75, including breakfast.

Harborview Boat & Breakfast (☎ *800-877-9330 voicemail*) offers berths on a 1947 classic Trumpy motor yacht. Rates start at $200 per couple and include a continental gourmet breakfast delivered to your vessel. The schooner *Woodwind* (☎ *410-263-7837*) also operates a boat-and-breakfast aboard a

74-foot yacht; rates of $200 per couple include a two-hour sail.

Historic Inns of Annapolis (☎ *410-263-2641, 800-847-8882*) offers lodging in period-furnished rooms within three historic buildings renovated to provide all modern amenities. The inns are the *Maryland Inn* (*16 Church Circle*), at the head of Main St, and two more residential properties: the *Governor Calvert House*, on State Circle between East St and Maryland Ave, and the *Robert Johnson House*, on State Circle south of School St. The Maryland Inn seems to be the most popular choice. Standard rates start at $189 for a double room in summer, but inquire about special package rates.

Hotels By staying downtown, you can walk, bike, or boat to any destination, but the lowest-price room downtown is around $75. For less expensive lodgings, there are chain motels clustered at Route 50 exit 22, including *Econo Lodge* (☎ *410-224-4317*) and *Days Inn* (☎ *410-224-2800, 800-638-5179*).

Gibson's Lodgings (☎ *410-268-5555, 110 Prince George St*) offers 21 rooms in three buildings. One building is an 18th-century Federal-Georgian house with a newer facade; another is a 19th-century structure; and the third is a modern annex. You will find the interior more modern than the facade suggests. The prices are good, and rooms are clean and tasteful. Rates start at $75.

Scot Laur Inn (☎ *410-268-5665, 165 Main St*), above Chick & Ruth's Delly, offers 10 rooms with TVs, air-con, phones, and private baths on the two upper floors. Room rates, which range from $75 to $95, include a full breakfast at the 'delly.' If no one answers the phone, ask at the restaurant downstairs.

There are also two modern hotels right downtown. *Loews Annapolis Hotel* (☎ *410-263-7777, 126 West St*) is a large corporate place with more than 200 rooms, a seven-story atrium, ballrooms, and good-size rooms with refrigerators. Rates start at $169. The 150-room *Marriott* (☎ *410-269-5864, 800-336-0072, 80 Compromise St*) features spacious waterfront rooms, some with balconies, right at City Dock. Rates start at $189 for singles or doubles. Sailboat and powerboat rentals are available from the dock fronting the hotel (see Sailing, earlier).

Places to Eat

The **Market House** (☎ 410-269-0941), at City Dock, offers many good and inexpensive choices for light meals, including brie-and-prosciutto sandwiches ($5), fresh produce, bakery goods, and a raw bar. Most food stalls are open 9 am to 7 pm, but you can find morning coffee and muffins starting at 7 am.

Open 24 hours, **Chick & Ruth's Delly** (☎ 410-269-6738, 165 Main St) is an Annapolis institution run by the second generation of the Levitt family. The service is friendly and the place is always full of regulars. All rise for the US Pledge of Allegiance at 8:30 am weekdays and 9:30 am weekends.

Tony's Pizza & Pasta (☎ 410-268-1631, 36 West St) has slices starting at $1.45, as well as subs, spaghetti, lasagna, eggplant parmigiana, and other entrees starting at $8.

The **Middleton Tavern** (☎ 410-263-3323, 2 Market Square), across from City Dock, has a raw bar and serves oyster shooters – oysters with a shot of beer – for 95¢ (don't stray too far from the shooters – they're the best item for the value). Horatio Middleton opened the tavern in 1740 for the 'seafaring man.' George Washington, Thomas Jefferson, and Ben Franklin found the pub to their liking. You'll find warming hearth fires in cold weather; tables on the porch offer the best people-watching in the city.

Riordan's Saloon & Restaurant (☎ 410-263-5449, 26 Market Space) offers a changing

---

The Art of Eating a Steamed Crab

More than a few connoisseurs have compared eating a Chesapeake Bay blue crab to exploring the mysteries of sex. But for the uninitiated, figuring out how to eat Marylanders' favorite food can be a daunting, clumsy enterprise. Learning the secret sources of the crab's sweet meat is something like a rite of passage in Chesapeake Bay country.

The key to getting started is having a paring knife in one hand and a small wooden mallet nearby. Your table should be broad and covered with paper to absorb the drips (eventually, you'll use the paper to wrap the fragments). Eating crab is a messy business, so roll up your sleeves.

Dainty eaters and strangers to Chesapeake Bay country often begin by snapping the legs off the body of their crab. They then make a career out of cracking open the claws with their mallets or knife handle and prying and sucking the meat out of the broken appendages. The initiated know that such pursuits yield little meat for all that effort and simply delay the main event – the attack on the body. Leave the claws and legs for later, when your appetite's waning.

If you want to eat a crab like a seasoned waterman or waterwoman, start first with the body. With thumb or knife point, pry off the 'apron' flap on the belly of the crab. The apron covers the crab's reproductive organs and opens the way to get inside the crab's shell

Second, use your thumb or knife point to pry the top shell off the body and discard it. Break off the toothed claws and set them aside for later.

Third, now that you have exposed the body, use the knife edge to scrape off the gills – called 'dead men' – and the mustard-colored fat. You will see a semitransparent membrane covering the meat, which is divided into chambers. These chambers fan out to the root of each leg.

Fourth, hold the crab's body on each side and break it apart at the center. Discard the legs.

Fifth, take your knife and slice lengthwise through the center of each body half. Now you have exposed succulent chunks of meat that you can push out of the chambered shell with your fingers or knife. Eat the meat as is or dip it in some vinegar and Old Bay spice. Depending on the size of the crab and your staying power, you will repeat the ritual five or 10 times before you feel totally satiated.

Cold beer and corn on the cob complement the feast.

variety of food and drink specials. Checkered tablecloths, a big window on City Dock, and the scent of steamed shrimp and beer make Riordan's a popular Sunday brunch place. The bar has a lively pickup scene for an upscale under-35 crowd at night.

McGarvey's Saloon & Oyster Bar (☎ 410-263-5700, 8 Market Space) is pretty much a Riordan's clone. Some of the sailing crowd hangs out here. *Buddy's Crabs & Ribs* (☎ 410-626-1100, 100 Main St) offers combination meals of ribs with shrimp, soft-shell crab or chicken strips for $15 to $16.

49 West (☎ 410-626-9796, 49 West St), wrapped around the corner at West and Cathedral Sts, serves three meals in a comfortable, arty, brick-walled dining room. For breakfast, there's eggs, waffles, and quiche (around $5), with soups, salads (blackened tuna Caesar salad is $7), and sandwiches available the rest of the day, along with appetizers late into the evening. At night, the alley corner features live entertainment, but the storefront dining room remains quiet enough for conversation. It's open 7:30 am to around midnight daily.

Galway Bay, on Maryland Ave at State Circle, is a welcoming Irish pub that serves traditional Irish stew for $9.50 and entrees such as Molly Malone's Cockles and Mussels for $14.

Entertainment

Annapolis has dozens of watering holes, and pub crawling is a favorite nighttime sport from Wednesday through Sunday. To keep the throngs of veterans engaged and challenged, the pubs offer endless promotions – such as extended happy hours, dollar beers, free hors d'oeuvres, sports paraphernalia, you name it – and draw a lot of musical talent from DC and Baltimore. On most nights, a survey will turn up at least a score of live acts playing the bars and restaurants around City Dock.

The *Ram's Head Tavern* (☎ 410-268-4545, 33 West St) houses the Fordham microbrewery and hosts live musicians most nights, including such nationally known performers as John Sebastian and Mose Allison. The

King of France Tavern (☎ 410-263-2641), in the Maryland Inn on Main St, also hosts nationally prominent jazz and folk acts. For serious rock, head for the *Acme Bar & Grill* (☎ 410-280-6486, 163 Main St) and join the mostly under-25 crowd.

At *Harry Browne's* (☎ 410-263-4332, 66 State Circle), gay and straight crowds mingle at a quiet bar above the posh restaurant.

Maryland Hall for the Creative Arts (☎ 410-263-5544, 801 Chase St) is the main center of performing arts. It hosts the opera; the Annapolis Chorale, a 150-person chorus and chamber orchestra that performs September to May; the Ballet Theater; and the Annapolis Symphony Orchestra. To find Maryland Hall head out of town on West St for about a mile and look for the signs.

Annapolis Summer Garden Theater (☎ 410-268-9212, 143 Compromise St) presents Broadway musicals at a 200-seat outdoor theater at City Dock in the summer.

Theater in the Round (108 East St) hosts five annual productions, including *A Christmas Carol*, by the Colonial Players (☎ 410-268-7373).

Apex Cinemas (☎ 410-224-1145) has two multiplex locations, at the Eastport Shopping Mall and the Annapolis Mall. Neither is within walking distance of downtown.

Getting There & Away

The nearest airport is Baltimore-Washington International Airport. SuperShuttle (☎ 800-258-3826) operates a shuttle between the airport and the larger Annapolis hotels and the Naval Academy for $28 per person.

The Baltimore Mass Transit Administration (☎ 800-543-9809) runs bus No 210 from downtown Baltimore to Annapolis. Greyhound (☎ 800-231-2222) has service to and from DC for $11.50. You'll find the bus stop at the 'Metro' sign near the football stadium at Rowe Blvd and Taylor Ave.

Annapolis is about 35 miles east of Washington, DC, and 35 miles south of Baltimore. From DC, take I-495 (the Beltway) to Route 50 east, and you will come right into town. From Baltimore, take I-695 to Route 2 south to Route 50 west.

Getting Around

Annapolis is compact and best navigated on foot. Annapolis Transit (☎ 410-263-7964 daytime, ☎ 410-263-7994 evenings and weekends) runs a bus or trolley from the Naval Academy stadium parking lot south on Rowe Blvd and Duke of Gloucester St to City Dock. Buses operate from 6:30 am to 7 pm. The fare is 75¢.

Parking can be difficult, especially during summer. Most streets have parking meters, and most spots are occupied. You're better off using a lot. There is free parking inside the Naval Academy from 9 am to sundown. This is technically for visitors to the academy, but people wander out into town as well. Enter at Gate 3 on Maryland Ave. There are several municipal and commercial lots in town.

SANDY POINT STATE PARK

This bayside park sits near the foot of the Chesapeake Bay Bridge, just off Route 50/301. If you're looking for an escape from Annapolis, Sandy Point (☎ 410-974-2149) is the closest place where you can try to beat the summer heat and humidity.

A broad beach overlooks an offshore lighthouse and the bay's main shipping lanes.

The state provides changing facilities, a vending area, boat ramps, and fishing jetties. Note: This place can be packed in July and August, and the Chesapeake's infamous stinging jellyfish – sea nettles – can make you wish you were in Alaska. Fees are $2 per adult from Memorial Day to Labor Day and $1 per car at other times.

Southern Maryland

South of Annapolis lies one of the least explored areas of the state. Calvert, St Mary's, and Charles Counties are a rural mix of farms, forest, marshland, and hundreds of miles of tidewater shore. The primary area of interest for travelers is the western shore of Chesapeake Bay, which provides closed-in bayside beaches and sheltered harbors for people unwilling to fight congestion out to the Eastern Shore.

The colony of Maryland was actually first founded on this peninsula, and remote Historic St Mary's City makes an interesting destination for colonial history buffs. Bicyclists will also find the flat, near-empty roads through the countryside ideal for bike touring.

Bass Fishing in Charles County

During the last few years, national television and outdoor magazine coverage has brought a lot of attention to the environmental revival of the Potomac River. Just a few years ago, this river was so polluted that environmentalists suggested the Potomac's nickname be changed from 'National River' to 'National Disgrace.' Since those sad days, better sewage treatment facilities and attention to agricultural runoff have improved the river's water quality dramatically. In addition, biologists have planted more than 40 miles of grass beds in the river, and these have drawn such huge schools of rockfish (striped bass) that Maryland's Charles County, with more than 100 miles of coastline along the tidal Potomac and its tributaries, is now recognized as a world-class fishing hole. Charles County is the site of the annual Bass Anglers Sportsman Society's multimillion-dollar bass-fishing tournament.

Boat ramps, marinas, restaurants, and camping and fishing complexes have opened along the river to meet the needs of anglers. One such facility is *Goose Bay Marina* (☎ 301-934-3812) in Welcome, on Route 6 west of La Plata. Campsites rent for $16, and boat-ramp use is $7. The marina store sells groceries, ice, fishing tackle, and marine supplies.

For a complete list of marina facilities, professional guides, and accommodations geared toward anglers, call the Charles County Tourism Office, Dept of Community Services (☎ 800-766-3386).

CHESAPEAKE BEACH

This small resort lies 25 miles south of Annapolis on the Chesapeake's western shore. In 1900, a tourist railroad called the Chesapeake Beach Railway Company completed a rail line from the District of Columbia to Chesapeake Beach (known as 'CB') and opened it to hordes of DC's middle-class residents, who were looking for an affordable escape from the capital's heat and humidity during summer.

CB reached its prime during the Roaring Twenties, when tens of thousands took the train to the beach to stroll the boardwalk, bathe, go fishing on party boats, listen to concerts at the casino, catch some thrills at an amusement park, and spend a few nights in the Grand Hotel.

But the depression of the 1930s, coupled with improved access to superior Atlantic beaches such as Ocean City, sent the resort into a decline that lasted until the 1980s; all the old attractions, except the railway station, vanished, and the cottage community grew ramshackle, largely populated by year-rounders looking for cheap rents.

With the recreational boating boom of the 1980s, sailors and anglers rediscovered Chesapeake Beach, its two sheltered harbors, and the rare (for the Chesapeake) sandy strand. Since this rediscovery, gentrification has brought a yacht basin and sportfishing charter-boat fleet, along with new condos and restaurants, to the year-round community of modest cottages and coffee shops.

Things to See & Do

Signs on Route 4 lead drivers east onto Route 260 into the heart of CB. A right turn south leads to the **Chesapeake Beach Railway Museum** (☎ 410-257-3892), a half-mile down the main road. Housed in the small historic depot at the water's edge, this museum includes a passenger car and a collection of photos and memorabilia depicting CB in its halcyon years.

The railway museum is open 1 to 4 pm daily in the peak summer season, and 1 to 4 pm on Saturday only in April and October; it's closed entirely in winter. There is no admission charge.

If you go left instead of right at the central intersection, the road leads north a mile or so to North Beach, where an expansive **boardwalk** provides a scenic promenade and access to a narrow stretch of sandy shore. Stinging sea nettles can be a problem here during the summer months, as they are in most of the Chesapeake.

The principal municipal beach is a couple of miles south of town at **Breezy Point Beach** (☎ 410-535-0259). Here, the beach is wider, and sea-nettle nets ease the stinging problem somewhat; there's also a bathhouse and campground. The day-use fee is $4 for adults, $2 for children, with many fee specials (Monday and Wednesday, children under 11 get in free). It's open May through October.

Places to Stay & Eat

Breezy Point Campground (☎ 410-535-0259), at the beach south of town, offers 13 sites ($25/20 with/without hookups).

The *Herrington Inn* (☎ 410-741-5100), on Route 261 a mile or so north of the North Beach boardwalk, operates a self-sufficient resort (it's as much of a resort as a pink concrete-block motel can be) on its own little point. It could be all you need in a getaway: modestly priced rooms, plenty of recreational rentals (boats, bikes, paddleboats, volleyball), and a restaurant next door at the resort's marina. Room rates range from $59 weekdays to a premium $139 for a weekend bay-front hot-tub room in peak summer season; rates include a continental breakfast and a complimentary cruise on a 22-passenger boat (Wednesday to Sunday only).

In town, locals gather at two coffee shops within a half-mile of each other on the main drag: *Wesley Snippets* (which has drive-thru liquor package sales) and the *Seabreeze*, across the street from the railway depot. Next to the depot, the waterfront *Rod 'N' Reel* (☎ 410-257-2735) draws the condo-weekend crowd with its bay views and seafood plates starting at $12; it hosts live entertainment in the bar out back on weekends.

FLAG PONDS NATURE PARK

Flag Ponds (☎ 410-586-1477), off Route 2/4 about 12 miles south of the town of Prince

Frederick, offers 327 acres of woods, marsh, and hay fields, including a 3-mile hiking trail, observation towers for bird watching, two ponds, extensive wildflowers such as the blue flag iris, a fishing and crabbing pier, indoor exhibits on wildlife, and the remnants of an active watermen's pound-net community that thrived here until the 1950s.

It's open seasonally – 9 am to 6 pm weekdays, to 8 pm weekends from Memorial Day to Labor Day. Admission is $6 per car.

CALVERT CLIFFS STATE PARK

This bayside state park (☎ 301-872-5688) is a few miles south of Flag Ponds off Route 2/4. Considering the size of the park (more than 500 acres) and its 40- to 100-foot cliffs, you might conclude that this is a place to come for a quiet walk on the beach, but you would be mistaken. The actual beach is quite small and prohibits swimming. Visitors come here to sift through the sand in search of fossils from the deep-sea creatures that were buried here during the Miocene Epoch, between 10 and 20 million years ago. Huge shark teeth are a common find, but more than 600 types of fossils have also been discovered. If you ask a park ranger for advice, odds are you will find your own fossil.

There are 13 miles of hiking trails, closed to bikes and horses, and kids will like the recycled-tire playground. The walk to the beach is 2 miles from the parking lot – a hot trip at the height of summer. Camping is not permitted. The park is open sunrise to sunset daily (inquire about hunting season schedules); admission is $3 per vehicle. It's south of the nuclear power plant.

JEFFERSON PATTERSON STATE PARK

If you like archaeology or harbor an interest in Native American life in Chesapeake country, you ought to visit this park on the Patuxent River. Given to the state in 1983 by Mrs Jefferson Patterson and listed on the National Register of Historic Places, Jefferson Patterson State Park (☎ 410-586-8500) includes 512 acres, 2½ miles of riverfront, and more than 70 archaeological sites, some under excavation. Follow the archaeological trail to see the evolution of native culture along the Patuxent over the last 12,000 years, from hunting-gathering tribes to a relatively sophisticated plantation community.

There are also nature trails, and the park **museum** displays artifacts from all periods of human habitation. The park is open 10 am to 5 pm Wednesday to Sunday from mid-April to mid-October. Admission is free. It's about 15 minutes from Prince Frederick via Route 2/4 south; follow the signs.

SOLOMONS ISLAND

About 25 years ago, Solomons Island was a sleepy watermen's town with a marine research station at the end of Route 2. It's separated from the mainland by a small tidal creek spanned by a very short highway bridge. Since it shelters a snug harbor, Solomons began to attract a yachting crowd that considered this the western shore's version of popular St Michaels on the Eastern Shore. Vacation and retirement homes sprung up, and a bridge across the Patuxent opened up the island to traffic headed to and from the large Patuxent River Naval Air Station across the river in Lexington Park. On warm weekends, the small narrow island and its single main-street loop may be jammed with visitors.

The Solomons Visitor Center (☎ 410-326-6027) is a resource for those visiting not only Solomons but also southern Maryland in general (pick up its great regional bike map). An easy first stop off the Route 2 Solomons exit, the center is open 9 am to 5 pm weekdays, to 7 pm weekends in summer, with reduced hours the rest of the year (currently Thursday to Sunday only).

Things to See & Do

The **Calvert Marine Museum** (☎ 410-326-2042), across the street from the visitor center and behind a picturesque Chesapeake Bay lighthouse, is the town's principal tourist attraction. For a nominal fee, visitors can view a collection of watermen's vessels, see displays about the changing environment and creatures of the Patuxent River and Chesapeake Bay, and watch river otters at play.

The **Riverwalk** promenade offers scenic views and bay breezes, along with access to the fishing and crabbing pier and small-boat rentals. Try Solomons Boat Rentals (☎ 800-535-2628), where 15-foot skiffs with 5hp motors rent for $17 per hour or $45 for a half-day (including fuel).

On Dowell Rd en route to the Calvert Marina (north of the island), **Annemarie's Garden** is a developing outdoor sculpture garden open to the public most daylight hours. Behind its mosaic gates, you'll come upon a central fountain with a huge statue of an oysterman in action. Trails lead off to a Stonehenge-like sculpture in the woods.

Places to Stay

The *Patuxent River Campsites* (☎ 410-586-9880, 4770 Williams Wharf Rd) in Broomes Island is about 8 miles by water and 15 miles north by highway (take Route 2/4, then follow Route 264) from Solomons Island. Here you will find 125 campsites, many on the river, with electricity and water. The facilities also include a bathhouse, pier, and boat ramp.

Sites run $18 to $25. Use of the boat launch costs $6. It's open May 1 to October 1.

At the *Locust Inn* (☎ 410-326-9817), on the main street across from the Riverwalk, proprietor Mrs English provides eight boarding house–style rooms, with rates starting at $59 for doubles, including continental breakfast. The inn's pool is open seasonally.

Holiday Inn (☎ 410-326-6311), located on Route 2 (not on the island), offers singles/ doubles starting at $105/115 on the weekend, with a seasonal pool, fitness center, restaurants, and marina.

Places to Eat

Edith's Place (☎ 410-326-1036), 1½ miles down Dowell Rd at Calvert Marina (beyond the 'private property' signs), serves breakfast and lunch to patrons fresh off the boats. Beginning at 6 am, Mrs Edith Taylor serves country-size breakfasts of eggs, sausage, grits, and pancakes; you can also find all the fixins for a picnic lunch.

The upscale spot for seafood is the *Lighthouse Inn Restaurant* (☎ 410-236-2444,

How to Catch a Blue Crab

Blue crabs scavenge the bottom of Chesapeake Bay for pungent morsels. Raw clams (out of their shells) or – better – uncooked chicken necks are ambrosia to a crab. So, if you want to catch a crab, use one or the other for bait.

Before you head to the dock or pier to start crabbing, stop by a hardware store or borrow your tools – a ball of twine (your fishing line), a long-handle dip net to land your catch, and a bucket for storage.

At the pier, tie a piece of bait to your line and drop the line into the water until you feel the bait touch the bottom. Pay out an additional 2 feet of line, then cut the line and tie it off a railing or the edge of the dock. To be efficient, you should deploy about a half-dozen lines in this fashion.

Next, watch your lines until they go taut. When you see a taut line, it means a crab has latched onto the bait with its claws and is trying to make off with the food.

Slowly reel in the line by hand. Grab your dip net and ease the net's basket about a foot beneath the surface of the water. You will see the crab hanging onto the bait as you reel the line to the surface. Before the crab and bait break the surface of the water, scoop up the crab with the dip net in one fluid swipe and lift the crab out of the water. Shake the net over the bucket, and the crab will drop in.

If you must pick up the crab, grab it at the joint between the back fin (paddle-shaped leg) and the shell so the crab can't give you a painful nip with its claws.

Store the crabs in a shady place or cover the bucket with a wet cloth to keep your catch alive until you can steam the crabs in a pot with Old Bay spice and beer.

14640 Solomons Island Rd), where the bar is a fully rigged skipjack and yachters pull up to its dock (entrees start at $13).

The best sunset view is from ***Solomons Pier Restaurant & Lounge*** on the Riverwalk.

SOTTERLY PLANTATION

Just 4 miles up the Patuxent River from Solomons Island, on the western bank, sits Sotterly (☎ 301-373-2280), an elegant colonial plantation. You can come in your own private boat and tie up at the plantation pier or take the 10-mile drive from Solomons. While Sotterly's manor house, built in 1717, is not on the scale of George Washington's Mount Vernon, the building does have its peculiar charms, which include being the oldest post-and-beam style house in the US. The plantation is still a working farm, and the slave quarters, house, and furnishings give a strong sense of pre-Revolutionary War America.

Sotterly is open 10 am to 4 pm Tuesday to Sunday from May to October. Admission is $7 for adults, $5 for children. To reach Sotterly from Solomons Island, cross over the Solomons Island bridge to the western shore of the Patuxent; take Route 235 north 3 miles, then turn right (east) on Route 245 and proceed to Sotterly Rd.

NAVAL AIR TEST & EVALUATION MUSEUM

This is not a stop for everyone, but you might want to visit this museum if you're curious about how the US Navy spends citizens' tax dollars, if you love military aircraft, or if you want a behind-the-scenes look into the best test-pilot school in the world.

Located at the North Gate of the Patuxent River Naval Air Station on Route 235, 5 miles south of Solomons Island in Lexington Park, the Naval Air Test & Evaluation Museum (☎ 301-863-7418) has a good collection of aircraft, hardware, and memorabilia profiling the program, whose graduates include celebrated astronauts such as Glenn, Shepard, Schirra, and Carpenter. Here you can examine a number of war birds, climb aboard an F-4 Phantom simulator, or look at failed prototypes, including an inflatable rubber airplane.

The museum is open 10 am to 5 pm Tuesday to Sunday; admission is free.

POINT LOOKOUT STATE PARK

At the very southern tip of Maryland lies Point Lookout, perched on a long peninsula jutting out between Chesapeake Bay and the Potomac River. The state park here (☎ 301-872-5688), open year-round, contains more than 1000 acres of wetlands and forest, including the best camping and recreation sites in southern Maryland. There are nature trails, a swimming beach, a pier for easy fishing and crabbing, and boat rentals. Ramparts date back to the Civil War, when the Fort Lincoln prisoner-of-war (POW) camp here housed Confederate prisoners; a small museum, open daily in summer, contains historic exhibits and memorials honoring the 3364 POWs who died here. Over the years, park rangers, campers, and psychics have reported regular sightings of Confederate ghosts.

In summer, an **excursion cruise** (☎ 410-425-2771) sails from here to Smith Island (see the Maryland's Eastern Shore chapter). Boats depart Wednesday to Sunday ($20 for adults). The state park charges day-use admission on weekends and holidays from May to September ($3 for those ages four and older).

The park offers *camping* as well. Rates for the 143-site campground are $15 for tents, $18 to $21 for sites with hookups. (Though the campground is open year-round, it shuts off the water in the winter; it's primitive camping only.)

ST MARY'S CITY

Maryland's first capital overlooks Horseshoe Bend on the St Mary's River from a promontory capped with historic buildings, stately trees, and lush fields. Near this spot in 1634, about 200 of Maryland's first colonists, led by Lord Baltimore's brother Leonard Calvert, stepped ashore St Clements Island and celebrated a thanksgiving mass. Thereafter, this mix of Catholic and Protestant colonists sailed aboard the Ark and the Dove to Horseshoe Bend, where they established St Mary's City on the site of a former Native American village.

Here, the colonists enjoyed peaceful relations with local Native Americans and formed the first European community in North America to guarantee all citizens the right to practice whatever religion they chose. The settlement was, nonetheless, a commercial venture, and it prospered, remaining the capital of Maryland until 1695, when the capital moved to Annapolis. The town all but vanished in subsequent centuries, but during the 1970s archaeologists began exploring the site and reconstructing the city to open it for public tours. A living-history attraction here called Historic St Mary's City (☎ 301-862-0990, 800-762-1634) preserves the original site where the first Marylanders landed. Historic St Mary's City is like a mini-Williamsburg, Virginia, with restorations and re-creations of several key buildings, including the reconstructed State House of 1675, a farmhouse, and Farthing's Ordinary, a tavern. There's also a Native American longhouse.

The town may be more evocative than the more touristy Williamsburg, for the surrounding region remains remote and sparsely inhabited, but it takes some imagination to picture the scattered buildings as a colonial capital. The site and interpretive museum are open seasonally, 10 am to 5 pm Wednesday to Sunday mid-March to November. Admission is $7.50 for adults, $3.50 to $6 for students, free for kids under five.

Maryland's Eastern Shore

The Eastern Shore – also called the Delmarva Peninsula (for Delaware, Maryland, and Virginia) – juts south from Wilmington, Delaware, to form the eastern border of Chesapeake Bay and a long stretch of Atlantic beaches. Maryland's portion is about 100 miles long by 65 miles wide. The state of Delaware takes up the upper northeastern wedge of the peninsula, and Virginia its southern tip. Maryland has most of the choice Chesapeake Bay waters.

Before 1952 and the construction of the William Preston Lane Jr Memorial Bridge (the Chesapeake Bay Bridge; Route 50) from Annapolis to Kent Island and the Eastern

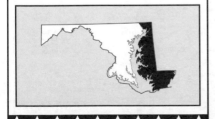

Shore, this long peninsula remained isolated from mainstream America. Because of this isolation, the descendants of shoremen (farmers) and watermen from the west coast of England, who settled the Eastern Shore 300 years ago, have held tight to their traditional lifestyles. On the Eastern Shore you will find some of Maryland's oldest towns and earliest ports, a vital seafood industry ('Maryland is for crabs'), pristine beaches, herds of wild horses, and one of the country's biggest beach resorts – Ocean City.

The Eastern Shore is flat farm country. Its beauty is almost impossible to see from the main highway (Route 50/301), which was designed to force-feed Ocean City with millions of tourists each year. You need to get onto the back roads or out on the tidal Chesapeake waterways to find the substantial charms that lurk here.

HAVRE DE GRACE

At the northernmost tip of Chesapeake Bay, less than an hour northeast of Baltimore, Havre de Grace could be considered the gateway to the Eastern Shore for folks traveling from Baltimore. Although not technically on the peninsula itself, the small waterfront town where the Susquehanna River meets the bay shares much in common with neighboring Shore communities.

The county tourism council (☎ 410-939-3336), 121 N Union St, distributes historic walking tour maps and other local information 9 am to 5 pm weekdays and 11 am to 4 pm Saturday, but it's easy enough to find your own way about.

Things to See & Do

The Havre de Grace **Decoy Duck Museum** (☎ 410-939-3739), at Giles and Market Sts on the south side of town, explains and displays the esteemed local art of crafting hunting decoys, which has made Havre de Grace the 'Decoy Capital of the World.' Carvers are on hand most weekends demonstrating their skill. The annual Decoy, Wildlife Art, and

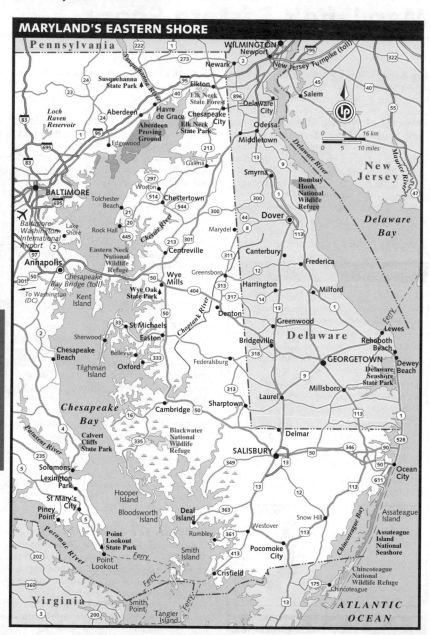

MARYLAND'S EASTERN SHORE

Sportsman Festival takes place the first weekend in May. The museum is open 11 am to 4 pm daily; admission is $4.

A quarter-mile **boardwalk promenade** leads from the decoy museum on a low bluff and winds its way down along the scenic Susquehanna Flats marsh (ideal for birding) to the historic **Concord Point Lighthouse** at the foot of Lafayette St. The tiny lighthouse, built in 1826, is open 1 to 5 pm weekends and holidays from April to October. Admission is free.

Across from the lighthouse, the new Havre de Grace **Maritime Museum** (☎ 410-939-4800), 100 Lafayette St, describes the town's maritime history and heritage and hosts boat-building classes.

The **Susquehanna Museum** (☎ 410-939-5780), at the north end of town within the 1840 lock house of the Susquehanna & Tidewater Canal, relates more local history, including claims that Spanish explorers checked out this area as early as 1588. The museum is open 1 to 5 pm weekends.

Susquehanna State Park (☎ 410-557-7994), 3 miles from Havre de Grace on the Susquehanna River west of I-95, holds a rural farm museum (☎ 410-939-2299) and a mill that operates weekends May to September or October.

The Chesapeake Heritage Conservancy (☎ 800-406-0766) offers 90-minute **skipjack rides** aboard the recently restored 1955 *Martha Lewis* from its dock at the foot of Congress St, several blocks north of the lighthouse. Those who want to go **bicycling** can rent bikes at Jody's Jalopies (☎ 410-939-2453), 843 Otsego St.

The town has recently become popular for its flea-market antiques. Each weekend, couples stroll through the compact downtown, surveying wares at dozens of antique shops and outside stands, and then celebrate their treasure-hunting at one of several comfortable family restaurants downtown.

Places to Stay & Eat

There are several B&Bs in town with around four rooms each (if you decide this place is more than a day trip). Rooms with private baths cost around $85, including breakfast.

The regal *Vandiver Inn* (☎ 410-939-5200, 301 S Union Ave) and the gabled *Spencer Silver Mansion* (☎ 410-939-1097, 200 S Union Ave) are grand Victorians on the main street downtown; the more modest *Currier Inn* (☎ 410-939-7886, 800 S Market St) is in a family home a block from the lighthouse.

There's also a *Super 8* (☎ 410-939-1880), on Route 40 south of town, with rates starting at $52/58 for a single/double.

Three restaurants are within a few blocks of one another downtown. *Ice Dreams* (☎ 410-939-1525, 209 N Washington St) offers more than its name might suggest. Around back, there's a bay-view seating area where you can order vegetarian sandwiches ($5 and up) and crab cakes.

MacGregor's (☎ 410-939-3003, 331 St John St), at the waterfront, is a big, friendly family restaurant and tavern serving pub appetizers, American plates around $10, and seafood.

Tidewater Grille (☎ 410-575-7045), at the foot of Franklin St, is the most refined option, where three sides of glass walls offer views from every table and seafood is the specialty of the house (entrees start at $10). For coffee, there's *Java by the Bay* (☎ 410-939-0227, 118 N Washington St).

CHESTERTOWN

On the upper Eastern Shore, 40 miles northeast across the bay from Annapolis, Chestertown (population 4000) is an architectural and historic gem. What makes it doubly attractive is that it's frequently overlooked by tourists in a hurry to get to the Eastern Shore's better-known destinations. Most visitors coming to Chestertown are professional people in search of a place to unwind and escape hectic lives and pressures in DC, Baltimore, Philadelphia, or New York – travelers clearly not seeking overstimulation but looking to kick back and pursue simple pleasures in a low-key historical setting.

Visiting Chestertown in 1774, a young traveler and Princeton University graduate by the name of Philip Vickers Fithian judged, 'A delightful part of the country...Chester-Town – this is a beautiful small Town on a River out of the bay navigable by Ships.' In

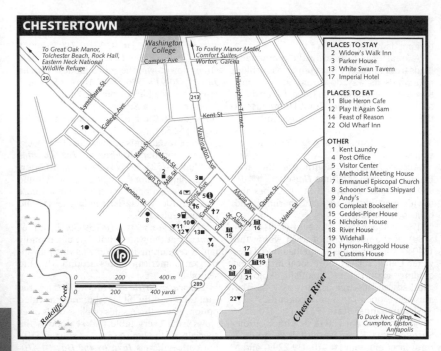

CHESTERTOWN

To Great Oak Manor,
Tolchester Beach, Rock Hall,
Eastern Neck National
Wildlife Refuge

Washington
College
Campus Ave

To Foxley Manor Motel,
Comfort Suites,
Worton, Galena

PLACES TO STAY
2 Widow's Walk Inn
3 Parker House
13 White Swan Tavern
17 Imperial Hotel

PLACES TO EAT
11 Blue Heron Cafe
12 Play It Again Sam
14 Feast of Reason
22 Old Wharf Inn

OTHER
1 Kent Laundry
4 Post Office
5 Visitor Center
6 Methodist Meeting House
7 Emmanuel Episcopal Church
8 Schooner Sultana Shipyard
9 Andy's
10 Compleat Bookseller
15 Geddes-Piper House
16 Nicholson House
18 River House
19 Widehall
20 Hynson-Ringgold House
21 Customs House

Chester River

To Duck Neck Camp,
Crumpton, Easton,
Annapolis

0   200   400 m
0   200   400 yards

the same year, Englishman George Chalmers toured Chestertown and remarked on the magnificent Queen Anne and Georgian mansions that stood as symbols of the town's trading wealth.

Chartered in 1706 as one of Maryland's 'ports of entry,' Chestertown had grown to a town of 200 houses when Fithian and Chalmers passed through. Here, colonists prospered through the exportation of corn and wheat from surrounding plantations. Meanwhile, Chestertown mariners and ships excelled in trade with the West Indies. Patriots stormed aboard the brigantine *Geddes* on May 13, 1774, and staged their own 'tea party' by dumping the vessel's cargo of tea into the river as a symbol of support for the Boston Tea Party patriots.

Today, the town's grand houses, along with some churches and public buildings, constitute a collection of restored colonial architecture to rival that of Annapolis. But Chestertown remains a quiet country town,

with culture that derives from its traditional place as the seat of Kent County government, centuries of well-traveled citizens, and Washington College. Visitors come to explore Kent County's 280 miles of bay shores, stay in historic B&Bs, and feel as if they're escaping into a carefree past. During colonial times, Chestertown's Hynson-Ringgold House was known as a 'home of the cavaliers,' where young English gentlemen ignored the troubles of the world at large and made Chestertown 'one of the gayest places in Maryland.' The spirit persists, particularly if you visit 'C-town' on a Friday or Saturday night.

Orientation

Most travelers approach Chestertown from Annapolis and points south. From this direction, Route 213 crosses a bridge over the Chester River and becomes Maple Ave and then Washington Ave in Chestertown. Planners laid out the municipality in a rectangular grid, with the heart of the town one block southwest of Maple Ave on High St. This main thoroughfare – High St – butts against the river to the southeast and stretches northwest about a mile toward Washington College. Kent County Courthouse marks the center of town, overlooking the small Fountain Park on High St between Cross and Court Sts.

Information

Kent County Tourism (☎ 410-778-0416, www.kentcounty.com) runs a visitor center at 100 N Cross St downtown. The post office (☎ 410-778-0690) is at 200 Spring Ave. A well-stocked, popular bookstore is the Compleat Bookseller (☎ 410-778-1480) at 301 High St. You will find Kent Laundry (☎ 410-778-3278) at the west end of town at 607 High St. The nearest hospital is Memorial Hospital (☎ 410-778-0603), 40 miles south in Easton.

Walking Tour

Begin with Chestertown's most famous landmark, the **Hynson-Ringgold House**, at the corner of Cannon and Water Sts in the southwest corner of town. Built in stages between 1735 and 1772, the mansion with its antler staircase is a good example of the evolution of Georgian-style architecture (named after England's four monarchs who ruled America from 1714 until the Revolution). In its early days, the house was a party site for young English gentry. The presidents of Washington College have lived here since 1944.

The **Customs House** sits a block north on Water St. Constructed in 1746 and embellished with Flemish Bond brickwork, this building served as both the customs office and a private residence around the same time the Chestertown Tea Party took place.

Just across High St, at No 101, sits one of Chestertown's most elaborate townhouses, **Widehall**. Kent County's wealthiest merchant, Thomas Smythe, built this house in 1770. Smythe became the head of Maryland's Revolutionary Provisional Government for the two years preceding the framing of the state constitution in 1776. His home is an example of the symmetry characteristic of Georgian architecture.

A few houses farther northeast along Water St, you will find the **River House**,

No 107. Built by Richard Smythe between 1784 and 1787, this 'English basement house' is an example of Federal-style architecture. The River House is one-room deep with no windows on the side, which is characteristic of Philadelphia townhouses.

One block inland, Queen St runs parallel to Water St. There are many fine Federal townhouses on this street. A particularly attractive example is **Nicholson House**, No 111. It belonged to Captain John Nicholson, who skippered the Revolutionary sloop of war *Hornet* and the frigate *Deane*. The *Deane* took the last naval prizes of the American Revolution and was the only frigate held by the Navy at the end of the war.

Open to the public for guided tours, the **Geddes-Piper House** (☎ 410-778-3499), 101 Church Alley (off Queen St), is the home of the Historical Society of Kent County. The Philadelphia-style townhouse is open noon to 4 pm Wednesday to Sunday from May to October (donations encouraged).

Heading back to High St and another block inland, you'll come to Fountain Park. On the corner of Park Row and Cross St is **Emmanuel Episcopal Church**, built from 1767 to 1772. Dr William Smith, the rector of this parish in 1780, founded Washington College and the Protestant Episcopal Church of the United States.

At the north end of Fountain Park stands the **Methodist Meeting House**. Built between 1801 and 1803, this meeting house attracted the attention of the first Methodist bishop of America. After his visit, Bishop Francis Ashbury judged Chestertown a 'very wicked place.' Apparently, the bishop had a different standard for conduct than the dominant sect of Episcopalians – some of the town's most lively taverns were right across High St from the meeting house.

One of the places that would have scandalized the bishop was the **White Swan Tavern**, 231 High St. Built as a residence in the 1730s, the building was expanded into an ale house by entrepreneurs in the 1790s. After almost two centuries of rough treatment and a zillion kegs of brew, the Swan reopened as a fully restored B&B in 1981 (see Places to Stay, later in the chapter).

MARYLAND

Washington College

In 1782, George Washington gave his name to this college, Maryland's first school of higher education. Washington was one of the school's first distinguished visitors. He served with the governors who chose the designs for the original buildings of Washington College and drafted a lottery to finance them: Washington sold the tickets around his home, Mount Vernon, in Alexandria, Virginia.

Washington College stands as the 10th-oldest college in America. The college enrolls 1200 students, many preparing for careers in law, medicine, business, and Chesapeake Regional Studies. Lacrosse and crew are distinctive sports at the college and draw sizable crowds to competitions.

– Randy Peffer

Activities

One popular pastime is **bicycling** along the rural broad-shouldered roads that fan out from Chestertown. The Kent County Tourism office publishes an excellent bicycling-tour guide with nine great rides. Call ☎ 410-778-0416 for a free guide.

Boating draws many people to the Chestertown area. Chartered sailing and powerboat cruises, fishing charters, and guided kayak tours operate out of Rock Hall, a bayside town 13 miles east of Chestertown (listed later in the chapter). For those interested in historic ships, the Shipbuilding School at the Schooner Sultana Shipyard (☎ 410-778-6461), 346 Cannon St, is putting together a replica of a 1767 schooner; inquire about public tours.

In Worton, north of Chestertown, visitors can go out on the water to experience the waterman's life at Echo Hill Outdoor School (☎ 410-348-5880). Echo Hill has a working skipjack, an oyster 'buy' boat, and an oyster tonger's bateau and can take you down the Chester River for a day of oystering (November to March). It also operates guided canoe trips throughout the year.

Organized Tours

Friendly and knowledgeable, Margaret Fallaw at Historic Chestertown & Kent County Tours (☎ 410-778-2829) conducts 90-minute walking tours by advance reservation ($7 for one or two people).

Special Events

If you'd like an inside view of Chestertown's historic homes. take the Maryland House and Garden Tour, held every other April (in odd-numbered years). The Chestertown Tea Party Festival in May takes place along the waterfront and High St. The Chester River Sailing Regatta in July features graceful three-sail-rigged log canoes and onetime oyster tonging boats. In September, the Candlelight Walking Tour lights up the streets, with columns of history lovers parading from house to house by the light of you-know-what.

Places to Stay

Campers can head for **Duck Neck Camp** (☎ 410-778-3070), 9 miles from Chestertown on the Chester River. Go south on Route 213 from Chestertown, turn left on Route 544 and proceed toward Millington for 4 miles; then go left on Double Creek Rd, following it for 1 mile, and turn left on Double Creek Point Rd. The arches to the camp are a quarter-mile farther. There are 10 tent sites for $19, plus 20 sites with full hookups for $21. The camp, which has a beach with jellyfish-free swimming, is open year-round.

On the low end of price and charm, **Foxley Manor Motel** (☎ 410-778-3200), on Washington Ave, less than a mile north of downtown on Route 213, has standard motel rooms that start at $45 on weekdays, $52 on weekends. Nearby, **Comfort Suites** (☎ 410-810-0555), on Route 213 behind the Chestertown Plaza, has an indoor pool and rooms that start at $70 on weekdays, $120 on weekends.

The best way to get a feel for the town is to stay in one of Chestertown's B&Bs. Two in the historic district charge less than $100 for rooms with a private bath (all rates include breakfast; expect higher weekend rates). **Widow's Walk Inn** (☎ 410-778-6455, 402 High St) operates out of a mammoth Victorian furnished in period antiques. This B&B stands out for its enormous country breakfasts and its reputation for having a friendly ghost. (We witnessed a staircase door mysteriously open and close all on its own.)

The *Parker House* (☎ 410-778-9041, 108 Spring Ave) offers comfortable rooms in an 1876 Victorian farmhouse in the center of town. Rates include a continental breakfast.

Ten minutes west of town, Jim and Tracy Stone rent out six rooms in their 1743 brick manor house overlooking Stoneybrook Pond. All rooms at the *Inn at Mitchell House* (☎ 410-778-6500) have colonial furnishings, and most have a private bath (doubles start at $85). Take Route 20 toward Rock Hall and turn west onto Route 21 to Tolchester Beach.

The town's deluxe B&Bs charge $100 and up for rooms with private bath. In town, *White Swan Tavern* (☎ 410-778-2300, 231 High St) operates from a former tavern dating to 1733 (see Walking Tour, earlier). The rooms are museum-quality showcases of 18th-century furnishings and decor. Guests can take sweet tea here daily at 4 pm (also open to walk-in visitors for $5).

A small Victorian gem, the *Imperial Hotel* (☎ 410-778-5000, 208 High St) provides such amenities as heated towel racks and console-concealing antique armoires along with period decor.

Eight miles north of town on Route 514, *Great Oak Manor* (☎ 410-778-5943) occupies 12 acres overlooking the Chesapeake. Built with bricks from ships' ballasts in the 18th century, this regal 25-room mansion features a circular staircase, library, and hunt room. Swimming, tennis, bicycling, and golf are available.

For houseboat rentals operating at the Worton Creek Marina north of Chestertown, call the Pennsylvania-based owners of *House Boat Rentals* (☎ 610-622-6723).

Places to Eat

The place to start for morning coffee, *Play It Again Sam* (☎ 410-778-2688, 108 S Cross St) also has sandwiches under $4, treats, and afternoon snacks. It features occasional live entertainment.

Feast of Reason (☎ 410-778-3828, 203 High St) is a small lunch place with fresh-baked bread made on the premises. It's somewhat upscale, but large beef, turkey, salmon, and vegetarian sandwiches cost less than $5.

At the foot of Cannon St, the family restaurant *Old Wharf Inn* (☎ 410-778-3566) has a nice view and standard American entrees ($10 and up) at dinner; there's also a salad bar and a Sunday brunch.

For fancier cuisine, *Blue Heron Cafe* (☎ 410-778-0188, 236 Cannon St) features such daily specials as grilled rockfish for lunch and dinner (entrees start at $18).

For pub food, try Andy's (see Entertainment, below), where the baked sausage and mozzarella-stuffed sandwich is less than $4. The kitchen opens at 4 pm.

Entertainment

Gone are the colonial days when every inn on High St was also a pub. But don't dismay: Washington College alumna Andy Goddard runs a world-class saloon. *Andy's* (☎ 410-778-6779, 337½ High St) attracts a crowd ranging from watermen and college students to travelers and older gentry. Andy always wanted to run a pub like Miss Kitty's Long Branch Saloon in the TV series *Gunsmoke*. From the moment you look over the bar and see the oil painting of Andy clad in a satin teddy and draped on a divan with a dreamy look in her eyes, you know how strongly she has stamped her personality on this establishment. In the front room, Andy has exotic brews on tap, current newspapers and magazines for browsing, shuffleboard, and light fare until midnight (also see Places to Eat, above).

The pub's back room looks like an elegant country living room built around a fireplace, but one corner has a dance floor and stage attracting the best acoustic, rock, and bluegrass performers from the Washington and Baltimore area almost every night. Andy's opens at 4 pm. There's a $3 cover daily except Thursday (when it gets packed), but there are so many specials – ladies' night, men's night, extended happy hour – that the cover seems insignificant. Single women will feel welcome and comfortable here.

MARYLAND

Shopping

Every Wednesday, people come from all over the East Coast to go to Dixon's Furniture Auction (☎ 410-928-3006) in nearby Crumpton (10 miles east at the intersection of Routes 544 and 290). It's one of the largest auctions of antique and country-estate furniture in the USA.

Getting There & Away

Coming from Annapolis by car, you approach Chestertown via the Chesapeake Bay Bridge (Route 50). Five miles after crossing the bridge, take Route 213 north about 20 miles.

From the north, follow I-95 to Route 213. Take Route 213 south to Galena and then southwest to Chestertown.

ROCK HALL

Calling itself the 'pearl of the Chesapeake,' this onetime ferry terminal off Route 20 about 13 miles west of Chestertown now has 12 marinas, six real-estate offices, and hundreds of vacation condos. Such booming development has changed the nature of this once-serene watermen's village, and every weekend the town is packed with tourists drawn to exploring Kent County's 280 miles of shoreline. In October, the Rock Hall Fallfest brings blues, bluegrass, and folk music to Main St.

Chartered sailing and powerboat cruises, fishing-boat charters, and guided kayak tours all operate from here. Try Haven Charters (☎ 410-639-7140), Sailing Emporium (☎ 410-778-1341), Eastern Neck Boat Rentals (☎ 410-639-7100), or Chester River Kayak Adventures (☎ 410-639-2001). The Kent County Tourism office in Chestertown has a full list.

Boaters take note: If you park or launch a trailer boat at one of Kent County's 30 public landings, you will need a landing permit. These are available at the Public Works Office (☎ 410-778-7439) in Chestertown and cost $35. However, most out-of-staters with boats choose to pay a small fee to use launch ramps at one of Rock Hall's marinas instead.

EASTERN NECK NATIONAL WILDLIFE REFUGE

This refuge (☎ 410-639-7056) lies just a few miles down the road beyond Rock Hall village on Route 445. At the confluence of the Chester River and the bay, Eastern Neck is a 2285-acre island refuge for migratory and wintering waterfowl. The island is also home to the endangered Delmarva fox squirrel and the southern bald eagle. Staff have documented peaks of more than 40,000 waterfowl on the island. Common species include Canada geese, tundra swans, canvasbacks, mallards, widgeons, and lesser ducks. There are also many species of wading birds, such as great blue heron, killdeer, sandpiper, and woodcock. Deer, beaver, red fox, raccoon, muskrat, and other indigenous mammals roam free.

You will find 6 miles of roads and trails to explore (including three wildlife trails) and an observation tower. This tower is one of the best places to get a sense of the vast wilderness typical of the Eastern Shore. The Ingleside Recreation Area within the refuge has facilities for crabbing and car-top boat launching from May 1 to September 30. Many people fish from the bridge at the entrance to the refuge. There are also picnic tables here.

EASTON

Established around a 17th-century Quaker meeting house and the 18th-century Talbot County Courthouse, both of which remain in use today, Easton (population 10,000) sits about halfway down the Eastern Shore. The town has traditionally called itself the 'Colonial Capital of the Eastern Shore' because the Maryland General Court met here during the Federal period.

Travelers often view Easton as the gateway to the nearby tourist destinations St Michaels and Oxford, but Easton is much more. It has remained the county seat as well as the commercial and cultural center of wealthy Talbot County for 200 years. Easton has a national reputation for its annual Waterfowl Festival in November, and the town is renowned around the globe for world-class duck hunting. When travelers get here, they discover a town with an 18th-century center that looks every bit as traditional as Annapolis or Chestertown.

The gentle climate and the subtle landscapes of corn fields, pine forests, and twisting tidal tributaries charm visitors. During the last two decades, Easton's historic architecture and the surrounding manors along the Tred Avon, Miles, and Wye Rivers have drawn wealthy refugees from mainstream America. The yachtsmen and the bicyclists are here too, from April to late November. Despite the tourist boom, the area still has a bedrock of ancestral farms, working watermen, great seafood, and small towns worth exploring (finding cheap accommodations is another matter – see Places to Stay, later).

Orientation
Easton is off Route 50 south of the Chesapeake Bay Bridge, 41 miles from Annapolis, 59 miles from Baltimore, and 73 miles from

DC. The highway, with its motels, gas stations, and fast-food franchises, skirts the town's eastern edge. The heart of Easton's historic district is less than a mile west, where six streets are laid out in a grid around the colonial courthouse.

Information
The Talbot County Chamber of Commerce (☎ 410-822-4606, fax 410-822-7922), 210 Marlboro Rd, off the Easton Bypass/Route 322 on the west side of town, is open 8:30 am to 5 pm weekdays year-round. Brochures and guides are also available at the Avalon Theatre (see Entertainment, later) and at the Easton Airport (see Getting There & Away, later).

The post office (☎ 410-822-0491) is at 116 E Dover St. Postal Suites Plus (☎ 410-819-0246) is in the Talbot Town Shopping Center, on Washington St at Harrison St on the south end of downtown.

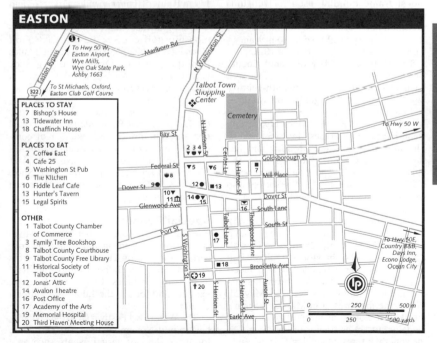

A small but select collection of local and best-selling titles can be found at Family Tree Bookshop (☎ 410-820-5252) 9 Goldsborough St. Jonas' Attic (☎ 410-820-8266), 4 E Dover St, described as a 'metaphysical five-and-dime,' has more-unusual titles. The News Center (☎ 410-822-7212), in the Talbot Town Shopping Center, has a large selection of newspapers, magazines, and mostly paperback books, along with local maps.

The Talbot County Free Library (☎ 410-822-1626), 100 W Dover St, has an extensive local history collection. (This is where author James Michener researched his best-seller *Chesapeake*.)

Memorial Hospital (☎ 410-822-1000) is at 219 S Washington St.

Things to See & Do
Built by the Society of Friends, the 1682 **Third Haven Meeting House** (☎ 410-822-2401), 405 S Washington St, is probably the oldest frame building used for religious meetings in the United States. William Penn preached here. Visitors are welcome to visit the quiet and peaceful spot from 9 am to 5 pm; there's a Sunday service at 10 am.

The **Historical Society of Talbot County** (☎ 410-822-0773), 25 S Washington St, runs a local history museum in its 19th-century headquarters and hosts guided tours of three 18th- and 19th-century houses, including the 1810 James Neall House and the 1795 Joseph Neall House, both homes of cabinetmakers. The museum is closed Monday and has shorter winter hours. Admission to the museum alone is $3; a three-home tour ticket is $3; a combo ticket is $5. The society also sponsors archaeological digs, lectures, painting and crafts classes, and neighborhood walking tours by reservation ($5 per person).

The original government building went up in 1712; **Talbot County Courthouse** (☎ 410-822-2401), 11 N Washington St, replaced it in 1794, and this was remodeled and expanded in 1958. It was here that Americans first expressed the 'Talbot Resolves' on May 24, 1774 – the first protest in Maryland against the British closing of the port of Boston – pledging 'to act as friends of liberty and to the general interest of mankind.' These same

sentiments later found their way into the American Declaration of Independence.

Built in 1921 as a vaudeville house, the 400-seat art deco **Avalon Theatre** (☎ 410-822-0345), at 40 E Dover St, in the heart of downtown, has been fully restored and now serves as a performing arts center. The theater has a year-round schedule of concerts, films, pageants, and other community events. There is a visitor kiosk in the lobby.

The **Academy of the Arts** (☎ 410-822-0455), 106 South St, houses a good collection of 19th- and 20th-century art in an 1820s schoolhouse. The academy also sponsors concerts and art classes. It's open 10 am to 4 pm Monday to Saturday year-round.

In 1881, four Protestant denominations built the hexagonal **No Corner for the Devil** and shared it on alternating Sundays. Its wide-angle design was made so 'the Devil would have no corner in which to sit and hatch evil.' It's on Route 50 between mile markers 67 and 68, about 3 miles south of Easton.

Easton attracts many golfers to its championship **golf** courses. Easton Club Golf Course (☎ 410-820-9800) is less than 2 miles from downtown on Oxford Rd. Hog Neck Golf Course (☎ 410-822-6079) is right on Route 50, across from the airport a few miles north of town.

Bicycling is one of the best ways to tour the Bay Hundred Peninsula (see the boxed text Bay Hundred). The chamber of commerce (see Information, earlier) distributes bike maps. Bike rentals are available in St Michaels, Oxford, and at the Bike Shop (☎ 410-822-8580), 8 miles south of Easton (call to reserve).

Special Events
The Eastern Shore Chamber Music Festival is a two-week event in June featuring concerts at the Avalon Theatre and other spots around town. The Talbot County Fair, held in mid-July, includes three days of games, exhibits, and food at the Talbot Agricultural Center.

The Waterfowl Festival (☎ 410-822-4567), held in mid-November, draws 20,000 people for three days of varied events, such as a decoy auction, retriever-dog demonstrations, a shooting exhibition, and many arts and crafts exhibits. Admission is $10 per day, $17 for all days.

Places to Stay

Rates for Easton and nearby towns are highest in the summer and during prime waterfowl-hunting season (October to January). Unless noted, all rates are high-season prices.

The least expensive stay in town is in a modest family B&B on the main highway 5 miles south of town. *Country B&B* (☎ 410-822-0587, 5991 Ocean Gateway) offers two comfortable rooms sharing one bath for $60 each, including breakfast.

Ocean Gateway (Route 50) near Goldsborough St, east of downtown Easton, is where you'll find franchise motels and fast food. Here, the *Days Inn* (☎ 410-822-4600) has standard doubles that start at $80 on weekdays, $93 on weekends. *Econo Lodge* (☎ 410-820-5555) charges $100 and up for singles and doubles.

For around the same price as a chain motel, you can stay in more intimate surroundings at a B&B in the historic district. *Chaffinch House* (☎ 410-822-5074, 800-861-5074, 132 S Harrison St) has six rooms in a huge Queen Anne Victorian with porches and a turret on every floor. The 'wedding room' is actually a suite decorated like a Victorian bridal chamber, complete with a bridal gown on a dressmaker's mannequin. There's also a sleeping porch for warm weather, as well as bicycles for borrowing. Innkeeper Laura Brandt seems like a gracious Victorian herself. Rooms start at $95.

The *Bishop's House* (☎ 410-820-7290, 800-223-7290, 214 Goldsborough St) is a nicely restored home built by a local steamboat captain for the former governor of Maryland. Later it was the home of the bishop of Easton. The house has high ceilings and old oak, walnut, and mahogany furniture, and fireplaces in most rooms. Each of the five guest rooms with private bath is $110 a night, including a full breakfast (two-night minimum stay). Bike rentals are available for guests by reservation.

The *Tidewater Inn* (☎ 410-822-1300, 800-237-8775, 101 E Dover St) is the replica of a brick inn in the Queen Anne style that led the way for historic preservation in downtown Easton. Rooms are modern but have traditional mahogany furnishings, such as four-poster beds. Diners and guests can get a free carriage tour of the town from the livery man waiting at curbside. Doubles start at $150; inquire about weekend packages that include dinner, breakfast, and champagne (see Hunter's Tavern under Places to Eat, below).

Some of the most deluxe accommodations in the region are in 18th-century manor houses north of town, such as the B&B *Ashby 1663* (☎ 410-822-4235, 800-458-3622, 27448 Ashby Dr). This spacious wooded estate dates to 1663 and has been used as a movie set. Inside you'll find chandeliers, fireplaces, a piano, panoramic views through wide glass doors, and other luxuries. Room rates start at $215 for a double year-round and include breakfast, cocktails, and other perks.

Places to Eat

Coffee East (☎ 410-819-6711, 5 Goldsborough St) is a bakery cafe serving baked goods (for example, corn muffins served with pepper cream cheese) and light lunches; it also offers Internet access.

Up the street, *Cafe 25* (☎ 410-822-9360, 25 Goldsborough St) is a comfortable spot for a full breakfast (starting at 7 am), Italian deli sandwiches, gourmet pizza, and a great seared-shrimp Caesar salad ($9), along with classic Italian plates. You can pick up $5 picnic sandwiches here, too, as well as at *Fiddle Leaf Cafe* (☎ 410-822-4353, W Dover St) and *The Kitchen* (☎ 410-819-6780, 22 Harrison St).

In tavern settings, you can find moderately priced burgers and sandwiches ($5 and up) at *Washington St Pub* (☎ 410-822-9011, 20 N Washington St) and at the speakeasy-style *Legal Spirits* (☎ 410-820-0033, 42 E Dover St), where pasta plates start at $10 at dinner.

Hunter's Tavern (☎ 410-822-1300, 101 E Dover St) is a comfortable restaurant within the refined Tidewater Inn. It serves a civilized breakfast and lunch ($11 for burgers). Fancy

MARYLAND

dinners include the likes of lobster thermidor ($60 for two).

Entertainment

The historic **Avalon Theatre** (*☎ 410-822-0345, 40 E Dover St*) hosts performances year-round; a recent season included a sea chantey concert, the Mrs Maryland pageant, Big Blow & the Bushwackers, and a visit by amazing savant Kim Peek of *Rainman* fame. The Washington St Pub (see Places to Eat, above) features live music, dancing, and a singles scene, along with 19 beers on tap.

Getting There & Away

Maryland Airlines (*☎ 410-822-0400*) and East Coast Flight Services (*☎ 410-820-6633*) run charter flights between the Easton Airport (*☎ 410-770-8055*) and Baltimore-Washington International or Ronald Reagan Washington National Airports, among other destinations. For a cab, call Mama's Taxi (*☎ 410-253-2394*).

Trailways buses (*☎ 410-822-3333*) stop at the Fast Stop Texaco station mini-mart on Route 50 across from the Easton Airport, a few miles north of town. Fares to/from Washington, DC, start at $17.

Coming from Annapolis by car, you approach Easton via the Chesapeake Bay Bridge and Route 50 south. Coming south from Chestertown, take Route 213 and join Route 50 at the town of Wye Mills.

AROUND EASTON
Wye Mill

The Wye Mill (*☎ 410-827-6909*), on Route 662 (off Route 50) north of Easton, is the oldest commercial building in continuous use in Maryland. Built in 1671 and rebuilt in 1720 and 1840, the mill provided flour for American troops during the Revolutionary War. The water-driven mill can be seen 11 am to 1 pm weekdays and 10 am to 4 pm weekends from mid-April to mid-November. The mill still grinds grist on the first and third Saturdays of the month, in season.

Wye Oak

The Wye Oak is also on Route 662 (off Route 50) near the Wye Mill and south of the town of Wye Mills. This 450-year-old white oak is Maryland's official tree. It's 95 feet high and 21 feet around and spreads out across 165 feet. The tree takes up most of Wye Oak State Park, the only one-tree state park in the country. Maryland residents can buy Wye Oak seedlings.

ST MICHAELS

Bay Hundred Peninsula thrusts into the Chesapeake like a crab claw from the bay's Eastern Shore near Easton. Along Bay Hundred's shores lie the sweeping manors and productive fishing ports that have typified Chesapeake life for three centuries. St Michaels, the so-called Town That Fooled the British, lies 9 miles west of Easton on Route 33. The nickname comes from events during the War of 1812. St Michaels' citizens rigged a forest with lanterns to trick British naval gunners into bombarding the wilderness while the actual town lay safe under a cloak of darkness.

St Michaels warrants exploration by boat, bike, and foot. From the water, St Michaels looks like a maze of coves. Beyond the town center, dominated by the lighthouse and spire on St Mary's Church, the shore is a mix of forest and a scattering of wharves leading to stately manor houses. Sometimes a fleet of the tall, three-sail log canoes will race out from the yacht club on Long Haul Creek like ghosts.

Thickly settled around a trio of coves on the Miles River, St Michaels (population 1200) has been a vital port on the Chesapeake since the 1700s. Today, the town main-

---

Bay Hundred

The term 'Bay Hundred' comes from the English division of Maryland into 'hundreds' for administrative and military purposes. Anglo Saxon hundreds were 10 families, 10 estates, or 100 fighting men. Colonists used the distinction of 'hundreds' in Maryland until after the American Revolution.

– Randy Peffer

MARYLAND

tains its colonial feel with red-brick Georgian buildings, gardens, and historic watercraft tied at the wharf of the Chesapeake Bay Maritime Museum. Less than 30 years ago, St Michaels was a backwater where many of the citizens earned a living as watermen, harvesting the bay's oysters from fall to winter and blue crabs from spring to summer. Landed gentry maintained vast manors outside the town and brought a patina of sophistication to the area with their fox hunts and sailboat races. People measured time in seasons, not by days or hours.

Life changed in St Michaels during the 1980s, when James Michener's novel *Chesapeake* popularized the area. The town is no longer one of those undiscovered gems of colonial America. Many shops along Talbot St have become self-consciously quaint and cater to expensive out-of-town tastes, and vacationing yachts from all over the Atlantic dominate the watermen's boats in the harbor.

Nevertheless, St Michaels celebrates its maritime heritage, and traces of its original watermen's community can still be seen. It's a beautiful spot.

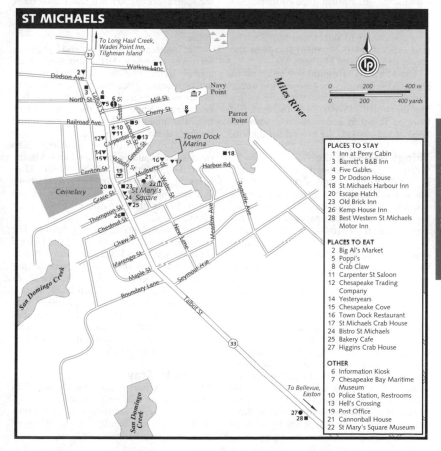

ST MICHAELS

PLACES TO STAY
1 Inn at Perry Cabin
3 Barrett's B&B Inn
4 Five Gables
9 Dr Dodson House
18 St Michaels Harbour Inn
20 Escape Hatch
23 Old Brick Inn
26 Kemp House Inn
28 Best Western St Michaels Motor Inn

PLACES TO EAT
2 Big Al's Market
5 Poppi's
8 Crab Claw
11 Carpenter St Saloon
12 Chesapeake Trading Company
14 Yesteryears
15 Chesapeake Cove
16 Town Dock Restaurant
17 St Michaels Crab House
24 Bistro St Michaels
25 Bakery Cafe
27 Higgins Crab House

OTHER
6 Information Kiosk
7 Chesapeake Bay Maritime Museum
10 Police Station, Restrooms
13 Hell's Crossing
19 Post Office
21 Cannonball House
22 St Mary's Square Museum

MARYLAND

Orientation

Route 33 runs right into the heart of St Michaels, where it becomes Talbot St, the main commercial thoroughfare. Many of the most popular restaurants and inns lie on Talbot St or on side streets between this thoroughfare and the harbor two blocks to the east. The Chesapeake Bay Maritime Museum, wharves, inns, and restaurants surround the three small coves that form the harbor.

Information

Information on St Michaels is available through the Talbot County Chamber of Commerce in Easton (see Information under Easton, earlier in the chapter). An occasionally staffed information kiosk sits near the corner of Talbot and Mill Sts. The post office (☎ 410-745-8616) stands at the corner of Talbot and Mulberry Sts.

The Memorial Hospital is 9 miles down Route 33 in Easton (see Information under Easton, earlier). The St Michaels Police Station (☎ 410-745-9500) is in the center of town on Talbot St, and public restrooms (in need of renovation) are behind the station.

Things to See & Do

Overlooking the harbor from Navy Point, the 1879 Hooper Strait octagonal lighthouse has become the image most people associate with Chesapeake Bay and is the focal point for the **Chesapeake Bay Maritime Museum** (☎ 410-745-2916). Surrounding the lighthouse on the 18-acre museum grounds are historic homes, a working boat shop, steamboats, and a prodigious collection of the Chesapeake's historic sailing craft, including a bugeye schooner, a skipjack, and log canoes. Special events include the Traditional Boat Race/Festival in September and the Mid-Atlantic Small Craft Festival in October. In addition, the museum sponsors frequent seminars on marine topics and Chesapeake heritage. The gift shop (☎ 410-745-2098) offers a complete selection of books on local history, maritime subjects, and the Chesapeake Bay. The museum is open daily (except major holidays) 9 am to 4 pm in winter, to 5 pm in spring and fall, to 6 pm in summer. Admission is $7.50 for adults, $3 for children six to 17.

St Mary's Square Museum (☎ 410-745-9561), on St Mary's Square, is part of a steam gristmill built around 1800 and exhibits furnishings, tools, and artifacts from St Michaels' colonial and Federal periods. The museum is open 10 am to 4 pm weekends only from May to October .

At the **Cannonball House**, on Mulberry St at St Mary's Square, a cannonball smashed through the roof during the War of 1812, rolled across the attic floor and then down the staircase. Legend has it that the dame of the house, one Mrs Merchant, felt that the devil himself pursued her as she fled the house.

The intersection of Locust and Carpenter Sts takes the name **Hell's Crossing**. Some legends assert that the nickname arose in the 19th century because of the noise from the shipyards, as well as the fire-and-fog bell near here. Others claim the name comes from the quantities of sin smoldering in the brothels that sprung up here.

If you're interested in **bicycling**, bike rentals are available at Town Dock Marina (☎ 410-745-2400, 800-678-8980), 305 Mulberry St, and at the St Michaels Harbour Inn marina (see Places to Stay, later). Several inns also provide bikes for their guests.

There are plenty of **boating** options. For one-hour narrated cruises along the historic shores of the Miles River, the *Patriot* (☎ 410-745-3100) leaves the Crab Claw dock four times a day. Tickets are $9 for adults, $5 for children. Rent boats at Town Dock Marina (see above) or canoes and aqua-bikes at St Michaels Harbour Inn (see Places to Stay, below; also call for transient slip-rental rates). You can rent kayaks at Loews Wharf (see Places to Stay, below).

Places to Stay

There are no budget accommodations in St Michaels, even relatively speaking.

A mile or so southeast of downtown St Michaels on Route 33, the 93-room

Chesapeake Bay Log Canoes

Looking nothing like their name, log canoes are tall, slender traditional racing sailboats with three sails, needle-bow sprits, and at least a half-dozen crew members. Before the mid-19th century, Chesapeake watermen built their oystering skiffs by clamping together two to five big logs, and then hollowing them out to make the hull of a boat. The results were narrow, sail-propelled vessels that could carry one or two men out to the shell-fishing bars to tong for oysters. Over the years, the boats grew to more than 30 feet in length, and a second mast was added, which allowed boats to carry more oysters and achieve more speed in racing home to get the best price from the oyster buyers. Racing log canoes for sport began in St Michaels in 1859, as an obsession with speed consumed Eastern Shore builders and watermen.

By 1925, gasoline engines had replaced the sails on the oyster tongers' boats, but the watermen and – increasingly – local gentry continued their obsession with these log canoes that, from a distance, look like majestic tall ships. To keep these narrow boats from upsetting under a press of sail in strong winds, captains recruit six to 10 crew members to help trim sails and ride like acrobats on staging planks that stretch out 10 feet on the windward side of the boat. Hence, watching the crew scampering to keep their sleek antique vessels upright in shifty winds is a spectacle that draws huge spectator fleets of pleasure craft, generally filled with plenty of foodstuffs and beer.

The log canoes race most weekends during July and August, around St Michaels, Oxford, and Chestertown, and spawn a carnival atmosphere on the water and shore after the races, when the crews tie up or beach their boats for cookouts and keg parties.

– Randy Peffer

Best Western St Michaels Motor Inn (☎ 410-745-3333, 800-528-1234) is the only franchise motel – actually it's the *only* motel – in town. It's on the highway near a supermarket shopping center and restaurant. Standard rooms run around $85 (single or double); there's a seasonal pool.

In Sherwood, 6 miles west on Route 33 and a half-mile down a dead-end road, ***Loews Wharf*** (☎ 410-745-6684) rents spartan rooms in a concrete block annex – an interesting way to go, but hardly a bargain at

$95/125 for a single/double. (Also see Entertainment, later in the chapter.)

Most lodging is available in B&Bs downtown, within short walking or biking distance of attractions and restaurants. Rates start at more than $100 a night. Peak season is May to October; spring and fall are shoulder seasons; winter is low season. Prices quoted are peak weekend rates for two people (rates are higher for special festival or holiday weekends). You can find discounts for weekdays and for shared baths at some inns.

Kemp House Inn (☎ *410-745-2243, 412 Talbot St)*, in a Federal-period home, features seven rooms (most with fireplaces, some with terraces) and a private cottage. Rates start at $105 and include a continental breakfast. **Five Gables** (☎ *410-745-0100, 201 N Talbot St)* offers eight rooms ($145) in a tidy blue clapboard house with an indoor pool.

Dr Dodson House (☎ *410-745-3691, 200 Cherry St)*, in a Federal brick house that once housed a tavern, offers canopy beds, antiques, and individual wood-burning fireplaces. Rates start at $160, including a gourmet breakfast, evening hors d'oeuvres, and bikes. **Barrett's B&B Inn** (☎ *410-745-3322, 204 N Talbot St)* features rooms with a double Jacuzzi in front of a fireplace. Rates start at $170.

The **Old Brick Inn** (☎ *410-745-3323, 401 S Talbot St)* is a newly restored two-story historic inn dating to 1816. It has 12 rooms (starting at $175) with all-modern conveniences.

Escape Hatch (☎ *410-745-6360, 310 S Talbot St)*, above Saltbox Antiques, offers a two-bedroom suite with a kitchen, living room, and porch ($185).

The **Wades Point Inn** (☎ *410-745-2500)* lies 5 miles west of town on a lane leading from Route 33. This is really a manor house set on a 120-acre farm overlooking Chesapeake Bay, and staying here is like joining the landed gentry. Betsy and John Feiler offer some rooms for as little as $110, including continental breakfast.

The 46-room **St Michaels Harbour Inn** (☎ *410-745-9001, 800-955-9001, 101 N Harbor Rd)* is a modern hotel on the water with scenic-view rooms, a seasonal pool, and a 60-slip marina popular with boat-in guests. It's a nice hotel to be sure, but its rates ($199 and up) illustrate how lodging costs in St Michaels have gone through the roof.

The 41-room **Inn at Perry Cabin** (☎ *410-745-2200)*, on Watkins Lane off Talbot St, a modern rendition of an English country home, was built by Sir Bernard Ashley to give St Michaels aristocratic (some locals say 'pretentious') accommodations. The inn, decorated lavishly in namesake Laura Ashley style, occupies a point overlooking the scenic cove and features an indoor pool,

fitness center, and many other deluxe amenities. Rooms at the deluxe resort start at $395 for garden-view accommodations.

Places to Eat

Try **Big Al's Market** (☎ *410-745-3151, 302 N Talbot St)*, which prepares steamed crabs for carry-out, has a deli, and sells bait. The **Bakery Cafe** (☎ *410-745-0200, 409 S Talbot St)* offers morning coffee and treats as well as light lunches, such as Chinese chicken salad ($5). **Chesapeake Trading Company** (☎ *410-745-9797, 102 N Talbot St)* has an espresso bar in addition to books and gifts; it's open long hours.

Poppi's (☎ *410-745-3158, 207 N Talbot St)*, in a happy little clapboard house with a few patio tables, is an inexpensive place that's popular with locals for breakfast (with all the B&Bs, few visitors are hunting down breakfast) and burgers at lunch. Poppi's opens at 7 am.

The classic local place is the **Carpenter St Saloon** (☎ *410-745-5111)*, Talbot St at Carpenter St. This smoky old corner bar is the most atmospheric place for conversation, burgers (from $2.50), and fried oyster 'poboy' sandwiches. It also has a light, airy place next door for civilized family dining (kids like the toy train). Both open at 7 am.

At **Town Dock Restaurant** (☎ *410-745-5577, 125 Mulberry St)*, you can enjoy the crab cake and Bloody Mary Sunday brunch, served al fresco on the harborside deck.

Bistro St Michaels (☎ *410-745-9111, 403 S Talbot St)* is the most glamorous place in town; you even need reservations for *lunch*. Inside a clapboard house, the tiny dining room is outfitted with gleaming wooden benches, mustard-colored walls, and giant Toulouse Lautrec posters. There's also a nice garden patio. Chef David Stein serves the inventive likes of roasted cod on crawfish risotto ($20 at dinner). The bistro also has a sophisticated wine selection, with several champagnes, and elegant desserts. It's closed Wednesday in summer, Tuesday and Wednesday the rest of the year.

Yesteryears (☎ *410-745-6206, 200 S Talbot St)* caters to throngs of weekend tourists with prime rib, broiled rockfish, and other daily chalkboard specials ($12 and up). Next door, **Chesapeake Cove** (☎ 410-745-3300) is a reasonable family place that attracts a nicely mixed crowd. You can get a good chicken dinner with all the fixins for around $10 (kids eat for $3.25). It's open daily for all three meals and does a brisk after-church business on Sunday.

The grand mammy of St Michaels restaurants remains the landmark **Crab Claw** (☎ 410-745-2900), perched on Navy Point adjacent to the Maritime Museum. The Crab Claw has served two generations of locals and travelers and was largely responsible for putting St Michaels on the tourist trail 30 years ago. Eating on the 2nd-floor deck, with its view of the entire town and harbor, is close to a religious experience (or at least a cultural ritual) for anyone caught up in the romance of the Chesapeake. You can feast for hours on trays mounded with blue crabs steamed in tangy Old Bay sauce and beer. The air fills with the swish and fizz of beer poured from pitchers, the slaps of crab mallets cracking open hundreds of shells, and the scent of plump meat from 'jimmy' (male) crabs. The price of crabs varies by season and availability, but plan on spending at least $20 for your feast. It's open daily from March to mid-December.

Two other crab houses in town also feed the multitudes. The waterfront **St Michaels Crab House** (☎ 410-745-3737), at the foot of Mulberry St, has a great patio. The Ocean City institution **Higgins Crab House** has opened up a local branch east of town, next to the Best Western hotel.

Entertainment

The Carpenter St Saloon (see Places to Eat, earlier) is a meeting place for restless gentry, watermen, and local youth. 'C St' can be a wild and woolly place on a Friday night, when St Michaels steps out – or as the locals say, 'goes down the road' – for a good time. The jukebox cranks out Garth Brooks and Reba McEntire anthems to a bar overflowing with laughter, dart throwers, tall tales, and draft beer. Police generally hover right outside the

door (the police station is the adjacent building) to keep the peace.

On weekends, the Inn at Perry Cabin (see Places to Stay, earlier) and the Town Dock Restaurant (see Places to Eat, earlier) feature dancing to live bands that cover mainstream rock music. Yesteryears (see Places to Eat, earlier) also has live music.

Loews Wharf in Sherwood (see Places to Stay, earlier) has a hideaway bar that's a great place for lively weekend entertainment and summer bonfires, or a nice quiet beer around the fireplace on weekdays and in the off season.

TILGHMAN ISLAND

Tilghman is a 3-by-½-mile island at the end of Route 33 – 't'end o' the road,' as the locals say – 14 miles southwest of St Michaels. This low bay island marks the northern juncture of the bay and the broad Choptank River. Connected to the mainland across Knapps Narrows by a counterbalance drawbridge, Tilghman is a thriving watermen's community. Here, you will find hundreds of oystering, clamming, fishing, and crabbing boats, along with the rough-and-ready men and women who, as they say, 'follow the water.'

Tilghman is the home port for a dozen of the remaining working skipjacks still dredging for Chesapeake oysters (see the boxed text The Chesapeake Bay Skipjack). It has become a cliché to say Tilghman Islanders (along with residents of other remote Eastern Shore islands) speak with the Elizabethan English accents of their ancestors. That's stretching the case, but the watermen and their families do have a distinctive way of speaking, which one visitor from Cornwall, England, said reminded him of the fisherfolk from home. On Tilghman, you'll hear some of the toughest men you've ever met call each other 'honey.' Tilghman Island has had various names in its history, including Great Choptank Island, but Gentleman William Tilghman inherited the island in 1775, and his family name remains.

For information on Tilghman Island, contact the Talbot County Chamber of

Commerce in Easton (see Information under Easton, earlier in the chapter).

Boating, Oystering & Crabbing

Several captains take visitors out on the bay aboard their work boats. Most skipjacks sail from Dogwood Harbor on the north end of the island. After crossing the drawbridge, drive for half a mile past the Fire Hall and Country Store; then look for the harbor about 100 yards ahead on your left. If you're fit, eager, and dressed to work, you might find a waterman who will take you out on the bay in exchange for your labor. Be respectful and ask one of the local bartenders to help you out with meeting watermen when they come ashore in the afternoons. Expect a long, hard day, but the rewards can

be the freshest seafood you will ever eat, shared beers after work, and perhaps lifelong friendships.

Captain Wade Murphy (☎ 410-886-2176) owns the *Rebecca T Ruark*, the oldest skipjack on the Chesapeake; parts of the boat date from 1886. For a price, Captain Murphy will take people oystering at dawn from November to March, crabbing from April to October, or just for a sail around the bay (starting at $30 per person). Or, call Captain Ed Farley (☎ 410-745-6080) for rides on his 32-passenger working skipjack, *HM Krentz*.

For fishing-boat charters, call Harrison's Chesapeake House (☎ 410-886-2121, 886-2109); see Places to Stay & Eat. There are 14 boats in Captain Buddy's navy, so if you want to fish and need a boat, come here.

The Chesapeake Bay Skipjack

The undisputed icon for the tradition and romance of the Chesapeake is the skipjack – the graceful, two-sail white sloops the watermen use for dredging (or as they say, 'drudging') oysters from the bay. These V-bottomed beauties with raked masts evolved during the 1880s as cheap and easy-to-build platforms for towing large dredges that scoop up oysters as the boats sail back and forth over the shellfish bars. More than 2000 of these vessels once sailed the bay for oysters. With colorful names like *Ruby G Ford*, *Rosie Parks*, *Lena Rose*, *Rebecca T Ruark*, and *Nellie Bird*, the skipjacks continue to ply the Maryland section of the Chesapeake Bay for oysters long after power work boats replaced sailboats in the rest of the country.

The skipjacks survive due to a Maryland conservation law that only permits dredging for oysters from a sailboat the size and shape of the skipjack. The average skipjack is about 45 feet long on deck and 15 feet wide. A 15-foot needle-nose bowsprit juts forward from the bows. The vessel hoists more than 1200 sq feet of sail and carries its load of oysters on deck. There is a small cabin aft, with a stove where the crew of four to six 'drudgers' can escape the weather and eat meals.

Old age and continuing poor oyster harvests (due to oyster blights) have steadily shrunk the ranks of the working skipjacks. While you may still see skipjacks tied at the wharves in Baltimore, Annapolis, and Chestertown, these boats now carry passengers. Only about a dozen skipjacks are still what the watermen call 'drudge boats' – ships that actually go out on the bay to catch a 'fair living' of oysters during the season that runs from November through March.

Today, most of the working skipjacks sail from Tilghman Island, where the tradition of independent watermen persists in spite of hard times, attempts to gentrify the island, and the lure of safer, better-paying jobs in the tourist industry. If you visit Tilghman during the winter season, you will hear the watermen's trucks roll up to the skipjacks at 4 am, the bluster of the push-boat motors, and the call 'away' as the watermen slip their lines and head out through the gloom to arrive on the drudging bars at sunrise. Bart Murphy, captain of the skipjack *Nellie Bird*, says, 'I wouldn't trade this life with no man, not the president or no man.' Murphy's son Little Bart, the mate on his father's drudge boat, says the same.

– Randy Peffer

Special Events

The Tilghman Island Seafood Festival, in late June, is a one-day celebration of music, crab races, crab picking, and a fireman's parade. Tilghman Island Day, held in late October, is an island-wide celebration of watermen, seafood, boat races, music, boat-docking contests, and other activities.

Places to Stay & Eat

The least expensive place is ***Norma's Guest House*** (☎ 410-886-2395), facing Dogwood Harbor, which offers modest lodging in an efficiency apartment ($65) or in a two-room cottage that sleeps four ($85).

Nearby, the ***Chesapeake Wood Duck Inn*** (☎ 410-886-2070), on Gibsontown Rd overlooking the skipjack fleet in Dogwood Harbor, is a onetime sailors' boarding house and bordello that has been restored as an elegant Victorian B&B. This is a six-room inn for romantics and discriminating travelers. Owner Dave Feith is a part-time waterman who can hook you up with people who might share their days on the bay with you. Rates start at $139 and include a gourmet breakfast.

Also on Dogwood Harbor, the ***Lazyjack Inn*** (☎ 410-886-2215, 800-690-5080) rents four rooms in a 160-year-old farmhouse. Room rates start at $145 for a double on weekends, including breakfast.

The century-old commercial hub of Tilghman Island remains ***Harrison's Chesapeake House*** (☎ 410-886-2121, 886-2109), about a mile south of the drawbridge. The Harrison family came to the Eastern Shore from England in the 18th century and began boarding visitors who were seeking refuge from the docks in Baltimore in the 1890s. Since then, the Harrisons have established an island dynasty that now consists of a 90-room motel and restaurant. It's down-home island-style – the Harrisons advertise their green-turf-carpeted front porch that's outfitted with wicker rockers as their 'exercise room.' But bicycle rentals and fishing-boat charters are available. Room rates are $95 to $110 for doubles; inquire about various package rates for fishing, lodging, and meals. Harrison's Chesapeake House serves a classic Eastern Shore dinner of fried chicken and crab cakes for $20, along with other seafood and steak plates.

If you're after more refined weekender ambiance, the ***Tilghman Island Inn*** (☎ 410-886-2141, 800-866-2141), on Coopertown Rd off the main road, is a modern two-story inn with lots of glass so you can see the fishing fleet coming in and out of Knapps Narrows. The inn offers tennis, fine dining, and a private marina. Rates start at $125 on weekends, including breakfast.

At the southern tip of the island on a 50-acre wildlife preserve, the ***Black Walnut Point Inn*** (☎ 410-886-2452, fax 410-886-2053), on Black Walnut Rd, offers four rooms in the main house starting at $120 and a one-bedroom cottage for $150 (all doubles). It also has a pool and resident Chesapeake Bay retrievers.

The restaurants on either side of the drawbridge have had an uneven history or have changed hands so often that's it's hard to know what to recommend – you can't go wrong with a drink and a view, in any case.

OXFORD

Travelers come to Oxford to absorb the feel of the Eastern Shore's genteel past and ride the village's historic ferry. Oxford lies on the third peninsula or 'neck' south of Easton, jutting into the Tred Avon River. Route 333 (Oxford Rd) runs 9 miles south from Easton past the estates and plantations of Talbot County's landed gentry and dead ends in Oxford village. Morris St, an extension of Route 333, runs north right through the center of the village to the Oxford-Bellevue Ferry landing at the intersection with the Strand.

The Talbot County Chamber of Commerce in Easton has information on the town (see Easton, earlier in the chapter). Or, try the Oxford Business Association at ☎ 410-226-5730.

History

European settlers arrived here in the early 1660s. In 1683, the Maryland General Assembly named Oxford as a seaport, and planners laid out a town. Meanwhile, English gentry developed tobacco plantations in the rich soil along the Tred Avon in response to England's voracious demand for the 'sot weed.' Ten years later, the General Assembly named Oxford as one of only two 'ports of entry' in Maryland, and the town thrived with its markets for tobacco and slaves. Many ancestors of the Eastern Shore's African Americans passed through the Oxford slave market and former tobacco plantations.

The town's prominence faded as other towns such as Baltimore grew after the Revolutionary War and as other regions usurped the tobacco trade. During the late 19th and early 20th centuries, Oxford boomed as a center for oyster buying, shucking, canning, and shipping until overfishing exhausted local oyster beds. The town's long periods of dormancy have left it free from the ravages of extensive development, and a collection of Federal-style homes under majestic shade trees overlooks the Tred Avon and Choptank Rivers. Above the Choptank, a grassy knoll called 'the Strand' is the most prestigious address on the Eastern Shore. 'Old money' families from the tobacco plantations, 'new money' from the oystering days a century ago, and newcomer wannabes have protected their community from development and commercialism.

The only dramatic changes in the town during the last 100 years have occurred around the harbors on Town Creek and Bachelor's Point. With no fewer than nine yacht yards and marinas, Oxford's biggest business is pleasure boating, but unlike Rock Hall and St Michaels, Oxford remains almost strictly residential.

Oxford had some famous early residents: Robert Morris Jr helped finance the Revolutionary War and was one of only two men to have signed the Declaration of Independence, the Articles of Confederation, and the Constitution. Other famous figures who resided here were Reverend Thomas Bacon, who compiled the first laws of Maryland, and Colonel Tench Tilghman, who was George Washington's aide-de-camp and the man who brought word of Cornwallis' surrender to the Continental Congress.

Things to See & Do

The **Oxford-Bellevue Ferry** (☎ 410-745-9023), begun in 1683, claims to be the oldest continuously running ferry operation in the USA. The car ferry crosses the Tred Avon River from Oxford to Bellevue in 10 minutes; from Bellevue, you can drive or bicycle 7 miles to St Michaels. There is always a cooling breeze and good view of Oxford's historic houses and of the manor houses on the farms farther up the river. The ferry runs every 25 minutes, beginning at 7 am weekdays and 9 am weekends and ending around sunset, March to November. The fare is $5 per car and driver one way, or $8 roundtrip; car passengers pay 50¢ each. Bicyclists pay $2 one way, $3 roundtrip. Pedestrians pay $1.

The small **Oxford Museum** (☎ 410-226-0191) is at the corner of Morris and Market Sts. It shows exhibits on the town's history from 2 to 5 pm Friday to Sunday. You'll find a replica of the 1694 **Oxford Customs House** at the foot of Morris St near the ferry.

If you want to go **bicycling**, Oxford Mews (☎ 410-820-8222), 105 Morris St, rents bikes for $3.50 an hour or $14 a day (closed Wednesday). There's a wonderful old market at the corner serving homemade muffins and cold drinks.

For **sailing**, Skylark Sailing Yachts (☎ 410-226-5654), at Shaws' Boat Yard on Myrtle St, has 16-foot Bullseye sloops. Qualified sailors might also try Maryland Yachts (☎ 410-226-5571) or Tred Avon Yacht Charters (☎ 410-226-5000), which maintains a fleet of yachts up to 39 feet, as well as day sailers.

Places to Stay

The ***Robert Morris Inn*** (☎ *410-226-5111*) is opposite the ferry landing on Morris St. Ship carpenters built the original part of the structure before 1710. (In 1750, the hotel's namesake, Robert Morris Sr, was hit in the arm by wadding flying out of a cannon fired in his honor. Morris died from his infected injuries and may be the only person to have ever been killed by a salute in his honor.) The inn consists of the original property (now expanded to 16 rooms, starting at $100) and the Sandaway (a 19-room mansion one block away, with rooms for $180 and up). At the inn, the most evocative rooms are those built in 1710. The Sandaway has a private strip of beach. The inn's high season is April to November; it's closed mid-winter and open weekends only from mid-February through March.

The *Oxford Inn* (☎ 410-226-5220, 504 S Morris St) offers 11 rooms, a sitting room with TV, and stamped-tin ceilings. Room rates are $90 for a double with shared bath and $100 to $150 for a room with private bath, including continental breakfast. It also has an on-site restaurant, Pope's Tavern.

The *1876 House* (☎ 410-226-5496, 110 N Morris St), in a Queen Anne Victorian house with wide-plank floors and Oriental carpets, has rooms for $108 year-round.

Places to Eat

The Robert Morris Inn (see Places to Stay, above) serves sandwiches for $6, along with such dinner dishes ($15 and up) as crab cakes, oyster sandwiches, and scallops, accompanied by crystal and linen. The restaurant is closed in winter.

Local gentry and yachters tend to favor *Latitude 38* (☎ 410-266-5303), located at the entrance to town on Route 333. It features such nouvelle-cuisine dishes as crab imperial and shrimp and pasta salad; entrees start at less than $10.

Set on the water at the foot of Tilghman St near the entrance to the yacht basin at Town Creek, *Schooner Landing* (☎ 410-226-0160) is a rambling restaurant built in an old oyster shucking house with indoor and outdoor decks. The blue-and-white decor of antique nautical memorabilia comes on strong, but the service is friendly and the restaurant overlooks the parade of yachts in and out of Town Creek. The made-to-order oyster stew is as good as it comes, and many lunches are less than $7. For entertainment, the tables are pushed back for dancing and live music on Friday nights. You can listen to acoustic music on the outdoor deck on weekends during warm weather. It's closed Tuesday year-round and shuts down altogether in January and February.

Around the corner from the yacht basin, *Le Zinc* (☎ 410-226-5776, 101 Mill St) offers 'down-home French country cooking,' cocktails, and an espresso bar in an attractive little garden spot. Pasta dishes are about $9. The *Chatterbox Cafe* next door has picnic supplies.

BLACKWATER NATIONAL WILDLIFE REFUGE

This 17,000-acre refuge (☎ 410-228-2677), 20 miles south of Easton, consists of tidal marshes set aside for migrating waterfowl. The visitor center on Key Wallace Drive is open 8 am to 4 pm weekdays, 9 am to 5 pm weekends.

The refuge is one of the major stopping points for Canada geese and has the greatest density of bald eagles in the eastern USA north of Florida. You can also see snow geese, peregrine falcons, blue herons, ospreys (nesting platforms are provided), and 20 duck species. The best time for bird watching is mid-October to mid-March.

Blackwater also has raccoons, otters, opossums, skunks, muskrats, red foxes, and fox squirrels. You might see white-tailed deer and Asian sika deer in the remaining wooded areas.

The 5-mile nature drive runs past ponds, woods, fields, and marshland. The entrance fee is $3 per car and $1 for bikers or pedestrians. From the north, take Route 50 south to Cambridge, and then take Route 16 south to State Rd 335. At the intersection of Key Wallace Drive, make a left and follow the signs to the entrance. The refuge is rife with insects in July and August, so bring repellent.

CRISFIELD

Crisfield (population 2900) is a flat, plain-looking town with few historical buildings, located on the southern tip of Maryland's Eastern Shore about 80 miles south of Easton. Ocean City lies 60 miles to the east. Come here if you love hanging around commercial fisherfolk, you can't resist seeing the annual Labor Day Hard Crab Derby, or you want to take a boat to Smith or Tangier Islands in the Chesapeake.

History

Local citizens like to say that Crisfield was built on oystering, literally and figuratively. A quiet fishing village known as Somers Cove for 200 years before the railroad arrived in 1867, Crisfield took its current name from a local entrepreneur who brought the railroad and turned the tiny village into a boomtown.

As oysters became the preferred delicacy among America's upper crust during the final decades of the 19th century, the Chesapeake's skipjack fleet grew to thousands of vessels. In response to the millions of bushels coming ashore from the 'drudge boats,' Crisfield turned into a maze of buyers' wharves, with shucking houses (for cleaning oyster meat from the shells) sprawled throughout town. The railroad shipped trainloads of canned and fresh oysters to diners in DC, Baltimore, Philadelphia, New York, and Boston. Empty oyster shells were used to fill in the marshes to make room for more wharves and seafood buyers, as well as to pave the roads.

More recently, with the continuing decline in the oyster harvest over the last 50 years, Crisfield likes to call itself the 'crab capital of the world' because its seafood buyers have all but cornered the market on Maryland's hard and soft-shell crabs, packing and shipping in excess of 125,000 bushels a year.

Information

The Somerset County Tourism Office (☎ 410-651-2968, 800-521-9189) is in a rest area at mile marker 19 on Route 13, north of Crisfield in Prince Ann. It's open 9 am to 6 pm daily in summer, with reduced hours in winter. The Crisfield Chamber of Commerce (☎ 410-968-2500), 906 W Main St, also provides information. It's open weekdays only year-round.

Things to See & Do

The **J Millard Tawes Museum** (☎ 410-968-2501), just off Main St at 8th St, traces the career of Crisfield native and former Maryland Governor J Millard Tawes. You could skip this one unless you're a J Millard Tawes fan. On the other hand, learning about one of the region's favorite sons can really shed light on the culture. It's open 9 am to 4 pm weekdays, 10 am to 2 pm weekends (closed Saturday in winter). Admission is $2.50 for adults, free for children 12 and under.

Contact the Somers Cove Marina (☎ 410-968-0925, 800-967-3474) for a list of 20 charter boat captains and **fishing** information.

Special Events

The annual Hard Crab Derby & Fair (☎ 410-968-2682, 800-782-3913) held on Labor Day weekend includes crab races, crab-picking contests, and crabs cooked in every possible way for consumers. Admission is $4. Hotels hike their rates and are usually booked for this weekend.

Places to Stay & Eat

The 40-room **Pines Motel** (☎ *410-968-0900, 129 N Somerset Ave*) has standard motel rooms ($60 for a double on weekends) and a seasonal pool. The **Somers Cove Motel** (☎ *410-968-1900*), on RR Norris Drive at the southern end of the Somers Cove Marina, is a two-story place overlooking the marina. It's nothing special, but it's clean and has a pool. Rates are $45 to $75; it's open year-round. **Leonora's Crisfield Inn** (☎ *410-968-2181, 209 W Main St*) offers three rooms in a family home. Rates start at $65, including breakfast. It's open May to October.

The **Dockside** (☎ *410-968-3464*), W Main St near 10th St, offers diner food daily year-round. The captains who run the boats to Smith and Tangier Islands come here for breakfast. At the north end of town on Maryland Ave (Route 413), just past the intersection with Standard St, is the **Big Belly Deli**, a modern sandwich place with no atmosphere but decent sandwiches.

The two seafood restaurants to try are the **Captain's Galley** (☎ *410-968-1636, 1021 W Main St*) and the **Watermen's Inn** (☎ *410-968-2119*), 9th and W Main Sts. Watermen's is run by culinary school graduates. Seafood dishes range from $10 to $20.

Getting There & Away

Crisfield is at the southern end of Route 413. To get there, take Route 13 south until you see signs for Route 413 and the town of

Westover. Follow Route 413 about 15 miles south until you hit Crisfield.

SMITH ISLAND

Twelve miles west of Crisfield in the middle of the Chesapeake lies Smith Island, actually several islands (due to the rise in bay waters during the last four centuries) and a marsh forming a ragged archipelago 8 miles long and 4 miles wide. Smith is the only island in Maryland that can be reached by boat only. There are three villages (total population 450): Ewell and Rhodes Point (which are on opposite sides of the largest island) and Tylerton. Passenger boats from Crisfield generally stop at Ewell but will stop at Tylerton on request. The island takes its name from Captain John Smith, who explored the Chesapeake in 1608, stopped here, and gave the site his name. For him, this place was an oasis.

Smith Islanders are exceptionally friendly and speak with an archaic Cornish accent that is even stronger than what you hear on Tilghman. Often described as 'historic' or 'rustic,' Smith Island has a tendency to disappoint day-trip visitors. Smith is important in soft-shell crab production, and many watermen live here, but the villages are not well-swept troves of historic architecture. Smith is dedicated to the 'water business,' not to looking good for travelers. Nondescript houses, aluminum siding, telephone wires, and abandoned cars (it's difficult to get dead vehicles off the island) are commonplace, and so are beer cans and plastic litter along Smith Island Rd, which runs between Ewell and Rhodes Point.

The joys of Smith Island can hardly be perceived, let alone explored, during an afternoon visit. The vast meadows of chartreuse

The Story of Jimmy & Sook

Although blue crabs live along most of the Atlantic Coast of the USA, they prefer estuaries where saltwater and freshwater mix. The Chesapeake Bay is ideal. The crab's Latin name is *Callinectes sapidus Rathbun*. The first two words translate as 'tasty beautiful swimmer.' The third, Rathbun, is from Dr Mary Rathbun, a Smithsonian carcinologist, who identified and described 1000 new crab species.

Blue crabs have an elaborate mating ritual. In fall, a courting jimmy (male) approaches a mature sook (female) and raises himself on his legs, weaving back and forth and waving his swimming legs. To make sure he gets the female's attention, he also digs up a storm of sand with his legs. The jimmy then grabs the sook and pulls her, right side up and face forward, under himself. He then cradle-carries her for at least two days, usually swimming for miles until she molts, which is the only time she may be fertilized. The pair, called 'doublers,' swim along the surface of the water and can easily be scooped up with a dip net that has a chicken-wire basket. After the female molts, the male carefully flips her over on her back and inserts his two pleopods into her genital pores. Coitus lasts five to 12 hours. When the lovemaking is over, the female saves the sperm until next spring and then uses it to fertilize the eggs she carries.

Sooks lay their eggs in the lower parts of the bay, generally from June to August, but the time and place vary. At hatching, crabs – called zoea – are 1/25 of an inch long and look like an insect. Only one in a million eggs produces an adult crab. The zoea sheds its carapace several times and begins to look like an adult crab, at which point it's called a 'megalops.' These young crabs begin to move north in the bay during the fall and keep molting – a total of about 20 times – until cold weather sets in and they bury themselves in the mud through the winter. When spring comes, the crabs continue migrating northward. In the few hours after molting, a crab is a soft-shell crab (a delicacy when pan-fried with spices and a few bread crumbs). The soft-shell crab is only about a third as large as its discarded shell.

– Randy Peffer

MARYLAND

marsh grass, stands of loblolly pine, and gatherings of waterfowl really deserve exploration by water. One person who took her kayak to Smith Island spent a week paddling around, camping on a remote islet one night. She said she thought she had found heaven until one of the Chesapeake's legendary thunder squalls ripped across the bay.

A small museum near the dock relates the island's history.

Places to Stay & Eat

A handful of places near the ferry dock in the small commercial district in Ewell are open for the temperate tourist season (call to confirm winter off-season availability).

For lodging, the **Ewell Tide Inn** (☎ 410-425-2141, 4063 Tyler Rd) has four rooms in a modern setting for around $85. Bike rentals are available. For meals, the **Bayside Inn** (☎ 410-425-2771) on the water serves standard seafood dishes for tourists; some boats dock here as well.

Up the block from the ferry dock, **Ruke's Seafood Deck** (☎ 410-425-2311) sells soda and sandwiches.

Getting There & Away

Smaller boats, including one that carries mail, run year-round from City Dock at the end of W Main St in Crisfield. You just show up and pay the captain. If you want to call ahead, try the *Captain Jason I & II* (☎ 410-425-5931, 425-4471) or the *Island Belle II* and *Island Princess* (☎ 410-968-3206). The trip to Smith Island costs $10 per person, half-price for children six to 12. It takes about 35 minutes. Boats generally leave Crisfield at 12:30 pm and return from Smith Island at 3:30 pm. Sometimes there are afternoon boats that stay overnight during the summer.

The 150-passenger *Captain Tyler II* (☎ 410-425-2771) departs from behind the J Millard Tawes Museum from Memorial Day to October. The fare is $20 roundtrip, half-price for children six to 12. From June to Labor Day, the same firm runs boats between Smith Island and Point Lookout, across Chesapeake Bay in southern Maryland. The fare is $22 for adults, $11 for children.

Another firm, Island and Bay Cruises (☎ 804-453-3430), runs boats between Smith Island and Smith Point in Reedville, Virginia, during the summer. There are no car ferries across the Chesapeake.

TANGIER ISLAND (VIRGINIA)

Tangier Island is 10 miles south of Smith Island, accessible only by boat, most readily from Crisfield. The island is barely a mile wide and 3 miles long and has the same unscrubbed ambiance you find on Smith Island, although there are no vehicles. There are gift shops, a few restaurants, and watermen's homes that cater to the tourist trade during temperate months (call to confirm availability during the winter off season).

You can eat home-cooked crab cakes, clam fritters, and country ham at **Hilda Crockett's Chesapeake House** (☎ 757-891-2331), in the small commercial district on the island. All-you-can-eat, family-style meals are $12.25 (crab cakes $2 extra), $6 for children under eight. Hilda's also has eight rooms for rent: $40 per person per day, including dinner and a full breakfast.

The **Islander Seafood Restaurant** (☎ 757-891-2249) charges $10 to $14 for seafood dinners; it also serves lunch. It's open daily in summer.

Tangier Island Cruises (☎ 410-968-2338) runs trips to the island from Somers Cove Marina in Crisfield. The hour-and-a-half ride, offered from May to October, is $20 for adults, free for children under 12.

OCEAN CITY

Founded as a vacation community four years after the Civil War, Ocean City ('OC') is Maryland's mammoth Atlantic shore beach resort. For most of its length, it's barely three blocks wide, yet it sprawls southward from the Delaware border along 10 miles of barrier beach lined with side-by-side hotels and motels. It's a Coppertone-scented town of bikini contests, waterslides, saltwater taffy, corn dogs, airbrushed T-shirts, go-carts, Skeeball, and miniature golf with story-high fantasyscapes floodlit for summer crowds late into the evening – all accompanied by a soundtrack of Jimmy Buffet and the Eagles.

A wide variety of accommodations cater to a range of tastes and budgets, from high-rise hotels to low-rent boarding houses, but Ocean City is predominantly a middle-class family resort.

The city's resident population of around 7500 swells to 300,000 with vacationers on summer weekends. From late May through June, Ocean City fills with recent high-school graduates and college students who provide much of the summer workforce, and the city takes on many aspects of a world-class fraternity party (several clubs cater to the under-21 crowd). July and August temper the scene a bit, with tens of thousands of families trying to beat the mid-Atlantic heat waves with one-or two-week vacations. Ocean City is nearly a ghost town from November to mid-April, when many businesses shut down and those still open offer bargain-basement specials.

The town originated at the southern tip of the Strand, now called 'the Inlet,' which retains a hint of Victorian flavor. Here, a 2½-mile boardwalk provides a pedestrian promenade that is the heart of the Ocean City experience (bikes allowed off-hours only). Across the Inlet is Assateague Island, famous for its herds of wild ponies (see Assateague Island, later in the chapter).

Orientation

Most travelers enter OC at the south end of town, via Route 50 from Easton and Salisbury, through a notorious, miles-long bottleneck on the mainland before you cross the Sinepuxent Bay bridge (officially called H Kelly Memorial Bridge) over to Ocean City. The two main north-south thoroughfares are Philadelphia and Baltimore Aves. Baltimore Ave – 'Motel Row' – runs closest to the beach. Endless traffic lights make travel along both streets slow during the summer season. A second bridge accesses the beach via Route 90 at 62nd St, a less-congested route for those headed to the visitor center or northern-side motels.

At the south end of town, blocks of east-west streets are named for Eastern Shore counties such as Talbot. Continuing north toward the Delaware border, east-west streets are numbered 1st to 146th St. The town is generally only two or three blocks wide, although there are condo developments on pieces of land that jut out into the bay.

Information

Tourist Offices The Convention and Visitors Bureau (☎ 410-289-8181, 800-626-2326), in the south end of the huge convention center (40th St at the Coastal Hwy), is a good first stop for travelers. It distributes maps, discount coupon booklets, and brochures on motels, restaurants, and recreation. A desk of the local hotel-and-restaurant association will help you find lodging if you've come to town without a reservation. The visitors bureau is open 8:30 am to 5 pm daily year-round, with extended evening hours in the summer.

The chamber of commerce (☎ 888-626-3386) distributes information from its office at 12320 Ocean Gateway in West Ocean City.

Post & Communications The main post office (☎ 410-289-7819) is on Philadelphia Ave at 5th St. There is a branch office (☎ 410-524-6039) at the north end of town at Montego Bay. A machine in the visitors bureau dispenses stamps.

Beachin.net (☎ 410-723-2702), 4100 Coastal Hwy at 41st St, provides Internet access and fax service. It's across from the convention center (under the sign 'Internet Cafe' – there's no cafe).

Internet Resources Check the website www.oceancity.com for general municipal information or www.ococean.com for more tourist-oriented information (including hotel and motel listings).

Bookstores At the heart of the action, Bookworld (☎ 410-289-7466), 1st St at the boardwalk, has both used and rare books. News Center (☎ 410-213-1440), on Route 50 in West OC near the outlet mall (see Shopping, later), has a large selection of periodicals and books for adults and kids. There's also a Book Warehouse in the outlet mall.

Media The most useful papers for travelers are free: Check out the *Ocean City Today*

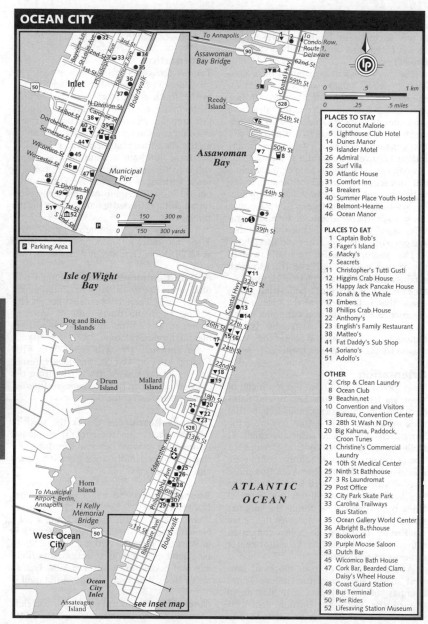

OCEAN CITY

PLACES TO STAY
4 Coconut Malorie
5 Lighthouse Club Hotel
14 Dunes Manor
19 Islander Motel
26 Admiral
28 Surf Villa
30 Atlantic House
31 Comfort Inn
34 Breakers
40 Summer Place Youth Hostel
42 Belmont-Hearne
46 Ocean Manor

PLACES TO EAT
1 Captain Bob's
3 Fager's Island
6 Macky's
7 Seacrets
11 Christopher's Tutti Gusti
12 Higgins Crab House
15 Happy Jack Pancake House
16 Jonah & the Whale
17 Embers
18 Phillips Crab House
22 Anthony's
23 English's Family Restaurant
38 Matteo's
41 Fat Daddy's Sub Shop
44 Soriano's
51 Adolfo's

OTHER
2 Crisp & Clean Laundry
8 Ocean Club
9 Beachin.net
10 Convention and Visitors
   Bureau, Convention Center
13 28th St Wash N Dry
20 Big Kahuna, Paddock,
   Croon Tunes
21 Christine's Commercial
   Laundry
24 10th St Medical Center
25 Ninth St Bathhouse
27 3 Rs Laundromat
29 Post Office
32 City Park Skate Park
33 Carolina Trailways
   Bus Station
35 Ocean Gallery World Center
36 Albright Bathhouse
37 Bookworld
39 Purple Moose Saloon
43 Dutch Bar
45 Wicomico Bath House
47 Cork Bar, Bearded Clam,
   Daisy's Wheel House
48 Coast Guard Station
49 Bus Terminal
50 Pier Rides
52 Lifesaving Station Museum

Inlet

Reedy
Island

Assawoman
Bay

Isle of Wight
Bay

Dog and Bitch
Islands

Drum
Island

Mallard
Island

Horn
Island

To Municipal
Airport, Berlin,
Annapolis

H Kelly
Memorial
Bridge

West Ocean
City

Ocean
City
Inlet

Assateague
Island

ATLANTIC
OCEAN

Municipal
Pier

P Parking Area

To Annapolis

Assawoman
Bay Bridge

To
Condo Row,
Route 1,
Delaware

see inset map

MARYLAND

and the *Maryland Coast Dispatch*. If you are just looking for food and entertainment, pick up *Oceana* or the *Beachcomber*.

Laundry 3 Rs is a 24-hour laundromat on the Coastal Hwy between 7th and 8th Sts. There's also Christine's Commercial Laundry (☎ 410-289-2269), 1607 N Philadelphia Ave; Crisp & Clean Laundry (☎ 410-524-5410), 106 64th St; Wicomico Bath House, on the beach side of Philadelphia Ave, north of Wicomico St in the Inlet; and 28th St Wash N Dry, at the Coastal Hwy.

Medical Services Atlantic General Hospital (☎ 410-641-1100) is at the junction of Route 50 (Ocean Gateway) and Route 113 in West Ocean City. Downtown, the 10th Street Medical Center (☎ 410-289-6241) can be found on the northwest corner of 10th St and Philadelphia Ave. On the north side, the 75th Street Medical Center (☎ 410-524-0075) is on the ocean side of the Coastal Hwy.

Emergency Call ☎ 911 for police, fire, or ambulance. The local police can be reached at ☎ 410-723-6610. The Coast Guard station (☎ 410-289-7579) is right at the corner of Philadelphia Ave and S Division St.

Beaches

Ocean City's 10 miles of beach are open to the public from 6 am to 10 pm. The sands are widest in front of the parking lot between the jetty at the Inlet and the pier on Wicomico St. The waves can get big here, so this is where surfers often congregate. Although the beach narrows as you follow it north from the pier, it is still broad enough to accommodate hundreds of thousands of sunbathers and swimmers without ever being even close to as crowded as, say, St Tropez, France, in August. Beach sports, including Frisbee and volleyball, are prohibited from 9 am to 5:30 pm. Pets, alcoholic beverages, and motor vehicles are always taboo. Lifeguards are on duty daily, and the beach is well groomed every night after 10 pm. The beach patrol will arrest you if they find you here after hours.

If you want to get away from the masses, try spreading out your blanket in front of

one of the hotels near the northern end of the Strand (though parking is a challenge). In spite of the crowds, you can walk for hours every morning along the edge of the sea without seeing anyone except the occasional surf anglers.

At the foot of Baltimore St, adjacent to the parking lot and the head of the boardwalk, Ocean City's **pier rides** (☎ 410-289-3031) are dominated by a roller coaster and a huge Ferris wheel, among many other games, arcades, and attractions.

As for **bathhouses**, Albright Bathhouse (☎ 410-289-7349), on N 1st St a few feet back from the boardwalk, is musty but clean (showers $5; soap and towels extra). Or there's the Ninth St Bathhouse (☎ 410-289-9189), Baltimore Ave at 9th St; and Wicomico Bath House (☎ 410-289-5025), north of Wicomico St next to the laundry, a block back from the boardwalk.

Boardwalk Promenade

The recently refurbished boardwalk is the heart of Ocean City. Residents built the first removable boardwalk in 1879, laying it out to protect their tender feet from the burning sand on the Fourth of July and packing it up in September for use again the next year. The city built the first permanent boardwalk in 1912, and the current wooden walkway extends 2½ miles from the Inlet to 27th St.

The popular promenade is lined with hotels, snack bars, trinket stores, and arcades, and it becomes a mob scene on hot summer nights. You can see the largest marlin and shark caught in Ocean City waters on display in Plexiglas cases at the southern end of the boardwalk, but watching the volume and variety of *Homo sapiens* flowing up and down the promenade can be a lot more fun.

A tram runs the length of the boardwalk in summer for 50¢. Bicycling and in-line skating on the boardwalk are restricted to less-congested hours, generally mornings – a nice ride. Rentals are readily available on and near the boardwalk.

Lifesaving Station Museum

This museum (☎ 410-289-4991) is in the 1891 lifesaving station at the southernmost tip of the Strand at 813 S Boardwalk. It has exhibits of items recovered from the sea by divers, photos of storms that have battered Ocean City, an exhibit on the lifesaving stations of the Delmarva coast, and a mermaid exhibit. It's open 11 am to 10 pm daily from June to September, to 4 pm daily in May and October, noon to 4 pm weekends in winter. Admission is $2 for adults, $1 for children.

Boating

Bayside marinas are the source of information about boat rentals, water-ski equipment, Jet Ski rentals, fishing charters, scenic cruises, and more. The midtown Bahia Marina (☎ 410-289-7438, 888-575-3625) is between 21st and 22nd Sts. Farther uptown, find Advanced Marina (☎ 410-723-2124) between 66th and 67th Sts. For 'head boats' (which charge by the person) and fishing charters, try the Talbot St Pier (☎ 410-289-9125, 289-3503), bayside in the Inlet.

Sailing Etc (☎ 410-723-1144, 800-468-9867), 46th St at the bay, rents sailboats for upwards of $30 an hour and offers sailing and windsurfing classes and equipment. It also rents kayaks and catamarans. Island Watersports (☎ 410-289-2896), 308 N 1st St at BJ's South, rents Jet Skis and parasailing craft.

Excursion cruises operate out of local marinas in Ocean City and the Shantytown Pier in West Ocean City, where the Bay Queen (☎ 410-213-0926) departs for hour-long bay and ocean cruises. Guided kayak and canoe ecotours can also be arranged at the Shantytown Pier through Ocean City Kayak (☎ 410-213-2818).

Surfing

From May to September, the city allows surfing on only two beaches per day, one each in northern and southern Ocean City. To find out which beaches, call the beach patrol (☎ 410-289-7556) or one of the surf shops. Designated surfing beaches are also announced on the radio and posted in local surf shops. Off season, you can surf anywhere. Cloud Break (☎ 410-723-0010), 58th St at the Coastal Hwy, is one of the friendliest and most helpful surf shops; it's open daily in summer.

Bicycling & In-Line Skating

Bicycles and in-line skates are permitted on the boardwalk during restricted times (usually mornings) from April through September and are unrestricted at other times of the year. Along the boardwalk, you will find an abundance of bike rentals. Some rental places aren't shops at all but just vendors with a fleet of bicycles lined up for your inspection. You can expect to pay an hourly rate of $4, or $10 daily, for a single-speed bike; mountain bikes, tandems, and in-line skates are also available.

Try Mike's Bikes (☎ 410-289-4637), 5 N 1st St and 10 N Division St, or Bike World (☎ 410-289-2587), at three locations: 10 Caroline St and on the boardwalk at 15th and 17th Sts. Darlene's on the Boards (☎ 410-289-6035) is on the boardwalk at 12th St. Skate Stop (☎ 410-289-8989), at 2nd St off the boardwalk, rents skates.

Skateboarding

A skate park in the City Park complex at 3rd St and St Louis Ave provides a bowl and half-pipe. For hours and regulations, call ☎ 410-289-2695. Skateboards are never permitted on the boardwalk.

Special Events

Springfest, held on the first weekend in May, and Sunfest in September last several days, with live music, food, and arts and crafts displays. The Fourth of July is also a big event, with beach music and a fireworks display over the Atlantic Ocean.

Places to Stay

Ten miles of beachfront are lined with places to stay, from spanking-new high-rises to funky old road motels. Altogether, more than 100 properties provide close to 10,000 guest rooms. If you want to be in the center of the action, boardwalk oceanfront rooms are considered the most desirable; but as you might imagine, these are also among the most expensive. Families might want to consider premium rooms east of Baltimore Ave to avoid crossing busy streets with water-winged kids in flip-flops – but prices drop west of Baltimore Ave. The uptown beach north of the boardwalk caters to more afflu-ent tastes, with luxury bayside hotels and 'Condo Row' between 94th and 118th Sts.

The Ocean City Hotel-Motel-Restaurant Association (☎ 410-289-6733, fax 410-289-5645), in the convention and visitors bureau (40th St at the Coastal Hwy), helps visitors with lodging and distributes hotel and motel listings. The staff know the price ranges and styles and will call the hotels for you.

Camping The nicest camping near OC is at Assateague Island, 12 miles from Ocean City (see Assateague Island, later in the chapter). The only campground in Ocean City is the year-round, 200-site *Ocean City Travel Park* (☎ 410-524-7601), 70th St at the Coastal Hwy, designed for RVs. All sites have full hookups ($37 to $47, depending on RV length; $32 for tents).

There are two other campgrounds in the area on the bay, both 4 miles away from OC: *Frontier Town* (☎ 410-641-0880, 800-228-5590), on Route 611 south of Route 50, has a campground and other shelters next to its Western Theme Park (can-can show, gun-fights, buffalo, etc). It charges $25 for tents and $28 and up for RVs ($50 for a premium spot on the bay). Its rental trailers have private bathrooms and rent for $710 a week; cabins without running water rent for $490. Both sleep six; bring linens. The place has a pool, showers, stores, and miniature golf. At *Bali-Hi RV Park* (☎ 410-352-5477), on St Martin's Neck Rd 2 miles north of Route 90 and west of the 62nd St Bridge, sites with hookups start at $25; there is emphatically no tent camping.

Hostels The *Summer Place Youth Hostel* (☎ 410-289-4542, 104 Dorchester St), between Baltimore and Philadelphia Aves, is the cheapest place in town at $25 a night, or $90 and up per week. The hostel, which is not HI-affiliated, is a cross between a mellow rooming house and a hostel. Kimberleigh and Van Duzee Flynn rent 10 rooms of varying sizes in their house (seven singles and three doubles). Guests have use of the kitchen, barbecue, sun deck, and – if you're real nice – the hot tub. The place often fills up

with folks working in town for the season, so your best bet is to visit in April or May.

Guesthouses A budget room in OC is any-thing less than $70 for a double in summer. These places tend to be at the southern end of town in the Inlet. Here, the *Belmont-Hearne* (☎ 410-289-8344, 800-638-2758, 4 Dorchester St), a few feet from the boardwalk and beach, offers the classic OC boardwalk-Inlet experi-ence. The friendly proprietor, Kate Jones Bunting, and her family run the operation. Kate was born and raised on her block and knows the history of Ocean City inside and out. The boarding house is actually three buildings, one of which has served as a hotel since the early 20th century, although it has been remodeled and redivided many times since. Air-conditioned single rooms with shared bath start at $50; doubles begin at $75. Most rooms have TVs. Inquire about longer-stay discounts and the annual weekend seafood and pig-roast package specials.

For B&B style, try the *Atlantic House* (☎ 410-289-2333), 5th St at Baltimore, which offers 11 rooms in a tidy Victorian house in the center of the action, with rates from $75 to $145, including a full breakfast buffet.

Hotels & Motels Between Philadelphia and Baltimore Aves, *Ocean Manor* (☎ 410-289-9050, 107 Wicomico St) has 18 rooms and a number of efficiencies and apartments open seasonally. The rooms are small, neat, and clean and start at $55 for a double (three-night minimum on weekends); effi-ciencies rent for $475 a week.

The *Surf Villa* (☎ 410-289-9434, 705 N Baltimore Ave) has 25 rooms with air-conditioning and TV and access to a kitchen. This hotel is a sunny, airy, and immaculate retreat a block from the beach. Rates start at $64 weekdays, $84 weekends.

The *Admiral* (☎ 410-289-6280, 800-292-6280) occupies the entire square block between 8th and 9th Sts and Baltimore and Philadelphia Aves. It includes a four-story hotel, a series of one-story motel buildings, and a pool. Rates start at $75 for average air-conditioned rooms with TVs and well-worn furniture.

The *Breakers* (☎ *410-289-9165*), 3rd St at the boardwalk, has 35 rooms in various sizes. Doubles range from $72 to $83, depending on day and view. Rooms are clean and sport newish motel furniture and some attempts at Victorian touches. It's a pretty good deal for the size and location. Or, try the *Islander Motel* (☎ *410-289-9179*), 20th St at Philadelphia Ave, which charges $70 and up for standard rooms; efficiencies cost extra.

Of the many chain motel lodgings available, the five-story *Comfort Inn* (☎ *410-289-5155, 800-282-5155*), between 5th and 6th Sts, is right on the boardwalk and nicely laid out, with a small pool facing the shore. Rates start at $99.

The Fager's Island complex (☎ *410-723-6100, 800-767-6060*), bayside from 56th to 60th Sts, includes a high-end restaurant and two hotels offering some of the most distinctive accommodations in town. Its landmark *Lighthouse Club Hotel*, a three-story replica of a traditional octagonal Chesapeake Bay lighthouse, has 23 rooms arranged in a circle, most with good bay views. The rooms have marble bathrooms with Jacuzzis. Fager's five-story, 85-room *Coconut Malorie* has a white-marble lobby and suites with Jacuzzis, marble bathrooms, and kitchenettes. Rates at both hotels are around $200 for doubles on the weekend.

All rooms face the ocean at the *Dunes Manor Hotel* (☎ *410-289-1100, 800-523-2888*), 28th St at Baltimore Ave, the large pink high-rise that looks like a mix of Victorian and Bauhaus. The hotel has an indoor-outdoor pool, a porch with rockers, and daily tea. Summer doubles start at $145.

For condominium style, the *Princess Royale* (☎ *410-524-7777*), 91st St at the Coastal Hwy, is a modern condo-hotel designed around a four-story atrium with a pool at its center. (Rooms on pool level look out at the people walking past your sliding-glass door.) Peak-season doubles start at more than $200.

Places to Eat

One visitors' guide advertises that there are more than 22,000 restaurant seats in Ocean City. Here, both purveyors and customers seem to judge dining by quantity. You will find a lot of seafood on the menus, and most larger restaurants serve all-you-can-eat meals, which can be economical for large appetites (children usually eat for half-price). Quality varies immensely, not just according to your choice of eatery but also according to how the day has been going for the college students preparing or serving your meal; there are few professionals in OC's food service industry.

Budget Budget travelers should look for the dizzying selection of daily specials – two-for-one deals, half-price prime rib night, free-appetizer happy hour, early bird discounts, etc. Find a poor local to fill you in on the current offerings; they'll often have their weeks' meals mapped out, bouncing from one special to the next.

For easy, cheap eats, OC's boardwalk offers a plethora of burgers, hot dogs, pizza, ice cream, candy, and snack foods. Nearby, you'll find cheap Mexican food at *Matteo's* (☎ *410-289-6409*), Baltimore Ave at Talbot St, which offers tacos, burritos, and chicken wings for less than $5.

Soriano's (☎ *410-289-6656, 310 S Baltimore Ave*), between Dorchester and Somerset Sts, serves breakfast all day and other inexpensive diner food. A block up the street, *Fat Daddy's Sub Shop*, at the corner of Talbot St and Baltimore Ave, serves cheese-steaks and sandwiches.

The 100-seat *Adolfo's* (☎ *410-289-4001*), at the Inlet end of Baltimore Ave, serves all-you-can-eat spaghetti and meatballs for $7.

For all-you-can-eat breakfasts under $10, head for two branches of *English's Family Restaurant* (☎ *410-289-7333*), at 15th and 137th Sts and the Coastal Hwy.

The family restaurant *Captain Bob's* (☎ *410-524-7070*), on the bay at 64th St, draws OC veterans for steaks, chicken, and side dishes such as peas, cole slaw, potato salad, and mashed potatoes. A half-chicken, two sides, and a roll costs less than $10.

Even farther uptown, *La Hacienda* (☎ *410-524-8080*), 80th St at the Coastal Hwy, offers economical Mexican fare starting at 5 pm; many dishes cost less than $10.

Despite all the efficiency apartments and kitchenettes, a decent market for provisions is hard to find. Mini-markets and several small grocery stores downtown offer slim pickings besides Rice-a-Roni, hot dogs, and other convenience foods. Meat-lovers like *Anthony's (☎ 410-289-9193, 1608 Philadelphia Ave)* for hand-carved carryout.

For a full-service supermarket, you need to head off the map to 94th St, where a shopping center on the Coastal Hwy has a *Super Fresh* supermarket offering an excellent produce selection, salad bar, and prepared deli foods. (There's also an Eckerd chain drugstore next door.)

Note that Berlin, 10 miles west of Ocean City, sponsors a *farmers' market*, featuring seafood and fresh produce, on Wednesday and Friday afternoons from June through October on Main St.

Mid-Range & Top End Despite its dopey name, *Seacrets (☎ 410-524-4900)*, 49th St at the bay, gets our vote for the best-time restaurant in Ocean City. Friendly people here serve good Jamaican-style food at reasonable prices to a mixed crowd in a great kitschy Pirates-of-the-Caribbean bayfront setting. Sandy pathways with rope handrails lead through bamboo groves to a rambling collection of shanty shacks strewn with rusty metal signs and skull-and-crossbones flags. The menu is written in pidgin English. Jerk chicken ('de house specialty') comes in appetizer portions for $6.25; there are also spicy Jamaican burgers, Jamaican pizza, gumbo, and jerk ribs (entrees around $14). It's also a great late-night bar, with frequent live entertainment (see Entertainment, later).

Fager's Island (☎ 410-524-5500), 60th St at the bay, is open daily year-round. It's known for its prime rib ($24 regular cut, $26 large) and fine dining upstairs, as well as a livelier bar and more-casual patio dining downstairs (Gulf shrimp quesadillas are $7.50). But it's perhaps best known for religiously playing the *1812 Overture* every night at sunset. The cannons blare just as the sun disappears behind the mainland, and the packed house applauds. (Also see Entertainment, later.)

Meanwhile, *Macky's (☎ 410-723-5565)*, on 53rd St at the bay, plays 'God Bless America.' It also serves Creole-inspired specials, and the tables are so close to the water that you can dip your feet in.

For crabs, try *Higgins Crab House (☎ 410-289-2581)*, 31st St at the Coastal Hwy. Your money goes a little further here than it does in many crab houses: Eat all-you-want steamed crabs, fried chicken, Alaskan crab legs, spiced shrimp, crab soup, and corn on the cob for about $15.

The oldest crab house is *Phillips Crab House (☎ 410-289-9121)*, at 21st St and Philadelphia Ave. Phillips started as a shack, and now, after countless additions, seats around 1500. All-you-can-inhale crabs cost around $20. Phillips has another oceanfront location at 13th St.

The Princess Royale hotel (see Places to Stay, earlier) serves a prime rib buffet for $22 and Sunday brunch buffet (11 am to 2 pm) for $11. *Embers (☎ 410-289-3322)*, 24th St at Philadelphia Ave, offers a seafood buffet for $23. Other places with buffets, which usually feature seafood, include the *Happy Jack Pancake House (☎ 410-289-7377)*, 26th St at the Coastal Hwy, and *Jonah & the Whale (☎ 410-524-2722)*, 26th St at the boardwalk.

The *Hobbit (☎ 410-524-8100)*, 81st St at the bay, is one of OC's better restaurants, without any all-you-can-stuff deals. Tables overlook the bay, and seafood entrees are around $20; the arty bar top depicts scenes from Tolkien's fanciful work. You can find upscale northern Italian food at *Christopher's Tutti Gusti (☎ 410-289-3318)*, 33rd St at the Coastal Hwy. The house fettucine comes with skiitake mushrooms. Pasta dishes cost about $11, meat entrees around $17.

Entertainment

Nightlife centers around the myriad bars and clubs.

Bars & Clubs The *Dutch Bar (☎ 410-289-5557)*, on the boardwalk, is a few doors north of Dorchester St near the Belmont-Hearne Hotel. The place is narrow, just wide enough for the bar and some stools, but

MARYLAND

widens at the back to accommodate a couple of pool tables and a jukebox stocked with heavy metal music. All the beer is in bottles or cans. Most clients are under 25.

A block up the boardwalk, the *Purple Moose Saloon* (☎ 410-289-6953), at the foot of Caroline St, has loud live music at the back and looks like the clubhouse for the University of Maryland men's and women's lacrosse teams.

Lined up on Wicomico St, right off the boardwalk and the pier, are the *Cork Bar*, the *Bearded Clam* and *Daisy's Wheel House*. These are three popular and rather sleazy local bars that offer a host of happy-hour deals to pack in an eclectic crowd – including a lot of day-trippers who park in the nearby public lot and take to the highways after tanking up. OC and state police are vigilant for speeders and drunk drivers, but in this party town the bad guys outnumber the good guys by thousands.

Seacrets (see Places to Eat, earlier) has the best atmosphere of any bar in town. The place is constructed on and around the bay and has five bars, including one in a wooden boat on the beach. Tables overlook the bay, and there are lots of palm trees (which are replaced every summer). During the day, you can chug your Red Stripe while sitting on small floating tubes in the shallow part of the bay. Seacrets features live music nightly in summer and three nights a week in winter. Bands cover perennial OC favorites such as Jimmy Buffett and Bruce Hornsby (a good ole Tidewater boy from Virginia). You can also hear some great reggae and ska from Jamaican bands out of Baltimore and DC.

The *Big Kahuna*, *Paddock*, and *Croon Tunes* (☎ 410-289-6331, 289-6335) are three connected nightspots at 18th St and Philadelphia Ave. If there is a cover, around $5 gets you into all three. Kahuna's has a surf-bar atmosphere, and the Paddock includes a large dance floor with half a Volkswagen embedded in the wall. Croon Tunes draws in some uninhibited karaoke singers.

Fager's Island (see Places to Eat, earlier) has five bars on the bay and a boardwalk across the water to a gazebo offshore. It offers rock music on weekends with no cover charge. The *Ocean Club* (☎ 410-524-7500), 49th St at the ocean, attracts a slightly older crowd for nightly live rock bands, as well as piano or acoustic music in peak season. It has its own bayside beach and an outdoor bar above the restaurant (the 'crow's nest') from which you can look out onto the ocean.

Gay & Lesbian Venues At first it seems strange that a resort the size of OC has no gay bars or entertainment, but OC has a distinctly 'hetero' character and publicizes itself as a mainstream family resort town. Gays and lesbians prefer the open, tolerant atmosphere at Rehoboth Beach, Delaware, a few miles north of OC. There, you'll find many gay-owned businesses and a substantial gay community (see the Delaware Seashore chapter).

Shopping

Joe Kroart runs the Ocean Gallery World Center (☎ 410-289-5300), 2nd St at the boardwalk (look for the wild wooden collage and mural along 2nd St). Billed as the gallery with the most paintings per square foot in the world, Ocean Gallery is a two-story building in which a lot of framed reproductions and poster art are piled on top of each other in a maze of passages.

Kite Loft (☎ 410-289-7855) sells a broad selection of kites and flying accessories. It has three locations: the boardwalk at 5th St, 45th St at the Coastal Hwy, and 131st St at the Coastal Hwy. These folks sponsor the dramatic kite-flying events that take place at Sunfest in September annually (see Special Events, earlier).

Ocean City Factory Outlets (☎ 800-625-6696), on Route 50 (Ocean Gateway) in West Ocean City, includes shops with such familiar name brands as Ann Taylor, Tommy Hilfiger, Levi's, and Reebok; there's also a Book Warehouse here.

Getting There & Away

Air Charter and private planes land at the Ocean City Municipal Airport (☎ 410-213-2471), 3 miles west of town on Route 611. There is a fair amount of traffic around OC, and it is not unreasonable to consider hitching a ride with a private pilot. Weekends are good days to meet pilots in transit.

US Airways (☎ 800-428-4322) serves the Salisbury-Wicomico County Regional Airport, 20 miles west of OC, with flights to DC and Baltimore.

For a cab from the airport, call Ocean City Taxicab at ☎ 410-289-8294 or ☎ 888-410-8294.

Bus The Carolina Trailways bus station (☎ 410-289-9307), 2nd St at Philadelphia Ave, offers regularly scheduled service to and from major cities in the region. Local buses use the downtown terminal, at the corner of S Division St and Baltimore Ave (note that N Division and S Division Sts are not close). You can catch a bus to Assateague Island from here.

Car Most people coming from the west take Route 50 from the Baltimore-Washington area across the Delmarva Peninsula and right into Ocean City at the Inlet. This is a notorious bottleneck, and traffic may be jammed for miles on Friday night and late Sunday afternoon. As an alternative, you can exit Route 50 onto Route 90 about 12 miles before entering Ocean City. This will bring you into OC at 62nd St and avoid some traffic. Ocean City is about three hours from Washington, DC.

Coming south on the Delmarva coast from the Delaware beaches, stay on Route 1, which enters Ocean City at 146th St and becomes the Coastal Hwy and then Philadelphia Ave.

If you're coming north from Virginia, take Route 13 to Route 113 in Maryland and follow this to Route 50, which then leads you into the Inlet.

Getting Around

Bus City buses (☎ 410-723-1607) run the length of the beach daily, traveling from the Inlet terminal at S Division St to the Delaware state line. Buses run south on the Coastal Hwy/Philadelphia Ave and north on Baltimore Ave to 17th St before jogging west one block and continuing north on Coastal Hwy/Philadelphia Ave. Buses run

about every 10 minutes during the summer and every half-hour otherwise. You can ride all day for $1.

Boardwalk Train The boardwalk 'train' is a chain of linked golf-cart-like cars pulled by a Jeep. The train operates from Easter to the first weekend in October and runs up and down the boardwalk about every 20 minutes from 11 am to 7 pm in peak season. The fare is $2 one way, $3 roundtrip. In shoulder seasons, it runs on weekends only.

Parking Meters are in effect 24 hours a day in peak season, and parking is a problem on summer weekends. The oceanfront parking lot at the southernmost tip of the strand fills quickly. There are municipal and private lots along Philadelphia Ave. You can park for free at the convention center at 40th St, but this is a long walk from everything. Hotels provide free parking for their guests.

ASSATEAGUE ISLAND

Assateague Island is one of the most pristine spots on the mid-Atlantic coast, and as an undeveloped barrier island, it provides a sharp contrast to the overdeveloped beach resorts that dominate the coast. Besides its natural appeal, the island is home to a legendary herd of wild horses – commonly called 'ponies' – which can be seen in dramatic silhouette as they race across the dunes (see the Wild Horses boxed text).

The name 'Assateague' is a corruption of an Indian name for 'marshy place across' – as in, across from the mainland. Before Hurricane Hazel carved out the Inlet in 1933, Assateague was part of OC. In the minds of nature lovers, the hurricane was an act of divine intervention.

Today, Assateague is protected as a national seashore and managed largely by the National Park Service, though a portion of the 37-mile-long island is a state park managed by the Maryland state park system, and the southern end of the island (across the Virginia border) is a national wildlife refuge managed by the US Fish & Wildlife Service. A bridge accesses the northern portion of the island, but roads do not go

MARYLAND

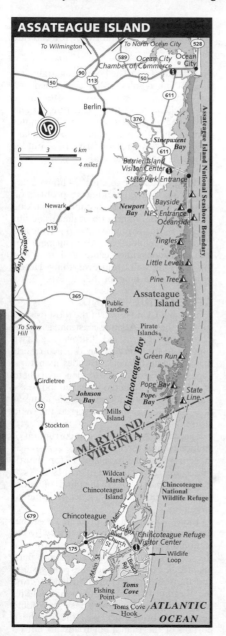

through beyond the state line. To drive from the northern end near Ocean City to the southern end at Chincoteague requires a circuitous inland detour that takes more than an hour (see Chincoteague Island in the Virginia's Chesapeake Bay chapter).

The island is a sanctuary where you can get away from the crowds of Ocean City and swim, bike, hike, fish, canoe, kayak, or camp with nothing but the sound of the surf and the wind whirring through the marsh as your companions. Clean bathhouses, small stores, snack bars, bike and boat rentals (in season) and other such services provide all you need for days of recreation.

Orientation & Information

Eleven miles south of Ocean City via Route 611, the Barrier Island Visitor Center (☎ 410-641-1441) serves as National Park Service (NPS) headquarters and is a good stop for first-time visitors. Here, an aquarium, touch tank, telescope, and hands-on shell exhibit entertain the kids, and short films relate the history of barrier island development as well as the horse story. You can also sign up for the Foster Horse program and learn perhaps more than you want to about horse contraception. Rangers provide maps and a schedule of such popular events as guided nature walks and surf-fishing demonstrations. The official national park handbook, *Assateague Island* by renowned marine biologist William H Amos, may be purchased here ($7), along with a nice selection of related books, horsey gifts, and fun books and games for children.

Once you cross over the bridge beyond the visitor center, you have two choices. You can enter the state park, which charges a fee of $2 per person per day whether you're in a car or on foot or bike. Or you can continue down the road a lick to the NPS gate; here they'll charge you $5 per vehicle, or $2 for bicyclists and pedestrians, but your pass is good for a full seven days.

The state park has a small store and short-order snack bar, and there is a market and restaurant on the mainland not far from the visitor center, but for most supplies, groceries, and restaurants, head for West Ocean

City. (Also note that the town of Berlin, 10 miles west of Ocean City, sponsors a farmers' market on Wednesday and Friday afternoons from June through October on Main St.)

Activities

Both the state park and NPS maintain lifeguard-staffed **swimming** areas with bathhouses. Note there's often a strong undertow.

Many visitors come to Assateague to go **fishing**, especially crabbing and shellfish collecting. Surf fishing for mackerel, blue fish, and striped bass (rockfish) is popular along the beaches. Inquire at the visitor center about surf-fishing demonstrations. Bait and tackle are available at the small store within the state park.

Flat, paved pathways along the island are ideal for leisurely **bicycling**. Bike rentals are available seasonally at the recreation outpost beyond the Bayside Campground (see Places to Stay, below). The outpost is open 9 am to 5 pm daily from Memorial Day to Labor Day, 9 am to 1 pm weekends only in shoulder seasons. The rates are $4 per hour, $8 for a half-day, $12 per day, or $50 weekly.

The protected marshland shores of Chincoteague Bay make for a great **canoeing** excursion. Four primitive canoe-in campgrounds are available along the bayside shore. Canoe rentals are available at the same recreation outpost listed above. The rates are $5 per hour, $12 for a half-day, $20 per day, or $90 weekly.

At the Maryland end, three half-mile nature trails provide **hiking** access to different island environments: dunes, marsh, and forest. The forest trail has the best viewing tower. At the Virginia end, 15 miles of trails wind through refuge marshes. Contact the visitor center for more information.

As for **bird watching**, the refuge's freshwater pools are home to a variety of herons, egrets, and other wading birds; late summer brings migrating shorebirds and peregrine

---

Wild Horses

Although most people use the word 'ponies' to describe the herds of wild hooved animals roaming Assateague, they are, in fact, horses. Folklore claims that the Assateague horses are the descendants of the four-legged cargo of a shipwrecked Spanish galleon. More likely, the herds' progenitors escaped from domestic stock that were grazing on the island during the 17th century. Livestock owners kept animals here to circumvent colonial laws requiring livestock to be fenced and taxed.

There are two herds of about 150 animals each on the island, separated by a fence at the Maryland-Virginia border. The National Park Service manages the Maryland herd and the Volunteer Fire Department in Chincoteague, Virginia, owns and manages the Virginia herd. Every year on the last Wednesday and Thursday of July, the fire department rounds up the Virginia herd and swims it across to Chincoteague, where a number of the foals and yearlings are auctioned off to pay the fire department's operating expenses. The rest of the horses swim back. The story of one such foal, *Misty of Chincoteague* by Marguerite Henry is a classic of American children's literature. The tale is largely responsible for canonizing Assateague's wild horses as symbols of mystery and freedom.

The highest bid so far for a pony was $3000 (in 1994), but the average is around $600. A carnival atmosphere pervades the week preceding 'pony penning.' There are pony races and other events. Many of the locals quip that the ponies are treated much better than the locals are, not only in July but at all times of the year.

You can see the Maryland herd roaming almost anywhere on Assateague, especially along the roads, in the parking areas, and near the beach in summer. In other seasons, look in the salt marsh.

Note: Every year several people get bitten or kicked because they ignored warnings not to approach the horses or try to feed or pet them. Leave these animals in peace!

– Randy Peffer

falcons. Thousands of waterfowl winter on the island, especially snow geese, black ducks, mallards, and pintails. Although you can see birds all over the island, birders find the highest concentrations at the national wildlife refuge at the southern end of the island. The Chincoteatue National Wildlife Refuge visitor center (see the Virginia's Chesapeake Bay chapter) provides bird lists; also inquire about wildlife bus tours.

For those keen to do some **off-road-vehicle driving**, ORVs are allowed along the beach from the end of the paved road to the Virginia border, but you must buy a 12-month permit for $60, issued by the NPS. Contact the visitor center, campground office, or ranger stations for more information.

Places to Stay

Although camping at Assateague amid the wild horses and flocking birds can be one of the region's best adventures (reserve early), campers should be prepared for island conditions. There is no shade, mosquitoes are present from mid-May to October, and high winds can pull short tent pegs out of the sand. Camping is not allowed in the Virginia portion of the national seashore, though private campgrounds are available in nearby Chincoteague (see the Virginia's Chesapeake Bay chapter).

The Assateague State Park (☎ 410-641-2120) maintains a 350-site seasonal *beachside campground* with 32 hookup sites. Bathhouses contain drinking water, hot showers, and flush toilets. The rates are $30 for sites with hookups, $20 without. For 24-hour reservations, call ☎ 888-432-2267; there's an $8 reservation surcharge.

The National Park Service maintains two year-round campgrounds for car-camping

on the island: 109 sites at *Oceanside Campground* and 49 sites (some limited shade) at *Bayside Campground*. Oceanside also has walk-in, tent-only sites 100 to 200 feet from parking. The campgrounds have chemical toilets, cold outdoor showers, and drinking water but no hookups. Sites can be reserved for summer dates up to five months in advance and cost $14 a night (call ☎ 800-365-2267 for reservations); the rest of the year, sites are first-come first-served and cost $10. Campers register at the NPS campground office (☎ 410-641-3030) on the island, which opens at 8 am every day year-round.

For *backcountry camping*, the NPS offers primitive hike-in and paddle-in campsites by permit only; some are seasonal, and some are open year-round. The sites have only picnic tables and a chemical toilet (no drinking water). They're 2 to 14 miles from the end of the road in the park. A $5 registration fee is required for each permit (in addition to the $5 entrance fee). Register at the NPS campground office on the island; it's first-come first-served. You'll want to pack insect repellent, sturdy shoes for sand walking, and hard-soled shoes for wading in the bay.

Getting There & Away

For campers, the Worcester County Ride Program (☎ 410-632-3232) provides an express bus that operates twice daily during peak season between Assateague Island (the state park ranger station) and Ocean City's S Division St bus terminal, downtown at the corner of S Division St and Baltimore Ave. The fare is $2 (exact change only).

By car, it's a 15- to 20-minute ride from Ocean City. Chincoteague is about an hour away via Routes 113, 13, and 175.

Western Maryland

To most eastern Marylanders, western Maryland is anything west of the Baltimore-Washington Parkway. In more precise geographic terms, western Maryland may be considered the part of the state west of the 'fall line,' where Appalachian rivers coursing down the Piedmont Plateau meet the lower coastal plain in a series of waterfalls and rapids.

Historically, as the fall line represented the extent of inland waterway navigation, river-port cities grew up on the plain east of this dividing line. The fertile central plateau became a farming region. West of the plateau, the Appalachian Mountains represented a formidable barrier until canals, roads, and then rail lines cut through the frontier toward the Ohio Valley. The scenic C&O Canal National Historic Park offers the opportunity to explore this historic corridor on a bike path through 185 miles of plain, plateau, and range, while hikers trace the ridgeline of the original frontier along the famous Appalachian Trail, often called the 'AT.'

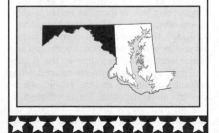

During the Civil War, Union and Confederate forces struggled to control the important mountain gap trade routes, and one of the war's bloodiest battles was fought here at Antietam. Nearby Frederick was inundated with the wounded and became a wartime medical center. Today, these two sites are landmarks on a popular Civil War historical touring route between Gettysburg, Pennsylvania and Harpers Ferry, West Virginia, notorious as the scene of radical abolitionist John Brown's 1859 raid. The tour continues farther south through Virginia's history-rich Shenandoah Valley.

In Maryland's remote 'back fin,' beyond where I-70 shoots north, I-68 closely follows the old National Road route cut a century ago. The surrounding backcountry remains largely wild, dotted with small towns nestled in mountain 'hollers.' Today, this isolated region is most noted for outdoor recreation, drawing summer crowds escaping Tidewater humidity to the cooler shores of Deep Creek Lake, while whitewater paddlers head down the Youghiogheny and Savage Rivers, and mountain bikers explore rugged trails all around. Come winter, western Maryland offers cross-country and downhill skiing.

State information centers in the region are open daily year-round. You'll find one off I-70 at South Mountain, between Frederick and Hagerstown (☎ 301-293-2526, 293-4161), and another off Route 15 at the Pennsylvania border near Emmitsburg (☎ 301-447-2553).

LOWER POTOMAC CORRIDOR

To travelers, the dominant feature of the lower Potomac corridor is the C&O Canal, which stretches from urban Washington, DC, through the outlying suburbs and Piedmont farms to the Appalachian foothills and beyond. Taking the canal route – by foot, by bike, or on horseback – travelers may remain blissfully unaware of the proximity of the huge Washington-Dulles International Airport to the south, as well as the

MARYLAND

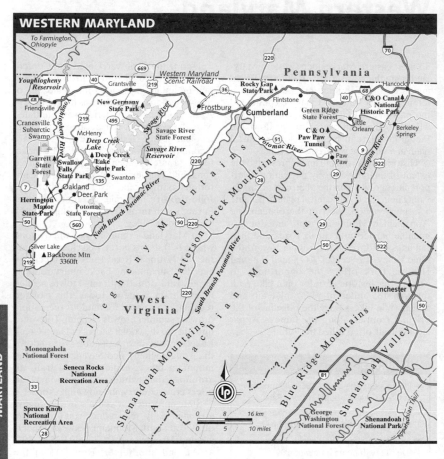

encroaching presence of aggressively up-scale suburban development on either side of the river.

C&O Canal National Historic Park

The historic C&O Canal runs 185 miles alongside the Potomac River between Georgetown in the District of Columbia to its Cumberland terminus in western Maryland. Begun in 1836, the canal was envisioned as a trade route through the rugged Appalachians to the Ohio Valley beyond, yet by 1850 the advent of the railroads had rendered it obsolete and construction was abandoned. For its short heyday, the canal left an enduring mark on western Maryland: Legends of the barge trade and boatsmen, engineering feats of their day, and near-ghost towns remain the canal's romantic legacy.

Today, the scenic canal corridor is preserved as a narrow national park and is a major recreational resource in the region. The most popular activities here are daylong bicycling excursions and the roughly three-day trip along the entire length of the dusty 12-foot-wide gravel towpath alongside the canal. Bicycle rentals are available in western Maryland at Swains Lock (17.2 miles west of

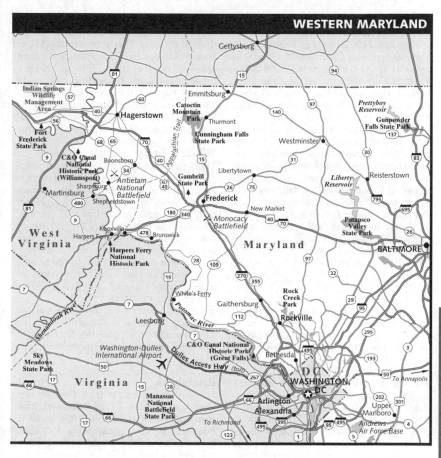

WESTERN MARYLAND

the Georgetown terminus), White's Ferry (35½ miles), across the river in Harpers Ferry (approximately 60 miles), and in Williamsport (100 miles). For bicycle rentals in DC, see Boating in the Washington, DC chapter.

The National Park Service (NPS) operates visitor centers at Georgetown, Great Falls Tavern, Williamsport, Hancock, and Cumberland. For maps and excursion guides listing campsites, bike-repair shops, and other resources along the route, contact park headquarters by calling ☎ 301-739-4200 or writing to Box 4, Sharpsburg, MD 21782.

Great Falls

Fourteen miles upriver from Georgetown, where the central Piedmont meets the Coastal Plain, the Potomac River cascades 77 feet in a series of beautiful, treacherous rapids. The C&O Canal was constructed to allow barge traffic to bypass this barrier, and today a widened unit of the C&O Canal National Historic Park is a popular spot for viewing the falls as well as for hiking, biking, and riding historic barges. The entrance to the park is south of the town of Potomac. Park admission is posted as $4 per car and $2 per pedestrian

MARYLAND

or bicyclist, but the gate appears to be staffed at peak periods only.

The **Great Falls Tavern**, first built as a lock house alongside the canal in 1828, remains in use today as a visitor center (☎ 301-299-2026), where exhibits demonstrate how the locks work. It's open 9 am to 4:30 pm daily. The best way to get a feel for the historic canal is aboard **barge rides** (☎ 301-299-3613), which run several times a day, Wednesday to Sunday from April to October. Fares are $7.50 for adults, $6 for seniors, $4 for children four to 14.

From the tavern, a half-mile walk down the towpath and across a series of bridges to Olmstead Island leads to the **falls overlook**, which offers a beautiful view of rugged rock and roaring rapids. For serious scramblers, the 2-mile **Billy Goat Trail** traverses these mountainous shards of rock, and the towpath provides an easy loop back. Other easy loop trails lead through the woods past the remains of gold-mine diggings, prospector's trenches, and overgrown Civil War earthworks. Inquire at the tavern about whitewater paddling and licensed outfitters. No bike or boat rentals are available at the park.

A small snack bar is open seasonally in the park, but the best place to eat is *Old Angler's Inn* (*☎ 301-365-2425, 10801 MacArthur Blvd*), just off the towpath at the southern tip of the park. It's French and it's expensive, but the lovely patio and gracious service are a deserved luxury after coming off the Billy Goat Trail or a long bike ride. It's open for lunch and dinner Tuesday to Sunday year-round. A plate of mussels runs $14 at lunch; a dinner of black sea bass is $23.

Note that Great Falls Park, also administered by the NPS, is across the river in Virginia. Admission paid at either side permits access to either park for seven days. See the Great Falls section in the Northern Virginia chapter.

Swains Lock

Sixteen miles upriver from Georgetown, Swains Lock has been operated by the Swain family for generations. Jesse Swain was lock tender from 1907 until the lock closed in 1924. Today, grandson Fred Swain and wife

Virginia run Swains Boathouse (☎ 301-299-9006) at a scenic bend of the river outside the town of Potomac. They rent bicycles ($5 per hour, $13 all day, including helmets; tandems are available for an additional charge), canoes, kayaks, and boats ($9 per hour, $19 all day). They also sell fishing tackle and bait and oversee a hiker/biker campground for towpath through-travelers. There's a small refreshment stand only; bring food with you.

White's Ferry

Thirty-five miles upriver from Georgetown, a car ferry continues to cross the Potomac River west of Poolesville. White's Ferry (☎ 301-349-5200) operates 5 am to 11 pm daily year-round. The car fare is $3 one way, $5 roundtrip; bicyclists pay $1; pedestrians cost 50¢. From late April through October, the ferry operator also rents canoes and provides shuttle service upriver (a canoe float from Brunswick runs seven to nine hours, for example). The seasonal store sells groceries, bait, and prepared foods.

Once across the river, historic downtown Leesburg, Virginia, is a short 4-mile ride west; it makes for a wonderful day outing or overnight detour (see the Northern Virginia chapter).

Brunswick

Fifty-five miles upriver from Georgetown, Brunswick is home to the **Brunswick Railroad Museum** (☎ 301-834-7100), at 40 W Potomac St, where elaborate HO-scale model railroads and exhibits aim to interpret life in a railroad town at the turn of the 20th century. It's open 10 am to 4 pm Saturday and 1 to 4 pm Sunday, April to December, with additional Thursday and Friday hours (10 am to 2 pm) in summer. Admission is $4 for adults, $2.50 for students, free for children five and under.

Compact downtown Brunswick is right off the towpath. Eastbound MARC commuter trains (☎ 800-325-7245 for schedules) en route from West Virginia to Washington, DC, stop in the morning, and westbound trains stop in the evening, weekdays only. A MARC shuttle bus (☎ 301-694-2065) runs between the train station and Frederick.

The **Brunswick Family Campground** (☎ 301-834-8050) is off the towpath.

Knoxville

Across the Potomac River east of Harpers Ferry, West Virginia, tiny Knoxville has no more than one road motel, one hostel, one 24-hour coffee shop, a market, a gas station, and a river outfitter, but it's all you need to put together plenty of adventure in this beautiful and historic region. The Appalachian Trail coincides here with the C&O Canal towpath and runs along Knoxville's riverbank. Many more trails in the area provide challenges for hikers, and the Potomac and Shenandoah Rivers provide opportunities for paddling excursions. An easy 2-mile walk west takes you to the Harpers Ferry National Historic Park, with its many attractions, restaurants, and rail service.

At River & Trail Outfitters (☎ 301-695-5177), 604 Valley Rd, Lee Baihly organizes river-rafting, canoeing, and kayaking trips on the Shenandoah and Potomac Rivers, tubing floats down Antietam Creek, hiking excursions, and winter cross-country ski tours.

The **HI Harpers Ferry** hostel (☎ 301-834-7652), Sandy Hook Rd, located at the near midpoint of the Appalachian Trail, offers dormitory lodging from April through November. Through-hikers swap tales and weather reports around the hostel's big kitchen table, in front of the stone fireplace, or out on the small deck. Three dormitory rooms (men, women, and 'other') are outfitted with 39 metal bunks and gender-specific toilets and showers. It's casually kept by the gracious manager, Andrew Hyman.

Lockout hours are technically 9:30 am to 5 pm. The rate is $11 for members, $14 for nonmembers; inquire about camping and shuttles. To reach the hostel by car, take Route 340 to Keep Tryst Rd; turn south toward the Hillside Motel and go a third of a mile uphill to Sandy Fork Rd; turn left and find the hostel around 100 yards up on the right. To reach it on foot, follow the steep hillside trail off the towpath/AT. This trail is not practical for bikes, so bicyclists should cross the railroad tracks earlier, head to the frontage road (there are several houses and

a tiny store), and take the road up to the hostel.

The no-frills **Hillside Motel** (☎ 301-834-8144, 19105 Keep Tryst Rd), on Route 180 facing Route 340, charges $26.

Cindy Dee's Restaurant (☎ 301-695-8181), across the street, serves good inexpensive breakfasts and other diner food around the clock (beware of over-generous portions of gravy); it's less than half a mile from the hostel.

Hikers may note that the Bears Den (HI-AYH) Hostel is 20 miles south along the Appalachian Trail. See Loudoun County in the Northern Virginia chapter.

Maryland Heights Trail

Two miles upriver from Knoxville, the Maryland Heights Trail leads uphill from the towpath to an area of major Union fortification during the Civil War. From here, hikers get a great view of the river gorges known as the Harpers Ferry Water Gap. The well-marked trailhead is just north of the AT Potomac River footbridge and across the frontage road. Several loop trails enable hikers to select hikes from 1.2 to 3.9 miles long.

HARPERS FERRY (WEST VIRGINIA)

Harpers Ferry packs a rich history and tremendous recreation onto a scenic spit of land, where the Shenandoah and Potomac Rivers meet to form the boundaries of three states. George Washington's 1794 federal armory here was the target of abolitionist John Brown's raid in 1859. Although Brown's ambition to arm slaves and spark a national rebellion against slavery died once he was caught and hanged (see the boxed text John Brown & the Raid on Harpers Ferry), the incident incited slaveholders' worst fears and helped precipitate the Civil War. Union and Confederate forces soon fought for control of the armory and town.

Today, tidy brick storefronts line the narrow lanes that climb the steep hill between the two roaring rivers, appearing little changed since the eve of the Civil War, when 3000 people lived in Harpers Ferry.

(The town now has a population of 400.) Downtown Harpers Ferry was declared a national historic park in 1986. The longest and most famous hiking path in the USA, the Appalachian Trail, passes through town, and the Appalachian Trail Conference is headquartered here (see the Appalachian Trail boxed text in the Activities chapter).

Orientation & Information

The historic district encompasses the entire three blocks of downtown Harpers Ferry along Shenandoah, Potomac, and High Sts. While a national park, it is also a living town where residents continue to live and do business and pedestrians are free to wander about the shops and cafes without paying admission. Parking, however, is severely restricted, and drivers will find it most practical

to park at the Harpers Ferry visitor center and take the shuttle downtown (free with admission). In the off season, you may find parking near the train station, but there are fewer than 20 spots.

The Jefferson County Visitor Bureau (☎ 304-535-2627, 800-848-8687), on Washington St at Route 340, distributes West Virginia highway maps and directories to local dining, lodging, and recreation.

The NPS visitor center (☎ 304-535-6298) is off Route 340 on a hill above town. The center and NPS attractions downtown are open 8:30 am to 6 pm daily in summer, to 5 pm the rest of the year. A charge of $5 per vehicle or $3 per pedestrian or bicyclist covers shuttle service to the historic district and admission to NPS buildings for seven consecutive days.

John Brown & the Raid on Harpers Ferry

Born the son of a leather tanner in Connecticut, John Brown tried his hand at tanning, farming, and land speculating in several northern states, from Ohio to Massachusetts. Considered a ne'er-do-well who took satisfaction in being a social rebel, Brown became an ardent abolitionist. In 1849, he and his family settled in an African American community in North Elba, New York, and his home became a station on the Underground Railroad.

In 1854, Brown and several of his sons moved to Kansas to join the fight to keep it a slavery-free territory. They settled in Osawatomie, and Brown organized a guerrilla band to fight pro-slavery settlers. In 1856, Brown and his guerrillas murdered five pro-slavery settlers at Pottawatomie Creek. After this incident, 'Old Osawatomie Brown' became a particularly feared figure. In Maryland in 1859, Brown planned to raid the federal arsenal in Harpers Ferry and incite a national uprising of slaves, amassing arms and ammunition at the Kennedy farmhouse (see Around Shepherdstown, later in the chapter).

With backing from northern abolitionists and a band of 21 men, black and white, Brown attacked the arsenal on October 16, 1859. They never gained the firearms they sought, nor did their raid incite a slave rebellion. Brown's troops barricaded themselves in the armory fire engine and guardhouse – since called 'John Brown's fort.'

On October 18, Colonel Robert E Lee and Lieutenant JEB Stuart, then serving in the US Army, stormed the building, killed 10 of Brown's men (including two of his sons), and captured Brown. Brown was tried for murder, treason, and conspiring with slaves to create an insurrection. A court found him guilty and sentenced him to death by hanging on December 2, 1859.

Despite the raid's quick end, it inspired many people in the North and outraged many in the South. On the day of his death, Brown wrote a note and gave it to his jailer. It read, 'I, John Brown, am now quite certain that the crimes of this guilty land will never be purged away but with blood. I had, as I now think, vainly flattered myself, that without very much bloodshed it might be done.' A little more than a year later, in April 1861, the Civil War began.

Harpers Ferry National Historic Park

To view the highlights of the historic district, start at **the Point** at the far side of the levee; it offers a beautiful view of the river junction. In Arsenal Square at the foot of town, **John Brown's Fort** was where Brown and his men barricaded themselves after attacking the armory. The 'fort' was the armory's fire engine house and originally stood north of Potomac St, across from Whitehall Tavern, but it has since been reconstructed and moved here.

Historic **Storer College** on Camp Hill was opened for freed slaves in 1868. The school was part of a nationwide effort by blacks, northern philanthropists, and the Freedmen's Bureau to educate thousands of freed slaves after the Civil War. Storer College continued to educate African Americans until the landmark 1955 *Brown v Board of Education* Supreme Court ruling that ended legal segregation – the subsequent cutoff in state funding resulted in the school's closing that same year. Exhibits also trace the town's African American history.

The **John Brown Museum** tells the story of Brown's raid in wax. Somewhat gory tableaux accompanied by raspy strains of 'John Brown's Body' (sung to the tune of 'Battle Hymn of the Republic') make this anachronistic display worth the price of admission ($4 for adults, $2 for children).

The **Master Armorer's House** on Shenandoah St was the 1858 home of the chief gunsmith of the armory. Displays explain how rifle technology developed here revolutionized the firearms industry. There are other historic buildings along Potomac, Shenandoah, and High Sts, including a confectionery, tavern, dry-goods store, and houses.

For another great river view, take the steep stone steps up from High St. Beyond historic **St Peter's Catholic Church** (which continues to hold services for its local congregation), continue along the footpath to **Jefferson Rock**. Here, Thomas Jefferson claimed the view of three states was 'worth a voyage across the Atlantic.'

Rangers lead public **walking tours** from Memorial Day to Labor Day. Shirley Dougherty leads lantern-lit nighttime ghost tours (☎ 304-725-8019) on weekends from early May to early November for $2 per person.

Restrooms are available at a park information center downtown on Shenandoah St.

Places to Stay

For camping, **Harpers Ferry KOA** (☎ 304-535-6895), off Route 340 south of town, has a pool and more than 200 sites ($32 with hookups, $26 without, $42 for cabins). It's open year-round. The HI Harpers Ferry hostel is located across the river in neighboring Maryland (see Knoxville, earlier in the chapter).

The only chain motel this side of Charles Town, West Virginia, the 50-room **Comfort Inn** (☎ 304-535-6391, 800-228-5150), Route 340 at Union St, is across from the NPS visitor center. Rooms start at $66, including continental breakfast. There's no pool.

At the 62-room **Hilltop House** (☎ 304-535-2132, 400 East Ridge St), the rooms and food are no match for the spectacular view. Rooms start at $49 on weekdays, $65 on weekends. Couch potatoes, be forewarned – there are no TVs.

A mile down Route 340 from town, the 100-room **Cliffside Inn** (☎ 304-535-6302, 800-782-9437) has indoor and outdoor pools. Decent rooms run $60 on weekdays, $76 on weekends for one or two people.

Several local families offer B&B lodging within Victorian-era homes in a tidy residential community about a mile from the downtown park district. Rates for rooms with private bath hover around $65 on weekdays, $80 on weekends, including a full breakfast. The **Harpers Ferry Guest House** (☎ 304-535-6955, 800 Washington St) offers spacious rooms in a two-story clapboard house and is catty-corner to Appalachian Trail Conference headquarters. Or, try one of these spots: the **Ranson-Armory House** (☎ 304-535-2142, 690 Washington St), which dates from 1830; **Briscoe House** (☎ 304-535-2416, 828 Washington St), which serves a 'full English breakfast'; or **Angler's Inn** (☎ 304-535-1239, 867 Washington St), which also offers deluxe fishing or floating excursions.

MARYLAND

Places to Eat

The *Anvil* (☎ 304-535-2582, 1270 Washington St), around a mile from the historic district, is the best restaurant in town, with seafood and steak entrees starting at $12 and 50¢ drafts during weekday happy hours. It's open for lunch and dinner 11 am to 9 pm Tuesday to Sunday (reduced winter hours January to March).

You'll find several sandwich-and-burger shops clustered in the three blocks of downtown Harpers Ferry, with fairly reasonable prices for a tourist zone (for example, $6 for a croissant turkey sandwich). Local snack shops sell ice cream, fudge, pretzels, and other treats.

Up Washington St near the West Virginia visitor center off Route 340, two home-style eateries cater to a local crowd: the *Country Cafe* for good breakfast and lunch and the publike *Mudfort Crest* for supper.

Shopping

The Harpers Ferry Historical Association (☎ 800-821-5206), on Shenandoah St, has an excellent bookstore with a wide selection of titles on the Civil War, John Brown, and Harpers Ferry. It's open daily year-round.

Molly the Rebel (☎ 304-535-2217), 144 High St, may seem like an unlikely place to buy stone Buddhas, but it actually sells these along with other icons, folk art, and toys.

The Outfitter (☎ 304-535-2087, 888-535-2087), 180 High St, two blocks from the train station, rents bikes and sells a wide variety of gear, including hiking boots, rock-climbing tools, and Patagonia clothing. It's open 10 am to sunset daily (closed mid-January to mid-February).

Besides antique furnishings and glassware, Stone House Antiques (☎ 304-535-6688), 181 Potomac St, across from the train station, has a 24-hour ATM.

Getting There & Away

Harpers Ferry is a rare rural destination well served by rail. Amtrak (☎ 800-872-7245) stops here on its *Capitol Limited* run between Chicago and Washington, DC. The fare is $9 to $17. From the same station, MARC commuter trains (☎ 800-325-7245) run between DC and Martinsburg (West Virginia), eastbound in the morning and westbound in the evening, weekdays only. The trip takes an hour and a half. Neither Amtrak nor MARC permit bikes. From the station, passengers can walk up the steep incline to downtown accommodations or hike the 2 miles to the hostel. Many places offer shuttles if reserved in advance.

SHEPHERDSTOWN (WEST VIRGINIA)

An unexpected little jewel, Shepherdstown (population 1800) is the oldest town in West Virginia. It was laid out by Thomas Shepherd on his land grant of 1734. In 1775, the legendary Bee Line March of Revolutionary volunteers set out from here to join Washington's forces in defense of Boston. In 1787, James Rumsey made the first public demonstration of a steamboat engine here, though history eclipsed Rumsey and credits Robert Fulton with the discovery. During the Civil War, this strategic river crossing became a sprawling hospital after the Battle of Antietam across the Potomac. Shepherd College, a state liberal arts school, was founded here in 1872.

Today, the sophisticated town boasts a good selection of restaurants and cafes, along with galleries and arty shops in historic brick row houses, all a short ride across the river from the Antietam Battlefield. Middle East peace talks brought Israeli and Syrian leaders to Shepherdstown in January 2000.

Orientation & Information

The main business district is in a compact, three-block stretch of German St, divided at the courthouse into E German St and W German St. Across from the courthouse, the 1800 Market House now houses the public library (note the Odd Fellows blue-and-yellow eye symbol up top). A few doors down, the visitor center (☎ 304-876-2786) distributes historic walking tour maps, gallery directories, and other useful local guides. It's open 11 am to 4 pm daily, depending on volunteer availability.

There's a post office a block behind the library. You will find local-interest books at

Four Seasons Books (☎ 304-876-3486), 116 W German St.

James Rumsey Monument

This monument, on the point at the head of town, pays tribute to the under-acclaimed inventor who first operated a steamboat here against the current of the Potomac River on December 3, 1787. It's a nice, quiet spot for a beautiful river view.

Bicycling

Shepherdstown makes a great biking destination along the C&O Canal towpath, 12 miles north of Harpers Ferry. Bike rentals are available at O'Hurley's General Store (☎ 304-876-6907), 205 E Washington St, on Route 230 a few blocks outside of the town's main business district. It's open 10 am to 7 pm Tuesday to Saturday, noon to 6 pm Sunday.

Places to Stay & Eat

The 1793 *Mecklenberg Inn* (☎ *304-876-2126)*, German St, offers three rooms in a historic building in the center of town, upstairs from its popular pub (see Entertainment). Rooms start at $55.

The *Thomas Shepherd Inn* (☎ *304-876-3715)*, at the corner of German and Duke Sts, is the town's preeminent inn. Originally built as a parsonage in the 1850s, the beautifully restored building now offers seven spacious guest rooms (starting at $85 weekdays, $95 weekends, including a great breakfast). It's two blocks from the center of town.

There are also two large hotels on the outskirts of town: the oddly Alpine *Bavarian Inn* (☎ *304-876-2551)*, on Route 480 north of town, with rooms starting at $85 weekdays, $115 weekends (chalets extra); and the 168-room *Clarion* (☎ *304-876-7000, 800-252-7466)*, on Route 480 south of town, with a health spa, a seasonal pool, and rates over $100.

Garth and Lissa from Boulder, Colorado, set the bohemian tone for the *Lost Dog Cafe* (☎ *304-876-0871, 134 E German St)*, a popular student hangout serving espresso drinks and bakery treats among weird art, local crafts, and music that 'pushes the envelope.'

Next door, the *Old Pharmacy Cafe* (☎ *304-876-2085)* offers gourmet sandwiches, salads, and pasta plates (starting at $7 for lunch, $12 for dinner), along with soda-fountain favorites, inside a 1911 building that once housed a pharmacy. The *Yellow Brick Bank Restaurant* (☎ *304-876-2208)*, 201 German St, serves roast pork loin and paella among the specialties of the house (starting at $15 for dinner); the wine cellar is in the former vault.

Ed's Tap Room (☎ *304-876-2930, 115 W German St)* makes good Italian deli sandwiches ($5 and up) and serves microbrews and a good selection of wines in its speakeasy back room (also see Entertainment).

Blue Moon Deli, a block off German St at Princess and High Sts, offers soups, salads, vegetarian dishes ($5 and up), and ice cream in a light, airy place that's open 11 am to 9 pm.

Tony's (☎ *304-876-2720)*, near the Lost Dog Cafe, is a casual place for good pizza. *Betty's* (☎ *304-876-6080)*, next door to the Mecklenberg Inn, is a down-home place for diner-style breakfast and lunch.

WB Lannum, across from the Opera House (see Entertainment, below), makes exquisite Swiss chocolates; it's only open Friday to Sunday. You can pick up fresh fruits and vegetables at the seasonal *farmers' market*, held behind the library on

MARYLAND

weekends; Sunday's the big day. A *super-market* a mile west of town on German St has a deli counter and a large produce section year-round.

Entertainment
Dominating the town with its campus, *Shepherd College* (☎ 304-876-5497), off German St, adjacent to the small commercial district downtown, hosts a wide variety of performances from ballet to poetry salons, including the acclaimed Contemporary American Theater Festival in summer. There's also a bowling alley on campus.

See movies at the restored 1909 *Opera House* (☎ 304-876-3704, 131 W German St). Local musicians perform at the Mecklenberg Inn (see Places to Stay & Eat) on weekends, and locals rave about open-mic nights on Tuesday. There's also an inviting little garden out back. Ed's Tap Room has live music on Wednesday nights and weekends (also see Places to Stay & Eat).

Getting There & Away
Amtrak and MARC trains stop at a whistle-stop 4 miles north of town. (Unfortunately, no trains stop at the nicely restored depot at the edge of town.)

AROUND SHEPHERDSTOWN
A winding route east along the Maryland bank of the Potomac River makes a beautifully scenic drive between Shepherdstown and Knoxville. From Shepherdstown, cross the bridge toward Sharpsburg and make an immediate right turn onto Canal Rd. Follow this route, which merges with other roads several times; keep veering right, and the road will wind in and out, climb up and down, through woods and pasturelands above the river and at the river's edge.

The **Kennedy farmhouse**, John Brown's 19th-century Unabomber shack on Sandy Hook Rd (see the boxed text John Brown & the Raid on Harpers Ferry) is identified with a historical marker. This route would be nearly impossible to follow after dark.

If you're heading west toward Cumberland, Route 9 is a scenic road through West Virginia's northern panhandle. Follow Route 9 through the interesting little spa town of Berkeley Springs and over to Paw Paw. From there, Route 51 leads north to the entrance of the historic Paw Paw Tunnel at the Maryland line.

ANTIETAM NATIONAL BATTLEFIELD
The hilly farmland on the extreme western edge of the Piedmont marks the site of the bloodiest single-day battle in the Civil War and US history. Northerners called it the Battle of Antietam (ann-**tee**-tum) after the nearby creek; Southerners called it the Battle of Sharpsburg after the nearby town. On September 17, 1862, more than 23,000 Union and Confederate soldiers fell dead or wounded or disappeared during General Robert E Lee's first invasion of the North, which ended as a tactical draw (see the boxed text The Battle of Antietam). Clara Barton, who later founded the American Red Cross, treated the battle's wounded.

The battlefield and surrounding area are surprisingly uncluttered, save for historic plaques and statues honoring the units that fought here. Antietam is a remarkable contrast to Gettysburg, where a string of fast-food restaurants mar the main entrance to the battlefield. Here, there are no wax museums, trinket shops, or tourist traps. Antietam seems a solemn, haunting place – as it should – as you drive along the roads past split-rail fences and monuments.

Orientation & Information
The Antietam National Battlefield Visitors Center (☎ 301-432-5124), on Route 65 north of Sharpsburg, is the place to find interpretive guides to the battlefield (alternatively, you can drive the public roads for free). The center is open 8:30 am to 6 pm daily in summer, to 5 pm the rest of the year. A $2-per-person, or $4-per-family, charge (good for three days) includes admission to the audio-visual shows, a driving-tour map (ask for 'the good map'), and seasonal ranger programs.

Year-round, rangers show the 26-minute film *Antietam Visit*, about Lincoln's visit to

The Battle of Antietam (1862)

The Battle of Antietam occurred when Confederate General Robert E Lee first attempted to take the Civil War to the North. Lee's 41,000 troops marched north from Virginia hoping to surprise Union General George B McClellan's encampment of 87,000. In addition to being on home turf, McClellan enjoyed a further advantage when, eight days before the battle, a Union soldier found a copy of the Confederate battle plan, known as 'Lee's Lost Dispatch' or 'Lee's Special Order No 191.'

The battle took place on September 17, 1862, over 12 sq miles and in three phases – early morning, midday, and afternoon. From about 6 am to 9 am, Union troops attacked and drove back Confederate troops dug in north of the current-day visitor center. Some of the most horrendous slaughter took place in the Miller cornfield (about half a mile north of the visitor center), as fighting raged back and forth across it for three hours. Union General Joseph Hooker noted, 'At the time I am writing, every stalk of corn in the northern and greater part of the field was cut as closely as could have been done with a knife and the slain lay in rows precisely as they had stood in their ranks a few moments before.'

During the midday phase (from 9:30 am to 1 pm), Union and Confederate infantry fought over the sunken road between the Roulette and Piper farms. The road (about half a mile southeast of the visitor center) became known as 'Bloody Lane' because of the 5000 casualties sustained there.

In the afternoon phase, Union General Burnside attacked across the Lower Bridge (a mile southeast of the town of Sharpsburg), but Confederate General AP Hill drove Burnside's men back to the bridge.

Lee's failure to bring the war successfully into the North likely prevented England from recognizing the Confederacy. The war continued for another two years, due in part to McClellan's extreme caution in committing his reserve troops and his refusal to pursue the Confederates back into Virginia. Had he acted decisively, he might have achieved an early end to the conflict.

Union General George B McClellan, on the hour and half-hour. You can also see a one-hour documentary at noon. During the summer, rangers offer talks and walking tours (no charge beyond admission) that bring the battle to life (you'd be lucky to catch Paul Chiles). Customized private tours are also available; ask rangers for a list of local historians happy to guide you through the site (for around $20). Or, you can rent audiotape tours (complete with recorder) for $5 at the visitor center.

Things to See & Do

Among the monumental memorials and broad vistas, a few landmarks in particular stand out. One is the octagonal **Maryland Monument**, one of the few monuments anywhere in the world to honor troops on both sides of battle. Another is the seldom-visited **West Woods**, right off Route 65. Here, Union General John Sedgwick's division lost more than 2200 men in less than half an hour in an ill-fated charge against Jackson's troops; a lion memorial evokes the sentiment of the day: 'Defiant even when wounded.' The third is at **Lower Bridge**, where a bust in a grove of trees commemorates the young officer who died among his charges.

Living-history reenactments take place several times a month from July to December. Held on the weekend closest to the battle anniversary, the **Sharpsburg Heritage Festival** includes three days of Civil War living history, music, crafts, and workshops. In early December, a **Memorial Illumination** features 23,110 lit candles that honor the battle's casualties. There are also celebrations on Memorial Day and Independence Day (including fireworks).

MARYLAND

FREDERICK

Forty-five miles north of DC, Frederick (population 50,000) is a convenient travelers' stop along I-70 and along the popular Route 15, a historical touring route. Downtown Frederick includes an attractive, 50-block historic district filled with restored 18th- and 19th-century Italian Renaissance, Greek revival, and Federal-period homes, churches, and public buildings.

Laid out in 1745 and named for Frederick Calvert, the sixth Lord Baltimore, Frederick was settled by German and English immigrants. Long before the Boston Tea Party, judges in Frederick committed one of the first acts of colonial protest when they permitted unstamped commercial and legal documents, in defiance of the 1765 Stamp Act imposed by the British Crown.

During the American Revolution, the Continental army brought British and Hessian (German mercenaries fighting for England) prisoners here, and Francis Scott Key, author of the national anthem, practiced law here.

But what draws most visitors is the town's Civil War history. During the war, hundreds of thousands of Union and Confederate troops passed through Frederick en route to the Battles of South Mountain and Antietam. Following the bloodbath at Antietam, Frederick served as a hospital for many of the wounded, a story related in exhibits at the town's Museum of Civil War Medicine.

Shortly after the Battle of Antietam, America's famous jurist and author Oliver Wendell Holmes traveled to Frederick to visit his son, who was wounded in the battle. Surveying the town, Holmes wrote 'How graceful, how charmingly its group of steeples nestles among the Maryland hills. The town had a poetical look from a distance, as if seers and dreamers might dwell there.'

Today, downtown Frederick retains much of this appeal, thanks to historic preservation and recent prosperity. A host of midsize, white-collar businesses have developed around the city's perimeter, prompting Frederick's population to double during the last decade. Frederick also has the dubious distinction of being the home of the US Army's Fort Detrick, the government research and storage facility for chemical and germ warfare – generating more than a little of the macabre humor that filters through Frederick's pubs.

Orientation

The main commercial center is along Market St, which runs north/south through the historic district; many restaurants and shops are located here, as well as along E Patrick St, one block north of the Carroll Creek plaza. A small knot of shops and cafes called 'Shab Row' has sprung up at the west end of downtown, off East St near E Church St.

Information

The visitor center (☎ 301-663-8687, 800-999-3613), 19 E Church St at Market St downtown, is open 9 am to 5 pm daily. It distributes maps and guides, maintains a binder of local restaurant menus, and validates parking for three hours at the adjacent lot (bring your ticket). Walking tours leave from here at 1:30 pm on weekends from April to December (and most Monday holidays). The charge for the 90-minute tour of the town's historic highlights is $4.50 for adults, $3.50 for seniors, free for children 12 and under. Inquire about carriage tours.

The main post office (☎ 301-662-2131), downtown on E Patrick St, is open 8:30 am to 5 pm weekdays, to 2 pm Saturday. Wonderbook & Video (☎ 301-694-5955), 1306 W Patrick St, has the city's most complete selection of books. The 7th St Laundromat is in the shopping plaza near the intersection of Route 15 and 7th St. Frederick Memorial Hospital (☎ 301-698-3300) is at 400 W 7th St.

Things to See & Do

The **Museum of Civil War Medicine** (☎ 301-695-1864), 48 E Patrick St, offers an interesting angle on Civil War history. A series of displays examines the health conditions and medical treatment of the time, moving through a soldier's recruitment to encampment conditions, battlefield medicine, and wartime hospitals. An informative self-guided tour brochure explains that while the majority of Civil War deaths resulted from

FREDERICK

PLACES TO STAY
1 Spring Bank B&B
7 Holiday Inn
8 Red Horse Motor Inn
9 Comfort Inn
13 Holiday Inn Express
14 Days Inn
15 Holiday Inn
16 Fairfield Inn
17 Hampton Inn
24 Tyler-Spite House
30 McNeery's Flat

PLACES TO EAT
19 Province
20 Brewer's Alley
21 La Paz
23 Frederick Coffee Company
26 44 North
27 Di Francesco's
29 Nido's
31 Tauraso's
32 Bentz St Raw Bar
35 Village Restaurant
36 Province II

OTHER
2 Rose Hill Manor
3 7th St Laundromat
4 Schifferstadt Architectural
    Museum
5 Frederick Memorial Hospital
6 Wonderbook & Video
10 Mount Olivet Cemetery
11 Harry Grove Stadium
12 Museum of Civil War
    Medicine (temporary)
18 Olde Towne Tavern
22 Visitor Center
25 Trinity Chapel
28 Historical Society of Frederick
33 Fritchie House
34 Weinberg Center for the Arts
37 Museum of Civil War
    Medicine (permanent)
38 Post Office
39 Brooke Taney House
40 Greyhound Bus Depot
41 Delaplaine Visual Arts Center
    & Community Bridge Mural

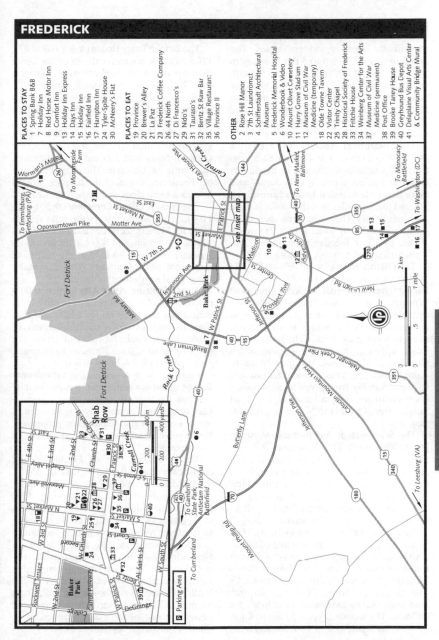

MARYLAND

disease rather than battle, changes in treatment during the war moved medicine from the middle ages to modern times. The museum is open 10 am to 5 pm Monday to Saturday and 11 am to 5 pm Sunday (with reduced winter hours). Admission is $5 for adults, $3 for children. Note that the museum returns to this downtown location in late 2000, after temporary relocation at a spot off I-70 during renovation.

The **Historical Society of Frederick** (☎ 301-663-1188), 24 E Church St across from the visitor center, opens its headquarters for guided tours. The Federal- and Georgian-style mansion houses furnishings, art, and memorabilia, as well as an extensive research library. There are often special exhibits of works by local artists. It's open 10 am to 4 pm Tuesday to Saturday, 1 to 4 pm Sunday year-round. Admission is $2.

The **Fritchie House** (☎ 301-698-0630), 154 W Patrick St, relates the history of Civil War heroine Barbara Fritchie. (John Greenleaf Whittier wrote a poem, 'Ballad of Barbara Fritchie,' about the 95-year-old woman who challenged the 'rebel hordes' to 'shoot if you must this old gray head.') The house is an exact replica of the heroine's home, which was destroyed by flood. It's open 10 am to 4 pm Monday to Thursday and Saturday, 1 to 4 pm Sunday from April to September; it's open 10 am to 4 pm Saturday, 1 to 4 pm Sunday from October to November. Admission is $2.

The **Schifferstadt Architectural Museum** (☎ 301-663-3885), 1110 Rosemont Ave, exhibits the oldest dwelling in town. Built in 1756, the house is a classic example of German colonial farmhouse architecture. It's open 10 am to 4 pm Monday to Saturday, noon to 4 pm Sunday from April to October. A $2 donation is encouraged.

Rose Hill Manor (☎ 301-694-1648), 1611 N Market St, is a pristine example of Georgian colonial architecture. The 1790s manor house belonged to Thomas Johnson, Revolutionary War statesman and Maryland's first elected governor. Costumed docents lead tours that include hands-on exhibits for children. The manor is open 10 am to 4 pm Monday to Saturday, 1 to 4 pm Sunday from April to October; it's open weekends only in November. Admission is $3.50.

The **Brooke Taney House** (☎ 301-663-8687), 121 S Bentz St, contains exhibits on the life of 'Star-Spangled Banner' composer, Francis Scott Key. It's open by appointment only.

The Evangelical Reformed Church's **Trinity Chapel** (☎ 301-662-2762), W Church St at N Market St, dates from 1763. Here, Francis Scott Key was baptized, Barbara Fritchie attended services, and Confederate General Stonewall Jackson prayed before the Battle of Antietam. The chapel has one of Frederick's graceful steeples, which houses a town clock and 10-bell chimes.

The **Mount Olivet Cemetery** (☎ 301-662-1164), 515 S Market St, is the final resting place for Francis Scott Key, Barbara Fritchie, Thomas Johnson, and 800 Union and Confederate soldiers who died at the battles of Antietam and Monocacy. You can make some good tombstone rubbings here.

The **Delaplaine Visual Arts Center** (☎ 301-698-0656), 40 Carroll St beside Carroll Creek, runs a fine-arts program for adults and children. Its galleries display changing exhibits of works by regional and national artists. It's open 10 am to 5:30 pm Thursday to Saturday, 1 to 4 pm Sunday. Admission is free.

Outside the arts center, the **Community Bridge mural** is a whimsical trompe l'oeil by William Cochran, the same artist responsible for several murals elsewhere around town. Look for the anamorphic projection, the angel image designed to be viewed from a sharp angle.

Three miles south of Frederick, the **Monocacy Battlefield** (☎ 301-662-3515), 4801 Urbana Pike, on Route 355, commemorates events of 1864. In early July, 5000 Union soldiers delayed 18,000 Confederates here, giving Union General Grant a chance to reinforce his regiments at Fort Stevens to protect Washington, DC, and to head off Confederate attempts to overrun the national capital. The surrounding farmland is virtually unchanged since the days of the battle. It's open 8 am to 4:30 pm daily from Memorial Day to Labor Day, with reduced hours the rest of the year (Wednesday to Sunday only from September to June).

Special Events

Frederick hosts the Maryland Civil War Show in late April, the Frederick Festival of the Arts in late June, Commemoration of the Battle of Monocacy during the second week in July, the Confederate Air Show in late August, and New Market Days (one of the largest antique fairs in the country) in late September.

Places to Stay

Five miles northwest of Frederick on Route 40, **Gambrill State Park** (☎ 301-271-7574) has three scenic overlooks, hiking and nature trails, fishing, and a 35-site seasonal campground. Sites cost $10 on weekdays, $14 on weekends ($5 to $7 extra for hookups). Call ☎ 888-432-2267 for reservations (open 24 hours); there's an $8 surcharge.

Six chain motels are off I-270, particularly around the Route 85 junction, including (roughly in ascending price order) a Days Inn, Fairfield Inn, Comfort Inn, Holiday Inn Express, a high-rise Hampton Inn, and two Holiday Inns. Rates run from around $65 to $85 for standard rooms. A lower-priced motel alternative is the 72-room **Red Horse Motor Inn** (☎ 301-662-0281, 800-245-6701, 996 W Patrick St), at the junction of Routes 40 and 15 near Fort Detrick. Rates start at $55; there's no pool. Look for the big red horse.

There are two great top-end places in the historic district: **McNeery's Flat** (☎ 301-620-2433, 800-774-7926, 121 E Patrick St) operates out of a spacious three-story townhouse painted in bold Charlestonian shades of maroon and orange inside. Proprietor Jutta Terrell, a former flight attendant from Denmark, offers gracious European hospitality and knows what makes travelers comfortable. Three large bedrooms and two suites have private baths and whimsical touches, such as classical statues in the bathroom. Rates start at $90 on weekdays, $100 on weekends, including a full breakfast.

The **Tyler-Spite House** (☎ 301-831-4455, 112 W Church St) is opulently decorated in 19th-century style. This Federal mansion has a parlor, library, music room, garden, and swimming pool. Inquire about high tea and horse-drawn carriage rides. Rooms start at $100 on weekdays, $180 on weekends.

Two other inns outside town charge $95 and up for rooms with private baths, full breakfast included. **Morningside Inn** (☎ 301-898-9147, 7477 McKaig Rd), 10 minutes east off Route 26 near Mount Pleasant, offers eight rooms in a converted hay barn on a 300-acre farm. **Spring Bank B&B** (☎ 301-694-0440, 7945 Worman's Mill Rd), north of the historic district on Route 15, operates from a house listed on the National Register of Historic Places.

Places to Eat

More than a dozen cafes and restaurants are located in a compact area downtown along N Market and E Patrick Sts. For starters, **Village Restaurant** (☎ 301-662-1944, 4 E Patrick St) is a popular local breakfast spot serving all-you-can-eat pancake breakfasts for under $5. **Province II** (☎ 301-663-3315, 12 E Patrick St) sells fresh-baked goods, sandwiches, soups, and salads. This can be a great stop for breakfast (under $5), lunch, or for a takeout picnic. The **Frederick Coffee Company** (☎ 301-698-0039, 100 East St), at Shab Row, makes a nice stop anytime for a coffee and bakery treat. It's open most days 7 am to 7 pm.

La Paz (☎ 301-694-8980, 18 Market Space), a Mexican restaurant tucked behind the intersection of Market and 2nd Sts, is a great place for fajitas and margaritas. Dinner plates start at $8.

Three brewpub-type places offer lunch, dinner, and friendly bar scenes. The comfortable and mild **44 North** (☎ 301-698-7327, 44 N Market St) serves burgers and sandwiches ($6) and such dinner entrees as pan-seared halibut ($17).

The newer and hotter **Brewer's Alley** (☎ 301-631-0089, 124 N Market St) offers such Creole-inspired specials as a fiery gumbo ($6), muffulettas, and spicy Cajun pizza with andouille sausage.

The most barlike is the **Bentz St Raw Bar** (☎ 301-694-9134, 6 S Bentz St), with such seafood specials as stuffed catfish or grilled salmon (starting at $13), as well as a by-the-piece raw bar. All three are open daily.

Frederick has three good, fairly upscale Italian restaurants that charge around $15 for most entrees but also have pasta plates under $10. *Nido's* (☎ *301-694-5939, 111 E Patrick St)* is perhaps the most romantic, with intimate candlelit tables in a small brick row house. *Tauraso's* (☎ *301-663-6600, 6 East St)*, on Everedy Square, has a great patio where you can enjoy wood-fired pizza; a bistro atmosphere prevails inside. *Di Francesco's* (☎ *301-695-5499, 26 N Market St)* offers classic Italian ambiance and cuisine; top-end entrees include veal saltimbocca and shrimp scampi.

For creative American cuisine, stop by *Province* (☎ *301-663-1441, 131 N Market St)*, set in a 1767 house decorated with contemporary works of local artists. Most daily seafood and steak specials cost around $20.

Entertainment

The *Weinberg Center for the Arts* (☎ *301-694-8585, 20 W Patrick St)* produces a continuous program of music, dance, and visual arts. It's also home to the Fredericktowne Players, a local theater group.

The pubs listed under Places to Eat, above, often host live entertainment on weekends; the Bentz St Raw Bar offers nightly bands and a raucous scene, with happy-hour discounts from 3:30 to 6 pm. The *Olde Towne Tavern*, N Market St at 3rd St, is a popular beer joint for the college crowd.

Spectator Sports

The Frederick Keys, a Class A farm team for the Baltimore Orioles, play minor-league baseball at *Harry Grove Stadium* (☎ *301-662-0013, 6201 New Design Rd)* from April to September. Tickets cost $6 for adults.

Shopping

During the last 50 years, Frederick and the surrounding townships have been quietly developing a vital art scene. Today, there are 16 studios and galleries in and around the city for shopping and browsing.

About 10 miles east of Frederick off I-70 is the Federal-era village of New Market. During the past 20 years, antique dealers by the dozens have reclaimed New Market's main street. Some collectors claim this little village is among the best places in the country to browse for antiques.

Getting There & Away

Frederick is at the junction of I-70, I-270, and Route 15. Any of the exits from the interstate highways lead to the historic district, but for drivers coming from Baltimore or DC, the Route 85N exit is the most direct.

Greyhound (☎ 301-663-3311) stops at the bus station at E All Saints St. MARC (☎ 800-325-7245) runs shuttle buses to and from the Brunswick train station, 15 miles southwest of Frederick, weekdays only (see Brunswick, earlier in the chapter).

On weekdays only, MTA buses (☎ 410-539-5000, 800-543-9809) travel between Frederick's Francis Scott Key Mall, 5500 Buckeystown Pike, off I-270 (exit 31, one exit south of the I-70 junction), and the Shady Grove Metro station, 15 miles south near the Potomac River.

Getting Around

There are four parking lots just south of the intersection of Patrick and Market Sts at the center of town. There is also a parking lot next to the downtown visitor center on E Church St. Transit Service of Frederick County (☎ 301-694-2065) runs buses within the city as well as to satellite communities. The fare is $1.

For a taxi, call City Cab (☎ 301-662-2250).

CATOCTIN MOUNTAIN & AROUND

The long narrow ridge of Catoctin Mountain spans the state of Maryland and forms the Appalachian front range, bordering the Piedmont Plateau. Though it's on the popular historical touring route from Gettysburg through Frederick, the region remains remote and is relatively undeveloped beyond highway exits – remote enough for a famous federal hideaway: The presidential retreat of Camp David is located deep within Catoctin Mountain Park.

Thurmont

Provisions, gas, and other basic necessities are available in this small town, which unfortunately holds little other appeal (it's the kind of town where a new franchise food outlet would be a welcome sign of a burgeoning local economy).

Many travelers end up at **Mountain Gate Family Restaurant** (☎ *301 271 4373, 133 Frederick Rd*), which offers all-you-can-eat buffets. Thurmont also has a **Super 8 Motel** (☎ *301-271-7888*), Route 15 exit 806, convenient for those passing through town.

From late spring to early fall, the seasonal Catoctin Mountain Visitors Center (☎ 301-271-3285) is open on Route 15 south of Thurmont.

Catoctin Mountain Park
This park (☎ 301-663-9388), administered by the National Park Service, and the adjacent state park together protect more than 10,000 acres of eastern hardwood climax forest. The visitor center distributes maps covering a total of 25 miles of hiking trails (skiing and snowshoeing in winter), some of which lead to waterfalls and beautiful mountain vistas.

The NPS maintains a remote **campground** ($12, no hookups) and rents individual walk-in rustic **cabins** with metal cots and electricity (no indoor plumbing) for $40. Cabins are available by advance reservation only (call ☎ 301 271 3140).

Cunningham Falls State Park
This state park (☎ 301-271-7574) features a popular lake for seasonal swimming, fishing, and boating (canoe rentals are available). Hunting Creek Lake has a sandy shore, a modern bathhouse, and a snack bar. There's a popular 139-site **campground** by the lake and another 31-site state campground right off Route 15, near the ruins of the ironworks that operated here from 1776 to 1904. Sites are $13 on weekdays, $17 on weekends (add $5 for hookups). Call ☎ 888-432-2267 for reservations (24 hours); there's an $8 surcharge.

St Elizabeth Ann Seton Landmarks
North of Thurmont, near the Pennsylvania border, two religious landmarks honor America's first saint. The National Shrine of St Elizabeth Ann Seton (☎ 301-447-6606, 447-3121), 333 S Seton St in Emmitsburg,

was named a 'minor basilica' by Pope John Paul II in 1991. The serene grounds include a 1770s farm house and the larger 'White House,' from which America's first saint led her heroic life of charity. It's open 10 am to 5 pm, with abbreviated hours in December and January (there's a daily Mass).

A few miles south, a rock crevice called the Grotto of Lourdes is tucked behind a peaceful 'prayer walk,' with nice mosaics and statues.

UPPER POTOMAC CORRIDOR
Beyond the midpoint of the C&O Canal, the Potomac River enters a more remote region.

Williamsport
Williamsport, southwest of the I-81 and I-70 junction, has a C&O Canal visitor center (☎ 301-582-0813) that distributes towpath maps and guides and information about local recreation. It's open Wednesday to Sunday.

Bike rentals are available from Potomac Pushbikes (☎ 301-582-4747), 11 E Potomac St, two blocks from the canal; it's open daily. Rooms at the local **Days Inn** (☎ *301-582-3500, 310 E Potomac St*) cost around $55.

Fort Frederick State Park
Located 112 miles up the canal, Fort Frederick State Park (☎ 301-842-2155) is centered around a stone stockade fort built in 1756 to defend English settlers against the French and Indians during the French and Indian War. The only time the fort ever actually saw battle was on Christmas Day, 1861, when Union troops inside fought off a small party of Confederate troops.

You can enjoy hiking, fishing, and boating in the 561-acre park, as well as biking and primitive camping along the towpath. Muzzle-loader shoots and military reenactments take place in the fort. It's a mile south of I-70 on Route 56.

Indian Springs Wildlife Management Area
This 6500-acre wildlife management area (☎ 301-842-2702) is centered in Clear Spring, 12 miles west of Hagerstown. The

top of Fairview Mountain was a Civil War signal post where messages were flashed to South Mountain across the Cumberland Valley. Visitors come here to fish and hunt for deer, turkey, grouse, rabbit, quail, and some waterfowl. The area includes a nature trail and two lakes stocked with trout. During the spring and fall, bird-dog clubs hold field trials for their canines.

Hancock & Berkeley Springs

Located 124 miles up the canal, Hancock has another C&O Canal visitor center (☎ 301-678-5463), 326 E Main St, where historical displays include a canal boat. It's open daily. Bike rentals are available at Pathfinders (☎ 301-678-6870), 6 S Pennsylvania Ave. There's a **Budget Motel** (☎ 301-678-7351) on E Main St downtown.

Across the river from Hancock, it's a 5-mile drive to Berkeley Springs, West Virginia, a small old-timey tourist town with mineral baths at Berkeley Springs State Park (☎ 304-258-2711).

About 5 miles west of Hancock, **Sideling Hill Road Cut** is worth a close look if you like geology. The cut, made in 1983 for the I-68 thoroughfare, exposes a 600-foot section of tightly folded 330-million-year-old rock in colors from tan to green to gray to red – a common sight in the American West but unusual for this area. The visitor center (☎ 301-842-2155), off I-68, is open 9 am to 5 pm daily.

Green Ridge State Forest

The state forest visitor center (☎ 301-478-3124), off I-68 exit 64 south of Flintstone, directs visitors to 38,811 acres of vast mountain wilderness. Wildlife is plentiful, with lots of turkeys, deer, and black bears. Trails are long and bushy, but the payoff comes with scenic overlooks, wild streams, and pristine primitive campsites ($6 per night).

This is not a place for the unfit, inexperienced, or ill-prepared. Always carry up-to-date topographic maps, a compass, and perhaps a hand-held GPS when hiking on any of Green Ridge's backcountry trails. Trails connect with the C&O Canal towpath, and the state forest service sponsors guided

canoe trips down a placid stretch of the Potomac River by advance reservation. In early October, the state mountain-biking championship is sometimes held here, along an 11½-mile trail.

Little Orleans

Off the towpath, you'll find the only business in downtown Little Orleans under the sign 'Mayor's Office.' Here, hunters, fishermen, and others wearing camouflage gear gather 'round a seven-stool bar at **Bill's Place** (☎ 301-478-2701) to swap tales. You'll find short-order food, cold sodas in the Coleman chest, nickel candy, and a game room out back that appears frozen in time from the late 1950s – a must-stop spot. Inquire about canoe rentals and shuttles.

Uphill on Orleans Rd, the **Little Orleans Campground** (☎ 301-478-2325) is primarily a residential RV park, but it also has tent sites up by the RVs on the hill (bathhouses here) and primitive tent sites down by the river (port-a-potties here) for $15 a night. Sites fill up on summer weekends; reservations are recommended.

Paw Paw Tunnel

Lying 28 miles downstream from Cumberland, the historic Paw Paw Tunnel, an engineering marvel when it was completed after 14 years of construction in 1850, goes 3118 feet through a mountain, permitting the canal and towpath to pass right through. You can hike through the inviting tunnel and return overland via the steep 2-mile Tunnel Hill Trail.

The tunnel lies near Route 51 and makes a good place for hikers and bikers to join or leave the towpath on a day trip to or from Cumberland. There's a primitive **campground** here for hikers, bicyclists, and paddlers.

ROCKY GAP STATE PARK

Surrounding 243-acre Lake Habeeb, about 15 miles east of Cumberland (off I-68 exit 50 in Flintstone), this state park (☎ 301-777-2139) encompasses the natural saddle formed by Evitt's and Martin's Mountains. This park is a good place for outdoor family adventures. In addition to hiking trails and campsites, Rocky Gap has launch ramps for boats, a swimming beach, and a bathhouse.

Within the park, the ***Rocky Gap Lodge & Golf Resort*** *(☎ 800-724-0828)* includes a six-story, 220-room hotel alongside the lake and an 18-hole golf course. Rates are $90 in winter, $120 in summer.

A 278-site *campground* charges $21 for sites with hookups, $16 without. Rustic seasonal cabins (outside kitchen, no private bathrooms, no linens) rent for $35. For minimum-stay requirements and camping or cabin reservations, call ☎ 888-432-2267 (24 hours); there's an $8 reservation surcharge.

CUMBERLAND

On the north shore of the Potomac River, about 135 miles from Washington, DC, Cumberland (population 24,000) has been a frontier outpost since young George Washington and General Braddock came through in colonial days. Washington used what was then known as Fort Cumberland as a spearhead into the wilderness during the French and Indian War.

As Cumberland stood on the dividing line between the civilized colonies to the east and the western territories, generations of explorers and pioneers made their way through here to the Ohio River Valley. The C&O Canal ended here, as did the first national pike (now Route 40 Alt). The western Maryland Railroad arrived in 1842, leading to the abandonment of the canal. Cumberland boomed as a shipping center in the 19th century and later found greater prosperity when miners began exploiting the rich bituminous coal fields beneath the surface of the Allegheny Mountains.

With improved routes to the west through Pennsylvania, plus a decline in demand for soft coal for homes and industries, Cumberland slipped into depression after WWII. The little city, with its stock of once-elegant Victorian homes and public buildings, became a place time seemingly forgot until the mid-1970s, when a new generation of explorers turned to the Allegheny wilderness as an oasis from the crowds, pollution, and crime in places like Washington, DC, and Baltimore.

Today, Cumberland is a ready base of operations for the thriving outdoor tourist industry in the region, as outfitters have made the forbidding Alleghenies accessible to hikers, campers, mountain bikers, skiers, boaters, and whitewater enthusiasts. On the first week in August, tens of thousands of people descend on the Cumberland area for the Rocky Gap Music Festival, held west of town – the 'Woodstock' of traditional bluegrass music.

Orientation & Information

The intersection of Baltimore and Centre Sts marks the heart of town, where there is now a pedestrian shopping mall.

The C&O Canal visitor center (☎ 301-722-8226), in the depot on Canal St downtown (via I-68 exit 43C), is at the terminus of the historic canal. The center distributes maps and guides for camping, lodging, and recreation along the canal. It also contains exhibits on the historical significance of the canal and the legendary bargemen and families who plied their trade on the canal during its brief heyday. The center is open 9 am to 5 pm daily in summer; it's closed Sunday and Monday in winter.

The Allegany County Visitors Bureau in Western Maryland Station Center (☎ 301-777-5905, 800-508-4748), at the foot of Canal St off Baltimore St (a block north of the I-68 bridge), is open 9 am to 5 pm weekdays, 10 am to 4 pm weekends.

The post office (☎ 301-722-8190), 215 Park St, is open 8 am to 4:30 pm weekdays, 9 am to noon Saturday. The Book Center (☎ 301-722-2284), 15-17 N Centre St, is a large independent bookstore with a local history section and a good supply of out-of-town newspapers. It's open daily. The Sunshine Central Laundromat (☎ 301-759-9711) is at 401 Green St downtown.

Memorial Hospital (☎ 301-777-4000) is at 600 Memorial Ave. Sacred Heart Hospital (☎ 301-759-4200) is at 900 Seton Drive.

Western Maryland Station Center

The grand, four-story 1913 depot, on Canal St downtown, is the center of much of the town's tourist activity. Standing at the head of a landscaped plaza between the railroad tracks and the canal, the depot is the starting point for steam-train rides and towpath adventures. Inside, the depot contains the local county visitors bureau, a C&O Canal visitor center, and the steam-train offices.

Exhibits at the seasonal **Transportation & Industrial Museum** (☎ 301-724-4398) here describe the railroad, canal, and industries that launched Cumberland's economic boom (donations encouraged).

Western Maryland Scenic Railroad

Rising from the ashes of the old mountain freight line, the WMSR (☎ 301-759-4400, 800-872-4650) runs three-hour roundtrip **steam-train rides**. Re-creating the boomtown days of Cumberland, a vintage 1916 steam locomotive pulls a train of coaches 1300 feet uphill 16 miles west, threading through ravines, forests, and a tunnel. After a pit stop at the terminus in Frostburg (see Frostburg, later in the chapter), the train crew turns the engine on a turntable and heads back down to Cumberland.

Excursion rides run Tuesday to Sunday from May to December, or daily during the popular fall-colors season in October (reservations recommended). Fares run $16 to $18 for adults (slight senior discounts), $10 for children two to 12. Special excursions include a murder mystery ride, dinner trains, and a Santa Express.

George Washington's Headquarters

The tiny log cabin at the foot of Greene St in Riverside Park served as Washington's headquarters (☎ 301-777-8214) during the French and Indian War. Looking through the window (it's lit around the clock), you can see the period furnishings. A push-button tape recording recounts frontier history. The cabin is open occasionally on holidays (no fee). A new pedestrian bridge nearby crosses the canal.

Emmanuel Episcopal Church

This stately church (☎ 301-777-3364) commands the bluff above the river on Washington St. The church was built in the 1850s over the earthworks of Fort Cumberland; remnants of the fort's 18th-century trenches are still visible in the catacombs below. The sanctuary itself holds beautiful opalescent Tiffany windows, and the parish hall holds a model of the fort. Guided tours are available by appointment only.

Victorian Historical District

Placed on the National Register of Historic Places in 1973, the elite neighborhood along Washington St west of the canal reflects Cumberland's prosperity in the early 20th century, when the canal, the railroads, and King Coal made fortunes for some of its citizens.

History House (☎ 301-777-8678), at 218 Washington St, is the 18-room mansion that belonged to the president of the C&O Canal after the Civil War. The county historical society offers guided tours Tuesday to Sunday ($3 for adults). Pick up walking tour maps, which describe more of the district's architectural highlights, at the depot visitor center.

Activities

Lots of people come to the Cumberland area for **hiking, biking, camping, canoeing**, and **kayaking** in the surrounding mountains and waterways. If you are planning outdoor adventuring, you can get up to speed on sites and itineraries, stock up on provisions, and find equipment by contacting an outfitter/guide service. Two good services in the Cumberland area are Allegany Adventures

---

Sssss – A Word about Snakes

The Allegheny Mountains are home to the eastern (timber) rattlesnake and the copperhead. Both species are large vipers with enough venom to kill a human. Watch for these serpents in the vicinity of boulder piles and fallen trees, where they like to nest. Hikers in the Alleghenies should always carry a walking staff to parry snakes, wear leather hiking boots (and possibly leg protection), and carry a snake-bite kit and/or an antitoxin vaccine.

(☎ 301-729-9708), 14419 National Highway (Route 40) in LaVale, and Allegheny Expeditions (☎ 301-722-5170, 800-819-5170), on Route 2 in Cumberland.

Particularly popular are mountain-biking excursions, but bicyclists need to bring their own bikes; there are currently no bike rentals available in town (though regional outfitters running trips from Cumberland provide all equipment).

Five miles south, at Lock 75, seasonal **barge rides** enable visitors to get a flavor for life on the canal.

Special Events
The premier regional event is the Rocky Gap Music Festival (☎ 301-724-2511, 800-424-2511), held the first weekend in August on the campus of Allegheny College, east of downtown (until a permanent site is developed at Rocky Gap State Park). The festival is a world-class party for Capital Region youth and lovers of the Scotch-Irish, foot-stomping fiddle and fife bluegrass music of Appalachian Mountain folk. Festivalgoers should reserve lodging or camping early (six months in advance is recommended).

Cumberland sees several other interesting events during the summer. During Heritage Days in early June, you can buy arts and crafts and watch historical reenactments. On the second weekend in July, there's the C&O Canal Boat Festival. During the Street Rod Roundup on Labor Day weekend, hundreds of classic hot rods descend on the town.

Places to Stay
Downtown, the *Inn at Walnut Bottom* (☎ 301-777-0003, 800-286-9718, 120 Green St) is a comfortable, simple Victorian boardinghouse with a grandmotherly common room and a hideaway restaurant (see Places to Eat). A dozen spacious rooms are outfitted with private modern baths, TVs, period furnishings, and hardwood floors. Rates start at $79 and include a full breakfast downstairs. The inn is a block off historic Washington St and two blocks from the river.

Chain motel lodging is available off the interstate. Located on Route 40 Alt, west of Cumberland in LaVale, the *Scottish Inn*

(☎ 301-729-2880, 1262 National Hwy) rents rooms for $42 and up, including a full breakfast next door at Denny's. The *Super 8 Motel* (☎ 301-729-6265, 1301 National Hwy) charges $55 and up.

Places to Eat
Locals say you haven't experienced Cumberland until you've had a hot dog from *Coney Island and Curtis* (☎ 301-759-9707, 15 & 35 N Liberty St), serving fully dressed dogs since 1918 (now $1.10). It's open daily 7 am to 10:30 pm.

The *Oxford House* (☎ 301-777-7101, 118 Greene St), within the Inn at Walnut Bottom, specializes in international cuisine. The popular chicken Annapolis (breasts stuffed with ham and crab meat) costs $16. The same owners operate the deli-style *Tivoli* (☎ 301-777-2885, 30 N Centre St), where the Philly cheese-steak sub costs $6.

Getting There & Away
US Air Commuter (☎ 800-428-4322) flies in and out of Cumberland Regional Airport, on Route 28, over the border in West Virginia.

Bus service is offered by Greyhound (☎ 301-722-6226), 201 Glenn St.

Amtrak (☎ 301-724-8890, 800-872-7245) offers limited passenger service to Cumberland's E Harrison St station.

By car, the most direct route to Cumberland is via I-68. For a more scenic and leisurely approach, try Route 9, which snakes its way through West Virginia's northern panhandle.

FROSTBURG
Sixteen miles west of Cumberland, Frostburg (population 7500) is the home of Frostburg State University. Originally founded as an outpost along the National Road, Frostburg developed into a coal-mining and brickmaking town. Today, the college town is the terminus of the steam-train excursion ride that originates in Cumberland. Its depot has a carriage museum, and the small village a half-mile uphill has restaurants, hotels, and bars catering to a large student population.

A modern local legend reveals the town's character: A couple of years back, the telemarketing firm Unitel abandoned their headquarters here because the locals were 'too friendly,' and the company needed to find employees willing to be more aggressive (they moved to Florida).

Things to See & Do

The only public four-year institution west of Baltimore County, **Frostburg State University** (☎ 301-687-4000, www.fsu.umd.edu) enrolls 4500 undergraduate students in four academic schools.

The **Thrasher Carriage Museum** (☎ 301-689-3380), in the depot at Mechanic and Harrison Sts, boasts the largest collection of horse-drawn carriages in the USA. A bequest of collector James R Thrasher, the collection includes President Theodore Roosevelt's inaugural carriage. It's open staggered hours from May through December to coincide with steam-train excursion trips from Cumberland, but it's open daily in October during the popular fall-colors season. Admission is $2 for adults, $1 for students 12 to 18, free for children under 12.

Adventure Sports (☎ 301-689-0345), 113 E Main St, is a local outfitter that sponsors guided recreational adventures for **hiking, biking, rafting, rock-climbing**, and **caving**.

Places to Stay

Across from the Tastee Freeze, **Charlie's Motel** (☎ 301-689-6557, 220 W Main St) is your best bet for cheap digs in all of western Maryland. There are 10 basic motel rooms with TVs and air-conditioning. A single bed costs $30, two beds $36.

For just a little more than the price of a Route 40 chain motel, you can stay in old-fashioned comfort at **Failinger's Hotel Gunter** (☎ 301-698-6511, 11 W Main St), a turn-of-the-19th-century Victorian hotel. The 17-room hotel at the head of Main St has been restored with private baths and an elevator, but it retains the original oak interiors with brass trim. In the basement, you can see the remains of an old jail, and the pit once used for cock fights is now a bar. Rooms, featuring canopy beds and some period antiques, start at $53/58 single/double.

Places to Eat

At the head of Main St, the **Princess Coffee Shop** (☎ 301-689-1680, 12 W Main St) offers cheap eats (steak burgers with fries for under $5) and is a good place to get the inside scoop on the area from friendly locals and students.

The **Tombstone Cafe** (☎ 301-689-5254, 60 E Main St) serves strong espresso, breakfast, and healthy sandwiches for lunch or dinner inside its arty cafe or on the sunny front patio. Try the havarti cheese and Granny Smith apple on multigrain bread (under $5). The cafe has imported beer and wine at reasonable prices as well. It's open 9 am to 11 pm (or later) Monday to Saturday.

Gandalf's (☎ 301-689-2010, 16 W Main St) draws a bohemian crowd for such inventive dishes as a Cantonese pita sandwich with steamed broccoli and marinated tofu ($3.50) and Thai red curry rice, along with seven microbrews on tap. The kitchen is open 5 to 10 pm Monday to Saturday.

Cafe 101 (☎ 301-689-1243, 101 E Main St) is a fairly new spot still finding its way, with vegetarian and some vegan dishes served in a spartan atmosphere. It does, however, draw an alternative crowd that likes to drink chai out on the back porch.

Lots of tourists who ride the Western Maryland Scenic Railroad to Frostburg eat lunch at the **Old Depot** (☎ 301-689-3676, 19 Depot St), a railroad-theme restaurant with burgers or chicken wings for $5. It's open April to December only.

Frostburg's top-end restaurant, **Au Petit Paris** (☎ 301-689-8946, 86 E Main St), has bistro-style decor and furnishings, including murals of French landscapes. The menu ranges from coq au vin to Châteaubriand. Some entrees run over $30.

Entertainment

According to the sign inside, Gandalf's (see Places to Eat) is not just a restaurant and bar but 'a social ecology within a small community where capital and all its entanglements are to be confronted rather than slept with' – a constitution that can lead to interesting bar talk. It also hosts regionally popular bands on Thursday and Friday nights for a $3 cover;

Wednesday's open-mic night draws an assortment of local musicians.

The *Spring St Saloon* (☎ *301-689-8085*), at the west end of Main St, is a sprightly tavern with good chicken wings.

GARRETT COUNTY

West of Frostburg, Maryland's westernmost county remains a rugged Appalachian region, where urban refugees mix with traditional Amish and Mennonite farmers in hardscrabble mountain towns designed to be practical, not picturesque. Coal remains a top industry. More than 70,000 acres of public wilderness include the Savage River State Forest south of Grantsville, as well as the Potomac and Garrett State Forests near Oakland. Deep Creek Lake is a popular outdoor recreation spot, offering boating, skiing, mountain biking, and more. The average summer temperature is 66° F; the average winter temperature is 22° F.

Grantsville

The little town of Grantsville (population 500), centered along Main St (Route 40, I-68 exit 19), is home to an Amish farming community carrying on its distinctive religious traditions and old-fashioned dress.

At the 1824 *Casselman Inn* (☎ *301-895-5055*), on Main St across from a thrift store and auto-parts shop, an Amish family maintains a 19th-century hostelry, renting modest rooms for $26 with shared bath, $35 with private bath. Rooms in a worn modern motel annex start at $23 with private bath. Their restaurant is known for its baked goods: fresh pastries, breads, pies, and cakes. It's open 7 am to 8 pm (closed Sunday).

Penn Alps (☎ 301-895-5985), a mile east on Route 40, has a full-service restaurant and handicraft shop surrounded by restored historic cabins that serve as studios for basket makers, weavers, potters, and other craftspeople in summer. The large restaurant features a soup-and-salad bar and reasonable buffets. It's open 7 am to 7 pm (or later) daily year-round. Its Summerfest, held the second full weekend in July, features crafts, storytelling, and music; also inquire about the summer concert series.

Yoder's Country Market (☎ *800-321-5148*), on Route 669, has a wonderful selection of fresh produce seasonally, along with locally produced maple syrup and other maple products.

New Germany State Park

Five miles southeast of Grantsville, in the heart of the Savage River Forest, the 462-acre New Germany State Park (☎ 301-895-5453) is a popular place for hikers and bikers to stay. The park has a 600-foot beach and a 13-acre lake (you can rent boats here). Ten miles of groomed Nordic ski trails are a big attraction during winter months.

There are 39 seasonal *campsites* ($12, no hookups) and 11 year-round furnished one-bedroom *cabins* (from $383 weekly). For reservations (accepted up to a year in advance), call ☎ 888-432-2267 (24 hours).

Savage River State Forest

With 53,000 acres of land, Savage River State Forest, south of Grantsville, is the largest of Maryland's public forests. It occupies part of the Appalachian Plateau in Garrett County and is headquartered (☎ 301-895-5759) south of Grantsville off I-68 exit 22. The staff distribute maps that outline trails for hiking, mountain biking, cross-country skiing, and off-road vehicles. They also sell local topographic maps. Primitive camping in the state forest carries a $2-per-night fee; backcountry campers check in at headquarters.

Deep Creek & Around

Twelve miles long, with 65 miles of shoreline, Deep Creek Lake is the heart of western Maryland's outdoor recreation area. Originally created as a hydroelectric reservoir in 1925, the lake is now under the management of the Maryland State Forest and Park Service. A good many vacation homes line the shores, and recreational boats fill the waters during the summer.

McHenry The town of McHenry, at the northern tip of the impoundment, comes closest to a commercial center, though motels, family restaurants, and recreational outlets pretty much surround the lake.

The seasonal visitor center (☎ 301-387-6171), on Route 219 south of the Deep Creek Bridge, distributes information about the lake and Garrett County. Look for the 'Adventure Sports' brochure put out by Garrett County Community College Adventuresports Institute (☎ 301-387-3013).

The Market Square shopping center, across from the visitor center, supplies all provisions, including gourmet groceries and an excellent selection of fresh produce, and has an espresso bar and a small cafeteria lunch counter.

Deep Creek Lake State Park This busy state park (☎ 301-387-5563), 868 State Park Rd off Route 219, is on the eastern side of the lake, 10 miles northeast of Oakland. Its 700-foot sandy beach is a popular spot for swimming (lifeguards on duty); the day-use fee is $2 per person (no charge for people over 62 or under 4). Boat rental is available; also inquire about scuba-diving lessons. (See Places to Stay & Eat, below, for camping information.)

Boating & Sailing Mile for mile, Deep Creek Lake seems more populated with watercraft than Chesapeake Bay. Water-skiing is probably the most popular activity on the lake, but small-boat sailing comes in a close second – the lake was home to the late Sandy Douglas, the designer and builder of the Olympic-class Flying Scot sloop.

Deep Creek Sailing School (☎ 301-387-4497) in Swanton offers sailing lessons in a variety of high-performance craft. You can rent motorboats at a number of marinas around the lake. Try Echo Marina (☎ 301-387-2628) if you want to ski or just to part the waters in a fast runabout.

Mountain Biking For mountain biking at Wisp Resort (see Skiing, below), call Rudy's Outdoor Adventures (☎ 301-387-4640) for rentals, maps, and trail access. Another outfitter to try is High Mountain Sports (☎ 301-387-4119) for bike rentals at two locations on Route 219: at Sang Run Rd and Trader's Landing.

Horseback Riding Western-style riding is one of the most popular ways to see western Maryland. The Deep Creek Lake area has three stables with trail rides: Small Oaks Riding Stables in Deer Park (☎ 301-334-5733, 334-4991); Sunny Slopes Stables in Oakland (☎ 301-334-4834), which has horses and cabin rentals; and Western Trails Riding Stables (☎ 301-387-6155), off Route 219 near Deep Creek Lake, which also offers camping.

Skiing Wisp Resort (☎ 301-387-4911) in McHenry is Maryland's only ski resort and just one of a handful of places for downhill skiing within day-tripping range of DC. Wisp Resort has a summit elevation of over 3000 feet and gets plenty of snow, but the vertical drop is only 610 feet. Wisp has big-mountain prices (all-day adult passes are $42 on weekdays, $70 on weekends), and there are more than enough skiers willing to pay to ride four chair lifts and ski 23 trails.

For cross-country skiing, Deep Creek Outfitters (☎ 301-387-6977), 1899 Deep Creek Dr, provides all rental equipment.

Places to Stay & Eat You'll find plenty of motels and restaurants around the lake and in McHenry.

A 112-site *campground* (☎ 888-432-2267 *for reservations 24 hours)* at Deep Creek Lake State Park is open from April to October. Sites start at $24 with hookups, $19 without. There are hot showers but no cabins.

The restaurant at the *Deer Park Inn* (☎ *301-334-2308)*, in Deer Park off Route 135, is considered the best in the area. Owner and chef Pascal Fountaine, formerly executive chef at the Westin Hotel and ANA Hotel in Washington, DC, serves French cuisine in what was once a historic hotel, originally built as a summer 'cottage' for a prominent Baltimore architect in 1889. Entrees start at about $20. It's open for dinner only (closed Sunday).

Youghiogheny River Gap

The 'Yough' (pronounced yock) threads between the mountains of western Pennsylvania and Maryland. One of the wildest and most scenic rivers in the eastern USA, the Yough flows north from Maryland's Garrett County into southern Pennsylvania, feeding into the Youghiogheny Reservoir near Friendsville, Maryland (west of Grantsville).

The river offers world-class **whitewater rafting**. The upper Yough has class V+ rapids near Friendsville; it has been the site of numerous national and international kayaking events. The lower parts of the river are more tame.

Most river-rafting outfitters are centered in Ohiopyle, Pennsylvania, just north of the Maryland border. White Water Adventurers (☎ 724-329-8850, 800-982-7238) runs three- to five-hour guided rafting trips (starting at $116 weekdays, $135 weekends) on the upper Yough around Friendsville. The company also rents inflatable boats and canoes. Alternatively, try Mountain Streams (☎ 800-723-8669) for guided whitewater rafting and rentals of rafts, boats, and bikes; or Laurel Highlands River Tours (☎ 800-472-3846).

The Youghiogheny, Casselman, and North Branch of the Potomac – called the 'Three Sisters' – are favorite rivers for **fly-fishing**; they've been featured in national TV shows on the sport. For a list of stocked streams and regulations, consult the *Maryland Sportfishing Guide*, available from sellers of fishing licenses. To inquire about seasons and limits,

check with the Maryland Department of Natural Resources (☎ 410-974-3771).

Also in the area, two houses designed by Frank Lloyd Wright are open to public tours. **Fallingwater** (☎ 724-329-8501), in Mill Run north of Ohiopyle, is a sandstone house built over a waterfall in 1939. It's open for tours from mid-March to mid-November. **Kentucky Knob** (☎ 412-329-1901), west of Ohiopyle, is open for tours most of the year.

The hostel *HI Ohiopyle (☎ 724-329-4476)*, at Ohiopyle State Park, offers 25 beds in dormitory lodging year-round and is near local outfitters.

Cranesville Subarctic Swamp

The Nature Conservancy (☎ 301-656-8673), a nonprofit foundation that buys up wilderness areas to protect their habitats and limit public use, owns and protects 500 acres of this boreal bog that formed during the Ice Age. A boardwalk allows visitors to pass through the swamp and observe rare flora and fauna that are usually only seen north of the Arctic Circle. The swamp is at the West Virginia border, 10 miles south of I-68.

Oakland

The county seat of Oakland (population 2000) is centered in a small village along Route 219, 10 miles south of Deep Creek Lake. The Deep Creek Lake-Garrett County Promotion Council (☎ 301-334-1948) is at 200 S 3rd St.

There's a great bookstore, Book Mark'et Mezzanine (☎ 301-334-8778), 11 S 2nd St, with a large children's selection.

Just outside town, the **Broadford Recreation Area** (☎ 301-334-9222) at Mountain Lake Park has a 700-foot beach.

Downtown, *Towne Restaurant (☎ 301-334-6144, 230 E Alder St)*, at Route 219, is a local spot that can't really be recommended for the food, but it's nearly always open. *Englander's Pharmacy (☎ 301-334-9455)* has soda-fountain treats; breakfast is served all day.

Fly-fishing the Three Sisters

Potomac & Garrett State Forests

The two state forests together comprise 18,000 acres of wilderness, including a number of attractions for hikers. Herrington Manor and Swallow Falls State Parks are more developed parts of this wilderness.

The Potomac State Forest, southeast of Oakland, features the 10½-mile Potomac River Trail (for hiking, mountain biking, and horseback riding) alongside the north branch of the Potomac River (whitewater rated class III-IV). Garrett State Forest (☎ 301-334-2038), northwest of Oakland, features a class I-II section of the Youghiogheny River.

Herrington Manor State Park Five miles northwest of Oakland, Herrington Manor State Park (☎ 301-334-9108) attracts the outdoor crowd with its 53-acre, trout-stocked lake. The facilities include a 400-foot beach, a concession stand, and boat rentals. The park maintains 10 miles of marked trails open to mountain biking in summer and cross-country skiing in winter (ski rentals are available).

Twenty furnished one-bedroom *cabins* are rented year-round for $75 a night; weekly rentals are available in summer only. Call ☎ 888-432-2267 for reservations (24 hours); there's an $8 surcharge.

Swallow Falls State Park In this state park (☎ 301-387-6938), located 9 miles north of Oakland near Herrington Manor State Park, trails lead to a number of scenic waterfalls and a tall hemlock forest. There's ice climbing here in winter.

The park has 65 seasonal *campsites* that cost $20 with hookups, $15 without (two-night minimum). Call ☎ 888-432-2267 for reservations (24 hours); there's an $8 surcharge.

Backbone Mountain

At 3360 feet (the highest point in Maryland), Backbone Mountain straddles the West Virginia border at the southwestern tip of the state. The mountain also serves as the Eastern Continental Divide – from here, the waters part to flow east to the Atlantic Ocean or west to the Gulf of Mexico. A mile-long hiking trail cut from an old lumber road reaches the summit, where a mailbox holds certificates congratulating hikers on their climb. The easier access is from the West Virginia side, on the east side of Route 219 just beyond Silver Lake (5 miles south of the Route 50 intersection in Redhouse, Maryland). The McHenry visitor center and the County Promotion Council in Oakland have maps.

Delaware

Facts about Delaware

What a difference a bay makes. Like Maryland and Virginia, Delaware is one of America's original 13 colonies, sharing strong roots with other Tidewater states; the three states also share the Delmarva Peninsula. But unlike its southern and western neighbors, Delaware does not face the sheltered meanders of the Chesapeake and its tributaries.

Instead, tucked into the northeastern corner of the peninsula, Delaware faces the rougher waters of the ocean and Delaware Bay, an estuary that lies exposed to the open Atlantic. A tugboat captain who tows barges through both the Delaware and the Chesapeake offered this perspective on the difference between the two bodies of water: 'The Chesapeake is a milk run in almost any weather – you can kick back and relax; the Delaware – when the wind comes hard against a tide – can be a test. This is not a place for your common Joe or the faint of heart.'

The captain might have been speaking of the state of Delaware as well. The wind and waves that have whipped the sand into huge dunes at Cape Henlopen have all but hewn Delaware's 100 miles of coast, Atlantic and bay alike, into one weathered piece. In keeping with the tough climes and landscapes, the state has long been a locus for rugged individualism, courage, extraordinary accomplishment, and – occasionally – sheer madness.

Although Delaware received its initial groups of immigrants from Europe, more recently, people have actually migrated from within the United States – from Pennsylvania or the Eastern Shore of Maryland. Today, only about half of Delaware's population was actually born in the state, with almost two-thirds living in northern New Castle County.

Ranking as America's second-smallest state (after Rhode Island), Delaware is often overlooked by all but shoppers searching for tax-free bargains (there's no sales tax) and entrepreneurs incorporating their businesses here to take advantage of the state's tax incentives and liberal incorporation laws.

Immigrants and travelers have all but forgotten about Delaware Bay, even though it is the second-largest estuary on the Atlantic Coast. And Delaware is better known for being the headquarters of chemical giant DuPont (as well as half the other Fortune 500 corporations) than as a destination for the wild at heart.

While receiving scant attention in most travel guides, Delaware remains a backwater full of challenge, mystery, and rewards for an explorer. The rewards include the forested Brandywine Valley, sometimes called 'America's chateau country,' which spans the Pennsylvania border with its collection of regal estates, formal gardens, and some of the best museums in America. Just south of the Brandywine and Wilmington, near the site where the Delaware River opens into the bay, you will find New Castle, the preserved colonial capital of the Dutch and English settlers, with at least as much long-ago and faraway ambiance as Annapolis and Chestertown, Maryland. A little farther 'down state' lies Odessa and the state capital of Dover, both replete with restored 18th-century historical centers.

If you follow the backroads along the bay and its tributaries, you will discover obscure fishing ports (such as Leipsic and Bowers Beach), vast marshlands, and Bombay Hook National Wildlife Refuge – a birder's paradise and one of Delaware's numerous wildlife preserves. Along Delaware's 28 miles of Atlantic beaches lie low-key, tolerant summer colonies where people of different races and sexual orientation mix without fuss or fanfare. Like Maryland's Eastern Shore, most of Delaware offers rich territory to the bicyclist, car-top boater, camper, and B&B enthusiast. But in Delaware, everything is a little less predictable.

HISTORY

Observers often cite Delaware's position at a geographical crossroads in America as a determining factor in the state's history.

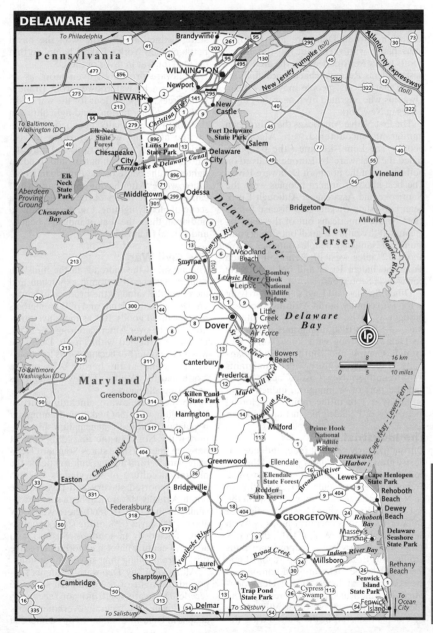

DELAWARE

Early Inhabitants & Immigrants

An often-told legend asserts that ancient Egyptians visited Delaware and brought lotus plants with them, but most evidence points to Native Americans as the area's earliest residents. Recent archaeological finds indicate that the first people may have been Owascos, who migrated from near the Finger Lakes in New York.

The first Native Americans that European immigrants encountered were Algonquin people. The Lenni Lenape ('the people'), called the 'Delaware' by Europeans, lived on both shores of the northern Delaware River. The best-known southern peoples were the Nanticoke and Assateague. Although European real-estate trickery and disease forced most Native Americans out of the state by the mid-18th century, a small but strong community of Nanticoke people continues to live about 12 miles west of Rehoboth Beach along the Indian River and holds a yearly powwow in September.

Dutch, Swedes, and English began arriving in the 17th century, as did Africans who were brought as slaves. A hundred years later, a wave of Scotch-Irish immigrants descended on Delaware, along with some Welsh and French. Central and southern Europeans came in the 19th century. Most immigrants went to northern New Castle County, which had the port of Wilmington, industry, and proximity to jobs in the rapidly developing metropolis of Philadelphia, just up the river.

The Industrial Age

During the early years of independence, industry grew around Wilmington, and the city became a major population center. In 1802, French immigrant Eleuthère Irénée du Pont de Nemours started a gunpowder mill on the fast-flowing Brandywine Creek – the birth of Delaware's famous chemical industry. With the outbreak of the War of 1812, du Pont's gunpowder factory began reaping enormous profits. The British navy tried to blockade the mouth of the Delaware and bombarded the settlement at Lewes (Cape Henlopen) when the Americans refused to resupply the enemy ships in 1813. No other military engagements occurred in the state during the War of 1812. However, a Delaware mariner, Captain Thomas Macdonough, brought his state distinction when he won the naval battle on New York's Lake Champlain that decided the war in favor of the US.

Delaware prospered even more as its mills, driven by waterpower from Brandywine Creek, supplied flour for the war effort and the growing nation. And agriculture in the south – especially peach orchards – thrived after the war. Returning to visit Delaware in 1824, the Marquis de Lafayette, who had been a French patron and freedom fighter for the cause of the American Revolution, wrote: 'After having seen nearly a half century ago the banks of the Brandywine a scene of bloody fighting, I am happy now to find upon them the seat of industry, beauty, and mutual friendship.'

The Civil War

The arrival of the railroads in the mid-19th century hastened economic expansion and increased the value of the produce of southern Delaware farmlands and of Wilmington's manufactured goods. But as the 'slave question' loomed over America during the 1850s, Delaware struggled within itself. Delaware was a slave state, but because of its location – like Maryland, at the border between the North and the South – Delaware's citizens had mixed allegiances.

Northern Delaware, including urban Wilmington, with its Quaker and immigrant population, favored emancipation and supported the North in the unfolding conflict between free and slave states. Southern Delaware, with its rural and agricultural ties to the plantation culture of Maryland's Eastern Shore, supported slavery and favored the South. Actually, slavery had been steadily declining in the state. In 1860, there were only about 1800 slaves (8% of the state's population, and mostly in southern Sussex), and late-17th-century laws had forbidden slave owners from selling their slaves out of state.

Although many Delaware residents supported the right of the Southern states to secede, Delaware itself did not secede. To ensure loyalty, the federal government took actions in Delaware similar to those imposed on Maryland: suspending the writ of habeas corpus, disarming questionable militia units, and supervising elections. Quaker residents and their allies helped escaped slaves make it to the North on the Underground Railroad, smuggling many blacks across Delaware Bay to Quaker, Free State outposts such as Greenwich, New Jersey.

During the Civil War, the state contributed proportionally more men under arms than any other Union state…and paid heavily. More than half of the Delaware troops at the bloody Battle of Antietam died in combat. (For more on that battle site, see the Western Maryland chapter.) Meanwhile, du Pont's gunpowder factories grew rich on the war effort, and 12,500 Confederate prisoners filled the Union prison at Fort Delaware on Pea Patch Island near the bay head at Delaware City. Before the fighting ended, 2700 of these prisoners had died from cholera, malaria, and other diseases spread by unsanitary conditions and the bay's fierce mosquitoes.

After the war, the federal government instituted various Reconstruction efforts to ensure African Americans' suffrage and equality. However, beginning in 1873, Delaware's postwar Democratic government disenfranchised blacks through state tax and literacy laws. The Democratic party said it was not 'morally bound' by any of the new national constitutional amendments that empowered blacks. African Americans' struggle to ensure the right to vote continued well into the 20th century, and racial segregation remained a fact of life in Delaware's two southern counties until the 1950s.

The 20th Century

Out-of-state corporations took over many Delaware companies in the late 19th and early 20th centuries. But the DuPont corporation's phenomenal growth kept the state's economy tracking at the forefront of the Industrial Revolution. By the outset of WWI, DuPont, known as the 'powder trust,' produced 90% of America's gunpowder, and heirs of the fortune were building châteaux in the style of French royalty all over the Brandywine Valley. Delaware prospered during WWI, largely due to DuPont and

other munitions manufacturers, who expanded into the field of chemicals, fertilizers, and synthetic products such as nylon.

Several of Delaware's du Pont millionaires spent money on improvements to the state. Thomas Coleman du Pont built a highway and donated it to the state (from 1911 to 1924), Alfred I du Pont set up a pension fund for the aged (1931), and Pierre S du Pont spent $2 million for African American schools when the state balked at doing so (1920s). Henry F du Pont built his fabulous estate, Winterthur, filled it with the largest and best collection of early American antiques in the country, and ultimately set up Winterthur as the nation's foremost museum of Americana.

Beyond the world of the du Ponts, advances in technology, particularly refrigeration, allowed southern Delaware to become increasingly integrated into the regional economy. Kent and Sussex Counties shipped poultry, dairy products, and vegetables widely. But, as in most parts of the US in the 20th century, farm employment declined, and more workers moved to DuPont, International Latex, and other firms. Production for WWII continued Delaware's prosperity, with huge oil refineries developing along the bay at places such as Delaware City.

While few people took notice during the mid-20th century, pollution from industry in Delaware, Pennsylvania, and New Jersey choked Delaware River and Bay, killing off the shad and sturgeon that had once made Delaware Bay the caviar capital of the world. Watermen on the bay continued to eke out a living by fishing for crabs, clams, and oysters, but the days when fleets of oystering and fishing schooners plied the bay had passed. So had the days when excursion steamers carried thousands of city folk down bay from Camden, Wilmington, and even Philadelphia for summer holidays at bay beaches. Once-thriving Delaware Bay fishing ports and resort beaches became virtual ghost towns. The bay had become an industrial sewer and a sea road for thousands of ships a year traveling to and from the industries lining the Delaware River.

In the 1950s, Delaware finally began integrating its public schools, but not without resistance from rural areas down state. This resistance presented a problem, since most political power in the state rested with southern legislators until the US Supreme Court ordered that the state legislature reapportion itself to fairly reflect the population. It did so in the 1960s, and most legislators are now elected by voters from more urban and liberal New Castle County, which has the largest population.

From 1950 to 1980, rapid population growth necessitated greater spending for schools, transportation, and government services. But Delaware has been reluctant to raise taxes, and it still has no state sales, real-estate, or personal-property tax. Many banks and companies continue to incorporate in the state because of its low taxes and central location.

Judging by the state's low 4% unemployment and the ever-expanding Wilmington-Newark suburbs, Delaware continues to ride the waves of chemical and commercial booms, but in recent years, the voices of environmentalists and preservationists have caught the attention of the state government and general citizenry. Environmental legislation has reversed trends of pollution: Shad,

for example, have returned to Delaware Bay in sizable numbers, and coastal zoning has protected hundreds of square miles of wetlands from development by petroleum companies seeking deep-water refineries along the southern coast of the bay. Once-shabby, forgotten towns such as New Castle, Odessa, and Lewes have embraced historic preservation. Downtown Wilmington, a victim of urban decay, has been revitalized with the Market St Mall – five blocks of the city's heart closed to all but pedestrian traffic. Plans are also in the works for a vibrant Avenue of the Arts on the banks of the Christina River.

GEOGRAPHY
Delaware's northern edge abuts Pennsylvania (the border is actually the arc of a perfect circle, with a 12-mile radius centered on the courthouse in New Castle); its western border splits the Delmarva Peninsula in half with Maryland, which lies to the south as well. The eastern border has 28 miles of beaches on the Atlantic, but most of the state's coast lies along 70 miles of Delaware Bay, with New Jersey on the opposite shore.

Delaware has a land mass of just 2044 sq miles, excluding the large Delaware Bay. The state stretches 96 miles north to south and 35 miles at its widest from east to west. Delaware's highest natural point – in Centreville, in the northwestern corner of the state – is just 442 feet.

The northern tip of the state lies on the Piedmont Plateau, but the rest of the state is on the Atlantic Coastal Plain, or Tidewater. The Christina River, which runs through Wilmington, separates the Piedmont from the Tidewater. The Piedmont contains many of the streams that powered early mills. The coastal plain is fairly flat, almost never higher than 80 feet above sea level, with marshes and beaches along the coast.

Delaware's soil is fertile but somewhat sandy. In northern New Castle, the soil is a two-layered clay and sand-gravel mixture. Moving south, the surface clay can be a sandy loam or a silt loam. Because the soils have been cultivated for more than 200 years, many farmers rely heavily on fertilizers.

Poor Little Rich Boy

In January 1996, another of the du Pont heirs, John E, brought international attention to his celebrated family. In a fit of paranoia, he murdered an Olympic wrestling champion who was his friend and a guest at du Pont's Brandywine Valley manor, just across the Pennsylvania border. Subsequent to the murder, du Pont, an able sharpshooter and gun collector, held local police at bay for three days before being captured. The murder and standoff created a media circus, with network TV newscasters raising questions about whether du Pont (who had apparently been delusional for some time) had been protected by his prominent family and tolerated by local law enforcers because of his wealth and connections.

DELAWARE

Delaware Bay

South of the Chesapeake & Delaware Canal, the Delaware River opens into Delaware Bay. This broad, shallow bay covers more than 1000 sq miles. Like the Chesapeake, Delaware Bay is the basin for a glacial river that once opened into the Atlantic at the edge of the Continental Shelf during the last ice age, 10,000 years ago. Shaped like the prehistoric horseshoe crab that breeds here by the hundreds of thousands, the bay sees more than 3000 ships a year – many of them oil tankers and auto carriers – pass through its waters. Currently, Wilmington-Philadelphia-Camden constitutes the second busiest port in America.

Before this almost-endless parade of ships filled the bay, it was a productive fishing ground to rival the Chesapeake. During the early part of the 20th century, mile-long nets stretched across the bay's shallows to catch sturgeon, which yielded the bulk of the world's caviar.

Until the 1950s, hundreds of schooners, twice the size of Chesapeake skipjacks, dredged for oysters in the Maurice River Cove and on the bars off the mouths of the Smyrna, Leipsic, and Mispillion Rivers. But then the Russians usurped the caviar business, a strange disease called MSX ravished the oyster beds, and the watermen dragged their schooners into the marshes to die. Today, after 25 years of environmental protection, Delaware Bay supports a small group of die-hard watermen who crab and catch oysters from small boats. A handful of the old oyster schooners remain, but all of them have been converted to power, their masts and sails long gone.

Today, few people experience the bay waters, although local anglers know that Delaware Bay is once again a great place to fish for weakfish (sea trout; so-named for their weak, fleshy mouths), shad, and rockfish (striped bass). Unlike the Chesapeake, with its dozens of charming harbors and bayside villages, Delaware Bay remains a much wilder place, with a coastline of broad marshlands, tidal creeks, and isolated beaches. Wading birds, turtles, and waterfowl love it. During the midsummer full moon, thousands upon thousands of horseshoe crabs – one of the earth's most primitive species – come ashore to lay their eggs. Watermen harvest the creatures for bait in eel and crab traps.

★★★★★★★★★★★★★★★★★★★★★★★★★★★★★★★

Most of the state's rivers rise in a watershed near the western border and flow east to the Delaware River and Bay (which link the state to New York, New Jersey, and Pennsylvania) or west to the Chesapeake. The largest of the important tributaries are the Christina River and Brandywine Creek. The Chesapeake & Delaware Canal crosses the state about 15 miles south of Wilmington and connects the Delaware River and Bay to the Chesapeake. Local lore maintains that the South begins below the canal.

DELAWARE

GOVERNMENT & POLITICS

Delaware has been governing itself under four different constitutions since the outbreak of the American Revolution in 1776, and earned its nickname the 'First State' because it was the first of the US states to ratify the national Constitution in 1787. Almost from the very beginning, Delaware's capital has been at Dover, in the middle of the state. As with each state in the American Union, Delaware's government has executive, legislative, and judicial branches. The state's chief executive is a governor, who is elected by popular vote to a four-year term of office, with a two-term limit.

The Senate and House of Representatives compose the state's General Assembly. The 21 members of the Senate are elected to four-year terms, with no term limits. Citizens elect 41 members to the House; these representatives serve two-year terms, with no term limits. Unlike any other state in the US, Delaware's legislators have the power to enact constitutional amendments with a popular vote. Five supreme-court justices oversee the state legal system. The governor appoints all judges; they serve 12-year terms after approval by the state Senate.

Three counties divide the state: New Castle (north), Kent (central), and Sussex (south). Each is governed by a council, sheriff, comptroller, and recorder of deeds.

On the national level, Delaware elects two senators and one representative to serve in the US congress. These three votes seem to give the state scant power in questions of national political debate. But the state's wealth and close association with some of the 'royalty' of US political-industrial dynasties (such as the du Ponts, who have been governors and US Senators) make Delaware's power felt in the legislative halls of Washington, DC.

Recently, Delaware's government found itself under national scrutiny, as tabloid journalism exploited the sensational details of a love affair that led to the murder of the governor's appointment secretary by a prominent Wilmington attorney, Thomas Capano. Investigative police and prosecutors alleged before the national media that Capano used his considerable political influence to inhibit the murder investigation.

ECONOMY

European settlers began planting tobacco in the late 17th century, but they had largely abandoned it for other products by the beginning of the Revolution. Initially, shipbuilders lumbered the state for its extraordinary stands of white oak, until they had all but depleted the forests; today, a small lumber industry still produces shingles, keels, and bark for tanning. Because of the state's waterfront, shipbuilding was common in early Delaware. As late as WWII, a single Wilmington shipyard was the state's largest employer. By the latter part of the 18th century, flour mills on the northern Brandywine Creek were well known.

Today there are more than 360,000 people in Delaware's labor force, primarily employed in five sectors: service (21%), manufacturing (21%), sales (20%), trade (18%), and government (12%).

Although farmland covers half the state, agriculture accounts for less than 2% of the state's gross product. In the 19th century, Delaware was known as the 'Peach State,' but after disease decimated the trees in the early 20th century, the crop declined to almost nothing. As in Maryland, broilers (five- to 12-week-old chickens) are the state's most important agricultural products, followed by dairy items. Soybeans are the leading crop. Some commercial fishing fleets work out of Lewes and small bay ports, with crab as their most important catch.

Chemicals rank first on the list of the state's manufactured products; specific items include nylon, drugs, plastics, and industrial chemicals. The largest producers are EI du Pont de Nemours & Co, Hercules, and ICI. Wilmington is the center of manufacturing in Delaware and is one of the largest chemical centers in the world (due more to research and corporate headquarters than to production). Newark has a huge auto-assembly plant for General Motors. Delaware's favorable tax laws and fees regarding corporations have encouraged more than 200,000 companies to incorporate here.

DELAWARE

Delaware's most famous corporation, DuPont, became so large that in 1912 the federal government forced the company to split into three companies to avoid monopolization. In spite of this, DuPont still maintains its monopoly in the production of smokeless gunpowder for national-security reasons.

POPULATION & PEOPLE

Only Alaska, Vermont, and Wyoming have fewer residents than Delaware, which has 680,000. The population is about 70% urban and 30% rural. Wilmington, with 72,000 residents, is the only large city; none of the others have more than 30,000 residents.

The ethnic breakdown is 80% white, 17% black, 1.5% Hispanic, 1.3% Asian, and 0.3% Native American. About 96% of all the state's residents are native-born US citizens.

ARTS

Delawareans are proud of the vigor and sophistication that characterizes their arts scene – and they should be. As Delaware rode the crest of the Industrial Revolution, its entrepreneurs amassed extraordinary wealth. And in the tradition of wealth begetting and attracting wealth, the Brandywine Valley spanning the Delaware-Pennsylvania border ranks up there with Florida's Palm

Tall Tales

If you take the time to explore Kent and Sussex Counties' secondary roads or tidal streams that run to the remote and marshy fringes of Delaware and Assawoman Bays, you may come across a solitary character known locally as a 'progger.' A progger is like a waterman; he makes a living from the bay fishing, catching turtles, crabbing, oystering, or trapping muskrats. But unlike a waterman, a progger is not much interested in earning more than a subsistence living. He often lives in a primitive shack along the tidewater and works only when he needs money, when the weather is 'right,' or when he just feels the urge. Proggers are notorious for two things – ignoring fish and game laws, and telling elaborate tall tales that are full of the mystery and hard times that typify the literature of Delaware. On the bay's shores, tale telling and game poaching often go hand in hand.

One day, while exploring the marshland in Bombay Hook National Wildlife Refuge by canoe, we came across a progger splashing around in an old boat on the edge of a tidal creek that feeds into the Leipsic River. He might have been setting an illegal net across the creek to catch fish on the ebb tide, but we had no time to look for the evidence. Eyeing us as if we might be conservation or game officers, the progger, who claimed he would be 82 next month, paddled his boat alongside our canoe, grabbed our gunwales and trapped us with a seriocomic tale of hard times along the road:

'Gave up perch fishin'. Several reasons. Got tired of the expense. Then I was fool enough to catch a lot of fish; had to clean 'em. Then I got to deliver 'em. Ones I had left someone took from my refrigerator. So no more of that. I quit bein' everybody's fool. Besides, weather's hot, and I can't take this here heat. Anyway, I don't like fish. Wouldn't give you a dime for three of 'em.'

As the yarn unraveled, the progger switched the subject away from fishing, and for several minutes he blasted the federal government for the high cost of construction:

'Why, I can't even build a doghouse without a permit. All our natural privileges is gone. Them dirty culprits down in Washington ought to be hung by the neck at sunrise….'

At last, the progger took his hands off the gunwale of our canoe and we paddled away, feeling somehow more informed, or at least less alone in the swamp, than we had before our encounter. The progger gave us a smile and a wave. As we turned a bend in the creek and started to lose sight of him, he began thrashing around with something beneath the stern of his boat that had all the markings of a perch net.

Beach as one of America's most financially and socially exclusive addresses.

Eschewing nearby Philadelphia and its populous traditions, the Brandywine's elite and wannabe elite have made Delaware – particularly Wilmington – their playground. First-class musicians, dramatists, and painters have recognized the possibilities for patronage in Delaware and have heeded the call. For most of the 20th century, the performing and visual arts have flourished in Wilmington… and the momentum continues to build. Down state, simpler pleasures prevail. Like Maryland's Eastern Shore, Kent and Sussex Counties are regions of storytellers.

Literature

A collection of mysteries by Wade B Fleetwood has been published locally. The novels include *Murder at the Henlopen*, *Murder in Bethany Beach*, *Murder in Rehoboth*, and *Murder on the Ocean City Pier*. JP Marquand's novels do a good job of prying into the private lives of Delaware's socialites.

For enthusiasts of sea stories or pirates, there are *Shipwrecks, Sea Stories & Legends of the Delaware Coast* (1989) and *Ghost Stories of the Delaware Coast* (1990), both by David Seibold and Charles Adams. Another author in this vein is Jack Beach, who wrote *Pirates on the Delmarva*.

Visual Arts

The Brandywine Valley's rolling farmland and light have inspired artists for generations and gave birth to one of America's best-known styles of painting, the so-called Brandywine School. Hailed as the 'Father of American Illustration' at the beginning of the 20th century, Wilmington's Howard Pyle pioneered the super-realistic, nostalgic, haunting style of painting. The definitive collection of Pyle's masterpieces is on display at the Delaware Art Museum, in Wilmington. The DAM also features the work of other 20th-century masters, such as Edward Hopper and Roy Lichtenstein, as well as the USA's largest collection of English pre-Raphaelite art.

While Pyle began the Brandywine School, it was his pupil NC Wyeth, and Wyeth's son

Andrew and grandson Jamie, who made the Brandywine School world famous. Their works hang at the Brandywine River Museum in Chadds Ford, Pennsylvania, along with the works of Maxfield Parrish (another celebrated Pyle protégé), Edward Moran, Asher Durand, and Thomas Nast.

The Delaware Center for the Contemporary Arts, in Wilmington, showcases the work of local, national, and international modern artists. Wilmington also has an active gallery scene, with many new openings.

In addition to supporting and collecting great art, Delaware's art patrons have provided two of the most spectacular sites for viewing art in America, as well as a world-class center of the horticultural arts. All three sites are Brandywine Valley estates. Nemours Mansion and Gardens is a Louis XVI–style mansion on 300 acres that preserves Alfred I du Pont's collections of antiques, carpets, tapestries, paintings, and automobiles. The celebrated Winterthur Museum (the country estate of another du Pont) displays the world's premier collection of American antiques and decorative arts in period room settings, and 30-acre Longwood Gardens contains 11,000 types of plants and flowers, which are displayed in conservatories and throughout the estate.

Music & Performing Arts

Comparable to the grandeur of Winterthur and Nemours, the Grand Opera House, in the heart of Wilmington, is America's finest remaining example of cast-iron architecture. Built in 1871 on the model of French Second Empire designs, the Grand is home to the nationally renowned Delaware Symphony Orchestra with Maestro Stephen Gunzenhauser. Barely two blocks from the Grand, the Playhouse Theatre in the Hotel du Pont has been hosting traveling Broadway productions for more than 80 years. Near the Christina River waterfront, the Delaware Theatre Company stages classic and contemporary serious drama.

Regional theater troupes include the Wilmington Drama League, often staging Broadway shows; the University of Delaware Center for Black Culture in Newark, showcasing African American arts; and the Media Theatre for the Performing Arts in nearby Media, Pennsylvania, where one can see musicals. Two dinner theaters thrive as well: the Candlelights Music Dinner Theatre and Three Little Bakers Dinner Theatre. The Russian Ballet Theatre of Delaware in Rockland (Greater Wilmington) stages classic and contemporary masterpieces each year and features dancers trained in Russia's finest academies.

Film

Delaware does not have a film industry per se. But as noted in the Facts for the Visitor chapter, historic Delaware towns such as New Castle and Dover have 'doubled' for colonial New England in a number of films, including *The Dead Poets' Society*. The area

is also great for period pieces, because the Georgian architecture, rolling countryside, family farms, and brilliant fall foliage replicate images of New England that hardly exist any longer in places like Boston.

INFORMATION

The area code for all of Delaware is ☎ 302.

The primary Delaware Tourism Office stands at 99 Kings Hwy, PO Box 1401, Dover, DE 19903 (☎ 302-739-4271, 800-441-8846). Delaware has no sales tax. The room tax in hotels is 8%.

In northern Delaware, most people read the *News Journal*. From Dover south, the most popular paper is the *Delaware State News*. You can find National Public Radio (NPR) in the Wilmington area on WHYY (Philadelphia) at 91.0 FM.

DELAWARE

Wilmington

Though Delaware's largest city (population 72,000) claims a long, proud history, Wilmington lacks a reputation as an architectural treasure (such as Annapolis) or as a major destination of day trippers (such as Baltimore). And frankly, viewed from an Amtrak train sliding along the Northeast corridor, or from the interstate highways that bound the city, Wilmington can look about as thrilling as Trenton, New Jersey. Hence, most of the world tends to dismiss Wilmington as little more than the home of corporations, banks, and industry, flooded with a sea of lawyers. But this small city can be well worth a stop, particularly if you are the kind of traveler who likes to get off the beaten path. Furthermore, Wilmington serves as a gateway to

the chateau country of the Brandywine Valley and historic New Castle. (For sights north of Wilmington, see the Northern Delaware chapter.)

By day, Wilmington is a bustling working city with more than its share of modern banks and corporate headquarters. Legions of professionals in pinstriped suits and Gucci shoes give downtown Wilmington a palpable vitality. But after work, the professional crowd trickles back to the suburbs, leaving the business district a bluesy sort of place for tavern-goers, the theater crowd, and business travelers staying in four major downtown hotels. The streets are well lighted, and public-safety officers wearing orange vests patrol the Market St Mall area. But almost all the shops and many restaurants in the mall area close at sunset, and the streets are virtually deserted after dark.

HISTORY

Sailing aboard the 220-ton pinnace *Kalmar Nyckel*, 22 Swedish traders and soldiers rode a fair tide up Delaware Bay and ghosted into the deep, sheltered mouth of the Christina River in 1638. The Europeans stepped ashore on an outcropping of blue rocks that made a natural wharf at present-day Wilmington and almost immediately began trading for the furs the Lenni Lenape brought by canoe to the European encampment. Here, on the Christina's natural harbor, the Swedes quickly built palisades and ramparts of earth, as well as log houses for shelter and for storing the furs. They named this site Fort Christina, after their young queen.

Subsequent expeditions to Fort Christina brought more Swedes, who prospered as traders and small-scale grain farmers. In 1655, the Dutch governor of New Amsterdam (New York City) arrived at Fort Christina with ships and soldiers and claimed the flourishing settlement for Holland. The English ousted the Dutch nine years later, but barely disturbed the lives of the settlers,

Highlights

- Brandywine Park – the green space, river, and breezes

- The Delaware Art Museum – showcasing American realists Homer, Eakin, and Wyeth

- Visiting the sailing replica of *Kalmar Nyckel* on the Christina River

- Inner-tubing past the historic sites on the Brandywine River

- The weekend restaurant and bar scene at Trolley Square

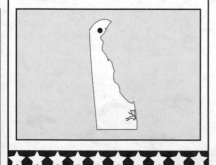

DELAWARE

who encouraged more waves of immigration from their homelands, especially Sweden.

For the next 50 years, the settlement at Christina Harbor thrived as a center for trade and shipping grain milled at waterworks poised along the steep descents of Brandywine Creek. By 1730, real-estate developers, including one Thomas Willing, mapped out an extended street plan for the village, divided up 10 acres of land into house lots, and named the first in a succession of Delaware subdivisions 'Willingtown.' Over the years, the name evolved into the present 'Wilmington.' Recognizing the potential for real-estate profits, a Quaker entrepreneur named William Shipley slipped into Willingtown in 1735, bought all of the land west of Market St, subdivided it, and doubled the number of houses in the town within a year. The settlement boomed as Shipley built a market house, wharf, and – to most people's delight – a brewery. Quakers from Pennsylvania moved here by the hundreds. The port gained momentum as a trading center where rigging gangs fitted out ships for the exportation of flour, butter, meat, and barrel staves for trade with the West Indies.

As America's troubles with England sharpened during the years just before the American Revolution, Wilmington became a center of patriotic sympathies. Locals feared that the English would close their port as they had done in Boston…and the citizens' fears proved well founded. In May 1776, the English frigates *Roebuck* and *Liverpool* positioned themselves in the Delaware River to blockade the entrance to the Christina River and the port of Wilmington. In one of the first naval battles of the Revolution, the fast and more maneuverable American schooner *Wasp*, together with several armed rowing galleys, thwarted the blockade. But Wilmington's independence proved short-lived. The war returned to Wilmington on August 25, 1777, when British General Howe landed his army of 18,000 men less than 20 miles away, on the Elk River at the head of the Chesapeake. Fearing that Howe planned to capture the all-important grain mills in the Brandywine Valley and then move on to attack the Revolutionary capital at Philadelphia,

General George Washington moved 11,000 soldiers – the main force of the Continental Army – to the southwestern edge of town to protect the port and the mills. Washington set up his headquarters in the home of Captain Joseph Bennett, a mariner, at 303 West St.

On September 11, Howe attacked and outflanked Washington's Continentals, driving them back to Chester, Pennsylvania. The next day, British forces took possession of Wilmington and engaged the citizens in tending to the needs of hundreds of wounded. The following day, the British captured Delaware's Revolutionary President John McKinly in the river aboard a sloop with state funds and crucial documents.

Following the Revolution, Wilmington mills and shipping once again prospered, and the town quickly grew to a population exceeding 5000. Before the Civil War, Wilmington's mills diversified to produce textiles, paper, and – of course – EI du Pont's gunpowder. By the middle of the century, Wilmington was building iron-hulled ships and railway cars to facilitate America's economic development. Wave after wave of immigrants arrived: first came the Irish, then the French, then the Italians and Jews. Blacks arrived as a consequence of the Underground Railroad, run by Wilmington's ardent abolitionist Quakers. Free-flowing money financed new neighborhoods of substantial brick townhouses.

A place of divided loyalties – as was Baltimore – during the Civil War, Wilmington suffered the same kind of isolation, with Union troops 'protecting' the city's crucial industries, such as the gunpowder mills. But after the war, Wilmington prospered again, with steel mills, the ever-growing DuPont empire, and a marine terminal to handle larger ships right on the Delaware River. The city reached its industrial peak as its mills ran 24 hours a day to supply the military needs of WWI, and the population ballooned for a time over 100,000.

Wilmington's heavy industry suffered during the depression of the 1930s and has never regained its former vigor. But, led by the various permutations of the DuPont chemical empire, Wilmington has evolved into something like an American Zurich. Delaware's tax incentives and liberal incorporation laws have transformed Wilmington into a commercial and banking capital that is trying to imitate Baltimore in revitalizing the heart of the city. Not only are the Market St Mall and the nascent Avenue of the Arts a start to reviving downtown, but in 1996, the city forged a deal with New York's prestigious Pratt Institute and DC's Corcoran School of Art to locate a professional college of art and design at 600 North Market St, in the former Delmarva Light and Power Building. Called the Delaware College of Art and Design, the school opened in September 1997, bringing talented art students into the heart of Wilmington. As this campus develops, the art students will no doubt add just what Wilmington is currently missing – downtown residents and a bohemian youth scene.

ORIENTATION

Wilmington stands at the confluence of Brandywine Creek, the Christina River, and the Delaware River, rising from former marshland in the east to a series of hills in the west. Planners laid out the streets in a roughly north-south, east-west grid on the delta of land between Brandywine Creek to the north and the Christina River to the south. Market St, running north-south, is the main artery bisecting the town and the locus for historical sites, daytime restaurants, shopping, and theater. Old Town Hall, at 512 Market St, marks the heart of the city.

Pennsylvania Ave and its offshoot, Delaware Ave, are the main arteries leading to the upscale restaurant, gallery, and bar scene at Trolley Square, in the West End. Little Italy's restaurants lie just south of Pennsylvania Ave on Lincoln St, in the West End. Pennsylvania Ave becomes Route 52 as it leaves the city and is the main route to the sites in the chateau country of the Brandywine Valley.

I-95 bisects the city and basically divides it into the business district to the east and residential neighborhoods to the west. The developing waterfront area along both sides of the Christina River stretches west from the Walnut St Bridge.

Because Wilmington is a small city with extensive industrial zones, there are some impoverished neighborhoods with desperate people where a traveler probably should not venture. Enjoying Wilmington depends on knowing where and when to walk. By night, the town is safest and most lively in the West End at Trolley Square (14th and Du Pont Sts). Little Italy has some good restaurants along the western end of Lancaster Ave. And there is an up-and-coming sports/nightclub scene in the south end of town around Frawley Stadium, where the Wilmington Blue Rocks play baseball. Neighborhoods grow more prosperous as you move north and west across the city. The area east of Walnut St downtown is not safe. This area includes the attractive Christina and Fort Christina Parks, which in recent years have become havens for the homeless.

INFORMATION
Tourist Offices

The best source for information is the Greater Wilmington Convention & Visitors Bureau's information center (☎ 302-737-4059) on I-95, just south of Wilmington between Routes 896 and 273. The travel counselors here are extremely helpful. Another reason to pay them a visit is that you can save money on several local motels when you book them at the center. It's open 8 am to 8 pm daily.

In downtown Wilmington, the Greater Wilmington Convention & Visitors Bureau (☎ 302-652-4088, 800-422-1181, ✉ info@wilmcvb.org) is at 100 W 10th St, Suite 20.

Post

Wilmington has a number of postal stations due to the large volume of business mail flowing to and from the city. You will find the central post office (☎ 302-656-0196) at 1101 King St, on Rodney Square, in the center of town.

Bookstores

Ninth Street Bookstore (☎ 302-652-3315) is at 104 W 9th St. Borders Books & Music (☎ 302-447-0361), 4221 Concord Pike, to the north of town, is the suburban outlet for a

WILMINGTON

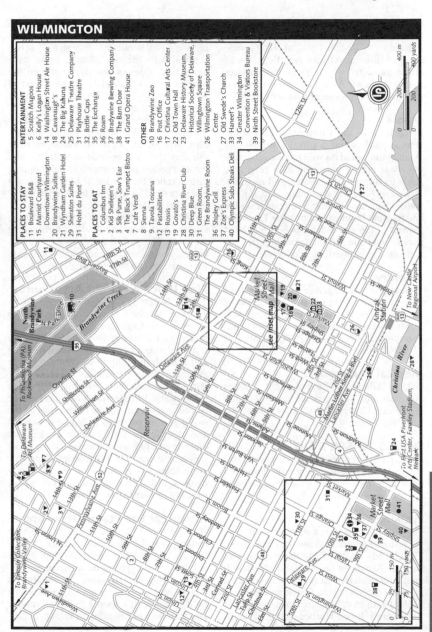

PLACES TO STAY
11 Boulevard B&B
15 Marriot Courtyard
    Downtown Wilmington
20 Brandywine Suites
21 Wyndham Garden Hotel
29 Sheraton Suites
31 Hotel du Pont

PLACES TO EAT
1 Columbus Inn
2 Kid Shelleen's
3 Silk Purse, Sow's Ear
4 The Black Trumpet Bistro
7 Cafe Verdi
8 Sienna
9 Tavola Toscana
12 Pastabilities
13 Rossis
19 Govato's
28 Christina River Club
30 Deep Blue
31 Green Room,
    The Brandywine Room
36 Shipley Grill
37 Zoe's Express
40 Olympic Subs Steaks Deli

ENTERTAINMENT
5 Scratch Magoos
6 Kelly's Logan House
14 Washington Street Ale House
18 Cavanaugh's
24 The Big Kahuna
25 Delaware Theatre Company
31 Playhouse Theatre
32 Bottle Caps
35 The Exchange
36 Roam
37 Bradywine Brewing Company
38 The Barn Door
41 Grand Opera House

OTHER
10 Brandywine Zoo
16 Post Office
17 Christina Cultural Arts Center
22 Old Town Hall
23 Delaware History Museum,
    Historical Society of Delaware,
    Willingtown Square
26 Wilmington Transportation
    Center
27 Old Swede's Church
33 Hanef's
34 Greater Wilmington
    Convention & Visitors Bureau
39 Ninth Street Bookstore

DELAWARE

chain of stores that carries mainstream fiction, history, and discount books and CDs. Haneef's (☎ 302-656-4193), at 911 Orange St, specializes in African American books and is connected with a series of businesses that include an African American newspaper, a clothing store, and an art gallery.

Media
In addition to the Convention & Visitors Bureau publications, a traveler stopping in Wilmington would do well to pick up a copy of *Out & About* magazine as a reference guide to current arts, theater, and nightlife. *Delaware Today*, a slick magazine for the whole state, has an extensive restaurant list and relevant features and profiles. The *News Journal* is the city's daily paper, but most people read the *Philadelphia Inquirer* for national and international coverage.

Laundry
Wilmington has a number of laundries, but most of them are in questionable areas of the city or on the fringes. One central, safe location stands out: Swan Cleaners and Laundromat (☎ 302-652-7607), located at 1710 W 4th St.

Medical Services
Greater Wilmington has more than a dozen hospitals. For emergencies, use Riverside Healthcare Center (☎ 302-765-4500), at 700 Lea Blvd; or call ☎ 911.

THINGS TO SEE & DO
For starters, Wilmington offers some impressive historical buildings, a very good art museum, progressive art galleries, a zoo, and an expansive riverside park.

Walking Tour
The best place to start a daytime stroll is at the restored Amtrak Station on S Market St. The city has begun calling the area west of here the Avenue of the Arts, and at last, Wilmington has started to act on long-heralded plans for reclaiming the Christina River waterfront with an urban mall along the lines of Baltimore's Inner Harbor. After years of

more talk than action, when the train station and the Delaware Theatre Company's building were just about the only sign of urban renewal here, the city added a promenade along both sides of the river between the Market St and Walnut St bridges. West of here, the large First USA Riverfront Arts Center opened in 1998 with much fanfare.

Head north on Market St and you will see the majority of Wilmington's historic and cultural sites. Six blocks of Market St, between 4th and 10th Sts, exclude auto traffic and create a pedestrian promenade and shopping district called the Market St Mall. You might end your stroll by stopping for refreshment at the Hotel du Pont. Or you can continue to the northern edge of town to explore Brandywine Park on both sides of the valley surrounding the creek. The park is a great place to find a bench, people watch, and catch some rays where the breeze blows through the valley.

First USA Riverfront Arts Center
This facility (☎ 302-777-1600, 888-395-0005), at 800 S Madison St, overlooking a sharp elbow in the Christina River, opened with much celebration in the fall of 1998. The center blends a restored industrial building and a modern addition to create a rather generic-looking convention venue. But the Arts Center actually is more high-brow than it looks and hosts a series of rather exotic traveling-museum shows from all over the world. Recent offerings include the Nicholas and Alexandra show, which evokes the lifestyle and history of Russia's last imperial family and features 14 galleries displaying more than 400 treasures of the Romanov dynasty. Admission prices for such shows vary, but expect to pay $12 or more.

Historical Society of Delaware
If you want to dig into the city's extensive history, visit the Historical Society (☎ 302-655-7161), at 505 Market St. The staff is very helpful, has pamphlets on many of the historical sights, and can offer you insights on how to best spend your time if you are on a tight schedule. It's open 1 to 9 pm Monday and 9 am to 5 pm Tuesday to Friday.

Delaware History Museum

This museum (☎ 302-656-0637) is run by and located next to the Historical Society, at 504 Market St. Here, you can see changing exhibits on topics from Delaware sports legends to Delaware in the Civil War. There is also a new interactive exhibit called 'Distinctively Delaware.' The museum is open noon to 4 pm weekdays and 10 am to 4 pm Saturday. Donations are accepted.

Old Town Hall

This building, at 512 Market St, marks the heart of town. Built from 1798 to 1800, the Old Town Hall was a center of political and social activities during the height of Wilmington's mercantile-milling economy. It operated as such until 1916, when the offices moved to a new city and county building.

Now, the Historical Society of Delaware runs Old Town Hall as a museum featuring changing exhibitions depicting Delaware's history, with displays of decorative arts, paintings, and toys. In the basement, restored jail cells indicate another of the building's former roles. It is open noon to 4 pm Tuesday to Friday from March to December; admission is free.

Willingtown Square

This collection of four stately, 18th-century homes surrounds a courtyard of cobblestone and brick at 506 Market St. Not open to the public, these buildings were moved here from other areas of the city by the Historical Society, which is next door.

Grand Opera House

The Grand Opera House (☎ 302-652-5346), 818 Market St, is the architectural showpiece of Wilmington. Built in 1871 and originally a Masonic temple, the Grand lives up to its name as a superb example of cast-iron architecture. Listed on the National Register of Historic Places, the building's interior is perhaps even grander than the facade, with ceiling frescoes, winding staircases, box seats, and felt and brass decor. Home to the Delaware Symphony Orchestra, the Grand opens its doors to visitors 11:30 am to 1:30 pm Thursdays.

Christina Cultural Arts Center

You will find the lively Christina Cultural Arts Center (☎ 302-652-0101) located at 705 Market St, between 7th and 8th Sts. The center is the Delaware Valley's premier community school of the arts celebrating African American culture. In addition to the variety of classes offered, the CCAC also features a schedule of theatrical, dance, and musical performances, as well as art exhibitions.

Old Swede's Church

This simple chapel (☎ 302-652-5629) rises near the Christina River at 606 Church St. Built in 1698 – one of the country's oldest churches – Old Swede's still has regular Episcopal services. You can take guided tours between 10 am and 4 pm Monday to Saturday; admission is $2.

Delaware Art Museum

Home to a renowned collection of American art, the Delaware Art Museum (☎ 302-571-9590) is at 2301 Kentmere Parkway. Dating from 1840 to the present, the collection includes the works of Winslow Homer, Thomas Eakins, Howard Pyle, NC Wyeth, Frank Schoonover, Andrew Wyeth, and John Sloan. America's largest collection of English pre-Raphaelite art can also be seen here. Except during special shows, the museum is open 9 am to 4 pm Tuesday to Saturday and 10 am to 4 pm Sunday. Admission is $5 for adults, $3 for seniors, and $2.50 for students.

Brandywine Park

Listed in the National Register of Historic Places and inspired by Frederick Law Olmstead, the creator of New York's Central Park, Brandywine Park is a long, narrow band of greenery lining both banks of the Brandywine Creek for about a mile and a half. Beginning at the Market St crossing of the Brandywine, just north of downtown, the park climbs from the lowlands to the steeps of the city and provides a relaxing escape from the traffic and concrete of the surrounding streets.

Brandywine Zoo

You will find Delaware's only zoo (☎ 302-571-7787) at 1001 N Park Drive. The zoo stands on 180 acres of Brandywine Park and features 140 animals native to North and South America. It's open 10 am to 4 pm daily. Admission is $3 for adults and $1.50 for seniors and children; from November to March, it's free.

Rockwood Museum

This 19th-century country estate owes its inspiration to the English country house. Built in the gothic style of architecture in 1851 by the merchant-banker Joseph Shipley, and standing on 72 of its original 300 acres, the museum consists of the porter's lodge, gardener's cottage, barn, and sundry outbuildings. A collection of English, Continental, and American decorative arts from the 17th to 19th centuries fill the manor house, while the grounds contain six acres of exotic foliage.

The Rockwood Museum (☎ 302-761-4340) is at 610 Shipley Road, in north Wilmington. It's open 11 am to 3 pm Tuesday to Saturday. Guided tours run every 30 minutes, and you can walk the grounds on your own. Admission is $5 for adults, $4 for seniors, and $1 for children. Since this museum is not easy to find, travelers should call for directions.

Kalmar Nyckel Foundation

This foundation (☎ 302-429-7447) offers a working 17th-century shipyard over at the extreme east end of 7th St. In 1998, shipwrights here finished building a replica of the 110-foot ship that brought the original Swedes to Delaware, and a similar project is under way to re-create the Delaware Valley's first permanent European settlement.

If you're interested, you can take a tour of the ship and the shipyard 10 am to 4 pm Monday to Saturday and noon to 4 pm Sunday. Admission is $6 for adults, $5 for seniors, and $4 for children. Sometimes the ship is docked at the shipyard; sometimes you will find it docked at the First USA Riverfront Arts Center.

Lincoln Collection of the University of Delaware

More than 2000 items that pertain to Abraham Lincoln's private and public life are presented here at the Goodstay Center (☎ 302-573-4500), 2600 Pennsylvania Ave (Route 52). The center is open by appointment. Admission is free.

Steam Train

Wilmington & Western Tourist Railroad (☎ 302-998-1930), Greenbank Station on Route 41, three blocks north of the junction with Route 2, features a ride through Red Clay Creek Valley aboard vintage trains. Many of the trains during the spring and fall have steam power; vintage diesels pull the summer trips. Train fares start at $8 for adults, $5 for children. Call for timetable information.

Canoeing & Inner-tubing

Wilderness Canoe Trips (☎ 302-654-2227), at 2111 Concord Pike, in the Fairfax Shopping Center, offers two- to six-hour canoe and tube trips down Brandywine Creek, passing many historical sites along the way.

SPECIAL EVENTS

Wilmington has its share of annual celebrations. An event you might catch no matter what time of year you are here is an Art on the Town Loop. Occurring the first Friday evening of every month except January and August, these popular events take the name 'loops' because free bus service loops around the city to connect the various galleries, restaurants, theaters, and bars hosting art openings and music.

The Christina Care Cup (date varies) is the lead-off event of the First Union Pro Cycling Series, drawing men's teams from a dozen countries. The Wilmington Classic race for women is an associated event.

Also look out for the following:

Holy Trinity Greek Festival (first week in June) Here you will find live Greek music, ozou, food stalls, and festival dancing on Broom St, between 8th and 9th Sts. The event runs for four nights and draws crowds of hundreds.

Clifford Brown Jazz Festival (week after Memorial Day) Named for the great trumpet player, this festival brings five days of world-class jazz to Rodney Square.

LPGA McDonald's Championship (early June) Golfers gather for this tournament in Wilmington.

St Anthony's Italian Festival (second week in June) People come in busloads for this one. The town closes some streets in the West End (Little Italy) to set up booths, carnival rides, beer stands, vino bars, live music, a bandstand, and an outdoor dance arena.

Rockwood Ice Cream Festival (July) This one-day event features museum staff dressed in Victorian costumes, old-time party games, and ice-cream bars galore at the Rockwood manor house, at 610 Shipley Rd.

PLACES TO STAY

When staying in Wilmington, you can choose from a downtown hotel, a B&B, or a moderately priced motel off I-95, in New Castle or in Newark. To save money, visit the Greater Wilmington Convention & Visitors Bureau's information center – you can enjoy special lower rates at certain properties when making reservations there (see Information, earlier).

The nearest campground is 17 miles south of Wilmington via Route 13. **Lums Pond State Park** (☎ 302-368-6989) is 2 miles south of Kirkwood on Route 71. There are 72 tent sites and a bathhouse, and there's no electricity or water at individual campsites. Tent sites are open April through October and cost $13 a night for Delaware residents and $15 for nonresidents. The Oceanmart, 2 miles away from the park in Kirkwood, is the closest place to shop.

A 10-minute drive south of downtown, the **Economy Inn** (☎ 302-656-9431, 1015 S Market St), Route 13, is a bit sleazy – for example, there's a free Playboy channel promotion. Singles or doubles run $40.

The lovely **Boulevard B&B** (☎ 302-656-9700, 1909 Baynard Blvd), between 19th and 20th Sts, is in one of Wilmington's tree-lined historic districts. Built in 1913 and listed on the National Register of Historic Places, the Boulevard is within walking distance of the downtown business district. Singles/doubles are $60/65 with shared bath and $80/85 with private bath; full breakfast is included.

The **Wyndham Garden Hotel** (☎ 302-655-0400, 700 King St) has an indoor pool and weekend specials for $89 that include a full buffet breakfast. Expect to pay about $110 during the week.

At **Brandywine Suites** (☎ 302-656-9300, 707 King St), two-room suites go for $99 with a continental breakfast.

The **Marriott Courtyard Downtown Wilmington** (☎ 302-429-7600, 1102 West St) has rooms for $129 during the week, but the tariff can drop to $69 on the weekend. The hotel offers such amenities as an exercise facility, an extensive continental breakfast, and microwave ovens in the rooms.

The **Sheraton Suites** (☎ 302-654-8300, 422 Delaware Ave) is an all-suite property with an indoor pool, sauna, and exercise room. Rates run $149 on weekdays but drop to $99 on weekends.

The **Hotel du Pont** (☎ 302-594-3100, 800-441-9019), at 11th and Market Sts, opened in 1913 to rival Europe's finest hotels. After undergoing a major renovation in 1993, its rooms have won a major design award. Even if you do not plan to stay or eat here, you should make a point of visiting, just to see the lobby's handcrafted furniture, oriental carpets, walnut reception desk, and paneling. Check out the Gold Ballroom, a testament to the craftsmanship and artistry that prevails in Delaware quarters where money is no object. Singles or doubles start at $179. Busy during the week with business travelers, the hotel offers good-value packages for weekends and holidays. These can include dining certificates, welcome gifts, and admission to museums or special events.

PLACES TO EAT

To sample the range of Wilmington's culinary offerings, the traveler will need a car to visit the three separate restaurant districts.

West End & Little Italy

For years, there was a healthy collection of restaurants along Lincoln St in this longtime Italian neighborhood, but slowly, the old standbys seem to be fading to memory. Still, a couple of remarkable options remain.

Pastabilities (☎ 302-656-9822, 415 N Lincoln) has to be Wilmington's most romantic place to eat. You enter through the kitchen, where chef/owner Luigi Vitrone sings along with the opera on the sound system as he dances between his coolers, chopping blocks, and burners. In the back of the building are eight tables under a funky starlit ceiling. Northern Italian entrees such as stuffed prawns cost about $16. Pastas are under $10; a glass of Chianti runs $3.50.

Rossis (☎ 302-655-8584, 1835 W 4th St) is a longtime favorite for Wilmington residents. You can get good veal and chicken for less than $15.

The Colonial-style *Columbus Inn (☎ 302-571-1492, 2216 Pennsylvania Ave)* is in one of the city's oldest buildings (1798). Set on a hill overlooking the main road to the Brandywine Valley, the Columbus Inn specializes in fresh seafood. It's open for lunch and dinner (jackets are required for men in the evening). Expect to pay at least $20 for an evening meal here.

Trolley Square

The north end of Lincoln St runs into a four-block area of gentrified townhouses just north of Pennsylvania Ave known as Trolley Square. Here you will find the most popular places in the city to window-shop among upscale boutiques, art galleries, cafes, and restaurants. While many of these restaurants look like they are quartered within the walls of old houses, most of them actually have backyard decks and patios that offer alfresco dining.

One spot in this area stands out for great cheap eats: *Cafe Verdi (☎ 302-656-5411)*, in the Trolley Square shopping plaza. On Monday and Tuesday, you can get a large pizza for $6.

Across the street, *Sienna (☎ 302-652-0653, 1616 Delaware Ave)* offers live jazz Wednesday to Saturday and Italian entrees,

such as Spinach Parpadella pasta for $17, in a dark, clubby setting.

Silk Purse (☎ 302-654-7666, 1307 N Scott St) is hidden on a quiet residential block and retains the feel of a private home. Serving new American cuisine with a Mediterranean emphasis, the owners also operate the simpler bistro *Sow's Ear* in the same building. You can get pan-roasted Arctic char in basil for about $19.

Another popular and romantic oasis in the neighborhood is the *Black Trumpet Bistro (☎ 302-777-0454, 1717 Delaware Ave)*. Consider the jumbo lump crab cake served with couscous and wasabi cream for $12.

Tavola Toscana (☎ 302-654-8001, 1412 N Dupont St) is a popular Northern Italian bistro with an open kitchen and extensive wine list. The place appeals to upscale suburbanites.

Kid Shelleen's (☎ 302-658-4600), at 14th and Scott Sts, is a charcoal house featuring grilled seafood and chicken, homemade soups, and a yuppie crowd. Entrees cost less than $10.

Downtown

In addition to the standard choice of fast-food outlets, there are several old-fashioned budget choices. *Govato's (☎ 302-652-4082, 800 N Market)* is a classic candy store and restaurant with daily specials, such as a chili burger on a bun with fries and coleslaw for under $5. Across the street, *Olympic Subs Steaks Deli (☎ 302-652-4677, 813 N Market St)* serves good-size sandwiches.

Zoe's Express (☎ 302-655-2326, 906 Orange St) is a newcomer to the deli trade, with mammoth turkey sandwiches for under $4.

The current rage among young, upscale diners is *Deep Blue (☎ 302-777-2040, 111 West 11th St)*. Dan Butler, creator of Tavola Toscana restaurant (see Trolley Square, earlier), opened this contemporary American fish house in late 1998. It features items such as Chilean sea bass with horseradish crust ($19). On many nights, live groups play acid jazz in the background.

Fair weather draws crowds to the waterside deck of the new *Christina River Club (☎ 302-652-4787, 201 A St)*, on the south side of the Christina River. Weekends bring bands and DJs playing '70s and '80s R&B. Entrees are steep at $19 and up, but you can get a bowl of crab soup for less than $5.

The Hotel du Pont (see Places to Stay, earlier) boasts two award-winning restaurants. The **Brandywine Room**, serving American Continental cuisine, is open for dinner Sunday to Thursday. The ornate **Green Room**, Wilmington's ultimate fine-dining experience, is open for lunch daily (around $30 per person) and for dinner on Friday and Saturday only ($60 to $80). A harpist plays from the balcony, and you can get a superb Sunday brunch here for slightly less than $30. You can also take afternoon tea (about $11) with Brandywine Valley matrons in the hotel's **Lobby Lounge** from 2:30 to 4:30 pm.

The **Shipley Grill** (☎ 302-652-7797, 913 Shipley St), between 9th and 10th Sts, is one of the city's nicest restaurants. You can enjoy lunch here for about $15 per person.

ENTERTAINMENT
Whether you're a barhopper or performing-arts enthusiast (or both), Wilmington has plenty to keep you entertained.

Theater
The **Playhouse Theatre** (☎ 302-656-4401), part of the du Pont Building (Hotel du Pont), at 10th and Market Sts, has been hosting traveling Broadway shows since the 1920s.

On the Avenue of the Arts, the **Delaware Theatre Company** (☎ 302-594-1100) faces the Christina River and stages classic and contemporary drama in a state-of-the-art facility. **Wilmington Drama League** (☎ 302-764-1172, 10 W Lea Blvd) is the oldest community theater in town, with more than 60 years of experience.

A company of Russian-trained dancers called the **Russian Ballet Theatre of Delaware** (☎ 302-764-2115) mounts four major productions a year at various venues.

Three Little Bakers Dinner Theatre (☎ 302-368-1616, 3540 Foxcroft Drive), near Pike Creek Shopping Center, off Route 7, offers a buffet with Broadway shows. In the village of Arden, another dinner-play option

is the **Candlelight Music Dinner Theatre** (☎ 302-475-2313), on Miller Rd off I-95.

Performing Arts
In addition to the annual jazz festival, jazz loops, and bar scene, Wilmington stages a mix of concerts.

The **Grand Opera House** (☎ 302-658-7897, 818 Market St) is Wilmington's restored Second Empire theater. The theater seats 1100 and hosts world-class jazz, classical, and popular artists. Director Stephen Gunzenhausen and the **Delaware Symphony Orchestra** (☎ 302-656-7442) perform at the Grand.

Opera Delaware (☎ 302-658-8063, 824 N Market St) has a reputation for bold productions that mix new works with a classical repertory. The Christina Cultural Arts Center (see the individual entry, earlier in this chapter) features live jazz, with a jam session at 7 pm on Thursday; admission is $3.

Bars & Clubs
Many of Wilmington's watering holes offer tasty, inexpensive food, as well as the usual liquid attractions and evening entertainment.

Cavanaugh's (☎ 302-656-4067, 703 Market Street), at 7th St, occupying the former Reynold's candy company building, is open 11 am to 1 am daily. The pub offers draft beer, wines, and a wide variety of food all day: sandwiches, salads, pasta, seafood, steaks, and snacks. There is a daily happy hour from 5 to 7 pm, including complimentary or cheap snacks.

Bottlecaps (☎ 302-427-9119, 216 9th St), between Orange and Tatnal Sts, features '99 bottles of beer' and great food with a daily happy hour from 4 to 8 pm. Sandwiches cost about $4, with some entrees in the $12 range. You will find pool tables here and live dance music Thursday to Saturday (with a $2 to $3 cover). It's closed Sunday. Bottlecaps hosts a monthly block party – the 9th Street Outdoor Cabaret, with eight or so local bands playing on two stages from 8 pm to 1 am. The crowd is under 25, and the cover is $5.

The **Barn Door** (☎ 302-655-7749, 845 Tatnal St), between 8th and 9th Sts, is rocking out to the jukebox these days, but they've finally gotten draft beer, with pints of the domestic beer running $2.

Two new pubs are attracting a crowd downtown. The **Washington Street Ale House** (☎ 302-658-2537, 1206 Washington St) pulls in a lot of young professionals Thursday to Saturday to sample 20 different brews on tap, nosh jerk-chicken sandwiches ($8), and rub their bodies against each other.

The **Brandywine Brewing Company** (☎ 301-655-8000), at the corner of Orange and 9th St, is a satellite of the brewpub that started its life north of town in one of the mini-malls of Greenville. It draws the same crowd as the Ale House, but the Brewing Company is more of a dinner-date scene. Drafts start at $3.50. The menu is standard pub fare, with the exception of a killer stuffed portabella and crab sandwich for $8.

South of downtown, across from Frawley Stadium, the **Big Kahuna** (☎ 302-571-8401, 550 S Madison St) is currently Wilmington's most popular club and a major-league strut, wiggle, and pickup scene for the 'big hair' crowd. The interior looks like a bad copy of a set from *Blue Lagoon*, but Kahuna's has a refreshing deck overlooking the river that attracts a mellower crowd, with national acts such as the Charlie Daniels Band and Black Rose.

If you're into barhopping and in the mood for good jazz and rock 'n' roll, head for Trolley Square. While the place does not jump on the same scale as similar venues in Baltimore or Annapolis, Trolley Square's bars attract thousands on weekend nights and have entertainment playing all week long.

On Friday nights, **Kelly's Logan House** (☎ 302-655-6426, 1701 Delaware Ave) draws a crowd of more than a thousand people, spreading out over two floors and a huge patio to listen to a really whacked mix of blues, reggae, alternative music, and rock.

Virtually next door to Kelly's, **Scratch Magoos** (☎ 302-651-9188, 1709 Delaware Ave) is another popular place for cheap beer, music, and lots of company. This place is without a doubt the best pickup scene in town Thursday to Saturday. Wild sandwiches, such as the Lumberjane (there's turkey in there), go for about $7.

Gay & Lesbian Venues

Upstairs from the Shipley Grill, at 913 Shipley St (between 9th and 10th Sts), **Roam** was long the center of gay nightlife in Wilmington, but it has gotten rather slow of late, since a new club has burst on the scene. Nevertheless, the drag shows on weekends and holidays can be a hoot.

The Exchange (☎ 302-777-7080, 914 Orange St) is the new rage in town. It hosts a major-league scene that is attracting folks from as far away as Philadelphia and the University of Delaware at Newark. Two bars, pool rooms, a wicked sound system, live dancers, and an industrial look draw the crowds to a packed dance floor. About 20% of the crowd is lesbian, 10% are straight, and the rest are gay or bisexual men. On Thursday night, beers run 69¢ with a $3 cover. On Friday, there is a college crowd, and the club admits nondrinkers over the age of 18. The club features heavy house music.

SPECTATOR SPORTS

Wilmington sports fans have much enthusiasm for their Class A baseball club, the **Wilmington Blue Rocks** (☎ 302-888-2015), a feeder team for the Kansas City Royals. Named after those blue rocks at Fort Christina, where the first Swedish settlers landed, and competing in the Carolina League, the team plays three or four home games a week at Frawley Stadium from mid-April to early September.

Delaware Park Race Course (☎ 302-994-2521) is in Stanton, on Route 7, off I-95 exit 4N. One of the country's most picturesque sports settings, this track features daytime thoroughbred racing from mid-April to November. Post time is 12:45 pm Tuesday, Wednesday, Saturday, and Sunday. And if the horses don't win for you, you can try your luck with the new banks of slot machines. Adults pay $2 for admission.

SHOPPING

The city's primary shopping district runs along the six-block pedestrian concourse of the Market St Mall (Shipley St), in the heart of town, and spills over into the three-block 9th St Plaza, west of Market. Artisan's III

DELAWARE

(☎ 302-656-7370), on the corner of 9th and Shipley Sts, sells gifts and clothing from Africa, Asia, and South America. You might find terrific used clothing at the Goodwill Boutique (☎ 302-654-6926), at 7th and Market Sts.

Wilmington has two major malls if you need to escape a heat wave, hurricane, or blizzard. The huge Christiana Mall is on Route 7 at exit 4S, in Newark. Concord Mall sprawls north of the city on Route 202N.

GETTING THERE & AWAY
Air
Philadelphia International Airport (PIA; ☎ 215-492-3181) is just a 30-minute drive away to the north. The following airlines serve PIA: British Airways, Continental Airlines, Delta Air Lines, Midway Airlines, US Airways, and United Airlines. (See the Getting There & Away chapter for toll-free phone numbers.)

There's an information desk and an ATM in every terminal, and Terminals A, B, and C each have a currency-exchange office.

Beginning in 1999, Shuttle America (☎ 888-999-3273) started operating a limited number of scheduled flights in and out of the New Castle Regional Airport, 5 miles south of Wilmington on Route 13. Currently, flights run between this airport and Norfolk, Virginia; Hartford, Connecticut; and Buffalo, New York.

Bus
Greyhound/Carolina Trailways provides daily service into the Wilmington Transportation Center (☎ 302-655-6111), 318 Market St, across Martin Luther King Jr Blvd from the Amtrak station. Service is from all major East Coast cities, as well as the Delaware coast. Typical of many American cities, the neighborhood around the bus station is not wonderful, nor is it too safe at night. There are 14 buses a day between Wilmington and Baltimore ($16).

Train
The handsome, restored Wilmington Amtrak station (☎ 302-658-1515) sits at Martin Luther King Blvd and King St. The city is on the main East Coast corridor between New York and Baltimore, with service to Philadelphia and DC. More than 25 Amtrak (☎ 800-872-7245) trains run daily between Wilmington and Baltimore/Washington. One-way fares are $29 to Baltimore, $37 to DC.

Car
I-95 cuts right through the center of Wilmington, running through DC and Maryland to the south and through New Jersey to the north. The Delaware Memorial Bridge connects the city to the New Jersey Turnpike. Route 13 links the city to southern Delaware and Virginia.

GETTING AROUND
Delaware Express (☎ 302-454-7800, 800-648-5466) and SuperShuttle (☎ 302-655-8878) run small shuttle buses between PIA and Wilmington. You must make reservations. Fares run from $21 to $23 per person, whether you are going to the distant Philadelphia airport or the nearby New Castle Airport.

Delaware Memorial Bridge: The World's Largest Twin Span

Carrying I-295 traffic over the Delaware River, the Delaware Memorial Bridge links the states of Delaware and New Jersey just south of Wilmington. Among the many highways that feed into the bridge are Routes 13 and 40, the New Jersey Turnpike, and the Delaware Turnpike. It is part of the direct route from Maine to Florida.

The bridge's main spans of 2150 feet make it the world's largest twin-suspension bridge. The original bridge, the New Jersey–bound span, opened in August 1951. The Delaware-bound bridge opened in September 1968. Tolls are collected in one direction only: Motorists pay $2 as they enter Delaware.

Beyond the Market St attractions, which can be easily covered on foot, you will need transportation to get around. Wilmington's local bus network is known as DART (Delaware Administration for Regional Transit). Blue-and-white signs indicate DART stops throughout the city. The buses can take you to major sites outside the city, such as the Brandywine Valley attractions and New Castle. For information about routes, call ☎ 302-577-3278 or 888-652-3278 (toll-free in state). Fares are $1.15 for travel within one zone and $1.90 for two zones; transfers cost an additional 10¢.

Yellow Cab Delaware (☎ 302-656-8151) is your safe and dependable carrier here. It will cost you $1.90 at flag-fall and $2.25 per mile.

If you have a car, there are a number of commercial lots for parking in the center of town.

Northern Delaware

The northern region of Delaware – New Castle County beyond Wilmington – includes the important tourist attractions of New Castle and the Brandywine Valley's chateau country. New Castle County holds the bulk of Delaware's population, most of its historic buildings, a vital visual- and performing-arts scene, museums, and the state's best selection of accommodations – including a number of attractive B&Bs. You will also find a lot of heavy industry marring beautiful landscapes (check out the Getty Oil refinery, at Delaware City, for an eyesore), maddening traffic, and a proliferation of housing developments. Depending on what roads you travel and where you stop, New Castle County will either seduce you or repulse you.

Highlights

- Winterthur, one of the great castles of the world
- The grounds at Nemours, which make you feel like you're lost in France
- Picnicking in Longwood Gardens
- The Brandywine River Museum, for generations of Wyeth paintings
- Historic New Castle's streets, for a trip back to the 18th century
- Rock concerts at the famous Stone Balloon in Newark

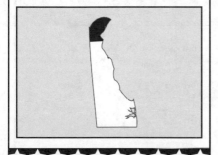

If you are a bicyclist or get nauseous at the sight of mini-malls, fast-food franchises, and filling stations, *avoid* Route 202 running north of Wilmington to West Chester, Pennsylvania; Route 2 between Wilmington and Newark is just as bad; Route 40 south of these two towns also makes for a hideous trip.

But Delaware's Ugly Highway Award goes to Route 13, running from the Pennsylvania state line in the north to Delaware's southern border with Maryland. When Coleman du Pont bankrolled this highway back in the 1910s, it was a lovely, straight thoroughfare traversing farm country and linking historic towns. Today, after 80 years of no apparent zoning, Route 13 is a commercial corridor plagued with an endless array of traffic lights, causing backups not only in Greater Wilmington, but also in minuscule towns along the way. Currently, the state is completing the final stretch of a parallel, limited-access highway, Route 1, to bypass the congestion on Route 13 between Greater Wilmington and Dover. Take Route 1 if you are headed north or south in a hurry, but realize that during the summer, this road is packed with cars headed to and from the Atlantic beaches.

Fortunately, you can escape these nightmares. Try exploring Routes 52, 82, and 100 as they wind through the Brandywine Valley area north of Wilmington. If you're heading south, follow Route 9 into New Castle then through the corn and soybean farms and along the marshy fringes of Delaware Bay. Bound east or west between Wilmington and Newark, your best bet by car is to take I-95 and just get the trip over with. Bicyclists will like the secondary roads that network through places such as Mermaid, Pleasant Hill, and Milford Crossing.

BRANDYWINE VALLEY
Fifteen miles wide and 35 miles long, the Brandywine Valley is a patchwork of rolling, wooded countryside, historic villages, ancient farmhouses, and chateau estates to rival the Loire Valley in France. The valley offers a

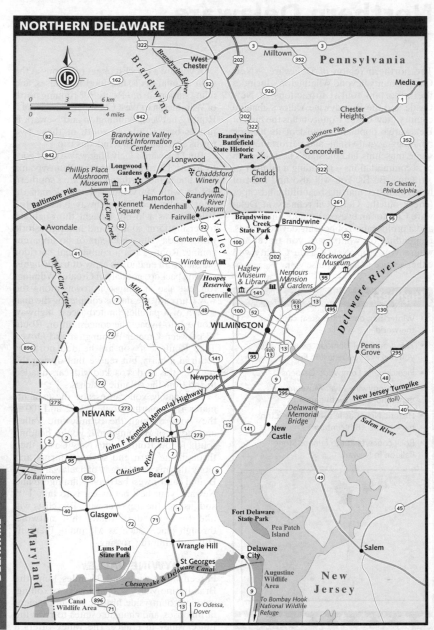

NORTHERN DELAWARE

wealth of attractions: mansions, gardens, museums, a winery, art collections, and some terrific country inns and restaurants. You don't have to go far out of your way to take in the best sights of the Brandywine, such as Winterthur and Hagley Museum. If time permits, also stop in at Nemours, Longwood Gardens, Rockwood, and the Brandywine River Museum.

Orientation

Straddling the Delaware-Pennsylvania state line, the Brandywine Valley's chateau country is northern Delaware's primary tourist destination. Most of the attractions are in Delaware, while the local places to stay and eat are in Pennsylvania. The Greater Wilmington Convention & Visitors Bureau promotes attractions on both sides of the border, including those sites in Wilmington's northern suburbs.

Information

The Brandywine Valley Tourist Information Center (☎ 610-388-2900, 800-228-9933) is located right outside the gates of Longwood Gardens, Route 1, in Kennett Square, Pennsylvania. Operated by Pennsylvania's Chester County Tourist Bureau, the center is open 10 am to 6 pm daily (it closes at 5 pm from October to March).

Winterthur

The Brandywine Valley's most famous attraction, Winterthur (☎ 302-888-4600, 800-448-3883) was the country estate of Henry Francis du Pont until he opened it to the public in 1951. For most of his life, du Pont collected American furniture. When he inherited Winterthur in 1927, he moved the best of his collection here, doubled the size of the existing house, and converted it into a showplace for the world's most important collection of early American decorative arts (1640–1860). During the next 20 years, du Pont continued to increase his collection…and the size of Winterthur.

The museum consists of two buildings, one with 175 period rooms and another with three exhibition galleries. There are more than 89,000 objects that were made or used in America between 1640 and 1860, including furniture, textiles, paintings, prints, pewter, silver, ceramics, glass, needlework, and brass. The museum is surrounded by 980 acres, of which 60 acres are beautifully planted with native and exotic plants.

General admission is $8 for adults, $6 for seniors and students, and $4 for children. Unless you are joining a special tour, you are free to stroll the galleries, explore the grounds or ride the year-round train (space permitting) at your leisure. For additional

Winterthur contains Henry du Pont's enormous art collection, surrounded by 980 acres.

DELAWARE TOURISM OFFICE

DELAWARE

fees, the following excellent guided tours (with groups of four to 10 people) are available (reservations are required): Introduction to Winterthur, a one-hour tour through selected period rooms ($5); Decorative Arts Tours, in-depth one- and two-hour guided tours of period rooms ($9 for one hour, $13 for two hours); and Garden Walks, which are available seasonally ($5). There are also other seasonal tours; ask at reception – or better still, call ahead, because all of the tours are popular and fill quickly.

The museum and garden hours are 9 am to 5 pm Monday to Saturday and noon to 5 pm Sunday. The garden is open until dusk, and the last tickets are sold at 3:45 pm. Winterthur is closed on New Year's Day, Thanksgiving, and Christmas Day.

You can have continental breakfast, lunch, Sunday brunch, and afternoon tea in the pleasant Visitors Pavilion. Reservations for tea and brunch are suggested (☎ 302-888-4826). Winterthur stands 6 miles northwest of Wilmington on Route 52, just 10 minutes off I-95 via exit 7 (Delaware Avenue, Route 52N).

Delaware Museum of Natural History

With more than 100 exhibits, ranging from local fauna to the wildlife of Mt Kenya, a walk across Australia's Great Barrier Reef, and an undersea world of exotic marine life, this museum (☎ 302-658-9111) has plenty of variety and has gained a certain degree of infamy since its founder, John E du Pont, ran amok on his nearby estate in 1996. Allow 45 minutes to an hour to tour on your own.

The museum is located on Route 52, 5 miles northwest of Wilmington, just before Winterthur (coming from Wilmington). It's open 9:30 am to 4:30 pm Monday to Saturday and noon to 5 pm Sunday. Admission is $4 for adults and $3 for seniors and children.

Hagley Museum & Library

Beautifully situated on the banks of the Brandywine River, Hagley is a must-see for visitors to the area. This 240-acre outdoor museum (☎ 302-658-2400) on the site of the birthplace of the DuPont company tells the story of the du Ponts as part of the broader history of America's Industrial Revolution.

Du Pont started operations here as a gunpowder manufacturer in 1802. You can explore the ruins of the original mills; tour Eleutherian Mills (the 1803 residence of EI du Pont); see the French-style garden; and visit restored buildings with exhibits, models, and live demonstrations.

Allow at least three to four hours for your visit. Hagley is a large site with great natural beauty and lots of things to see and do. It is open 9:30 am to 4:30 pm daily from March 15 to January 1 and 9:30 am to 4:30 pm weekends from January 2 to March 14. Weekday ticket sales are at 1 pm; there is one guided tour of the site from 1:30 to 4 pm. It's closed Thanksgiving, Christmas, and New Year's Eve. Admission is $9.75 for adults and $7.50 for students and seniors.

The museum is on Route 141 in north Wilmington. From I-95, take exit 7 to Route 52N, to Route 100N, to Route 141N; or take exit 8 from I-95 (Route 202N) to Route 141S, and follow the signs to Hagley Museum.

Nemours Mansion & Gardens

This is the estate of Alfred I du Pont, named after the site of the family's ancestral home in north-central France. Surrounded by 300 acres of gardens and natural woodlands, the Louis XVI–style chateau (☎ 302-651-6912) was built in 1909–1910 and has 102 rooms. Today it contains fine examples of antique furniture, oriental rugs, tapestries, and paintings dating back to the 15th century. Nemours exhibits items illustrating the du Ponts' lavish lifestyle, including vintage cars, a billiard room, a bowling alley, and rooms for making ice and bottling sparkling water. The French gardens, stretching almost one-third of a mile along the main vista from the mansion, are generally considered to be among the finest of their kind in America.

Located on Rockwood Rd in north Wilmington, Nemours is open May to November with the following guided-tour schedule: 9 and 11 am, 1 and 3 pm Tuesday to Saturday; 11 am, 1 and 3 pm Sunday. Admission is $10. Nobody under 16 is admitted. Tours take a minimum of two hours and include a guided

Mr Gunpowder

The biography of Eleuthère Irénée du Pont de Nemours is not your average American immigrant rags-to-riches story. Du Pont arrived on the shores of Delaware with a bundle of money; after he got here, he made plenty more – enough to make the state of Delaware his family's virtual principality for generations to come. The keys to his success were an uncommon education, plenty of investment capital, and a legacy of entrepreneurial skills that put him in a position to deliver to Americans something they crave like hamburger.

Born into the wealthy family of a French economist and publisher in 1771, EI du Pont grew up on the ancestral estate in Nemours and had the good fortune to study with the noted chemist Antoine Lavoisier. From Lavoisier, du Pont learned the secrets of making gunpowder and perfected his talents working in the royal powder mills in Essone. While gunpowder was what du Pont loved, he felt a filial duty to work in his father's printing business during the 1790s, until the French Revolution made things too hot for royalists such as the du Ponts. Like political refugees the world over, du Pont and his father grabbed what they could of the family fortune and split for America.

It didn't take the young du Pont long to see that while Americans loved their shooting irons, their gunpowder was just as bad as the local wine. Figuring he had a better shot at improving the gunpowder situation – rather than the American viniculture industry – du Pont returned to France, appropriated plans and models of superior French gunpowder machinery, secured some additional financial backing, and returned to the US to start EI du Pont de Nemours and Co.

The rest, as they say, is history. Du Pont made gunpowder that went snap-bang when guys like Daniel Boone required it – without huge clouds of sulfurous smoke. And Americans got themselves into an endless series of armed conflicts (including an obsession to tame the frontier) that made du Pont's gunpowder a household word. By the time du Pont died in 1834, he had monopolized the American gunpowder industry and might have taken some credit for the deaths of hundreds of thousands of his fellow Homo sapiens and a whole lot more lions and tigers and bears.

tour through a series of rooms on three floors of the mansion, followed by a bus tour through the gardens. Visitors need to arrive at reception a good 15 minutes before the start of the tour. Reservations are recommended for individuals; the office is open 8:30 am to 4:30 pm weekdays. Finding this mansion is complicated, so call for directions.

Longwood Gardens

For many fans of horticulture, Longwood (☎ 610-388-1000) is America's ultimate garden, with 1050 outdoor acres and 20 indoor gardens presenting 'a never-ending cavalcade of exquisite bloom.' There are 11,000 different kinds of plants, roses, and orchids in bloom year-round, an indoor Children's Garden with a maze, an Idea Garden for home gardeners, the historic Pierce du Pont House, and one of the world's mightiest pipe organs. Each season brings another range of colors, while the heated conservatory and seasonal festivals and concerts add dimensions to the spectacle. At night, displays of illuminated fountains in the summer and festive lights at Christmas are breathtaking.

Longwood Gardens lies along Route 1, in Kennett Square, Pennsylvania. The outdoor gardens open at 9 am, and conservatories open at 10 am daily. They all close at 6 pm from April to October, and at 5 pm from November to March. Admission is $12 for adults, $6 for youth ages 15 to 20, and $2 for children 5 to 14. On Tuesday, adults pay $8.

Phillips Place Mushroom Museum

A unique collection of exhibits explaining the history, lore, and mystique of mushrooms (mushroom farming is a local tradition), Phillips Place (☎ 610-388-6082) features film,

DELAWARE

slides, and nutritional charts. It's located half a mile south of Longwood Gardens on Route 1, in Kennett Square, Pennsylvania, and it's open 10 am to 6 pm daily. Admission is $1.25.

Chadds Ford

If the Brandywine Valley is really chateau country, then there must be a winery…and here it is. Operating from a renovated 18th-century barn, the **Chaddsford Winery** (☎ 610-388-6221) is located on Route 1, 5 miles south of Route 202.

Producing small lots of varietal wines with grapes imported from the surrounding area, Chaddsford offers free guided and self-guided tours to see the grapes being crushed, fermented, barrel-aged, and bottled. For $5, you can taste seven or eight of the wines (and you get to keep your logo glass). Their white wines include Chardonnay, sauvignon blanc, and vidal blanc. For reds, Chaddsford offers cabernet sauvignon, merican (a cabernet sauvignon-cabernet Franc blend), and some chambourcins. There are tables for picnics outside around the barn. It's open noon to 6 pm Monday to Saturday most of the year, but it's closed Monday during winter months.

A renowned showcase of American art, the **Brandywine River Museum** (☎ 610-388-2700), at Routes 1 and 100, presents a fine collection of works by three generations of the Wyeth family. Housed in a 19th-century gristmill, the galleries also feature other American artists, such as Howard Pyle, Maxfield Parrish, William Trost Richards, Horace Pippin, and hundreds of others. The museum is open 9:30 am to 4:30 pm daily. Admission is $5 for adults and $2.50 for seniors and students.

The Brandywine River Museum also maintains the **NC Wyeth House & Studio** nearby. The house and studio reflect 1945, the year of the artist's death. You must take a shuttle bus (wheelchair-accessible) from the museum to get there. The hour-long tours ($3 in addition to museum fee) take place 10 am to 3:15 pm from April 1 to November 19.

The **John Chadds House** (☎ 610-388-7376), on Route 100 at the junction with Route 1, was the home of John Chadds – ferryman, farmer, and tavern keeper. There is a demonstration of

baking in a beehive oven. Built around 1725, the home is open noon to 6 pm weekends May to September. Admission is $3.

The **Barns-Brinton House** (☎ 610-388-7376), on Route 1 at the junction with Route 100, was originally built as a tavern in 1714 and has been restored to its original appearance by the Chadds Ford Historical Society. It is open noon to 6 pm weekends May to September. Admission is $3.

Brandywine Battlefield State Historic Park

This park (☎ 610-459-3342), which includes the farmhouses that served as headquarters for George Washington and his French comrade the Marquis de Lafayette, lies on the north side of Route 1 just after you cross the Chadds Ford Bridge heading east.

The chief reasons to stop here are to pick up pamphlets on the battle that took place on farms north of the park, to see a reenactment of the battle, or to visit the restored headquarters of the Revolutionary generals who came close to losing their bid for American independence at Brandywine. Hours are 9 am to 5 pm Tuesday to Saturday and noon to 5 pm Sunday. Park visits are free, but tours of the headquarters cost $3.50, or $2.50 for seniors and AAA members.

Special Events

From Thanksgiving to New Year, Christmas exhibitions and events occur at most Brandywine Valley museums. The following are other events held throughout the year:

Welcome Spring Indoors Celebration (January to April) Longwood Gardens features fragrant bulbs, acacias, orchids, and organ concerts.

Acres of Spring (April to May) Longwood celebrates outdoors with daffodils, flowering cherries, tulips, irises, and wisteria.

Antique Show (May) Brandywine River Museum is host to this annual antiques show.

Point to Point Race (May) This race takes place at Winterthur (also see Special Events in the Wilmington chapter).

Festival of Fountains (June to September) Longwood Gardens holds evening fountain displays, fireworks, outdoor concerts, roses, and water lilies.

Winterthur Craft Festival (Labor Day weekend)
This event draws hundreds of crafters in jewelry, wood, metal, toys, stained glass, sculpture, pottery, basketry, carving, furniture, and more. Food stalls and a pops concert are other highlights of this two-day event.

Revolutionary Times at Brandywine (September)
This is a reenactment of the Battle of Brandywine; there are crafts and food too.

Chrysanthemums Festival (October) Longwood Gardens celebrates fall foliage with organ concerts.

Hoots, Howls & Haunts Halloween Carnival (October) The Delaware Museum of Natural History stages an annual carnival.

Places to Stay

Accommodations in Wilmington and New Castle, and even Philadelphia, are within easy reach of the Brandywine Valley. However, some options are even closer. Route 202 (Concord Pike) has a larger selection of accommodations, whereas there is only one on Route 52 (Kennett Pike). Most motels and hotels offer good value packages (especially on weekends) that include admission to Brandywine Valley museums.

Right before the Pennsylvania border, the *Tally-Ho Motor Lodge* (☎ 302-478-0300, 5209 Concord Pike) has singles/doubles for

The Battle of Brandywine (1777)

The English army nearly ended the American Revolution when it attacked and overwhelmed the Continental forces at Brandywine Creek on September 11, 1777.

Weeks before the actual battle, General George Washington knew that a confrontation of major proportions was brewing. In late August, Washington learned that British General William Howe had landed 13,000 British troops and 5000 Hessian mercenaries at the head of the Chesapeake Bay and had been advancing slowly through Delaware, gathering intelligence and securing supply lines for an attack on Philadelphia, the new capital of the rebellious United States.

In defense of Philadelphia, Washington moved 11,000 Continentals to the Wilmington area. Realizing that the Brandywine presented a geographical obstacle to Howe, Washington and his French supporter, the Marquis de Lafayette, set up the bulk of their defenses along the high ground east of the creek at Chadds Ford, the most likely place for the British to cross the Brandywine. In addition, American troops covered two other fords on the Brandywine in hopes of forcing Howe to fight at Chadds Ford.

Howe anticipated Washington's plans and, using intelligence from local British sympathizers, sent the bulk of his troops on a long march to the north to round Washington's right flank under the cover of darkness and fog on September 11. Meanwhile, when the fog lifted at Chadds Ford, Howe's generals made a decoy attack and marched a few columns back and forth among the hills to give Washington's scouts the impression that the main British force was gathering at Chadds Ford for a charge. Preoccupied at Chadds Ford, Washington did not realize until mid-afternoon that Howe and 11,000 Redcoats had rounded the Continental right flank and nearly encircled the Americans. After brutal fighting, the remains of the American force escaped to Chester, Pennsylvania. British troops suffered 600 dead and wounded; the Continentals had 900 casualties and lost 400 men as prisoners of war.

Fifteen days later, Howe's troops marched into Philadelphia unopposed, but Washington was regrouping to fight again. Although Washington's attack on Howe at Germantown in October failed, and he had to suffer a long, cold winter encamped at Valley Forge, history shows that Washington's escape from the near catastrophe at Brandywine Creek gave the United States the hope and manpower to continue the revolution. As Washington reported to Congress following the Battle of Brandywine, 'Notwithstanding the misfortune of the day, I am happy to find the troops in good spirits; and I hope another time we shall compensate for the losses now sustained.'

$45/60. On Route 202, the **Best Western Brandywine Valley Inn** (☎ 800-537-7772, 1807 Concord Pike), 1 mile north of I-95 exit 8, has rooms starting at $69.

In the same area and similarly priced is the **Holiday Inn of Wilmington – North** (☎ 302-478-2222, 4000 Concord Pike). Farther north, the **Radisson Hotel Wilmington** (☎ 302-478-6000, 4727 Concord Pike) has singles for $60 to $90 and doubles for $85 to $109.

In Pennsylvania, there is a selection of country-style inns and B&Bs. **Pace One** (☎ 610-459-3702), at Thornton and Glen Mills Rds, is a combination restaurant (see Places to Eat, later) and B&B in a 250-year-old restored barn. Doubles are $75 to $95. All seven rooms are decorated in different colors, with Lancaster oak queen beds, original watercolors of local scenes, and private bath/shower. From Route 52 near Chadds Ford, head east on Route 1 and then left on Thornton Rd. The inn is on your right.

The **Brandywine River Hotel** (☎ 610-388-1200), on Route 1 at Route 100, Chadds Ford, has 40 rooms with doubles from $125, and suites for $169. Built in 1987, this hotel is not a piece of antiquity, but it is nicely designed to blend in with the surroundings, and it has a Colonial-style interior.

The luxurious **Fairville Inn** (☎ 610-388-5900), on Route 52, Mendenhall, is a delightful establishment run by Ole and Patricia Retlev. The main house was built in 1826, and there is a rear carriage house and barn. Eight of the 15 rooms have fireplaces (11 have decks), and the entire place is beautifully decorated. Prices range from $140 to $190, and there are two suites for $180. A substantial continental breakfast and a light but delicious afternoon tea are included. From Route 1 west of Chadds Ford, take Route 52S to Mendenhall; the Fairville Inn is almost a mile past Mendenhall on the left side.

The **Inn at Montchanin Village** (☎ 302-888-0389), at Route 100 and Rockland Rd, in Montchanin, is a newcomer to the luxury-inn trade. This historic property has 33 rooms and suites, with prices ranging from $170 to $500. (Also see Places to Eat, next.)

Places to Eat

In Greenville, on Route 52 and convenient for many of the Brandywine attractions, there are a couple of nice establishments in the Powder Mill Square shopping complex. **Brew ha ha!** (☎ 302-658-6336) is an espresso cafe serving soup, sandwiches, and salads along with the coffee. **Cromwell's** (☎ 302-571-0561) is an upscale tavern serving such specialties as crab cakes, chicken winglets, and daily specials. It's open 11 am to 1 am daily (but it closes at 10 pm Sunday).

For local brews and hearty food, you can head across the street to the **Brandywine Brewing Company** (☎ 302-655-8000), in the Greenville Center, at the intersection of Routes 52 and 141. Consider the thick corn-and-crab chowder for less than $5. Draft beers brewed in house run $3.50 and up. This is a popular dinner spot for an upscale crowd of all ages Thursday to Sunday, so you might want to make reservations.

Krazy Kat's Restaurant, at the Inn at Montchanin Village (see Places to Stay, earlier) offers an eclectic menu with specials such as mahi mahi for $24 and an extensive wine list in a 19th-century blacksmith shop.

Buckley's Tavern (☎ 302-656-9776, 5812 Kennett Pike), Route 52, in Centreville, is one of the region's most popular drinking spots. There is a small pub with a dining room and garden room at the back. Locals of all stripes, from gentry to farmers, are regulars here, and the place is usually packed. There is a small menu featuring good food, with dishes ranging from $5 to $15. It's open daily.

Chadds Ford Inn (☎ 610-388-7361), on Route 1 at Route 100 in Chadds Ford, Pennsylvania, dates back to the 18th century. The house was built by Francis Chadsey, an English Quaker who had bought the land from William Penn's commissioner of land grants. In 1736, his eldest son turned the house into a tavern, which through the centuries has evolved into a popular restaurant furnished with antiques and colonial memorabilia. The international cuisine served is up-to-date, though, as are prices, with lunch costing $5 to $11 and dinner costing $10 to $25. It's open daily.

Another popular historic restaurant is *Dilworthtown Inn* (☎ 610-399-1390), on Old Wilmington Pike at Brinton Bridge Rd, in Dilworthtown, Pennsylvania. Open daily for dinner ($29 for the top-end lobster thermidor), this wood, stone, and brick structure with fireplaces and gas lamps dates to 1758 and serves continental cuisine with French and Asian influences. To find the inn, head north on Route 1 from the junction with Route 202. After a mile and a half, turn left at the second traffic light and continue for another mile and a half. Go straight when you reach the stop sign, and the restaurant is the second on your right.

Pace One (see Places to Stay, earlier) has a restaurant that is open daily (no lunch Saturdays, extensive brunch Sundays). Lunch entrees such as scampi cost $15, and a dinner of veal tenderloin stuffed with crabmeat costs about $25. Artwork and vases of fresh flowers decorate a dimly lit interior room with stucco walls, bare floors, and a low ceiling. There is also a brighter, porchlike outer room.

Shopping

Concord Mall, on Route 202N, is home to the Strawbridge & Clothier department store, Sears, Boscov's, and more than 90 specialty stores. Most of the region's museums operate gift shops offering a wide range of gifts and souvenirs. Winterthur also has a popular mail-order catalog. There are several attractive upscale shopping options along Route 52, from Fairville through Centreville to Greenville.

Getting There & Away

Routes 52 and 202 form the general eastern and western borders of the Brandywine Valley, accessible from Wilmington. If you're coming from Philadelphia, take I-95 to join either road.

FORT DELAWARE STATE PARK

In the Delaware River, Pea Patch Island lies a mile from the shore of Delaware City. On the island, Fort Delaware State Park (☎ 302-834-7941) surrounds a granite fortress that served as a detention center during the Civil War. Of the 12,500 prisoners

incarcerated here during the war, 2700 perished from cholera and other diseases, which were spread by unsanitary conditions and mosquitoes.

Visitors can see 19th-century cells in the museum here, along with other artifacts from the period. There is also an audiovisual presentation. The park itself is popular with birders, as the island is a nesting spot for egrets, herons, and other marsh fowl. There is an observation tower for bird watchers, along with nature trails, fishing, and picnic facilities. It's open 10 am to 6 pm Wednesday to Friday from mid-June to August. The fort may be also open some weekends during the spring and fall.

The only way to reach Pea Patch Island is via a 10-minute ride on the passenger ferry *Delafort* from Delaware City. The ride costs $6 for adults and $4 for children; there is no additional charge to enter the park or museum or to continue on to Fort Mott on the New Jersey side of the river.

The state of Delaware has been planning to open a B&B at Fort Delaware, a truly intriguing possibility. The park is open weekends and holidays from late April through the fall and some weekdays from mid-June to Labor Day – call for specifics. Delaware City can be reached via Route 9.

NEW CASTLE

Historic New Castle (population 4800), the longtime colonial capital of Delaware, lies 7 miles south of Wilmington on the Delaware River, near the spot where the river begins to widen into the bay. With rough, cobblestone streets and unbroken blocks of 18th-century townhouses and public buildings, the heart of New Castle remains much as it was in colonial times. The oldest courthouse in the United States is here, and surveyors Mason and Dixon measured the arc of Delaware's northern boundary with Pennsylvania from the courthouse cupola.

Historic New Castle is the real thing. Beyond visiting the museums, admiring the architecture, exploring the shops, taking in the view of the Delaware River, and enjoying a drink, snack, or meal in one of the pleasant establishments here, what truly completes the picture is the air of authenticity provided by all the little touches in the residents' private homes.

As you look around, notice the heraldic flags and banners hanging from numerous homes, the painted signs, the lamp fixtures, the window frames, and other period details. Due to a strict code controlling these items, the town truly does allow you to step back in time. Architectural examples of the Dutch, Colonial, French, Georgian, Federal, and Empire periods exist here. If you can, try to visit on A Day in Old New Castle (see Special Events, later), held every year in May, when residents open up their homes to visitors and the town celebrates the rites of spring.

Surprisingly, there are no hordes of tourists here, and New Castle can be just the antidote for the nearby bustle of traffic racing along the highways of America's Northeast corridor. You can come to New Castle for the day, or you can check into one of the town's B&Bs and disconnect from the modern world indefinitely. The Visitors Bureau has dubbed it 'The Little Williamsburg on the Delaware River,' and New Castle actually lives up to its billing.

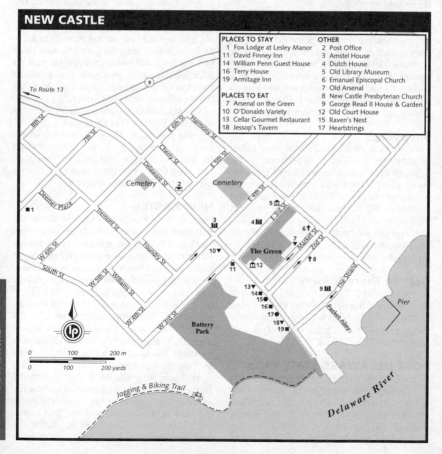

NEW CASTLE

PLACES TO STAY
1 Fox Lodge at Lesley Manor
11 David Finney Inn
14 William Penn Guest House
16 Terry House
19 Armitage Inn

PLACES TO EAT
7 Arsenal on the Green
10 O'Donalds Variety
13 Cellar Gourmet Restaurant
18 Jessop's Tavern

OTHER
2 Post Office
3 Amstel House
4 Dutch House
5 Old Library Museum
6 Emanuel Episcopal Church
7 Old Arsenal
8 New Castle Presbyterian Church
9 George Read II House & Garden
12 Old Court House
15 Raven's Nest
17 Heartstrings

History

Originally named Fort Casimir by the Dutch, the settlement was founded by Peter Stuyvesant in 1651 to provide a position from which to command river traffic. Due to its strategic location on the Delaware River, the Dutch, Swedish, and English all fought and gained control of the town at one time or another. After defeating the Dutch, the English renamed the settlement and gave the town to William Penn. In 1682, Penn came ashore at the foot of Delaware St to take possession, adding the three counties of what is now Delaware to his lands in America. Dissatisfied with life under Penn, these counties won the privilege of electing their own legislature in 1704, and New Castle became the colonial capital of Delaware. The town also served as the first state capital until its vulnerability to British naval attack caused the government to move to Dover in 1777.

An ideal transfer point for trips up and down the coast, New Castle thrived during the 18th and early 19th centuries. The courts and general assembly that functioned here attracted numerous judges, lawyers, and government officials, who built grand homes, many of which have been restored today. Five signers of the Declaration of Independence – George Read, George Ross Jr, Thomas McKean, Charles Thompson, and Francis Hopkin – were New Castle citizens. Although the great fire of 1824 destroyed many of the inns and warehouses on The Strand, some were rebuilt, and the rest of the village has remained intact.

New Castle today has two identities. It is both the historical center and the sprawling modern town that virtually surrounds it. Most passersby do not make a point of stopping and only see the thoughtless commercial development along Route 13.

Orientation & Information

The historical part of New Castle consists of several blocks of cobblestone streets and brick sidewalks laid out in a grid around the village courthouse and a small park called 'The Green.' Once you have parked, you can explore on foot. The main street is Delaware St, running from west to east toward the Delaware River, where you will find the post office and most of the gift shops, banks, and B&Bs. Side streets and alleyways can be easily explored, since the grid system makes it hard to get lost. The Strand is the street of mansions that face the river.

For additional information, contact the Historic New Castle Visitors Bureau (☎ 302-322-8411, 800-758-1550), PO Box 465, New Castle, DE 19720.

Amstel House

On 4th and Delaware Sts, this 1830s house (☎ 302-322-2794) was the home of Governor Van Dyke. It's open 11 am to 4 pm Tuesday to Saturday and 1 to 4 pm Sunday from March to December. Admission is $2.25, or $4 when combined with the Dutch House.

Old Arsenal

On Market St and The Green, and now home to the Arsenal on The Green restaurant (see Places to Eat & Drink, later), this building was built by the federal government in 1809 in preparation for the War of 1812. Note the bas-relief of an American eagle perched on a gun on the south wall.

Old Churches & Cemeteries

On The Green in the center of the village are two early-18th-century churches – Emanuel Episcopal Church and New Castle Presbyterian Church – and their cemeteries, which date from the 17th century. They are usually open every day, and admission is free.

Old Court House

Built in 1732, this is the oldest surviving courthouse (☎ 302-323-4453) in the US. The colonial assembly met here until 1777, when Dover became the capital. The courthouse, on Delaware St, remained the seat of the New Castle County government until 1881, when the county government moved to Wilmington. It is open 10 am to 3:30 pm Tuesday to Saturday and 1:30 to 4:30 pm Sunday; admission is free.

Dutch House

On The Green, the Dutch House (☎ 302-322-2794) is one of Delaware's oldest brick houses and remains virtually unchanged since it was built, which was around 1700. The house is furnished as it would have been by the early Dutch settlers. It's open 11 am to 4 pm Tuesday to Saturday and 1 to 4 pm Sunday from March to December. Admission is $2.25, or $4 when combined with the Amstel House.

Old Library Museum

This hexagonal library (☎ 302-322-2794), at 40 E 3rd St, was commissioned by the New Castle Library Company and was built in 1892 by Frank Furness, a noted Philadelphia architect. It is now home to the New Castle Historical Society. It's open 11 am to 4 pm Saturday and 1 to 4 pm Sunday, as well as on Thursday and Friday whenever a docent can be there. Admission is free.

Packet Alley

Leading off The Strand, this is one of several little pathways that can be found in the town. It is named after the many packet boats that traveled to New Castle in the late 18th and early 19th centuries. On the side wall next to the alley is one of the oldest surviving Ivory Soap billboards.

George Read II House & Garden

On The Strand, at No 42, this beautiful Federal mansion (☎ 302-322-8411) is furnished in the early-19th-century style. The surrounding gardens still maintain much of the original 1840s plan. It's open 10 am to 4 pm Saturday and noon to 4 pm Sunday in January and February; it's open 10 am to 4 pm Tuesday to Saturday and noon to 4 pm Sunday from March to December. Admission is $4.

Riverfront & Battery Park

At the foot of Delaware St, be sure to enjoy the cooling breezes and lovely views of the Delaware River from the wharf. There is a children's playground, a 2½-mile jogging and bicycle trail, and picnic tables.

Organized Tours

The Historical Society of Delaware offers guided walking tours of historic New Castle. Lasting about one hour, tours cost $4 per person and are available every day except Monday. Reservations are required. Contact the Society at George Read II House & Garden (☎ 302-322-8411) as far in advance as possible.

Special Events

Throughout the year, New Castle hosts special events, including the following:

May Market (1st weekend in May) A plant and flower sale takes place in the Market Square.

A Day in Old New Castle (3rd Saturday in May) This is New Castle's biggest event. Some 60 private homes open up to the public. Thousands of visitors come for Maypole dancing, carriage rides, music performances, and a bell-ringing concert. Tickets cost $10 and are available on the day of the event from the Old Court House. Proceeds go toward the preservation and continued restoration of the site.

Separation Day (1st or 2nd Saturday in June) It's a day-long celebration of Delaware's separation from England, ending with fireworks.

Battery Park Antique Show (last Sunday in August)

Art on The Green (4th Saturday in September) Arts, crafts, and music fill The Green.

Candlelight Tours of Old New Castle (2nd and 4th weekends in December) The tours celebrate Christmas by visiting decorated museums, churches, and public buildings, and they often include live performances by musical ensembles.

Places to Stay

The best way to soak up the slow-paced congeniality of historic New Castle is to spend a night or two in the historic district at a B&B. As space is limited, reservations are recommended to secure preferred weekend dates (usually a month or so in advance, but up to a year before for the weekend of A Day in New Castle). As this guide goes to press, new B&Bs are in the works, and travelers might want to consult the New Castle Visitors Bureau (see Orientation & Information, earlier) for listings.

The *William Penn Guest House* (☎ 302-328-7736, 206 Delaware St) offers a less-expensive alternative. William Penn actually slept in this house, which dates from 1682. The four rooms share two bathrooms. Rates are $60 to $85, with continental breakfast included. They accept cash or checks only.

The **Terry House** (☎ 302-322-2505, 130 Delaware St) is a Federal townhouse (1869) overlooking Battery Park and the Delaware River. With 12-foot-high ceilings and Chippendale or Queen Anne furniture (some of it authentic), the four spacious rooms each have private baths, air-conditioning, cable TV, and queen-size beds. Rates are $69 to $98, depending on the season. Continental breakfast is included. Visa, MasterCard, and Discover are accepted.

The **Armitage Inn** (☎ 302-328-6618, No 2 on The Strand) has the grandest location, fronting right on the park, with the river vistas just 100 yards away. Steve and Rina Marks recently restored this colonial townhouse, which was built in 1732, to its original splendor and beyond. The public rooms are a treasure trove of antiques, family heirlooms, and an eclectic collection of original art. The four guest rooms feature elegant colonial reproductions, canopy beds, and private baths. The homemade kugel (a sweet noodle pudding) and carefully brewed gourmet coffee make for a rich breakfast. Rates are $105 to $135.

For a Victorian manor experience, try the **Fox Lodge at Lesley Manor** (☎ 302-328-0768, 123 West 7th St). This Gothic Revival mansion features a five-story tower, 13-foot ceilings, and three guest rooms with rates from $105 to $185. One other thing: ask owner Elaine Class about the frequent sightings of ghosts in the house – including a mysterious aviator – or post a watch yourself.

After being closed by a devastating fire, the Colonial-style **David Finney Inn** (☎ 302-322-6367, 219 Delaware St) reopened at the end of 1998. Two suites above the restaurant with fireplaces and kitchens are available for $225. A bedroom runs $175.

If you're unable to find a vacancy in the historic district, or if you want something else, head 2 miles west of the village to Route 13 (Du Pont Hwy), where you will find a variety of motels. Among the cheapest is **Hollywood Motel** (☎ 302-322-3070, 145 S Du Pont Hwy), with singles or doubles for $25 and a two-bed room for $35. Next door, **Super 8 Motel**

(☎ 302-322-9480, 215 S Du Pont Hwy) has singles/doubles for $44/51.

The **Econo Lodge** (☎ 302-322-4500, 232 S Du Pont Hwy) has singles/doubles for $49/54 with continental breakfast. **Rodeway Inn** (☎ 302-328-6246, 111 S Du Pont Hwy) is probably the nicest motel along this stretch. Rooms start at $59 and include a fridge and microwave, as well as continental breakfast.

Places to Eat & Drink

If you are just out for a stroll, stop in at the ice-cream bar at **O'Donalds Variety** (☎ 302-322-4272, 308 Delaware St) to get a cone for the road (under $2). The **Cellar Gourmet Restaurant** (☎ 302-323-0999, 208 Delaware St) is the place to go for a cup of coffee or for a variety of light meals, such as quiches, salads, sandwiches, ice creams, waffles, and other desserts for $3 to $7. It's open daily.

For something grander, try the **Arsenal on The Green** (☎ 302-328-1290), on Market St. Housed in the 1809 Arsenal, this restaurant offers an elegant but informal setting. Afternoon tea is served on Friday and Saturday from 2:30 to 4:30 pm. Sunday brunch is served 11:30 am to 2:30 pm. Lunch (around $20 per person) and dinner ($30 and up) are served daily.

Jessop's Tavern (☎ 302-322-6111, 114 Delaware St) has replaced the Green Frog. This is the town's English pub (built in 1724). The tavern is open 9 am to 1 am Monday to Saturday and is a friendly place for pub fare such as fish and chips ($11) – it won a Best of Delaware award. A bowl of oyster chowder runs $5. There is a lively mixed crowd here on weekend nights, and there is Celtic music with a harp, flute and tin whistle at least once a week. The David Finney Inn (see Places to Stay, earlier) is just up the street and has good dinner values, such as the grilled chicken breast platter for $8.

On Route 13, **Lone Star Steakhouse & Saloon** (☎ 302-322-3854, 113 S Du Pont Hwy) has become a popular spot with locals and visitors alike. This casual, cowboy-theme restaurant with sawdust on the floor serves up burgers, ribs, and steaks. Meal prices vary from $10 to $20 per person. Along this same busy stretch of Route 13, you will find an array of other chain and fast-food restaurants.

Shopping

More than 10 attractive shops along Delaware St justify a browse. You will find few bargains, but you might discover something you like for yourself or as a gift. Heartstrings, on the 2nd floor of No 116, near Jessop's Tavern (see Places to Eat & Drink, earlier), has four rooms of antiques and collectibles. Raven's Nest, at No 204, also has antiques and estate jewelry.

Getting There & Away

Wilmington's DART (☎ 800-652-3278) bus system provides a service to and from New Castle. Take the No 15 bus ($1.15) for the 15-minute ride.

If coming by car from the south on I-95, take exit 5, Route 141S, toward New Castle. Continue past the overpass of Routes 13 and 40. At the intersection of Routes 9 and 273, turn left onto Route 9N. Go half a mile to the next light, and bear right onto Delaware St to enter historic New Castle (look for the River Plaza Shopping Center on your left).

Approaching from the north on I-95, follow I-295 toward New Jersey. Take the last exit before paying the toll, Route 9S to New Castle. Follow Route 9S for about 2 miles. At the first stop sign, go straight ahead into New Castle, and turn left onto Delaware St at the first light (look for the River Plaza Shopping Center on your right).

Approaching from New Jersey on I-295 and the NJ Turnpike, take the Delaware Memorial Bridge into Delaware. At the first exit after paying the toll, take Route 9S to New Castle as detailed above.

NEWARK

Pronounced 'New Ark,' this is the home of the University of Delaware's main campus, as well as auto-assembly plants. It is also New Castle County's second-largest city. Newark (population 25,000) is primarily a college town and has little else to justify a visit. However, you might find that this is a great place to stay if you crave the strong coffee, heady conversations, cheap beer, and great

rock 'n' roll that go along with thousands of bright, young adults trying to squeeze excitement out of every moment.

The University of Delaware began here in 1765 and has bloomed into a 1000-acre campus with more than 16,000 full-time undergraduate and graduate students. You can find everything you might expect in the way of a university education here…as well as some things you might not expect – such as an experimental farm and a program in ice-skating science for Olympic hopefuls. Dozens of fraternities and sororities enroll 16% of the student body. More than half the students come from out of state; 89% are white; and women outnumber men seven to six.

Orientation

Main St east of the university is a one-way thoroughfare (westbound traffic) and is the heart of Newark's commercial life. Along this stretch of town lie stores, a post office, several banks, a shopping mall (the Newark Shopping Center, with a cinema), and various eating, drinking, and live-music venues. There is also an inexpensive motel here.

Places to Stay

Allowing you to step outside and stroll along Main St makes the ***Travelodge*** (☎ 302-737-5050, 268 E Main St) attractive. Standard motel-type singles/doubles are $45/55.

Two other motels in Newark are less centrally located. ***Howard Johnson*** (☎ 302-368-8521, 1119 S College Ave) is just off the intersection of I-95 at exit 1B (Route 896). Singles and doubles cost $55. Across the road, the ***Comfort Inn*** (☎ 302-368-8715, 1120 S College Ave) has singles/doubles for $54/61.

Places to Eat

The popular ***Klondike Kate's Saloon & Restaurant*** (☎ 302-737-6100, 158 E Main St) serves a wide selection of foods and has specials; meat loaf, pastas, pizza, burgers, and salads run from $6 to $20. It's open 11 am to 1 am daily.

Try the ***Post House Restaurant*** (☎ 302-368-3459), on E Main St, for breakfast under $3 and lunch for less than $5.50. It's not open for dinner.

Deer Park Tavern (☎ *302-731-5315, 108 W Main St*) has a history of its own. On this site, a log cabin was built in 1747. Called the St Patrick's Inn, it existed for nearly 100 years and served, among others, the surveyors Mason and Dixon (1764) and the writer Edgar Allan Poe (1843). The present building went up in 1851 and was named after the surrounding farmland, known as Deer Park. It was home to a women's seminary, a ballroom, a polling place, a barbershop, and also one of the region's finest hotels. This was the site of women's suffrage movements in 1913, and it became a forum for student activists in the 1960s.

Today's students still flock here, along with others who enjoy the somewhat rundown surroundings, the bar, and the primarily Mexican menu. Meals cost $2 to $7, and the very good Sunday brunch is $6 to $10. It is open 9 am to 1 am daily; you can hear live music most nights.

East End Cafe (☎ *302-738-0880, 270 E Main St*), next to the Travelodge, specializes in grilled burgers, chicken, and tuna sandwiches for under $6 and live entertainment every day except Monday and Tuesday. It's closed Sunday.

Crab Trap (*57 Elkton Rd*) claims to feature Newark's largest selection of draft beers, sandwiches for $4 to $5, and seafood entrees for $6 to $10. It's open 11 am to 1 am daily.

The Trap's competition is Newark's new brewpub, ***Iron Hill Brewery & Restaurant*** (☎ *302-277-9000, 147 E Main St*). This place is very popular with legions of the university alums who come back to town to relive their college days. Beers such as the Pig Iron Porter go for $3.50, but Wednesday night, you can get half-price pizza and pitchers (under $5). Sandwiches, such as the black-pepper chicken, go for $7. Catch the jazz brunch on Sunday.

Rainbow Books & Music (☎ *302-368-7738, 54 E Main St*) is a cafe selling a good selection of books and music.

Entertainment

The ***Stone Balloon Tavern & Concert Hall*** (☎ *302-368-2000, 115 E Main St*) has been rocking here for more than 25 years. This is one of the Capital Region's top music venues, with nationally renowned bands regularly featured here. Tickets vary from $5 to $12, depending on the artist.

Other places for live music along Main St are Deer Park Tavern (never a cover charge), the East End Cafe, and Iron Hill Brewery (Wednesday nights). See Places to Eat, earlier, for more information on these three places.

Getting There & Away

Newark is best reached by car. From I-95, take exit 1B to Newark. If you want to get here by bus, you can take DART (☎ 800-652-3278) bus Nos 6 or 33 from Wilmington for $1.90.

Central Delaware

South of the Chesapeake & Delaware Canal lies the heart of Delaware Bay country. Largely ignored by tourists rushing to and from Delaware's Atlantic beaches, central Delaware is a quilt of family farms and marshes. Amish people travel the roads by horse and buggy; bayside fishing communities endure; swamps spread to the edge of the bay; tidal rivers snake throughout the countryside; and important wildlife refuges shelter tens of thousands of migratory Canada and snow geese. Here you will discover funky fishing ports, as well as historic settlements – including Brigadoon-like Odessa and the state capital of Dover, with its village Green and 18th-century public buildings.

Life in central Delaware is distinctly slower, more rural, and more conservative than you will find at either end of the state. Here in bay country, a soft drawl similar to that heard on Maryland's Eastern Shore (clearly a kindred region) replaces the Pennsylvania twang you hear in the speech of people living north of the canal. The traditional lifestyles of the waterman, farmer, and progger persist. For fun, people head to the fairs, hunt all types of beasts and fowl, or go fishing. But the 21st century is never far away. Dover has a NASCAR raceway and an active air-transport base flying gigantic C-5 Galaxies.

Much like southern Maryland, central Delaware has a hundred curious backwaters unknown to all but local citizens…and they're ripe for exploration by bicycle or small boat.

COASTAL HERITAGE GREENWAY

This is a spectacular backroad tour of bayside Delaware, which essentially follows Route 9 (also known as the River Rd) south from New Castle to where it joins Route 1/113 south of Dover. From here, the Greenway follows Routes 1 and 113 south to Lewes and Cape Henlopen. The Greenway is well marked with signs that plot your course along a narrow, blacktop road that winds through farmland, marsh meadows, and wildlife refuges. Along the way you will see historic farmhouses, watermen's wharves, and a whole village that is on the National Register of Historic Places.

For an excellent 40-page collection of maps and narratives relevant to the Greenway, call the Department of Natural Resources and Environmental Control (☎ 302-739-5285) or stop by the Greater Wilmington Convention Center and Visitors Bureau Information Center at milepost No 6 on I-95 between Wilmington and Newark.

Bring your insect repellent for any jaunts into the field you plan along the way: From the first hint of warm weather in the spring, Delaware's marshy lowlands breed fierce mosquitoes and no-see-ums.

Highlights

- Biking along the Heritage Greenway to discover coastal wilderness and funky ports
- Eating steamed crabs at Sambo's Tavern on the Leipsic River
- Bird watching during the fall or spring migration at Bombay Hook National Wildlife Refuge
- Public buildings from the 17th and 18th centuries around The Green in Dover

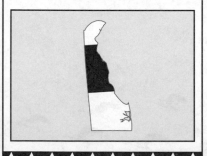

DELAWARE

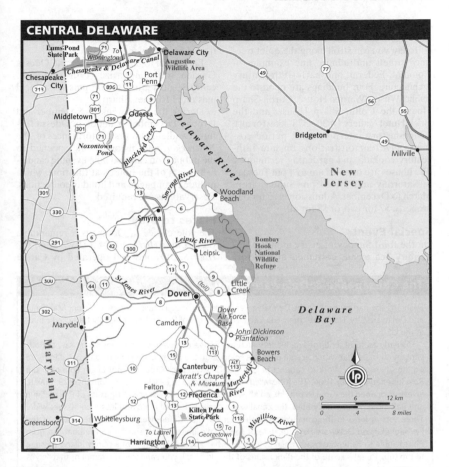

CENTRAL DELAWARE

ODESSA

About halfway between Wilmington and Dover, on Route 1/13, the village of Odessa, with its concentration of 18th- and early-19th-century buildings, can on a foggy morning appear like a mirage from another century. All of the village is on the National Register of Historic Places, and while most of the homes are private, Winterthur Museum owns three sites and opens them to the public.

Odessa is a great retreat for bicyclists, birders, and car-top boaters exploring the Greenway, tidewater creeks, and vast marsh-lands that stretch all the way from Delaware Bay to the doorsteps of Odessa's citizens.

Historic Houses

Originally settled by the Dutch and known in the 18th century as Cantwell's Bridge, Odessa was a busy grain-shipping port. In an effort to give the community world prominence as a grain port, citizens renamed their town in 1885 after the Ukrainian seaport that enjoyed international celebrity as a grain center. The public-relations maneuver did not work, and Odessa became another Delaware Bay port that time forgot until preservationists began

DELAWARE

to reclaim the decaying trove of historic buildings in the 1930s.

Today, you can stroll along the quiet tree-lined streets and admire fine examples of Colonial, Federal, and early-19th-century architecture. Four buildings are open to the public: Wilson-Warner House, Corbit-Sharp House, the Collin Sharp House, and the Brick Hotel Gallery (☎ 302-378-4069 for all). Living-history interpreters in period costumes give demonstrations on late-18th-century cooking and gardening techniques. The houses are open 10 am to 4 pm Tuesday to Saturday and 1 to 4 pm Sunday from March to December. Admission is $5 for one property, $7 for two, or $8 for all.

Special Events
On the third Sunday of every month, 18th-Century Tea means costumed interpreters prepare traditional afternoon snacks in the Collins-Sharp House. Reservations are required for the event.

Late April to late September, the Odessa Garden Tour emphasizes 19th- and 20th-century gardening techniques of a local master, H Rodney Sharp.

During the third week in November and through December, Yuletide in Odessa features candlelight tours, performances of *The Nutcracker*, and historic homes opened to the public. You can also take evening candlelight tours of the houses at this time, which include champagne and holiday confections. Reservations are required.

Places to Stay
The sole choice in Odessa is a remarkable B&B, *Cantwell House* (☎ *302-378-4179, 107 High St*). Owned and operated by Carole

---

The Chesapeake & Delaware Canal

Spanning the narrow neck of the Delmarva Peninsula for about 12 miles between Elkton, Maryland, and Delaware City, Delaware, the C&D Canal is one of the oldest and most heavily trafficked canals in the US.

As early as 1654, enterprising leaders such as Delaware's Swedish Governor Rising saw the advantage to trade that would accrue once the colonies on the Delaware were linked by canal to those on the Chesapeake. Work to connect St Georges Creek to Back Creek did not begin until after the Revolutionary War, in 1804. The job stalled for decades due to a lack of funds, but in 1829, private investors opened the canal to provide an all-water route between the swelling cities of Philadelphia and Baltimore. As originally built, the canal was a shallow 10 feet deep and less than 50 feet wide. Three sets of locks in the canal compensated for the tidal differences between the waters of the Chesapeake and Delaware Bays. In spite of the canal's limitations, it shortened the boat trip from Philadelphia to Baltimore by as much as a week, while adding the safety of a purely inland passage to the trip. To get a sense of the dimensions of the old canal, you can look at a remnant that serves as a boat basin in Delaware City today.

In 1919, the federal government bought the canal and began a 17-year project to widen and deepen the ditch. Today's canal is 450 feet wide with a controlling depth of 33 feet. Thousands of ships, seagoing tugs, and tows pass through the C&D every year. A good place to watch the action is at Schaefer's Canal House (☎ 410-855-2200), on Bank St, in North Chesapeake City, Maryland (like Delaware City, this place is really a village). At Schaefer's, you will see launches racing alongside passing ships, picking up and dropping off pilots to guide the ships through the Chesapeake and Delaware Bays.

The C&D Canal Museum (☎ 410-885-5622), at 2nd St and Bethel Rd, in Chesapeake City, features the old lock pump house and historical exhibits. It's open 8 am to 4:15 pm Monday to Saturday from Easter to Thanksgiving and 10 am to 6 pm Sunday; it's closed on holidays and Sunday in the winter. Admission is free.

★★★★★★★★★★★★★★★★★★★★★★★★★★★★★★★★

Coleman, it's a restored 1840 three-story house with four rooms. The rooms vary in size, and just one has a private bathroom. They cost $65 to $150, depending on the room and day of the week. A continental breakfast with home-baked items is included. High St is one block up the hill from the historic properties on Main St, and Cantwell House is the second house down from the library.

Getting There & Away
Odessa is about 23 miles south of Wilmington and 26 miles north of Dover. Route 13 runs past the western edge of the village; the historic houses lie a few blocks to the east. Route 299 makes a short link from Odessa to Route 9 and the Greenway.

LEIPSIC
Farther south on Route 9 is another small village that is home to a legendary eating place. *Sambo's Tavern* (☎ 302-674-9724), on Front St, in Leipsic, is one of the East Coast's most renowned crab houses. This place is friendly and informal, with newspaper-covered tables overlooking the meanders of the Leipsic River. There are also a few stools at the bar, a pool table, and a jukebox. A map of the world on one wall allows visitors to hang name-and-place tags to illustrate that people from far and wide continue to eat here. Crabs served in the shell are the main event. Expect to spend about $25 for a dozen steamed crabs. The menu also features crab cakes, shrimp, oysters, and various sandwiches, all from $3 to $16.

Sambo's is open 9 am (the kitchen is ready by 11 am) to 11 pm (with last orders at 10 pm) Monday to Saturday from April until the Saturday before Thanksgiving. The place can fill up during the summer, as well as whenever there is a major speedway event at Dover Downs or bird watching at Bombay Hook, so make reservations. Heading north 6 miles from Dover, Leipsic's one main street veers east off Route 9.

BOMBAY HOOK NATIONAL WILDLIFE REFUGE
This beautiful 15,918-acre site (☎ 302-653-9345) is a haven for migrating and resident

Spot a great blue heron at Bombay Hook.

waterfowl, primarily ducks and geese. Three-quarters of the refuge is tidal salt marsh. A visitor center encourages the public to visit the refuge for wildlife observation, nature study, and photography throughout the year. Very well organized, with informative signs posted throughout, the refuge is a joy to explore. You will find an auto tour route, observation towers, and nature trails. Call ahead to inquire about special events. Birders travel from all over the country, even the world, to watch the Canada and snow geese, heron, eagles, and other species that migrate or nest here.

The visitor center is open 8 am to 4 pm weekdays year-round. During the spring and summer, the center is also open 9 am to 5 pm weekends. The refuge itself is open from sunrise to sunset every day of the year. Admission is $4 per vehicle and $2 per person without a vehicle. To reach Bombay Hook headquarters, go about a mile north of the village of Leipsic on Route 9, then head east on Whitehall Neck Rd for 2 miles and look for the signs.

Standing on the northern edge of the refuge beside Route 9, **Allee House** is one of the best-preserved 18th-century brick farmhouses in the state. Believed to have been built in 1753, the house was restored in the 1960s and is now open to the public 2 to 5 pm weekends. Admission is free, and the

DELAWARE

house can be reached via the refuge auto tour or from Route 9, which is north of the entrance to the visitor center.

The *Mallard Lodge* on the property offers canoes and fishing gear, as well as cooking facilities and basic accommodations (36 bunks) for school groups and professional researchers who come to study the habitat. The facility rents for $50 for the day; it costs $50 extra if you stay the night.

LITTLE CREEK
Reached by the Greenway (Route 9), Little Creek is a small village of watermen, farmers, and their descendents on the Mahon and Little Rivers. The settlement lies about 4 miles east of Dover and the mammoth Dover Air Force Base. But Little Creek is a world of agricultural fields, farm stands, and crab traps stacked in front yards.

Roseland Estates
This farm (☎ 302-734-5277) lies about a mile south of Little Creek on Route 9. Here, Roseline Busch cultivates her raspberry vineyard and makes jellies, jams, cordials, brandies, and syrups. Prices for the jellies range from about $3 to $6.

Places to Stay & Eat
In 1999, Carol and Bobby Thomas opened the *Little Creek Inn Bed & Breakfast* (☎ *302-730-1300, 2623 Little Creek Rd*), about 2½ miles east of Dover. This is an Italianate frame farmhouse dating from the 1860s and listed on the National Register of Historic Places. Decorated with period furnishings, the rooms are nonetheless modern, with private baths (two with Jacuzzis), private phones, and satellite TV. There is a pool and sundeck behind the house, which stands on 8 acres of land amid cultivated fields. The most spectacular thing about staying here is that you get a gourmet dinner and breakfast included in the rate of $100 per person.

The *Village Inn* (☎ *302-734-3245*) is the place to come for beamed ceilings and candlelit dinners. Look for it on the west side of Route 9, south of the bridge crossing Little Creek. Chicken Chesapeake (sautéed breast topped with crabmeat) costs $17.

Entertainment
If you like the idea of catching a drink with the watermen and farmers after work, stop by the *Laughing Gull* (☎ *302-674-3171*), right next to the bridge on Main St. Duffy, the 70-plus-year-old woman who keeps bar, will serve you up a shot and a beer for less than $3, to the tunes of Willie Nelson and his country cousins.

DOVER
In the midst of central Delaware's farm country, Dover (population 32,000), the state capital, is an attractive town with a historical center and a collection of small museums. It is also a potential jumping-off point for historical and natural sights nearby. But in spite of the attractions, Dover does not draw flocks of tourists except during a few key weeks each year, when it is totally overwhelmed. These moments of chaos coincide with NASCAR racing events at the local speedway and the state fair in nearby Harrington.

During the rest of the year, the comings and goings of Air Force personnel to Dover AFB accounts for the bulk of Dover's transient clientele.

Despite being a state capital, Dover remains something of a farm town with the feel of one of those rural all-American communities where almost everyone knows everybody and life is just a little simpler than it is in the rest of the USA. It is not uncommon to hear the state governor and a police officer greet each other by their first names.

History
Originally planned as the courthouse seat for Kent County, Dover became the state capital in 1777, when the Delaware legislature wanted a safer location inland as an alternative to New Castle. This arrangement became permanent in 1792. On December 7, 1787, Dover Green was the site of the Delaware convention that ratified the Federal Constitution, making Delaware the first state to do so and thus giving the state ceremonial precedence in national ceremonies.

DOVER

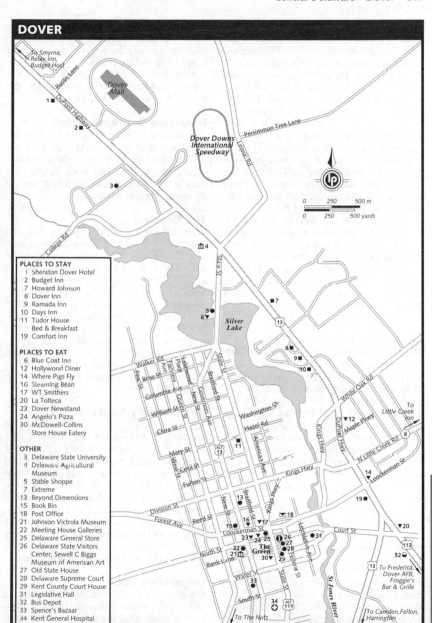

PLACES TO STAY
1 Sheraton Dover Hotel
2 Budget Inn
7 Howard Johnson
8 Dover Inn
9 Ramada Inn
10 Days Inn
11 Tudor House
    Bed & Breakfast
19 Comfort Inn

PLACES TO EAT
6 Blue Coat Inn
12 Hollywood Diner
14 Where Pigs Fly
16 Steaming Bean
17 WT Smithers
20 La Tolteca
23 Dover Newstand
24 Angelo's Pizza
30 McDowell-Collins
    Store House Eatery

OTHER
3 Delaware State University
4 Delaware Agricultural
    Museum
5 Stable Shoppe
7 Extreme
13 Beyond Dimensions
15 Book Bin
18 Post Office
21 Johnson Victrola Museum
22 Meeting House Galleries
25 Delaware General Store
26 Delaware State Visitors
    Center, Sewell C Biggs
    Museum of American Art
27 Old State House
28 Delaware Supreme Court
29 Kent County Court House
31 Legislative Hall
32 Bus Depot
33 Spence's Bazaar
34 Kent General Hospital

DELAWARE

Orientation

Located almost literally in the center of the state, Dover is 45 miles south of Wilmington, 86 miles southeast of Baltimore, and 77 miles south of Philadelphia. Visitors will spend most of their time in the downtown area and along Route 13 and Route 113. The downtown area is focused on Loockerman St, the main commercial street, with The Green, two blocks south, being the center of the historic government complex. There is free two-hour parking downtown, and there are several convenient parking lots for longer stays around Loockerman St. From any of these, you can stroll around the government buildings, shop, and eat.

Loockerman St runs west from Route 13. Virtually all accommodations and most restaurants stand along the commercial strip of Route 13 that separates the old town from the Air Force base and housing subdivisions that lie east of the highway. Route 13 runs between Dover and Wilmington. Route 113 and the new high-speed artery, Route 1, link Dover to the state's Atlantic beaches.

Information

The Delaware State Visitors Center (☎ 302-739-4266) is behind the Old State House, at 406 Federal St. It's open 8:30 am to 4:30 pm Monday to Saturday. In addition to general tourist information, the center also has a gallery of changing exhibits and a gift shop. Upstairs is the Sewell C Biggs Museum of American Art. Admission is free. There is also the Smyrna Information Center (☎ 302-653-8910), on Route 13 north of Smyrna, about 12 miles north of Dover; it's open 7 am to 8 pm daily on summer weekends and until 5 pm the rest of the year.

The main post office (☎ 302-734-5821) has the cryptic address of '55 the Plaza,' but it is actually on Loockerman St east of City Hall. It's open 8 am to 5 pm weekdays and 8 am to 3 pm Saturday.

Book Bin (☎ 302-678-9091), 207 Loockerman St, west of S Governors Ave, sells and trades used books. It's open 11 am to 5 pm Wednesday to Friday and 10 am to 2 pm Saturday. It sells national papers and magazines, and it also has coffee, breakfast, sandwiches, and soups to go. On Route 13, the Atlantic Book Warehouse, just south of the Dover Mall, has a large selection of popular titles at lower-than-average prices.

Coin Laundry (☎ 302-736-5002) is at 431 New St, and Kent General Hospital (☎ 302-674-4700) is at 640 S State St.

Delaware Supreme Court

The Supreme Court Building (☎ 302-739-4155) stands at No 55 on The Green. Built between 1909 and 1912, the courthouse was separated from the Old State House next door in 1974. It's open to the public 9 am to 4 pm weekdays and is free.

The Green

William Penn laid out this park in 1722, and little has changed here since. Then, as now, The Green was the center of life as the county seat, and it has always been the site of fairs and markets. Today's main events on The Green are the Old Dover Days celebrations and political rallies. It was here in 1775 that Delaware's Continental Regiment mustered before marching to join Washington's troops. In 1776, the Declaration of Independence was read to the public here. During the joyful celebration that immediately followed, there was a public burning of King George III's portrait.

Kent County Court House

At No 38 on The Green, this building was erected in 1874 on the site of the Court House of 1691. That was itself a replacement of an even earlier version that the court had ordered 'Burnt to get ye naiules [nails].' From about 1722 to 1863, a tavern occupied this site. A legend claims that the tavern had a portrait of King George III on its sign until patriotic yearnings caused the king's portrait to be painted out and replaced with a likeness of George Washington. It's open to the public 9 am to 4 pm weekdays. Admission is free.

Legislative Hall

Standing on Legislative Ave and built in 1932, this is where Delaware's General Assembly, made up of the Senate and House of Representatives, meets on the 1st floor. The governor's offices are on the 2nd floor. It's open 8:30 am to 4:30 pm weekdays. Admission is free.

Old State House

On S State St and The Green, you will find the country's second-oldest state house in continuous use; it was built in 1792. Guided tours provide information about legislative and judicial activities, as well as the period and reproduction furnishings and accessories on display. Visitors can also see an 18th-century courtroom and legislative chamber. It's open 10 am to 3:30 pm Tuesday to Saturday. Admission is free. For a free guided tour, inquire at the visitor center.

Johnson Victrola Museum

On Bank Lane and New St, this museum is a very interesting tribute to Eldridge R Johnson, who grew up in Dover and became a leading pioneer in the development of the talking machine and, subsequently, the record

business. He founded what is today RCA. (See the boxed text for more on Johnson.)

Set up like a 1920s Victrola dealer's store, the museum has an extensive collection of talking machines, early recordings (by the likes of Enrico Caruso), and an exhibit with Johnson's famous company trademark 'His Master's Voice,' featuring Nipper the dog. There is a small gift shop. It's open 10 am to 3:30 pm Tuesday to Saturday. Admission is free.

Meeting House Galleries

Located in a 1790s Presbyterian church at 316 S Governors Ave is Meeting House Gallery I, with an exhibition of 12,000 years of Dover's archaeological heritage.

Right next door to the former church, in an 1880s Sunday school, is Meeting House Gallery II, presenting a look at 'Main Street Delaware' – an exhibit on small-town life. With authentic displays incorporating original fixtures, you can see re-creations of a

Eldridge R Johnson: The RCA Legend

Born in Wilmington and raised in Dover, Eldridge R Johnson (1867–1945) became one of America's greatest individual business success stories. While it was Thomas Edison who invented the talking machine, Johnson invented many patented improvements on the basic design. Johnson is remembered today for his business acumen and vision, which greatly contributed to bringing music to the masses via records. He founded the Victor Talking Machine Co in Camden, New Jersey, the forerunner of today's RCA. The company's famous 'His Master's Voice' trademark, featuring Nipper the dog, became recognized around the world.

Johnson received a posthumous Grammy in 1985 and was cited for his contribution to the record industry with his invention of the first motor that allowed a disc talking machine to operate at uniform speed. The Academy said that Johnson transformed the talking machine 'from a scientific toy to a commercial article of great value.'

post office, a general store, a drugstore, a print shop, and carpentry from the 18th and 19th centuries. Both meeting houses are open 10 am to 3:30 pm Tuesday to Saturday; admission is free.

Sewell C Biggs Museum of American Art

If you go to 406 Federal St (upstairs from the main visitor center), you will find this museum, which houses a personal collection devoted to local artists. It's open 10 am to 4 pm Wednesday to Saturday and 1:30 to 4:30 pm Sunday. Admission is free.

Delaware Agricultural Museum

With the recent addition of another wing, this museum (☎ 302-734-1618), 866 N Du Pont Hwy (Route 13), is bigger and better. You can see two centuries of life on the farm portrayed here. An indoor display of farmer Americana includes a Swedish log house, vintage farm equipment and vehicles, dairy paraphernalia, and numerous other objects.

Outside, behind the exhibit hall, are life-size re-creations of an 1890s village and a 19th-century farmstead. The village includes a barbershop, general store, train station, school, and blacksmith and wheelwright's shop. The farmstead includes a farmhouse, garden, henhouse, privy, granary, animal pen, and corn house. The museum is open 10 am to 4 pm Tuesday to Saturday and 1 to 4 pm Sunday. Admission is $3 for adults and $2 for seniors and children.

Dover Air Force Base & Museum

Dover AFB is the second-largest industry in town (after state government). The base is the home for squadrons of the Military Airlift Command's giant C-5 Galaxy, one of the world's largest operational aircraft, and while you are in Dover, you will most likely see one of these monsters lumbering to or from the airfield.

But the C-5 is not the feature that distinguishes the base in the minds of most Americans. Dover AFB is the US military morgue – and as such it is known to hundreds of millions of TV watchers as the place seen on the evening news every time the US

government reclaims a dead American's body. It is the home of the flag-draped coffin, the sound of a rifle salute, and the trumpet dirge of 'Taps.' Victims of Guyana's Jonestown Massacre ended up here (in storage for months), as have political hostages, Gulf War casualties, and the bones of MIAs uncovered in Vietnam. Hang around with local citizens long enough, and you are sure to hear about all sorts of ghostly sightings.

The base museum (☎ 302-677-5938) is not a house of horrors, however. Here you will find an expanding collection of vintage planes, such as a B-17 Flying Fortress. Sometimes you can go aboard a C-5 Galaxy or sit in the cockpit of a C-141. The museum is open 9 am to 3 pm Monday to Saturday. Admission is free. To get there, take Route 113 for 2 miles south of Dover and follow signs to the main base gate. The security police will give you directions from there.

John Dickinson Plantation

John Dickinson was one of Delaware's leading statesmen during the Revolutionary and Federal periods. Built around 1740, his boyhood home is furnished with family pieces and antiques. Farm outbuildings and a log dwelling have been built to present an 18th-century plantation of the region. The museum (☎ 302-732-1808) is east of Route 113, 4 miles south of Dover. It's open 10 am to 4 pm Tuesday to Saturday and 1 to 4 pm Sunday. Admission is free.

Organized Tours

Dover Heritage Trail, Inc (☎ 302-678-2040), PO Box 1628, Dover, DE 19903, offers two good two-hour walking tours: Old Dover Historic District and Victorian Dover. Each costs $2 per person; call ahead for reservations.

Special Events

The following are special events in Dover you may want to plan your visit around:

Old Dover Days (early May) Here you have two days of celebrating Dover's heritage with a parade, Maypole dancing, arts & crafts, a Civil War military encampment, historic house tours, country dancing, a costume ball, and a re-creation of 19th-century baseball – a great time to visit.

NASCAR racing (early June and late September) Dover Downs International Speedway packs in more than 200,000 fans to bathe in the roar of supercharged Fords and Chevys.

Delaware State Fair (end of July) Hundreds of thousands of people descend on the little town of Harrington, about 4 miles west of Dover, for a monumental agricultural fair and carnival.

Indy Car Racing at Dover Downs (first weekend in August) This is Woodstock for East Coast speed demons and their groupies.

Bombay Hook Annual Field Day (early November) Grab your binoculars and head for the fresh salt air of the refuge marshes to watch tens of thousands of migratory geese and ducks.

Places to Stay

All of Dover's accommodations, except the B&Bs, are along a 1-mile stretch of Route 13, and there are a lot of chain motels from which to choose. But if you are coming here while a speedway event is being staged at Dover Downs, make reservations as far ahead as possible to secure a place to stay. (The major speedway races take place during the first weekend in June and the third weekend in September.) You will find modern, comfortable rooms with singles/doubles for around $40/50 at any of the following motels: the *Relax Inn* (☎ 302-734-8120); *Dover Inn* (☎ 302-674-4011); or the *Budget Host* (☎ 302-678-0161).

With more modern facilities and singles/doubles at $50/60, four motels stand out: *Budget Inn* (☎ 302-734-4433); *Comfort Inn* (☎ 302-674-3300); *Howard Johnson* (☎ 302-678-8900); and *Days Inn* (☎ 302-674-8002).

The *Sheraton Dover Hotel* (☎ 302-678-8500) has singles/doubles for $75/85. Facilities include an indoor pool, health club, and a hot tub. In addition to the Little Creek Inn Bed & Breakfast (see Little Creek, earlier in this chapter), two other inns have recently come to the Dover area.

The *Tudor House Bed & Breakfast* (☎ 302-736-1763, 228 N State St), near the center of town, has four rooms with private baths and air-conditioning. There is a pool and hot tub. No pets or kids are permitted; cats live here, too. Rooms run $75.

The *Rose Tower* (☎ 302-698-9033, 228 E Camden-Wyoming Ave), in Camden, is a rambling 18th-century mansion in the heart of the village of Camden, which is 4 miles southwest of Dover on the edge of Amish country farms. There are three rooms with private baths and air-conditioning for $76.

Places to Eat

The *Dover Newsstand*, on Loockerman St, serves coffee, breakfast, sandwiches, and soups to go, with items under $3. You pay about the same for similar fare at the *Steaming Bean*, across the street. *McDowell-Collins Store House Eatery (408 S State St)*, by The Green, is open weekdays. The Store House has just two tables and serves breakfast, bagels, and various snacks, mainly to go.

Hollywood Diner is an authentic 1950s diner run by an efficient team of women on the east side of Route 13, north of Junction 8. Breakfast runs about $4; the standard diner menu offers dishes mainly in the $4 to $7 range. It's open 24 hours.

WT Smithers (☎ 302-674-8875, 140 S State St) is named after the man whose childhood home this bar now occupies. William T Smithers (1876–1948) lived an eventful life as an orphan, sportsman, politician, soldier, lawyer, investor, and used-car salesman. Draft beer, wine, and food are available all day, such as appetizers, sandwiches, salads, pizza, seafood, steaks, and chicken. Sandwiches run $5 to $9, and dinner entrees cost $10 to $19. A Sunday jazz brunch runs noon to 3 pm.

If you want to see how central Delaware does Mexican, try *La Tolteca* (☎ 302-734-3444, 245 S Du Pont Hwy), where the Tex-Mex is served in a hacienda-style dining area. A chicken chimichanga for lunch costs about $5.

Locals say that *Angelo's Pizza* (☎ 302-678-9650, 20 Loockerman St) tops the list of pizza and sub vendors in town. Subs go for $5, and a large cheese pizza costs $9.

Where Pigs Fly (☎ 302-678-0586, 617 E Loockerman St), in the Edgehill Shopping Center, off Route 13, is Dover's place for ribs and barbecue. You can get a half rack of baby-back ribs here for under $7 at lunch; dinner entrees run about $9.

The posh, Colonial-style *Blue Coat Inn* (☎ 302-674-1776, 800 N State St) is beautifully situated overlooking Silver Lake, and its food tastes just as good as the place looks. Set in a former colonial home with stone fireplaces and antiques, the inn serves delicacies such as stuffed lobster tail for lunch ($11) and shrimp Rockefeller ($18) for dinner.

Some diners claim that Harry and David Thomas, at *The Nuts (☎ 302-678-0988, 1068 S State St)*, serve up the best steaks in Dover. The restaurant stands just before the spot where State St joins Route 13, south of downtown. With specialties such as Norwegian salmon and beef Wellington, dinner prices can exceed $18. It's open for lunch weekdays and for dinner Monday to Saturday.

Entertainment

WT Smithers (see Places to Eat, earlier) has a daily happy hour from 4:30 to 7 pm, with complimentary appetizers Wednesday and Friday. Smithers brings in a variety of cover bands on Thursday to Saturday nights and charges a $3 cover. The place is very popular with people of various ages, and the patio and deck out back get packed on warm weekend evenings.

Extreme (☎ 302-678-8118), at the Howard Johnson on Route 13, is currently one of Dover's hottest nightspots. It's open until 1 am nightly and attracts an under-25 crowd with rock, house, and hip-hop music. The cover charge varies, but plan on $5 or more; women get in free on Wednesday.

Froggie's Bar & Grille (☎ 302-678-1117, 348 Route 113) opened in the late '90s and immediately became popular with Dover's young crowd and Air Force personnel. This place features live rock 'n' roll five nights a week. The cover charge (after 10 pm) varies, but expect to pay $5 and up. When driving down Route 113 from Dover, stay to the left and follow the Route 10W signs. The club is on the left just after the overpass (look for the pizza sign). Be sure to turn off at the small exit road before the club. The next exit leads to another highway, with no exits for miles.

Spectator Sports

The *Dover Downs International Speedway (☎ 302-674-4600)*, east of Route 13 and just

north of the city center, is the host of popular NASCAR racing events in June and September. The raceway now has 215,000 seats and is in the process of adding even more. Nevertheless, you need to plan far ahead (a year is not unreasonable) to get good seats and a place to stay on these weekends.

Harness racing runs from November to March at Dover Downs, and there are slot machines on the premises.

Shopping

Spence's Bazaar, on New and Queen Sts, is a wonderful combination of flea market, farmers' market, and antique market. Established half a century ago, it operates from around 8 am to 4 pm each Tuesday and Friday. Some of the local Amish community participate. On Tuesday evenings, there are auctions starting at around 5:30 pm and lasting until 9 pm. Items found here range from furniture, antiques, and farm produce to tools, cars, and farm equipment.

Delaware General Store (☎ 302-736-1419) is in a delightful 18th-century house at 214 S State St. A showcase for local manufacturers, the store specializes in Delaware-made products. The Stable Shoppe, on N State St, is a lovely country store crammed with a wide selection of gifts and collectibles.

Beyond Dimensions (☎ 302-674-9070), 59 S Governors Ave, in a residential block, is a gift shop specializing in American-made handcrafted items. The shop has a slight New Age emphasis, but it has some traditional styles, too.

Rose Valley Quilt Shop is an Amish craft shop west of Dover. Take Route 8 (head west along Loockerman St) for about 5 miles. Turn left on Route 198 immediately after Byler's Country Store (☎ 302-674-1689), where you can buy craft items made by the local Mennonite Community. After a mile or so, you will see the quilt shop on your left. It's open 9 am to 6 pm weekdays except Thursday and 9 am to 5 pm Saturday.

Dover Mall, on Route 13, the capital's largest, is home to 100 stores, including JC Penney and Sears.

Getting There & Away

Greyhound/Trailways (☎ 302-734-1417, 800-231-2222) has two buses a day to and from Wilmington and the beaches. The bus station is at 650 Bay Court Plaza, south of town off Route 113.

DART (☎ 302-577-3278, 888-652-3278 toll-free in state) runs several buses (No 301) between Dover and Wilmington. A Dover-Wilmington ticket costs $4 – about half the Greyhound fare.

You can connect with DART buses in Dover that head south to the seashore (see Getting There & Away for Rehoboth Beach & Dewey Beach, in the Delaware Seashore chapter), but the connections involve long waits and several bus changes. A better way to go is to take the Greyhound ($7 to Lewes, $9 to Rehoboth).

By car, Route 13 from the north and Route 113 from the south are the major roads to and from the state capital.

BOWERS BEACH

About 8 miles south of Dover, off Route 113, at the end of Bowers Beach Rd, lies one of the most unforgettable fishing ports in the Capital Region. Bowers Beach squats at the mouth of the Murderkill River like a town dreamed up by Alfred Hitchcock. Rows of tilted, weathered Victorian structures line the main street, Hubbard Ave. Fifty-passenger party-fishing boats tie up along rickety wharves.

And when the boats return after seven-hour trips into the bay for weakfish (sea trout), bluefish, and flounder, the long rows of cleaning tables that overlook the wharves get packed with what the local captains call 'meat hunters.' Mostly men, these people are generally a mix of African Americans and Amish farmers who come with 50lb coolers to catch anything and everything – from toadfish to sharks – that the bay will provide.

If you'd like to go fishing, popular party boats run from Donavan's Dock (☎ 302-335-3500). Another option is to contact the Tradewinds (☎ 302-422-3474), a local party boat that carries fishers. A day of fishing will cost about $24. Rod rentals run $5.

Tony Cadiz is a friendly guy with the cheapest rooms within 75 miles of Bowers Beach at his **Bowers Old Inn** (☎ 302-335-3085, 46 Hubbard Ave). Tony has 10 simple rooms with double beds and a shared bath for $32 a night.

Where Hubbard Ave meets the docks on the river, you will find **JP's Wharf Seafood Restaurant** (☎ 302-335-4035). This modern seafood house has indoor dining, as well as outdoor dining on the deck overlooking the river. You can get fresh grilled yellow-fin tuna with two side orders for $13.

When all the fish have been cleaned, and the whole town smells like fish guts, a fair percentage of the crowd retires to the **Bay View Inn** (☎ 302-335-4201), on Hubbard Ave at Murderkill Ave. This gin mill looks like a cantina from a David Lynch film. Inside, the light is orange, and draft beer costs 75¢. Men in jeans and women in tight sweaters shoot pool, tell fish stories, drink beer, and listen to Elvis Presley on the jukebox until there is not a care in the world.

BARRATT'S CHAPEL & MUSEUM

Eleven miles south of Dover, on the east side of Route 113 and north of Frederica, this chapel (☎ 302-335-5544) is the 'cradle of Methodism' in America. Built in 1780 by local landowner Philip Barratt, the chapel is where the Methodists established the New World chapter of their congregation in 1784. It's open 10 am to 3:30 pm Tuesday to Saturday and 1:30 to 4:30 pm Sunday; it's closed on Sunday in January and February. Admission is always free.

Delaware's Diminishing Amish

Kent County has been home for a community of Old Order Amish since 1915. Not as well known as their Pennsylvania counterparts, the present population is an estimated 1200. Increased development west of Dover has impinged on Amish land, and families have been slowly relocating farther west to Kentucky, Missouri, and Kansas.

DELAWARE

Delaware Seashore

Delaware has 28 miles of sandy beaches on the Atlantic Ocean, running south from Cape Henlopen State Park, at the junction of the Delaware River and the ocean, to the Maryland border. State parks protect nearly half of the coastline from development, distinguishing the Delaware seashore from the New Jersey coastline to the north and Maryland's crowded Ocean City just down the coast to the south. Delaware's beach towns – Lewes, Rehoboth Beach, Bethany Beach, and Fenwick Island – each have a distinctive character. While it would be stretching the case to call these towns 'quaint,' each of Delaware's resorts seems like something of an oasis in comparison to the huge New Jersey and Maryland resort towns.

Highlights

- Browsing the shops and cafes in Lewes
- The sand dunes and beaches of Cape Henlopen
- People-watching and strolling on the Rehoboth Boardwalk
- Gourmet food in more than 40 Rehoboth restaurants
- The gay and lesbian scene in Rehoboth
- The nonstop beach-party scene in Dewey
- Miles of empty beach at Delaware Seashore State Park

Many of Washington, DC's more affluent and celebrated citizens have summer homes on the Delaware coast, and you will also find the small but proud Nanticoke tribe of Native Americans living on the fringe of the inshore bays here. During recent years, Rehoboth Beach has become popular with gay and lesbian vacationers, and a respectful atmosphere of open-mindedness has taken root. While families on one- or two-week vacations constitute half the resorts' visitors during the summer, Delaware's beaches have become romantic getaways for couples during the spring and fall. Lewes and Rehoboth have exceptional restaurants that far exceed the standard offerings of most American beach resorts. Like Ocean City, Maryland, Delaware's resorts – particularly Rehoboth Beach – are good places for a traveler with working papers to stop and get some seasonal employment to refill the kitty.

LEWES

Long considered by vacationers as simply the southern terminus of the Cape May–Lewes ferry and a gateway to Delaware's and Maryland's Atlantic beaches, Lewes (pronounced **loo**-is; population 2600) is an often-overlooked waterside retreat for upscale travelers and people who eschew populous beach resorts and like to surround themselves with a sense of history.

The town has a good beach on Delaware Bay, a number of historic buildings, some attractions, and a small but inviting eating and shopping district with shady Bradford pear trees – all within a half-mile radius of the center. Unlike the neighboring beach resorts, Lewes has the feel of a town that was here long before tourism: For centuries, Lewes has been the home of mariners and Delaware Bay pilots who guide ships up and down the bay and river.

In the same maritime spirit, Lewes is the site of the College of Marine Studies of the University of Delaware, which maintains a coastal park, harbor, and research vessels

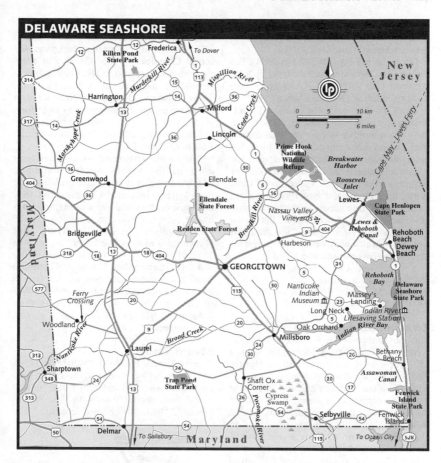

DELAWARE SEASHORE

here. There are good marinas for yachts, and sport-fishing boats that stage billfishing tournaments every summer.

History

The Dutch began to dispossess the resident Lenni Lenape with a whaling settlement at Lewes in 1631. The Native Americans killed the first settlers, but other Europeans followed to take advantage of the good natural harbor here behind the dunes of Cape Henlopen. Lewes is called the 'First Town in the First State' because of the original Dutch settlement, Zwaanendael (Valley of the Swans).

Mariners have sought shelter here ever since. For a short time, the port bore the name 'Whorekill,' testimony to rough days here.

Information

The Lewes Chamber of Commerce and Visitors Bureau (☎ 302-645-8073), at 120 Kings Hwy, in the 1730 Fisher-Martin house, behind the Zwaanendael Museum, distributes a useful guide to the town's buildings and businesses. They also provide a walking-tour map. The chamber is open year-round 10 am to 4 pm weekdays; during the summer, it's also open 10 am to 2 pm Saturday.

The post office takes up a small block in the commercial center of town, on Front St between Bank St and Neil Alley.

Books by the Bay (☎ 302-645-2304), 103 2nd St, is an expanding store owned by John Allwood that sells new books and has a good selection of Delaware history.

The *Cape Gazette* is the seashore's comprehensive weekly newspaper. In addition, there are a number of free weeklies distributed up and down the coast, with the usual entertainment information and ads for restaurants, motels, and every other kind of business. You can pick these up in most stores, restaurants, and motel lobbies along the coast. The free papers – which come and go – include the *Beachcomber*, the *Coast Press*, *Delaware Beach Guide*, and the *Delaware Wave*, which has more news than restaurant and activity information.

You can find Quick Wash (☎ 302-645-8542) at 411 Kings Hwy.

Beebe Memorial Hospital (☎ 302-645-3300) is at 424 Savannah Rd.

Zwaanendael Museum

This museum (☎ 302-645-1148), at the intersection of Kings Hwy and Savannah Rd, is a 1931 replica of the town hall in Hoorn, Holland. The small museum has several professionally curated exhibits, the largest of which is a collection of items retrieved from the sunken treasure brig *deBraak*, which went down in 1798 and was excavated in 1984. The museum also has a collection of period household items. It's open 10 am to 4:30 pm Tuesday to Saturday and 1:30 pm to 4:30 pm Sunday. Admission is free.

Nassau Valley Vineyards

If you wind your way to 36 Nassau Commons (take Route 1N to the Nassau Bridge, then follow the signs), you will find the vineyard cellars and sales building of Nassau Valley Vineyards (☎ 302-645-9463). This is a great place to bring a picnic, as it is surrounded by an orchard and picnic tables. You can get a tour and tasting of five wines, including Chardonnay and rosé, for free. Bottles run $7 to $12. Hours are 11 am to 5 pm Tuesday to Saturday and noon to 5 pm Sunday.

Historic Buildings

Seven structures built during the 17th and 18th centuries are collected at the **Lewes Historical Complex** (☎ 302-645-7670), at Shipcarpenter Square and 3rd St. They include a farmhouse, a store, and a doctor's office. There is also a reading room with material on Delaware history. Admission is $4, or $5 for a guided tour. It's open 10 am to 3 pm Tuesday to Friday and to 12:30 pm Saturday from mid-June until Labor Day.

The Lewes Historical Society maintains most of the town's historic buildings. The following two important buildings are outside the Historical Complex, but they are open at the same times as the buildings in the complex and are accessible on the same admission ticket. The **Ryves Holt House**, at 2nd and Mulberry Sts, built in 1665, is probably the oldest house in the state. The **Cannonball House**, at Front and Bank Sts, is celebrated because the British fired a cannonball into it during the War of 1812. (A lot of towns celebrate their cannonball houses.) It now has a marine museum inside.

Steam Train

Queen Anne's Railroad (☎ 302-644-1720), 730 Kings Hwy, runs one-hour daytime excursions over 18 miles of track, as well as 2½-hour dinner trips, with their steam-powered locomotive and coaches. The

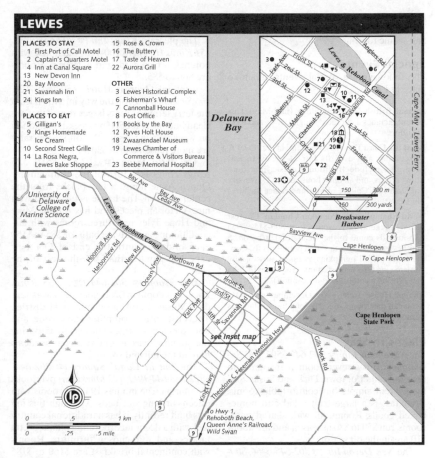

LEWES

PLACES TO STAY
1 First Port of Call Motel
2 Captain's Quarters Motel
4 Inn at Canal Square
13 New Devon Inn
20 Bay Moon
21 Savannah Inn
24 Kings Inn

PLACES TO EAT
5 Gilligan's
9 Kings Homemade Ice Cream
10 Second Street Grille
14 La Rosa Negra, Lewes Bake Shoppe
15 Rose & Crown
16 The Buttery
17 Taste of Heaven
22 Aurora Grill

OTHER
3 Lewes Historical Complex
6 Fisherman's Wharf
7 Cannonball House
8 Post Office
11 Books by the Bay
12 Ryves Holt House
18 Zwaanendael Museum
19 Lewes Chamber of Commerce & Visitors Bureau
23 Beebe Memorial Hospital

excursions run four days a week and cost $9 for adults and $7 for children (bring a picnic lunch). Dinner trains with full dining service, plus murder-mystery theater, cost $115 per couple and run most weekend nights during the summer (Saturday only through New Year's Day).

Fishing

Party and charter boats leave from Fisherman's Wharf on the east side of the Lewes & Rehoboth Canal (☎ 302-645-8862). The marina also rents small fishing boats for about $75 a day.

Dolphin & Whale Watching

Pappy's Lady and other vessels usually run a daily whale-watching trip and a dolphin-watching trip out of Fisherman's Wharf (☎ 302-645-8862) June through September. The dolphin-watching trip last two hours and costs $12 for adults and $7 for children; the whale-watching trip last four hours and costs $21 for adults and $11 for children.

Bicycling

If you didn't bring a bike, you can get one at Lewes Cycle Sports (☎ 302-645-4544), 514 Savannah Rd. Bikes cost $9 to $14 per day

DELAWARE

and are a better deal at $23 to $39 a week. The town streets and paths make for quiet and scenic touring.

Special Events

The following are special events that take place in Lewes:

Annual British Motorcar Show (mid-May) This event includes a parade through Lewes and food vendors.

Boast the Coast Day (first weekend in October) A street fair and a crafts fair at the historical complex include traditional music, maritime tower tours, and an open house at the University of Delaware College of Marine Science facilities in Lewes.

World Championship Pumpkin Chunkin' Contest (first weekend in November; ☎ 800-515-9095) Thousands come to the village of Harbeson, 5 miles west of Lewes, to watch pumpkins fly. Contestants propel pumpkins as far as possible by any means. One winner chunked a pumpkin 2655 feet (using a compressed-air cannon).

Annual House Tour (early December) For $10, you can participate in a day-long tour of famous houses in town.

Places to Stay

The *Savannah Inn* (☎ 302-645-5592, 330 Savannah Rd) is a seven-room year-round inn near the center of town. Dick and Susan Stafursky rent simple but comfortable rooms. Breakfast is a large fruit salad and home-baked goods. Rooms, all with shared bathrooms, run $50 to $80 in season and are about $10 less in the off season.

The *New Devon Inn* (☎ 302-645-6466, 800-824-8754) is a restored 1920s brick hotel on the corner of 2nd and Market Sts. The 25 rooms come in three sizes, are decorated with antiques, and have private modern bathrooms (no televisions, but there is a TV room). Rates include a bed turndown with cordials and breakfast. In-season rates are $50 to $175; off-season rates are $45 to $110.

First Port of Call Motel (☎ 302-645-2126), in a not very enticing location across from the ferry terminal, rents small, standard motel rooms with air-conditioning and television for $55 in season. It also sells sandwiches and bait and tackle. The management here is so laid back that they don't always answer knocks on the office door.

The pleasant *Kings Inn* (☎ 302-645-6438, 151 Kings Hwy) is a 100-year-old house with porches, a backyard, and a Jacuzzi. Rooms are $60 to $85.

Captain's Quarters Motel (☎ 302-645-7924, 406 Savannah Rd), on the way into town from the ferry terminal, rents larger rooms that are clean but musty for $60 on weekdays and $85 on weekends in season. The off-season rates are more reasonable at $30/40.

The *Wild Swan* (☎ 302-645-8550, 525 Kings Hwy) is a turn-of-the-19th-century Queen Anne house a few blocks from the center of town. The house is furnished with nice Victorian pieces and has a pool. Mike and Hope Tyler rent three rooms with air-conditioning and private bath for $85 to $150 each mid-May until the end of October; expect to pay less than $80 the rest of the year.

Bay Moon (☎ 302-644-1802, 128 Kings Hwy) is a popular B&B near the Zwaanendael Museum and the commercial district. The hosts offer complimentary wine and hors d'oeuvres. Rates start at $105 during the summer season, but you can get deals here in the fall and spring.

The *Inn at Canal Square* (☎ 302-644-3377, 888-644-1911, 122 Market St) overlooks the marina. The inn has 19 large rooms with queen- or king-size beds. Although this inn was built recently, it has a traditional country feel, with a decor incorporating plants, pretty fabrics, and well-chosen furniture. Rooms with continental breakfast are $160 to $185 in season and $85 to $125 off season.

Places to Eat & Drink

The *Lewes Bake Shoppe* (124 2nd St) is a small coffee shop where you can get your breakfast caffeine and sugar fix for under $3. The shop also sells coffee beans and baked goods to go. *Kings Homemade Ice Cream* (201 2nd St) is a must-stop if you have a sweet tooth.

If you want a neighborhood diner with high-quality home-style cooking, head for the *Aurora Grill* (☎ 302-645-2327, 329 Savannah Rd), across from the Savannah Inn (see Places to Stay, earlier). The menu offers breakfast all day; lima-bean soup made with large, locally grown beans; and sandwiches and subs ($2.75 to $5).

Gilligan's (☎ *302-645-7866*) is an intimate little place with a deck and waterfront view of the canal at the end of Market St. You can get sandwiches and salads for lunch ($6 to $8); dinner entrees such as ginger-rubbed sea bass run in the $15 to $24 range.

There are several places to eat among the shops on 2nd St. The *Second Street Grille* (☎ *302-644-4121, 115 2nd St*) is an upscale sandwich ($6) and entree place with a lot of seafood on the menu, but the specialty of the house is the grilled lamb chops and venison in dry cherry Grand Marnier sauce ($26).

The *Rose & Crown* (☎ *302-645-2373, 108 2nd St*) is a modern bar and restaurant that looks like something out of the Gay Nineties, with gold-painted tin ceiling, brass rails, and etched glass. Sandwiches go for $5 to $7. Dinners such as stuffed flounder run $16. Live rock is offered on weekends, when there is a youngish but mixed crowd. Usually there is no cover.

The Buttery (☎ *302-645-7755*) is a bistro-style restaurant in a restored Victorian house with dining porch at the corner of Savannah Rd and 2nd St. The menu here features nouvelle cuisine. If you come before 6:30 pm, you can eat prix-fixe specials, such as Norwegian salmon for $15.

Once just a popular cafe and deli, *Taste of Heaven* (☎ *302-644-1992, 107 Savannah Rd*) has gone upscale and moved. This place remains a popular lunch spot where you can sit on the porch of a compact Victorian house, sip a latte ($2.50) and munch a porta-bella mushroom sandwich on a French baguette ($7). Candlelit dinners feature international cuisine in the $20 range.

La Rosa Negra (☎ *302-645-1980, 128 2nd St*) is a romantic Italian bistro with a chef who gets rave reviews from the locals. The menu constantly evolves, but try the black sesame-and peanut-crusted tuna steak ($20) if you can get it. If you are planning on this place for a weekend evening during the summer, you will need a reservation.

Getting There & Away
Greyhound/Trailways (☎ 302-734-1417, 800-231-2222) has one bus a day to and from Wilmington and Dover. The fare is $14 to Wilmington and $7 to Dover. The stop is in front of the Ace Hardware building at the intersection of Route 1 and Route 9. Lewes is tucked right behind Cape Henlopen at the entrance to Delaware Bay. It is accessible by Routes 1 or 9.

Travelers exploring the mid-Atlantic coast can take the Cape May–Lewes Ferry (☎ 800-643-3779 for schedules, ☎ 800-717-7245 for car reservations) to save themselves the hours it takes to drive around Delaware Bay from the beaches of Cape May, New Jersey, to reach the Delaware beaches. The ferry has daily year-round service between the two points. The trip lasts 70 minutes and can have the pitching and rolling associated with an ocean voyage, because the ferries transit the often rough, open mouth of Delaware Bay: If you are prone to seasickness, you may want to consider a morning passage, when the wind and seas are generally at their calmest. The five new enormous ferries can carry more than 800 passengers and 100 cars. There is onboard dining (not just snacks) on the Lido Deck and sometimes even entertainment.

The fare is $6.50 one way ($12 roundtrip) for adults and $3.50 one way or roundtrip for children under 12. Vehicles cost $20 to $65 (one way) according to length; bikes cost $7; motorcycles cost $17. All rates are decreased December to March. The Lewes ferry terminal (☎ 302-664-6030) is next to the Cape Henlopen State Park entrance, a mile from the center of Lewes; follow the signs.

Getting Around
The Jolly Trolley (☎ 302-645-6800) runs people from the ferry terminal in and around Lewes for $2 from May to September.

DART runs buses from Lewes to Rehoboth and Dewey Beaches, making frequent stops along Business Route 9 and Routes 1 and 1A. The buses run from around 7 or 8 am to around 10 or 11 pm Memorial Day to Labor Day. For $1, you get a pass good for riding from 7 am to 4 pm.

CAPE HENLOPEN STATE PARK

This 3143-acre park is on the Atlantic coast east of Lewes. In the 19th century, part of Cape Henlopen served as a quarantine station for immigrants. Later, the cape was a major coastal defense to protect Delaware Bay from attack by German submarines during WWII. There was no state park here until the Department of Defense gave the land to the state in 1964; consequently, the park is festooned with abandoned bunkers, gun emplacements, buildings, and other military fixtures. Some small active Navy buildings still remain.

Most of the cape is now a park, but the overall effect is of a reclaimed place, rather than of an eternally pristine one. The landscape includes a lot of small pine trees, high dunes, and dune grass. In addition to the unpopulated bay and sea shores, some of the park's most interesting geographical features are the so-called walking dunes, which are actually migrating through the pine forest. Gordon's Pond Wildlife Area has a big lagoon at its heart that is a good place for bird watching. Recently, the park has added biking paths, and the White Bike Program offers free bikes to visitors who did not bring their own.

The park is open 8 am to dusk daily. Fees ($2.50 for Delaware license plates, $5 for others) are collected from Memorial Day to Labor Day and on weekends in April, September, and October.

Information

You can pick up information at the park office (☎ 302-645-8983), about 800 feet south of the fee-collection booth on the way in. The office is open 8 am to 4:30 pm daily from April to October and weekdays only the rest of the year.

The Seaside Nature Center (☎ 302-645-6852) is on the left side of the road running straight past the fee booth. The nature center has an extensive series of educational programs, hikes, and educational courses for visitors. The staff also sponsors concerts, a Halloween spook trail, and bird watching, and they distribute pamphlets for self-guided trails.

Things to See & Do

On the coast near the shore is the huge **Great Dune**, one of the tallest sand dunes on the Atlantic Coast. You can climb the 105 steps of the observation tower in the middle of the park for a view of Cape May, New Jersey; the Atlantic; and the beach resorts.

There are **swimming** areas with lifeguards, bathrooms, etc at the northern and southern ends of the park. Each end also has a food concession.

The park has a **fishing** pier with a bait and tackle shop, Hoss's Pier One (☎ 302-645-2612), right next to it.

Places to Stay

The *campground* (☎ 302-645-2103) has 159 sites that are rented out on a first-come, first-served basis at the center of the park at $16 per site. There is also a 'primitive' youth camping area with minimal services. The rates are the same.

REHOBOTH BEACH & DEWEY BEACH

Delaware's most popular beach, Rehoboth, is a small coastal town 8 miles south of Lewes that swells to become the state's second-largest city each summer, when its permanent population of 4000 explodes to 50,000. Starting in June, vacationers arrive from DC, Baltimore, Wilmington, Philadelphia, and central Pennsylvania.

By comparison to Ocean City, Maryland, 20 miles south of here, Rehoboth is still small enough to have some charm. The town can be a great place to stroll or bike, with tree-lined streets, duck ponds, lagoons, and green spaces among neighborhoods of beach houses trimmed in clapboard and cedar shingles. There are small, neat yards and lots of flowers. Modern oceanfront resort motels and hotels break some of Rehoboth's spell as you get closer to the waterfront.

The commercial strip along Rehoboth Ave has something of a honky-tonk feel, with T-shirt emporiums, fast-food stands, and a thousand short-term parking spaces. However, a 'Main Street Restoration Project' is under way with hopes of restoring Rehoboth Ave to its appearance of a hundred years ago.

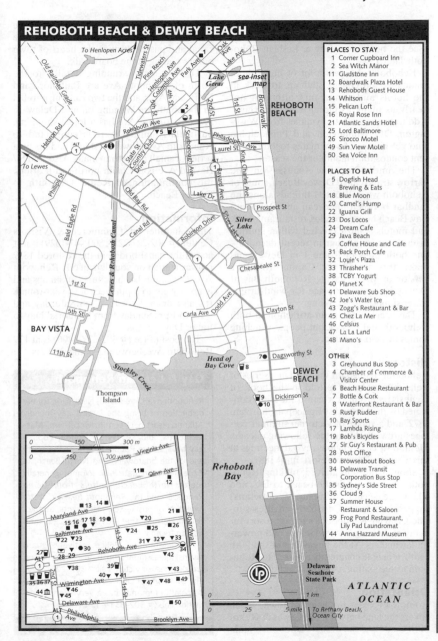

REHOBOTH BEACH & DEWEY BEACH

PLACES TO STAY
1 Corner Cupboard Inn
2 Sea Witch Manor
11 Gladstone Inn
12 Boardwalk Plaza Hotel
13 Rehoboth Guest House
14 Whitson
15 Pelican Loft
16 Royal Rose Inn
21 Atlantic Sands Hotel
25 Lord Baltimore
26 Sirocco Motel
49 Sun View Motel
50 Sea Voice Inn

PLACES TO EAT
5 Dogfish Head
   Brewing & Eats
18 Blue Moon
20 Camel's Hump
22 Iguana Grill
23 Dos Locos
24 Dream Cafe
29 Java Beach
   Coffee House and Cafe
31 Back Porch Cafe
32 Louie's Pizza
33 Thrasher's
38 TCBY Yogurt
40 Planet X
41 Delaware Sub Shop
42 Joe's Water Ice
43 Zogg's Restaurant & Bar
45 Chez La Mer
46 Celsius
47 La La Land
48 Mano's

OTHER
3 Greyhound Bus Stop
4 Chamber of Commerce &
   Visitor Center
6 Beach House Restaurant
7 Bottle & Cork
8 Waterfront Restaurant & Bar
9 Rusty Rudder
10 Bay Sports
17 Lambda Rising
19 Bob's Bicycles
27 Sir Guy's Restaurant & Pub
28 Post Office
30 Browseabout Books
34 Delaware Transit
   Corporation Bus Stop
35 Sydney's Side Street
36 Cloud 9
37 Summer House
   Restaurant & Saloon
39 Frog Pond Restaurant,
   Lily Pad Laundromat
44 Anna Hazzard Museum

DELAWARE

Rehoboth's clientele is a genial mix of white families and a sizable gay community. (See the boxed text Gay & Lesbian Rehoboth, later.)

Rehoboth also gets a lot of high-school graduates and college students to work in the hotels and restaurants, although not nearly as many as Ocean City, Maryland. Add to this mix a lot of yuppies from Washington, DC, Wilmington, and Philadelphia who get groups of soul mates together and rent condos for a month or the season.

The under-30 scene focuses on the narrow strand called Dewey Beach, south of Rehoboth where Route 1 threads along the sandbar between the ocean and Rehoboth Bay. Beach houses, condos, restaurants, bars, and motels – most erected within spitting distance of each other in recent decades – line both sides of Route 1 in Dewey and make this strand the Capital Region's version of Margaritaville. Rehoboth Bay at Dewey is a popular place for windsurfing, water-skiing, and Jet Skiing.

The beach is the main attraction in both Rehoboth and Dewey, but people-watching comes in a close second.

History

Rehoboth (named for the third in a series of wells dug by Isaac, as told in the book of Genesis) started as a camp meeting convened by the Methodist Episcopal Church in 1872, and a village of Victorian summer cottages grew quickly in the following decade. Methodists held religious revival meetings at this 'Christian seaside resort' until 1881.

Soon, a rail line arrived, making Rehoboth the closest Atlantic beach to DC, and when the secular influence (politicians) slipped into town, Christian activities subsided, leaving Rehoboth a summer resort for many of America's most famous and powerful lawmakers. At the beginning of the 20th century, people commonly referred to Rehoboth as the 'nation's summer capital.'

Orientation

Route 1 bypasses the heart of town, which covers the land between the Lewes & Rehoboth Canal and the ocean. Rehoboth's main east-west avenue is called Rehoboth Ave (Route 1A); it crosses a bridge over the canal and passes through the heart of town before ending at the boardwalk.

The two streets running parallel to the north of Rehoboth Ave are Baltimore and Maryland Aves, and the two running parallel to the south are Wilmington and Delaware Aves. Baltimore Ave has a lot of shopping, particularly antiques. It is connected to Rehoboth Ave between 1st and 2nd Sts by a series of small pedestrian malls. Also, 2nd St/Bayard Ave is the main north-south artery, the continuation of Route 1A south to Dewey Beach.

Information

The Chamber of Commerce & Visitors Center (☎ 302-227-2233, 800-441-1329) is just across the canal bridge in the restored 1879 railway station on your left, at 501 Rehoboth Ave. The center has brochures and maps and is open 9 am to 5 pm weekdays year-round. It's also open 9 am to 2 pm Saturday and 9 am to 1 pm Sunday from Memorial Day to Labor Day.

The post office (☎ 302-227-8406) is at 179 Rehoboth Ave, between 1st and 2nd Sts.

Gay & Lesbian Rehoboth

Rehoboth rivals Fire Island, New York, for the distinction of being the largest gay-friendly Atlantic resort between Provincetown, Massachusetts, and Key West, Florida. Popular gay beaches are Poodle Beach, at the south end of the boardwalk, and North Beach, in Cape Henlopen State Park. Women generally prefer North Beach. *Letters from Camp Rehoboth* and the *Rehoboth Beach Gazette* have lists of businesses, restaurants, and accommodations that advertise as gay and lesbian friendly.

The Rehoboth Police actively guard against harassment and hate crimes. If you are a witness or victim, call ☎ 302-227-2577. The University of Delaware Lesbian, Gay, and Bisexual Community has a very useful information line (☎ 302-831-4114).

In addition to the giveaway shore papers, *Letters from Camp Rehoboth* is a free paper with more than 32 pages put out by members of Rehoboth's gay community. It has articles and advertisements and 'seeks to create a more positive environment of cooperation and understanding among all people.' The *Rehoboth Beach Gazette* is another gay-oriented paper that has made the scene in recent years. Lambda Rising (☎ 302-227-6969), 39 Baltimore Ave, stocks many gay and lesbian books, periodicals, and videos.

Browseabout Books (☎ 302-227-0905), at 133 Rehoboth Ave, has a complete stock of mainstream fiction and nonfiction.

For laundry, try the centrally located Lily Pad Laundromat (☎ 302-227-2234), at 5 1st St. The Frog Pond restaurant, next door, manages the Lily Pad, and more than a few patrons come for lunch or a beer while their laundry cycles itself clean.

For medical help, you will find Beebe Memorial Hospital (☎ 302-645-3300) in Lewes, at 424 Savannah Rd.

Facts & Fiction of Clam Digging

Some seaside wags will tell you that you can only 'catch' clams on a moonlit night, with a sharp rake that looks like a trenching tool. Others will tell you that the way to catch a Delaware clam is to wade into the ocean, then start to feel around in the sand with your toes until they curl around something hard and smooth. Well…maybe. But the success of such efforts is far from guaranteed.

Two kinds of clams live along the Delmarva coast – hard-shell clams, sometimes called 'cherrystones,' and soft-shell clams, called 'steamers.' Hard-shell clams are by far the more prevalent of the two.

Delaware's conservation laws permit nonresident visitors to catch and keep up to 50 clams, and you can rent clam rakes and buckets from bait-and-tackle shops around Rehoboth Bay. But if you really want to get the thrill of catching your own clams – which has an addicting allure – forget the rake and be prepared for dirty fingernails: You will be using your hands.

Before you go, you might want to consult with a bait shop or check at the state parks for maps that tell you where the productive clam beds are. Next, get a plastic beach bucket to carry your catch, or wear shorts or a swimsuit with big pockets, and head for Rehoboth Bay at low tide. Try to find a place where the water is about 2 feet deep and the bottom is a composite of mud and sand.

When you're in a spot where the bottom has a silty texture, bend over and dig your fingers into the bottom to a depth of about your middle knuckles. Then begin squeezing your fingers together with your thumbs as if you were kneading bread dough.

Start close to your feet and explore the bottom in quadrants within a radius of 2 feet around you. When you find a clam, it might try to burrow away from you, so hang on. This clam is probably a hard clam, and you will likely find it among a colony of others, so don't lose your spot. After you have caught your clam, put it in your pocket and keep hunting until your pockets are full.

Most people will eat six to 12 clams, so harvest accordingly. If you buy a clam knife, you can open the cherrystones (don't try this without instruction) and eat the clams raw with a dash of lemon or lime or Tabasco. (Travelers with a weakened immune system should consult a doctor before indulging in raw clams, as the rare clam carries a parasite that can exacerbate an illness.) To steam your catch, fill the steamer pot with about 3 inches of liquid and steam for about 15 minutes, or until the clams have opened (*never* eat a steamed clam that hasn't opened unless you want really nasty food poisoning). Steaming with water – even seawater – is fine, but adding at least a touch of beer, white wine, and herbs will enhance the taste of the steamers. You can also dip the meat in melted butter, teriyaki sauce, or whatever you fancy.

Before you go clamming, make certain to check with the local shellfish warden or bait shops to learn where the clams are safe from diseases such as red tide.

Anna Hazzard Museum

The museum (☎ 302-226-1119) is in a former camp-meeting tent that was moved to its present location at the fork of Christian St and Wilmington Ave. The museum has items from the history of Rehoboth. It's open weekend afternoons from Memorial Day to Labor Day. Donations are encouraged.

Rehoboth Art League

This organization (☎ 302-227-8408), at 12 Dodds Lane, north of town in Henlopen Acres, sponsors summer and winter art classes, exhibitions, a 'Cottage Art Tour,' and performing-arts events. The Homestead mansion, one of the oldest homes in the area, is frequently the site of special events and exhibits.

Beach & Boardwalk

The beach is narrow in spots, but reclamation is ongoing. The boardwalk runs about a mile between Prospect and Surfside Sts, but the mellow commercial section is between Laurel and Olive Sts. It has a few arcades, some small indoor rides, and boardwalk food stalls. But compared with Maryland's Ocean City, the boardwalk here is a very subdued scene.

Water-sports enthusiasts will love Rehoboth.

DELAWARE TOURISM OFFICE

Jet Skiing & Boating

Bay Sports (☎ 302-227-7590), in the Ruddertowne complex, at the west end of Dickinson St in Dewey Beach, rents Jet Skis, sailboats, and sailboards. Jet Skis rent half-hourly for $40 to $60 and hourly for $60 to $90. Sailboats rent by the hour for $45 and by the day for $160. Kayaks rent for $10 a half-hour, $15 an hour, and $45 a day. You can also rent a RAVE here for $55 a half-hour, $85 an hour: These are large trampolines strung across huge inflatable tubes and moored in the bay like miniature islands.

Bicycling

Bob's Bicycles (☎ 302-227-7966), on 1st St between Baltimore and Maryland Aves, rents adult bikes by the hour ($3), day ($9), and week ($28); mountain bikes are $3 an hour and $9 to $10 a day. They also have tandems and one- and two-seat surreys for $15 an hour.

Golf

There are several courses in the seacoast area, and more are under development. Baywood Greens (☎ 302-947-9800), a 15-minute drive from Rehoboth off Route 24 in Long Neck, is a popular championship course that recently added a back nine. During the week, 18 holes will cost you $48; on weekends, $54. A cart is included in the price.

Organized Tours

Jolly Trolley (☎ 302-227-1197) offers narrated trolley tours of Rehoboth for six or more individuals. Expect to pay $5.

Special Events

June through August, band concerts are held weekend evenings, as well as some weekdays. Crowds of couples and families assemble at the bandstand on Rehoboth Ave. Concerts start at 8 pm – check a local paper for listings.

The following are some other events worth noting:

Rehoboth Art League Tour of Homes (July) Many of the more attractive cottages open their doors to guests.

Rehoboth Jazz Festival (a four-day weekend in October)

DELAWARE

Rehoboth Beach Independent Film Festival (early November) This centers around the huge multiplex theater at the Rehoboth Mall, with screenings, the obligatory parties, and workshops.

Places to Stay

You'll find that accommodations here are easy to come by.

Camping The *Big Oaks Campground* (☎ 302-645-6838) is 3 miles from Rehoboth. It's open May 1 to October 1. Tent sites are $27 daily and $170 weekly; for RVs, the cost is $32 daily and $205 weekly. Take Route 1N from Rehoboth to County Rd 270 (just before Route 24). Go right, and the campground is on your left. Coming south on Route 1, go past Route 24, make a U-turn onto Route 1N, and then go right on Road 270.

Guesthouses James and Doris Downs have run the *Lord Baltimore* (☎ 302-227-2855, 16 Baltimore Ave) for more than 35 years. The front portion of the building dates to the latter half of the 19th century, and the whole house has the feel of your great aunt's seaside cottage. There are 12 rooms in this rambling building, and there is plenty of parking half a block from the beach at the center of town. Rates are $35 to $55 off season and $40 to $70 in season – small rooms with air-conditioning, television, and shared bath are at the low end of the price range; larger rooms with a private bath with cost you more. The friendly Downses also rent apartments and efficiencies. They're open year-round.

The *Sea Voice Inn* (☎ 302-226-9435, 800-637-2862, 14 Delaware Ave) is a B&B and retreat house. A group of 30 women who had been coming to the beach to stay at a YWCA cottage bought the house in 1926. They formed a corporation called the Bettie Neumann Girls Club – named after the social secretary of the YWCA cottage. Men could come for vacation, but could not become members of the club. The club disbanded in 1984, and the house was sold, although former members still come for vacation. Jeff and Susie Bond rent 11 rooms in the house at rates of $58 to $95. Call ahead to make sure a retreat group is not in residence.

The *Gladstone Inn* (☎ 302-227-2641, 3 Olive Ave) is one building away from the beach. Some guests find the furniture cheesy, but it's serviceable. Eight rooms with air-conditioning and shared baths or outside showers go for $75. Apartments that sleep six are $700 to $750 a week.

Rehoboth Guest House (☎ 302-227-4117, 40 Maryland Ave) is a gay-owned and -operated beach house that is open year-round. The floors and walls are painted wood; there is a mix of beach furniture, a roof sundeck, and two outdoor showers. All rooms have air-conditioning. Rates include a continental breakfast, and the owners stage a wine and cheese gathering in the backyard on Saturday nights in season. Off-season rates are $40 to $55, and in-season rates are $65 to $105. The cheapest room is a small one up on the dormered top floor.

The *Royal Rose Inn* (☎ 302-226-2535, 41 Baltimore Ave) is another nice place. It is a beach bungalow with eight air-conditioned rooms, and rates include a continental breakfast with homemade food. In-season rates are $85 to $115 weekdays and $105 to $140 weekends. The lower rates get you a room with a shared bath.

Lisa Myers and Lauren Romig opened the *Pelican Loft* (☎ 302-226-5080, 45 Baltimore Ave) in 1999 for both straight and lesbian couples. There is a trendy gift shop in the front of this restored summer cottage. Rooms with shared bath start at $55 off season and rise to $105 during the summer. You will find a large deck out back, an outdoor shower, air-conditioning, and cable TV.

The *Corner Cupboard Inn* (☎ 302-227-8553, 50 Park Ave) calls itself the 'inn that was an inn before inns were in.' Its rambling colonial structure and wooded surroundings certainly recall a classic country inn, yet the inn is just a three-minute walk from the quietest section of Rehoboth Beach. There are 18 rooms here, all with air-conditioning and private bath. There is also a full-service restaurant on the premises, and you can bring your own libations. Single rooms run $115 to $215 per day; doubles are $140 to $250. Ask about off-season rates.

Dennis Santangini and Nancy Warrington have done an over-the-top restoration of the monumental Victorian *Sea Witch Manor* (☎ 302-226-9482, 71 Lake St), near the center of town. There are six rooms here, all furnished with period pieces and fabrics. All have private baths, and one has a Jacuzzi. You get a gourmet breakfast in the formal dining room. Rates in season are a value at $135 to $170; they're $99 to $135 off season.

Hotels & Motels The *Whitson* (☎ 302-227-7966, 30 Maryland Ave) has basic rooms with a sink and shared bath for $42 on the 1st floor. As you ascend to the floors above, prices go up to $65 for rooms with refrigerators and private bath. All rates include a continental breakfast. It's open from mid-May to the end of September.

The *Sun View Motel* (☎ 302-227-3651), at Wilmington Ave and the boardwalk, was built in 1963 after the 1962 hurricane wiped out the coast. Not much has changed since then – walls are paneled, and the carpet is thick. This place is not fancy, but it's clean and right on the ocean. All 18 rooms have air-conditioning, TVs, microwaves, and refrigerators. Summer rates are $85 to $105; off-season (until June 24) rates are $70 to $85. You can add $10 to these rates on weekends. It's open May 1 to the end of September.

Every one of the eight rooms in the *Sirocco Motel* (☎ 302-227-9324), on Baltimore Ave and the boardwalk, faces the ocean. The furnishings are older motel-style – paneling, veneer furniture, and dropped ceilings. Take a room on the 3rd floor; those on the 2nd have an overwhelming view of the asphalt roofs of boardwalk shops. All rooms have TVs and refrigerators but no phones. In-season rates are $120 weekdays and $145 weekends; off season, they're between $60 and $88.

The *Atlantic Sands Hotel* (☎ 302-227-2511, 800-422-0600) is on the north side of Baltimore Ave and the boardwalk. You will find recently renovated rooms with a pool, hot tub, and gas grills. In-season rates are $145 to $230 during the week and $200 to $285 on weekends.

The *Boardwalk Plaza Hotel* (☎ 302-227-7169, 800-332-3224), at Olive Ave and the boardwalk, opened in 1991. The hotel has an indoor-outdoor Jacuzzi, a fitness room, and a sundeck. Rooms have antique or reproduction furniture, microwaves, coffeemakers, and air-conditioning. Rates start at $64 in the very low season and go up to $399 for a suite on summer weekends.

Places to Eat

During the 1990s, Rehoboth began building an astounding collection of ethnic, gourmet eateries that now number more than 40, and each year sees new additions to the mix. One of the best ways to survey your eating options is to pick up the Rehoboth Beach Restaurant Association Dining Guide (☎ 302-366-8565) at your place of lodging or at a local restaurant. Here you will find a list of menus from all of the most popular restaurants.

Budget The Rehoboth Beach boardwalk has a few sandwich places, candy stores, and other fast-food purveyors.

At *Louie's Pizza* (☎ 302-227-6002, 11 Rehoboth Ave), a slice costs $2. *Thrasher's* (7 Rehoboth Ave) sells fries to go, with vinegar and salt only – no ketchup. There are several other imitators on the block that are just as good, but Thrasher's is 'the original' resort chip vendor, having been around for more than 80 years and still drawing long lines in season.

TCBY Yogurt (60 Rehoboth Ave) sells cups and cones of the cold and creamy for less than $2; smoothies cost about $3. Try *Joe's Water Ice* (24 Rehoboth Ave) for something else to cool you off. A small cup of orange velvet costs $1.25.

The *Delaware Sub Shop* (☎ 302-227-0440), at 1st St and Wilmington Ave, makes overstuffed subs (you can't close the bread because there is so much meat) in the $7 to $8 range.

Dream Cafe (☎ 302-226-3233, 26 Baltimore Ave) has good coffee, muffins, and French breads. They also serve lunch salads and sandwiches for around $5. The only drawback is that you sit below street level and have to look up for natural light.

The *Java Beach Coffee House and Cafe* (☎ 302-226-3373, 167 Rehoboth Ave), next to the post office, has some attractive eye-openers, such as the bagel with veggies or strawberry cream cheese for $1.50. Lunch salads, such as the smoked turkey, cost less than $6, as do most of the huge sandwiches. Cheesecake costs $3.50 a slice.

Dos Locos (☎ *302-227-5626)*, on the south side of Baltimore Ave between 1st and 2nd Sts, is a small Mexican place. The cooks make their own sauces, taco shells, and tortilla chips, and the food tastes better because of it. Quesadillas, tacos, burritos, and chimichangas (including vegetarian) cost less than $9.

Mid-Range A bit more upscale, ***Mano's*** (☎ *302-227-6707, 10 Wilmington Ave)* has seafood for $11 to $13. The crab cakes are especially good – they're lumpy with crab meat, not flour. Mano's also has a bar, and a real mix of people hang out here.

Zogg's Restaurant & Bar (☎ *302-227-7660, 1 Wilmington Ave)* brings Tex-Mex and Cajun cooking to Rehoboth. Soft tacos run $8, as does the killer blackened-tuna sandwich.

The ***Camel's Hump*** (☎ *302-227-0947, 21 Baltimore Ave)*, across the street from the Lord Baltimore, has Middle Eastern food in a converted beach house. If you aren't adverse to paying $10 for a gyro or $8 for falafel, this is the place.

Dogfish Head Brewing & Eats (☎ *302-226-2739, 320 Rehoboth Ave)* is the beach's new microbrewery. You can get hickory-smoked pizza for under $10.

Veggie lovers flock to ***Planet X*** (☎ *302-226-1928, 35 Wilmington Ave)*, a 'hip cafe with cosmic decor' *(Washington Post)*. This eclectically decorated conversion of a beach house offers delights such as organic kale sautéed with soy and mírín for $5. The artichoke enchilada ($15) is extremely popular.

For a total Mexican cantina experience with lots of outdoor seating on the porch, head for the ***Iguana Grill*** (☎ *302-227-0948, 52 Baltimore Ave)*. You can eat light here on the salads or quesadillas for about $7. Most entrees, such as the grilled boneless pork chops, are under $13.

Top End The ***Back Porch Cafe*** (☎ *302-227-3674, 59 Rehoboth Ave)* has a brunch menu if you want to escape from the bacon-and-eggs breakfast routine. The menu includes a salmon-and-cream omelet ($7.50) and shirred eggs with ham and asparagus ($8.50). Dinner choices include mahi mahi ($21), jerk pork ($17), and duck in Thai green curry ($24). They also have a bar and serve wine by the glass.

The ***Blue Moon*** (☎ *302-227-6515, 35 Baltimore Ave)* is a beach house that has been converted into a restaurant. The eatery has an extensive wine list and entrees such as sautéed shrimp, lobster, and scallops in a salmon nest for $22.

Chez La Mer (☎ *302-227-6494, 201 2nd St)*, at Wilmington Ave, has a changing menu that includes appetizers such as baked brie with a roasted-garlic puree topping ($7) and mussel and mushroom bisque ($4.50). Entrees include duck with Indian spices ($21) and bouillabaisse ($28).

La La Land (☎ *302-227-3887, 22 Wilmington Ave)* is one of the best restaurants in the state. You sit in chairs painted gold, green, purple, and blue. It's elegant without being stuffy. The entrees are in the $19 to $28 range and include dishes such as Thai-spiced swordfish, lamb tamales, teriyaki catfish, and salmon lasagna with dill and black pepper pasta.

La La Land's rival is ***Celsius*** (☎ *302-227-5767, 50C Wilmington Ave)*. The chef cooks American cuisine with a California flair, featuring dishes such as chops from naturally raised lambs. You'll probably spend more than $25 here.

Entertainment

Rehoboth and Dewey Beach are party towns. During the summer season, the action is hot and heavy every night. Whether you are straight or gay, 21 or 51, you can find many kindred spirits to help you get your groove on.

Bars & Clubs In addition to the bars at restaurants like Mano's, the Back Porch Cafe, and Blue Moon, there are a few places with live music.

Without a doubt, the best dance and pickup scene for the 30-to-50 crowd is Sue Krick's ***Summer House Restaurant & Saloon*** (☎ *302-227-3895, 228 Rehoboth Ave)*.

DELAWARE

After 10 pm, this place drops its guise as a family-oriented chicken and pasta house and turns into a premier meat market as the DJ spins out classic rock and top 40 music that gets a whole lot of people dancing. Sunday afternoons draw a younger crowd, including a lot of the town's studliest lifeguards, for the daiquiri party.

Sir Guy's Restaurant & Pub (☎ *302-227-7616, 243 Rehoboth Ave*) has live music on weekends year-round without any cover charge. It's generally reggae on Saturday and variations on rock other nights. The crowd tends to be in their mid-20s and up.

Sydney's Side Street (☎ *302-227-1339, 25 Christian St*) is a small bar-restaurant. Sydney's brings in live music nightly during the summer and on weekends in the off season. The music is always jazz or blues, and the cover, if any, is usually $5 or less. Sydney's also offers wine and liquor tastings, and you can order entrees in small ('grazing') portions.

The *Bottle & Cork* (☎ *302-227-8545*), on Route 1 in Dewey Beach, bills itself as 'the greatest rock and roll bar in the world.' Having passed its 65th anniversary, this ersatz Tudor-style roadhouse must be doing something right. The rock is continuous, the dance floors are a mob scene, and the crowd is mostly over 30.

The *Rusty Rudder* (☎ *302-227-3888, 113 Dickinson St*), in Dewey Beach, sits right on the edge of the bay. This venue is a big Southern California kind of place with a deck that holds 500 people. The Rudder does a quick change every night from restaurant to club. The after-beach crowd shows up for drinks and steel drums everyday from 4 to 9 pm. Wednesday through Friday, top regional bands play a mix of oldies, progressive, and rock. Saturday night, separate DJs work the indoor and deck venues. The crowd here includes plenty of tan, young hardbodies – mostly straight and with few inhibitions: college kids during the week, yuppies on the weekends. This is the place to come if you like to dance or wish to pursue a torrid but brief romantic adventure.

Nearby the *Waterfront Restaurant & Bar* (☎ *302-227-9292*), at McKinley St on the bay, does a similar number. There is a DJ here on Friday, Saturday, and Sunday playing pop oldies for the 25- to 35-year-old crowd.

Gay & Lesbian Venues The *Renegade* (☎ *302-227-4713*), on Route 1, is a huge nightspot with a pool and multiple bars and dance floors. This is Rehoboth's premier gay entertainment venue for both men and women. There is live music and dancing every night in season, as well as occasional drag revues.

Cloud 9 (☎ *302-226-1999, 234 Rehoboth Ave*), next to Sydney's, is a bistro with a lively happy hour and a DJ and dancing on weekends. The Cloud is popular with a mix of gays and lesbians. There is a tea dance on some Sundays.

The *Frog Pond Restaurant* (☎ *302-227-2234*), 1st St at Rehoboth Ave, has live music five nights a week. This place brings in many female bands, and on those nights, the scene draws a lot of lesbians to kick up their heels.

Another popular bar scene for lesbians is the *Beach House Restaurant* (☎ *302-227-4227, 316 Rehoboth Ave*), which has a popular pool room off the upscale dining room.

Shopping

There are a lot of resort-wear shops in the pedestrian walkways between Baltimore and Rehoboth Aves. Rehoboth Ave from 2nd St to the boardwalk has a lot of shops selling 'family' items, such as T-shirts, jewelry, toys, T-shirts, Christmas ornaments, candy, T-shirts, clothing, and more T-shirts.

The big thrill for the shopping crowd is the ever-growing Ocean Outlets (☎ 302-227-6860) shopping malls just north of town on Route 1. At this writing, there are more than 150 factory outlet stores in these complexes, and the number is rising. Almost all of the big apparel manufacturers are here, including Izod, LL Bean, Eddie Bauer, and Reebok. Whether you like these kinds of malls or not, Ocean Outlets is the closest one to a major travelers' attraction in all of the Capital Region. You really can get some good deals, saving up to 40% off the normal prices on clothing and everyday accessory items.

Getting There & Away

Greyhound/Trailways (☎ 302-734-1417, 800-231-2222) has one bus a day to and from Wilmington and Dover. The fare is $14 to Wilmington and $9 to Dover. The bus stops in front of the Wilgus Glamorama dry cleaners (☎ 302-227-7223), 251 Rehoboth Ave, near 4th St. There is one bus a day to and from DC; the cheapest weekend rate is $25.

Delaware Transit Corporation (☎ 302-739-3278, 800-652-3278) runs weekdays to Wilmington by way of Dover and other intermediate stops and transfers that can make this trip an odyssey. The bus stops at Rehoboth Ave and the boardwalk.

By car, Route 1 runs straight from Wilmington and continues down the coast to Ocean City, Maryland. Despite the fact that Route 1 expands to six lanes in the vicinity of Rehoboth, stoplights as well as beach and outlet traffic make for slow driving during the summer and sunny weekends year-round.

Getting Around

Bus DART (☎ 302-739-3278, 800-553-3278) runs buses between Lewes, Rehoboth Beach, and Dewey Beach along Business Route 9 and Routes 1 and 1A. There are three buses each day between around 7 am and around 4 pm from Memorial Day to Labor Day. The fare is $1.

The Jolly Trolley (☎ 302-227-1197) has shuttle service between central Rehoboth Beach (Rehoboth Ave and the boardwalk) and Dewey Beach (near the Ruddertowne complex) from 8 am until 2 am daily. Trolleys depart Rehoboth on the hour and half-hour. They leave Dewey at a quarter past and at a quarter to the hour. The fare is $1.50 until midnight, after which you pay $3.

Park & Ride When the approach to town gets untenable, you can drop your car at the 24-hour lot off Route 1 about a mile north of town and take a free shuttle bus from there to the beach. For more information, call ☎ 302-226-2001. The bus runs from 7 am until 2:30 am, and parking is $5 a day.

Be aware that the Park & Ride lot is not currently well marked. To find it, turn west after you pass Outlet Two and the Exxon station on Route 1. The lot will be on your left, less than a quarter of a mile ahead.

NANTICOKE INDIAN MUSEUM

The Nanticokes are the last remaining Native American people in Delaware. The museum (☎ 302-945-7022) is in a schoolhouse at the intersection of Route 24 and County Rd 297, about 12 miles west of Rehoboth. Inside is one large room of exhibits, which include artifacts and replicas from the Nanticokes and other Native American peoples. The museum is open 9 am to 4 pm Tuesday to Friday, 10 am to 4 pm Saturday, and noon to 4 pm Sunday. Admission is $1 for adults and 50¢ for children.

A **powwow** occurs yearly in September (usually the first weekend after Labor Day) at a wooded site near the museum. The gathering includes two days of singing, dancing, drumming, and storytelling. There are a lot of booths selling silver and turquoise jewelry and feather items. You can also buy 'fry bread,' on which you sprinkle confectionery sugar or honey (Italian *zeppole* is a rounder version of this bread). The powwow gets crowded. Parking is in a large field near the site, but the traffic backs up nearby. Parking with admission costs $5; walk-ins are $1.

Take Route 1N from Rehoboth to Route 24. Take Route 24 heading southwest about 9 miles, to the intersection with County Rd 297, and look for the signs directing you to parking.

INDIAN RIVER LIFESAVING STATION

Built in 1876, this building was the post of 'surfmen,' who rescued mariners and their passengers from ships wrecked along this bold coast. The new museum in the restored station evokes the lives, gear, and dramatic rescue of the US Lifesaving Service. It's open 10 am to 5 pm Tuesday to Sunday. It's located south of Dewey Beach off Route 1 in Delaware Seashore State Park.

DELAWARE SEASHORE STATE PARK

Delaware Seashore State Park is a 10-mile-long, half-mile-wide peninsula stretching along the coast between the towns of Dewey Beach to the north and Bethany Beach to the south. The beach on the ocean side is long, straight, and clean – and, unlike Cape Henlopen, it is unmarred by abandoned military installations. The park takes up the entire thin peninsula, with Route 1 running down its center.

The park office (☎ 302-227-2800) is at the southern end of the park on the west side of Route 1, north of the Indian River Inlet Bridge. It's open 8 am to 4:30 pm daily year-round. Usage fees are charged if you want to stop and use the park, but you can drive through for free. The fee for Delaware-registered vehicles is $2.50; for all others, it's $5. The fee is collected daily from Memorial Day to Labor Day, and it's collected on weekends and holidays in May, September, and October.

Hiking

You will find a looping 1½-mile hike onto Burton's Island, west of the marina. There are 13 points on the trail marked to correspond with an interpretive pamphlet that you can pick up at the park office.

Swimming

Guarded swimming areas are on the ocean at the northern end (Tower Road Ocean) and at the southern end (Southeast Day Area) of the park. There are also access roads to unguarded beaches in between.

Fishing

The Indian River Inlet Marina (☎ 302-227-3071) is west of the park office. More than 30 charter fishing boats run out of the marina. Book one by calling ☎ 302-947-1924.

Places to Stay

There are three campgrounds (☎ 302-539-7202), all around the Indian River Inlet. The *New Camp*, south of the inlet, has sites with water, electricity, and sewage for $21. The *Old Camp*, next to it, has sites without hookups for $14. There is also *Overflow Camp*, on the north side of the inlet, which has sites without hookups for $14. This is used when the others fill up.

The land on both sides of the inlet is crowded with the campgrounds, park office, a coast-guard station, picnic and swimming areas, and the marina. There are also power lines overhead, and the view of the highway bridge from below doesn't add much to one's sense of getting back to nature. But once you get to the ocean, you can forget about the camping conditions and walk in virtual privacy for miles.

BETHANY BEACH & FENWICK ISLAND

These two beach towns bill themselves together as the 'quiet resorts.' Bethany Beach is the first community on the coast south of Delaware Seashore State Park. Immediately south of Bethany is Fenwick Island State Park (which runs for 3 miles along the coast). Next comes the town of Fenwick Island. If you look at a map, you'll see what appears to be a long barrier peninsula, with the two towns and the park on it. You will also see that the Assawoman Canal runs north-south behind Bethany Beach, and that the towns are actually on an island because the canal separates the beach communities from the mainland.

Bethany is a popular upper-middle-class summer resort (the town's permanent population of 350 balloons to more than 4000 in summer) with several hundred expensive beach houses – many built on stilts to withstand hurricanes. But while the homes are large and lovely, the lots are tiny, creating a visual contradiction and undermining Bethany's pretensions. Nevertheless, Bethany is exclusive enough to draw vacationers the likes of actor Denzel Washington, Vice President Al Gore, and many other prominent government officials and media celebrities.

Bethany Beach remains quiet because it is a community of housing developments with few places for travelers to stay. Nonetheless, Bethany Beach has evolved quite a bit from its origins as a camp-meeting town of 'seaside assembly for the Christian churches of this country.' (The Biblical town of Bethany was the home of Lazarus, who Jesus raised from the dead.) Fenwick Island is something of a small-scale Bethany, with fewer glitzy homes.

The center of the village of Fenwick Island, along Route 1, is more commercial, but seems like an oasis when compared with Ocean City, across the border in Maryland. Parking is difficult, but there are metered lots just north and south of Garfield Pkwy near the beach along Atlantic Ave.

Information

The Bethany-Fenwick Area Chamber of Commerce (☎ 302-539-2100, 800-962-7873) is in a large wooden beach house on stilts on the eastern side of Route 1, at the line between Fenwick Island and Fenwick Island State Park. From June to November, it is open 9 am to 5 pm weekdays and 10 am to 2 pm weekends. In the off season, the weekday hours are 10 am to 4 pm.

Things to See & Do

There isn't much besides the quiet beach and largely noncommercial **boardwalk** in Bethany. There are some beach-clothing stores, a market, and a few places to eat along Garfield Pkwy (off of Route 1), which is the main road and leads to the center of the boardwalk.

Fenwick Island doesn't have a boardwalk, but the beach has clean, hard sand that's good for walking. **Fenwick Lighthouse** is at the south end of town, just west of Route 1 before you enter Maryland. It's visible from the highway, and you can drive up to look at it, but you can't go inside.

Steen's Beach Service (☎ 302-539-9160), on the beach near the boardwalk, rents umbrellas and chairs. Bethany Rental Service (☎ 302-539-6244/2244), at 201 Central Ave, part of Harry's Bait & Tackle, rents equipment, from bicycles and boats to microwaves, blenders, and typewriters. The Fenwick Islander bike shop (☎ 302-537-2021), Route 1 and Virginia Ave, also rents bikes.

Places to Stay

Bethany Beach The *Sandy Cove Campsite* (☎ 302-539-6245) is in Ocean View, 4 miles inland from Bethany. Tent sites with water and electricity cost $25, or $27.50 if you bring an RV.

The cedar-shingle house *Journey's End* (☎ 302-539-9502) is on Atlantic Ave near the corner of Parkwood St. The house was built for John Addy, a plumber and one of the original founders of Bethany Beach. It was the first house to have indoor plumbing in town, and it used to sit closer to the shore, but it was moved back to avoid erosion. It's a pleasant, airy beach house thanks to its 67 doors and 100 windows. Most rooms have two single beds and rent for about $55 in June and September and $80 in July and August. Guests share bathrooms and must take showers outside.

The *Addy Sea* (☎ 302-539-3707) sits right on the beach, at the end of Ocean View Pkwy, although it was moved back from its original location to escape the surf. This Victorian inn has been a guest house since 1935. The rates in season start at about $75; they're $55 out of season.

The *Blue Surf Motel* (☎ 302-539-7531) is at the ocean end of Garfield Pkwy. It has reasonably large rooms with low-end but unworn furniture and decklike wood floors outside between the rooms that give it an earthy motel feeling. In-season rates are $120 to $145; it's more for an oceanfront view. Off-season rates are between $48 and $66.

The *Bethany Arms Motel* (☎ 302-539-9603) stands at Hollywood St and the ocean. It has five buildings – two oceanfront, one with ocean view, and two with no view. In-season rates are $115 to $175, depending on whether you get a sea view. Off-season rates run $55 to $85. Add $15 per night if you come on a summer weekend.

Fenwick Island The *Treasure Beach RV Park & Campground* (☎ 302-436-8001) is on Route 54. There are 80 sites. Tent sites cost $20; full hookups cost $30. You'll probably need reservations here in season.

There are a few motels with unsurprising decor on Route 1 in Fenwick Island. The *Sands Motel* (☎ 302-539-7745, 302-539-8200) has '70s furnishings and a beach view that is partially obscured by houses. Get a room on the 2nd floor, because the lower rooms look out onto a weedy lot. Rooms are clean and come without phones. The cheapest rates are $29 off season and $71 in season. Larger rooms go up to about $100; add $20 for weekends.

DELAWARE

The *Fenwick Islander* (☎ 302-539-2333), on Route 1 and South Carolina Ave, is one of the newer (1985) motels around. Off-season rates for two people in a room are $36 for weekdays and $50 on weekends; in-season rates are $99 weekdays and $139 weekends. The lowest rates are in October.

Places to Eat
Neither Bethany nor Fenwick Island may excite you with delicious food, and they can be a particular letdown if you've come south from Lewes and Rehoboth.

Bethany Beach In the small pedestrian mall on the southern side of Garfield Pkwy, *Surf's Up Subs & Steaks* has been a fixture in town for decades, and repeat visitors don't feel as if they've truly returned to Bethany until they have sampled a Surf's Up Philly cheesesteak sub on a 17-inch roll ($8).

Another popular place is *La Pizzeria* (☎ 302-539-8314, 109 Garfield). This is an intimate little Italian place with good values, such as lasagna for under $7.50.

If you are in the mood for a cheap feast, you might consider driving 2 miles west on Route 26 (which is Garfield Pkwy in town) to get to *Bootsie's Bar-B-Q* (☎ 302-539-9529). This restaurant is a small, brown, wooden building standing alone on your right. The chicken and pork ribs are good, but ignore the chopped pork barbecue unless you like Sloppy Joes. Half a barbecued chicken with potato salad, coleslaw, and roll costs about $6. A rack of ribs runs about $8; sandwiches are generally under $5. Food is only available for take-out.

Upscale diners now head for *Mango Mike's* (☎ 302-537-6621), at the corner of Garfield and the boardwalk. This is a popular spot for sea views, tropical drinks, and cuisine with a Caribbean flair, such as conch cakes for $8 and jerked or coconut chicken for $18. The all-you-can-eat Sunday brunch buffet runs $14.

Fenwick Island A 'family restaurant,' *Warren's Station* (☎ 302-539-7156) is on Route 1 across from the Sands Motel. It serves diner-style sandwiches (under $5) and fish and meat dishes ($6 to $12).

There are a few large seafood places in Fenwick serving up the usual. *Harpoon Hanna's* (☎ 302-539-3095) lies just west of Route 1 before Ocean City (watch for the signs) and serves shrimp and chicken dishes ($14) and fish ($14 to $20).

The *Fenwick Crab House* (☎ 302-539-2500) is on Route 1 near Delaware Ave. The crab house offers the usual seafood, crab imperial and crab cakes ($16), as well as jambalaya ($15).

Getting There & Away
Bus DART (☎ 302-739-3278, 800-652-3278) runs buses that connect cities on the coast with inland northern Delaware, but expect a tortured trip with a lot of changes. The stop in Bethany is at Central Blvd and Pennsylvania Ave.

Greyhound Carolina Trailway (☎ 800-231-2222) stops at Harry's Bait & Tackle, at the corner of Central Blvd and Pennsylvania Ave in Bethany Beach. To Dover you pay $11; to Wilmington, $19; to DC, $39.

In Fenwick Island, DART (☎ 302-739-3278, 800-652-3278) runs buses to stops at the state park entrance and at Ocean Hwy (Route 1), at the corner of Lighthouse Rd (Route 54) on the southern end of town. Buses also go into Ocean City, just across the state line in Maryland, where they stop at Ocean Hwy and 145th St.

Car Bethany Beach and Fenwick Island lie along the Route-1 beach highway between Rehoboth and Ocean City, Maryland. During the summer season, this route can be packed with slow-moving traffic. If you are coming from the west and just want to get to one of these quiet resorts, try taking a couple of back roads. Route 26 runs through swamp country to Bethany; Route 54 will bring you to the coast a few miles farther south, at Fenwick Island.

FENWICK ISLAND STATE PARK
Fenwick Island State Park (☎ 302-539-9060) is a 3-mile strip bordered on the east by the Atlantic Ocean and on the west by Little

Assawoman Bay. And as with Delaware Seashore State Park, you can drive through on Route 1 without paying a usage fee. However, if you pull off at the southern end's guarded swimming beach, you will have to pay $2.50 if you have Delaware license plates and $5 if you don't. The park has a good 3-mile Atlantic beach, although the only access if you're driving is at the southern end, and you'll have to pay. There are a couple of surf-fishing access points, but to drive onto the beach at these, you need a surf-fishing permit. The charge for Delaware-registered vehicles is $50; for out-of-state ones, it's $100.

Coastal Kayaks (☎ 302-227-7167, 539-7999), on the bay side of the park, across Route 1 from the guarded beach, rents water-sports equipment. Kayaks go for $15 an hour, $25 for two hours, and $45 for the day. Sailboats (such as Hobie Cats) rent by the hour for $45 and by the day for $115.

Acknowledgments

Many thanks to the travelers who used *Washington, DC & the Capital Region* and wrote to us with helpful hints, useful advice, and anecdotes:

Adam Simmons, Alice H Davenport, Allan Parker, Amelie Cherlin, Ben Dorman, Brian and Pat Holbrook, David Roland, Erith French, Ian C Story, Ian Nightingale, James Collier, Jettie Van Caenegem, Jo Ann Berlin, John Borg, John Witten, Linda C Pearl, Lisa Hatle, Marcia and Gary Tyeryar, Michael La Place, Mike Borger, Peter M Smith, Ross Geraghty, Thomas J Reiser, Tim Grutzner, Tony Dragon

LONELY PLANET

You already know that Lonely Planet produces more than this one guidebook, but you might not be aware of the other products we have on this region. Here is a selection of titles which you may want to check out as well:

USA
ISBN 0 86442 513 9
US$24.95 • UK£14.99 • 180FF

New York, New Jersey & Pennsylvania
ISBN 1 86450 138 3
US$21.99 • UK£13.99 • 159FF

New York City
ISBN 1 86450 180 4
US$16.99 • UK£10.99 • 129FF

Washington, DC city map
ISBN 1 86450 078 6
US$5.95 • UK£3.99 • 39FF

Available wherever books are sold.

Index

Bold indicates maps.

Boxed Text

MAP LEGEND

BOUNDARIES

- ▪·▬·▪·▬· International
- ▬·▪·▬·▪· Province
- ▬ ▬ ▬ ▬ County

HYDROGRAPHY

Water

Coastline

Beach

River, Waterfall

Swamp, Spring

ROUTES & TRANSPORT

Freeway

Toll Freeway

Primary Road

Secondary Road

Tertiary Road

Unpaved Road

Pedestrian Mall

Trail

Walking Tour

Ferry Route

Railway, Train Station

Mass Transit Line & Station

ROUTE SHIELDS

- 95 Interstate
- 10 State Highway
- 1 US Highway
- 229 Country Road

AREA FEATURES

- Building
- Cemetery
- Ecological Reserve
- Golf Course
- Park
- Plaza

- ✪ **NATIONAL CAPITAL**
- ◉ **State, Provincial Capital**
- ● **LARGE CITY**
- ● **Medium City**
- ● Small City
- ● Town, Village
- ○ Point of Interest

- ▪ Place to Stay
- ⚠ Campground
- ⊕ RV Park

- ▼ Place to Eat
- ▮ Bar (Place to Drink)

MAP SYMBOLS

✝ Airfield	▲ Monument
✈ Airport	⚲ Mosque
∴ Archaeological Site, Ruins	▲ Mountain
❺ Bank	🏛 Museum
✕ Battlefield	🔭 Observatory
⟫ Beach	← One-Way Street
🚲 Bike Path	♣ Park
⊖ Bus Depot, Bus Stop	ℙ Parking
🚌 Cathedral	⋂ Picnic Area
⌂ Cave	★ Police Station
✝ Church	🏊 Pool
◣ Dive Site	✉ Post Office
◗ Embassy	❖ Shopping Mall
⟩⟨ Footbridge	⚡ Skiing (Alpine)
✿ Garden	⚡ Skiing (Nordic)
⛽ Gas Station	🏛 Stately Home
⊕ Hospital, Clinic	✡ Synagogue
❶ Information	▣ Tomb
🛆 Lighthouse	🕴 Trailhead
♪ Live Music	❧ Winery
✳ Lookout	🐘 Zoo

Note: Not all symbols displayed above appear in this book.

LONELY PLANET OFFICES

Australia
PO Box 617, Hawthorn 3122, Victoria
☎ 03 9819 1877 fax 03 9819 6459
email talk2us@lonelyplanet.com.au

USA
150 Linden Street, Oakland, California 94607
☎ 510 893 8555, TOLL FREE 800 275 8555
fax 510 893 8572
email info@lonelyplanet.com

UK
10A Spring Place, London NW5 3BH
☎ 020 7428 4800 fax 020 7428 4828
email go@lonelyplanet.co.uk

France
1 rue du Dahomey, 75011 Paris
☎ 01 55 25 33 00 fax 01 55 25 33 01
www.lonelyplanet.fr

World Wide Web: www.lonelyplanet.com *or* AOL keyword: lp
Lonely Planet Images: lpi@lonelyplanet.com.au